Professional SQL Server 7.0 Programming

Robert Vieira

Wrox Press Ltd. ®

Professional SQL Server 7.0 Programming

First published: Sept 1999

Reprinted: Dec 1999

Reprinted: March 2000

Published by Wrox Press Ltd, Arden House, 1102 Warwick Road, Acock's Green,
Birmingham, B27 6BH, UK
Printed in the United States
ISBN 1-861002-31-9

Trademark Acknowledgements

Credits

Author
Robert Vieira

Additional Material
Frank Miller
Rachelle Reese
Sakhr Youness

Technical Reviewers
Michael Ask
Jody Baty
Mark Bell
Robert Chang
Jason Cropley
Steve Danielson
Robin Dewson
Pete Dixon
Steven M. Fowler
Tony Greening
Hope Hatfield
Ron Landers
Wendy Sarrett
Craig Utley

Cover
Chris Morris

Technical Editors
Catherine Alexander
Craig A. Berry
Nessa Bellingham
Kate Hall
Frances Olesch

Managing Editor
Joanna Mason

Development Editor
Dominic Lowe

Project Manager
Tony Berry

Index
Alessandro Ansa

Design/Layout
Tom Bartlett
Mark Burdett
Jonathan Jones
John McNulty

Technical Diagrams
David Boyce
William Fallon

About the Author

Experiencing his first bout with computing in 1978, Robert Vieira knew right away that this was something "really cool". In 1980 he began immersing himself into the computing world more fully – splitting time between building and repairing computer kits, and programming in BASIC as well as Z80 and 6502 assembly. In 1983, he began studies for a degree in Computer Information Systems, but found the professional mainframe environment too rigid for his tastes, and dropped out in 1985 to pursue other interests. Later that year, he caught the "PC bug" and began the long road of programming in database languages from dBase to SQL Server. Rob completed a degree in Business Administration in 1990, and, has since typically worked in roles that allow him to combine his knowledge of business and computing. Beyond his Bachelors degree, he has been certified as a Certified Management Accountant as well as Microsoft Certified as a Solutions Developer (MCSD), Trainer (MCT), and Database Administrator (MCDBA).

Rob currently works in a number of different roles ranging from requirements gathering, to database and general systems architecture as well as project management. He resides with his wife Nancy and daughter Ashley in Vancouver, WA.

Author Acknowledgements

At the beginning of many books you read, you get one of those sappy dedications that tell you how much various people mean to the author. I'm not normally all that much of a sap, but I'm going to follow tradition (and my heart), and get sappy now.

This book is dedicated to my wife Nancy and daughter Ashley, who put up with me "disappearing" into my home office for days at a time during the several months that I worked on this book. I know that I can never repay them for the time I've lost that could have been spent with them, yet they have been nothing but supportive through it all. To them I offer in print, for all the world to see, my continued undying love and devotion.

I also want to pay special thanks to several people at Wrox Press:

- Dominic Shakeshaft – who kept gently prodding me to write this book until I had no choice but to submit.
- Dominic Lowe – who saw me on my way, and then stayed around to find extra help when needed.
- Tony Berry – who was nothing but understanding when some unexpected personal matters delayed release of this book.
- Kate Hall – who, although she was probably ready to kill me by the end of it, somehow guided me through the edit process to build a better book.
- The rest of the edit and technical review team – who made sure that every "i" was dotted and every "t" was crossed.

There are enough other people who deserve mention that I'm sure I'll miss one or two – if you're among those missed, please accept my humblest apologies and my assurance that your help was appreciated. That said, people who deserve some additional thanks include Sakhr Youness, Frank Miller, Rachelle Reese, Kristin Engstrom, Chris Randall, Itzik Ben-Gan, Hal Berenson, and Richard Waymire

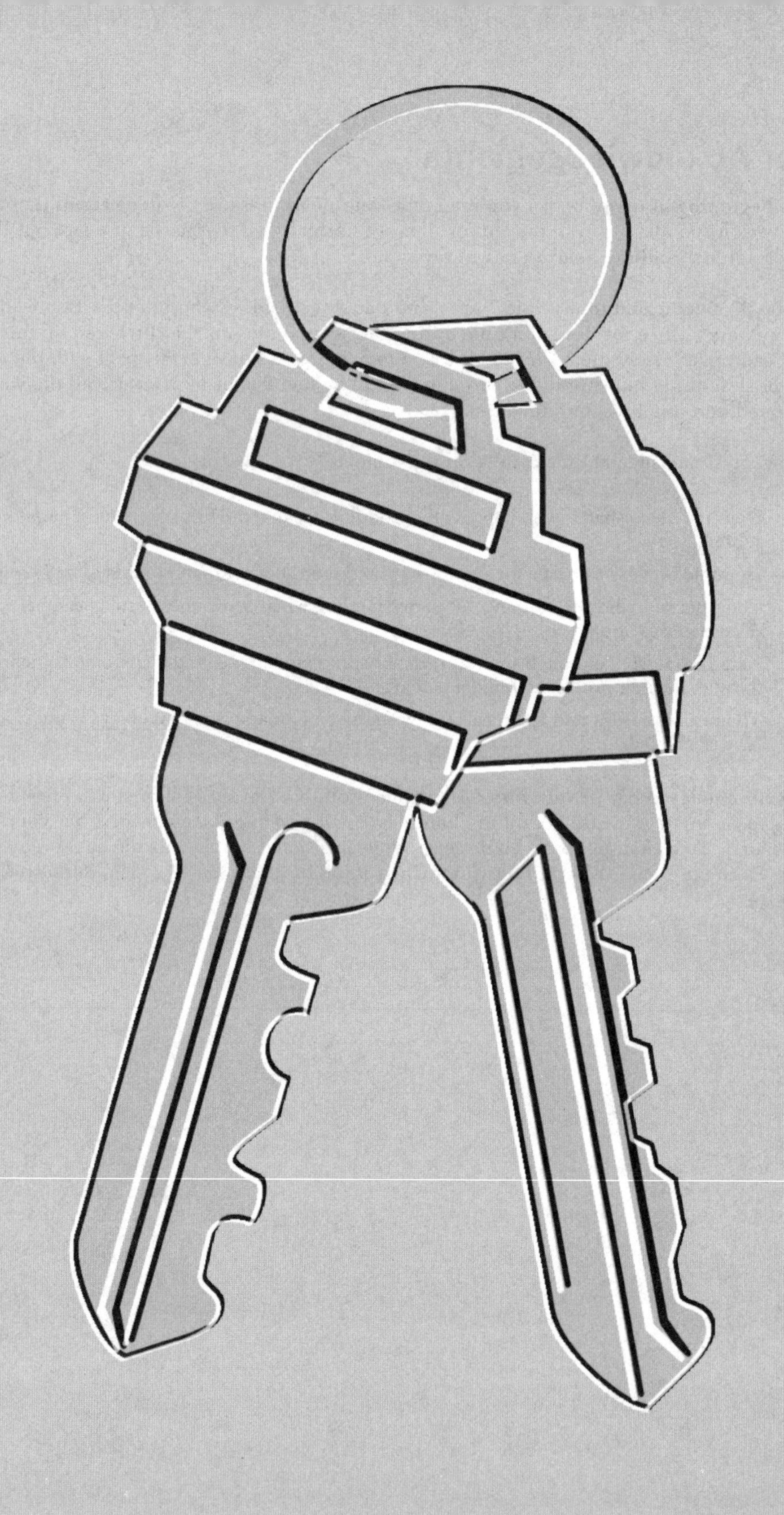

Table of Contents

Chapter 3: Tools of the Trade 45

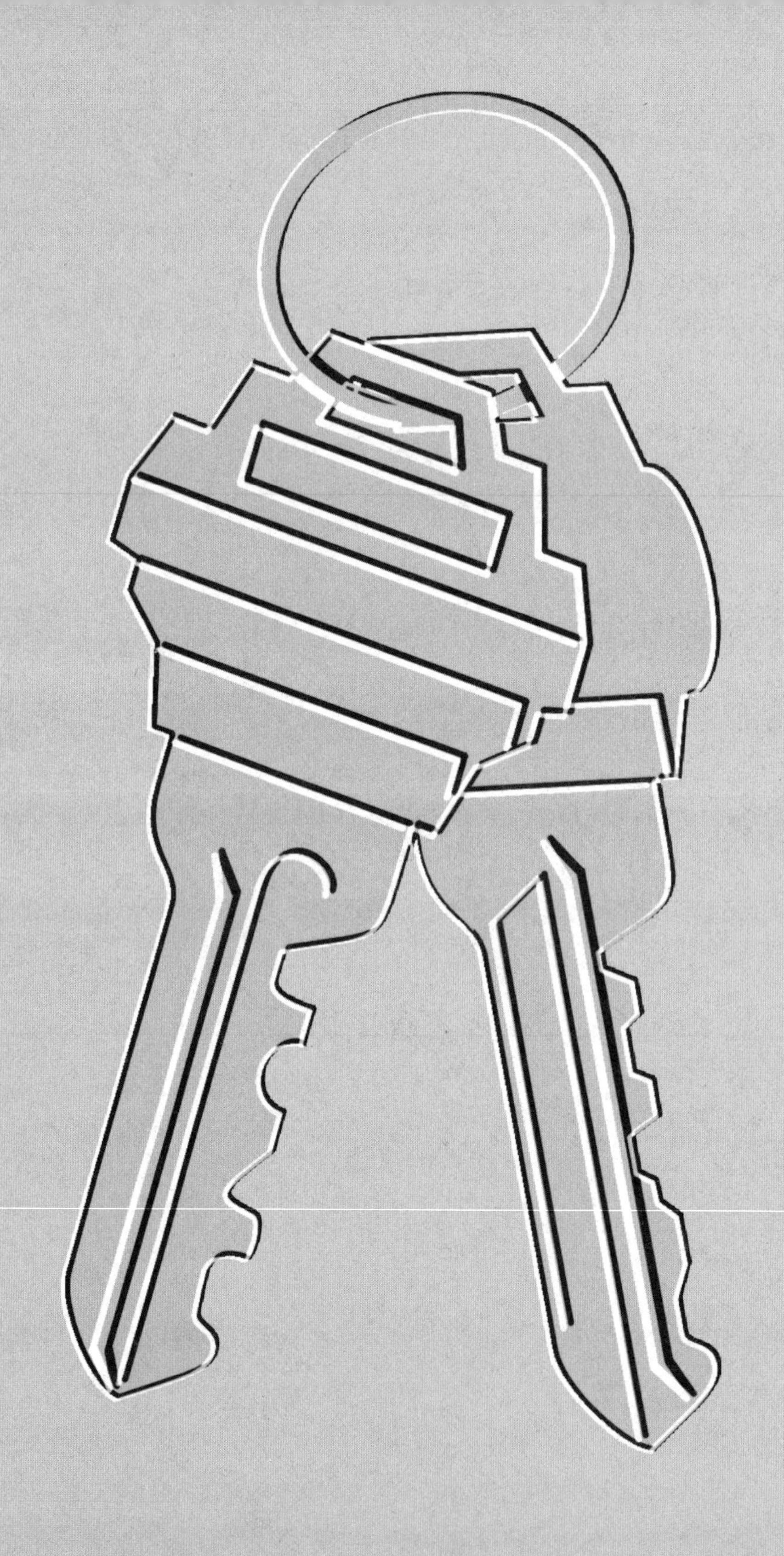

Introduction

SQL Server 7.0 is a major leap forward from SQL Server 6.5. There is a cornucopia of new features and tools available to the database developer - everything from new Transact-SQL statements, such as `ALTER TABLE` and `DENY` to Data Transformation Services (DTS) to utilities such as OLAP Services and Full-Text Search (and the list could go on still).

Even developers who have used SQL Server for years have a lot to get to grips with. Whether you're coming to SQL Server 7.0 from another relational database management system, are upgrading your existing system, or perhaps want to add programming skills to your DBA knowledge, you'll find what you need in this book. *Professional SQL Server 7.0 Programming* provides a comprehensive guide to programming with SQL Server 7.0, from a tutorial on Transact-SQL, to an in-depth discussion of more advanced topics, such as English Query, Data Transformation Services and replication.

What's Covered in this Book

The book is designed to become progressively more advanced as you progress through it, but, from the very beginning, I'm assuming that you are already an experienced developer – just not necessarily with databases. In order to make it through this book you do need to already have an understanding of programming basics such as variables, data types, and procedural programming. You do not have to have ever seen a query before in your life (though I suspect you have).

This book is something of a blend of both the beginning and the advanced in the SQL Server database development world. If you're already familiar with RDBMS systems – SQL Server in particular – then several of the early chapters may be sort of "Ho Humm" to you. I would still strongly suggest reading Chapters 2 and 3, but Chapter 4 may be worth skipping. From there, we're getting into areas where SQL Server 7.0 has some variance from other RDBMS products and vs. version 6.5 of SQL Server.

The focus of the book is highly developer-oriented. This means that we will, for the sake of both brevity and sanity, sometimes gloss over or totally ignore items that are more the purview of the database administrator than the developer. We will, however, remember administration issues as they either affect the developer or as they need to be thought of during the development process – we'll also take a brief look at several administration related issues in Chapter 25.

I've made an attempt to keep this book relatively language independent outside of SQL Server's own Active Scripting (used with DTS) and T-SQL (SQL Server's own brand of SQL) language requirements. Several items are pointed out with references to similarities and differences vs. two of the more popular programming languages today – C++ and Visual Basic. In a few places, particularly Chapter 22, we are forced to make a decision for example purposes. In these cases, we will use Visual Basic since it is typically a bit easier to understand for the generic reader of this book (I find that C programmers tend to read VB better than VB programmers tend to read C).

So let's take a brief look at the chapters of this book:

Chapter 1 provides some background information on the history of SQL Server along with a comparison of the features of the various SQL Server editions and data access technologies.

In *Chapter 2*, we explore the **database objects** present in SQL Server 7. We'll look in detail at the databases installed by default, and more generally, at the other objects including stored procedures, rules and views.

Chapter 3 introduces the tools used by a developer working in SQL Server 7. By the time you finish this chapter you'll be familiar with the **Enterprise Manager**, **Performance Monitor** and **Query Analyzer** (among others).

Chapter 4 begins the **Transact-SQL** tutorial with an introduction to basic queries.

Chapter 5 follows on from the previous chapter and introduces the concept of **joins** (`INNER`, `OUTER`, `FULL` and `CROSS`).

Chapter 6 deals with **tables**, both creating and altering them.

Chapter 7 introduces **constraints**. Included in this chapter are explanations and examples of primary keys, foreign keys as well as rules and defaults.

In *Chapter 8*, we turn our attention to **database design** and consider normalization. We will discuss the 3 normal forms (as well as few extra rarely used and academic forms).

Chapter 9 is another theoretical chapter and covers the **index structures** used in SQL Server as well as rules of thumb as to when to use indexes and when not to.

In *Chapter 10*, we'll turn our attention to **views** - virtual tables that allow you to partition off parts of your tables from readers.

Chapter 11 discusses SQL **scripts** and **batches**. We'll look at the `USE` and `GO` statements and wrap up the chapter with a discussion of **OSQL**.

Chapter 12 is concerned with **stored procedures** - one of the fundamental tools of a database developer's kit - we see how to create, alter and drop stored procedures. The chapter will conclude with a brief discussion of **extended stored procedures**.

Chapter 13 covers **transactions** and **locks**. We'll discuss the `BEGIN`, `COMMIT`, `ROLLBACK` and `SAVE TRAN` statements. Then we'll see the **SQL Server log** works before moving on to a discussion of the various forms of lock and how to deal with deadlocks.

In *Chapter 14* we'll cover **triggers**, we'll discuss how to create and alter them and also when to use them and when to avoid them.

Chapter 15 introduces concepts behind advanced queries. We'll look at how to create **nested subqueries** and **correlated subqueries**.

In *Chapter 16*, we'll discuss **distributed transactions** and queries and the role of **linked** and **remote servers**.

In *Chapter 17*, we'll see how to navigate a recordset using **cursors**.

We'll see how to move large chunks of data around in *Chapter 18*. We'll begin by discussing the **bulk copy program**, but then move on to **Data Transformation Services** (new to SQL Server 7).

Chapter 19 is devoted to **replication**, after discussing what it is and why you might need to use it, we'll run through all the replication wizards supplied with SQL Server 7.

Chapter 20 deals with advanced database design issues such as advanced diagramming, dealing with large file-based information and sub-categories.

Chapter 21 provides an introduction to the **OLAP Services** that are provided with SQL Server 7.

In *Chapter 22* we'll look at two new technologies we can use to query our database - **English Query** and **Full-Text Search**.

Chapter 23 is concerned with **security**. We'll consider NT security as well as that provided by SQL Server itself.

Chapter 24 covers a mix of issues. The core principle behind it, though, is **performance tuning** and you'll find that all the topics mentioned will need to be considered to get the most out of your SQL Server.

We'll wrap up the book with an overview of **administration** in *Chapter 25*.

Version Issues

This book was written from the ground up with SQL Server version 7.0 in mind. As such, if you're running 6.5, I may not have covered every detail for which you're looking. That being said, I have tried to make a point of stating the obvious gotchas between versions. SQL Server 7.0 brought about many changes, but very few of them are to the detriment of code and designs that were developed under previous versions. I have tried to point out the exceptions.

What You Need to Use This Book

Nearly everything discussed in this book has examples with it. All the code is written out and there are plenty of screen shots where appropriate. However, you'll want to make sure that you have a system available (and by that I mean one that you can have administrative-level access to) to run the examples on, in order to get the most out of it. Your system should be equipped with:

- SQL Server 7.0
- Windows NT 4.0 or better (Win 9x will work, but you'll miss out on some things)

Conventions Used

I've used a number of different styles of text and layout in the book, to help differentiate between different finds of information. Here are some of the styles I've used and an explanation of what they mean:

> **These boxes hold important, not-to-be forgotten, mission-critical details that are directly relevant to the surrounding text.**

Background information, asides and references appear in text like this.

- **Important Words** are in a bold font
- Words that appear on the screen, such as menu options, are in a similar font to the one used on screen, for example, the Tools menu
- All object names, function names and other code snippets are in this style: `SELECT`

Code that is new or important is presented like this:

```
SELECT CustomerID, ContactName, Phone
FROM Customers
```

Whereas code that we've seen before or has little to do with the matter being discussed, looks like this:

```
SELECT ProductName FROM Products
```

In Case of a Crisis...

There are number of places you can turn to if you encounter a problem:

- Books Online
- `http://www.wrox.com` - for the downloadable source code and support
- `http://www.microsoft.com/sql/` - for up-to-the-minute news and support
- `http://www.ProfessionalSQL.com` - for source code and examples
- My e-mail address – `robv@ProfessionalSQL.com`

Feedback

I've tried, as best as possible, to write this book as though we were sitting down next to each other going over this stuff. I've made a concerted effort to keep it from getting "too heavy" while still maintaining a fairly quick pace. I'd like to think that I've been successful at it, but I encourage you to e-mail me and let me know what you think one way or the other. Constructive criticism is always appreciated, and can only help future versions of this book. You can contact me either by email (`feedback@wrox.com`) or the Wrox website.

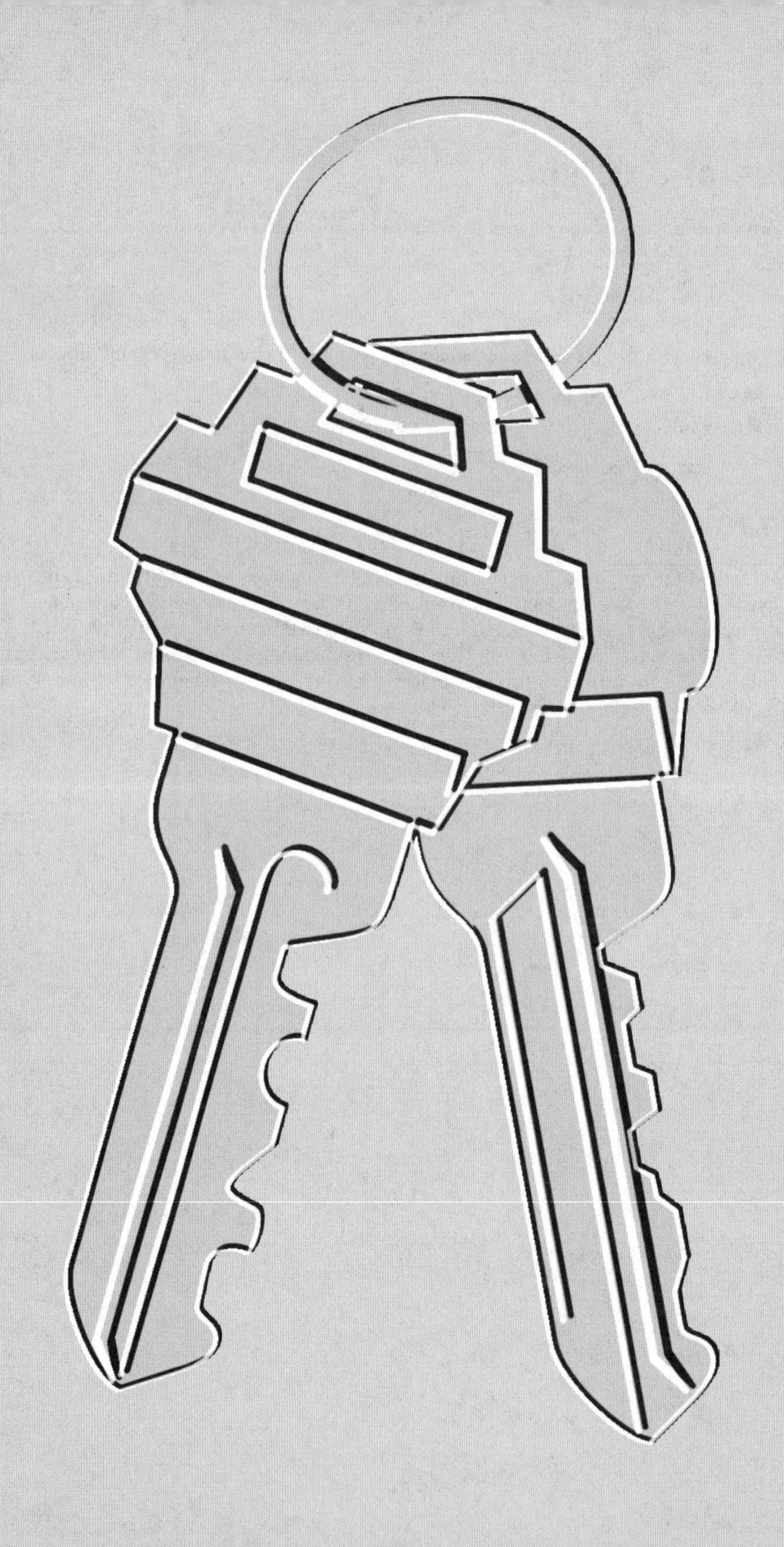

1

SQL Server 7.0 - Particulars and History

So you want to learn something about **databases** - **SQL Server** in particular. That's great! Databases are pervasive – they are everywhere, though you may not have really thought about things that way up until now.

In this chapter we'll be looking at some of the different varieties and brands of databases available both today and throughout history. We'll look into some of the advantages and disadvantages of each, and how they fit into the grand picture of life, so to speak.

Moving on from there, we'll take a look at SQL Server specifically – the different editions that are currently available and what each does or doesn't include.

In addition, we'll take some time to examine the database development process and how it fits into your overall development cycle. In this same section, we'll talk at an entry level about some system architecture issues and how that affects our database thinking.

Finally, we'll look at what you'll need to take the best advantage of what the book has to offer. We'll also take a small amount of time to look into the Microsoft exam process and how this book fits into any study plans you may have for your Microsoft certification.

A Brief History of Databases

SQL Server is a **RDBMS** – or **Relational Database Management System**. RDBMS systems are at the pinnacle of their popularity at the moment – using a RDBMS as the basis for data storage is just plainly "the way it's done" for most applications nowadays – but it wasn't always this way.

In this section, we're going to take a look back in time and examine some of the other databases used in the past. We'll try not to dwell on this "Old News", but it's critical to understand where you came from if you want to understand where you're going and why.

Types of Databases

Databases are not just limited to the computer-based systems that we typically think about when we hear the term – they are much, much more. A database is really any collection of *organized* data. Even Webster's puts a qualifier on any computer notion:

> *Database: A usually large collection of data organized especially for rapid search and retrieval (as by a computer).*

The file drawers in your office are really something of a database (that is, if they are better organized than mine at home). In fact, databases have existed throughout most of the history of the "civilized" world going back to the days of the early philosophers and academics (Socrates, Aristotle, Hippocrates, etc.).

That being said, there's a reason why databases are so closely associated with computers. It's because for most database situations (virtually, but not quite, all of them) computers are simply the fastest and most efficient way to store data. Indeed, the term database is thought to have originated from the computing community in 1962 or so.

Databases, then, fall into a number of common categories:

- Paper-based: **These, although often not thought of as databases, probably still make up the largest** number of databases in the world today. There are literally billions and billions of tons of paper out there which are still meticulously organized, but haven't been anywhere near a computer.
- **Legacy mainframe** – often **VSAM** (**Virtual Storage Access Method** – common to IBM mainframes) databases: Don't underestimate the number of and importance of these still out there. Connectivity to host systems and the vast amounts of data they still contain is one of the major opportunity areas in database and systems development today. There are still many situations where I recommend a host system solution rather than a client-server or web based model. It's worth noting though that I still believe in using a true RDBMS – albeit that it's located on a host system.

- **dBase** and other file based databases: Typically, these include any of the older **Inline Sequential Access Method** – or **ISAM** – databases. These typically use a separate file for each table, but the ISAM name comes from the physical way the data is stored and accessed more than anything else. Examples of ISAM databases that are still in widespread legacy use – and even some new developments in certain cases – include dBase, FoxPro, Excel, Paradox, and Access. (Yes, Access is an ISAM with a relational feel and several relational features– it is not, however, a true relational database system.) These systems had their heyday well before RDBMS systems (there is something of a paradox in this since RDBMS systems appeared first). These systems are still quite often great for small, stand-alone databases where you will never have more than one user accessing the data at a time.

- **RDBMS systems**: Data for the masses, but with much better data integrity. These systems do more than just store and retrieve data. They can be thought of as actually caring for the integrity of the data. Whereas VSAM and ISAM databases typically stored data very well, the database itself had no control over what went in and out of the database (OK, Access has some, but not like a true RDBMS) – the programs that used the database were responsible for implementing any data integrity rules. RDBMS systems take the level of responsibility right down to the database level. Before, if five programs were accessing the data, you'd better have made sure they all were programmed correctly. RDBMS systems bring the data integrity rules right into the database – you still want your programs to know about the data integrity rules to avoid getting errors from the database, but the database now takes some level of responsibility itself – the data is much more safe.

- **Object-oriented databases**: These have been around for a while now, but are only recently beginning to make a splash. They are really a completely different way of thinking about your data, and, to date, have only found fairly specialized use. Examples would be something similar to a document management system – instead of storing the document in several tables, the document would be stored as a single object, and would have properties whose state would be maintained. **ODBMS** systems often provide for such object-oriented concepts as inheritance and encapsulation.

RDBMS systems are clearly king these days. They are designed from the ground up with the notion that they are not going to be working with just one table that has it all, but with data that relates to data in a completely different table. They facilitate the notion of combining data in many different ways. They eliminate the repetitive storage of data and increase speed in transactional environments.

The Evolution of Relational Databases

The principles behind relational database structures and a **Structured English QUEry Language** – or **SEQUEL** - were first introduced by **E.F. Codd** of IBM back in the late 1960's (the name was later shortened to just **Structured Query Language** or **SQL**). The concept was actually pretty simple – increase data integrity and decrease costs by reducing repetitive data as well as other database problems that were common at the time.

Nothing really happened in the relational world as far as a "real" product was concerned until the mid to late 70's though. Around that time, companies such as Oracle and Sybase became the first to create true relational database systems. It might surprise you to learn that these systems got their start in mainframe – not Client/Server – computing. These systems offered a new way of looking at database architecture, and, since they ran on multiple platforms, they also often offered a higher potential to share data across multiple systems.

In the 80's, the **American National Standards Institute** (**ANSI**) finally weighed in with a specification for SQL, and **ANSI-SQL** was born. This was actually a rather powerful moment in RDBMS computing because it meant that there would be better compatibility between vendors. That, in turn, meant that more of the expertise built up in one RDBMS was also usable in a competing system. This has greatly aided the process of trying to increase the number of developers in the SQL community. The ANSI spec called for several different levels of compliance. Most of the major RDBMS products available today are classified as being **Entry-Level ANSI compliant** (SQL Server, for example, is Entry-Level compliant).

ANSI compliance is a double-edged sword. I'm going to encourage you to make use of ANSI compliant code where feasible – it's particularly important if you may be migrating your code between different database servers. But you also need to realize that many of the performance and functionality features that each of the high performance database vendors offer are not ANSI compliant. Each vendor extends their product beyond the ANSI spec in order to differentiate their product and meet needs that ANSI hasn't dealt with yet. This leaves you with a choice – ANSI compliance or performance.

Use ANSI compliance not as a religion, but rather where it makes sense. Go for ANSI code where it makes little or no difference in performance (such as queries), but also don't be afraid to make judicious use of specialized features that may offer some functionality or performance gain that ANSI can't give you. Just document these areas where you use them so that, if you are faced with porting to a new RDBMS, you know where to look for code that may not run on the new system.

Microsoft SQL Server (referred to in this book as simply **SQL Server**) was originally born from Sybase SQL Server (referred to in this book simply as **Sybase**). Microsoft partnered with Sybase in 1989 to develop a version of SQL Server for, of all things, OS/2. SQL Server was migrated to Windows NT back in 1993 with version 4.2. The relationship ended with the release of version 6.0. From 6.5 forward, SQL Server has been a Microsoft-alone product. Version 7.0 represents what is essentially a complete rewrite of the product and is the first version available for Windows 9x (there is now virtually no Sybase code left in SQL Server).

While there are unmistakable similarities, there are now substantial differences in implementation and feature support between version 4.21 (the oldest version you're likely to actually find installed somewhere) and version 7.0. Version 6.0 added such things as cursor support. Version 6.5 added distributed transactions, replication, and ANSI compatibility.

About SQL Server 7.0

SQL Server 7.0 comes with far more than just the usual RDBMS – It has additional components added in that would, for many products, be sold entirely separately or with add-on pricing. Instead, Microsoft has seen fit to just toss in these extras at no additional charge.

SQL Server 7.0 is available in four **editions** (Desktop, Small Business (SBE), Standard and Enterprise) which are discussed in more detail later.

The full suite that makes up SQL Server 7.0 includes:

System/Subsystem	Description	Editions
SQL Server 7.0 (The Main RDBMS)	This is the "guts" of the system, and is required for anything else to work. It is a very robust relational database system. This part of the system also includes several different services and utilities such as the **SQL Server Agent** (Scheduler); the **Distributed Transaction Coordinator** (**DTC**); the **SQL Server Profiler** (trouble-shooting); and the **Enterprise Manager** (**EM**) - one of the best built-in management tools in the business regardless of price-range. If you're coming from the Access world or some other desktop database, strap on your seatbelt, because you have just scratched the surface of what's possible.	Desktop Standard Enterprise
Full Text Search	This is an optional part of the main install, but you have to select it. If you want this functionality, you need to actively choose it – it's not installed by default. **Full Text Search** provides the functionality to support more robust word lookups. If you've used an Internet search engine and been left in awe of the words and phrases that you can find, Full Text Search is the tool for you. It ranges from being able to quickly locate small phrases in large bodies of text to being able to tell that drink is pretty much the same word as drunk or that swam is just the past tense version of that word swim you were looking for. This one is not available in the Desktop version (Win 9x) of SQL Server. We'll look at it extensively in Chapter 22.	Standard Enterprise
English Query	Also featured in Chapter 22, **English Query** allows you to develop applications for even the most non-technical of users. English Query, or EQ, allows users to ask questions or give commands in plain English and have them translated into a query that's usable by SQL Server. A great tool, but keep in mind that this is a completely separate install from the rest of SQL Server.	Standard Enterprise Desktop
OLAP Server (AKA Plato)	Yet another tool that isn't part of the main install and isn't part of the Desktop version, but gives great extras to the product. **OLAP** stands for **OnLine Analytical Processing**. It's something that many companies try and do from their main server – we'll look into why that's a mistake and how to make use of SQL Server's OLAP services in detail in Chapter 21.	Standard Enterprise

There are a few additional differences between the various editions of SQL Server 7.0. These include:

- **Symmetric Multiprocessing** (**SMP**) Support for up to two processors in the Desktop version (Though Win 9x can't take advantage of this). Support for up to four processors in the Standard edition if installed on NT Server or Enterprise. Support for up to 8 processors with the Enterprise edition, provided that it is installed on NT Enterprise Edition.

  SMP distributes the workload of the server over multiple processors symmetrically – that is, it tries to balance the load as opposed to running on just one CPU per process.
- **Clustering Support** (Enterprise Edition Only): Clustering allows for load-balancing across servers and automatic fail-over support (if one server dies, another one automatically picks up where the other left off). Currently, you can only cluster 2 servers, but that is expected to be expanded in a future release of Windows 2000.

Which Edition Should You Use?

The answer is like the answer to most things in life: It depends.

Each of the various editions has a particular target "market" that it's designed for. Usually, I have some exception to the rule on how I think things should be used, but, for these products, I would say that what Microsoft designed them for is really the best use. Let's take a quick look at them one-by-one.

Desktop Edition

This is new with SQL Server 7.0, and it's really a great addition. It was created to serve a couple of purposes: provide a more robust desktop database solution than provided with Access (even on Windows 9x), and to provide a version of SQL Server that could be used in "unplugged" situations. The latter is the big one – it is proving to be really big in situations like a sales rep who is on the road all the time. They can have their own version of the customer database, and just "synchronize" using replication when they are able to connect back up with the network.

Contrary to popular belief, this is not truly a different version of SQL Server – the **Desktop Edition** uses the same binary executable that the Standard Edition uses. The difference is more in which auxiliary services are supported.

The Desktop Edition is excellent when you want a small stand-alone database or when you have the need to be disconnected from a central data source, but want to be able to take some of that data with you. You could also use the Desktop Edition to run a small server on Window NT – this later configuration even has support for 2 processors. Keep in mind though, that, even with multiprocessing active, there is no support for parallel queries (which runs different parts of the same query at the same time).

I'm told (I haven't tried it myself), that several of the tools which are not supposed to work with the Desktop Edition actually do work just fine – particularly if you're running under NT Workstation. I strongly discourage you from implementing things this way. If you need the extra features, then use the right O/S to support them. Otherwise, you may find that everything works OK for a while, but you'll also find that you have no support from Microsoft when you want to ask why something broke.

Small Business Edition

This one only comes as part of the Back Office – **Small Business Edition** (**SBE**) suite of products. This is, in most respects, the same as the Standard Edition is except that it has had several restrictions placed on it. To be more specific, SBE:

- Has a maximum database size of 10GB
- Does not support OLAP
- Will not run on an operating system other than Windows NT – Small Business Edition

SQL Server SBE has a particular time that it's the right choice – when running with Back Office SBE.

Standard Edition

The **Standard Edition** is the mainstream edition of SQL Server. This is the edition that's going to be installed for the majority of major SQL Server users, and is essentially the edition that equates to previous versions of SQL Server. This is the "lowest" edition of SQL Server that officially supports most of the interesting tools that you hear about (OLAP etc.). In addition, Standard Edition supports multiprocessing of up to four CPUs.

This should be your default installation – if you're not sure what edition to install, choose this one.

Enterprise Edition

To run this, you must have NT **Enterprise Edition** installed. SQL Server Enterprise Edition adds support for multiprocessing of up to 32 CPU's, clustering (where two separate servers provide fail-over and can otherwise share a workload), and also allows for user-defined cubes in OLAP Services (cubes are fully described in Chapter 21).

Whether to go with Enterprise Edition or not is usually a relatively easy decision because the outcome is almost always made for you based on a requirement for one of the Enterprise Edition features. If you need clustering, then you need Enterprise Edition. If you need support for more than 4 processors, then you need Enterprise Edition. It's that simple.

Hardware Requirements

The stated **minimum hardware requirements** for SQL Server are pretty easy to reach these days:

- Pentium 166 or better (Alpha is also an option, but MS has stated there will be no future development for that platform).
- 32MB Memory (64MB for the Enterprise Edition)
- 65MB hard disk space (minimum install) or 180MB (full install)
  You also need 50MB if you want to install OLAP services, and another 12MB for English Query.
- Windows 9x or NT Workstation with SP4 (Desktop version only: eliminates some SQL Server features), Windows NT Server with SP4 (Standard or Desktop versions), or Windows NT Enterprise with SP4 (SQL Enterprise Edition)
- IE 4.01 or later

In reality, you'll want to have a bit of a beefier machine than the recommendation. Even for a stand-alone development server, I recommend a minimum of 128MB of RAM and a Pentium II 233 or better processor.

Building Database Connected Systems

At this juncture, we're probably ready to go into the "holy-war territory" of architectural issues. It seems like everybody's got an idea of what the best architecture is for everything.

Before we even get too deep into this I'll give you my first soapbox diatribe and my slant on things.

The perfect architecture to use is the one that is right for the particular solution you are working towards. There are very few easy answers in life, and what system architecture to use for a project is rarely one of them. Don't let anyone ever make you fall into the trap of thinking "You should always use n-tier architecture" or that "The mainframe is dead – anyone who installs a host-based system today is nuts!"

I have a definite belief in the power and flexibility of the n-tier approach we'll be talking about shortly – but don't believe for a minute that I think it's the only solution. The moment you let yourself be backed into thinking one approach is the right one for everything, will be the moment that you start turning out substandard work. Both traditional client/server and host technology still very much have their place, and I'll try and address some of the wheres and whys as we go through this section.

There have been a few models to come around through the years, but today we usually group them depending on how they handle three groups of **services**:

- **User Services**: This usually includes things like drawing the User Interface (U/I) and basic formatting and field rules. Examples of things that might be handled by User Services would be proper formatting of a date – including making known that a given field is a date field and pre-validating that any value entered into this field is actually a date. User services is all about presentation and making sure that each field has at least the type of data it's supposed to have in it.
- **Business Services**: This is the part of things that knows about various business rules. An example of a business service would be one that connects with your credit card company to validate a customer's credit card purchase. In a 3-tier or n-tier system, the Business Services objects may reside on a server to themselves, be split across several servers, or, in smaller installations, share a server with Data Services.
- **Data Services**: This is all about storage and retrieval of data. Data services know about data integrity rules (say, that an inventory value can't go below zero), but don't care where the credit card approval came from. This is where SQL Server fits in.

Let's take a look at some of the classic architectures used both past and present and see how our services fit in.

Single Tier (Host) Systems

This is the old mainframe and mini-computer model. There was virtually no logic at the desktop – instead, there was a dumb terminal. All that was sent down the wire to the terminal was the screen layout information.

Advantages	Disadvantages
Requires very little bandwidth on your network in order to have fast response times – great for international or WAN situations where bandwidth can be expensive.	Very expensive hardware wise. In the old days, these often even required special plumbing for cooling water, although I'm not aware of any systems which still require that being produced today.
Also exceptionally reliable. You'll find mainframes out there that haven't been "down" in literally years.	Typically proprietary in nature – much more difficult to share information with other systems.
Deployment of new software is extremely easy – just install on the host system, and every user has the new version – no running from machine to machine for the upgrade.	Very limited number of "off-the shelf" software packages available. Since the number of potential customers is few, the cost of these packages tends to be extremely high.

2-Tier Architecture (Client/Server)

2-tier, or **client/server** systems first started becoming popular in the early nineties. There were actually two sub-types to this architecture: client-centric (smart client) and server-centric (smart server).

Client-Centric

The **client-centric** version of client/server lived on the notion that PCs are cheap (the driving force behind most client/server development) and that you're going to get the most power when you distribute the computing requirements as much as possible. As such, whenever possible, only the data services piece of things was performed on the server. The business and U/I side of things was performed at the client – thus ensuring that no one system had to do all that much of the work. Every computer sort of did their fair share (at least, that was the idea).

Traditional Client/Server
(Client-Centric)

Client
Server
Data Services
User & Business Services
Database

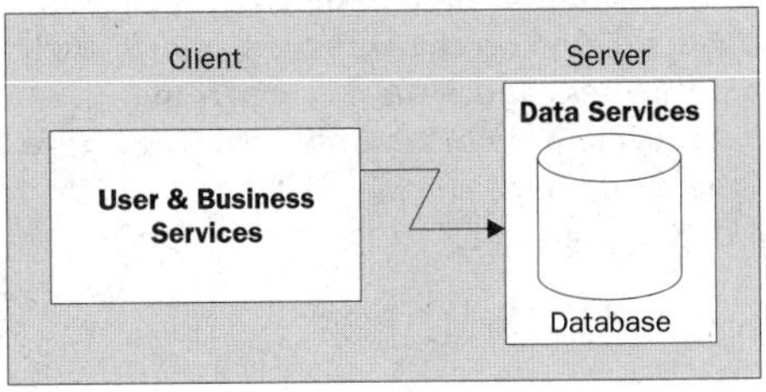

The big problem with client-centric client/server was and is bandwidth. If all the business logic is on the client, there tends to be a very large number of round trips (network send and receives) between the client and the server. Frequently, large chunks of raw data are sent to the client – quickly clogging the network and slowing down everyone else trying to get their own huge blocks of data back and forth.

Advantages	Disadvantages
Distributes the workload to a large number of relatively cheap clients.	Is a terrible bandwidth hog - clogs networks up very quickly.
If you have one user who needs more speed, you can purchase a faster system just for them rather than a large expensive host system that everyone is going to take a piece of.	Installations are time-consuming and difficult to coordinate. New software or versions of software must be installed on multiple machines. Version upgrades can be particularly problematic since old clients are not always compatible with the new server components and vice versa. All clients may have to be upgraded at one time which can create quite a serious logistics problem.
The same money that buys the computing power on the client side also buys power for other productivity applications such as word processing and spreadsheet applications.	

Server-Centric

This one still lives on the notion that computing power is cheaper in PCs than in host systems, but tries to gain some of the advantages of centralized systems. Only user services are distributed to the client. Only information that actually needs to be displayed on the screen is sent to the client. Business and data services remain at the server. Network bandwidth is far more host-system like.

Traditional Client/Server (Server-Centric)

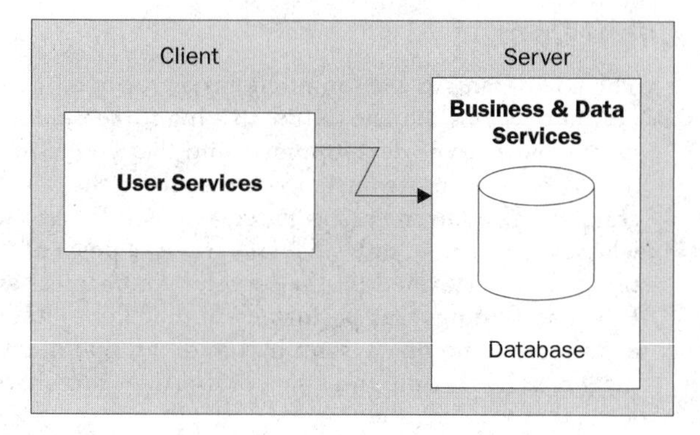

Advantages	Disadvantages
Some upgrades can be done entirely at the server level.	Other upgrades still require a "touch" on every client computer – upgrades and new installs are both very tedious and difficult logistically.
A large number of homogeneous products are available off-the-shelf – pre-made software is cheap.	Long-running and heavy-load jobs by one user affect all users.
Since only the information to be displayed is sent on the network, there is little network bandwidth comparatively to the client-centric model.	Large servers grow exponentially in price. Some are every bit as expensive as host systems.
	Though the model starts to look like a host system model, there is considerably more downtime.

Three-Tier

This model and the closely related one that follows (n-tier) are the hyped up architectures for the day. If you hear someone talking today about how everything needs to be done one way regardless of what it is – they are almost certainly talking **three-tier** or n-tier computing.

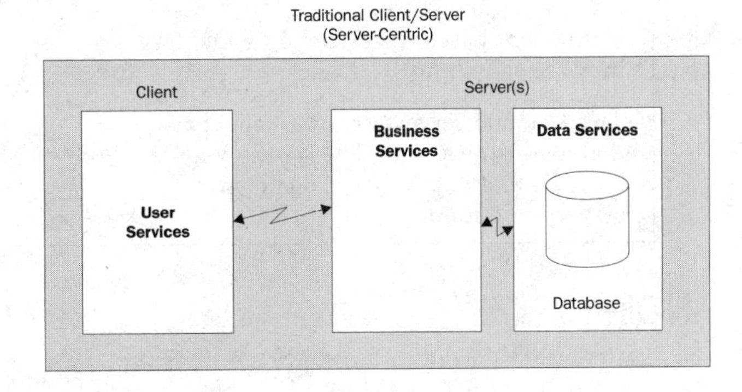

This model takes the approach of breaking up all three service levels into completely separate logical models. Clients are responsible for U/I issues only – just as they were under server-centric client/server. The difference is that the business and data services are logically separated from each other. In addition, this approach moves the logical model into a distinctly separate realm from the physical model. This means that they can run on the same server, but do not have to. This adds a significant level of stability and scalability since you can split the workload onto two (and, depending on how it's done, more) servers. In addition, this model has a tendency to be more extensible, since changes and additions affect smaller pieces of code (instead of one huge build of everything, you can just rebuild the affected components).

Since everything is component-based, you can, if you use DCOM, take an approach where you distribute the components over many servers. If you use Microsoft Transaction Server (MTS), you can even keep copies of the same component on multiple servers for load balancing.

Advantages	Disadvantages
Some upgrades can be done entirely at the server level.	Other upgrades still require a "touch" on every client computer – upgrades and new installs are both very tedious and difficult logistically.
An increasing number of homogeneous products are available off the shelf – pre-made software is cheap.	There is typically still considerably more down time than in a host system.
Since only the information to be displayed is sent on the network, there is little network bandwidth comparative to the client-centric model. The load may, however, be higher between the business-logic and data-services systems if they are on different servers.	
Allows for (actually encourages) component-based development which *can* increase reusability.	
Two medium servers are often cheaper than one large server. The separation of business and data services makes two servers an option.	

N-Tier

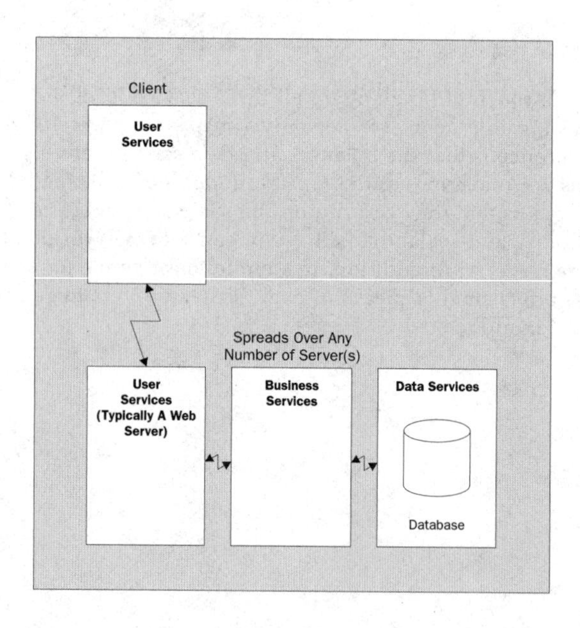

Essentially like 3-tier, and theoretically the best of all worlds. Frankly, I like this model a lot, but I still have to caution you about taking the "one size fits all" approach. This model gets serious about implementing what looks like a three-tier model logically, but instead breaks the components down to their smallest reasonable logical unit of work. If the data services layer is done properly, even the database can be spread across multiple servers and moved around as needed. The only impact is on the data services components that provide information to the moved data. The business services components are oblivious to the move (less re-development here folks!), since they only need to know the name of the data services component that supplies the data and what specific method to call.

Similarly, you can change U/I implementations fairly easily – you only need to redevelop the U/I. You still call the same business logic components regardless of what U/I (say, web vs true client?) you are using.

Advantages	Disadvantages
Even more upgrades can be done entirely at the server level.	Often increases the number of network connections (which are frequently the most slow and unreliable part of your system).
An increasing number of homogeneous products are available off-the-shelf – pre-made software is cheap.	There is typically still considerably more downtime than in a host system.
Since only the information to be displayed is sent on the network (rather than an entire, not yet filtered, dataset), there is little network bandwidth comparative to the client-centric model. The load may, however, be higher between the business-logic and data-services systems if they are on different servers.	
Allows for (actually encourages) component-based development which can increase reusability.	
Multiple medium servers are often cheaper than one large server. The separation of business and data services makes two servers an option.	

Data Access Models

Certainly one of the biggest issues to deal with these days is how to access your database within the various options in Microsoft's "Alphabet Soup" of **data access architectures**. Which models are available in what circumstances varies – depending primarily on the version of SQL Server, the choice and version of your programming language.

There are five different access models that Microsoft considers being up to date for accessing SQL Server. These include:

- **RDO**: **Remote Data Objects**. This is actually a very thin wrapper around ODBC. It was built specifically with VB in mind, but is also usable in J++. RDO is very, very easy to use in comparison to programming to the ODBC API directly, but doesn't lose all that much in the speed category.

  There is a ton of legacy code in place using this technology – it is fast and very reliable. That being said, I would recommend against using this technology for future development. It's OK to continue using it in legacy code where it already exists, but Microsoft – although still calling it current - picks no bones about the fact that they will not be investing any more research and development dollars into this model. As such, you have to figure that its days are numbered as far as active support goes (though the fact that so many legacy applications use it means that it may still be supported for some time to come).

- **ADO**: **ActiveX Data Objects**. The new RDO – or at least that's what Microsoft would like you to believe. Don't – ADO is its own animal. Each version (2.0 was the third version, and it's already obsolete) seems to improve performance and add new features, but ADO still can't be compared on a one-to-one basis to RDO. RDO had a few features that will never be in ADO. (ODBC handles, for example, can't be added because of OLE DB being in-between ADO and ODBC), and ADO has some really cool features with persistent recordsets, filters, sorts (without going back to the server), and others that RDO never had.

  Unlike RDO, which was based on ODBC, ADO is based on OLE DB. This provides a level of flexibility that ODBC alone can't offer, but it comes with more than just a few headaches. Note that ADO can still indirectly use ODBC for connectivity by using the OLE DB provider for ODBC.

  It's tough to take just a brief look at ADO, but since I have to, I'll say this much: ADO is now competitive, if not faster, in speed compared to RDO and has a very robust feature set. It is still nowhere near RDO in reliability as of writing this, but Microsoft has made and continues to make a substantial investment in ADO and OLE DB. This is where they are saying the future is, and I would suggest any new non-C++ based development use this access method (More for the C++ crowd shortly).

- **ODBC**: **Open Database Connectivity**. If you've been developing for any length of time at all (say, for more than a week?), you just about have to have heard of ODBC before. It is a Microsoft pushed standard, but it is most definitely a standard – and a very good one at that. ODBC provides a way of gaining cross-platform access to database information. It is quite fast (often as fast or faster than the native driver for your database) and allows you to use most of the mainstream standard SQL statements regardless of what the back-end expects for syntax. In short, ODBC is very cool. The major shortcoming for ODBC is that it is very much oriented to tabular data (columns and rows), and doesn't deal with non-standard data such as a directory structure or a multi-sheet database.

- **OLE DB**: The primary competitor to ODBC at this point, OLE DB is an attempt at having an open standard to communicate with both tabular and non-tabular data. OLE DB uses what is called a **provider**. A provider is a lot like an ODBC driver except that it is relatively self-describing. That is, it is able to tell the application which uses it what kind of functionality it supports. As mentioned earlier, OLE DB is the foundation under ADO. It is very fast indeed when not used with ADO (that extra layer adds some overhead), but, since it deals with a number of items that aren't compatible with VB, you'll typically only see OLE DB being used directly by C++ programmers. It is far more of a pain to program in than ADO, but it is much faster by itself than when used in conjunction with ADO. If you're a non-C++ programmer, stick with ADO at this point, but, if you're a C++ programmer, you're going to need to figure out whether or not the speed is worth the hassle
- **Java Database Connectivity (JDBC)**: OK, so I said there were five, and there are, but I have to say that JDBC is still something of an outcast at this point. This is being used primarily in the web arena and by non-Microsoft users. The last time I saw much of anything done with it, it was fairly simple to use, but had very little functionality and was very slow. In short – unless for some reason you absolutely have to, don't go there.

- In addition to these current object models, there are a few others that you may run across and should know:

- **DB-Lib**: Prior to version 7.0, this was the native way in which SQL Server did all of its talking between the main host and client and utility applications (SQL Server now uses OLE DB natively in this role). It is still actively supported, but will only be enhanced to the extent necessary to maintain backward compatibility as SQL Server moves forward. Microsoft has said that they will pull support for this access method at some point in the future, but they also acknowledge that there are too many legacy applications out there using DB-Lib to figure on dropping support for it anytime soon.
- **VB-SQL**: This was only briefly available, but still found its way into several applications. This was based on an old wrapper that was written for VB to make many DB-Lib functions available for VB programmers.

  If you're still using VB-SQL, move off it as soon as possible. It is slow and, if it breaks, you'll get no help with it.
- **DAO: Data Access Objects**. This is actually native to Microsoft Access (more specifically, the Jet database which is at the heart of Access. There are a lot of applications written in VB and Access that use this technology – too bad. This object model can be considered clunky, slow, and just plain outdated (believe me, I'm being nice and not saying what I really think). It's still the fastest way to access things if you're using a JET (Access) database, but if you're using this technology to access SQL Server, I would suggest putting some serious effort into migrating away from it as soon as possible. Microsoft was calling DAO a "Legacy" model more than a year before the end of the Office '97 lifecycle. They want people to stop using it, and I have to agree with them.

There are several books out there on accessing SQL Server and the data access side of the database relationship – I'm going to leave you to look through those for more information, but I will recommend that you check out Bill Vaughn's *The Hitchhikers Guide To Visual Basic And SQL Server*. It is the relative bible of the connectivity side of Visual Basic programming. Another source you may want to check out is *Professional Visual Basic 6 Databases* from Wrox Press. There really isn't nearly as dominant a book for the C++ crowd, so I'll leave you to your own devices if you're looking for the C++ variety of book.

Microsoft Certification

Microsoft has three SQL Server related exams that participate in different certifications which Microsoft offers. These include exams on **development**, **administration**, and **data warehousing**.

Each of these exams has some relevance to the MCP, MCSD, MCDBA & MCSE certifications. Indeed, the development and administration exams are core to the MCDBA certification process.

This book was not purposely written to address any Microsoft exam – it is focused on trying to successfully prepare you to develop applications using SQL Server 7.0. That being said, the 70-029 (development) exam was written to try and test to see if you are ready to do just that – develop and implement applications using SQL Server 7.0 - most everything I can think of that's covered in the exam is addressed somewhere in this book.

I am not going to tell you that if you read this book you will pass that exam. I participated in the authoring of that exam, and I have had to take it myself – it is one seriously nasty exam. Still, the topics covered in this book happen to speak right to the heart of the exam – if you do well going through this book, the odds are you'll do just fine on the exam (sorry folks, this isn't exam cram, so no guarantees on that!).

Summary

Well, we've gotten a start and talked briefly about where the database world has been, database access, who the book is for, and a few other miscellaneous items. These are really just conducting some bookkeeping and prep to get you seriously ready to go.

In our next few chapters, we're going to take a deeper look into many of the basics of building and making use of a SQL Server database. I strongly encourage you to run through the many examples in this book. As I mentioned earlier, there are very few concepts in this book that do not have specific examples associated with them – take advantage of that and you'll be taking full advantage of this book.

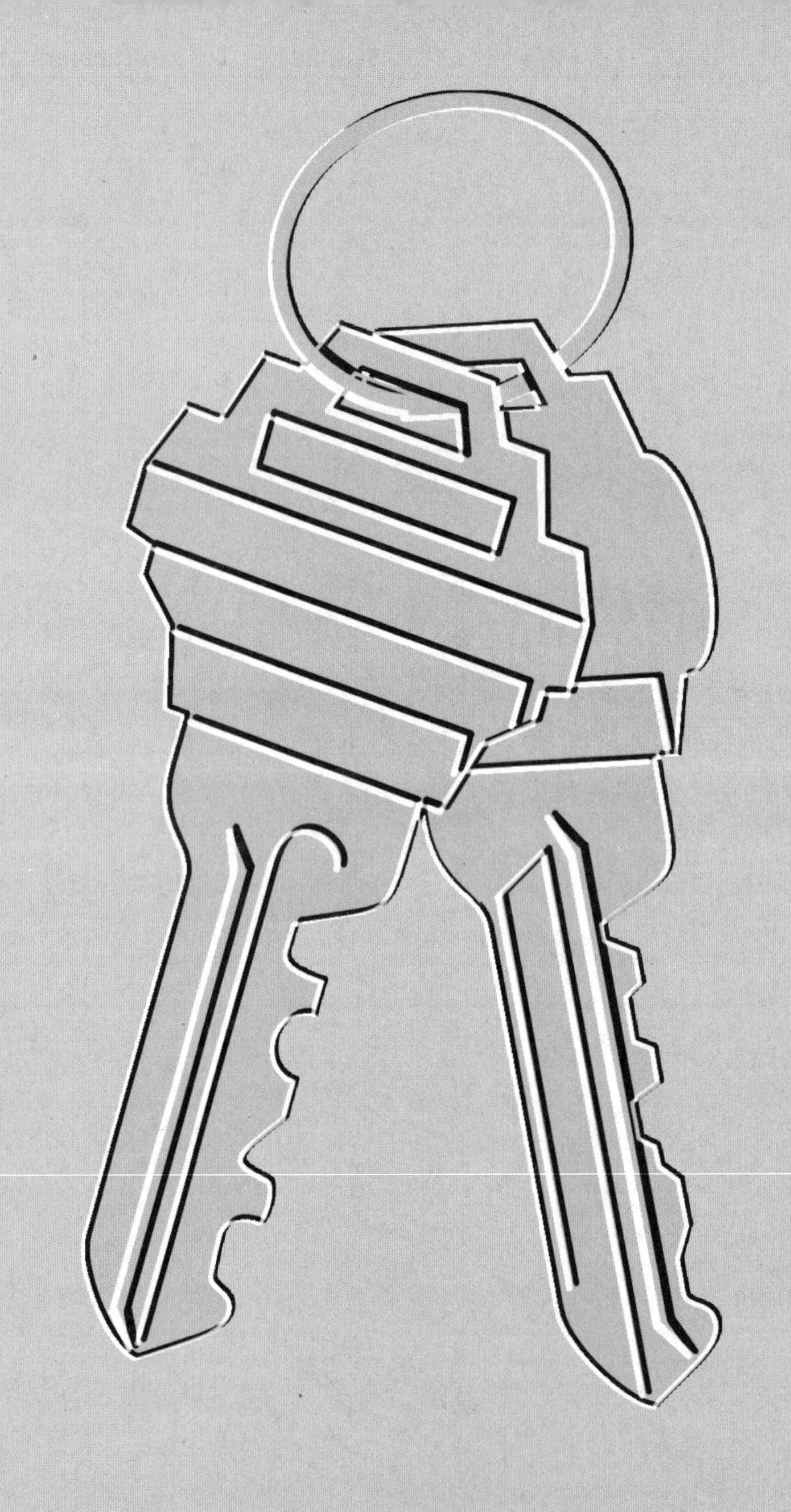

2

RDBMS Basics: What Makes Up a SQL Server Database?

What makes up a database? Data for sure (what use is a database that doesn't store anything?), but in a **Relational Database Management System** (**RDBMS**), it is actually much more. Today's advanced RDBMS systems not only store your data, they also manage that data for you - restricting what kind of data can go into the system, and also facilitating getting data out of the system. If all you wanted was to tuck the data away somewhere safe, you could use just about any system. RDBMS systems allow you to go beyond the storage of the data into the realm of defining what that data should look like, or the **business rules** of the data.

Don't confuse what I'm calling the "business rules of data" as being the more generalized business rules that drive your entire system (e.g. someone can't see anything until they've logged on, or automatically adjusting the current period in an accounting system on the first of the month). Those types of rules can be enforced at virtually any level of the system (these days, it's usually in the middle tier of a n-tier system). Instead, what we're talking about here are the business rules that specifically relate to the data, such as that you can't have a negative order. With an RDBMS, we can incorporate these rules right into the integrity of the database itself.

This chapter will provide an overview to the rest of the book. Everything discussed in this chapter will be covered again in later chapters, but this chapter is intended to provide you with a roadmap or plan to bear in mind as we progress through the book. Therefore, in this chapter, we will take a high-level look into:

- Database objects
- Data types
- Other database concepts that ensure data integrity

An Overview of Database Objects

An RDBMS such as SQL Server contains many **objects**. Object purists out there may quibble with whether Microsoft's choices of what to call an object (and what not to) actually meets the normal definition of an object, but, for SQL Server's purposes, the list of database objects can be said to contain:

- The database itself
- The log
- Tables
- Filegroups
- Diagrams
- Views
- Stored procedures
- Users
- Roles
- Rules
- Defaults
- User-defined data types
- Full-text catalogs

The Database Object

The database is effectively the highest-level object that you can refer to within a given SQL Server (technically speaking, the server itself can be considered to be an object). Most, but not all, other objects in a SQL Server are children of the database object.

> *If you are already familiar with SQL Server you may now be saying, "What? What happened to logins? What happened to Remote Servers and SQL Executive Tasks?" SQL Server has several other objects (as listed above) that exist on the periphery of the database. With the exception of linked servers, and perhaps DTS packages, these are primarily the domain of the database administrator (they are programmable via something called the SQL Distributed Management Objects (SQL-DMO) object model, but are usually set up manually), and as such, we generally do not give them significant thought during the design and programming processes.*

A database is typically a group of at least a set of table objects and, more often than not, other objects (such as stored procedures and views) that pertain to the particular grouping of data that is stored in the tables of that database.

What types of tables do we store in just one database and what in a separate database? We'll discuss that in some detail later in the book, but for now we'll take the simple approach of saying that any data that is generally thought of as belonging to just one system, or is significantly related, will be stored in a single database. An RDBMS such as SQL Server may have multiple databases on just one server, or it may have only one. How many will reside on one SQL Server will depend on such factors as capacity (CPU power, disk I/O limitations, memory, etc.), autonomy (you want one person to have management rights to the server this system is running on, and someone else to have admin rights to a different server), or just how many databases your company has. Many servers only have one production database, others may have many.

When you first load SQL Server, you begin with six databases installed by default:

- `master`
- `model`
- `msdb`
- `tempdb`
- `pubs`
- `Northwind`

Some of them have to be there or your SQL Server won't run. Others are there to give you sample databases to work with. Let's look at these one by one.

The master Database

Every SQL Server, regardless of version or custom modifications, has the **master** database. This database holds a special set of tables (system tables) that keep track of the system as a whole. For example, when you create a new database on the server, an entry is placed in the `sysobjects` table in the `master` database. All extended stored procedures, regardless of what database they are intended for use with, are stored in this database. Obviously, since almost everything that describes your server is stored in here, this database is critical to your system and cannot be deleted.

The `master` database can be, in a pinch, extremely useful. It can allow you to determine whether certain objects exist already before you perform operations on them. For example, if you try to create a table that already exists in the database, you will get an error. If you want to force the issue, you could test to see whether the table already has an entry in `sysobjects`. If it does, then you would delete that table before re-creating it.

> **If you're quite cavalier, you may be saying to yourself, "Cool, I can't wait to mess around in there!"** ***Don't go there!*** **Using the system tables in any form is fraught with peril. Microsoft has recommended against using the system tables for at least the last two versions of SQL Server. They make absolutely no guarantees about compatibility in the `master` database between versions - indeed, they virtually guarantee that they will change. The worst offense comes when performing updates on objects in the `master` database. Trust me when I tell you that altering these tables in any way is asking for a SQL Server that no longer functions.**
>
> **All that said, there are still times where nothing else will do. We will discuss a few situations where you can't avoid using the system tables, but in general, you should consider them to be evil cannibals from another tribe and best left alone.**

The model Database

The `model` database is aptly named, in the sense that it's the model on which a copy can be based. The `model` database forms a template for any new database that you create. This means that you can, if you wish, alter the `model` database if you want to change what the standard, newly created database looks like. For example, you could add a set of audit tables that you include in every database you build. You could also include a few user groups that would be cloned into every new database that was created on the system. Note that, since this database serves as the template for any other database, it is a required database and must be left on the system – you cannot delete it.

There are several things to keep in mind when altering the `model` database. First, any database you create has to be at least as large as the `model` database. That means that if you alter the `model` database to be 100MB in size, you can't have any database be smaller than 100MB. There are several other similar pitfalls. As such, for 99.99% of installations, I strongly recommend leaving this one alone.

The msdb Database

Up until now, the databases that were installed along with SQL Server were required - if you delete `master` or `model` your system will fail. `msdb` is different.

`msdb` is where the **SQL Agent** process and task manager stores any system tasks. If you schedule backups to be run on a database nightly, then there is an entry in `msdb`. Schedule a stored procedure for one time execution - yes, it has an entry in `msdb`. `msdb` can, however, be deleted and not cause a complete system crash. You will lose any of your scheduled task entries though, and will not be able to use SQL Agent.

If you remove it and then decide that you want to re-install it, good luck. The one time I had to re-install it, it messed my server up pretty well (can you say, "Complete Reload?"). In short, while you can remove this, I would strongly suggest you don't.

The tempdb Database

`tempdb` is one of the key working areas for your server. Whenever you issue a complex query that SQL Server needs to build interim tables to solve – it does so in `tempdb`. Whenever you create a temporary table of your own – it is created in `tempdb` (even though you think you're creating it in the current database). Whenever you create quite a wide variety of situations where data needs to be stored temporarily, the data is probably stored in `tempdb`.

`tempdb` is very different from any other database in that, not only are the objects within it temporary, the database itself is temporary. It has the distinction of being the only database in your system that is completely rebuilt from scratch every time you start your SQL Server.

Technically speaking, you can actually create objects yourself in `tempdb` – I strongly recommend against this practice. You can create temporary objects from within any database you have access to in your system – they will be stored in `tempdb`. Creating objects directly in `tempdb` gains you nothing, but adds the confusion of referring to things across databases. This is another of those, "Don't go there!" kind of things.

The pubs Database

Ahhhh pubs! It's almost like an old friend. pubs is now installed mostly to support training articles and books like this. pubs has absolutely nothing to do with the operation of SQL Server. It is merely there to provide a consistent place for your training and experimentation. We will make use of pubs occasionally in this book.

pubs can be deleted with no significant consequences. Indeed, many database administrators delete it from their production database servers. Since it takes up such a small amount of space, I usually leave it. (It comes in quite handy for doing small proof of concept experiments. These are better done on a non-production server, but the production server is often the only server, particularly in small shops.)

This brings up the point of test databases. If possible, you really want to have a complete copy of your database available to serve as nothing more than a test bed for making changes or working on new procedures before you try them in the "live" database.

The Northwind Database

If your past programming experience has involved Access or Visual Basic, then you are probably already somewhat familiar with the Northwind database. Northwind is new to SQL Server with version 7.0. It is, like pubs, a training database. The advantage of Northwind is that it is significantly more complex than pubs. That means that you can explore SQL Server more fully than with pubs. This turns out to be something of a good news/bad news story. It's a much better training ground, but it also takes up more space. Still, by default, it only takes up about 4MB for both the database and the log, so in this age of cheap hard drives, I usually leave it in place. The Northwind database will serve as one of the major testing grounds for this book

The Transaction Log

Believe it or not, the database file itself isn't where most things happen. While the data is certainly read in from there, any changes you make don't initially go to the database itself – instead, they are written serially to the **transaction log**. At some later point in time, the database is issued a **checkpoint** – it is at that point in time that all the changes in the log are propagated to the actual database file.

The database is in a random access arrangement, but the log is serial in nature. While the random nature of the database file allows for speedy access, the serial nature of the log allows things to be tracked in the proper order. The log accumulates changes that are deemed as having been committed, and then writes several of them to the database file at a time.

We'll take a much closer look at how things are logged in our chapter on transactions and locking, but for now, remember that the log is the first place on disk that the data goes, and it is only propagated to the actual database at a later time – you need both files in order to have a functional database.

The Most Basic Database Object - Table

Databases are made up of many things, but none are more central to the makeup of a database than tables. A table can be thought of as equating to an accountant's ledger or an Excel spreadsheet. It is made up of what is called **domain** data (columns) and **entity** data (rows). The actual data for the database is stored in the tables.

Each table definition contains the **meta data** (descriptive information about data) that describes the nature of the data it is to contain. Each column has its own set of rules about what can be stored in that column. A violation of the rules of any one column can cause the system to reject an inserted row or an update to an existing row, or prevent the deletion of a row.

Let's take a look at the `publishers` table in the `pubs` database:

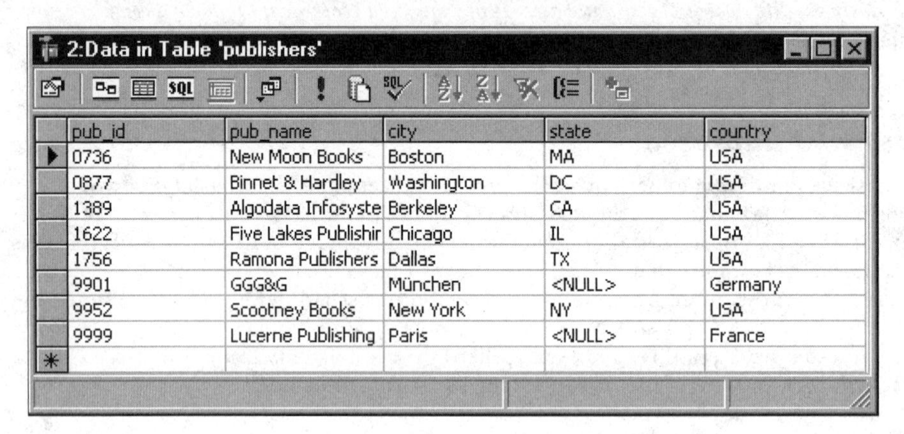

2:Data in Table 'publishers'

pub_id	pub_name	city	state	country
0736	New Moon Books	Boston	MA	USA
0877	Binnet & Hardley	Washington	DC	USA
1389	Algodata Infosyste	Berkeley	CA	USA
1622	Five Lakes Publishir	Chicago	IL	USA
1756	Ramona Publishers	Dallas	TX	USA
9901	GGG&G	München	<NULL>	Germany
9952	Scootney Books	New York	NY	USA
9999	Lucerne Publishing	Paris	<NULL>	France

This table is made up of five columns of data. The number of columns remains constant regardless of how much data (even zero) is in the table. Currently, the table has eight records. This will go up and down as we add or delete data, but the nature of the data in each record (or row) will be described and restricted by the **data type** of the column. Let's look at the definition for this table:

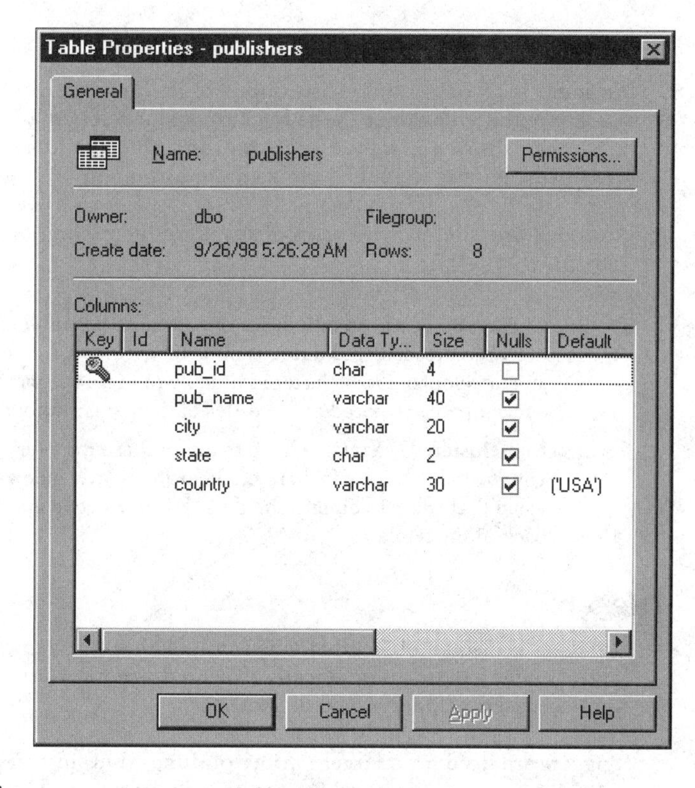

Working from left to right, we can tell:

- Whether a column is part of the **primary key** for the table
- Whether it is an **IDENTITY** column
- The column's name
- The data type for the column
- The size in bytes that the column takes up
- Whether the column allows NULL values or not
- Whether the column has a default value (in case one isn't provided during an insert)

We will discuss the meaning of each of these and the other column choices in Chapter 6.

I'm going to take this as my first opportunity to launch into a diatribe on the naming of objects in SQL Server 7.0. New to this version is the ability to embed spaces in names, and in some cases, to use keywords as names. Resist the temptation to do this! Columns with embedded spaces in their name have nice headers when you make a `SELECT` statement, but there are other ways to achieve the same result. Using embedded spaces and keywords for column names is literally begging for bugs, confusion and other disasters. I'll discuss later why Microsoft has elected to allow this, but for now, just remember to associate embedded spaces or keywords in names with evil empires, torture and certain death. (This won't be the last time you hear from me on this one.)

Indexes

An **index** is an object that exists only within the framework of a particular table. An index works much like the index does in the back of an encyclopedia – there is some sort of lookup (or "key") value that is sorted in a particular way, and, once you have that, you are provided with another key which you can use to lookup the actual information you were after.

An index provides us with ways of speeding the lookup of our information. Indexes fall into two categories:

- **Clustered** – You can only have one of these per table. If an index is clustered, then that means that the table the clustered index is on is physically sorted according to that index. If you were indexing an encyclopedia, the clustered index would be the page numbers; the information in the encyclopedia is stored in the order of the page numbers.
- **Non-clustered** – You can have many of these for every table. This is more along the lines of what you probably think of when you hear the word "index". This kind of index points to some other value that will let you find the data. For our encyclopedia, this would be the keyword index at the back of the book.

Triggers

A **trigger** is also an object that exists only within the framework of a table. Triggers are pieces of logical code that are automatically executed when certain things happen to your table (you decide between inserts, updates, and deletes).

Triggers are used for a larger variety of things, but, in general, these all boil down to either copying data as it is entered or checking the change over to make sure that it meets some criteria.

Constraints

A **constraint** is yet another object that only exists within the confines of a table. Constraints are much like they sound – they confine the data in your table to meeting certain conditions. Constraints, in a way, compete with triggers as possible solutions to data integrity issues. They are not, however, the same thing – each has its own distinct advantages.

Filegroups

Filegroups are probably the closest thing that version 7 has to previous versions' concepts of devices and segments. By default, all your tables and everything else about your database (except the log) are stored in a single file. That file is a member of what's called the **primary filegroup**. However, you are not stuck with this arrangement.

SQL Server allows you to define a virtually unlimited number of **secondary files**. These secondary files can be made part of the primary filegroup or a secondary filegroup. While there is only one primary filegroup (and it is actually called "Primary"), you can have any number of **secondary filegroups**. A secondary filegroup is created the first time that you reference it in a `CREATE TABLE` command (we'll learn how to use this command in a later chapter) – you can then place multiple files within that group. If you don't specify a particular file or filegroup, then your table or index will be automatically placed in whatever filegroup has been designated as the **default filegroup** (unless you change this, it will be the Primary).

If you worked with SQL Server 6.5 devices, but didn't use multiple devices in one database, you may be saying something like, "Hey, we got rid of devices – Hallelujah! Why would we need anything similar to those?" If only it were as simple as that.

Devices were indeed a rather nasty pain in the neck for perhaps 95% or more of all installations. For the other 5% or so, they were a saving grace. Devices allowed you to break up the database onto multiple physical devices – to spread out the I/O loading and improve performance. With 7.0, we now use files – which are generally easier to manage, but filegroups give us the ability to group together our files for administrative purposes – it means that we can easily back up an entire group rather than one file at a time. In short, they are here to make our lives easier – honest!

Diagrams

The ability to make database diagrams is new to SQL Server 7.0. We will discuss database diagramming in some detail when we discuss normalization and database design, but for now, suffice to say that a database diagram is a visual representation of the database design, including the various tables, the column names in each table, and the relationships between tables. Prior to this version, you had very few choices in making what's referred to as an **entity-relationship** (or ER) diagram. In an ER diagram the database is divided into two parts - entities (such as "supplier" and "product") and relations (such as "supplies", "purchases").

One could say that we still have few choices in making ER diagrams. The database design tools that are part of Enterprise Manager (EM) in SQL Server 7.0 are considered sparse by those of us who are fortunate enough to work with a more serious database design tool. Indeed, the diagramming methodology the tools use does not adhere to any of the accepted standards in ER diagramming.

Still, the new diagramming tools, or the "da Vinci Tools" as they are known within Microsoft, are light years ahead of what we had in version 6.5 – which is to say that we didn't have anything. I have had jobs were I would have killed for anything as much as the da Vinci tools provide, still, if you're doing any serious design work, I strongly suggest paying for a more serious ER diagramming tool.

Below is a diagram that shows the various tables that make up the `Northwind` database. The diagram also describes many other properties about the database. Notice the tiny icons for keys and the infinity sign. These depict the nature of the relationship between two tables. We'll talk about relationships extensively in Chapters 6 and 7 and we'll look further into diagrams later in the book.

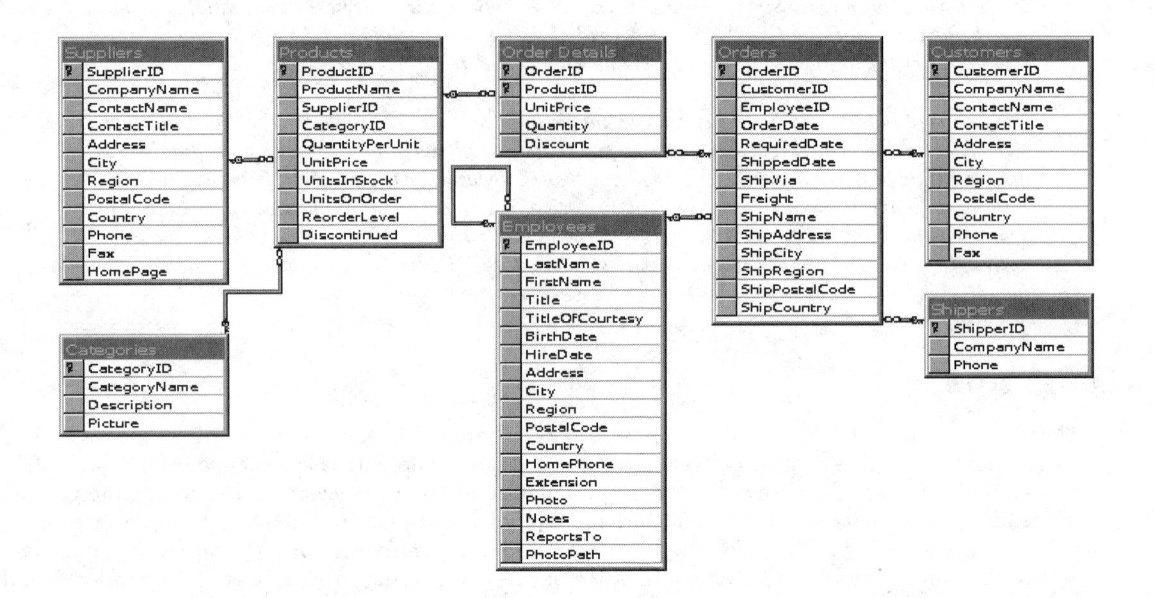

Views

A view is something of a virtual table. A view, for the most part, is used just like a table, except that it doesn't contain any data itself. Instead, a view is merely a preplanned mapping and representation of the data stored in tables. The plan is stored in the database in the form of a query. This query calls for data from some columns (but not necessarily all columns) to be retrieved from one or more tables. The data retrieved may or may not (depending on the view definition) have to meet special criteria in order to be shown as data in that view.

The purpose of views is to control what the user of the view sees. This has two major impacts - security and ease of use. With views you can control what the users see, if there is a section of a table that should be accessed by only a few users (e.g. salary details), you can create a view that includes only those columns to which everyone is allowed access. In addition, the view can be tailored so that the user does not have to search through any unneeded information.

Stored Procedures

Stored procedures (or **sprocs**) are the bread and butter of programmatic functionality in SQL Server. Stored procedures are an ordered series of Transact-SQL (the language used to query Microsoft SQL Server) statements bundled up into a single logical unit. They allow for variables and parameters as well as selection and looping constructs. Sprocs offer several advantages over just sending all the code to the server in the sense that they:

- Are referred to using short names, rather than a long string of text, therefore less network traffic is required in order to run the code within the sproc
- Are pre-optimized and pre-compiled, saving a small amount of time each time the sproc is run
- Can be called from other sprocs, thus making them reusable in a somewhat limited sense

In short, sprocs are the closest things that SQL Server has to a "program".

There has been something of a trend in recent years to "avoid sprocs at all costs!" This has been brought about by the popularity of 3- and n-tier architectures, and a move towards portability. I have to say that I disagree with this point of view.

Many developers erroneously believe that they should just pass through raw SQL to the server, that way it won't matter what the server is as long as it is ANSI (American National Standards Institute) compliant - and all major RDBMSs are. Good n-tier development says that your data layer should insulate the middle tier(s) from the actual implementation of the database. This is certainly true and doing so limits, for the most part, the risks involved with moving to a new platform to just the data layer. However, this can be done with a component approach. You should create a component that knows how to get the most out of your back-end. For SQL Server, that way is by using sprocs.

N-tier purists may scowl nastily at me for saying so, but you're nuts if you don't use every reasonable optimization available to whatever backend you choose – regardless of what back-end that is. If you're building an n-tier system, you should build your middle tier(s) to talk to a data tier. This lets the data tier know the best way to talk to the database. You'll get a faster performing system, and the only thing that will have to be developed if you change back-ends (or decide to support more than one) is just the data components.

Users and Roles

These two go hand in hand. Prior to SQL Server 7.0, their equivalents were referred to as logins and groups, but they were not exactly the same as their current version counterparts. **Users** are pretty much the equivalent of logins. In short, this object represents an identifier for someone to login into the SQL Server. Anyone logging into SQL Server has to map (directly or indirectly depending on the security model you're using) to a user. Users, in turn, belong to one or more **roles**. Rights to perform certain actions in SQL Server can then be granted either directly to a user or to a role to which that one or more users belong.

If you are familiar with the NT security arena, you may be noticing that the new format has a striking resemblance to NT groups – this is not by accident. Microsoft is making a serious effort to increase the security compatibility within the BackOffice suite of products. The new roles concept in SQL Server moves solidly into the NT camp in the way that it's implemented. Perhaps the nicest side though is that they actually made things both simpler and more flexible in the process.

Rules

Rules and constraints provide restriction information on what can go into a table. If an updated or inserted record violates a rule, then that insertion or update will be rejected. In addition, a rule can be used to define a restriction on a **user-defined data type**. (Unlike rules, constraints are not really an object unto themselves, but rather a piece of metadata describing a particular table.)

Defaults

There are two types of defaults. The default that is an object unto itself, and the default that is not really an object, but rather metadata describing a particular column in a table. They both serve the same purpose. If, when inserting a record, you don't provide the value of a column and that column has a default defined, then a value will be inserted automatically as defined in the default.

User-Defined Data Types

User-defined data types are extensions to the system-defined data types. You can take a system-defined data type, such as integer, and bind a rule to it. For example, you could create a rule that states that a value must be greater than 5000, bind that rule to a user-defined data type built using an integer, and you would wind up with a data type that automatically ensures that any column where that data type is used will always have a value greater than 5000.

User-defined data types are limited in scope to just the database in which they are created.

> **This is one of those odd areas where it can actually make sense to modify the `model` database. If your development group has a data type that they use consistently across all their databases, then you could create the user-defined data type in the `model` database of all the servers you want to ensure have this data type. The data type would then be automatically added to any new database you created.**

Full-Text Catalogs

These are mappings of data that speed the search for specific blocks of text within columns that have had full-text searching enabled. While these objects are tied at the hip to the tables and columns that they map, they are separate objects, and are therefore not automatically updated when changes happen to the database.

SQL Server Data Types

Now that you're familiar with the base objects of a SQL Server database, let's take a look at the options that SQL Server has for one of the fundamental items of any environment that handles data - data types. Note that, since this book is intended for developers, and that no developer could survive for 60 seconds without an understanding of data types, I'm going to assume that you already know how data types work, and just need to know the particulars of SQL Server data types.

SQL Server has the following intrinsic data types:

Data Type Name	Class	Size in Bytes	Nature of the Data
`Bit`	Integer	1	The size is somewhat misleading. The first `bit` data type in a table takes up 1 byte; the next seven make use of the same byte. Allows nulls for the first time in SQL Server 7.0, although allowing nulls causes an additional byte to be used.
`Int`	Integer	4	Whole numbers from -2,147,483,648 to 2,147,483,647.
`SmallInt`	Integer	2	Whole numbers from -32,768 to 32,767.
`TinyInt`	Integer	1	Whole numbers from 0 to 255.
`Decimal` or `Numeric`	Decimal/ Numeric	Varies	Fixed precision and scale from $-10^{38}-1$ to $10^{38}-1$. The two names are synonymous.
`Money`	Money	8	Monetary units from -2^{63} to 2^{63} plus precision to four decimal places. Note that this could be any monetary unit, not just dollars. While you still can't use commas when entering data into a money field, the values returned from a money field will be formatted with whatever separators (such as a comma) are specified by the language and local information for the server.
`SmallMoney`	Money	4	Monetary units from -214,748.3648 through +214,748.3647.
`Float` (also a synonym for ANSI `Real`)	Approximate Numerics	Varies	Accepts an argument (e.g. `Float(20)`) that determines size and precision. Note that the argument is in bits, not bytes. Ranges from -1.79E + 308 to 1.79E + 308.

Table Continued on Following Page

Data Type Name	Class	Size in Bytes	Nature of the Data
`DateTime`	Date/Time	8	Date and time data from January 1, 1753 to December 31, 9999 with an accuracy of three-hundredths of a second. Allows nulls for the first time in SQL Server 7.0.
`SmallDateTime`	Date/Time	4	Date and time data from January 1, 1900, through June 6, 2079, with an accuracy of one minute.
`Cursor`	Special Numeric	1	Pointer to a cursor.
`Timestamp`	Special Numeric	8	Special value that is unique within a given database. Value is set by the database itself automatically every time the record is either inserted or updated – even if the timestamp column wasn't referred to by the `UPDATE` statement.
`UniqueIdentifier`	Special Numeric	16	Special Globally Unique Identifier. Is guaranteed to be unique across space and time.
`Char`	Character	Varies	Fixed length character data. Values shorter than the set length are padded with spaces to the set length. Data is non-Unicode. Maximum length is 8,000.
`VarChar`	Character	Varies	Variable length character data. Values are not padded with spaces. Data is non-Unicode. Maximum length is 8,000 characters.
`Text`	Character	Varies	Maximum length is 2,147,483,647 characters. Data is non-Unicode. Space is allocated in 8K pages.
`NChar`	Unicode	Varies	Fixed length Unicode character data. Values shorter than the set length are padded with spaces. Maximum length is 4,000 characters.

Data Type Name	Class	Size in Bytes	Nature of the Data
`NVarChar`	Unicode	Varies	Variable length Unicode character data. Values are not padded. Maximum length is 4,000 characters.
`Ntext`	Unicode	Varies	Variable length Unicode character data, maximum of 1,073,741,823 characters. Data is allocated in 8K pages.
`Binary`	Binary	Varies	Fixed-length binary data with a maximum length of 8,000 bytes.
`VarBinary`	Binary	Varies	Variable-length binary data with a maximum length of 8,000 bytes.
`Image`	Binary	Varies	Variable-length binary data with a maximum length of 2^{31} - 1 (2,147,483,647) bytes. Data is allocated in 8K pages. Don't confuse this with the word "image" as used in a picture. While pictures could be stored in an image field, so can any other binary data, or even text data – it's an all purpose kind of data type but has huge overhead.

Most of these have equivalent data types in other programming languages. For example, an `int` in SQL Server is equivalent to a `Long` in Visual Basic, and for most systems and compiler combinations in C++, is equivalent to an `int`.

In general, SQL Server data types work much as you would expect given experience in most other modern programming languages. Adding numbers yields you a sum, but adding strings concatenates them. When you mix the usage or assignment of variables or fields of different data types, there are a number of types that convert implicitly (or automatically). Most other types can be converted explicitly (you specifically say what type you want to convert to). A few cannot be converted between at all. Below is a chart that shows the various possible conversions:

From: \ To:	binary	varbinary	char	varchar	nchar	nvarchar	datetime	smalldatetime	decimal	numeric	float	real	int(INT4)	smallint(INT2)	tinyint(INT1)	money	smallmoney	bit	timestamp	uniqueidentifier	image	ntext	text
binary		◐	◐	◐	◐	◐	◐	◐	◐	◐	○	○	◐	◐	◐	◐	◐	◐	◐	◐	◐	○	○
varbinary	◐		◐	◐	◐	◐	◐	◐	◐	◐	○	○	◐	◐	◐	◐	◐	◐	◐	◐	◐	○	○
char	●	●		◐	◐	◐	◐	◐	◐	◐	◐	◐	◐	◐	◐	●	●	◐	●	◐	◐	◐	◐
varchar	●	●	◐		◐	◐	◐	◐	◐	◐	◐	◐	◐	◐	◐	●	●	◐	●	◐	◐	◐	◐
nchar	●	●	◐	◐		◐	◐	◐	◐	◐	◐	◐	◐	◐	◐	●	●	◐	●	◐	○	◐	◐
nvarchar	●	●	◐	◐	◐		◐	◐	◐	◐	◐	◐	◐	◐	◐	●	●	◐	●	◐	○	◐	◐
datetime	●	●	◐	◐	◐	◐		◐	●	●	●	●	●	●	●	●	●	●	●	○	○	○	○
smalldatetime	●	●	◐	◐	◐	◐	◐		●	●	●	●	●	●	●	●	●	●	●	○	○	○	○
decimal	◐	◐	◐	◐	◐	◐	◐	◐	*	*	◐	◐	◐	◐	◐	◐	◐	◐	◐	○	○	○	○
numeric	◐	◐	◐	◐	◐	◐	◐	◐	*	*	◐	◐	◐	◐	◐	◐	◐	◐	◐	○	○	○	○
float	◐	◐	◐	◐	◐	◐	◐	◐	◐	◐		◐	◐	◐	◐	◐	◐	◐	○	○	○	○	○
real	◐	◐	◐	◐	◐	◐	◐	◐	◐	◐	◐		◐	◐	◐	◐	◐	◐	○	○	○	○	○
int(INT4)	◐	◐	◐	◐	◐	◐	◐	◐	◐	◐	◐	◐		◐	◐	◐	◐	◐	◐	○	○	○	○
smallint(INT2)	◐	◐	◐	◐	◐	◐	◐	◐	◐	◐	◐	◐	◐		◐	◐	◐	◐	◐	○	○	○	○
tinyint(INT1)	◐	◐	◐	◐	◐	◐	◐	◐	◐	◐	◐	◐	◐	◐		◐	◐	◐	◐	○	○	○	○
money	◐	◐	●	●	●	●	◐	◐	◐	◐	◐	◐	◐	◐	◐		◐	◐	◐	○	○	○	○
smallmoney	◐	◐	●	●	●	●	◐	◐	◐	◐	◐	◐	◐	◐	◐	◐		◐	◐	○	○	○	○
bit	◐	◐	◐	◐	◐	◐	◐	◐	◐	◐	◐	◐	◐	◐	◐	◐	◐		◐	○	○	○	○
timestamp	◐	◐	◐	◐	○	○	◐	◐	◐	◐	○	○	◐	◐	◐	◐	◐	◐		○	◐	○	○
uniqueidentifier	◐	◐	◐	◐	◐	◐	○	○	○	○	○	○	○	○	○	○	○	○	○		○	○	○
image	◐	◐	○	○	○	○	○	○	○	○	○	○	○	○	○	○	○	○	◐	○		○	○
ntext	○	○	●	●	◐	◐	○	○	○	○	○	○	○	○	○	○	○	○	○	○	○		○
text	○	○	◐	◐	●	●	○	○	○	○	○	○	○	○	○	○	○	○	○	○	○	○	

● Explicit Conversion

◐ Implicit Conversion

○ Conversion not allowed

* Requires CONVERT when loss of precision or scale will occur

Why would we have to convert a data type? Well, let's try a simple example. If I wanted to output the phrase, "Today's date is ##/##/####", where ##/##/#### is the current date, I could write it like this:

```
SELECT "Today's date is " + GETDATE()
```

We will discuss Transact-SQL statements such as this in much greater detail later in the book, but the expected results of the above example should be fairly obvious to you.

The problem is that this statement would yield the following result:

```
Server: Msg 241, Level 16, State 1, Line 1
Syntax error converting datetime from character string.
```

Not exactly what we were after, is it? Now let's try it with the `CONVERT()` function:

```
SELECT "Today's date is " + CONVERT(varchar(12), GETDATE(),101)
```

This yields something like:

```
-----------------------------------
Today's date is 01/01/1999

(1 row(s) affected)
```

Date and time data types (such as the output of the `GETDATE()` function) are not implicitly convertible to a string data type (such as `"Today's date is "`), yet we run into these conversions on a regular basis. Fortunately, the `CONVERT()` function allows us to convert between many SQL Server data types. We will discuss the `CONVERT()` function more in a later chapter.

In short, data types in SQL Server perform much the same function that they do in other programming environments. They help prevent programming bugs by ensuring that the data supplied is of the same nature (remember 1/1/1980 means something different as a date than as a number) that the data is supposed to be and ensures that the kind of operation performed is what you expect.

NULL Data

What if you have a row where you don't have any data for a particular column - that is, what if you simply don't know the value? For example, let's say that we have a record that is trying to store the company performance information for a given year. Now, imagine that one of the fields is a percentage growth over the prior year, but you don't have records for the year before the first record in your database. You might be tempted to just enter a zero in the `PercentGrowth` column. Would that provide the right information though? People who didn't know better might think that it meant you had zero percent growth, when the fact is that you simply don't know the value for that year.

Values that are indeterminate are said to be **NULL**. It seems that every time I teach a class in programming, at least one student asks me to define the value of NULL. Well, that's a tough one, because, by definition, a NULL value means that you don't know what the value is. It could be 1, it could be 347, it could be -294 for all we know. In short, it means "undefined".

Prior to version 7.0, several data types did not accept NULL values. For example, bit fields didn't accept NULLs. This was very problematic. Typically, the way this was handled was to define an arbitrary number to serve as the "I don't know" value. The problem with this is that you are assigning a specific value to something and the specific value that you've assigned is wrong! By rule, you are sticking inaccurate data into your database! Thankfully, all data types now accept NULLs.

> *When I first received the production version of SQL Server 7.0, I thought I had missed something. I've been tracking this product since nearly a year before its release and one of the simplest features I was excited about was that you could have a NULL value in a bit field. Imagine my surprise when I went to create a nullable bit field using Enterprise Manager and found it wouldn't let me.*
>
> *With a little experimentation, I discovered that Enterprise Manager had a bug in it. It will not let you create nullable bit fields, but you can create them using the more manual* `CREATE TABLE` *statement that we will look into in Chapter 6.*

SQL Server Identifiers for Objects

Now you've heard all sorts of things about objects in SQL Server. You've even heard my first soapbox diatribe on column names. But let's take a closer look at naming objects in SQL Server.

What Gets Named?

Basically, everything has a name in SQL Server. Here's a partial list:

Stored procedures	Tables	Columns
Views	Rules	Constraints
Defaults	Indexes	Filegroups
Triggers	Databases	Servers
Logins	Roles	Full-text catalogs

And the list goes on. Most things I can think of except rows (which aren't really objects) have a name. The trick is to make every name both useful and practical.

Rules for Naming

As I mentioned earlier in the chapter, the rules for naming in SQL Server are substantially more relaxed than they used to be. Like most freedoms, however, it's easy to make some bad choices and get yourself into trouble.

In SQL Server 6.5, you were usually limited to 20 characters for object names. This often generated problems in creating clear names that truly described the object that was being named. For example, let's say we had tables called `Organization` and `Characteristic`. If we created a linking table between these tables, we might want to call it something like `OrganizationCharacteristic` – that is, simply combine the names of the significant tables that we are linking. The problem would make itself apparent rather quickly when we got a message indicating that the identifier was too long (26 characters). In comes SQL Server version 7.0 and the length limitation is practically eliminated. The new limit is 128 characters for normal objects and 116 for temporary objects. It should be a very rare day indeed when you run into a problem with that limit – we'll explore this in more detail later.

Here are the main rules:

- The name of your object must start with any letter as defined by the specification for Unicode 2.0. This will include the letters most westerners are used to – A-Z and a-z. Whether "A" is different to "a" will depend on how you have your server configured, but either makes for a valid beginning to an object name. After that first letter, you're pretty much free to run wild – almost any character will do.
- Any names that are the same as SQL Server keywords or contain embedded spaces must be enclosed in either double quotes (`" "`) or square brackets (`[]`). What words are considered to be keywords will vary depending on the compatibility level to which you have set your database.

These rules are generally referred to as the rules for identifiers and are in force for any objects you name in SQL Server. Additional rules may exist for specific object types.

Summary

Like most things in life, the little things do matter when thinking about an RDBMS. Sure, almost anyone who knows enough to even think about picking up this book at least has an idea of the *concept* of storing data in columns and rows (even if they don't know that these groupings of columns and rows should be called "tables"), but a few tables seldom make a real database. The things that make today's RDBMSs great are the extra things - the objects that allow you to place both functionality and business rules that are associated with data, right into the database with the data.

Database data has type - just as any other programming environment does. Most things that you do in SQL Server are going to have at least some consideration of type. Review the types that are available, and think about how these types map to the data types in whatever programming environment with which you are familiar.

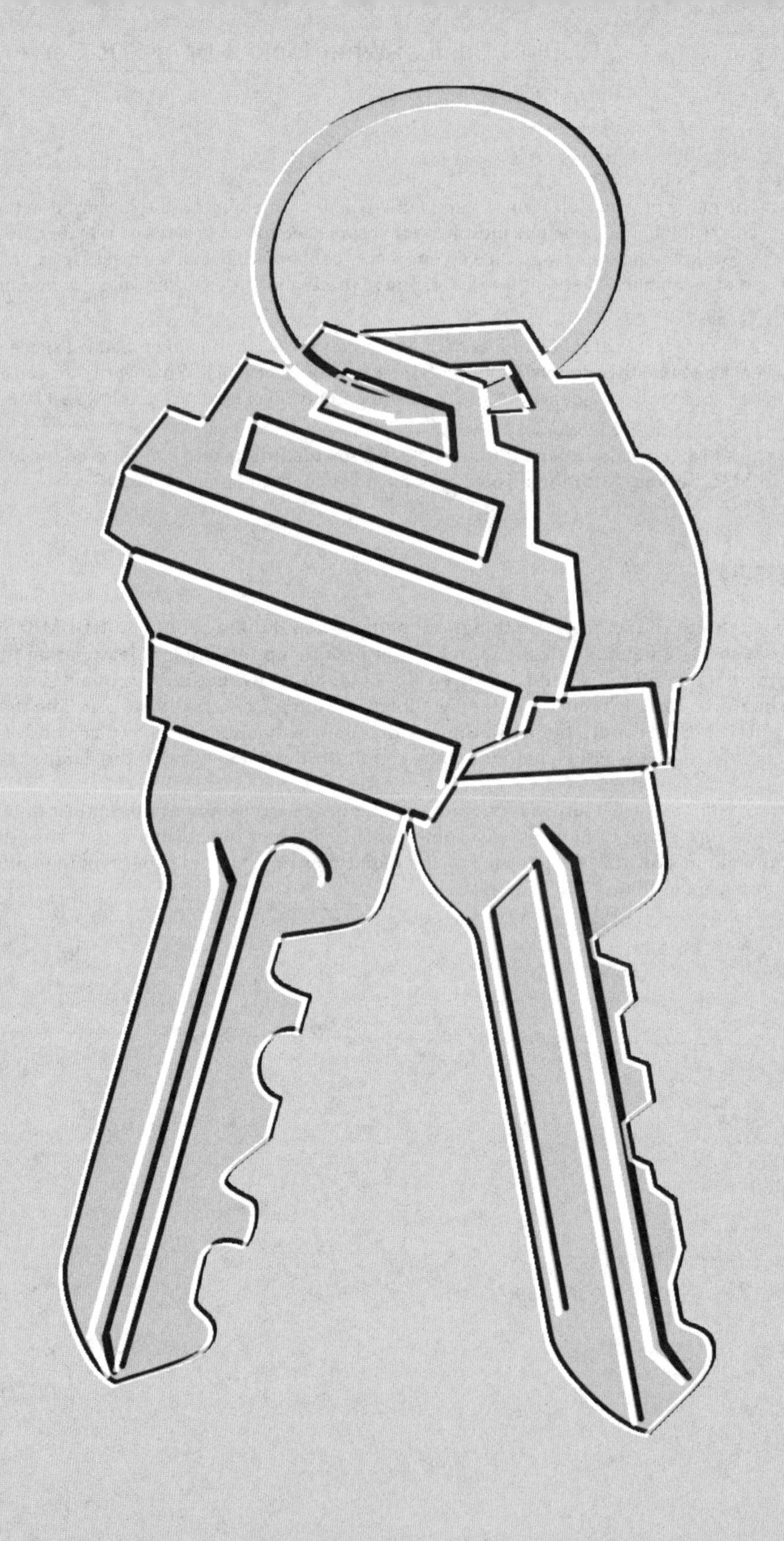

3

Tools of the Trade

Now that we know something about the many types of objects that exist on SQL Server, we probably should get to know something about how to find these objects, and how to monitor our system in general.

In this chapter, we will look into the tools that SQL Server has to offer. Some of them offer only a small number of highly specialized tasks - others do many different things.

The tools we will look at in this chapter include:

- SQL Server Books Online
- The Client and Server Network Utilities
- The Enterprise Manager
- Data Transformation Services (DTS)
- MS DTC Administrative Console
- Performance Monitor
- Profiler
- Query Analyzer
- OSQL
- Service Manager

Books Online

Is **Books Online** a tool? I think so. Let's face it, it doesn't matter how many times you read this or any other book on SQL Server, you're not going to remember everything you'll ever need to know about SQL Server. SQL Server is one of my mainstay products, and I still can't remember it all. I work with someone who practically lives and breathes SQL Server databases, and he can't remember it all - there's simply too much! In short, Books Online is simply one of the most important tools you're going to find in SQL Server.

My general philosophy about books or any other reference material related to programming is that I can't have enough of it. I first began programming in 1980 or so, and back then it was possible to remember most things (but not everything). Today, it's simply impossible. If you have any diversification at all (something that is, in itself, rather difficult these days), there are just too many things to remember, and the things you don't use everyday get lost in dying brain cells.

Here's a simple piece of advice: Don't even try to remember it all. Remember what you've seen as possible. Remember what is an integral foundation to what you're doing. Remember what you work with everyday. Then remember to build a good reference library (starting with this book) for the rest.

Books Online in SQL Server uses a version of the interface that is becoming something of a standard among the Microsoft technical product line (Back Office, MSDN, Visual Studio):

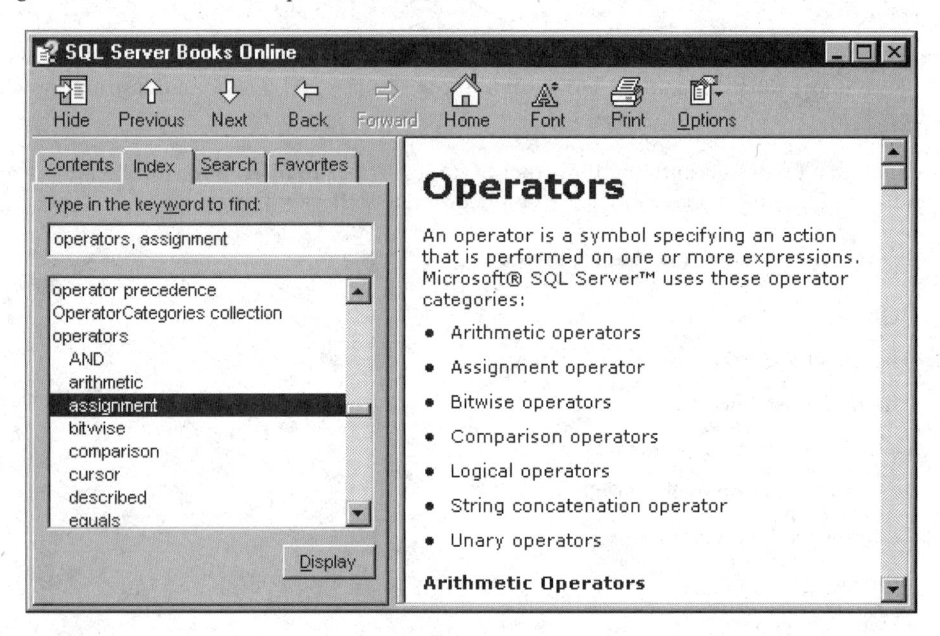

Everything works pretty much as one would expect here, so I'm not going to go into the details of how to operate a help system. Suffice to say that SQL Server Books Online is a great quick reference that follows you to whatever machine you're working on at the time. Books Online also has the added benefit of often having information that is more up to date than the printed documentation.

Technically speaking, it's quite possible that not every system that you move to will have the Books Online (BOL) installed. This is because you can manually de-select BOL at the time of installation. Even in tight space situations however, I strongly recommend that you always install the BOL. It really doesn't take up all that much space when you consider cost per megabyte these days, and it can save you a fortune in time by having that quick reference available wherever you are running SQL Server.

The Client and Server Network Utilities

These tools are something that will be used more by the people who set up the clients that will be connecting to the server hosting your database, but it is still important to understand them yourself. A fair percentage of the time, the connectivity issues that I run into, come back to the client network configuration and how that configuration matches with that of the server.

SQL Server provides several of what are referred to as **Net-Libraries** (network libraries) - or **NetLibs**. These are dynamic-link libraries (DLLs) that SQL Server uses to communicate with certain **network protocols**. The NetLibs supplied with SQL Server 7.0 include:

- Named Pipes
- TCP/IP
- Multiprotocol
- NWLink IPX/SPX
- AppleTalk
- Banyan VINES
- Shared Memory

NetLibs serve as something of an insulator between your client application and the network protocol (which is essentially the language that one network card uses to talk to another) that is to be used – they serve the same function at the server end too.

The same NetLib must be available on both the client and server computers so that they can communicate with each other via the network protocol. Choosing a client NetLib that is not supported on the server will result in your connection attempt failing (with a Specified SQL Server Not Found error).

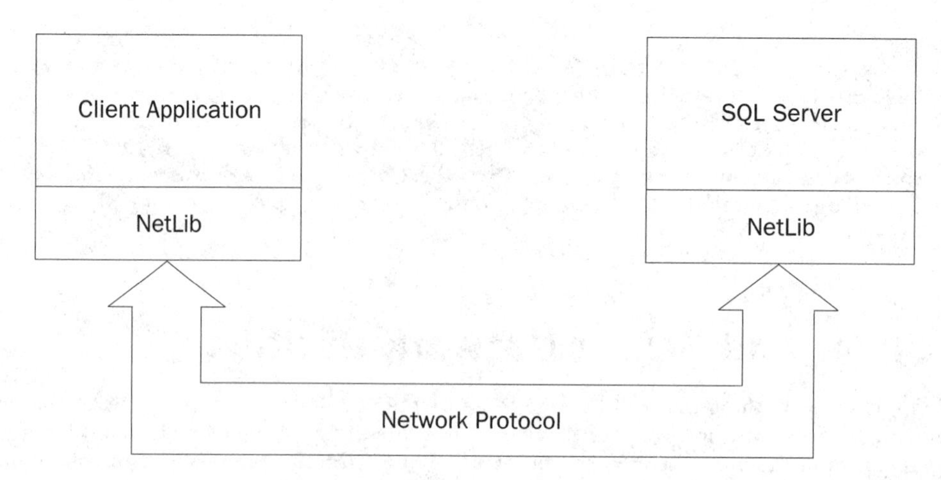

Regardless of the data access method and the kind of driver used (ODBC, OLE DB, or DB-Lib), it will always be the driver that talks to the NetLib. The process works like this:

1. The client app talks to the driver (DB-Lib, ODBC, or OLE DB)
2. The driver calls the client NetLib
3. This NetLib calls the appropriate network protocol and transmits the data to a server NetLib
4. The server NetLib then passes the requests from the client to the SQL Server

The reply from SQL Server to the client follow the same sequence, but in reverse.

Prior to SQL Server 7.0, the default was Named Pipes (which is the default used by NT networks). With version 7.0, the TCP/IP and Multiprotocol NetLibs are also activated on the server by default.

In case you're familiar with TCP/IP, the default port that the IP NetLib will listen on is 1433. A port can be thought of as being like a channel on the radio – signals are bouncing around on all sorts of different frequencies, but they only do you any good if you re "listening" on the right channel. 'We'll go into the importance of ports further when we talk about Security later in the book.

For now, what we're interested in is what libraries our client and server each have available, and which one(s) they are actually using.

The Protocols

Let's start off with that, "What are the available choices?" question. If you run the Server Network Utility under the Microsoft SQL Server 7.0 program group on the Start menu, you'll see something like this:

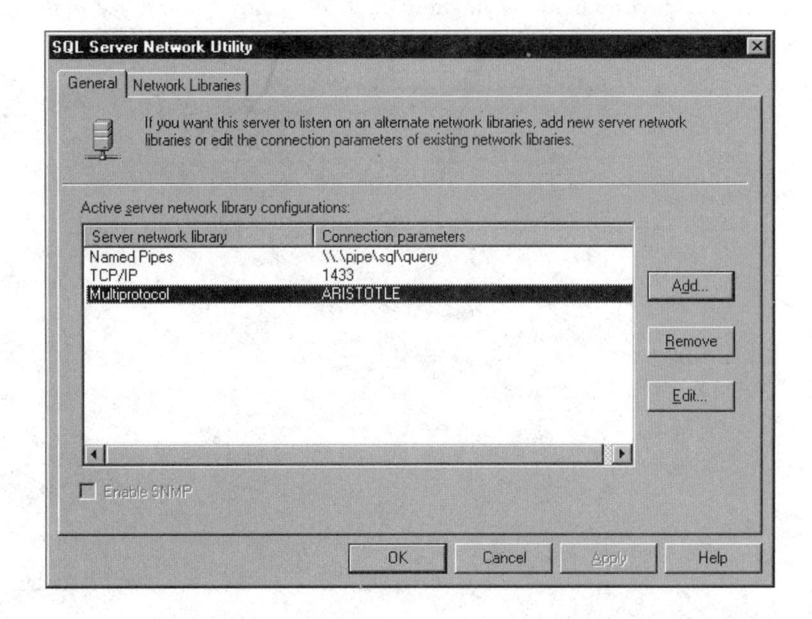

Notice the original three default protocols installed - this is with Windows NT. For Windows 95/98 we get Shared Memory instead of Named Pipes (the other two remain the same).

Now let's see what our server *could* be listening for:

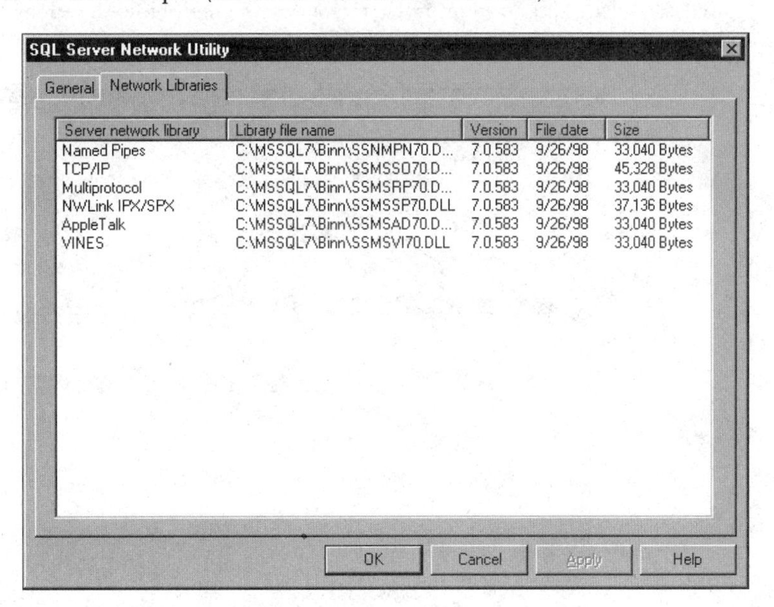

Keep in mind that, in order for your client to gain a connection to the server, the server has to be listening for the protocol with which the client is trying to communicate. Therefore, if we were in a Novell environment, we might need to add a new library. To do that, we would go back to the General tab, and click on Add. We would then see the following dialog:

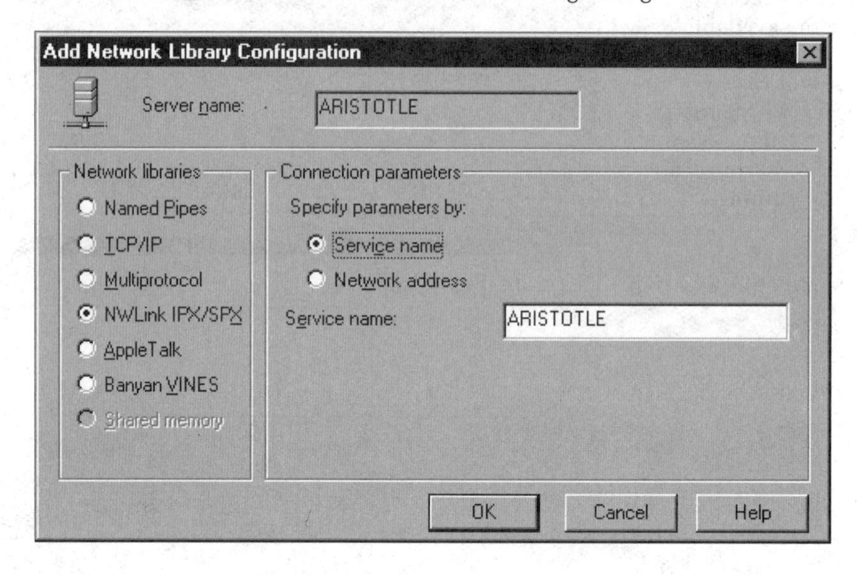

We can identify our server to the Novell world by either Service name or Network Address. For now, I'm just going to identify by my service name (which happens to be the same as my computer - Aristotle) and move on. Now, in the General tab, I see this:

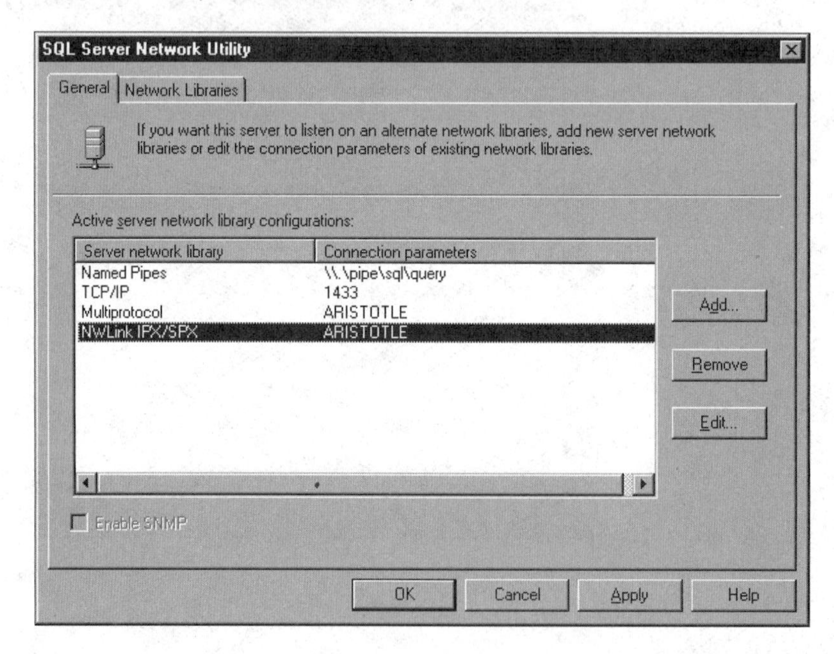

You can see that we can easily add and remove different NetLibs from the list of NetLibs to which the server listens.

> *At this point, you might be tempted to say, "Hey, why don't I just enable every NetLib? Then I won't have to worry about it." This situation is like anything you add onto your server - more overhead. In this case, it would both slow down your server (not terribly, but every little bit counts) and expose you to unnecessary openings in your security gauntlet (why leave an extra door open if nobody is supposed to be using that door?).*

OK, now let's take a look at what we can support and why we would want to choose a particular protocol.

Named Pipes

Named Pipes is (for an NT server installation at least) not only a default, but also a requirement. Named Pipes is not supported at all for server installations running under Windows 9x (It is, however, supported for client use in Win 9x). The requirement under NT lasts, however, only until SQL Server is actually installed, and then the NetLib can, if you choose, be removed. Named Pipes can be very useful in situations where TCP/IP is either not available, or where there is no Domain Name Service (DNS) server to allow naming of servers under TCP/IP.

Although you don't have to physically choose them yourself (SQL Server decides for you) Named Pipes comes in two flavors: **Local Pipes** and **Network Pipes**. Local Pipes are used when you run the client using Named Pipes to a server that is located on the same machine. It is extremely fast and is the best choice for NT clients local to the server machine (Under Win 9x, the Shared Memory NetLib is the best option). Network Pipes are used when using Named Pipes over a Local Area Network (LAN) environment. It will resolve server locations by the server name, and can be a very easy-to-use connection option.

TCP/IP

TCP/IP has become something of the de-facto standard networking protocol, and is now one of the default NetLibs installed with SQL Server. IP has the advantages of both running on any server type (NT or Windows 9x - being the default for 9x) and of out-performing Named Pipes in situations where the client and server are on different boxes (which is the case most of the time).

Multiprotocol

Multiprotocol rides on top of the other protocols that are currently installed - just automating the process of what protocol needs to be selected for which server. Multiprotocol is handy in two instances:

- You have multiple servers that do not have consistent NetLib support. (Multiprotocol will essentially figure out what NetLib to use for you in this case.)
- You want to be able to access your SQL Server directly over the Internet through a firewall.

We will cover the second instance further in the Security chapter later in the book, along with another very special capability that Multiprotocol offers - encryption (this is not available for Windows 95/98).

Keep in mind that, when using Multiprotocol, you are still using the other base protocols - this means that Multiprotocol adds overhead in order to figure out which NetLib to use when connecting to a server. Personally, I like the idea of just taking the time to explicitly configure the NetLib to use for connections to each server.

NW Link IPX/SPX

IPX equates to Novell. If you're running on a Novell network, then you're going to want to check with your network administrator to see if they are using IPX. If they support both IPX and IP (as many Novell networks now do), then I would suggest that you configure for IP and don't even activate the IPX NetLib. The performance is better under IP, and you avoid a series of bugs that have plagued the IPX NetLib over the years.

AppleTalk

This one is pretty close to self-descriptive, but let's hit the highlights anyway. Use this one for older Macintosh networks that are still only utilizing **AppleTalk**. The AppleTalk NetLib is not supported on Windows 95/98.

There was no small amount of talk before SQL Server 7.0 came out that Microsoft was going to terminate support for the AppleTalk NetLib. They didn't, but the fact that the talk was there should give you a head's up for what may be inevitable. If you are thinking of using SQL Server in an environment that has a Macintosh presence, then you may want to verify that your Mac environment is not limited to AppleTalk for communication. Most Mac's have had IP support added, but it's a question worth asking up front.

Banyan VINES

Hard to believe, but not that long ago, this was a very mainstream networking product. It is currently dying a rather slow death, but, fortunately, it still has support under SQL Server. In short, if your network is running **VINES**, then this NetLib is for you.

Shared Memory

This lovely gem is new with version 7.0, but is only available for Win 9x clients (NT can do the same thing via Named Pipes). In short, **shared memory** removes the need for inter-process marshaling (which is a way of packaging information before transferring it across process boundaries) between the client and the server if they are running on the same box. The client has direct access to the same memory mapped file where the server is storing data. This removes a substantial amount of overhead and is *very* fast.

On to the Client

Now, we've seen all the possible protocols and we know how to choose which ones to offer. Once we know what's being offered by our server, we can go and configure the client. Most of the time, the defaults are going to work just fine, but let's take a look at what we've got. Select Client Network Utility from the Microsoft SQL Server 7.0 program group:

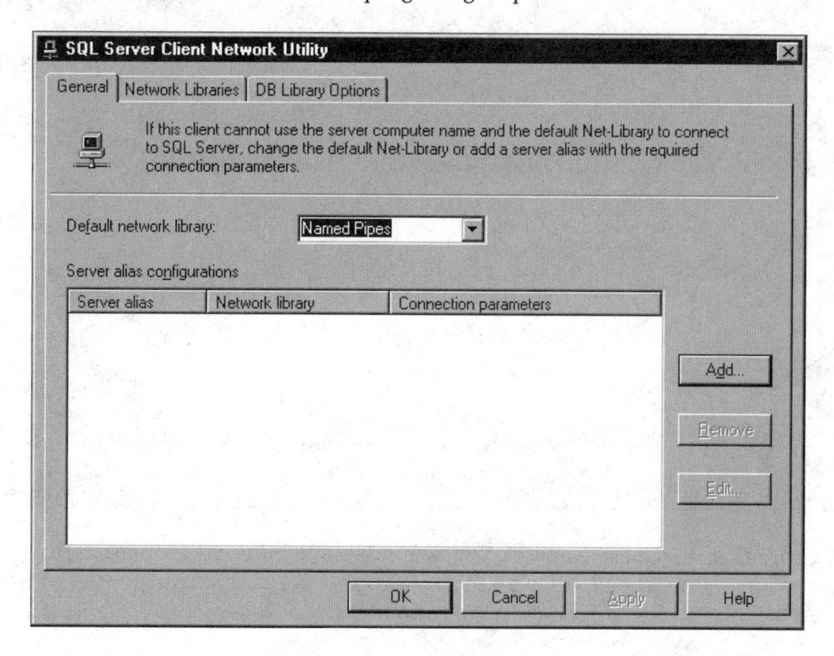

As you can see, we are again (by default) using Named Pipes. Unless you change the default, Named Pipes is the NetLib that will be used for connections to any server not listed in the Server alias configurations list.

If you have TCP/IP support on your network, leave your server configured to use it and change your client's default to TCP/IP. IP has fewer overheads and just plain runs faster - there is no reason not to use it unless your network doesn't support it. It's worth noting, that for local servers, the Local Pipes/Shared Memory NetLibs will be quicker, as you do not need to go across the network to view your local SQL server.

The Server alias configurations list is a listing of all the servers where you have defined a specific NetLib to be used when contacting that particular server. This means that you can contact one server using IP and another using IPX - whatever you need to get to that particular server. In this case, we've configured our client to use the NW Link NetLib for requests from the server named ARISTOTLE, and to use Named Pipes for contact with any other SQL Server:

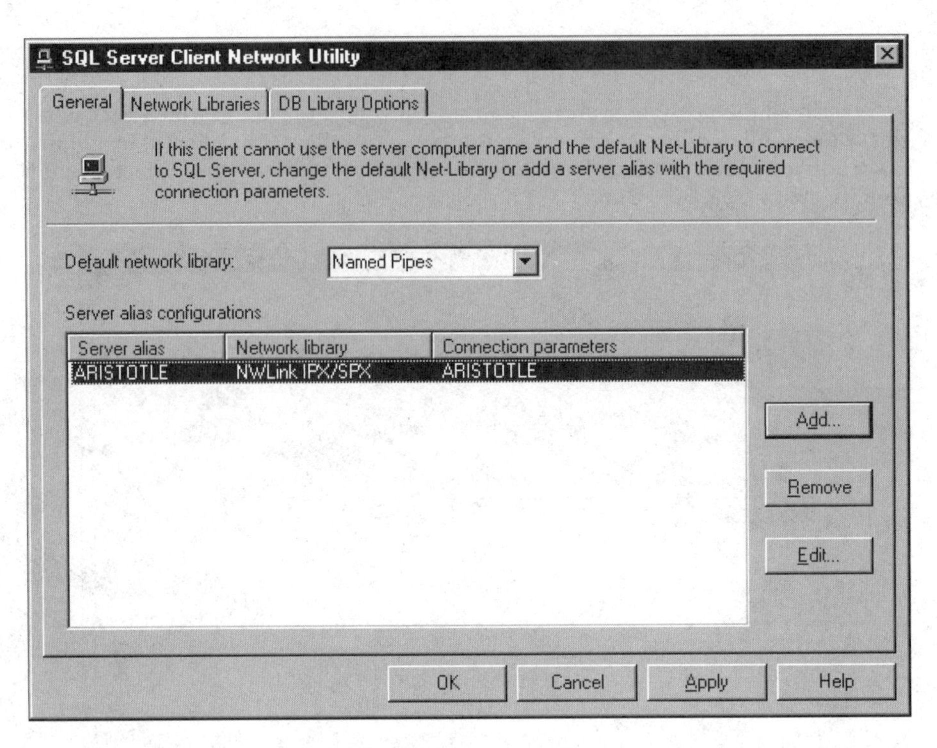

Again, remember that the Client Network Utility on the network machine must either have a default protocol that matches one provided for on the server, or it must have an entry in the Server alias configurations to specifically choose a NetLib supported by that server.

The Enterprise Manager

The **Enterprise Manger**, or **EM**, is pretty much home base when administering a SQL Server. It provides a variety of functionality to manage your server using a relatively easy to use graphical user interface. With version 7.0, it also has tools to assist the development side of the equation. EM now supports **Entity Relationship** (**ER**) **diagramming** (which we'll look into in Chapter 8 and again in Chapter 20 - albeit with somewhat non-standard ER diagrams) as well as greatly improved tools for creating tables, views, triggers and stored procedures. In addition, EM supports access to most of the other tools covered in this chapter.

For the purposes of this book, we're not going to cover everything that EM has to offer, but let's take a quick run down of the things you can do from EM:

- Create, edit and delete databases and database objects
- Create, edit and delete Data Transformation (DTS) packages
- Manage scheduled tasks such as backups and the execution of DTS package runs
- Display current activity, such as who is logged on, what objects are locked, and from which client they are running

- Setup web publishing jobs
- Manage security, including such items as roles, logins, and remote and linked servers
- Initiate and manage the SQL Mail Service
- Create and manage Full-Text Search Catalogs
- Manage configuration settings for the server
- Create and manage both publishing and subscribing databases for replication

In addition to the tasks that truly belong to EM, you can also run several of the other SQL Server tools, such as the Query Analyzer and the SQL Server Profiler from EM menu choices.

We will be seeing a great deal of the EM throughout this book.

Data Transformation Services (DTS)

Your friend and mine - that's what **DTS** is. I simply sit back in amazement every time I look at this addition to SQL Server. To give you a touch of perspective here, I've done a couple of Decision Support Systems (DSS) projects over the years. (These are usually systems that don't have online data going in and out, but instead pull data together to help management make decisions.) They have gathered data from a variety of sources and pumped them into one centralized database to be used for centralized reporting.

These projects can get very expensive very quickly, as they attempt to deal with the fact that not every system calls what is essentially the same data by the same name. There can be an infinite number of issues to be dealt with. These can include data integrity (what if the field has a `NULL` and we don't allow `NULL`s?) or differences in business rules (one system deals with credits by allowing a negative order quantity, another doesn't allow this and has a separate set of tables to deal with credits). The list can go on and on - so can the expense.

With the advent of DTS, a tremendous amount of the coding that had to be done for these situations can either be eliminated or, at least, simplified. DTS allows you to take data from any data source that has an OLE DB provider, and pump it into a SQL Server table.

> **While DTS depends on OLE DB to perform data transfer, be aware that there is a special OLE DB provider for ODBC. This provider allows you to map your OLE DB access directly to an ODBC driver – that means anything that ODBC can access can also be accessed by OLE DB (and, therefore, DTS).**
>
> **While we're at it, it's also worth pointing out that DTS, while part of SQL Server, can work against any OLE DB source and any OLE DB destination – that means that SQL Server doesn't need to be involved in the process at all other than providing the data pump. You could, for example, pump data from Oracle to Excel, or event Sybase to DB/2.**

While transferring our data, we can also apply what are referred to as **transformations** to that data. Transformations essentially alter the data according to some logical rule(s). The alteration can be as simple as changing a column name, or as complex as an analysis of the integrity of the data and application of rules to change it if necessary. To think about how this is applied, consider the example I gave earlier of taking data from a field that allows nulls and moving it to a table that does not allow nulls. With DTS, you can, during the transfer process, automatically change out any null values to some other value you choose (for a number, that might be zero, or, for a character, it might be something like "unknown").

We will be looking into DTS in some depth in Chapter 18.

MS DTC Administrative Console

What is the **Distributed Transaction Coordinator** (**DTC**) you ask? Well, the Reader's Digest version is that DTC makes sure that a group of statements that you're running either happen in their entirely, or are "rolled back" such that they appear to never have happened at all. SQL Server has it's own way of managing this kind of stuff, but DTC is special in that can deal with more than one data source – even non-SQL Server data sources.

Let's say that you're running a bank. You want to transfer $100 from account "A" in your bank to account "B" in another bank. You wouldn't want the $100 dollars to be removed from the account in your bank unless it really is *for sure* going to be deposited in the other bank account - right? DTC is all about being sure that it happens this way.

The MS DTC Admin Console is actually more of a monitoring application than something that allows you to change much. Mostly, it just allows you to see what transactions are going through the DTC, and change the rules for logging transactions. (A **transaction** is a group of things that you want to apply this "all or nothing" rule to - either all succeed or they all fail.)

I know I'm repeating myself here - but we will learn much more about transactions and DTC in Chapter 16.

Performance Monitor

Those of you who are familiar with NT's **Performance Monitor** will immediately recognize this tool. Much like the DTC, the performance monitor is really not about setting things - it allows you to understand how your current settings are affecting the system's performance. The Performance Monitor allows you to check out things like what percentage of reads are coming from cache as opposed to needing to be read off the hard disk. (Reads from the hard disk can be as much as hundreds of times slower than a read from cache.) In short, the SQL Server Performance Monitor is exactly the same as the NT Performance Monitor; save that it starts up by default with several SQL-related measurements - for example, the percentage of reads coming from the data cache.

SQL Server Profiler

I can't tell you how many times this one has saved my bacon by telling me what was going on with my server when nothing else would. It's not something a developer (or even a DBA for that matter) will tend to use everyday, but it's extremely powerful, and can be your salvation when you're sure nothing can save you.

SQL Server Profiler is, in short, a real-time tracing tool. Those of you who are already familiar with a prior version of SQL Server will recognize this as being the descendant of SQL Trace. Whereas the Performance Monitor is all about tracking what's happening at the macro level-system configuration stuff - the Profiler is concerned with tracking specifics. This is both a blessing and a curse. The Profiler can, depending on how you configure your trace, give you the specific syntax of every statement executed on your server. Now, imagine that you are doing performance tuning on a system with 1000 users - I'm sure you can imagine the reams of paper that would be used to print out the statements executed by so many people in just a minute or two. Fortunately, the Profiler has a vast array of filters to help you narrow things down and track more specific problems. For example, long running queries, or the exact syntax of a query being run within a stored procedure (which is nice when your procedure has conditional statements that cause it to run different things under different circumstances).

We will be looking into SQL Server Profiler in some detail in our chapter on Performance Tuning.

The Query Analyzer

This, or an offshoot of this, will be your home base as a developer and when you're trouble shooting. The **Query Analyzer** is your tool for interactive sessions with a given SQL Server. It is where you can execute statements using **Transact SQL** (**T-SQL**). T-SQL (I pronounce it "Tee-Sequel") is the native language of SQL Server. It is a dialect of the Structured Query Language (SQL), and is "entry-level" ANSI SQL 92 compliant. "Entry-level" means that SQL Server meets a first tier of requirements that a product needs to meet to be called ANSI compliant. You'll find that most RDBMS products only support ANSI to "entry-level".

Again, those of you who have some experience with prior versions of SQL Server may recall this under a different name - **ISQL/W**. Microsoft has renamed this tool to make the name more representative of its purpose. In addition, there have been substantial enhancements to the Query Analyzer in version 7.0.

Since the Query Analyzer is where we will spend a fair amount of time in this book, let's take a more in depth look at this tool and get familiar with how to use it.

Getting Connected

Well, we've been doing plenty of talking about things in this book, and it's high time we started doing something. To that end, start the Query Analyzer by selecting it from the Microsoft SQL Server 7.0 program group on the Start menu. When it first starts up, you should see something like this:

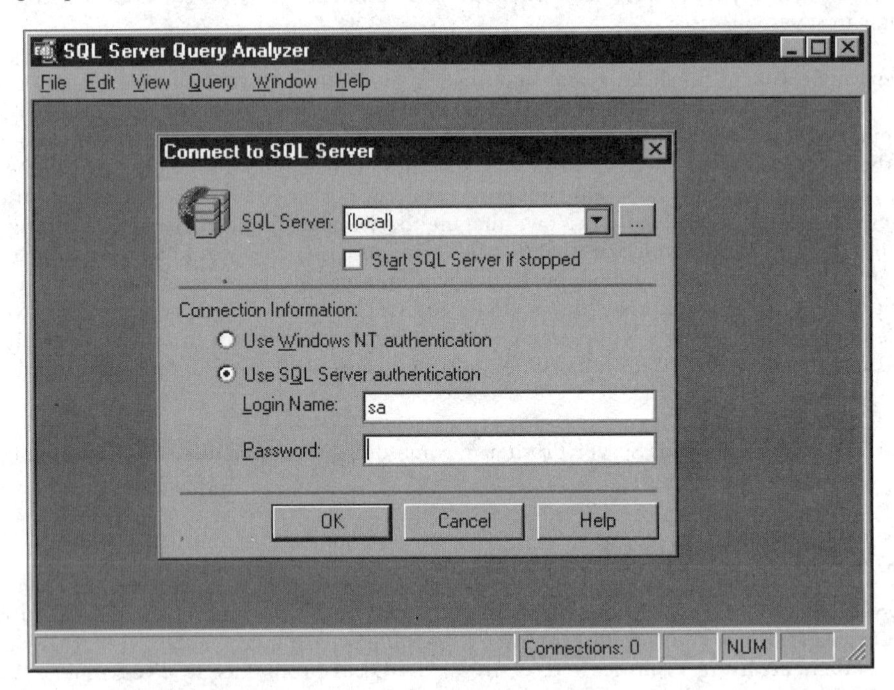

Your login screen may look a little bit different than this depending on whether you've logged in before, what machine you logged into, and what login name you used. Most of these are pretty self-descriptive, but let's look at a couple in more depth.

SQL Server

As you might guess, this is the SQL Server into which you're asking to be logged. In our illustration, we have chosen (local). This doesn't mean that there is a server named (local), but rather that we want to log into the SQL Server that is on this same machine, regardless of what it is named. Selecting (local) not only automatically identifies which server you want to use, but also how you're going to get there.

As you might have inferred from this statement, you can only have one SQL Server running per server. I have heard it directly from several of the SQL Server product managers (for different segments of the product) that they are trying to migrate to a model where you can have multiple instances running on the same server,. There is currently no estimate as to what version this will become available in (don't look for it before version 8.0, and it may be well beyond that).

Note that your server will almost certainly be named the same as your machine is named on the network. There are ways to change the server name after the time of install (when it will automatically be named the same as your server's NT or Win 9x computer name), but they are problematic at best, and deadly to your server at worst.

You may recall when we were discussing NetLibs that the Named Pipes option would vary in the method it actually used to connect depending on whether you were connecting to the same machine or going out over the network. If you select (local), then your system will use Local Pipes (one brand of Named Pipes – it bypasses the network stack), regardless of what NetLib you have selected. This is a bad news/good news story. The bad news is that you give up a little bit of control. The good news is that you don't have to remember what server you're on, and you get a high-performance option for work on the same machine. If you use a specific server's name, then your communications will still go through the network stack and incur the overhead associated with that just as if you were communicating with another system.

Now, what if you can't remember the name of the server you want? If you look just to the right of the server name box, you'll see an ellipsis (...) - try clicking on it. You should see a box come up with a list of servers:

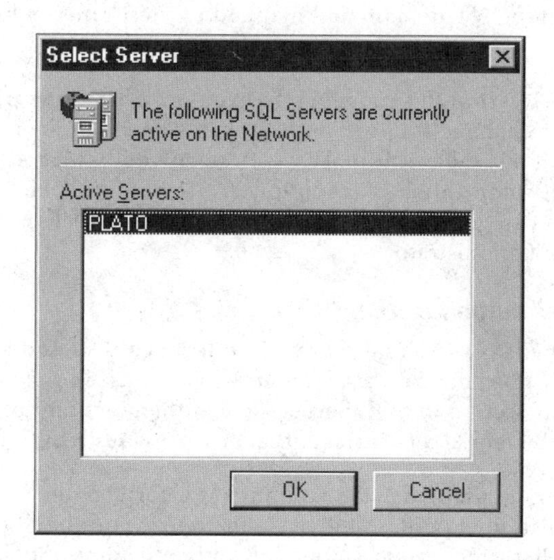

You can select one of these servers and click OK, or just double-click the one you want.

Watch out when using the server selection dialog. While it is usually pretty reliable, there are ways of configuring a SQL Server so that it doesn't "broadcast". When a server has been configured this way, it won't show up in the list. Also, servers that are only listening on the TCP/IP NetLib and do not have a DNS entry will also not show up. You must, in this case, already know your IP address and refer to the server using the IP address.

Start SQL Server if Stopped

This one pretty much does as it says, but you have to have administrative control over the target server in order to do this.

Authentication Type

You can choose between **NT authentication** and **SQL Server authentication**. Prior versions of SQL Server also had an option called "Mixed" security. Beginning with SQL Server 7.0, NT authentication is always active on the server side of the equation and SQL Server authentication is optional. This means that SQL Server authentication is now pretty much what Mixed used to be (it gave you the option of using either approach). The SQL Server default is SQL Server authentication (which is essentially Mixed), though, beginning with version 7.0, Microsoft has begun recommending the use of NT authentication. This recommendation will likely become somewhat stronger and louder when SQL Server is running with Windows 2000.

NT Authentication

It is, pretty much, just as it sounds. You have NT users. Those NT users are mapped into SQL Server "Roles" in their NT user profile. When they attempt to log into SQL Server, they are validated through the NT domain and mapped to these roles, which in turn identify what the user is allowed to do.

The best part of this model is that you only have one password (if you change it in the NT domain, then it's changed for your SQL Server logins too). You pretty much don't have to fill in anything to log in (it just takes it from how you're currently logged into the NT network), and that the administrator only has to administer users in one place. The downside is that mapping out this process can get complex and, to administer the NT user side of things, it requires that you are a domain administrator.

SQL Server Authentication

This one is really about more micro-level control and is the only option for Windows 95/98. The security does not care at all about what the user's rights to the network are, but rather what you have explicitly set up in SQL Server. The authentication process does not take into account the current network login at all - instead, the user provides a SQL Server specific login and password.

This can be nice since the administrator for a given SQL Server does not need to be a domain administrator in order to give rights to users on the SQL Server. The process also tends to be somewhat simpler than under NT authentication. Finally, it means that one user can have multiple logins that give them different rights to different things.

> **Under SQL Server 7.0, giving a user multiple logins is much less desirable than before. It used to be a common practice to do this. A user would have one login for utilizing the full power of an application (including insert, update, and delete rights) and another, read-only login for doing reporting. The latter didn't really make any serious security improvement (the user could always use the login they use with an application and gain full access). It did, however, give the user an alternative "safety" login that, by only allowing read-only access, provided them a safe login for building reports and looking directly at data without fear of corrupting that data.**
>
> **This was a major security risk, but it was very frequently used due to how simple it was to implement. Under version 7.0, we can now automatically grant different rights to a user depending on whether they are logged in directly, or whether they are using the login in an application role.**

We will discuss authentication types and application roles further in our chapter on security.

Making the Connection

Let's get logged on. If you are starting up your SQL Server for the first time, set everything just is it is in our example screen. Choose the (local) option for the SQL Server, select Use SQL Server authentication, a Login Name of sa (which stands for **System Administrator** - remember this), and an empty password box. On case-sensitive servers, the login is also case-sensitive, so makes sure you enter it in lowercase. If you're connecting to an installation that has been installed by someone else, or where you have changed the default information, then you will need to provide login information that matches those changes. After you click OK, you should see the main Query Analyzer screen:

Don't forget to change the password for the "sa" user. This is a super-user with full access to everything. If you don't place any kind of security on it, then you're opening yourself up to just anyone coming into your system with full rights to add and drop objects or insert, update, and delete data.

Curious about how many people forget to do this? To date, about 25% of the active production SQL Servers I have come across still have the "sa" password left null. That is to say that 25% of the servers I've come across effectively had no security.

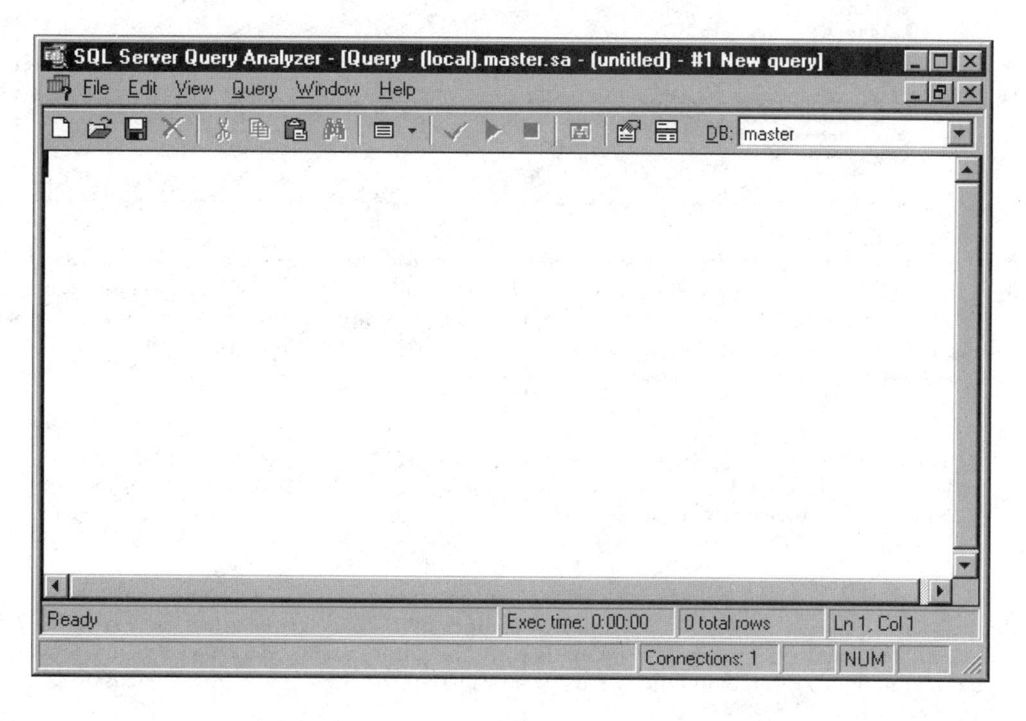

Again, many of the items here (New, Open, Save, Cut, Paste, etc.) are things that you will have seen plenty of from Windows, and should be familiar with, but there's also a fair amount that's specific to SQL Server. We'll look at these shortly, but let's get our very first query out of the way.

Type the following code into the main window of the Query Analyzer:

```
SELECT * FROM INFORMATION_SCHEMA.TABLES
```

Now click on the green arrow in the tool bar. The Query Analyzer changes a bit:

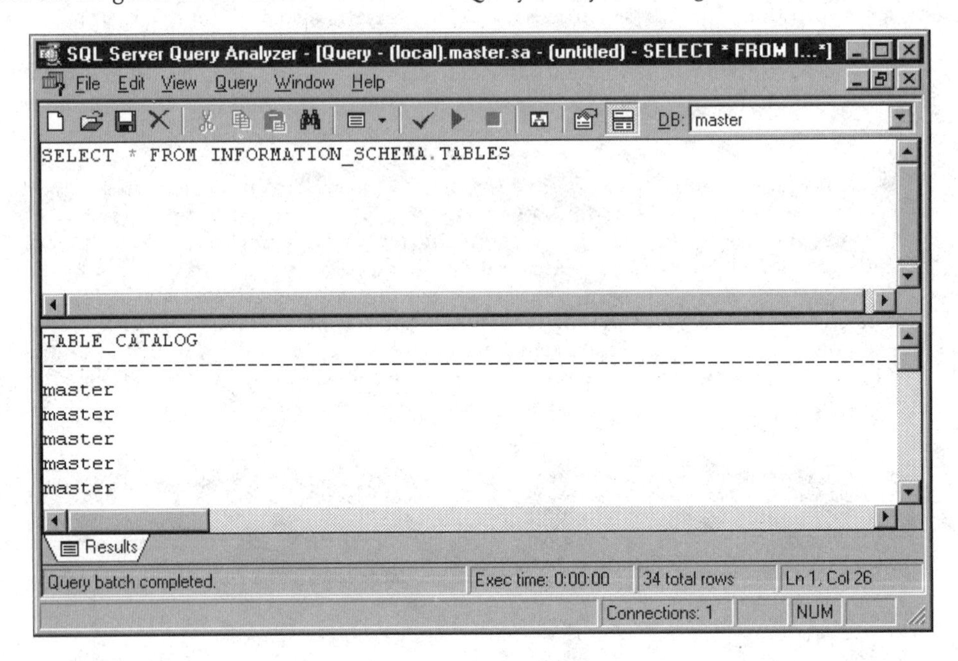

Notice that the window has been automatically divided into two panes. The top is your original query text; the bottom is called the **results pane**. In addition, notice that the results pane has a tab at the bottom of it. Later on, after we've run queries that return multiple sets of data, you'll see that we can get each of these results on separate tabs - this can be rather handy since you often don't know how long each set of data, or **result set**, is.

> **The words result set and recordset are frequently used to refer to a set of data that is returned as a result of some command being run. You can think of these words as being relatively interchangeable.**

Now, let's change a setting or two and see how what we get varies. Click on the small down arrow on the toolbar (right after the icon of a window with lines in it). This lets us select our execute mode for the query. The same choice can also be made from the Query menu. We have three choices: Results in text (the default), Results in Grid (what I prefer 99% of the time) and Show Execution Plan. Let's look at each of these.

Results in Text

This is the default, and, while I almost never use this choice, I also can find no way to change what the default is. Each time you start up Query Analyzer, you have to change this if you want to get results in a grid. This option takes all the output from your query and puts it into one page of text results. The page can be a virtually infinite length (limited by the available memory in your system).

I use this output method in a couple of different scenarios:

- When I'm only getting one result set and the results have only fairly narrow columns
- When I want to be able to easily save my results in a single text file
- When I'm going to have multiple result sets, but the results are expected to be small, and I want to be able to see more than one result set on the same page

Results in Grid

This one divides up the columns and rows into a grid arrangement. It also takes each result set and puts it into its own tab.

Before discussing this further, let's re-run that last query using this option and see what we get. Choose the Results in Grid option and re-run the previous query by clicking on the green arrow:

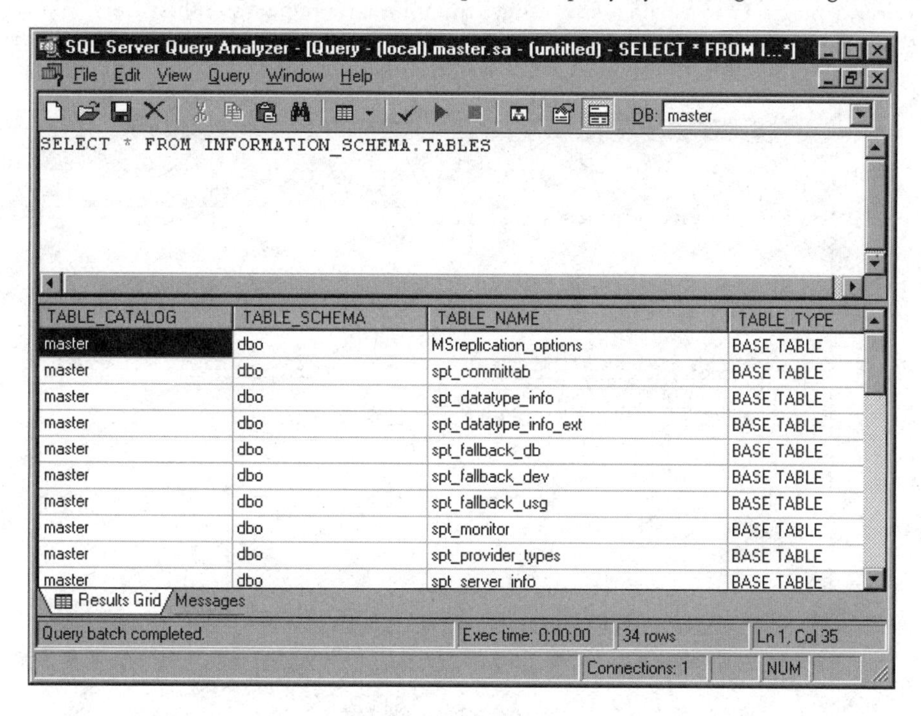

The data that we get back is exactly the same - it's just given to us in a somewhat different format. Specific things that this option gives us that the Results in Text doesn't, include:

- You can resize the column by hovering your mouse on the right border of the column header, and then clicking and dragging the column border to its new size. Double-clicking on the right border will result in the auto-fit for the column.
- If you select several cells, and then cut and paste them into another grid (say, Microsoft Excel), they will be treated as individual cells (under the Results in Text option, the cut data would have been pasted all into one cell).
- You can select just one or two columns of multiple rows (under Results in Text, if you select several rows all of the inner rows have every column selected - you can only select in the middle of the row for the first and last row selected).
- You can instantly move between result sets by simply selecting the tab you want.

I use this option for almost everything since I find that I usually want one of the above benefits.

Show Execution Plan

Every time you run a query, SQL Server parses your query into its component parts and then sends it to the **query optimizer**. The query optimizer is the part of SQL Server that figures out what is the best way to run your query to balance fast results with minimum impact to other users. When you use the Show Execution Plan option, you receive a graphical representation and additional information on how SQL Server plans to run your query. Let's see what one looks like on our query:

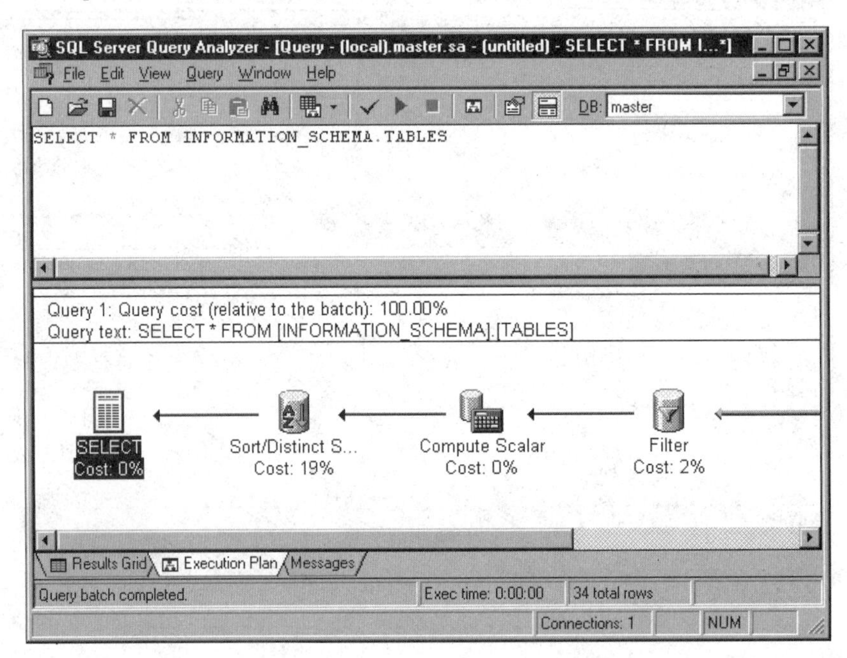

Note that you have to actually click on the Execution Plan tab for it to come up, and that your results are still displayed in whichever way you had selected.

We won't spend any more time on the Show Execution Plan option right here, other than to point out that there is another execution plan option on the toolbar - the Estimated Execution Plan. This toolbar button will give you the same output as a Show Execution Plan with two exceptions:

- You get the plan immediately rather than after your query executes.
- While what you see is the actual "plan" for the query, all the cost information is estimated, and the query is not actually run. Under Show Query Plan, the query was physically executed and the cost information you get is actual rather than estimated.

The DB Combo Box

Finally, let's take a look at the **DB combo box**. In short, this is where you select the default database that you want your queries to run against for the current window. Initially, it will come up with whatever the default database is for the user that's logged in (for sa, that is the master database unless someone has changed it on your system). You can then change it to any other database that the current login has permission to access. Since we're using the sa user ID, every database on the current server should have an entry in the DB combo box.

Let's change our current database to Northwind and re-run the query:

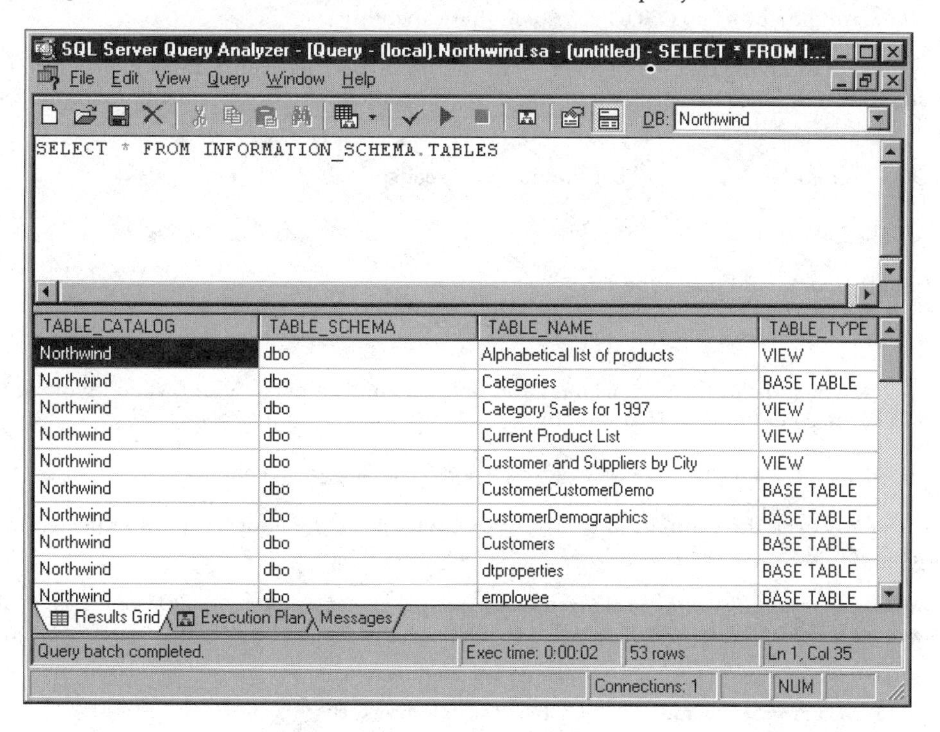

As you can see, the data has changed to represent the data from the newly queried database.

There is one more thing that I want to mention about the Query Analyzer. In SQL Server 7.0, the Query Analyzer has enhanced tools for debugging. The most obvious of these is the coloring of words and phrases as you type them into the code window. Statement keywords should appear in blue; unidentifiable items, such as column and table names (these vary with every table in every database on every server), are in black; and statement arguments and connectors are in red. Pay attention to how these work and learn them - they can help you catch many bugs before you've even run the statement (and seen the resulting error). The other simple debugging item is represented by the check mark icon on the toolbar. This item quickly parses the query for you without the need to actually attempt to run the statement - if there are any syntax errors, this should catch them before you see error messages.

OSQL

You won't see this one in your SQL Program Group. Indeed, it's amazing how many people don't even know that this utility (or it's older brother - `ISQL`) is around. That's because it's a Console rather than a Windows program.

This is the tool to use when you want to include SQL commands and management tasks in command line batch files. Prior to version 7.0 and the advent of DTS, this tool was often used in conjunction with the **Bulk Copy Program** (**BCP**), to manage the import of data from external systems. I suspect that most of this type of use is going to go away as administrators and developers everywhere learn the power and simplicity of DTS. Even so, there are occasionally items that you want to script into a larger command line process. **OSQL** gives you that capability.

Just for the sake of saying that we've been there and done that, let's run a quick query from the command line, and place the results into a text file (presumably to be used for some report in another system).

Get a DOS box going. Make sure that the dos path reads:

```
C:\MSSQL7\Binn
```

Then from the command line, type this:

```
OSQL /?
```

This will give you a list of the various flags and options you can make use of when invoking OSQL. Now, let's get to something more productive:

```
OSQL -U sa -Q "SELECT * FROM Orders" -d NorthWind -o output.txt -P
```

Now, if you go check the contents of `output.txt`, you'll see the information we selected in our query has been placed in the file.

For those more familiar with the Windows environment, but who want to see DOS in action, here are a few useful commands:

❑ `cd ..`	To go back a directory
❑ cd directory name	Go forwards a directory
❑ `dir`	View the contents of a directory
❑ `edit output.txt`	To view the contents of `output.txt` (in a scrollable format)

OSQL can be very handy - but keep in mind that there are usually tools that can do what you're after from OSQL much more effectively, and with a user interface that is more consistent with the other things you're doing with your SQL Server.

The Service Manager

This one is as simple as they come. Depending on the options you chose when installing your SQL Server, you have anywhere from two to four services available that are SQL Server related. These are:

- The **SQL Server Service**: This is the main service that forms the backbone of SQL Server. It is what stores and retrieves data.
- **SQL Agent**: Formerly known as SQL Executive, this is the task scheduler for SQL Server. This service watches the clock and runs backups, replication publishing, and other items you have set the SQL Server to do on an automated schedule.
- **MS DTC** (the **Distributed Transaction Coordinator**): This is installed with SQL Server or Microsoft Transaction Server. We've already hit the highlights of this one, so we'll just point out here that you can use the Service Manager to start and stop MS DTC.
- **Full Text Search**: The engine that provides the full text search capabilities that come with version 7.0 of SQL Server is actually an entirely separate service. Actually, these services are provided by **Microsoft Index Server** (which originally came with Site Server), but a high level of integration has been established, so they let you not only install it with SQL Server, but also manage that service from the SQL Server tools as well. Index Server was originally designed to make searching of file based text content (largely on web pages, but also in things like Word documents, text files, or any other supported format) easy. When installed as part of SQL Server, it adds some integration that has greatly enhanced SQL Server's power with respect to large blocks of text.

The SQL Server Service Manager really has only one function - to allow you to start, stop, or pause any of these services. It can be selected either from the Microsoft SQL Server 7.0 program group or via the icon for the service that SQL Server sets up on the far right of the Windows Task Bar by default. Just right-click on it and a list of options will come up.

Summary

Most of the tools that you've been exposed to here are not ones you'll use every day. Indeed, for the average developer, only the Query Analyzer and Enterprise Manager will get daily use. Nonetheless, it is important to have some idea of the role that each one can play. Each has something significant to offer you. We will wind up seeing each of these tools again in our journey through this book.
Note that there some other utilities available that don't have shortcuts on your Start menu, (Connectivity tools, Server Diagnostics and Maintenance utilities) which are mostly Admin related.

In the next chapter, we will begin the Transact-SQL tutorial with a look at basic queries.

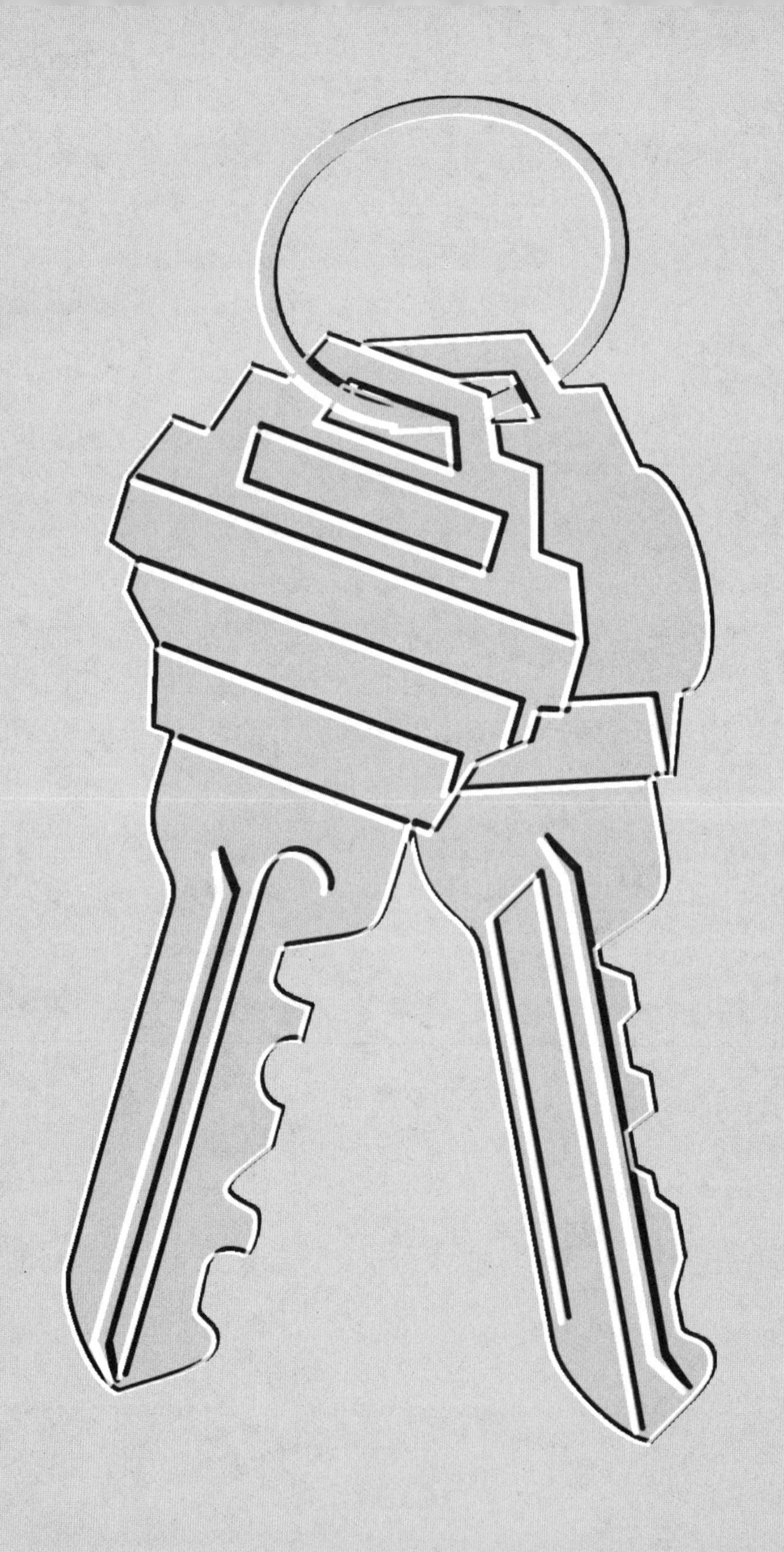

4

The Foundation Statements of T-SQL

At last! We've finally disposed of the most boring stuff. It doesn't get any worse than basic objects and tools, does it? Unfortunately, we have to lay down a foundation before we can build the house. The nice thing is that the foundation is now down. Having used the clichéd example of building a house, I'm going to turn it all upside down by talking about the things that let you enjoy living in it before we've even talked about the plumbing. You see, when working with databases, you have to get to know something about how data is going to be accessed before you can learn all that much about the best ways to store it.

In this chapter, we will discuss the most fundamental **Transact-SQL** (or **T-SQL**) statements. T-SQL is SQL Server's own dialect of **Structured Query Language** (or **SQL**). The T-SQL statements that we will learn in this chapter are:

- `SELECT`
- `INSERT`
- `UPDATE`
- `DELETE`

These four statements are the bread and butter of SQL. We'll learn plenty of other statements as we go along, but these statements make up the basis for T-SQL's **Data Manipulation Language** – or DML. Since you'll, in general, issue far more commands meant to manipulate (that is, read and modify) data than another other type of command (such as those to grant user rights or create a table), you'll find that these will become like old friends in no time at all.

In addition, SQL provides many operators and keywords that help refine your queries. We'll learn some of the most common of these in this chapter.

While T-SQL is unique to SQL Server, the statements you use most of the time are not. T-SQL is entry-level ANSI SQL-92 compliant, which means that it complies up to a certain level of a very wide open standard. What this means to you as a developer is that much of the SQL you're going to learn in this book is directly transferable to other SQL-based database servers such as Sybase (which used to share the same code base as SQL Server), Oracle and Informix. Be aware, however, that every RDBMS has different extensions and performance enhancements that it uses above and beyond the ANSI standard. I will try to point out the ANSI vs. non-ANSI ways of doing things where applicable. In some cases, you'll have a choice to make – performance vs. portability to other RDBMS systems. Most of the time, however, the ANSI way is as fast as any other option. In such a case, the choice should be clear – stay ANSI compliant.

Getting Started with a Basic SELECT Statement

If you haven't used SQL before, or don't really feel like you've really understood it yet -pay attention here! The `SELECT` statement and the structures used within it form the basis for the lion's share of all the commands we will perform with SQL Server. Let's look at the basic syntax rules for a `SELECT` statement:

```
SELECT <column list>
[FROM <source table(s)>]
[WHERE <restrictive condition>]
[GROUP BY <column name or expression using a column in the SELECT list>]
[HAVING <restrictive condition based on the GROUP BY results>]
[ORDER BY <column list>]
```

Wow - that's a lot to decipher, so let's look at the parts.

The SELECT Statement and FROM Clause

The "verb" - in this case a `SELECT` - is the part of the overall statement that tells SQL Server what we are doing. A `SELECT` indicates that we are merely reading information, as opposed to modifying it. What we are selecting is identified by an expression or *`column list`* immediately following the `SELECT` - you'll see what I mean by this in a moment.

Next, we add in more specifics, such as `FROM` where we are getting this data. The `FROM` statement specifies the name of the table or tables from which we are getting our data. With these, we have enough to create a basic `SELECT` statement. Fire up the Query Analyzer and let's take another look at the `SELECT` statement we ran during the last chapter:

```
SELECT * FROM INFORMATION_SCHEMA.TABLES
```

Let's look at what we've asked for here. We've asked to SELECT information - you can also think of this as requesting to display information. The * may seem odd, but it actually works pretty much as * does everywhere - it's a wildcard of sorts. When we say SELECT *, we're saying we want to select every column from the table. Next, the FROM indicates that we've finished saying what items to output, and that we're about to say what the source of the information is supposed to be - in this case, INFORMATION_SCHEMA.TABLES.

> **INFORMATION_SCHEMA is a special access path that is used for displaying metadata about your system's databases and their contents. INFORMATION_SCHEMA has several parts that can be specified after a period, such as INFORMATION_SCHEMA.CATALOGS or INFORMATION_SCHEMA.VIEWS. These special access paths to the metadata of your system are new to SQL Server and have been put there so you won't have to use what are called "system tables".**

Let's play around with this some more. Change the current database to be the Northwind database. Recall that, to do this, you need only select the Northwind entry from the combo box at the top right of the Query Analyzer window:

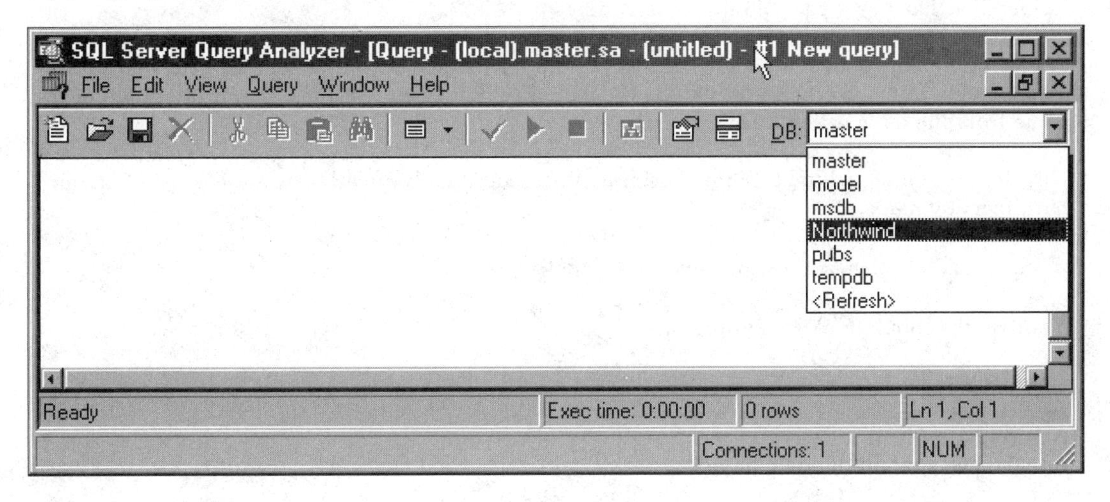

Now that we have the Northwind database selected, let's start looking at some real data from our database. Try this query:

```
SELECT * FROM Customers
```

This query will list every column of data from the Customers table in the current database (in our case, Northwind). If you haven't altered any of the settings on your system or the data in the Northwind database before you ran this query, then you should see the following information line after the data:

```
(91 row(s) affected)
```

Note that if you're viewing the data in grid format, you'll need to click on the Messages tab to view this line.

For a `SELECT` statement, the number shown here is the number of rows that your query returned.

Let's look at a few specifics of our line of code. Notice that I capitalized the `SELECT` and `FROM`. This is not a requirement of SQL Server - we could run them as `SeLeCt` and `frOM` and they would work just fine. I capitalized them purely for purposes of convention and readability. You'll find that many SQL coders will use the convention of capitalizing all commands and keywords, while using mixed case for table, column and non-constant variable names. The standards you choose or have forced upon you may vary, but live by at least one rule - be consistent.

> *OK, time for my next soapbox diatribe. Nothing is more frustrating for the person that has to read your code or remember your table names than lack of consistency. When someone looks at your code or, more importantly, uses your column and table names, it shouldn't take him or her long to guess most of the way you do things just by experience with the parts that he or she has already worked with. Being consistent is one of those incredibly simple things that has been missed to at least some degree in almost every database I've ever worked with. Break the trend - be consistent.*

The `SELECT` is telling the Query Analyzer what we are doing and the `*` is saying what we want (remember that `*` = every column). Then comes the `FROM`.

A `FROM` statement leads into just what it says - that is, the place from which our data should come. Immediately following the `FROM` will be the names of one or more tables. In our query, all of the data came from the table called `Customers`.

Now let's try taking a little bit more specific information. Let's say all we want is a list of all our customers by name:

```
SELECT CompanyName FROM Customers
```

Your results should look something like:

```
CompanyName
-----------------------------------------------
Alfreds Futterkiste
Ana Trujillo Emparedados y helados
...
...
Wilman Kala
Wolski  Zajazd

(91 row(s) affected)
```

Note that I've snipped the rows out of the middle for brevity - you should have 91 rows there. Since the name of each customer is all that we want, that's all that we've selected.

*Many SQL writers have the habit of cutting their queries short and always selecting every column by using a * in their selection criteria. This is another one of those habits to resist. While typing in a * saves you a few moments of typing out the column names that you want, it also means that more data has to be retrieved than is really necessary. You would be surprised at just how much this can drag down your application's performance and that of your network. In short, a good rule to live by is to select what you need - that is, exactly what you need. No more, no less.*

Let's try another simple query. How about:

```
SELECT ProductName FROM Products
```

Again, assuming that you haven't modified the data that came with the sample database, SQL Server should respond by returning a list of 77 different products that are available in the `Northwind` database:

```
ProductName
----------------------------------------
Alice Mutton
Aniseed Syrup
...
...
Wimmers gute Semmelknödel
Zaanse koeken

(77 row(s) affected)
```

The columns that you have chosen right after your `SELECT` clause are known as the **SELECT list**. In short, the `SELECT` list is made up of the columns that you have requested to be output from your query.

The WHERE Clause

Well, things are starting to get boring again, aren't they? So let's add in the `WHERE` clause. The `WHERE` clause allows you to place conditions on what is returned to you. What we have seen thus far is unrestricted information in the sense that every row in the table specified has been included in our results. Unrestricted queries such as these are very useful for populating things like list boxes and combo boxes, and in other scenarios where you are trying to provide a **domain listing**.

> **For our purposes, don't confuse a domain listing with that of an NT domain. A domain listing is an exclusive list of choices. For example, if you want someone to provide you with information about a state in the US, you might provide them with a list that limits the domain of choices to just the fifty states. That way, you can be sure that the option selected will be a valid one. We will see this concept of domains further when we begin talking about database design.**

Now we want to try looking for more specific information. We don't want a listing of customer names - we want information on a specific customer. Try this - see if you can come up with a query that returns the customer name, contact name and phone number for a customer with the customer number `"ROMEY"`.

Let's break it down and build a query one piece at a time. First, we're asking for information to be returned, so we know that we're looking at a SELECT statement. Our statement of what we want indicates that we would like all of the customer name, contact name and phone number, so we're going to have to know what the column names are for these pieces of information. We're also going to need to know out of which table or tables we can retrieve these columns.

Now, we'll take a look at the tables that are available. Since we've already used the Customers table once before, we know that it's there. For now, we'll just make use of that fact, but later on in the chapter, we'll take a look at how we could find out what tables are available if we didn't already know. The Customers table has several columns. To give us a quick listing of our column options we can study the design view of the Customers table from Enterprise Manager. To open this screen in EM, click on the Tables member underneath the Northwind database. Then right-click on the Customers table (in the right-hand pane of EM) and choose Design Table. Again, we'll see some other methods of finding this information a little later in the chapter.

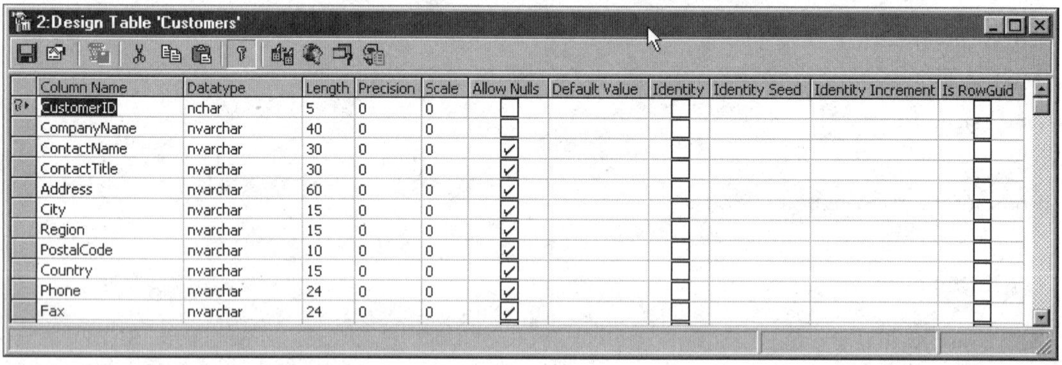

2:Design Table 'Customers'

Column Name	Datatype	Length	Precision	Scale	Allow Nulls	Default Value	Identity	Identity Seed	Identity Increment	Is RowGuid
CustomerID	nchar	5	0	0	☐		☐			☐
CompanyName	nvarchar	40	0	0	☐		☐			☐
ContactName	nvarchar	30	0	0	☑		☐			☐
ContactTitle	nvarchar	30	0	0	☑		☐			☐
Address	nvarchar	60	0	0	☑		☐			☐
City	nvarchar	15	0	0	☑		☐			☐
Region	nvarchar	15	0	0	☑		☐			☐
PostalCode	nvarchar	10	0	0	☑		☐			☐
Country	nvarchar	15	0	0	☑		☐			☐
Phone	nvarchar	24	0	0	☑		☐			☐
Fax	nvarchar	24	0	0	☑		☐			☐

We don't have a column called customer number, but we do have one that's probably what we're looking for: CustomerID. The other two columns are, save for the missing space in between the two words, pretty easy to identify.

Therefore, our Customers table is going to be the place we get our information FROM, and the CompanyName, ContactName and Phone columns will be the specific columns from which we'll get our information:

```
SELECT CompanyName, ContactName, Phone
FROM Customers
```

This query, however, still won't give us the results that we're after – it will still return too much information. Run it – you'll see that it still returns every record in the table rather than just the one we want.

If the table only has a few records and all we want to do is take a quick look at it, this might be fine. After all, we can look through a small list ourselves – right? But that's a pretty big "if" there. In any significant system, very few of your tables will have small record counts. You don't want to have to go scrolling through 10,000 records. What if you had 100,000 or 1,000,000? Even if you felt like scrolling through them all, the time before the results were back would be increasing dramatically. Finally, what do you do when you're designing this into your application and you need a quick result that gets straight to the point?

What we're after is a conditional statement that will limit the results of our query to just one customer – "ROMEY". That's where the WHERE clause comes in. The WHERE clause immediately follows the FROM clause and defines what conditions a record has to meet before it will be shown. For our query, we would want the CustomerID to be equal to "ROMEY", so let's finish our query:

```
SELECT CompanyName, ContactName, Phone
FROM Customers
WHERE CustomerID = 'ROMEY'
```

Run this query against the Northwind database and you should come up with:

```
CompanyName              ContactName                  Phone
------------------------ ---------------------------- -----------------
Romero y tomillo         Alejandra Camino             (91) 745 6200

(1 row(s) affected)
```

This time we've gotten back precisely what we wanted – nothing more, nothing less. In addition, this query runs much faster than the first query.

Let's take a look at all the operators we can use with the WHERE clause:

Operator	Example Usage	Effect
=, >, <, >=, <=, <>, !=, !>, !<	*<Column Name>* = *<Other Column Name>* *<Column Name>* = 'Bob'	Standard Comparison Operators – these work as they do in pretty much any programming language with a couple of notable points: 1. What constitutes "greater than", "less than" and "equal to" can change depending on the collation order you have selected for your SQL Server. For example, "ROMEY" = "romey" on a server where case-insensitive sort order has been selected, but "ROMEY" <> "romey" on a case sensitive server. 2. != and <> both mean "not equals". !< and !> mean "not less than" and "not greater than" respectively.
AND, OR, NOT	*<Column1>* = *<Column2>* AND *<Column3>* >= *<Column 4>* *<Column1>* != "MyLiteral" OR *<Column2>* = "MyOtherLiteral"	Standard Boolean logic. You can use these to combine multiple conditions into one WHERE clause. Note that XOR is not supported.

Table Continued on Following Page

<table>
<tr><th>Operator</th><th>Example Usage</th><th>Effect</th></tr>
<tr><td>BETWEEN</td><td><<em>Column1</em>> BETWEEN 1 AND 5</td><td>Comparison is true if the first value is between the second and third values inclusive. It is the functional equivalent of A>=B AND A<=C. Any of the specified values can be column names, variables or literals.</td></tr>
<tr><td>LIKE</td><td><<em>Column1</em>> LIKE "ROM%"</td><td>Uses the % (all) and _ characters for wildcarding. % indicates a value of any length can replace the % character. _ indicates any one character can replace the _ character.</td></tr>
<tr><td>IN</td><td><<em>Column1</em>> IN (<em>List of Numbers</em>)

<<em>Column1</em>> IN ("A", "b", "345")</td><td>Returns true if the value to the left of the IN keyword matches any of the values in the list provided after the IN keyword. This is frequently used in sub queries, which we will look at in Chapter 15.</td></tr>
<tr><td>ALL, ANY, SOME</td><td><<em>column|expression</em>> (<em>comparision operator</em>) <ANY|SOME> (<em>subquery</em>)</td><td>These return true if any or all (depending on which you choose) values in a subquery meet the comparison operator (e.g. <, >, =, >=) condition. ANY and SOME are functional equivalents.</td></tr>
<tr><td>EXISTS</td><td>EXISTS (subquery)</td><td>Returns true if at least one row is returned by the subquery. Again, we'll look into this one further in Chapter 15.</td></tr>
</table>

ORDER BY

In the queries that we've run thus far, most of them have come out in something resembling alphabetical order. Is this by accident? Actually, the answer to that is yes. If you don't say you want a specific sorting on the results of a query, then you get the data as SQL Server decides to give it to you. This will always be based on what SQL Server decided was the lowest cost way to gather the data. It will usually be based either on the physical order of a table, or on one of the indexes SQL Server used to find your data.

Think of an ORDER BY clause as being a "sort by". It gives you the opportunity to define the order in which you want your data to come back. You can use any combination of columns in your ORDER BY clause as long as they are columns (or derivations of columns) found in the tables within your FROM clause.

Let's look at this query:

```
SELECT CustomerID, ContactName, Phone
FROM Customers
```

This will produce the following results:

```
CustomerID  ContactName                              Phone
----------  ---------------------------------------  ------------------
ALFKI       Maria Anders                             030-0074321
ANATR       Ana Trujillo                             (5) 555-4729
...
WILMK       Matti Karttunen                          90-224 8858
WOLZA       Zbyszek Piestrzeniewicz                  (26) 642-7012

(91 row(s) affected)
```

As it happened, our query result set was sorted in `CustomerID` order. Why? Because SQL Server decided that the best way to look at this data was by using an index that sorts the data by `CustomerID`. That just happened to be what created the lowest cost (in terms of CPU and I/O) query. Were we to run this exact query when the table had grown to a much larger size, SQL Server might have chosen an entirely different execution plan, and therefore might sort the data differently. We could force this sort order by changing our query to this:

```
SELECT CustomerID, ContactName, Phone
FROM Customers
ORDER BY CustomerID
```

Note that the `WHERE` clause isn't required. It can either be there or not depending on what you're trying to accomplish – just remember that if you do have a `WHERE` clause it goes before the `ORDER BY` clause.

Unfortunately, that last query doesn't really give us anything different, so we don't see what's actually happening. Let's change the query to sort the data differently – by the `ContactName`:

```
SELECT CustomerID, ContactName, Phone
FROM Customers
ORDER BY ContactName
```

Now our results are quite different. It's the same data, but it's been substantially rearranged:

```
CustomerID  ContactName                              Phone
----------  ---------------------------------------  --------------------
ROMEY       Alejandra Camino                         (91) 745 6200
MORGK       Alexander Feuer                          0342-023176
ANATR       Ana Trujillo                             (5) 555-4729
TRADH       Anabela Domingues                        (11) 555-2167
...
...
LAUGB       Yoshi Tannamuri                          (604) 555-3392
OCEAN       Yvonne Moncada                           (1) 135-5333
WOLZA       Zbyszek Piestrzeniewicz                  (26) 642-7012

(91 row(s) affected)
```

SQL Server still chose the least cost method of giving us our desired results, but the method it actually used changed somewhat because the nature of the query changed.

We can also do our sorting using numeric fields. Let's try one on the `Products` table of `Northwind`:

```
SELECT ProductID, ProductName, UnitsInStock, UnitsOnOrder
FROM Products
WHERE UnitsOnOrder > 0
AND UnitsInStock < 10
ORDER BY UnitsOnOrder DESC
```

This one results in:

```
ProductID      ProductName                              UnitsInStock       UnitsOnOrder
-------------- ---------------------------------------- ------------------ ------------------
66             Louisiana Hot Spiced Okra                4                  100
31             Gorgonzola Telino                        0                  70
45             Rogede sild                              5                  70
21             Sir Rodney's Scones                      3                  40
32             Mascarpone Fabioli                       9                  40
74             Longlife Tofu                            4                  20
68             Scottish Longbreads                      6                  10

(7 row(s) affected)
```

Notice several things in this query. First, we've made use of many of the things that we've talked about up to this point. We've combined multiple `WHERE` clause conditions and we also have an `ORDER BY` clause in place. Second, we've added something new in our `ORDER BY` clause – the `DESC` keyword. This tells SQL Server that our `ORDER BY` should work in descending order, rather than the default of ascending. (If you want to explicitly state that you want it to be ascending, use `ASC`).

OK, let's do one more, but this time, let's sort based on multiple columns. To do this, all we have to do is add a comma followed by the next column by which we want to sort.

Suppose, for example, that we want to get a listing of every order that was placed between December 10th and 20th in 1996. To add a little bit to this though, let's further say that we want the orders sorted by date, and we want a secondary sort based on the `CustomerID` on days where there was more than one order. Just for grins, we'll toss in yet another little twist: we want the `CustomerIDs` sorted in descending order.

Our query would look like this:

```
SELECT OrderDate, CustomerID
FROM Orders
WHERE OrderDate BETWEEN '12-10-1996' AND '12-20-1996'
ORDER BY OrderDate, CustomerID DESC
```

This time, we get data that is sorted two ways.

```
OrderDate                          CustomerID
---------------------------------- ---------------
1996-12-10 00:00:00.000            FOLKO
1996-12-11 00:00:00.000            QUEDE
1996-12-12 00:00:00.000            LILAS
1996-12-12 00:00:00.000            HUNGO
1996-12-13 00:00:00.000            ERNSH
1996-12-16 00:00:00.000            BERGS
1996-12-16 00:00:00.000            AROUT
1996-12-17 00:00:00.000            SPLIR
1996-12-18 00:00:00.000            SANTG
1996-12-18 00:00:00.000            FAMIA
1996-12-19 00:00:00.000            SEVES
1996-12-20 00:00:00.000            BOTTM

(12 row(s) affected)
```

Our dates, since we didn't say anything to the contrary, were still sorted in ascending order (the default), but, if you look at the 16th as an example, you can see that our `CustomerIDs` were indeed sorted last to first – descending order.

> **While we usually sort the results based on one of the columns that we are returning, it's worth noting that the `ORDER BY` clause can be based on any column in any table used in the query regardless of whether it is included in the `SELECT` list.**

Aggregating Data Using the GROUP BY Clause

With `ORDER BY`, we have kind of taken things out of order compared with how the `SELECT` statement reads at the top of the chapter. Let's review the overall statement structure:

```
SELECT <column list>
[FROM <source table(s)>]
[WHERE <restrictive condition>]
[GROUP BY <column name or expression using a column in the SELECT list>]
[HAVING <restrictive condition based on the GROUP BY results>]
[ORDER BY <column list>]
```

Why, if `ORDER BY` comes last, did we look at it before the `GROUP BY`? There are two reasons:

- `ORDER BY` is used far more often than `GROUP BY`, so I want you to have more practice with it
- I want to make sure that you understand that you can mix and match all of the clauses after the `FROM` clause as long as you keep them in the order that SQL Server expects them (as defined in the syntax definition)

The GROUP BY clause is used to aggregate information. Let's look at a simple query without a GROUP BY. Let's say that we want to know how many parts were ordered on a given set of orders:

```
SELECT OrderID, Quantity
FROM [Order Details]
WHERE OrderID BETWEEN 11000 AND 11002
```

This yields a result set of:

```
OrderID         Quantity
--------------- -----------
11000           25
11000           30
11000           30
11001           60
11001           25
11001           25
11001           6
11002           56
11002           15
11002           24
11002           40

(11 row(s) affected)
```

Even though we've only asked for three orders, we're seeing each individual line of detail from the order. We can either get out our adding machine, or we can make use of the GROUP BY clause with an aggregator – in this case we'll use SUM():

```
SELECT OrderID, SUM(Quantity)
FROM [Order Details]
WHERE OrderID BETWEEN 11000 AND 11002
GROUP BY OrderID
```

Note the use of the square brackets in this query. Remember back from Chapter 2 that, if a object name (a table in this case) has embedded spaces in it, we must delimit the name by using either square brackets or double quotes – this lets SQL Server know where the start and the end of the name is.

This gets us what we were looking for:

```
OrderID
--------------- -----
11000           85
11001           116
11002           135

(3 row(s) affected)
```

We can also group based on multiple columns. To do this, we just add a comma and the next column name.

Let's say, for example, that we're looking for the number of orders each employee has taken for customers with CustomerIDs between A and AO. We can use both the EmployeeID and CustomerID columns in our GROUP BY (I'll explain how to use the COUNT() function shortly):

```
SELECT CustomerID, EmployeeID, COUNT(*)
FROM Orders
WHERE CustomerID BETWEEN 'A' AND 'AO'
GROUP BY CustomerID, EmployeeID
```

This gets us counts, but the counts are pulled together based on how many orders a given employee took from a given customer:

```
CustomerID  EmployeeID
----------  -------------  --
ALFKI       1              2
ANTON       1              1
ALFKI       3              1
ANATR       3              2
ANTON       3              3
ALFKI       4              2
ANATR       4              1
ANTON       4              1
ALFKI       6              1
ANATR       7              1
ANTON       7              2

(11 row(s) affected)
```

Note that, once we use a GROUP BY, every column in the SELECT list has to either be part of the GROUP BY or it must be an aggregate. What does this mean? Let's find out.

Aggregates

When you consider that they usually get used with a GROUP BY clause, it's probably not surprising that aggregates are functions that work on groups of data. For example, in one of the queries above, we got the sum of the Quantity column. The sum is calculated and returned on the selected column for each group defined in the GROUP BY clause – in this case, just OrderID. There are a wide range of aggregates available, but let's play with the most common.

> **While aggregates show their power when used with a GROUP BY clause, they are not limited to grouped queries – if you include an aggregate without a GROUP BY, then the aggregate will work against the entire table. The catch here is that, when not working with a GROUP BY, some aggregates can only be in the SELECT list with other aggregates (for example, AVG can't be paired with a column name in the SELECT list unless you have a GROUP BY), others have no problem being mixed with non-aggregates.**

AVG

This one is for computing averages. Let's try running that same query we ran before, only now we'll modify it to return the average quantity per order rather than the total for each order:

```
SELECT OrderID, AVG(Quantity)
FROM [Order Details]
WHERE OrderID BETWEEN 11000 AND 11002
GROUP BY OrderID
```

Notice that our results changed substantially:

```
OrderID
--------------- ---
11000           28
11001           29
11002           33

(3 row(s) affected)
```

You can check the math – on order number 11000 there were three line items totaling 85 altogether. $85 \div 3 = 28.33$. I can just hear some of you out there squealing right now. You're probably saying something like, "Hey, if it's 28.33, then why did it round the value to 28?" Good question. The answer lies in the rules of **casting**. If you're from the C++ world, then you probably understand casting very well. Those of you from the Visual Basic camp may not be as well versed in it. We'll cover casting in some detail in the chapter on advanced query topics (Chapter 15), but for now just realize that since the number that we were calculating the average on was an integer, then the result is an integer.

MIN/MAX

Bet you can guess these two. Yes, these grab the minimum and maximum amounts for each grouping for a selected column. Again, let's use that same query modified for the MIN function:

```
SELECT OrderID, MIN(Quantity)
FROM [Order Details]
WHERE OrderID BETWEEN 11000 AND 11002
GROUP BY OrderID
```

Which gives us the following results:

```
OrderID
--------------- ---
11000           25
11001           6
11002           15

(3 row(s) affected)
```

Modify it one more time for the MAX function:

```
SELECT OrderID, MAX(Quantity)
FROM [Order Details]
WHERE OrderID BETWEEN 11000 AND 11002
GROUP BY OrderID
```

And you come up with this:

```
OrderID
--------------- ---
11000           30
11001           60
11002           56

(3 row(s) affected)
```

What if, however, we wanted both the MIN and the MAX? Simple! Just use both in your query:

```
SELECT OrderID, MIN(Quantity),MAX(Quantity)
FROM [Order Details]
WHERE OrderID BETWEEN 11000 AND 11002
GROUP BY OrderID
```

Now, this will yield you an additional column and a bit of a problem:

```
OrderID
--------------- --------- ----
11000           25        30
11001           6         60
11002           15        56

(3 row(s) affected)
```

Can you spot the issue here? We've gotten back everything that we've asked for, but now that we have more than one aggregate column, we have a problem identifying which column is which. Sure, in this particular example, we can be sure that the columns with the largest numbers are the columns generated by the MAX and the smallest by the MIN, but the answer to which column is which is not always so apparent. So let's make use of an **alias**. An alias allows you to change the name of a column in the result set, and is created by using the AS keyword:

```
SELECT OrderID, MIN(Quantity)AS Minimum, MAX(Quantity) AS Maximum
FROM [Order Details]
WHERE OrderID BETWEEN 11000 AND 11002
GROUP BY OrderID
```

Now our results are somewhat easier to make heads or tails of:

```
OrderID         Minimum             Maximum
--------------- ------------------- -------------
11000           25                  30
11001           6                   60
11002           15                  56

(3 row(s) affected)
```

It's worth noting that the AS keyword is actually optional. Indeed, prior to version 6.5, it wasn't even a valid keyword. If you like, you can execute the same query as before, except remove the two AS keywords from the query – you'll see that you wind up with exactly the same results. It's also worth noting that you can alias any column (and even, as we'll see in the next chapter, table names) – not just aggregates.

Let's re-run this last query, but this time we'll not use the `AS` keyword in some places, and we'll alias every column:

```
SELECT OrderID AS "Order Number", MIN(Quantity) Minimum, MAX(Quantity) Maximum
FROM [Order Details]
WHERE OrderID BETWEEN 11000 AND 11002
GROUP BY OrderID
```

Despite the `AS` keyword being missing in some places, we've still changed the name output for every column:

```
Order Number        Minimum         Maximum
------------------  --------------  ---------
11000               25              30
11001               6               60
11002               15              56

(3 row(s) affected)
```

I must admit that I usually don't include the `AS` keyword in my aliasing, but I would also admit that it's a bad habit on my part. I've been working with SQL Server since before the `AS` keyword was available and have unfortunately got set in my ways about it (I simply forget to use it). I would, however, strongly encourage you to go ahead and make use of this "extra" word. Why? Well, first, because it reads somewhat more clearly, and second because it's the ANSI standard way of doing things.

So then, why did I even tell you about it? Well, I got you started doing it the right way – with the `AS` keyword – but I want you to be aware of alternate ways of doing things so that you aren't confused when you see something that looks a little different.

COUNT(Expression | *)

The `COUNT(*)` function is about counting the rows in a query. To begin with let's go with one of the most common varieties of queries. If you don't already have the Query Analyzer running, fire it up and make the `Northwind` database the current database. Then try the following query:

```
SELECT COUNT(*)
FROM Employees
WHERE EmployeeID = 5
```

The recordset you get back looks a little different from what you're used to from earlier queries:

```
-----------
1

(1 row(s) affected)
```

Let's look at the differences. First, as with all columns that are returned as a result of a function call, there is no default column name – if you want there to be a column name, then you need to supply an alias. Next, you'll notice that we haven't really returned much of anything. So what does this recordset represent? It is the number of rows that matched the `WHERE` condition in the query for the table(s) in the `FROM` clause.

> **Keep this query in mind. This is a basic query that you can use to verify that the exact number of rows that you expect to be in a table and match your `WHERE` condition, are indeed in there.**

Just for fun, try running the query without the `WHERE` clause:

```
SELECT COUNT(*)
FROM Employees
```

If you haven't done any deletions or insertions into the `Employees` table, then you should get a recordset that looks something like this:

```
-----------
9

(1 row(s) affected)
```

What is that number? It's the total number of rows in the `Employees` table. This is another one to keep in mind for future use.

Now, we're just getting started! If you look back at the header for this section (the `COUNT` section), you'll see that there are two different ways of using `COUNT`. We've already discussed using `COUNT` with the `*` option. Now it's time to look at it with an expression – usually a column name.

First, try running the `COUNT` the old way, but against a new table:

```
SELECT COUNT(*)
FROM Customers
```

This is a slightly larger table, so you get a higher count:

```
-----------
91

(1 row(s) affected)
```

Now alter your query to select the count for a specific column:

```
SELECT COUNT(Fax)
FROM Customers
```

You'll a result that is a bit different to the one before:

```
-----------
69

(1 row(s) affected)

Warning: Null value eliminated from aggregate.
```

This new result brings with it several possible questions. Most, if not all, of them surround why, since the `Fax` column exists for every row, there would be a different count for `Fax` than there is for the row count in general. The answer is fairly obvious when you stop to think about it – there isn't a value, as such, for the `Fax` column in every row. In short, the `COUNT`, when used in any form other than `COUNT(*)`, ignores `NULL` values. Let's verify that `NULL` values are the cause of the discrepancy:

```
SELECT COUNT(*)
FROM Customers
WHERE Fax IS NULL
```

This should yield you the following recordset:

```
-----------
22

(1 row(s) affected)
```

Now, let's do the math:

69 + 22 = 91

That's 69 records with a defined value in the `Fax` field and 22 rows where the value in the `Fax` field is `NULL`, making a total of 91 rows.

> **Actually, all aggregate functions ignore `NULL`s except for `COUNT(*)`. Think about this for a minute –it can have a very significant impact on your results. Many users expect `NULL` values in numeric fields to be treated as zero when performing averages, but a `NULL` does not equal zero, and as such, shouldn't be used as one. If you perform an `AVG` or other aggregate function on a column with `NULL`s, the `NULL` values will not be part of the aggregation unless you manipulate them into a non-`NULL` value inside the function. We'll explore this further in Chapter 15, but beware of this when coding in T-SQL and when designing your database.**
>
> **Why does it matter in your database design? Well, it can have a bearing on whether you decide to allow `NULL` values in a field or not by thinking about the way that queries are likely to be run against the database and how you want your aggregates to work.**

Before we go away from this one, we had better see it in action with the GROUP BY clause.

Let's say our boss has asked us the number of employees that report to each manager. The statements that we've done this far would either count up all the rows in the table (`COUNT(*)`) or all the rows in the table that didn't have null values (`COUNT(`*`ColumnName`*`)`). When we add a `GROUP BY` clause, these aggregators perform exactly as they did before, except that they return a count for each grouping rather than the full table – we can use this to get our number of reports:

```
SELECT ReportsTo, COUNT(*)
FROM Employees
GROUP BY ReportsTo
```

Notice that we only are grouping by the `ReportsTo` – the `COUNT()` is an aggregator, and therefore does not have to be included in the `GROUP BY` clause.

```
ReportsTo
--------------- --
NULL          1
2             5
5             3

(3 row(s) affected)
```

Our results tell us that the manager with 2 as his/her `ManagerID` has five people reporting to him or her, and that three people report to the manager with `ManagerID` 5. We are also able to tell that one `Employees` record had a `NULL` value in the `ReportsTo` field – this employee apparently doesn't report to anyone (hmmm, president of the company I suspect?).

Now that we've seen how to operate with groups, let's move on to one of the concepts that a lot of people have problems with. Of course, after reading the next section, you'll think it's a snap.

Placing Conditions on Groups with the HAVING Clause

Up to now, all of our conditions have been against specific rows. If a given column in a row doesn't have a specific value or isn't within a range of values, then the row is left out. All of this happens before the groupings are really even thought about.

What if we want to place conditions on what the groups themselves look like? In other words, what if we want every row to be added to a group, but then we want to say that only after the groups are fully accumulated are we ready to apply the condition. Well, that's where the `HAVING` clause comes in.

The `HAVING` clause is only used if there is also a `GROUP BY` in your query. Whereas the `WHERE` clause is applied to each row before they even have a chance to become part of a group, the `HAVING` clause is applied to the aggregated value for that group.

Let's start off with a slight modification to the `GROUP BY` query we used at the end of the last section - the one that tells us the number of employees assigned to each manager's `EmployeeID`:

```
SELECT ReportsTo AS Manager, COUNT(*) AS Reports
FROM Employees
GROUP BY ReportsTo
```

Now let's look at the results again:

```
Manager         Reports
--------------- --
NULL            1
2               5
5               3

(3 row(s) affected)
```

In the next chapter, we'll learn how to put names on the EmployeeIDs that are in the Manager column. For now though, we'll just note that there appear to be two different managers in the company. Apparently, everyone reports to these two people except for one person who doesn't have a manager assigned – that is probably our CEO (we could write a query to verify that, but we'll just trust in our assumptions for the time being).

We didn't put a WHERE clause in this query, so the GROUP BY was operating on every row in the table and every row is included in a grouping. To test out what would happen to our counts, let's add a WHERE clause:

```
SELECT ReportsTo AS Manager, COUNT(*) AS Reports
FROM Employees
WHERE EmployeeID != 5
GROUP BY ReportsTo
```

This yields us one slight change that we probably expected:

```
Manager         Reports
--------------- ---------
NULL            1
2               4
5               3

(3 row(s) affected)
```

The groupings were relatively untouched, but one row was eliminated before the GROUP BY clause was even considered. You see, the WHERE clause filtered out the one row where the EmployeeID was 5. As it happens, EmployeeID 5 reports to ManagerID 2. When EmployeeID 5 was no longer part of the query, the number of rows that were eligible to be in ManagerID 2's group was reduced by one.

I want to look at things a bit differently though. See if you can work out how to answer the following question. Which managers have more than four people reporting to them? You can look at the query without the WHERE clause and tell by the count, but how do you tell programmatically? That is, what if we need this query to return only the mangers with more than four people reporting to them? If you try to work this out with a WHERE clause, you'll find that there isn't a way to return rows based on the aggregation – the WHERE clause is already completed by the system before the aggregation is executed. That's where our HAVING clause comes in:

```
SELECT ReportsTo AS Manager, COUNT(*) AS Reports
FROM Employees
GROUP BY ReportsTo
HAVING COUNT(*) > 4
```

Try it out and you'll come up with something a little bit more like what we were after:

```
Manager        Reports
-------------- ----------
2              5

(1 row(s) affected)
```

There is only one manager that has more than four employees reporting to him or her.

As I mentioned before – we could have gone and picked this out of the original listing fairly quickly, but the list is not always so short, and when dealing with things programmatically, you often need an exact answer that requires no further analysis.

Let's try a somewhat larger possible recordset, and then we'll leave this topic until we look at multi-table queries in the next chapter. If we want a query that will look at the total quantity of items ordered on each order in the system, it's a reasonably easy query:

```
SELECT OrderID, SUM(Quantity) AS Total
FROM [Order Details]
GROUP BY OrderID
```

```
OrderID        Total
-------------- -------
10248          27
...
...
11075          42
11076          50
11077          72

(830 row(s) affected)
```

Unfortunately, it's somewhat difficult to do analysis on such a large list. So, let's have SQL Server do some paring down of this list to help us do our analysis. Assume that we're only interested in larger order quantities. Can you modify the query to return the same information, but limited to orders where the total quantity of product ordered was over 300? It's as easy as adding the `HAVING` clause:

```
SELECT OrderID, SUM(Quantity) AS Total
FROM [Order Details]
GROUP BY OrderID
HAVING SUM(Quantity) > 300
```

Now we get a substantially shorter list:

```
OrderID        Total
-------------- -------
10895          346
11030          330

(2 row(s) affected)
```

As you can see, we can very quickly pare the list down to just the few in which we are most interested. We could perform additional queries now specifically searching for `OrderIDs` 10895 and 11030, or as you'll learn in later chapters, we can `JOIN` the information from this query with additional information to yield information that is even more precise.

The DISTINCT and ALL Predicates

There's just one more major concept to get through and we'll be ready to move on to action statements. It has to do with repeated data.

Let's say, for example, that we wanted a list of all of the suppliers of all of the products that we have in stock currently. We can easily get that information from the `Products` table with the following query:

```
SELECT SupplierID
FROM Products
WHERE UnitsInStock > 0
```

What we get back is one row matching the `SupplierID` for every row in the `Products` table:

```
SupplierID
--------------
1
1
1
2
3
3
3
...
...
12
23
12

(72 row(s) affected)
```

While this meets our needs from a technical standpoint, it doesn't really meet our needs from a reality standpoint. Look at all those duplicate rows! As we've seen in other queries in this chapter, this particular table is small, but the number of rows returned and the number of duplicates can quickly become overwhelming. Like the problems we've discussed before – we have an answer. It comes in the form of the `DISTINCT` predicate on your `SELECT` statement.

Try re-running the query with a slight change:

```
SELECT DISTINCT SupplierID
FROM Products
WHERE UnitsInStock > 0
```

Now you come up with a true list of the SupplierIDs from which we currently have stock:

```
SupplierID
--------------
1
2
3
...
...
27
28
29

(29 row(s) affected)
```

As you can see, this cut down the size of our list substantially and made the contents of the list more relevant. Another side benefit of this query is that it will actually perform better than the first one. Why? Well, we'll go into that later in the book when we discuss performance issues further, but for now, suffice to say that not having to return every single row means that SQL Server doesn't have to do quite as much work in order to meet the needs of this query.

As the old commercials on television go: But wait! There's more! We're not done with DISTINCT yet. Indeed, the next part is one that you might be able to use as a party trick to impress your programmer friends. You see, this is one that an amazing number of SQL programmers don't even realize you can do – DISTINCT can be used as more than just a predicate for a SELECT statement. It can also be used in the expression for an aggregate. What do I mean? Let's compare three queries.

First, grab a row count for the Order Details table:

```
SELECT COUNT(*)
FROM [Order Details]
```

If you haven't modified the Order Details table, this should yield you 2,155 rows.

Now run the same query using a specific column to count:

```
SELECT COUNT(OrderID)
FROM [Order Details]
```

Since the OrderID column is part of the key for this table, it can't contain any NULLs (more on this in the chapter on constraints). Therefore, the net count for this query is always going to be the same as the COUNT(*) – in this case, it's 2,155.

Key is a term used to describe a column or combination of columns that can be used to identify a row within a table. There are actually several different kinds of keys (we'll see much more on these in Chapters 7-9), but the when the word key is used by itself, it is usually referring to the table's primary key. A primary key is a column or group of columns that are effectively the unique name for that row – when you refer to a row using its primary key, you can be certain that you will only get back one row, because no two rows are allowed to have the same primary key within the same table.

Now for the fun part. Modify the query again:

```
SELECT COUNT(DISTINCT OrderID)
FROM [Order Details]
```

Now we get a substantially different result:

```
-----------
830

(1 row(s) affected)
```

All duplicate rows were eliminated before the aggregation occurred, so you have substantially fewer rows.

> **Note that you can use DISTINCT with any aggregate function, though I question whether many of the functions have any practical use for it. For example, I can't imagine why you would want an average of just the DISTINCT rows.**

That takes us to the ALL predicate. With one exception, it is a very rare thing indeed to see someone actually including an ALL in a statement. ALL is perhaps best understood as being the opposite of DISTINCT. Where DISTINCT is used to filter out duplicate rows, ALL says to give every row. ALL is the default for any SELECT statement except for situations where there is a UNION. We will discuss the impact of ALL in a UNION situation in the next chapter, but for now, realize that ALL is happening any time you don't ask for a DISTINCT.

Adding Data with the INSERT Statement

By now, you should have pretty much got the hang of basic SELECT statements. We would be doing well to stop here save for a pretty major problem – we wouldn't have very much data to look at if we didn't have some way of getting it into the database in the first place. That's where the INSERT statement comes in.

The basic syntax for an INSERT statement looks like this:

```
INSERT [INTO] table_name [(column_list)] data_values
```

Let's look at the parts:

INSERT is the action statement. It tells SQL Server what it is that we're going to be doing with this statement and everything that comes after this keyword is merely spelling out the details of that action.

The INTO keyword is pretty much just fluff. Its sole purpose in life is to make the overall statement more readable. It is completely optional, but I highly recommend its use for the very reason that they added it to the statement – it makes things much easier to read. As we go through this section, try a few of the statements both with and without the INTO keyword. It's a little less typing if you leave it out, but it's also quite a bit stranger to read – it's up to you.

Next comes the table into which you are inserting. Until this point, things have been pretty straightforward – now comes the part that's a little more difficult.

Now comes the column list. An explicit column list (where you specifically state the columns to receive values) is optional – if you don't provide one, then the list will be assumed to match up with the column list of the table in order, and a value must be supplied for every column (you'll see more about what I mean shortly). In summary, this will be a list of one or more columns that you are going to be providing data for in the next part of the statement.

Finally, you'll supply the values to be inserted. There are two ways of doing this, but for now, we'll focus on single line inserts that use data that you explicitly provide. To supply the values, we'll start with the `VALUES` keyword, and then follow that with a list of values, separated by commas and enclosed in parentheses. The number of items in the value list must exactly match the number of columns in the column list. The type of each value must be similar to the type of the column with which it matches (they are taken in order).

Whew! That's confusing, so let's practice with some examples. Let's make use of the `pubs` database. This is a different database than we've been using, so don't forget to make the change:

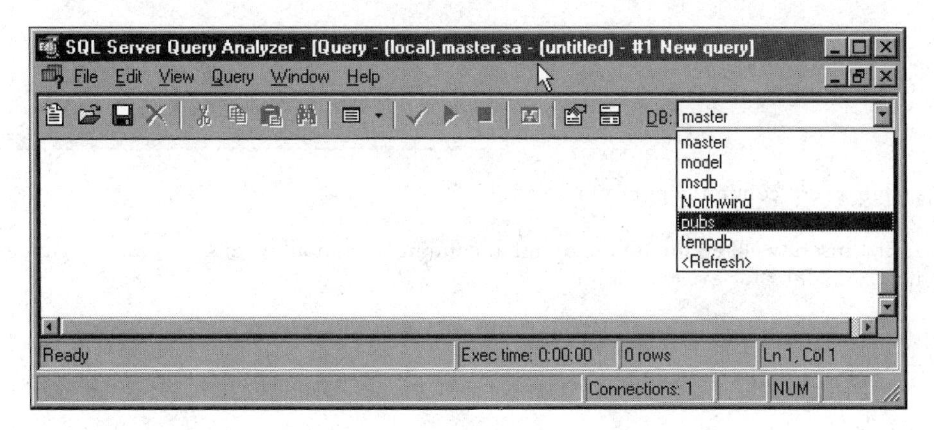

OK, most of the inserts we're going to do in this chapter will be to the `stores` table, so let's take a look at the properties for that table. To do this, click on the Tables node of the pubs database. Then, in the right-hand pane of EM (which should now have a list of all the tables in `pubs`), double-click on the `stores` table:

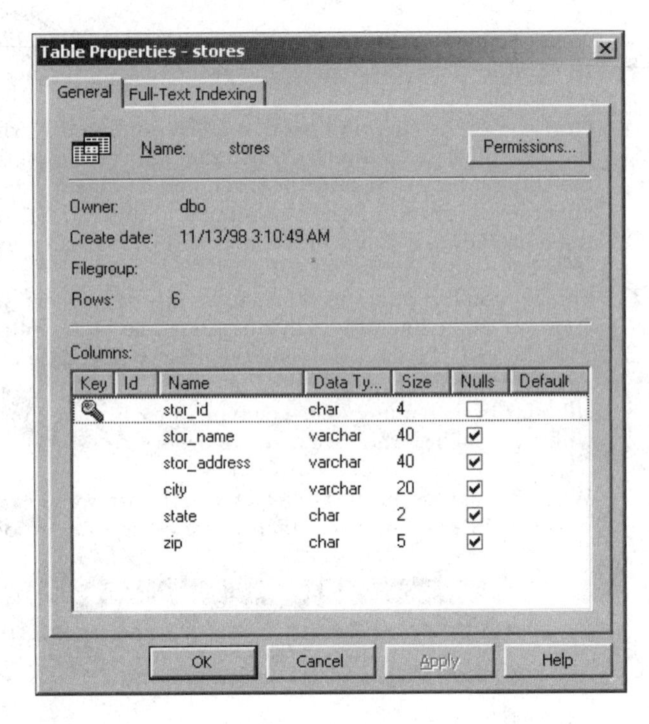

In this table, every column happens to be a `char`.

For our first insert, we'll eliminate the optional column list and allow SQL Server to assume we're providing something for every column:

```
INSERT INTO stores
VALUES
   ('TEST', 'Test Store', '1234 Anywhere Street', 'Here', 'NY', '00319')
```

As stated earlier, unless we provide a different column list (we'll cover how to provide a column list shortly), all the values have to be supplied in the same order as the columns are defined in the table. After executing this query, you should see a statement that tells you that one row was affected by your query. Now, just for fun, try running the exact same query a second time. You'll get the following error:

Server: Msg 2627, Level 14, State 1, Line 1
Violation of PRIMARY KEY constraint 'UPK_storeid'. Cannot insert duplicate key in object 'stores'.
The statement has been terminated.

Why did it work the first time and not the second? Because this table has a primary key that does not allow duplicate values for the `stor_id` field. As long as we changed that one field, we could have left the rest of the columns alone and it would have taken the new row. We'll see more of primary keys in the chapters on design and constraints.

So let's see what we inserted:

```
SELECT *
FROM stores
WHERE stor_id = 'TEST'
```

This query yields us exactly what we inserted.

```
stor_id    stor_name     stor_address              city    state   zip
---------- ------------- ------------------------- ------- ------- -------
TEST       Test Store    1234 Anywhere Street      Here    NY      00319

(1 row(s) affected)
```

Note that I've trimmed a few spaces off the end of each column to help it fit on a page neatly, but the true data is just as we expected it to be.

Now let's try it again with modifications for inserting into specific columns:

```
INSERT INTO stores
   (stor_id, stor_name,  city, state, zip)
VALUES
   ('TST2', 'Test Store', 'Here', 'NY', '00319')
```

Note that, on the line with the data values, we've changed just two things. First, we've changed the value we are inserting into the primary key column so it won't generate an error. Second, we eliminated the value that was associated with the `stor_address` column since we have omitted that column in our column list. For now, we're just taking advantage of the fact that the `stor_address` column is not a required column – that is, it accepts `NULL`s. Since we're not providing a value for this column and since it has no default (we'll see more on defaults later on), this column will be set to `NULL` when we perform our insert.

Let's verify that by re-running our check `SELECT` statement with one slight modification:

```
SELECT *
FROM stores
WHERE stor_id = 'TST2'
```

Now we see something a little different:

```
stor_id    stor_name     stor_address    city     state    zip
---------- ------------- --------------- -------- -------- -------
TST2       Test Store    NULL            Here     NY       00319

(1 row(s) affected)
```

Notice that a `NULL` was inserted for the column that we skipped.

Note that the columns have to be **nullable** in order to do this. What does that mean? Pretty much what it sounds like – it means that you are allowed to have NULL values for that column. Believe me, we will be discussing the nullability of columns to great length in this book, but for now, just realize that some columns allow NULLs and some don't. We can always skip providing information for columns that allow NULLs. If, however, the column is not nullable, then one of two conditions must exist, or we will receive an error and the INSERT will be rejected. The first option is that the column has been defined with a default value. A default is a constant value that is inserted if no other value is provided. We will learn how to define defaults in a later chapter. The second option is, of course, that we supply a value for the column.

Just for posterity, let's perform one more INSERT statement. This time, we'll insert a new sale into the sales table. To view the properties of the sales table, we can either open its Properties dialog as we did with stores, or we can run a system stored procedure called sp_help. sp_help will report information about any database object, user-defined data type or SQL Server data type. The syntax for using sp_help is as follows:

```
EXEC sp_help <name>
```

To view the properties of the sales table, we just have to type the following into the Query Analyzer:

```
EXEC sp_help sales
```

Which returns (among other things):

```
Column_name          Type              Length  Nullable
-------------------------------------------------------------------------
stor_id              char              4       no
ord_num              varchar           20      no
ord_date             datetime          8       no
qty                  smallint          2       no
payterms             varchar           12      no
title_id             tid               6       no
```

The sales table has six columns in it, but pay particular attention to the qty and ord_date columns – they are of types that we haven't done inserts with up to this point (title_id column is of type tid, but that is actually just a user defined type, which is still a character type with a length of 6).

What you need to pay attention to in this query is how to format the types as you're inserting them. Any numeric value does *not* use quotes as we have with our character data. However, the datetime data type does require quotes:

```
INSERT INTO sales
   (stor_id, ord_num, ord_date, qty, payterms, title_id)
VALUES
   ('TEST', 'TESTORDER', '01/01/1999', 10, 'NET 30', 'BU1032')
```

This gets us back the now familiar (1 row(s) affected) message.

> **Note that, while I've used the MM/DD/YYYY format that is popular in the US, you can use a wide variety of other formats (such as the internationally more popular YYYY-MM-DD) with equal success.**

Changing What You've Got with the UPDATE Statement

The UPDATE statement, like most SQL statements, does pretty much what it sounds like it does – it updates existing data. The structure is a little bit different from a SELECT, though you'll notice definite similarities. Let's look at the syntax:

```
UPDATE <table name>
SET <column> = <value> [,<column> = <value>]
[FROM <source table(s)>]
[WHERE <restrictive condition>]
```

An UPDATE can be created from multiple tables, but can only effect one table. What do I mean by that? Well, we can build a condition, or retrieve values from any number of different tables, but only one table at a time can be the subject of the update action. Don't sweat this one too much – we haven't looked at joining multiple tables yet (next chapter folks!), so we won't get into complex UPDATE statements here. For now, we'll look at simple updates.

Let's start off by doing some updates to the data we inserted in the previous section. Let's re-run that query to look at one row of inserted data:

```
SELECT *
FROM stores
WHERE stor_id = 'TEST'
```

Which returns the following to us:

stor_id	stor_name	stor_address	city	state	zip
TEST	Test Store	1234 Anywhere Street	Here	NY	00319

Let's update the value in the city column:

```
UPDATE stores
SET city = 'There'
WHERE stor_id = 'TEST'
```

Much like when we ran the INSERT statement, we don't get much back from SQL Server:

(1 row(s) affected)

Yet, when we again run our SELECT statement, we see that the value has indeed changed:

stor_id	stor_name	stor_address	city	state	zip
TEST	Test Store	1234 Anywhere Street	There	NY	00319

Note that we could have changed more than one column just by adding a comma and the additional column expression. For example, the following statement would have updated both columns:

```
UPDATE stores
SET city = 'There', state = 'CA'
WHERE stor_id = 'TEST'
```

If we choose, we can use an expression for the SET clause (e.g. a calculation) instead of the explicit values we've used thus far.

For example, take a look at a few records from the titles table of the pubs database:

```
SELECT title_id, price
FROM titles
WHERE title_id LIKE 'BU%'
```

Our LIKE operator used here is going to provide us with the rows that start with BU, but which have any value after that (since we've used a %). Assuming you haven't been playing around with the data in the pubs database, you should end up with results similar to these:

```
title_id        price
--------------- -----------
BU1032          19.9900
BU1111          11.9500
BU2075          2.9900
BU7832          19.9900

(4 row(s) affected)
```

Now that we've seen what the data looks like, let's try a somewhat different update to our previous one, by using an expression in our UPDATE statement:

```
UPDATE titles
SET price = price * 1.1
WHERE title_id LIKE 'BU%'
```

After executing that update, run the SELECT statement again:

```
SELECT title_id, price
FROM titles
WHERE title_id LIKE 'BU%'
```

You should see the price increased by 10% for every title ID that starts with BU:

```
title_id        price
--------------- -----------
BU1032          21.9890
BU1111          13.1450
BU2075          3.2890
BU7832          21.9890

(4 row(s) affected)
```

Let's take this a little further to show you how much we can manipulate our results. For example, let's say that we have a business rule that says our prices need to be evenly payable with US currency. The prices we came up with don't meet our criteria, so we need to do something to get our prices rounded to the nearest whole penny (for overseas readers, that's 0.01 dollars). From the point that we're at, we could round to the nearest penny by running another update that does the rounding, but let's go back to the beginning. First, let's undo our last update:

```
UPDATE titles
SET price = price / 1.1
WHERE title_id LIKE 'BU%'
```

Notice that we only had to change just the one line of code. After you execute this, the SELECT statement should yield you the results with which we started:

```
title_id        price
--------------- -----------
BU1032          19.9900
BU1111          11.9500
BU2075          2.9900
BU7832          19.9900

(4 row(s) affected)
```

Now we're ready to start from the beginning with a more advanced query. This time, we're going to perform pretty much the same update, but we'll round the updated data:

```
UPDATE titles
SET price = ROUND(price * 1.1, 2)
WHERE title_id LIKE 'BU%'
```

We've actually performed two mathematical operations before the UPDATE is actually written to each record. First, we perform the equivalent of our first query (increasing the price by 10%). Then we round it to match our business rule (must be to the penny) by indicating that our ROUND() function should round data off to two decimal places (hence the number 2 right after our 1.1,). The great thing is that we've been able to do this in just one operation rather than two.

Let's verify that result:

```
title_id        price
--------------- -----------
BU1032          21.9900
BU1111          13.1500
BU2075          3.2900
BU7832          21.9900

(4 row(s) affected)
```

As you can see, a single UPDATE statement can be fairly powerful. Even so, this is really just the beginning. We'll see even more advanced updates in later chapters.

> **While SQL Server is nice enough to let us update pretty much any column (there are a few that we can't, such as timestamps), be very careful about updating primary keys. Doing so puts you at very high risk of "orphaning" other data (data that has a reference to the data you're changing).**
>
> **For example, the stor_id field in the stores table of the pubs database is a primary key. If we decide to change stor_id 10 to 35 in stores, then any data in the sales table that relates to that store may be orphaned and lost to us if the stor_id value in all of the records relating to stor_id 10 is not also updated to 35.**

The DELETE Statement

The version of the DELETE statement that we'll cover in this chapter may be one of the easiest statements of them all. There's no column list – just a table name and, usually, a WHERE clause. The syntax couldn't be much easier:

```
DELETE <table_name>
[WHERE <search condition>]
```

The WHERE clause works just like all of the WHERE clauses we've seen thus far. We don't need to provide a column list because we are deleting the entire row (you can't delete half a row for example).

Since this is so easy, we'll only perform a couple of quick deletes that are focused on cleaning up the inserts that we performed earlier in the chapter. First, let's run a SELECT to make sure the first of those rows is still there:

```
SELECT *
FROM stores
WHERE stor_id = 'TEST'
```

If you haven't already deleted it, you should come up with a single row that matches what we added with our original INSERT statement. Now let's get rid of it:

```
DELETE stores
WHERE stor_id = 'TEST'
```

Note that we've run into a situation where SQL Server is refusing to delete this row due to referential integrity violations:

```
Server: Msg 547, Level 16, State 1, Line 1
DELETE statement conflicted with COLUMN REFERENCE constraint
'FK__sales__stor_id__1BFD2C07'. The conflict occurred in database 'pubs', table 'sales', column
'stor_id'.
The statement has been terminated.
```

SQL Server won't let us delete a row if it is referenced as part of a foreign key constraint. We'll see much more on foreign keys in Chapter 7, but for now, just keep in mind that, if one row references another row (either in the same or a different table – it doesn't matter) using a foreign key, then the referencing row must be deleted before the referenced row can be deleted. Our last INSERT statement inserted a record into the sales table that had a stor_id of 'TEST' - this record is referencing the record we have just attempted to delete.

Before we can delete the record from our stores table, we must delete the record referencing it in the sales table:

```
DELETE sales
WHERE stor_id = 'TEST'
```

Now we can successfully rerun the first DELETE statement:

```
DELETE stores
WHERE stor_id = 'TEST'
```

You can do two quick checks to verify that the data was indeed deleted. The first happens automatically when the DELETE statement was executed – you should get a message telling you that one row was affected. The other quick check is to re-run the SELECT statement – you should get zero rows back.

For one more easy practice DELETE, we'll also kill off that second row by making just a slight change:

```
DELETE stores
WHERE stor_id = 'TST2'
```

That's it for simple deletes! Like the other statements in this chapter, we'll come back to the DELETE statement when we're ready for more complex search conditions.

Summary

T-SQL is SQL Server's own brand of ANSI SQL or Structured Query Language. T-SQL is entry-level ANSI 92 compliant, but it also has a number of its own extensions to the language – we'll see more of those in later chapters.

Even though, for backward compatibility, SQL Server has a number of different syntax choices that are effectively the same, wherever possible, you ought to use the ANSI form. Where there are different choices available, I will usually show you all of the choices, but again, stick with the ANSI version wherever possible. This is particularly important for situations where you think your back-end – or database server – might change at some point. Your ANSI code will, more than likely, run on the new database server - however, code that is only T-SQL definitely will not.

In this chapter, you have gained a solid taste of making use of single table statements in T-SQL, but the reality is that you often need information from more than one table. In the next chapter, we will learn how to make use of JOINs to allow us to use multiple tables.

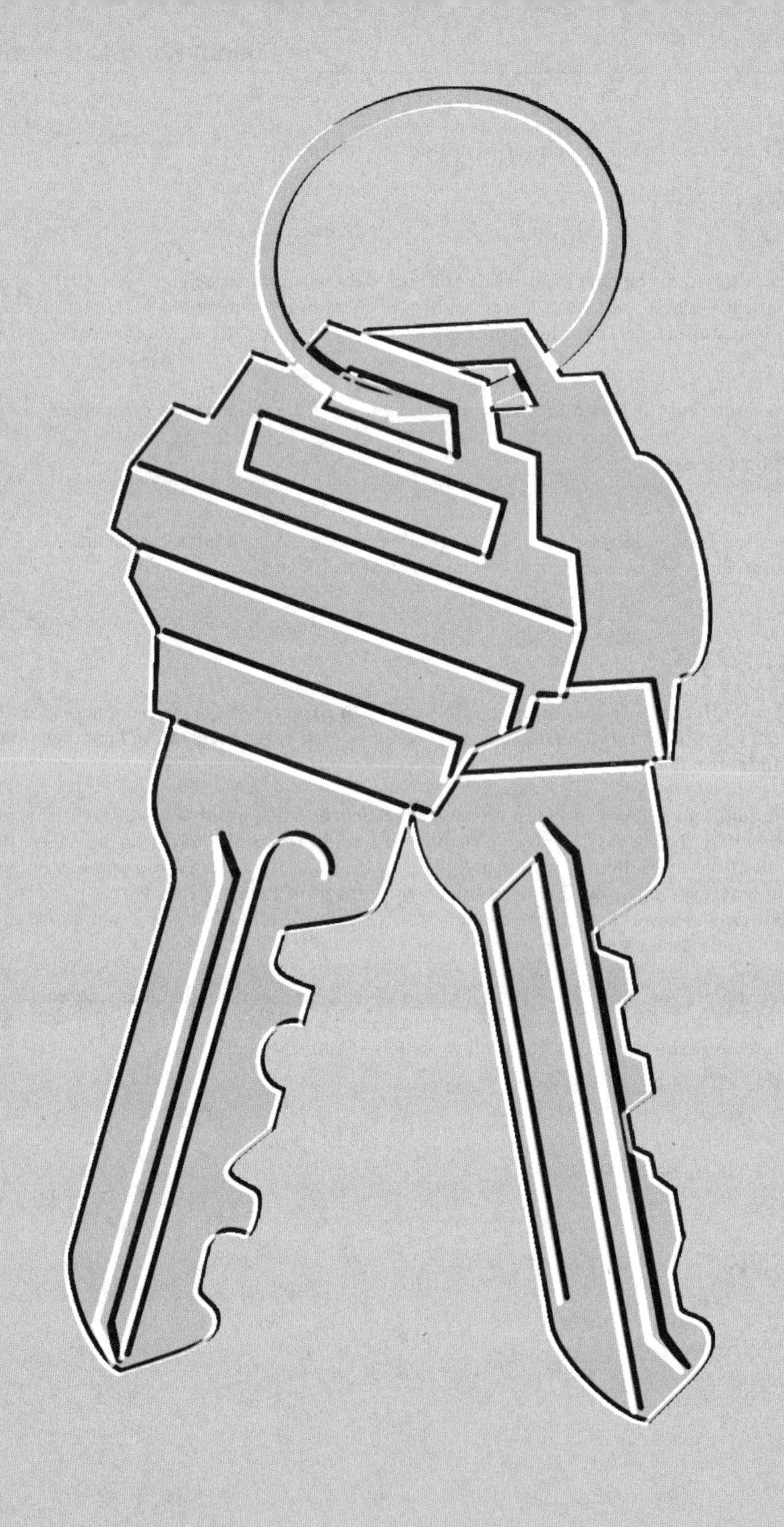

5

Joining Tables

As the Carpenters said in the 70s – we've only just begun. We've now got the basic statements under our belt, but they are only a small part of the bigger picture of the statements we will run. Simply put, there's often not that much you can do with just one table – especially in a highly normalized database.

A **normalized** database is one where the data has been broken out from larger tables into many smaller tables for the purpose of eliminating repeating data, saving space, increasing performance, and increasing data integrity. It's great stuff and vital to relational databases; however, it also means that you wind up getting your data from here, there and everywhere.

> *We will be looking into the concepts of normalization extensively in Chapter 8. For now though, just keep in mind that, the more normalized your database is, the more likely that you're going to have to join multiple tables together in order to get all the data you want.*

In this chapter, we're going to introduce you to the process of combining tables into one result set by using the various forms of the `JOIN` clause. These will include:

- `INNER JOIN`
- `OUTER JOIN` (both `LEFT` and `RIGHT`)
- `FULL JOIN`
- `CROSS JOIN`

We'll also learn how there is more than one syntax available to use for joins, but why one particular syntax is the right choice. In addition, we'll take a look at the `UNION` operator, which allows us to combine the results of two queries into one.

JOINs

When we are operating in a normalized environment, we frequently run into situations where not all of the information that we want is in one table. In other cases, all the information we want returned is in one table, but the information we want to place conditions on is in some other table. That's where the JOIN clause comes in.

A JOIN does just what it sounds like – it puts the information from two tables together into one result set. We can think of a result set as being a "virtual" table. It has both columns and rows, and the columns have data types. Indeed, in Chapter 15, we'll see how to treat a result set just as if it was a table and use it for other queries.

How exactly does a JOIN put the information from two tables into a single result set? Well, that depends on how you tell it to put the data together – that's why there are four different kinds of JOINs. The thing that all JOINs have in common is that they match one record up with one or more other records to make a record that is a superset created by the combined columns of both records.

For example, let's take a record from a table we'll call Films:

FilmID	FilmName	YearMade
1	My Fair Lady	1964

Now let's follow that up with a record from a table called Actors:

FilmID	FirstName	LastName
1	Rex	Harrison

With a JOIN, we could create one record from two records found in totally separate tables:

FilmID	FilmName	YearMade	FirstName	LastName
1	My Fair Lady	1964	Rex	Harrison

This JOIN (at least apparently) joins records in a one-to-one relationship. We have one Films record joining to one Actors record.

Let's expand things just a bit and see if you can see what's happening. I've added another record to the Actors table:

FilmID	FirstName	LastName
1	Rex	Harrison
1	Audrey	Hepburn

Now let's see what happens when we join that to the very same (only one record) `Films` table:

FilmID	FilmName	YearMade	FirstName	LastName
1	My Fair Lady	1964	Rex	Harrison
1	My Fair Lady	1964	Audrey	Hepburn

As you can see, the effect has changed a bit – we are no longer seeing things as being one-to-one, but rather one-to-two, or even more appropriately, what we would call one-to-many. We can use that single record in the `Films` table as many times as necessary in order to have complete (joined) information about the matching records in the `Actors` table.

Have you noticed how they are matching up? It is, of course, by matching up the `FilmID` field from the two tables to create one record out of two.

The examples that we have used here with such a limited data set, would actually yield the same results no matter what kind of `JOIN` we have. Let's move on now and look at the specifics of the different `JOIN` types.

INNER JOINs

`INNER JOIN`s are far and away the most common kind of `JOIN`. They match records together based on one or more common fields, as do most `JOIN`s, but an `INNER JOIN` returns only the records where there are matches for whatever field(s) you have said are to be used for the `JOIN`. In our previous examples, every record has been part of the result set at least one time, but it often does not work that way in real-life data.

Let's modify our tables and then see what we would get with an `INNER JOIN`. Here's our `Films` table:

FilmID	FilmName	YearMade
1	My Fair Lady	1964
2	Unforgiven	1992

And our `Actors` table:

FilmID	FirstName	LastName
1	Rex	Harrison
1	Audrey	Hepburn
2	Clint	Eastwood
5	Humphrey	Bogart

Using an INNER JOIN, our result set would look like this:

FilmID	FilmName	YearMade	FirstName	LastName
1	My Fair Lady	1964	Rex	Harrison
1	My Fair Lady	1964	Audrey	Hepburn
2	Unforgiven	1992	Clint	Eastwood

Notice that Bogey was left out of this result set. That's because he didn't have a matching record in the Films table. If there isn't a match in both tables, then the record isn't returned. Enough theory – let's try this out in code.

The preferred code for an INNER JOIN looks something like this:

```
SELECT <select list>
FROM <first_table>
<join_type> <second_table>
        [ON <join_condition>]
```

This is the ANSI syntax, and you'll have much better luck with it on non-SQL Server database systems than you will with the proprietary syntax that was the way things had to be done through version 6.0. We'll take a look at the other syntax later in the chapter.

Fire up the Query Analyzer and take a test drive of INNER JOINs using the following code against Northwind:

```
SELECT *
FROM Products
INNER JOIN Suppliers
        ON Products.SupplierID = Suppliers.SupplierID
```

The results of this query are too wide to actually print in this book, but if you run this, you should get something on the order of 77 rows back. There are several things worth noting about the results:

- The SupplierID column appears twice, but there's nothing to say which one is from which table
- All columns were returned from both tables
- The first columns listed were from the first table listed

We can figure out which SupplierID is which just by looking at what table we selected first and matching it with the first SupplierID column that shows up, but this is tedious at best, and at worst, prone to errors. That's one of many reasons why using the plain * operator in JOINs is ill advised. In the case of an INNER JOIN though, it's not necessarily such a big deal since we know that both SupplierID columns, even though they came from different tables, will be exact duplicates of each other. How do we know that? Think about it – since we're doing an INNER JOIN on those two columns, they have to match or the record wouldn't have been returned! Don't get in the habit of counting on this though. When we look at other JOIN types, we'll find that we can't depend on the JOIN values being equal.

As for all columns being returned from both tables, that is as expected. We used the * operator, which as we've learned before is going to return all columns to us. As I mentioned earlier, use of the * operator, is a bad habit. It's quick and easy, but it's also dirty, and prone to create poor performance and errors.

> *One habit to get into early is to select what you need, and need what you select. What I'm getting at here is that every additional record or column that you return takes up additional network bandwidth, and often, additional query processing on your SQL Server. The upshot is that selecting unnecessary information hurts performance not only for the current user, but also for every other user of the system and for users of the network on which the SQL Server resides.*
>
> *Select only the columns that you are going to be using and make your* `WHERE` *clause as restrictive as possible.*

If you must insist on using the * operator at least take a look at using it only for the tables from which you need all the columns. That's right – the * operator can be used on a per table basis. For example, if we wanted all of our product information, but only the name of the supplier, we could have changed our query to read:

```
SELECT Products.*, CompanyName
FROM Products
INNER JOIN Suppliers
        ON Products.SupplierID = Suppliers.SupplierID
```

If you scroll over to the right in the results of this query, you'll see that most of the supplier information is now gone. Indeed, we also only have one instance of the `SupplierID` column. What we got in our result set was all the columns from the `Products` table (since we used the * qualified for just that table – our one instance of `SupplierID` came from this part of the `SELECT` list) and the only column that had the name `CompanyName` (which happened to be from the `Suppliers` table). Now let's try it again, with only one slight change:

```
SELECT Products.*, SupplierID
FROM Products
INNER JOIN Suppliers
        ON Products.SupplierID = Suppliers.SupplierID
```

Uh, oh – this is a problem. We get an error back:

```
Server: Msg 209, Level 16, State 1, Line 3
Ambiguous column name 'SupplierID'.
```

Why did `CompanyName` work and `SupplierID` didn't? For just the reason SQL Server has indicated – our column name is ambiguous. While `CompanyName` only exists in the `Suppliers` table, `SupplierID` appears in both tables. SQL Server has no way of knowing which one we want. All the instances where we have returned `SupplierID` up to this point have been resolvable. That is, SQL Server could figure out which table was which. In the first query (where we used a plain * operator), we said to return everything – that would include *both* `SupplierID` columns, so no name resolution is necessary. In our second example (where we qualified the * to be only for `Products`), we again said nothing specifically about which `SupplierID` column to use – instead, we said pull everything from the `Products` table and `SupplierID` just happened to be in that list. `CompanyName` was resolvable because there was only one `CompanyName` column, so that must be the one we want.

When we want to refer to a column where the column name exists more than once in our `JOIN` result, we must **fully qualify** the column name. We can do this in one of two ways:

- Provide the name of the table that the desired column is from, followed by a period and the column name (*`Table.ColumnName`*)
- Alias the tables, and provide that alias, followed by a period and the column name (*`Alias.ColumnName`*)

The task of providing the names is straightforward enough – we've already seen how that works with the qualified * operator - but let's try our `SupplierID` query again with a qualified column name:

```
SELECT Products.*, Suppliers.SupplierID
FROM Products
INNER JOIN Suppliers
        ON Products.SupplierID = Suppliers.SupplierID
```

Now things are working again and we have the `SupplierID` from the `Suppliers` table added back to the far right-hand side of the result set.

Aliasing the table is only slightly trickier, but can cut down on the wordiness and help the readability of your query. It works almost exactly the same as aliasing a column in the simple `SELECT`s that we did in the last chapter – right after the name of the table, we simply state the alias we want to use to refer to that table. Note that, just as with column aliasing, we can use the `AS` keyword (but for some strange reason, this hasn't caught on in practice):

```
SELECT p.*, s.SupplierID
FROM Products p
INNER JOIN Suppliers s
        ON p.SupplierID = s.SupplierID
```

Run this code and you'll see that we receive the exact same results as we did in the last query.

Be aware that using an alias is an all or nothing proposition. Once you decide to alias a table, you must use that alias in every part of the query. This is on a table-by-table basis, but try running some mixed code and you'll see what I mean:

```
SELECT p.*, Suppliers.SupplierID
FROM Products p
INNER JOIN Suppliers s
        ON p.SupplierID = s.SupplierID
```

This seems like it should run fine, but it will give you an error:

Server: Msg 107, Level 16, State 3, Line 3
The column prefix 'Suppliers' does not match with a table name or alias name used in the query.

Again, you can mix and match which tables you choose to use aliasing on and which you don't, but once you make a decision, you have to be consistent.

Well, let's move on to the third of the three bullet items we had when we noticed things about our original query – the columns from the first table listed in the JOIN were the first columns returned. Take a break for a moment and think about why that is, and what you might be able to do to control it. After the few examples we've done looking at the other bullet items, I'm betting that you can make some pretty good guesses.

SQL Server always uses a column order that is the best guess it can make at how you want the columns returned. In our first query, we used one global * operator, so SQL Server didn't have much to go on. In that case, it goes on the small amount that it does have – the order of the columns as they exist physically in the table, and the order of tables that you specified in your query. The nice thing is that it is extremely easy to reorder the columns – we just have to be explicit about it. The simplest way to reorder the columns would be to change which table is mentioned first, but we can actually mix and match our column order by simply explicitly stating the columns that we want (even if it is every column), and the order in which we want them. Let's try a smaller query to demonstrate the point:

```
SELECT p.ProductID, s.SupplierID, p.ProductName, s.CompanyName
FROM Products p
INNER JOIN Suppliers s
        ON p.SupplierID = s.SupplierID
WHERE p.ProductID < 4
```

This yields a pretty simple resultset:

ProductID	SupplierID	ProductName	CompanyName
1	1	Chai	Exotic Liquids
2	1	Chang	Exotic Liquids
3	1	Aniseed Syrup	Exotic Liquids

(3 row(s) affected)

Again, the columns have come out in exactly the order that we've specified in our SELECT list.

How an INNER JOIN is Like a WHERE Clause

In the INNER JOINs that we've done this far, we've really been looking at the concepts that will work for any JOIN type – the column ordering and aliasing is exactly the same for any JOIN. The part that makes an INNER JOIN different from other JOINs is that it is an **exclusive join** – that is, it excludes all records that don't have a value in both tables (the first named, or left table, and the second named, or right table).

Our first example of this was with our imaginary Films and Actors tables. Bogey was left out because he didn't have a matching movie in the Films table. Let's look at a real example or two of how this works.

We have a Customers table, and it is full of customer names and addresses. This does not mean, however, that the customers have actually ordered anything. Indeed, I'll give you a hint up front and tell you that there are some customers that have *not* ordered anything, so let's take a question and turn it into a query – the question I've picked calls for an INNER JOIN, but we'll see how slight changes to the question will change our choice of JOINs later on.

Here's a question you might get from a sales manager: "Can you show me all the customers who have placed orders with us?"

You can waste no time in saying, "Absolutely!" and starting to dissect the parts of the query. What are the things we need? Well, the sales manager asked about both customers and orders, so we can take a guess that we will need information from both of those tables. The sales manager only asked for a list of customers, so the CompanyName and perhaps the CustomerID are the only columns we need. Note that while we need to include the Orders table to figure out whether a customer has ordered anything or not, we do not need to return anything from it to make use of it (that's why it's not in the SELECT list). The sales manager has asked for a list of customers where there has been an order, so the question calls for an answer where there is both a Customers record and an Orders record – that's our INNER JOIN scenario, so we should now be ready to write the query:

```
SELECT DISTINCT c.CustomerID, c.CompanyName
FROM Customers c
INNER JOIN Orders o
        ON c.CustomerID = o.CustomerID
```

If you haven't altered any data in the Northwind database, this should yield you 89 rows. Note that we used the DISTINCT keyword because we only need to know that the customers have made orders (once was sufficient), not how many orders. Without the DISTINCT, a customer who ordered multiple times would have had a separate record returned for each Orders record to which it joined.

Now let's see if we got all the customers back. Try running a simple COUNT query:

```
SELECT COUNT(*) AS "No. Of Records" FROM Customers
```

And you'll get back a different count on the number of rows:

```
No. Of Records
--------------------
91

(1 row(s) affected)
```

Where did the other two rows go? As expected, they were excluded from the result set because there were no corresponding records in the Orders table. It is for this reason that an INNER JOIN is comparable to a WHERE clause. Just as an INNER JOIN will exclude rows because they had no corresponding match in the other table, the WHERE clause also limits the rows returned to those that match the criteria specified.

Just for a little more proof and practice, consider the following tables from the pubs database:

authors	titles	titleauthor
au_id	title_id	au_id
au_lname	title	title_id
au_fname	type	au_ord
phone	pub_id	royaltyper
address	price	
city	advance	
state	royalty	
zip	ytd_sales	
contract	notes	
	pubdate	

What we're looking for this time is a query that returns all the authors that have written books and the titles of the books that they have written. Try coming up with this query on your own for a few minutes, then we'll dissect it a piece at a time.

The first thing to do is to figure out what data we need to return. Our question calls for two different pieces of information to be returned: The author's name and the book's title. The author's name is available (in two parts) from the `authors` table. The book's title is available in the `titles` table, so we can write the first part of our `SELECT` statement:

```
SELECT au_lname + ", " + au_fname AS "Author", title
```

What we need now is something to join the two tables on, and that's where we run into our first problem – there doesn't appear to be one. The tables don't seem to have anything in common on which we can base our `JOIN`.

This brings us to the third table listed. Depending on which database architect you're talking to, a table like `titleauthor` will be called a number of different things. The most common names that I've run across for this type of table are **linking table** or **associate table**.

A linking table is any table for which the primary purpose is not the storage of its own data, but rather to relate the data stored in other tables. You can consider it to be "linking" or "associating" the two or more tables. These tables are used to get around the common situation where you have what is called a "many-to-many" relationship between the tables. This is where two tables relate, but either table can have many records that match potentially many records in the other table. SQL Server can't implement this directly, so the linking table breaks down the relationship into two "one-to-many" relationships – which SQL Server can handle. We will see much more on this subject in Chapter 8.

This particular table doesn't meet the criteria for a linking table in the strictest sense of the word, but it still serves that general purpose, and I, not being a purist, consider it such a table. By using this third table, we are able to indirectly join the `authors` and `titles` tables by joining each to the linking table, `titleauthor`. `authors` can join to `titleauthor` based on `au_id`, and `titles` can join to `titleauthor` based on `title_id`. Adding this third table into our `JOIN` is no problem – we just keep on going with our `FROM` clause and `JOIN` keywords (don't forget to switch the database to `pubs`):

```
SELECT a.au_lname + ", " + a.au_fname AS "Author", t.title
FROM authors a
JOIN titleauthor ta
  ON a.au_id = ta.au_id
JOIN titles t
  ON t.title_id = ta.title_id
```

Notice that, since we've used aliases on the tables, we had to go back and change our `SELECT` clause to use the aliases, but our `SELECT` statement with a three-table join is now complete! If we execute this (I'm using the grid mode here), we get:

Author	Title
Bennet, Abraham	The Busy Executive's Database Guide
Blotchet-Halls, Reginald	Fifty Years in Buckingham Palace Kitchens
Carson, Cheryl	But Is It User Friendly?
DeFrance, Michel	The Gourmet Microwave
del Castillo, Innes	Silicon Valley Gastronomic Treats
Dull, Ann	Secrets of Silicon Valley
Green, Marjorie	The Busy Executive's Database Guide
Green, Marjorie	You Can Combat Computer Stress!
Gringlesby, Burt	Sushi, Anyone?
Hunter, Sheryl	Secrets of Silicon Valley
Karsen, Livia	Computer Phobic AND Non-Phobic Individuals: Behavior Variations
Locksley, Charlene	Net Etiquette
Locksley, Charlene	Emotional Security: A New Algorithm
MacFeather, Stearns	Cooking with Computers: Surreptitious Balance Sheets
MacFeather, Stearns	Computer Phobic AND Non-Phobic Individuals: Behavior Variations
O'Leary, Michael	Cooking with Computers: Surreptitious Balance Sheets
O'Leary, Michael	Sushi, Anyone?

Author	Title
Panteley, Sylvia	Onions, Leeks, and Garlic: Cooking Secrets of the Mediterranean
Ringer, Albert	Is Anger the Enemy?
Ringer, Albert	Life Without Fear
Ringer, Anne	The Gourmet Microwave
Ringer, Anne	Is Anger the Enemy?
Straight, Dean	Straight Talk About Computers
White, Johnson	Prolonged Data Deprivation: Four Case Studies
Yokomoto, Akiko	Sushi, Anyone?

If we were to do a simple `SELECT *` against the `authors` table, we would find that several authors were left out because, although they have been entered into the `authors` table, they apparently haven't written any matching books (at least not that we have in our database). Indeed, we've even left one title out because we can't match it up with an author.

> **Notice that we did not use the `INNER` keyword in this last query. That is because an `INNER JOIN` is the default `JOIN` type. Schools of thought vary on this, but I believe that because leaving the `INNER` keyword out has dominated the way code is written for so long, that it is almost more confusing to leave it in – that's why you won't see me use it again in this book.**

Once again, the key to `INNER JOIN`s is that they are exclusive.

OUTER JOINs

This type of `JOIN` is something of the exception rather than the rule. Definitely not because they don't have their uses, but rather because:

- We, more often than not, want the kind of exclusiveness that an `INNER JOIN` provides
- Many SQL writers learn `INNER JOIN`s and never go any farther – they simply don't understand the `OUTER` variety
- There are other ways to accomplish the same thing
- They are often simply forgotten about as an option

Where `INNER JOIN`s are exclusive in nature; `OUTER` and, as we'll see later in this chapter, `FULL JOIN`s are inclusive. It's a tragedy that people don't get to know how to make use of `OUTER JOIN`s, because they make seemingly difficult questions simple. They can also often speed performance when used instead of nested subqueries (which we will also look into).

Earlier in this chapter, we briefly introduced the concept of a JOIN having sides – a left and a right. With INNER JOINs these are a passing thought at most, but with OUTER JOINs, understanding your left from your right is absolutely critical. When you look at it, it seems very simple because it is very simple, yet many query mistakes involving OUTER JOINs stem from not thinking through your left from your right.

To learn how to construct OUTER JOINs correctly, we're going to use two syntax illustrations. The first deals with the simple scenario of a two-table OUTER JOIN. The second will deal with the more complex scenario of mixing OUTER JOINs with any other JOIN.

The Simple OUTER JOIN

The first syntax situation is the easy part – most people get this part just fine.

```
SELECT <SELECT list>
FROM <the table you want to be the "LEFT" table>
<LEFT|RIGHT> [OUTER] JOIN <table you want to be the "RIGHT" table>
                        ON <join condition>
```

In the examples, you'll find that I tend to use the full syntax – that is, I include the OUTER keyword (e.g. LEFT OUTER JOIN). Note that the OUTER keyword is optional – you need only include the LEFT or RIGHT (e.g. LEFT JOIN).

What I'm trying to get across here is that the table that comes before the JOIN keyword is considered to be the LEFT table, and the table that comes after the JOIN keyword is considered to be the RIGHT table.

OUTER JOINs are, as we've said, inclusive in nature. What specifically gets included depends on which side of the join you have emphasized. A LEFT OUTER JOIN includes all the information from the table on the left, and a RIGHT OUTER JOIN includes all the information from the table on the right. Let's put this in practice with a small query to see what I mean.

Let's say we want to know what all our discounts are, the amount of each discount, and which stores use them. Looking over our pubs database, we have tables called discounts and stores as follows:

discounts	**stores**
discounttype	stor_id
stor_id	stor_name
lowqty	stor_address
highqty	city
discount	state
	zip

We can directly join these tables based on the stor_id. If we did this using a common INNER JOIN, it would look something like:

```
SELECT discounttype, discount, s.stor_name
FROM discounts d
JOIN stores s
  ON d.stor_id = s.stor_id
```

This yields us just one record:

```
discounttype          discounts        stor_name
--------------------  ---------------  -----------
Customer Discount     5.00             Bookbeat

(1 row(s) affected)
```

Think about this though – it doesn't answer the question. We wanted results based on the discounts we have – not which ones were actually in use. This query only gives us discounts that we have matching stores for – it doesn't answer the question!

What we need is something that's going to return every discount and the stores where applicable. In order to make this happen, we only need to change the JOIN type in the query:

```
SELECT discounttype, discount, s.stor_name
FROM discounts d
LEFT OUTER JOIN stores s
             ON d.stor_id = s.stor_id
```

This yields us somewhat different results:

```
discounttype          discounts        stor_name
--------------------  ---------------  -----------
Initial Customer      10.50            NULL
Volume Discount       6.70             NULL
Customer Discount     5.00             Bookbeat

(3 row(s) affected)
```

If you were to perform a SELECT * against the discounts table, you'd quickly find that we have included every row from that table. We are doing a LEFT JOIN, and the discounts table is on the left side of the JOIN. But what about the stores table? If we are joining, and we don't have a matching record for the stores table, then what happens? Since it is not on the inclusive side of the join (in this case, the LEFT side), SQL Server will fill in a NULL for any value that comes from the opposite side of the join if there is not at least one match with the inclusive side of the join. In this case, all but one of our rows has a stor_name that is NULL. What we can discern from that is that two of our discounts records (the two with NULLs in the column from the stores table) do not have matching store records – that is, no stores are using that discount type.

We've answered the question then; of the three discount types, only one is being used (Customer Discount) and it is only being used by one store (Bookbeat).

Now, just for grins, let's see what happens if we change the join to a RIGHT OUTER JOIN:

```
SELECT discounttype, discount, s.stor_name
FROM discounts d
RIGHT OUTER JOIN stores s
            ON d.stor_id = s.stor_id
```

Even though this seems like a very small change, it actually changes our results rather dramatically:

```
discounttype        discountstor_name
------------------  ---------------  ------------------------------------------
NULL                NULL             Eric the Read Books
NULL                NULL             Barnum's
NULL                NULL             News & Brews
NULL                NULL             Doc-U-Mat: Quality Laundry and Books
NULL                NULL             Fricative Bookshop
Customer Discount   5.00             Bookbeat

(6 row(s) affected)
```

Similar to before, if you were to perform a SELECT * on the stores table, you would find that all of the records from stores have been included in the query. Where there is a matching record in discounts, the appropriate discount record is displayed. Everywhere else, the columns that are from the discounts table are filled in with NULLs. Assuming that we always name the discounts table first, and the stores table second, then we would use a LEFT JOIN if we want all the discounts, and a RIGHT JOIN if we want all the stores.

Finding Orphan or Non-Matching Records

We can actually use the inclusive nature of OUTER JOINs to find non-matching records in the exclusive table. What do I mean by that? Let's express it by example.

Let's change our discount question. We want to know the store name for all the stores that do not have any kind of discount record. Can you come up with a query to perform this based on what we know this far? Actually, the very last query we ran has us 90% of the way there. Think about it for a minute; an OUTER JOIN returns a NULL value in the discounts-based columns wherever there is no match. What we are looking for is pretty much the same result set as we received in the last query, except that we want to filter out any records that do have a discount, and we only want the store name. To do this, we simply change our SELECT list and add a WHERE clause. To make it a touch prettier to give to our manager, we also alias the stor_name field to be the more expected "Store Name":

```
SELECT s.stor_name AS "Store Name"
FROM discounts d
RIGHT OUTER JOIN stores s
            ON d.stor_id = s.stor_id
WHERE d.stor_id IS NULL
```

As expected, we have exactly the same stores that had NULL values before:

```
Store Name
--------------------------------------------------
Eric the Read Books
Barnum's
News & Brews
Doc-U-Mat: Quality Laundry and Books
Fricative Bookshop

(5 row(s) affected)
```

There is one question you might come up with that I want to anticipate, so that you're sure you understand why this will always work. Ask yourself this, "What if the discount record actually has a NULL value?" Well, that's why we built a WHERE clause on the same field that was part of our join. If we are joining based on the stor_id columns in both tables, then only three conditions can exist:

- If the stores.stor_id column has a non-NULL value, then, by definition of the ON operator of the JOIN clause, if a discounts record exists, then discounts.stor_id must also have the same value as stores.stor_id (look at the ON d.stor_id = s.stor_id).
- If the stores.stor_id column has a non-NULL value, then, by definition of the ON operator of the JOIN clause, if a discounts record does not exist, then discounts.stor_id will be returned as NULL.
- If the stores.stor_id happens to have a NULL value, and discounts.stor_id also has a NULL value – there will be no join, and discounts.stor_id will return NULL because there is no matching record.

A value of NULL does not join to a value of NULL. Why? Think about what we've already said about comparing NULLs - a NULL does not equal NULL. Be extra careful of this when coding. One of the more common questions I am asked is, "Why isn't this working?" in a situation where people are using an "equal to" operation on a NULL – it simply doesn't work because they are not equal. If you want to test this, try executing some simple code:

```
IF (NULL=NULL)
   PRINT "It Does"
ELSE
   PRINT "It Doesn't"
```

If you execute this, you'll get the answer to whether your SQL Server thinks a NULL equals a NULL.

This is actually a change of behavior vs. prior versions of SQL Server. Be aware that if you are running in SQL Server 6.5 compatibility mode, or if you have ANSI_NULLS set to off, then you will get a different answer (your server will think that a NULL equals a NULL). This is considered non-standard at this point. It is a violation of the ANSI standard, and it is no longer compatible with the default configuration for SQL Server. (Even the Books Online will tell you a NULL is not equal to a NULL.)

Let's use this notion of being able to identify non-matching records to identify some of the missing records from some of our earlier INNER JOINs. Remember these two queries which we ran against Northwind?

```
SELECT DISTINCT c.CustomerID, c.CompanyName
FROM Customers c
INNER JOIN Orders o
        ON c.CustomerID = o.CustomerID
```

And...

```
SELECT COUNT(*) AS "No. Of Records" FROM Customers
```

The first was one of our queries where we explored the INNER JOIN. We discovered by running the second query that the first had excluded (by design) some rows. Now let's identify the excluded rows by using an OUTER JOIN.

We know from our SELECT COUNT(*) query that our first query is missing some records from the Customers table. (It may also be missing records from the Orders table, but we're not interested in that at the moment.) The implication is that there are records in the Customers table that do not have corresponding Orders records. While our manager's first question was about all the customers that had placed orders, it would be a very commonplace question to ask just the opposite, "What customers haven't placed an order?" That question is answered with the same result as asking the question, "What records exist in Customers that don't have corresponding records in the Orders table?" The solution has the same structure as our query to find stores without discounts:

```
SELECT c.CustomerID, CompanyName
FROM Customers c
LEFT OUTER JOIN Orders o
            ON c.CustomerID = o.CustomerID
WHERE o.CustomerID IS NULL
```

Just that quick we are able to not only find out how many customers haven't placed orders, but now we know which customers they are (I suspect the sales department will contact them shortly...):

```
CustomerID  CompanyName
----------  ----------------------------------------
FISSA       FISSA Fabrica Inter. Salchichas S.A.
PARIS       Paris spécialités

(2 row(s) affected)
```

Note that whether you use a LEFT or a RIGHT JOIN doesn't matter as long as the correct table or group of tables is on the corresponding side of the JOIN. For example, we could have run the above query using a RIGHT JOIN as long as we also switched which sides of the JOIN the Customers and Orders tables were on. For example this would have yielded exactly the same results:

```
SELECT c.CustomerID, CompanyName
FROM Orders o
RIGHT OUTER JOIN Customers c
              ON c.CustomerID = o.CustomerID
WHERE o.CustomerID IS NULL
```

When we take a look at even more advanced queries, we'll run into a slightly more popular way of finding records that exist in one table without corresponding records in another table. Allow me to preface that early by saying that using JOINs is usually our best bet performance wise. There are exceptions to the rule that we will cover as we come across them, but in general, the use of JOINs will be the best when faced with multiple options.

Dealing with More Complex OUTER JOINs

Now we're on to our second illustration and how to make use of it. This scenario is all about dealing with an OUTER JOIN being mixed with some other JOIN (no matter what the variety).

It is when mixing an OUTER JOIN with other JOINs that the concept of sides becomes even more critical. What's important to understand here is that everything to the "left" – or before – the JOIN in question will be treated just as if it was a single table for the purpose of inclusion or exclusion from the query. The same is true for everything to the "right" – or after – the JOIN. The frequent mistake here is to perform a LEFT OUTER JOIN early in the query and then use an INNER JOIN late in the query. The OUTER JOIN includes everything up to that point in the query, but the INNER JOIN may still create a situation where something is excluded! My guess is that you will, like most people (including me for a while), find this exceptionally confusing at first, so let's see what we mean with some examples. Since none of the databases that come along with SQL Server has any good scenarios for demonstrating this, we're going to have to create a database and sample data of our own.

If you want to follow along with the examples, the example database called Chapter5DB can be created by running Chapter5.sql from the downloadable source code.

What we are going to do is to build up a query step-by-step and watch what happens. The query we are looking for will return a vendor name and the address of that vendor. The example database only has a few records in it; so let's start out with selecting all the choices from the central item of the query – the vendor. We're going to go ahead and start aliasing from the beginning, since we will want to do this in the end:

```
SELECT v.VendorName
FROM Vendors v
```

This yields us a scant three records:

```
VendorName
------------------------------------
Don's Database Design Shop
Dave's Data
The SQL Sequel

(3 row(s) affected)
```

These are the names of every vendor that we have at this time. Now, let's add in the address information – there are two issues here. First, we want the query to return every vendor no matter what, so we'll make use of an OUTER JOIN. Next, a vendor can have more than one address and vice versa, so the database design has made use of a linking table. This means that we don't have anything to directly join the Vendors and Address tables – we must instead join both of these tables to our linking table, which is called VendorAddress. Let's start out with the logical first piece of this join:

```
SELECT v.VendorName
FROM Vendors v
LEFT OUTER JOIN VendorAddress va
          ON v.VendorID = va.VendorID
```

Since VendorAddress doesn't itself have the address information, we're not including any columns from that table in our SELECT list. VendorAddress' sole purpose in life is to be the connection point of a many-to-many relationship (one vendor can have many addresses, and, as we've set it up here, an address can be the home of more than one vendor). Running this, as we expect, gives us the same results as before:

```
VendorName
------------------------------------
Don's Database Design Shop
Dave's Data
The SQL Sequel

(3 row(s) affected)
```

Let's take a brief time out from this particular query just to check on the table against which we just joined. Try selecting out all the data from the VendorAddress table:

```
SELECT *
FROM VendorAddress
```

Just two records are returned:

```
VendorID     AddressID
--------------  -------------
1            1
2            3

(2 row(s) affected)
```

We know, therefore, that our OUTER JOIN is working for us. Since there are only two records in the VendorAddress table, and three vendors are returned, we must be returning at least one row from the Vendors table that didn't have a matching record in the VendorAddress table. While we're here, we'll just verify that by briefly adding one more column back to our vendors query:

```
SELECT v.VendorName, va.VendorID
FROM Vendors v
LEFT OUTER JOIN VendorAddress va
          ON v.VendorID = va.VendorID
```

Sure enough, we wind up with a NULL in the VendorID column from the VendorAddress table:

```
VendorName                                   VendorID
-------------------------------------------- --------------
Don's Database Design Shop                   1
Dave's Data                                  2
The SQL Sequel                               NULL

(3 row(s) affected)
```

The vendor named "The SQL Sequel" would not have been returned if we were using an INNER or RIGHT JOIN. Our use of a LEFT JOIN has ensured that we get all vendors in our query result.

Now that we've tested things out a bit though, let's return back to our original query, and then add in the JOIN to get the actual address information. Since we don't care if we get all addresses, no special JOIN is required – at least, it doesn't appear that way at first...

```
SELECT v.VendorName, a.Address
FROM Vendors v
LEFT OUTER JOIN VendorAddress va
          ON v.VendorID = va.VendorID
JOIN Address a
  ON va.AddressID = a.AddressID
```

We get back the address information as expected, but there's a problem:

```
VendorName                                   Address
-------------------------------------------- ----------------------
Don's Database Design Shop                   1234 Anywhere
Dave's Data                                  567 Main St.

(2 row(s) affected)
```

Somehow, we've lost one of our vendors. That's because SQL Server is applying the rules in the order that we've stated them. We have started with an OUTER JOIN between Vendors and VendorAddress. SQL Server does just what we want for that part of the query – it returns all vendors. The issue comes when it applies the next set of instructions. We have a result set that is all inclusive of vendors, but we now apply that result set as part of an INNER JOIN. Since an INNER JOIN is exclusive to both sides of the JOIN, only records where the result of the first JOIN has a match with the second JOIN will be included. Since only two records match up with a record in the Address table, only two records are returned in the final result set. We have two ways of addressing this:

- Add yet another OUTER JOIN
- Change the ordering of the JOINs

Let's try it both ways. We'll add another OUTER JOIN first:

```
SELECT v.VendorName, a.Address
FROM Vendors v
LEFT OUTER JOIN VendorAddress va
            ON v.VendorID = va.VendorID
LEFT OUTER JOIN Address a
            ON va.AddressID = a.AddressID
```

And now we get to our expected results:

```
VendorName                                  Address
------------------------------------------  ---------------------
Don's Database Design Shop                  1234 Anywhere
Dave's Data                                 567 Main St.
The SQL Sequel                              NULL

(3 row(s) affected)
```

Now let's do something slightly more dramatic and reorder our query:

```
SELECT v.VendorName, a.Address
FROM VendorAddress va
JOIN Address a
  ON va.AddressID = a.AddressID
RIGHT OUTER JOIN Vendors v
            ON v.VendorID = va.VendorID
```

And we still get our desired result:

```
VendorName                                  Address
------------------------------------------  ---------------------
Don's Database Design Shop                  1234 Anywhere
Dave's Data                                 567 Main St.
The SQL Sequel                              NULL

(3 row(s) affected)
```

The question you should be asking now is, "Which way is best?" Quite often in SQL, there are several ways of executing the query without one having any significant advantage over the other – this is not one of those times.

I would most definitely steer you to the second of the two solutions. The reason has to do with going as succinctly to your data as possible. If you keep adding OUTER JOINs not because of what's happening with the current table you're trying to add in, but because you're trying to carry through an earlier JOIN result, you are much more likely to include something you don't intend, or make some sort of mistake in your overall logic. The second solution addresses this by only using the OUTER JOIN where necessary – just once. You can't always create a situation where the JOINs can be moved around to this extent, but you often can. The rule of thumb is to get all of the INNER JOINs you can out of the way first, and you will then find yourself using the minimum number of OUTER JOINs, and decreasing the number of errors you have.

I can't stress enough how often I see errors with `JOIN` *order. It is one of those areas that just seems to give developers fits. Time after time I will get called in to look over a query that someone has spent hours verifying each section of, and it seems that at least half the time I get asked whether I know about this SQL Server "bug". The bug isn't in SQL Server in this case – it's with the developer. If you take anything away from this section, I hope it is that this is one of the first places to look for errors when the results aren't coming up as you expect.*

Seeing Both Sides with FULL JOINs

Like many things in SQL, a `FULL JOIN (also known as a FULL OUTER JOIN)` is basically what it sounds like – it is a matching up of data on both sides of the `JOIN` with everything included no matter what side of the `JOIN` it is on.

`FULL JOINs` are one of those things that seem really cool at the time you learn it and then almost never get used. You'll find an honest politician more often than you'll find a `FULL JOIN` in use. Their main purpose in life is when you want to look at the complete relationship between data without giving one side or the other favoritism. You want to know about every record on both sides of the equation – with nothing left out.

A `FULL JOIN` is perhaps best expressed as what you would get if you could do a `LEFT JOIN` and a `RIGHT JOIN` in the same `JOIN`. You get all the records that match, based on the `JOIN` field(s). You also get any records that exist only in the left side, with `NULLs` being returned for columns from the right side. Finally, you get any records that exist only in the right side, with `NULLs` being returned for columns from the left side. Note that, when I say "finally", I don't mean to imply that they'll be last in the query. The result order you get will (unless you use an `ORDER BY` clause) depend entirely on what SQL Server thinks is the least cost way to retrieve your records.

Let's just get right to it by looking back at our last query from our section on `OUTER JOINs`:

```
SELECT v.VendorName, a.Address
FROM VendorAddress va
JOIN Address a
  ON va.AddressID = a.AddressID
RIGHT OUTER JOIN Vendors v
              ON v.VendorID = va.VendorID
```

What we want to do here is take it a piece at a time again, and add some fields to the `SELECT` list that will let us see what's happening. First, we'll take the first two tables using a `FULL JOIN`:

```
SELECT a.Address, va.AddressID
FROM VendorAddress va
FULL JOIN Address a
       ON va.AddressID = a.AddressID
```

As it happens, a `FULL JOIN` on this section doesn't yield us any more than a `RIGHT JOIN` would have:

```
Address                   AddressID
------------------------- -------------
1234 Anywhere             1
567 Main St.              3
999 1st St.               NULL
1212 Smith Ave            NULL
364 Westin                NULL

(5 row(s) affected)
```

But wait – there's more! Now let's add in the second `JOIN`:

```
SELECT a.Address, va.AddressID, v.VendorID, v.VendorName
FROM VendorAddress va
FULL JOIN Address a
       ON va.AddressID = a.AddressID
FULL JOIN Vendors v
       ON va.VendorID = v.VendorID
```

Now we have everything:

```
Address                   AddressID           VendorID            VendorName
------------------------- ------------------- ------------------- -----------------------------------
1234 Anywhere             1                   1                   Don's Database Design Shop
567 Main St.              3                   2                   Dave's Data
999 1st St.               NULL                NULL                NULL
1212 Smith Ave            NULL                NULL                NULL
364 Westin                NULL                NULL                NULL
NULL                      NULL                3                   The SQL Sequel

(6 row(s) affected)
```

As you can see, we have the same two rows that we would have had with an `INNER JOIN` clause. Those are then followed by the three `Address` records that aren't matched with anything in either table. Last, but not least, we have the one record from the `Vendors` table that wasn't matched with anything.

Again, use a `FULL JOIN` when you want all records from both sides of the `JOIN` – matched where possible, but included even if there is no match.

CROSS JOINs

CROSS JOINs are very strange critters indeed. A CROSS JOIN differs from other JOINs in that there is no ON operator, and that it joins every record on one side of the JOIN with every record on the other side of the JOIN. In short, you wind up with a Cartesian product of all the records on both sides of the JOIN. The syntax is the same as any other JOIN except that it uses the keyword CROSS (instead of INNER, OUTER or FULL), and that it has no ON operator. Here's a quick example:

```
SELECT v.VendorName, a.Address
FROM Vendors v
CROSS JOIN Address a
```

Think back now – we had three records in the Vendors table, and five records in the Address table. If we're going to match every record in the Vendors table with every record in the Address table, then we should end up with 3 x 5 = 15 records in our CROSS JOIN:

```
VendorName                              Address
-------------------------------------   --------------------
Don's Database Design Shop              1234 Anywhere
Don's Database Design Shop              567 Main St.
Don's Database Design Shop              999 1st St.
Don's Database Design Shop              1212 Smith Ave
Don's Database Design Shop              364 Westin
Dave's Data                             1234 Anywhere
Dave's Data                             567 Main St.
Dave's Data                             999 1st St.
Dave's Data                             1212 Smith Ave
Dave's Data                             364 Westin
The SQL Sequel                          1234 Anywhere
The SQL Sequel                          567 Main St.
The SQL Sequel                          999 1st St.
The SQL Sequel                          1212 Smith Ave
The SQL Sequel                          364 Westin

(15 row(s) affected)
```

Indeed, that's exactly what we get.

Every time I teach a SQL class, I get asked the same question about CROSS JOINs, "Why in the world would you use something like this?" I'm told there are scientific uses for it – this makes sense to me since I know there are a number of high-level mathematical functions that make use of Cartesian products. I presume that you could read a large number of samples into table structures, then perform your CROSS JOIN to create a Cartesian product of your sample. There is, however, a much more frequently occurring use for CROSS JOINs – the creation of test data.

When you are building up a database, that database is quite often part of a larger scale system that will need substantial testing. A reoccurring problem in the testing of large-scale systems is the creation of large amounts of test data. By using a `CROSS JOIN`, you can do smaller amounts of data entry to create your test data in two or more tables, and then perform a `CROSS JOIN` against the tables to produce a much larger set of test data. You have a great example in our last query – if you needed to match a group of addresses up with a group of vendors, then that simple query yields 15 records from 8. Of course, the numbers can become far more dramatic. For example, if we created a table with 50 first names, and then created a table with 250 last names, we could `CROSS JOIN` them together to create a table with 12,500 unique name combinations. By investing in keying in 300 names, we suddenly get a set of test data with 12,500 names.

Exploring Alternative Syntax for Joins

What we're going to look at in this section is what many people still consider to be the "normal" way of coding joins. Until SQL Server 6.5, the alternate syntax we'll look at here was the only join syntax in SQL Server, and what is today called the "standard" way of coding joins wasn't even an option.

Until now, we have been using the ANSI syntax for all of our SQL statements. I'm going to hold the Microsoft party line on this one and recommend that you use the ANSI method since it should, over the long run, have much better portability between systems and is also much more readable. The funny thing about this is that the old syntax is actually very well supported across platforms at the current time.

The primary reason I am covering the old syntax at all is that there is absolutely no doubt that, sooner or later, you will run into it in legacy code. I don't want you staring at that code saying, "What the heck is this?"

That being said, it is my strong recommendation that you use the ANSI syntax wherever possible. It is substantially more readable and Microsoft has indicated that they may not continue to support the old syntax indefinitely. I find it very hard to believe, given the amount of legacy code out there, that Microsoft will dump the old syntax anytime soon, but you never know.

Perhaps the biggest reason is that it is actually more functional. Under old syntax, it was actually possible to create ambiguous query logic – where there was more than one way to interpret the query. The new syntax eliminates this problem.

Remember when I compared a `JOIN` to a `WHERE` clause earlier in this chapter? Well, there was a reason. The old syntax expresses all of the `JOIN`s within the `WHERE` clause.

The old syntax supports all of the joins that we've done using ANSI with the exception of a `FULL JOIN`. If you need to perform a full join, I'm afraid you'll have to stick with the ANSI version.

An Alternative INNER JOIN

Let's do a déjà vu thing and look back at the first INNER JOIN we did in this chapter:

```
SELECT *
FROM Products
INNER JOIN Suppliers
        ON Products.SupplierID = Suppliers.SupplierID
```

This got us 77 rows back (again, assuming that Northwind is still as it was when it was shipped with SQL Server). Instead of using the ANSI JOIN though, let's write it over using a WHERE clause based join syntax. It's actually quite easy – just eliminate the words INNER JOIN and add a comma, and replace the ON operator with a WHERE clause:

```
SELECT *
FROM Products, Suppliers
WHERE Products.SupplierID = Suppliers.SupplierID
```

It's a piece of cake, and it yields us the same 77 rows we got with the other syntax.

An Alternative OUTER JOIN

The alternative syntax for OUTER JOINs works pretty much the same as the INNER JOIN, except that, since we don't have the LEFT or RIGHT keywords (and no OUTER or JOIN for that matter), we need some special operators especially built for the task. These look like this:

Alternative	ANSI
*=	LEFT JOIN
=*	RIGHT JOIN

Let's pull up the first OUTER JOIN we did this chapter. It made use of the pubs database and looked something like this:

```
SELECT discounttype, discount, s.stor_name
FROM discounts d
LEFT OUTER JOIN stores s
             ON d.stor_id = s.stor_id
```

Again, we just lose the words LEFT OUTER JOIN, and replace the ON operator with a WHERE clause:

```
SELECT discounttype, discount, s.stor_name
FROM discounts d, stores s
WHERE d.stor_id *= s.stor_id
```

Sure enough, we wind up with the same results as before:

```
discounttype                 discountstor_name
---------------------------- ---------------- ------------
Initial Customer             10.50            NULL
Volume Discount              6.70             NULL
Customer Discount            5.00             Bookbeat

(3 row(s) affected)
```

A RIGHT JOIN looks pretty much the same:

```
SELECT discounttype, discount, s.stor_name
FROM discounts d, stores s
WHERE d.stor_id =* s.stor_id
```

Again, we come up with the same six rows we would have under the ANSI syntax.

An Alternative CROSS JOIN

This is far and away the easiest of the bunch. To create a cross join using the old syntax, you just do nothing. That is, you don't put anything in the WHERE clause of the form: *TableA.ColumnA = TableB.ColumnA*.

So, for an ultra quick example, let's take our example from the CROSS JOIN section earlier in the chapter. The ANSI syntax looked like this:

```
SELECT v.VendorName, a.Address
FROM Vendors v
CROSS JOIN Address a
```

To convert it to the old syntax, we just strip out the CROSS JOIN keywords and add a comma:

```
SELECT v.VendorName, a.Address
FROM Vendors v, Address a
```

Just as with the other examples in this section, we get back the same results that we got with the ANSI syntax:

```
VendorName                                    Address
--------------------------------------------  --------------------
Don's Database Design Shop                    1234 Anywhere
Don's Database Design Shop                    67 Main St.
Don's Database Design Shop                    999 1st St.
Don's Database Design Shop                    1212 Smith Ave
Don's Database Design Shop                    364 Westin
Dave's Data                                   1234 Anywhere
Dave's Data                                   567 Main St.
Dave's Data                                   999 1st St.
Dave's Data                                   1212 Smith Ave
Dave's Data                                   364 Westin
The SQL Sequel                                1234 Anywhere
The SQL Sequel                                567 Main St.
The SQL Sequel                                999 1st St.
The SQL Sequel                                1212 Smith Ave
The SQL Sequel                                364 Westin

(15 row(s) affected)
```

The UNION

UNION is a special operator we can use to cause two or more queries to generate one result set.

A UNION isn't really a JOIN, like the previous options we've been looking at – instead it's more of an appending of the data from one query right onto the end of another query (functionally, it works a little different than this, but this is the easiest way to look at the concept). Where a JOIN combined information horizontally (adding more columns), a UNION combines data vertically (adding more rows).

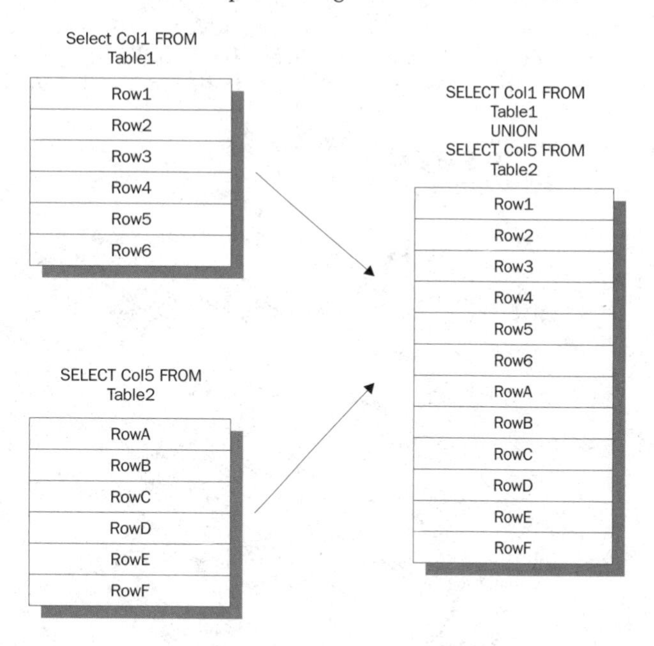

When dealing with queries that use a UNION, there are just a few key points:

- All the UNIONed queries must have the same number of columns in the SELECT list. If your first query has three columns in the SELECT list, then the second (and any subsequent queries being UNIONed) must also have three columns. If the first has five, then the second must have five too. Regardless of how many columns are in the first query, there must be the same number in the subsequent query(s).
- The headings returned for the combined result set will be taken only from the first of the queries. If your first query has a SELECT list that looks like `SELECT Col1, Col2 AS Second, Col3 FROM...`, then, regardless of how your columns are named or aliased in the subsequent queries, the headings on the columns returned from the UNION will be Col1, Second and Col3 respectively.
- The data types of each column in a query must be implicitly compatible with the data type in the same relative column in the other queries. Note that I'm not saying they have to be the same data type – they just have to be implicitly convertible (a conversion table that shows implicit vs. explicit conversions can be found in Chapter 2). If the second column in the first query is of type char(20), then it would be fine that the second column in the second query is varchar(50); however, since things are based on the first query, any rows longer than 20 would be truncated for data from the second result set.
- Unlike non-UNION queries, the default return option is DISTINCT rather than ALL. This can really be confusing to people. In our other queries, all rows were returned regardless of whether they were duplicated with another row or not, but the results of a UNION do not work that way. Unless you use the ALL keyword in your query, then only one of any repeating rows will be returned.

As always, let's take a look at this with an example or two.

First, let's look at a UNION that has some practical use to it (it's something I could see happening in the real world – albeit not all that often). For this example, we're going to assume that it's time for the holidays, and we want to send out a New Year's card to everyone that's involved with the Northwind. We want to return a list of full addresses to send our cards to including our employees, customers and suppliers. We can do this in just one query with something like this:

```
SELECT CompanyName AS Name,
       Address,
       City,
       Region,
       PostalCode,
       Country
FROM Customers

UNION

SELECT CompanyName,
       Address,
       City,
       Region,
       PostalCode,
       Country
FROM Suppliers

UNION

SELECT FirstName + " " + LastName,
       Address,
       City,
       Region,
       PostalCode,
       Country
FROM Employees
```

This gets us back just one result set, but it has data from all three queries:

Name	Address	City	Region	Postal Code	Country
Alfreds Futterkiste	Obere Str. 57	Berlin	NULL	12209	Germany
Ana Trujillo Emparedados y helados	Avda. de la Constitución 2222	México D.F.	NULL	5021	Mexico
Andrew Fuller	908 W. Capital Way	Tacoma	WA	98401	USA
...					
...					
...					
Wilman Kala	Keskuskatu 45	Helsinki	NULL	21240	Finland
Wolski Zajazd	ul. Filtrowa 68	Warszawa	NULL	01-012	Poland
Zaanse Snoepfabriek	Verkoop Rijnweg 22	Zaandam	NULL	9999 ZZ	Netherlands

We've got something for everyone here. Alfreds is a customer, Andrew Fuller is an employee, and Zaanse is a supplier. We have our one result set from what would have been three. Again, notice that the headings for the returned columns all came from the `SELECT` list of the first of the queries.

As I played with this, I got some rather inconsistent results on the sorting of the query, so don't be surprised if the order of your query looks a lot different from mine. The big thing is that you should have approximately 129 rows depending on what modifications you've made to the `Northwind` *database previously. If you want the results to be returned in a specific order, then don't forget the* `ORDER BY` *clause.*

Moving on to a second example, I want to show you how a `UNION` deals with duplicate rows – it's actually just backwards of a normal query in that it assumes you want to throw out duplicates (in our previous queries, the assumption was that you wanted to keep everything unless you used the `DISTINCT` keyword). This demo has zero real-world potential, but it's quick and easy to run and see how things work.

In this case, we are creating two tables from which we will select. We'll then insert three rows into each table, with one row being identical between the two tables. If our query is performing an `ALL`, then every row (six of them) will show up. If the query is performing a `DISTINCT`, then it will only return five rows (tossing out one duplicate):

```
CREATE TABLE UnionTest1
(
   idcol    int        IDENTITY,
   col2     char(3),
)

CREATE TABLE UnionTest2
(
   idcol    int        IDENTITY,
   col4     char(3),
)

INSERT INTO UnionTest1
VALUES
   ("AAA")

INSERT INTO UnionTest1
VALUES
   ("BBB")

INSERT INTO UnionTest1
VALUES
   ("CCC")

INSERT INTO UnionTest2
VALUES
   ("CCC")

INSERT INTO UnionTest2
VALUES
   ("DDD")

INSERT INTO UnionTest2
VALUES
   ("EEE")

SELECT col2
FROM UnionTest1

UNION

SELECT col4
FROM UnionTest2

PRINT "Divider Line--------------------------"

SELECT col2
FROM UnionTest1

UNION ALL

SELECT col4
FROM UnionTest2


DROP TABLE UnionTest1
DROP TABLE UnionTest2
```

Now, let's look at the heart of what's returned (you'll see some one rows affected in there – just ignore them until you get to where the results of your query are visible):

```
col2
------
DDD
EEE
AAA
BBB
CCC

(5 row(s) affected)

Divider Line-------------------------
col2
-----
AAA
BBB
CCC
CCC
DDD
EEE

(6 row(s) affected)
```

The first result set returned was a simple `UNION` statement with no additional parameters. You can see that one row was eliminated – even though we inserted "CCC" into both tables, only one makes an appearance since the duplicate record is eliminated by default.

The second return changed things a bit. This time we used a `UNION ALL` and the `ALL` keyword ensured that we get every row back. As such, our eliminated row from the last query suddenly reappears.

Summary

In RDBMS systems, the data we want is quite frequently spread across more than one table. `JOINs` allow us to combine the data from multiple tables in a variety of ways:

- Use an `INNER JOIN` when you want to exclude non-matching fields.
- Use an `OUTER JOIN` when you want to retrieve matches wherever possible, but also want a fully inclusive data set on one side of the `JOIN`.
- Use a `FULL JOIN` when you want a to retrieve matches wherever possible, but also want a fully inclusive data set of both sides of the `JOIN`.
- Use a `CROSS JOIN` when you want a Cartesian product based on the records in two tables. This is typically used in scientific environments and when you want to create test data.
- Use a `UNION` when you want the combination of the result of a second query appended to the first query.

There are two different forms of `JOIN` syntax available for `INNER` and `OUTER JOINs`. We provided the legacy syntax here to help you deal with legacy code, but the newer ANSI format presented through most of this chapter is highly preferable, as it is more readable, is not prone to the ambiguities of the older syntax, and will be supported in SQL Server for the indefinite future.

Over the course of the next few chapters, we will be learning how to build our own tables and "relate" them to each other. As we do this, the concepts of knowing what columns to join on will become even clearer.

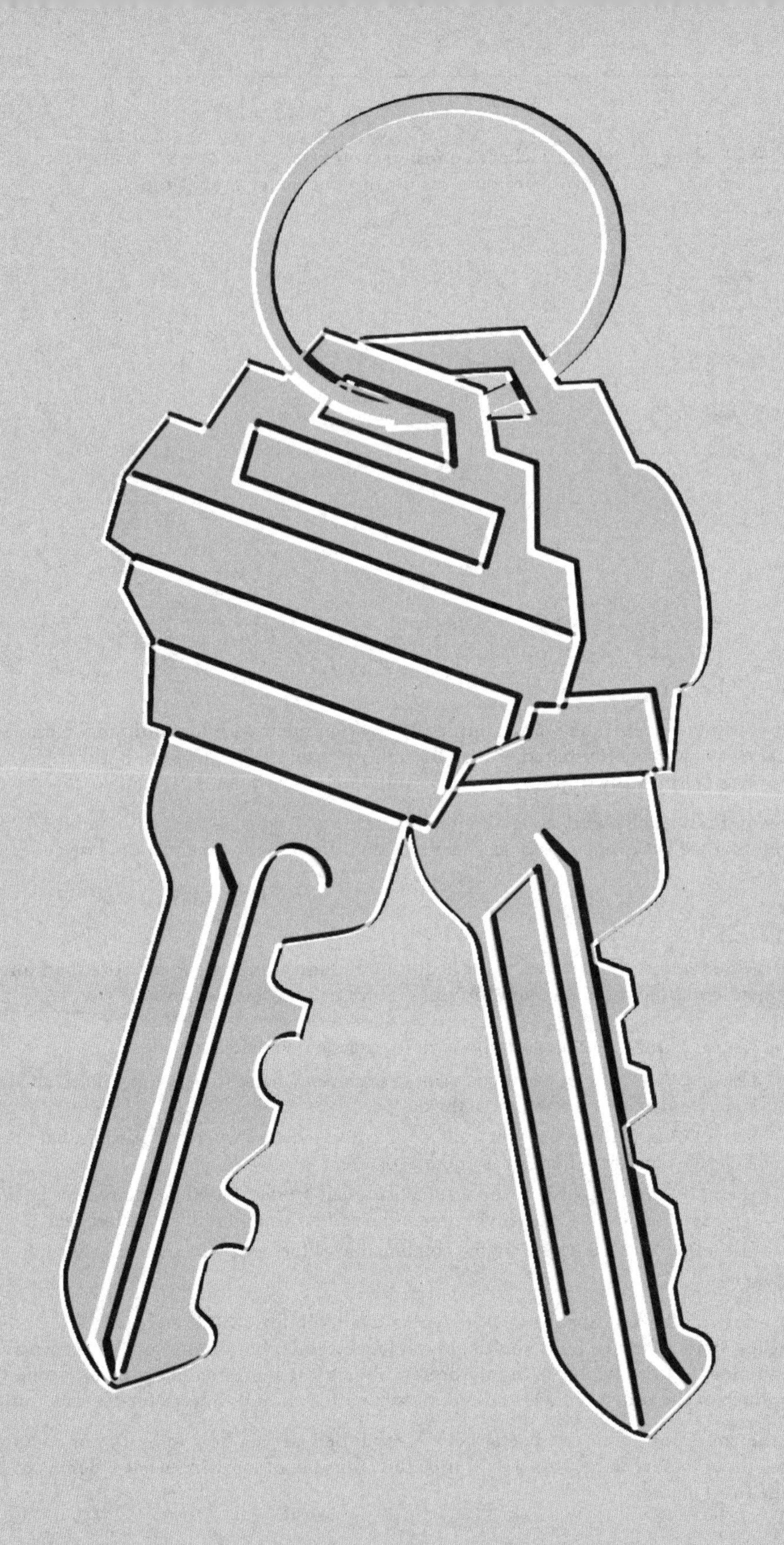

6

Creating and Altering Tables

Every time I teach the T-SQL code for creating databases, tables, keys and constraints, I am asked the same question, "Can't you just do this in the GUI tool?" The answer is an unequivocal - yes! Therefore, the next question usually follows quite shortly behind, "Then why are we spending all this time learning stuff I'll never use?" The answer is just as unequivocal – you will use the regular syntax on a quasi-regular basis. The reality is you probably won't actually write the code from scratch that often, but you'll verify and edit it on the majority of all larger database projects you work on – that means that you had better know how it works.

In this chapter, we will be studying the syntax to create our own tables. We will also take a look at how to make use of the new and improved – at least for this task – Enterprise Manager to help us with this (after we know how to do it for ourselves).

However, before we get too deep in the actual statements that create tables and other objects, we need to digress far enough to deal with the convention for a fully qualified name, and, to a lesser extent, ownership.

Object Names in SQL Server

In all the queries that we've been performing so far in this book, you've seen simple naming at work. I've had you switch the active database in the Query Analyzer before running any queries and that has helped your queries to work. How? Well, SQL Server only looks at a very narrow scope when trying to identify and locate the objects you name in your queries and other statements. For example, we've only been providing the names of tables without any additional information, but there are actually four levels in the naming convention for any SQL Server table (and any other SQL Server object for that matter). A fully qualified name is as follows:

```
[ServerName.[DatabaseName.[OwnerName.]]]ObjectName
```

You must provide an object name whenever you are performing an operation on that object, but all parts of the name to the left of the object name are optional. Indeed, most of the time, they are not needed, and are therefore left off. Still, before we start creating objects, it's a good idea for us to get a solid handle on each part of the name. So let's move from the object name left.

Ownership

Ownership of objects is a sticky one. If I thought I could get away with it, I'd skip it entirely and try to keep you from even knowing it exists. Some people really like using ownership, but I'm definitely not one of them. It's my personal experience that use of ownership always creates *far* more problems than solutions. Why? Well, we'll get to that in due time. For now, let's instead worry about what it is and how it works.

Ownership is actually a great deal like what it sounds – it is a recognition, right within the fully qualified name, of who "owns" the object. Usually, this will be either the person who created the object or the database owner (more commonly referred to as the `dbo` – I'll get to describing the `dbo` shortly).

By default, only users who have the `sysadmin` system role or the `db_owner`, or `db_ddladmin` `database` roles can create objects in a database.

> *The roles mentioned here are just a few of many system and database roles that are built into SQL Server with version 7.0. These roles have a logical set of permissions granted to them according to how that role might be used. When you assign a particular role to someone, you are giving that person the ability to have all the permissions that the role has. This is looked into much more extensively in Chapter 23.*

Individual users can also be given the right to create certain types of both database and system objects. If such individuals do indeed create an object, then they will be assigned as the owner for that object.

> **We'll talk much more about this in the chapter on security, but let me say that just because a feature is there it doesn't mean it should be used! Giving `CREATE` authority to individual users is nothing short of nightmarish. Trying to keep track of who created what, when, and for what reason becomes near impossible. As we'll see in this and later chapters, you start a wild mix of ownership chains (where someone owns an object, which refers to an object that is owned by someone else, which refers to an object that is owned by a third person, and so on) that will break people's will, their minds, and most of all, their queries. In short, keep `CREATE` access limited to the `sa`, or at the very most, `sa` plus one or two `db_owner` role members.**

Ownership by Default: The dbo

Whoever creates the database is considered to be the owner, or dbo, of that database. Any objects that they create within that database shall be listed with an ownership of dbo rather than their individual user name. Any objects created by anyone else will have an ownership listed with that user's login name.

For example, let's say that I am an everyday user of a database, my login name is GIJoe, and I have been granted CREATE TABLE authority to a given database. If I create a table called MyTable, the owner qualified object name would be GIJoe.MyTable. Note that, since the table has a specific owner, any user of GIJoe.MyTable would need to provide the owner qualified name in order for SQL Server to resolve the table name.

Now let's say, that there is also a user with a login name of Fred. Fred is the database owner. If Fred creates a table called MyTable using an identical CREATE statement to that used by GIJoe, the owner qualified table name will be dbo.MyTable. In addition, as dbo also happens to be the default owner, any user could just refer to the table as MyTable.

It's worth pointing out that sa (or members of the sysadmins role) always aliases to the dbo. That is, no matter who actually owns the database, sa will always have full access as if it was the dbo, and any objects created by the sa login will show ownership belonging to the dbo.

Personally, I create all objects using sa whenever possible. It removes any doubt about who the dbo is, and keeps things cleaner. With version 7, I'm finding that my attitude seems to be shifting to having specific logins for each user - even for your system administrator - and then assigning them the db_owner role for any databases for which they are responsible. If they need full-blown sa-level access, then you can assign them the sysadmins role. You can find your own way on what works best for you.

Why the change? Well, in some ways it isn't a change. I've always tried to set things up where every user – including people with system administrator roles – had their own logins. If they needed sa-level access, then they should log in separately as sa, do what they need to do, then log out. This is a hassle, but it makes it much easier to audit who's doing what in the system (if five people are all logged in as sa, then how do you tell who's who?). Still, that meant a lot of people spent a lot of time logged in as sa (if they are a sysadmin, then they frequently need that level of access). With 7.0, we can now assign sa-level access to someone other than the sa account. This means we can safely put sa to bed, and let our system administrators use their own accounts together with the sysadmins role.

The Database Name

The next item in the fully qualified naming convention is the database name. Prior to SQL Server 7.0, this was actually the top of the name hierarchy, but more on that shortly.

Sometimes you want to retrieve data from a database other than the default, or current, database. Indeed, you may actually want to `JOIN` data from across databases. A database-qualified name gives you that ability. For example, if you were logged in with `pubs` as your current database, and you wanted to refer to the `Orders` table in the `Northwind` database, then you could refer to it by `Northwind.dbo.Orders`. Since `dbo` is the default owner, you could also use `Northwind..Orders`. If the login `GIJoe` owns a table named `MyTable` in `MyDatabase`, then you could refer to that table as `MyDatabase.GIJoe.MyTable`. Remember that the current database is always the default, so, if you only want data from the current database, then you do not need to include the database name in your fully qualified name.

Naming by Server

Beginning with SQL Server 7.0, the server name is now the top of the fully qualified name game. With 7.0 came the possibility of linked servers (do not confuse these with remote servers). Linked servers give you the capability to perform a `JOIN` across not just different databases, but different servers. We'll see much more about this later in the book, but for now, just realize that there is one more level in our naming hierarchy, and that it works pretty much like the database and ownership levels work.

Let's just add to our previous example. If we want to retrieve information from a server we have created a link with called `MyServer`, a database called `MyDatabase`, and a table called `MyTable` owned by `GIJoe`, then the fully qualified name would be `MyServer.MyDatabase.GIJoe.MyTable`.

Reviewing the Defaults

So let's look one last time at how the defaults work at each level of the naming hierarchy from right to left:

- Object Name: There isn't a default – you must supply an object name
- Ownership: You can leave this off, in which case it will resolve using `dbo`
- Database Name: This can also be left off, in which case SQL Server will substitute in the name of the current database
- Server Name: You can provide the name of a linked server here, but most of the time you'll just leave this off which will cause SQL Server to default to the server you are logged into

If you want to skip something in the middle, but still provide information to the left of what you are skipping, then you must still provide the extra "." for the level of the hierarchy you are skipping. For example, if we are logged in using the `Northwind` database on our local server, but want to refer to the `Orders` table in the `Northwind` database on a linked server called `MyOtherServer`, then we could refer to that table by using `MyOtherServer...Orders`. Since we didn't provide a specific database name, it will assume that the name of the current database on the local server is also the name of the database we want on the other server.

The CREATE Statement

In the bible, God said, "Let there be light!" And there was light. Unfortunately, creating things isn't quite as simple for us mere mortals. We need to provide a well-defined syntax in order to create the objects in our database. To do that, we make use of the `CREATE` statement.

Let's look at the full structure of a `CREATE` statement, starting with the utmost in generality. You'll find that all the `CREATE` statements start out the same, and then get into the specifics. The first part of the `CREATE` will always look like:

```
CREATE <object type> <object name>
```

This will be followed by the details that will vary by the nature of the object that you're creating.

CREATE DATABASE

For this part of things, we'll need to create a database called `Accounting` that we will also use when we start to create tables. The most basic syntax for the `CREATE DATABASE` statement looks like the example above.

```
CREATE DATABASE <database name>
```

It's worth pointing out that, when you create a new object, no one can access it except for the person that created it, the system administrator and the database owner (which, if the object created was a database, is the same as the person that created it). This allows you to create things and make whatever adjustments you need to make before you explicitly allow access to your object. We will look further into how to "grant" access and security in general in Chapter 23.

It's also worth noting that you can only use the `CREATE` statement to create objects on the local server (adding in a specific server name doesn't work).

This will yield a database that looks exactly like your `model` database (we discussed the `model` database in Chapter 2). The reality of what you want is almost always different, so let's look at a fuller syntax listing:

```
CREATE DATABASE <database name>
[ON [PRIMARY]
   ([NAME = <'logical file name'>,]
    FILENAME = <'file name'>
   [, SIZE = <size in megabytes or kilobytes>]
   [, MAXSIZE = <size in megabytes or kilobytes>]
   [, FILEGROWTH = <No of megabytes or kilobytes|percentage>])]
[LOG ON
   ([NAME = <'logical file name'>,]
    FILENAME = <'file name'>
   [, SIZE = <size in megabytes or kilobytes>]
   [, MAXSIZE = <size in megabytes or kilobytes>]
   [, FILEGROWTH = <No of megabytes or kilobytes|percentage>])]
```

There's a lot there, so let's break down the parts.

ON

`ON` is used in two places: To define the location of the file where the data is stored, and to define the same information for where the log is stored. You'll notice the `PRIMARY` keyword there - this means that what follows is the primary (or main) filegroup in which to physically store the data. You can also store data in what are called secondary filegroups, but we'll defer discussion of those until we get to performance tuning. For now, stick with the default notion that you want everything in one file.

> **SQL Server allows you to store your database in multiple files; furthermore, it allows you to cluster those files into logical groupings called filegroups. Filegroups are there to make life easier in the backup process by allowing you to treat blocks of files as though they were one.**

NAME

This one isn't quite what it sounds like. It is a name for the file you are defining, but only a logical name - that is, the name that SQL Server will use internally to refer to that file. You will use this name when you want to resize (expand or shrink) the database and/or file.

FILENAME

This one is what it sounds like - the physical name on the disk of the actual operating system file that the data and log (depending on what section you're defining) will be stored in. The default here (assuming you used the simple syntax we looked at first) depends on whether you are dealing with the database itself or the log. Your file will be located in the `\Data` subdirectory under your main `MSSQL7` directory (or whatever you called your main SQL Server directory if you changed it at install). If we're dealing with the physical database file, it will be named the same as your database with an `.mdf` extension. If we're dealing with the log, it will be named the same as the database file only with a suffix of `_Log` and an `.ldf` extension. You are allowed to specify other extensions if you explicitly name the files, but I strongly encourage you to stick with the defaults of `mdf` (database) and `ldf` (log file).

Keep in mind that, while `FILENAME` is an optional parameter, it is only optional as long as you go with the extremely simple syntax that I introduced first. If you provide any of the additional information, then you must include an explicit file name - be sure to provide a full path.

> *Prior to version 7.0, SQL Server used a very different paradigm for the physical storage of both the data and log information. The old method made use of what was called a device, and actually operated somewhat outside the realm of the normal operating storage system. Thank fully, this way of doing things has gone the way of the dinosaur.*
>
> *Devices were not automatically created when you created a database – indeed, you needed to make sure that you created them in advance of your `CREATE DATABASE` statement. You could potentially store many databases in one device.*
>
> *Perhaps the trickiest issue regarding the old device concept was that the physical operating system file for the device was not deleted from the system when the logical SQL Server device was. You needed to go to Windows Explorer and manually delete the operating system file. This often led to very large disk drives being inexplicably full.*

SIZE

No mystery here. It is what it says – the size of the database. By default, the size is in megabytes, but you can make it kilobytes by using a `KB` instead of `MB` after the numeric value for the size. Keep in mind that this value must be at least as large as the `model` database is, or you will receive an error. If you do not supply a value for `SIZE`, then the database will initially be the same size as the `model` database.

> **The value you supply for size (if any) is exactly the size that will be taken up by your `CREATE` statement – this is unlike previous versions that used to round the size of your device to a set increment level.**

MAXSIZE

This one is still pretty much what it sounds like, with only a slight twist vs. the `SIZE` parameter. SQL Server has a mechanism to allow your database to automatically allocate additional disk space (to grow) when necessary. `MAXSIZE` is the maximum size to which the database can grow. Again, the number is, by default, in megabytes, but it can be set in kilobytes by using the `KB` suffix. The slight twist is that there is no firm default. If you don't supply a value for this parameter, then there is considered to be no maximum – the practical maximum becomes when your disk drive is full.

If your database reaches the value set in the `MAXSIZE` parameter, your users will start getting errors back saying that their inserts can't be performed. If your log reaches its maximum size, you will not be able to perform any logged activity (which is most activities) in the database. Personally, I recommend setting up what is called an **alert**. You can use alerts to tell you when certain conditions exist (such as a database or log that's almost full). We'll see how to create alerts in Chapter 25.

> **I recommend that you always include a value for `MAXSIZE`, and that you make it at least several megabytes smaller than would fill up the disk. I suggest this because a completely full disk can cause situations where you can't commit any information to permanent storage. If the log was trying to expand, the results could potentially be disastrous. In addition, even the operating system can occasionally have problems if it runs completely out of disk space.**
>
> **One more thing – if you decide to follow my advice on this issue, be sure to keep in mind that you may have multiple databases on the same system. If you size each of them to be able to take up the full size of the disk less a few megabytes, then you will still have the possibility of a full disk (if they all expand).**

FILEGROWTH

Where `SIZE` set the initial size of the database, and `MAXSIZE` determined just how large the database file could get, `FILEGROWTH` essentially determines just how fast it gets to that maximum. You provide a value that indicates how many megabytes (or kilobytes) at a time you want the file to be enlarged. Alternately, you can provide a percentage value by which you want the database to increase. With this option, the size will go up by the stated percentage of the current database size. Therefore, if you set a database to start out at 1GB with a `FILEGROWTH` of 20%, then the first time it expands it will grow to 1.2GB, the second time to 1.44, and so on.

LOG ON

The `LOG ON` option allows you to establish that you want your log to go in a different filegroup than the database itself.

Building a Database

At this point, we're ready to begin building our database. Below is the statement to create it, but keep in mind that the database itself is only one of many objects that we will create on our way to a fully functional database:

```
CREATE DATABASE Accounting
ON
   (NAME = 'Accounting',
    FILENAME = 'c:\mssql7\data\Accounting_Data.mdf',
    SIZE = 10,
    MAXSIZE = 50,
    FILEGROWTH = 5)
LOG ON
   (NAME = 'AccountingLog',
    FILENAME = 'c:\mssql7\data\Accounting_Log.ldf',
    SIZE = 5MB,
    MAXSIZE = 25MB,
    FILEGROWTH = 5MB)

GO
```

Now is a good time to start learning about some of the informational utilities that are available with SQL Server. We saw `sp_help` in Chapter 4, but in this case, let's try running a command called `sp_helpdb`. This one is especially tailored for database structure information, and often provides better information if we're more interested in the database itself than the objects it contains. `sp_helpdb` takes one parameter – the database name:

```
sp_helpdb 'Accounting'
```

This actually yields you two separate result sets. The first is based on the combined (data and log) information about your database:

name	db_size	owner	dbid	created	status
Accounting	15.00 MB	sa	9	Jan 01 1999	no options set

The second provides specifics about the various files that make up your database – including their current size and growth settings:

name	fileid	filename	filegroup	size	maxsize	growth	usage
Accounting	1	c:\mssql7\data\Accounting.mdf	PRIMARY	10240 KB	51200 KB	5120 KB	data only
AccountingLog	2	c:\mssql7\data\AccountingLog.ldf	NULL	5120 KB	25600 KB	5120 KB	log only

After you create tables and insert data, the database will begin to automatically grow on an as-needed basis – this is much different from version 6.5, and is one of the many features added to SQL Server in version 7.0 that is meant to make life easier for the database administrator.

CREATE TABLE

The first part of creating a table is pretty much the same as creating any object – remember that line I showed you? Well, here it is again:

```
CREATE <object type> <object name>
```

Since a table is what we want, we can be more specific:

```
CREATE TABLE Customers
```

With `CREATE DATABASE`, we could have stopped with just these first three keywords, and it would have built the database based on the guidelines established in the `model` database. With tables however, there is no `model`, so we need to provide some more specifics in the form of columns, data-types and special operators.

Let's look at more extended syntax:

```
CREATE TABLE [database_name.[owner].]table_name
({column_name data_type
[[DEFAULT constant_expression]
   |[IDENTITY [(seed, increment) [NOT FOR REPLICATION]]]]
   [ROWGUIDCOL]
   [NULL|NOT NULL]
   [<column constraints>]
   |[column_name AS computed_column_expression]
   |[<table_constraint>]}
   [,...n]
)
[ON {<filegroup>|DEFAULT}]
[TEXTIMAGE_ON {<filegroup>|DEFAULT}]
```

Now that's a handful – and it still has sections taken out of it for simplicity's sake! As usual, let's look at the parts, starting with the second line (we've already seen the top line).

Table and Column Names

What's in a name? Frankly – a lot. You may recall that one of my first soapbox diatribes was back in Chapter 2 and was about names. I promised then that it wouldn't be the last you heard from me on the subject, and this won't be either.

The rules for naming tables and columns are, in general, the same rules that apply to all database objects. The SQL Server documentation will refer to these as the **rules for identifiers**, and they are the same rules we looked at the end of Chapter 2. The rules are actually pretty simple: What we want to touch on here though, are some notions about how exactly to name your objects – not specific rules of what SQL Server will and won't accept for names, but how you want to go about naming your tables and columns so that they are useful and make sense.

There are a ton of different "standards" out there for naming database objects – particularly tables and columns. My rules are pretty simple:

- Capitalize the first letter and use small case for the remaining letters of each word in the name.
- Keep the name short, but make it long enough to be descriptive.
- Limit use of abbreviations. The only acceptable use of abbreviations is when the chosen abbreviation will be recognized by anyone. Examples of abbreviations I use include "ID" to take the place of identification, "No" to take the place of number, and "Org" to take the place of organization. Keeping your names of reasonable length will sometimes require you to be more cavalier about your abbreviations at some times than others, but keep in mind that, first and foremost, you want clarity in your names.
- When building tables based on other tables (usually called linking or associate tables), you should include the names of all of the parent tables in your new table name. For example, say you have a movie database where many stars can appear in many movies. If you have a `Movies` table and a `Stars` table, you may want to tie them together using a table called `MovieStars`.
- When you have two words in the name, do not use any separators (run the words together) – use the fact that you capitalize the first letter of each new word to figure out how to separate words.

I can't begin to tell you the battles I've had with other database people about naming issues. You will find that a good many people believe that you should separate the words in your names with an underscore (_). Why don't I do it that way? Well, it's an ease of use issue. Underscores present a couple of different problems:

- First, many people have a difficult time typing an underscore without taking their hand away from the proper keyboard position – this leads to lots of typos.
- Second, in documentation it is not uncommon to run into situations where the table or column name is underlined. Underscores are, depending on the font, impossible to see when the text is underlined – this leads to confusion and more errors.
- Finally (and this is a nit pick), it's just more typing.

Beginning with SQL Server 7.0, it is also an option to separate the words in the name using a regular space. If you recall my first soapbox diatribe back in Chapter 2, you'll know that isn't really much of an option – it is extremely bad practice and creates an unbelievable number of errors. It was added to facilitate Access upsizing, and I curse the person(s) who decided to put it in – I'm sure they were well meaning, but they will be part of the cause for much grief in the database world.

This list is certainly not set in stone, rather it is just a reader's digest version of the rules I use when naming tables. I find that they save me a great deal of grief. I hope they'll do the same for you.

Consistency, consistency, consistency. Every time I teach, I always warn my class that it's a word I'm going to repeat over and over, and in no place is it more important than in naming. If you have to pick one rule to follow, then pick a rule that says that, whatever your standards are – make them just that: standard. If you decide to abbreviate for some reason, then abbreviate that word every time (the same way). Regardless of what you're doing in your naming, make it apply to the entire database consistently. This will save a ton of mistakes, and it will save your users time in terms of how long it takes for them to get to know the database.

Data Types

There isn't much to this – the data types are as I described them in Chapter 2. You just need to provide a data type immediately following the column name – there is no default data type.

DEFAULT

We'll cover this in much more detail in our chapter on constraints, but for now, suffice to say that this is the value to want to be used for any rows that are inserted without a value for this particular column. The default, if you use one, should immediately follow the data type.

IDENTITY

The concept of an **identity** value is a very important concept in database design. We will cover how to use identity columns in some detail in our chapters on design. What is an identity column? Well, when you make a column an identity column, SQL Server automatically assigns a sequenced number to this field with every row you insert. The number that SQL Server starts counting from is called the **seed value**, and the amount that the value increases with each row is called the **increment**. The default is for a seed of 1 and an increment of 1, and most designs call for it to be left that way. As an example though, you could have a seed of 3 and an increment of 5. In this case, you would start counting from 3, and then add 5 each time for 8, 13, 18, 23, and so on.

An identity column must be numeric, and it is almost always implemented with an integer data type. You can use a fixed length numeric field if you need to use larger numbers than an integer allows for. The usage is pretty simple; you simply include the `IDENTITY` keyword right after the data type for the column. An identity option cannot be used in conjunction with a default constraint. This makes sense if you think about it - how can there be a constant default if you're counting up every time?

It's worth noting that an identity column works sequentially. That is, once you've set a seed (the starting point) and the increment, your values only go up. There is no automatic mechanism to go back and fill in the numbers for any rows you may have deleted. If you want to fill in blanks spaces like that, you need to use `SET IDENTITY_INSERT ON`, which allows you to turn off the identity process for inserts from the current connection.

The most common use for an identity column is to ensure a unique identifier for each row – that is, identity columns are commonly used to create a primary key for a table.

If you've come from the Access world, you'll notice that an `IDENTITY` column is much like an AutoNumber field. The major difference is that you have a bit more control over it in SQL Server.

NOT FOR REPLICATION

This one is very tough to deal with at this point, so I am, at least in part, going to skip it until we come to the chapter on replication.

> **Briefly, replication is the process of automatically doing what, in a very loose sense, amounts to copying some or all of the information in your database to some other database. The other database may be on the same physical machine as the original, or it may be located remotely.**

The `NOT FOR REPLICATION` parameter determines whether a new identity value for the new database is assigned when the column is published to another database (via replication), or whether it keeps its existing value. There will be much more on this at a later time.

ROWGUIDCOL

This is also replication related and, in many ways, is the same in purpose to an identity field. We've already seen how using an identity column can provide you with an easy way to make sure that you have a value that is unique to each row and can, therefore, be used to identify that row. However, this can be a very error-prone solution when you are dealing with replicated or other distributed environments.

Think about it for a minute – while an identity column will keep counting upwards from a set value, what's to keep the values from overlapping on different databases? Now, think about when you try to replicate the values such that all the rows that were previously in separate databases now reside in one database – uh oh! You now will have duplicate values in the column that is supposed to uniquely identify each row!

Over the years, the common solution for this was to use separate seed values for each database you were replicating to and from. For example, you may have database A which starts counting at 1, database B starts at 10,000, and database C starts at 20,000. You can now publish them all into the same database safely – for a while. As soon as database A has more than 9,999 records inserted into it, you're in big trouble.

"Sure," you say, "why not just separate the values by 100,000 or 500,000?" If you have tables with a large amount of activity, you're still just delaying the inevitable – that's where a `ROWGUIDCOL` comes into play.

What is a `ROWGUIDCOL`? Well, it's quite a bit like an identity column in that it is usually used to uniquely identify each row in a table. The difference is to what degree the system goes to make sure that the value used is truly unique. Instead of using a numerical count, SQL Server instead uses what is known as a **GUID**, or a **Globally Unique Identifier**. While an identity value is usually (unless you alter something) unique across time, it is not unique across space. Therefore, we can have two copies of our table running, and have them both assigned an identical identity value. While this is just fine to start with, it causes big problems when we try to bring the rows from both tables together as one replicated table. A GUID is unique across both space and time.

GUIDs are actually in increasingly widespread use in computing today. For example, if you check the registry, you'll find tons of them. A GUID is a 128bit value – for you math types, that's 38 zeros in decimal form. If I generated a GUID every second, it would, theoretically speaking, take me millions of years to generate a duplicate given a number of that size.

GUIDs are generated using a combination of information - each of which is designed to be unique in either space or time. When you combine them, you come up with a value that is guaranteed, statistically speaking, to be unique across space and time.

There is a Win32 API call to generate a GUID in normal programming, but, in addition to the `ROWGUIDID` option on a column, SQL has a special function to return a GUID – it is called the `NEWID()` function, and can be called at any time.

NULL/NOT NULL

This one is pretty simple - it states whether the column in question accepts `NULL` values or not. The default, when you first install SQL Server, is to set a column to `NOT NULL` if you don't specify nullability. There are, however, a very large number of different settings that can effect this default, and change its behavior. For example, setting a value by using the `sp_dbcmptlevel` stored procedure or setting ANSI-compliance options can change this value.

I highly recommend explicitly stating the `NULL` option for every column in every table you ever build. Why? As I mentioned before, there are a large number of different settings that can effect what the system uses for a default for the nullability of a column. If you rely on these defaults, then you may find later that your scripts don't seem to work right (because you, or someone else, has changed a relevant setting without realizing its full effect).

Column Constraints

We have a whole chapter coming up on constraints, so we won't spend that much time on it here. Still, it seems like a good time to review the question of what column constraints are – in short, they are restrictions and rules that you place on individual columns about the data that can be inserted into that column.

For example, if you have a column that's supposed to store the month of the year, you might define that column as being of type `tinyint` – but that wouldn't prevent someone from inserting the number 54 in that column. Since 54 would give us bad data (it doesn't refer to a month), we might provide a constraint that says that data in that column must be between 1 and 12. We'll see how to do this in a later chapter.

Computed Columns

New with version 7.0 is the ability to have what amounts to a "virtual" column. That is, a column that doesn't have any data of its own, but whose value is derived on the fly from other columns in the table. This is something of a boon for many applications.

For example, let's say that we're working on an invoicing system. We want to store information on the quantity of an item we have sold, and at what price. It used to be fairly commonplace to go ahead and add columns to store this information, along with another column that stored the extended value (price times quantity). However, that leads to unnecessary wasting of disk space and maintenance hassles associated with when the totals and the base values get out of synch with each other. With a computed column, we can get around that by defining the value of our computed column to be whatever value is created by multiplying price by quantity.

Let's look at the specific syntax:

```
column_name AS computed_column_expression
```

The first item is a little different – we're providing a column name to go with our value. This is simply the alias that we're going to use to refer to the value that is computed, based on the expression that follows the `AS` keyword.

Next comes the computed column expression. The expression can be any normal expression that uses either literals or column values from the same tables. Therefore, in our example of price and quantity, we might define this column as:

```
ExtendedPrice AS Price * Quantity
```

For an example using a literal, let's say that we always charge a fixed markup on our goods that is 20% over our cost. We could simply keep track of cost in one column, and then use a computed column for the `ListPrice` column:

```
ListPrice AS Cost * 1.2
```

Pretty easy eh? There are a few caveats and provisos though:

- The expression value is not nearly as flexible as a `WHERE` clause expression is.
- You cannot use a subquery, and the values cannot come from a different table.
- You cannot use a computed column as any part of a key (primary, foreign or unique) or with a default constraint.
- Since the value is derived not explicit, you cannot create an index on, insert a value into, or update a computed column. Hence, a computed field is not the best choice for a column that is frequently searched.

We'll look at specific examples of how to use computed columns a little later in this chapter.

I'm actually surprised I haven't heard much debate about the use of computed columns. Rules for normalization of data say that we should not have a column in our table for information that can be derived from other columns – that's exactly what a computed column is!

I'm glad the religious zealots of normalization haven't weighed into this one much, as I like computed columns as something of a compromise. You aren't storing the data twice, and you don't have issues with the derived values not agreeing with the base values because they are calculated on the fly directly from the base values. However, you still get the end result you wanted. This isn't the way to do everything related to derived data, but it sure is an excellent helper for most situations.

Table Constraints

Table constraints are quite similar to column constraints, in that they place restrictions on the data that can be inserted into the table. What makes them a little different is that they may be based on more than one column.

Again, we will be covering these in the constraints chapter, but examples of table-level constraints include `PRIMARY` and `FOREIGN KEY` constraints, as well as `CHECK` constraints.

> **OK, so why is a `CHECK` constraint a table constraint? Isn't it a column constraint since it effects what you can place in a given column? The answer is that it's both. If it is based on solely one column, then it meets the rules for a column constraint. If, however (as `CHECK` constraints can) it is dependent on multiple columns, then you have what would be referred to as a table constraint.**

ON

Remember when we were dealing with database creation, and we said we could create different filegroups? Well, the `ON` clause in a table definition is a way of specifically stating on which filegroup (and, therefore, physical device) you want the table located. You can place a given table on a specific device, or, as you will want to do in most cases, just leave the `ON` clause out, and it will be placed on whatever the default filegroup is (which will be the `PRIMARY` unless you've set it to something else). We will be looking at this usage extensively in our chapter on performance tuning.

TEXTIMAGE_ON

This one is basically the same as the `ON` clause we just looked at, except that it lets you move a very specific part of the table to yet a different filegroup. This clause is only valid if your table definition has `text`, `ntext`, or `image` column(s) in it. When you use the `TEXTIMAGE_ON` clause, you move only the `BLOB` information into the separate filegroup – the rest of the table stays either on the default filegroup or with the filegroup chosen in the `ON` clause.

> **There can be some serious performance increases to be had by splitting your database up into multiple files, and then storing those files on separate physical disks. When you do this, it means you get the I/O from both drives. We'll look into this more in Chapter 24, but, for now, I would suggest you leave well enough along unless you know exactly why you're going to move things.**

Creating a Table

All right, we've seen plenty; we're ready for some action, so let's build a few tables.

When we started this section, we looked at our standard `CREATE` syntax of:

```
CREATE <object type> <object name>
```

And moved that on to a more specific start (indeed, it's the first line of our statement that will create the table) on creating a table called `Customers`:

```
CREATE TABLE Customers
```

Our `Customers` table is going to be the first table in a database we will be putting together to track our company's accounting. We'll be looking at designing a database in a couple of chapters, but we'll go ahead and get started on our database by building a couple of tables to learn our `CREATE TABLE` statement. We'll look at most of the concepts of table construction in the section, but we'll save a few for later on in the book. That being said, let's get started building the first of several tables.

I'm going to add in a `USE <database name>` line prior to my `CREATE` code so that I'm sure that, when I run the script, the table is created in the proper database. We'll then follow up that first line that we've already seen with a few columns.

Any script you create for regular use with a particular database should include a `USE` *command with the name of that database. This ensures that you really are creating, altering and dropping the objects in the database you intend. More than once have I been the victim of my own stupidity when I blindly opened up a script and executed it only to find that the wrong database was current, and any tables with the same name had been dropped (thus losing all data) and replaced by a new layout. You can also tell when other people have done this by taking a look around the* `master` *database – you'll often find several extraneous tables in that database from people running* `CREATE` *scripts that were meant to go somewhere else.*

```
USE Accounting
CREATE TABLE Customers
(
   CustomerNo     int                IDENTITY  NOT NULL,
   CustomerName   varchar(30)                  NOT NULL,
   Address1       varchar(30)                  NOT NULL,
   Address2       varchar(30)                  NOT NULL,
   City           varchar(20)                  NOT NULL,
   State          char(2)                      NOT NULL,
   Zip            varchar(10)                  NOT NULL,
   Contact        varchar(25)                  NOT NULL,
   Phone          char(15)                     NOT NULL,
   FedIDNo        varchar(9)                   NOT NULL,
   DateInSystem   smalldatetime                NOT NULL
)
```

This is a somewhat simplified table versus what we would probably use in real life, but there's plenty of time to change it later (and we will).

Once we've built the table, we want to verify that it was indeed created, and that it has all the columns and types that we expect. To do this, we can make use of several commands, but perhaps the best is one that will seem like an old friend before you're done with this book: `sp_help`. The syntax is simple:

```
EXEC sp_help <object name>
```

Alternatively, to specify the table object that we currently want to look at, try executing the following code:

```
EXEC sp_help Customers
```

The `EXEC` command is used in two different ways. This rendition is used to execute a stored procedure – in this case, a system stored procedure. We'll see the second version later when we are dealing with advanced query topics and stored procedures.

> **Technically speaking, you can execute a stored procedure by simply calling it (without using the `EXEC` keyword). The problem is that this only works if there are absolutely no other commands in the stretch of code that you're running. Just having `sp_help Customers` would have worked in the place of the code above, but if you tried to run an `SELECT` statement before or after it – it would blow up on you.**

Try executing the command, and you'll find that you get back several result sets one after another. The information retrieved includes separate result sets for:

- Table name
- Column names and types
- The identity column (if one exists)
- The RowGUIDCol (if one exists)
- Filegroup information
- Index names, types and included columns
- Constraint names, types and included columns
- Foreign key (if any) names and columns

Now that we're certain that we have our table created, let's take a look at creating yet another table – the `Employees` table. This time, let's talk about what we want in the table first, and then see how you do trying to code the `CREATE` script for yourself.

The `Employees` table is another fairly simple table. It should include information on:

- The employee's ID – this should be automatically generated by the system
- First name
- Optionally, middle initial
- Last name
- Title
- Social Security Number
- Salary
- The previous salary

- The amount of the last raise
- Date of hire
- Date terminated (if there is one)
- The employee's manager
- Department

Start off by trying to figure out a layout for yourself.

Before we start looking at this together, let me tell you not to worry too much if your layout isn't exactly like mine. There are as many database designs as there are database designers – and that all begins with table design. We all can have different solutions to the same problem. What you want to look for is whether you got all the concepts that needed to be addressed. That being said, let's take a look at one way to build this table.

We have a special column here. The `EmployeeID` is to be generated by the system and therefore is an excellent candidate for either an identity field or a RowGUIDCol. There are several reasons you might want to go one way or the other between these two, but we'll go with an identity field for a couple of reasons:

- It's going to be used by an average person. (Would you want to have to remember a GUID?)
- It incurs lower overhead.

We're now ready to start constructing our script:

```
CREATE TABLE Employees
(
   EmployeeID         int              IDENTITY  NOT NULL,
```

For this column, the `NULL` option has essentially been chosen for us by virtue of our use of an `IDENTITY` column. You cannot allow `NULL` values in an `IDENTITY` column. Note that we still need to include our `NOT NULL` option (if we leave it to the default we'll get an error, as the default allows `NULL`s), but we don't really have to think about which we want it to be.

Next up, we want to add in our name fields. I usually allow approximately 25 characters for names. Most names are far shorter than that, but I've bumped into enough that were rather lengthy (especially since hyphenated names have become so popular) that I allow for the extra room. In addition, I make use of a variable length data type for two reasons:

- To recapture the space of a field that is defined somewhat longer than the actual data usually is (retrieve blank space)
- To simplify searches in the `WHERE` clause – fixed length fields are padded with spaces which requires extra planning in your `WHERE` clause

The exception in this case is the middle initial. Since we really only need to allow for one character here, recapture of space is not an issue. Indeed, a variable length data type would actually use more space in this case, since a `varchar` needs not only the space to store the data, but also a small amount of overhead space to keep track of how long the data is. In addition, ease of search is also not an issue since, if we have any value in the field at all, there isn't enough room left for padded spaces.

Since a name for an employee is a critical item, we will not allow any NULL values in the first and last name columns. Middle initial is not nearly so critical (indeed, some people don't have a middle name), so we will allow a NULL for that field only:

```
    FirstName           varchar(25)         NOT NULL,
    MiddleInitial       char(1)             NULL,
    LastName            varchar(25)         NOT NULL,
```

Next up is the employee's title. We must know what they are doing if we're going to be cutting them a paycheck, so we will also make this a required field:

```
    Title               varchar(25)         NOT NULL,
```

In that same paycheck vein, we must know their Social Security Number (or similar identification number outside the US) in order to report for taxes. In this case, we'll use a varchar and allow up to eleven characters, as these identification numbers are different lengths in different countries. If you know your application is only going to require SSNs from the US then you'll probably want to make it char(11) instead:

```
    SSN                 varchar(11)         NOT NULL,
```

We must know how much to pay the employees – that seems simple enough – but what comes next is a little different. When we add in the prior salary and the amount of the last raise, we get into a situation where we could use a computed column. The new salary is the sum of the previous salary and the amount of the last raise. The Salary amount is something that we might use quite regularly – indeed we might want an index on it to help with ranged queries. Since we can't have indexes on computed columns, I'm going to choose one of the other two columns to derive. In this case, we'll compute the amount of the last raise, but we could have just as easily computed the previous salary by subtracting the amount of the raise from the Salary column:

```
    Salary              money               NOT NULL,
    PriorSalary         money               NOT NULL,
    LastRaise AS Salary - PriorSalary,
```

If we hired them, then we must know the data of hire – so that will also be required:

```
    HireDate            smalldatetime       NOT NULL,
```

Note that I've chosen to use a smalldatetime data type rather than the standard datetime to save space. The datetime data type will store information down to additional fractions of seconds, plus it will save a wider range of dates. Since we're primarily interested in the date of hire, not the time, and since we are dealing with a limited range of calendar dates (say, back 50 years and ahead a century or two), the smalldatetime will meet our needs and take up half the space.

> **Date and time fields are somewhat of a double-edged sword. On one hand, it's very nice to save storage space and network bandwidth by using the smaller data type. On the other hand, you'll find that `smalldatetime` is incompatible with some other language data types (including Visual Basic). Even going with the normal `datetime` is no guarantee of safety from this last problem though – some data access models pretty much require you to pass a date in as a `varchar` and allow for implicit conversion to a `datetime` field.**

The date of termination is something we may not know (we'd like to think that some employees are still working for us), so we'll need to leave it nullable:

```
    TerminationDate  smalldatetime           NULL,
```

We absolutely want to know who the employee is reporting to (somebody must have hired them!) and what department they are working in:

```
    ManagerEmpID     int                     NOT NULL,
    Department       varchar(25)             NOT NULL
)
```

So, just for clarity, let's look at the entire script to create this table:

```
USE Accounting

CREATE TABLE Employees
(
   EmployeeID        int           IDENTITY  NOT NULL,
   FirstName         varchar(25)             NOT NULL,
   MiddleInitial     char(1)                 NULL,
   LastName          varchar(25)             NOT NULL,
   Title             varchar(25)             NOT NULL,
   SSN               varchar(11)             NOT NULL,
   Salary            money                   NOT NULL,
   PriorSalary       money                   NOT NULL,
   LastRaise AS Salary - PriorSalary,
   HireDate          smalldatetime           NOT NULL,
   TerminationDate   smalldatetime           NULL,
   ManagerEmpID      int                     NOT NULL,
   Department        varchar(25)             NOT NULL
)
```

Again, I would recommend executing `sp_help` on this table to verify that the table was created as you expected.

Save the scripts for this and the `Customers` table, and then drop the `Accounting` database:

```
USE master

DROP DATABASE Accounting
```

You should see the following in the **Results** pane:

Deleting database file 'c:\mssql7\data\Accounting_Data.mdf'.
Deleting database file 'c:\mssql7\data\Accounting_Log.ldf'.

You may run into a situation where you get an error that says that the database cannot be deleted because it is in use. If this happens, check a couple of things:

- Make sure that the database that you have as current in Query Analyzer is something other than the database you're trying to drop (that is, make sure you're not using the database as you're trying to drop it).
- Ensure you don't have any other connections open that are showing the database you're trying to drop as the current database.

I usually solve the first one just as we did in the code example – I switch to using the `master` database. The second you have to check manually – I usually close other sessions down entirely just to be sure.

Using the GUI Tool

We've just spent a lot of time pounding in perfect syntax for creating a database and a couple of tables – that's enough of that for a while. Let's take a look at the graphical tool in Enterprise Manager (EM) that allows us to build and relate tables. From this point on, we'll not only be dealing with code, but with the tool that can generate much of that code for us.

Creating a Database Using EM

If you run EM and expand the Databases tree, you should see something like this:

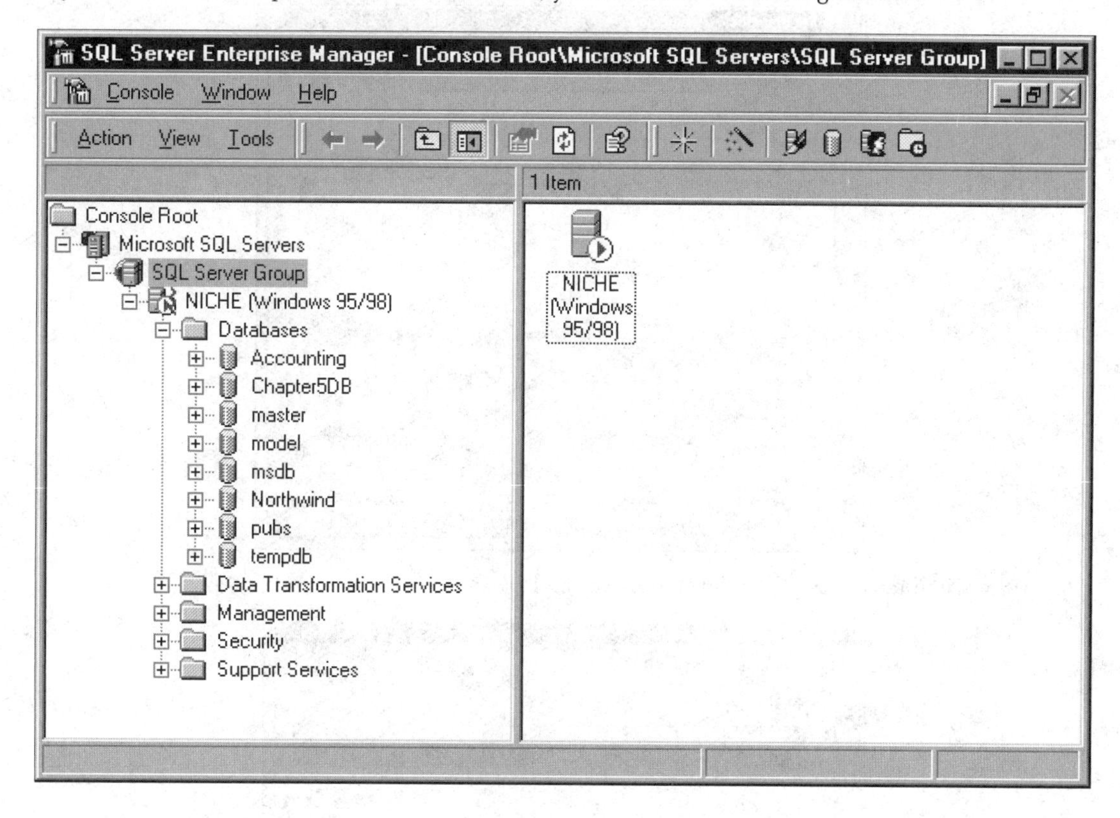

If you look closely at this screen shot, you'll see that my `Accounting` *database is still showing even though we just dropped it in the previous example. You may or may not wind up seeing this, depending on whether you already had EM open when you dropped the database or you opened EM after you dropped the database in QA.*

Why the difference? Well, before version 7.0, the EM used to refresh information such as the available databases regularly. Now it only updates when it knows it has a reason to (for example, you deleted something by using EM instead of QA, or perhaps you explicitly chose to refresh). The reason for the change was performance. The old EM used to be a slug performance wise because it was constantly making round trips to the server. The new EM performs much better, but doesn't necessarily have the most up-to-date information.

The bottom line on this is that, if you see something in EM that you don't expect to, try pressing F5 (refresh), and it should update things for you.

Now try right-clicking on the Databases node, and choose the New Database... option:

This will pull up the Database Properties dialog box, and allow you to fill in the information on how you want your database created. We'll use the same choices that we did when we created the `Accounting` database at the beginning of the chapter. First comes the information about the database itself:

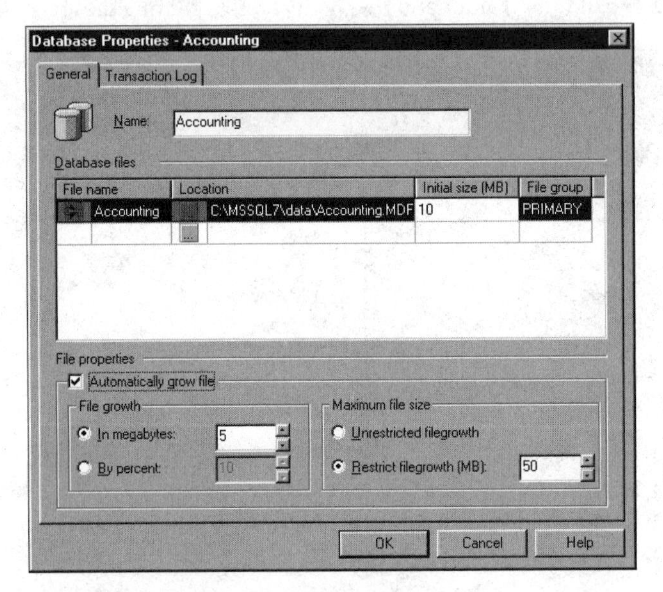

Then we switch tabs to see the information on the log:

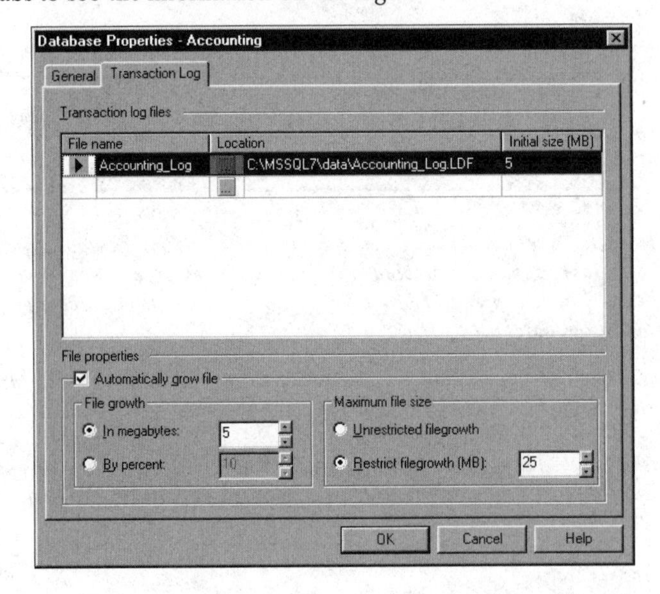

Click OK and, after a brief pause to actually create the script, you'll see your new database added to the tree:

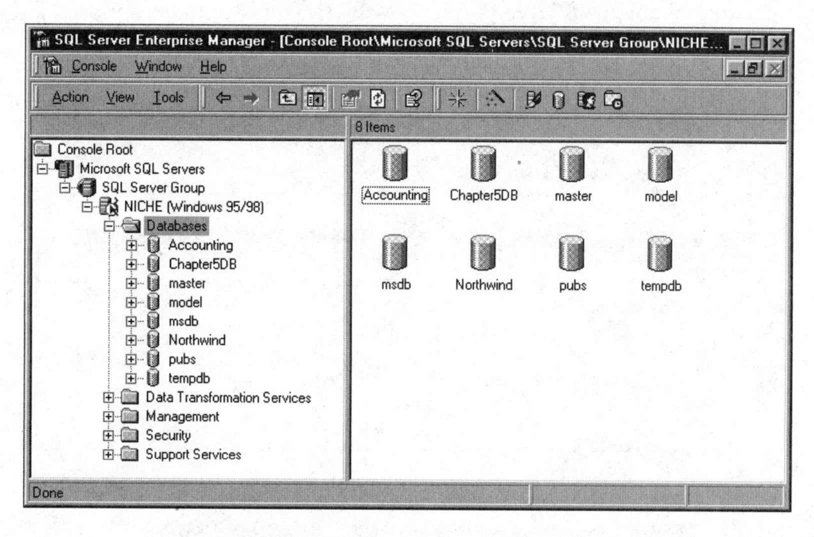

Now expand the tree to show the various items underneath the Accounting node, and select the Diagrams node. Right-click it, and choose the New Database Diagram menu choice.

SQL Server tries to build you a diagram, but then figures out that there aren't any tables that it can add to a diagram, so you get a dialog message:

There are no tables to be added to the diagram. You can create new tables from within the diagram.

After clicking OK, you get the diagram screen:

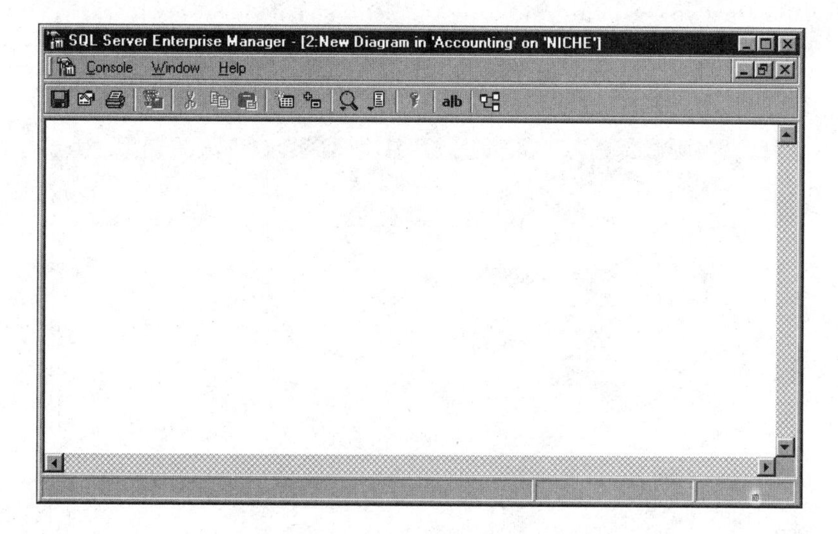

It can't be much less interesting than that. The nice part is that you can add a table by either right-clicking and choosing the appropriate option, or by clicking on the New table icon in the tool bar. When you choose to add a new table, SQL Server will ask you for the name you want to give your new table. You will then you get a rather helpful dialog box that lets you fill in your table one piece at a time – complete with labels for what you need to fill out:

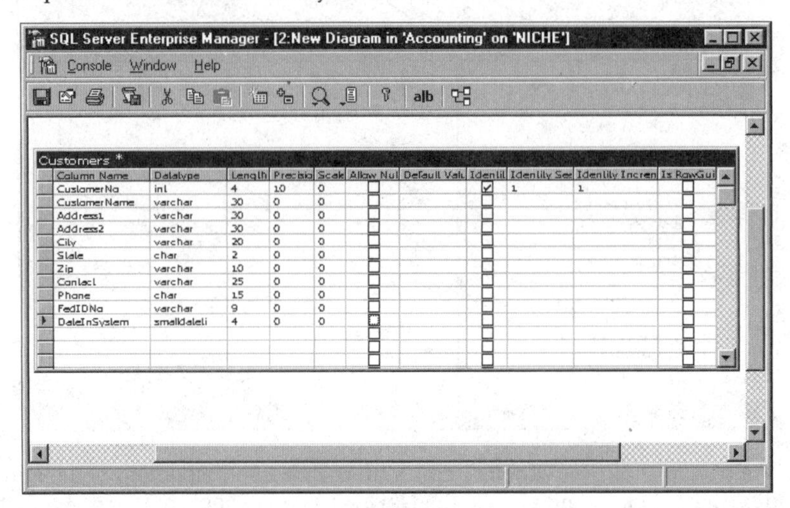

Once you have the table filled out, you can save the changes, and that will create your table for you.

This is really a point of personal preference, but I prefer to set the view down to just column names at this point. You can do this by clicking on the Show *icon on the toolbar or, as I prefer, by right-clicking the table and choosing* Column Names*. I find that this saves a lot of screen real-estate, and makes more room for me to work on additional tables.*

After you add in the `Employees` table, you'll see a different response when you go to save it – it will want confirmation that you want to add the new table. I have no idea why it asks you this time (and every subsequent time for that matter) when it didn't on the first save, but it is actually a nice confirmation of what you wanted to do before going on. After accepting that dialog's question, your diagram should have two tables in it:

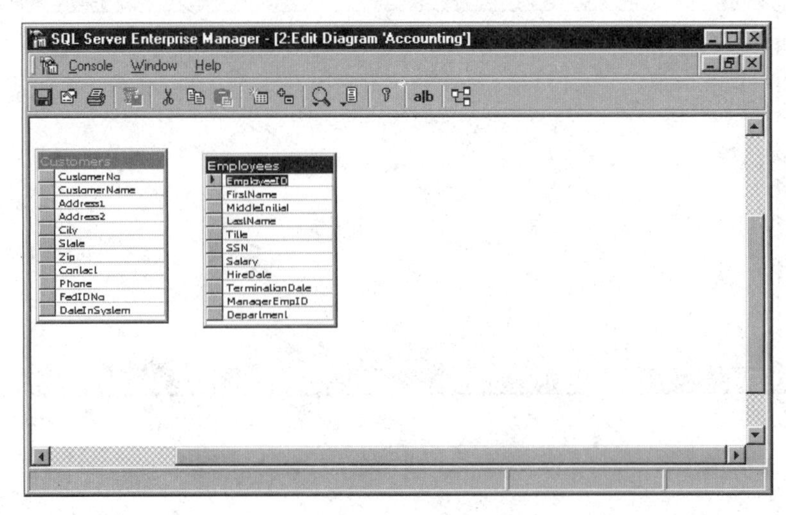

It's worth noting that you can bring up similar dialogs by going to the tables section in EM (right-click on the Tables node and select New Table) rather than the diagrams. The reason I wanted you to use the dialogs screen is that it will become your home for doing more advanced database development as we continue through this book.

The diagramming tool that is included with SQL Server (you may sometimes hear this tool and the similar tools that show up in Microsoft's development suites referred to as "The da Vinci Tools") is not designed to be everything to everyone.

Presumably, since you are reading this book, you are just starting out on your database journey – this tool will probably be adequate for you for a while. Eventually, you may want to take a look at some more advanced (and far more expensive) tools to help you with your database design.

Backing into the Code: The Basics of Creating Scripts with EM

One last quick introduction before we exit this chapter– we want to see the basics of having EM write our scripts for us. For now, we are going to do this as something of a quick and dirty introduction. Later on, after we've learned about the many objects that the scripting tool references, we will take a more advanced look.

To generate scripts, we go into EM and right-click on the database for which we want to generate scripts. (In this case, we're going to generate scripts on our `Accounting` database.) On the pop-up menu, choose All Tasks, and then choose Generate SQL Scripts. EM brings up a special dialog:

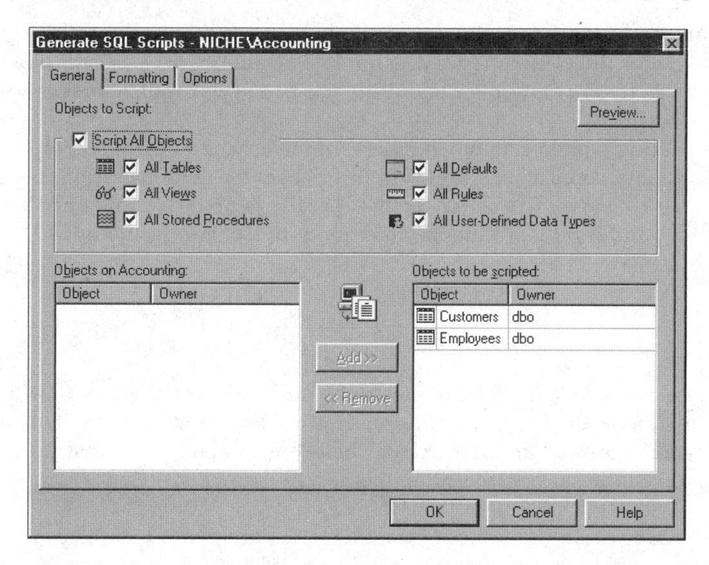

The default is to script all of our objects, so our `Customers` and `Employees` tables are already in our list of objects to be scripted. We could, if we chose, de-select the Script All Objects checkbox, and select our objects one at a time. For now, we'll just preview the script EM will generate by clicking Preview... in the upper right-hand corner of the dialog box.

In addition to our CREATE statements, by default SQL Server also generates some code to drop our two objects, if they already exist, before trying to run the new CREATE code. Let's ignore those two IF statements for now, and focus on the CREATE statements:

```
CREATE TABLE [dbo].[Customers] (
   [CustomerNo]         [int]       IDENTITY(1, 1)  NOT NULL ,
   [CustomerName]       [varchar](30)               NOT NULL ,
   [Address1]           [varchar](30)               NOT NULL ,
   [Address2]           [varchar](30)               NOT NULL ,
   [City]               [varchar](20)               NOT NULL ,
   [State]              [char](2)                   NOT NULL ,
   [Zip]                [varchar](10)               NOT NULL ,
   [Contact]            [varchar](25)               NOT NULL ,
   [Phone]              [char](15)                  NOT NULL ,
   [FedIDNo]            [varchar](9)                NOT NULL ,
   [DateInSystem]       [smalldatetime]             NOT NULL
) ON [PRIMARY]
GO

CREATE TABLE [dbo].[Employees] (
   [EmployeeID]         [int]       IDENTITY(1, 1)  NOT NULL ,
   [FirstName]          [varchar](25)               NOT NULL ,
   [MiddleInitial]      [char](1)                   NULL ,
   [LastName]           [varchar](25)               NOT NULL ,
   [Title]              [varchar](25)               NOT NULL ,
   [SSN]                [varchar](11)               NOT NULL ,
   [Salary]             [money]                     NOT NULL ,
   [HireDate]           [smalldatetime]             NOT NULL ,
   [TerminationDate]    [smalldatetime]             NOT NULL ,
   [ManagerEmpID]       [int]                       NOT NULL ,
   [Department]         [varchar](25)               NOT NULL
) ON [PRIMARY]
GO
```

If you go back and compare these to the scripts that we wrote by hand, you'll see that they are nearly identical, with the major differences related to qualified naming. SQL Server likes to use the squared brackets every time so there is no doubt about the use of keywords as names or embedded spaces.

As you can see, scripting couldn't be much easier. Indeed, once you get a complex database put together, it still isn't quite as easy as it seems in this particular demonstration, but it is a lot easier than writing it all out by hand. The reality is that it really is pretty simple once you learn what the scripting options are, and we'll learn much more about those later in the book.

Summary

At this point, you're ready to start getting into some hardcore details about how to lay out your tables, and a discussion on the concepts of normalization and more general database design. I'm actually going to make you wait another chapter before we get there, so that we can talk about constraints and keys somewhat before hitting the design issues.

In this chapter, we've covered the basics of the CREATE statement as it relates to creating a database and tables. There are, of course, many other renditions of CREATE that we will cover as we continue through the book. We have also taken a look at the wide variety of options that we can use in databases and tables to have full control over our data. Finally, we have begun to see the many things that we can use the Enterprise Manager for in order to simplify our lives, and make design and scripting simpler.

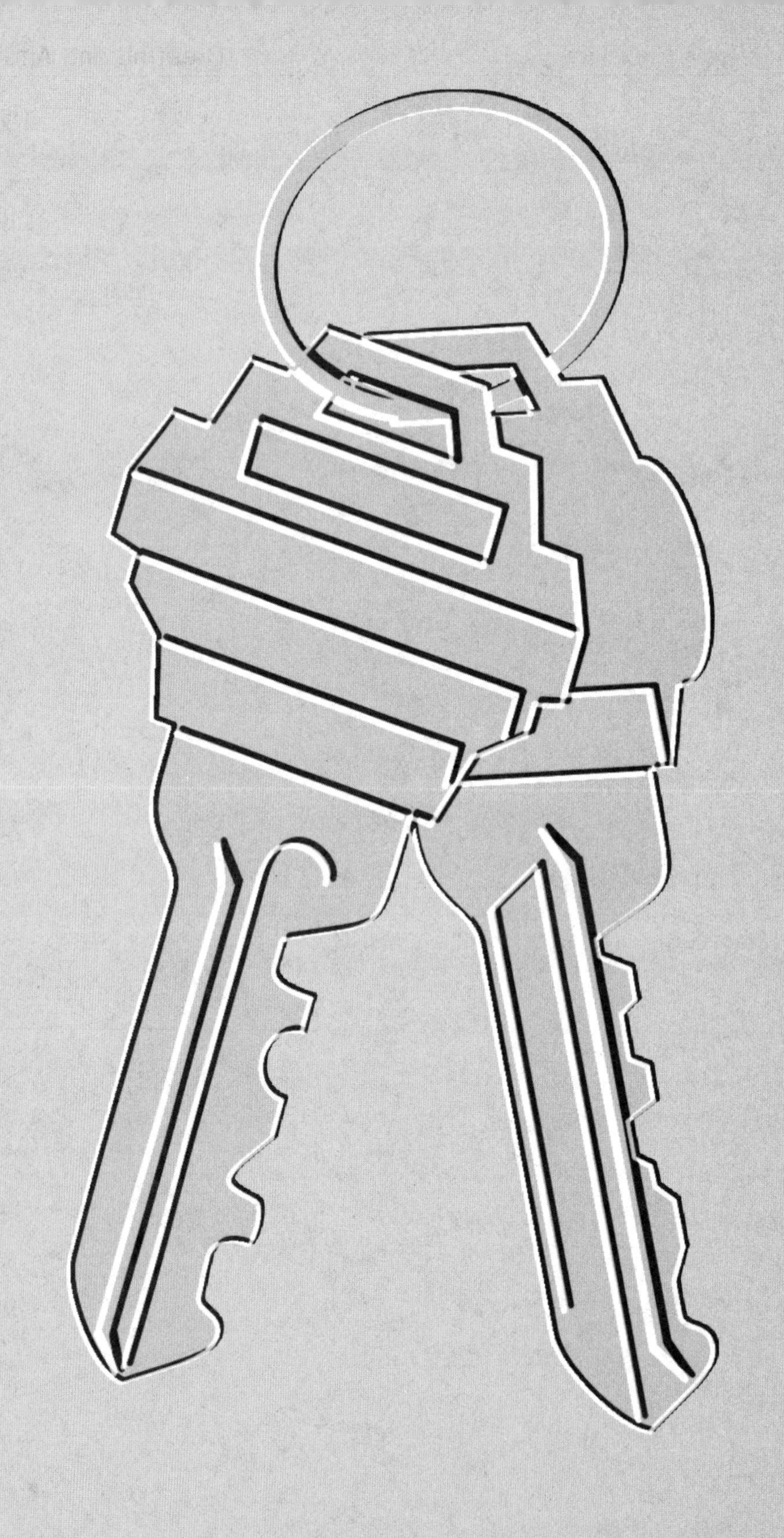

7

Constraints

You've heard me talk about them, but now it's time to look at them seriously - it's time to deal with constraints. We've talked a couple of times already about what constraints are, but let's review in case you decided to skip straight to this chapter.

A constraint is a restriction. Placed at either column or table level, a constraint ensures that your data meets certain data integrity rules.

This gets back to the notion that I talked about back in Chapters 1 and 2, where ensuring data integrity is no longer the responsibility of the programs that use your database, but rather the responsibility of the database itself. If you think about it, this is really cool. Data is inserted, updated and deleted from the database by many sources. Even in stand-alone applications - situations where only one program accesses the database - the same table may be accessed from many different places in the program. It doesn't stop there though. Your database administrator (that might mean you if you're a dual role kind of person) may be altering data occasionally to deal with problems that arise. In more complex scenarios, you can actually run into situations where literally hundreds of different access paths exist for altering just one piece of data, let alone your entire database.

Moving the responsibility for data integrity into the database itself has been revolutionary to database management. There are still many different things that can go wrong when you are attempting to insert data into your database, but your database is now *proactive* rather than *reactive* to problems. Many problems with what a program allows through to the database, are now caught much earlier in the development process because, although the client program allows the data through, the database rejects it. How does it do it? Primarily with constraints (data types and triggers are among the other worker bees of data integrity). Well, let's take a look.

In this chapter, we'll be looking at the three different types of constraints at a high level:

- Entity constraints
- Domain constraints
- Referential integrity constraints

At a more specific level, we'll be looking at the specific methods of implementing each of these types of constraints, including:

- `PRIMARY KEY` constraints
- `FOREIGN KEY` constraints
- `UNIQUE` constraints (also known as alternate keys)
- `CHECK` constraints
- `DEFAULT` constraints
- Rules
- Defaults (similar, yet different than `DEFAULT` constraints)

We'll also take a very cursory look at triggers and stored procedures (there will be much more on these later) as a method of implementing data integrity rules.

Types of Constraints

There are a number of different ways to implement constraints, but each of them falls into one of three categories – entity, domain, or referential integrity constraints:

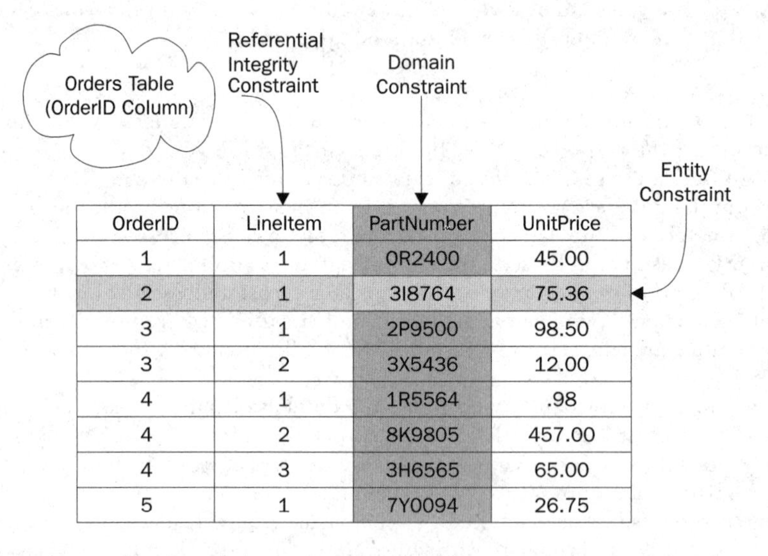

OrderID	LineItem	PartNumber	UnitPrice
1	1	0R2400	45.00
2	1	3I8764	75.36
3	1	2P9500	98.50
3	2	3X5436	12.00
4	1	1R5564	.98
4	2	8K9805	457.00
4	3	3H6565	65.00
5	1	7Y0094	26.75

Domain Constraints

Domain constraints deal with one or more columns. What we're talking about here is ensuring that a particular column or set of columns meet a particular criteria. When you insert or update a row, the constraint is applied without respect to any other row in the table - it's the column data you're interested in.

For example, if we want to confine the `UnitPrice` column only to values that are greater than or equal to zero, that would be a domain constraint. While any row that had a `UnitPrice` that didn't meet the constraint would be rejected, we're actually enforcing integrity to make sure that entire column (no matter how many rows) meets the constraint. The domain is the column, and our constraint is a domain constraint.

We'll see this kind of constraint in dealing with `CHECK` constraints, rules, defaults and `DEFAULT` constraints.

Entity Constraints

Entity constraints are all about individual rows. This form of constraint doesn't really care about a column as a whole, it's interested in this particular row, and would best be exemplified by a constraint that requires every row to have a unique value for some column.

"What," you say, "a unique column? Doesn't that mean it's a domain constraint?" No, it doesn't. We're not saying that a column has to meet any particular format, or that the value has to be greater or less than anything. What we're saying is that for *this* row, the same value can't already exist in some other row.

We'll see this kind of constraint in dealing with `PRIMARY KEY` and `UNIQUE` constraints.

Referential Integrity Constraints

This is created when a value in one column must match the value in another column - either in the same table or, far more typically, a different table.

Let's say that we are taking orders for a product, and that we accept credit cards. In order to be paid by the credit card company, we need to have some form of merchant agreement with that company. We don't want our employees to take credit cards from companies from which we're not going to be paid back. That's where referential integrity comes in – it allows us to build what we would call a **domain table**. A domain table is a table whose sole purpose in life is to provide a limited list of acceptable values. In our case, we might build a table that looks something like this:

CreditCardID	CreditCard
1	VISA
2	MasterCard
3	Discover Card
4	American Express

We can then build one or more tables that **reference** the CreditCardID column of our domain table. With referential integrity, any table (such as our Orders table) that is defined as referencing our CreditCard table will have to have a column that matches up to the CreditCardID column of our CreditCard table. For each row that we insert into the referencing table, it will have to have a value that is in our domain list (it will have to have a corresponding row in the CreditCard table).

We'll see more of this as we learn about FOREIGN KEY constraints later in this chapter.

Constraint Naming

Before we get down to the nitty gritty of constraints, I'll digress for a moment and address the issue of naming constraints.

For each of the different types of constraints that we will be dealing with in this chapter, you can elect not to supply a name - that is, you can have SQL Server provide a name for you. Resist the temptation to do this. You'll quickly find that when SQL Server creates its own name it isn't particularly useful.

An example of a more useful name might be something like PK__Employees__145C0A3F. This is a SQL Server generated name for a primary key on the Employees table of the Accounting database, which we will create later in the chapter - the PK is for primary key, the Employees is for the Employees table that it is on, and the rest is a randomly generated value to ensure uniqueness.

That one isn't too bad, but you get less help on other constraints, for example, a CHECK constraint used later in the chapter might generate something like CK__Customers__22AA2996. From this, we know that it's a CHECK constraint, but we know nothing of what the nature of the CHECK is.

Since we can have multiple CHECK constraints on a table, you could wind up with all these as names of constraints on the same table:

```
CK__Customers__22AA2996
CK__Customers__25869641
CK__Customers__267ABA7A
```

Needless to say, if you needed to edit one of these constraints, it would be a pain to figure out which was which.

Personally, I either use a combination of type of constraint together with a phrase to indicate what it does or the names of the column(s) it effects. For example, I might use CKPriceExceedsCost if I have a constraint to ensure that my users can't sell a product at a loss, or perhaps something as simple as CKCustomerPhoneNo on a column that ensures that phone numbers are formatted properly.

As with the naming of anything that we'll use in this book, how exactly you name things is really not all that important. What is important is that you:

- Be consistent
- Make it something that everyone can understand
- Keep it as short as you can while still meeting the above rules
- Did I mention to be consistent?

Key Constraints

There are four different types of common keys that you may hear about in your database endeavors. These are primary keys, foreign keys, alternate keys and inversion keys. For this chapter, we'll only take a look at the first three of these, as they provide constraints on the database.

An inversion key is basically just any index (we cover indexes in Chapter 9), that does not apply some form of constraint to the table (primary key, foreign key, unique). Inversion keys, rather than enforcing data integrity, are merely an alternate way of sorting the data.

Keys are one of the cornerstone concepts of database design and management, so fasten your seatbelt and hold on tight - this will be one of the most important concepts you'll read about in this book, and will become absolutely critical as we move on to normalization.

PRIMARY KEY Constraints

Before we define what a primary key actually is, let's digress slightly into a brief discussion of relational databases. Relational databases are constructed on the idea of being able to "relate" data. Therefore, it becomes critical in relational databases for most tables (there are exceptions, but they are very rare) to have a unique identifier for each row. A unique identifier allows you to accurately reference a record from another table in the database - so forming a relation between those two tables.

This is a wildly different concept than we had with our old mainframe environment or the ISAM databases (dBase, FoxPro, Clipper, etc.) of the 80's and early 90's. In those environments, we dealt with one record at a time – we would generally open the entire table, and go one record at a time until we found what we were looking for.

Primary keys are the unique identifiers for each row. They must contain unique values (and hence cannot be `NULL`). Due to their importance in relational databases, primary keys are the most fundamental of all keys and constraints.

Don't confuse the primary key, which uniquely identifies each row in a table, with a GUID, which is a more generic tool to identify something (more than just rows) across all space and time. While a GUID can certainly be used as a primary key, they incur some overhead, and are usually not called for when we're only dealing with the contents of a table. Indeed, the only common place that a GUID becomes particularly useful in a database environment is as a primary key when dealing with replicated or other distributed data. We'll see more about this in the replication chapter.

A table can have a maximum of one primary key. As I mentioned earlier, it is rare to have a table on which you don't want a primary key.

When I say "rare" here - I mean very rare. A table that doesn't have a primary key severely violates the concept of relational data - it means that you can't guarantee that you can relate to a specific record. The data in your table no longer has anything that gives it distinction.

Situations where you can have multiple rows that are logically identical are actually not that uncommon, but that doesn't mean that you don't want a primary key. In these instances, you'll want to take a look at fabricating some sort of key - this approach is most often implemented using an identity column.

A primary key ensures uniqueness within the columns declared as being part of that primary key, and that unique value serves as identifier for each row in that table. How do we create a primary key? Actually, there are two ways. You can create the primary key either in your `CREATE TABLE` command or with an `ALTER TABLE` command.

Before version 7.0, there was yet another method for establishing a primary key. This method used a stored procedure called `sp_primarykey`. Microsoft has been warning for some time now that `sp_primarykey` (and a similar option for foreign keys) would go away - and it has. I only mention it here in case you see it in legacy code.

Creating the Primary Key at Table Creation

Let's review one of our `CREATE TABLE` statements from the last chapter:

```
CREATE TABLE Customers
(
   CustomerNo      int    IDENTITY    NOT NULL,
   CustomerName    varchar(30)        NOT NULL,
   Address1        varchar(30)        NOT NULL,
   Address2        varchar(30)        NOT NULL,
   City            varchar(20)        NOT NULL,
   State           char(2)            NOT NULL,
   Zip             varchar(10)        NOT NULL,
   Contact         varchar(25)        NOT NULL,
   Phone           char(15)           NOT NULL,
   FedIDNo         varchar(9)         NOT NULL,
   DateInSystem    smalldatetime      NOT NULL
)
```

This `CREATE` statement should seem old hat by now, but it's missing a very important piece – our `PRIMARY KEY` constraint. We want to identify `CustomerNo` as our primary key. Why `CustomerNo`? Well, we'll look into what makes a good primary key in the next chapter, but for now, just think about it a bit - do we want two customers to have the same `CustomerNo`? Definitely not - it makes perfect sense for a `CustomerNo` to be used as an identifier for a customer. Indeed, such a system has been used for years, so there's really no sense in re-inventing the wheel here.

To alter our `CREATE TABLE` statement to include a `PRIMARY KEY` constraint, we just add in the constraint information right after the column(s) that we want to be part of our primary key. In this case, we would use:

```
CREATE TABLE Customers
(
   CustomerNo      int    IDENTITY    NOT NULL
      PRIMARY KEY,
   CustomerName    varchar(30)        NOT NULL,
   Address1        varchar(30)        NOT NULL,
```

```
    Address2        varchar(30)      NOT NULL,
    City            varchar(20)      NOT NULL,
    State           char(2)          NOT NULL,
    Zip             varchar(10)      NOT NULL,
    Contact         varchar(25)      NOT NULL,
    Phone           char(15)         NOT NULL,
    FedIDNo         varchar(9)       NOT NULL,
    DateInSystem    smalldatetime    NOT NULL
)
```

Note that, if you want to try out this code, you may need to first DROP the existing table by issuing a DROP TABLE Customers command. Notice that we altered one line (all we did was remove the comma), and added some code on a second line for that column. In a word - it was easy! Again, we just added one simple keyword (OK, so it's two words, but they operate as one), and we now have ourselves a primary key.

Creating a Primary Key on an Existing Table

Now, what if we already have a table and we want to set the primary key? That's also easy - we'll do that for our Employees table:

```
USE Accounting

ALTER TABLE Employees
   ADD CONSTRAINT PK_EmployeeID
   PRIMARY KEY (EmployeeID)
```

Our ALTER command tells SQL Server:

- That we are adding something to the table (we could also be dropping something from the table if we so chose)
- What it is that we're adding (a constraint)
- What we want to name the constraint (to allow us to address the constraint directly later)
- The type of constraint (PRIMARY KEY)
- The column(s) that the constraint applies to

FOREIGN KEY Constraints

Foreign keys are both a method of ensuring data integrity and a manifestation of the relationships between tables. When you add a foreign key to a table, you are creating a dependency between the table for which you define the foreign key (the **referencing** table), and the table your foreign key references (the **referenced** table). After adding a foreign key, any record you insert into the referencing table must either have a matching record in the referenced column(s) of the referenced table, or the value of the foreign key column(s) must be set to NULL. This can be a little confusing, so let's do it by example.

Let's create another table in our Accounting database called Orders. One thing you'll notice in this CREATE script is that we're going to use both a primary key and a foreign key. A primary key, as we will see as we continue through design, is a critical part of a table. Our foreign key is added to the script in almost exactly the same way as our primary key was, except that we must say what we are referencing. The syntax goes on the column or columns that we are placing our FOREIGN KEY constraint on, and looks something like this:

```
<column name> <datatype> <nullability>
FOREIGN KEY REFERENCES <table name>(<column name>)
```

Therefore, for our `Orders` table, the script looks something like this:

```
USE Accounting

CREATE TABLE Orders
(
   OrderID       int    IDENTITY    NOT NULL
      PRIMARY KEY,
   CustomerNo    int                NOT NULL
      FOREIGN KEY REFERENCES Customers(CustomerNo),
   OrderDate     smalldatetime      NOT NULL,
   EmployeeID    int                NOT NULL
)
```

Note that you must have a primary key defined on the referenced table or the creation of your foreign key will fail. In addition, the actual column being referenced must have either a `PRIMARY KEY` or a `UNIQUE` constraint defined on it (we'll discuss `UNIQUE` constraints later in the chapter).

> *It's also worth noting that primary and foreign keys can exist on the same column. You can see an example of this in the `Northwind` database with the `Order Details` table. The primary key is comprised of both the `OrderID` and `ProductID` columns - each of these are also foreign keys, and reference the `Orders` and `Products` tables respectively.*

Once you have successfully run the above code, run `sp_help` and you should see your new constraint reported under the constraints section of the `sp_help` information. If you want to get even more to the point, you can run `sp_helpconstraint` - the syntax is easy:

```
EXEC sp_helpconstraint <table name>
```

Run `sp_helpconstraint` on our new `Orders` table, and you'll get information back giving you the names, criteria and status for all the constraints on the table. At this point, our `Orders` table has one `FOREIGN KEY` constraint and one `PRIMARY KEY` constraint.

Unlike primary keys, we are not limited to just one foreign key on a table. We can have between 0 and 253 foreign keys in each table. The only limitation is that a given column can only be involved in referencing one foreign key. However, you can have more than one column participate in a single foreign key. A given column that is the target of a reference by a foreign key can also be referenced by many tables.

Adding a Foreign Key to an Existing Table

Just like with primary keys, or any constraint for that matter, we have situations where we want to add our foreign key to a table that already exists. This process is similar to creating a primary key.

Let's add another foreign key to our `Orders` table to restrict the `EmployeeID` field (which is intended to have the ID of the employee that entered the order) to valid employees as defined in the `Employees` table. To do this, we need to be able to uniquely identify a target record in the referenced table. As I've already mentioned, you can do this by either referencing a primary key or a column with a `UNIQUE` constraint. In this case, we'll make use of the existing primary key that we placed on the `Employees` table earlier in the chapter:

```
ALTER TABLE Orders
   ADD CONSTRAINT FK_OrderEmployee
   FOREIGN KEY (EmployeeID) REFERENCES Employees(EmployeeID)
```

Now execute `sp_helpconstraint` again against the `Orders` table and you'll see that our new constraint has been added.

Making a Table be Self-Referencing

What if the column you want to refer to isn't in another table, but is actually right within the table in which you are building the reference? Can a table be both the referencing and the referenced table? You bet! Indeed, while this is far from the most common of situations, it is actually used with regularity. In an `ALTER` situation, this works just the same as any other foreign key definition. We can try this out against our `Employees` table:

```
ALTER TABLE Employees
   ADD CONSTRAINT FK_EmployeeManagerID
   FOREIGN KEY (ManagerEmpID) REFERENCES Employees(EmployeeID)
```

There is one difference with a `CREATE` statement. The only trick to it is that you can (but you don't have to) leave out the `FOREIGN KEY` phrasing and just use the `REFERENCES` clause. We already have our `Employees` table set up at this point, but if we were creating it from scratch, here would be the script (pay particular attention to the foreign key on the `ManagerEmpID` column):

```
CREATE TABLE Employees (
   EmployeeID          int    IDENTITY    NOT NULL
      PRIMARY KEY,
   FirstName           varchar (25)       NOT NULL,
   MiddleInitial       char (1)           NULL,
   LastName            varchar (25)       NOT NULL,
   Title               varchar (25)       NOT NULL,
   SSN                 varchar (11)       NOT NULL,
   Salary              money              NOT NULL,
   HireDate            smalldatetime      NOT NULL,
   TerminationDate     smalldatetime      NULL,
   ManagerEmpID        int                NOT NULL
      REFERENCES Employees(EmployeeID),
   Department          varchar (25)       NOT NULL
)
```

Other Things to Think about with Foreign Keys

There are some other things to think about before we're done with foreign keys. We will be coming back to this subject over and over again throughout the book, but for now, I just want to get in a couple of more fine points:

- What makes values in foreign keys required versus optional
- How foreign keys are bi-directional
- Cascading updates and deletes

What Makes Values in Foreign Keys Required versus Optional

By the nature of a foreign key itself, you have two possible choices on what to fill into a column or columns that have a foreign key defined for them:

- Fill the column in with a value that matches the corresponding column in the referenced table
- Do not fill in a value at all and leave the value `NULL`

You can make the foreign key completely required (limit your users to just the first option above) by simply defining the referencing column as `NOT NULL`. Since a `NULL` value won't be valid in the column and the foreign key requires any non-`NULL` value to have a match in the referenced table, you know that every row will have a match in your referenced table. In other words, the reference is required.

Allowing the referencing column to have `NULL`s will create the same requirement, except that the user will also have the option of supplying no value - even if there is not a match for `NULL` in the referenced table, the insert will still be allowed.

How Foreign Keys are Bi-Directional

When defining foreign keys, you need to be aware that they can place restrictions on *both* tables. Up to this point, we've been talking about things in terms of the referencing table; however, once the foreign key is defined, the referenced table must also live by a rule:

> **You cannot delete a record from a referenced table if that record is referenced from the dependent table.**

Let's illustrate this.

We just defined a couple of foreign keys for the `Orders` table. One of those references the `EmployeeID` columns of the `Employees` table. Let's say, for instance, that we have an employee with an `EmployeeID` of 10 who takes many orders for us for a year or two, and then decides to quit and move on to another job. Our tendency would probably be to delete the record in the `Employees` table for that employee, but that would create a rather large problem – we would get what are called **orphaned** records in the `Orders` table. Our `Orders` table would have a large number of records with an `EmployeeID` of 10. If we are allowed to delete `EmployeeID` 10 from the `Employees` table, then we will no longer be able to tell which employee entered in all those orders – the value for the `EmployeeID` column of the `Orders` table will become worthless!

Now let's take this example one step further. Say now, that the employee did not quit. Instead, for some unknown reason, we wanted to change that employee's ID number. If we made the change (via an `UPDATE` statement) to the `Employees` table, but did not make the corresponding update to the `Orders` table, then we would again have orphaned records – we would have records with a value of 10 in the `EmployeeID` column of the `Orders` table with no matching employee.

Now, let's take it one more step further! Imagine that someone comes along and inserts a new record with an `EmployeeID` of 10 – we now have a number of records in our `Orders` table that will be related to an employee that didn't take those orders.

Instead of allowing orphaned records, SQL Server restricts us from deleting or updating records from the referenced table (in this case, the `Employees` table) unless any dependent records have already been deleted from or updated in the referencing (in this case, `Orders`) table.

As you can see, even though the foreign key is defined on one table, it actually placed restrictions on both tables (if the foreign key is self-referenced, then both sets of restrictions are on the one table).

Cascading Updates and Deletes

Those readers who are coming to SQL Server from some other database platform such as Oracle, or even Access, may be familiar with the concept of cascading updates and deletes. Unfortunately, these are not supported under the **declarative form** of referential integrity (which means to use foreign keys) for SQL Server.

When we talked about how foreign keys are bi-directional, we talked about the situation where we are not allowed to delete a record because it has dependent records in another table. Sometimes, however, we would rather automatically delete any dependent records rather than prevent the deletion of the referenced record. The same notion applies to updates to records where we would like the dependent record to automatically reference to the newly updated record.

The process of making such automatic deletions and updates is known as **cascading**. This process, especially for deletes, can actually run through several layers of dependencies (where one record depends on another, which depends on another, and so on). Amazingly, this process is not inherently supported in SQL Server's declarative referential integrity (even Access has this!) – that's the bad news. The good news is that it can be done another way in SQL Server – unfortunately, the only way to do it is with triggers, and there are several caveats.

How exactly to implement cascading updates and deletes is far beyond the level of information you have been given at this point. It is, however, important that you understand that such concepts exist, and that they can indeed be done on SQL Server if you jump through the right hoops.

UNIQUE Constraints

These are relatively easy. `UNIQUE` constraints are essentially the younger sibling of primary keys in that they require a unique value throughout the named column (or combination of columns) in the table. You will often hear `UNIQUE` constraints referred to as **alternate keys**. The major differences are that they are not considered to be *the* unique identifier of a record in that table (even though you could effectively use it that way) and that you *can* have more than one `UNIQUE` constraint (remember that you can only have one primary key per table).

Once you establish a `UNIQUE` constraint, every value in the named columns must be unique. If you go to update or insert a row with a value that already exists in a column with a unique constraint, SQL Server will raise an error and reject the record.

> **Unlike a primary key, a `UNIQUE` constraint does not automatically prevent you from having a `NULL` value. Whether `NULL`s are allowed or not depends on how you set the `NULL` option for that column in the table. Keep in mind though that, if you do allow `NULL`s, you will only be able to insert one of them (although a `NULL` doesn't equal another `NULL`, they are still considered to be duplicate from the perspective of a `UNIQUE` constraint).**

Since there is nothing novel about this (we've pretty much already seen it with primary keys), let's get right to the code. Let's create yet another table in our Accounting database – this time, it will be our Shippers table:

```
CREATE TABLE Shippers
(
   ShipperID      int    IDENTITY    NOT NULL
      PRIMARY KEY,
   ShipperName    varchar(30)        NOT NULL,
   Address        varchar(30)        NOT NULL,
   City           varchar(25)        NOT NULL,
   State          char(2)            NOT NULL,
   Zip            varchar(10)        NOT NULL,
   PhoneNo        varchar(14)        NOT NULL
      UNIQUE
)
```

Now run sp_helpconstraint against the Shippers table, and verify that your Shippers table has been created with the proper constraints.

Creating UNIQUE Constraints on Existing Tables

Again, this works pretty much the same as with primary and foreign keys. We will go ahead and create a UNIQUE constraint on our Employees table:

```
ALTER TABLE Employees
   ADD CONSTRAINT AK_EmployeeSSN
   UNIQUE (SSN)
```

A quick run of sp_helpconstraint verifies that our constraint was created as planned, and on what columns the constraint is active.

CHECK Constraints

The nice thing about CHECK constraints is that they are not restricted to a particular column. They can be related to a column, but they can also be essentially table-related in that they can check one column against another as long as all the columns are within a single table. They may also check that any combination of column values meets a criterion.

The constraint is defined using the same rules that you would use in a WHERE clause. Examples of the criteria for a CHECK constraint include:

Goal	SQL
Limit Month column to appropriate numbers	BETWEEN 1 AND 12
Proper SSN formatting	LIKE [0-9][0-9][0-9]-[0-9][0-9]-[0-9][0-9][0-9][0-9]
Limit to a specific list of Shippers	IN ('UPS', 'Fed Ex', 'USPS')
Price must be positive	UnitPrice >= 0
Referencing another column in the same row	ShipDate >= OrderDate

This really only scratches the surface and the possibilities are virtually endless. Virtually anything you could put in a WHERE clause you can also put in your constraint. What's more, CHECK constraints are very fast performance-wise as compared to the alternatives (rules and triggers).

Still building on our Accounting database, let's add a modification to our Customers table to check for a valid date in our DateInSystem field (you can't have a date in the system that's in the future):

```
ALTER TABLE Customers
   ADD CONSTRAINT CN_CustomerDateInSystem
   CHECK
   (DateInSystem <= GETDATE ())
```

Now try to insert a record that violates the CHECK constraint, you'll get an error:

```
INSERT INTO Customers
   (CustomerName, Address1, Address2, City, State, Zip, Contact,
    Phone, FedIDNo, DateInSystem)
VALUES
   ('Customer1', 'Address1', 'Add2', 'MyCity', 'NY', '55555',
    'No Contact', '555-1212', '930984954', '12-31-2049')
```

Server: Msg 547, Level 16, State 1, Line 1
INSERT statement conflicted with COLUMN CHECK constraint 'CN_CustomerDateInSystem'. The conflict occurred in database 'Accounting', table 'Customers', column 'DateInSystem'.
The statement has been terminated.

Now if we change things to use a DateInSystem that meets the criterion used in the CHECK (anything with today's date or earlier), the INSERT works fine.

DEFAULT Constraints

This will be the first of two different types of data integrity tools that will be called something to do with "default". This is, unfortunately very confusing, but I'll do my best to make it clear (and I think it will become so).

We'll see the other type of default when we look at Rules and Defaults later in the chapter.

A DEFAULT constraint, like all constraints, becomes an integral part of the table definition. It defines what to do when a new row is inserted that doesn't include data for the column on which you have defined the default constraint. You can either define it as a literal value (say, setting a default salary to zero or "UNKNOWN" for a string column) or as one of several system values such as GETDATE().

The main things to understand about a DEFAULT constraint are that:

- Defaults are only used in INSERT statements – they are ignored for UPDATE and DELETE statements
- If any value is supplied in the INSERT, then the default is not used
- If no value is supplied, the default will always be used

Defaults are only made use of in INSERT statements. I cannot express enough how much this is a confusion point for many SQL Server beginners. Think about it this way - when you are first inserting the record, SQL Server doesn't have any kind of value for your column except what you supplied (if anything) or the default. If neither of these are supplied, then SQL Server will either insert a NULL (essentially amounting to "I don't know"), or, if your column definition says NOT NULL, then SQL Server will reject the record. After that first insert, however, SQL Server already has some value for that column. If you are updating that column, then it has your new value. If the column in question isn't part of an UPDATE statement, then SQL Server just leaves what is already in the column.

If a value was provided for the column, then there is no reason to use the default – the supplied value is used.

If no value is supplied, then the default will always be used. Now this seems simple enough until you think about the circumstance where a NULL value is what you actually wanted to go into that column for a record. If you don't supply a value on a column that has a default defined, then the default will be used. What do you do if you really wanted it to be NULL? Say so – insert NULL as part of your INSERT statement.

Defining a DEFAULT Constraint in Your CREATE TABLE Statement

At the risk of sounding repetitious, this works pretty much like all the other constraints we've dealt with thus far. You just add it to the end of the column definition.

To work an example, start by dropping the existing Shippers table that we created earlier in the chapter. This time, we'll create a simpler version of that table including a default:

```
CREATE TABLE Shippers
(
   ShipperID      int    IDENTITY    NOT NULL
      PRIMARY KEY,
   ShipperName    varchar(30)        NOT NULL,
   DateInSystem   smalldatetime      NOT NULL
      DEFAULT GETDATE ()
)
```

After you have run your CREATE script, you can again make use of sp_helpconstraint to show you what you have done. You can then test out how your default works by inserting a new record:

```
INSERT INTO Shippers
   (ShipperName)
VALUES
   ('United Parcel Service')
```

Then run a SELECT statement on your Shippers table:

```
SELECT * FROM Shippers
```

The default value has been generated for the DateInSystem column since we didn't supply a value ourselves:

```
ShipperID     ShipperName                DateInSystem
------------  -------------------------  ---------------------
1             United Parcel Service      1999-05-17 23:28:00

(1 row(s) affected)
```

Adding a DEFAULT Constraint to an Existing Table

While this one is still pretty much more of the same, there is a slight twist. We make use of our ALTER statement and ADD the constraint as before, but we add a FOR operator to tell SQL Server what column is the target for the DEFAULT:

```
ALTER TABLE Customers
   ADD CONSTRAINT CN_CustomerDefaultDateInSystem
      DEFAULT GETDATE() FOR DateInSystem
```

And an extra example:

```
ALTER TABLE Customers
   ADD CONSTRAINT CN_CustomerAddress
      DEFAULT "UNKNOWN" FOR Address1
```

As with all constraints except for a PRIMARY KEY, we are able to add more than one per table.

> **You can mix and match any or all of these constraints as you choose – just be careful not to create constraints that have mutually exclusive conditions. For example, don't have one constraint that says that `col1 > col2` and another one that says that `col2 > col1`. SQL Server will let you do this, and you wouldn't see the issues with it until run-time.**

Disabling Constraints

Sometimes we want to eliminate the constraint checking, either just for a time or permanently. It probably doesn't take much thought to realize that SQL Server must give us some way of deleting constraints, but SQL Server also allows us to just deactivate a FOREIGN KEY or CHECK constraint while otherwise leaving it intact.

The concept of turning off a data integrity rule might seem rather ludicrous at first. I mean, why would you want to turn off the thing that makes sure you don't have bad data? The usual reason is the situation where you already have bad data. This data usually falls into two categories:

- Data that's already in your database when you create the constraint
- Data that you want to add after the constraint is already built

> **You cannot disable `PRIMARY KEY` or `UNIQUE` constraints.**

Ignoring Bad Data When You Create the Constraint

All this syntax has been just fine for the circumstances where you create the constraint at the same time as you create the table. Quite often however, data rules are established after the fact. Let's say, for instance, that you missed something when you were designing your database, and you now have some records in an Invoicing table that show a negative invoice amount. You might want to add a rule that won't let any more negative invoice amounts into the database, but at the same time, you want to preserve the existing records in their original state.

To add a constraint, but have it not apply to existing data, you make use of the WITH NOCHECK option when you perform the ALTER TABLE statement that adds your constraint. As always, let's look at an example.

The Customers table we created in the Accounting database has a field called Phone. The Phone field was created with a data type of char because we expected all of the phone numbers to be of the same length. We also set it with a length of 15 in order to ensure that we have enough room for all the formatting characters. However, we have not done anything to make sure that the records inserted into the database do indeed match the formatting criteria that we expect. To test this out, we'll insert a record in a format that is not what we're expecting, but might be a very honest mistake in terms of how someone might enter a number:

```
INSERT INTO Customers
    (CustomerName,
     Address1,
     Address2,
     City,
     State,
     Zip,
     Contact,
     Phone,
     FedIDNo,
     DateInSystem)
VALUES
    ("MyCust",
     "123 Anywhere",
     "",
     "Reno",
     "NV",
     80808,
     "Joe Bob",
     "555-1212",
     "931234567",
     GETDATE ())
```

Now let's add a constraint to control the formatting of the Phone field:

```
ALTER TABLE Customers
   ADD CONSTRAINT CN_CustomerPhoneNo
   CHECK
  (Phone LIKE "([0-9][0-9][0-9]) [0-9][0-9][0-9]-[0-9][0-9][0-9][0-9]")
```

When we run this, we have a problem:

Server: Msg 547, Level 16, State 1, Line 1
ALTER TABLE statement conflicted with COLUMN CHECK constraint 'CN_CustomerPhoneNo'.
The conflict occurred in database 'Accounting', table 'Customers', column 'Phone'.

SQL Server will not create the constraint unless the existing data meets the constraint criteria. To get around this long enough to install the constraint, either we need to correct the existing data or we must make use of the `WITH NOCHECK` option in our `ALTER` statement. To do this, we just add `WITH NOCHECK` to the statement as follows:

```
ALTER TABLE Customers
   WITH NOCHECK
   ADD CONSTRAINT CN_CustomerPhoneNo
   CHECK
   (Phone LIKE "([0-9][0-9][0-9]) [0-9][0-9][0-9]-[0-9][0-9][0-9][0-9]")
```

Now if we run our same `INSERT` statement again (remember it inserted without a problem last time), the constraint works and the data is rejected:

```
Server: Msg 547, Level 16, State 1, Line 1
INSERT statement conflicted with COLUMN CHECK constraint 'CN_CustomerPhoneNo'. The
conflict occurred in database 'Accounting', table 'Customers', column 'Phone'.
The statement has been terminated.
```

However, if we modify our `INSERT` statement to adhere to our constraint and then re-execute it, the row will be inserted normally:

```
INSERT INTO Customers
   (CustomerName,
    Address1,
    Address2,
    City,
    State,
    Zip,
    Contact,
    Phone,
    FedIDNo,
    DateInSystem)
VALUES
   ("MyCust",
    "123 Anywhere",
    "",
    "Reno",
    "NV",
    80808,
    "Joe Bob",
    "(800) 555-1212",
    "931234567",
    GETDATE ())
```

Try running a `SELECT` on the `Customers` table at this point. You'll see data that both does and does not adhere to our `CHECK` constraint criterion:

```
SELECT CustomerNo, CustomerName, Phone FROM Customers
```

```
CustomerNo CustomerName  Phone
---------------- -------------------- --------------------
5          MyCust        555-1212
7          MyCust        (800) 555-1212

(2 row(s) affected)
```

The old data is retained for backward reference, but any new data is restricted to meeting the new criteria.

> **Keep in mind that the constraint now applies to any inserted or *modified* row in the table. What this means is that any row that is changed in any way must meet the new criteria. If you execute an `UPDATE` statement on a row that does not meet the new criteria, but was grandfathered in with the `WITH NOCHECK` clause, then the record is now required to meet the `CHECK` constraint – even if the constrained column was not the column updated.**
>
> **If it becomes critical for you to modify data in your old rows, but you don't want to have to update the constrained column to meet the constraint, then you can turn the constraint off for the duration of the update as described in the next section.**

Temporarily Disabling an Existing Constraint

All right – so you understand why we need to be able to add new constraints that do not check old data, but why would we want to temporarily disable an existing constraint? Why would we want to let data that we know is bad be added to the database? Actually, the most common reason is basically the same reason that we make use of the `WITH NOCHECK` for – old data.

Old data doesn't just come in the form of data that has already been added to your database. It may also be data that you are importing from a legacy database or some other system. Whatever the reason, the same issue still holds - you have some existing data that doesn't match up with the rules, and you need to get it into the table.

Certainly one way to do this would be to drop the constraint, add the desired data, and then add the constraint back using a `WITH NOCHECK`. But what a pain! Fortunately, we don't need to do that. Instead, we can run an `ALTER` statement with an option called `NOCHECK` that turns off the constraint in question. Here's the code that disables the `CHECK` constraint that we just added in the last section:

```
ALTER TABLE Customers
   NOCHECK
   CONSTRAINT CN_CustomerPhoneNo
```

Now we can run that `INSERT` statement again – the one we proved wouldn't work if the constraint was active:

```
INSERT INTO Customers
    (CustomerName,
     Address1,
     Address2,
     City,
     State,
     Zip,
     Contact,
     Phone,
     FedIDNo,
     DateInSystem)
VALUES
    ("MyCust",
```

```
"123 Anywhere",
"",
"Reno",
"NV",
80808,
"Joe Bob",
"555-1212",
"931234567",
GETDATE())
```

Once again, we are able to INSERT non-conforming data to the table.

By now, the question may have entered your mind asking how do you know whether you have the constraint turned on or not. It would be pretty tedious if you had to create a bogus record to try and insert in order to test whether your constraint is active or not. Like most (but not all) of these kinds of dilemmas, SQL Server provided a procedure to indicate the status of a constraint, and it's a procedure we've already seen, sp_helpconstraint. To execute it against our Customers table is easy:

```
EXEC sp_helpconstraint Customers
```

The results are a little too verbose to fit into the pages of this book, but the second result set this procedure generates includes a column called status_enabled. Whatever this column says the status is can be believed – in this case, it should currently be Disabled.

When we are ready for the constraint to be active again, we simply turn it back on by issuing the same command with a CHECK in the place of the NOCHECK:

```
ALTER TABLE Customers
   CHECK
   CONSTRAINT CN_CustomerPhoneNo
```

If you again run the INSERT statement to verify that the constraint is again functional, you will see a familiar error:

```
Server: Msg 547, Level 16, State 1, Line 1
INSERT statement conflicted with COLUMN CHECK constraint 'CN_CustomerPhoneNo'. The
conflict occurred in database 'Accounting', table 'Customers', column 'Phone'.
The statement has been terminated.
```

Our other option, of course, is to run sp_helpconstraint again, and check out the status_enabled column. If it shows as Enabled, then our constraint must be functional again.

Rules and Defaults – Cousins of Constraints

Rules and **defaults** have been around much longer than CHECK and DEFAULT constraints have been. They are something of an old SQL Server stand-by, and are definitely not without their advantages.

That being said, I'm going to digress from explaining them long enough to recommend that you look them over for backward compatibility and legacy code familiarity only. Rules and defaults are not ANSI compliant (bringing about portability issues), and they do not perform as well as constraints do. As if that's not enough, they are described in the Books Online as "a backward compatibility feature" – not an encouraging thing if you're asking yourself whether this feature is going to continue to be supported in the future. I wouldn't go so far as to suggest that you start sifting through and replacing any old code that you may already have in place, but you should use constraints for any new code you generate.

The primary thing that sets rules and defaults apart from constraints is in their very nature; constraints are features of a table – they have no existence on their own – while rules and defaults are actual objects in and of themselves. Whereas a constraint is defined in the table definition; rules and defaults are defined independently and are then "bound" to the table after the fact.

The independent object nature of rules and defaults gives them the ability to be reused without being redefined. Indeed, rules and defaults are not limited to being bound to just tables; they can also be bound to data types – vastly improving your ability to make highly functional user-defined data types. Let's look at them individually.

Rules

A rule is incredibly similar to a `CHECK` constraint. The only difference beyond those I've already described is that rules are limited to working with just one column at a time. You can bind the same rule separately to multiple columns in a table, but the rule will work independently with each column, and will not be aware of the other columns at all. A constraint defined as (`QtyShipped <= QtyOrdered`) would not work for a rule (it refers to more than one column), whereas `LIKE ([0-9][0-9][0-9])` would (it applies only to whatever column the rule is bound to).

Let's define a rule so that you can see the differences first hand:

```
CREATE RULE SalaryRule
   AS @Salary > 0
```

Notice that what we are comparing is shown as a variable – whatever the value is of the column being checked, that is the value that will be used in the place of `@Salary`. Thus, in this example, we're saying that any column our rule is bound to, would have to have a value greater than zero.

If you want to go back and see what your rule looks like, you can make use of `sp_helptext`:

```
EXEC sp_helptext SalaryRule
```

And it will show you your exact rule definition:

```
Text
------------------------------------
CREATE RULE SalaryRule
   AS @Salary > 0
```

Now we've got a rule, but it isn't doing anything. If we tried to insert a record in our `Employees` table, we could still insert any value right now without any restrictions beyond data type.

In order to activate the rule, we need to make use of a special stored procedure called sp_bindrule. We want to bind our SalaryRule to the Salary column of our Employees table. The syntax looks like this:

```
sp_bindrule <'rule'>, <'object_name'>, [<'futureonly_flag'>]
```

The *rule* part is simple enough – that's the rule we want to bind. The *object_name* is also simple enough – it's the object (table or user-defined data type) to which we want to bind the rule. The only odd parameter is the *futureonly_flag* and it applies only when the rule is bound to a user-defined data type. The default is for this to be off. However, if you set it to True or pass in a 1, then the binding of the rule will only apply to new columns to which you bind the user-defined data type. Any columns that already have the data type in its old form will continue to use that form.

Since we're just binding this rule to a table, our syntax only requires the first two parameters:

```
sp_bindrule 'SalaryRule', 'Employees.Salary'
```

Take a close look at the *object_name* parameter – we have both Employees and Salary separated by a "." – why is that? Since the rule isn't associated with any particular table until you bind it, you need to state the table and column to which the rule will be bound. If you do not use the *tablename.column* naming structure, then SQL Server will assume that what you're naming must be a user-defined data type – if it doesn't find one, you'll get back an error that can be a bit confusing if you hadn't intended to bind the rule to a data type:

```
Server: Msg 15105, Level 16, State 1, Procedure sp_bindrule, Line 185
You do not own a data type with that name.
```

In our case, trying to insert or update an Employees record with a negative value violates the rule and generates an error.

If we want to remove our rule from use with this column, we make use of sp_unbindrule:

```
EXEC sp_unbindrule 'Employees.Salary'
```

The *futureonly_flag* parameter is again an option, but doesn't apply to this particular example. If you use sp_unbindrule with the *futureonly_flag* turned on, and it is used against a user-defined data type (rather than a specific column), then the unbinding will only apply to future uses of that data type – existing columns using that data type will still make use of the rule.

Defaults

Defaults are even more similar to their cousin – a default constraint – than a rule is to a CHECK constraint. Indeed, they work identically, with the only real differences being in the way that they are attached to a table and the default's (the object, not the constraint) support for a user-defined data type.

> **The concept of defaults vs. DEFAULT constraints is wildly difficult for a lot of people to grasp. After all, they have almost the same name. If we refer to "default", then we are referring to either the object-based default (what we're talking about in this section), or as shorthand to the actual default value (that will be supplied if we don't provide an explicit value). If we refer to a "DEFAULT constraint", then we are talking about the non-object based solution – the solution that is an integral part of the table definition.**

The syntax for defining a default works much as it did for a rule:

```
CREATE DEFAULT <default name>
AS <default value>
```

Therefore, to define a default of zero for our Salary:

```
CREATE DEFAULT SalaryDefault
   AS 0
```

Again, a default is worthless without being bound to something. To bind it we make use of sp_bindefault, which is, other than the procedure name, identical syntax to the sp_bindrule procedure:

```
EXEC sp_bindefault 'SalaryDefault', 'Employees.Salary'
```

To unbind the default from the table, we use sp_unbindefault:

```
EXEC sp_unbindefault 'Employees.Salary'
```

Keep in mind that the *futureonly_flag* also applies to this stored procedure, it is just not used here.

Determining What Tables and Data Types Use a Given Rule or Default

If you ever go to delete or alter your rules or defaults, you may first want to take a look at what tables and data types are making use of them. Again, SQL Server comes to the rescue with a system stored procedure. This one is called sp_depends. Its syntax looks like this:

```
EXEC sp_depends <object name>
```

`sp_depends` provides a listing of all the objects that depend on the object you've requested information about.

> **Beginning with version 7.0, using `sp_depends` is no longer a sure bet to tell you about every object that depends on a parent object. SQL Server 7.0 supports something called "deferred name resolution". Basically, deferred name resolution means that you can create objects (primary stored procedures) that depend on another object – even before the second (target of the dependency) object is created. For example, SQL Server will now allow you to create a stored procedure that refers to a table even before the said table is created. In this instance, SQL Server isn't able to list the table as having a dependency on it. Even after you add the table, it will not have any dependency listing if you use `sp_depends`.**

Triggers for Data Integrity

We've got a whole chapter coming up on triggers, but any discussion of constraints, rules and defaults would not be complete without at least a mention of triggers.

One of the most common uses of triggers is to implement data integrity rules. Since we have that chapter coming up, I'm not going to get into it very deep here other than to say that triggers have a very large number of things they can do data integrity wise that a constraint or rule could never hope to do. The downside (and you knew there had to be one) is that they incur substantial additional overhead and are, therefore, much (very much) slower in almost any circumstance. They are procedural in nature (which is where they get their power), but they also happen after everything else is done, and should only be used as a relative last resort.

Choosing What to Use

Wow. Here you are with all these choices, and now how do you figure out what the right one to use is. Some of the constraints are fairly independent (`PRIMARY` and `FOREIGN KEY`s, `UNIQUE` constraints) – you are using either them or nothing. The rest have some level of overlap with each other and it can be rather confusing when making a decision on what to use. You've got some hints from me as we've been going through this chapter about what some of the strengths and weaknesses are of each of the options, but it will probably make a lot more sense if we look at them all together for a bit.

Restriction	Pros	Cons
Constraints	Fast. Can reference other columns. Happens before the command occurs.	Must be re-defined for each table. Can't reference other tables. Can't be bound to data types.
Rules, Defaults	Independent objects. Reusable. Can be bound to data types. Happens before the command occurs.	Slightly slower. Can't reference across columns. Can't reference other tables.
Triggers	Ultimate flexibility. Can reference other columns and other tables.	Happens after the command occurs. High overhead.

The main time to use rules and defaults is if you are implementing a rather robust logical model, and are making extensive use of user-defined data types. In this instance, rules and defaults can provide a lot of functionality and ease of management without much programmatic overhead – you just need to be aware that they may go away in a future release someday. Probably not soon, but someday.

Triggers should only be used when a constraint is not an option. Like a constraint, they are attached to the table, and must be re-defined with every table you create. On the bright side, they can do most things that you are likely to want to do data integrity wise. Indeed, they can even take the place of foreign keys if required (I don't recommend this unless you need cascading updates and deletes, again for performance reasons). We will cover these in some detail later in the book.

That leaves us with constraints, which should become your data integrity solution of choice. They are fast and not that difficult to create. Their downfall is that they can be limiting (not being able to reference other tables except for a `FOREIGN KEY`), and they can be tedious to re-define over and over again if you have a common constraint logic.

Regardless of what kind of integrity mechanism that you're putting in place (keys, triggers, constraints, rules, defaults), the thing to remember can best be summed up in just one word – balance.

Every new thing that you add to your database adds additional overhead, so you need to make sure that whatever you're adding honestly has value to it before you stick it in your database. Avoid things like redundant integrity implementations (for example, I can't tell you how often I've come across a database that has both foreign keys defined for referential integrity and triggers to do the same thing). Make sure you know what constraints you have before you put the next one on, and make sure you know exactly what you hope to accomplish with it.

Summary

The different types of data integrity mechanisms described in this chapter are the backbone of a sound database. Perhaps the biggest power of RDBMS systems is that the database can now take responsibility for data integrity rather than depending on the application. This means that even ad hoc queries are subject to the data rules, and that multiple applications are all treated equally with regard to data integrity issues.

In the chapters to come, we will look at the tie between some forms of constraints and indexes, along with taking a look at the advanced data integrity rules than can be implemented using triggers.

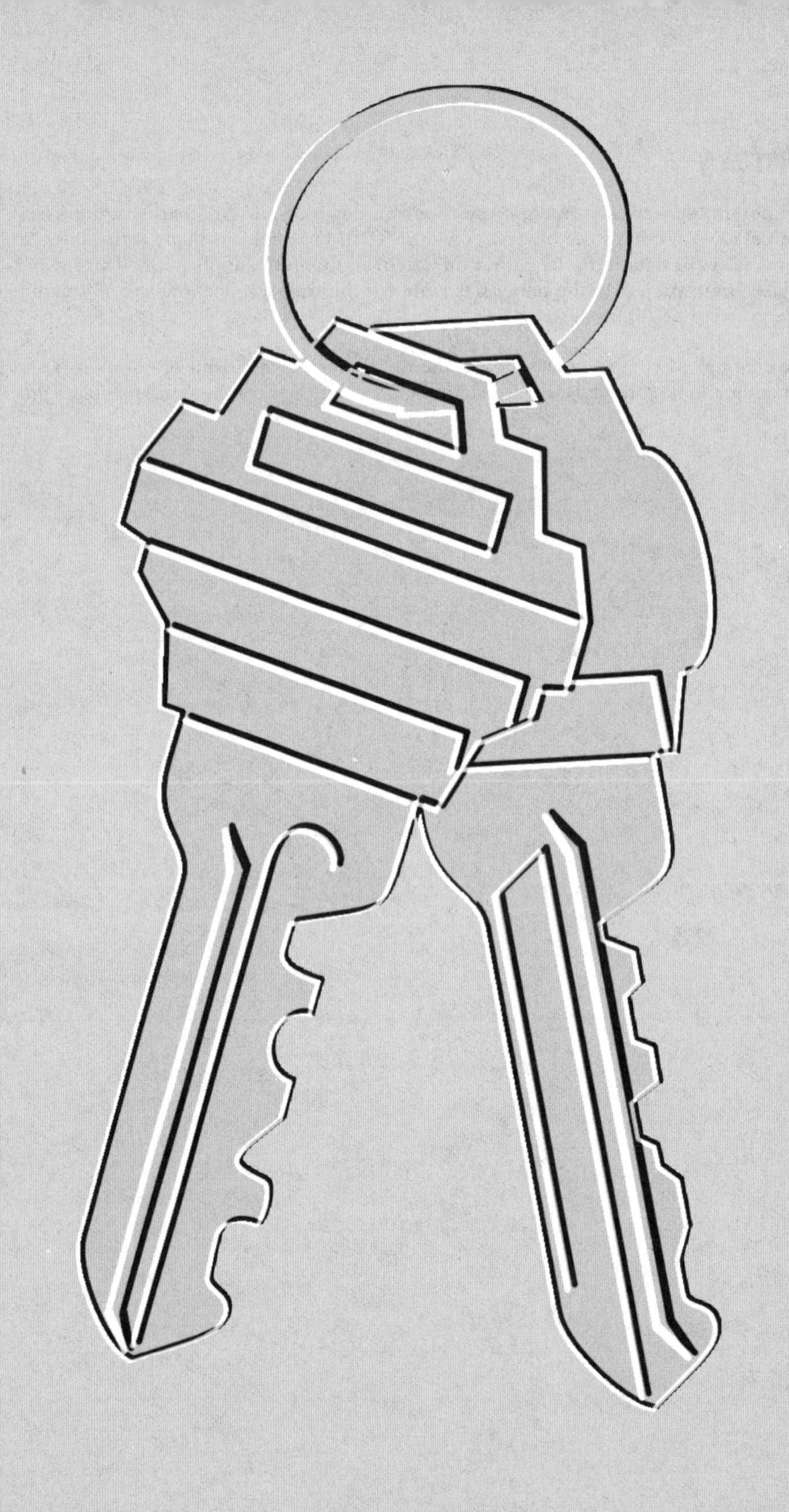

8

Normalization and Other Basic Design Issues

If this book is your first real foray into databases, then I can imagine you being somewhat perplexed about the how and why of some of the tables we've constructed thus far. With the exception of a chapter or two, this book is being primarily focused on an **Online Transaction Processing**, or **OLTP**, environment.

OLTP is far and away the most common type of database. If you're working with a database, unless you've specifically been told otherwise, the odds are overwhelming that it is OLTP in nature. OLTP databases are designed, as their name says, with transaction processing in mind. They attempt to eliminate all redundancy for both performance and data integrity reasons.

OLAP (**Online Analytical Processing**) databases are typically a polar opposite to that notion. OLAP databases are for analysis – reporting – as such, they tend to think about things in a different light (little or no updating of data, lots of reading of data for example). With OLAP, we are primarily only reading data, so redundancy doesn't typically hurt us – indeed, it can actually help us. Keep OLAP databases in mind, and we'll revisit them in Chapter 21, but, in the real world, you'll find that these are only a small faction of the total number of databases you'll come across.

My point is that you will, in most of the examples, be seeing a table design that is optimized for the most common kind of database – OLTP. As such, you will typically have a database layout that is, for the most part, **normalized** to what is called the 3rd normal form.

So what is "normal form?" We'll be taking a very solid look at that in this chapter, but, for the moment, let's just say that it means that your data has been broken out into a logical, non-repetitive format that can easily be reassembled back into the whole. In addition to normalization, we'll also be examining the characteristics of OLTP and OLAP databases. And, as if we didn't have enough between those two topics, we'll also be looking at many examples of how the constraints we've already seen are implemented in the overall solution.

This is probably going to be one of the toughest chapters in the book to grasp because of a paradox in what to learn first. Some of the concepts used in this chapter refer to things we'll be covering later – such as triggers and stored procedures. On the other hand, it is difficult to relate those topics without understanding their role in database design.

I strongly recommend reading this chapter through, and then coming back to it again after you've read several of the subsequent chapters (perhaps through Chapter 16).

Tables

This is going to seem beyond basic, but let's make a brief review of what exactly a table is. We're obviously not talking about the kind that sits in your kitchen, but, rather, the central object of any database.

A table is a collection of instances of data that have the same general **attributes**. These instances of data are organized into **rows** and **columns** of data. A table should represent a "real-world" collection of data – or **entity**, and will have **relationships** with information in other tables. A drawing of the various entities (tables) and relationships (how they work together) is usually referred to as an Entity-Relationship Diagram – or **ER Diagram**. Sometimes the term ER Diagram will even be shorten further down to ERD.

By connecting one or more tables through their various relationships, you are able to temporarily create other tables as needed from the combination of the data in both tables (we've already seen this to some degree in Chapters 4 and 5). A collection of related entities are then grouped together into a database.

Time for Therapy – Keeping Your Data "Normal"

Normalization is something of the cornerstone model of OLTP database design. Normalization first originated along with the concept of relational databases. Both came from the work of E.F. Codd (IBM) in 1969. Codd put forth the notion that a database "consists of a series of unordered tables that can be manipulated using non-procedural operations that return tables". Several things are key about this:

- Order must be unimportant
- The tables would be able to "relate" to each other in a non-procedural way (indeed, Codd called tables "relationships")
- That, by relating these base tables, you would be able to create a virtual table to meet a new need

Normalization was a natural off-shoot of the design of a database of "relations."

> *The concept of normalization has to be one of most over referenced and yet misunderstood concepts in programming. Everyone thinks they understand it, and many do in at least its academic form. Unfortunately, it also tends to be one of those things that many database designers wear like a cross – it is somehow their symbol that they are a "real" database architect.*
>
> *What it really is, is a symbol that they know what the normal forms are – and that's all. Normalization is really just one piece of a larger database design picture. Sometimes you need to normalize your data – then again, sometimes you need to deliberately de-normalize your data. Even within the normalization process, there are often many ways to achieve what is technically a normalized database.*
>
> *My point in this latest soapbox diatribe is that normalization is a theory, and that's all it is. Once you choose to either implement a normalized strategy or not, what you have is a database – hopefully the best one you could possibly design. Don't get stuck on what the books (including this one) say you're supposed to do – do what's right for the situation that you're in. As the author of this book, all I can do is relate concepts to you – I can't implement them for you. You need to pick and choose between these concepts in order to achieve the best fit and the best solution. Now, excuse me while I put that soapbox away, and we'll get on to talking about the normal forms and what they purportedly do for us.*

Let's start off by saying that there are six normal forms. For those of you who have dealt with databases and normalization before, that number may come as a surprise – you are very likely to hear that a fully normalized database is one that is normalized to the third normal form. Doesn't it then follow that there must be only three normal forms? Perhaps it will make those same people who thought there were only three normal forms feel better that we're only going to be looking at the three forms you've heard about to any extent in this book, as they are the only three that are put to any regular use in the real world. I will, however, take a brief (very brief) scan over the other three forms just for posterity.

We've already looked at how to create a primary key and some of the reasons for using one for our tables – if we want to be able to act on just one row, then we need to be able to uniquely identify that row. The concepts of normalization are highly dependent on issues surrounding the definition of the primary key and what columns are dependent on it. One phrase you might hear frequently in normalization is:

The key, the whole key, and nothing but the key.

Or, if you like, you can try out the rather amusing new version of this I recently heard:

The key, the whole key, and nothing but the key, so help me Codd.

This is a super-brief summarization of what normalization is about out to the 3rd normal form. When you can say that all your columns are dependent only on the whole key and nothing more or less, then you are at 3rd normal form.

Let's take a look at the various normal forms, and what each does for us.

Before the Beginning

You actually need to begin by getting a few things in place even before you try to get your data into first normal form. You have to have a thing or two in place before you can even consider the table to be a true entity in the relational database sense of the word:

- The table should describe one entity (no trying to short cut and combine things!)
- All rows must be unique, and there must be a primary key
- The column and row order must not matter

Since a table should describe one entity, we probably ought to look more closely at what exactly an entity is. I mentioned earlier that an entity is a "real-world collection of data". To get more specific though, that collection of data should describe a specific thing – or, to use a word from English class – a noun. An entity should be a "person, place or thing" that you want to record data about. Avoid the temptation to mix different things in one entity (Customers and Orders for example).

The place to start, then, is by identifying the right entities to have. Some of these will be fairly obvious, others will not. Many of them will be exposed and refined as you go through the normalization process. At the very least, go through and identify all the obvious entities. If you're familiar with object-oriented programming, then you can liken the most logical top level entities to objects in an object model.

Let's think about a hyper simple model – our sales model again. To begin with, we're not going to worry about the different variations possible, or even what columns we're going to have – instead, we're just going to worry about identifying the basic entities of our system.

First, think about the most basic process. What we want to do is create an entity for each atomic unit for which we want to maintain data about in the process. Our process then, looks like this: A customer calls or comes in. They talk to an employee who takes and order.

A first pass on this might have one entity: Orders.

> *As you become more experienced at normalization, your first pass at something like this is probably going to yield you quite a few more entities right from the beginning. For now though, we'll just take this one and see how the normalization process shows us which others we need.*

Assuming you've got your concepts down of what you want your entities to be, the next place to go is to figure out your beginning columns and, from there, a primary key. Remember that a primary key provides a unique identifier for each row.

We can peruse our list of columns and come up with **key candidates**. Your list of key candidates should include any column that can potentially be used to uniquely identify each row in your entity. There is, otherwise, no hard and fast rule on what column has to be the primary key (this is part of why you'll see such a wide variation in how people design databases that are meant to contain the same basic information). In some cases, you will not be able to find even one key candidate, and you will need to make one up (remember Identity and rowguid() columns?).

We've already created an `Orders` table in the last chapter, but for example purposes let's take a look at a very common implementation of an `Orders` table in the old flat file design:

Orders
OrderNo
CustomerNo
CustomerName
CustomerAddress
CustomerCity
CustomerState
CustomerZip
OrderDate
ItemsOrdered
Total

Since this is an `Orders` table, and logically, an order number is meant to be one to an order, I'm going go with `OrderNo` as my primary key.

OK, so now we have a basic entity. Nothing about this entity cares about the ordering of columns (tables are, by convention, usually organized as having the primary key as the first column(s), but, technically speaking, it doesn't have to be that way). Nothing in the basic makeup of this table cares about the ordering of the rows. The table, at least superficially, describes just one entity. In short, we're ready to begin our normalization process (actually, we sort of already have).

The First Normal Form

The first normal form (1NF) is all about eliminating repeating groups of data and guaranteeing atomicity (the data is self-contained and independent). At a high level, it works by creating a primary key (which we already have), then moving any repeating data groups into new tables, creating new keys for those tables, and so on. In addition, we break out any columns that combine data into separate rows for each piece of data.

In the more traditional flat file designs, repeating data was commonplace – as were multiple pieces of information in a column – this was rather problematic in a number of ways:

- At that time, disk storage was extremely expensive. Storing data multiple times means wasted space. Data storage has become substantially less expensive, so this isn't as big of an issue as it once was.
- Repetitive data means more data to be moved, and larger I/O counts. This means that performance is hindered as large blocks of data must be moved through the data bus and/or network. This, even with today's much faster technology, can have a substantial negative impact on performance.
- The data between what should be repeated rows often did not agree, creating something of a data paradox and a general lack of data integrity.

- If you wanted to query information from a column that contained combined data, then you had to first come up with a way to parse the data in that column (this was extremely slow).

Now, there are a lot of columns in our table, and I probably could have easily tossed in a few more. Still, the nice thing about it is that I could query everything out of one place when I wanted to know about orders.

Just to explore what this means, though, let's take a look at what some data in this table might look like. Note that I'm going to cut out a few columns here just to help things fit on a page, but I think you'll still be able to see the point:

Order No	Order Date	Customer No	Customer Name	Customer Address	ItemsOrdered
100	1/1/1999	54545	ACME Co	1234 1st St.	1A4536, Flange, 7lbs, $75; 4-OR2400, Injector, .5lbs, $108; 4-OR2403, Injector, .5lbs, $116; 1-4I5436, Head, 63lbs, $750
101	1/1/1999	12000	Sneed Corp.	555 Main Ave.	1-3X9567, Pump, 5lbs, $62.50
102	1/1/1999	66651	ZZZ & Co.	4242 SW 2nd	7-8G9200; Fan, 3lbs, $84; 1-8G5437, Fan, 3lbs, $15; 1-3H6250, Control, 5lbs, $32
103	1/2/1999	54545	ACME Co	1234 1st St.	40-8G9200, Fan, 3lbs, $480; 1-2P5523, Housing, 1lbs, $165; 1-3X9567, Pump, 5lbs, $42

I have a number of issues to deal with in this table if I'm going to normalize it. While I have a functional primary key (yes, these existed long before relational systems), I have problems with both of the main areas of the first normal form:

- I have repeating groups of data (customer information). I need to break that out into a different table.
- The `ItemsOrdered` column does not contain data that is atomic in nature. That is, it's only one column, but it contains multiple values (you might hear this called "multi-valued") – each of these should be stored distinctly.

I can start by moving several columns out of the table:

Order No (PK)	Order Date	Customer No	ItemsOrdered
100	1/1/1999	54545	1A4536, Flange, 7lbs, $75; 4-OR2400, Injector, .5lbs, $108; 4-OR2403, Injector, .5lbs, $116; 1-4I5436, Head, 63lbs, $750
101	1/1/1999	12000	1-3X9567, Pump, 5lbs, $62.50
102	1/1/1999	66651	7-8G9200; Fan, 3lbs, $84; 1-8G5437, Fan, 3lbs, $15; 1-3H6250, Control, 5lbs, $32
103	1/2/1999	54545	40-8G9200, Fan, 3lbs, $480; 1-2P5523, Housing, 1lbs, $165; 1-3X9567, Pump, 5lbs, $42

And putting it into its own table:

Customer No (PK)	Customer Name	Customer Address
54545	ACME Co	1234 1st St.
12000	Sneed Corp.	555 Main Ave.
66651	ZZZ & Co.	4242 SW 2nd

There are several things to notice about both the old and new tables:

- I have to have a primary key for my new table to ensure that each row is unique. For our `Customers` table, there are two candidate keys – `CustomerNo` and `CustomerName`. `CustomerNo` was actually created just to serve this purpose and seems the logical choice – after all, it's entirely conceivable that you could have more than one customer with the same name (for example, there have to be hundreds of AA Auto Glass companies in the US), so you would want to rule it out.
- Although I've moved the data out of the orders table, I still need to maintain a reference to the data in the new `Customers` table; otherwise, we wouldn't be able to "relate" an order back to who ordered it. This is why you still see the `CustomerNo` (the primary key) column in the `Orders` table. Later on, when we build our references, we'll create a `FOREIGN KEY` constraint to force all orders to have valid customer numbers.
- We were able to eliminate an instance of the information for ACME Co. That's part of the purpose of moving data that appears in repetitive groups – just to store it once. This saves us both space and prevents conflicting values.
- We only moved repeating *groups* of data. We still see the same order date several times, but it doesn't really fit into a group – it's just a relatively random piece of data that has no relevance outside of this table.

Next, we are ready to move on to the second violation of first normal form – atomicity. If you take a look at the ItemsOrdered column, you'll see that there are actually several different pieces of data there:

- Anywhere from 1 to many individual part numbers
- Quantity weight information on each of those parts

Part Number, Weight, and Price are each atomic pieces of data if kept to themselves, but combined into one lump grouping, you no longer have atomicity.

> **Believe it or not, things were sometimes really done this way. At first glance, it seemed the easy thing to do – paper invoices often had just one big boxed area for writing up what the customer wanted. When computer-based systems came along, they were often as much of a clone to paper as someone could make it – if you didn't have distinct values on the paper, then you weren't going to get one in the database.**

We'll go ahead and break things up – and, while we're at it – we'll add in a new piece of information in the form of a unit price. The problem is that, once we break up this information, our primary key no longer uniquely identifies our rows – our rows are still unique, but the primary key is now inadequate:

Order No (PK)	Order Date	Customer No	Part No	Description	Qty	Unit Price	Total Price	Wt
100	1/1/1999	54545	1A4536	Flange	5	15	75	6
100	1/1/1999	54545	OR2400	Injector	4	27	108	.5
100	1/1/1999	54545	OR2403	Injector	4	29	116	.5
100	1/1/1999	54545	4I5436	Head	1	750	750	3
101	1/1/1999	12000	3X9567	Pump	1	62.50	62.50	5
102	1/1/1999	66651	8G9200	Fan	7	12	84	3
102	1/1/1999	66651	8G5437	Fan	1	15	15	3
102	1/1/1999	66651	3H6250	Control	1	32	32	5
103	1/2/1999	54545	8G9200	Fan	40	12	480	3
103	1/2/1999	54545	2P5523	Housing	1	165	165	1
103	1/2/1999	54545	3X9567	Pump	1	42	42	5

For now, we'll address this by adding a line item number to our table so we can, again, uniquely identify our rows:

Order No (PK)	Line Item (PK)	Order Date	Customer No	Part No	Description	Qty	Unit Price	Total Price	Wt
100	1	1/1/1999	54545	1A4536	Flange	5	15	75	6
100	2	1/1/1999	54545	OR2400	Injector	4	27	108	.5
100	3	1/1/1999	54545	OR2403	Injector	4	29	116	.5
100	4	1/1/1999	54545	4I5436	Head	1	750	750	3
101	1	1/1/1999	12000	3X9567	Pump	1	62.50	62.50	5
102	1	1/1/1999	66651	8G9200	Fan	7	12	84	3
102	2	1/1/1999	66651	8G5437	Fan	1	15	15	3
102	3	1/1/1999	66651	3H6250	Control	1	32	32	5
103	1	1/2/1999	54545	8G9200	Fan	40	12	480	3
103	2	1/2/1999	54545	2P5523	Housing	1	165	165	1
103	3	1/2/1999	54545	3X9567	Pump	1	42	42	5

Rather than create another column as I did here, I also could have taken the approach of making `PartNo` part of my `Primary Key`. The fallout from this would have been that we could not have had the same part number appear twice in the same order. We'll briefly discuss keys based on more than one column – or composite keys – in our next chapter.

At this point, we meet our criteria for first normal form. We have no repeating groups of data, and all columns are atomic. We do have issues with data having to be repeated within a column (because it's the same for all rows for that primary key), but we'll deal with that shortly.

The Second Normal Form

The next phase in normalization is to go to the second normal form (2NF). Second normal form further reduces the incidence of repeated data (not necessarily groups).

Second normal form has two rules to it:

- The table must meet the rules for first normal form (normalization is a building block kind of process – you can't stack the third block on if you don't have the first two there already).
- Each column must depend on the *whole* key.

Our example has a problem – actually, it has a couple of problems – in this area. Let's look at the first normal form version of our `Orders` table again – is every column dependent on the whole key? Are there any that only need part of the key?

Order No (PK)	Line Item (PK)	Order Date	Customer No	Part No	Description	Qty	Unit Price	Total Price	Wt
100	1	1/1/1999	54545	1A4536	Flange	5	15	75	6
100	2	1/1/1999	54545	OR2400	Injector	4	27	108	.5
100	3	1/1/1999	54545	OR2403	Injector	4	29	116	.5
100	4	1/1/1999	54545	4I5436	Head	1	750	750	3
101	1	1/1/1999	12000	3X9567	Pump	1	62.50	62.50	5
102	1	1/1/1999	66651	8G9200	Fan	7	12	84	3
102	2	1/1/1999	66651	8G5437	Fan	1	15	15	3
102	3	1/1/1999	66651	3H6250	Control	1	32	32	5
103	1	1/2/1999	54545	8G9200	Fan	40	12	480	3
103	2	1/2/1999	54545	2P5523	Housing	1	165	165	1
103	3	1/2/1999	54545	3X9567	Pump	1	42	42	5

The answers are no and yes respectively. There are two columns that only depend on the `OrderNo` column – not the `LineItem` column. The columns in question are `OrderDate` and `CustomerNo`, both are the same for the entire order regardless of how many line items there are. Dealing with these requires that we introduce yet another table. At this point, you, for the first time, run across the concept of a **header** vs. a **detail** table.

What I'm choosing to call header and detail tables here also are called other things depending on the shop you work in. Master vs. detail tables and parent vs. child tables are also common terminologies. The key is to remember what the nature of the relationship is – you have one header (or master, or parent) to at least one, and possibly many, detail (or child) records. This type of relationship is called a one-to-many relationship, and we will look at this kind of relationship and more later in the chapter.

Sometimes what is, in practice, one entity still needs to be broken out into two tables and, thus, two entities. The header is a bit like the parent table of the two tables in the relationship. It contains information that only needs to be stored once while the detail table stores the information that may exist in multiple instances. The header usually keeps the name of the original table, and the detail table usually has a name that begins with the header table name and adds on something to indicate that it is a detail table (for example, `OrderDetails`). For every one header record, you usually have at least one detail record and may have many, many more.

So let's take care of this by splitting our table again. We'll actually start with the detail table since it's keeping the bulk of the columns. From this point forward, we'll call this table `OrderDetails`:

Order No (PK)	Line Item (PK)	Part No	Description	Qty	Unit Price	Total Price	Wt
100	1	1A4536	Flange	5	15	75	6
100	2	OR2400	Injector	4	27	108	.5
100	3	OR2403	Injector	4	29	116	.5
100	4	4I5436	Head	1	750	750	3
101	1	3X9567	Pump	1	62.50	62.50	5
102	1	8G9200	Fan	7	12	84	3
102	2	8G5437	Fan	1	15	15	3
102	3	3H6250	Control	1	32	32	5
103	1	8G9200	Fan	40	12	480	3
103	2	2P5523	Housing	1	165	165	1
103	3	3X9567	Pump	1	42	42	5

Then we move the remaining columns to what, although you could consider it to be the new table of the two, will serve as the header table and thus keep the `Orders` name:

Order No (PK)	Order Date	Customer No
100	1/1/1999	54545
101	1/1/1999	12000
102	1/1/1999	66651
103	1/2/1999	54545

So, now we have second normal form. All of our columns depend on the entire key. I'm sure you won't be surprised to hear that we still have a problem or two though – we'll deal with them next.

The Third Normal Form

This is the relative end of the line. There are technically levels of normalization beyond this, but none that get much attention outside of academic circles. We'll look at those extremely briefly next, but first we need to finish the business at hand.

I mentioned at the end of our discussion of second normal form that we still had problems – we still haven't reached third normal form (3NF). Third normal form deals with the issue of having all the columns in our table not just be dependent on something – but the right thing. Third normal form has just three rules to it:

- The table must be in 2NF (I told you this was a building block thing)
- No column can have any dependency on any other non-key column.
- You cannot have derived data

We already know that we're in second normal form, so let's look at the other two rules.

First, do we have any columns that have dependencies other than the primary key? That's a big "Yes!" Actually, there are a couple of columns that are dependent on the part number as much or more than the primary key of this table. `Weight` and `Description` are both entirely dependent on the `PartNo` column – we again need to split into another table.

Your first tendency here might be to also lump `UnitPrice` into this category, and you would be partially right. The `Products` table that we will create here can and should have a `UnitPrice` column in it – but it will be of a slightly different nature. Indeed, perhaps it would be better named `ListPrice`, as it is the cost we have set in general for that product. The difference for the `UnitPrice` in the `OrderDetails` table is twofold: First, we may offer discounts that would change the price at time of sale. This means that the price in the order detail record may be different from the planned price that we will keep in the `Products` table. Second, the price we plan to charge will change over time with factors such as inflation, but changes in future prices will not change what we have charged on our actual orders of the past. In other words, Price is one of those odd circumstances where there are really two flavors of it – one dependent on the PartNo, and one dependent on the primary key for the `OrderDetails` table (i.e., `OrderID` and `LineItem`).

First, we need to create a new table (we'll call it `Products`) to hold our part information. This new table will hold the information that we had in `OrderDetails` that was more dependent on `PartNo` than on `OrderID` and `LineItem`.

Part No (PK)	Description	Wt
1A4536	Flange	6
OR2400	Injector	.5
OR2403	Injector	.5
4I5436	Head	3
3X9567	Pump	5
8G9200	Fan	3
8G5437	Fan	3
3H6250	Control	5
8G9200	Fan	3
2P5523	Housing	1
3X9567	Pump	5

We can then chop all but the foreign key out of the `OrderDetails` table:

Order No (PK)	Line Item (PK)	Part No	Qty	Unit Price	Total Price
100	1	1A4536	5	15	75
100	2	OR2400	4	27	108
100	3	OR2403	4	29	116
100	4	4I5436	1	750	750
101	1	3X9567	1	62.50	62.50
102	1	8G9200	7	12	84
102	2	8G5437	1	15	15
102	3	3H6250	1	32	32
103	1	8G9200	40	12	480
103	2	2P5523	1	165	165
103	3	3X9567	1	42	42

That takes care of problem #1 (cross-column dependency), but doesn't deal with derived data. We have a column called `TotalPrice` that contains data that can actually be derived from multiplying `Qty` * `UnitPrice`. This is a no-no in normalization.

Derived data is one of the places where you'll see me "de-normalize" data the most often. Why? Speed. A query that reads "`WHERE TotalPrice > $100`" runs faster than one that reads "`WHERE Qty * UnitPrice > 50`".

On the flip side of this, however, I'll probably be doing a bit more of a hybrid version with SQL Server 7.0 and beyond. SQL Server now supports computed columns (virtual columns that are defined as being computed from the contents of other columns). While I suspect that physically storing `TotalPrice` would still be faster in very large query sets, I am not seeing an appreciable difference in smaller sets and do not expect the difference to be worth it even in large datasets.

So, to reach third normal form, we just need to drop off the `TotalPrice` column and compute it when needed.

Other Normal Forms

There are a few other forms out there that are considered, at least by academics, to be part of the normalization model. These include:

- Boyce-Codd (considered to really just be a variation on third normal form). This one tries to address situations where you have multiple overlapping candidate keys. This is typically a situation where any number of solutions work, and almost never gets logically thought of outside the academic community.
- Fourth Normal Form: This one tries to deal with issues surrounding multi-valued dependence.
- Fifth Normal Form: Deals with non-loss and loss decompositions. In short, this one deals with the goal of having your database to the point where splitting your tables any further would create a situation where you can't reconstruct the original table by joining the two tables you created (the decomposition of the original table has "lost" the ability to recreate the original table).
- Sixth Normal Form – or Domain-Key Normal Form: This is achieved only when you have eliminated any possibility of modification anomalies (where modifying in one place propagates the change everywhere needed with no risk of being out of sync with other data in the system). This is virtually impossible in the real world.

This is, of course, just a quick look at these – and that's deliberate on my part. The main reason to know these in the real world is either to impress your friends (or prove to them you're a know-it-all) or to not sound like an idiot when some database guru comes to town and starts talking about them.

Again, the big point to remember in all this are the first through third normal forms. Think of them as being steps to your goal:

- 1st NF: Eliminate all non-atomic (multi-valued) attributes or repeating groups.
- 2nd NF: Eliminate any partial or functional dependencies – that is, make sure every column is dependent on the *entire* key.
- 3rd NF: Eliminate any dependencies on any thing except for the key (don't depend on any non-key columns), plus eliminate any columns that are derived from other data.

Relationships

Well, I've always heard from women that men immediately leave the room if you even mention the word "relationship". With that in mind, I hope that I didn't just lose about half my readers.

I am, of course, kidding – but not by as much as you might think. Experts say the key to successful relationships is that you know the roles of both parties and that everyone understands the boundaries and rules of the relationship that they are in. I can be talking about database relationships with that statement every bit as much as people relationships.

There are 3 different kinds of major relationships:

- One-to-One
- One-to-Many
- Many-to-Many

Each of these has some variations depending on whether one side of the relationship is nullable or not. For example, instead of a one-to-one relationship, you might have a zero or one-to-one relationship.

One-to-One

This is exactly what it says it is. A one-to-one relationship is one where the fact that you have a record in one table means that you have exactly one matching record in another table.

To illustrate a one-to-one relationship, let's look at a slight variation of our earlier example. Imagine that you have customers – just as we did in our earlier example. This time, however, we're going to imagine that we are a subsidiary of a much larger company. Our parent company wants to be able to track all of its customers, and to be able to tell the collective total of each customer's purchases – regardless of which subsidiary(s) the customer made purchases with.

Even if all the subsidiaries run from one server at the main headquarters, there's a very good chance that the various subsidiaries would be running with their own databases. One way, however, to track all customer information in a way that would facilitate combining it later, would be to create a master customer database owned by the parent company. The subsidiaries would then maintain their own customer table, but do so with a one-to-one relationship to the parent company's customer table. Any customer record created in the parent company would imply that you needed to have one in the subsidiaries also. Any creation of a customer record in a subsidiary would require that one was also created in the parent company's copy.

A second example – one that used to apply frequently to SQL Server prior to version 7.0 – is the situation where you have too much information to fit in one row. Remember that the maximum row size for SQL Server is 8060 bytes of non-BLOB data. That's a lot harder to fill than version 6.5's 1962 bytes, but you can still have situations where you need to store a very large number of columns or even just a few very wide columns. One way to get around this problem was to actually create two different tables and split our rows between the tables. We could then impose a one-to-one relationship. The combination of the matching rows in the two tables then meets our larger rowsize requirement.

> **SQL Server has no inherent method of enforcing a true one-to-one relationship. You can say that table A requires a matching record in table B, but, when you then add that table B must have a matching record in table A, you create a paradox – which table gets the record first? If you need to enforce this kind of relationship in SQL Server, the best you can do is to force all inserts to be done via stored procedure. The stored procedure can have the logic to insert into both tables or neither table. Both `FOREIGN KEY` constraints and triggers cannot handle this circular relationship.**

Zero or One-to-One

SQL Server can handle the instance of zero or one-to-one relationships. This is essentially the same as a one-to-one, only one side of the relationship has the option of either having a record or not.

Going back to our parent company vs. subsidiary example, you might prefer to create a relationship where the parent company needs to have a matching record for each subsidiary's records, but the subsidiary doesn't need the information from the parent. You could, for example, have subsidiaries that have very different customers (such as a railroad and a construction company). The parent company wants to know about all the customers regardless of what business they came from, but your construction company probably doesn't care about your railroad customers. In such a case, you would have zero or one construction customers to one parent company customer record.

Zero or one-to-one relationships can be enforced in SQL Server through:

- A combination of a `UNIQUE` or `PRIMARY KEY` with a `FOREIGN KEY` constraint: A `FOREIGN KEY` constraint can enforce that *at least* one record must exist in the "one" (or parent company in our example) table, but it can't ensure that *only* one exists (there could be more than one). Using a `PRIMARY KEY` or `UNIQUE` constraint would ensure that one was indeed the limit.
- Triggers: Note that triggers would be required in both tables.

The reason SQL Server can handle a zero or one-to-one, but not a one-to-one is due to the "which goes first" problem. In a true one-to-one relationship, you can't insert into either table because the record in the other table isn't there yet – it's a paradox. But with a zero or one-to-one, you can insert into the required table first (the "one"), and the optional table (the zero or one), if desired, second. This same problem will hold true for one-to-one or many and one-to-zero, one or many.

One-to-One or Many

This is one form of your run of the mill, average, every-day foreign key kind of relationship. Usually, this is found in some form of header/detail relationship. A great example of this would be our Orders situation. Order details (the "one or many" side of the relationship) don't make much sense without an order header to belong to (does it do you much good to have an order for a part if you don't know who the order is for?). Likewise, it doesn't make much sense to have an order if there wasn't anything actually ordered (e.g., "Gee, look, ACME company ordered absolutely nothing yesterday.").

Order No (PK)	Order Date	Customer No
100	1/1/1999	54545
101	1/1/1999	12000
102	1/1/1999	66651
103	1/1/1999	54545

Order No (PK)	Line Item (PK)	Part No	Qty	Unit Price	Total Price
100	1	1A4536	5	15	75
100	2	OR2400	4	27	108
100	3	OR2403	4	29	116
100	4	4I5436	1	750	750
101	1	3X9567	1	62.50	62.50
102	1	8G9200	7	12	84
102	2	8G5437	1	15	15
102	3	3H6250	1	32	32
103	1	8G9200	40	12	480
103	2	2P5523	1	165	165
103	3	3X9567	1	42	42

This one, however, gives us the same basic problem that we had with one-to-one relationships. It's still that chicken or egg thing – which came first? Again, in SQL Server, the only way to fully implement this is by restricting all data to be inserted or deleted via stored procedures.

One-to-Zero, One, or Many

ShipperID	CompanyName	Phone
1	Speedy Express	(503) 555-9831
2	United Package	(503) 555-3199
3	Federal Shipping	(503) 555-9931

OrderID	OrderDate	CustomerID	ShipperID	ShipToAddress
10500	1997-04-09	LAMAI	1	1 rue Alsace-Lorraine
10501	1997-04-09	BLAUS	3	Forsterstr. 57
10502	1997-04-10	PERIC	1	Calle Dr. Jorge...

This is the other, and perhaps even more common, form of the run of the mill, average, every-day foreign key relationship. The only real difference in implementation here is that the referencing field (the one in the table that has the foreign key constraint) is allowed to be null – that is, the fact that you have a record in the "one" table, doesn't necessarily mean that you have any instances of matching records in the referencing table.

An example of this can be found in the `Northwind` database in the relationship between `Suppliers` and `Orders`. `Orders` tracks which shipper was used to ship the order – but what if the order was picked up by the customer? If there is a shipper, then we want to limit it to our approved list of shippers, but it's still quite possible that there won't be any shipper at all.

> **This kind of relationship usually sets up what is called a** domain **relationship. A domain is a limited list of values that the dependent table must choose from – nothing outside the domain list is considered a valid option. The table that holds the rows that make up the domain list is commonly referred to as a** domain table. **Nearly any database you create is going to have at least one, and probably many, domain tables in it. Our `Shippers` table is a** domain table **(also sometimes called a** lookup table **or** type table**) – the purpose of having it isn't just to store the information on the name and phone number of the shipper, but to also limit the list of possible shippers in the `Orders` table.**

In SQL Server, we can enforce this kind of relationship through two methods:

- `FOREIGN KEY` constraint: You simply declare a `FOREIGN KEY` constraint on the table that serves as the "Many" side of the relationship, and reference the table and column that is to be the "One" side of the relationship (you'll be guaranteed of only one in the referenced table since you must have a `PRIMARY KEY` or `UNIQUE` constraint on the column(s) referenced by a foreign key).
- Triggers: Actually, for all the early versions of SQL Server, this was the only option for true referential integrity. You actually need to add two triggers – one for each side of the relationship. Add a trigger to the table that is the "many" side of the relationship and check that any row inserted or changed in that table has a match in the table it depends on (the "one" side of the relationship). Then, you add a delete trigger to the other table – this trigger checks records that are being deleted from the referenced table to make sure that is isn't going to orphan (make it so it doesn't have a reference). Though a bit slower than the declarative form of referential integrity (usually called DRI, and implemented in SQL Server through the use of `FOREIGN KEY` constraints), triggers have the advantage of being able to create cascading deletes and cascading updates. When you cascade a change, then the change you make to a parent record (delete, update the related field) is automatically propagated to the child record(s).

We've previously discussed the performance ramifications of the choices between the two in our chapter on constraints. Using a `FOREIGN KEY` constraint is generally faster – particularly in a rollback situation (rollbacks are discussed in Chapter 13). That being said, triggers may still be the better option in situations where you're going to have a trigger executing anyway (or some other special constraint need).

Many-to-Many

In this type of relationship, both sides of the relationship may have several records – not just one – that match. An example of this would be the relationship of products to orders. A given order may contain many different products. Likewise, any given product may be ordered many times. We still may, however, want to relate the tables in question – for example, to ensure that an order is for a product that we know about (it's in our `Products` table).

SQL Server has no way of establishing a many-to-many relationship, so we cheat by having an intermediate table to organize the relationship. Some tables create our many-to-many relationships almost by accident as a normal part of the normalization process – others are created entirely from scratch for the sole purpose of establishing this kind of relationship. This latter "middleman" kind of table is often called either a **linking table** or an **associate table**. Let's look at both instances.

First, let's look at a many-to-many relationship that is created in the normal course of normalization. An example of this can be found in our `OrderDetails` table, which creates a many-to-many relationship between our `Orders` and `Products` tables:

Order No (PK)	Order Date	Customer No
100	1/1/1999	54545
101	1/1/1999	12000
102	1/1/1999	66651
103	1/2/1999	54545

Order No (PK)	Line Item (PK)	Part No	Qty	Unit Price	Total Price
100	1	1A4536	5	15	75
100	2	OR2400	4	27	108
100	3	OR2403	4	29	116
100	4	4I5436	1	750	750
101	1	3X9567	1	62.50	62.50
102	1	8G9200	7	12	84
102	2	8G5437	1	15	15
102	3	3H6250	1	32	32
103	1	8G200	40	12	480
103	2	2P5523	1	165	165
103	3	3X9567	1	42	42

Part No (PK)	Description	Wt
1A4536	Flange	6
OR2400	Injector	.5
OR2403	Injector	.5
4I5436	Head	3
3X9567	Pump	5
8G9200	Fan	3
8G5437	Fan	3
3H6250	Control	5
2P5523	Housing	1

By using the join syntax we learned back in Chapter 5, we can relate one product to the many orders that it's been part of, or we can go the other way and relate an order to all the products on that order.

Let's move on to our second example – one where we create an associate table from scratch just so we can have a many to many relationship. We'll take the example of a user and a group of rights that a user can have on the system.

We might start with a `Permissions` table that looks something like this:

PermissionID	Description
1	Read
2	Insert
3	Update
4	Delete

Then we add a `Users` table:

UserID	Full Name	Password	Active
JohnD	John Doe	Jfz9..nm3	1
SamS	Sam Spade	klk93)md	1

Now comes the problem – how do we define which users have which permissions? Our first inclination might be to just add a column called `Permissions` to our `Users` table:

UserID	Full Name	Password	Permissions	Active
JohnD	John Doe	Jfz9..nm3	1	1
SamS	Sam Spade	klk93)md	3	1

This seems fine for only a split second, then a question begs to be answered – what about the situation when our users have permission to do more than one thing?

In the older, flat file days, you might have just combined all the permissions into the one cell, like:

UserID	Full Name	Password	Permissions	Active
JohnD	John Doe	Jfz9..nm3	1,2,3	1
SamS	Sam Spade	klk93)md	1,2,3,43	1

This violates our first normal form, which said that the values in any column must be atomic. In addition, this would be very slow because you would have to procedurally parse out each individual value within the cell.

What we really have between these two tables, `Users` and `Permissions`, is a many-to-many relationship – we just need a way to establish that relationship within the database. We do this by adding an associate table. Again, this is a table that, in most cases doesn't add any new data to our database other than establishing the association between rows in two other tables:

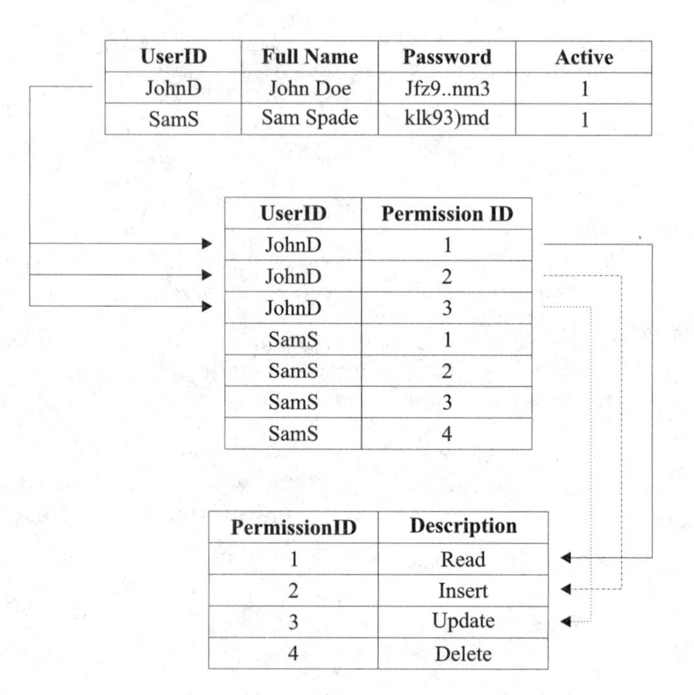

UserID	Full Name	Password	Active
JohnD	John Doe	Jfz9..nm3	1
SamS	Sam Spade	klk93)md	1

UserID	Permission ID
JohnD	1
JohnD	2
JohnD	3
SamS	1
SamS	2
SamS	3
SamS	4

PermissionID	Description
1	Read
2	Insert
3	Update
4	Delete

With the addition of our new table (we'll call it `UserPermissions`), we can now mix and match our permissions to our users.

Note that, for either example, the implementation of referential integrity is the same – each of the base tables (the tables holding the underlying data and have the many-to-many relationship) has a one-to-many relationship with the associate table. This can be done via a trigger or a `FOREIGN KEY` constraint.

Diagramming

Entity Relationship Diagrams – or ERDs – are an important tool in good database design. Small databases can usually be easily created from a few scripts and implemented directly without drawing things out at all. The larger your database gets, however, the quicker it becomes very problematic to just do things "in your head." ERD's solve a ton of problems because they allow you to quickly visualize and understand both the entities and their relationships.

Before writing this section, I debated for a long while about how I wanted to handle this. On one hand, serious ER Diagramming is usually done with a application that is specifically designed to be an ER Diagramming tool (we talk about a few of these in Appendix C). These tools almost always support at least one of a couple of industry standard diagramming methods. Even some of the more mass-market diagramming tools – such as Visio – support a couple of ERD methodologies. With SQL Server version 7.0 and beyond, Microsoft has given you an option for diagramming right within Enterprise Manager (EM) – and therein lies the problem.

The tools included in EM are a variation on a tool set that appears in a number of other Microsoft development products, and has been code named the da Vinci tools. The problem is that the da Vinci tools don't comply with any ERD standard. After thinking about this for some time now, I've decided to stick with what I know that you have – the da Vinci tools. I will, however, provide a bit more information on standards and other tools in Appendix C.

The da Vinci Tools

You can open up the da Vinci tools in Enterprise Manager by navigating to the Diagrams node of your database (expand your server first, then the database).

The da Vinci tools don't give you all that many options, so you'll find that you'll get to know them fairly quickly. Indeed, if you're familiar with the relationship editor in Access, then much of the da Vinci tools will look very familiar.

Let's start by opening up the diagram that comes with the Northwind database. If you navigate to click on Diagrams under the Northwind database, you should see one entry (called Relationships) show up in the right hand pane of EM. Simply double-click on it and it should open up to show you a diagram of most of the tables and relationships in Northwind databases:

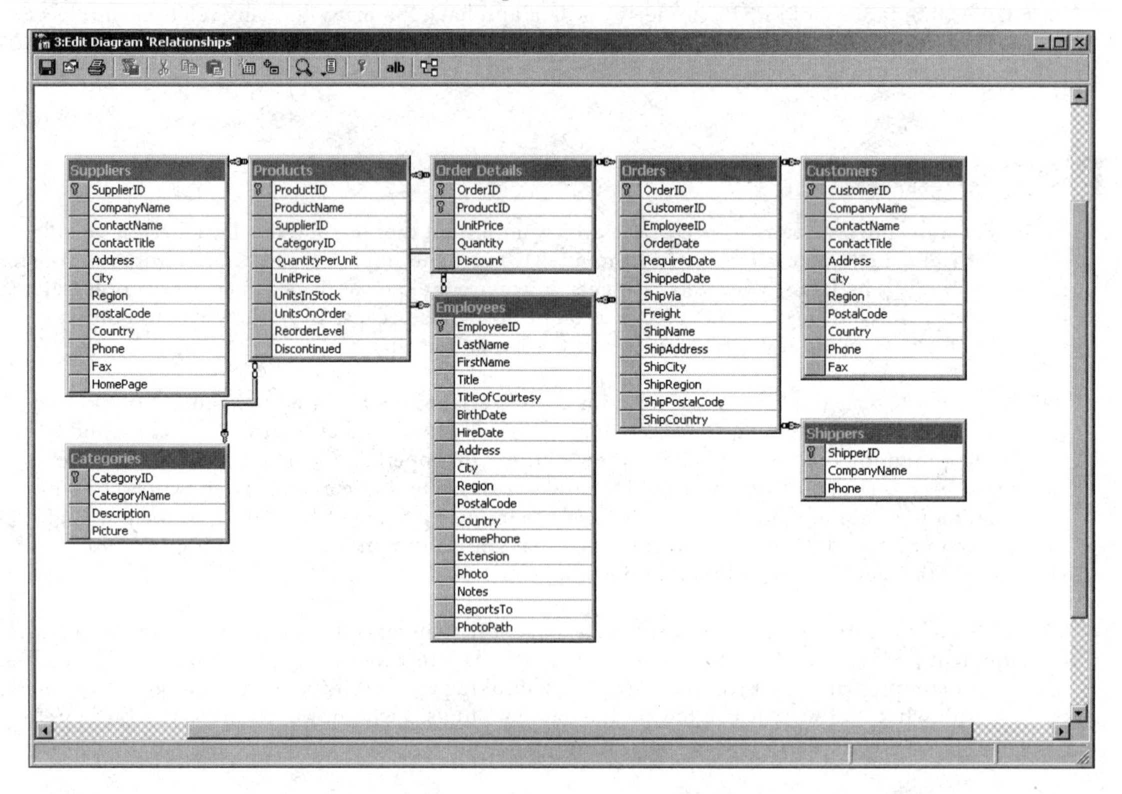

We'll use this existing diagram as a launching point for explaining how the diagramming tool works and building a few tables here and there.

Tables

Each table has its own window you can move around. The primary key is shown with the little symbol of a key in the column to the left of the name:

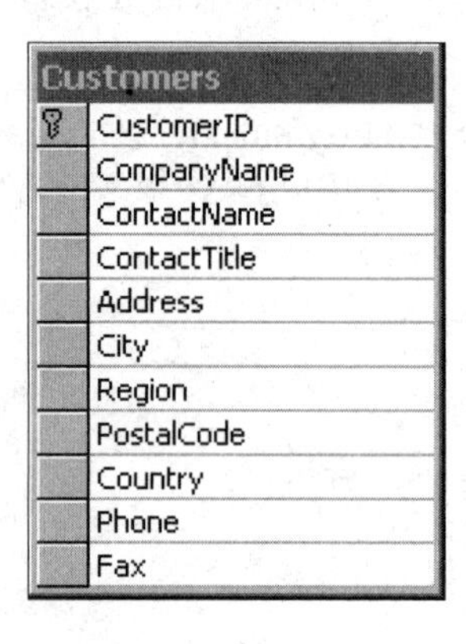

This is just a default view for a table though – you can select from several others that allow you to edit the very makeup of the table: To check out your options for views of a table, just right-click on the table that you're interested in:

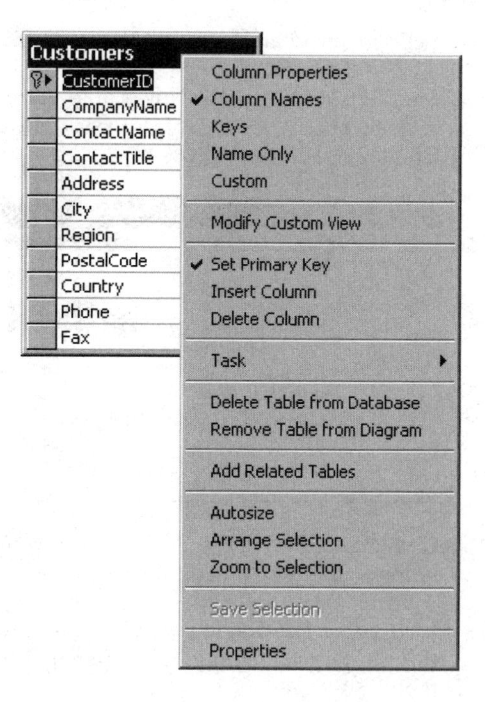

The default is Column Names, but you should also take an interest in the choice of Column Properties - this is what you would use when you want to edit the table from right within the diagram (yep, you can do that!).

Adding and Deleting Tables

You can add a new table to the diagram in one of two ways:

If you have a table that already exists in the database (but not in the diagram), and now you want to add it to your diagram, simply click the Add Table button on the diagramming window's toolbar. You'll be presented with a list of all the tables in the database – just choose the one that you want to add, and it will appear along with any relationships it has to other tables in the diagram. Note that, even though tables that are already in the diagram will appear in the table list, you cannot add them to the diagram a second time.

If you want to add a completely new table, click on the New Table on the diagramming window's toolbar or right-click in the diagram and choose New Table...– you'll be asked for a name for the new table, and the table will be added to the diagram in Column Properties view. Simply edit the properties to have the column names, data types, etc. that you want, and you have a new table in the database.

> **Let me take a moment to point out a couple of gotchas in this process.**
>
> **First, don't forget to add a primary key to your table. SQL Server does not automatically do this, nor does it even prompt you (as Access does). This is a somewhat less than intuitive process. To add a primary key, you must select the columns that you want to have in the key. Then right-click and choose Set Primary Key.**
>
> **Next, be aware that your new table is not actually added to the database until you choose to save – this is also true of any edits that you make along the way.**

Let's go ahead and add a table to our database just to show how it works.

Start by clicking on the New Table button in the diagramming window's toolbar. When prompted for a name, choose a name of `CustomerNotes`. You should then get a new window table up using the Column Properties view:

CustomerNotes

Column Name	Datatype	Length	Precision	Scale	Allow Nulls	Default Value	Identity	Identity Seed	Identity Increment	Is RowGuid
CustomerID	nchar	5	0	0						
NoteDate	datetime	8	0	0						
EmployeeID	int	4	10	0						
Note	varbinary	8000	0	0						

If you don't have all the columns showing up in the editor like I do, just resize the window – the size it comes up to by default doesn't show you everything you need to see.

Notice that I've added several columns to my table along with a primary key. Before you click to save this, let's try something out – open up Query Analyzer, and try and run a query against your new table:

```
SELECT * FROM CustomerNotes
```

Back comes an error message:

```
Server: Msg 208, Level 16, State 1, Line 1
Invalid object name 'CustomerNotes'.
```

Now, switch back to EM and right-click in the white space (not on a table or relationship) of the diagram window. Notice that there are two save options:

- Save: This saves the changes to both the diagram and to the database.
- Save Change Script: This saves the changes to a script so it can be run at a later time.

Go ahead and just choose Save, and you'll be prompted for confirmation (after all, you're about to alter your database – there's no "undo" of this):

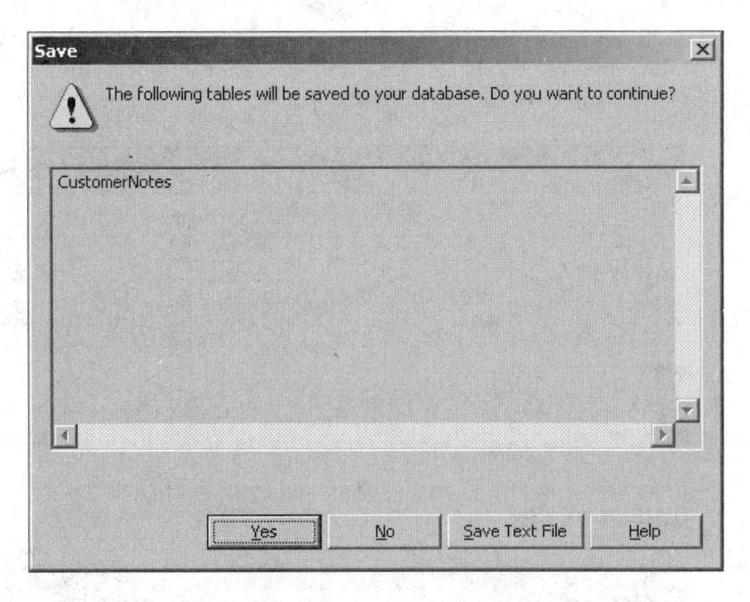

Go ahead and confirm the changes, and try running that query again against your `CustomerNotes` table. You should not receive an error this time since the table has now been created (you won't get any rows back, but the query should still run).

OK, we've got our `CustomerNotes` table into the database, but now we notice a problem – the way our primary key is declared, we can only have one note per customer. More than likely, we are going to keep taking more and more notes on the customer over time. That means we need to change our primary key, and leaves us with a couple of options depending on our requirements:

- Make the date part of our primary key: This is problematic from two standpoints. First, we're tracking what employee took the note – what if two different employees wanted to add notes at the same time? We could, of course, potentially address this by also adding `EmployeeID` to the primary key. Second, what's to say that even the same employee wouldn't want to enter two completely separate notes on the same day? Oops, now even our `EmployeeID` being in the key doesn't help us.
- Add another column to help with the key structure. We could either do this by adding a counter column for each note per customer, Or, as another alternative, we could just add an identity column to ensure uniqueness – it means that our primary key doesn't really relate to anything, but that isn't always a big deal (though it does mean that we have one more index that has to be maintained) and it does allow us to have a relatively unlimited number of notes per customer.

I'm going to take the approach of adding a column, I'll call `Sequence`, to the table. By convention (it's not a requirement and not everyone does it this way), primary keys are normally the first columns in your table. If we were going to be doing this by script ourselves, we'd probably just issue an `ALTER TABLE` statement and `ADD` the column – this would stick our new column down at the end of our column list. If we wanted to fix that, we'd have to copy all the data out to a holding table, drop any relationships to or from the old table, drop the old table, `CREATE` a new table that has the columns and column order we want, then re-establish the relationships and copy the data back in (a long and tedious process). With the da Vinci tools, however, SQL Server takes care of all that for us.

To insert a new row in the middle of everything, I just right-click on the row that is to immediately follow the row I want to insert, and then choose Insert Column. The tool is nice enough to shift everything down for me to create space:

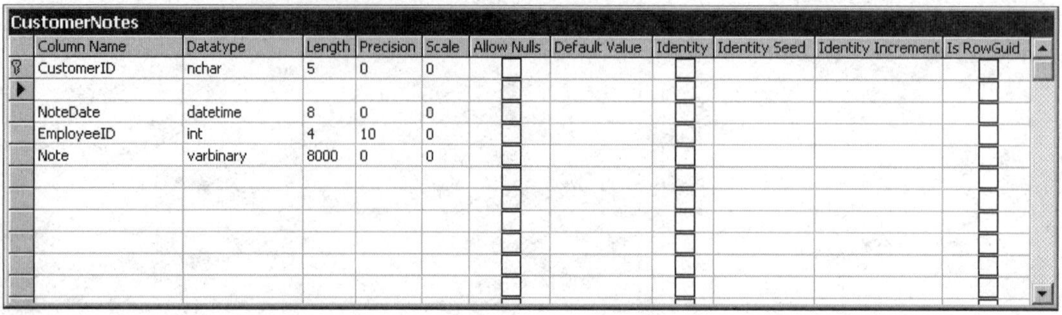

CustomerNotes

Column Name	Datatype	Length	Precision	Scale	Allow Nulls	Default Value	Identity	Identity Seed	Identity Increment	Is RowGuid
CustomerID	nchar	5	0	0						
NoteDate	datetime	8	0	0						
EmployeeID	int	4	10	0						
Note	varbinary	8000	0	0						

I can then add in my new column, and reset the primary key (select both rows, right-click and choose Set Primary Key):

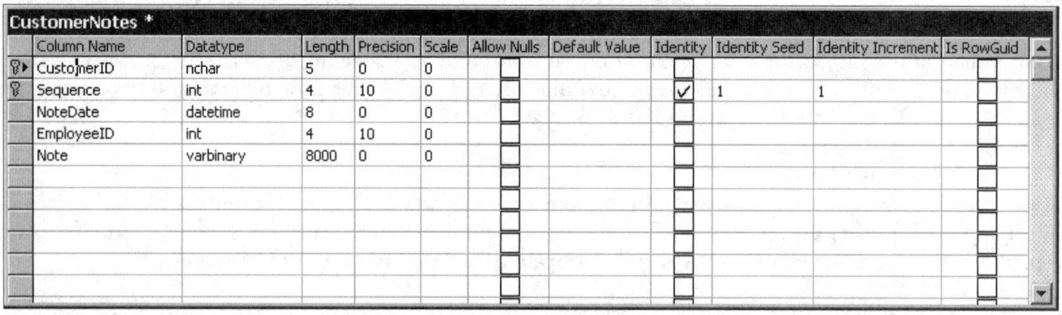

CustomerNotes *

Column Name	Datatype	Length	Precision	Scale	Allow Nulls	Default Value	Identity	Identity Seed	Identity Increment	Is RowGuid
CustomerID	nchar	5	0	0						
Sequence	int	4	10	0			✓	1	1	
NoteDate	datetime	8	0	0						
EmployeeID	int	4	10	0						
Note	varbinary	8000	0	0						

Now just save, and you have a table with the desired column order. Just to verify this, try using `sp_help`:

```
EXEC sp_help CustomerNotes
```

You'll see that we have the column order we expect:

```
....
CustomerID
Sequence
NoteDate
EmployeeID
Note
....
```

> **Making things like column order changes happens to be one area in which the da Vinci tools positively excel. I've used a couple of other ERD tools, and they all offered the promise of synchronizing a change in column order between the database and the diagram – the success has been pretty hit and miss (in other words, be very careful about doing it around live data). The tools are getting better, but this is an area where the da Vinci tools show some of the genius of their namesake.**
>
> **Also, under the heading of "one more thing" – use the scripting option rather than the live connection to the database to make changes like this if you're operating against live data. That way you can fully test the script against test databases before risking your real data. Be sure to also fully back up your database before making this kind of change.**

Editing Table Properties

Beyond the basic attributes that we've looked at thus far, we can also edit many other properties of our table. To check these out, right-click on our table and select Properties from the menu. You get a dialog with a ton of information we hadn't seen up to this point:

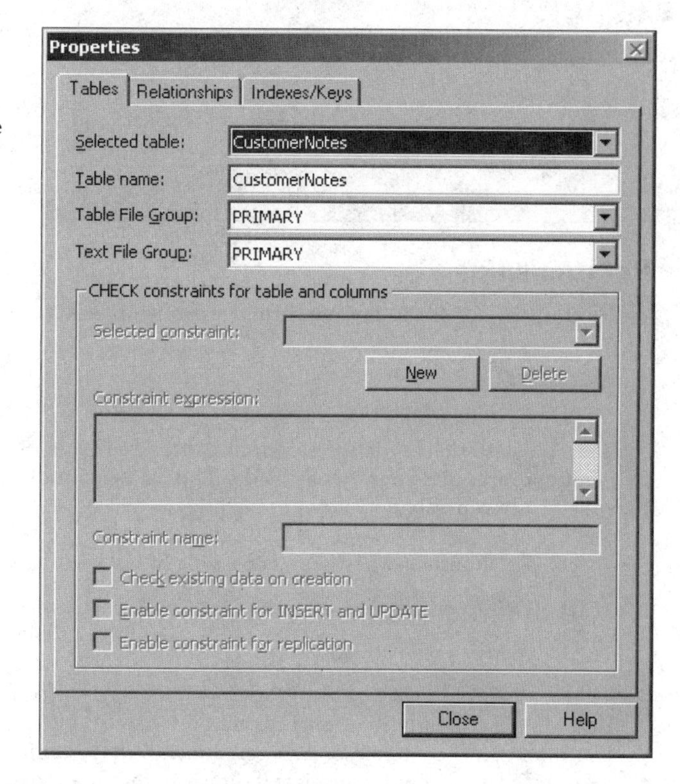

This is the dialog where you can make changes to the more obscure information about your table. From the Tables tab, you can change the filegroups that both your BLOB and non-BLOB information are stored on. In addition, you can create `CHECK` constraints on your table. I'm going to skip the Relationships tab for the moment (we'll look at it in the next subsection), but click over to the Indexes/Keys tab:

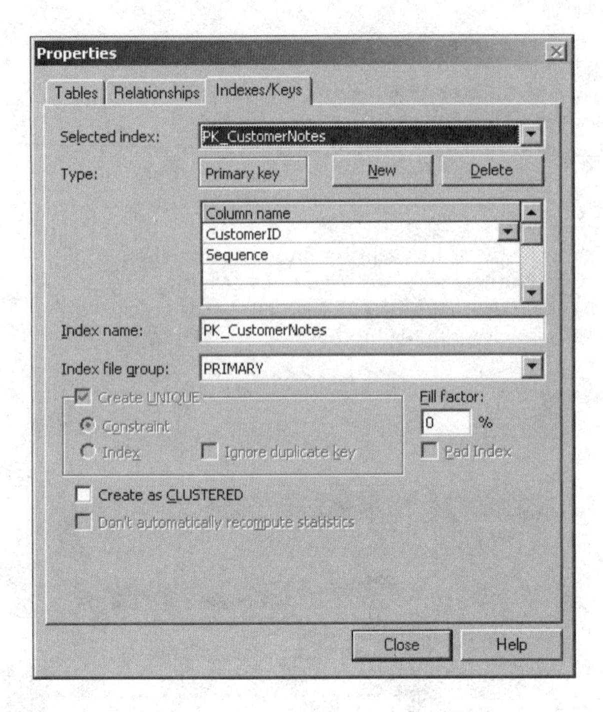

From here, you can create, edit, and delete indexes. You can also establish what filegroup you want the index to be stored on (in most instances, you'll just want to leave this alone). We'll look further into indexes in our next chapter.

Relationships

Next up on our list to review is the relationship line:

The side with the key is the side that is the "one" side of a relationship. The side that has the infinity symbol represents your "many" side. The da Vinci tools have no relationship line available to specifically represent:

- Relationships where zero is possible (it still uses the same line)
- One-to-one relationships
- Many-to-many relationships.

In addition, the only relationships that actually show in the diagram are ones that are declared using `FOREIGN KEY` constraints. Any relationship that is enforced via triggers – regardless of the type of relationship – will not cause a relationship line to appear.

Looking at our `Northwind` diagram again, try right-clicking on the relationship line between the `Customers` and `Orders` tables. You'll be given the option to either delete the relationship, or to view the properties. Choose Properties, and you'll get the same properties dialog box that we saw in the last section – it lets us edit a variety of things about our table as well as its indexes and relationships. This time around, we're interested in the Relationships tab:

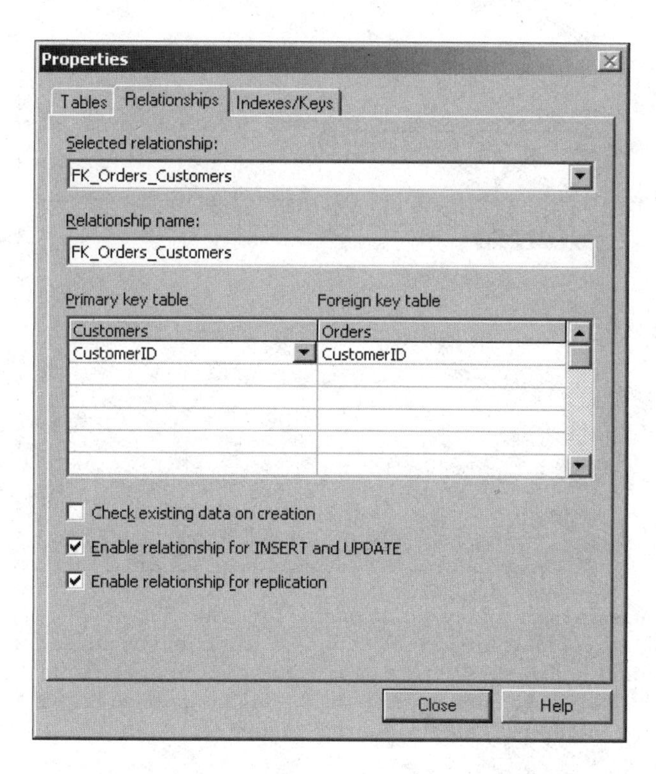

From here, we can edit the nature of our relationship. We can also disable it (for example, if we want to deliberately add data in that violates the relationship). Last, but not least, we can change the name of the relationship.

Database designers seem to vary widely in their opinion regarding names for relationships. Some don't care what they are named, but I prefer to use a verb phrase to describe my relationships – for example, in our `Customers/Orders` relationship, I would probably name it `CustomerHasOrders` or something of that ilk. It's nothing critical – most of the time you won't even use it – but I find that it can be really helpful when I'm looking at a long object list.

Adding Relationships in the Diagramming Tool

Just drag and drop – it's that easy. The only trick is making sure that you start and end your drag in the places you meant to. If in doubt, select the column(s) you're interested in before starting your drag.

Let's add a relationship between our new `CustomerNotes` table (we created it in the last section) and the `Customers` table – after all, if it's a customer note we probably want to make sure. To do this, click and hold in the gray area to the left of the `CustomerID` column in the `Customers` table, then drag your mouse until it is pointing at the `CustomerID` column in the `CustomerNotes` table. A dialog box should pop up to confirm the column mapping between the related tables:

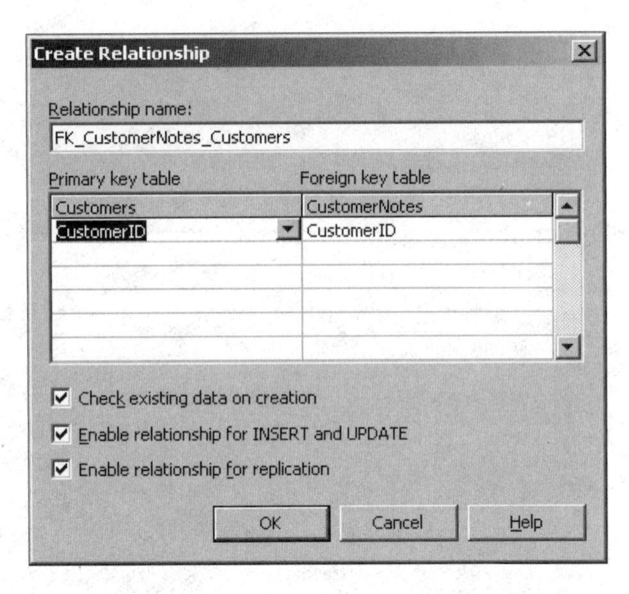

Don't worry too much about it if the names on both columns didn't come up right – just click the combo box for the table you want to change columns for and select the new column. For mine, I'm changing the name of the relationship from the default of `FK_CustomerNotes_Customers` to `CustomerHasNotes`. As soon as I click OK, I'll see the new relationship line in my diagram – if I hover over that relationship, I'll even see a tooltip with the relationship's name and nature:

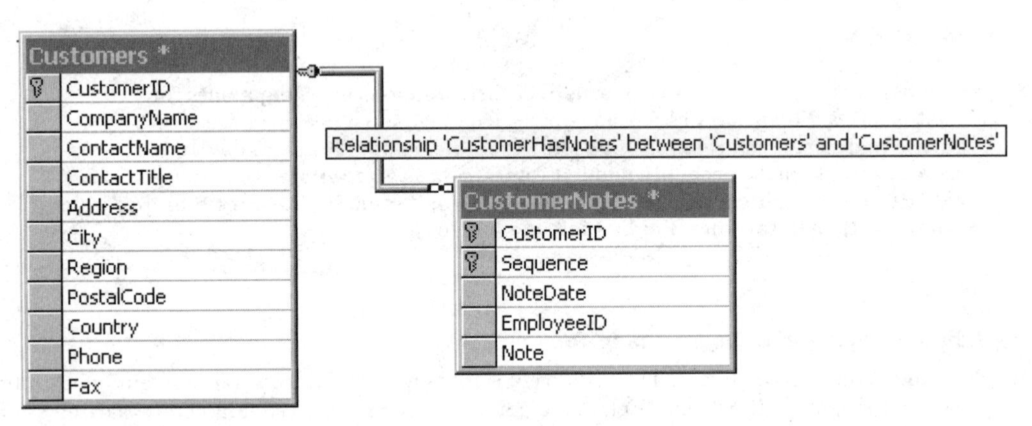

De-Normalization

I'm going to keep this relatively short since we'll be dealing with this issue again in both the advanced design chapter and the OLAP chapter, but remember not to get carried away with the normalization of your data.

As I stated early in this chapter, normalization is one of those things that database designers sometimes wear like a cross. It's somehow turned into a religion for them, and they begin normalizing data for the sake of normalization rather than for the good things it does to their database. Here are a couple of things to think about in this regard:

- If declaring a computed column or storing some derived data is going to allow you to run a report more effectively, then, by all means, put it in. Just remember to take into account the benefit vs. the risk (for example, what if your "summary" data gets out of synch with the data it can be derived from? – how will you determine that it happened, and how will you fix it if it does happen?).
- Sometimes, but including this one de-normalized column in a table, you can eliminate or significantly cut down the number the joins necessary to retrieve information. Watch for these scenarios – they actually come up reasonably frequently. I've dealt with situations where adding one column to one commonly used base table cut a nine-table join down to just three, and cut the query time by about 90% in the process.
- If you are keeping historical data – data that will largely go unchanged and just be used for reporting – then the integrity issue becomes a much smaller consideration. Once the data is written to a read-only area and verified, you can be reasonably certain that you won't have the kind of out of sync problems that is one of the major things that data normalization addresses. At that point, it may be much nicer (and faster) to just "flatten" (de-normalize) the data out into few tables, and speed things up.
- The fewer tables that have to be joined, the happier your users who do their own reports are going to be. The user base out there continues to get more and more savvy with the tools they are using. More and more often, users are coming to their DBA and asking for direct access to the database to be able to do their own custom reporting. For these users, a highly normalized database can look like a maze and become virtually useless. De-normalizing your data can make life much easier for these users.

All that said, if in doubt, normalize things. There is a reason why that is the way relational systems are typically designed. When you err on the side of normalizing, you are erring on the side of better data integrity, and on the side of better performance in a transactional environment.

Beyond Normalization

In this section, we're going to look into a basic set of "beyond normalization" rules of the road in design. Very few of these are hard and fast kind of rules – they are just things to think about. The main point to understand here is that, while normalization is a big thing in database design, it is not the only thing.

Keep it Simple

I run into people in the development on a regular basis that have some really slick way to do things differently than it's ever been done before. Some of the time, I wind up seeing some ideas that are incredibly cool and incredibly useful. Other times I see ideas that are incredibly cool, but not very useful. As often as not though, I see ideas that are neither – they may be new, but that doesn't make them good.

Before I step too hard on your creative juices here, let me clarify what I'm trying to get across – don't just accept the "because we've always done it that way" approach to things, but also recognize that the tried and true probably continue to be tried for a reason – they usually work.

Try and avoid instilling more complexity in your database than you really need to. A minimalist approach usually (but not always) yields something that is not only easier to edit, but also runs a lot faster.

Choosing Data Types

In keeping with the minimalist idea, choose what you need, but only what you need.

For example, if you're trying to store months (the number, 1-12) – those can be done in a single byte by using a `tinyint` . Why then, do I regularly come across databases where a field that's only going to store a month is declared as an int (4 bytes)? Don't use an `nchar` or `nvarchar` if you're never going to do anything that requires Unicode – these data types take up two bytes for every one as compared to their non-Unicode cousins.

> **There is a tendency to think about this as being a space issue. When I bring this up in person, I sometimes here the argument "Ah, disk space is cheap these days!" Well, beyond the notion that a name-brand SCSI hard drive still costs more than I care to throw away on laziness, there's also a network bandwidth issue. If you're passing an extra 100 bytes down the wire for every row, and you pass a 100 record result, then that's about 10K worth of extra data you just clogged your network with. Still not convinced? Now, say that you have just 100 users performing 50 transactions per hour – that's over 50MB of wasted network bandwidth per hour.**
>
> **The bottom line is, most things that happen with your database will happen repetitively – this means that small mistakes snowball and can become rather large.**

Err on the Side of Storing Things

There was an old movie called *The Man Who Knew Too Much* – Hitchcock I believe – that man wasn't keeping data.

Every time that you're building a database, you're going to come across the question of, "are we going to need that information later?" Here's my two bit advice on that – if in doubt, keep it. You see, most of the time you can't get back the data that has already come and gone. I guarantee that at least once (and probably many, many more times than that), there will be a time where a customer (remember, customers are basically anyone who needs something from you – there is such a thing as an internal customer, not just the ones in accounts receivable) will come to you and say something like, "Can you give me a report on how much we paid each non-incorporated company last year? OK, so are you storing information on whether your vendor is a corporation or not? You had better be if you are subject to US tax law (1099 reporting).

OK, so you say you can handle that, and the customer replies, "Great! Can you print that out along with their address as of the end of the year?" Ooops – I'm betting that you don't have past addresses, or, at the very least, aren't storing the date on which the address changed. In short, you never know what a user of your system is going to ask for – try and make sure you have it. Just keep in mind that you don't want to be moving unnecessary amounts of data up and down your network wire (see my comments on choosing a data type). If you're storing the data just for posterity, then make sure you don't put it in any of your application's `SELECT` statements if it isn't needed. (Actually this should be your policy regardless of why you're storing the data.)

If you think that there may be legal ramifications either way (both in keeping it and in getting rid of it), consult your attorney (sometimes you're legally obligated to keep data for a certain amount of time, other times attorneys would rather that you got rid of information as soon as legally possible – people can't subpoena information from you that you don't have).

Drawing Up a Quick Example

Let's walk quickly through the process of designing our `Invoicing` database that we've already started during our section on normalization. For the most part, we're just going to be applying the da Vinci tools to what we've already designed, but we'll also toss in a few new issues to show how they affect our design.

Creating the Database

Unlike a lot of the third party diagramming tools out there, the da Vinci tools will not create the database for you – you have to have already created it in order to get as far has having the diagram available to work with.

We're not going to be playing with any data to speak of, so just create a small database called `Invoice`. Feel free to use either T-SQL or EM. I'll go ahead and use EM for the sake of an example.

I'll right-click on the databases node of my server in EM and select New Database... I'm going to enter information in for a database called `Invoice` that I'll set up as 3MB in size.

Since we've already had a chapter on creating databases, and for the sake of brevity, I'm just going to accept the defaults on all the other options:

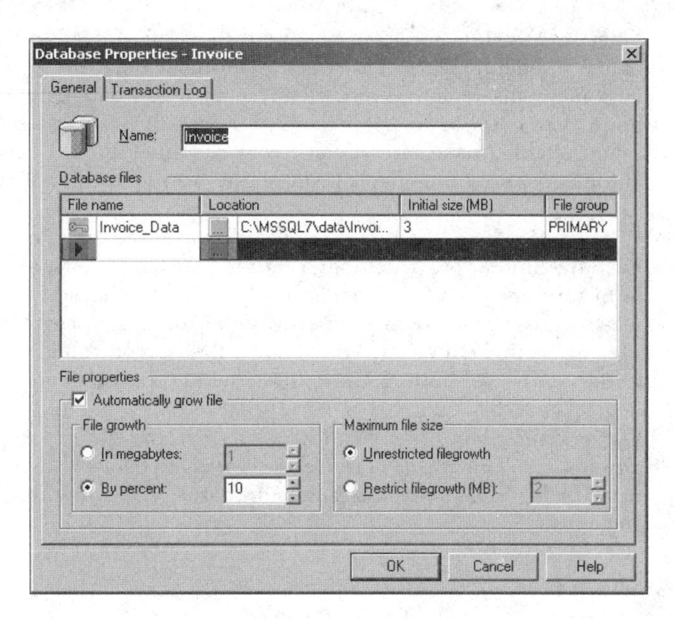

Adding the Diagram and Our Initial Tables

In order to add the diagram, I'll expand the node for our database (it should have been added underneath the databases node). I'll then right-click on diagrams and select New Diagram... SQL Server will give me a warning that there aren't currently any tables in the database (if we had some, it would try and start up a wizard to help us build a diagram after the fact):

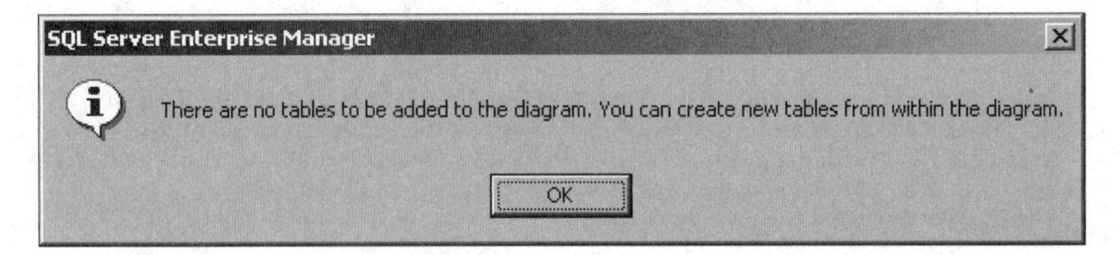

Now we're ready to start adding new tables. You can either click the New Table icon on the toolbar, or right-click anywhere in the diagram and select New Table... I'm going to start off by adding in the `Orders` table:

Orders *

Column Name	Datatype	Length	Precision	Scale	Allow Nulls	Default Value	Identity	Identity Seed	Identity Increment	Is RowGuid
OrderID	int	4	10	0			✓	1	1	
OrderDate	datetime	8	0	0		(GETDATE())				
CustomerNo	int	4	10	0						

Let's stop long enough to look at a couple of the decisions that I made here. While we had addressed the issue of normalization, we hadn't addressed any of the other basics yet. First up of those was the question of data types.

Since `OrderID` is my primary key for the table, I need to be sure that I allow enough room for my values to be unique as I insert more and more data. If this was a table I wasn't going to be making very many inserts into, I might choose a smaller data type, but since it is my `Orders` table (and I hope to be entering lots of orders!), I'll push the size up a bit. In addition, numeric order numbers seem suitable (make sure you ask your customer about issues like this!) and facilitate the use of an automatic numbering mechanism in the form of an Identity column.

With `OrderDate`, the first thing to come to mind was a `smalldatetime` field. After all, we don't need the kind of precision that a `datetime` field offers, and we also don't need to go back all that far in history (maybe a few years at most?). Why, then, did I still go for `datetime` rather than `smalldatetime`? To show mercy on Visual Basic programmers. VB throws fits when you start playing around with `smalldatetime` fields. You can get around the problems, but it's a pain. I went to `datetime` for nothing more than making the client coding easy.

Our customer has told us (and we've seen in the earlier sample data), that `CustomerNo` is five digits, all numeric. This is one of those areas where you start saying to your customer, "Are you sure you're never going to be alpha characters in there?" Assuming the answer is yes, then you go with an integer since it is:

- Faster on lookups
- Smaller in size – 4 bytes will cover a five digit number easily, but it takes 5 bytes minimum (six if you're using variable length fields) to handle five characters.

> *Note that I'm kind of cheating on this one – realistically, the customer number for this table is really being defined by the relationship we're going to be building with the `Customers` table. Since that's the last table we'll see in this example, I'm going ahead and filing in the blanks for this field now.*

After data types, I also had to decide the size of the column – this was a no-brainer for this particular table since all the data types have fixed sizes.

Next on the hit list is whether the rows can be null or not. In this case, we're pretty sure that we absolutely want all this information and that it should be available at the time we enter the order, so we won't allow nulls.

> *I've touched on this before, but you just about have to drag me kicking and screaming in order to force me into allowing nulls in my databases. There are situations where you just can't avoid it – "undefined" values are legitimate. I'll still often fill text fields with actual text saying "Value Unknown" or something like that.*
>
> *The reason I do this is because nullable fields promote errors in much the same way that undeclared variables do. Whenever you run across null values in the table you wind up asking yourself, "Gee, did I mean for that to be there, or did I forget to write a value into the table for that row" – that is, do I have a bug in my program?*

The next issue I faced was default values. After looking things over, I couldn't have a default for `OrderID` because I'm making it an identity column (the two are mutually exclusive). For `OrderDate`, however, a default made some level of sense. If an `OrderDate` isn't provided, then I'm going to assume that the order date is today. Last, but not least, is the `CustomerNo` – which customer would I default to? Nope – can't do that here.

Next up was the issue of an identity column. `OrderId` is an ideal candidate for an identity column – the value has no meaning other than keeping the rows unique. Using a counter like an identity field gives us a nice, presentable and orderly way to maintain that unique value. I don't have any reason to change the identity seed and increment, so I won't. We'll leave it starting at one and incrementing by one.

Last, but not least, is `IsRowGuid`. This is whether I want to automatically use the `NewID()` function to generate a GUID for each row. I don't have a GUID data type in there, so this is pretty much a self answering question. Without a GUID data type, I must not be planning on using the `IsRowGuid`.

Now I'm ready to move on to my next table – the OrderDetails table.

OrderDetails

	Column Name	Datatype	Length	Precision	Scale	Allow Nulls	Default Value	Identity	Identity Seed	Identity Increment	Is RowGuid
🔑▸	OrderID	int	4	10	0	☐		☐			☐
🔑	LineItem	int	4	10	0	☐		☐			☐
	PartNo	char	6	0	0	☐		☐			☐
	Qty	int	4	10	0	☐		☐			☐
	UnitPrice	money	8	19	4	☐		☐			☐

For this table, the OrderID column is going to have a foreign key to it, so my data type is decided for me – it must be of the same type and size as the field it's referencing, so it's going to be an int.

The LineItem is going to start over again with each row, so we probably could have got as little as a tinyint here. I'm still going to go with an int on this one just for safety's sake (I've had people exceed limits that have been set on this sort of thing before).

PartNo is, for this table, actually going to be defined by the fact it need to match up with the PartNo in the Products table. It's going to be a char(6) in that table (we'll come to it shortly), so that's what I'll make it here.

Quantity is guesswork. The question is, what's the largest order you can take as far as quantity for one line-time goes? Since we don't know what we're selling, we can't really make a guess on a maximum quantity (for example, if we were selling barrels of oil, it might be bought literally millions of barrels at a time).

Moving along, I'm again (no surprise here), considering all data fields to be required, no I'm not allowing nulls anywhere.

No defaults seem to make sense for this table, so I'm skipping that part also.

Identity? The temptation might be to mark OrderID as an identity column again – Don't do that! Remember thar OrderID is a value that we're going to match up to column in another table. That table already will have a value (as it happens, set by identity, but it didn't necessarily have to be that way), so setting our column to identity would cause a collision – we would be told that we can't do our insert because we're trying to set an identity value. All the other columns either get their data from another table or require user input of the data. IsRowGuid again does not apply.

That takes us to our Products and Customers tables.

Products *

	Column Name	Datatype	Length	Precision	Scale	Allow Nulls	Default Value	Identity	Identity Seed	Identity Increment	Is RowGuid
🔑	PartNo	char	6	0	0	☐		☐			☐
	Description	varchar	15	0	0	☐		☐			☐
	Weight	tinyint	1	3	0	☐		☐			☐
	UnitPrice	money	8	19	4	☐		☐			☐

Customers *

	Column Name	Datatype	Length	Precision	Scale	Allow Nulls	Default Value	Identity	Identity Seed	Identity Increment	Is RowGuid
🔑▸	CustomerNo	int	4	10	0	☐		☐			☐
	CustomerName	varchar	50	0	0	☐		☐			☐
	CustomerAddress	varchar	50	0	0	☐		☐			☐

Let's hit the highlights on the choices here and move on.

`PartNo` has been defined by the data that we saw when we were looking at normalization. It's a numeric, followed by an alpha, followed by four numerics. That's 6 characters, and it seems to be fixed. We would want to hold the customer to the cross about the notion that the size of the part number can't get any larger, but, assuming that's OK, I'd probably go with a `char(6)` here. That's because a `char` takes up slightly less overhead than a `varchar`, and we know that the length is going to always remain the same (i.e., there's no benefit from the variable size).

`Description` is one of those guessing games. Sometimes a field like this is going to be driven by your user interface requirements (don't make it wider than can be displayed on the screen), other times you're just going to be truly guessing at what is "enough" space. I'm choosing a variable length `char` over a regular `char` for two reasons:

- To save a little space.
- So I don't have to deal with trailing spaces (look at the `char` vs. `varchar` data types back in Chapter 2 if you have questions on this).

I didn't choose a `nchar` or `nvarchar` because this is a little rinky dink invoicing system, and I'm not concerned about localization issues.

`Weight` is similar to description in that it is going to be somewhat of a guess. I've chosen a `tinyint` here because I believe that my `Products` have no chance to ever be over 256 pounds. Note that I am also preventing myself from keeping decimal places in my weight (integers only).

`UnitPrice` is a currency kind of thing, so I'm going with the `money` data type. Note that this `UnitPrice` is a little bit different from the one we put in the `OrderDetails` table. This unit price is the current list price for our product, where as the `UnitPrice` in `OrderDetails` is the price that was actually charged when we made the sale.

We already described the `CustomerNo` field back when we were doing the `Orders` table.

`CustomerName` and `CustomerAddress` are pretty much the same situation as description – the question is, how much is enough? But you need to be sure that you don't do too much....

I'm again considering all fields to be required (no nulls in either table) and no defaults to be called for. `Identity` columns also do not seem to fit the bill here (both the customer number and part number have special formats that do not lend themselves to automatic number like an identity provides).

Adding the Relationships

OK, to make this part easy, I've gone through all four of my tables and changed the view on them down to just Column Names. You can do this by simply right-clicking on the table and selecting the Column Names menu choice.

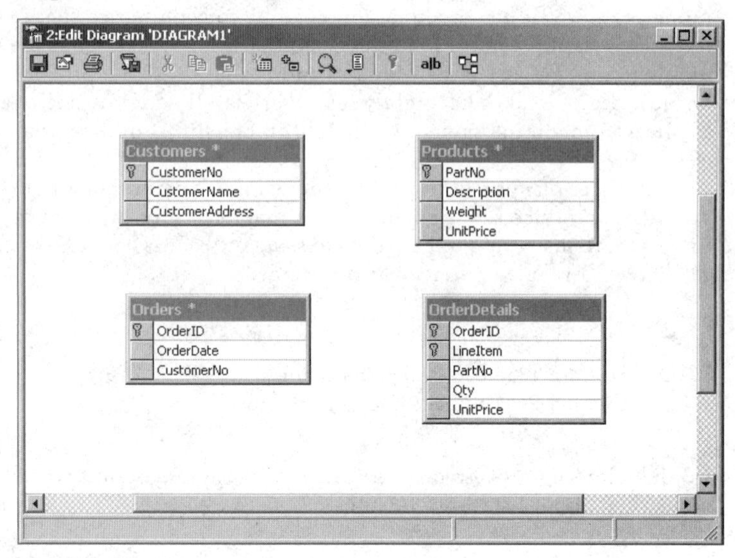

I've wound up with a diagram that looks like this:

I'm ready to start adding relationships, but I probably need to stop and think about what kind of relationships I need.

All the relationships that I draw with the relationship lines in our SQL Server diagram tool are going to be one-to-zero, one, or many relationships. SQL Server doesn't really know how to do any other kind implicitly. As we discussed earlier in the chapter, you can add things like unique constraints and triggers to augment what SQL Server will to naturally with relations, but, assuming you don't do any of that, you're going to wind up with a one-to-zero, one, or many relationship.

> *The bright side is that this is by far, the most common kind of relationship out there. In short, don't worry if SQL Server doesn't cover every base here. The standard foreign key constraint (which is essentially what our reference line represents) fits the bill for most things that you need to do, and the rest can usually be simulated via some other means.*

I'm going to start with the central table in our system – the `Orders` table. First, I'll look at any relationships that it may need. In this case, I have one – it needs to reference the `Customers` table. This is indeed going to be a one-to-many relationship with `Customers` as the parent (the one) and `Orders` as the child (the many) table.

To build the relationship (and a foreign key constraint to serve as foundation for that relationship), I'm going to simply click and hold in the leftmost column of the `Customers` table (in the gray area) right where the `CustomerNo` column is. I'll then drag to same position (the gray area) next to the `CustomerNo` column in the `Orders` table and let go. SQL Server promptly pops up with a dialog to confirm the configuration of this relationship:

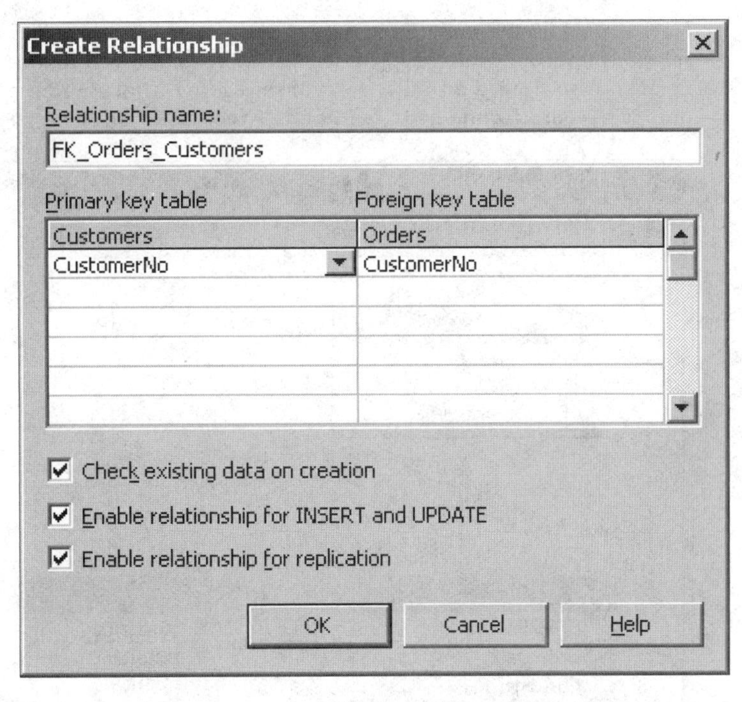

As I pointed out earlier in the chapter, don't worry if the names that come up don't match what you intended – just use the combo boxes to change them back so both sides have `CustomerNo` *in them. Note also that the names don't have to be the same - keeping the same just helps ease confusion in situations where they really are the same.*

As soon as I click OK, I have my first relationship in my new database:

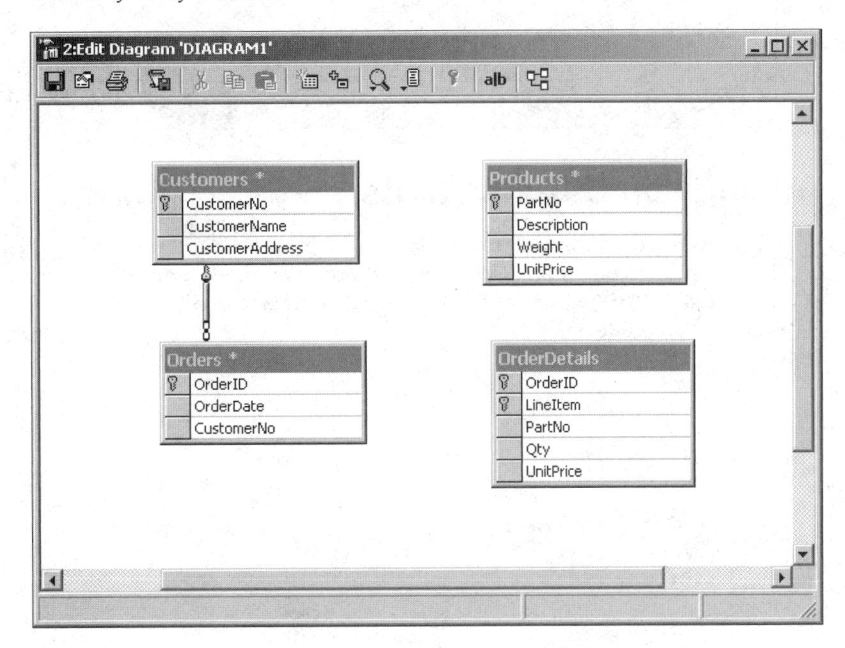

Now I'll just do the same thing for my other two relationships. I need to establish a one-to-many relationship from `Orders` to `OrderDetails` (there will be one order header for one or more order details). Also, I need a similar relationship going from `Products` to `OrderDetails` (there will be one part record for many `OrderDetail` records):

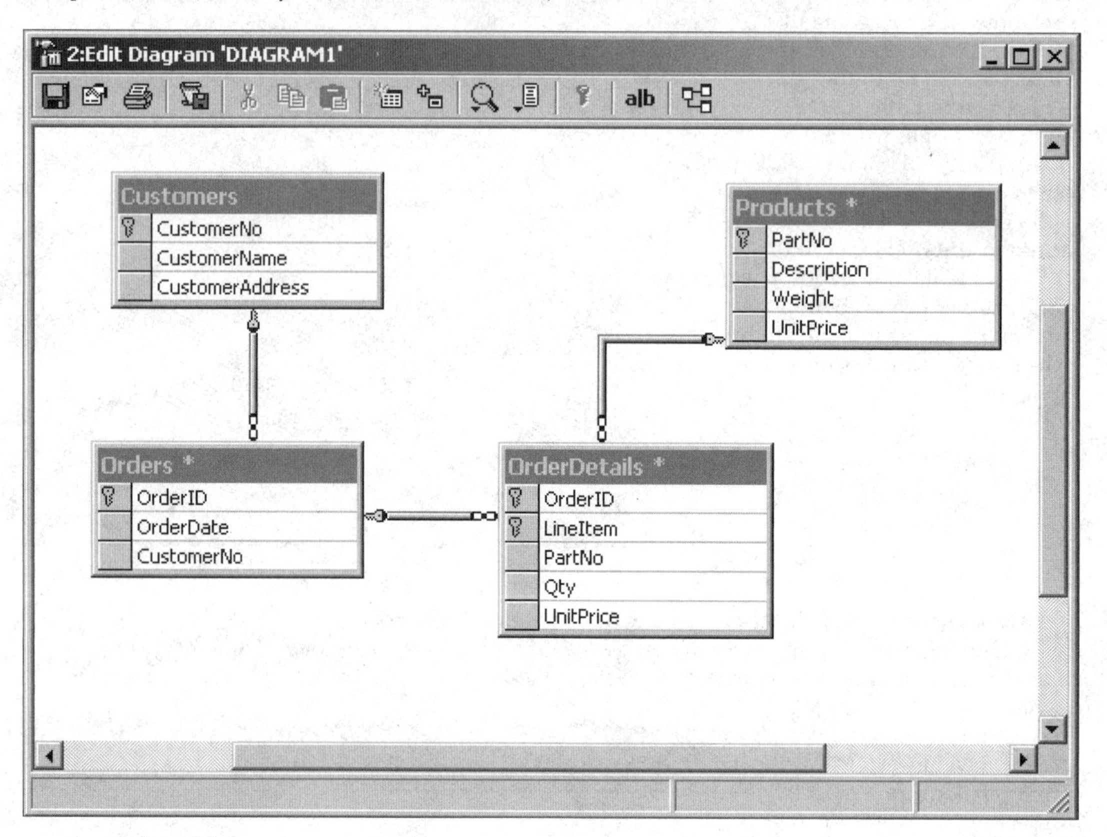

Adding some Constraints

As we were going through the building of our tables and relationships, I mentioned a requirement that we still haven't addressed. This requirement needs a constraint to enforce it: The part number is formatted as 9A9999 where "9" indicates a numeric digit 0-9 and "A" indicates an alpha (non-numeric) character.

Let's add that requirement now by right-clicking on the `Products` table and selecting Properties. This will bring up a dialog box.

When it first comes up, the dialog will be on the tab we need, but most of what we want (the constraints stuff) will be grayed out. That's because there aren't currently any constraints to show. We can fix this by clicking on the New button.

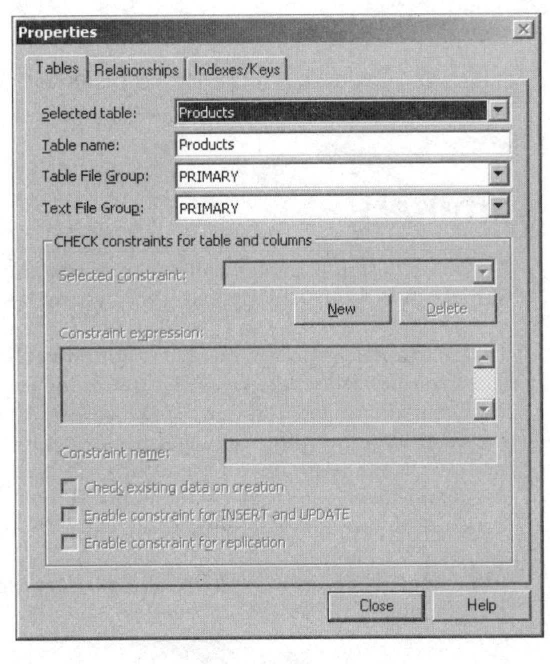

It is at this point that we are given the opportunity to define our constraint. In order to restrict part numbers entered to the format we've established, we're going to need to make use of the `LIKE` operator:

```
(PartNo LIKE [0-9][A-Z][0-9][0-9][0-9][0-9])
```

This will essentially evaluate each character that the user is trying to enter in the PartNo column of our table. The first character will have to be zero through nine (a numeric digit), the second "A" through "Z" (and alpha), and the next four will again have to be numeric digits (the zero through nine thing again). We just enter this into the large text box: In addition, I'm going to change the default name for our constraint from `CK_Products` to `CK_PartNo`:

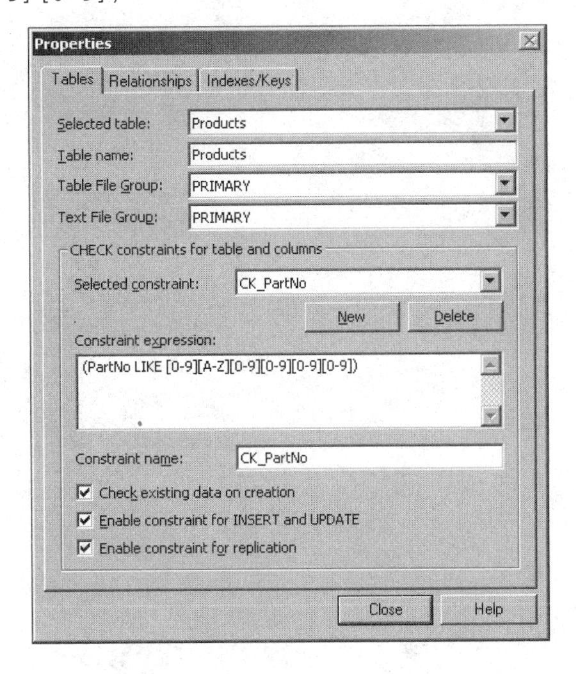

So, that didn't take use too long – and we now have our first database that we designed!!!

This was, of course, a relatively simple model – but you've now done the things that make up perhaps 90% or more of the actual data architecture.

Summary

Database design is a huge concept, and one that has many excellent books dedicated to it as their sole subject. It is essentially impossible to get across every database design notion in just a chapter or two.

In this chapter, we have, however, gotten you off to a solid start. We've seen that data is considered to be normalized when we take it out to the third normal form. At that level, repetitive information has been eliminated and our data in entirely dependent on our key – in short, the data is dependent on, "The key, the whole key, and nothing but the key." We've seen that normalization is, however, not always the right answer – strategic de-normalization of our data can simplify the database for users and speed reporting performance. Finally, we've looked at some non-normalization related concepts in our database design, plus how to make use of the da Vinci tools to design our database.

In our next chapter, we will be taking a very close look at how SQL Server stores information and how to make the best use of indexes.

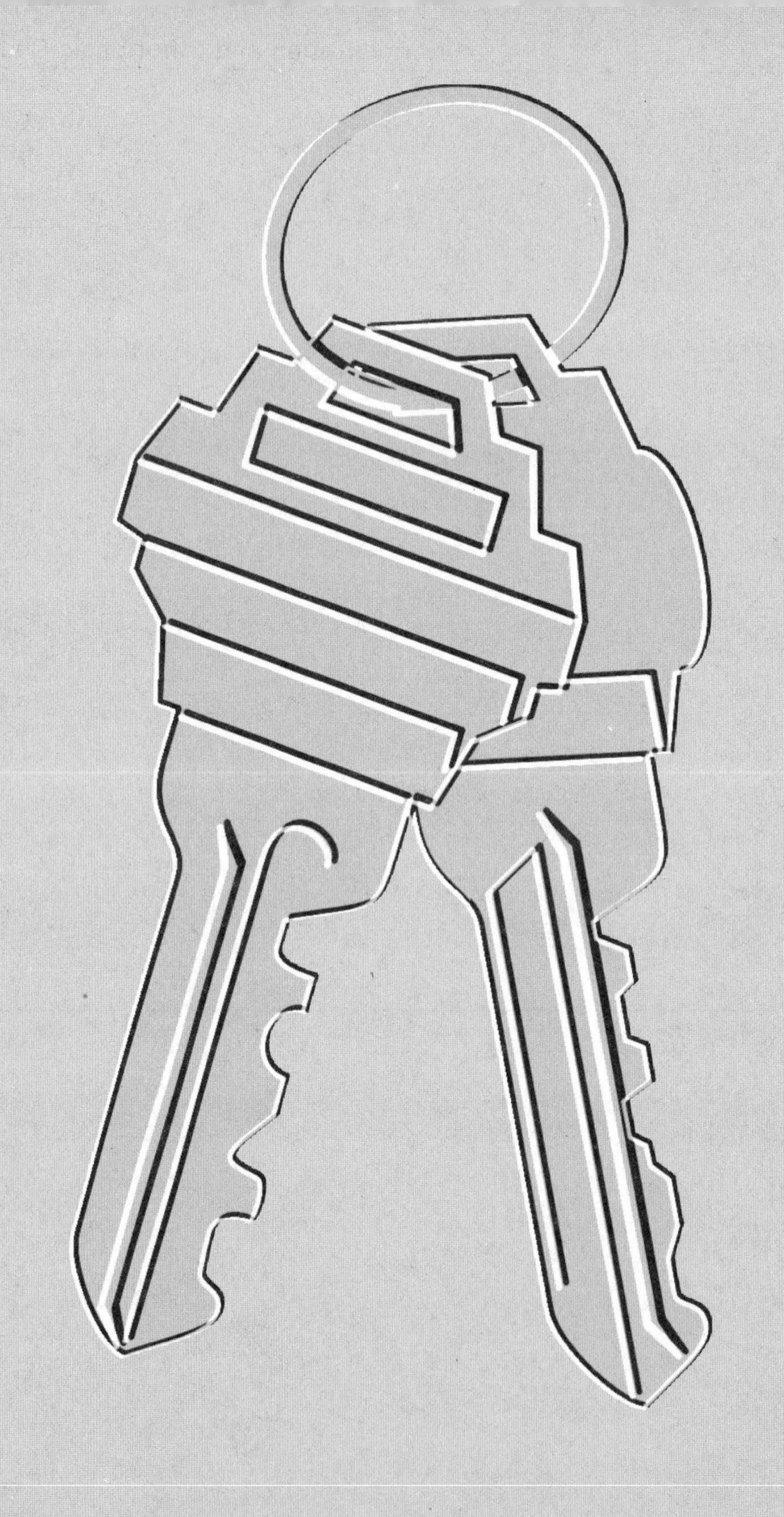

9

Speeding Performance: SQL Server Storage and Index Structures

Indexes are a critical part of your database planning and system maintenance. They provide SQL Server (and any other database system for that matter) with additional ways to look up data and take short cuts to that data's physical location. Adding the right index can cut huge percentages of time off your query executions. Unfortunately, too many indexes, or poorly planned ones, can actually increase the time it takes for your query to run. Indeed, indexes tend to be one of the most misunderstood objects that SQL Server offers, and, therefore, also tend to be one of the most mismanaged.

We will be studying indexes rather closely in this chapter from both a developer's and an administrator's point of view, but in order to fully understand indexes you also need to understand how data is stored in SQL Server. For that reason, we will also take a look at data storage past and present in SQL Server.

SQL Server Storage: Past and Present

The method of physically storing data to disk that was used for SQL Server prior to version 7.0 had been around for perhaps 20 years or more. While there's something to be said for time tested technologies, this particular technology is not ideally suited to either the NT storage or security systems, nor would it have been a good choice for building a Windows 9x capable product. Something had to be done if Microsoft was to provide some of the featureset they wanted to supply for SQL Server 7.0 and beyond.

Many users of SQL Server today do not realize that the product, until version 7.0, was deeply rooted in Sybase. Microsoft and Sybase did form a cooperative to offer SQL Server on OS/2 back in the days before NT was even around. Indeed, it wasn't until version 4 of SQL Server that it came to Windows NT. After version 6.0 (which, incidentally, is what came after version 4.21), Sybase and Microsoft decided to go their separate ways. Microsoft kept the NT version of SQL Server, Sybase kept the UNIX version and all the other non-NT based versions. (They then came out with their own NT version.)

Prior to the split, Microsoft had decided they wanted to be a serious player in the enterprise database management market. Essentially, they wanted to take Oracle and Informix head on, but they didn't feel they had the product to do it with, so they embarked on a complete and utter re-write of the product.

Re-writing a mission critical system like SQL Server is no small task, nor is it a short one. Especially when you consider that you're going to have to deal with issues of backward-compatibility as well as adding new features (not too many customers will buy something just because you've entirely re-written it – you have to throw them a bone in the form of new featureset). This being the case, Microsoft decided to throw out an interim release – SQL Server 6.5. This version offered a number of bug fixes from version 6.0 (and added a few new bugs for that matter), plus added replication (which didn't work very well), the Microsoft Distributed Transaction Coordinator (MS DTC), and several ANSI compatibility changes (most notably the new JOIN syntax).

Now, of course, we have SQL Server 7.0. In building this product, Microsoft went out in search of the best and brightest RDBMS systems designers the world had to offer. The Sphinx (what SQL Server 7.0 code was named in development) team was and is an amazing collection of integral people who were hired away from the likes of Oracle, IBM, Informix, SAP and more. A totally new approach was needed, and Microsoft went after the people that could give it to them. By the time Sphinx became SQL Server 7.0, they had totally redesigned and rebuilt the Storage Engine, the Relational Engine, and the Query Engine – in short, they had re-written everything. I don't know what the end number is in the released product, but I was told by a Microsoft VP in September of 1997 (about 16 months before the release of the product) that Sphinx would be over 98% Microsoft code – amazing when you consider that 6.0 was essentially 100% Sybase code.

What's the point of this lengthy study in history? We've looked at the development history, and we'll look at storage in 6.5 so that you are better equipped to understand the various differences you are going to run into with the product. SQL Server already has a very large installed base, and I suspect you will see legacy code from 4.x and 6.x developed apps for many years into the future. That being said, let's take a look at how both the 6.5 and below versions, as well as the 7.0 version handle storage.

SQL Server Storage – What All Versions Have in Common

Even with all the changes that we will investigate between SQL Server storage past and present, it's worth noting that they actually have a large number of things in common. Primarily, these similarities are in the logical way that data is stored. The data can be thought of in both new and old versions as existing in something of a hierarchy of structures.

The hierarchy is pretty simple. Some of the objects within the hierarchy are things that you will deal with directly, and will therefore know easily. A few others exist under the covers, and, while they can, in most cases, be directly addressed, they usually are not. Let's take a look at them one by one.

The Database

OK – this one is easy. I can just hear people out there saying, "Duh! I knew that." Yes, you probably did, but I point it out as a unique entity here because it is the highest level that storage is defined for in a given server which is common to both new and old storage paradigms. How exactly the storage space for the database is defined is actually one of the biggest areas of change between the new and old versions of the product. This is the highest level that a **lock** can be established at, although you cannot explicitly create a database-level lock.

A lock is something of both a hold and a place marker that is used by the system. As you do development using SQL Server – or any other database for that matter – you will find that understanding and managing locks is absolutely critical to your system.

We will be looking into locking extensively in Chapter 13, but we will see the lockability of objects within SQL Server discussed in passing as we look at storage.

The Extent

An **extent** is the basic unit of storage used to allocate space for tables and indexes. It is made up of 8 continuous data **pages**. When you create the first table in your database, at least one extent is created; the size of which varies by version (16K for 6.5 and prior, 64K for 7.0). Additional space is never allocated by less than an extent at a time.

The concept of allocating space based on extents, rather than actual space used, can be somewhat difficult to understand for people used to operating system storage principles. For those of you who are indeed familiar with the concept of clustered storage, you can think of extents as being somewhat similar to a cluster. The important points about an extent include:

- Once an extent is full, the next record will take up not just the size of the record, but the size of a whole new extent. Many people who are new to SQL Server get tripped up in their space estimations in part due to the allocation of an extent at a time rather than a record at a time.
- By pre-allocating this space, SQL Server saves the time of allocating new space with each record.
- Extents are lockable resources – locking less than a table, but more than a page of data.

It may seem like a waste that a whole extent is taken up just because one too many rows were added to fit on the currently allocated extent(s), but the amount of space wasted in this cause is typically not that bad. Still, it can add up – particularly in a highly fragmented environment – so it's definitely something of which you should be aware.

The good news in taking up all this space is that SQL Server skips some of the allocation time overhead. Instead of worrying about allocation issues every time it writes a row, SQL Server only deals with additional space allocation when a new extent is needed.

Don't confuse the space that an extent is taking up with the space that a database takes up. Whatever space is allocated to the database (or device prior to version 7.0) is what you'll see disappear from your disk drive's available space number. An extent is merely how things are, in turn, allocated within the total space reserved by the database.

An extent is also a lockable resource. If you have an extent lock, then you have a lock on all the data within that extent. Data may be part of the same table as that in the extent, but still be available (not have a lock on it) as long as it is not in the locked extent.

A Page

Much like an extent is a unit of allocation within the database, a page is the unit of allocation within a specific extent. There are 8 pages to every extent, though the size of those pages (and the extent for that matter) depends on what version of the product you are running (pre, or post 7.0).

A page is the last level you get to before you are at the actual data row. Whereas the number of pages per extent is fixed, the number of rows per page is not – that depends entirely on the size of the row, which can vary. You can think of a page as being something of a container for both table and index row data. A row is not allowed to be split between pages.

A page is made up of several components beyond the individual rows: the header, the actual row data, and the row offsets. Here is a good illustration of this:

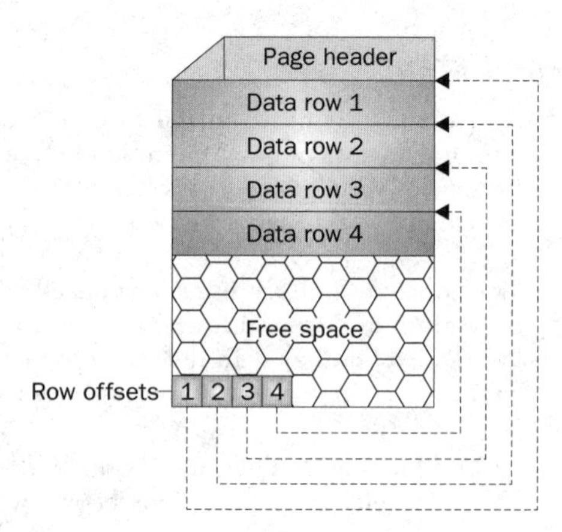

Note that there are a number of different **page types**:

- Data
- Index
- Binary Large Objecct (BLOB) (for text, ntext, and image data)
- Global and shared Allocation Map (GAM, or SGAM)
- Page Free Space (PFS)
- Index Allocation Map (IAM)

Data Pages

Data pages are pretty self explanatory – they are the actual data in your table, with the exception of any BLOB data. In the case of a row that has a column that contains BLOB data, the regular data is stored in a data page along with a 16-byte pointer to where to find the BLOB page that contains the binary information that makes up the BLOB.

Index Pages

Index pages are also pretty straightforward: they hold both the non-leaf and leaf level pages (we'll examine what these are later in the chapter) of a non-clustered index, as well as the non-leaf level pages of a clustered index. These index types will become much more clear as we continue through this chapter.

BLOB Pages

BLOB pages are for storing Binary Large Objects. For SQL Server, these amount to any data stored in a text, ntext, or image field. BLOB pages are special as far as data storage pages go, in that they don't have any rows as such. Since a BLOB can be as large as 2GB, they have to be able to go on more than one page – for this portion of things it doesn't matter what the version is. SQL Server will allocate as many pages as it needs in order to store the entire BLOB, but there is no guarantee that these pages will be contiguous – the pages could be located anywhere within the database file(s).

As mentioned before, the connection between the non-BLOB data for a row and any BLOB related to that row comes in the form of a pointer. The nature of that pointer and how SQL Server navigates to the BLOB data was changed for version 7.0 of SQL Server. In version 6.5 and before, the BLOB pages were put together in a chain – similar to a linked list. In order to find any page that was part of the BLOB, you needed to start at the beginning and navigate through the BLOB page by page. If you were trying to perform some form of text or binary search, this kind of arrangement was deadly, given that you were forced into a serial scan of the data. Beginning with version 7.0, however, the pages are organized into a B-Tree structure (which we will discuss fully a little later in the chapter). B-Trees provide more of a branching structure, and, therefore, a more direct path for larger BLOBs. This has made quite a difference in how quickly text operations can be performed.

Even with the significant improvements made in version 7.0, BLOBs are very slow performance wise, so we will talk about alternative storage methods when we look at advanced design issues later on.

Global Allocation Map, Shared Global Allocation Map, and Page Free Space Pages

Global Allocation Map (GAM), Shared Global Allocation Map (SGAM), and Page Free Space (PFS) page types are involved with figuring out which extents and pages are in use, and which are not. Essentially, these pages store records that indicate where there is space available. Understanding these page types is not really necessary in order to do high quality development or systems administration, and are beyond the scope of this book. If, however, you're just dying to know about them (or you're having problems with insomnia), then you can find more information on them in the Books Online – just look up GAM in the index.

Page Splits

When a page becomes full, it splits. This means more than just a new page is being allocated – it also means that approximately half the data from the existing page is moved to the new page.

The exception to this process is when a clustered index is in use. If there is a clustered index, and the next inserted row would be physically located as the last record in the table, then the new page is created and the new row is added to the new page without relocating any of the existing data. We will see much more on page splits as we investigate indexes.

Now that we have an idea of what the versions of SQL Server have in common, let's look at the specifics.

SQL Server Storage in Version 6.5 and Below

Since this book is focused on SQL Server 7.0, I am not going to go into every detail of how 6.5 did things. Still, we need to have a generalized understanding of prior versions of SQL Server if we are to be able to deal with the many legacy servers out there – not to mention a very large amount of legacy code that will try to do things that version 7.0 won't like.

In 7.0, the database is the absolute highest level of space allocation that you have available. I mention that here because 6.5 doesn't work that way at all. 6.5 had its own brand of space allocation, and we'll see how that winds up making a large difference in the way things are stored.

The Device

In version 6.5 and earlier, there was the concept of a **device**. A device was something like another pre-allocation of space, but, in this case, SQL Server was telling the operating system (remember, this goes back to the Sybase days, so we're talking a couple of different operating systems) to set aside disk space in what amounted to a named storage area. SQL Server was then responsible for what did and didn't go into that area. It could be one database, a database and its log, or multiple databases and logs – any mix of data and logs was fine, as long as there was still room in the device. The trick was that you needed to say how much of that device you wanted to allocate to each database or log. When you ran out of space in your database, you needed to allocate additional space to it. If there was no room left in the device, then you needed to either expand the device, or create a new one and put a portion of your database into the new device.

Particularly tricky was that any restore from backup had to be done using the same device names in the same sizes and order of creation as was originally performed. For many shops, there was a sad day when they had a good set of backups, but didn't know what the device names, sizes, or creation order was. This rendered the backups relatively useless if you lacked the information to rebuild the device structures to be exactly as they were.

> *This goes in the "way back" files, but, if you have a 6.5 server and run into this "We don't know what or when" device issue, there are system tables (`sysdevices`, `sysobjects`, and `sysdatabases`) that you can query to find the information you need as long as you still have the original `master` database.*

The Database

Because 6.5 and earlier versions of SQL Server used the notion of devices, databases were a somewhat simpler animal in terms of definition than they are under 7.0. At creation time, everything was defined in terms of what device the database and log were going on, and how much of that space you wanted to take up. In short, you were dealing only with the logical device, rather than the physical component that you reference in 7.0 (in 7.0, you refer to the physical file rather than a logical device). In practice though, we had to deal with two different things (a device and a database), which actually made things quite a pain. 7.0, while being more complex in the actual database definition, actually simplifies things when you compare it to the combination of device and database in 6.5 and prior.

In most other ways though, pre-7.0 databases work just as the 7.0 databases do from a storage standpoint. The database is full of extents, pages, and so on. The database is a lockable resource – nothing has changed save for how you actually create the database, and that a 6.5 database works on devices rather than files.

Extents and Pages

Extents in 6.5 and earlier, held 8 pages just as version 7.0 does, but the pages were only 2KB in size, and so the extent was only 16KB in size. Any table you created meant that you also created at least one extent – extents were limited to dealing with one table at a time.

BLOB data was stored in special pages, but any BLOB page would be referring to data for only one record. That record may have many pages of BLOB data associated with it, but the reverse was not true – if your BLOB information was only 10 bytes in size, it still took up an entire 2KB page.

BLOB information in SQL Server 6.5 and earlier was stored using a chain approach. This is actually a beneficial approach from a raw I/O standpoint, but also creates what was and is extremely poor performance for string manipulation exercises.

Both extents and pages were lockable resources.

Rows

The primary difference in the area of rows has to do with size and lockability.

The rule of rows not spanning pages (except for BLOB data) meant that the maximum row size was a little less than 2KB (1,962 bytes, the rest of the 2048 bytes contained page header and row-offset information).

Rows were only a quasi-lockable resource. You will read many things about how row-level locking wasn't available in SQL Server 6.5 and prior. While this is true of 6.0 and earlier databases, version 6.5 did have a limited form of row-level locking. The limitation was to `INSERT` statements only. What's more, by default, row-level locking on inserts was turned off. Indeed, most people didn't realize it had been added. Those who knew about it usually didn't make use of it because it required some special syntax usage in your `INSERT` statement. In short, you could lock at the row level, but only on inserts, only if you had turned on the option, and only if you used the required syntax.

SQL Server Storage in 7.0

The Device

Hooray! There aren't any. Everything the device did in prior versions is either no longer necessary, or has been incorporated directly into the database and/or database file(s).

The Database

We've already seen how the database in 7.0 becomes the center point for declaring physical space needs. Beyond that, it works much as it did in 6.5. The database is still a lockable resource.

For those of you who are coming from the 6.5 and earlier versions of SQL Server, be aware that deleting a database in 7.0 also deletes the physical files. This is a significant change from how deleting a device worked in 6.5.

The File

Files are probably the closest thing that version 7.0 has to a device. If, however, you notice the way that I'm presenting things here (which is following a hierarchy), you'll notice that we're talking about files after the database rather than before.

Whereas with devices, you could have multiple databases, with files it works the other way around – that is, you can have multiple files for one database. A file cannot hold multiple databases.

By default, your database has two files associated with it:

- The first is the primary physical database file – that's where your data is ultimately stored. This file should be named with a `*.mdf` extension (this is a recommendation, not a requirement – but I think you'll find doing it in other ways will become confusing over time).
- The second is something of an offshoot to the database file – the log. We'll dive into the log quite a bit when we deal with transactions and locks in Chapter 13, but you should be aware that it resides in its own file (which should end with a `*.ldf` extension), and that your database will not operate without it. The log is the serial recording of what's happened to your database since the last time that data was "committed" to the database. The database isn't really your complete set of data. The log isn't your complete set of data. Instead, if you start with the database and "apply" (add in all the activities from) the log, you have your complete set of data.

There is no restriction about where these files are located relative to each other. It is possible (actually, it's even quite desirable) to place each file on a separate physical device. This not only allows for the activity in one file not to interfere with that in the other file, but it also creates a situation where losing the file with the database does not cause you to lose your work – you can restore a backup and then re-apply the log (that was safe on the other drive). Likewise, if you lose the drive with the log, you'll still have a valid database up through the time of the last checkpoint.

The Extent

Under 7.0, an extent has several changes to it. Prior to this release, there was only a table to one or many extents – that's been slightly changed.

SQL Server no longer considers an extent to be exclusive to one table. Instead, we now have two different kinds of extents:

- Shared Extents
- Uniform Extents

Shared extents are extents that can have up to eight different objects in them (up to eight different objects on the eight different pages that exist within the extent). New tables and indexes start off with shared extents. Once they have at least eight pages then they are moved to uniform extents.

Uniform extents are just that – uniform. Every page in the extent is from the exact same object. Here's an example of how shared and uniform extents might have data allocated:

Page	Shared Extent	Uniform Extent
1	MyTable1	MyTable1
2	1st Index on MyTable1	MyTable1
3	2nd Index on MyTable1	MyTable1
4	MyTable2	MyTable1
5	MyTable3	MyTable1
6	1st Index on MyTable3	MyTable1
7	4th Index on MyTable1	MyTable1
8	1st Index on MyTable2	MyTable1

This new way of doing things has some advantages over the previous method:

- First, you save space. If SQL Server was still using the one table or index per extent rule that was in place under 6.5, then the objects listed in our table on shared extent usage would have taken up to 8 times as much space as with the new system. Think about that for a moment – if SQL Server 7.0 has 64KB extents, then that means that you would save over 400KB (8 x 64K for the 8 extents, minus 8 x 8K for the 8 pages actually in use) for every shared extent.
- Second, you gain speed. Fewer extents means that you switch between extents less often, which, in turn, means that you have fewer reads. Fewer reads mean less time taken performing reads, which, in turn, means that you take less time on whatever task you are performing.

The larger extent and page sizes do, however, increase the risk of was is called **fragmentation**. Fragmentation creates a situation where you have small amounts of data residing on lots of otherwise empty pages. This means that you end up incurring the overhead of switching between pages and extents for even small record counts. Fragmentation occurs in situations where you are doing a lot of deletions in your database, and is discussed further later in the chapter when we deal with the concept of a fill factor.

Pages

Pages are another area of huge change in the way that version 7.0 works as compared to previous versions. Some of the major changes include:

- Size now 8KB instead of 2KB
- BLOB pages can now be used for more than one row's data
- The method of linking to BLOB pages has changed.

The 8KB size change has to be the biggest in terms of everyday effect. The rule on a given row not spanning a page it still in effect, so a bigger page means the potential for bigger rows. In addition, the larger size cuts down on the number of page changes, which in turn cuts down on logical reads. Fewer logical reads usually means less time and effort spent in I/O, and better performance.

There is a downside to larger pages however. First, it means that, even when SQL Server knows what page your data is on, is has more rows to sift through in order to find the specific row (Microsoft has, however, implemented some ways around this problem). More importantly though, is that you have a larger number of rows within the page, and, therefore, a larger number of rows that are included when you lock the page. We will see more about how this can negatively impact us when we look at locks.

As for BLOB data, we now have the potential for more than one row to have data on the same BLOB page. Indeed, the data on that page is all stored in something of a general BLOB format, and does not need to even be of the same type – you can mix text, ntext, and image data with no problems.

In 7.0, Microsoft has changed the storage method to make use of what is essentially a **Balanced Tree** structure. For those of you who are not familiar with **B-Trees** (which is probably most of you), we will take a look at them shortly as we deal with indexes. The abbreviated version of how it works, in this case, is that a text pointer is stored with the actual data row. That text pointer does not point to the actual data, but, rather, to what is called a **root structure**. This root structure is the first place that might actually point to the real data, but, if the BLOB is too large, then the root structure may need to point at what is called an **intermediate node**. The larger the BLOB, the larger the B-Tree. If the B-Tree gets too large (more than 32KB), then the tree must split, and additional layers of the tree will need to be navigated in order to get to the end data. As the BLOB gets larger and larger, the number of tree-branch level nodes also grows.

As you might expect, there was a purpose in going with this new design. The fact is that text operations should run much faster in this structure, since SQL Server can navigate to a particular point within the structure just by traversing the B-Tree. Under 6.5, you would have had to go page by page, in order, until you got to the page you wanted.

Rows

If there is a single area where Microsoft is hearing the best things about the changes made in version 7.0, it has to be due to the changes surrounding rows. The biggest changes are:

- Rows can be up to 8KB
- Row level locking is now supported on all statements - in 6.5, you could only have row level locking on `INSERT` statements, and then only if you knew the right set of hoops to jump through.

Larger Row Sizes

Rows can now be up to slightly less than 8KB (8060 bytes to be more specific) in size. This is just over 4 times as large as under 6.5, and it has a much larger impact on table and database design than many people realize.

Under 6.5, it was not at all uncommon to have tables that needed to be broken out into a one-to-one relationship just so you had enough room to store everything. This was problematic both in terms of database complexity and in the performance costs needed to perform a join in order to get at data that should have all been in one table. While this can still certainly be a problem under 7.0, it is far less likely.

Another benefit of the larger row sizes becomes apparent when you realize that the maximum length of many field types also went up. Under 6.5 for example, the maximum length for a non-BLOB character type was 255 characters. This was very problematic – for even things as common as a description field on a form quite often need more than 255 characters to be of any use whatsoever. By allowing these to now be up to 8060 characters, we can often avoid needing to use text fields, which are both slower and more unwieldy than char, varchar, nchar, or nvarchar.

In addition to the limit of 8060 characters, there is also a maximum of 1024 columns (up from just 250 in version 6.5). In practice, you'll find it very unusual to run into a situation where you run out of columns before you run into the 8060 character limit. 1024 gives you an average column width of 8 bytes. For most uses, you'll easily exceed that. The exception to these tends to be in measurement and statistical information – where you have a large number of different things that you are storing numeric samples of. Still, even those applications will find it a rare day when they bump into the 1024 column count limit.

Row-Level Locking

As I've mentioned before, we have an entire chapter coming up on the subject of locking, but I want to point this piece out here because of its sheer importance. Locking at row level means that we are placing a hold on only that one row – not all the rows on a page or in the extent. This becomes a huge issue when we start to talk about contention issues in Chapter 13. For now though, what I want you to understand is that the concept of row-level locking applies not only to the actual data, but also to the index rows we will be working with throughout this chapter.

Understanding Indexes

Webster's dictionary defines an index as:

A list (as of bibliographical information or citations to a body of literature) arranged usually in alphabetical order of some specified datum (as author, subject, or keyword).

I'll take a simpler approach in the context of databases, and say it's a way of potentially getting to data a heck of a lot quicker. Still, the Webster's definition isn't too bad – even for our specific purposes.

Perhaps the key thing to point out in the Webster's definition is the word "usually" that's in there. The definition of alphabetical order changes depending on a number of rules. For example, in SQL Server, we have a number of different collation options available to us. Among these options are:

- Binary: Sorts by the numeric representation of the character (for example, in ASCII, a space is represented by the number 32, the letter "D" is 68, but the letter "d" is 100). Because everything is numeric, this is the fastest option – unfortunately, it's also not at all the way in which people think, and can really raise havoc with your comparisons in your `WHERE` clause.
- Dictionary order: This sorts things just as you would expect to see in a dictionary, with a twist – you can set a number of different additional options to determine sensitivity to case, accent, and character set.

It's fairly easy to understand that, if we tell SQL Server to pay attention to case, then "A" is not going to be equal to "a". Likewise, if we tell it to be case insensitive, then "A" will be equal to "a". Things get a tad more confusing when you add accent sensitivity – that is, does SQL Server pay attention to diacritical marks, and therefore the idea that "a" is different from "á", which is different from "à". Where many people get even more confused is in how collation order affects not only the equality of data, but also the sort order (and, therefore, the way it is stored in indexes).

By way of example, let's look at the equality of a couple of collation options, and what they do to our sort order and equality information:

Collation Order	Comparison Values	Index Storage Order
Dictionary order, case-insensitive, accent-insensitive (the default)	A = a = à = á = â = Ä = ä = Å = å	a, A, à, â, á, Ä, ä, Å, å
Dictionary order, case-insensitive, accent-insensitive, uppercase preference	A = a = à = á = â = Ä = ä = Å = å	A, a, à, â, á, Ä, ä, Å, å
Dictionary order, case-sensitive	A ≠ a, Ä ≠ ä, Å ≠ å, a ≠ à ≠ á ≠ â ≠ ä ≠ å, A ≠ Ä ≠ Å	A, a, à, á, â, Ä, ä, Å, å

The point here is that what happens in your indexes depends on the collation information you have established for your server. Perhaps even more importantly though, the behavior of your system may see some rather radical changes if a server is installed as case-sensitive rather than insensitive. If you're going to assume that your server is case-insensitive, then you need to be sure that the documentation for your system deals with this. Imagine, if you're an independent software vendor (ISV), and you sell your product – now imagine that your customer installs it on their existing server (which is going to seem like an entirely reasonable thing to them), but that existing server happens to be case-sensitive. You're going to get a support call from one very unhappy customer.

Once the collation order has been set for your server, it is a major pain to change it, so be certain of the collation order you want before you set it. Once your server has been set up with a certain collation order, then to change it you must bulk copy the data out of the databases (sorry, a backup won't do), rebuild the `master` database, and then bulk copy the data back in – Yuck!

B-Trees

The concept of a **Balanced Tree**, or **B-Tree**, is certainly not one that was created with SQL Server. Indeed, B-Trees are used in a very large number of indexing systems both in and out of the database world.

A B-Tree simply attempts to provide a consistent and relatively low cost way of finding your way to a particular piece of information. The "Balanced" in the name is pretty much self-descriptive – a B-Tree is, with the odd exception, self-balancing, meaning that every time the tree branches, approximately half the data is on one side, and half on the other side. The "Tree" in the name is also probably pretty obvious at this point (hint, tree, branch – see a trend here?) – it's there because, when you draw the structure, then turn it upside down, it has the general form of a tree.

A B-Tree starts at the **root node** (another stab at the tree analogy there, but not the last). This root node can, if there is a small amount of data, point directly to the actual location of the data. In such a case, you would end up with a structure that looked something like this:

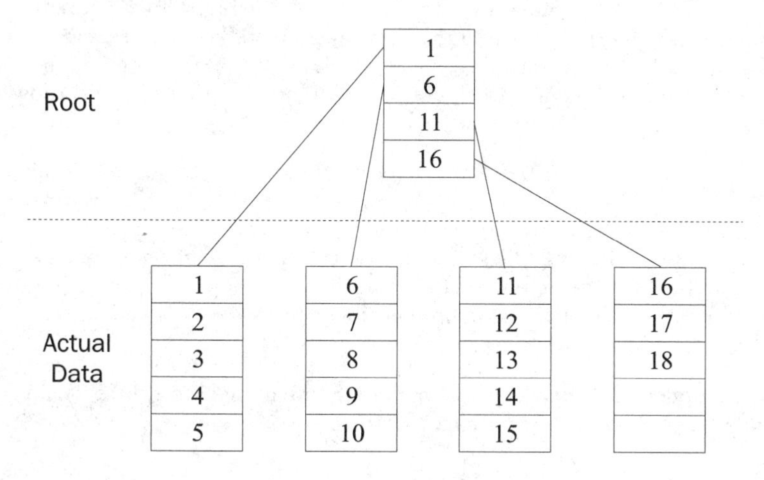

So, we start at the root and look through the records until we find the last page that starts with a value less than what we're looking for. We then obtain a pointer to that node, and look through it until we find the row that we want.

In most situations though, there is too much data to reference from the root node, so the root node points at intermediate nodes – or what are called **non-leaf level** nodes. Non-leaf level nodes are nodes that are somewhere in between the root and the node that tells you where the data is physically stored. Non-leaf level nodes can then point to other non-leaf level nodes, or to **leaf level** (last tree analogy reference – I promise) nodes. Leaf level nodes are the nodes where you obtain the real reference to the actual physical data. Much like the leaf is the end of the line for navigating the tree, the node we get to at the leaf level is the end of the line for our index – from here, we can go straight to the actual data node that has our data on it:

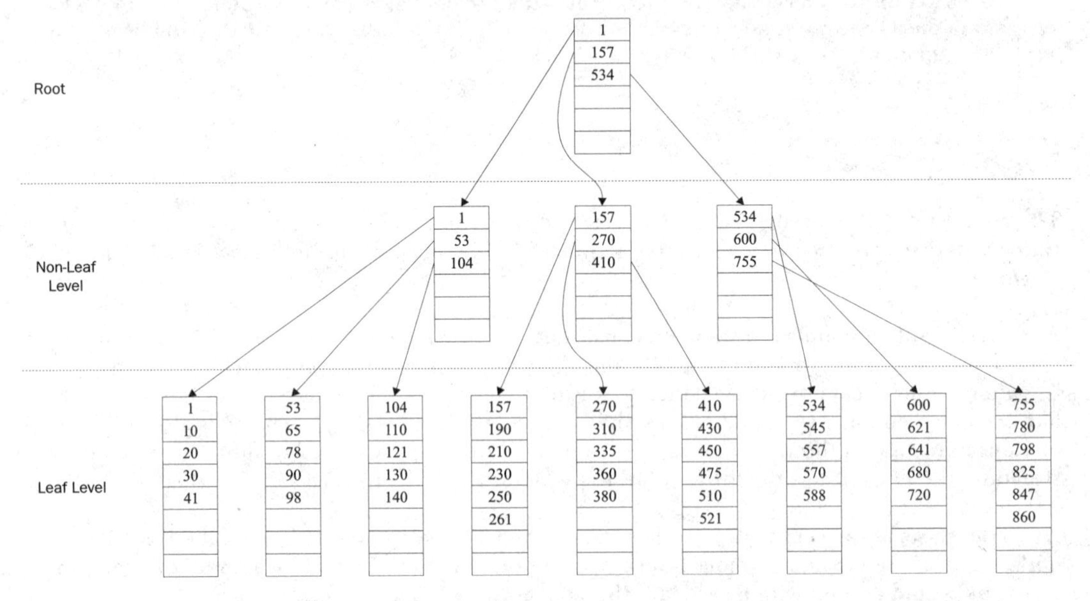

Again, we start with the root node, then move to the node that starts with the highest value that is equal to or less than what we're looking for and is also in the next level down. We then repeat the process – look for the node that has the highest starting value at or below the value we're looking for. We keep doing this level by level down the tree until we get to the leaf level – from there we know the physical location of the data, and can quickly navigate to it.

Page Splits – A First Look

All of this works quite nicely on the read side of the equation – it's the insert that gets a little tricky. Recall that the "B" in B-Tree stands for "balanced". You may also recall that I mentioned that a B-Tree is balanced because about half the data is on either side every time you run into a branch in the tree. B-Trees are sometimes referred to as **self-balancing** because the way new data is added to the tree prevents them from becoming lopsided.

When data is added to the tree, a node will eventually become full, and will need to split. Since, in SQL Server, a node equates to a page – this is called a **page split**.

When a page split occurs, data is automatically moved around to keep things balanced. The first half of the data is left on the old page, and the rest of the data is added to a new page – thus you have about a 50-50 split, and your tree remains balanced:

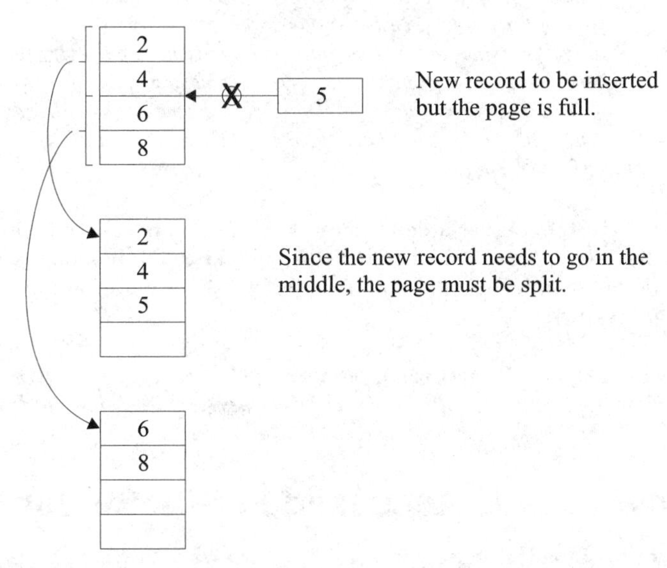
Ordered Insert as middle record
in a Cluster Key
2
4
6
8
5
New record to be inserted
but the page is full.
2
4
5
Since the new record needs to go in the
middle, the page must be split.
6
8

If you think about this split process a bit, you'll realize that it adds a substantial amount of overhead at the time of the split. Instead of inserting just one page, you are:

- Creating a new page
- Migrating rows from the existing page to the new page
- Adding your new row to one of the pages
- Adding another entry in the parent node

But the overhead doesn't stop there. Since we're in a tree arrangement, you have the possibility for something of a cascading action. When you create the new page (because of the split), you need to make another entry in the parent node. This entry in the parent node also has the potential to cause a page-split at that level, and the process starts all over again. Indeed, this possibility extends all the way up to and can even affect the root node.

If the root node splits, then you actually end up creating two additional pages. Since there can only be one root node, the page which was formerly the root node is split into two pages, and becomes a new intermediate level of the tree. An entirely new root node is then created, and will have two entries (one to the old root-node, one to the split page).

Needless to say, page splits can have a very negative impact on system performance, and are characterized by behavior where your process on the server seems to just pause for a few seconds (while the pages are being split and re-written).

We will talk about page-split prevention before we're done with this chapter.

> *While page splits at the leaf level are a common fact of life, page splits at intermediate nodes happen far less frequently. As your table grows, every layer of the index will experience page splits, but, since the intermediate nodes only have one entry for several entries on the next lower node, the number of page splits gets less and less frequent as you move further up the tree. Still, for a split to occur above the leaf level, there must have already been a split at the next lowest level – this means that page splits up the tree are cumulative (and expensive performance-wise) in nature.*

Every SQL Server index form makes use of this B-Tree approach in some way or another. Indeed, they are all very similar in structure thanks to the flexible nature of a B-Tree. Still, we shall see that there are indeed some significant differences, and these can have an impact on the performance of our system.

> *For a SQL Server index, the nodes of the tree come in the form of pages, but you can actually apply this concept of a root node, the non-leaf level, the leaf level and the tree structure to more than just SQL Server or even just databases.*

How Data is Accessed in SQL Server

In the broadest sense, there are only two ways in which SQL Server retrieves the data you request:

- A table scan
- Use of an index.

Which method SQL Server will use to run your particular query will depend on what indexes are available, what columns you are asking about, what kind of joins you are doing, and the size of your tables.

Use of Table Scans

A table scan is a pretty straightforward process. When a table scan is performed, SQL Server starts at the physical beginning of the table looking through every row in the table. As it finds rows that match the criteria of your query, it includes them in the result set.

You may hear lots of bad things about table scans, and, in general, they will be true. However, table scans can actually be the fastest method of access in some instances. Typically, this is the case when retrieving data from rather small tables. The exact size where this becomes the case will vary widely according to the width of your table and what the specific nature of the query is.

> *Think about how this works for a bit. See if you can spot why the use of* `EXISTS` *in the* `WHERE` *clause of your queries has so much to offer performance-wise where it fits the problem. If you recall our discussion of the* `EXISTS` *option, you should remember that SQL Server stops as soon as it find one record that matches the criteria. If you had a 1 million record table, and it found a matching record on the third record, then use of the* `EXISTS` *option would have saved you the reading of 999,997 records! Also, don't forget the* `NOT EXISTS` *works the same way.*

Use of Indexes

When SQL Server decides to use an index, the process actually works somewhat similarly to a table scan, but with a few shortcuts.

During the query parsing process, the optimizer takes a look at all the available indexes and chooses the best one (this is primarily based on the information you specify in your joins and `WHERE` clause). Once that index is chosen, SQL Server navigates the tree structure to the point of data that matches your criteria and again extracts only the records it needs. The difference is that, since the data is sorted, the query engine knows when it has reached the end of the current range it is looking for. It can then end the query, or move on to the next range of data as necessary.

If you've read ahead in the query topics at all (to Chapter 15 specifically), you may notice some striking resemblances to how the `EXISTS` option worked. The `EXISTS` keyword allows a query to quit running the instant that it finds a match (that's what `EXISTS` is about – seeing if there is a match of any kind or not – so once it finds a match, it's done). The performance gains are similar or even better since the process can work in a similar fashion – that is, the server is able to know when there is nothing left that's relevant, and can stop things right there. Even better, however, is that by using an index, we don't have to limit ourselves to Boolean situations (did I find it – yes or no). We can apply this same notion to both the beginning and end of a range – we are able to gather ranges of data with essentially the same benefits of an index. What's more, we can do a very fast lookup (called a seek) of our data rather than hunting through the entire table.

Don't get the impression from my comparing what indexes do for us to the `EXISTS` operator that indexes replace the `EXISTS` operator altogether(or vice versa). The two are not mutually exclusive – they can be used together, and often are. I mention them here together only because they have the similarity of being able to tell when their work is done, and quit before getting to the physical end of the table.

Index Types and Index Navigation

Although there are nominally two types of indexes in SQL Server (**Clustered** and **Non-Clustered**), there are actually, internally speaking, three different types:

- Clustered Indexes
- Non-Clustered Indexes – which include:
  - Non-Clustered Indexes on a Heap
  - Non-Clustered Indexes on a Clustered Index

The way the physical data is stored varies between clustered and non-clustered indexes. The way SQL Server traverses the B-Tree to get to the end data varies between all three index types.

All SQL Server indexes have leaf level, and non-leaf level pages. As we mentioned when we discussed B-Trees, the leaf level is the level that holds the "key" to identifying the record, and the non-leaf level pages are guides to the leaf level.

The indexes are built over either a **clustered table**, or what is called a **heap**.

A clustered table is any table that has a clustered index on it. Clustered indexes are discussed in detail shortly, but what they mean to the table is that the data is physically stored in a designated order. Individual rows are uniquely identified through the use of the **cluster-key** – the columns which define the clustered index.

> *This should bring to mind the question of, "What if the clustered index is not unique?" That is, how can a clustered index be used to uniquely identify a row if the index is not a unique index? The answer lies under the covers – SQL Server forces any clustered indexes to be unique – even if you don't define it that way. Fortunately, it does this in a way that doesn't change how you use the index. You can still insert duplicate rows if you wish, but SQL Server will add a suffix to the key internally to ensure that the row has a unique identifier.*

A heap is any table that does not have a clustered index on it. In this case, a unique identifier, or Row ID (RID) is created based on a combination of the extent, pages, and row offset (places from the top of the page) for that row. A RID is only necessary if there is no cluster key available (no clustered index).

Clustered Indexes

A clustered index is a "one of a kind" for any given table – you can only have one per table. You don't have to have a clustered index, but you'll find it to be one of the most commonly chosen as the first index, for a variety of reasons which shall become apparent as we look at our index types.

What makes a clustered index special is that the leaf level of a clustered index is the actual data – that is, the data is re-sorted to be stored in the same physical order that the index sort criteria state. This means that, once you get to the leaf level of the index, you're done – you're at the data. Any new records are inserted according to its correct physical order in the clustered index. How new pages are created changes depending on where the record needs to be inserted.

In the case of a new record that needs to be inserted into the middle of the index structure, a normal page split occurs. The last half of the records from the old page are moved to the new page and the new record is inserted into the new or old page as appropriate.

In the case of a new record that is logically at the end of the index structure, a new page is created, but only the new record is added to the new page:

Ordered Insert as last record in a Cluster Key

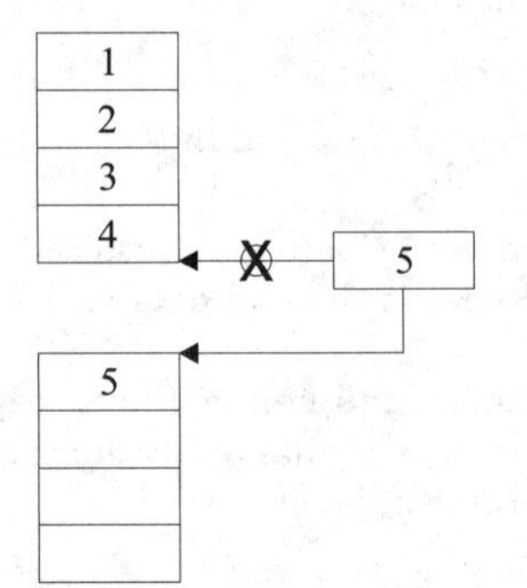

New record to be inserted but the page is full. Since it is last, it is added to an entirely new page without disturbing the existing data.

Navigating the Tree

As I've indicated previously, even the indexes in SQL Server are stored in a Balanced – or B-Tree. Theoretically, a B-Tree always has half of the remaining information in each possible direction as the tree branches. Let's take a look at a visualization of what a B-Tree looks like for a clustered index:

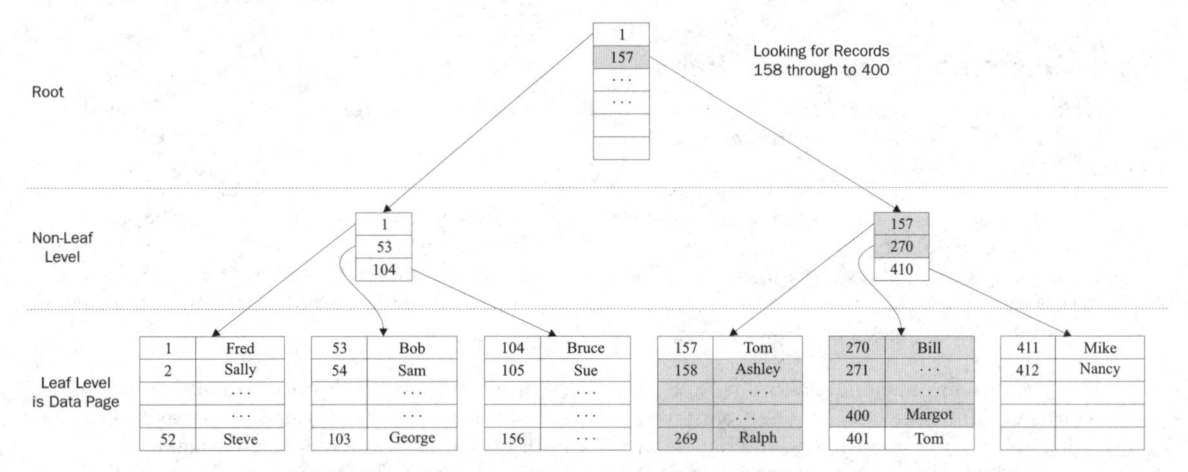

As you can see, it looks essentially identical to the more generic B-Trees we discussed earlier in the chapter. In this case, we're doing a range search (something clustered indexes are particularly good at) for numbers 158-400. All we have to do is:

Navigate to the first record, and include all remaining records on that page – we know we need the rest of that page because the information from one node up lets us know that we'll also be needing data from a few other pages. Since this is an ordered list, we can be sure it's continuous – that means if the next page has records which should be included, then the rest of this page must be included. We can just start spewing out data from those pages without having to do the verification side of things.

We start off by navigating to the root node. SQL Server is able to locate the root node based on an entry that is kept in the system table called `sysindexes`.

> **Every index in your database has an entry in `sysindexes`. This system table is part of your database (as opposed to being in the `master` database), and stores the location information for all the indexes in your database and what columns they are based on.**

By looking through the page that serves as the root node, we can figure out what the next page we need to examine is (the second page on the second level as we have it drawn here). We then continue the process. With each step we take down the tree, we are getting to smaller and smaller subsets of data.

Eventually, we will get to the leaf level of the index. In the case of our clustered index, getting to the leaf level of the index means that we are also at our desired row(s) and our desired data.

> **I can't stress enough the importance of the distinction that, with a clustered index, when you've fully navigated the index, that means that you've fully navigated to your data. How much of a performance difference this can make will really show its head as we look at non-clustered indexes – particularly when the non-clustered index is built over a clustered index.**

Non-Clustered Indexes on a Heap

Non-clustered indexes on a heap work very similarly to clustered indexes in most ways. They do, however, have a few notable differences:

The leaf level is not the data – instead, it is the level at which you are able to obtain a pointer to that data. This pointer comes in the form of the RID, which, as we described earlier in the chapter, is made up of the extent, page, and row offset for the particular row being pointed to by the index. Even though the leaf level is not the actual data (instead, it has the RID), we only have one more step than with a clustered index – because the RID has the full information on the location of the row, we can go directly to the data.

Don't, however, misunderstand this "one more step" to mean that there's only a small amount of overhead difference, and that non-clustered indexes on a heap will run close to as fast as a clustered index. With a clustered index, the data is physically in the order of the index. That means, for a range of data, when you find the row that has the beginning of your data on it, there's a good chance that the other rows are on that page with it (that is, you're already physically almost to the next record since they are stored together). With a heap, the data is not linked together in any way other than through the index. From a physical standpoint, there is absolutely no sorting of any kind. This means that, from a physical read standpoint, your system may have to retrieve records from all over the file. Indeed, it's quite possible (possibly even probable) that you will wind up fetching data from the same page several separate times – SQL Server has no way of knowing it will have to come back to that physical location because there was no link between the data. With the clustered index, it knows that's the physical sort, and can, therefore, grab it all in just one visit to the page.

Here's the same search we did with the clustered index, only with a non-clustered index on a heap this time:

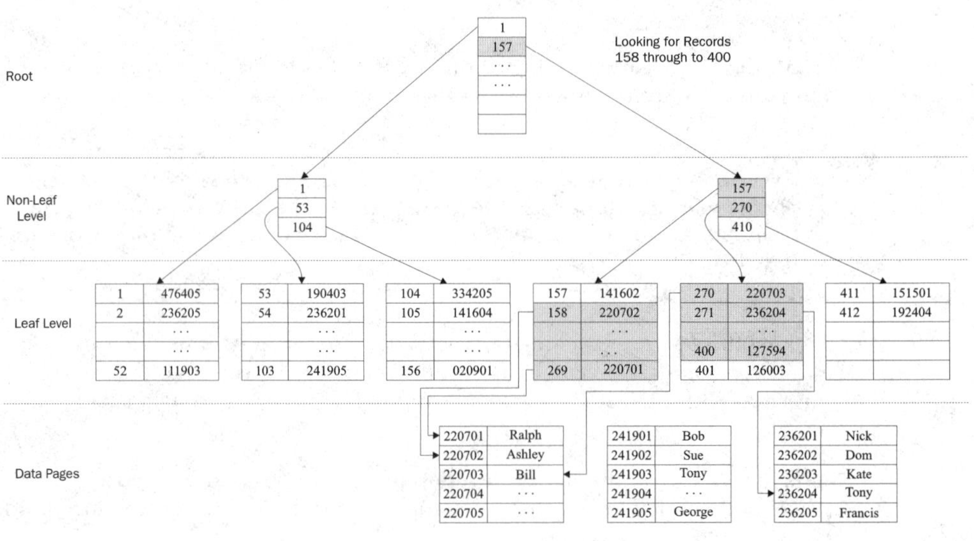

Through most of the index navigation, things work exactly as they did before. We start out at the same root node, and we traverse the tree dealing with more and more focused pages until we get to the leaf level of our index. This is where we run into the difference. With a clustered index, we could have stopped right here, but, with a non-clustered index, we have more work to do. If the non-clustered index is on a heap, then we have just one more level to go. We take the Row ID from the leaf level page, and navigate to it - it is not until that point that we are at our actual data.

Non-Clustered Indexes on a Clustered Table

With non-clustered indexes that are built on a table that has a clustered index, the similarities continue – but so do the differences. Just as with non-clustered indexes on a heap, the non-leaf level of the index looks pretty much as it did for a clustered index. The difference does not come until we get to the leaf level.

At the leaf level, we have a rather sharp difference from what we've seen with the other two index structures – we have yet another index to look over. With clustered indexes, when we got to the leaf level, we found the actual data. With non-clustered indexes on a heap, we didn't find the actual data, but did find an identifier that let us go right to the data (we were just one step away). With non-clustered indexes on a clustered table, we find the cluster-key. That is, we find enough information to go and make use of the clustered index.

We end up with something that looks like this:

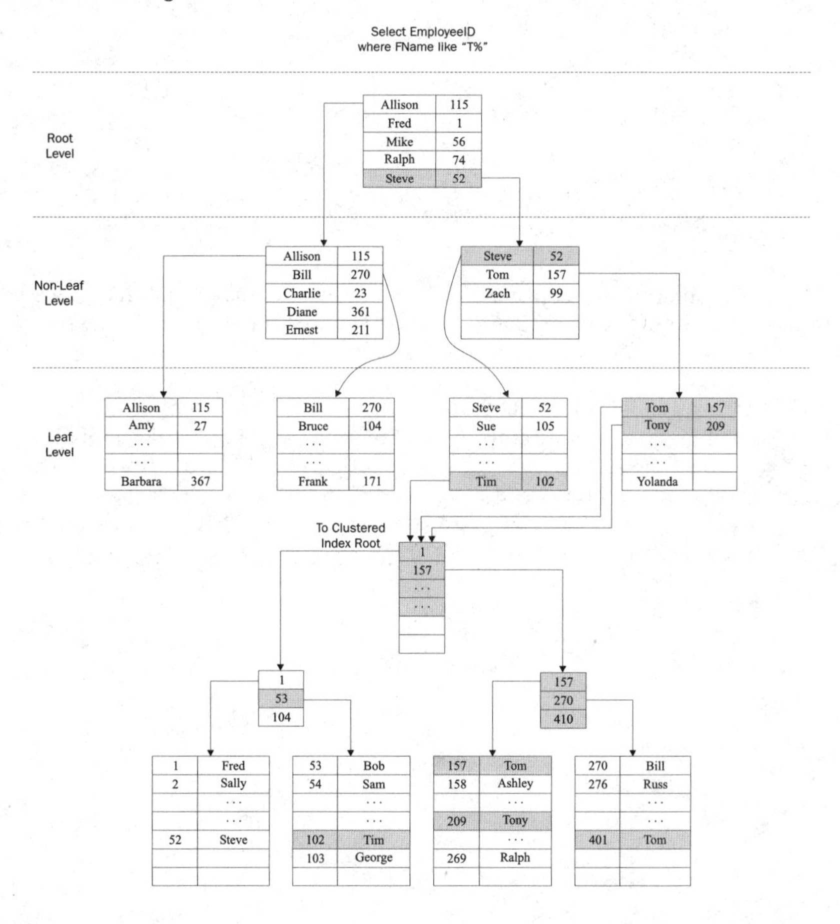

What we end up with is two entirely different kinds of lookups.

In the example from our diagram, we start off with a ranged search – we do one single lookup in our index and are able to look through the non-clustered index to find a continuous range of data that meets our criteria (`LIKE 'T%'`). This kind of lookup, where we can go right to a particular spot in the index, is called a **seek**.

The second kind of lookup then starts – the lookup using the clustered index. This second lookup is very fast; the problem lies in the fact that it must happen multiple times. You see, SQL Server retrieved a list from the first index lookup (a list of all the names that start with "T"), but that list doesn't logically match up with the cluster key in any continuous fashion – each record needs to be looked up individually.

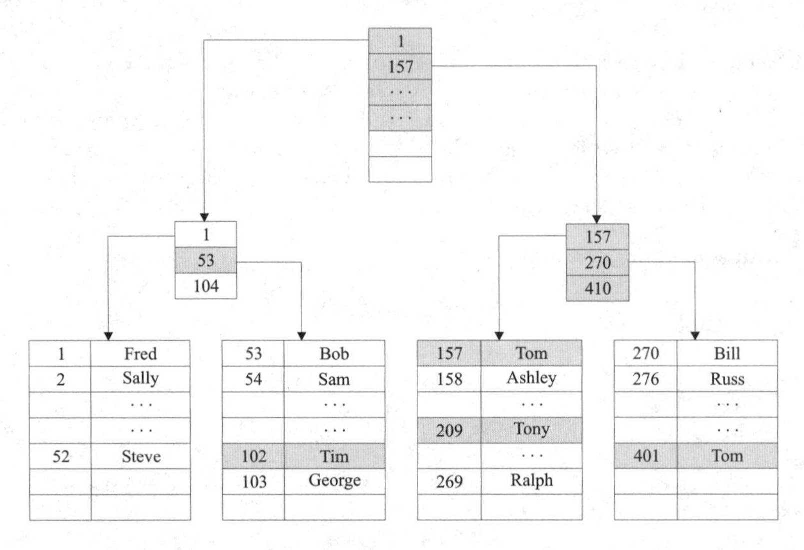

Needless to say, this multiple lookup situation introduces more overhead than if we had just been able to use the clustered index from the beginning. The first index search – the one through our non-clustered index – is going to require very few logical reads.

For example, if I have a table with 1,000 bytes per row, and I did a lookup similar to the one in our drawing (say, something that would return 5 or 6 rows), it would only take something to the order of 8-10 logical reads to get the information from the non-clustered index. However, that only gets me as far as being ready to look up the rows in the clustered index. Those lookups would cost approximately 3-4 logical reads *each*, or 15-24 additional reads. That probably doesn't seem like that big a deal at first, but look at it this way:

Logical reads went from 3 minimum to 24 maximum – that's an 800% increase in the amount of work that had to be done.

Now expand this thought out to something where the range of values from the non-clustered index wasn't just 5 or 6 rows, but 5 or 6 thousand, or 5 or 6 *hundred* thousand rows – that's going to be a huge impact.

> *Don't let the extra overhead vs. a clustered index scare you – the point isn't meant to scare you away from using indexes, but rather to recognize that a non-clustered index is not going to be as efficient as a clustered index from a read perspective (it can, in some instances, actually be a better choice at insertion time). An index of any kind is usually (there are exceptions) the fastest way to do a lookup. We'll explain what index to use and why later in the chapter.*

Creating and Dropping Indexes

You might have noticed that there is no `ALTER` option listed in that section title – that's because there is no `ALTER` statement that goes with indexes. You can create them and drop them, but, to change them, you must first drop the index, then recreate it.

Indexes have two ways in which they can be created:

- Through an explicit `CREATE INDEX` command
- As an implied object when a constraint is created

Each of these has its own quirks about what it can and can't do, so let's look at both them individually.

The CREATE INDEX Statement

The `CREATE INDEX` statement does exactly what it sounds like – it creates an index on the specified table based on the stated columns. Note that tables are the only thing you can create indexes on – views don't contain any data of their own (they only point to data in tables), so there's nothing to index.

The syntax to create an index is somewhat drawn out, and introduces several items that we haven't really talked about up to this point:

```
CREATE [UNIQUE] [CLUSTERED|NONCLUSTERED]
INDEX <index name> ON <table name>(<column name> [,...n])
[WITH
[PAD_INDEX]
[[,] FILLFACTOR = <fillfactor>]
[[,] IGNORE_DUP_KEY]
[[,] DROP_EXISTING]
[[,] STATISTICS_NORECOMPUTE]
]
[ON filegroup]
```

Loosely speaking, this statement follows the same `CREATE <Object type> <Object name>` that we've seen plenty of already (and will see even more of). The primary hitch in things is that we have a few intervening parameters that we haven't seen elsewhere.

Just as we'll see with views in our next chapter, we do have to add an extra clause onto our `CREATE` statement to deal with the fact that an index isn't really a stand-alone kind of object. It has to go together with a table, and we need to say what that table our column(s) are "on."

After the `ON <table name>(<column name>)` clause, everything is optional. These options can have a significant impact on system performance and behavior, so let's look at them one by one.

WITH

Easy one – just tell SQL Server that you will indeed be supplying one or more of the options that follow.

PAD_INDEX

In the syntax list,this one comes first – but that will seem odd when you understand what `PAD_INDEX` does. In short, it determines just how full (what percentage) the non-leaf level pages of your index are going to be as the index is first created. You don't state a percentage on `PAD_INDEX` because it will use whatever percentage was specified in the `FILLFACTOR` option that follows. `PAD_INDEX` is meaningless without a `FILLFACTOR` (thus why it seems odd that it comes first). This will become clearer when we look deeper into page splits, fragmentation and fillfactors later in the chapter.

FILLFACTOR

When SQL Server first creates an index, the pages are, by default, filled as full as they can be, minus two records. You can set the `FILLFACTOR` to be any value between 1 and 100. This number will be how full, as a percentage, your pages are once index construction is completed. Keep in mind though that, as your pages split, your data will still be distributed 50-50 between the two pages – you cannot control the fill percentage on an ongoing basis other than regularly rebuilding the indexes (something you should do – setting up a maintenance schedule for this is covered in Chapter 25).

We use a `FILLFACTOR` when we need to adjust the page densities. We will discuss the issue of page densities shortly, but, for now, think about things this way:

- If it's an OLTP system, you want the `FILLFACTOR` to be low.
- If it's an OLAP or other very stable (in terms of changes – very few additions and deletions) system, you would want the `FILLFACTOR` to be as high as possible.
- If you have something that has a medium transaction rate and a lot of report type queries against it, then you probably want something in the middle (not too low, not too high).

If you don't provide a value, then SQL Server will fill your pages to two rows short of full, with a minimum of one row per page (for example, if your row is 8000 characters wide, you can only fit one row per page – so leaving things two rows short wouldn't work).

IGNORE_DUP_KEY

This one is a way of doing little more than circumventing the system. In short, it causes a UNIQUE constraint to have a slightly viewpoint than it would otherwise have.

Normally, a unique constraint, or unique index, does not allow any duplicates of any kind – if a transaction tries to create a duplicate based on a column that is defined as unique, then that transaction would be rolled back and rejected. Once you set the IGNORE_DUP_KEY option, however, you'll get something of a mixed behavior. You will still receive an error, but the error will only be of a warning level – the record is still not inserted.

This last line – "the record is still not inserted" - is a critical concept from an IGNORE_DUP_KEY standpoint. A rollback isn't issued for the transaction (the error is a warning error rather than a critical error), but the duplicate row will have been rejected.

Why would you do this? Well, it's a way of storing unique values, but not disturbing a transaction that tries to insert a duplicate. For whatever process is inserting the would-be duplicate, it may not matter at all that it's a duplicate row (no logical error from it). Instead, that process may have an attitude that's more along the lines of, "Well, as long as I know there's one row like that in there, I'm happy – I don't care whether it's the specific row that I tried to insert or not."

DROP_EXISITING

No rocket science here. If you specify this option, any existing index with the name in question will be dropped prior to construction of the new index.

STATISTICS_NORECOMPUTE

Under version 7.0, SQL Server attempts to automate the process of updating the statistics on your tables and indexes. By selecting the STATISTICS_NORECOMPUTE option, you are saying that you will take responsibility for the updating of the statistics. In order to turn this option off, you would need to drop and rebuild the index.

I recommend highly against using this option. Why? Well, the statistics on your index are what the query optimizer uses to figure out just how helpful your index is going to be for a given query. The statistics on an index are changing constantly as the data in your table goes up and down in volume and as the specific values in a column change. When you combine these two facts, you should be able to see that not updating your statistics means that the query optimizer is going to be running your queries based on out-of-date information. Leaving the automatic statistics feature on means that the statistics will be updated regularly (just how often depends on the nature and frequency of your updates to the table). Conversely, turning automatic statistics off means that you will either be out of date, or you will need to set up a schedule to manually run the UPDATE STATISTICS command.

ON <FileGroup>

SQL Server gives you the option of storing your indexes separately from the data. This can be nice from a couple of perspectives:

- The space that is required for the indexes can be spread across other drives
- The I/O for index operations does not burden the physical data retrieval

You can mix and match these options. Many of them are seldom used, but some, such as FILLFACTOR, can be a major issue with performance – we will discuss these later in the chapter.

Implied Indexes Created with Constraints

I guess I call this one "Index by accident." It's not that the index shouldn't be there – these have to be there if you want the constraint that created the index. It's just that I've seen an awful lot of situations where the only indexes on the system were those created in this fashion. Usually, this implies that the administrators and/or designers of the system are virtually oblivious to the concept of indexes.

However, you'll also find yet another bizarre twist on this one – the situation where the administrator or designer knows how to create indexes, but doesn't really know how to tell what indexes are already on the system and what they are doing. This kind of situation is typified by duplicate indexes. As long as they have different names, SQL Server will be more than happy to create them for you.

Implied indexes are created when one of two constraints are added to a table:

- A `PRIMARY KEY`
- A `UNIQUE` constraint (aka, an "alternate" key)

We've seen plenty of the `CREATE` syntax up to this point, so I won't belabor it – however, it should be noted that all the options except for `FILLFACTOR` are not allowed when creating as an implied index to a constraint.

Choosing Wisely: Deciding What Index Goes Where and When

By now, you're probably thinking to yourself, "Geez, I'm always going to create clustered indexes!" There are plenty of good reasons to think that way. Just keep in mind that there are also some reasons not to.

Choosing what indexes to include and what not to can be a tough process, and, in case that wasn't enough, you have to make some decisions about what type you want them to be. The latter decision is made simultaneously easier and harder in the fact that you can only have one clustered index. It means that you have to choose wisely to get the most out of it.

Selectivity

Indexes, particularly non-clustered indexes, are primarily beneficial in situations where there is a reasonably high level of **selectivity** within the index. By selectivity, I'm referring to the percentage of values in the column that are unique. The higher the percentage of unique values within a column, the higher the selectivity is said to be, and the greater the benefit of indexing.

If you think back to our sections on non-clustered indexes – particularly the section on non-clustered indexes over a clustered index – you will recall that the lookup in the non-clustered index is really only the beginning. You still need to make another loop through the clustered index in order to find the real data. Even with the non-clustered index on a heap, you still end up with multiple physically separate reads to perform.

If one lookup in your non-clustered index is going to generate multiple additional lookups in a clustered index, then you are probably better off with the table scan. The exponential effect that's possible here is actually quite amazing. Consider that the looping process created by the non-clustered index is not worth it if you don't have somewhere in the area of 95% uniqueness in the indexed column.

Clustered indexes are substantially less affected by this, since, once you're at the start of your range of data – unique or not – you're there. That is, no additional index pages to read. Still, more than likely, your clustered index has other things that it could be put to greater use on.

One other exception to the rule of selectivity has to do with foreign keys. If your table has a column that is a foreign key, then, in all likelihood, you're going to benefit from having an index on that column. Why foreign keys and not other columns? Well, foreign keys are frequently the target of joins with the table they reference. Indexes, regardless of selectivity, can be very instrumental in join performance because it allows what is called a "merge join". A merge join obtains a row from each table and compares them to see if they match the join criteria (what you're joining on). Since there are indexes on the related columns in both tables, the seek for both rows is very fast.

The point here is that selectivity is not everything, but it is a big issue to consider. If the column in question is not in a foreign key situation, then it is almost certainly the biggest issue you need to consider.

Watching Costs: When Less Is More

Remember that, while indexes speed up performance when reading data, they are actually very costly when modifying data. Indexes are not maintained by magic. Every time that you make a modification to your data, any indexes related to that data also need to be updated.

When you insert a new row, a new entry must be made into every index on your table. Remember too that, when you update a row, this is handled as a delete and insert – again, your indexes have to be updated. (Feeling like a late night infomercial here.) But wait! There's more! When you delete records – again, you must update all the indexes too – not just the data. For every index that you create, you are creating one more block of entries that have to be updated.

Notice, by the way, that I said "entries" plural – not just one. Remember that a B-Tree has multiple levels to it. Every time that you make a modification to the leaf level, there is a chance that a page split will occur, and that one or more non-leaf level pages must also be modified to have the reference to the proper leaf page.

Sometimes – quite often actually – not creating that extra index is the thing to do. Sometimes, the best thing to do is choose your indexes based on the transactions that are critical to your system and use the table in question. Does the code for the transaction have a `WHERE` clause in it? What column(s) does it use? Is there a sorting required?

Choosing that Clustered Index

Remember that you can only have one, so you need to choose it wisely.

By default, your primary key is created with a clustered index. This is often the best place to have it, but not always (indeed, it can seriously hurt you in some situations), and if you leave things this way, you won't be able to use a clustered index anywhere else. The point here is don't just accept the default. Think about it when you are defining your primary key – do you really want it to be a clustered index?

If you decide that you indeed want to change things – that is, you don't want to declare things as being clustered, just add the NONCLUSTERED keyword when you create your table. For example:

```
CREATE TABLE MyTableKeyExample
(
   Column1    intIDENTITY
      PRIMARY KEY NONCLUSTERED,
   Column2    int
)
```

Once the index is created, the only way to change it is to drop and rebuild it, so you want to get it set correctly up front.

Keep in mind that, if you change which column(s) your cluster index is on, SQL Server will need to do a complete resorting of your entire table (remember, for a clustered index, the table sort order and the index order are the same). Now, consider a table that you have that is 5,000 characters wide and has a million rows in it – that is an awful lot of data that has to be reordered. Several questions should come to mind from this:

- How long will it take: It could be a long time, and there really isn't a good way to estimate that time).
- Do I have enough space: Figure that, in order to do a resort on a clustered index, you will, on average, need an *additional* 1.2 times (working space plus the new index) the amount of space your table is already taking up. This can turn out to be a very significant amount of space if you're dealing with a large table – make sure you have the room to do it in. All this activity will, by the way, happen in the database itself – so this will also be affected by how you have your maximum size and growth options set for your database.

The Pros

Clustered indexes are best for queries when the column(s) in question will frequently be the subject of a ranged query. This kind of query is typified by use of the BETWEEN statement or the < or > symbols. Queries that use a GROUP BY and make use of the MAX, MIN, and COUNT aggregators are also great examples of queries that use ranges and love clustered indexes. Clustering works great here because the search can go straight to a particular point in the physical data, keep reading until it gets to the end of the range, and then stop. It is extremely efficient.

Clusters can also be excellent when you want your data sorted (ORDER BY) based on the cluster key.

The Cons

There are two situations where you don't want to create that clustered index. The first is fairly obvious – when there's a better place to use it. I know I'm sounding repetitive here, but don't just use a clustered index on a column just because it seems like the thing to do (primary keys are the common culprit here) – be sure that you don't have another column that it's better suited to first.

Perhaps the much bigger no-no use for clustered indexes, however, is when you are going to be doing a lot of inserts in a non-sequential order. Remember that concept of page splits? Well, here's where it can come back and haunt you big time.

Imagine this scenario: You are creating an accounting system. You would like to make use of the concept of a transaction number for your primary key in your transaction files, but you would also like those transaction numbers to be somewhat indicative of what kind of transaction it is (it really helps troubleshooting for your accountants). So you come up with something of a scheme - you'll place a prefix on all the transactions indicating what sub-system they come out of. They will look something like this:

ARXXXXXX	Accounts Receivable Transactions
GLXXXXXX	General Ledger Transactions
APXXXXXX	Accounts Payable Transactions

*Where XXXXXX will be a sequential numeric value

This seems like a great idea, so you implement it, leaving the default of the clustered index going on the primary key.

At first look, everything about this setup looks fine. You're going to have unique values, and the accountants will love the fact that they can infer where something came from, based on the transaction number. The clustered index seems to make sense since they will often be querying for ranges of transaction IDs.

Ahhh, but if only it were that simple. Think about your `INSERT`s for a bit. With a clustered index, we originally had a nice mechanism to avoid much of the overhead of page splits. When a new record was inserted that was to be inserted after the last record in the table, then, even if there was a page split, only that record would go to the new page - SQL Server wouldn't try and move around any of the old data. Now we've messed things up though.

New records inserted from the General Ledger will wind up going on the end of the file just fine (GL is last alphabetically, and the numbers will be sequential). The AR and AP transactions have a major problem though - they are going to be doing non-sequential inserts. When AP000025 gets inserted and there isn't room on the page, SQL Server is going to see AR000001 in the table, and know that it's not a sequential insert. Half the records from the old page will be copied to a new page before AP000025 is inserted.

The overhead of this can be staggering. Remember that we're dealing with a clustered index, and that the clustered index is the data. The data is in index order. This means that, when you move the index to a new page, you are also moving the data. Now imagine that you're running this accounting system in a typical OLTP environment (you don't get much more OLTP like than an accounting system) with a bunch of entry people keying in vendor invoices or customer orders as fast as they can. You're going to have page splits occurring constantly, and, every time you do, you're going to see a brief hesitation for users of that table while the system moves data around.

Fortunately, there are a couple of ways to avoid this scenario:

- Choose a cluster key that is going to be sequential in its inserting. You can either create an identity column for this, or you may have another column that logically is sequential to any transaction entered regardless of system.
- Choose not to use a clustered index on this table. This is often the best option in a situation like in this example, since a non-clustered index on a heap is usually faster than one on a cluster key.

This one is perhaps one of the best examples of why I have gone into so much depth as to how things work. You need to think through how things are actually going to get done before you have a good feel for what the right index to use (or not use) is.

Column Order Matters

Just because an index has two columns in it doesn't mean that the index is useful for any query that refers to either column.

An index is only considered for use if the first column listed in the index is used in the query. The bright side is that there doesn't have to be an exact one-for-one match to every column – just the first. Naturally, the more columns that match, the better, but only the first creates a do-not-use situation.

Think about things this way. Imagine that you are using a phone book. Everything is indexed by last name, and then first name – does this sorting do you any real good if all you know is that the person you want to call is named Fred? On the other hand, if all you know is that his last name is Blake, the index will still serve to narrow the field for you.

One of the more common mistakes that I see in index construction is to think that one index that includes all the columns is going to be helpful for all situations. Indeed, what you're really doing is storing all the data a second time. The index will totally be ignored if the first column of the index isn't mentioned in the `ORDER BY` or `WHERE` clauses of the query.

You Made the Mess, Now Clean it Up: Dropping Indexes

If you're constantly re-analyzing the situation and adding indexes, don't forget to drop indexes too. Remember the overhead on inserts – it doesn't make much sense to look at the indexes that you need and not also think about what indexes you do not need. Always ask yourself, "Can I get rid of any of these?"

The syntax to drop an index is pretty much the same as dropping a table. The only hitch is that you need to qualify the index name with the table it is attached to:

```
DROP INDEX <table name>.<index name>
```

And it's gone.

Use the Index Tuning Wizard

It would be my hope that you'll learn enough about indexes not to need the Index Tuning Wizard, but it still can be quite handy. It works by taking a workload file, which you generate using the SQL Server Profiler (discussed in Chapter 24), and looking over that information for what indexes will work best on your system.

The Index Tuning Wizard is found as part of the Wizards option within the Tools menu of Enterprise Manager. Like all wizards, I don't recommend using this tool as the sole way you decide what indexes to build, but it can be quite handy in terms of making some suggestions that you may not have thought of.

Maintaining Your Indexes

As developers, we often tend to forget about our product after it goes out the door. For many kinds of software, that's something you can get away with just fine – you ship it, you move on to the next product or next release. With database driven projects, however, it's virtually impossible to get away with. You need to take responsibility for the product well beyond the delivery date.

Please don't take me to be meaning that you have to go serve a stint in the tech support department – I'm actually talking about something even more important: Maintenance Planning.

There are really two issues to be dealt with in terms of maintenance of indexes:

- Page Splits
- Fragmentation

Both are related to page density, and, while the symptoms are substantially different, the trouble-shooting tool is the same, as is the cure.

Fragmentation

We've already talked about page splits quite a bit, but we haven't really touched on fragmentation. I'm not talking quite the same fragmentation that you may have heard of with your O/S files, and the defrag tool you use for that won't help with database fragmentation.

Fragmentation happens when your database grows, pages split, then data is eventually deleted. While the B-Tree mechanism is really not that bad at keeping things balanced from a growth point of view, it doesn't really have a whole lot to offer as you delete data. Eventually, you may get down to a situation where you have one record on this page, a few records on that page – just a situation where many of your data pages are holding only a small fraction of the amount of data that they could hold.

The first problem with this is probably the first you would think about – wasted space. Remember that SQL Server allocates an extent of space at a time. If only one page has one record on it, then that extent is still allocated.

The second problem is the one that is more likely to cause you grief – records that are spread out all over the place cause additional overhead in data retrieval. Instead of just loading up one page and grabbing the 10 needed rows, SQL Server may have to load 10 separate pages in order to get that same information. It isn't just reading the row that causes effort – SQL Server has to read that page in first. More pages = more work on reads.

That being said, database fragmentation does have its good side – OLTP systems positively love fragmentation. Any guesses as to why? Page splits. Pages that don't have much data in them can have data inserted with little or no fear of page splits.

So, high fragmentation equates to poor read performance, but it also equates to excellent insert performance. As you might expect, this means that OLAP systems really don't like fragmentation, but OLTP systems do.

Identifying Fragmentation vs. Likelihood of Page Splits

SQL Server gives us a command to help us identify just how full the pages and extents in our database are. We can then use that information to make some decisions about what we want to do to maintain our database. The command is actually an option for the Database Consistency Checker – or DBCC.

The syntax is pretty simple:

```
DBCC SHOWCONTIG ([<table object id>], [<index id>])
```

The only real tricky part is that `SHOWCONTIG` is looking for the table ID and index ID values rather than their names. In order to get that, we have to use the `OBJECT_ID(<object name>)` function for the table, and we have to get the index ID out of `sysindexes`. I usually run `SHOWCONTIG` as part of a script to package everything up, or, on some systems, I've just packaged it up into a stored procedu.re for more frequent use. For example, to get the information from the `PK_Order_Details` index in the `Order Details` table, we would run a script like this:

```
USE Northwind
GO

-- Declare my holding variables
DECLARE @ID int,
@IdxID int,
@IndexNamevarchar(128)

-- Set what I'm looking for
SELECT @IndexName = 'PK_Order_Details'
SET @ID = OBJECT_ID('Order Details')
-- Get the index id valeus
SELECT @IdxID = IndID
FROM sysindexes
WHERE id = @ID
   AND name = @IndexName

-- Get the info I'm really after
DBCC SHOWCONTIG (@id, @IdxID)
GO
```

As an exercise, once you've read the stored procedure chapter, you should try and convert this one over to be a sproc. In the mean time, all you have to do is save this as a script, and just change two lines (the ones with the table and index names) to re-execute it.

The output is not really all that self-describing:

```
DBCC SHOWCONTIG scanning 'Order Details' table...
Table: 'Order Details' (661577395); index ID: 1, database ID: 6
TABLE level scan performed.
```

```
- Pages Scanned................................:          9
- Extents Scanned..............................:          6
- Extent Switches..............................:          5
- Avg. Pages per Extent........................:          1.5
- Scan Density [Best Count:Actual Count].......: 33.33% [2:6]
- Logical Scan Fragmentation ..................:          0.00%
- Extent Scan Fragmentation ...................:          33.33%
- Avg. Bytes Free per Page.....................:          664.3
- Avg. Page Density (full).....................:          91.79%
DBCC execution completed. If DBCC printed error messages, contact your system administrator.
```

Oh, some of it is probably pretty straightforward, but let's walk through what everything means:

Stat	What it means
Pages Scanned	The number of pages in the table (for a clustered index) or index.
Extents Scanned	The number of extents in the table or index. This will be a minimum of page/8 rounded up. The more extents for the same number of pages, the higher the fragmentation.
Extent Switches	The number of times DBCC moved from one extent to another as it traversed the pages of the table or index. This is another one for fragmentation – the more switches it has to make to see the same amount of pages, the more fragmented we are.
Avg. Pages per Extent	The average number of pages per extent. A fully populated extent would have 8.
Scan Density [Best Count: Actual Count]	The best count is the ideal number of extent changes if everything is perfectly linked. Actual count is the actual number of extent changes. Scan density is the percentage of best count divided by actual count.
Logical Scan Fragmentation	The percentage of pages that are out-of-order as checked by scanning the leaf pages of an index. Only relevant to scans related to a clustered table. An out of order page is one for which the next page indicated in the index allocation map (IAM) is different than that pointed to by the next page pointer in the leaf page.
Extent Scan Fragmentation	This one is telling whether an extent is not physically located next to the extent that it is logically located next to. This just means that the leaf pages of your index are not physically in order (though they still can be logically), and just what percentage of the extents this problem pertains to.

Table Continued on Following Page

Stat	What it means
Avg. Bytes free per page	Average number of free bytes on the pages scanned. This number can get artificially high if you have large row sizes. For example, if your row size was 4040 bytes, then every page could only hold one row, and you would always have an avg free bytes of about 4020 bytes. That would seem like a lot, but, given your row size, it can't be any less than that.
Avg. Page density (full)	Average page density (as a percentage). This value takes into account row size and is, therefore, a more accurate indication of how full your pages are. The higher the percentage, the better.

So, now the question is, how to we use this information once we have it. The answer is, of course, it depends.

Using the output from our `SHOWCONTIG`, we have a decent idea of whether our database is full, fragmented, or somewhere in between (the latter is, most likely, what we want to see). If we're running an OLAP system, then seeing our pages full would be great – fragmentation would bring on depression. For an OLTP system, we would want much the opposite (although only to a point).

So, how do we take care of the problem? To answer that we need to look into the concept of index rebuilding and fill factors.

DBREINDEX and FILLFACTOR

As we saw earlier in the chapter, SQL Server gives us an option for controlling just how full our leaf level pages are, and, if we choose, another option to deal with non-leaf level pages. Unfortunately, these are proactive options – they are applied once, and then you need to re-apply them as necessary by rebuilding your indexes and reapplying the options.

To rebuild indexes, we can either drop them and create them again, or make use of `DBREINDEX`. `DBREINDEX` is another DBCC command, and the syntax looks like this:

```
DBCC DBREINDEX (<'database.owner.table_name'>[,<index name>
[,<fillfactor>]]]
)  [WITH NO_INFOMSGS]
```

Executing this command completely rebuilds the requested index. If you supply a table name with no index name, then it rebuilds all the indexes for the requested table. There is no single command to rebuild all the indexes in a database.

Rebuilding your indexes restructures all the information in those indexes, and re-establishes a base percentage that your pages are full. If the index in question is a clustered index, then the physical data is also reorganized.

By default, the pages will be reconstituted to be full minus two records. Just as with the `CREATE TABLE` syntax, you can set the `FILLFACTOR` to be any value between 1 and 100. This number will be the percent full that your pages are once the database reorganization is complete. Remember though that, as your pages split, your data will still be distributed 50-50 between the two pages – you cannot control the fill percentage on an on-going basis other than regularly rebuilding the indexes.

We use a `FILLFACTOR` when we need to adjust the page densities. As we've already discussed, lower page densities (and, therefore, lower `FILLFACTORs`) are ideal for OLTP systems where there are a lot of insertions – this helps avoid page splits. Higher page densities are desirable with OLAP systems (fewer pages to read, but no real risk of page splitting due to few to no inserts).

If we wanted to rebuild the index that serves as the primary key for the `Order Details` table we were looking at earlier with a fill factor of 65; we would issue a DBCC command as follows:

```
DBCC DBREINDEX ([Order Details], PK_Order_Details, 65)
```

We can then re-run the `DBCC SHOWCONTIG` to see the effect:

```
DBCC SHOWCONTIG scanning 'Order Details' table...
Table: 'Order Details' (661577395); index ID: 1, database ID: 6
TABLE level scan performed.
- Pages Scanned................................:          13
- Extents Scanned..............................:          2
- Extent Switches..............................:          1
- Avg. Pages per Extent........................:          6.5
- Scan Density [Best Count:Actual Count].......: 100.00% [2:2]
- Logical Scan Fragmentation ..................:          0.00%
- Extent Scan Fragmentation ...................:          50.00%
- Avg. Bytes Free per Page.....................:          2950.4
- Avg. Page Density (full).....................:          63.55%
DBCC execution completed. If DBCC printed error messages, contact your system administrator.
```

The big one to notice here is the change in Avg. Page Density. The number didn't quite reach 65% because SQL Server has to deal with page and row sizing, but it gets as close as it can.

Several things to note about `DBREINDEX` and `FILLFACTOR`:

- If a `FILLFACTOR` isn't provided, then the `DBREINDEX` will use whatever the index was built using before. If one has never been specified, then the fillfactor will make the page full less two records (which is too full for most situations).
- If a `FILLFACTOR` is provided, then that value becomes the default `FILLFACTOR` for that index.
- While `DBREINDEX` can be done live, I highly recommend against it – it locks resources and has a host of problems it can cause.

Summary

Indexes are sort of a cornerstone topic in SQL Server or any other database environment, and are not something to be taken lightly. They can drive your performance successes, but they can also drive your performance failures.

Top level things to think about with indexes:

- Clustered indexes are usually faster than a non-clustered index (one could come very close to saying always, but there is an exception).
- Only place non-clustered indexes on columns where you are going to get a high level of selectivity (that is, 95% or more of the rows are unique).
- All data manipulation language (DML: `INSERT`, `UPDATE`, `DELETE`, `SELECT`) statements can benefit from indexes, but inserts and updates (remember, they use a delete and insert approach) are also slowed by indexes. The lookup part of a query is helped by the index, but anything that modifies data will have extra work to do (to maintain the index in addition to the actual data).
- Indexes take up space.
- Indexes are only used if the first column in the index is relevant to your query.
- Indexes can hurt as much as they help – know why you're building the index, and don't build indexes you don't need.

When you're thinking about indexes, ask yourself these questions:

Question	Response
Are there a lot of inserts or modifications to this table?	If yes, keep indexes to a minimum. This kind of table usually has modifications done through single record lookups of the primary key – usually, this is the only index you want on the table. If the inserts are non-sequential, think about not having a clustered index.
Is this a reporting table? That is, not many inserts, but reports run lots of different ways?	More indexes are fine. Target the clustered index to frequently used information that is likely to be extracted in ranges. OLAP installations will often have many times the number of indexes seen in an OLTP environment.
Is there a high level of selectivity on the data?	If yes, and it is frequently the target of a `WHERE` clause, then add that index.
Have I dropped the indexes I no longer need?	If not, why not?
Do I have a maintenance strategy established?	If not, why not?

In our next chapter, we'll be looking at views. While you cannot build an index over a view, they do share minor similarities in syntax and in the fact that they are both objects that are subsidiary to the table.

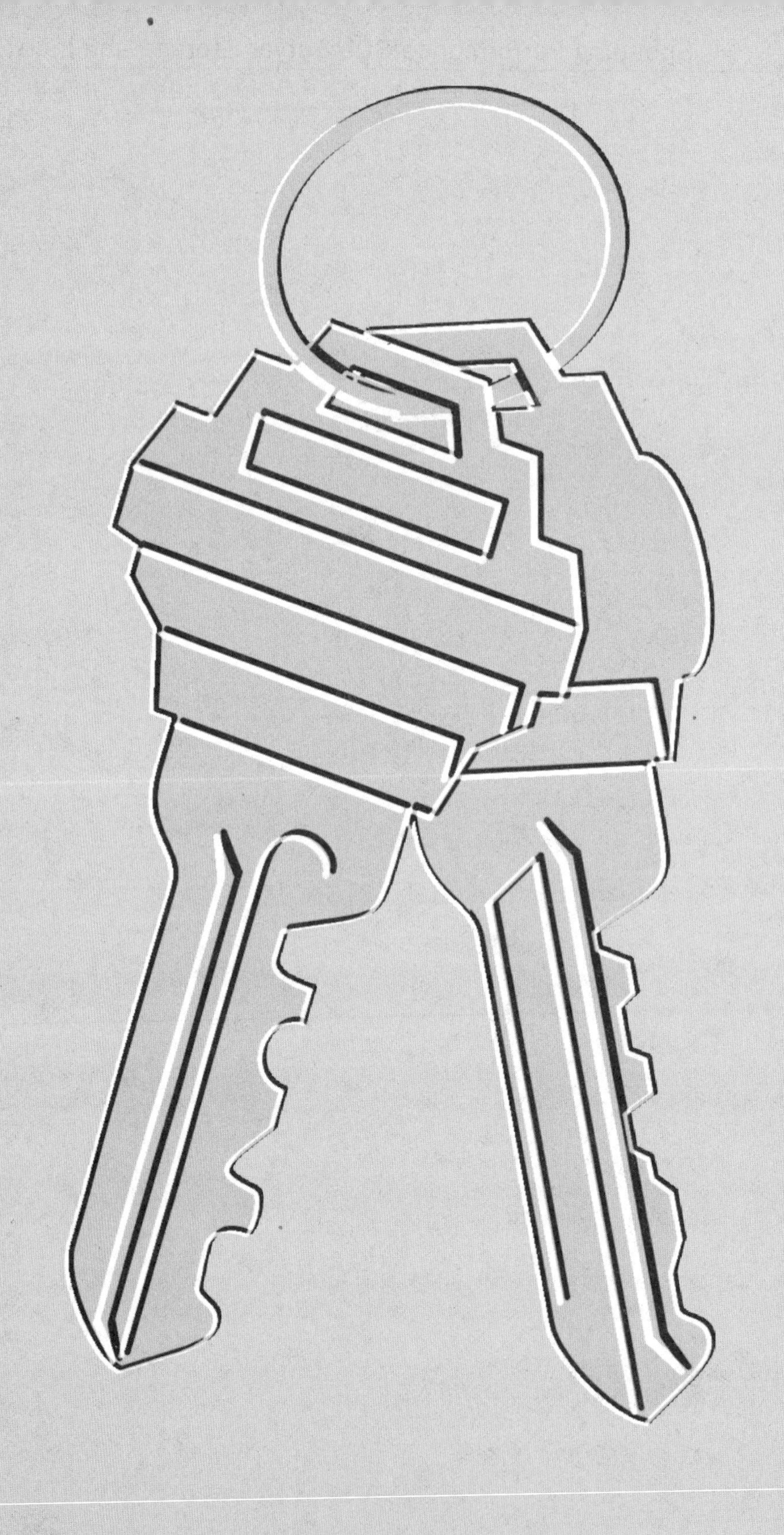

10

Views

Up to this point, we've been dealing with base objects – objects that have some level of substance of their own. In this chapter, we're going to go virtual, and take a look at views.

Views have a tendency to be used either too much, or not enough – rarely just right. When we're done with this chapter, you should be able to use views to:

- Reduce apparent database complexity for end users
- Prevent sensitive columns from being selected, while still affording access to other important data

A **view** is, at its core, really nothing more than a stored query. What's great is that you can mix and match your data from base tables to create what will essentially function just like another base table. You can create a simple query that selects from only one table and leaves some columns out, or you can create a complex query that joins several tables and makes them appear as one.

Simple Views

The syntax for a view, in its most basic form, is a combination of a couple of things we've already seen in the book – the basic `CREATE` statement that we saw back in Chapter 6, plus a `SELECT` statement like we've used over and over again:

```
CREATE VIEW <view name>
AS
    <select statement>
```

Let's go ahead and dive right in with an extremely simple view. We'll call this one our customer phone list, and create it as `CustomerPhoneList_vw` in our `Accounting` database:

```
CREATE VIEW CustomerPhoneList_vw
AS
   SELECT CustomerName, Contact, Phone
   FROM Customers
```

Notice that when you execute the `CREATE` statement in the Query Analyzer, it works just like all the other `CREATE` statements we've done – it doesn't return any rows. It just lets us know that the view has been created:

```
The command(s) completed successfully.
```

Now switch to using the grid view to make it easy to see more than one result set. Then run a `SELECT` statement against your view – using it just as you would a table – and another against the `Customers` table directly:

```
SELECT * FROM CustomerPhoneList_vw

SELECT * FROM Customers
```

What you get back looks almost identical – indeed, in the columns that they have in common, the two result sets are identical. To clarify how SQL Server is looking at your query on the view, let's break it down logically a bit.

The `SELECT` statement in your view is defined as:

```
SELECT CustomerName, Contact, Phone
FROM Customers
```

So when you run:

```
SELECT * FROM CustomerPhoneList_vw
```

You are essentially saying to SQL Server:

"Give me all of the rows and columns you get when you run the statement `SELECT CustomerName, Contact, Phone FROM Customers`."

We've created something of a passthrough situation. What's nice about that is that we have reduced the complexity for the end user. In this day and age, where we have so many tools to make life easier for the user, this may not seem like all that big of deal – but to the user, it is.

> **Be aware that there is nothing special done for a view. The view runs just as if it were run from the command line – there is no pre-optimization of any kind. This means that you are adding one more layer of overhead between the request for data and the data being delivered. That means that a view is never going to run as fast as if you had just run the underlying `SELECT` statement directly.**

Let's go with another view that illustrates what we can do in terms of hiding sensitive data. For this example, let's go back to our `Employees` table in our `Accounting` database. Take a look at the table layout:

Employees
EmployeeID
FirstName
MiddleInitial
LastName
Title
SSN
Salary
HireDate
TerminationDate
ManagerEmpID
Department

Federal law protects some of this information – we must limit access to a "need to know" basis. Other columns though are free for anyone to see. What if we want to expose the unrestricted columns to a group of people, but don't want them to be able to see the general table structure or data? One solution would be to keep a separate table that includes only the columns that we need:

Employees
EmployeeID
FirstName
MiddleInitial
LastName
Title
HireDate
TerminationDate
ManagerEmpID
Department

While on the surface this would meet our needs, it is extremely problematic:

- We use disk space twice
- We have a synchronization problem if one table gets updated and the other doesn't
- We have double I/O operations (you have to read and write the data in two places instead of one) whenever we need to insert, update, or delete records

Views provide an easy and relatively elegant solution to this problem. By using a view, the data is only stored once (in the underlying table or tables) – eliminating all of the problems described above. Instead of building our completely separate table, we can just build a view that will function in a nearly identical fashion.

Our `Employees` table is currently empty. To add some records to it, load the `Chapter10.sql` file (supplied with the source code) into Query Analyzer and run it. Then add the following view to the `Accounting` database:

```
CREATE VIEW Employees_vw
AS
SELECT    EmployeeID,
          FirstName,
          MiddleInitial,
          LastName,
          Title,
          HireDate,
          TerminationDate,
          ManagerEmpID,
          Department
FROM Employees
```

We are now ready to let everyone have access – either directly or indirectly – to the data in the `Employees` table. Users who have the "need to know" can now be directed to the `Employees` table, but we continue to *deny* access to other users. Instead, the users who do not have that "need to know" can have access to our `Employees_vw` view. If they want to make use of it, they do it just the same as they would for a table:

```
SELECT *
FROM Employees_vw
```

This actually gets into one of the sticky areas of naming conventions. Because I've been using the _vw suffix, it's pretty easy to see that this is a view and not a table. Sometimes, you'd like to make things a little more hidden than that, so you might want to deliberately leave the _vw off. Doing so means that you have to use a different name (`Employees` is already the name of the base table), but you'd be surprised how many users won't know that there's a difference if you do it this way.

Views as Filters

This will probably be one of the shortest sections in the book. Why? Well, it doesn't get much simpler that this.

You've already seen how to create a simple view – you just use an easy `SELECT` statement. How do we filter the results of our queries? With a `WHERE` clause. Views are no different.

Let's take our `Employees_vw` view from the last section, and beef it up a bit by making it a list of only current employees. To do this, there are really only two changes that need to be made.

First, we have to filter out employees that no-longer work for the company. Would a current employee have a termination date? Probably not, so, if we limit our results to records with a NULL TerminationDate, then we've got what we're after.

The second change illustrates another simple point about views that work just like queries – the column(s) contained in the WHERE clause do not need to be included in the SELECT list. In this case, it doesn't make any sense to include the termination date in the result set as we're talking about current employees.

With these two things in mind, let's create a new view by changing our old view around just a little bit:

```
CREATE VIEW CurrentEmployees_vw
AS
SELECT    EmployeeID,
          FirstName,
          MiddleInitial,
          LastName,
          Title,
          HireDate,
          ManagerEmpID,
          Department
FROM Employees
WHERE TerminationDate IS NULL
```

In addition to the name change and the WHERE clause we've added, note that we've also eliminated the TerminationDate column from the SELECT list.

Let's test out how this works a little bit by running a straight SELECT statement against our Employees table and limiting our SELECT list to the things that we care about:

```
SELECT    EmployeeID,
          FirstName,
          LastName,
          TerminationDate
FROM Employees
```

This gets us back a few columns from all the rows in the entire table:

EmployeeID	FirstName	LastName	TerminationDate
1	Joe	Dokey	NULL
2	Peter	Principle	NULL
3	Steve	Smith	1997-01-31 00:00:00
4	Howard	Kilroy	NULL
5	Mary	Contrary	1998-06-15 00:00:00
6	Billy	Bob	NULL

(6 row(s) affected)

Now let's check out our view:

```
SELECT    EmployeeID,
          FirstName,
          LastName
FROM CurrentEmployees_vw
```

Our recordset has become a bit smaller:

```
EmployeeID  FirstName           LastName
----------  ------------------  ------------
1           Joe                 Dokey
2           Peter               Principle
4           Howard              Kilroy
6           Billy               Bob

(4 row(s) affected)
```

A few people are missing versus our first select – just the way we wanted it.

More Complex Views

Even though I use the term "complex" here – don't let that scare you. The toughest thing in views is still, for the most part, simpler than most other things in SQL.

What we're doing with more complex views is really just adding joins and summarization.

> *For those of you who will be applying this information to versions of SQL Server prior to 7.0, be aware that there is a limit to the number of joins that you can do. This might bring in the question of, "What has that to do with views?" Everything!*
>
> *As I've mentioned before, views are nothing more than stored queries. For versions prior to 7.0, your queries that are part of views (and all queries for that matter) are limited to 16 joins. It doesn't stop there though – when you do a query that makes use of views, the joins that happen inside the view also count toward your 16 table limit. That means that if you try to join 4 views that each join 5 tables, you're at 20 joins, and you're over the limit. Version 7.0 does not have this limit.*
>
> *You can get around this limit by performing multiple queries and creating temporary working tables that summarize some of the joins in your query. In the end, you join the working tables for a final result.*

Perhaps one of the most common uses of views is to flatten data – that is, the removal of complexity that we outlined at the beginning of the chapter. Imagine that we are providing a view for management to make it easier to check on sales information. No offense to managers who are reading this book, but managers that write their own complex queries are still a rather rare breed – even in the information age.

For an example, let's briefly go back to using the `Northwind` database. Our manager would like to be able to do simple queries that will tell him (or her) what orders have been placed for what parts and who placed them. So, we create a view that they can perform very simple queries on – remember that we are creating this one in `Northwind`:

```
CREATE VIEW CustomerOrders_vw
AS
SELECT    cu.CompanyName,
          o.OrderDate,
          od.ProductID,
```

```
        p.ProductName,
        od.Quantity,
        od.UnitPrice,
        od.Quantity * od.UnitPrice AS ExtendedPrice
FROM    Customers AS cu
INNER JOIN   Orders AS o
      ON cu.CustomerID = o.CustomerID
INNER JOIN   [Order Details] AS od
      ON o.OrderID = od.OrderID
INNER JOIN   Products AS p
      ON od.ProductID = p.ProductID
```

Now do a SELECT:

```
SELECT *
FROM CustomerOrders_vw
```

You wind up with a bunch of rows – over 2000 – but you also wind up with information that is far simpler for the average manager to comprehend and sort out. What's more, with not that much training, the manager (or whichever user) can get right to the heart of what they are looking for:

```
SELECT CompanyName, ExtendedPrice
FROM CustomerOrders_vw
WHERE OrderDate = '9/3/1996'
```

The user didn't need to know how to do a four-table join – that was hidden in the view. Instead, they only need limited skill (and limited imagination for that matter) in order to get the job done.

```
CompanyName                       ExtendedPrice
--------------------------------  ------------------
LILA-Supermercado                 201.6000
LILA-Supermercado                 417.0000
LILA-Supermercado                 432.0000

(3 row(s) affected)
```

However, we could make our query even more targeted. Let's say that we only want our view to return yesterday's sales. We'll make only slight changes to our query:

```
CREATE VIEW YesterdaysOrders_vw
AS
SELECT  cu.CompanyName,
        o.OrderID,
        o.OrderDate,
        od.ProductID,
        p.ProductName,
        od.Quantity,
        od.UnitPrice,
        od.Quantity * od.UnitPrice AS ExtendedPrice
FROM    Customers AS cu
INNER JOIN   Orders AS o
      ON cu.CustomerID = o.CustomerID
INNER JOIN   [Order Details] AS od
      ON o.OrderID = od.OrderID
INNER JOIN   Products AS p
      ON od.ProductID = p.ProductID
WHERE CONVERT(varchar(12),o.OrderDate,101) =
      CONVERT(varchar(12),DATEADD(day,-1,GETDATE()),101)
```

All the dates in the Northwind database are old enough that this view wouldn't return any data, so let's add a record to test it. Execute the following script all at one time:

```
USE Northwind

DECLARE @Ident int

INSERT INTO Orders
(CustomerID,OrderDate)
VALUES
('ALFKI', DATEADD(day,-1,GETDATE()))

SELECT @Ident = @@IDENTITY

INSERT INTO [Order Details]
(OrderID, ProductID, UnitPrice, Quantity)
VALUES
(@Ident, 1, 50, 25)

SELECT 'The OrderID of the INSERTed row is ' + CONVERT(varchar(8),@Ident)
```

I'll be explaining all of what is going on here in our chapter on scripts and batches. For now, just trust me that you'll need to run all of this in order for us to have a value in Northwind that will come up for our view. You should see a result from the Query Analyzer that looks something like this:

```
(1 row(s) affected)


(1 row(s) affected)


------------------------------------------
The OrderID of the INSERTed row is 11082

(1 row(s) affected)
```

The OrderID might vary, but the rest should hold pretty true.

Now let's run a query against our view and see what we get:

```
SELECT CompanyName, OrderID, OrderDate FROM YesterdaysOrders_vw
```

In my case, I've actually added two rows, but you can see that the 11082 does indeed show up:

```
CompanyName          OrderID          OrderDate
--------------------------------------------------------------------------------
Alfreds Futterkiste  11081            1999-05-28 16:04:00.657
Alfreds Futterkiste  11082            1999-05-28 16:04:36.677

(2 row(s) affected)
```

> **Don't get stuck on the notion that your OrderID numbers are going to be the same as mine – these are set by the system (since OrderID is an identity column), and are dependent on just how many records have already been inserted into the table. As such, your numbers will vary.**

The DATEADD and CONVERT Functions

The join, while larger than most of the ones we've done this far, is still pretty straightforward. We keep adding tables, joining a column in each new table to a matching column in the tables that we've already named. As always, note that the columns do not have to have the same name – they just have to have data that relates to one another.

Since this was a relatively complex one, let's take a look at what we are doing in the query that supports this view.

The `WHERE` clause is where things get interesting. It's a single comparison, but we have several functions that are used to come up with our result.

It would be very tempting to just compare the `OrderDate` in the `Orders` table to `GETDATE()` (today's date) minus one day – the subtraction operation is what the `DATEADD` function is all about. `DATEADD` can add (you subtract by using negative numbers) any amount of time you want to deal with. You just tell it what date you want to operate on, what unit of time you want to add to it (days, weeks, years, minutes, etc.). On the surface, you should just be able to grab today's date with `GETDATE()` and then use `DATEADD` to subtract one day. The problem is that `GETDATE()` includes the current time of day, so we would only get back rows from the previous day that happened at the same time of day down to a one-thousandth of a second – not a likely match. So we took things one more step and used the `CONVERT` function to equalize the dates on both sides of the equation to the same time-of-day-less format before comparison. Therefore, the view will show any sale that happened any time on the previous date.

Using a View to Change Data

As we've said before, a view works *mostly* like a table does from an in-use perspective (obviously, creating them works quite a bit differently). Now we're going to come across some differences though.

It's surprising to many, but you can run `INSERT`, `UPDATE`, and `DELETE` statements against a view successfully. There are several things, however, that you need to keep in mind when changing data through a view:

- ❑ If the view contains a join, you won't be able to `INSERT`, `UPDATE` or `DELETE` the data (there are circumstances where you will be able to update records if only one of the base tables is being modified, but inserting into views can lead to problems)
- ❑ When inserting data, all the required fields in the table must be exposed in the view or have defaults
- ❑ You can, to a limited extent, restrict what is and isn't inserted or updated in a view

No Changing Joined Data

If the view has more than one table, then using a view to modify data is out – sort of anyway (more on this in a moment). Since it creates some ambiguities in the key arrangements, Microsoft has decided to just lock you out when there are multiple tables. (Personally, I don't agree with this, but they didn't ask me what I thought, so...) Now, what did I mean by "sort of..."? Well, technically you can't use a view to update data when you have multiple tables in the underlying query. The instance that keeps this from being completely true is if you open a view in the Enterprise Manager. It seems that SQL Server bypasses the view in EM when doing updates and, instead, goes directly to the tables. This "going directly to the table" business creates some problems (also known as bugs) when using the `WITH CHECK` option that we'll be discussing in the next section.

Required Fields Must Appear in the View or Have Default Value

If you are using a view to insert data (must be a single table SELECT in the underlying query), then you must be able to supply some value for all required (doesn't allow NULLs) fields. Note that by "supply some value" I don't mean that it has to be in the SELECT list – a default covers the bill rather nicely. Just be aware that any columns that do not have defaults and do not accept NULL values will need to appear in the view in order to perform INSERTs through the view.

Limit What's Inserted into Views – WITH CHECK OPTION

The WITH CHECK OPTION is one of those lesser to almost completely unknown features in SQL Server. The rules are simple – in order to update or insert data using the view, the resulting row must qualify to appear in the view results. Restated, the inserted or updated row must meet any WHERE criterion that's used in the SELECT statement that underlies your view.

To illustrate this, let's continue working with the Northwind database, and create a view to show only Oregon shippers. We only have limited fields to work with in our Shippers table, so we're going to have to make use of the Area Code in order to figure out where the shipper is from (make sure that you use Northwind):

```
CREATE VIEW OregonShippers_vw
AS
SELECT   ShipperID,
         CompanyName,
         Phone
FROM     Shippers
WHERE Phone LIKE '(503)%'
WITH CHECK OPTION
```

Run a SELECT * against this view, and, as it happens, you return all the rows in the table (because all the rows in the table meet the criteria):

```
ShipperID      CompanyName                    Phone
-------------- ------------------------------ --------------------
1              Speedy Express                 (503) 555-9831
2              United Package                 (503) 555-3199
3              Federal Shipping               (503) 555-9931

(3 row(s) affected)
```

Now try to update one of the rows using the view – set the phone value to have anything other than a value starting with (503):

```
UPDATE OregonShippers_vw
SET Phone = '(333) 555 9831'
WHERE ShipperID = 1
```

SQL Server promptly tells you that you are a scoundrel, and that you should be burned at the stake for your actions – well, not really, but it does make its point...

```
Server: Msg 550, Level 16, State 1, Line 1
The attempted insert or update failed because the target view either specifies WITH CHECK
OPTION or spans a view that specifies WITH CHECK OPTION and one or more rows resulting
from the operation did not qualify under the CHECK OPTION constraint.
The statement has been terminated.
```

Sort of reminds one of an old Arnold Schwarzenegger flick – doesn't it? Since our update wouldn't meet the WHERE clause criteria, it is thrown out; however, if we insert the row right into the base table:

```
UPDATE Shippers
SET Phone = '(333) 555 9831'
WHERE ShipperID = 1
```

SQL Server is a lot more friendly:

(1 row(s) affected)

The restriction applies only to the view – not to the underlying table. This can actually be quite handy in a rare circumstance or two. Imagine a situation where you want to allow some users to insert or update data in a table, but only when the updated or inserted data meets certain criteria. We could easily deal with this restriction by adding a CHECK constraint to our underlying table – but this might not always be an ideal solution.

Imagine now that we've added a second requirement – we still want other users to be able to INSERT data into the table without meeting this criterion. Uh oh, the CHECK constraint will not discriminate between users. By using a view together with a WITH CHECK OPTION, we can point the restricted users to the view, and let the unrestricted users make use of the base table or a view that has no such restriction.

Just for confirmation – this works on an INSERT too. Run an INSERT that violates the WHERE clause:

```
INSERT INTO OregonShippers_vw
VALUES
('My Freight Inc.', '(555) 555-5555')
```

And you see your old friend, the "terminator" error, exactly as before:

Server: Msg 550, Level 16, State 1, Line 1
The attempted insert or update failed because the target view either specifies WITH CHECK OPTION or spans a view that specifies WITH CHECK OPTION and one or more rows resulting from the operation did not qualify under the CHECK OPTION constraint.
The statement has been terminated.

A student in one of my SQL Server courses discovered a bug in Release Candidate 1 that still existed in the released product. The issue is only with editing and inserting of data through views while using Enterprise Manager.

Despite the fact that you open the view, EM still does its inserts and updates directly to the underlying table. This means that the `WITH CHECK OPTION` is bypassed when using EM to edit data through a view. Perhaps an even bigger issue with this use of the underlying table instead of the actual view is that if the user does not have rights to update or insert into the underlying table, then any editing through EM will fail – even if they have the proper rights to the view.

The bug has been reported and acknowledged, but I have no idea when it will be fixed – test your release before you depend on this feature in EM.

Editing Views with T-SQL

The main thing to remember when you edit views with T-SQL is that you are completely replacing the existing view. The only differences between using the `ALTER VIEW` statement and the `CREATE VIEW` statement are:

- `ALTER VIEW` expects to find an existing view, where `CREATE` doesn't
- `ALTER VIEW` retains any permissions that have been established for the view

The latter of these two is the biggy. If you perform a `DROP`, and then use a `CREATE`, you have *almost* the same effect as using an `ALTER VIEW` statement. The problem is that you will need to entirely re-establish your permissions on who can and can't use the view.

Dropping Views

It doesn't get much easier than this:

```
DROP VIEW <view name>
```

And it's gone.

Creating and Editing Views in EM

For people that really don't know what they are doing, this has to be a rather cool feature in EM. Building views is a snap, and you really don't have to know all that much about queries in order to get it done.

To take a look at this; fire up EM, open up the Northwind database sub-node of the Databases node and click on Views:

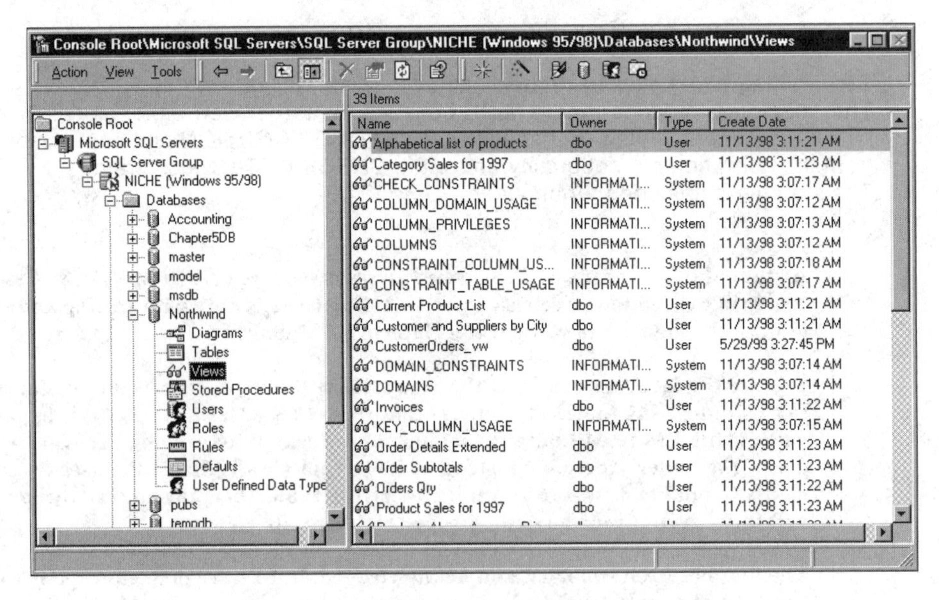

Now right-click on Views and select New View...:

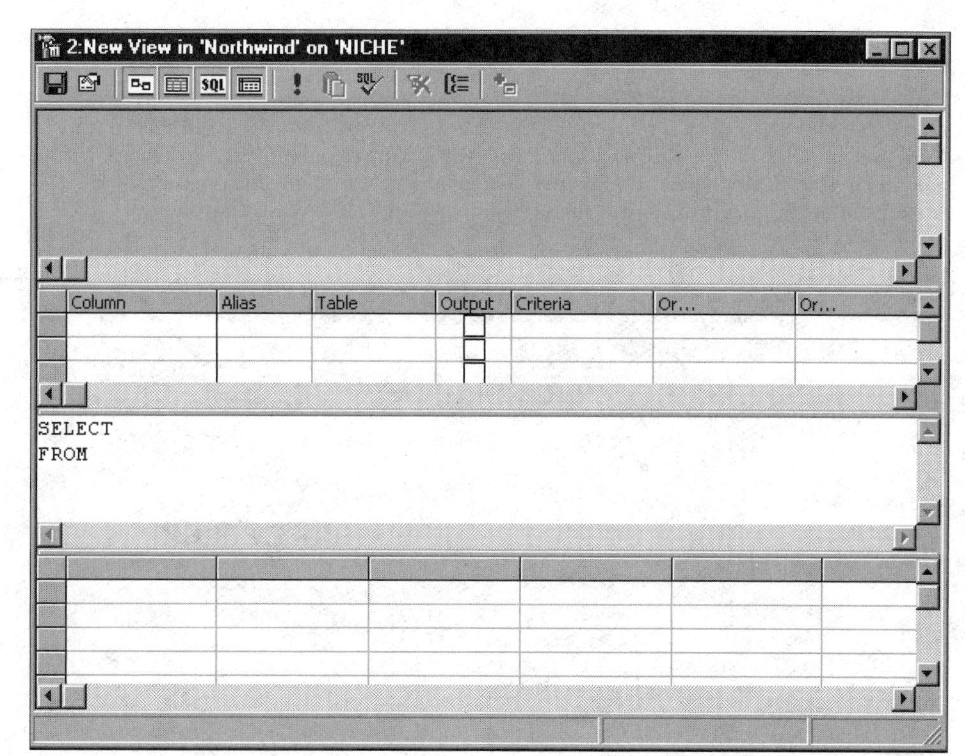

This new View Builder is part of the da Vinci tools that are now part of SQL Server. There are four panes – each of which can be independently turned on or off:

- The Diagram pane
- The Grid pane
- The SQL pane
- The Results pane

For those of you who have worked with Access at all, the Diagram pane works much as it does in Access queries. You can add and remove tables, and even define relationships. Each of those added tables, checked columns, and defined relationships will automatically be reflected in the SQL pane in the form of the SQL required to match the diagram. To identify each of the icons on the toolbar, just hover your mouse over them for a moment or two, and you will get a Tooltip that indicates the purpose of each button.

For demonstration purposes, add the `Customers`, `Orders`, `Order Details`, and `Products` tables.

> **You can add tables by either right-clicking in the Diagram pane (the top one in the picture above) or by clicking on the Add table toolbar button (the rightmost one). Note that, in order to be able to add a table, the Diagram pane must be the active pane. If in doubt, just click your mouse somewhere inside the Diagram pane – the Add table toolbar button should then become enabled (if it wasn't already).**

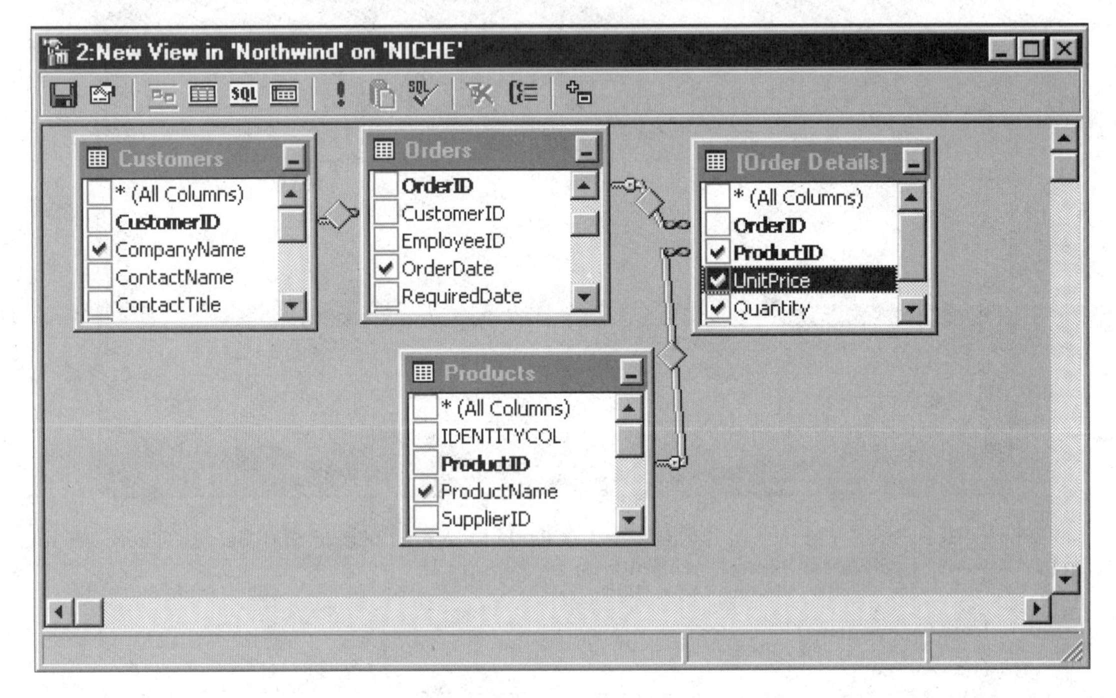

Note that I turned off the Grid, SQL, and Results panes to save space here. I then went through and checked the boxes for the columns that I wanted to include. If I had the Grid pane up, then you would have seen each column appear in the Grid pane as I selected it. With the SQL pane up, you would have also seen it appear in the SQL code.

In case you haven't recognized it yet, we're building the same view that we built as our first complex view (`CustomerOrders_vw`). The only thing that's tricky at all is the computed column (`ExtendedPrice`). To do that one, either we have to manually type the equation into the SQL pane, or we can type it into the **Column** column in the Grid pane along with its alias:

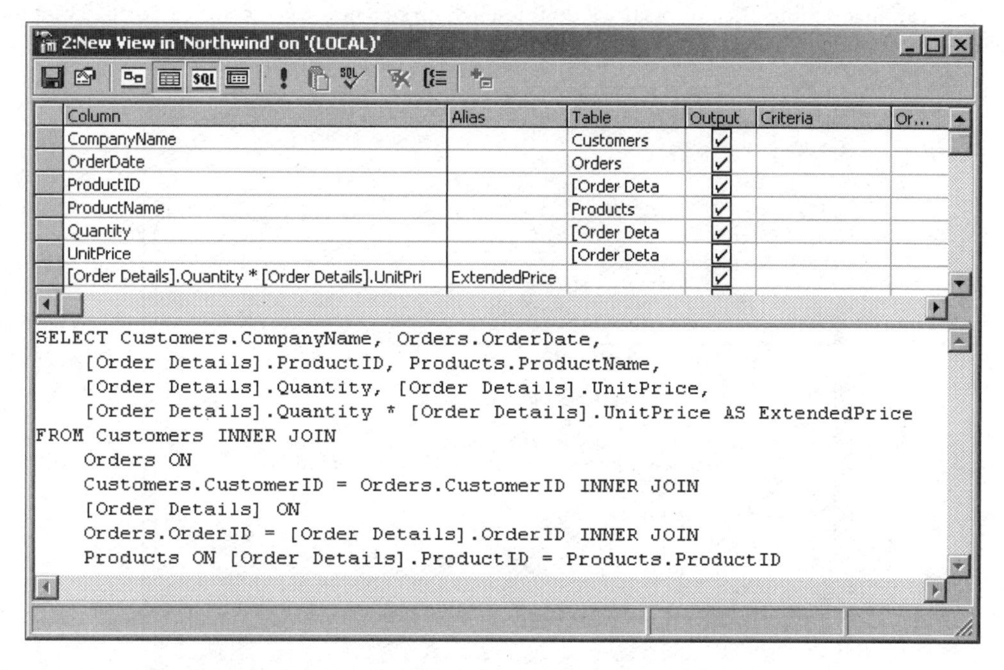

When all is said and done, the view builder gives us the following SQL code:

```
SELECT Customers.CompanyName, Orders.OrderDate,
    [Order Details].ProductID, Products.ProductName,
    [Order Details].Quantity, [Order Details].UnitPrice,
    [Order Details].Quantity * [Order Details].UnitPrice AS ExtendedPrice
FROM Customers INNER JOIN
    Orders ON
    Customers.CustomerID = Orders.CustomerID INNER JOIN
    [Order Details] ON
    Orders.OrderID = [Order Details].OrderID INNER JOIN
    Products ON
    [Order Details].ProductID = Products.ProductID
```

While it's not formatted the same, if you look it over, you'll find that it's basically the same code we wrote by hand!

> **If you've been struggling with learning your T-SQL query syntax, you can use this tool to play around with the syntax of a query. Just drag and drop some tables into the Diagram pane, select the column you want from each table, and, for the most part, SQL Server will build you a query – you can then use the syntax from the view builder to learn how to build it yourself next time.**

Now go ahead and save it as `CustomerOrders2_vw` and close the view builder.

Editing Views in EM

To edit a view, we have a couple of choices.

First, we can just double-click on it. If we double-click on our new `CustomerOrders2_vw` view, we'll get something a little different from what we might expect at this point:

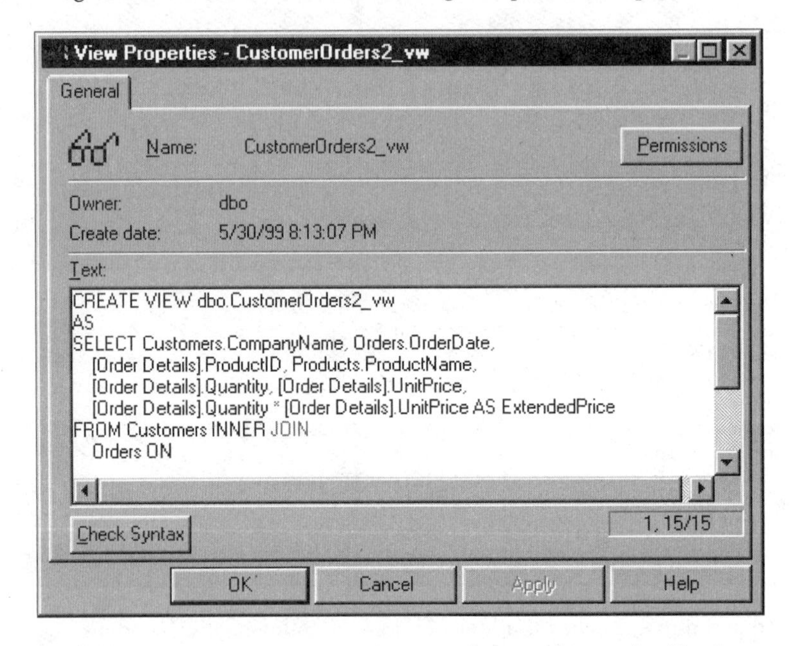

We're back to straight code. From a user interface standpoint, this stinks. Not because we're back to code, but that we have an inconsistent interface. Oh well, again – they didn't consult with me first....

You can edit the code as you see fit, then just click OK or Apply in order to make the change.

Your other option is probably going to be a bit more appealing – it's back to the editor we used the first time around. To use this, just right-click on your view and choose Design View. You'll be greeted with the same friendly query designer that we used to create our query.

Auditing: Displaying Existing Code

What do you do when you have a view, but you're not sure what it does? The first option should be easy at this point – just go into EM like you're going to edit the view. Go to the Views sub-node and double-click. You'll see the code behind the view complete with color-coding.

Unfortunately, we don't always have the option of having EM around to hold our hand through this stuff. The bright side is that we have two ways of getting at the actual view definition:

- `sp_helptext`
- The `syscomments` system table

Using sp_helptext is highly preferable, as when new releases come out, it will automatically be updated for changes to the system tables.

Let's run sp_helptext against one of the supplied views in the Northwind database – Alphabetical List of Products:

```
EXEC sp_helptext "Alphabetical List of Products"
```

SQL Server obliges us with the code for the view:

```
Text
-----------------------------------------------------------
create view "Alphabetical list of products" AS
SELECT Products.*, Categories.CategoryName
FROM Categories INNER JOIN Products ON
Categories.CategoryID = Products.CategoryID
WHERE (((Products.Discontinued)=0))
```

I must admit to finding this one of the more peculiar examples that Microsoft supplies – I attribute it to this database being migrated from Access. Why? Well, the one seemingly simple thing that we *cannot* do in views is use an ORDER BY clause. Microsoft say this view is in alphabetical order, but there is no guarantee of that. Indeed, if you run the query, odds are it won't come out in alphabetical order!

Note that the restriction on using the ORDER BY clause only applies to the code within the view. Once the view is created, you can still use an ORDER BY clause when you reference the view in a query.

Now let's try it the other way – using syscomments. Beyond the compatibility issues with using system tables, using syscomments (and most other system tables for that matter) comes with the extra added hassle of everything being coded in object IDs.

Object IDs are SQL Server's internal way of keeping track of things. They are integer values rather than the names that you're used to for your objects.

Fortunately, you can get around this by joining to the sysobjects table:

```
SELECT sc.text FROM syscomments sc
JOIN sysobjects so
   ON sc.id = so.id
WHERE so.name = 'Alphabetical list of products'
```

Again, you get the same exact block of code (indeed, all `sp_helptext` does is run what amounts to this same query):

```
Text
----------------------------------------------------------------
create view "Alphabetical list of products" AS
SELECT Products.*, Categories.CategoryName
FROM Categories INNER JOIN Products
ON Categories.CategoryID = Products.CategoryID
WHERE (((Products.Discontinued)=0))

(1 row(s) affected)
```

I can't stress enough my recommendation that you avoid the system tables where possible – but I do like you to know your options.

Protecting Code: Encrypting Views

If you're building any kind of commercial software product, odds are you're interested in protecting your source code. Views are the first place we see the opportunity to do just that.

All you have to do to encrypt your view is use the `WITH ENCRYPTION` option. This one has a couple of tricks to it if you're used to the `WITH CHECK OPTION` clause:

- `WITH ENCRYPTION` goes after the name of the view, but *before* the `AS` keyword
- `WITH ENCRYPTION` does not use the `OPTION` keyword

In addition, remember that if you use an `ALTER VIEW` statement, you are entirely replacing the existing view except for access rights. This means that the encryption is also replaced. If you want the altered view to be encrypted, then you must use the `WITH ENCRYPTION` clause in the `ALTER VIEW` statement.

Let's do an `ALTER VIEW` on our `CustomerOrders_vw` view that we created in `Northwind`. If you haven't yet created the `CustomerOrders_vw` view, then just change the `ALTER` to `CREATE` (don't forget to run this against `Northwind`):

```
ALTER VIEW CustomerOrders_vw
WITH ENCRYPTION
AS
SELECT    cu.CompanyName,
          o.OrderDate,
          od.ProductID,
          p.ProductName,
          od.Quantity,
          od.UnitPrice,
          od.Quantity * od.UnitPrice AS ExtendedPrice
FROM      Customers AS cu
INNER JOIN    Orders AS o
      ON cu.CustomerID = o.CustomerID
INNER JOIN    [Order Details] AS od
      ON o.OrderID = od.OrderID
INNER JOIN    Products AS p
      ON od.ProductID = p.ProductID
```

Now do an sp_helptext on our CustomerOrders_vw:

```
EXEC sp_helptext CustomerOrders_vw
```

SQL Server promptly tells us that it can't do what we're asking:

```
The object comments have been encrypted.
```

The heck you say, and promptly go to the syscomments table:

```
SELECT sc.text FROM syscomments sc
JOIN sysobjects so
  ON sc.id = so.id
WHERE so.name = 'CustomerOrders_vw'
```

But that doesn't get you very far either:

```
text
----------------------------------------------------------------------------------------------------
????????????????????????????????????u??????????????????????u??????

(1 row(s) affected)
```

Note that I've chopped off the right hand side of this for brevity's sake, but I think you get the point – the data is pretty useless.

In short – your code is safe and sound. Even if you pull it up in EM you'll find it useless.

> **Make sure you store your source code somewhere before using the `WITH ENCRYPTION` option. Once it's been encrypted, there is no way to get it back. If you haven't stored your code away somewhere and you need to change it, then you're going to be re-writing it from scratch.**

Summary

Views tend to be either the most over or most under-used tools in most of the databases I've seen. Some people like to use them to abstract seemingly everything (often forgetting that they are adding another layer to the process when they do this). Others just seem to forget that views are even an option. Personally, like most things, I think you should use it when it's the right tool to use – not before, not after. Things to remember with views include:

- Stay away from building views based on views – instead, adapt the appropriate query information from the first view into your new view.
- Remember that a view using the `WITH CHECK OPTION` provides some flexibility that can't be duplicated with a normal `CHECK` constraint.
- Encrypt views when you don't want others to be able to see your source code – either for commercial product or general security reasons.
- Prior to 7.0, there was a 16 table join limit – any query that includes views needs to include the tables within those views as being part of the table count.
- Using an `ALTER VIEW` completely replaces the existing view other than permissions. This means you must include the `WITH ENCRYPTION` and `WITH CHECK OPTION` clauses in the `ALTER` statement if you want encryption and restrictions to be in effect in the altered view.
- Use `sp_helptext` to display the supporting code for a view – avoid using the system tables.
- Minimize the user of views for production queries – they add additional overhead and hurt performance.

Common uses for views include:

- Filtering rows
- Protecting sensitive data
- Reducing database complexity
- Abstracting multiple physical databases into one logical database

In our next chapter, we'll take a look at batches and scripting. We got a brief taste of it when you ran the `INSERT` script in this chapter to insert a record into the `Orders` table, and then use information from the freshly inserted record in an insert into the `Order Details` table. Batches and scripting will lead us right into stored procedures – the closest thing that SQL Server has to its own programs.

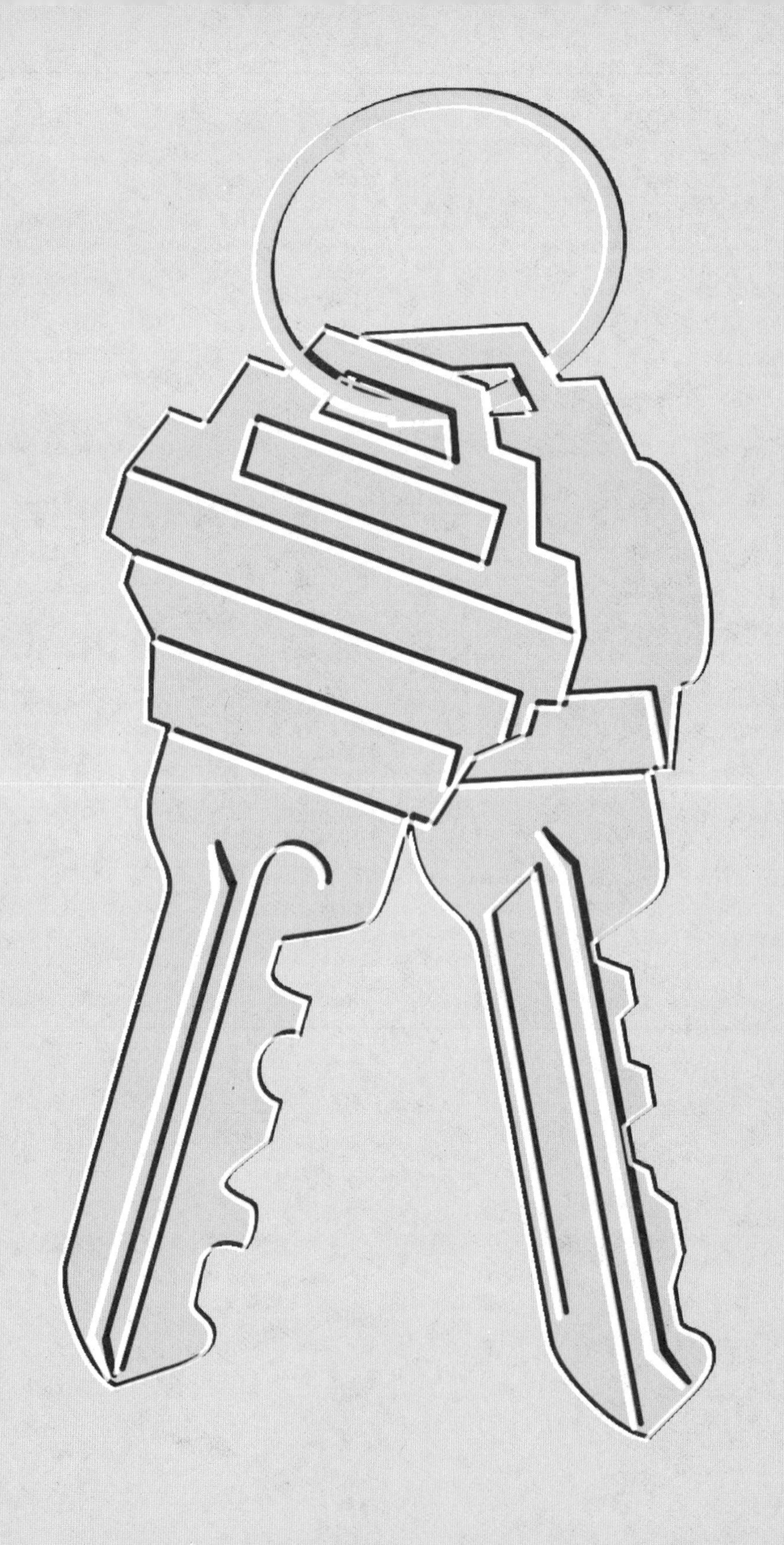

11

Writing Scripts & Batches

Whether you've realized it or not, you've already been writing SQL **scripts**. Every CREATE statement that you write, every ALTER, every SELECT is all (if you're running a single statement) or part (multiple statements) of a script. It's hard to get excited though over a script with one line in it – could you imagine Hamlet's, "To be, or not to be…?" if it had never had the following lines – we wouldn't have any context for what the heck he was talking about.

SQL scripts are much the same way. Things get quite a bit more interesting when we string several commands together into a longer script – a full play or at least an act to finish our Shakespeare analogy.

Scripts are generally stored with a unified goal. That is, all the commands that are in the script are usually building up to one overall purpose. Examples include scripts to build a database (this might be used for a system installation), system maintenance (backups, Database Consistency Checker utilities (DBCCs)) – anything where several commands are usually run together.

We will be looking into scripts during this chapter, and adding in the notion of **batches** – which control how SQL Server groups your commands together. In addition, we will take a look at **OSQL** – the command line utility, and how it relates to scripts.

Script Basics

A script technically isn't a script until you store it in a file where it can be pulled up and re-used. SQL scripts are stored as text files and, prior to 7.0, many of the people I knew actually wrote their scripts in Notepad rather than the ISQL/W utility. The case against that now is pretty high given that the new ISQL/W (now called the Query Analyzer, but still `isqlw.exe` on the executable) has so many things to help you edit your code. Color-coding, parse without executing, graphical query plan display – these are just a few of the things that were either added to this version, or have been made easier to use. If you do elect not to use the Query Analyzer, then you might take a look at the increasing number of SQL editing tools that are available. Some of these give you something just short of a fully-fledged programming environment similar to what you would see in Visual Basic or Visual C++.

Scripts are usually treated as a unit. That is, you are normally executing the entire script or nothing at all. They can make use of both global and local variables. As an example, let's look at the script that we used to `INSERT order` records in our chapter on views:

```
USE Northwind

DECLARE @Ident int

INSERT INTO Orders
(CustomerID,OrderDate)
VALUES
('ALFKI', DATEADD(day,-1,GETDATE()))

SELECT @Ident = @@IDENTITY

INSERT INTO [Order Details]
(OrderID, ProductID, UnitPrice, Quantity)
VALUES
(@Ident, 1, 50, 25)

SELECT 'The OrderID of the INSERTed row is ' + CONVERT(varchar(8),@Ident)
```

We have six distinct commands working here covering a range of different things that we might do in a script. We're using both global and local variables, the `USE` statement, `INSERT` statements, and both assignment and regular versions of the `SELECT` statement.

The USE Statement

The `USE` statement sets the current database. This affects any place that we are making use of default values for the database portion of our fully qualified object name. In this particular example, we have not indicated what database the tables in our `INSERT` or `SELECT` statements are from, but, since we've included a `USE` statement prior to our `INSERT` and `SELECT` statements, they will use that database (in this case, `Northwind`). Without our `USE` statement, we would be at the mercy of whoever executes the script to make certain that the correct database was current when the script was executed.

Don't take this as meaning that you should always include a `USE` statement in your script – it depends on what the purpose of the script is. If your intent is to have a general-purpose script, then leaving out the `USE` statement might actually be helpful.

Usually, if you are naming database-specific tables in your script (that is, non-system tables), then you want to use the `USE` command. I also find it very helpful if the script is meant to modify a specific database – I can't tell you how many times I've accidentally created a large number of tables in the `master` database that were intended for a user database.

Next up we have a `DECLARE` statement to declare a variable. We've talked about `DECLARE` statements briefly before, but let's expand on this some.

Declaring Variables

The `DECLARE` statement has a pretty simple syntax:

```
DECLARE @<variable name> <variable type>[,
        @<variable name> <variable type>[,
        @<variable name> <variable type>]]
```

You can declare just one variable at a time, or several. It's not at all uncommon to see people re-use the `DECLARE` statement with each variable they declare, rather than using the comma separated method. It's up to you, but no matter which method you choose, the value of your variable will always be `NULL` until you explicitly set it to some other value.

In our case, we've declared a local variable called `@ident` as an integer. Technically, we could have got away without declaring this variable – instead, we could have chosen to just use `@@IDENTITY` directly. `@@IDENTITY` is a **global** variable. It is always available, and supplies the last identity value that was assigned in the current connection. As with most global variables, you should make a habit of explicitly moving the value in `@@IDENTITY` to a local variable. That way, you're sure that it won't get changed accidentally. There was no danger of that in this case, but, as always, be consistent.

I like to move a value I'm taking from a global into my own variable. That way I can use the value and know that it's only being changed when I change it. With the global variable itself, you sometimes can't be certain when it's going to change because most global variables are not set by you, but by the system. That creates a situation where it would be very easy to have the system change a value at a time you weren't expecting it, and wind up with the most dreaded of all computer terms: unpredictable results.

Setting the Value in Your Variables

Well, we now know how to declare our variables, but the question that follows is, "How do we change their value?" There are currently two ways to set the value in a variable. You can use a SELECT statement or a SET statement. Functionally, they work almost the same, except that a SELECT statement has the power to have the source value come from a column within your SELECT statement.

So why have two ways of doing this? Actually, I don't know (though I'm sure some reader out there will find out and send me the answer), but there are some differences in the way they are typically put to use.

Setting Variables Using SET

SET is usually used for setting variables in the fashion that you would see in more procedural languages. Examples of typical uses would be:

```
SET @TotalCost = 10
SET @TotalCost = @UnitCost * 1.1
```

Notice that these are all straight assignments that use either explicit values or another variable. With a SET, you cannot assign a value to a variable from right within the query – you have to separate the query from the SET. For example:

```
USE Northwind

DECLARE @Test money

SET @Test = MAX(UnitPrice) FROM [Order Details]
SELECT @Test
```

Causes an error, but:

```
USE Northwind

DECLARE @Test money

SET @Test = (SELECT MAX(UnitPrice) FROM [Order Details])
SELECT @Test
```

Works just fine.

Although this later syntax works, by convention, code is never implemented this way. Again, I don't know for sure why it's "just not done that way", but I suspect that it has to do with readability – you want a SELECT statement to be related to retrieving table data, and a SET to be about simple variable assignments.

Setting Variables Using SELECT

SELECT is usually used to assign variable values when the source of the information you're storing in the variable is from a query. For example, our last illustration above would be far more typically done using a SELECT:

```
USE Northwind

DECLARE @Test money

SELECT @Test = MAX(UnitPrice) FROM [Order Details]
SELECT @Test
```

Notice that this is a little cleaner (it takes less verbiage to do the same thing).

So again, the convention on when to use which goes like this:

- Use SET when you are performing a simple assignment of a variable – where your value is already known in the form of an explicit value or some other variable.
- Use SELECT when you are basing the assignment of your variable on a query.

I'm not going to pick any bones about the fact that you'll see me violate this last convention in many places in this book. Using SET for variable assignment is a new thing (you couldn't do it before), and I must admit that I haven't completely adapted yet. Nonetheless, this seems to be something that's really being pushed by Microsoft and the SQL Server community, so I strongly recommend that you start out on the right foot and adhere to the convention.

Reviewing Global Variables

There are over 30 global variables (also called "parameterless system functions") available. Some of the ones you should be most concerned with are in the table that follows.

Variable	Purpose	Gotchas
@@CURSOR_ROWS	How many rows are currently in the last cursor set opened on the current connection.	SQL Server 7 can populate cursors asynchronously. Be aware that the value in this variable may change if the cursor is still in the process of being populated.
@@DATEFIRST	Returns what is currently set as the first day of the week (say, Sunday vs Monday).	Is a system wide setting – if someone changes the setting, you may not get the result you expect.
@@DBTS	Returns the last used timestamp for the current database.	The value changes based on any change in the database, not just the table you're working on. The value is more of a true global than is @@IDENTITY – *any* timestamp change in the database is reflected, not just those for the current connection.

Table Continued on Following Page

Variable	Purpose	Gotchas
@@ERROR	Returns the error number of the last T-SQL statement executed on the current connection. Returns 0 if no error.	Is reset with each new statement. If you need the value preserved, move it to a local variable immediately after the execution of the statement for which you want to preserve the error code.
@@FETCH_STATUS	Used in conjunction with a FETCH statement.	Returns 0 for valid fetch, -1 for beyond end of cursor set, -2 for a missing (deleted) row. Typical gotcha is to assume that any non-zero value means you are at the end of the cursor – a –2 may just mean only one missing record.
@@IDENTITY	Returns the last identity value inserted as a result of the last INSERT or SELECT INTO statement.	Is set to NULL if no identity value was generated. This is true even if the lack of an identity value was due to a failure of the statement to run. If multiple inserts are performed by just one statement, then only the last identity value is returned.
@@LANGID and @@LANGUAGE	Returns the language or the ID of the language currently in use.	Handy for localization situations.
@@LOCK_TIMEOUT	Returns the current amount of time in milliseconds before the system will time-out waiting on a blocked resource.	Connection default is system default, but unless you manually set it, the value returned is –1. Use SET LOCK_TIMEOUT if you want to change it for the current connection.
@@NESTLEVEL	Returns the current nesting level for nested stored procedures.	Returns 1 for non-nested stored procedures, and a higher number for each additional nesting level. You cannot nest beyond 32 levels.
@@OPTIONS	Returns information about options that have been set using the SET command.	Since you only get one value back, but can have many options set, SQL Server uses binary flags to indicate what values are set. In order to test whether the option you are interested is set, you must use the option value together with a bitwise operator.

Variable	Purpose	Gotchas
@@REMSERVER	Used only in stored procedures. Returns the value of the server that called the stored procedure.	Handy when you want the sproc to behave differently depending on the remote server (often a geographic location) from which the sproc was called.
@@ROWCOUNT	One of the most used globals. Returns the number of rows effected by the last statement.	Commonly used in non run-time error checking. For example, if you go to DELETE a row using a WHERE clause, and no rows are effected, then that would imply that something unexpected happened. You can then raise an error manually.
@@SERVERNAME	Returns the name of the local server that the script is running from.	Can be changed by using sp_addserver and then restarting SQL Server, but rarely required.
@@TRANCOUNT	Returns the number of active transactions – essentially the transaction nesting level – for the current connection.	A ROLLBACK TRAN statement decrements @@TRANCOUNT to 0 unless you are using savepoints. BEGIN TRAN increments @@TRANCOUNT by 1, COMMIT TRAN decrements @@TRANCOUNT by 1.
@@VERSION	Returns the current version of SQL Server as well as the date, processor and OS architecture.	Unfortunately, this doesn't return in the information into any kind of structured field arrangement, so you have to parse it if you want to use it to test for specific information.

Don't worry if you don't recognize some of the terms in a few of these. They will become clear in due time, and you will have this table to look back on for reference at a later date. The thing to remember is that there are sources you can go to in order to find out a whole host of information about the current state of your system and your activities.

Using @@IDENTITY

@@IDENTITY is one of the most important of all the global variables. Remember when we saw identity values all the way back in Chapter 6? An identity column is one where we don't supply a value, and SQL Server inserts a numbered value automatically.

In our example case, we obtain the value of @@IDENTITY right after performing an insert into the Orders table. The issue is that we don't supply the key value for that table – it's automatically created as we do the insert. Now we want to insert a record into the Order Details table, but we need to know the value of the primary key in the associated record in the Orders table (remember, there is a foreign key constraint on the Order Details table that references the Orders table). Since SQL Server generated that value instead of us supplying it, we need to have a way to retrieve that value for use in our dependent inserts later on in the script. @@IDENTITY gives us that automatically generated value since it was the last statement run.

In the case of our example, we could have easily gotten away with not moving @@IDENTITY to a local variable – we could have just referenced it explicitly in our next INSERT query. I make a habit of always moving it to a local variable though to avoid errors on the occasions that I do need to keep a copy. An example of this kind of situation would be if we had yet another INSERT that was dependent on the identity value from the INSERT into the Orders table. If I hadn't moved it into a local variable, then it would be lost when I did the next INSERT. Instead, it would have been overwritten with the value from the Order Details table, which, since Order Details has no identity column, means that @@IDENTITY would have been set to NULL). Moving the value of @@IDENTITY to a local variable also lets me keep the value around for the statement where I printed out the value for later reference.

Let's create a couple of tables to try this out:

```
CREATE TABLE TestIdent
(
   IDCol    int    IDENTITY
   PRIMARY KEY
)

CREATE TABLE TestChild1
(
   IDcol    int
   PRIMARY KEY
   FOREIGN KEY
           REFERENCES TestIdent(IDCol)
)

CREATE TABLE TestChild2
(
   IDcol    int
   PRIMARY KEY
   FOREIGN KEY
           REFERENCES TestIdent(IDCol)
)
```

What we have here is a parent table – it has an identity column for a primary key (as it happens, that's the only column it has at all). We also have two child tables. They each are the subject of an identifying relationship – that is, they each take at least part (in this case all) of their primary key by placing a foreign key on another table (the parent). So what we have is a situation where the two child tables need to get their key from the parent. Therefore, we need to insert a record into the parent first, and then retrieve the identity value generated so we can make use of it in the other tables.

Now that we have some tables to work with, we're ready to try a little test script:

```
/*******************************************
* This script illustrates how the identity
* value gets lost as soon as another INSERT
* happens
******************************************* */

DECLARE @Ident   int  -- This will be a holding variable
                      -- We'll use it to show how we can
                      -- move values from globals into a
                      -- safe place.

INSERT INTO TestIdent
       DEFAULT VALUES

SET @Ident = @@IDENTITY
PRINT "The value we got originally from @@IDENTITY was " +
      CONVERT(varchar(2),@Ident)
PRINT "The value currently in @@IDENTITY is " + CONVERT(varchar(2),@@IDENTITY)

/* On this first INSERT using @@IDENTITY, we're going to get lucky.
** We'll get a proper value because there is nothing between our
** original INSERT and this one. You'll see that on the INSERT that
** will follow after this one, we won't be so lucky anymore. */
INSERT INTO TestChild1
VALUES
      (@@IDENTITY)

PRINT "The value we got originally from @@IDENTITY was " +
      CONVERT(varchar(2),@Ident)
IF (SELECT @@IDENTITY) IS NULL
   PRINT "The value currently in @@IDENTITY is NULL"
ELSE
   PRINT "The value currently in @@IDENTITY is " + CONVERT(varchar(2),@@IDENTITY)

-- The next line is just a spacer for our print out
PRINT ""

/* The next line is going to blow up because the one column in
** the table is the primary key, and primary keys can't be set
** to NULL. @@IDENTITY will be NULL because we just issued an
** INSERT statement a few lines ago, and the table we did the
** INSERT into doesn't have an identity field. Perhaps the biggest
** thing to note here is when @@IDENTITY changed - right after
** the next INSERT statement. */
INSERT INTO TestChild2
VALUES
      (@@IDENTITY)
```

What we're doing in this script, is seeing what happens if we depend on `@@IDENTITY` directly rather than moving the value off to a safe place. When we execute the script above, everything's going to work just fine until the final `INSERT`. That final statement is trying to make use of `@@IDENTITY` directly, but the preceding `INSERT` statement has already changed the value in `@@IDENTITY`. Since that statement is on a table with no identity column, the value in `@@IDENTITY` is set to `NULL`. Since we can't have a `NULL` value in our primary key, the last `INSERT` fails.

```
(1 row(s) affected)

The value we got originally from @@IDENTITY was 5
The value currently in @@IDENTITY is 5
```

(1 row(s) affected)

The value we got originally from @@IDENTITY was 5
The value currently in @@IDENTITY is NULL

Server: Msg 515, Level 16, State 2, Line 43
Cannot insert the value NULL into column 'IDcol', table 'Northwind.dbo.TestChild2'; column does not allow nulls. INSERT fails.
The statement has been terminated.

If we make just one little change (to save the original @@IDENTITY value):

```
/*****************************************
* This script illustrates how the identity
* value gets lost as soon as another INSERT
* happens
***************************************** */

DECLARE @Ident   int     -- This will be a holding variable
                         -- We'll use it to show how we can
                         -- move values from globals into a
                         -- safe place.

INSERT INTO TestIdent
       DEFAULT VALUES

SET @Ident = @@IDENTITY
PRINT "The value we got originally from @@IDENTITY was " +
      CONVERT(varchar(2),@Ident)
PRINT "The value currently in @@IDENTITY is " + CONVERT(varchar(2),@@IDENTITY)

/* On this first INSERT using @@IDENTITY, we're going to get lucky.
** We'll get a proper value because there is nothing between our
** original INSERT and this one. You'll see that on the INSERT that
** will follow after this one, we won't be so lucky anymore. */
INSERT INTO TestChild1
VALUES
      (@@IDENTITY)

PRINT "The value we got originally from @@IDENTITY was " +
      CONVERT(varchar(2),@Ident)
IF (SELECT @@IDENTITY) IS NULL
   PRINT "The value currently in @@IDENTITY is NULL"
ELSE
   PRINT "The value currently in @@IDENTITY is " + CONVERT(varchar(2),@@IDENTITY)

-- The next line is just a spacer for our print out
PRINT ""

/* This time all will go fine because we are using the value that
** we have placed in safekeeping instead of @@IDENTITY directly.*/
INSERT INTO TestChild2
VALUES
      (@Ident)
```

This time everything runs just fine:

(1 row(s) affected)

The value we got originally from @@IDENTITY was 1
The value currently in @@IDENTITY is 1

```
(1 row(s) affected)

The value we got originally from @@IDENTITY was 1
The value currently in @@IDENTITY is NULL


(1 row(s) affected)
```

> **In this example, it was fairly easy to tell that there was a problem because of the attempt at inserting a `NULL` into the primary key. Now, imagine a far less pretty scenario – one where the second table did have an identity column – you could easily wind up inserting bogus data into your table and not even knowing about it (at least not until you already had a very serious data integrity problem on your hands!)**

Batches

Batches are a grouping of T-SQL statements into one logical unit. All of the statements within a batch are combined into one execution plan, so all statements are parsed together and must pass a validation of the syntax or none of the statements will execute. Note, however, that this does not prevent run-time errors from happening. In the event of a run-time error, any statement that has been executed prior to the run-time error will still be in effect. To summarize, if a statement fails at parse-time, then nothing runs – if a statement fails at run-time, then all statements until the statement that generated the error have already run.

All the scripts we have run up to this point are made up of one batch each. Even the script we've been analyzing so far this in chapter is just one batch. To separate a script into multiple batches, we make use of the `GO` statement. The `GO` statement:

- Must be on its own line (nothing other than a comment can be on the same line). There is an exception to this discussed below, but think of a `GO` as needing to be on a line to itself.
- Causes all statements since the beginning of the script or the last `GO` statement (whichever is closer) to be compiled into one execution plan and sent to the server independent of any other batches.
- Is not a T-SQL command, but, rather, a command recognized by the various SQL Server command utilities (osql, isql and the Query Analyzer).

A Line to Itself

The `GO` command should stand alone on its own line. Technically, you can start a new batch on the same line after the `GO` command, but you'll find this puts a serious damper on readability. T-SQL statements cannot precede the `GO` statement, or the `GO` statement will often be misinterpreted and cause either a parsing error or other unexpected result. For example, if I use a `GO` statement after a `WHERE` clause:

```
SELECT * FROM Customers WHERE CustomerID = 'ALFKI' GO
```

The parser becomes somewhat confused:

```
Server: Msg 170, Level 15, State 1, Line 1
Line 1: Incorrect syntax near 'GO'.
```

Each Batch is Sent to the Server Separately

Because each batch is processed independently, an error in one batch does not preclude another batch from running. To illustrate, take a look at some code:

```
USE Northwind

DECLARE @MyVarchar varchar(50)   --This DECLARE only lasts for this batch!

SELECT @MyVarchar = "Honey, I'm home..."

PRINT 'Done with first Batch...'

GO

PRINT @MyVarchar   --This generates an error since @MyVarchar
                   --isn't declared in this batch
PRINT 'Done with second Batch'

GO

PRINT 'Done with third batch'    -- Notice that this still gets executed
                                 -- even after the error

GO
```

If there were any dependencies between these batches, then either everything would fail – or, that the very least, everything after the point of error would fail – but it doesn't. Look at the results if you run the above script.

```
Done with first Batch...
Server: Msg 137, Level 15, State 2, Line 2
Must declare the variable '@MyVarchar'.
Done with third batch
```

Again, each batch is completely autonomous from the other in terms of run-time issues. Keep in mind though that you can build in dependencies in the sense that one batch may try to perform work that depends on the first batch being complete – we'll see some of this in the next section when we talk about what can and can't span batches.

GO is Not a T-SQL Command

Thinking this way is a common mistake. GO is a command that is only recognized by the editing tools (Query Analyzer, Enterprise Manager). If you use a third party tool, then it may or may not support the GO command.

When the editing tool (ISQL, OSQL, or the Query Analyzer) encounters a GO statement, it sees it as a flag to terminate that batch, package it up, and send it as a single unit to the server – *without* including the GO. That's right, the server itself has absolutely no idea what GO is supposed to mean.

If you try and execute a GO command in a pass through query using ODBC, OLE DB, ADO, DB-LIB, or any other access method, you'll get an error back from the server. The GO is merely an indicator to the tool that it is time to end the current batch, and time, if appropriate, to start a new one.

Errors in Batches

Errors in batches fall into two categories:

- Syntax errors
- Run-time errors

If the query parser finds a **syntax error**, processing of that batch is cancelled immediately. Since syntax checking happens before the batch is compiled or executed, a failure during the syntax check means none of the batch will be executed – regardless of the position of the syntax error within the batch.

Run-time errors work quite a bit differently. Any statement that has already executed before the run-time error was encountered is already done, so anything that statement did will remain intact unless it is part of an uncommitted transaction (transactions are covered in Chapter 13, but the relevance here is that they imply and all or nothing situation). What happens beyond the point of the run-time error depends on the nature of the error. Generally speaking, run-time errors will terminate execution of the batch from the point where the error occurred to the end of the batch. Some run-time errors, such as a referential-integrity violation will only prevent the offending statement from executing – all other statements in the batch will still be executed. This later scenario is why error checking is so important – we will cover error checking in full in our chapter on stored procedures.

When to Use Batches

Batches have several purposes, but they all have one thing in common – they are used when something has to happen either before or separately from everything else in your script.

Statements that Require their Own Batch

There are several commands that absolutely must be part of their own batch. These include:

- `CREATE DEFAULT`
- `CREATE PROCEDURE`
- `CREATE RULE`
- `CREATE TRIGGER`
- `CREATE VIEW`

If you want to combine any of these statements with other statements in a single script, then you will need to break them up into their own batch by using a `GO` statement.

> **Note that, if you `DROP` an object, you may want to place the `DROP` in its own batch or at least with a batch of other `DROP` statements. Why? Well, if you're going to later create an object with the same name, the `CREATE` will fail during the parsing of your batch unless the `DROP` has already happened. That means you need to run the `DROP` in a separate and prior batch to it will be complete when the batch with the `CREATE` statement executes.**

Using Batches to Establish Precedence

Perhaps the most likely scenario for using batches is when precedence is required – that is, you need one task to be completely done before the next task starts. Most of the time, SQL Server deals with this kind of situation just fine – the first statement in the script is the first executed, and the second statement in the script can rely on the server being in the proper state when the second statement runs. There are times however, when SQL Server can't resolve this kind of issue.

Let's take the example of creating a database together with some tables:

```
CREATE DATABASE Test

CREATE TABLE TestTable
(
   col1   int,
   col2   int
)
```

Execute this and, at first, it appears that everything has gone well:

```
The CREATE DATABASE process is allocating 0.75 MB on disk 'TEST'.
The CREATE DATABASE process is allocating 0.49 MB on disk 'TEST_log'.
```

However, things are not as they seem – check out the `INFORMATION_SCHEMA` in the `Test` database, and you'll notice something is missing:

```
SELECT TABLE_CATALOG FROM INFORMATION_SCHEMA.TABLES WHERE TABLE_NAME =
   'TestTable'
```

```
TABLE_CATALOG
--------------------------------------------------------------------------------------------
master


(1 row(s) affected)
```

Hey! Why was the table created in the wrong database? The answer lies in what database was current when we ran the `CREATE TABLE` statement. In my case, it happened to be the `master` database, so that's where my table was created.

> *Note that you may have been somewhere other than the master database when you ran this, so you may get a different result than I did. That's kind of the point though – you could be in pretty much any database. That's why making use of the `USE` statement is so important.*

When you think about it, this seems like an easy thing to fix – just make use of the `USE` statement, but before we test our new theory, we have to get rid of the old (OK, not that old) database:

```
USE MASTER
DROP DATABASE Test
```

We can then run our newly modified script:

```
CREATE DATABASE Test

USE Test

CREATE TABLE TestTable
(
   col1   int,
   col2   int
)
```

Unfortunately, this has its own problems:

```
Server: Msg 911, Level 16, State 1, Line 3
Could not locate entry in sysdatabases for database 'TEST'. No entry found with that name. Make
sure that the name is entered correctly.
```

The parser tries to validate your code and finds that you are referencing a database with your `USE` command that doesn't exist. Ahh, now we see the need for our batches. We need the `CREATE DATABASE` statement to be completed before we try and use the new database:

```
CREATE DATABASE Test
GO

USE Test

CREATE TABLE TestTable
(
   col1   int,
   col2   int
)
```

Now things work a lot better. Our immediate results look the same:

```
The CREATE DATABASE process is allocating 0.75 MB on disk 'Test'.
The CREATE DATABASE process is allocating 0.49 MB on disk 'Test_log'.
```

But when we run our `INFORMATION_SCHEMA` query, things are confirmed:

```
TABLE_CATALOG
--------------------------------------------------------------------------------
Test

(1 row(s) affected)
```

Let's move onto another example that shows an even more explicit need for precedence.

When you use an `ALTER TABLE` statement that significantly changes the type of a column or adds columns, you cannot make use of those changes until the batch that makes the changes has completed.

If we add a column to our `TestTable` table in our `Test` database and then try to reference that column without ending the first batch:

```
USE Test

ALTER TABLE TestTable
   ADD col3 int

INSERT INTO TestTable
(col1, col2, col3)
VALUES
(1,1,1)
```

We get an error – SQL Server cannot resolve the new column name, and therefore complains:

```
Server: Msg 207, Level 16, State 1, Line 1
Invalid column name 'col3'.
```

Add one simple `GO` statement after the `ADD col3 int` though and everything is working fine:

```
(1 row(s) affected)
```

OSQL

OSQL – usually spoken as "OH-Sequel" – is a utility that allow you to run scripts from a command prompt in an NT command box or Win 9x DOS prompt. This can be very nice for executing conversion or maintenance scripts, as well as a quick and dirty way to capture a text file.

OSQL replaces the older ISQL with a new 32-bit engine. ISQL is still included with SQL Server for backward compatibility only.

The syntax for running OSQL from the command line includes a ton of different switches, and looks like this:

```
osql -U <login id> [-e] [-E] [-p] [-n] [-d <database name>]
[-Q "query text"] [-q "query text"] [-c <cmd terminator>]
[-h <headers>] [-w <column width>] [-s <column separator>]
[-t <time out>] [-m <error level>] [-I] [-L] [-?] [-r {0 | 1}]
[-H <workstation name>] [-P <password>] [-R] [-S <server name>]
[-i <input file>] [-o <output file>] [-u] [-a <packet size>]
[-b] [-O] [-l <time out>]
```

The single biggest thing to keep in mind with these flags is that many of them (but, oddly enough, not all of them) are case sensitive. For example, "-Q" and "-q" both will execute queries, but the first will exit OSQL when the query is complete, and the second won't. The other big thing in running OSQL is to run the arguments for each flag right against the flag (don't put a space in between). The exception to this later rule is when the parameter argument is quoted, it which case you do want a space between the parameter and the first quote, for example:

```
oqsl -URobV -PMyPassword -Q "My Query"
```

So, let's try a quick one query direct from the command line. Again, remember that this is meant to be run from the NT command prompt or a DOS box in Win9x (don't try it in QA):

```
osql -Usa -P -Q "SELECT * FROM Northwind..Shippers"
```

If you run this from a command prompt, you should get something like:

```
C:\>Osql -Usa -P -Q "SELECT * FROM Northwind..Shippers"
ShipperID     CompanyName                  Phone
------------- ---------------------------- ------------------
1             Speedy Express               (503) 555-9831
2             United Package               (503) 555-3199
3             Federal Shipping             (503) 555-9931

(3 rows affected)

C:\>
```

Now, let's create a quick text file to see how it works when including a file. At the command prompt (or DOS box on Win9x), type the following:

```
C:\>copy con testsql.sql
```

This should take you down only a black line (no prompt of any kind), where you can enter in this:

```
SELECT * FROM Northwind..Shippers
```

Then press *F6* and return (this ends you creating our text file). You should get back a message like:

```
1 file(s) copied.
```

Now let's retry out earlier query using a script file this time. The command line at the prompt only has a slight change to it:

```
C:\>Osql -Usa -P -i testsql.sql
```

This should get us the exact same results as we had when we ran the query using `-Q`. The major difference is, of course, that we took the command from a file. The file could have had hundreds – if not thousands – of different commands in it.

There are a wide variety of different parameters, but the biggies are the login, the password, and the one that says what you want to do (straight query or input file).

Summary

Understanding scripts and batches is the cornerstone to understand programming with SQL Server. The concepts of scripts and batches lay the foundation for a variety of functions from scripting complete database builds to programming stored procedures and triggers.

Local variables have scope for only one batch. Even if you have declared the variable within the same overall script, you will still get an error if you don't re-declare it (and start over with assigning values) before referencing it in a new batch.

There are over 30 global variables. We provided a listing of some of the most useful globals, but there are many more. Try checking out the Books Online or the appendix at the back of this book for some of the more obscure globals. Globals do not need to be declared, and are always available. Some are scoped to the entire server, while others return values specific to the current connection.

You can use batches to create precedence between different parts of your scripts. The first batch starts at the beginning of the script, and ends at the end of the script or the first `GO` statement – whichever comes first. The next batch (if there is another) starts on the line after the first one ends and continues to the end of the script or the next `GO` statement – again, whichever comes first. The process continues to the end of the script. The first batch from the top of the script is executed first; the second is executed second, and so on. All commands within each batch must pass validation in the query parser, or none of that batch will be executed; however, any other batches will be parsed separately and will still be executed (if it passes the parser).

In the next couple of chapters, we well take the notions of scripting and batches to the next level, and apply them to stored procedures and triggers – the closest things that SQL Server has to actual programs.

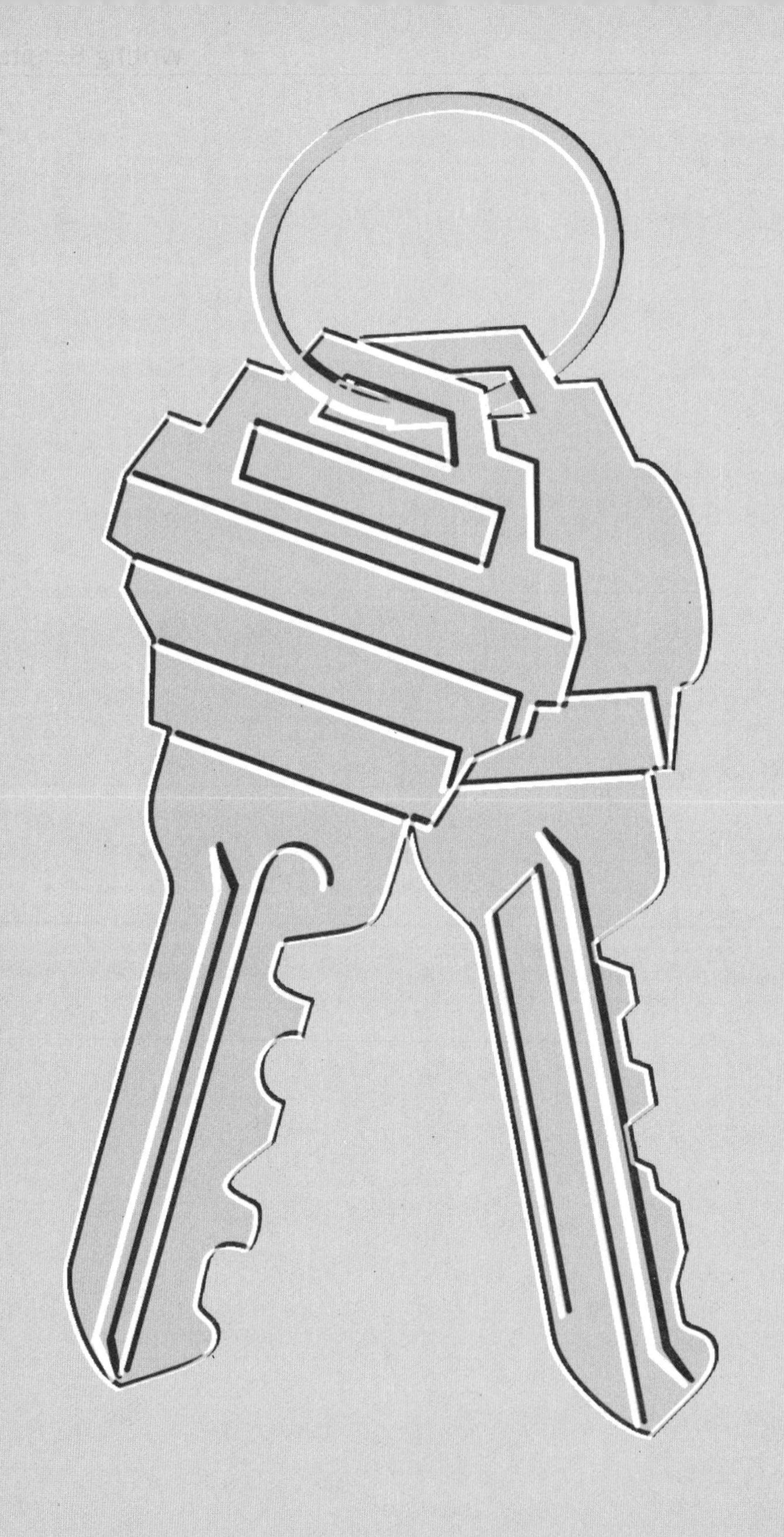

12

Code Storage: Stored Procedures

Ahhh, the good stuff. If you're a programmer coming from a procedural language, then this is probably the part you've been waiting for. It's time to get down to the "code" of SQL Server, but before we get going too far down that road, I need to prepare you for what lies ahead – probably a lot less than you're expecting, and, at the very same time, a whole lot more.

You see, a **stored procedure**, sometimes referred to as a **sproc**, is really just something of a script – more exactly speaking, a **batch** – that is stored in the database rather than in a separate file. Now this comparison is not an exact one by any means – sprocs have some things like input parameters, output parameters, and return values that a script doesn't really have, but the comparison is not that far off either.

SQL Server's only "programming" language is T-SQL, and that leaves us miles short of the kind of procedural horsepower that you expect when you think of a true programming language. T-SQL blows C, C++, Visual Basic, Java, Delphi, or whatever away when it comes to what T-SQL is supposed to do – work on data definition, manipulation, and access. T-SQL's horsepower stops right about there though – data access and management. From there, it has an adequate amount of power to get most simple things done, but it's not always the place to do it.

For this chapter, however, we're not going to worry all that much about T-SQL's downfalls – instead, we'll focus on how to get the most out of T-SQL. We'll take a look at parameters, return values, control of flow, looping structures, both basic and advanced error trapping, and more. In short, this is a big chapter that deals with many subjects. All of the major subject areas are broken up into their own sections, so you can take them one step at a time, but let's start right out with the basics of getting a sproc created.

Creating the Sproc: Basic Syntax

Creating a sproc works pretty much the same as creating any other object in a database, save that it has the AS keyword that you first saw when we took a look at views. The basic syntax looks like this:

```
CREATE PROCEDURE|PROC <sproc name>
   [<parameter name> <parameter type> [= <default value>] INPUT|OUTPUT[,
    <parameter name> <parameter type> [= <default value>] INPUT|OUTPUT[,
    ...
    ...
      ]]
[WITH
   RECOMPILE|ENCRYPTION|RECOMPILE, ENCRYPTION]
[FOR REPLICATION]
AS
   <code>

GO
```

As you can see, we still have our basic CREATE <Object Type> <Object Name> syntax that is the backbone of every CREATE statement. The only oddity here is the choice between PROCEDURE and PROC – either works just fine, but, as always, I recommend that you be consistent on which one you choose (personally, I like the saved steps of PROC). The name of your sproc must follow the rules for naming as outlined in Chapter 2.

After the name comes a list of parameters. Parameterization is optional, and we'll defer that discussion until a little later in the chapter.

Last, but not least, comes your actual code following the AS keyword.

An Example of a Basic Sproc

Perhaps the best example of sproc syntax is to get down to the most basic of sprocs – a sproc that returns all the columns in all the rows on a table – in short, everything to do with a table's data.

I would hope that, by now, you have the query that would return all the contents of a table down cold (HINT: SELECT * FROM ...) – if not, then I would suggest a return to the chapter on basic query syntax. In order to create a sproc that performs this basic query, we just add the query in the code area of a sproc syntax:

```
USE Northwind

GO
CREATE PROC spShippers
AS
   SELECT * FROM Shippers
```

Not too rough – eh? If you're wondering why I put the GO keyword in before the CREATE syntax (if we were just running a simple SELECT statement, we wouldn't need it), it's because most non-table CREATE statements cannot share a batch with any other code. Indeed, even with a CREATE TABLE statement leaving out the GO can become rather dicey. In this case, having the USE command together with our CREATE PROC statement would have been a no-no, and would have generated an error.

Now that we have our sproc created, let's execute it to see what we get:

```
EXEC spShippers
```

We get exactly what we would have got if we had run the `SELECT` statement that's embedded in the sproc:

```
ShipperID      CompanyName                  Phone
-------------- ---------------------------- ------------------
1              Speedy Express               (503) 555-9831
2              United Package               (503) 555-3199
3              Federal Shipping             (503) 555-9931

(3 row(s) affected)
```

You've just written your first sproc. It was easy of course, and frankly, sproc writing isn't nearly as difficult as most database people would like to have you think (job preservation), but there are lots of possibilities, and we've only seen the beginning.

Changing Stored Procedures with ALTER

I'm going to admit something here – I cut and pasted almost all the text you're about to read in this and the next (Dropping) section from the chapter on views. What I'm pointing out by telling you this is that they work almost identically from the standpoint of what an `ALTER` statement does.

The main thing to remember when you edit sprocs with T-SQL is that you are completely replacing the existing sproc. The only differences between using the `ALTER PROC` statement and the `CREATE PROC` statement are:

- `ALTER PROC` expects to find an existing proc, where `CREATE` doesn't
- `ALTER PROC` retains any permissions that have been established for the proc

The latter of these two is the biggy.

> **If you perform a `DROP` and then use a `CREATE`, you have almost the same effect as using an `ALTER PROC` statement with one rather big difference – if you `DROP` and `CREATE` then you will need to entirely re-establish your permissions on who can and can't use the sproc.**

Dropping Sprocs

It doesn't get much easier than this:

```
DROP PROC|PROCEDURE <sproc name>
```

And it's gone.

Parameterization

A stored procedure gives you some procedural capability, and also gives you a performance boost (more on that later), but it wouldn't be much help in most circumstances if it couldn't accept some data to tell it what to do. For example, it doesn't do much good to have an `spDeleteShipper` stored procedure if we can't tell it what shipper we want to delete so we use an **input parameter**. Likewise, we often want information back out of the sproc – not just one or more recordsets of table data, but also information that is more direct. An example here might be where we update several records in a table and we'd like to know just how many we updated. Often, this isn't easily handed back in recordset form, so we make use of an **output parameter**.

From outside of the sproc, parameters can be passed in either by position or by reference. From the inside, it doesn't matter which way they come in – they are declared the same either way.

Declaring Parameters

Declaring a parameter requires two to four pieces:

- The name
- The type
- The default
- The direction

The syntax is:

```
@parameter_name datatype [= default|NULL] [VARYING] [OUTPUT]
```

The name has a pretty simple set of rules to it. First, it must start with the @ sign. Other than that, the rules for naming are pretty much the same as the rules for naming described in Chapter 2, save for the fact they can't have embedded spaces.

The type, much like the name, must be declared just as you would for a variable – with a valid SQL Server data type. The one special thing in declaring the data type is to remember that, when declaring a parameter of type `CURSOR`, you must also use the `VARYING` and `OUTPUT` options. Use of this type of parameter is pretty unusual. We will take a good look at output parameters in this chapter, but we will defer our look at outputting cursors until our chapter on cursors later in the book.

The default is the first place we start to see any real divergence from variables. Where variables are always initialized to a `NULL` value, parameters are not. Indeed, if you don't supply a default value, then the parameter is assumed to be required, and a beginning value must be supplied when the sproc is called. To supply a default, you simply add an = sign after the type and then provide the default value. Once you've done this, the users of your sproc can decide to supply no value for that parameter, or they can provide their own value.

Let's create another sproc, only this time we'll make use of a few input parameters to create a new record in the Shippers table:

```
USE Northwind
GO

CREATE PROC spInsertShipper
   @CompanyName    nvarchar(40),
   @Phone          nvarchar(24)
AS
   INSERT INTO Shippers
   VALUES
      (@CompanyName, @Phone)
```

Our last sproc told us what data is currently in the Shippers table, but let's use our new sproc to insert something new:

```
EXEC spInsertShipper 'Speedy Shippers, Inc.', '(503) 555-5566'
```

If this is executed from the Query Analyzer, we see the results of our stored procedure run just as if we had run the INSERT statement ourselves:

(1 row(s) affected)

Now let's run our first sproc again and see what we get:

```
EXEC spShippers
```

```
ShipperID       CompanyName                    Phone
--------------- ------------------------------ ------------------
1               Speedy Express                 (503) 555-9831
2               United Package                 (503) 555-3199
3               Federal Shipping               (503) 555-9931
4               Speedy Shippers, Inc.          (503) 555-5566
```

(4 row(s) affected)

Sure enough, our record has been inserted, and a new identity has been filled in for it.

Since we didn't supply any default values for either of the parameters, both parameters are considered to be required. That means that, in order to have success running this sproc, we *must* supply both parameters. You can easily check this out by running the query again with only one or no parameters supplied:

```
EXEC spInsertShipper 'Speedy Shippers, Inc.'
```

SQL Server wastes no time in informing you of the error of your ways:

Server: Msg 201, Level 16, State 1, Procedure spInsertShipper, Line 0
Procedure 'spInsertShipper' expects parameter '@Phone', which was not supplied.

Supplying Default Values

To make a parameter optional, you have to supply a default value. To do this, you just add an = together with the value you want to use for a default after the type but before the comma.

Let's try building our INSERT sproc again, only this time we won't require the phone number:

```
USE Northwind
GO

CREATE PROC spInsertShipperOptionalPhone
   @CompanyName    nvarchar(40),
   @Phone          nvarchar(24) = NULL
AS
   INSERT INTO Shippers
   VALUES
      (@CompanyName, @Phone)
```

Now we're ready to re-issue our command, only using the new sproc this time:

```
EXEC spInsertShipperOptionalPhone 'Speedy Shippers, Inc'
```

This time everything works just fine, and our new row is inserted:

(1 row(s) affected)

```
EXEC spShippers
```

ShipperID	CompanyName	Phone
1	Speedy Express	(503) 555-9831
2	United Package	(503) 555-3199
3	Federal Shipping	(503) 555-9931
4	Speedy Shippers, Inc.	(503) 555-5566
5	Speedy Shippers, Inc.	NULL

(5 row(s) affected)

In this particular case, we set the default to NULL, but the value could have been anything that was compatible with the data type of the parameter for which we are establishing the default. Also, notice that we didn't have to establish a default for both values – we can make one have a default, and one not – we decide which parameters are required (have no default), and which are not (have a default).

Creating Output Parameters

Sometimes, you want to pass non-recordset information out to whatever called your sproc. One example of this would create a modified version of our last two sprocs.

Let's say, for example, that you are performing an insert into a table (like we just did in the last example), but you are planning to do additional work based on the inserted record.

For example, maybe we're inserting a new record into our `Orders` table in `Northwind`, but we also need to insert detail records in the `Order Details` table. In order to keep the relationship intact, we have to know the identity of the `Order` record before we can do our inserts into the `Order Details` table. The sproc will look almost exactly like our `spInsertShipper` did, except that it will have parameters that match up with the different columns in the table and, most importantly of all, it will have an output parameter for the identity value that is generated by our insert:

```
USE Northwind
GO

CREATE PROC spInsertOrder
   @CustomerID       nvarchar(5),
   @EmployeeID       int,
   @OrderDate        datetime       = NULL,
   @RequiredDate     datetime       = NULL,
   @ShippedDate      datetime       = NULL,
   @ShipVia          int,
   @Freight          money,
   @ShipName         nvarchar(40)   = NULL,
   @ShipAddress      nvarchar(60)   = NULL,
   @ShipCity         nvarchar(15)   = NULL,
   @ShipRegion       nvarchar(15)   = NULL,
   @ShipPostalCode   nvarchar(10)   = NULL,
   @ShipCountry      nvarchar(15)   = NULL,
   @OrderID          int       OUTPUT

AS
   /* Create the new record */
   INSERT INTO Orders
   VALUES
      (
         @CustomerID,
         @EmployeeID,
         @OrderDate,
         @RequiredDate,
         @ShippedDate,
         @ShipVia,
         @Freight,
         @ShipName,
         @ShipAddress,
         @ShipCity,
         @ShipRegion,
         @ShipPostalCode,
         @ShipCountry
      )

/* Move the identity value from the newly inserted record into
   our output variable */
SELECT @OrderID = @@IDENTITY
```

Now, let's try this baby out, only this time, let's set our parameter values by reference rather than position. In order to see how our output parameter is working, we'll also need to write a little bit of test code in the script that executes the sproc:

```
USE Northwind
GO

DECLARE   @MyIdent   int

EXEC spInsertOrder
     @CustomerID = 'ALFKI',
     @EmployeeID = 5,
     @OrderDate = '5/1/1999',
     @ShipVia = 3,
```

```
        @Freight = 5.00,
        @OrderID = @MyIdent OUTPUT

    SELECT @MyIdent AS IdentityValue

    SELECT OrderID, CustomerID, EmployeeID, OrderDate, ShipName
    FROM Orders
    WHERE OrderID = @MyIdent
```

Notice that we didn't supply all of the parameters. Some of them were optional, and we decided to leave some of those off – just taking the optional value. If we had been calling the sproc and passing values in using positional parameters, then we would have had to address each position in the parameter list at least until the last parameter for which we wanted to supply a value.

Let's see what this gives us – keep in mind that your identity value may vary from mine depending on what modifications you already made in the `Orders` table:

```
(1 row(s) affected)

IdentityValue
-----------------
11078

(1 row(s) affected)

OrderID         CustomerID           EmployeeID           OrderDate                      ShipName
--------------- -------------------- -------------------- ------------------------------ --------------
11078           ALFKI                5                    1999-05-01 00:00:00.000        NULL

(1 row(s) affected)
```

The first row affected line is really feedback from the sproc itself – it inserted one row. The second result set provides us with the identity value that was inserted – for me, this value was 11078 – this is positive proof that our identity value was indeed passed out of the sproc by the output parameter. Finally, we selected several columns from that row in the `Orders` table to verify that the row was indeed inserted using the data we expected.

There are several things that you should take note of between the sproc itself, and the usage of it by the calling script:

- The `OUTPUT` keyword was required for the output parameter in the sproc declaration.
- The `INPUT` keyword was, however, not required for input parameters as it is the default – you can include it if you choose, but I have never seen this in practice (not even once).
- You must use the `OUTPUT` keyword when you call the sproc, much as you did when you declared the sproc. This gives SQL Server advance warning about the special handling that parameter will require. Be aware, however, that forgetting to include the `OUTPUT` keyword won't create a run-time error (you won't get any messages about it), but the value for the output parameter won't be moved into your variable (you'll just wind up with what was already there – most likely a `NULL` value). This means that you'll have what I consider to be the most dreadful of all computer terms: unpredictable results.
- The variable you assign the output result to does *not* have to have the same name as the internal parameter in the sproc.

- The EXEC (or EXECUTE) keyword was required since the call to the sproc wasn't the first thing in the batch (you can leave off the EXEC if the sproc call is the first thing in a batch) – personally, I recommend that you train yourself to use it regardless.

Control of Flow Statements

Control of flow statements are a veritable must for any programming language these days. I can't imagine having to write my code where I couldn't change what commands to run depending on a condition. T-SQL offers most of the classic choices for control of flow situations, including:

- IF...ELSE
- CASE (aka SELECT CASE, DO CASE, and SWITCH/BREAK in other languages)
- GOTO
- WHILE
- WAITFOR

The IF...ELSE Statement

IF...ELSE statements work much as they do in any language, though I equate them closest to C in the way they are implemented. The basic syntax is:

```
IF <Expression>
   <SQL statement> | BEGIN <code series> END
[ELSE
   <SQL statement> | BEGIN <code series> END]
```

The expression can be pretty much any expression that evaluates to a Boolean. If the value of the expression is non-Boolean in nature, then zero or NULL will be treated a FALSE and any non-zero value will be treated as TRUE.

This brings us to back to one of the most common traps that I see SQL programmers fall into – improper user of NULLs. I can't tell you how often I have debugged stored procedures only to find a statement like:

```
IF @myvar = NULL
```

This will, of course, never be true on most systems (see below), and will wind up bypassing all their NULL values. Instead, it needs to read:

```
IF @myvar IS NULL
```

Don't forget that NULL doesn't equate to anything – not even NULL. Use IS instead of =.

The exception to this is dependent on whether you have set the ANSI_NULLS option set ON or OFF. The default is that this is ON, in which case you'll see the behavior described above. You can change this behavior by setting ANSI_NULLS to OFF. I strongly recommend against this since it violates the ANSI standard (it's also just plain wrong).

Note that, unless you explicitly put your statements into code blocks using BEGIN...END, then only the very next statement after the IF will be considered to be conditional (as per the IF). You can include multiple statements as part of your control of flow block using BEGIN...END, but we'll discuss that one a little later in the chapter.

Let's create a new edition of our last query, and deal with the situation where someone supplies an OrderDate that is older than we want to accept.

Our sales manager is upset because someone has been putting in orders long after she has already completed her sales analysis for the time-period in which that order is. She has established a new policy that says that an order must be entered into the system within seven days after the order is taken, or the order date is considered to be invalid and must be set to NULL.

How to change the value of the order date? That's where our IF...ELSE statement comes in.

We need to perform a simple test, and to do it, we'll need to make use of the DATEDIFF function. The syntax for DATEDIFF is:

```
DATEDIFF(<datepart>, <startdate>, <enddate>)
```

DATEDIFF compares our two dates – in this case the supplied order date and the current date. It can actually compare any part of the datetime data supplied from the year down to the millisecond. In our case, a simple dd for day will suffice, and we'll put it together with an IF statement:

```
IF DATEDIFF(dd, @OrderDate, GETDATE()) > 7
```

In the event that our returned value is over 7 – that is, over 7 days old – then we want to change the value that we insert:

```
   SELECT @OrderDate = NULL
```

Now that we've got ourselves set with our IF statement, let's write that new version of the spInsertOrder sproc:

```
USE Northwind
GO

CREATE PROC spInsertDateValidatedOrder
   @CustomerID        nvarchar(5),
   @EmployeeID        int,
   @OrderDate         datetime      = NULL,
   @RequiredDate      datetime      = NULL,
   @ShippedDate       datetime      = NULL,
   @ShipVia           int,
   @Freight           money,
   @ShipName          nvarchar(40)  = NULL,
   @ShipAddress       nvarchar(60)  = NULL,
   @ShipCity          nvarchar(15)  = NULL,
   @ShipRegion        nvarchar(15)  = NULL,
   @ShipPostalCode    nvarchar(10)  = NULL,
   @ShipCountry       nvarchar(15)  = NULL,
   @OrderID           int       OUTPUT

AS

/* Test to see if supplied date is over seven days old, if so
   replace with NULL value                                    */
IF DATEDIFF(dd, @OrderDate, GETDATE()) > 7
```

```
    SELECT @OrderDate = NULL

/* Create the new record */
INSERT INTO Orders
VALUES
(
    @CustomerID,
    @EmployeeID,
    @OrderDate,
    @RequiredDate,
    @ShippedDate,
    @ShipVia,
    @Freight,
    @ShipName,
    @ShipAddress,
    @ShipCity,
    @ShipRegion,
    @ShipPostalCode,
    @ShipCountry
)

/* Move the identity value from the newly inserted record into
      our output variable */
SELECT @OrderID = @@IDENTITY
```

Now let's run that same test script as we used for the original `spInsertOrder` sproc with only a minor modification to deal with our new situation:

```
USE Northwind
GO

DECLARE   @MyIdent   int

EXEC spInsertDateValidatedOrder
    @CustomerID = 'ALFKI',
    @EmployeeID = 5,
    @OrderDate = '5/1/1999',
    @ShipVia = 3,
    @Freight = 5.00,
    @OrderID = @MyIdent OUTPUT

SELECT @MyIdent AS IdentityValue

SELECT OrderID, CustomerID, EmployeeID, OrderDate, ShipName
FROM Orders
WHERE OrderID = @MyIdent
```

This time, even though most of the sproc is the same, we change what we put into the database, and therefore, what we see in our selected results:

```
(1 row(s) affected)

IdentityValue
-----------------
11079

(1 row(s) affected)

OrderID        CustomerID          EmployeeID          OrderDate          ShipName
-------------- ------------------- ------------------- ------------------ -------------
11079          ALFKI               5                   NULL               NULL

(1 row(s) affected)
```

Even though we supplied the same date as last time (5/1/1999) that isn't the value that was inserted – our IF statement picked off the illegal value and changed it before the insert.

The ELSE Clause

Now this thing about being able to change the data on the fly is just great, but it doesn't really deal with all the scenarios we might want to deal with. Quite often – indeed, most of the time – when we deal with an IF condition, we have specific statements we want to execute not just for the true condition, but also a separate set of statements that we want to run if the condition is false – or the ELSE condition.

The ELSE statement works pretty much as it does in any other language. The exact syntax may vary slightly, but the nuts and bolts are still the same – the statements in the ELSE clause are executed if the statements in the IF clause are not.

To expand out example just a bit, let's look at the oldest records that are currently in the Northwind Orders table:

```
USE Northwind
GO

SELECT TOP 5 OrderID, OrderDate
FROM  Orders
WHERE OrderDate IS NOT NULL
ORDER BY OrderDate
```

There's something interesting about the results:

```
OrderID         OrderDate
--------------- ------------------------------
10248           1996-07-04 00:00:00.000
10249           1996-07-05 00:00:00.000
10250           1996-07-08 00:00:00.000
10251           1996-07-08 00:00:00.000
10252           1996-07-09 00:00:00.000

(5 row(s) affected)
```

None of the dates have a time component – OK, technically they're all at midnight, but I suspect you get the picture. It's likely that this was done on purpose, as it makes date (without time) comparisons much easier.

What we want to do is convert our sproc to make sure that we store all dates as just dates – no times. The current sproc won't work because it will insert the entire date, including time - but to verify that, let's test it out:

```
USE Northwind
GO

DECLARE   @MyIdent    int
DECLARE   @MyDate     smalldatetime

SELECT @MyDate = GETDATE()
```

```
EXEC spInsertDateValidatedOrder
   @CustomerID = 'ALFKI',
   @EmployeeID = 5,
   @OrderDate  = @MyDate,
   @ShipVia    = 3,
   @Freight = 5.00,
   @OrderID = @MyIdent OUTPUT

SELECT @MyIdent AS IdentityValue

SELECT OrderID, CustomerID, EmployeeID, OrderDate, ShipName
FROM Orders
WHERE OrderID = @MyIdent
```

When we insert our date, the time comes along with it:

```
(1 row(s) affected)

IdentityValue
-----------------
11080

(1 row(s) affected)

OrderID         CustomerID          EmployeeID          OrderDate                      ShipName
--------------- ------------------- ------------------- ------------------------------ -------------
11080           ALFKI               5                   1999-06-06 12:55:00.000 NULL

(1 row(s) affected)
```

So, what we have is an either/or situation. Either we now want the date changed to NULL, or we want the time truncated from the date. Unfortunately, SQL Server doesn't give us a function that does it automatically (another severe let down in my not so humble opinion). Fortunately, however, we again have a work around.

Truncating the Time from a Datetime Field

In order to truncate a date, we can either take the date apart piece by piece and reassemble it without the time, or, as I prefer, we can use the CONVERT function on it to convert it to a timeless day and then convert it back.

CONVERT() is just one of many functions that are available to us in SQL Server. Originally, it was the one and only method to convert data between data types. These days, CONVERT should be getting much less use in scripts because much of its functionality is duplicated by CAST(), which is ANSI-compliant (CONVERT isn't). Still, CONVERT has some special date formatting capabilities that can't be duplicated by CAST.

CONVERT works with this syntax:

```
CONVERT(<target data type>, <expression to be converted>, <style>)
```

The first two parameters are pretty self-describing, but the last one isn't – it only applies when dealing with dates and its purpose is to tell SQL Server in which format you want the date to be. Examples of common date formats include 1, for standard US mm/dd/yy format and 12 for the standard ISO format (yymmdd). Adding 100 to any of the formats adds the full century to the date scheme (for example, standard US format with a four digit year – mm/dd/yyyy – has a style of 101).

For example, it would look something like this for the GETDATE function:

```
SELECT CONVERT(datetime,(CONVERT(varchar,GETDATE(),112)))
```

This takes things to an ANSI date format and then back again:

```
---------------------------------
1999-06-06 00:00:00.000

(1 row(s) affected)
```

Implementing the ELSE Statement in Our Sproc

Now that we've figured out how to do the pieces, it's time to move that into our actual sproc. This time, however, we're going to make use of the ALTER command rather than creating a separate procedure. Remember that, even when using an ALTER statement, we must entirely re-define the procedure:

```
USE Northwind
GO

ALTER PROC spInsertDateValidatedOrder
   @CustomerID      nvarchar(5),
   @EmployeeID      int,
   @OrderDate       datetime       = NULL,
   @RequiredDate    datetime       = NULL,
   @ShippedDate     datetime       = NULL,
   @ShipVia         int,
   @Freight         money,
   @ShipName        nvarchar(40)  = NULL,
   @ShipAddress     nvarchar(60)  = NULL,
   @ShipCity        nvarchar(15)  = NULL,
   @ShipRegion      nvarchar(15)  = NULL,
   @ShipPostalCode nvarchar(10)  = NULL,
   @ShipCountry     nvarchar(15)  = NULL,
   @OrderID         int       OUTPUT

AS

/* I don't like altering input parameters - I find that it helps in debugging
** if I can refer to their original values at any time. Therefore, I'm going
** to declare a separate variable to assign the end value we will be
** inserting into the table.                                                */
DECLARE   @InsertedOrderDate    smalldatetime

/* Test to see if supplied date is over seven days old, if so
** replace with NULL value
** otherwise, truncate the time to be midnight                              */
IF DATEDIFF(dd, @OrderDate, GETDATE()) > 7
   SELECT @InsertedOrderDate = NULL
ELSE
   SELECT @InsertedOrderDate =
      CONVERT(datetime,(CONVERT(varchar,@OrderDate,112)))

   /* Create the new record */
INSERT INTO Orders
VALUES
(
   @CustomerID,
   @EmployeeID,
   @InsertedOrderDate,
   @RequiredDate,
   @ShippedDate,
   @ShipVia,
   @Freight,
```

```
        @ShipName,
        @ShipAddress,
        @ShipCity,
        @ShipRegion,
        @ShipPostalCode,
        @ShipCountry
    )

    /* Move the identity value from the newly inserted record into
          our output variable */
    SELECT @OrderID = @@IDENTITY
```

Now, if we re-run the original batch, we have the effect we were after:

```
(1 row(s) affected)

IdentityValue
----------------
11082

(1 row(s) affected)

OrderID          CustomerID          EmployeeID          OrderDate                     ShipName
---------------- ------------------- ------------------- ----------------------------- -------------
11082            ALFKI               5                   1999-06-06 00:00:00.000  NULL

(1 row(s) affected)
```

We now have a sproc that handles the insert differently depending on the specific values that are given to the sproc.

> **If you look closely, you'll note that I changed more than just the `IF...ELSE` statement for this version of the sproc – I also changed things so that a holding variable was declared for the order date.**
>
> **The purpose behind this has to do with a general philosophy I have about changing input parameter values. With the exception of where you are changing parameter values for the express purpose of passing out a changed value, I don't think you should change parameter values. Why? Well, part of it is a clarity issue – I don't want people to have to look in multiple places for where my variables are declared if possible. The other reason is perhaps a more convincing one – debugging. I like to retain my input values for as long as possible so that, when I need to debug, I can easily check my input value against the various places in the code I make use of the input value. That is, I want to simplify being able to tell if things are working correctly.**

Grouping Code into Code Blocks

Sometimes you need to treat a group of statements as though they were all one statement (if you execute one, then you execute them all – otherwise, you don't execute any of them). For instance, the IF statement will, by default, only consider the very next statement after the IF to be part of the conditional code. What if you want the condition to require several statements to run? Life would be pretty miserable if you had to create a separate IF statement for each line of code you wanted to be held to the condition.

Thankfully, SQL Server gives us a way to group code into blocks that are considered to all belong together. The block is started when you issue a BEGIN statement, and continues until you issue an END statement. It works like this:

```
IF <Expression>
BEGIN    --First block of code starts here - executes only if
         --expression is TRUE
   Statement that executes if expression is TRUE
   Additional statements
   ...
   ...
   Still going with statements from TRUE expression
   IF <Expression>    --Only executes if this block is active
      BEGIN
         Statement that executes if both outside and inside
            expressions are TRUE
         Additional statements
         ...
         ...
         Still statements from both TRUE expressions
      END
   Out of the condition from inner condition, but still
      part of first block
END   --First block of code ends here
ELSE
BEGIN
   Statement that executes if expression is FALSE
   Additional statements
   ...
   ...
   Still going with statements from TRUE expression
END
```

Notice our ability to nest blocks of code. In each case, the inner blocks are considered to be part of the outer block of code. I have never heard of there being a limit to how many levels deep you can nest your BEGIN...END blocks, but I would suggest that you minimize them. There are definitely practical limits to how deep you can keep them readable – even if you are particularly careful about the formatting of your code.

Just to put this notion into play, let's make yet another modification to our last order insert query. This time, we're going to provide a little bit of useful information to our user as we go through code that alters what the caller of the sproc has provided. This can act as something of a lead in for the upcoming section on error handling.

Anytime we decide to change the data we're inserting to be something other than what the user supplied, then we also need to inform the user of exactly what we're doing. We'll use a `PRINT` statement to output the specifics of what we've done. We'll add these `PRINT` statements as part of the code in our `IF...ELSE` statement so the information can be topical. Note that a `PRINT` statement doesn't generate any kind of error – it just provides textual information regardless of error status. We'll discuss this further in the error handling section.

```
USE Northwind
GO

ALTER PROC spInsertDateValidatedOrder
   @CustomerID        nvarchar(5),
   @EmployeeID        int,
   @OrderDate         datetime      = NULL,
   @RequiredDate      datetime      = NULL,
   @ShippedDate       datetime      = NULL,
   @ShipVia           int,
   @Freight           money,
   @ShipName          nvarchar(40)  = NULL,
   @ShipAddress       nvarchar(60)  = NULL,
   @ShipCity          nvarchar(15)  = NULL,
   @ShipRegion        nvarchar(15)  = NULL,
   @ShipPostalCode    nvarchar(10)  = NULL,
   @ShipCountry       nvarchar(15)  = NULL,
   @OrderID           int       OUTPUT

AS

/* I don't like altering input paramters - I find that it helps in debugging
** if I can refer to their original value at any time. Therefore, I'm going
** to declare a separate variable to assign the end value we will be
** inserting into the table.                                              */
DECLARE   @InsertedOrderDate   smalldatetime

/* Test to see if supplied date is over seven days old, if so
** replace with NULL value
** otherwise, truncate the time to be midnight*/
IF DATEDIFF(dd, @OrderDate, GETDATE()) > 7
BEGIN
   SELECT @InsertedOrderDate = NULL
   PRINT 'Invalid Order Date'
   PRINT 'Supplied Order Date was greater than 7 days old.'
   PRINT 'The value has been reset to NULL'
END
ELSE
BEGIN
   SELECT @InsertedOrderDate =
      CONVERT(datetime,(CONVERT(varchar,@OrderDate,112)))
      PRINT 'The Time of Day in Order Date was truncated'
END

/* Create the new record */
INSERT INTO Orders
VALUES
(
   @CustomerID,
   @EmployeeID,
   @InsertedOrderDate,
   @RequiredDate,
   @ShippedDate,
   @ShipVia,
   @Freight,
   @ShipName,
   @ShipAddress,
   @ShipCity,
```

```
        @ShipRegion,
        @ShipPostalCode,
        @ShipCountry
    )

    /* Move the identity value from the newly inserted record into
        our output variable */
    SELECT @OrderID = @@IDENTITY
```

Now when we execute our test batch, we get slightly different results. Note that we've deleted the identity only `SELECT` out of the test batch for brevity's sake:

First, the test batch using the current date:

```
USE Northwind
GO

DECLARE    @MyIdent    int
DECLARE    @MyDate     smalldatetime

SELECT @MyDate = GETDATE()

EXEC spInsertDateValidatedOrder
    @CustomerID = 'ALFKI',
    @EmployeeID = 5,
    @OrderDate  = @MyDate,
    @ShipVia    = 3,
    @Freight    = 5.00,
    @OrderID    = @MyIdent OUTPUT

SELECT OrderID, CustomerID, EmployeeID, OrderDate, ShipName
FROM Orders
WHERE OrderID = @MyIdent
```

And we can see that our value was truncated both in terms of the actual data, but we also have the message that explicitly tells us:

```
The Time of Day in Order Date was truncated

(1 row(s) affected)

OrderID         CustomerID           EmployeeID           OrderDate                      ShipName
--------------- -------------------- -------------------- ------------------------------ --------------
11080           ALFKI                5                    1999-08-30 00:00:00.000        NULL

(1 row(s) affected)
```

Next, we run the older version of the test batch that manually feeds an older date:

```
USE Northwind
GO

DECLARE   @MyIdent    int

EXEC spInsertDateValidatedOrder
    @CustomerID = 'ALFKI',
    @EmployeeID = 5,
    @OrderDate  = '1/1/1999',
    @ShipVia    = 3,
    @Freight    = 5.00,
    @OrderID    = @MyIdent OUTPUT
```

```
SELECT OrderID, CustomerID, EmployeeID, OrderDate, ShipName
FROM Orders
WHERE OrderID = @MyIdent
```

Again we see an explicit indication of what happened to our data:

```
Invalid Order Date
Supplied Order Date was greater than 7 days old.
The value has been reset to NULL

(1 row(s) affected)

OrderID         CustomerID          EmployeeID          OrderDate           ShipName
--------------- ------------------- ------------------- ------------------- -------------
11085           ALFKI               5                   NULL                NULL

(1 row(s) affected)
```

The CASE Statement

The CASE statement is essentially the equivalent of one of several different statements depending on the language from which you're coming. Names for other statements that work like CASE include:

- Switch - C, C++, Delphi
- Select Case - Visual Basic
- Do Case - Xbase
- Evaluate - COBOL

I'm sure there are others – these are just from the languages that I've worked with in some form or another over the years.

A CASE statement works similar to an IF...ELSE, except that it allows for multiple evaluations. You can base your CASE on one or more criteria depending on what you're doing and how you format the CASE statement.

Note that, as implied by "depending on how you format", there is more than one way to write a CASE statement – with an input expression or a Boolean expression.

The first option is to use an input expression that will be compared with the value used in each WHEN clause. The SQL Server documentation refers to this as a "simple" CASE:

```
CASE <input expression>
WHEN <when expression> THEN <result expression>
[...n]
[ELSE <result expression>]
END
```

Option number two is to provide an expression with each `WHEN` clause that will evaluate to `TRUE/FALSE`. The docs refer to this as a "searched" `CASE`:

```
CASE
WHEN <Boolean expression> THEN <result expression>
[...n]
[ELSE <result expression>]
END
```

Perhaps what's nicest about `CASE` is that you can use it "inline" with (that is, as an integral part of) a `SELECT` statement. This can actually be quite powerful.

Let's move away from our previous example for the time being (don't worry, we'll be back to it), and look at a `CASE` statement from a couple of different perspectives.

A Simple CASE

A simple `CASE` takes an expression that equates to some value. The expression could evaluate to `TRUE` or `FALSE`, but can also equate to 5, "5", "Fred" – any valid SQL Server expression is OK. Let's get right to an example:

```
USE Northwind
GO

SELECT TOP 10 OrderID, OrderID % 10 AS 'Last Digit', Position =
CASE OrderID % 10
   WHEN 1 THEN 'First'
   WHEN 2 THEN 'Second'
   WHEN 3 THEN 'Third'
   WHEN 4 THEN 'Fourth'
   ELSE 'Something Else'
END
FROM Orders
```

For those of you who aren't familiar with it, the `%` operator is for a **modulus**. A modulus works the same math that a divide by (/) does, but it only gives you the remainder. Therefore, 16 % 4 = 0 (4 goes into 16 evenly), but 16 % 5 = 1 (16 divided by 5 has a remainder of 1). In the example, since we're dividing by ten, using the modulus is giving us the last digit of the number we're evaluating.

Let's see what we got with this:

```
OrderID         Last Digit           Position
--------------- -------------------- --------------------
10249           9                    Something Else
10251           1                    First
10258           8                    Something Else
10260           0                    Something Else
10265           5                    Something Else
10267           7                    Something Else
10269           9                    Something Else
10270           0                    Something Else
10274           4                    Fourth
10275           5                    Something Else

(10 row(s) affected)
```

Notice that whenever there is a matching value in the list, the THEN clause is invoked. Since we have an ELSE clause, any value that doesn't match one of the previous values will be assigned whatever we've put in our ELSE. If I had left the ELSE out, then any such value would be given a NULL.

Let's go with one more example that expands on what we can use as an expression. This time, we'll use another column from our query:

```
USE Northwind
GO

SELECT TOP 10 OrderID % 10 AS "Last Digit",
    ProductID,
    "How Close?" = CASE OrderID % 10
       WHEN ProductID THEN 'Exact Match!'
       WHEN ProductID - 1 THEN 'Within 1'
       WHEN ProductID + 1 THEN 'Within 1'
       ELSE 'More Than One Apart'
    END
FROM [Order Details]
WHERE ProductID < 10
ORDER BY OrderID DESC
```

Notice that I've used equations at every step of the way on this one, yet it still works...

```
Last Digit      ProductID           How Close?
--------------- -------------------- ----------------------------
7               8                   Within 1
7               7                   Exact Match!
7               6                   Within 1
7               4                   More Than One Apart
7               3                   More Than One Apart
7               2                   More Than One Apart
6               6                   Exact Match!
5               2                   More Than One Apart
2               2                   Exact Match!
1               7                   More Than One Apart

(10 row(s) affected)
```

As long as the expression evaluates out to a specific value that is of a compatible type to the input expression, then it can be analyzed, and the proper THEN clause applied.

A Searched CASE

This one works pretty much the same as a simple CASE, with only two slight twists:

- There is no input expression
- The WHEN expression must evaluate to a Boolean value

Perhaps what I find the coolest about this kind of CASE is that we can completely change around what is forming the basis of our expression – mixing and matching column expressions depending on our different possible situations.

As usual, I find the best way to get across how this works is via an example:

```
USE Northwind
GO

SELECT TOP 10 OrderID % 10 AS "Last Digit",
   ProductID,
   "How Close?" = CASE
      WHEN (OrderID % 10) < 3 THEN 'Ends With Less Than Three'
      WHEN ProductID = 6 THEN 'ProductID is 6'
      WHEN ABS(OrderID % 10 - ProductID) <= 1 THEN 'Within 1'
      ELSE 'More Than One Apart'
   END
FROM [Order Details]
WHERE ProductID < 10
ORDER BY OrderID DESC
```

This is substantially different from our simple CASE examples, but it still works:

```
Last Digit     ProductID         How Close?
-------------- ----------------- ---------------------------------
7              8                 Within 1
7              7                 Within 1
7              6                 ProductID is 6
7              4                 More Than One Apart
7              3                 More Than One Apart
7              2                 More Than One Apart
6              6                 ProductID is 6
5              2                 More Than One Apart
2              2                 Ends With Less Than Three
1              7                 Ends With Less Than Three

(10 row(s) affected)
```

There are a couple of things to pay particular attention to in how SQL Server evaluated things:

- Even when two conditions are true, (the second to last row, for example, meets both the first and third conditions) only the first condition is given. For many languages, this is the way this kind of statement always works. If you're from the C world though, you'll need to remember this when you are coding. There is no "break" statement required – it always terminates after one condition is met.
- You can mix and match what fields you're using in your condition expressions. In this case, we used OrderID, ProductID, and both together.
- You can perform pretty much any expression as long as, in the end, it evaluates to a Boolean result.

Let's try this out with a slightly more complex example. In this example, we're not going to do the mix and match thing – instead, we'll stick with just the one column we're looking at (we could change columns being tested – but, most of time, we won't need to). Instead, we're going to deal with a more real-life scenario that I helped solve for a rather large ecommerce site.

The scenario is this: marketing people really like nice clean prices. They hate it when you apply a 10% markup over cost, and start putting out prices like $10.13, or $23.19. Instead, they like slick prices that end in number like 49, 75, 95, or 99. In our scenario, we're supposed to create a possible new price list for analysis, and they want it to meet certain criteria.

If the new price ends with less than 50 cents (such as our $10.13 example above), then marketing would like the price to be bumped up to the same dollar amount but ending in 49 cent ($10.49 for our example). Prices ending with 50¢ to 75¢ should be changed to end in 75¢, and prices ending with more than 75¢ should be changed to end with 95¢. Let's look at some examples of what they want:

If the New Price Would Be	Then It Should Become
$10.13	$10.49
$17.57	$17.75
$27.75	$27.75
$79.99	$79.95

Technically speaking, we could do this with nested `IF...ELSE` statements, but:

- It would be much harder to read – especially if the rules were more complex
- We would have to implement the code using a cursor (BAD!!!) and examine each row one at a time

In short – YUCK!

A `CASE` statement is going to make this process relatively easy. What's more, we're going to be able to place our condition inline to our query and use it as part of a set operation – this almost always means that we're going to get much better performance than we would with a cursor.

Our marketing department has decided they would like to see what things would look like if we increased prices by 10%, so we'll plug a 10% markup into a `CASE` statement, and, together with a little extra analysis, we'll get the numbers we're looking for:

```
USE Northwind
GO

/* I'm setting up some holding variables here. This way, if we get asked
** to run the query again with a slightly different value, we'll only have
** to change it in one place.
*/
DECLARE @Markup     money
DECLARE @Multiplier money

SELECT @Markup = .10                -- Change the markup here
SELECT @Multiplier = @Markup + 1    -- We want the end price, not the amount
                                    -- of the increase, so add 1


/* Now execute things for our results. Note that we're limiting things
** to the top 10 items for brevity - in reality, we either wouldn't do this
** at all, or we would have a more complex WHERE clause to limit the
** increase to a particular set of products
*/
SELECT TOP 10 ProductID, ProductName, UnitPrice,
   UnitPrice * @Multiplier AS "Marked Up Price", "New Price" =
   CASE WHEN FLOOR(UnitPrice * @Multiplier + .24)
             > FLOOR(UnitPrice * @Multiplier)
                     THEN FLOOR(UnitPrice * @Multiplier) + .95
        WHEN FLOOR(UnitPrice * @Multiplier + .5) >
             FLOOR(UnitPrice * @Multiplier)
```

```
                    THEN FLOOR(UnitPrice * @Multiplier) + .75
        ELSE FLOOR(UnitPrice * @Multiplier) + .49
    END
FROM Products
ORDER BY ProductID DESC         -- Just because the bottom's a better example
                                -- in this particular case
```

The FLOOR function you see here is a pretty simple one – it takes the value supplied and rounds down to the nearest integer.

Now, I don't know about you, but I get very suspicious when I hear the word "analysis" come out of someone's lips – particularly if that person is in a marketing or sales role. Don't get me wrong – those people are doing their jobs just like I am. The thing is, once they ask the question one way, they usually want to ask the question another way. That being the case, I quit when ahead and set this up as a script – now all we need to do when they decide they want to try it with 15% is make a change to the initialization value of @Markup. Let's see what we got this time with that 10% markup though:

```
ProductId       ProductName                              UnitPrice            Marked Up Price      New Price
--------------- ---------------------------------------- -------------------- -------------------- ----------------
77              Original Frankfurter grüne Soße          13.0000              14.3000              14.4900
76              Lakkalikööri                             18.0000              19.8000              19.9500
75              Rhönbräu Klosterbier                     7.7500               8.5250               8.7500
74              Longlife Tofu                            10.0000              11.0000              11.4900
73              Röd Kaviar                               15.0000              16.5000              16.7500
72              Mozzarella di Giovanni                   34.8000              38.2800              38.4900
71              Flotemysost                              21.5000              23.6500              23.7500
70              Outback Lager                            15.0000              16.5000              16.7500
69              Gudbrandsdalsost                         36.0000              39.6000              39.7500
68              Scottish Longbreads                      12.5000              13.7500              13.7500

(10 row(s) affected)
```

Look these over for a bit, and you'll see that the results match what we were expecting. What's more, we didn't have to build a cursor in to do it.

Now, for one final example with this CASE statement, and to put something like this more into the context of sprocs, let's convert this to something the Marketing department can call themselves.

In order to convert something like this to a sproc, we need to know what information is going to be changing each time we run it. In this case, the only thing that will change will be the markup percentage. That means that only the markup percent needs to be accepted as a parameter – any other variables can remain internal to the sproc.

To change this particular script then, we only need to change one variable to a parameter, add our CREATE statements, and we should be ready to go. However, we are going to make just one more change to clarify the input for the average user:

```
USE Northwind
GO

CREATE PROC spMarkupTest
   @MarkupAsPercent   money
AS
```

```
    DECLARE @Multiplier money

-- We want the end price, not the amount
SELECT @Multiplier = @MarkupAsPercent / 100 + 1 /*of the increase, so add 1

** Now execute things for our results. Note that we're limiting things
** to the top 10 items for brevity - in reality, we either wouldn't do this
** at all, or we would have a more complex WHERE clause to limit the
** increase to a particular set of products
*/
SELECT TOP 10 ProductId, ProductName, UnitPrice,
   UnitPrice * @Multiplier AS "Marked Up Price", "New Price" =
   CASE WHEN FLOOR(UnitPrice * @Multiplier + .24)
              > FLOOR(UnitPrice * @Multiplier)
                      THEN FLOOR(UnitPrice * @Multiplier) + .95
        WHEN FLOOR(UnitPrice  * @Multiplier + .5) >
              FLOOR(UnitPrice * @Multiplier)
                      THEN FLOOR(UnitPrice * @Multiplier) + .75
        ELSE FLOOR(UnitPrice * @Multiplier) + .49
   END
FROM Products
ORDER BY ProductID DESC     -- Just because the bottom's a better example
                            -- in this particular case
```

Now, to run our sproc, we only need to make use of the EXEC command and supply a parameter:

```
EXEC spMarkupTest 10
```

Our results should be exactly as they were when the code was in script form. By putting it into sproc form though, we:

- Simplified the use for inexperienced users
- Sped up processing time

The simplified use for the end user seems pretty obvious. They probably would be pretty intimidated if they had to look at all that code in the script – even if they only had to change just one line. Instead, they can enter in just three words – including the parameter value.

The performance boost is actually just about nothing in an interactive scenario like in this case, but, rest assured, the process will run slightly faster (just milliseconds in many cases – longer in others) as a sproc – we'll look into this much further before the chapter's done.

Confirming Success or Failure with Return Values

You'll see return values used in a couple of different ways. The first is to actually return data, such as an identity value or the number of rows that the sproc affected. Consider that use to be an evil practice from the dark ages. Instead, move on to the way that return values should be used and what they are really there for – determining the execution status of your sproc.

If it sounds like I have an opinion on how return values should be used, it's because I most definitely do. I was actually originally taught to use return values as a "trick" to get around having to use output parameters – in effect, as a shortcut. Happily, I overcame this training. The problem is that, like most shortcuts, you're cutting something out, and, in this case, what you're cutting out is rather important.

Using return values as a means of returning data back to your calling routine clouds the meaning of the return code when you need to send back honest to goodness error codes. In short – don't go there!

Return values are all about indicating success or failure of the sproc, and even the extent or nature of that success or failure. For the C programmers among you, this should be a fairly easy strategy to relate to – it is a common practice to use a function's return value as a success code, with any non-zero value indicating some sort of problem. If you stick with the default return codes in SQL Server, you'll find that the same rules hold true.

How to Use RETURN

Actually, your program will receive a return value whether you supply one or not. By default, SQL Server automatically returns a value of zero when your procedure is complete.

To pass a return value back from our sproc to the calling code, we simple use the RETURN statement:

```
RETURN [<integer value to return>]
```

Note that the return value must be an integer.

Perhaps the biggest thing to understand about the RETURN statement is that it unconditionally exits from your sproc. That is, no matter where you are in your sproc, not one single more line of code will execute after you have issued a RETURN statement.

By unconditionally, I don't mean that a RETURN statement is executed regardless of where it is in code – on the contrary, you can have many RETURN statements in your sproc, and they will only be executed when the normal conditional structure of your code issues the command. Once that happens however, there is no turning back.

Let's illustrate this idea of how a RETURN statement affects things by writing a very simple test sproc:

```
USE Northwind
GO

CREATE PROC spTestReturns
AS
   DECLARE @MyMessage          varchar(50)
   DECLARE @MyOtherMessage     varchar(50)

   SELECT @MyMessage = "Hi, it's that line before the RETURN"
   PRINT @MyMessage
   RETURN
   SELECT @MyOtherMessage = "Sorry, but we won't get this far"
   PRINT @MyOtherMessage
RETURN
```

OK, now we have a sproc, but we need a small script to test out a couple of things for us. What we want to see is:

- What gets printed out
- What value does the RETURN statement return

In order to capture the value of a RETURN statement, we need to assign it to a variable during our EXEC statement. For example, the following code would assign whatever the return value is to @ReturnVal:

```
EXEC @ReturnVal = spMySproc
```

Now let's put this into a more useful script to test out our sproc:

```
DECLARE @Return int

EXEC @Return = spTestReturns
SELECT @Return
```

Short but sweet – when we run it, we see that the RETURN statement did indeed terminate the code before anything else could run:

```
Hi, it's that line before the RETURN

-----------
0

(1 row(s) affected)
```

We also got back the return value for our sproc, which was zero. Notice that the value was zero even though we didn't specify a specific return value – that's because the default is always zero.

> **Think about this for a minute – if the default return value is zero, then that means that the default return is also, in effect, "No Errors". This has some serious dangers to it. The key point here is to make sure that you always explicitly define your return values – that way, you are reasonably certain to be returning the value you intended rather than something by accident.**

Now, just for grins, let's alter that sproc to verify that we can send whatever integer value we want back as the return value:

```
USE Northwind
GO

ALTER PROC spTestReturns
AS
   DECLARE @MyMessage         varchar(50)
   DECLARE @MyOtherMessage    varchar(50)
```

```
    SELECT @MyMessage = "Hi, it's that line before the RETURN"
    PRINT @MyMessage
    RETURN 100
    SELECT @MyOtherMessage = "Sorry, but we won't get this far"
    PRINT @MyOtherMessage
RETURN
```

Now re-run your test script, and you'll get the same result save for that change in return value:

```
Hi, it's that line before the RETURN

-----------
100

(1 row(s) affected)
```

The WAITFOR Statement

There are often things that you either don't want to or simply can't have happen right this moment, but you also don't want to have to hang around waiting for the right time to execute something.

No problem – use the WAITFOR statement and have SQL Server wait for you. The syntax is incredibly simple:

```
WAITFOR
   DELAY <'time'> | TIME <'time'>
```

The WAITFOR statement does just exactly what it says it does – that is, it waits for whatever you specify as the argument to occur. You can specify either an explicit time of day for something to happen, or you can specify an amount of time to wait before doing something.

The DELAY Parameter

The DELAY parameter choice specifies an amount of time to wait. You cannot specify a number of days – just time in hours, minutes, and seconds. The maximum allowed delay is 24 hours. So, for example:

```
WAITFOR DELAY '01:00'
```

Would run any code prior to the WAITFOR, then reach the WAITFOR statement and stop for one hour, after which execution of the code would continue with whatever the next statement was.

The TIME Parameter

The TIME parameter choice specifies to wait until a specific time of day. Again, we cannot specify any kind of date – just time of day using a 24-hour clock. Once more, this gives us a one day time limit for the maximum amount of delay. For example:

```
WAITFOR TIME '01:00'
```

Would run any code prior to the WAITFOR, then reach the WAITFOR statement and stop until 1AM, after which execution of the code would continue with whatever the next statement was after the WAITFOR.

Looping with the WHILE Statement

This is one of those Catch 22 kinds of statements. It's a control of flow statement, so I need to address it here. At the same time, the WHILE statement is rarely used in SQL except when dealing with cursors, so it makes a lot of sense to address it there.

We're going to do a little of both. We'll get the basics down here and go through an example of where we might want to make use of a WHILE in a non-cursor construct.

The WHILE statement works much as it does in other languages to which you have probably been exposed. Essentially, a condition is tested each time you come to the top of the loop. If the condition is still TRUE, then the loop executes again – if not, you exit.

The syntax looks like this:

```
WHILE <Boolean expression>
      <sql statement> |
[BEGIN
      <statement block>
      [BREAK]
      <sql statement> | <statement block>
      [CONTINUE]
END]
```

While you can just execute one statement (much as you do with an IF statement), you'll almost never see a WHILE that isn't followed by a BEGIN...END with a full statement block.

The BREAK statement is a way of exiting the loop without waiting for the bottom of the loop to come and the expression to be re-evaluated.

> *I'm sure I won't be the first to tell you this, but using a BREAK is generally thought of as something of bad form in the classical sense. I tend to sit on the fence on this one. I avoid using them if reasonably possible. Most of the time, I can indeed avoid them just by moving a statement or two around while still coming up with the same results. The advantage of this is usually more readable code. It is simply easier to handle a looping structure (or any structure for that matter) if you have a single point of entry and a single exit. Using a BREAK violates this notion.*
>
> *All that being said, sometimes you can actually make things worse by reformatting the code to avoid a BREAK. In addition, I've seen people write much slower code for the sake of not using a BREAK statement – bad idea.*

The CONTINUE statement is something of the complete opposite of a BREAK statement. In short, it tells the WHILE loop to go back to the beginning. Regardless of where you are in the loop, you immediately go back to the top and re-evaluate the expression (exiting if the expression is no longer true).

We'll go ahead and do something of a short example here just to get our feet wet. As I mentioned before, WHILE loops tend to be rare in non-cursor situations, so forgive me if this example seems kind of lame.

What we're going to do is create something of a monitoring process using our WHILE loop and a WAITFOR command. We're going to be automatically updating our statistics once per day:

```
WHILE 1 = 1
BEGIN
   WAITFOR TIME '01:00'
   EXEC sp_updatestats
   RAISERROR('Statistics Updated for Database', 1, 1) WITH LOG
END
```

This would update the statistics for every table in our database every night at 1AM and write a log entry of that fact to both the SQL Server log and the Windows NT application log. If you want test to see that this works, leave this running all night and then check your logs in the morning.

Note that a loop like this isn't the way that you would normally want to schedule a task. If you want something to run everyday, set up a job in EM. In addition to not keeping a connection open all the time (which the above example would do), you also get the capability to make follow up actions dependent on the success or failure of your script. Also, you can e-mail or net-send messages regarding the completion status.

Dealing with Errors

Sure. You won't need this section. I mean, our code never has errors, and we never run into problems, right? OK, well, now that we've had our moment of fantasy for today, let's get down to reality – things go wrong. It's just the way that life in the wonderful world of software engineering works. Fortunately, we can do something about it. Unfortunately, you're probably not going to be happy with the tools you have. Fortunately again, there are ways to make the most out of what you have, and ways to hide many of the inadequacies of error handling in the SQL world.

Three common error types can happen in SQL Server:

- Errors that create run-time errors and stop your code from proceeding further.
- Errors that SQL Server knows about, but that don't create run-time errors such that your code stops running. These can also be referred to as "in-line" errors.
- Errors that are more logical in nature and that SQL Server is essentially oblivious to.

The first thing to understand about handling errors in SQL Server is that there is no "error handler" mechanism available. You don't have an option that essentially says, "If any error happens, go run this code over in this other spot." This is probably going to be something of a real shock for you if you've come from a more modern procedural or event-driven programming language. Errors that have enough severity to generate a run-time error are problematic from the SQL Server side of the equation. The bright side is that all the current data access object models pass through the message on such errors, so you know about them in your client application and can do something about them there. This leaves us with the other two kinds of errors.

Handling In-Line Errors

In-line errors are those pesky little things where SQL Server keeps running as such, but hasn't, for some reason, succeeded in doing what you wanted it to do. For example, let's insert a record into the `Order Details` table that doesn't have a corresponding record in the `Orders` table:

```
USE Northwind
GO

INSERT INTO [Order Details]
   (OrderID, ProductID, UnitPrice, Quantity, Discount)
VALUES
   (999999,11,10.00,10, 0)
```

SQL Server won't perform this insert for us because there is a `FOREIGN KEY` constraint on `Order Details` that references the `PRIMARY KEY` in the `Orders` table. Since there is no record in the `Orders` table with an `OrderID` of 999999, the record we are trying to insert into `Order Details` violates that constraint and is rejected:

```
Server: Msg 547, Level 16, State 1, Line 1
INSERT statement conflicted with COLUMN FOREIGN KEY constraint 'FK_Order_Details_Orders'.
The conflict occurred in database 'Northwind', table 'Orders', column 'OrderID'.
The statement has been terminated.
```

Pay attention to that error 547 up there – that's something of which we can make use.

Making Use of @@ERROR

We've already talked some about this bad boy when we were looking at scripting, but it's time to get a lot friendlier with this particular global variable.

To review, `@@ERROR` contains the error number of the last T-SQL statement executed. If the value is zero, then no error occurred.

> **The caveat with `@@ERROR` is that it is reset with each new statement – this means that if you want to defer analyzing the value, or you want to use it more than once, you need to move the value into some other holding bin – a local variable that you have declared for this purpose.**

Let's play with this just a bit using our `INSERT` example:

```
USE Northwind
GO

DECLARE   @Error   int

-- Bogus INSERT - there is no OrderID of 999999 in Northind
INSERT INTO [Order Details]
   (OrderID, ProductID, UnitPrice, Quantity, Discount)
VALUES
   (999999,11,10.00,10, 0)

-- Move our error code into safe keeping. Note that, after this statement,
-- @@Error will be reset to whatever error number applies to this statement
SELECT @Error = @@ERROR
```

```
-- Print out a blank separator line
PRINT ''

-- The value of our holding variable is just what we would expect
PRINT 'The Value of @Error is ' + CONVERT(varchar, @Error)

-- The value of @@ERROR has been reset - it's back to zero
PRINT 'The Value of @@ERROR is ' + CONVERT(varchar, @@ERROR)
```

Now execute our script, and we can examine how `@@ERROR` is affected:

```
Server: Msg 547, Level 16, State 1, Line 0
INSERT statement conflicted with COLUMN FOREIGN KEY constraint 'FK_Order_Details_Orders'.
The conflict occurred in database 'Northwind', table 'Orders', column 'OrderID'.
The statement has been terminated.

The Value of @Error is 547
The Value of @@ERROR is 0
```

This illustrates pretty quickly the issue of saving the value from `@@ERROR`. The first error statement is only informational in nature. SQL Server has thrown that error, but hasn't stopped our code from executing. Indeed, the only part of that message that our sproc has access to is the error number. That error number resides in `@@ERROR` for just that next T-SQL statement – after that it's gone.

> **Notice that `@Error` and `@@ERROR` are two separate and distinct variables, and can be referred to separately. This isn't just because of the case difference (depending on how you have your server configured, case sensitivity can affect your variable names), but rather because of the difference in scope. The `@` or `@@` is part of the name, so just the number of `@` symbols on the front makes each one separate and distinct from the other.**

Using @@ERROR in a Sproc

Let's go back to our `spInsertValidatedOrder` stored procedure that we started back when we were dealing with `IF...ELSE` statements. All the examples we worked with in that sproc ran just fine. Of course they did - they were well controlled examples. However, that's not the way things work in the real world. Indeed, you never have any idea what a user is going to throw at your code. The world is littered with the carcasses of programmers who thought they had thought of everything only to find that their users had broken something (you might say they thought of something else) within the first few minutes of operation.

We can break that sproc in no time at all by just changing one little thing in our test script:

```
USE Northwind
GO

DECLARE    @MyIdent    int
DECLARE    @MyDate     smalldatetime

SELECT @MyDate = GETDATE()
```

```
EXEC spInsertDateValidatedOrder
   @CustomerID = 'ZXZXZ',
   @EmployeeID = 5,
   @OrderDate  = @MyDate,
   @ShipVia    = 3,
   @Freight    = 5.00,
   @OrderID    = @MyIdent OUTPUT

SELECT OrderID, CustomerID, EmployeeID, OrderDate, ShipName
FROM Orders
WHERE OrderID = @MyIdent
```

This seemingly simple change creates all kinds of havoc with our sproc:

```
The Time of Day in Order Date was truncated
Server: Msg 547, Level 16, State 1, Procedure spInsertDateValidatedOrder, Line 44
INSERT statement conflicted with COLUMN FOREIGN KEY constraint 'FK_Orders_Customers'.
The conflict occurred in database 'Northwind', table 'Customers', column 'CustomerID'.
The statement has been terminated.
OrderID     CustomerID     EmployeeID     OrderDate     ShipName
----------- -------------- -------------- ------------- ---------

(0 row(s) affected)
```

Our row wasn't inserted. It shouldn't have been – after all, isn't that why we put in constraints – to ensure that bad records don't get inserted into our database?

The ugly thing here is that we get a big ugly message that's almost impossible for the average person to understand. What we need to do is test the value of `@@ERROR` and respond accordingly.

We can do this easily using an `IF...ELSE` statement together with either `@@ERROR` (if we can test the value immediately and only need to test it once), or we can move `@@ERROR` into a local variable and then test the local variable.

> *Personally, I like my code to be consistent, so I always move it into a local variable and then do all my testing with that – even when I only need to test it once. I have to admit to being in the minority on that one though. Doing this when you don't need to takes up slightly more memory (the extra variable) and requires an extra assignment statement (to move @@ERROR to your local variable). Both of these pieces of overhead are extremely small and I gladly trade them for the idea of people who read my code knowing that they are going to see the same thing done the same way every time.*

In addition, it doesn't make much sense to still select out the inserted row, so we'll want to skip that part since it's irrelevant.

So let's add a couple of changes to deal with this referential integrity issue and skip the code that doesn't apply in this error situation:

```
USE Northwind
GO

ALTER PROC spInsertDateValidatedOrder
   @CustomerID       nvarchar(5),
   @EmployeeID       int,
```

```
    @OrderDate          datetime      = NULL,
    @RequiredDate       datetime      = NULL,
    @ShippedDate        datetime      = NULL,
    @ShipVia            int,
    @Freight            money,
    @ShipName           nvarchar(40)  = NULL,
    @ShipAddress        nvarchar(60)  = NULL,
    @ShipCity           nvarchar(15)  = NULL,
    @ShipRegion         nvarchar(15)  = NULL,
    @ShipPostalCode     nvarchar(10)  = NULL,
    @ShipCountry        nvarchar(15)  = NULL,
    @OrderID            int       OUTPUT

AS

-- Declare our variables
DECLARE   @Error                 int
DECLARE   @InsertedOrderDate     smalldatetime

/* Test to see if supplied date is over seven days old, if so
** replace with NULL value
** otherwise, truncate the time to be midnight*/
IF DATEDIFF(dd, @OrderDate, GETDATE()) > 7
BEGIN
   SELECT @InsertedOrderDate = NULL
   PRINT 'Invalid Order Date'
   PRINT 'Supplied OrderDate was greater than 7 days old.'
   PRINT 'The value has been reset to NULL'
END
ELSE
BEGIN
   SELECT @InsertedOrderDate =
      CONVERT(datetime,(CONVERT(varchar,@OrderDate,112)))
      PRINT 'The Time of Day in Order Date was truncated'
END

/* Create the new record */
INSERT INTO Orders
VALUES
(
   @CustomerID,
   @EmployeeID,
   @InsertedOrderDate,
   @RequiredDate,
   @ShippedDate,
   @ShipVia,
   @Freight,
   @ShipName,
   @ShipAddress,
   @ShipCity,
   @ShipRegion,
   @ShipPostalCode,
   @ShipCountry
)

-- Move it to our local variable and check for an error condition
SELECT @Error = @@ERROR

IF @Error != 0
BEGIN
    -- Uh, oh - something went wrong.

   IF @Error = 547
   -- The problem is a constraint violation. Print out some informational
   -- help to steer the user to the most likely problem.
   BEGIN
      PRINT 'Supplied data violates data integrity rules'
      PRINT 'Check that the supplied customer number exists'
      PRINT 'in the system and try again'
   END
```

```
    ELSE
    -- Oops, it's something we haven't anticipated, tell them that we
    -- don't know, print out the error.
    BEGIN
       PRINT 'An unknown error occurred. Contact your System Administrator'
       PRINT 'The error was number ' + CONVERT(varchar, @Error)
    END
    -- Regardless of the error, we're going to send it back to the calling
    -- piece of code so it can be handled at that level if necessary.
    RETURN @Error
END

/* Move the identity value from the newly inserted record into
      our output variable */
SELECT @OrderID = @@IDENTITY

RETURN
```

Now we need to run our test script again, but it's now just a little inadequate to test our sproc – we need to accept the return value so we know what happened. In addition, we have no need to run the query to return the row just inserted if the row couldn't be inserted – so we'll skip that in the event of error:

```
USE Northwind
GO

DECLARE   @MyIdent   int
DECLARE   @MyDate    smalldatetime
DECLARE   @Return    int

SELECT @MyDate = GETDATE()

EXEC @Return = spInsertDateValidatedOrder
   @CustomerID = 'ZXZXZ',
   @EmployeeID = 5,
   @OrderDate  = @MyDate,
   @ShipVia    = 3,
   @Freight    = 5.00,
   @OrderID    = @MyIdent OUTPUT

IF @Return = 0
   SELECT OrderID, CustomerID, EmployeeID, OrderDate, ShipName
   FROM Orders
   WHERE OrderID = @MyIdent
ELSE
   PRINT 'Value Returned was ' + CONVERT(varchar, @Return)
```

Realistically, not much changed – just five lines. Nonetheless, our behavior is quite a bit different when we have an error. Run this script, and we wind up with a different result than before we had our error checking:

```
The Time of Day in Order Date was truncated
Server: Msg 547, Level 16, State 1, Procedure spInsertDateValidatedOrder, Line 42
INSERT statement conflicted with COLUMN FOREIGN KEY constraint 'FK_Orders_Customers'.
The conflict occurred in database 'Northwind', table 'Customers', column 'CustomerID'.
The statement has been terminated.
Supplied data violates data integrity rules
Check that the supplied customer number exists
in the system and try again
Value Returned was 547
```

We didn't have an error handler in the way most languages operate these days, but we were able to handle it nonetheless.

Handling Errors before they Happen

Sometimes you have errors that SQL Server doesn't really have an effective way to even know about, let alone tell you about. Other times we want to prevent the errors before they happen. These we need to check for and handle ourselves.

Sticking with the main example sproc we've used for this chapter, let's address some business rules that are logical in nature, but not necessarily implemented in the database. For example, we've been allowing nulls in the database, but maybe we don't want to do that as liberally anymore. We've decided that we should no longer allow a null `OrderDate`. We still have records in there that we don't have values for, so we don't want to change over the column to disallowing nulls at the table level. What to do?

The first thing we need to take care of is editing our sproc to no longer allow null values. This seems easy enough – just remove the `NULL` default from the parameter, right? That has two problems to it:

- SQL Server will generate an error if the parameter is not supplied, but will still allow a user to explicitly supply a `NULL`
- Even when the user fails to provide the parameter, the error information is vague

We get around these problems by actually continuing our `NULL` default just as it is, but this time we're testing for it. If the parameter contains a `NULL`, we then know that one was either not supplied or the value supplied was `NULL` (which we don't allow anymore) – we then act accordingly. So the question becomes, "How do I test to see if it's a `NULL` value?" Simple, just the way we did in our `WHERE` clauses in queries:

```
IF @OrderDate IS NULL
   <abort the INSERT and print a message>
```

Let's make the modifications to our now very familiar sproc:

```
USE Northwind
GO

ALTER PROC spInsertDateValidatedOrder
   @CustomerID        nvarchar(5),
   @EmployeeID        int,
   @OrderDate         datetime = NULL,
   @RequiredDate      datetime = NULL,
   @ShippedDate       datetime = NULL,
   @ShipVia           int,
   @Freight           money,
   @ShipName          nvarchar(40)  = NULL,
   @ShipAddress       nvarchar(60)  = NULL,
   @ShipCity          nvarchar(15)  = NULL,
   @ShipRegion        nvarchar(15)  = NULL,
   @ShipPostalCode    nvarchar(10)  = NULL,
   @ShipCountry       nvarchar(15)  = NULL,
   @OrderID           int      OUTPUT

AS

-- Declare our variables
DECLARE   @Error                 int
DECLARE   @InsertedOrderDate     smalldatetime
```

```
/* Here we're going to declare our constants. SQL Server doesn't really
** have constants in the classic sense, but I just use a standard
** variable in their place. These help your code be more readable
** - particularly when you match them up with a constant list in your
** client.                                                          */

DECLARE   @INVALIDDATE   int

/* Now that the constants are declared, we need to initialize them.
** Notice that SQL Server ignores the white space in between the
** variable and the "=" sign. Why I put in the spacing would be more
** obvious if we had several such constants - the constant values
** would line up nicely for readability
*/
SELECT @INVALIDDATE = 60000

/* Test to see if supplied date is over seven days old, if so
** it is no longer valid. Also test for NULL values.
** If either case is true, then terminate sproc with error
** message printed out.                                          */
IF DATEDIFF(dd, @OrderDate, GETDATE()) > 7 OR @OrderDate IS NULL
BEGIN
   PRINT 'Invalid Order Date'
   PRINT 'Supplied Order Date was greater than 7 days old '
   PRINT 'or was NULL. Correct the date and resubmit.'
   RETURN @INVALIDDATE
END

-- We made it this far, so it must be OK to go on with things.
SELECT @InsertedOrderDate =
   CONVERT(datetime,(CONVERT(varchar,@OrderDate,112)))
   PRINT 'The Time of Day in Order Date was truncated'

/* Create the new record */
INSERT INTO Orders
VALUES
(
   @CustomerID,
   @EmployeeID,
   @InsertedOrderDate,
   @RequiredDate,
   @ShippedDate,
   @ShipVia,
   @Freight,
   @ShipName,
   @ShipAddress,
   @ShipCity,
   @ShipRegion,
   @ShipPostalCode,
   @ShipCountry
)

-- Move it to our local variable, and check for an error condition
SELECT @Error = @@ERROR

IF @Error != 0
BEGIN
   -- Uh, oh - something went wrong.

   IF @Error = 547
   -- The problem is a constraint violation. Print out some informational
   -- help to steer the user to the most likely problem.
   BEGIN
      PRINT 'Supplied data violates data integrity rules'
      PRINT 'Check that the supplied customer number exists'
      PRINT 'in the system and try again'
   END
```

```
    ELSE
    -- Oops, it's something we haven't anticipated, tell them theat we
    -- don't know, print out the error.
    BEGIN
       PRINT 'An unknown error occurred. Contact your System Administrator'
       PRINT 'The error was number ' + CONVERT(varchar, @Error)
    END
    -- Regardless of the error, we're going to send it back to the calling
    -- piece of code so it can be handled at that level if necessary.
    RETURN @Error
END

/* Move the identity value from the newly inserted record into
        our output variable */
SELECT @OrderID = @@IDENTITY

RETURN
```

We're going to want to test this a couple of different ways, first, we need to put back in a valid customer number, then we need to run it. Assuming it succeeds, then we can move on to supplying an unacceptable date:

```
USE Northwind
GO

DECLARE    @MyIdent    int
DECLARE    @MyDate     smalldatetime
DECLARE    @Return     int

SELECT @MyDate = '1/1/1999'

EXEC @Return = spInsertDateValidatedOrder
   @CustomerID = 'ALFKI',
   @EmployeeID = 5,
   @OrderDate = @MyDate,
   @ShipVia = 3,
   @Freight = 5.00,
   @OrderID = @MyIdent OUTPUT

IF @Return = 0
   SELECT OrderID, CustomerID, EmployeeID, OrderDate, ShipName
   FROM Orders
   WHERE OrderID = @MyIdent
ELSE
   PRINT 'Value Returned was ' + CONVERT(varchar, @Return)
```

This time, when we run it, we get an error:

```
Invalid Order Date
Supplied Order Date was greater than 7 days old
or was NULL. Correct the date and resubmit.
Value Returned was -1000
```

Note that this wasn't a SQL Server error – as far as SQL Server's concerned, everything about life is just fine. What's nice though is that, if we were using a client program (say one you wrote in VB, C++, or some other language), we would be able to track the –1000 against a known constant and send a very specific message to the end user.

Manually Raising Errors

Sometimes we have errors that SQL Server doesn't really know about, but we wish it did. For example, perhaps in our previous example we don't want to return –1000. Instead, we'd like to be able to create a run-time error at the client end that the client would then use to invoke an error handler and act accordingly. To do this, we make use of the RAISERROR command in T-SQL. The syntax is pretty straightforward:

```
RAISERROR (<msg id | msg str>, <severity>, <state>
[, <argument>
[,<...n>]] )
[WITH option[,...n]]
```

Message ID/Message String

The message ID or message string you provide determines what message is sent out to the client.

Using a message ID creates a manually raised error with the ID that you specified and the message that is associated with that ID as found in the sysmessages table in the master database.

There is a complete listing of all of the standard error messages included in an appendix of this book. However, it will obviously not include any custom error messages you create. If you want to see what your SQL Server has as predefined messages, you can always perform a SELECT * FROM master..sysMessages. *This will include any messages that have been manually added to your system using the* sp_addmessage *stored procedure or through the Enterprise Manager.*

You can also just supply a message string in the form of ad hoc text without creating a more permanent message in sysmessages. For example:

```
RAISERROR ("Hi there, I'm an error", 1, 1)
```

Raises a rather simple error:

```
Msg 50000, Level 1, State 50000
Hi there, I'm an error
```

Notice that the assigned message number, even though we didn't supply one, is 50000. This is the default error value for any ad hoc error. It can be overridden using the WITH SETERROR option.

Severity

For those of you already familiar with NT, severity should be an old friend. Severity is an indication of just how bad things really are based on this error. They can range from essentially being informational (severities 0-18), to being considered as system level (19-25), to essentially catastrophic (20-25). If you raise an error of severity 19 or higher (system level), then the WITH LOG option must also be specified.

State

State is an ad hoc value. It is something that recognizes that the same exact error may occur at multiple places within your code. The notion is that this gives you an opportunity to send something of a place marker for where exactly the error occurred.

As of this writing, there was a bug in SQL Server that always supplies a state value that is the same as the error number when you use `RAISERROR`*. Hopefully this will be fixed in a service pack somewhere along the way.*

State values can be between 1 and 128. If you are troubleshooting an error with Microsoft, they apparently have some arcane knowledge that hasn't been shared with us of what some of these mean. I'm told that, if you make a tech support call to MS, they are likely to ask and make use of this state information.

Error Arguments

Some pre-defined errors will accept arguments. These allow the error to be somewhat more dynamic in nature by changing to the specific nature of the error. You can also format your error messages to accept arguments.

When you want to make use of dynamic information in what is otherwise a static error message, you need to format the fixed portion of your message such that it leaves room for the parameterized section of the message. This is done using placeholders. If you're coming from the C or C++ world, then you'll recognize the parameter placeholders immediately – they are very similar to the `printf` command arguments. If you're not from the C world, these may seem a little odd to you. All of the placeholders start with the `%` sign, and are then coded for what kind of information you'll be passing to them:

Placeholder Type Indicator	Type of value
`d`	Signed Integer – note that Books On Line also indicates that `i` is an OK choice, but I've had problems getting it to work as expected.
`o`	Unsigned octal
`p`	Pointer
`s`	String
`u`	Unsigned integer
`x` or `X`	Unsigned hexadecimal

In addition, there is the option to prefix any of these placeholder indicators with some additional flag and width information:

Flag	What it does
- (dash or minus sign)	Left Justify – only makes a difference when you supply a fixed width.
+ (plus sign)	Indicate the positive or negative nature if the parameter is a signed numeric type.

Flag	What it does
0	Tells SQL Server to pad the left side of a numeric value with zeroes until it reaches the width specified in the width option.
# (pound sign)	Only applies to Octal and Hex values. Tells SQL Server to use the appropriate prefix (0 or 0x) depending on whether it is Octal or Hex
' '	Pad the left of a numeric value with spaces if positive.

Last, but not least, you can also set the width, precision, and long/short status of a parameter:

- Width: Set by simply supplying an integer value for how much space we want to hold for the parameterized value. You can also specify a `*`, in which case SQL Server will automatically determine the width depending on the value you've set for precision.
- Precision: Determines the maximum number of digits output for numeric data.
- Long/Short: Set by using an `h` (short) or `I` (long) when the type of the parameter is an integer, octal or hex value.

To use this in an example:

```
RAISERROR ("This is a sample parameterized %s, along with a zero
padding and a sign%+010d",1,1, "string", 12121)
```

If you execute this, you get back something that looks a little different than what's in the quotes:

```
Msg 50000, Level 1, State 50000
This is a sample parameterized string, along with a zero
padding and a sign+000012121
```

The extra values supplied were inserted, in order, into our placeholders, with the final value being reformatted as specified.

WITH <option>

There are currently three options that you can mix and match when you raise an error:

- `LOG`
- `SETERROR`
- `NOWAIT`

WITH LOG

This tells SQL Server to log the error to the SQL Server error log as well as the NT application log (the later applies to installations on NT only).

WITH SETERROR

By default, a `RAISERROR` command does not set `@@ERROR` with the value of the error you generated – instead, `@@ERROR` reflects the success or failure of your actual `RAISERROR` command. `SETERROR` overrides this and sets the value of `@@ERROR` to be equal to your error ID.

WITH NOWAIT

Immediately notifies the client of the error.

Adding Your Own Custom Error Messages

We can make use of a special system stored procedure to add messages to the system. The sproc is called `sp_addmessage`, and the syntax looks like this:

```
sp_addmessage [@msgnum =] <msg id>,
[@severity =] <severity>,
[@msgtext =] <'msg'>
[, [@lang =] <'language'>]
[, [@with_log =] [TRUE|FALSE]
[, [@replace =] 'replace']
```

All the parameters mean pretty much the same thing that they did with `RAISERROR`, except for the addition of the language and replace parameters and a slight difference with the `WITH LOG` option.

@lang

This specifies the language to which this message applies. What's cool here is that you can specify a separate version of your message for any language supported in `syslanguages`.

@with_log

This works just the same as it does in `RAISERROR` in that, if set to true the message will be automatically logged to both the SQL Server error log and the NT application log when raised (the latter only when running under NT). The only trick here is that you indicate that you want this message to be logged by setting this parameter to `TRUE` rather than using the `WITH LOG` option.

Be careful of this one in Books Online. Depending on how you read it, it would be easy to interpret it as saying that you should set `@with_log` to a string constant of `'WITH_LOG'`, when you should set it to `TRUE`. Perhaps even more confusing is that the `REPLACE` option looks much the same, and it must be set to the string constant rather than `TRUE`.

@replace

If you are editing an existing message rather than creating a new one, then you must set the `@replace` parameter to `'REPLACE'`. If you leave this off, you'll get an error if the message already exists.

Creating a set list of additional messages for use by your applications can greatly enhance reuse, but more importantly, it can significantly improve readability of your application. Imagine if every one of your database applications made use of a constant list of custom error codes. You could then easily establish a constants file (a resource or include library for example) that had a listing of the appropriate errors – you could even create an include library that had a generic handling of some or all of the errors. In short, if you're going to be building multiple SQL Server apps in the same environment, consider using a set list of errors that is common to all your applications.

Using sp_addmessage

As has already been indicated, `sp_addmessage` creates messages in much the same way as we create ad hoc messages using `RAISERROR`.

As an example let's add our own custom message that tells the user about the issues with their order date:

```
sp_addmessage
    @msgnum = 60000,
    @severity = 10,
    @msgtext = '%s is not a valid Order date.
Order date must be within 7 days of current date.'
```

Execute the sproc and it confirms the addition of the new message:

(1 row(s) affected)

New message added.

> **No matter what database you're working with when you run `sp_addmessage`, the actual message is actually added to the `sysmessages` table in the `master` database. The significance of this is that, if you migrate your database to a new server, the messages will need to be added again to that new server (the old ones will still be in the `master` database of the old server). As such, I strongly recommend keeping all your custom messages stored in a script somewhere so they can easily be added into a new system.**
>
> **It's also worth noting that you can add and delete custom messages using Enterprise Manager (right-click on a server, then go to All Tasks | Manage SQL Server messages). While this is quick and easy, it makes it more problematic to create and test the scripts I recommend in the paragraph above. In short, I don't recommend its use.**

Removing an Existing Custom Message

To get rid of the custom message, use:

```
sp_dropmessage <msg num>
```

Putting Our Error Trap to Use

Now it's time to put all the different pieces we've been talking about to use at once.

First, if you tried out the `sp_dropmessage` on our new error 60000 – quit that! Add the message back so we can make use of it in this example.

What we want to do is take our sproc to the next level up. We're going to again modify our sproc so that it takes advantage of the new error features we know about. When we're done, we'll be able to generate a trappable run-time error in our client so we can take appropriate action at that end.

All we need to do is replace our PRINT statement with a RAISERROR:

```
USE Northwind
GO

ALTER PROC spInsertDateValidatedOrder
   @CustomerID        nvarchar(5),
   @EmployeeID        int,
   @OrderDate         datetime      = NULL,
   @RequiredDate      datetime      = NULL,
   @ShippedDate       datetime      = NULL,
   @ShipVia           int,
   @Freight           money,
   @ShipName          nvarchar(40)  = NULL,
   @ShipAddress       nvarchar(60)  = NULL,
   @ShipCity          nvarchar(15)  = NULL,
   @ShipRegion        nvarchar(15)  = NULL,
   @ShipPostalCode    nvarchar(10)  = NULL,
   @ShipCountry       nvarchar(15)  = NULL,
   @OrderID           int       OUTPUT

AS

-- Declare our variables
DECLARE    @Error                  int
DECLARE    @BadDate                varchar(12)
DECLARE    @InsertedOrderDate      smalldatetime

/* Test to see if supplied date is over seven days old, if so
** it is no longer valid. Also test for null values.
** If either case is true, then terminate sproc with error
** message printed out.                                        */
IF DATEDIFF(dd, @OrderDate, GETDATE()) > 7 OR @OrderDate IS NULL
BEGIN
   --RAISERROR doesn't have a date data type, so convert it first
   SELECT @BadDate = CONVERT(varchar, @OrderDate)
   RAISERROR (60000,1,1, @BadDate) WITH SETERROR
   RETURN @@ERROR
END

-- We made it this far, so it must be OK to go on with things.
SELECT @InsertedOrderDate =
   CONVERT(datetime,(CONVERT(varchar,@OrderDate,112)))
   PRINT 'The Time of Day in Order Date was truncated'

/* Create the new record */
INSERT INTO Orders
VALUES
(
   @CustomerID,
   @EmployeeID,
   @InsertedOrderDate,
   @RequiredDate,
   @ShippedDate,
   @ShipVia,
   @Freight,
   @ShipName,
   @ShipAddress,
   @ShipCity,
   @ShipRegion,
   @ShipPostalCode,
   @ShipCountry
)

-- Move it to our local variable, and check for an error condition
SELECT @Error = @@ERROR
```

```
IF @Error != 0
BEGIN
   -- Uh, Oh - something went wrong.

   IF @Error = 547
   -- The problem is a constraint violation. Print out some informational
   -- help to steer the user to the most likely problem.
   BEGIN
      PRINT 'Supplied data violates data integrity rules'
      PRINT 'Check that the supplied customer number exists'
      PRINT 'in the system and try again'
   END
   ELSE
   -- Oops, it's something we haven't anticipated, tell them theat we
   -- don't know, print out the error.
   BEGIN
      PRINT 'An unknown error occurred. Contact your System Administrator'
      PRINT 'The error was number ' + CONVERT(varchar, @Error)
   END
   -- Regardless of the error, we're going to send it back to the calling
   -- piece of code so it can be handled at that level if necessary.
   RETURN @Error
END

/* Move the identity value from the newly inserted record into
         our output variable */
SELECT @OrderID = @@IDENTITY

RETURN
```

What a Sproc Offers

Now that we've spent some time looking at how to build a sproc, we probably ought to ask the question as to why to use them. Some of the reasons are pretty basic, others may not come to mind right away if you're new to the RDBMS world. The primary benefits of sprocs include:

- Making processes that require procedural action callable
- Security
- Performance

Creating Callable Processes

As I've already indicated, a sproc is something of a script that is stored in the database. The nice thing is that, since it is a database object, we can call to it – you don't have to manually load it from a file before executing it.

Sprocs can call to other sprocs (called nesting). For SQL Server 7, you can nest up to 32 levels deep. This gives you the capability of re-using separate sprocs much as you would make use of a subroutine in a classic procedural language. The syntax for calling one sproc from another sproc is exactly the same as it is calling the sproc from a script. As an example, let's create a mini sproc to perform the same function as the test script that we've been using for most of this chapter:

```
USE Northwind
GO

CREATE PROC spTestInsert
   @MyDate    smalldatetime
AS
DECLARE   @MyIdent   int
DECLARE   @Return    int

EXEC @Return = spInsertDateValidatedOrder
   @CustomerID = 'ALFKI',
   @EmployeeID = 5,
   @OrderDate  = @MyDate,
   @ShipVia    = 3,
   @Freight    = 5.00,
   @OrderID    = @MyIdent OUTPUT

IF @Return = 0
   SELECT OrderID, CustomerID, EmployeeID, OrderDate, ShipName
   FROM Orders
   WHERE OrderID = @MyIdent
ELSE
   PRINT 'Error Returned was ' + CONVERT(varchar, @Return)
```

Now just call the sproc supplying a good date, then a bad date (to test the error handling). First the good date:

```
DECLARE @Today smalldatetime

SELECT @Today = GETDATE()

EXEC spTestInsert
   @MyDate = @Today
```

Using today's date gets what we expect:

```
The Time of Day in Order Date was truncated

(1 row(s) affected)

OrderID      CustomerID     EmployeeID     OrderDate                     ShipName
-----------  -------------  -------------  ----------------------------  ---------
11097        ALFKI          5              1999-06-06 00:00:00.000NULL

(1 row(s) affected)
```

Then a bad date:

```
EXEC spTestInsert '1/1/1999'
```

Again, this yields us what we expect – in this case an error:

```
Msg 60000, Level 1, State 60000
Jan  1 1999  is not a valid Order date.
Order date must be within 7 days of current date.
Error Returned was 60000
```

Note that local variables are just that – local to each sproc. You can have five different copies of `@MyDate`, one each to five different sprocs and they each are independent of each other.

Using Sprocs for Security

Many people don't realize the full use of sprocs as a tool for security. Much like views, we can create a sproc that returns a recordset without having to give authority to the underlying table. Granting someone the right to execute a sproc implies that they can perform any action within the sproc provided that the action is taken within the context of the sproc. That is, if we grant someone authority to execute a sproc that returns all the records in the `Customers` table, but not access to the actual `Customers` table, then the user will still be able to get data out of the `Customers` table provided that they do it by using the sproc (trying to access the table directly won't work).

What can be really handy here is that we can give someone access to modify data through the sproc, but then only give them read access to the underlying table. They will be able to modify data in the table provided that they do it through your sproc (which will likely be enforcing some business rules). They can then hook directly up to your SQL Server using Excel, Access, or whatever to build their own custom reports with no risk of "accidentally" modifying the data.

> **Setting users up to directly link to a production database via Access or Excel has to be one of the most incredibly powerful and yet stupid things you can do to your system. While you are empowering your users, you are also digging your own grave in terms of the resources they will use and long running queries they will execute (naturally, they will be oblivious to the havoc this causes your system).**
>
> **If you really must give users direct access, then consider using replication or backup and restores to create a completely separate copy of the database for them to use. This will help insure you against record locks, queries that bog down the system, and a whole host of other problems.**

Sprocs and Performance

Generally speaking, sprocs can do a lot to help the performance of your system. Keep in mind though that, like most things in life, there are no guarantees – indeed, some processes can be created in sprocs that will substantially slow the process if the sproc hasn't been designed intelligently.

Where does that performance come from? Well, when we create a sproc, the process works something like this:

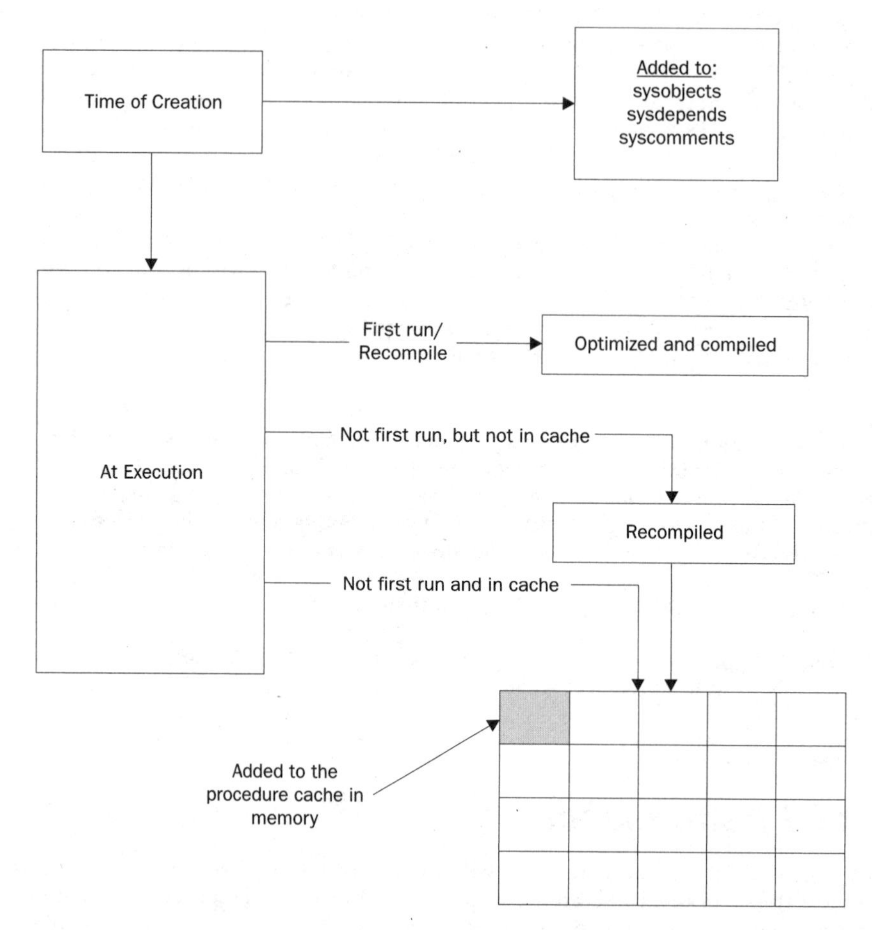

We start by running our `CREATE PROC` procedure. This parses the query to make sure that the code should actually run. The one difference versus running the script directly is that the `CREATE PROC` command can make use of what's called **deferred name resolution**. Deferred name resolution ignores the fact that you may have some objects that don't exist yet. This gives you the chance to create these objects later.

After the sproc has been created, it sits in waiting until the first time that the sproc is executed. At that time, the sproc is optimized and a query plan is compiled and cached on the system. Subsequent times that we run our sproc will, unless we specify otherwise using the `WITH RECOMPILE` option, use that cached query plan rather than creating a new one. This means that whenever the sproc is used it can skip much of the optimization and compilation process. Exactly how much time this saves varies depending on the complexity of the batch, the size of the tables involved in the batch, and the number of indexes on each table. Usually, the amount of time saved is seemingly small – say perhaps one second top for most scenarios – yet that difference can really add up in terms of percentage (1 second is still 100% faster than 2 seconds). The difference can become even more extreme when we have the need to make several calls or when we are in a looping situation.

When a Good Sproc Goes Bad

Perhaps one of the most important things to recognize on the down side of sprocs is that, unless you manually interfere (using the `WITH RECOMPILE` option) they are optimized based on either the first time that they run, or when the statistics have been updated on the table(s) involved in any queries.

That "optimize once, use many times" strategy is what saves the sproc time, but it's a double-edged sword. If our query is dynamic in nature (builds the query up as it goes using the `EXEC` command), then the sproc may be optimized for the way things ran the first time, only to find that things never run that way again – in short, it may be using the wrong plan!

It's not just dynamic queries in sprocs that can cause this scenario either. Imagine a web page that lets us mix and match several criteria for a search. For example, let's say that we wanted to add a sproc to the `Northwind` database that would support a web page that allows users to search for an order based on:

- Customer number
- Order ID
- Product ID
- Order date

The user is allowed to supply any mix of the information, with each new piece of information supplied making the search a little more restricted and theoretically faster.

The approach we would probably take to this would be to have more than one query, and select the right query to run depending on what was supplied by the user. The first time that we execute our sproc, it is going to run through a few `IF...ELSE` statements and pick the right query to run. Unfortunately, it's just the right query for that particular time we ran the sproc (and an unknown percentage of the other times). Any time after that first time the sproc selects a different query to run, it will still be using the query plan based on the first time the sproc ran. In short, the query performance is really going to suffer.

Using the WITH RECOMPILE Option

We can choose to use the security and compartmentalization of code benefits of a sproc but still ignore the pre-compiled code side of things. This lets us get around this issue of not using the right query plan because we're certain that a new plan was created just for this run. To do this, we make use of the `WITH RECOMPILE` option, which can be included in two different ways.

First, we can include the `WITH RECOMPILE` at run-time. We simply include it with our execution script:

```
EXEC spTestInsert '1/1/1999'
   WITH RECOMPILE
```

This tells SQL Server to throw away the existing execution plan, and create a new one – but just this one time. That is, just for this time that we've executed the sproc using the `WITH RECOMPILE` option.

We can also choose to make things more permanent by including the `WITH RECOMPILE` option right within the sproc. If we do things this way, we add the `WITH RECOMPILE` option immediately before our `AS` statement in our `CREATE PROC` or `ALTER PROC` statements.

If we create our sproc with this option, then the sproc will be recompiled each time that it runs regardless of other options chosen at run-time.

Extended Stored Procedures (XPs)

There are times where basic T-SQL and the other features of SQL Server just won't give you what you need. These are usually situations where you need to communicate with something outside of your SQL Server installation, but there may also be situations where you want to provide a level of procedural functionality you just can't get from T-SQL. For these times, there are **extended stored procedures**.

Where standard sprocs have a naming convention that usually includes an `sp` somewhere in the title of the sproc, extended stored procedures make use of an `xp` to show that they are different. However, perhaps the biggest thing to know about extended stored procedures is that they can only exist in the `master` database – this has several impacts:

- If the `master` database is not current when you run the XP, then you will need to fully qualify the XP (e.g. `master..xp_sendmail`)
- If you move your application's database, you will need to re-run any scripts to build the XPs on the new server (the existing XPs will have been left behind in the old server's `master` database)
- Rights to execute the `XP` are granted in the `master` database rather than your application database

XPs are actually created outside of your SQL Server using some form of low-level programming language. Currently, the only language that is actively supported is C++. The SQL Server API does not currently support Visual Basic in any way. XPs run in-process (in the same memory space) to your SQL Server and can be very fast.

XPs are only rarely used these days, as there is almost always an alternative that is both easier to code and fits better with today's modern architectures. Most things that might have been created as an XP in the past, are now created as a client-side COM object instead.

XPs are a broad topic, and require a serious understanding of C++. Since they very complex and only apply to a very small subset of the users of SQL Server, we will consider XPs to be out of the scope of this book other than to point out a useful example.

xp_cmdshell

You can use `xp_cmdshell` to run O/S command line commands from within SQL Server. Since this one requires no special setup, let's go ahead and run a quick example. The syntax looks like this:

```
xp_cmdshell <'command_string'> [, no_output]
```

The *`command_string`* is exactly what you would have typed into the command line were you at the DOS prompt in Win 9x or in a command box in NT. The `no_output` parameter suppresses any results that would have been returned (this lets you execute a command without any feedback that might, in some cases, confuse the user).

Therefore, if we wanted to run a quick directory listing of the main SQL directory, we could do that by issuing a simple command through `xp_cmdshell`:

```
EXEC master..xp_cmdshell 'Dir C:\MSSQL7'
```

The results pane of the Query Analyzer would quickly show us the same thing as if we had been at a command prompt:

```
output
-----------------------------------------------------------------
 Volume in drive C has no label.
 Volume Serial Number is F8D5-17EC
NULL
 Directory of C:\MSSQL7
NULL
07/22/99  11:39p      <DIR>            .
07/22/99  11:39p      <DIR>            ..
08/19/99  11:03p      <DIR>            BACKUP
08/21/99  04:41p      <DIR>            Binn
07/22/99  11:35p      <DIR>            Books
08/25/99  09:57p      <DIR>            Data
07/22/99  11:33p      <DIR>            DevTools
07/22/99  11:37p      <DIR>            FTDATA
07/22/99  11:35p      <DIR>            HTML
07/22/99  11:37p      <DIR>            Install
07/22/99  11:39p      <DIR>            JOBS
09/01/99  11:19p      <DIR>            LOG
07/22/99  11:39p      <DIR>            REPLDATA
11/13/98  01:23a             106,496 sqlsun.dll
07/22/99  11:40p             440     sqlsunin.ini
07/23/99  08:48a             113,410 Uninst.isu
07/22/99  11:33p      <DIR>            Upgrade
       3 File(s)      220,346 bytes
      14 Dir(s)       5,288,349,696 bytes free

(24 row(s) affected)
```

We could also run any other command that is legal from the command prompt – including any executables we may feel the need to execute.

BEWARE OF THIS XP. I usually lock this XP down because of the potential security risk associated with it. Quite often, we will give the account that SQL Server runs under a lot of authority in our network. Now, keep in mind that `xp_cmdshell` runs in the security context that SQL Server is running under. That may mean that a user that would have no rights of their own could have major access available through `xp_cmdshell` if you're not careful. How bad can this get? Well, let me make an admission just to prove a point.

A few years ago, I used to work very closely with a SQL Server DBA for a product that I was supporting and augmenting. That DBA had gone to reasonable lengths to make sure that his server was well protected from users accidentally (or deliberately) deleting files off the server. You can imagine the DBA's frustration when he kept finding files moved, deleted or totally new files added to the server. Who could have been doing all that? How could they do that (no one had rights but the aforementioned DBA)? Well, someone (I'm not admitting – uh, saying – who) was actually issuing the commands through `xp_cmdshell` as part of a joke on our DBA. I finally had to tell him to close that loophole.

> **In this example, things were pretty innocuous, but it could have easily been very important files that were deleted or altered in some way. Think about this before you leave `xp_cmdshell` open.**

Summary

Wow! That's a lot to have to take in for one chapter. Still, this is among the most important chapters in the book in terms of being able to function as a developer in SQL Server.

Sprocs are something of the backbone of code in SQL Server. You can create reusable code, and get improved performance and flexibility at the same time. You have a variety of programming constructs that you might be familiar with from other languages, but sprocs aren't meant for everything.

Pros to sprocs include:

- Usually better performance
- Possible use as a security insulation layer (control how a database is accessed and updated)
- Reusable code
- Compartmentalization of code (can encapsulate business logic)
- Flexible execution depending on dynamics established at run-time

Cons to sprocs include:

- Not portable across platforms (Oracle, for example has a completely different kind of implementation of sprocs)
- May get locked into the wrong execution plan in some circumstances (actually hurting performance)

Sprocs are not the solution to everything, but they are still the cornerstones of SQL Server programming.

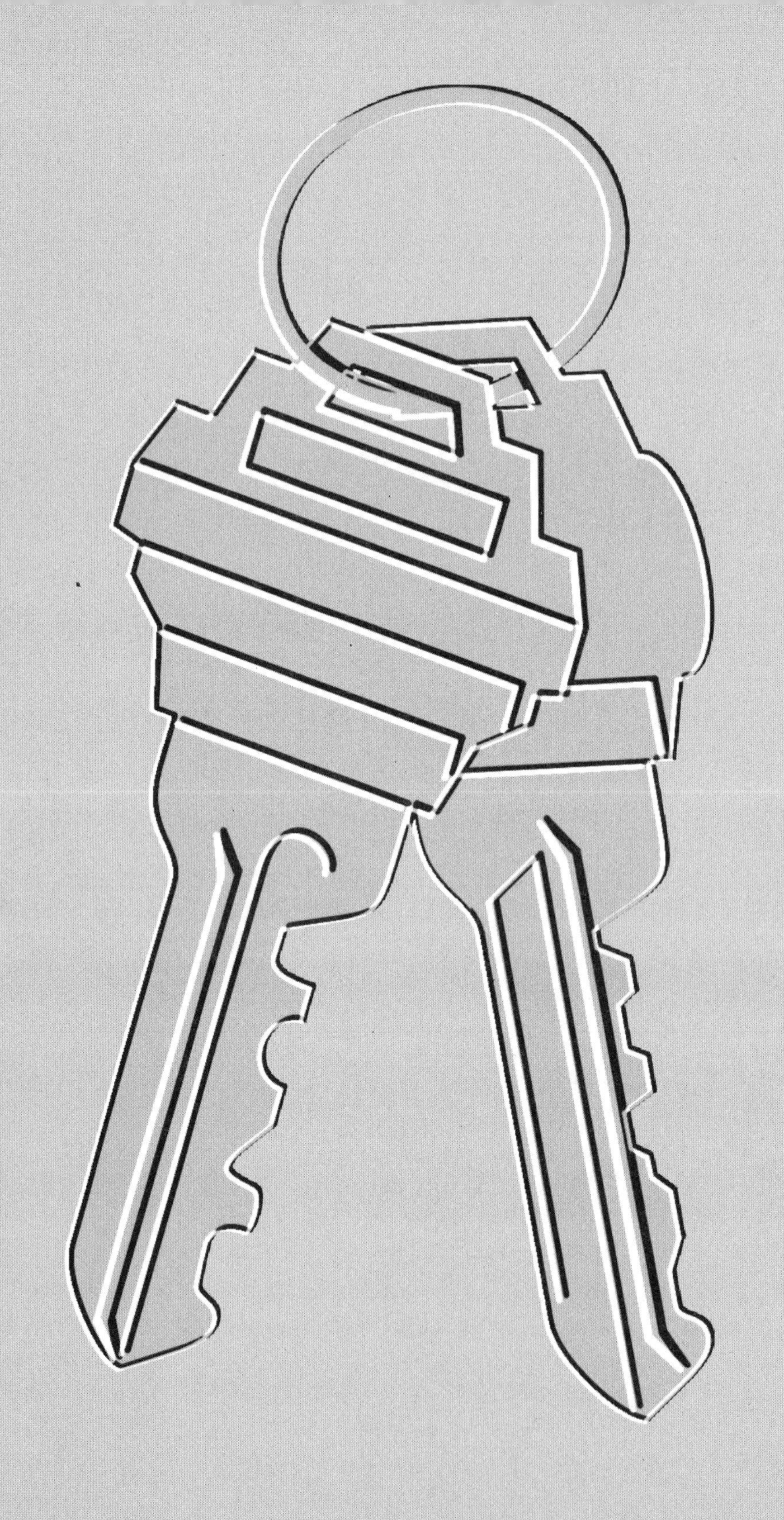

13

Transactions and Locks

This is one of those chapters that, when you go back to work, makes you sound like you've had your Wheaties today. Nothing in what we're going to cover in this chapter is wildly difficult, yet transactions and locks tend to be two of the most misunderstood areas in the database world.

In this chapter, we're going to:

- Demystify transactions
- Examine how the SQL Server log works
- Unlock your understanding of locks

We'll learn why these topics are so closely tied to each other, and how to minimize problems with each.

Transactions

Transactions are all about **atomicity**. Atomicity is the concept that something should act as a unit. From our database standpoint, it's about the smallest grouping of one or more statements that should be considered to be "all or nothing".

Often, when dealing with data, we want to make sure that if one thing happens, another thing happens or neither of them happen. Indeed, this can be carried out to the degree where 20 things all have to happen together or nothing happens. Let's look at a classic example:

Imagine that you are a banker. Sally comes in and wants to transfer $1000 from checking to savings. You are, of course, happy to oblige, so you process her request.

Behind the scenes, we have something like this happening:

```
UPDATE checking
   SET Balance = Balance - 1000
   WHERE Account = 'Sally'
UPDATE savings
   SET Balance = Balance + 1000
   WHERE Account = 'Sally'
```

This is a hyper-simplification of what's going on, but it captures the main thrust of things: you need to issue two different statements – one for each account.

Now, what if the first statement executes and the second one doesn't? Sally would be out of a thousand dollars! That might, for a short time, seem OK from your perspective (heck, you just made a 1000 bucks!), but not for long. By that afternoon you'd have a steady stream of customers leaving your bank – it's hard to stay in business with no depositors.

What you need is a way to be certain that, if the first statement executes, then the second statement executes. There really isn't a way that we can be certain of that – all sorts of things can go wrong from hardware failures to simple things like violations of data integrity rules. Fortunately though, there is a way to do something that serves the same overall purpose – we can essentially forget that the first statement ever happened. We can enforce the notion that if one thing didn't happen, then nothing happened – at least within the scope of our **transaction**.

In order to capture the notion of a transaction though, we need to be able to define very clear-cut boundaries. A transaction has to have very definitive begin and end points. Actually, every `SELECT`, `INSERT`, `UPDATE`, `DELETE` statement you issue in SQL Server is part of a transaction. Even if you only issue one statement that one statement is considered to be a transaction – everything about the statement will be executed, or none of it will. Indeed, by default, that is the length of a transaction – one statement.

But what if we need to have more than one statement be all or nothing – such as our bank example above? On such an occasion, we need a way of marking the beginning and end of a transaction, as well as the success or failure of that transaction. To that end, there are several T-SQL statements that we can use to "mark" these points in a transaction. We can:

- `BEGIN` a transaction – set the starting point
- `COMMIT` a transaction – make the transaction a permanent, irreversible part of the database
- `ROLLBACK` a transaction – essentially saying that we want to forget that it ever happened
- `SAVE` a transaction – establishing a specific marker to allow us to do only a partial rollback

Let's look over all of these individually before we put them together into our first transaction.

BEGIN TRAN

The beginning of the transaction is probably one of the easiest concepts to understand in the transaction process. Its sole purpose in life is to denote the point that is the beginning of a unit. If for some reason we are unable to or do not want to commit the transaction, this is the point which all database activity will be rolled back to. That is, everything beyond this point that is not eventually committed, will effectively be forgotten as far as the database is concerned.

The syntax is:

```
BEGIN TRAN[SACTION] [<transaction name>|<@transaction variable>]
```

COMMIT TRAN

The committing of a transaction is the end of a completed transaction. At the point that you issue the `COMMIT TRAN` the transaction is considered to be what is called **durable**. That is, the effect of the transaction is now permanent, and will last even if you have a system failure (as long as you have a backup or the database files haven't been physically destroyed). The only way to "undo" whatever the transaction accomplished is to issue a new transaction that, functionally speaking, is a reverse of your first transaction.

The syntax for a `COMMIT` looks pretty similar to a `BEGIN`:

```
COMMIT TRAN[SACTION] [<transaction name>|<@transaction variable>]
```

ROLLBACK TRAN

Whenever I think of a `ROLLBACK`, I think of the movie The Princess Bride. If you've ever seen the film (if you haven't, I highly recommend it), you'll know that the character Vizzini (considered a genius in the film) always said, "If anything goes wrong – go back to the beginning." That was some mighty good advice. A `ROLLBACK` does just what Vizzini suggested – it goes back to the beginning. In this case, it's your transaction that goes back to the beginning. Anything that happened since the associated begin statement is effectively forgotten about. The only exception to going back to the beginning is through the use of what are called **savepoints** – which we'll describe next.

The syntax again looks pretty much the same, with the exception of allowance for a savepoint.

```
ROLLBACK TRAN[SACTION] [<transaction name>|<savepoint name>|<@transaction
variable>|<@savepoint variable>]
```

SAVE TRAN

To save a transaction is essentially to create something of a bookmark. You establish a name for your bookmark (you can have more than one). After this "bookmark" is established, you can reference it in a rollback. What's nice about this is that you can rollback to the exact spot in the code that you want to – just by naming a savepoint to rollback to. This is truly great if you have a long process that gets an error at the end. You could, for example, use a `WAITFOR` and wait briefly before trying again (for example, if the problem was a deadlock – or two transactions fighting over the same record - odds are a second try will get your transaction through). The syntax is simple enough:

```
SAVE TRAN[SACTION] [<savepoint name>| <@savepoint variable>]
```

The thing to remember about savepoints is that they are cleared on `ROLLBACK` – that is, even if you save five savepoints, once you perform one `ROLLBACK` they are all gone. You can start setting new savepoints again, and rolling back to those, but whatever savepoints you had when the `ROLLBACK` was issued are gone.

Savepoints were something of a major confusion area for me when I first came across them. Books Online indicates that, after rolling back to a savepoint, you must run the transaction to a logical conclusion (this is technically correct). Where the confusion came was an implication in the way that Books Online was written that seemed to indicate that you had to go to a `ROLLBACK` or `COMMIT` without using any more savepoints. This is not the case – you just can't use the savepoints that we declared prior to the `ROLLBACK` – savepoints after this are just fine.

Let's test this out with a bit of code to see what happens when we mix the different types of `TRAN` commands. Type the following code in and then we'll run through an explanation of it:

```
-- Start the transaction
BEGIN TRAN TranStart

-- Insert our first piece of data using default values.
-- Consider this record No1. It is also the 1st record that stays
-- after all the rollbacks are done.
INSERT INTO Orders
   DEFAULT VALUES

-- Create a "Bookmark" to come back to later if need be
SAVE TRAN FirstPoint

-- Insert some more default data (this one will disappear
-- after the rollback).
-- Consider this record No2.
INSERT INTO Orders
   DEFAULT VALUES

-- Roll back to the first savepoint. Anything up to that
-- point will still be part of the transaction. Anything
-- beyond is now toast.
ROLLBACK TRAN FirstPoint

-- Insert some more default data.
-- Consider this record No3 It is the 2nd record that stays
-- after all the rollbacks are done.

INSERT INTO Orders
   DEFAULT VALUES

-- Create another point to roll back to.
SAVE TRAN SecondPoint

-- Yet more data. This one will also disappear,
-- only after the second rollback this time.
-- Consider this record No4.
INSERT INTO Orders
   DEFAULT VALUES

-- Go back to second savepoint
ROLLBACK TRAN SecondPoint

-- Insert a little more data to show that things
-- are still happening.
-- Consider this record No5. It is the 3rd record that stays
-- after all the rollbacks are done.
INSERT INTO Orders
   DEFAULT VALUES

-- Committ the transaction
COMMIT TRAN TranStart

-- See what records were finally committed.
SELECT TOP 3 OrderID
FROM Orders
ORDER BY OrderID DESC
```

First, we begin the transaction. This starts our grouping of "all or nothing" statements. We then `INSERT` a row. At this juncture, we have just one row inserted:

```
-- Start the transaction
BEGIN TRAN TranStart

-- Insert our first piece of data using default values.
-- Consider this record No1. It is also the 1st record that stays
-- after all the rollbacks are done.
INSERT INTO Orders
   DEFAULT VALUES
```

Next we establish a savepoint called `FirstPoint`, and insert yet another row. At this point, we have two rows inserted, but remember, they are not committed yet, so the database doesn't consider them to really be part of the database:

```
-- Create a "Bookmark" to come back to later if need be
SAVE TRAN FirstPoint

-- Insert some more default data (this one will disappear
-- after the rollback).
-- Consider this record No2.
INSERT INTO Orders
   DEFAULT VALUES
```

We then `ROLLBACK` – explicitly saying that it is *not* the beginning that we want to rollback to, but just to `FirstPoint`. With the `ROLLBACK`, everything between our `ROLLBACK` and the `FirstPoint` savepoint is undone. Since we have one `INSERT` statement between the `ROLLBACK` and the `SAVE`, that statement is rolled back. At this juncture, we are back down to just one row inserted. Any attempt to reference a savepoint would now fail since all savepoints have been reset with our `ROLLBACK`:

```
-- Roll back to the first savepoint. Anything up to that
-- point will still be part of the transaction. Anything
-- beyond is now toast.
ROLLBACK TRAN FirstPoint
```

We add another row, putting us back up to a total of two rows inserted at this point. We also create a brand new savepoint. This is perfectly valid, and we can now refer to this savepoint since it is established after the `ROLLBACK`:

```
-- Insert some more default data.
-- Consider this record No3 It is the 2nd record that stays
-- after all the rollbacks are done.

INSERT INTO Orders
   DEFAULT VALUES

-- Create another point to roll back to.
SAVE TRAN SecondPoint
```

Time for yet another row to be inserted, bringing our total number of still-valid inserts up to three:

```
-- Yet more data. This one will also disappear,
-- only after the second rollback this time.
-- Consider this record No4.
INSERT INTO Orders
   DEFAULT VALUES
```

Now we perform another ROLLBACK – this time referencing our new savepoint (which happens to be the only one valid at this point since FirstPoint was reset after the first ROLLBACK). This one undoes everything between it and the savepoint it refers to – in this case just one INSERT statement. That puts us back at two INSERT statements that are still valid:

```
-- Go back to second savepoint
ROLLBACK TRAN SecondPoint
```

We then issue yet another INSERT statement, bringing our total number of INSERT statements that are still part of the transaction back up to three:

```
-- Insert a little more data to show that things
-- are still happening.
-- Consider this record No5. It is the 3rd record that stays
-- after all the rollbacks are done.
INSERT INTO Orders
   DEFAULT VALUES
```

Last (for our transaction anyway), but certainly not least, we issue the COMMIT TRAN statement that locks our transaction in and makes it a permanent part of the history of the database:

```
-- Committ the transaction
COMMIT TRAN TranStart

-- See what records were finally committed.
SELECT TOP 3 OrderID
FROM Orders
ORDER BY OrderID DESC
```

Note that if either of these ROLLBACK statements had not included the name of a savepoint, or had included a name that had been set with the BEGIN statement, then the entire transaction would be rolled back, and the transaction would be considered to be closed.

The end of our script is just a little statement that shows us our three rows. When you look at this, you'll be able to see what's happened in terms of rows being added and then removed from the transaction:

```
OrderID
----------
11148
11146
11144

(3 row(s) affected)
```

Sure enough, every other row was inserted.

Some of you will likely be confused why the `OrderID` number skipped some numbers. After all, doesn't the Identity field automatically insert numbers sequentially for us – keeping track of which one was last?

Indeed, it does just that, but you have to remember that we did have a couple of other rows – they were just "undone." The change in identity value cannot be reversed since other inserts may (and, in this case have) already drawn the next value out before the `ROLLBACK` occurred. The inserted record was reversed – essentially removed from any history – but not without a trace. Identity and timestamp values are still incremented.

How the SQL Server Log Works

You definitely must have the concept of transactions down before you get into trying to figure out the way that SQL Server tracks what's what in your database. You see, what you *think* of as being your database is only rarely a complete version of all the data. Except for rare moments when it happens that everything has been written to disk, the data in your database is made up of not only the data in the physical database file(s), but also any transactions that have been committed to the log since the last checkpoint.

In the normal operation of your database, most activities that you perform are "logged" to the **transaction log** rather than written directly to the database. A **checkpoint** is a periodic operation which forces all **dirty pages** for the database currently in use to be written to disk. Dirty pages are log or data pages that have been modified after they were read into the cache, but the modifications have not yet been written to disk. Without a checkpoint the log would fill up and/or use all the available disk space. The process works something like this:

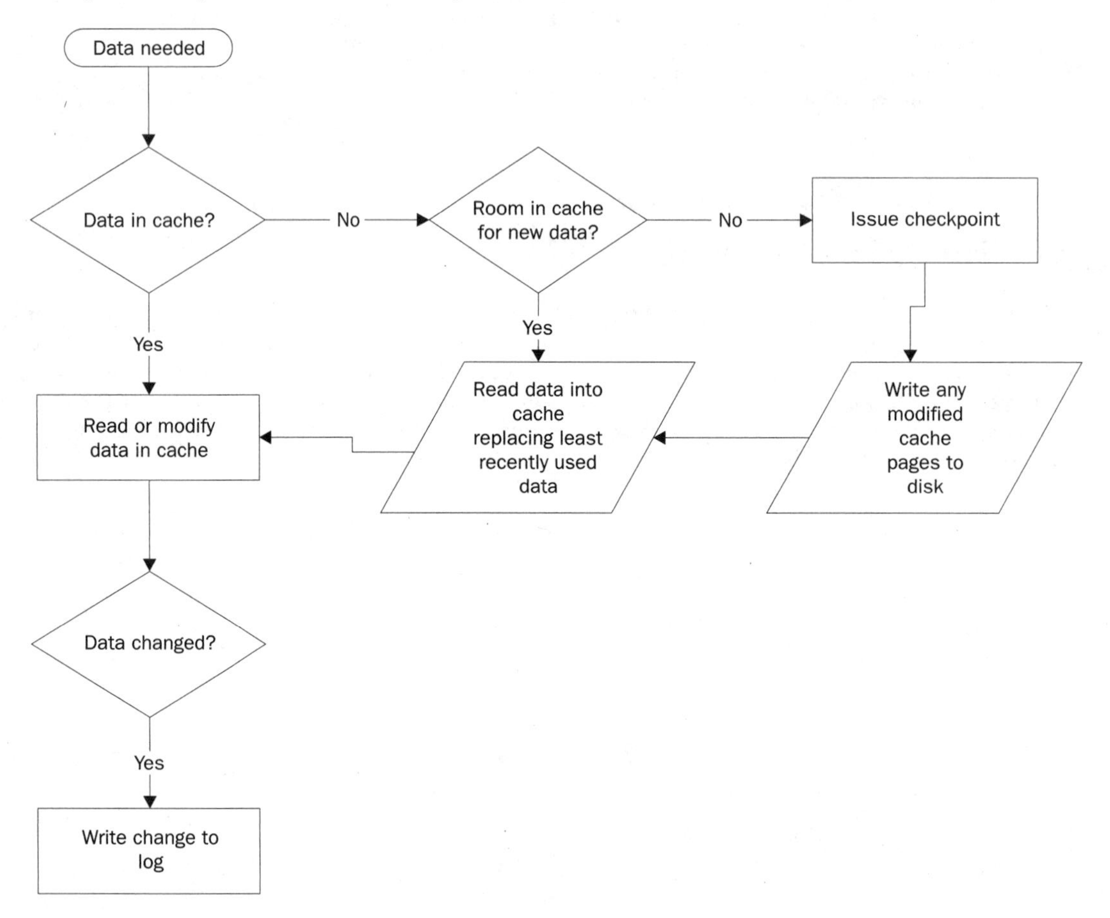

Don't mistake all this as meaning that you have to do something special to get your data out of the cache. SQL Server handles all of this for you. This information is only provided here to facilitate your understanding of how the log works, and, from there, the steps required to handle a transaction. Whether something is in cache or not can make a big difference in performance, so understanding when things are logged and when things go in and out of the cache can be a big deal when you are seeking maximum performance.

Note that data being read into a full cache is not the only reason that a checkpoint would be issued. Checkpoints can come from:

- Manual statement – using the `CHECKPOINT` command
- During recovery if the setting of the Checkpoint on Recovery option in the server options is set to true
- At normal shutdown of the server (unless the `WITH NOWAIT` option is used)
- When you change any database option (e.g. – single user only, dbo only, etc.)
- The database option Truncate On Checkpoint is set, and the log becomes 70% full
- The amount of data in the log since the last checkpoint (often called the "**active**" portion of the log) exceeds the size that the server could recover in the amount of time specified in the **recovery interval** option.

Using the CHECKPOINT Command

One way – but probably the least often used way – for the database to have a checkpoint issued is for it to be done manually. You can do this anytime by just typing in the word:

```
CHECKPOINT
```

It's just that simple.

SQL Server does a very good job of managing itself in the area of checkpoints, so the times when issuing a manual checkpoint makes sense would be fairly rare.

One place that I will do this is during the development cycle when I have the Truncate On Checkpoint option turned on for my database (you would not want that option active on a production database). It's not at all uncommon during the development stage of your database to perform actions that are long running and fill up the log rather quickly. While I could always just issue the appropriate command to trucate the log myself, `CHECKPOINT` is a little shorter and faster and, when Truncate On Checkpoint is active, has the same effect.

CHECKPOINT on Recovery

Every time you start your server, it goes through period called **recovery** (covered in the next section). Turning on the Checkpoint on Recovery option means just what it says: A checkpoint will be issued every time your database does a recovery – which is going to be anytime your server starts up.

Generally speaking, I recommend against the use of this option. Since a checkpoint is automatically issued at normal system shutdown, there really shouldn't be anything that needs to be the subject of a checkpoint. Having this option on means that your server still needs to go through the process though, and that will slow down your start up times – not much since their usually won't be any data to commit to the main database file, but it still slows things down.

At Normal Server Shutdown

Ever wonder why SQL Server can sometimes take a very long time to shut down? Besides the deallocation of memory and other destructor routines that have to run to unload the system, SQL Server must also first issue a checkpoint before the shutdown process can begin. This means that you'll have to wait for any data that's been committed in the log to be written out to the physical database before your shutdown can continue. Checkpoints also occur when the server is stopped:

- Using Service Manager
- Using EM
- Using the `net stop mssqlserver` NT command on the command prompt
- Using the services icon in the NT control panel, selecting the mssqlserver service, and clicking the stop button

> **Unlike Checkpoint on Recovery, this is something that I like. I like the fact that all my committed transactions are in the physical database (not split between the log and database), which just strikes me as being cleaner, with less chance of data corruption.**

There is a way you can get around the delay if you so choose. To use it, you must be shutting down using the `SHUTDOWN` command in T-SQL. To eliminate the delay associated with the checkpoint (and the checkpoint itself for that matter), you just add the `WITH NO WAIT` key phrase to your shutdown statement:

```
SHUTDOWN [WITH NO WAIT]
```

Note that I recommend highly against using this unless you have some programmatic need to shut down your server. It will cause the subsequent restart to take a longer time than usual to recover the databases on the server.

At a Change of Database Options

A checkpoint is issued anytime you issue a change to your database options regardless of how the option gets changed (using `sp_dboption`). The checkpoint is issued prior to making the actual change in the database.

When the Truncate on Checkpoint Option is Active

If you have turned on the Truncate On Checkpoint database option (which is a common practice during the development phase of your database), then SQL Server will automatically issue a checkpoint any time the log becomes more than 70% full.

When Recovery Time Would Exceed the Recovery Interval Option Setting

As we saw briefly earlier (and will see more closely next), SQL Server performs a process called recovery every time the SQL Server is started up. SQL Server will automatically issue a checkpoint anytime the estimated time to run the recovery process would exceed the amount of time set in a database option called recovery interval. By default, the recovery interval is set to zero – which means that SQL Server will decide for you (in practice, this means about 1 minute).

Failure and Recovery

A recovery happens every time that SQL Server starts up. SQL Server takes the database file, and then applies (by writing them out to the physical database file) any committed changes that are in the log since the last transaction. Any changes in the log that do not have a corresponding commit are rolled back – that is, they are essentially forgotten about.

Let's take a look at how this pans out depending on how transactions have occurred in your database. Imagine five transactions that span the log as pictured:

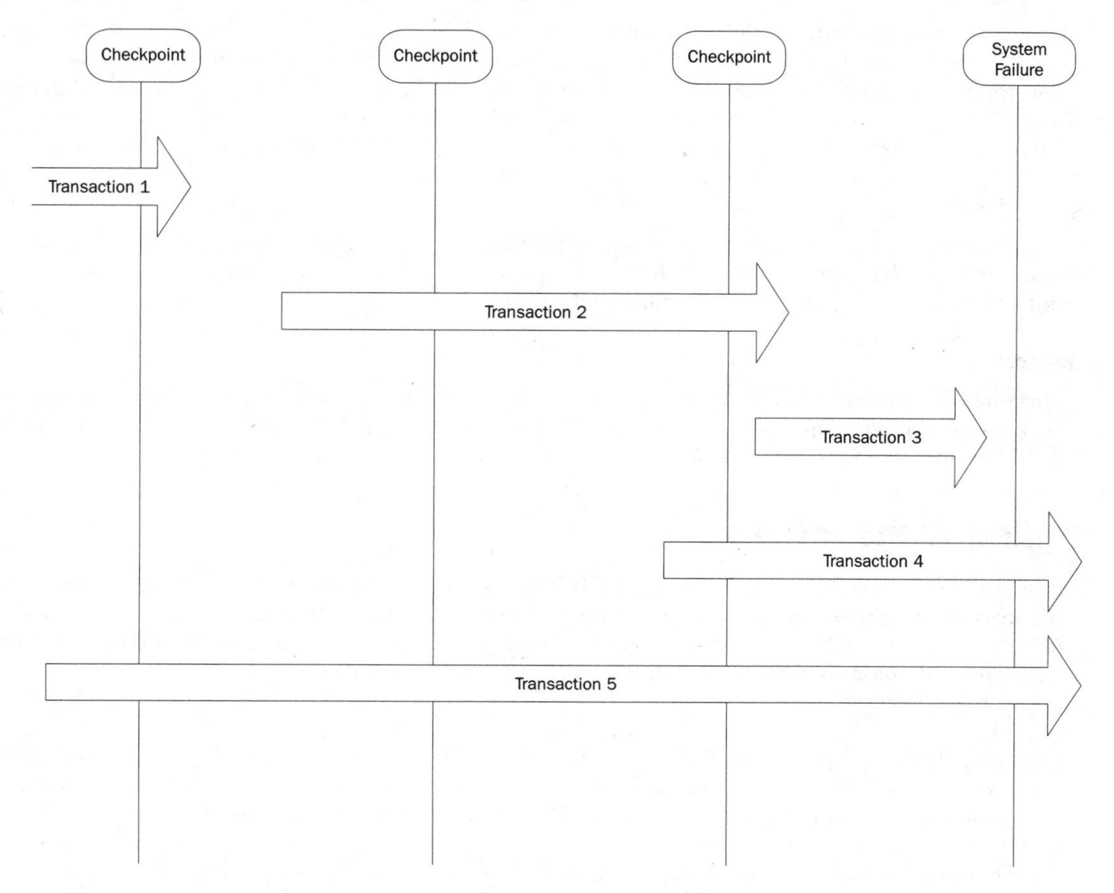

Let's look at what would happen to these transactions one by one.

Transaction 1

Absolutely nothing would happen. The transaction has already been through a checkpoint, and has been fully committed to the database. There is no need to do anything at recovery, because any data that is read into the data cache would already reflect the committed transaction.

Tranaction 2

Even though the transaction existed at the time that a checkpoint was issued, the transaction had not been committed (the transaction was still going). Without that commitment, the transaction does not actually participate in the checkpoint. This transaction would, therefore, be "rolled forward." This is just a fancy was of saying that we would need to read all the related pages back into cache, and then use the information in the log to re-run all the statements that we run in this transaction. When we're done, the transaction should look exactly as it did before the system failed.

Transaction 3

It may not look the part, but this transaction is exactly the same as Transaction 2 from the standpoint of what needs to be done. Again, because Transaction 2 wasn't finished at the time of the last checkpoint, it did not participate in that checkpoint just like Transaction 3 didn't. The only difference is that Transaction 3 didn't even exist at that time, but, from a recovery standpoint, that makes no difference – it's where the commit is issued that makes all the difference.

Transaction 4

This transaction wasn't completed at the time of system failure, and must, therefore, be rolled back. In effect, it never happened from a row data perspective. The user would have to re-enter any data, and any process would need to start from the beginning.

Transaction 5

This one is no different than Transaction 4. It appears to be different because the transaction has been running longer, but that makes no difference. The transaction was not committed at the time of system failure, and must therefore be rolled back.

Implied Transactions

Primarily for compatibility with other major RDBMS systems such as Oracle or DB2, SQL Server supports the notion of what is called an **implied transaction**. Implied transactions do not require a `BEGIN TRAN` statement – instead, they are automatically started with your first statement. They then continue until you issue a `COMMIT TRAN` or `ROLLBACK TRAN` statement. The next transaction then begins with your next statement.

Theoretically, the purpose behind this is to make sure that every statement is part of a transaction. SQL Server also wants every statement to be part of a transaction, but, by default, takes a different approach – if there is no `BEGIN TRAN`, then SQL Server assumes you have a transaction of just one statement, and automatically begins and ends that transaction for you. With some other systems though, you'll find the implied transaction approach. Those systems will assume that any one statement is only the beginning of the transaction, and therefore require that you explicitly end the every transaction with a `COMMIT` or `ROLLBACK`.

By default, the `IMPLICIT_TRANSACTIONS` option is turned off. (and the connection is in autocommit transaction mode) You can turn it on by issuing the command:

```
SET IMPLICIT_TRANSACTIONS ON
```

After that, any of the following statements will initiate a transaction:

- `CREATE`
- `ALTER TABLE`
- `GRANT`
- `REVOKE`
- `CREATE`
- `SELECT`
- `UPDATE`
- `DELETE`
- `INSERT`
- `TRUNCATE TABLE`
- `DROP`
- `OPEN`
- `FETCH`

The transaction will continue until you `COMMIT` or `ROLLBACK`. Note that the implicit transactions option will only effect the current connection – any other users will still have the option turned off unless they have also executed the `SET` statement.

> **Implicit transactions is something of a dangerous territory, and I highly recommend that you leave this option off unless you have a very specific reason to turn it on (such as compatibility with code written in another system).**
>
> **Here's a common scenario: A user calls up as says, "I've been inserting data for the last half hour, and none of my changes are showing." So, you go run a `DBCC OPENTRAN` (see the admin chapter), and discover that there's a transaction that's been there for a while – You can take a guess at what's happened. The user has a transaction open, and his or her changes won't appear until that transaction is committed. They may have done it using an explicit `BEGIN TRANS` statement, but they may also have executed some code that turned implicit transactions on, and then didn't turn it off. A mess follows....**

Locks and Concurrency

Concurrency is a major issue for any database system. It addresses the notion of two or more users all trying to interact with the same object at the same time. The nature of that interaction may be different for each user (updating, deleting, reading, inserting), and the ideal way to handle the competition for control of the object changes depending on just what all the users in question are doing and just how important their actions are. The more users – more specifically the more transactions – that you can run with reasonable success at the same time the higher your concurrency is said to be.

In the OLTP environment that is usually the first thing we deal with in data (OLAP is usually something of an afterthought – it shouldn't necessarily be that way, but it is) and is the focus of most of the database notions put forward in this book. Dealing with the issue of concurrency can be critical to the performance of your system. At the foundation of dealing with concurrency in databases is a process called **locking**.

Locks are a mechanism for preventing a process from performing an action on an object that conflicts with something already being done to that object. That is, there are some things you can't do to an object if someone else got there first. What you can and can't do depends on what the "someone else" is doing. It is also a means of describing what is being done, so the system knows if the second process action is compatible with the first process or not. For example, 1, 2, 10, 100, 1000, or whatever number of user connections the system can handle are usually all able to share the exact same piece of data at the exact same time as long as they all only want the record for a read-only basis. Think of it as being like a crystal shop – lots of people can be in looking at things – even the same things – as long as they don't go to move it, buy it, or otherwise change it. If more than one person does that at the same time, you're liable to wind up with broken crystal. That's why the shopkeeper usually keeps a close eye on things, and they will usually decide who gets to handle it first.

The SQL Server **lock manager** is that shopkeeper. When you come into the SQL Server "store", the lock manager asks what is your intent – what is it you're going to be doing. If you say "just looking," and no one else already there is doing anything but "just looking," then the lock manager will let you in. If you want to "buy" (update or delete) something, then the lock manager will check to see if anyone's already there. If so, then you must wait, and everyone who comes in behind you will also wait. When you are let in to "buy", no one else will be let in until you are done.

By doing things this way, SQL Server is able to help us avoid a mix of different problems that can be created by concurrency issues. We will examine the possible concurrency problems and how to set an isolation level that will prevent each, but for now, let's move on to what can and can't be locked, and what kinds of locks are available.

What Problems Can Be Prevented by Locks

There are four major problems that locks can address:

- Dirty reads
- Unrepeatable reads
- Phantoms
- Lost updates

Each of these presents a separate set of problems, and can be handled by mix of solutions that usually include proper setting of the **transaction isolation level**. Just to help make things useful as you look back at this chapter later, I'm going to include information on what transaction isolation level is appropriate for each of these problems. We'll take a complete look at isolation levels shortly, but for now, let's first make sure that we understand what each of these problems is all about.

Dirty Reads

Dirty reads occur when a transaction reads a record that is part of another transaction that isn't complete yet. If the first transaction completes normally, then it's unlikely there's a problem. But what if the transaction was rolled back? You would have information from a transaction that never happened from the database's perspective!

Let's look at it in an example series of steps:

Trans 1 Command	Trans 2 Command	Real Database Value	Uncommitted Database Value	What Trans 2 Shows
`BEGIN TRAN`		3		
`UPDATE col = 5`	`BEGIN TRAN`	3	5	
`SELECT anything`	`SELECT @var = col`	3	5	5
`ROLLBACK`	`UPDATE anything`	3		5
	`SET whatever = @var`			
		Oops – Problem!!!		

Transaction 2 has now made use of a value that isn't valid! If you try to go back and audit to find where this number came from, you'll wind up with no trace and an extremely large headache.

Fortunately, this scenario can't happen if you're using the SQL Server default for the transaction isolation level (`READ COMMITTED`).

Unrepeatable Reads

It's really easy to get this one mixed up with a dirty read. Don't worry about that – it's just terminology. Just get the concept.

An **unrepeatable read** is caused when you read the record twice in a transaction, and a separate transaction alters the data in the interim. For this one, let's go back to our bank example. Remember that we don't want the value of the account to go below 0 dollars.

Transaction 1	Transaction 2	@Var	Value in Table
`BEGIN TRAN`		NULL	125
`SELECT @Var = value FROM table`	`BEGIN TRAN`	125	125
`IF @Var >=100`	`UPDATE value, SET value = value - 50`		75

Table Continued on Following Page

Transaction 1	Transaction 2	@Var	Value in Table
`UPDATE value, SET value = value - 100`	`END TRAN`	125	75
(Finish wait for lock to clear, then continue)		125	-25 (No `CHECK`) 547 Error (`CHECK`)

Again we have a problem. Transaction 1 has pre-scanned (which can be a good practice in some instances) to make sure that the value is valid, and that the transaction can go through (there's enough money in the account). The problem is that, before the `UPDATE` was made, transaction 1 has been beaten to the punch by transaction 2. If there isn't any `CHECK` constraint on the table to prevent the negative value, then it would indeed be set to a negative 25 – even though logically it appears that we prevent that through the use of our `IF` statement.

We can only prevent this problem two ways:

- Create our `CHECK` and monitor for the 547 Error
- Set our `ISOLATION LEVEL` to be `REPEATABLE READ` or `SERIALIZABLE`

The `CHECK` constraint seems fairly obvious. The thing to realize here is that you are taking something of a reactive rather than proactive approach with this method. Nonetheless, in most situations we have a potential for unrepeatable reads, so this would be my preferred choice in most circumstances.

We'll be taking a full look at isolation levels shortly, but for now, suffice to say that there's a good chance that setting it to `REPEATABLE READ` or `SERIALIZABLE` is going to cause you as many headaches (or more) as it solves. Still – it's an option.

Phantoms

No – we're not talking the "of the opera" kind here – what we're talking about are records that appear mysteriously, as not having been affected by an `UPDATE` or `DELETE` statement that you've issued. This can happen quite legitimately in the normal course of operating your system, and doesn't require any kind of elaborate scenario to illustrate. Here's a classic example of how this happens:

Let's say you are running a fast food restaurant. If you're typical of that kind of establishment, you probably have a fair number of employees working at the "minimum wage" as defined by the government. The government has just decided to raise the minimum wage from $5.00 to $5.50 per hour, and you want to run an update on the `Employees` table to move anyone making less than $5.50 per hour up to the new minimum wage. No problem you say, and you issue the rather simple statement:

```
UPDATE Employees
SET HourlyRate = 5.50
WHERE HourlyRate < 5.50

ALTER TABLE Employees
   ADD ckWage CHECK (HourlyRate >= 5.50)

GO
```

That was a breeze, right? WRONG! Just for illustration, we're going to say that you get an error back:

```
Server: Msg 547, Level 16, State 1, Line 1
ALTER TABLE statement conflicted with COLUMN CHECK constraint 'ckWage'. The conflict
occurred in database 'FastFood', table 'Employees', column 'HourlyRate'.
```

So you run a quick `SELECT` statement checking for values below $5.50, and sure enough you find one. The question is likely to come rather quickly – "How did that get there! I just did the `UPDATE` which should have fixed that!" You did run the statement, and it ran just fine – you just got a **phantom**.

The instances of a phantom read are rare, and require just the right circumstances to happen. In short, someone performed an `INSERT` statement at the very same time your `UPDATE` was running. Since there was an entirely new row, it didn't have a lock on it, and it proceeded just fine.

The only cure for this is setting your transaction isolation level to `SERIALIZABLE`, in which case any updates to the table must not fall within your `WHERE` clause, or they will be locked out.

Lost Updates

Lost updates happen when one update is successfully written to the database, but is accidentally overwritten by another transaction. I can just hear you right about now, "Yikes! How could that happen?"

Lost updates can happen when two transactions read an entire record, then one writes updated information back to the record, then the other writes updated information back to the record. Let's look at an example:

Let's say that you are a credit analyst for your company. You get a call that customer X has reached their credit limit, and would like an extension, so you pull up their customer information to take a look. You see that they have a credit limit of $5,000, and that they appear to always pay on time.

While you're looking, Sally, another person in your credit department, pulls up customer X's record to enter a change in the address. The record she pulls up also shows the credit limit of $5,000.

At this point, you decide to go ahead and raise customer X's credit limit to $7,500, and press enter. The database now shows $7,500 as the credit limit for customer X.

Sally now completes her update to the address, but she's using the same edit screen that you are – that is, she updates the entire record. Remember what her screen showed as the credit limit? $5,000. Oops, the database now shows customer X with a credit limit of $5,000 again. Your update has been lost!

The solution to this depends on your code somehow recognizing that another connection has updated your record between when you read the data and when you went to update it. How this recognition happens varies depending on what access method you're using.

Detecting Updates Using ADO

Detecting that someone else has updated things under ADO is about as easy as it gets – do nothing. Well, sort of nothing – you just need to set an error handler. You see, ADO will raise an error when you issue an `UPDATE` or `UpdateBatch` command and one or more records in your recordset have already been updated. Indeed, it can even detect whether the particular columns you're updating have been changed – if the column you're updating wasn't the one changed, it can then just do the update without any errors or any problems.

There are complete books on ADO alone, so I'm not going to go deep down that alley here, but keep in mind that it has some nice features in this regard.

Detecting Updates Using non-ADO Access Methods

Some of the other data access models have their own methods for helping to detect changes in the data before your edit is applied, but the most common method makes use of the timestamp data type.

Remember that a timestamp is a number based on the activity of your server, and is guaranteed to be unique within any given database (it's actually very unlikely that you'd find duplicates on the same server, but Microsoft only promise it to the database level). What's even more unique about this data type is that the column of this type (you can only have one per table) in a table is automatically updated whenever any change is made to a row. Checking for change then, is not a problem – you just read the timestamp in with the rest of the data, and, before updating the row, make sure that the timestamp hasn't changed. If the timestamp has changed, then someone else has beaten you to the row, and you'll want to abort the update – usually giving the user the chance to either see the exact change or to start over after refreshing to the new data.

Lockable Resources

There are six different **lockable resources** for SQL Server, and they form something of a hierarchy. The higher level the lock, the less **granularity** it has (that is, you're choosing a higher and higher number of objects to be locked in something of a cascading action just because the object that contains them has been locked). These include, in descending order of granularity:

Database

The entire database is locked. This happens usually during database schema changes.

Table

The entire table is locked. This includes all the data related objects associated with that table including the actual data rows (every one of them) and all the keys in all the indexes associated with the table in question.

Extent

The entire extent is locked. Remember than an extent is made up of eight pages, so an extent lock means that the lock has control of the extent, the eight data or index pages in that extent, and all the rows of data in those eight pages.

Page

All the data or index keys on that page are locked.

Key

A lock on a particular or series of keys in an index. Other keys in the same index page may be unaffected.

Row or Row Identifier (RID)

The addition of this little gem may be the most celebrated feature enhancement in version 7.0 of SQL Server. Although the lock is technically placed on the row identifier (an internal SQL Server construct), it essentially locks the entire row.

Lock Escalation and Lock Effects on Performance

For years developers using SQL Server have been asking – no, pleading – for row-level locking. You see, in prior versions the granularity only went down to page level locking. This meant that if you were placing a lock to do with one row, you were actually affecting all the other rows on that same page. This led to a lot of contentious issues where users were prevented from accessing a record that wasn't even in use because the page that the desired row was on had another record that was in use by another user.

Microsoft had a classic marketing answer to this, and, like most Microsoft marketing ploys, it had some basis in reality (all right, sometimes that basis might be a little thin, but there's usually some basis for it). The answer to the row-level locking question went something like this:

Locking a page takes up fewer resources than locking a row. If you lock the page, then you don't need to check every row in a page to see whether it's locked or not – if the page is locked the row is locked. What's more, if you only lock the page, then you don't waste the memory, CPU, and other resources associated with keeping track of every row on the page that's locked – you just keep track of the one page.

That argument didn't hold a lot of water with those of us trying to fight off contentious issues related to two separate rows in a table. Still, it has a lot of relevance in terms of thinking about performance and understanding the concept of escalation.

Escalation is all about recognizing that maintaining a smaller level of granularity (say a row-lock instead of a page lock) makes a lot of sense when the number of items being locked is small. But as we get more and more items locked, then the overhead associated with maintaining those locks actually hinders performance. It can cause the lock to be in place longer (thus creating contentious issues – the longer the lock is in place, the more likely that someone will want that particular record). When you think about this for a bit, you'll realize there's probably a balancing act to be done in there somewhere, and that's exactly what the lock manager uses escalation to do.

When the number of locks being maintained reaches a certain threshold, then the lock is escalated to the next highest level, and the lower level locks do not have to be so tightly managed (freeing resources, and helping speed over contention).

Note that the escalation is based on the number of locks rather than the number of users. The importance here is that you can single-handedly lock a table by performing a mass update – a row-lock can graduate to a page lock which escalates to an extent lock and finally to a table lock. That means that you could potentially be locking every other user out of the table. If your query makes use of multiple tables, it's actually quite possible to wind up locking everyone out of all of those tables.

While you certainly would prefer not to lock all the other users out of your object, there are times where you still need to perform updates that are going to have that effect. There is very little you can do about escalation other than to keep your queries as targeted as possible. Recognize that escalations will happen, so make sure you've thought about what the possible ramifications of your query are.

Lock Modes

Beyond considering at just what resource level you're locking, you also should consider what mode lock your query is going to acquire. Much like there are a variety of resources to lock, there is also a variety of **lock modes**. Particular modes are exclusive of each other (they don't work together). Some modes do nothing more than essentially modify other modes. Whether modes can work together is based on whether they are **compatible**. The table below shows the compatibility of the resource lock modes (listed in increasing lock strength). Existing locks are shown by the columns; requested locks by the rows.

	IS	**S**	**U**	**IX**	**SIX**	**X**
Intent Shared (IS)	YES	YES	YES	YES	YES	NO
Shared (S)	YES	YES	YES	NO	NO	NO
Update (U)	YES	YES	NO	NO	NO	NO
Intent Exclusive (IX)	YES	NO	NO	YES	NO	NO
Shared with Intent Exclusive (SIX)	YES	NO	NO	NO	NO	NO
Exclusive (X)	NO	NO	NO	NO	NO	NO

Also:

- The schema stability lock (Sch-S) is compatible with all lock modes except the schema modification lock (Sch-M).
- The schema modification lock (Sch-M) is incompatible with all lock modes.
- The bulk update (BU) lock is compatible only with schema stability and other bulk update locks.

Compatibility varies, certain lock modes are compatible with most other locks; while the exclusive lock, just as it's name suggests, is not compatible with any other lock.

Just as we did with lockable resources, let's take a look at lock modes one by one.

Shared

This is the most basic type of lock there is. A **shared lock** is for when you only need to read the data – you won't be changing anything. A shared lock wants to be your friend, as it is compatible with other shared locks. That doesn't mean that it still won't cause you grief – while a shared lock doesn't mind any other kind of lock, there are other locks that don't like share locks.

Shared locks tell other locks that you're out there. It's the old, "Look at me! Ain't I special?" thing. Meaningless, yet you can't really ignore it either.

Update

Update locks are something of a hybrid between shared locks and the next lock we'll look at – exclusive locks. Update locks are compatible only with shared locks and intent shared locks – they don't even like other update locks. That is, you can't place an update lock on a resource that already has an update lock on it.

An update lock is something of a special kind of placeholder. Think about it – in order to do an `UPDATE`, you need to validate your `WHERE` clause (assuming there is one) to figure out just what rows you're going to be updating. That means you only need a shared lock, until you actually go to make the physical update. At the time of the physical update, you'll need an exclusive lock.

Update locks indicate that you have a shared lock that's going to become an exclusive lock after you've done your initial scan of the data to figure out what exactly needs to be updated. This acknowledges the fact that there are two distinct stages to an update: First, the stage where you are figuring out what meets the `WHERE` clause criteria (what's going to be updated) – this is the part of an update query that has an update lock. Secondly, the stage where if you are actually decide to perform the update the lock is upgraded to an exclusive lock. Otherwise the lock is converted to a shared lock. What's nice about this is that it forms a barrier against one variety of deadlock. A deadlock is not a type of lock in itself, but rather a situation where a paradox has been formed. One lock can't do what it needs to do in order to clear because another lock is holding that resource – the problem is that the opposite resource is itself stuck waiting for the lock to clear on the first transaction.

Without update locks, this kind of problem would crop up all the time. Two update queries would be running in shared mode. Query A completes its query and is ready for the physical update. It wants to escalate to an exclusive lock, but it can't because query B is finishing its query. Query B then finished the query, except that it needs to do the physical update. In order to do that, Query B must escalate to an exclusive lock, but it can't because Query A is still waiting. This creates something of an impasse – or a deadlock.

Instead, an update lock prevents any other update locks from being established. The instant that the second transaction attempts to achieve an update lock, they will be put into a wait status for whatever the lock timeout is – the lock will not be granted. If the first lock clears before the lock time-out is reached, then the lock will be granted to the new requester, and that process can continue. If not, an error will be generated.

Exclusive

Exclusive locks are just what they sound like. Exclusive locks are not compatible with any other lock. They cannot be achieved if any other lock exists, nor will they allow a new lock of any form to be created on the resource while the exclusive lock is still active. This prevents two people from updating, deleting, or whatever at the same time.

Intent

An **intent lock** is a true placeholder, and is meant to deal with the issue of object hierarchies. Imagine a situation where you have a lock established on a row, but someone wants to establish a lock on a page, extent, or let's say modify a table. You wouldn't want the other transaction going around yours by going higher up the hierarchy, would you?

Without intent locks, the higher level objects wouldn't even know that you had the lock at the lower level. Intent locks improve performance, as SQL Server needs to examine intent locks only at the table level, and not check every row or page lock on the table, to determine if a transaction can safely lock the entire table. Intent locks come in three different varieties:

- Intent Shared – A shared lock has or is going to be established at some lower point in the hierarchy. For example, a page is about to have a row level shared lock established on it. This type of lock only applies to tables and pages.
- Intent Exclusive – Same as intent shared, but with an exclusive lock about to be placed on the lower level item.
- Shared with Intent Exclusive – A share lock has or is about to be established lower down the object hierarchy, but the intent is to modify data, so it will become an intent exclusive at some point.

Schema

These come in two flavors - both deal with the issues of **schema** modifications:

- Sch-M – A schema change is being made to the object. No queries or other `CREATE`, `ALTER`, `DROP` statements can be run against this object for the duration of the Sch-M lock.
- Sch-S- Very similar to a share lock, this lock's sole purpose is to prevent a Sch-M since there are already some for other queries or `CREATE`, `ALTER`, `DROP` statements active on the object. Compatible with all other lock types.

Bulk Load

A **bulk load lock** is really just a variant of a table lock. The only real difference is an indication of the cause/source of the table lock (the BCP utility or DTS is bulk copying data into your table).

Specifying a Specific Lock Type – Optimizer Hints

Sometimes you want to have more control over how the locking goes either in your query, or perhaps in your entire transaction. You can do this by making use of what are called **optimizer hints**.

Optimizer hints are ways of explicitly telling SQL Server to escalate a lock to a specific level. They are included right after the table that they are to effect, and are designated as follows:

Hint	Description
SERIALIZABLE/ HOLDLOCK	Once a lock is established by a statement in a transaction, that lock is not released until the transaction is ended (via ROLLBACK or COMMIT). Inserts are also prevented if the inserted record would match the criteria in the WHERE clause in the query that established the lock (no phantoms). This is the highest isolation level, and guarantees absolute consistency of data.
READUNCOMMITTED/ NOLOCK	Obtains no lock (not even a shared lock), and does not honor other locks. While a very fast option, it can generate what are called "Dirty Reads" as well as a host of other problems.
READCOMMITTED	The Default. Honors all locks, but releases any locks held as soon as the object in question is no longer needed. Performs the same as the READ COMMITTED isolation level.
REPEATABLEREAD	Once a lock is established by a statement in a transaction, that lock is not released until the transaction is ended (via ROLLBACK or COMMIT). New data can be inserted however.
READPAST	Rather than waiting for a lock to clear, skips all locked rows. The skip is limited to row-locks (still waits for page, extent, and table locks), and can only be used with a SELECT statement.
ROWLOCK	First introduced in 6.5, this tells SQL Server to use row-level locking instead of page locks for inserts. For 7.0, it forces the initial level of the lock to be at the row-level even if the optimizer would have otherwise selected a less granular locking strategy. It does not prevent the lock from being escalated to those less granular levels if the number of locks reaches the system's lock threshold.
TABLOCK	Forces a full table lock rather than whatever the lock manager would have used. Can really speed up known table scan situations, but creates big contention problems if other users want to modify data in the table.
TABLOCKX	Similar to TABLOCK, but creates an exclusive lock – locks all other users out of the table for the duration of the statement or transaction depending on how the TRANSACTION ISOLATION LEVEL is set.
UPDLOCK	Uses an Update lock instead of a shared lock. This is a highly under-utilized tool in the war against deadlocks, as it still allows other users to obtain shared locks, but ensures that no data modification (other update locks) are established until you end the statement or transaction (presumably after going ahead and updating the rows).

Most of these have times where they can be very useful, but, before you get too attached to using these, make sure that you also check out the concept of isolation levels later in the chapter.

The syntax for using them is fairly easy – just add it after the table name, or after the alias if you're using one:

```
....
FROM <table name> [AS <alias>][[WITH](<hint>)]
```

So to put this into a couple of examples, any of these would be legal, and all would force a table lock (rather than the more likely key or row lock) on the `Orders` table:

```
SELECT * FROM Orders AS ord WITH (TABLOCKX)
```

```
SELECT * FROM Orders AS ord (TABLOCKX)
```

```
SELECT * FROM Orders WITH (TABLOCKX)
```

```
SELECT * FROM Orders (TABLOCKX)
```

Now look at it from a multiple table perspective. The queries below would do the same thing as those above in terms of locking – they would force an exclusive table lock on the `Orders` table. The thing to note though, is that they do *not* place any kind of special lock on the `Order Details` table – the SQL Server lock manager still is in complete control of that table.

```
SELECT *
FROM Orders AS ord WITH (TABLOCKX)
JOIN [Order Details] AS od
  ON ord.OrderID = od.OrderID
```

```
SELECT *
FROM Orders AS ord (TABLOCKX)
JOIN [Order Details] AS od
  ON ord.OrderID = od.OrderID
```

```
SELECT *
FROM Orders WITH (TABLOCKX)
JOIN [Order Details] AS od
  ON Orders.OrderID = od.OrderID
```

```
SELECT *
FROM Orders (TABLOCKX)
JOIN [Order Details] AS od
  ON Orders.OrderID = od.OrderID
```

Using sp_lock – and an Extra Surprise

Sometimes you want to know which locks are active in the system. If you go ask your buddy who's already a DBA, then he'll probably tell you, "No, Problem! Use `sp_lock`." I have one word for that DBA – yuck! Let's look at `sp_lock` and I think you'll see what I mean.

We'll open two separate query windows in the Query Analyzer, and use one of the queries that we just used to illustrate optimizer hints. (OK, so I'm cheating here with two demos in one, but hey, it works and it's probably how you'd check things in real life.)

In the first Query Analyzer window, we'll set up our query:

```
SELECT *
FROM Orders AS ord (TABLOCKX)
JOIN [Order Details] AS od
  ON ord.OrderID = od.OrderID
```

Now, in the second window, run the `sp_lock` system stored proc:

```
EXEC sp_lock
```

Make sure that both windows are visible. Execute the first window (the query), and then, while the first command is still executing, switch to the second window and execute `sp_lock`. Your `sp_lock` return should look something like this:

```
spid dbid     ObjId             IndId     Type Resource                 Mode     Status
---------------  ------------------  ---------  ---------------------------  --------  ----------
1     1        0                 0         DB                           S        GRANT
6     1        0                 0         DB                           S        GRANT
7     6        0                 0         DB                           S        GRANT
8     6        0                 0         DB                           S        GRANT
8     6        661577395         1         PAG 1:281                    IS       GRANT
8     6        661577395         0         TAB                          IS       GRANT
8     6        357576312         0         TAB                          X        GRANT
8     6        661577395         1         KEY (4a2b0610ad00)           S        GRANT
9     1        0                 0         DB                           S        GRANT
9     2        0                 0         DB                           S        GRANT
9     6        0                 0         DB                           S        GRANT
9     1        117575457         0         TAB                          IS       GRANT
```

It doesn't take a rocket scientist to figure out that this isn't, immediately speaking, much help. It does, however, take a rocket scientist to figure out what it all means – well, not really, but it seems like it.

Part of it is relatively easy. The Type tells us whether it's a table, database, row, page, extent, etc. The Mode tells us whether it's a shared, update, exclusive, etc., with and "I" in the front indicating that it's an intent lock. Finally (as far as the easy stuff goes), it tells the status – almost always that's going to be that the lock has actually been `GRANT`ed, though it may still be pending.

Now things become more difficult – what exactly has these locks on it? The information is there, but you have to know how to get it. You need to decipher the **dbid** (the database ID) by querying the sysdatabases in the master database; and the **ObjId** (the object ID) and **IndId** (the index ID) by querying the sysobjects and sysindexes tables respectively in the appropriate database.

Using spDBLocks

I find all that deciphering rather annoying, so I'm giving you a little present on the Wrox website. The present is called `spDBLocks`. Just pull up the script and run it. I'd like it to be a system stored procedure (so you could call it everywhere after only creating it once), but it can't be, so you'll need to add it to whatever database from which you want to run it. Personally, I recommend just adding it to the `master` database and running it fully qualified (`master..spDBLocks`) when you need it. The specific syntax is (assuming you build it in the `master` database):

```
EXEC master..spDBLocks '<database name>'[, '<object name>']
```

If you run the previous example using this new sproc you get a little more useful result:

```
Resource Locks for Database Northwind
spid dbid   ObjId       ObjectName     IndId  Type Resource        Mode  Status
---------------------------------------------------------------------------------
8    6      661577395   Order Details  1      PAG 1:177            IS    GRANT
8    6      661577395   Order Details  0      TAB                  IS    GRANT
8    6      357576312   Orders         0      TAB                  X     GRANT
8    6      661577395   Order Details  1      KEY (7f284dc8a000)   S     GRANT

(4 row(s) affected)
```

Notice that it knew what database we were interested in (on a production server, a mix of databases and larger user counts can make using `sp_lock` a real nightmare). That's because I told it what database to check. Optionally, we could tell it the object in which we're interested.

If you like, you can modify the sproc to eliminate information that you may not be interested in (such as the `dbid`, or, if you're not looking to track the lock to a particular process, the `spid`).

The reason I build this sproc is pretty simple – I wanted to be able to trim the list down to just the database I was interested in, and, if necessary, just the object I was interested in. When I'm looking for a block, I'd like to see the object name rather than the object ID – maybe Microsoft will "borrow" this code and give us something more useful next time...

If you go ahead and analyze the results, you'll also see a nice example of why locking with less granularity can actually be a good thing if contention isn't your concern – it takes fewer resources. Even in this rather brief example where we aren't using a `HOLDLOCK` (which means that as soon as the resource is not needed any more, the lock is released), we still have 3 locks related to the `Order Details` table, but only one for the `Orders` table. In a transaction situation, this could be even more dramatic.

Because we started out with a table lock on the `Orders` table, there were no intent locks required. Even if we touched 20,000 rows, the single table lock would be enough to protect our cause. The `Order Details` table, however, has to establish either a rowID lock (if there's no cluster key) or a key lock (cluster key available), plus the intent locks for the page and table. In short, we can see that, by obtaining the table lock straight off the bat, we were able to save resources – that usually translates into a somewhat faster query - exactly how much depends on the query (usually not much, but every little bit helps).

Determining Locks Using EM

Perhaps the nicest way of all to take a look at your locks is by using the Enterprise Manager. EM will show you locks in two different sorts – by **Process ID**, or by **Object**.

To make use of EM's lock display, just navigate to the Management|Current Activity node of your server:

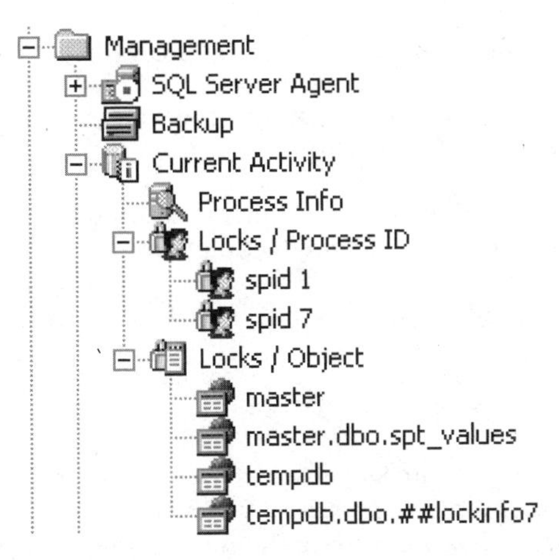

Just expand the node that you're interested in (the Process ID or the Object), and you'll see various locks.

> **Perhaps the coolest feature in this shows itself when you double-click on a specific lock in the right hand pane of EM. You'll get a dialog box that will come up and tell you the last statement that was run by that Process ID. This can be very handy when you are troubleshooting deadlock situations.**

Setting the Isolation Level

We've seen the several different kinds of problems that can be prevented by different locking strategies. We've also seen what kinds of locks are available and how they impact the availability of resources. Now it's time to take a closer look at how these process management pieces work together to ensure overall data integrity – to make certain that you can get the results you expect.

The first thing to understand about the relationship between transactions and locks is that they are inextricably linked with each other. By default, any lock that is data modification related will, once created, be held for the duration of the transaction. If you have a long transaction, that means your locks may be preventing other processes from accessing the objects you have a lock on for a rather long time. It probably goes without saying that this can be rather problematic.

But that's only the default. In fact, there are actually four different **isolation levels** that you can set:

- READ COMMITTED (Default)
- READ UNCOMMITTED
- REPEATABLE READ
- SERIALIZABLE

The syntax for switching between them is pretty straightforward:

```
SET TRANSACTION ISOLATION LEVEL <READ COMMITTED|READ UNCOMMITTED
    |REPEATABLE READ|SERIALIZABLE>
```

The change in isolation level will affect only the current transaction – so you don't need to worry about adversely affecting other users (or them affecting you).

Let's start by looking at the default situation (READ COMMITTED) a little more closely.

READ COMMITTED

With READ COMMITTED, any shared locks you create will be automatically released as soon as the statement that created them is complete. That is, if you start a transaction, run several statements, run a SELECT statement, and then run several more statements, the locks associated with the SELECT statement were freed as soon as the SELECT statement was complete – SQL Server didn't wait for the end of the transaction.

Action queries (UPDATE, DELETE, and INSERT) are a little different. If your transaction performs a query that modifies data, then those locks will be held for the duration of the transaction (in case you need to rollback).

By keeping this level of default, with READ COMMITTED, you can be sure that you have enough data integrity to prevent dirty reads. Unrepeatable reads and phantoms can still occur.

READ UNCOMMITTED

This is the most dangerous of all isolation level choices, but also the highest performance in terms of speed.

Setting the isolation level to READ UNCOMMITTED tells SQL Server not to set any locks, and also not to honor any locks. With this isolation level, it is possible to experience any of the various concurrency issues we discussed earlier in the chapter (most notably a dirty read).

Why would one ever want to risk a dirty read? When I watch the newsgroups on usenet, I see the question come up on a regular basis. It's surprising to a fair number of people, but there are actually good reasons to have this isolation level, and they almost always surround reporting.

In an OLTP environment, locks are both your protector and your enemy. They prevent data integrity problems, but they also often prevent, or block, you from getting at the data you want. It is extremely commonplace to see a situation where management wants to run reports regularly, but the data entry people are often prevented from or slowed in entering data because of locks held by the manager's reports.

By using `READ UNCOMMITTED`, you can often get around this problem – at least for reports where the numbers don't have to be exact. For example, let's say that a sales manager wants to know just how much has been done in sales so far today. Indeed, we'll say he's a micro manager, and asks this same question (in the form of re-running the report) several times a day.

If the report happened to be a long-running report, then the chances that his running the report would damage the productivity of other users would be high due to locking considerations. What's nice about this report though, is that it is a truly nebulous report – the exact values are probably meaningless. The manager is really just looking for ball-park numbers.

By having an isolation level of `READ UNCOMMITTED`, we do not set any locks, so we don't block any other transactions. Our numbers will be somewhat suspect (because of the risk of dirty reads), but we don't need exact numbers anyway, and we know that the numbers are still going to be close even on the off chance that a dirty read is rolled back.

You can get the same effect as `READ UNCOMMITTED` by adding the `NOLOCK` optimizer hint in your query. The advantage to setting the isolation level is that you don't have to use a hint for every table in your query, or use it in multiple queries. The advantage to using the `NOLOCK` optimizer hint is that you don't need to remember to set the isolation level back to the default for the connection.

REPEATABLE READ

This escalates your isolation level somewhat, and provides an extra level of concurrency protection by preventing not only dirty reads (the default already does that), but also preventing unrepeatable reads.

That prevention of unrepeatable reads is a big upside, but holding even shared locks until the end of the transaction can block users' access to objects, and, therefore, hurt productivity.

Personally, I prefer to use other data integrity options (such as a `CHECK` constraint together with error handling) rather than this choice, but it remains an available option.

The equivalent optimizer hint for the `REPEATABLE READ` isolation level would be `REPEATABLEREAD` (these are the same, only no space).

SERIALIZABLE

This is something of the fortress of isolation levels. It prevents all forms of concurrency issues except for a lost update. Even phantoms are prevented.

When you set your isolation to `SERIALIZABLE`, you're saying that any `UPDATE`, `DELETE` or `INSERT` to the table or tables used by your transaction must not meet the `WHERE` clause of any statement in that transaction. Essentially, if the user was going to do something that your transaction would be interested in, then it must wait until your transaction has been completed.

The SERIALIZABLE isolation level can also be simulated by using the SERIALIZABLE/HOLDLOCK optimizer hint in your query. Again, like the READ UNCOMMITTED and NOLOCK debate, the options of not having to set it every time versus not having to remember to change the isolation level back is the big issue.

> *Going with a isolation level of SERIALIZABLE would, on the surface, appears to be the way you want to do everything. Indeed, it does provide your database the highest level of what is called* ***consistency*** *– that is, the update process works the same for multiple users as it would if all your users did one transaction at a time (processed things serially).*
>
> *As with most things in life, however, there is a tradeoff. Consistency and concurrency can, from a practical sense, be thought of as polar opposites. Making things SERIALIZABLE can prevent other users from getting to the objects they need – that equates to lower concurrency. The reverse is also true – increasing concurrency (by going to a REPEATABLE READ for example) reduces the consistency of your database.*
>
> *My personal recommendation on this is to stick with the default (READ COMMITTED) unless you have a specific reason not to.*

Dealing with Deadlocks (aka "A 1205")

OK, so now you've seen locks, and you've also seen transactions. Now that you've got both, we can move on to the rather pesky problem of dealing with **deadlocks**.

As we've already mentioned, a deadlock is not a type of lock in itself, but rather a situation where a paradox has been formed by other locks. Like it or not, you'll bump into these on a regular basis (particularly when you're just starting out), and you'll be greeted with an **error number 1205**. So prolific is this particular problem that you'll hear many a database developer refer to them simply by the number.

Deadlocks are caused when one lock can't do what it needs to do in order to clear because a second lock is holding that resource, and vice versa. When this happens, somebody has to win the battle, so SQL Server chooses a deadlock "**victim.**" The deadlock victim's transaction is then rolled back and is notified that this happened through the 1205 error. The other transaction can continue on normally (indeed, it will be entirely unaware that there was a problem).

How SQL Server Figures out there's a Deadlock

SQL Server checks every 5 seconds all the current transactions for what locks they are waiting on but haven't yet been granted. As it does this, it essentially makes a note that the request exists. It will then re-check the status of all open lock requests again, and, if one of the previous requests has still not been granted, it will recursively check all open transactions for a circular chain of lock requests. If it finds such a chain, then one or more deadlock victims will be chosen.

How Deadlock Victims Are Chosen

By default, a deadlock victim is chosen based on the "cost" of the transactions involved. The transaction that costs the least (SQL Server has to do the least number of things to undo it) to rollback will be chosen. However, you can override this by setting the `DEADLOCK_PRIORITY` to `LOW` for your connection. The syntax is pretty simple:

```
SET DEADLOCK_PRIORITY <LOW|NORMAL>
```

If you set your `DEADLOCK_PRIORITY` to `LOW`, then any transactions on the current connection will be treated as a preferred choice to become the deadlock victim. If there is a deadlock, and there is only one connection that has a low priority, then that will be the one chosen. If there are two at the same priority, then the standard least-cost method will be used between those connections. `NORMAL specifies the default deadlock-handling mechanism.`

> **Setting the `DEADLOCK_PRIORITY` can be a problematic if not used properly. Since the `SET` option applied to the entire connection, and other transactions run for this connection will also adhere to that priority setting. As such, I would classify it as nothing short of critical that you make sure to change the option back prior to exiting your sproc. Make certain that, if you have multiple exit points, that you reset this option prior to each one.**

Avoiding Deadlocks

Deadlocks can't be avoided 100% of the time in complex systems, but you can almost always totally eliminate them from a practical standpoint – that is, make them so rare that they have little relevance to your system.

To cut-down or eliminate deadlocks, follow these simple (OK, usually simple) rules:

- Use your objects in the same order
- Keep your transactions as short as possible and in one batch
- Use the lowest transaction isolation level necessary
- Do not allow open-ended interruptions (user interactions, batch separations) within the same transaction
- In controlled environments, use bound connections (described briefly below)

Nearly every time I run across deadlocking problems, at least one (usually more) of these rules has been violated. Let's look at each one individually.

Use Objects in the Same Order

This is the most common problem area within the few rules that I consider to be basic. What's great about using this rule is that it almost never costs you anything to speak of – it's more a way of thinking. You decide early in your design process how you want to access your database objects – including order – and it becomes a habit in every query, procedure, or trigger you write for that project.

Think about it for a minute – if our problem is that our two connections each have what the other wants, then it implies that we're dealing with the problem too late in the game. Let's look at a simple example.

Consider that we have two tables: `Suppliers` and `Products`. Now say that we have two processes that make use of both of these tables. The first process accepts inventory entries, and updates `Products` with the new amount of product on hand, and updates `Suppliers` with the total amount of product that we've purchased. The second process records sales. It updates the total amount of product sold in the `Suppliers` table, and then decreases the inventory quantity in `Products`.

If we run these two processes at the same time, we're begging for trouble. Process 1 will grab an update lock on the `Products`. Process 2 grabs an update lock on the `Suppliers` table. Process 1 then attempts to grab a lock on the `Suppliers` table, but it will be forced to wait for Process 2 to clear its existing lock. In the mean time, Process 2 tries to create a lock on the `Products` table, but it will have to wait for Process 1 to clear its existing lock. We now have a paradox – both processes are waiting on each other. SQL Server will have to pick a deadlock victim.

Now rearrange that scenario, only with Process 2 rearranged to first decrease the inventory quantity in `Products`, and then update the total amount of product sold in the `Suppliers` table. This is a functional equivalent to the first way we worked the process, and it will cost us nothing to perform it this new way. The impact though, will be stunning – no more deadlocks (at least not between these two processes)! Let's walk through what will now happen.

When we run these two processes at the same time, Process 1 will grab an update lock on the `Products` table (so far, it's the same). Process 2 then also tries to grab a lock on the `Products` table, but will be forced to wait for Process 1 to finish (notice that we haven't done anything with `Suppliers` yet). Now Process 1 finished with the `Products` table, but doesn't release the lock because the transaction isn't complete yet. Process 2 is still waiting for the lock on `Products` to clear. Process 1 now moves on to grab a lock on the `Suppliers` table. Process 2 continues to wait for the lock to clear on `Products`. Process 1 finishes and commits or rolls back the transaction as required, but frees all locks in either case. Process 2 now is able to obtain its lock on the `Products` table, and moves through the rest of its transaction without further incident.

Just swapping the order in which these two queries are run has eliminated a potential deadlock problem. Keep things in the same order wherever possible and you too shall experience far less in the way of deadlocks.

Keeping Transactions as Short as Possible

This is another of the basics. Again, it should become just an instinct – something you don't really think about, something you just do.

This is one that never has to cost you anything really. Put what you need to put in the transaction, and keep everything else out – it's just that simple. Why this works isn't rocket science - the long the transaction is open, and the more it touches (within the transaction), then the higher the likelihood that you''re going to run into some other process that wants one or more of the objects that you're using (reducing concurrency). If you keep your transaction short, then you minimize the number of objects that can potentially cause a deadlock, plus to cut down on the time that you have your lock on them. It's just as simple as that.

Keeping transactions in one batch minimizes network roundtrips during a transaction, reducing possible delays in completing the transaction and releasing locks.

Use the Lowest Transaction Isolation Level Possible.

This one is considerably less basic, and requires some serious thought. As such, it isn't surprising just how often it isn't thought of at all. Consider it Rob's axiom – that which requires thought is likely not to be thought of. Be different – think about it.

We have several different transaction isolation levels available. The default is `READ COMMITTED`. Using a lower isolation level holds shared locks for a shorter duration than a higher isolation level, thereby reducing locking contention.

No Open-Ended Transactions

This is probably the most common sense out of all the recommendations here – but it's one that's often violated due to past practices.

One of the ways we used to prevent lost updates (mainframe days here folks!), was just grab the lock and hold it until you were done with it. I can't tell you how problematic this was (can you say YUCK!)!

Imagine this scenario (it's a real-life example): Someone in your service department likes to use update (exclusive locks) screens instead of display (shared locks) screens to look at data. They go into to look at a work order. Now their buddy calls and asks if they're ready for lunch. "Sure!" comes the reply, and the service clerk heads off to a rather long (1½-2hr) lunch. Everyone who is interested in this record is now locked out of it for the duration of this clerk's lunch.

Wait – it gets worse. In the mainframe days, you used to see the concept of queuing far more often (it actually can be quite efficient). Now someone submits a print job (which is queued) for this work order. It sits in the queue waiting for the record lock to clear. Since it's a queue environment, every print job your company has for work orders now piles up behind that first print job (which is going to wait for that person's lunch before clearing).

This is a rather extremely example – but I'm hoping that it clearly illustrates the point. Don't ever create locks that will still be open when you begin some form of open-ended process. Usually we're talking user interaction (like our lunch lover), but it could be any process that has an open-ended wait to it.

Bound Connections

Hmm. I had to debate even including this one, because it's something of a can of worms. Once you open it, you're never going to get them all back in. I'll just say that this is one is used extremely rarely, and is not for the faint of heart.

It's not that it doesn't have its uses, it's just that things can become rather convoluted rather quickly, so you need to manage things well. It's my personal opinion that there is usually a better solution.

That brings on the question of what is a bound connection. Bound connections are connections that have been associated together, and are allowed to essentially share the same set of locks. What that means is that the two transactions can operate in tandem without any fear of deadlocking each other or being blocked by one another. The flip side of that is that it means that you essentially are on your own in terms of dealing with most concurrency issues – locks aren't keeping you safe anymore.

Given my distaste for these for 99.9% of situations, we're going to forget that these exist now that we've seen that they are an option. If you're going to insist on using them, just remember that you're going to be dealing with an extremely complex relationship between connections, and you need to manage the activities in those connections rather closely if you are going to maintain data integrity within the system.

Summary

Transactions and locks are both cornerstone items to how SQL Server works, and, therefore, to maximizing your development of solutions in SQL Server.

By using transactions, you can make sure that everything you need to have happen as a unit happens, or none of it does. SQL Server's use of locks make sure that we avoid the pitfalls of concurrency to the maximum extent possible (you'll never avoid them entirely, but it's amazing how close you can come with a little - OK a lot – of planning). By using the two together, you are able to pass what the database industry calls the **ACID** test. If a transaction is ACID, then it has:

- **Atomicity**: The transaction is all or nothing.
- **Consistency**: All constraints and other data integrity rules have been adhered to, and all related objects (data pages, index pages) have been updated completely.
- **Isolation**: Each transaction is completely isolated from any other transaction. The actions of one transaction can not be interfered with by the actions of a separate transaction.
- **Durability**: After a transaction is completed, its effects are permanently in place in the system. The data is "safe", in the sense that things like a power outage or other non-disk system failure will not lead to data that is only half written.

In short, by using transactions and locks, you can minimize deadlocks, ensure data-integrity, and improve the overall efficiency of your system.

In our next chapter, we'll be looking at triggers. Indeed, we'll see that, for many of the likely uses of triggers, the concepts of transactions and rollbacks shall be at the very center of the trigger.

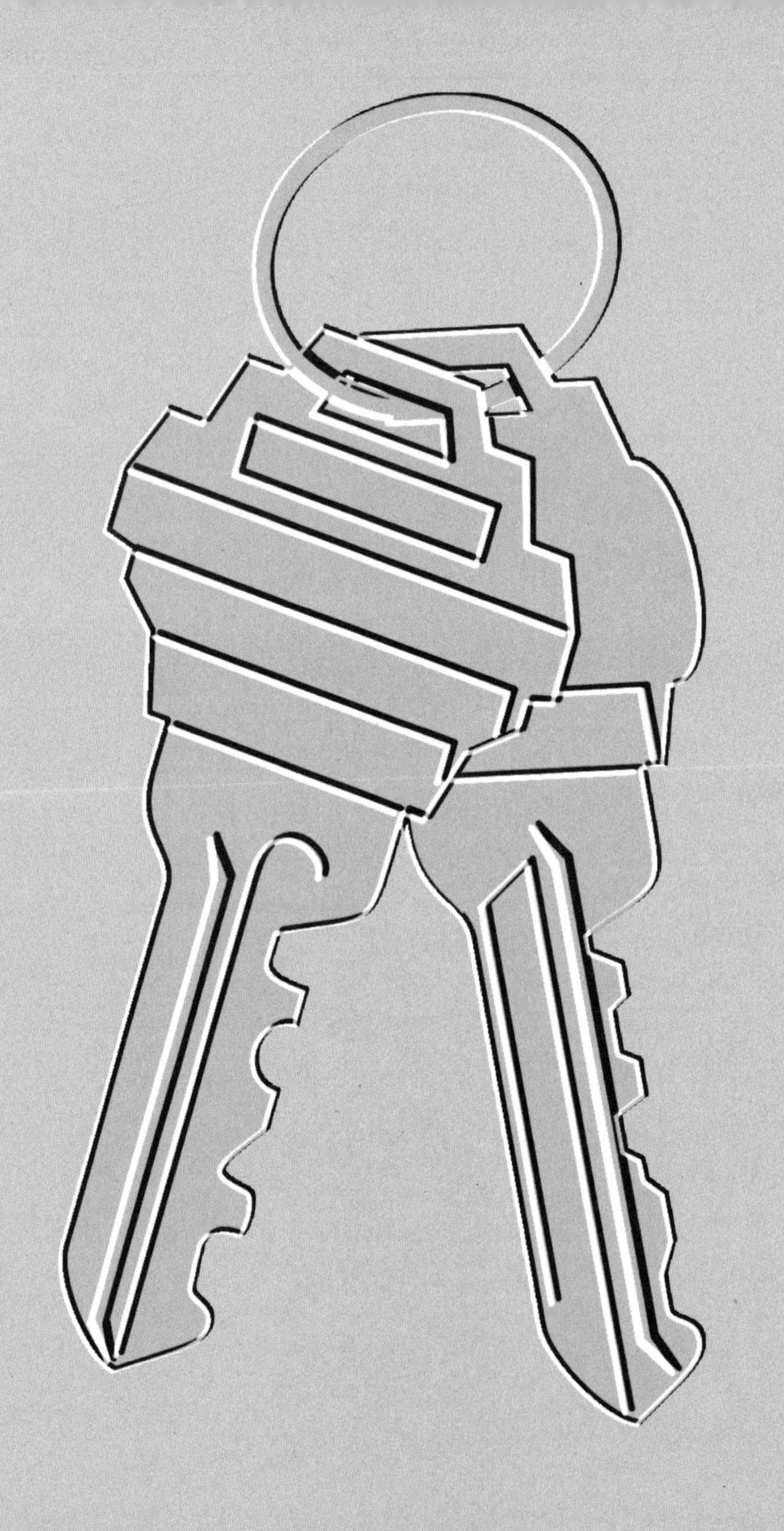

14

Triggers

Ahhh triggers. Triggers are cool, triggers are neat and triggers are our friends. At the very same time, triggers are evil, triggers are ugly and triggers are our enemy. In short, I am often asked, "should I use triggers?" The answer is like most things in SQL, only worse – "It depends". There's little that's black and white in the wonderful world of SQL Server – triggers are definitely a very plain shade of gray.

In this chapter, we'll try to look at triggers in all of their colors – from black all the way to white and a whole lot in between. The main issues we'll be dealing with include:

- What is a trigger?
- Using triggers instead of DRI (declarative referential integrity)
- Using triggers for more flexible referential integrity
- Using triggers to create flexible data integrity rules
- Other common uses for triggers
- Performance considerations

By the time we're done, you should have an idea of just how complex your decision of when to use triggers and when not to can be. You'll also have an inkling of just how powerful and flexible they can be.

Most of all, if I've done my job right, you won't be a trigger extremist (which *sooooo* many SQL Server people I meet are) – with the distorted notion that triggers are evil and should never be used. Neither will you side with the other end of the spectrum which thinks that triggers are the solution to all the world's problems. The right answer in this respect is that they can do a lot for you, but they can also cause a lot of problems. The trick is to use them when they are the right thing to use, and not use them when they aren't.

Some common uses of triggers include:

- Referential Integrity: Though I recommend using DRI whenever possible, there are many things that DRI won't do (e.g. referential integrity across databases or even servers, many types of relationships, etc.) Triggers have the flexibility to do these while DRI won't.
- Creating Audit Trails: Writing records out that keep track of not just the most current data, but the actual change history for each record.
- Functionality similar to a CHECK constraint: But that work across tables.

And these are just a few.

So, with no further ado, let's look at exactly what a trigger is.

What is a Trigger?

A **trigger** is a special kind of stored procedure that responds to specific events.

Triggers are pieces of code that you attach to a particular table. Unlike sprocs, where you needed to explicitly invoke the code, the code in triggers is automatically run whenever the event(s) you attached the trigger to occur in the table – indeed, you can't explicitly invoke triggers. The only way is by performing the action in the table that they are assigned to.

Beyond not being able to explicitly invoke a trigger, you'll find two other things that exist for sprocs but are missing from triggers: parameters and return codes.

While triggers take no parameters, they do have a mechanism for figuring out what records they are supposed to act on (we'll investigate this further later in the chapter). And, while you can use the RETURN keyword, you can not return a specific return code (since you didn't explicitly call the trigger – what would you return a return code to?).

What events can you attach triggers to? They are the three "action" query types you use in SQL – that means, there are three types of triggers, plus hybrids that come from mixing and matching the events that fire them:

- INSERT triggers
- DELETE triggers
- UPDATE triggers
- A mix and match of any of the above

It's worth noting that there are times when a trigger will not fire – even though it seems that the action that you are performing falls into one of the above listed categories. At issue is whether the operation you are doing is a logged activity or not. For example, a DELETE statement is a normal, logged activity that would fire any delete trigger, but a TRUNCATE TABLE , which has the affect of deleting rows, just deallocates the space used by the table – there is no individual deletion of rows logged, and no trigger is fired.

Data inserted into tables from the Bulk Copy Program (BCP) used to also work this way (no triggers fired). With SQL Server 7.0, you now have the option to log BCP activity, which in turn causes your triggers to fire.

The syntax for creating triggers looks an awful lot like all of our other CREATE syntax, except that it has to be attached to a table – a trigger can't stand on its own. It is also worth noting that triggers can't be invoked against views.

```
CREATE TRIGGER <trigger name>
   ON <table>
   [WITH ENCRYPTION]
   FOR <[DELETE] [,] [INSERT] [,] [UPDATE]>
   [WITH APPEND]
   [NOT FOR REPLICATION]
AS
   <sql statements
   ...
   ...
   ...>
```

As you can see, the all too familiar CREATE <object type> <object name> is still there – we've just added the ON clause to indicate the table to which this is going to be attached.

WITH ENCRYPTION

This works just as it does for views and sprocs. If you add this option, you can be certain that no one will be able to view your code (not even you!). This is particularly useful if you are going to be building software for commercial distribution, or if you are concerned about security and don't want your users to be able to see what data you're modifying or accessing.

As with views and sprocs, the thing to remember when using the `WITH ENCRYPTION` option is that you must re-apply it every time you `ALTER` your trigger. If you make use of an `ALTER TRIGGER` statement and do not include the `WITH ENCRYPTION` option, then the trigger will no longer be encrypted.

The FOR Clause

The FOR clause indicates under what type of action(s) you want this trigger to fire. You can have the trigger fire whenever there is an `INSERT`, `UPDATE`, or `DELETE`, or any mix of the three. So, for example, your `FOR` clause could look something like:

```
FOR INSERT, DELETE
```

Or:

```
FOR UPDATE, INSERT
```

Or:

```
FOR DELETE
```

INSERT Triggers

The code for any trigger that you mark as being `FOR INSERT` will be executed anytime that someone inserts a new row into your table. For each row that is inserted, SQL Server will create a copy of that new row, and insert it in a special table that exists only within the scope of your trigger. That table is called `Inserted`, and we'll see much more of it over the course of this chapter. The big thing to understand is that the `Inserted` table only lives as long as your trigger does. Think of it as not existing before your trigger started, and as no longer existing after your trigger completes.

DELETE Triggers

This works much the same as an `INSERT` trigger does, save that the `Inserted` table is not created – instead, a copy of each record that was deleted is inserted into another table called `Deleted`, which, like the `Inserted` table, is limited in scope to just the life of your trigger.

UPDATE Triggers

More of the same, save for a twist. The code in a trigger declared as being `FOR UPDATE` will be fired whenever an existing record in your table is changed. The twist is that there's no such table as `Updated`. Instead, SQL Server treats each row as if the existing record had been deleted, and a totally new record was inserted. As you can probably guess from that, a trigger declared as `FOR UPDATE` contains not one, but two special tables called `Inserted` and `Deleted`.

WITH APPEND

`WITH APPEND` is something of an oddball, and, in all honesty, you're pretty unlikely to use it; nonetheless, we'll cover it here for that "just-in-case" kind of scenario. `WITH APPEND` only applies when you are running in 6.5 compatibility mode (which can be set using `sp_dbcmptlevel`).

SQL Server 6.5 and prior did not allow for the possibility of having multiple triggers of the same type on any single table. For example, if you had already declared a trigger called `trgCheck` to enforce data integrity on updates and inserts, then you couldn't create a separate trigger for cascading updates. Once one update (or insert, or delete) trigger was created, that was it – you couldn't create another trigger for the same type of action.

This was a real pain. It meant that you had to combine logically different activities into one trigger. Trying to get what amounted to two entirely different procedures to play nicely together could, at times, be quite a challenge. In addition, it made reading the code something of an arduous task.

Along comes SQL Server 7.0, and the rules have changed substantially. No longer do we have to worry about how many triggers we have for one type of action query – you can have several if you like. When running our database in 6.5 compatibility mode though, we run into a problem – our database is still working on the notion that there can only be one trigger of a given type on a given table.

`WITH APPEND` gets around this problem by explicitly telling SQL Server that we want to add this new trigger even though we already have a trigger of that type on the table. It's a way of having something of both worlds.

NOT FOR REPLICATION

Adding this option slightly alters the rules for when the trigger is fired. With this option in place, the trigger will not be fired whenever a replication related task modifies your table.

AS

Exactly as it was with sprocs, this is the meat of the matter. The `AS` keyword tells SQL Server that your code is about to start. From this point forward, we're into the scripted portion of your trigger.

Using Triggers for Referential Integrity

Up to this point, the only way presented to perform **referential integrity** checks has been through the use of declarative referential integrity– or DRI – but that's not the only option. Indeed, DRI wasn't even an option until SQL Server 6.5. Before that everything was done with triggers.

Triggers are still often an excellent choice for your referential integrity needs. While they are a bit slower (more on that later), they are considerably more flexible in the way they enforce data integrity. As such, there are actually some types of relationships that can only be enforced by means of a trigger – there are no similar options in DRI. There are also some treatments to relationships that can only be handled through the use of triggers.

Examples of relationship uses where triggers shine include:

- One-to-one relationships
- Exclusive sub-typing
- Cascades – both updates and deletes

As game show announcers often say, there are "these and many, many more!" It just sort of depends on your particular requirements. That's what's great about triggers – they are the ultimate in flexibility.

Using Triggers for Simple Referential Integrity

Besides all those tricky things we just listed, triggers can be used for the same plain and simple referential integrity that DRI can. Generally speaking, this isn't the way you want to do things, but there are times when it's the thing to do, or you might just want to understand how they work in case you bump into these kinds of triggers in legacy code.

Let's not waste any more time with the theory, and instead get right to the code. Before we create the actual trigger though, we'll need to create a test area. What we'll do is make use of a copy of the `Northwind` database that doesn't have any DRI in it. Indeed, when we start, it won't have any referential integrity at all.

Make sure you've downloaded the file `NorthwindTriggers.dts` from `www.wrox.com` or my personal website `www.ProfessionalSQL.com` before you start working with this example.

To create NorthwindTriggers – our test database for triggers – you'll want to go to the Data Transformation Services node in EM, and right-click:

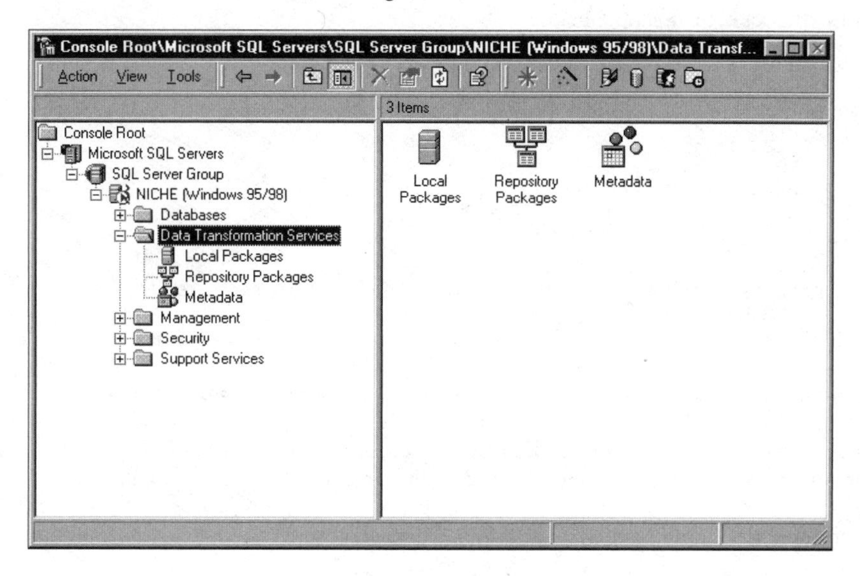

Select the All Tasks menu choice, and then Open Package. Open the file NorthwindTriggers.dts, and then execute it (by clicking on the green arrow).

> **If you've changed your sa password away from the default of blank (which I actually recommend that you do – even for a test machine), this DTS package will fail. Just double click on each of the two icons called Connection, enter your correct sa password, and then execute the package again.**

Now that we've got something to work with, let's go for one of the relationships that was performed with DRI before. What we're going to do is add back the relationship between Customers and Orders. First though, let's make sure that the old integrity isn't there:

```
INSERT Orders
   DEFAULT VALUES
```

When we run this, we get exactly what we expect, but also exactly what we don't want – an inserted record that doesn't meet our CustomerID constraint (that doesn't exist at the moment as far as the database is concerned).

(1 row(s) affected)

Now we'll create a simple trigger to take care of this:

```
CREATE TRIGGER OrderHasCustomer
   ON Orders
   FOR INSERT, UPDATE
AS
   IF EXISTS
      (
       SELECT 'True'
       FROM Inserted i
       LEFT JOIN Customers c
          ON i.CustomerID = c.CustomerID
       WHERE c.CustomerID IS NULL
      )
   BEGIN
      RAISERROR('Order Must Have Valid CustomerID',16,1)
      ROLLBACK TRAN
   END
```

This will actually catch two different situations. First, if the user or any sproc tries to insert a record without a matching `CustomerID`, the insert will fail. Second, if they try to update an existing order to a `CustomerID` that doesn't exist, then that will also fail. We are enforcing the very same one-to-zero, one, or many relationship that DRI did in the original `Northwind` database.

Let's try to insert that data now that the trigger is in place:

```
INSERT Orders
   DEFAULT VALUES
```

This time we get an error:

```
Server: Msg 50000, Level 16, State 1, Line -1074284106
Order Must Have Valid CustomerID
```

Ahhh. Isn't life grand?

But wait – this error is quite uninformative. It doesn't tell the user much about what actually constitutes a valid `CustomerID`.

This is actually one of the nice things about using triggers instead of DRI – you're in control of how the error message reads. If you're in a client/server environment, this isn't always a big thing (you'll often use some form of resource file to change the actual text of the error that the user sees anyway), but in some instances you really like to be able to just pass through the text of the error to the end-user. With triggers, we can easily do this with custom messages – just as we did with our sprocs.

Let's go ahead and enter in a custom message for use with our sproc above:

```
sp_addmessage 60000, 16, 'Error. Value for field %s in table %s must have matching
value in field %s of table %s'
```

Notice that our new custom message accepts four parameters corresponding to the column and table names for the relevant fields in each of our two tables. Also note that, if we were dealing with a composite key (two or more fields in the key), we would need to create a separate message for those or modify this message to be a bit more flexible yet.

Let's alter our trigger to make use of this new error. Note that the syntax for the `ALTER TRIGGER` command is exactly the same as the `CREATE TRIGGER` save that there isn't any need for the `WITH APPEND` option.

```
ALTER TRIGGER OrderHasCustomer
   ON Orders
   FOR INSERT, UPDATE
AS
   IF EXISTS
      (
       SELECT 'True'
       FROM Inserted i
       LEFT JOIN Customers c
          ON i.CustomerID = c.CustomerID
       WHERE c.CustomerID IS NULL
      )
   BEGIN
      RAISERROR(60000,16,1,'CustomerID','Orders','CustomerID','Customers')
      ROLLBACK TRAN
   END
```

Now we'll run our little test again:

```
INSERT Orders
   DEFAULT VALUES
```

And, sure enough, we get our new error:

```
Server: Msg 60000, Level 16, State 1, Line -1074284106
Error. Value for field CustomerID in table Orders must have matching value in field CustomerID of
table Customers
```

Now let's move on to dealing with the other direction. DRI doesn't just deal with records being inserted into the destination table – it also deals with the concept of orphans by dealing with deletions from the referenced table (in our case, `Customers`). This is one of the minor pitfalls of triggers – in order to ensure that we do not create orphan records in a one-to-one table relationship, we have to prevent an insertion and/or deletion procedure that results in a one-to-zero relationship. For triggers this often means placing a trigger at both ends of the relationship.

Let's get right to it again by adding in a trigger to prevent deletions from the `Customers` table:

```
CREATE TRIGGER CustomerHasOrders
   ON Customers
   FOR DELETE
AS
   IF EXISTS
      (
       SELECT 'True'
       FROM Deleted d
       JOIN Orders o
          ON d.CustomerID = o.CustomerID
      )

      BEGIN
         RAISERROR('Customer has Order History. Delete failed!',16,1)
         ROLLBACK TRAN
      END
```

And test it out by trying to delete a customer that has orders:

```
DELETE Customers
   WHERE CustomerID = 'WHITC'
```

We get the expect error – and the record is not deleted:

```
Server: Msg 50000, Level 16, State 1, Line -1074284106
Customer has Order History. Delete failed!
```

It's just that simple. The only additional trick would be if our relationships were a one-to-zero or many-to-many rather than a one-to-many. In that case we would need to modify our triggers to only run the test query if `CustomerID` in the inserted table was `NOT NULL`.

Note that, just like with our previous trigger, we could have (and should have) created a custom error message to use with the `DELETE` statement – I'll leave that for you to experiment with on your own.

Using Triggers for More Flexible Referential Integrity

Plain old DRI enforces only two kinds of relationships: one-to-one or many; or one-to-zero, one, or many – that's it. Another instance of a common requirement that can't be met with DRI would be that of an **exclusive sub-type relationship**. In this relationship, the parent table holds information that is similar between several possible child tables, but for each row in the parent, there is a match in only one of the child tables (We look at sub-types in Chapter 20)– you definitely can't deal with that using DRI.

For these types of relationships, triggers are our only answer. While you'll hear me push DRI for performance reasons, DRI doesn't deal with the oddball stuff. Triggers become our salvation, and they actually do quite well at it.

One-to-One Relationships

Exact one-to-one relationships are far from the most common kind of relationship you'll find – but they aren't at all unheard of either. Perhaps the most common usage of one-to-one relationships is to establish a point of commonality between two separate systems.

For example, let's say that you have a system that is tracking all purchases that you make with your vendors. To further complicate this though, add the notion that you are a conglomerate - running several smaller companies that each have their own systems suited to their specific business. You want your top level system to make sure that you know all the things that you're buying so that you can make sure to use that information when bargaining with your vendors.

To do this, you would probably want to make sure that each system was using the same vendor numbers as well as the same part numbers for items that are the same. You want to make sure that your subsidiaries don't add records that you don't know about, and you want to make sure that they know what all the options are that the parent company already knows about.

The implementation of this is a set of tables (one to each system for each of the vendors and part numbers) that all have a one-to-one relationship with the copy of the table on the master system. Every system gets a certain level of local performance and control over their tables, and they get to run the table within the context of their particular system. Still, you are certain that each system is working from some level of common ground.

For an example, we're going to pretend that our `NorthwindTriggers` database has a second system to which it's relating. First, we'll create a second `Orders` table to relate to:

```
CREATE TABLE Orders2 (
   OrderID           int            NOT NULL,
   CustomerID        nchar (5)      NULL,
   EmployeeID        int            NULL,
   OrderDate         datetime       NULL,
   RequiredDate      datetime       NULL,
   ShippedDate       datetime       NULL,
   ShipVia           int            NULL,
   Freight           money          NULL
      CONSTRAINT DF_Orders2_Freight DEFAULT (0),
   ShipName          nvarchar (40) NULL,
   ShipAddress       nvarchar (60) NULL,
   ShipCity          nvarchar (15) NULL,
   ShipRegion        nvarchar (15) NULL,
   ShipPostalCode    nvarchar (10) NULL,
   ShipCountry       nvarchar (15) NULL,
      CONSTRAINT PK_Orders2 PRIMARY KEY  CLUSTERED
      (OrderID)
)
GO
```

Note that we've removed the `IDENTITY` option from the `OrderID` column since the `Orders` table will drive this table in the master system.

Next we'll populate it with some data from the existing `Orders` table:

```
INSERT INTO Orders2
SELECT * FROM Orders
```

And just that quick we have something to play with.

Now, in a one-to-one relationship, there are a couple of ways things can work. We can either have one table be a true master (as we will here), where all the inserting happens in one table, and then is propagated out to the other tables, or we can allow both tables to accept inserts and propagate to the other tables.

As I just indicated, we're going to take the model of having the `Orders` table be the master table, and the `Orders2` table be a dependent table. We want `Orders2` to reject any inserts that aren't already in the `Orders` table. Likewise, we need the `Orders` table to insert any new records it receives into the `Orders2` table as well. To do this, we'll actually need to create two triggers – one for each table:

```
CREATE TRIGGER OrdersFeedsOrder2
   ON Orders
   FOR INSERT, UPDATE, DELETE
AS
   DECLARE @Count int
   SELECT @Count = COUNT(*) FROM DELETED

   IF @Count  > 0
   BEGIN
      DELETE FROM Orders2
         FROM DELETED i
         JOIN Orders2 o2
            ON i.OrderID = o2.OrderID
   END

   IF @@ERROR != 0
      ROLLBACK TRAN

   SELECT @Count = COUNT(*) FROM Inserted

   IF @Count > 0
   BEGIN
      INSERT INTO Orders2
         SELECT i.*
         FROM Inserted i
         LEFT JOIN Orders2 o2
            ON i.OrderID = o2.OrderID
         WHERE o2.OrderID IS NULL
   END

   IF @@ERROR != 0
      ROLLBACK TRAN
```

```
CREATE TRIGGER Order2DependsOnOrders
   ON Orders2
   FOR INSERT, UPDATE, DELETE
AS
   DECLARE @Count int

   SELECT @Count = COUNT(*) FROM DELETED
   IF @Count > 0
   BEGIN
      IF NOT EXISTS
         (
          SELECT 'True'
          FROM Deleted d
          LEFT JOIN Orders o
             ON d.OrderID = o.OrderID
          WHERE o.OrderID IS NULL
         )
      BEGIN
         RAISERROR('Record Exists In Orders Table. Delete Cancelled.',16,1)
         ROLLBACK TRAN
      END
   END

   IF @@ERROR != 0
      ROLLBACK TRAN
   SELECT @Count = COUNT(*) FROM INSERTED
   SELECT 'Count is ' + CONVERT(varchar,@Count) + ' Before Delete'
   IF @Count > 0
   BEGIN
      IF EXISTS
         (
          SELECT 'True'
          FROM Inserted i
          LEFT JOIN Orders o
             ON i.OrderID = o.OrderID
          WHERE o.OrderID IS NULL
         )
      BEGIN
         RAISERROR('Inserted Record Must exist in the Orders Table',16,1)
         ROLLBACK TRAN
      END
   END
   IF @@ERROR != 0
      ROLLBACK TRAN
```

Now we're ready to do some testing again. Let's start with an insert into the `Orders` table, and make sure that it propagates to the `Orders2` table:

```
INSERT Orders
   (CustomerID, OrderDate)
VALUES
   ('ALFKI', '1/1/2000')
```

Then select back the values from both tables:

```
SELECT OrderID, CustomerID FROM Orders WHERE OrderDate = '1/1/2000'
SELECT OrderID, CustomerID FROM Orders2 WHERE OrderDate = '1/1/2000'
```

And we see that, even though we only inserted the value into the `Orders` table, we also had data inserted into the other table:

```
OrderID          CustomerID
---------------- ---------------
11098            ALFKI

(1 row(s) affected)

OrderID          CustomerID
---------------- ---------------
11098            ALFKI

(1 row(s) affected)
```

Now let's test out a couple of deletes – first from the `Orders2` table:

```
DELETE Orders2
WHERE  OrderDate = '1/1/2000'
```

Yields us an error:

```
Server: Msg 50000, Level 16, State 1, Line -1074284106
Record Exists In Orders Table. Delete Cancelled.

(0 row(s) affected)
```

The deletion was rejected since we've set things up such that it has to go through the master table.

Now we'll delete it from the master table by just changing our last delete query:

```
DELETE Orders
WHERE  OrderDate = '1/1/2000'
```

And then re-run our search for our two records:

```
SELECT OrderID, CustomerID FROM Orders WHERE OrderDate = '1/1/2000'
SELECT OrderID, CustomerID FROM Orders2 WHERE OrderDate = '1/1/2000'
```

```
OrderID          CustomerID
---------------- ----------------

(0 row(s) affected)

OrderID          CustomerID
---------------- ----------------

(0 row(s) affected)
```

Note that this whole example is just one of many possible one-to-one examples.

Exclusive Sub-Typing

Back when we were working on design issues, we discussed the notion of an exclusive sub-type. Remember that these are when you have a base type that provides the basic information about a certain class of item, and then sub-types that are built on and extend that base type. This kind of relationship can only be enforced through the use of triggers.

We're going to build a hyper-simple example since `Northwind` doesn't really have anything to offer us in this regard. We'll just say that we have a concept of an `Activity`. This `Activity` has a few common pieces of information, and looks like this:

```
CREATE TABLE Activity
(
   ActivityID          int    IDENTITY (1, 1)    NOT NULL,
   ActivityType        int                       NOT NULL,
   ActivityDate        datetime                  NOT NULL,
   ActivityComplete    bit NOT                   NULL,
   CONSTRAINT PK_Activity
      PRIMARY KEY  NONCLUSTERED (ActivityID)
)
```

Football and Softball are both activities that are exclusive sub-types of activities – that is, you can have one or the other, but not both. We'll create them like this:

```
CREATE TABLE ActivityFootball
(
   ActivityID         int         NOT NULL,
   InstantReplay      bit         NOT NULL,
   FlagTackle         bit         NOT NULL,
   TwoPointPlay       bit         NOT NULL
   CONSTRAINT PK_ActivityFootball
      PRIMARY KEY  NONCLUSTERED (ActivityID)
)
GO

CREATE TABLE ActivitySoftball
(
   ActivityID         int         NOT NULL,
   NoOfRefs           tinyint     NOT NULL,
   DiamondSize        tinyint     NOT NULL,
   StealingAllowed    bit         NOT NULL
   CONSTRAINT PK_ActivitySoftball
      PRIMARY KEY  NONCLUSTERED (ActivityID)
)
GO
```

Now we're ready to deal with enforcing our exclusive sub-type relationship. First, we'll add a trigger to the `ActivityFootball` table. It will look a lot like our standard referential integrity trigger, except that it will take its check one step further and make sure there aren't any softball records:

```
CREATE TRIGGER FootballIsExclusiveActivity
   ON ActivityFootball
   FOR INSERT, UPDATE
AS
--Check for ActivityID (Must Be In Activity Table)
   IF EXISTS
      (
       SELECT 'True'
       FROM Inserted i
       LEFT JOIN Activity a
          ON i.ActivityID = a.ActivityID
       WHERE a.ActivityID IS NULL
      )
   BEGIN
      RAISERROR('Football item Must Have Corresponding Activity',16,1)
      ROLLBACK TRAN
   END
--Check for Softball Record (Must NOT be one)
   IF EXISTS
      (
       SELECT 'True'
       FROM Inserted i
       LEFT JOIN ActivitySoftball asb
          ON i.ActivityID = asb.ActivityID
       WHERE asb.ActivityID IS NOT NULL
      )
   BEGIN
      RAISERROR('Matching Softball Record Exists.',16,1)
      ROLLBACK TRAN
   END
```

Now we need a near identical trigger for Softball:

```
CREATE TRIGGER SoftballIsExclusiveActivity
   ON ActivitySoftball
   FOR INSERT, UPDATE
AS
--Check for ActivityID (Must Be In Activity Table)
   IF EXISTS
      (
       SELECT 'True'
       FROM Inserted i
       LEFT JOIN Activity a
          ON i.ActivityID = a.ActivityID
       WHERE a.ActivityID IS NULL
      )
   BEGIN
      RAISERROR('Softball item Must Have Corresponding Activity',16,1)
      ROLLBACK TRAN
   END
--Check for Football Record (Must NOT be one)
   IF EXISTS
      (
       SELECT 'True'
       FROM Inserted i
       LEFT JOIN ActivityFootball afb
          ON i.ActivityID = afb.ActivityID
       WHERE afb.ActivityID IS NOT NULL
      )
   BEGIN
      RAISERROR('Matching Football Record Exists.',16,1)
      ROLLBACK TRAN
   END
```

Now we're ready to go. Let's insert a couple of records:

```
DECLARE @Identity int

INSERT Activity
VALUES
   (1,'1/1/1980',1)

SELECT @Identity = @@IDENTITY

INSERT ActivityFootball
VALUES
   (@Identity, 0,0,0)

SELECT 'New ActivityID is ' + CONVERT(varchar,@Identity)
```

This gets us started. Both records should go in just fine, and we get back some information about what the `ActivityID` assigned was. Now we'll run an `INSERT` on the `SoftballActivity` table to get our expected failure (since a record already exists in `FootballActivity`):

```
INSERT ActivitySoftball
VALUES
   (1,3,90,1)
```

Note that the value inserted into the first column may change – fill it in with whatever the previous command said was the identity value used. When you do that, you should get an error message saying that your insert into `ActivitySoftball` has failed:

```
Server: Msg 50000, Level 16, State 1, Line -1074284106
Matching Football Record Exists.
```

This is something we could never do with DRI.

Using Triggers for Data Integrity Rules

Much as a trigger can enforce relationships like a Foreign Key constraint can (aka DRI), a trigger can also perform the same functionality as a `CHECK` constraint or even a `DEFAULT`. Again, as with triggers vs. DRI, the triggers vs. `CHECK` constraints question is one of "it depends." If a `CHECK` can do the job, then it's probably (but not always) the preferable choice. There are times, however, where a `CHECK` constraint just won't do the job, or where something inherent in the `CHECK` process makes it less desirable than a trigger. Examples of where you would want to use a trigger over a `CHECK` include:

- Your business rule needs to reference data in a separate table
- When your business rule needs to check the delta (difference between before and after) of an update
- You require a customized error message

A summary table of when to use what type of data integrity mechanism is provided at the end of Chapter 7.

These really just scratch the surface of things. Since triggers are highly flexible, deciding when to use them really just comes down to whenever you need something special done.

Dealing with Requirements Sourced from Other Tables

CHECK constraints are great – fast and efficient – but they don't do everything you'd like them to. Perhaps the biggest shortcoming shows up when you need to verify data across tables.

To illustrate this, let's take a look at the Products and Order Details tables in the NorthwindTriggers database that we created earlier in the chapter. If we still had our DRI in place, the relationship looks like this:

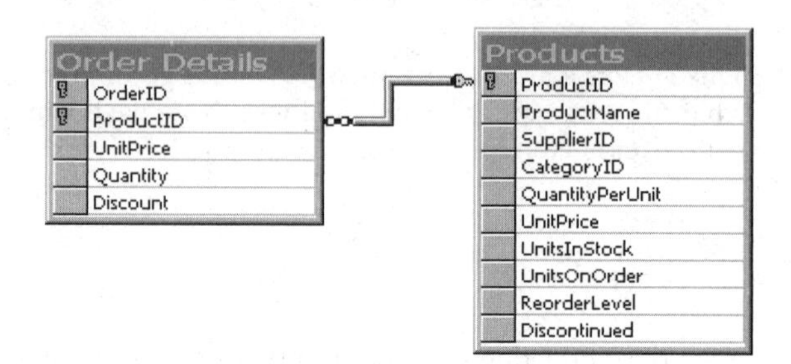

So, under DRI (which we've removed for this chapter), you could be certain that no Order Detail item could be entered into the Order Details table unless there was a matching ProductID in the Products table.

Since we have removed our declarative referential integrity, we'll go ahead and quickly add back in the referential integrity side of things before dealing with our constraint:

```
CREATE TRIGGER OrderDetailIsProduct
   ON [Order Details]
   FOR INSERT, UPDATE
AS
   IF EXISTS
      (
       SELECT 'True'
       FROM Inserted i
       LEFT JOIN Products p
          ON i.ProductID = p.ProductID
       WHERE p.ProductID IS NULL
      )
   BEGIN
      RAISERROR('Order Item Must Be a Valid Product',16,1)
      ROLLBACK TRAN
   END
```

OK. Now that we have got that little item out of the way, let's deal with our business requirements that can't be met with a CHECK constraint.

Our Inventory department has been complaining that our Customer Support people keep placing orders for products that are marked discontinued. They would like to have such orders rejected before they get into the system.

We can't deal with this using a `CHECK` constraint because the place where we know about the discontinued status (the `Products` table) is in a separate table from where we are placing the restriction (the `Order Details` table). Don't sweat it though – you can tell the Inventory department, "No problem!" You just need to use a trigger:

```
CREATE TRIGGER OrderDetailNotDiscontinued
   ON [Order Details]
   FOR INSERT, UPDATE
AS
   IF EXISTS
      (
       SELECT 'True'
       FROM Inserted i
       JOIN Products p
          ON i.ProductID = p.ProductID
       WHERE p.Discontinued = 1
      )
   BEGIN
      RAISERROR('Order Item is discontinued. Transaction Failed.',16,1)
      ROLLBACK TRAN
   END
```

Notice that this trigger is entirely separate from the previous trigger that we wrote on this table. Under 6.5 and previous versions, we could not have written this separate trigger as there was already one trigger for either insert or for update (in this case, it was both). We would have had to combine all the logic into one trigger. In this case, that probably wouldn't have been that big a deal, but, for complex triggers, it can really make the trigger convoluted and difficult to debug. Thankfully, under 7.0, we can just go ahead and add the additional trigger.

Let's go ahead and test out our handy work. First, we need a record or two that will fail when it hits our trigger:

```
SELECT ProductID, ProductName FROM Products WHERE Discontinued = 1
```

```
ProductID       ProductName
--------------- ----------------------------------------
5               Chef Anton's Gumbo Mix
9               Mishi Kobe Niku
17              Alice Mutton
24              Guaraná Fantástica
28              Rössle Sauerkraut
29              Thüringer Rostbratwurst
42              Singaporean Hokkien Fried Mee
53              Perth Pasties

(8 row(s) affected)
```

So let's go ahead an add an `Order Details` item that violates this constraint:

```
INSERT [Order Details]
   (OrderID, ProductID, UnitPrice, Quantity, Discount)
VALUES
   (10000, 5, 21.35, 5, 0)
```

This gets the rejection that we expect:

```
Server: Msg 50000, Level 16, State 1, Line -1074284106
Order Item is discontinued. Transaction Failed.
```

Remember that we could, if desired, also create a custom error to raise instead of the ad hoc message that we used with the `RAISERROR` command.

Quantifying the Changes: Using Triggers to Check the Delta of an Update

Sometimes, you're not interested as much in what the value was or is as you are in just how much it changed. While there isn't any one column or table that gives you that information, you can calculate it by making use of both the `Inserted` and `Deleted` tables in your trigger.

To check this out, let's take a look at the `Products` table again. `Products` has a column called `UnitsInStock`. Recently, there has been a rush on several products, and `Northwind` has been selling out of several things. Since `Northwind` needs more than just a few customers to stay in business in the long run, it has decided to institute a rationing system on their products. The Inventory department has requested that we prevent orders from being placed that try to sell more than half of the units in stock for any particular product.

To implement this, we make use of both the `Inserted` and `Deleted` tables:

```
CREATE TRIGGER ProductIsRationed
   ON Products
   FOR UPDATE
AS
   IF EXISTS
      (
       SELECT 'True'
       FROM Inserted i
       JOIN Deleted d
          ON i.ProductID = d.ProductID
       WHERE (d.UnitsInStock - i.UnitsInStock) > d.UnitsInStock / 2
          AND d.UnitsInStock - i.UnitsInStock > 0
      )
   BEGIN
      RAISERROR('Cannot reduce stock by more than 50%% at once.',16,1)
      ROLLBACK TRAN
   END
```

Before we test this out, let's analyze what we're doing here.

First, we're making use of an `IF EXISTS` just as we have all throughout this chapter. We only want to do the rollback if something exists that meets the evil, mean, and nasty criteria that we'll be testing for within.

Then we join the `Inserted` and `Deleted` tables together – this is what gives us the chance to compare the two.

Our `WHERE` clause is the place that things might become a bit confusing. The first line of it is pretty straightforward. It implements the nominal statement of our business requirement; updates to the `UnitsInStock` column that are more than half the units we previously had on hand will meet the criteria, and set up for the transaction to be rejected.

The next line, though, is not quite so straightforward. As with all things in programming, we need to think beyond the nominal statement of the problem, and think about other ramifications. The requirement really only applies to reductions in orders – we certainly don't want to restrict how many units be put *in* stock – so we make sure that we only worry about updates where the number in stock after the update is less than before the update.

If both (over 50%, and a reduction rather than addition to the inventory) of these conditions have been met, then we raise the error. Notice the use of two, rather than one, `%` signs in the `RAISERROR`. Remember that a `%` sign works as a placeholder for a parameter, so one `%` sign by itself won't show up when your error message comes out. By putting two in a row, we let SQL Server know that we really did want to print out a percent sign.

OK – let's check out how it works. We'll just pick a record and try to do an update that reduces the stock by more than 50%:

```
UPDATE Products
    SET UnitsInStock = 2
    WHERE ProductID = 8
```

I just picked out "Northwoods Cranberry Sauce" as our victim, but you could have chosen any `ProductID` as long as you set the value to less than 50% of its previous value. If you do, you'll get the expected error:

Server: Msg 50000, Level 16, State 1, Line -1074284106
Cannot reduce stock by more than 50% at once.

Note that we could have also implemented this in the `Order Details` table by referencing the actual order quantity against the current `UnitInStock` amount, but we would have run into several problems:

- Is the process that's creating the `Order Details` record updating `Products` before or after the `Order Details` record? That makes a difference in how we make use of the `UnitsInStock` value in the `Products` table to calculate the effect of the transaction.
- Updates that change the inventory external to the `Order Details` table updates would not be affected – they could still reduce the inventory by more than half (this may actually be a good thing in many circumstances, but it's something that has to be thought about).

Using Triggers for Custom Error Messages

We've already touched on this in some of our other examples, but remember that triggers can be handy for when you want control over the error message or number that gets passed out to your user or client application.

With a CHECK constraint for example, you're just going to get the standard 547 error along with its rather nondescript explanation of the error. As often as not, this is less than helpful in terms of the user really figuring out what went wrong – indeed, your client application often doesn't have enough information to make an intelligent and helpful response on behalf of the user.

In short, sometimes you create triggers when there is already something that would give you the data integrity that you want, but won't give you enough information to handle it.

Other Common Uses for Triggers

In addition to the straight data integrity uses, triggers have a number of other uses. Indeed, the possibilities are fairly limitless, but here are a few common examples:

- Updating summary information
- Feeding de-normalized tables for reporting
- Setting condition flags

Updating Summary Information

Sometimes we like to keep aggregate information around to help with reporting, or to speed performance when checking conditions.

Take, for instance, the example of a customer's credit limit vs. their current balance. The limit is a fairly static thing, and is easily stored with the rest of the customer information. The current balance is another matter. We can always figure out the current balance by running a query to total all of the unpaid balances for any orders the customer has, but think about that for a moment. Let's say that you work for Sears & Robuck, and you do literally millions of transactions every year. Now think about how your table is going to have many millions of records for your query to sort through, and that you're going to be competing with many other transactions in order to run your query. Things would perform an awful lot better if we could just go to a single place to get that total – but how to maintain it?

We certainly could just make sure that we always use a stored procedure for adding and paying order records, and then have the sproc update the customer's current balance. But that would mean that we would have to be sure that every sproc that has a potential effect on the customer's balance would have the update code. If just one sproc leaves it out, then we have a major problem, and figuring out which sproc is the offending one is a hassle at best, and problematic at worst. By using a trigger, however, the updating of the customer balance becomes pretty easy.

We'll go ahead and implement an extremely simplified version of this. It probably isn't quite the way we'd build our tables in a real life accounts receivable situation, but it will have all the basics.

First, we need to add a current balance column to our `Customers` table:

```
ALTER TABLE Customers
   ADD CurrentBalance money NOT NULL
   CONSTRAINT CurrentBalanceDefault
   DEFAULT 0 WITH VALUES
```

Make sure you get all four lines in, or you'll wind up with null values in the `CurrentBalance` column. That wouldn't be that big a deal, except that when we go to do math on the column later, a `NULL` plus anything equals a `NULL` – so we wouldn't get far.

Now we'll add a trigger to our `Order Details` table to adjust the balance:

```
CREATE TRIGGER OrderDetailAffectsCustomerBalance
   ON [Order Details]
   FOR INSERT, UPDATE, DELETE
AS
   UPDATE c
      SET c.CurrentBalance = c.CurrentBalance + i.UnitPrice * i.Quantity *
          (1 - Discount)
   FROM Customers c
   JOIN Orders o
      ON c.CustomerID = o.CustomerID
   JOIN Inserted i
      ON o.OrderID = i.OrderID

   UPDATE c
      SET c.CurrentBalance = c.CurrentBalance - d.UnitPrice * d.Quantity *
          (1 - d.Discount)
   FROM Customers c
   JOIN Orders o
      ON c.CustomerID = o.CustomerID
   JOIN Deleted d
      ON o.OrderID = d.OrderID
```

Before we get going here, we should probably also initialize our values for `CurrentBalance` in the `Customers` table. Note that this isn't quite the way things would be in reality since we're going to assume that none of our customers has ever made a payment (we wouldn't stay in business long if that were the case!):

```
SELECT c.CustomerID, CAST(SUM(od.UnitPrice * od.Quantity * (1 - Discount))
                          AS Money) AS CurrentBalance
INTO #Totals
   FROM Customers c
   JOIN Orders o
      ON c.CustomerID = o.CustomerID
   JOIN [Order Details] od
      ON o.OrderID = od.OrderID
GROUP BY c.CustomerID

UPDATE c
SET c.CurrentBalance = t.CurrentBalance
FROM Customers c
JOIN #Totals t
   ON c.CustomerID = t.CustomerID
```

OK, so you should now have some data in the `CurrentBalance` column of the `Customers` table. So we're ready to do something more real. We'll start by figuring out what the existing balance is of a customer:

```
SELECT CustomerID, CurrentBalance
FROM Customers
WHERE CustomerID = 'BLAUS'
```

It turns out that Blauer See Delikatessen has a balance of $3,329.80:

```
CustomerID  CurrentBalance
----------------  --------------------
BLAUS       3239.8000

(1 row(s) affected)
```

Now let's modify an existing order. Blauer See Delikatessen already has an order 10614 with three line items on it for a total of $464:

```
SELECT o.CustomerID, ProductID, od.Quantity * od.UnitPrice AS ExtendedPrice
FROM Orders o
JOIN [Order Details] od
   ON o.OrderID = od.OrderID
WHERE o.OrderID = 10614
COMPUTE  SUM( od.Quantity * od.UnitPrice)
```

```
CustomerID  ProductID            ExtendedPrice
----------------  --------------------  -------------------
BLAUS       11                   294.0000
BLAUS       21                   80.0000
BLAUS       39                   90.0000

sum
===========
464.0000


(4 row(s) affected)
```

Now we'll make an addition to this order:

```
INSERT [Order Details]
   (OrderID, ProductID, UnitPrice, Quantity, Discount)
VALUES
   (10614, 1, 18.00, 5, 0)
```

If everything worked right, then we should have a current balance that is $90 ($18x5) higher than it was before – or $3,329.80. Let's find out:

```
SELECT CurrentBalance
FROM Customers
WHERE CustomerID = 'BLAUS'
```

Hooray! We get what we're looking for:

```
CurrentBalance
--------------------
3329.8000

(1 row(s) affected)
```

Now we'll make sure that the deletion part of the query is working OK:

```
DELETE [Order Details]
WHERE OrderID = 10614 AND ProductID = 1
```

Rerun the SELECT statement again, and we see this puts us right back where we started (as it should be):

```
CurrentBalance
--------------------
3239.8000

(1 row(s) affected)
```

Now we will know that we always have up-to-date information on the customer's current balance.

We can do something like this for pretty much any aggregation of which we want to keep track. Keep in mind, however, that every trigger that you add increases the amount of work that has to be done to complete your transactions. That means that you are placing an additional burden on your system and increasing the chances that you will run into deadlock problems.

Feeding Data into De-normalized Tables for Reporting

I'm going to start right off by saying this isn't the way you should do things in most circumstances. Usually, this kind of data transfer should be handled as part of a batch process run at night or during non-peak hours for your system – depending on the nature of what you are moving, replication may also be an excellent answer. We will be discussing replication in detail in Chapter 19.

That being said, sometimes you need the data in your reporting tables to be right up-to-the-minute. The only real way to take care of this is to either modify all your sprocs and other access points into your system to update the reporting tables at the same time as they update the OLTP tables (YUCK!), or to use triggers to propagate any updates to records.

I'm going to skip the specific example on this one because it works pretty much the same as our last example for aggregation – just copy the data to the new table rather than aggregating it.

What's nice about using this method to propagate data is that you are always certain to be up-to-the-minute on what's happening in the OLTP tables. That being said, it defeats a large part of the purpose of keeping separate reporting tables. While keeping the data in a de-normalized format can greatly improve query performance, one of its main goals, in most installations, is to clear reporting needs out of the main OLTP database and minimize concurrency issues. If all your OLTP updates still have to update information in your reporting tables, then all you've done is to move which database the actual deadlock or other concurrency issue is happening in. From the OLTP standpoint, you've added work without gaining any benefits.

The thing you have to weigh up here is whether you're going to gain enough performance in your reporting to make it worth the damage you're going to do to performance on your OLTP system.

Setting Condition Flags

This situation is typically used as much as aggregation is – to maintain a flag as changes are made rather than having to look for a certain condition across a complete table. Lookup flags are one of the little things that, while they usually break the rules of normalization (you're not supposed to store data that can be derived elsewhere), can really boost system performance substantially.

For our example on this topic, let's assume that we maintain a variety of information on the products that we sell. Material Safety Data Sheets (MSDS), nutritional information, information on suppliers – imagine there can be an unlimited number of different documents that all provide some sort of information on our products. Now, further imagine that we have something more than the mere 77 products that are in the `Northwind` database. The number of possible informational records could get extremely high.

We want to be able to put a flag on our Customer Support screens that tell the order taker whether there is any additional information available for this product. If we were living by the rules of a normalized database, we would have to look in the `ProductInformation` table to see if it had any records that matched up with our `ProductID`.

Rather than do that lookup, we can just place a bit field in our `Products` table that is a yes/no indicator on whether other information is available. We would then put a trigger on the `ProductInformation` table that updates the bit flag in the `Products` table. If a record is inserted into `ProductInformation`, then we set the bit flag to `TRUE` for the corresponding product. When a `ProductInformation` record is deleted, we look to see whether it was the last one, and, if so, set the bit flag in the `Products` table back to `FALSE`.

Again, this looks an awful lot like our aggregation update, so we'll go for an ultra quick example. First, we need to set up a bit by creating the bit flag field and `ProductInformation` table:

```
CREATE TABLE ProductInformation
(
   InformationID    int              NOT NULL   IDENTITY
      PRIMARY KEY,
   ProductID        int              NOT NULL
      REFERENCES Products(ProductID),
   Information      varchar(7500)    NOT NULL
)

ALTER TABLE Products
   ADD Information  Flagbit   NOT NULL
   CONSTRAINT InformationFlagDefault
      DEFAULT 0 WITH VALUES
```

Then we're ready to add our trigger:

```
CREATE TRIGGER InformationBelongsToProduct
   ON ProductInformation
   FOR INSERT, DELETE
AS
   DECLARE @Count   int

   SELECT @Count = COUNT(*) FROM Inserted

   IF @Count > 0
      BEGIN
         UPDATE Products
            SET InformationFlag = 1
            FROM Inserted i
            JOIN Products p
               ON i.ProductID = p.ProductID
   END

   IF @@ERROR != 0
      ROLLBACK TRAN

   SELECT @Count = COUNT(*) FROM Deleted
   IF @Count > 0
   BEGIN
      UPDATE Products
         SET InformationFlag = 0
         FROM Inserted i
         RIGHT JOIN Products p
            ON i.ProductID = p.ProductID
         WHERE i.ProductID IS NULL
   END

   IF @@ERROR != 0
      ROLLBACK TRAN
```

And we're ready to test:

```
INSERT ProductInformation
   (ProductID, Information)
VALUES
   (1, 'Yatta, Yatta, Yatta')

SELECT InformationFlag
FROM Products
WHERE ProductID = 1
```

Yields us the proper update:

```
InformationFlag
--------------------
1

(1 row(s) affected)
```

And the delete:

```
DELETE ProductInformation
WHERE InformationID = 1

SELECT InformationFlag
FROM Products
WHERE ProductID = 1
```

Again gets up the proper update:

```
InformationFlag
--------------------
0

(1 row(s) affected)
```

Now we can find out whether there's `ProductInformation` right in the very same query with which we grab the base information on the product. We won't incur the overhead of the query to the `ProductInformation` table unless there really is something out there for us to retrieve.

Other Trigger Issues

Ahh, you have most of it now, but if you are thinking you are finished with triggers, then think again. As I indicated early in the chapter, triggers create an awful lot to think about. The sections below attempt to point out some of the biggest issues you need to think about with triggers plus provide some information on additional trigger features and possibilities.

Triggers Can Be Nested

A **nested trigger** is one that did not fire directly as a result of a statement that you issued, but rather because of a statement that was issued by another trigger.

This can actually set off quite a chain of events – with one trigger causing another trigger to fire which, in turn, causes yet another trigger to fire and so on. Just how deep the triggers can fire depends on:

- Whether nested triggers are turned on for your system (this is a system wide, not database level option. It is set using EM or `sp_configure`, and defaults to on).
- There is a limit of nesting to 32 levels deep.
- A trigger can, by default, only be fired once per trigger transaction. Once fired, it will ignore any other calls as a result of activity that is part of the same trigger action. Once you move on to an entirely new statement (even within the same overall transaction), the process can start all over again.

In most circumstances, you actually want your triggers to nest (thus the default), but you need to think about what's going to happen if you get into something of a circle of triggers firing triggers. If it comes back around to the same table twice, then the trigger will not fire the second time, and something you think is important may not happen. It's also worth noting that, if you do a ROLLBACK anywhere in the nesting chain, then entire chain is rolled back.
In other words, the entire nested trigger chain behaves as a transaction.

Triggers Can Be Recursive

Recursive triggers are rare. Indeed, by default, recursive triggers are turned off. This is, however, a way of dealing with the situation where you are nesting triggers and you want the update to happen the second time around. Recursion, unlike nesting, is a database level option, and can be set using `sp_dboption` system sproc.

What is a recursive trigger? A trigger is said to be recursive when something the trigger does eventually causes that same trigger to be fired. It may be directly (by an action query done to the table the trigger is set on), or indirectly (through the nesting process).

The danger in recursive triggers is that you'll get into some form of unintended loop. As such, you'll need to make sure that you get some form of recursion check in place to stop the process if necessary.

Debugging Triggers

Debugging triggers is a hassle at best. Since you have something of a level of indirection (you write a statement that causes the trigger to fire, rather than explicitly firing it yourself), it always seems like you have to second guess what's going on.

The big things to remember when trying to debug triggers are:

Use `PRINT` and `SELECT` statements to output your values in the triggers. Beyond telling you what your variables are doing along the way, they can also tip you off to recursion and, in some cases nesting, problems.

> *Nesting issues can be one of the biggest gotchas of trigger design. You will find it not at all uncommon to see situations where you execute a command and wind up with unexpected results because you didn't realize how many other triggers were, in turn, going to be fired. What's more, if the nested triggers perform updates to the initiating table, the trigger will not fire a second time – this creates data integrity problems in tables where you are certain that your trigger is correct in preventing them. It probably has the right code for the first firing, but it doesn't even run the second time around in a nested situation.*

You can also make use of `SELECT @@NESTLEVEL` to show just how deep into a nesting situation you've got.

Keep in mind though, that PRINT and result set generating SELECT statements don't really have anywhere to send their data to other than the screen (in the Query Analyzer), or as an informational message (data access models). This is usually far more confusing than anything else is. As such, I highly recommend removing these statements once you've finished debugging, and before you go to production release.

Triggers Don't Prevent Architecture Changes

This is a classic good news/bad news story.

This is positively great from an ease of making the change standpoint. Indeed, I often use triggers for referential integrity early in the development cycle (when I'm more likely to be making lots of changes to the design of the database), and then change to DRI late in the cycle when I'm close to production.

When you want to drop a table and re-create it using DRI, you must first drop all of the constraints before dropping the table. This can create quite a maze in terms of dropping multiple constraints, making your changes, and then adding back the constraints again. It can be quite a wild ride trying to make sure that everything drops that is supposed to so that your changed scripts will run. Then it's just as wild a trip to make sure that you've got everything back on that needs to be. Triggers take care of all this because they don't care that anything has changed until they actually run.

There's the rub though – when they run. You see, it means that you may change architecture and break several triggers without even realizing that you've done it. It won't be until the first time that those triggers try and address the object(s) in question before you find the error of your ways. By that time, you may have a difficult time piecing together just what exactly you did and why you did it.

Both sides have their hassles - just keep the hassles in mind no matter which method you're employing.

Triggers Can Be Turned Off Without Being Removed

Sometimes, just like with CHECK constraints, you want to turn off the integrity feature so you can do something that will violate the constraint, but still has a valid reason for happening (importation of data is probably the most common of these).

Another common reason for doing this is when you are performing some sort of bulk insert (importation again), but you are already 100% certain the data is valid. In this case, you may want to turn off the triggers to eliminate their overhead, and speed up the insert process.

You can turn the trigger off and on by using an ALTER TABLE statement. The syntax looks like this:

```
ALTER TABLE <table name>
   <ENABLE|DISABLE> TRIGGER <ALL|<trigger name>>
```

As you might expect, my biggest words of caution in this area are: Don't forget to re-enable your triggers!

One last thing: If you're turning them off to do some form of mass importation of data, I highly recommend that you kick out all your users and go either to single-user mode, dbo only mode, or both. This will make sure that no one sneaks in behind you while you had the triggers turned off.

Performance Considerations

I've seen what appear almost like holy wars happen over the pros and cons, evils and goods, and the light and dark of triggers. The worst of it tends to come from purists – people who love the theory, and that's all they want to deal with, or people that have figured out how flexible triggers are and want to use them for seemingly everything.

My two bits worth on this is, as I stated early in the chapter, use them when they are the right things to use. If that sounds sort of non-committal and ambiguous – good! Programming is rarely black and white, and databases are almost never that way. I will however, point out some facts for you to think about.

Triggers Are Reactive Rather than Proactive

What we mean here is that triggers happen after the fact. By the time that your trigger fires, the entire query has run and your transaction has been logged (but not committed and only to the point of the statement that fired your trigger). This means that, if the trigger needs to roll things back, it has to undo what is potentially a ton of work that's already been done. Can you say SLOW! Keep this knowledge in balance though. How big an impact this adds up to depends strongly on how big your query is.

"So what?" you say. Well, compare this to the notion of constraints, which are proactive – that is, they happen before your statement is really executed. That means that they prevent things that will fail happening before the majority of the work has been done. This will usually mean that they will run at least slightly faster – much faster on more complete queries. Note that this extra speed really only shows itself to any significant extent when a rollback occurs.

What's the end analysis here? Well, if you're dealing with very few rollbacks, and/or the complexity and run-time of the statements affected are small, then there probably isn't much of a difference between triggers vs. constraints. There's some, but probably not much.

Triggers Do Not Have Concurrency Issues with the Process that Fires Them

You may have noticed throughout this chapter that we often make use of the `ROLLBACK` statement, even though we don't issue a `BEGIN TRAN`. That's because a trigger is always implicitly part of the same transaction as the statement that caused the trigger to fire.

If the firing statement was not part of an explicit transaction (there was a `BEGIN TRAN`), then it would still be part of its own one-statement transaction. In either case, a `ROLLBACK TRAN` issued inside the trigger will still rollback the entire transaction.

Another upshot of this part of the same transaction business is that triggers inherit the locks already open on the transaction they are part of. This means that we don't have to do anything special to make sure that we don't bump into the locks created by the other statements in the transaction. We have free access within the scope of the transaction, and we see the database based on the modifications already placed by previous statements within the transaction.

We Can Tell Exactly What Columns Were Updated: Using IF UPDATE()

In an UPDATE trigger, we can often limit the amount of code that actually executes within the trigger by checking to see whether the column(s) we are interested in are the ones that have been changed. To do this, we make use of the UPDATE() function.

Let's run a quick example of this by modifying one of our earlier triggers:

```
ALTER TRIGGER ProductIsRationed
   ON Products
   FOR UPDATE
AS
   IF UPDATE(UnitsInStock)
   BEGIN
   IF EXISTS
      (
       SELECT 'True'
       FROM Inserted i
       JOIN Deleted d
          ON i.ProductID = d.ProductID
       WHERE (d.UnitsInStock - i.UnitsInStock) > d.UnitsInStock / 2
          AND d.UnitsInStock - i.UnitsInStock > 0
      )
   BEGIN
      RAISERROR('Cannot reduce stock by more than 50%% at once.',16,1)
      ROLLBACK TRAN
   END
   END
```

With this change, we will now limit the rest of the code to only run when the UnitsInStock column (the one we care about) has been changed. The user can change the value of any other column, and we don't care. This means that we'll be executing less lines of code, and, therefore, will perform more quickly than our previous version.

Keep it Short and Sweet

I feel like I'm stating the obvious here – and for good reason (I am stating the obvious) – but it's a necessary evil.

I can't tell you how often I see bloated, stupid code in sprocs and triggers. I don't know whether it's that people get in a hurry, or if they just think that the medium they are using is fast anyway, so it won't matter.

Remember that a trigger is part of the transaction that the statement which called it is in. This means the statement is not complete until your trigger is complete. Think about it – if you write long running code in your trigger, then you're going to have a long running trigger, which in turns means that every piece of code that you create that causes that trigger to fire will in turn be long running. This can really cause heartache in terms of trying to figure out why your code is taking so long to run. You write what appears to be a very efficient sproc, but it performs terribly. You may spend weeks and yet never figure out that your sproc is fine – it just fires a trigger that isn't.

Don't Forget Triggers when Choosing Indexes

Another common mistake. You look all through your sprocs and views figuring out what the best mix of indexes is – and totally forget that you have significant code running in your triggers.

This is the same notion as the "Short and Sweet" section – long running queries make for long running statements, which in turn lead to long running everything. Don't forget your triggers when you optimize!

JOINs in Triggers Count towards the Pre-7.0 Table Limit

It doesn't apply in 7.0, but you had a limit of 16 tables involved in a query at one time when using any SQL Server version prior to 7.0. If you're working with a prior version, make sure to include tables you access in your trigger in your table count.

Try Not to Rollback within Triggers

This one's hard since rollbacks are so often a major part of what you want to accomplish with your triggers.

Just remember that triggers happen after most of the work is already done – that means a rollback is expensive. This is where DRI picks up almost all of its performance advantage. If you are using many `ROLLBACK TRAN` statements in your triggers, then make sure that you pre-process looking for errors before you execute the statement that fires the trigger. That is, since SQL Server can't be proactive in this situation, be proactive for it. Test for errors beforehand rather than waiting for the rollback.

Order of Firing is Not Guaranteed

Remember that you can now (you couldn't in 6.5 and before) have multiple triggers of the same type on the same table.

One of the most common questions I get about this is, "How do I set up which trigger is fired first?" The answer is that you don't – the triggers can multi-thread (run at the same time) if SQL Server so chooses, and you never know which one SQL Server is going to decide to run first. This means that you must not create triggers that are dependent on each other. If you have logic that is dependent on something happening first, then encapsulate it all in one trigger where you can control execution order easily.

Dropping Triggers

Dropping triggers is as easy as it has been for almost everything else this far:

```
DROP TRIGGER <trigger name>
```

And it's gone.

Summary

Triggers are an extremely powerful tool that can add tremendous flexibility to both your data integrity and the overall operation of your system. That being said, they are not something to take lightly. Triggers can greatly enhance the performance of your system if you use them for proper summarization of data; but they can also be the bane of your existence - they are very difficult to debug, and poorly written triggers affect not only the trigger itself, but any statement that causes that trigger to fire.

Before you get too frustrated with triggers – or before you get too bored with the couple of trigger templates that fill about 90% of your trigger needs – keep in mind that there are a large number of tools out there that will auto-generate triggers for you that meet certain needs. We will be looking at this a bit further in Appendix C of this book.

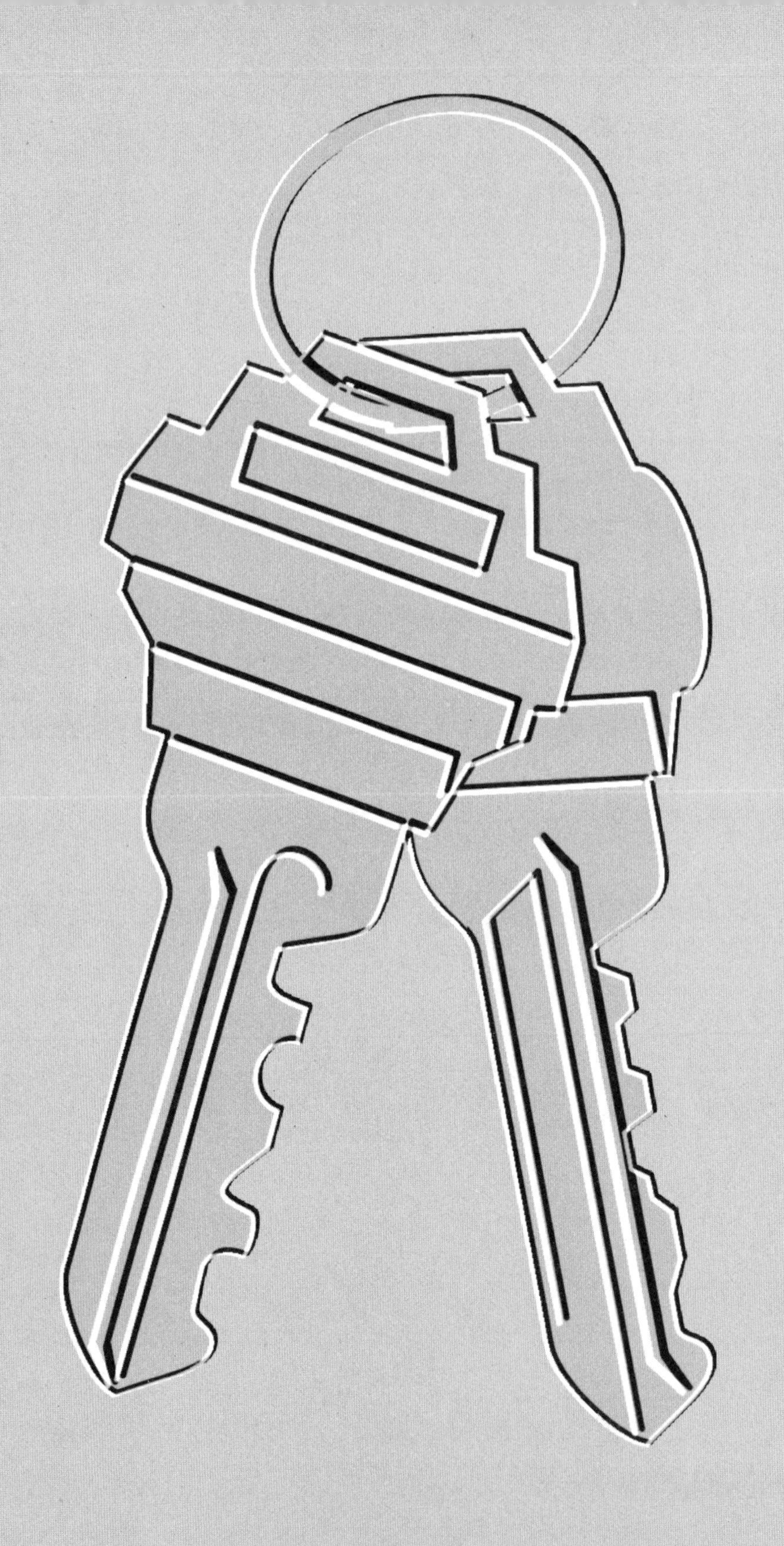

15

Asking a Better Question: Advanced Queries

It was a tough decision. Advanced query design before cursors, or cursors before advanced query design? You see, it's something of a chicken and egg thing (which came first?). Not that you need to know anything about cursors to make sure of the topics covered in this chapter, but rather because we'll be discussing some benefits of different query methods that avoid cursors – and it really helps to understand the benefits if you know what you're trying to avoid.

That said, I went for the advanced queries first notion. In the end, I figured I wanted to try to get you thinking about non-cursor based queries as much as possible before we start talking cursors. Since I figure that a large percentage of the readers of this book will already have experience in a programming language, I know that you're going to have a natural tendency to think of things in a procedural fashion rather than a "set" fashion. Since cursors are a procedural approach, the odds are you're going to think of the more complex problems in terms of cursors first rather than how you could do it in a single query.

Suffice to say that I want to challenge you in this chapter. Even if you don't have that much procedural programming experience, the fact is that your brain has a natural tendency to break complex problems down into their smaller subparts (sub-procedures – logical steps) as opposed to as a whole (the "set", or SQL way). My challenge to you is to try and see the question as its whole first. Be certain that you can't get it in a single query. Even if you can't think of a way, quite often you can break it up into several small queries and then combine them one at a time back into a larger query that does it all in one task. Try to see it as a whole, and, if you can't, then go ahead and break it down, but then recompile it into the whole again to the largest extent possible.

In this chapter, we're going to be looking at ways to ask what amounts to multiple questions in just one query. Essentially, we're going to look at ways of taking what seems like multiple queries and placing them into something that will execute as a complete unit. In addition, we'll also be taking a look at query performance, and what you can do to get the most out of them.

Among the topics we'll be covering in this chapter are:

- Nested subqueries
- "Correlated" subqueries
- Making use of the `EXISTS` operator
- Optimizing query performance

We'll see how using subqueries, we can make the seemingly impossible completely possible, and how an odd tweak here and there can make a big difference in your query performance.

What is a Subquery?

A **subquery** is a normal T-SQL query that is nested inside another query, using parentheses - created when you have a `SELECT` statement that serves as the basis for either part of the data or the condition in another query.

Subqueries are generally used to fill one of a couple of needs:

- Break a query up into a series of logical steps
- Provide a listing to be the target of a `WHERE` clause together with [`IN`|`EXISTS`|`ANY`|`ALL`]
- To provide a lookup driven by each individual record in a parent query

Some subqueries are very easy to think of and build, but some are extremely complex – it usually depends on the complexity of the relationship between the inner (the sub) and outer (the top) query.

It's also worth noting that most subqueries (but definitely not all) can also be written using a join. In places where you can use a join instead, the join is usually the preferable choice.

I once got into a rather lengthy (perhaps 20 or 30 e-mails flying back and forth with examples, reasons, etc. over a few days) debate with a co-worker over the joins vs. subqueries issue.

Traditional logic says to always use the join, and that was what I was pushing (due to experience rather than traditional logic – you've already seen several places in this book where I've pointed out how traditional thinking can be bogus). My co-worker was pushing the notion that a subquery would actually cause less overhead – I decided to try it out.

What I found was essentially (as you might expect), that we were both right in certain circumstances. We will explore these circumstances fully towards the end of the chapter after you have a bit more background.

Now that we know what a subquery theoretically is, let's look at some specific types and examples of subqueries.

Building a Nested Subquery

A **nested subquery** is one that goes in only *one* direction – returning either a single value for use in the outer query, or perhaps a full list of values to be used with the IN operator. In the event that you want to use an explicit = operator, you're going to be using a query that returns a single value – that means one column from one row. If you are expecting a list back, then you'll need to use the IN operator with your outer query.

In the loosest sense, your query syntax is going to look something like one of these two syntax templates:

```
SELECT <SELECT list>
FROM <SomeTable>
WHERE <SomeColumn> = (
          SELECT <single column>
          FROM <SomeTable>
          WHERE <condition that results in only one row returned>)
```

Or:

```
SELECT <SELECT list>
FROM <SomeTable>
WHERE <SomeColumn> IN (
          SELECT <single column>
          FROM <SomeTable>
          [WHERE <condition>)]
```

Obviously, the exact syntax will vary. Not for just substituting the select list and exact table names, but also because you may have a multi-table join in either the inner or outer queries – or both.

Nested Queries Using Single Value SELECT Statements

Let's get down to the nitty-gritty with an explicit example. Let's say, for example, that we wanted to know the ProductIDs of every item sold on the first day any product was purchased from the system.

If you already know the first day that an order was placed in the system, then it's no problem, the query would look something like this:

```
SELECT DISTINCT o.OrderDate, od.ProductID
FROM Orders o
JOIN [Order Details] od
  ON o.OrderID = od.OrderID
WHERE OrderDate = "7/4/1996"  --This is first OrderDate in the system
```

This yields us the correct results:

```
OrderDate                          ProductID
---------------------------------- -------------
1996-07-04 00:00:00.000            11
1996-07-04 00:00:00.000            42
1996-07-04 00:00:00.000            72

(3 row(s) affected)
```

But let's say, just for instance, that we are regularly purging data from the system, and we still want to ask this same question as part of an automated report.

Since it's going to be automated, we can't run a query to find out what the first date in the system is and manually plug that into our query.

No problem, you say. Just add in a variable and make it part of a batch:

```
DECLARE @FirstDate smalldatetime

SELECT @FirstDate = MIN(OrderDate) FROM Orders

SELECT DISTINCT o.OrderDate, od.ProductID
FROM Orders o
JOIN [Order Details] od
  ON o.OrderID = od.OrderID
WHERE o.OrderDate = @FirstDate
```

While this works (you should get back the exact same results), we can actually clean things up a bit by putting it all into one statement:

```
SELECT DISTINCT o.OrderDate, od.ProductID
FROM Orders o
JOIN [Order Details] od
  ON o.OrderID = od.OrderID
WHERE o.OrderDate = (SELECT MIN(OrderDate) FROM Orders)
```

It's just that quick and easy. The inner query `(SELECT MIN...)` retrieves a single value for use in the outer query. Since we're using an equals sign, the inner query absolutely must return only one column from one single row, or you will get a run-time error.

Nested Queries Using Subqueries that Return Multiple Values

Perhaps the most common of all subqueries that are implemented in the world are those that retrieve some form of domain list and use it as a criterion for a query.

For this one, let's switch over to using the `Pubs` database as we did in Chapter 5 (Joins). What we want is a list of all the stores that have discount records. The stores are, not surprisingly, in a table called `Stores`. The discounts are in a table called, appropriately enough, `discounts`.

We might write something like this:

```
USE PUBS

SELECT stor_id AS "Store ID", stor_name AS "Store Name"
FROM Stores
WHERE stor_id IN (SELECT stor_id FROM Discounts)
```

As it happens, this only gets us back one row – but what's interesting is that it is exactly the same row we saw doing an inner join in a query in Chapter 5:

```
Store ID         Store Name
---------------- ---------------
8042             Bookbeat

(1 row(s) affected)
```

Queries of this type almost always fall into the category of one that can be done using an inner join rather than a nested SELECT. For example, we could get the same results as the subquery above by running this simple join:

```
SELECT s.stor_id AS "Store ID", stor_name AS "Store Name"
FROM Stores s
JOIN Discounts d
  ON s.stor_id = d.stor_id
```

For performance reasons you want to use the join method as your default solution if you don't have a specific reason for using the nested SELECT – we'll discuss this more before the chapter's done.

Using a Nested SELECT to Find Orphaned Records

This type of nested SELECT is nearly identical to our previous example, except that we add the NOT operator. The difference this makes when you are converting to join syntax is that you are equating to an outer join rather than an inner join.

Before we do the nested SELECT syntax, let's review one of our examples of an outer join from Chapter 5. In this query, we were trying to identify all the stores in the pubs database that didn't have matching discount records:

```
USE Pubs

SELECT s.Stor_Name AS "Store Name"
FROM Discounts d
RIGHT OUTER JOIN Stores s
              ON d.Stor_ID = s.Stor_ID
WHERE d.Stor_ID IS NULL
```

This got us 5 rows back:

```
Store Name
--------------------------------------------------
Eric the Read Books
Barnum's
News & Brews
Doc-U-Mat: Quality Laundry and Books
Fricative Bookshop

(5 row(s) affected)
```

This is the way that, typically speaking, things should be done. I can't say, however, that it's the way that things are usually done. The join usually takes a bit more thought, so we usually wind up with the nested SELECT instead.

See if you can write this nested SELECT on your own – but I'll warn you, this one has something of a gotcha in it. Once you're done, come back and take a look below.

It should wind up looking like this:

```
SELECT stor_id AS "Store ID", stor_name AS "Store Name"
FROM Stores
WHERE stor_id NOT IN
    (SELECT stor_id FROM Discounts WHERE stor_id IS NOT NULL)
```

This yields us exactly the same five records. I'm guessing though, that you probably didn't use the NOT NULL comparison in the inner query the first time you tried it.

Whether you need to include the NOT NULL qualification or not depends on whether your table accepts NULLs and what exactly you want for results. In our case, if we leave the comparison off, we will, in error, wind up thinking that there aren't any stores that don't have discounts (when there really are). The reason has to do with how NULLs compare – you need to be extremely careful when dealing with the possibility of NULL values in your IN list.

The ANY, SOME and ALL Operators

Up to this point, we've only been looking for an item that was IN a list – that is, where at least one value in the list was an exact match to what we were looking for. Ahh, but life isn't that simple. What if we want to do something other than an exact match – something that isn't quite equivalent to an equals (=) sign? What if we want a more complete list of operators? No problem!

But "Wait, hold on!" you say. "What if I want to see if *every* value in a list matches something – what then?" Again – no problem!

ANY and SOME

ANY and SOME are functional equivalents; if you choose to use one of them (you'll see later why I don't recommend them), then I would suggest using SOME, as it is the ANSI compliant one of the two. In all honesty, for the rest of this section, I'm only going to use SOME, but feel free to substitute ANY in any place – you should get the same results.

The ANY and SOME operators allow you to use a more broad range of other operators against the lists created by your subqueries. They can also be used with any of the other operators you would typically use for comparisons (such as >=, <=, <>, !>, etc.).

Taking > as an example, >SOME means greater than *any one value*, i.e. greater than the minimum. So >SOME (1, 2, 3) means greater than 1. If you use them with an equals sign (=), then they are a functional equivalent of the IN operator.

Let's try this out with a simple rehash of the NOT IN query we just looked at. We'll use this one to show how close SOME is to the IN operator, but then we'll play with it to see the additional flexibility SOME gives us. The syntax only requires two changes (NOT IN becomes != SOME):

```
SELECT stor_id AS "Store ID", stor_name AS "Store Name"
FROM Stores
WHERE stor_id != SOME
   (SELECT stor_id FROM Discounts WHERE stor_id IS NOT NULL)
```

Run this and you should get the same 5 rows back yet again:

```
Store ID         Store Name
---------------- --------------------------------------------------
6380             Eric the Read Books
7066             Barnum's
7067             News & Brews
7131             Doc-U-Mat: Quality Laundry and Books
7896             Fricative Bookshop

(5 row(s) affected)
```

That works fine, but let's mess around with it some and see how we can change things. This time, we'll change our comparison:

```
SELECT stor_id AS "Store ID", stor_name AS "Store Name"
FROM Stores
WHERE stor_id < SOME
(SELECT stor_id FROM Discounts WHERE stor_id IS NOT NULL)
```

This gets us back five rows:

```
Store ID         Store Name
---------------- --------------------------------------------------
6380             Eric the Read Books
7066             Barnum's
7067             News & Brews
7131             Doc-U-Mat: Quality Laundry and Books
7896             Fricative Bookshop

(5 row(s) affected)
```

The results of this one would be any stores that have a `stor_id` that is less than the largest `stor_id` with no discount.

> *Actually, I'm not a big fan of this keyword. The reason is that I find it functionally useless. The things you can do with* `SOME` *(or* `ANY`*) fall into two categories. The first of these is that there isn't anything you can do with* `SOME` *that you can't do with some other syntax (the other syntax has always been more succinct in my experience). The only exception to this is the case of* `<> SOME`*. Where the* `NOT IN (A, B, C)` *clause gets you a logical expansion of* `<>A AND <> B AND <> C`*,* `<> SOME` *gets you* `<>A OR <> B OR <> C`*. This last option is a positively useless construct. Think about it for a minute – any comparison you run against* `<>ANY` *is going to yield you a non-filtered list. By definition, anything that is* `= A` is `<> B`*.*
>
> *In short, if you find a reason to use this, great – but, to date, I haven't seen anything done with* `SOME` *that can't be done more clearly and with better performance using a different construct (which one depends on the nature of the* `SOME` *you're trying to match).*

ALL

The `ALL` operator is similar to the `SOME` and `ANY` operators in allowing you to work with a broader range of comparison operators. However, applying our previous > example to the `ALL` statement, we see the difference. `>ALL` means greater than *every value*, i.e. greater than the maximum. `So >ALL (1, 2, 3)` means greater than 3.

Correlated Subqueries

Two words for you on this section: Pay Attention! This is another one of those little areas that, if you truly "get it" can really set you apart from the crowd. By "get it" I don't just mean that you understand how it works, but also that you understand how important it can be.

Correlated subqueries are one of those things that make the impossible possible. What's more, they often turn several lines of code into one, and often create a corresponding increase in performance. The problem with them is that they require a substantially different style of thought than you're probably used to. Correlated subqueries are probably the single easiest concept in SQL to learn, understand, then promptly forget because it simply goes against the grain of how you think. If you're one of the few who choose to remember it as an option, then you will be one of the few who figure out that hard to figure out problem. You'll also be someone with a far more complete tool set when it comes to squeezing every ounce of performance out of your queries.

How Correlated Subqueries Work

What makes correlated subqueries different from the nested subqueries we've been looking at is that the information travels in *two* directions rather than one. In a nested subquery, the inner query is only processed once, and that information is passed out for the outer query, which will also execute just once – essentially providing the same value or list that you would have provided if you had typed it in yourself.

With correlated subqueries, however, the inner query runs on information provided by the outer query, and vice versa. That may seem a bit confusing (that chicken or the egg thing again), but it works in a 3 step process:

- The outer query obtains a record, and passes it into the inner query
- The inner query executes based on the passed in value(s)
- The inner query then passes the values from its results back out to the outer query, which uses them to finish its processing

Correlated Subqueries in the WHERE Clause

I realize that this is probably a bit confusing, so let's look at it in an example.

We'll go back to the `Northwind` database and look again at the query where we wanted to know the orders that happened on the first date that an order was placed in the system. However, this time we want to add a new twist: we want to know the `OrderID`(s) and `OrderDate` of the first order in the system for each customer. That is, we want to know the first day that a customer placed an order and the IDs of those orders. Let's look at it piece by piece.

First, we want the `OrderDate`, `OrderID`, and `CustomerID` for each of our results. All of that information can be found in the `Orders` table, so we know that our query is going to be based, at least in part, on that table.

Next, we need to know what the first date in the system was for each customer. That's where the tricky part comes in. When we did this with a nested subquery, we were only looking for the first date in the entire file – now we need a value for each individual customer.

This wouldn't be that big a deal if we were to do it in two separate queries – we could just create a temporary table, and then join back to it – like this:

```
USE Northwind

SELECT CustomerID, MIN((OrderDate)) AS OrderDate
INTO #MinOrderDates
FROM Orders
GROUP BY CustomerID
ORDER BY CustomerID

SELECT o.CustomerID, o.OrderID, o.OrderDate
FROM Orders o
JOIN #MinOrderDates t
  ON o.CustomerID = t.CustomerID
  AND o.OrderDate = t.OrderDate
ORDER BY o.CustomerID

DROP TABLE #MinOrderDates
```

We get back 89 rows:

```
(89 row(s) affected)

CustomerID OrderID          OrderDate
---------- ---------------- ----------------------------
ALFKI      10643            1997-08-25 00:00:00.000
ANATR      10308            1996-09-18 00:00:00.000
ANTON      10365            1996-11-27 00:00:00.000
AROUT      10355            1996-11-15 00:00:00.000
BERGS      10278            1996-08-12 00:00:00.000
...
...
...
WHITC      10269            1996-07-31 00:00:00.000
WILMK      10615            1997-07-30 00:00:00.000
WOLZA      10374            1996-12-05 00:00:00.000

(89 row(s) affected)
```

As previously stated, don't worry if your results are slightly different from those shown here.

The fact that we are building two completely separate result sets here is emphasized by the fact that you see two different row(s) affected in the results. That, more often that not, has a negative impact on performance. We'll explore this further after we consider our options some more.

Sometimes using this two query approach is simply the only way to get things done without using a cursor – this is not one of those times.

OK, so if we want this to run in a single query, we need to find a way to lookup each individual. We can do this by making use of an inner query that performs a lookup based on the current `CustomerID` in the outer query. We will then need to return a value back out to the outer query so it can match things up based on the earliest order date.

It looks like this:

```
SELECT o1.CustomerID, o1.OrderID, o1.OrderDate
FROM Orders o1
WHERE o1.OrderDate = (SELECT Min(o2.OrderDate)
                      FROM Orders o2
                      WHERE o2.CustomerID = o1.CustomerID)
ORDER BY CustomerID
```

With this, we get back the same 89 rows:

```
CustomerID  OrderID             OrderDate
----------  ------------------  ------------------------------
ALFKI       10643               1997-08-25 00:00:00.000
ANATR       10308               1996-09-18 00:00:00.000
ANTON       10365               1996-11-27 00:00:00.000
AROUT       10355               1996-11-15 00:00:00.000
BERGS       10278               1996-08-12 00:00:00.000
...
...
...
WHITC       10269               1996-07-31 00:00:00.000
WILMK       10615               1997-07-30 00:00:00.000
WOLZA       10374               1996-12-05 00:00:00.000

(89 row(s) affected)
```

There are a couple of key things to notice in this query:

- We see only one row(s) affected line – giving us a good clue that only one query plan had to be executed.
- The outer query (in this example) looks pretty much just like a nested subquery. The inner query, however, has an explicit reference to the outer query (notice the use of the `o1` alias).
- Aliases are used in both queries – even though it looks like the outer query shouldn't need one – because they are required whenever you explicitly refer to a column from the other query (inside refers to a column on the outside or vice versa).

> **The latter point of needing aliases is a big area of confusion. The fact is that sometimes you need them, and sometimes you don't. While I don't tend to use them at all in the types of nested subqueries that we looked at in the early part of this chapter, I alias everything when dealing with correlated subqueries.**
>
> **The hard and fast "rule" is that you must alias any table (and its related columns) that's going to be referred to by the other query. The problem is that this can quickly become very confusing. The way to be on the safe side is to alias everything – that way you can be positive about which table you're getting your information from, and in which query.**

We only see that 89 row(s) affected once. That's because it only affected 89 rows one time. Just by observation, we can guess that this version probably runs faster than the two query version, and, in reality, it does. Again, we'll look into this a bit more shortly.

In this particular query, the outer query only references the inner query in the `WHERE` clause – it could also have requested data from the inner query to include in the `SELECT` list.

Normally, it's up to us whether we want to make use of an alias or not, but, with correlated subqueries, they are required. This particular query is a really great one for showing why because the inner and outer queries are based on the same table. Since both queries are getting information from each other, without aliasing, how would they know which instance of the table data that you were interested in?

Correlated Subqueries in the SELECT List

Subqueries can also be used to provide a different kind of answer in your selection results. This kind of situation is often found where the information you're after is fundamentally different from the rest of the data in your query (for example, you want an aggregation on one field, but you don't want all the baggage from that to affect the other fields returned).

To test this out, let's just run a somewhat modified version of the query we used in the last section. What we're going to say we're after here is just the name of the customer and the first date on which they ordered something.

This one creates a somewhat more significant change than is probably apparent at first. We're now asking for the customer's name, which means that we have to bring the `Customers` table into play. In addition, we no longer need to build any kind of condition in – we're asking for all customers (no restrictions), we just want to know when their first order date was.

The query actually winds-up being a bit simpler than the last one, and it looks like this:

```
SELECT cu.CompanyName,
   (SELECT Min(OrderDate)
          FROM Orders o
          WHERE o.CustomerID = cu.CustomerID)
          AS "Order Date"
FROM Customers cu
```

This gets us data that looks something like this:

```
CompanyName                                     Order Date
----------------------------------------------- ------------------------------
Alfreds Futterkiste                             1997-08-25 00:00:00.000
Ana Trujillo Emparedados y helados              1996-09-18 00:00:00.000
Antonio Moreno Taquería                         1996-11-27 00:00:00.000
Around the Horn                                 1996-11-15 00:00:00.000
Berglunds snabbköp                              1996-08-12 00:00:00.000
Blauer See Delikatessen                         1997-04-09 00:00:00.000
...
...
...
White Clover Markets                            1996-07-31 00:00:00.000
Wilman Kala                                     1997-07-30 00:00:00.000
Wolski Zajazd                                   1996-12-05 00:00:00.000

(91 row(s) affected)
```

Note that, if you look down through all the data, there are a couple of rows that have a NULL in the Order Date column. Why do you suppose that is? The cause is, of course, because there is no record in the Orders table that matches the current record in the Customers table (the outer query).

This brings us to a small digression to take a look at a particularly useful function for this situation – ISNULL().

Dealing with NULL Data – the ISNULL Function

There are actually a few functions that are specifically meant to deal with NULL data, but the one of particular use to us at this point is ISNULL(). ISNULL() accepts a variable or expression and tests it for a null value. If the value is indeed NULL, then the function returns some other pre-specified value. If the original value is not NULL, then the original value is returned. This syntax is pretty straightforward:

ISNULL(*<expression to test>*, *<replacement value if null>*)

So, for example:

ISNULL Expression	Value Returned
ISNULL(NULL, 5)	5
ISNULL(5, 15)	5
ISNULL(@MyVar, 0) WHERE @MyVar IS NULL	0
ISNULL(@MyVar, 0) WHERE @MyVar =3	3
ISNULL(@MyVar, 0) WHERE @MyVar ='Fred Farmer'	Fred Farmer

Now let's see this at work in our query:

```
SELECT cu.CompanyName,
   ISNULL(CONVERT(varchar,(SELECT MIN(o.OrderDate)
           FROM Orders o
           WHERE o.CustomerID = cu.CustomerID)), "  NEVER ORDERED")
           AS "Order Date"
FROM Customers cu
```

Now, in our two lines that we had problems with, we go from:

```
...
FISSA Fabrica Inter. Salchichas S.A.  NULL
...
Paris spécialités                     NULL
...
```

To something substantially more useful:

```
...
FISSA Fabrica Inter. Salchichas S.A.  NEVER ORDERED
...
Paris spécialités                     NEVER ORDERED
...
```

Notice that I also had to put the `CONVERT()` function into play to get this to work. The reason has to do with casting and implicit conversion. Since the first row starts off returning a valid date, the column `Order Date` is assumed to be of type `DateTime`. However, when we get to our first `ISNULL`, there is an error generated since `NEVER ORDERED` can't be converted to the `DateTime` datatype. Keep `CONVERT()` in mind – it can help you out of little troubles like this one. This is covered further later in the chapter.

So, at this point, we've seen correlated subqueries that provide information for both the `WHERE` clause, and for the select list. You can mix and match these two in the same query if you wish.

The EXISTS Operator

I call `EXISTS` an operator, but all you'll hear the Books Online call it is a keyword. That's probably because it defies description in some senses. It's both an operator much like the `IN` keyword is, but it also looks at things just a bit differently.

When you use `EXISTS`, you don't really return data – instead, you return a simple `TRUE/FALSE` regarding the existence of data that meets the criteria established in the query which the `EXISTS` statement is operating against.

Let's go right to an example, so you can see how this gets applied. What we're going to query here is a list of customers that have placed at least one order (we don't care how many):

```
SELECT CustomerID, CompanyName
FROM Customers cu
WHERE EXISTS
   (SELECT OrderID
          FROM Orders o
          WHERE o.CustomerID = cu.CustomerID)
```

This gets us what amounts to the same 89 records that we've been dealing with throughout this chapter:

```
CustomerID            CompanyName
--------------------- ---------------------------------------
ALFKI                 Alfreds Futterkiste
ANATR                 Ana Trujillo Emparedados y helados
ANTON                 Antonio Moreno Taquería
AROUT                 Around the Horn
BERGS                 Berglunds snabbköp
BLAUS                 Blauer See Delikatessen
...
...
...
WHITC                 White Clover Markets
WILMK                 Wilman Kala
WOLZA                 Wolski Zajazd

(89 row(s) affected)
```

We could have easily done this same thing with a join:

```
SELECT DISTINCT cu.CustomerID, cu.CompanyName
FROM Customers cu
JOIN Orders o
  ON cu.CustomerID = o.CustomerID
```

This join based syntax, for example, would have yielded us exactly the same results (subject to possible sort differences). So why, then, would we need this new syntax? Performance – plain and simple.

When you use the EXISTS keyword, SQL Server doesn't have to perform a full row by row join. Instead, it can look through the records until it finds the first match, and stop right there. As soon as there is a single match, the EXISTS is true, so there is no need to go further.

Let's take a brief look at things the other way around – that is, what if our query wanted the customers who had not ordered anything? Under the join method that we looked at back in Chapter 5, we would have had to make some significant changes in the way we went about getting our answers. First, we would have to use an outer join. Then we would perform a comparison to see whether any of the Order records were NULL.

It looked like this:

```
USE Northwind

SELECT c.CustomerID, CompanyName
FROM Customers c
LEFT OUTER JOIN Orders o
             ON c.CustomerID = o.CustomerID
WHERE o.CustomerID IS NULL
```

And it returned two rows.

To do the same change over when we're using EXISTS we only add one word – NOT:

```
SELECT CustomerID, CompanyName
FROM Customers cu
WHERE NOT EXISTS
   (SELECT OrderID
          FROM Orders o
          WHERE o.CustomerID = cu.CustomerID)
```

And we get back those exact same two rows:

```
CustomerID           CompanyName
-------------------- ----------------------------------------
FISSA                FISSA Fabrica Inter. Salchichas S.A.
PARIS                Paris spécialités

(2 row(s) affected)
```

The performance difference here is even more marked then with the inner join. SQL Server just applies a little reverse logic vs. the straight EXISTS statement. In the case of the NOT we're now using, SQL Server can still stop looking as soon as it finds one matching record – the only difference is that it knows to return FALSE for that lookup rather than TRUE. Performance wise, everything else about the query is the same.

Using EXISTS in Other Ways

If you use the Enterprise Manager to create any scripts, one of the options it gives you is whether to include DROP statements. Assuming you select that option, you'll notice something peculiar that it adds to the creation script for each table. It will look something like this:

```
IF EXISTS (SELECT * FROM sysobjects WHERE id =
object_id(N'[dbo].[Shippers]') AND OBJECTPROPERTY(id, N'IsUserTable') = 1)
DROP TABLE [dbo].[Shippers]
GO

CREATE TABLE [dbo].[Shippers] (
    [ShipperID] [int] IDENTITY (1, 1) NOT NULL ,
    [CompanyName] [nvarchar] (40) NOT NULL ,
    [Phone] [nvarchar] (24) NULL
)
GO
```

Actually, it's kind of funny that they still do it this way vs. using the INFORMATION SCHEMA as they tell you to, but it's still handy for illustrating a very common use for EXISTS – that is, with an IF...ELSE statement, as we'll see later.

Since EXISTS returns nothing but TRUE or FALSE, that means it works as an excellent conditional expression. The above example will only run the DROP TABLE code if the table exists; otherwise, it skips over that part and moves right into the CREATE statement. This avoids one of two errors showing up when you run the script. Firstly, that it can't run the CREATE statement (which would probably create other problems if you were running this in a script where other tables were depending on this being done first) because the object already exists. Secondly, that it couldn't DROP the table (this pretty much just creates a message that might be confusing to a customer who installs your product) because it didn't exist. You're covered for both.

As for an instance of this, let's write our own CREATE script for something that's often skipped in the automation effort – the database. Because EM will generate the table scripts for you (assuming that you've already created the table with the New Table... command, or previous scripts, or whatever), that part tends to get done – it's easy, so people are willing to do it. But creation of the database is often left as part of some cryptic directions that say something like "create a database called 'xxxx'". The fun part is when the people who are actually installing it (who often don't know what they're doing) start including the quotes, or create the database too small, or a host of other possible and very simple errors to make. This is the point where I hope you have a good tech support department.

Instead, we'll just build a little script to create the database object that could go with Northwind. For safety's sake, we'll call it NorthwindCreate. We'll also keep the statement to a minimum since we're interested in the EXISTS rather than the CREATE command:

```
USE master

GO

IF NOT EXISTS (SELECT 'True' FROM INFORMATION_SCHEMA.SCHEMATA WHERE CATALOG_NAME =
'NorthwindCreate')
BEGIN
   CREATE DATABASE NorthwindCreate
   ON
   ( NAME = NorthwindCreate,
     FILENAME = 'c:\mssql7\data\NorthwindCreate.mdf' )
END
ELSE
BEGIN
   PRINT 'Database already exists. Skipping CREATE DATABASE Statement'
END
GO
```

The first time you run this, there won't be any database called `NorthwindCreate` (unless by sheer coincidence you created something called that before we got to this point), so you'll get a response back that looks like this:

```
The CREATE DATABASE process is allocating 0.75 MB on disk 'NorthwindCreate'.
The CREATE DATABASE process is allocating 0.49 MB on disk 'NorthwindCreate_log'.
```

If the sizes seem small, that's because we didn't specify a size, so the files were created from what the `model` database had. In a real life situation, you'd specify whatever size was appropriate.

Now run the script a second time, and you'll see a change:

```
Database already exists. Skipping CREATE DATABASE Statement
```

So, without much fanfare or fuss, we've added a rather small script in that will make things much more usable for the installers of your product. That may be an end user who bought your off-the-shelf product, or it may be you – in which case it's even better that it's fully scripted.

The long and the short of it is that `EXISTS` is a very handy keyword indeed. It can make some queries run much faster, and it can also simplify some queries and scripts.

Mixing Data Types: CAST and CONVERT

You'll see both `CAST` and `CONVERT` used frequently. Indeed, we've touch briefly on both of these in several places throughout the book. This seems like a good time, however, to look a little closer at what these two functions can do for you.

Both `CAST` and `CONVERT` perform data type conversions for you. In most respects, they both do the same thing, with the exception that `CONVERT` also does some date formatting conversions that `CAST` doesn't offer.

> *So, the question probably quickly rises to your mind – hey, if `CONVERT` does everything that `CAST` does, and `CONVERT` also does date conversions, why would I ever use `CAST`? I have a simple answer for that – ANSI compliance. `CAST` is ANSI compliant, and `CONVERT` isn't – it's that simple.*

Let's take a look for the syntax for each:

```
CAST (expression AS data_type)
```

```
CONVERT(data_type, expression[, style])
```

With a little flip-flop on which goes first, and the addition of the formatting option on `CONVERT` (with the *`style`* argument), they have basically the same syntax.

`CAST` and `CONVERT` can deal with a wide variety of data type conversions that you'll need to do when SQL Server won't do it implicitly for you. For example, converting a number to a string is a very common need. To illustrate:

```
SELECT "The Customer has an Order numbered " + OrderID
FROM Orders
WHERE CustomerID = "ALFKI"
```

Will yield an error:

```
Server: Msg 245, Level 16, State 1, Line 1
Syntax error converting the varchar value 'The Customer has an Order numbered ' to a column of data type int.
```

But change the code to convert the number first:

```
SELECT "The Customer has an Order numbered " + CAST(OrderID AS varchar)
FROM Orders
WHERE CustomerID = "ALFKI"
```

And you get a very different result:

```

----------------------------------------------------------
The Customer has an Order numbered 10643
The Customer has an Order numbered 10692
The Customer has an Order numbered 10702
The Customer has an Order numbered 10835
The Customer has an Order numbered 10952
The Customer has an Order numbered 11011

(6 row(s) affected)
```

The conversions can actually get a little less intuitive also. Assume, for example, that you wanted to convert a `timestamp` column into a regular number. A `timestamp` is just a binary number, so the conversion isn't any really big deal. This code:

```
CREATE TABLE ConvertTest
(
   ColID   int   IDENTITY,
   ColTS   timestamp
)

INSERT INTO ConvertTest
   DEFAULT VALUES

SELECT ColTS AS "Unconverted", CAST(ColTS AS int) AS "Converted" FROM ConvertTest
```

Yields us something like this (your exact numbers will vary):

(1 row(s) affected)

```
Unconverted                           Converted
------------------------------------- -------------
0x00000000000000C9                    201

(1 row(s) affected)
```

We can also convert dates:

```
SELECT OrderDate, CAST(OrderDate AS varchar) AS "Converted"
FROM Orders
WHERE OrderID = 11050
```

This yields us something similar to the following (your exact format may change depending on the system date configuration):

```
OrderDate                             Converted
------------------------------------- ----------------------------
1998-04-27 00:00:00.000               Apr 27 1998 12:00AM

(1 row(s) affected)
```

Notice that `CAST` can still do date conversion, you just don't have any control over the formatting as you do with `CONVERT`. For example:

```
SELECT OrderDate, CONVERT(varchar(12), OrderDate, 111) AS "Converted"
FROM Orders
WHERE OrderID = 11050
```

Yields us:

```
OrderDate                             Converted
------------------------------------- ---------------
1998-04-27 00:00:00.000               1998/04/27

(1 row(s) affected)
```

Which is quite a bit different from what `CAST` did. Indeed, we could have converted to any one of thirty-four two-digit or four-digit year formats. This query:

```
SELECT OrderDate, CONVERT(varchar(12), OrderDate, 5) AS "Converted"
FROM Orders
WHERE OrderID = 11050
```

Gives us:

```
OrderDate                             Converted
------------------------------------- -------------
1998-04-27 00:00:00.000               27-04-98

(1 row(s) affected)
```

All you need is to supply a code at the end of the CONVERT function (111 in the above example gives us the JAPAN standard, with a four-digit year; and 5 the Italian standard, with a two-digit year) that specifies what format you want. Anything in the 100s is a four-digit year; anything less than 100, with a few exceptions, is a two-digit year. The available formats can be found in Books Online under the topic of CONVERT or CASE.

Keep in mind that some changes have needed to be made to things to deal with the infamous Y2K issue. One of the changes is that you can now set a split point that SQL Server will use to determine whether a 2 digit year should be have a 20 added on the front or a 19. The default breaking point is 49/50 – a two-digit year of 49 or less will be converted using a 20 on the front. Anything higher will use a 19. These can be changed using sp_configure*, or by setting them in the* Server Settings *tab of the* Properties *dialogue for your server in EM.*

Performance Considerations

We've already touched on some of the macro-level "what's the best thing" to do stuff as we've gone through the chapter, but, like most things in life, it's not as easy as all that. What I want to do here is provide something of a quick reference for performance issues for your queries. I'll try and steer you towards the right kind of query for the right kind of situation.

Yes, it's time again folks for one of my now famous soapbox diatribes. At issue this time, is the concept of blanket use of blanket rules.

What we're going to be talking about in this section is about the way that things ***usually*** *work. The word usually is extremely operative here. There are very few rules in SQL that will be true 100% of the time. In a world full of exceptions, SQL has to be at the pinnacle of that – exceptions are a dime a dozen when you try and describe the performance world in SQL Server.*

In short, you need to gauge just how important the performance of a given query is. If performance is critical, then don't take these rules too seriously – instead, use them as a starting point, and then ***TEST, TEST, TEST!!!***

JOINs vs. Subqueries

This is that area I mentioned earlier in the chapter that I had a heated debate with a coworker over. And, as you might expect when two people have such conviction in their point of view, both of us were correct up to a point (and it follows, wrong up to a point).

The long standing, traditional viewpoint about subqueries has always been that you are much better off to use joins instead if you can. This is absolutely correct – sometimes. In reality, it depends on a large number of factors. Here is a table that discusses some of the issues that the performance balance will depend on, and which side of the equation they favor:

Situation	Favors
The value returned from a subquery is going to be the same for every row in the outer query	Pre-query. Declaring a variable, and then selecting the needed value into that variable will allow the would-be subquery to be executed just once rather than once for every record in the outer table.
Both tables are relatively small (say 10,000 records or less)	Subqueries. I don't know the exact reasons, but I've run several tests on this, and it held up pretty much every time. I suspect that the issue is the lower overhead of a lookup vs. a join.
The match, after considering all criteria, is only going to return one value	Subqueries. Again, there is much less overhead in going and finding just one record and substituting it, than having to join the entire table.
The match, after considering all criteria, is only going to return relatively few values and there is no index on the lookup column	Subqueries. A single lookup or even a few lookups will usually take less overhead than a hash join.
The lookup table is relatively small, but the base table is large	Nested subqueries if applicable; joins if vs. a correlated subquery. With subqueries the lookup will only happen once, and has relatively low overhead. With correlated subqueries, however, you will be cycling the lookup many times – in this case, the join would be a better choice in most cases.
Correlated subquery vs. join	Join. Internally, a correlated subquery is going to create a nested loop situation. This can create quite a bit of overhead. It is substantially faster than cursors in most instances, but slower than other options that might be available.
`EXISTS` vs. whatever	`EXISTS`. It does not have to deal with multiple lookups for the same match – once it finds one match for that particular row, it is free to move onto the next lookup – this can seriously cut down on overhead.

These are just the highlights. The possibilities of different mixes and additional situations are positively endless.

Now let's briefly quantify this in very simplistic terms (I can just hear people out there saying, "Yes, but how much of a difference?"). The proviso here is that you have to remember that these are very small samples and are generalizations – every situation will be somewhat different.

To quantify, we'll look back at a couple of the queries in the chapter. It will illustrate some of the balancing acts you have to do between relatively clean and compact code vs. raw performance. For most of these, I have compared performance using a looping structure to perform multiple executions. This is a good news, bad news story in terms of accuracy. It means that they are being run under ideal circumstances (after the first loop, all data is going to be in cache). The impacts may be somewhat different if you're in a situation where you're paging data in and out of cache often (if you are, you might think of investing in a little more RAM for your system).

The first query we'll look at is the first subquery in the chapter – looking up order detail items from the date of the first order in the system. This had a join, which required multiple statements, vs. a subquery, which could do it in just one statement.

Even though the join requires a variable declaration, a separate query to find the earliest date in the system, and then the actual join, it still runs on the order of 40% faster than the subquery. The subquery is cleaner, but pre-querying is significantly faster. Just how much faster will depend on the number of loops that the subquery will be affected by – the larger the number of rows in the outer query, the larger the difference will be between the two.

Next, let's look at the outer join vs. `NOT EXISTS` syntax on the query to identify non-matching records. It would be real easy to fall into the trap of thinking (because of reading too many books with not enough practice) that a join is always faster if you can do it that way – but the `NOT EXISTS` syntax actually runs more than twice as fast.

As I mentioned before, this is generalization at its worst, yet it gives you an inkling of what the different choices to perform what is apparently the same query can mean. These couple of examples really just scratch the surface.

> **I can't stress enough how important it is, when in doubt – heck, even when you're not in doubt but performance is everything – to make reasonable tests of competing solutions to the problem. Most of the time the blanket rules will be fine, but not always. By performing reason tests, you can be certain you've made the right choice.**

Summary

The query options you learned back in Chapters 4 & 5 cover perhaps 80% or more of the query situations that you run into, but it's that other 20% that can kill you. Sometimes the issue is whether you can even find a query that will give you the answers you need. Sometimes it's that you have a particular query or sproc that has unacceptable performance. Whatever the case, you'll run across plenty of situations where simple queries and joins just won't fit the bill. You need something more, and, hopefully, the options covered in this chapter have given you a little extra arsenal to deal with those tough situations.

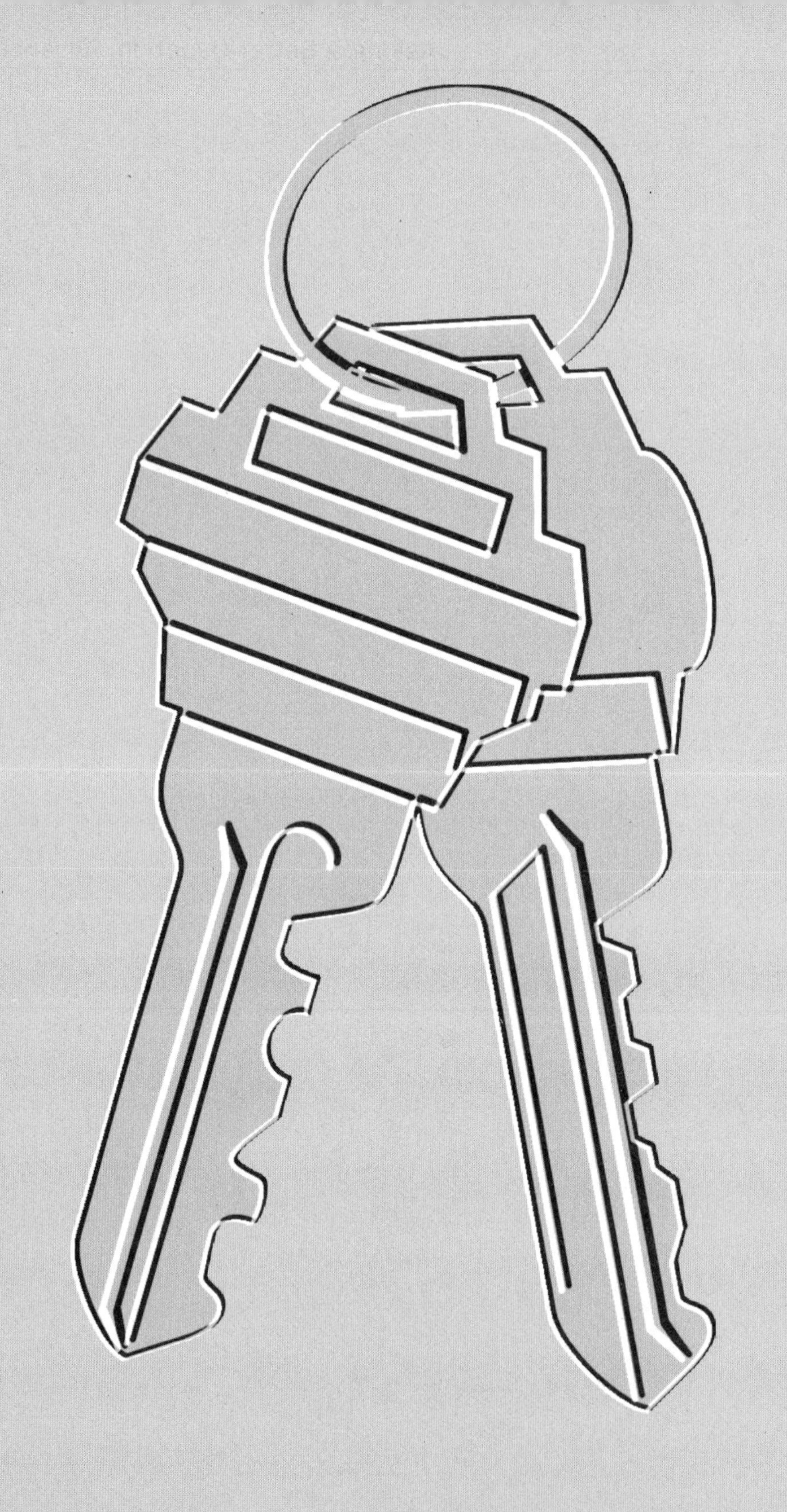

16

Spreading Things Out: Distributed Queries and Transactions

Wouldn't it be nice if everything everywhere could run on just one machine? Of course, everyone would need to have bandwidth to the machine such that it seemed local. And security - oops, that would be a problem. And this is, of course, just the start of things. Nope – we don't want every application for everyone running on the same server at all.

Indeed, sometimes dealing with multiple servers is a must. Reasons for operating on separate servers include geographical requirements, loading (too much for one machine), redundancy (not all your eggs in one basket as the old saying goes), and more. Often we can let those servers live in their own little autonomous world, but quite often we keep things separate because it seems like too much of a hassle to bring them together.

You can think of a distributed transaction as any transaction where you need the same transactional features (remember that "all or nothing" stuff?) we've already discussed using on SQL Server, but you now need to have that same reliability across multiple servers. SQL Server 7.0 continues the support for distributed transactions that was added in version 6.5.

In addition to that continued support for distributed transactions, version 7.0 added features that make querying information across servers – re-phrase that – data sources extremely easy. You can now perform heterogeneous (mixed data source) joins on SQL Server. That means that you can query information from SQL Server A and SQL Server B, and join that information with any OLE DB data source – including Excel, Access, dBase, Active Directory – anything that has an OLE DB provider.

In this chapter, we'll take a look at both of these distributed features.

Distributed Transactions

To make use of all the basic SQL Server transaction features (`BEGIN`, `SAVE`, `ROLLBACK`, `COMMIT`); the transaction must only deal with objects local to the server on which the transaction is running.

SQL Server does, however, offer another choice for transactions that is especially made for situations where you need to have absolute assurance that data is committed at both ends of an unreliable connection. (Phone lines can easily go down even in the same city – imagine if your line is from Virginia to Malaysia. You would definitely want a safety net.) It is called **Microsoft Distributed Transaction Coordinator** (MS DTC) and comes with not only SQL Server, but also with Microsoft Transaction Server (MTS). DTC can be described as a "vote collector" and co-ordinator of transactions between different servers and different RDBMSs.

MS DTC makes use of what is called a two-phase commit protocol (2PC). Much as its name implies, a 2PC has two distinct phases to guarantee that a transaction that is indicated as committed really did get committed at both ends:

- Prepare
- Commit

The Prepare Phase

In the prepare phase of the transaction, the server (more technically, the transaction manager for that server – for SQL Server, it will be DTC) that is the source of the request for a transaction sends a command to the other servers involved in the transaction. These other servers do not need to be SQL Servers as such, but can actually be any other server that provides a transaction manager which supports a protocol used by MTS (X/Open and OLE Transactions are currently supported) – which is pretty much all of the mainstream data sources.

At the point that the prepare command is received by the remote servers, those servers do whatever is necessary to create the transaction at their end – including ensuring the durability and atomicity of the transaction. When this is completed, a confirmation or failure message is sent to the originating server as appropriate. As each remote server completes the prepare phase, it returns success or failure of the prepare to the originating server.

The Commit Phase

Assuming that all remote servers involved in the transaction reply with a success message, then the transaction can proceed. The originating server will then send out a message that signals to go ahead and commit the transaction. The remote servers then commit the transaction, and again report back the success or failure of the transaction. Assuming that all remote servers return a success message to the commit command, then the originating server will report the transaction as complete.

If at any point in this process one of the servers fails to send the required reply, then the entire transaction is terminated, and, if it has gotten far enough to require it, rolled back.

If any of the remote servers fail to respond to DTC in the prepare phase, as a result of a failed connection between the two servers, for instance, the other remote servers which have signaled their readiness to commit, are said to be in doubt. This situation can be resolved by forcing the in-doubt transactions to abort.

Unfortunately, starting out a distributed transaction is a little bit different than it was for regular transactions. On the bright side though, the commands to invoke the distributed transaction engine look almost like those for the regular SQL Server transaction engine. The comparison looks like this:

SQL Server Native Command	Distribution Command
`BEGIN TRAN`	`BEGIN DISTRIBUTED TRAN`
`SAVE TRAN`	(Not Supported)
`ROLLBACK TRAN`	`ROLLBACK TRAN`
`COMMIT TRAN`	`COMMIT TRAN`

Notice that things are almost the same. The `BEGIN` just requires an extra word. The commands are otherwise syntactically the same except for the lack of support for saved transactions.

There are, however, some other differences to be aware of:

- Distributed transactions cannot be nested.
- Local transactions can automatically be escalated if you issue a distributed query – use `sp_configure` with the remote `proc trans` option to set your preference.
- MS DTC must be running locally to your SQL Server in order to use distributed transactions with it.
- The remote server must support transactions in order for the transaction process to succeed. DTC will attempt to manage this for you, and even provides a level of transitioning not inherent in the base product in some instances. There are, however, instances where transactions will not be an option with a given data source.

Other than that, distributed transactions work pretty much as regular transactions do.

Distributed Queries

Along with SQL Server 7.0 came a whole host of new features, and what they've done in the way of querying distributed data is quite a gift. If you're coming from the Access world, then a lot of this will look somewhat familiar – definitely not the same, but definitely familiar.

There are a couple of new features in this realm. Amongst them are the ability to:

- "Link" to another server and reference its objects directly by merely qualifying the object with a server name.
- Open a query on the fly – without using a linked server – and join the result set of that query with other objects in yet another query.
- Open a query on a linked server making use of a pass-through query to avoid certain compatibility issues.

Let's take a look at each of these in turn.

Creating Linked Servers

This is probably the least interesting part of this whole chapter, but it's a necessary evil on your way to putting some great horsepower in your query options.

To create a "linked" server is essentially to inform the SQL Server to which you're connected how to make contact with another individual server. What this amounts to is telling your server how to become a client to yet another server. I guess you could say that you're creating something of a controlled schizophrenia.

To create a linked server and make it usable involves two steps:

- Telling SQL Server the name and contact information for the new linked server
- Providing login mapping information to the new server

Using sp_addlinkedserver

To add a linked server, you execute a special stored procedure called `sp_addlinkedserver`. This special sproc stores away the information on where to find and how to connect with another data source. It accepts up to seven parameters, although only one is actually required. The syntax looks like this:

```
sp_addlinkedserver [@server =] '<server>'
[, [@srvproduct =] '<product name>']
[, [@provider =] '<provider name>']
[, [@datasrc =] '<data source path>']
[, [@location =] '<location>']
[, [@provstr =] '<connection string>']
[, [@catalog =] '<database>']
```

Let's take a look at each of the parameters:

Parameter	Required?	Description
`@server`	Yes	Internal name for the linked server you are creating. This will be the name you use when referring to this linked server in queries. For example: `NorthwindRemote.Northwind.dbo.Orders`
`@srvproduct`	No	A user friendly name for `@provider` below. For example, SQL Server OLEDB Provider or Oracle OLEDB Provider.
`@provider`	No	OLEDB provider name (PROGID). For example, `MSSQL` is the OLEDB name for the SQL Server provider and `MSDAORA` is the name for the Oracle OLEDB provider.
`@datasrc`	No	Name of the data source as interpreted by the OLEDB provider. For Access, this will be the full path to the `.mdb` file. For Oracle and SQL Server, this would be the name of the server. For the ODBC provider, this would be the name of the ODBC data source.

Parameter	Required?	Description
@location	No	The location of the data source as interpreted by the OLEDB provider (exact meaning varies).
@provstr	No	Any connection string information required by your OLEDB provider.
@catalog	No	The catalog as interpreted by the OLEDB provider. For many providers, this is used to change the default database (the one that is set to current when you fist log on) for the connection.

I've seen a variety of documentation on this, and about half of it was wrong on the parameter names. This isn't that big a deal if you're passing your parameters positionally, but, if you're passing them by name, then it could cause you lots of grief. The parameter names listed here are taken directly from the `sp_addlinkedserver` system sproc, and are accurate at least through Service Pack 1 of Version 7.0 – I suspect they'll keep these names forever at this point.

Note that, even though there's only one required parameter (the name that you will refer to the server by internally), this sproc is pretty much useless without some of the other parameters – most notably `@provider` and `@datasrc`. If you're using the OLEDB provider for ODBC, then the `@provstr` parameter is also very important.

Deleting a Linked Server

Deleting a linked server entry is pretty straightforward – just execute the `sp_dropserver` sproc and supply the name of the linked server you want to drop.

Using sp_addlinkedsrvlogin

In addition to providing the link to the actual server, you must also provide a mapping of what user information to use on the remote server. SQL Server provides us with a reasonably easy means of doing this through the use of a system sproc called `sp_addlinkedsrvlogin`. It accepts five parameters:

Parameter	Required?	Description
@rmtsrvname	Yes	Name of the remote server as you defined it in `sp_addlinkedserver`.
@useself	No	If true, automatically maps all the current user information straight through to the remote server. In this case, the remaining parameters become irrelevant.
@locallogin	No	The name of the user for which you are creating the map. Whatever login ID you specify here will be, when contacting the server named in the first parameter above, aliased to the login ID and password supplied in the next two parameters.
@rmtuser	No	Name of the alias that you want to use when the user supplied in `@locallogin` performs a linked query to the server supplied in `@rmtsrvname`.
@rmtpassword	No	Password that goes with `@rmtuser`.

The default for everything is for `@useself` to be true – that is, if you don't set up any kind of linked server login information, then SQL Server will still try to contact the remote server using the current user's login ID and password such as it is on the local system.

> **This is an area where using NT integrated security really shines. Think about it for a moment – imagine managing the user names and passwords for 1000 users. Not a big deal – right? Now imagine that all 1000 users need to be able to link to 10 servers – that's 10,000 logins to maintain, right? Wrong! Actually, you're going to be maintaining 19,000 login entries. The 10,000 logins local to each server, plus 9 linked server login entries for each user – or another 9,000.**
>
> **Of course, you can just make sure that they have the same login ID on every server, and that the password is the same on every server, then just keep the `@useself` option set to `True`. However, I think you'll find keeping all those passwords in synch will be quite a chore.**
>
> **Thankfully, SQL Server's integration with NT security is MUCH better than it has been in the past. If you just use NT security, then you only have to worry about the one user ID and one password in NT – you get to avoid all the work associated with setting up additional logins for every SQL Server you have.**

Deleting Linked Server Login Information

Deleting an entry made by `sp_addlinkedsrvlogin` is easy – just use the `sp_droplinkedsrvlogin` sproc and supply the name of the linked server along with the local login ID.

Seeing What You Already Have

In order to verify your linked server exists (or check out what's already there), use the `sp_linkedservers` system sproc. The syntax looks like this:

```
EXEC sp_linkedservers
```

No parameters, so it's an easy one.

Using a Linked Server

Let's go ahead and work a quick example by actually linking to another SQL Server. Since I'm guessing you are going to have to work on this at home (if you're like me, you learn lots of new stuff at work, but never get the chance to do it as formally as working through the examples in a book), you probably don't have the resources to have multiple machines at home to test with, so it's worth noting that this example will work looping back to your original. In other words, if you use your own server name in the `@datasrc` field below, you'll get a loop back to yourself that should work just fine for limited testing purposes.

Let's start our example by getting the linked server definition in place. Remember that this is what tells SQL Server where to go to find the local name we're going to create:

```
EXEC sp_addlinkedserver @Server = 'MyLocalServer',
   @srvproduct = 'SQLServer OLEDB Provider',
   @provider = 'SQLOLEDB',
   @datasrc  = 'Aristotle'
```

To verify that your new server was added, just use `sp_linked servers`:

```
EXEC sp_linkedservers
```

And you'll quickly see the servers you have available for linked queries.

If you're looped back to your own server (for example, if I was running this on Aristotle), then you could actually stop right here – you know that your own login is going to work fine on your own machine. Indeed, this example is usable right away as long as the remote server (Aristotle in this case) has a matching login and password to the current user on the local machine (remember that the current login information is passed to the linked server automatically if you haven't set something specific up using `sp_addlinkedsrvlogin`).

Let's test it out:

```
SELECT CustomerID, CompanyName
FROM MyLocalServer.Northwind.dbo.Customers
WHERE CustomerID < 'C'
```

Notice, since I wanted to go to the linked server rather than the local server, I needed to explicitly provide the server's name. If I don't fully qualify the name, then the query parser will assume I want the local server. OK, that being said, we can see that we do indeed get data back!

```
CustomerID  CompanyName
----------- --------------------------------------------
ALFKI       Alfreds Futterkiste
ANATR       Ana Trujillo Emparedados y helados
ANTON       Antonio Moreno Taquería
AROUT       Around the Horn
BERGS       Berglunds snabbköp
BLAUS       Blauer See Delikatessen
BLONP       Blondesddsl père et fils
BOLID       Bólido Comidas preparadas
BONAP       Bon app'
BOTTM       Bottom-Dollar Markets
BSBEV       B's Beverages

(11 row(s) affected)
```

But it doesn't stop there. We could also join information together from two different servers – even if both servers were linked:

```
SELECT mnw.CustomerID, mnw.CompanyName, nw.OrderID
FROM MyLocalServer.Northwind.dbo.Customers mnw
JOIN Northwind..Orders nw
   ON mnw.CustomerID = nw.CustomerID
WHERE mnw.CustomerID LIKE 'AN%'
```

This gets us:

```
CustomerID  CompanyName                                 OrderID
----------  ----------------------------------------    ----------
ANATR       Ana Trujillo Emparedados y helados          10308
ANATR       Ana Trujillo Emparedados y helados          10625
ANATR       Ana Trujillo Emparedados y helados          10759
ANATR       Ana Trujillo Emparedados y helados          10926
ANTON       Antonio Moreno Taquería                     10365
ANTON       Antonio Moreno Taquería                     10507
ANTON       Antonio Moreno Taquería                     10535
ANTON       Antonio Moreno Taquería                     10573
ANTON       Antonio Moreno Taquería                     10677
ANTON       Antonio Moreno Taquería                     10682
ANTON       Antonio Moreno Taquería                     10856

(11 row(s) affected)
```

Now this example was really dealing with the simplest of worlds – so perhaps we'd better get a reality check.

In this scenario, I'm assuming that you are actually linking back to yourself – this doesn't have even the slightest hint of real life to it, other than seeing that you can link to a server. The cold hard facts are that you are always going to be linking to some other server – which is going to have its own login information.

To check out how to deal with that, we need to add another user to our remote server. Even if your remote server is the same as your local server (the home test if you will), you still, for testing purposes at least, want to create a separate user to which you can map. Then we'll test out that user with some special permissions to see how things work.

First, we have to create the user and give it a slightly different permission set than is the default for `Northwind` users:

```
EXEC sp_addlogin 'rmtuser','rmtpass'

USE Northwind

EXEC sp_adduser 'rmtuser'

EXEC sp_addrolemember 'db_denydatawriter','rmtuser'
```

These are all sprocs that help us set up and manage users in the system. For the time being, I'm not going to elaborate on exactly how they work (they are covered in our chapter on security). If you really feel the need to know exactly how they work, feel free to skip ahead to Chapter 23. Otherwise, just take my word for it that you need to run the code above to get our test users added.

You should now have a new user called rmtuser added to the Northwind database. It will have the same rights that everyone belonging to the public (default) group has, save that this user also belongs to db_denydatawriter – which means that they can't do any kind of updates to the Northwind database.

Before we implement the rest of this though – let's verify that, before we make the changes, we have the authority to make an update:

```
SELECT OrderID, ProductID, Quantity, UnitPrice
FROM MyLocalServer.Northwind.dbo.[Order Details]
WHERE OrderID = 10250

UPDATE MyLocalServer.Northwind.dbo.[Order Details]
SET Quantity = Quantity + 5
WHERE OrderID = 10250
AND ProductID = 41

SELECT OrderID, ProductID, Quantity, UnitPrice
FROM MyLocalServer.Northwind.dbo.[Order Details]
WHERE OrderID = 10250
```

This should show you a before and after shot for that order:

```
OrderID         ProductID            Quantity             UnitPrice
--------------- -------------------- -------------------- -------------
10250           41                   10                    7.7000
10250           51                   35                   42.4000
10250           65                   15                   16.8000

(3 row(s) affected)


(1 row(s) affected)

OrderID         ProductID            Quantity             UnitPrice
--------------- -------------------- -------------------- ------------
10250           41                   15                   7.7000
10250           51                   35                   42.4000
10250           65                   15                   16.8000

(3 row(s) affected)
```

That pretty well proves that we currently have the right to update the records – even though we haven't explicitly provided the remote server with any users. We can now be pretty sure that it has just passed through our existing user and login information - that the same information (login ID and password) exists on the remote server (it does in this case, since the remote and the local are the same system) - and that the login ID in question has update rights.

Now let's bring sp_addlinkedsrvlogin into the picture by mapping our current user to the different role:

```
EXEC sp_addlinkedsrvlogin MyLocalServer, FALSE, 'sa', 'rmtuser', 'rmtpass'
```

Now we re-run our query:

```
SELECT OrderID, ProductID, Quantity, UnitPrice
FROM MyLocalServer.Northwind.dbo.[Order Details]
WHERE OrderID = 10250

UPDATE MyLocalServer.Northwind.dbo.[Order Details]
SET Quantity = Quantity + 5
WHERE OrderID = 10250
AND ProductID = 41

SELECT OrderID, ProductID, Quantity, UnitPrice
FROM MyLocalServer.Northwind.dbo.[Order Details]
WHERE OrderID = 10250
```

Only we get a different result this time

```
OrderID         ProductID            Quantity             UnitPrice
--------------- -------------------- -------------------- ------------
10250           41                   15                   7.7000
10250           51                   35                   42.4000
10250           65                   15                   16.8000

(3 row(s) affected)

Server: Msg 7399, Level 16, State 1, Line 1
OLE DB provider 'SQLOLEDB' reported an error. The provider indicates that the user did not have
the permission to perform the operation.
[OLE/DB provider returned message: Permission denied.]
```

So, things have indeed changed – but what? Even though we're logged in locally as `sa`, that is not the login id that is being used on the linked server. Instead, the linked server is now using the security context of `rmtuser` – the login that we used `sp_addlinkedsrvlogin` to map our `sa` user to.

It's worth noting that there isn't any way to update an existing linked server login. The only option is to drop the current instance and create an entirely new one.

Executing Sprocs on a Linked Server

You can also execute stored procedures that reside on your remote server. There really isn't any significant trick to it – you just need to fully qualify the sproc when you run your `EXEC` statement.

Before we can make use of this though, we need to enable remote procedure calls (RPC). This is done by enabling one or both of two server options. The `'rpc'` option enables RPC calls for the local server, and the `'rpc out'` option enables RPC for the remote server. We'll go ahead and turn them both on:

```
EXEC sp_serveroption 'MyLocalServer', 'rpc', TRUE
EXEC sp_serveroption 'MyLocalServer', 'rpc out', TRUE
```

We are then ready to run our sproc:

```
EXEC MyLocalServer.Northwind.dbo.CustOrderHist 'BLAUS'
```

This sproc lists the product by product order history for our customer:

```
ProductName                          Total
------------------------------------ -------
Camembert Pierrot                    21
Carnarvon Tigers                     10
Chartreuse verte                     5
Lakkalikööri                         14
Manjimup Dried Apples                8
Queso Cabrales                       14
Ravioli Angelo                       4
Rössle Sauerkraut                    3
Sir Rodney's Scones                  23
Sirop d'érable                       4
Tourtière                            20
Zaanse koeken                        14

(12 row(s) affected)
```

It's easy as can be.

Gathering Metadata Information from the Remote Server

Now all of this is well and good so far – but how do you deal with the situation where you don't really know (or more likely, can't remember the specifics of) what the linked server has to offer?

You see, most of the system sprocs that we use in order to retrieve metadata don't work against a remote data source. Fortunately, SQL Server offers a series of separate sprocs that are meant to deal with just this situation. Here's a list of the main sprocs for retrieving information about linked servers:

Sproc Name	Syntax	Description
`sp_linkedservers`	`sp_linkedservers`	Lists all the servers that currently have linked server entries on the local system.
`sp_catalogs`	`sp_catalogs <linked server name>`	Lists all the databases (catalogs is the ANSI term, and also fits well in that it doesn't necessarily mean quite the same thing as a database) that exist on the linked server.
`sp_tables_ex`	`sp_tables_ex <linked server>, <catalog to list tables from>`	Lists all the tables in the requested server and catalog.

Table Continued on Following Page

Sproc Name	Syntax	Description
sp_columns_ex	sp_columns_ex [*server name*] [, <'*table name*'>] [, <'*owner*'>] [, <'*catalog*'>] [, <'*column*'>] [, <'*ODBCVer*'>]	Lists all the columns and data types for the server. If you leave off parameters, then all values for that parameter will be included. Do *not* leave out the catalog name. It will run without it – but it may never end (very long running) and won't respond to a stop request.
sp_table_privileges_ex	sp_table_privileges_ex '<table server>' [, '<table name>'] [, '<owner>' [, '<database>']	Provides a listing of what security permissions have been established on a specific table on a linked server.
sp_columnprivileges	sp_column_privileges_ex '<table server'> [, '<table name>'] [, '<table owner>'] [, 'table catalog>'] [,'<column name>']	Provides column level permissions for a table on a linked server.
sp_primarykeys	sp_primarykeys <'*server name*'> [, <'*table name*'>] [, <'*owner*'>] [, <'*catalog*'>]	Provides the name of the column(s) that serve as the primary key for the requested table.
sp_foreignkeys	sp_foreignkeys <'*server name*'> [, <'*pk table name*'>] [, <'*pk table owner*'>] [, <'*pk table catalog*'>] [, <'*fk table name*'>] [, <'*fk table owner*'>] [, <'*fk table catalog*'>]	This one is somewhat similar to `sp_primarykeys` except that it is focused on foreign keys rather than primary keys. As such, you may see it return entirely separate key values (since you can have more than one), whereas all of `sp_primarykeys` output would relate to just one key.
sp_indexes	sp_indexes <'*server name*'> [, <'*table name*'>] [, <'*table owner*'>] [, <'*catalog*'>] [, <'*index_name*'>] [, <'*is_unique*'>]	Lists one or more of the indexes on the requested table (if one – otherwise on all tables). Listing can also be limited by whether a unique constraint (unique or primary key) is imposed or not.

You can mix and match these to obtain a wide variety of information about the schema on your linked servers.

> *In reality, you would pretty much only want to use these for non-SQL Server data sources and when you need to get some sort of result set back programmatically. Beyond these needs, I'm sure you'll find it much easier – not to mention more informative – to register the linked server in EM and examine things from there.*

Creating and Using Pass-Through Queries

Sometimes you've have the need to send a command directly through to the linked server without any pre-processing by the local server. The reasons for this vary, but the most common would be that you need to issue a command that is completely valid to the remote server, but does not pass the SQL Server query parser (legal on the remote server, but not on the local server). What's nice is that, if your command produces a result set, that result set can be joined to and otherwise treated as though it were a table.

To perform these pass-throughs, we make use of a command called `OPENQUERY`. The syntax looks a little odd in use, but it works like this:

```
OPENQUERY(<linked server name>, <'query string'>)
```

It's quite strange to see this in a `SELECT` statement since it gets used just like a table, but doesn't really look like one. Here's a very simple example using our `MyLocalServer` linked server:

```
SELECT *
FROM OPENQUERY(MyLocalServer, "SELECT CustomerID, CompanyName
                              FROM Northwind.dbo.Customers
                              WHERE CustomerID < 'b'")
```

Yields us four quick rows:

```
CustomerID  CompanyName
----------- ----------------------------------------
ALFKI       Alfreds Futterkiste
ANATR       Ana Trujillo Emparedados y helados
ANTON       Antonio Moreno Taquería
AROUT       Around the Horn

(4 row(s) affected)
```

We can also join results with objects from the local server – or even with another pass-through query:

```
SELECT ptq.CustomerID, ptq.CompanyName, o.OrderID, o.OrderDate
FROM OPENQUERY(MyLocalServer, "SELECT CustomerID, CompanyName
                               FROM Northwind.dbo.Customers
                               WHERE CustomerID < 'b'") ptq
JOIN Orders o
  ON ptq.CustomerID = o.CustomerID
WHERE YEAR(o.OrderDate) = 1998
```

CustomerID	CompanyName	OrderID	OrderDate
ALFKI	Alfreds Futterkiste	10835	1998-01-15 00:00:00.000
ALFKI	Alfreds Futterkiste	10952	1998-03-16 00:00:00.000
ALFKI	Alfreds Futterkiste	11011	1998-04-09 00:00:00.000
ANATR	Ana Trujillo Emparedados y helados	10926	1998-03-04 00:00:00.000
ANTON	Antonio Moreno Taquería	10856	1998-01-28 00:00:00.000
AROUT	Around the Horn	11016	1998-04-10 00:00:00.000
AROUT	Around the Horn	10864	1998-02-02 00:00:00.000
AROUT	Around the Horn	10920	1998-03-03 00:00:00.000
AROUT	Around the Horn	10953	1998-03-16 00:00:00.000

(9 row(s) affected)

This is really cool stuff – particularly when you are dealing with more unorthodox data sources, such as say Active Directory or Index Server.

Notice, by the way, that we had multiple `WHERE` clauses in operation. The first was with the pass-through query. This `WHERE` executes with the pass-through query, and effects the pass-through related recordset before it is available for the join. The second belongs to the outer query, and is the last filter to run in this particular query.

> *You can also include pass-through queries as the target in action statements (`INSERT`, `UPDATE`, `DELETE`). The trick here is whether your OLEDB provider will allow it or not. SQL Server will; others, such as Access, will as long as the query is formatted right (some are considered updateable, some aren't).*

Play with this – there are odd instances where these and a close relative (which we'll discuss next) can be lifesavers.

Using Ad Hoc Queries Against Remote Data Sources

Pass-through queries and linked servers are all well and good. They refer to something that is essentially a constant connection (it isn't, but whether it's connected or not is relatively invisible to the query, so, from the query's standpoint, it appears to be a constant connection). Sometimes, however, that just doesn't fit the bill. Occasionally, you need something that's going to go together better in an "on the fly situation" – the situation where your query is more ad hoc, and you want to create the connection manually at the time it's needed. `OPENQUERY` has a close relative that was made for just this kind of situation.

The most flexible, albeit tedious, query option is achieved through the use of a command called OPENROWSET. The syntax looks like a cross between sp_addlinkedserver, sp_addlinkedsrvlogin, and OPENQUERY – and it is indeed a little bit of all of these. It looks like this:

```
OPENROWSET
(
   <'provider name'>,
   <'data source'>;<'login ID'>,<'password'>,'provider string',
   <'query'>
)
```

Just like with a pass-through query, this should return a tabular result set that can be used in a join or otherwise much like a table. What's different is that there isn't any information stored about the server that you're connecting to – you're basically making things up as you go along.

Here's the final pass-through query that we did, redone to be an ad hoc query:

```
SELECT ptq.CustomerID, ptq.CompanyName, o.OrderID, o.OrderDate
FROM OPENROWSET('SQLOLEDB', 'ARISTOTLE'; 'rmtuser'; 'rmtpass',
                "SELECT CustomerID, CompanyName
                 FROM Northwind.dbo.Customers
                 WHERE CustomerID < 'b'") ptq
JOIN Orders o
  ON ptq.CustomerID = o.CustomerID
WHERE YEAR(o.OrderDate) = 1998
```

Execute it, and you probably won't be surprised to see the same nine rows.

Pretty much all the same rules apply. You can perform action queries on the OPENROWSET results as long as your OLEDB provider supports it, and, as we've shown with this example, you can also perform joins against the results.

Other Distributed Query Points to Ponder

There are some other things to think about when running distributed queries. The biggies among these are:

- Some activities can't be done on a remote server
- Collation Compatibility
- Shared names with "remote" servers

Let's quickly look at each one of these.

Some Activities Can't Be Done Via Links

Some commands can't be executed via a linked server arrangement. These include:

- DDL Statements (CREATE, DROP, ALTER), or anything that implies any one of these (SELECT INTO for example).
- In some cases, ORDER BY statements. ORDER BYs are fine as long as your query doesn't include a BLOB field. Note that it doesn't matter whether the BLOB is part of the ORDER BY (you can't even do that in a local server – at least without pulling some tricks). If the BLOB is part of the query at all, then the query cannot have an ORDER BY.
- Use any of the BLOB related statements (READTEXT, WRITETEXT, UPDATETEXT).

These are situations that you shouldn't run into that often, so I wouldn't worry about them much – still, you need to be aware that they exist.

Collation Compatibility

By default, the Collation Compatibility option is turned off. What this gem does for you is tell SQL Server that the local and remote servers both play by the same rules when it comes to sort order and accent sensitivity. This may not seem like that big of a deal – but it can be.

Normally (without Collation Compatibility set), the local SQL Server requests all the data to be returned to the local server (the WHERE clause isn't applied until the data arrives at the local server). This is because the local server has to make sure that the query is playing by the local rules (since that's where the query came from). If, however, the local server knows that the remote server plays by the right set of rules (has the same collation order), then it can defer the comparison testing to the remote server.

The benefits of this should be readily apparent. First, since the comparisons are happening at the remote server, only the data that meets the comparison criteria needs to be passed back to the local server – that means an awful lot less data transfer over the network. Second, is the whole notion of distributed work. If the remote server can do a portion of the analysis work, then you're taking some load off your local server – it can work on other things while it's waiting. Since SQL Server can run queries asynchronously, the distribution factor alone may help speed up your query.

To turn on collation compatibility, use the sp_serveroption system sproc. The syntax looks like this:

```
EXEC sp_serveroption '<server name>', 'collation compatible',
'true'
```

Making a "Remote" Server also Act as a Linked Server

"What?" you say. "I thought a linked server *was* a remote server." It is – sort of. It is a remote server in that it is a separate box from the local server. In SQL Server however, we also have the notion of a "remote" server – this is a type of server used with replication (we'll look at replication in Chapter 19). Remote servers are registered with the system in much the same way as linked servers are. Just because you have a server configured as being a remote server that does not also make it configured to be a linked server (only linked servers have all the various remote querying that we've looked at in this chapter). It's a bit early for the whole remote server game, but suffice to say for now that you can configure a remote server to also work as a linked server.

If you have a server that you've been using in replication which you want to now also show as a linked server, just execute `sp_serveroptions` and set the data access option to `True`.

Adding a Linked Server Using EM

Adding a linked server in EM is, as you might expect, a little easier (but you can't script it, so keep `sp_addlinkedserver` in mind).

Linked servers can be found inside the Security node for your server. Just right-click on the Linked Server sub-node and choose New Linked Server... You should get a dialog box that looks something like this:

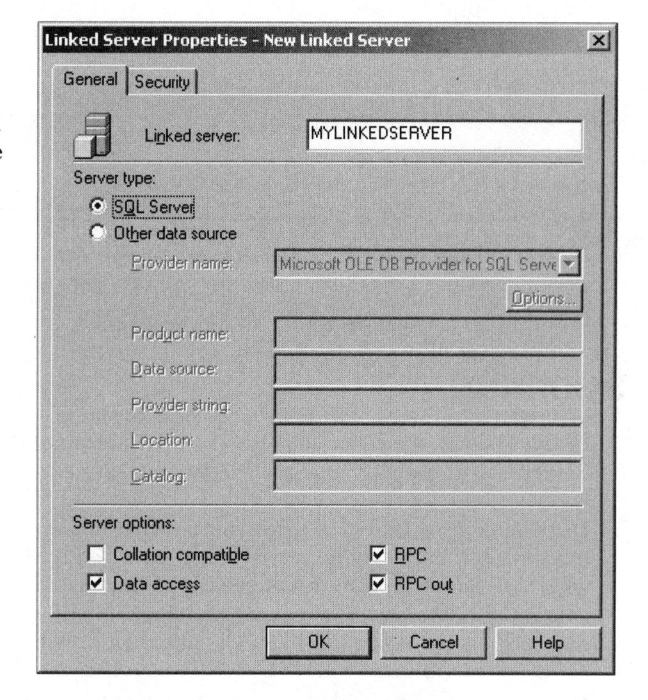

The information matches up well to `sp_addlinkedserver`. If you want to link a SQL Server, just check that option box and most of the other parameter boxes will be grayed out (SQL Server already knows how to fill them in). If you want to link to something other than a SQL Server, then choose Other data source and select the appropriate OLEDB provider.

Adding a Linked Server Login Using EM

This is just another tab on the linked server dialog box you've already seen:

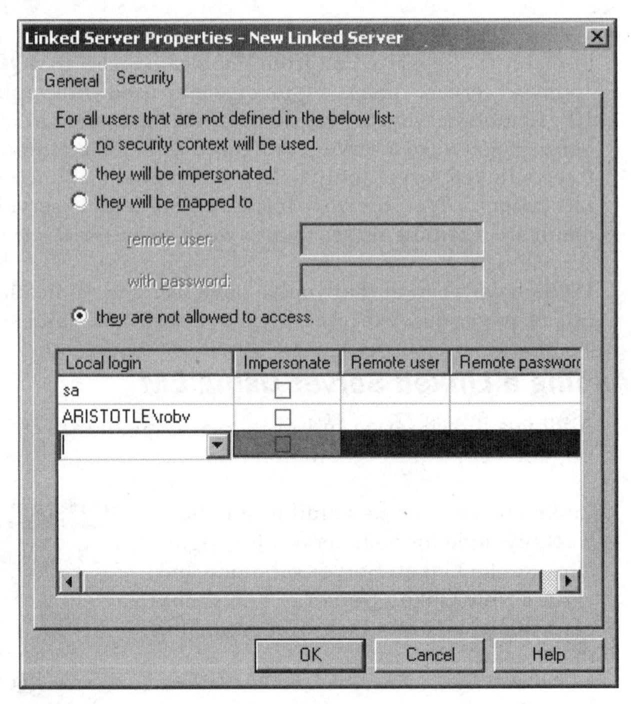

Again, you can do all the same things that you can do using the `sp_addlinkedsrvlogin`, but, again, you can't script this, so, if you need to have an install script, EM is out of the question.

Summary

In this chapter, we've looked closely at the notion of distributed environments as they relate to SQL Server in a transaction and query context.

Distributed transactions are transactions that in any way cross the boundary to operate outside of the local system. For SQL Server, they are managed by MSDTC (which, in addition to being included with SQL Server, is also installed with MTS). Distributed transactions make use of a two-phase commit (2PC) to ensure atomicity and durability even across unreliable connections. Transactions that start out as local can be "escalated" to be distributed automatically.

SQL Server 7.0 also added a whole new means of making use of distributed transactions. Developers now have the option to make use of linked servers for a semi-permanent connection, and `OPENROWSET` when they need a more "ad hoc" query.

We will be seeing more and more about working with data outside SQL Server in the chapters to come, but first, we need to take a look at a somewhat different concept – cursors.

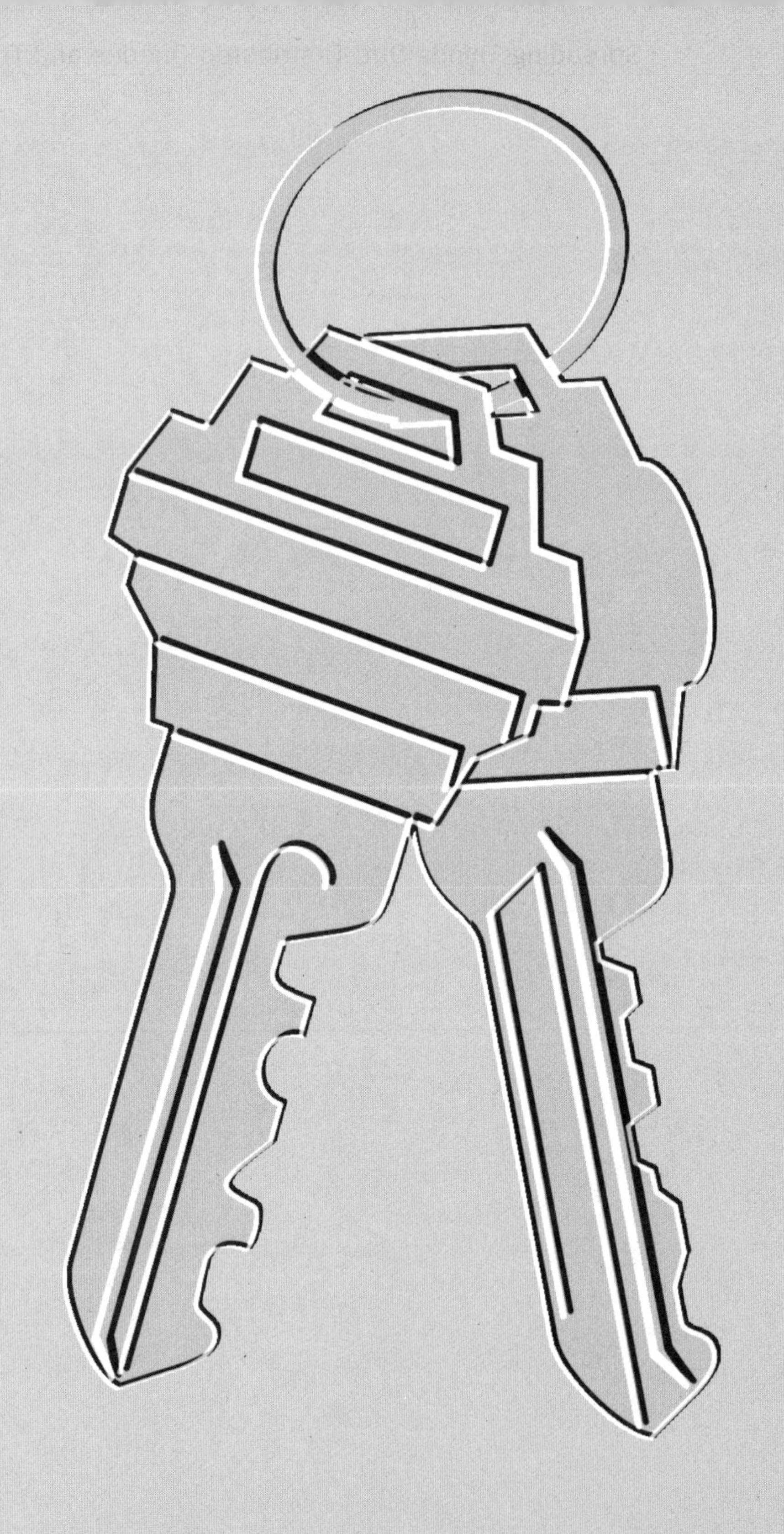

17

SQL Cursors

It was a tough decision. Advanced query design before cursors, or cursors before advanced query design? Well, I guess that we've already seen how I answered that question.

Throughout this book thus far, we've been dealing with data in sets. This tends to go against the way that the more procedure-driven languages go about things. Indeed, when the data gets to the client end, they almost always have to take our set, and then deal with it row by row. What they are dealing with is a **cursor**.

In this chapter, we will be looking at:

- What a cursor is
- The lifespan of a cursor
- Cursor types (sensitivity and scrollability)
- Uses for cursors

We'll discover that there's a lot to think about when creating cursors.

> **Perhaps the biggest thing to think about when creating cursors is, "Is there a way I can get out of doing this?" If you ask yourself that question every time you're about to create a cursor, then you will be on the road to a better performing system. That being said, we shall see that there are times when nothing else will do.**

What Is A Cursor?

Cursors are a way of taking a set of data, and being able to interact with a single record at a time in that set. It doesn't happen nearly as often as one tends to think, but there are indeed times where you just can't obtain the results you want to by modifying or even selecting the data in an entire set. The set is generated by something all of the rows have in common (as defined by a SELECT statement), but then you need to deal with those rows on a one by one basis.

The result set that you place in a cursor has several distinct features that set it apart from a normal SELECT statement:

- You declare the cursor separately from actually executing it
- The cursor and, therefore its result set, is named at declaration – you then refer to it by name
- The result set in a cursor, once opened, stays open until you close it
- Cursors have a special set of commands used to navigate the record set

While SQL Server has its own engine to deal with cursors, there are actually a few different object libraries that can also create cursors in SQL Server:

- OLE DB (used by ADO)
- ODBC (used by RDO, DAO and in some cases, OLE DB/ADO)
- DB-Lib (used by VB-SQL)

These are the libraries that client applications will typically use to access individual records. Each provides it own syntax for navigating the record set and otherwise managing the cursor. Each, however, shares in the same set of basic concepts, so, once you have got one object model down for cursors, you're most of the way there for all of them.

Every data access API out there (ADO, RDO, ODBC, OLE DB, etc) returns data to a client application or component in a cursor – it's simply the only way that non-SQL programming languages can currently deal with things. This is the source of a big difference between this kind of cursor and SQL Server cursors. With SQL Server cursors, you usually have a choice to perform things as a set operation, which is what SQL Server was designed to do. With the API based cursors, all you have is cursors, so you don't have the same cursor vs no cursor debate that you have in your server side activities.

The client side part of your data handling is going to be done using cursors – that's a given, so don't worry about it. Instead, worry about making the server side of your data access as efficient as possible – that means not using cursors on the server side if you can possibly help it.

The Lifespan of a Cursor

Cursors have lots of little pieces to them, but I think that it's best if we get right into looking at the most basic form of cursor, and then build up from there.

Before we get into the actual syntax though, we need to understand that using a cursor requires more than one statement – indeed, it takes several. The main parts include:

- The declaration
- Opening
- Utilizing/navigating
- Closing
- Deallocating

That being said, the basic syntax for declaring a cursor looks like this:

```
DECLARE <cursor name> CURSOR
FOR <select statement>
```

Keep in mind that this is the super simple rendition – create a cursor using defaults wherever possible. We'll look at more advanced cursors a little later in the chapter.

The cursor name is just like any other variable name, and must obey the rules for SQL Server naming accordingly. The `SELECT` statement can be any valid `SELECT` statement that returns a result set. Note that some result sets will not, however, be updateable. (For example, if you use a `GROUP BY` then what part of the group is updated? The same holds true for calculated fields for much the same reason.)

We'll go ahead and start building a reasonably simple example. For now, we're not really going to use it for much, but we'll see later that it will be the beginning of a rather handy tool for administering your indexes:

```
DECLARE @TableName varchar(255)
DECLARE TableCursor CURSOR FOR
   SELECT TABLE_NAME FROM INFORMATION_SCHEMA.TABLES
      WHERE TABLE_TYPE = 'BASE TABLE'
```

Note that this is just the beginning of what we will be building. One of the first things you should notice about cursors is that they require a lot more code than the usual `SELECT` statement.

We've just declared a cursor called `TableCursor` that is based on a `SELECT` statement that will select all of the tables in our database. We also declare a holding variable that will contain the values of our current row while we are working with the cursor.

Just declaring the cursor isn't enough though – we need to actually open it:

```
OPEN TableCursor
```

This actually executes the query that was the subject of the `FOR` clause, but we still don't have anything in place we can work with. For that, we need to do a couple of things:

- Grab – or `FETCH` - our first record
- Loop through, as necessary, the remaining records

We issue our first `FETCH` – this is the command that says to retrieve a particular record. We must also say into what variable we want to place the value:

```
FETCH NEXT FROM TableCursor INTO @TableName
```

Now that we have a first record, we're ready to move onto performing actions against the cursor set:

```
WHILE @@FETCH_STATUS = 0
BEGIN
   PRINT @TableName
   FETCH NEXT FROM TableCursor INTO @TableName
END
```

You may remember `@@FETCH_STATUS` from our brief discussion of globals earlier in the book. Every time we fetch a row, `@@FETCH_STATUS` is updated to tell us how our fetch went. The possible values are:

- 0 Fetch succeeded – everything's fine.
- -1 Fetch failed - record missing (you're not at the end, but a record has been deleted since you opened the cursor). We'll look at this closer, later in the chapter.
- -2 Fetch failed – this time it's because you're beyond the last (or before the first) record in the cursor. We'll also see more of this later in the chapter.

Once we exit this loop, we are, for our purposes, done with the cursor, so we'll close it:

```
CLOSE TableCursor
```

Closing the cursor, does not, however, free up the memory associated with that cursor. It does free up the locks associated with it. In order to be sure that you've totally freed up the resources used by the cursor, you must deallocate it:

```
DEALLOCATE TableCursor
```

So let's bring it all together just for clarity:

```
DECLARE @TableName varchar(255)
DECLARE TableCursor CURSOR FOR
   SELECT TABLE_NAME FROM INFORMATION_SCHEMA.TABLES
      WHERE TABLE_TYPE = 'BASE TABLE'
OPEN TableCursor
FETCH NEXT FROM TableCursor INTO @TableName
WHILE @@FETCH_STATUS = 0
BEGIN
   PRINT @TableName
   FETCH NEXT FROM TableCursor INTO @TableName
END
CLOSE TableCursor
DEALLOCATE TableCursor
```

As we've created it at the moment, it's really nothing more than if we had just run the `SELECT` statement by itself (technically, this isn't true since we can't "`PRINT`" a `SELECT` statement, but you could do what amounts to the same thing). What's different is that, if we so chose, we could have done nearly anything to the individual rows. Let's go ahead and illustrate this by completing our little utility.

In SQL Server there is, unfortunately, no single statement that will rebuild all the indexes in your system, yet there are several reasons that you might want to do this (if you don't recall any, take a look back at the chapter on indexes, or look forward to the performance tuning round up).

The only real tool that you have for rebuilding our indexes is to either drop and recreate them, or use `DBCC DBREINDEX`. The syntax for the latter looks like this:

```
DBCC DBREINDEX ('<table name>' [, index_name [, fillfactor ] ] )
```

The problem with trying to use this statement to rebuild all the indexes on all of your tables is that it is designed to work on one table at a time. You can leave off the index name if you want to build all the indexes for a table, but you can't leave off the table name to build all the indexes for all the tables.

Our cursor can get us around this by just dynamically building the `DBCC` command:

```
DECLARE @TableName varchar(255)
DECLARE TableCursor CURSOR FOR
   SELECT TABLE_NAME FROM INFORMATION_SCHEMA.TABLES
      WHERE TABLE_TYPE = 'BASE TABLE'
DECLARE @Command varchar(255)

OPEN TableCursor
FETCH NEXT FROM TableCursor INTO @TableName
WHILE @@FETCH_STATUS = 0
BEGIN
   PRINT "Reindexing " + @TableName
   DBCC DBREINDEX(@TableName)
   FETCH NEXT FROM TableCursor INTO @TableName
END
CLOSE TableCursor
DEALLOCATE TableCursor
```

We've now done what would be impossible using only set based commands. The `DBCC` command is expecting a single argument – providing a recordset won't work. We get around the problem by combining the notion of a set operation (the `SELECT` that forms the basis for the cursor), with single data point operations (the data in the cursor).

In order to mix these set based and individual data point operations, we had to walk through a series of steps. First, we declared the cursor and any necessary holding variables (in this case just one, but we'll see more in use at one time as we continue through the chapter). We then "opened" the cursor – it was not until this point that the data was actually retrieved from the database. Next, we utilized the cursor by navigating through it. In this case, we only navigated forward, but, as we shall see, we could have created a cursor that can scroll forwards and backwards. Moving on, we closed the cursor (any locks were released at this point in time), but memory continues to be allocated for the cursor. Finally, we deallocated the cursor. At this point, all resources in use by the cursor are freed for use by other objects in the system.

So quick as that, we have our first cursor. Still, this is really only the beginning. There is much more to cursors than meets the eye in this particular example. Next, we'll go on and take a closer look at some of the powerful features that give cursors additional flexibility.

Types of Cursors and Extended Declaration Syntax

Cursors come in a variety of different flavors (we'll visit them all before we're done). The default cursor is forward-only (you can only move forwards through the records, not backwards) and read-only, but cursors can also be scrollable and updateable. They can also have a varying level of sensitivity to changes that are made to the underlying data by other processes.

The forward-only, read-only cursor is the default type of cursor in not only the native SQL Server cursor engine, but from pretty much all the cursor models I've ever bumped into. It is extremely low in overhead, by comparison, to the other cursor choices, and is usually referred to as being a "firehose" cursor because of the sheer speed with which you can enumerate the data. Firehose cursors simply blow away the other cursor-based options in most cases, but don't mistake this as a performance choice over set operations – even a firehose cursor is slow by comparison to most equivalent set operations.

Let's start out by taking a look at a more extended syntax for cursors, and then we'll look at all of the options individually:

```
DECLARE <cursor name> CURSOR
[LOCAL|GLOBAL]
[FORWARD_ONLY|SCROLL]
[STATIC|KEYSET|DYNAMIC|FAST_FORWARD]
[READ_ONLY|SCROLL_LOCKS|OPTIMISTIC]
[TYPE_WARNING]
FOR <SELECT statement>
[FOR UPDATE [OF <column name >[,...n]]]
```

At first glance, it really looks like a handful, and indeed, there are a good many things to think about when declaring cursors (as I've said, probably the most important is along the lines of, "Do I really need to be doing this?"). The bright side is that several of these options imply one another, so once you've made one choice the others often start to fall into place quickly.

Let's go ahead and apply the specific syntax in a step-by-step manner that attaches each part to the important concepts that go with it.

Scope

The LOCAL vs GLOBAL option determines the scope of the cursor, that is, what connections and processes can "see" the cursor. Most items that have scope will default to the more conservative approach, that is, the minimum scope (which would be LOCAL in this case). SQL Server cursors are something of an exception to this – the default is actually GLOBAL. Before we get too far into the ramifications of the LOCAL vs GLOBAL scope question, we had better digress for a moment as to what I mean by local and global in this context.

We are already dealing with something of an exception in that the default scope is set to what we're calling global rather than the more conservative option of local. The exception doesn't stop there though. In SQL Server, the notion of something being global vs local usually indicates that it can be seen by all connections rather than just the current connection. For the purposes of our cursor declaration, however, it refers to whether all processes (batches, triggers, sprocs) in the current connection can see it vs just the current process.

The figure below illustrates this:

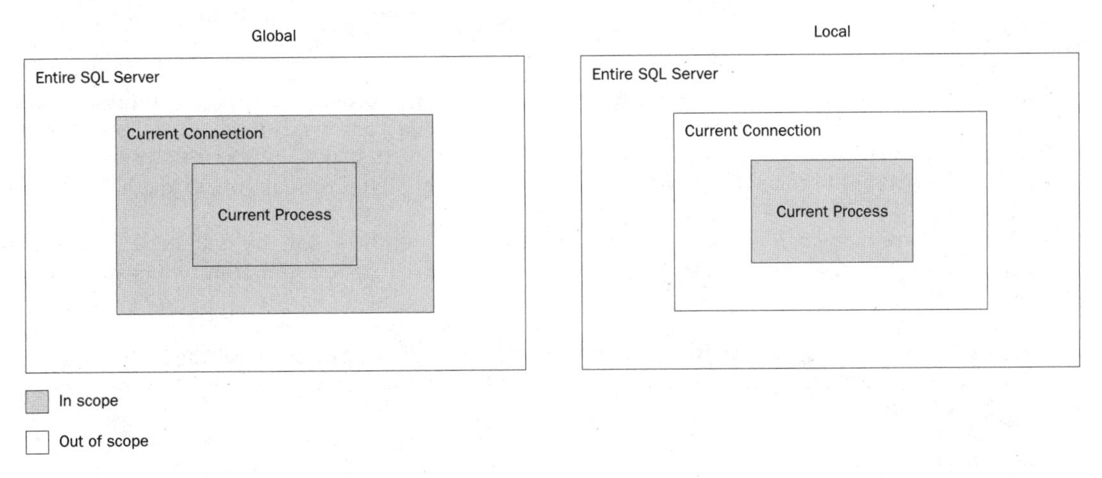

Now let's think about what this means, and test it out.

The ramifications to the global default fall, as you might expect, on both the pro and the con side of the things. Being global, it means that you can create a cursor within one sproc and refer to it from within a separate sproc – you don't necessarily have to pass references to it. The down side of this though is that, if you try to create another cursor with the same name, you're going to get an error.

Let's test this out with a brief sample. What we're going to do here is create a sproc that will create a cursor for us:

```
USE Northwind
GO

CREATE PROCEDURE spCursorScope
AS

DECLARE @Counter       int,
        @OrderID       int,
        @CustomerID    varchar(5)


DECLARE CursorTest  CURSOR
GLOBAL
FOR
   SELECT OrderID, CustomerID
   FROM Orders
```

```
SELECT @Counter = 1
OPEN CursorTest
FETCH NEXT FROM CursorTest INTO @OrderID, @CustomerID
PRINT "Row " + CONVERT(varchar,@Counter) + " has an OrderID of " +
   CONVERT(varchar,@OrderID) + " and a CustomerID of " + @CustomerID

WHILE (@Counter<=5) AND (@@FETCH_STATUS=0)
BEGIN
   SELECT @Counter = @Counter + 1
   FETCH NEXT FROM CursorTest INTO @OrderID, @CustomerID
   PRINT "Row " + CONVERT(varchar,@Counter) + " has an OrderID of " +
   CONVERT(varchar,@OrderID) + " and a CustomerID of " + @CustomerID
END
```

Notice several things in this sproc. First, I've declared holding variables to do a few things for us. The first, `@Counter`, will just keep tabs on things so we only have to move through a few records rather than moving through the entire recordset. The second and third, `@OrderID` and `@CustomerID` respectively, will hold the values retrieved from the query as we go row by row through the resultset.

Next, we declare the actual cursor. Note that I've explicitly set the scope. By default, if I had left off the `GLOBAL` keyword, then I would have still receive a cursor that was global in scope

You do not have to live by this default. You can use `sp_dboption` to set the "default to local cursor" option to `True` (set it back to `False` if you want to go back to global).

This happens to be yet another great example of why it makes sense to always explicitly state the options that you want – don't rely on defaults. Imagine if you were just relying on the default of `GLOBAL`, and then someone changed that option in the system! I can hear plenty of you out there saying, "Oh, no one would ever change that." WRONG! This is exactly the kind of "small change" that people make to fix some problem somewhere. Depending on the obscurity of your cursor usage, it may be weeks before you run into the problem – by which time you've totally forgotten that the change was made.

We then go ahead and open the cursor and step through several records. Notice, however, that we do not close or deallocate the cursor – we just leave it open and available as we exit the sproc.

I can't help but think of the old show "Lost in Space" here, with the robot constantly yelling "DANGER Will Robinson! DANGER!" Leaving cursors open willy nilly like this will lead you to a life of sorrow, frustration, and severe depression.

I'm doing it here to fully illustrate the concept of scope, but you want to be extremely careful about this kind of usage. The danger lies in the notion that you would call this sproc without realizing that it doesn't clean up after itself. If you don't clean up (close and deallocate) the cursor outside the sproc, then you will create something of a resource leak in the form of this abandoned, but still active cursor. You will also expose yourself to the possibility of errors should you call the same sproc again (it will try to declare and open the cursor again, but it already exists).

When we look into declaring our cursor for output, we will see a much more explicit and better choice for situations where we want to allow outside interaction with our cursors.

Now that we've enumerated several records and proven that our sproc is operating, we will then exit the sproc (remember, we haven't closed or deallocated the cursor). We'll then refer to the cursor from outside the sproc:

```
EXEC spCursorScope

DECLARE @Counter      int,
        @OrderID      int,
        @CustomerID   varchar(5)

SET @Counter=6

WHILE (@Counter<=10) AND (@@FETCH_STATUS=0)
BEGIN
     PRINT "Row " + CONVERT(varchar,@Counter) + " has an OrderID of " +
     CONVERT(varchar,@OrderID) + " and a CustomerID of " + @CustomerID
     SELECT @Counter = @Counter + 1
     FETCH NEXT FROM CursorTest INTO @OrderID, @CustomerID
END

CLOSE CursorTest
DEALLOCATE CursorTest
```

OK, so let's walk through what's happening here.

First, we execute the sproc. As we've already seen, this sproc builds the cursor and then enumerates several rows. It exits leaving the cursor open.

Next, we declare the very same variables that were declared in the sproc. Why do we have to declare them again, but not the cursor? Because it is only the cursor that is global by default. That is, our variables went away as soon as the sproc went out of scope – we can't refer to them anymore, or we'll get a variable undefined error. We must redeclare them.

The next code structure looks almost identical to one in our sproc – we're again looping through to enumerate several records.

Finally, once we've proven our point that the cursor is still alive outside the realm of the sproc, we're ready to close and deallocate the cursor. It is not until we close the cursor that we free up the memory or `tembdb` space from the result set used in the cursor, and it is not until we deallocate that the memory taken up by the cursor variable and its query definition is freed.

Now, go ahead and create the sproc in the system (if you haven't already) and execute the script. You should wind up with a result that looks like this:

```
Row 1 has an OrderID of 10248 and a CustomerID of VINET
Row 2 has an OrderID of 10249 and a CustomerID of TOMSP
Row 3 has an OrderID of 10250 and a CustomerID of HANAR
Row 4 has an OrderID of 10251 and a CustomerID of VICTE
Row 5 has an OrderID of 10252 and a CustomerID of SUPRD
Row 6 has an OrderID of 10253 and a CustomerID of HANAR

Row 7 has an OrderID of 10254 and a CustomerID of CHOPS
Row 8 has an OrderID of 10255 and a CustomerID of RICSU
Row 9 has an OrderID of 10256 and a CustomerID of WELLI
Row 10 has an OrderID of 10257 and a CustomerID of HILAA
```

So, you can see that the cursor stayed open, and our loop outside the sproc was able to pick up right where the code inside the sproc had left off.

Now let's see what happens if we alter our sproc to have local scope:

```
ALTER PROCEDURE spCursorScope
AS

DECLARE @Counter      int,
        @OrderID      int,
        @CustomerID   varchar(5)


DECLARE CursorTest cursor
LOCAL
FOR
   SELECT OrderID, CustomerID
   FROM Orders

SELECT @Counter = 1
OPEN CursorTest
FETCH NEXT FROM CursorTest INTO @OrderID, @CustomerID
PRINT "Row " + CONVERT(varchar,@Counter) + " has an OrderID of " +
      CONVERT(varchar,@OrderID) + " and a CustomerID of " + @CustomerID

WHILE (@Counter<=5) AND (@@FETCH_STATUS=0)
BEGIN
     SELECT @Counter = @Counter + 1
     FETCH NEXT FROM CursorTest INTO @OrderID, @CustomerID
     PRINT "Row " + CONVERT(varchar,@Counter) + " has an OrderID of " +
     CONVERT(varchar,@OrderID) + " and a CustomerID of " + @CustomerID
END
```

It seems like only a minor change, but the effects are significant when we execute our script again:

```
Row 1 has an OrderID of 10248 and a CustomerID of VINET
Row 2 has an OrderID of 10249 and a CustomerID of TOMSP
Row 3 has an OrderID of 10250 and a CustomerID of HANAR
Row 4 has an OrderID of 10251 and a CustomerID of VICTE
Row 5 has an OrderID of 10252 and a CustomerID of SUPRD
Row 6 has an OrderID of 10253 and a CustomerID of HANAR

Server: Msg 16916, Level 16, State 1, Line 13
A cursor with the name 'CursorTest' does not exist.
Server: Msg 16916, Level 16, State 1, Line 16
A cursor with the name 'CursorTest' does not exist.
Server: Msg 16916, Level 16, State 1, Line 17
A cursor with the name 'CursorTest' does not exist.
```

Things ran just as they did before until we got out of the sproc. This time the cursor was no longer in scope as we came out of the sproc, so we were unable to refer to it, and our script ran into several errors. Later on in the chapter, we'll take a look at how to have a cursor with local scope, but still be able to access it from outside the procedure in which it was created.

The big thing that you should have gotten out of this section is that you need to think about the scope of your cursors. They do not behave quite the way that other items for which you use the `DECLARE` statement do.

Scrollability

Like most of the concepts we'll be talking about throughout this chapter, **scrollability** applies to pretty much any cursor model you might face. The notion is actually fairly simple: Can I navigate in relatively any direction, or am I limited to only moving forward? The default is no – you can only move forward.

FORWARD_ONLY

A forward-only cursor is exactly what it sounds. Since it is the default method, it probably doesn't surprise you to hear that it is the only type of cursor that we've been using up to this point. When you are using a forward-only cursor, the only navigation option that is valid is `FETCH NEXT`. You need to be sure that you're done with each record before you move onto the next because, once it's gone, there's no getting back to the previous record unless you close and reopen the cursor.

SCROLLABLE

Again, this is just as it sounds. You can "scroll" the cursor backwards and forwards as necessary. If you're using one of the APIs (ODBC, OLE DB, DB-Lib), then, depending on what object model you're dealing with, you can often navigate right to a specific record. Indeed, with ADO you can even easily re-sort the data and add additional filters.

The cornerstone of scrolling is the `FETCH` keyword. You can use `FETCH` to move forward and backward through the cursor, as well as move to specific positions. The main arguments to `FETCH` are:

- `NEXT` – Move to the next record
- `PRIOR` – Move to the previous record
- `FIRST` – Move to the first record
- `LAST` – Move to the last record

We'll take a more in-depth look at `FETCH` later in the chapter, but, for now, be aware that `FETCH` exists and is what controls your navigation through the cursor set.

Let's do a brief example to get across the concept of a scrollable cursor. We'll actually just use a slight variation of the sproc we created a little earlier in the chapter:

```
CREATE PROCEDURE spCursorScroll
AS

DECLARE @Counter       int,
        @OrderID       int,
        @CustomerID    varchar(5)


DECLARE CursorTest cursor
LOCAL
SCROLL
FOR
   SELECT OrderID, CustomerID
   FROM Orders
```

```
SELECT @Counter = 1
OPEN CursorTest
FETCH NEXT FROM CursorTest INTO @OrderID, @CustomerID
PRINT "Row " + CONVERT(varchar,@Counter) + " has an OrderID of " +
      CONVERT(varchar,@OrderID) + " and a CustomerID of " + @CustomerID

WHILE (@Counter<=5) AND (@@FETCH_STATUS=0)
BEGIN
     SELECT @Counter = @Counter + 1
     FETCH NEXT FROM CursorTest INTO @OrderID, @CustomerID
     PRINT "Row " + CONVERT(varchar,@Counter) + " has an OrderID of " +
     CONVERT(varchar,@OrderID) + " and a CustomerID of " + @CustomerID
END

WHILE (@Counter>1) AND (@@FETCH_STATUS=0)
BEGIN
     SELECT @Counter = @Counter - 1
     FETCH PRIOR FROM CursorTest INTO @OrderID, @CustomerID
     PRINT "Row " + CONVERT(varchar,@Counter) + " has an OrderID of " +
     CONVERT(varchar,@OrderID) + " and a CustomerID of " + @CustomerID
END

CLOSE CursorTest
DEALLOCATE CursorTest
```

The big differences are:

- The cursor is declared with the SCROLL option
- We added a new navigation keyword – PRIOR – in the place of NEXT
- We went ahead and closed and deallocated the cursor in the sproc rather than using an outside procedure (been there, done that)

The interesting part comes in the results. This one doesn't require the fancy test script – simply execute it:

```
EXEC spCursorScroll
```

And you'll see how the order values scroll forward and back:

```
Row 1 has an OrderID of 10249 and a CustomerID of TOMSP
Row 2 has an OrderID of 10251 and a CustomerID of VICTE
Row 3 has an OrderID of 10258 and a CustomerID of ERNSH
Row 4 has an OrderID of 10260 and a CustomerID of OTTIK
Row 5 has an OrderID of 10265 and a CustomerID of BLONP
Row 6 has an OrderID of 10267 and a CustomerID of FRANK
Row 5 has an OrderID of 10265 and a CustomerID of BLONP
Row 4 has an OrderID of 10260 and a CustomerID of OTTIK
Row 3 has an OrderID of 10258 and a CustomerID of ERNSH
Row 2 has an OrderID of 10251 and a CustomerID of VICTE
Row 1 has an OrderID of 10249 and a CustomerID of TOMSP
```

As you can see, we were able to successfully navigate not only forward, as we did before, but also backwards.

A forward-only cursor is far and away the more efficient choice of the two options. Think about the overhead for a moment - if it is read only, then SQL Server really only needs to keep track of the next record – à la linked list. In a situation where you may reposition the cursor in other ways, extra information must be stored in order to reasonably seek out the requested row. How exactly this is implemented depends on the specific cursor options you choose.

Some types of cursors imply scrollability, others do not. Some types of cursors are sensitive to changes in the data, and some are not. We'll look at some of these issues in the next section.

Cursor Types

The various APIs generally break cursors into four types:

- Static
- Keyset-driven
- Dynamic
- Forward-only

How exactly these four types are implemented (and what, they're called) will sometimes vary slightly between the various APIs and object models, but the general nature of them is usually pretty much the same.

What makes the various cursor types different is their ability to be scrollable and their **sensitivity** to changes in the database over the life of the cursor. We've already seen what scrollability is all about, but the term "sensitivity" probably sounds like something you'd be more likely to read in *Men are from Mars, Women are from Venus* than in a programming book. Actually though, the concept of sensitivity is a rather critical one to think about when choosing your cursor type.

Whether a cursor is sensitive or not defines whether it notices changes in the database or not after the cursor is opened. It also defines what it does about it once the change is detected. Let's look at this in its most extreme versions – static vs dynamic cursors. The static cursor, once created, is absolutely oblivious to any change to the database. The dynamic cursor, however, is effectively aware of every change (inserted records, deletions, updates, you name it) to the database as long as the cursor remains open. We'll explore the sensitivity issue as we look at each of the cursor types.

Static Cursors

A static cursor is one that represents a "snapshot" in time. Indeed, at least one of the data access object models refers to it as a snapshot recordset rather than a static one.

When a static cursor is created, the entire recordset is created in what amounts to a temporary table in `tempdb`. After the time that it's created, a static cursor changes for no one and nothing. That is, it is set in stone. Some of the different object models will let you update information in a static cursor, some won't, but the bottom line is always the same: You cannot write updates to the database via a static cursor.

Before we get too far into this brand of cursor, I'm going to go ahead and tell you that the situations where it makes sense to use a static cursor on the server-side are extremely rare. I'm not saying they don't exist – they do – but they are very rare indeed.

Before you get into the notion of using a static cursor on the server side, ask yourself:

- Can I do this with a temporary table?
- Can I do this entirely on the client side?

Remember that a static cursor is kept by SQL Server in a private table in `tempdb`. If that's how SQL Server is going to be storing it anyway, why not just use a temporary table yourself? There are times when that won't give you what you need (record rather than set operations). However, if you are just after the concept of a snapshot in time, rather than record-based operations, build your own temp table using `SELECT INTO` and save yourself (and SQL Server) a lot of overhead.

If you're working in a client-server arrangement, static cursors are often better dealt with on the client side. By moving the entire operation to the client, you can cut the number of network round-trips to the server substantially. Since you know that your cursor isn't going to be affected by changes to the database (after all, isn't that why you chose a static cursor in the first place), there's no reason to make contact with the server again regarding the cursor after it is created.

OK, so let's move onto an example of a static cursor. What we're going to do in this example is play around with the notion of creating a static cursor, then make changes and see what happens. We'll play with variations of this throughout the remainder of this part of the chapter as we look at each cursor type.

We'll start with building a table to test with, then we'll build our cursor and manipulate it to see what's in it. Don't forget that, since we're using a `SELECT INTO` here, you'll need to have the `SELECT INTO/BULK COPY` option turned on (`sp_dboptions`) for the `Northwind` database:

```
USE Northwind
/* Build the table that we'll be playing with this time */
SELECT OrderID, CustomerID
INTO CursorTable
FROM Orders
WHERE OrderID BETWEEN 10701 AND 10705

-- Declare our cursor
DECLARE CursorTest CURSOR
GLOBAL                    -- So we can manipulate it outside the batch
SCROLL                    -- So we can scroll back and see the changes
STATIC                    -- This is what we're testing this time
FOR
SELECT OrderID, CustomerID
FROM CursorTable

-- Declare our two holding variables
DECLARE @OrderID       int
DECLARE @CustomerID    varchar(5)

-- Get the cursor open and the first record fetched
OPEN CursorTest
FETCH NEXT FROM CursorTest INTO @OrderID, @CustomerID

-- Now loop through them all
WHILE @@FETCH_STATUS=0
BEGIN
     PRINT CONVERT(varchar(5),@OrderID) + '    ' +  @CustomerID
     FETCH NEXT FROM CursorTest INTO @OrderID, @CustomerID
END
```

```
-- Make a change. We'll see in a bit that this won't affect the cursor.
UPDATE CursorTable
      SET CustomerID = 'XXXXX'
      WHERE OrderID = 10703

-- Now look at the table to show that the update is really there.
SELECT OrderID, CustomerID
FROM CursorTable

-- Now go back to the top. We can do this since we have a scrollable cursor
FETCH FIRST FROM CursorTest INTO @OrderID, @CustomerID

-- And loop through again.
WHILE @@FETCH_STATUS=0
BEGIN
     PRINT CONVERT(varchar(5),@OrderID) + '    ' +  @CustomerID
     FETCH NEXT FROM CursorTest INTO @OrderID, @CustomerID
END

-- Now it's time to clean up after ourselves
CLOSE CursorTest

DEALLOCATE CursorTest

DROP TABLE CursorTable
```

Let's take a look at what this gets us:

```
(5 row(s) affected)

10701       HUNGO
10702       ALFKI
10703       FOLKO
10704       QUEEN
10705       HILAA

(1 row(s) affected)

OrderID     CustomerID
----------- ----------
10701       HUNGO
10702       ALFKI
10703       XXXXX
10704       QUEEN
10705       HILAA

(5 row(s) affected)

10701       HUNGO
10702       ALFKI
10703       FOLKO
10704       QUEEN
10705       HILAA
```

There are several things to notice about what happened during the run on this script.

First, even through we had a result set open against the table, we were still able to perform the update. In this case, it's because we have a static cursor – once it was created, it was disconnected from the actual records and no longer maintains any locks.

Second, although we can clearly see that our update did indeed take place in the actual table, it did not affect the data in our cursor. Again, this is because, once created, our cursor took on something of a life of its own – it is no longer associated with the original data in any way.

Under the heading of "one more thing," you could also notice that we made use of a new argument to the `FETCH` keyword – this time we went back to the top of our result set by using `FETCH FIRST`.

Keyset-Driven Cursors

When we talk about keysets with cursors, we're not talking your local locksmith. Instead, we're talking about maintaining a set of data that uniquely identifies the entire row in the database.

Keyset-driven cursors have the following high points:

- Require a unique index to exist on the table in question
- Only the keyset is stored in `tempdb` – not the entire dataset
- They are sensitive to changes to the rows that are already part of the keyset including the possibility that they have been deleted
- They are, however, not sensitive to new rows that are added after the cursor is created
- Keyset cursors can be used as the basis for a cursor that is going to perform updates to the data

Given that it has a name of "keyset" and that I've already said that the keyset uniquely identifies each row, it probably doesn't shock you in any way that you must have a unique index of some kind (usually a primary key, but it could also be any index that is explicitly defined as unique) to create the keyset.

The keys are all stored in a private table in `tempdb`. SQL Server uses this key as a method to find its way back to the data as you ask for a specific row in the cursor. The point to take note of here is that the actual data is being fetched, based on the key, at the time that you issue the `FETCH`. The great part about this is that the data for that particular row is up-to-date as of when the specific row is fetched. The downside (or upside depending on what you're using the cursor for), is that it uses the keyset that is already created to do the lookup. This means that, once the keyset is created that is all the rows that will be included in your cursor. Any rows that were added after the cursor was created – even if they meet the conditions of the `WHERE` clause in the `SELECT` statement – will not be seen by the cursor. The rows that are already part of the cursor can, depending on the cursor options you chose, be updated by a cursor operation.

Let's modify our earlier script to illustrate the sensitivity issue when we are making use of keyset-driven cursors:

```
USE Northwind
/* Build the table that we'll be playing with this time */
SELECT OrderID, CustomerID
INTO CursorTable
FROM Orders
WHERE OrderID BETWEEN 10701 AND 10705

-- Now create a unique index on it in the form of a primary key
ALTER TABLE CursorTable
      ADD CONSTRAINT PKCursor
      PRIMARY KEY (OrderID)

/* The IDENTITY property was automatically brought over when
** we did our SELECT INTO, but I want to use my own OrderID
** value, so I'm going to turn IDENTITY_INSERT on so that I
** can override the identity value.
*/
SET IDENTITY_INSERT CursorTable ON

-- Declare our cursor
DECLARE CursorTest CURSOR
GLOBAL                  -- So we can manipulate it outside the batch
SCROLL                  -- We can scroll back to see if the changes are there
KEYSET                  -- This is what we're testing this time
FOR
SELECT OrderID, CustomerID
FROM CursorTable

-- Declare our two holding variables
DECLARE @OrderID       int
DECLARE @CustomerID    varchar(5)

-- Get the cursor open and the first record fetched
OPEN CursorTest
FETCH NEXT FROM CursorTest INTO @OrderID, @CustomerID

-- Now loop through them all
WHILE @@FETCH_STATUS=0
BEGIN
     PRINT CONVERT(varchar(5),@OrderID) + '    ' +  @CustomerID
     FETCH NEXT FROM CursorTest INTO @OrderID, @CustomerID
END

-- Make a change. We'll see that it does affect the cursor this time.
UPDATE CursorTable
       SET CustomerID = 'XXXXX'
       WHERE OrderID = 10703

-- Now we'll delete a record so we can see how to deal with that
DELETE CursorTable
       WHERE OrderID = 10704

-- Now Insert a record. We'll see that the cursor is oblivious to it.
INSERT INTO CursorTable
       (OrderID, CustomerID)
VALUES
       (99999, 'IIIII')

-- Now look at the table to show that the update is really there.
SELECT OrderID, CustomerID
FROM CursorTable

-- Now go back to the top. We can do this since we have a scrollable cursor
FETCH FIRST FROM CursorTest INTO @OrderID, @CustomerID
```

```
/* And loop through again.
** This time, notice that we changed what we're testing for.
** Since we have the possibility of rows being missing (deleted)
** before we get to the end of the actual cursor, we need to do
** a little bit more refined testing of the status of the cursor.
*/
WHILE @@FETCH_STATUS != -1
BEGIN
     IF @@FETCH_STATUS = -2
     BEGIN
          PRINT '  MISSING! It probably was deleted.'
     END
     ELSE
     BEGIN
          PRINT CONVERT(varchar(5),@OrderID) + '    ' + @CustomerID
     END
     FETCH NEXT FROM CursorTest INTO @OrderID, @CustomerID
END

-- Now it's time to clean up after ourselves
CLOSE CursorTest

DEALLOCATE CursorTest

DROP TABLE CursorTable
```

The changes aren't really all that remarkable. We've gone ahead and added the required unique index. I happened to choose to do it as a primary key since that's what matches up best with the table we got this information out of, but it also could have been a unique index without the primary key. We also added something to insert a row of data so we can clearly see that the keyset doesn't see the row in question.

Perhaps the most important thing that we've changed is the condition for the `WHILE` loop on the final run through the cursor. Technically speaking, we should have made this change to both loops, but there is zero risk of a deleted record the first time around in this example, and I wanted the difference to be visible right within the same script.

The change was made to deal with something new we've added – the possibility that we might get to a record only to find that it's now missing. More than likely, someone has deleted it.

Let's take a look then at the results we get after running this:

```
(5 row(s) affected)

10701        HUNGO
10702        ALFKI
10703        FOLKO
10704        QUEEN
10705        HILAA

(1 row(s) affected)


(1 row(s) affected)
```

```
(1 row(s) affected)

OrderID         CustomerID
--------------- ---------------
10701           HUNGO
10702           ALFKI
10703           XXXXX
10705           HILAA
99999           IIIII

(5 row(s) affected)

10701           HUNGO
10702           ALFKI
10703           XXXXX
  MISSING! It probably was deleted.
10705           HILAA
```

OK, let's walk through the highlights here.

Everything starts out pretty much as it did before. We see the same five rows in the first result set as we did last time. We then see an extra couple of "affected by" messages – these are for the `INSERT`, `UPDATE` and `DELETE` statements that we added. Next comes the second result set. It's at this point that things get a bit more interesting.

In this next result set, we see the actual results of our `UPDATE`, `INSERT` and `DELETE` statements. Just as we think we're done, `OrderID` 10704 has been deleted, and a new order with the `OrderID` of 9999 has been inserted. That's what's in the table, but things don't appear quite as cosy in the cursor.

The next (and final) result set tells the tale on some differences in the way that things are presented in the cursor vs actually re-running the query. As it happens, we have exactly five rows – just like we started out with and just like our `SELECT` statement showed are in the actual table. But that's entirely coincidental.

In reality, there are a couple of key differences between what the cursor is showing and what the table is showing. The first presents itself rather boldly - our result set actually knows that a record is missing. You see, the cursor continues to show the key position in the keyset, but, when it went to do the lookup on the data, the data wasn't there anymore. Our `@@FETCH_STATUS` was set to `-2`, and we were able to test for it and report it. The `SELECT` statement showed us what data was actually there without any remembrance of the record ever having been there. The `INSERT`, on the other hand, is an entirely unknown quantity to the cursor. The record wasn't there when the cursor was created, so the cursor has no knowledge of its existence – it doesn't show up in our result set.

Keyset cursors can be very handy for dealing with situations where you need some sensitivity to changes in the data, but don't need to know about every insert right up to the minute. They can, depending on the nature of the result set you're after and the keyset, also provide some substantial savings in the amount of data that has to be duplicated and stored into `tempdb` – this can have some favorable performance impacts for your overall server.

> **WARNING!!! If you define a cursor as being of type `KEYSET` but do so on a table with no unique index, then SQL Server will implicitly convert your cursor to be `STATIC`. The fact that the behavior gets changed would probably be enough to ruffle your feathers a bit, but it doesn't stop there – it doesn't tell you about it. That's right, by default you get absolutely no warning about this conversion. Fortunately, you can watch out for this sort of thing by using the `TYPE_WARNING` option in your cursor. We'll look at this option briefly towards the end of the chapter.**

DYNAMIC Cursors

Don't you just wish that you could be on a quiz show and have them answer a question like, "What's so special about a dynamic cursor?" Hmmm, then again, I suppose their pool of possible contestants would be small, but those that decided to go for it would probably have the answer right away, "They are **dynamic** – right?" Exactly.

Well, almost exactly. Dynamic cursors fall just short of what I would call dynamic in the sense that they won't proactively tell you about changes to the underlying data. What gets them close enough to be called dynamic is that they are sensitive towards all changes to the underlying data. Of course, like most things in life, all this extra power comes with a high price tag.

If you want inserted records to be added to the cursor – no problem. If you want updated rows to appear properly updated in the cursor – no problem. If you want deleted records to be removed from the cursor set – no problem (although you can't really tell that something's been deleted since you won't see the missing record that you saw with a keyset cursor type). If, however, you want to have concurrency – uh oh, big problem (you're holding things open longer, so collisions with other users are more likely). If you want this to be a low overhead – uh oh, big problem again (you are effectively requerying with every `FETCH`). Yes, dynamic cursors can be the bane of your performance existence, but, hey, that's life isn't it?

The long and the short of it is that you usually should avoid dynamic cursors.

Why all the hype and hoopla? Well, in order to understand some of the impacts that a dynamic cursor can have, you just need to realize a bit about how they work. You see, with a dynamic cursor, your cursor is essentially rebuilt every single time you issue a `FETCH`. That's right, the `SELECT` statement that forms the basis of your query, complete with its associated `WHERE` clause is effectively re-run. Think about that when dealing with large data sets. It brings just one word to mind – ugly. Very ugly indeed.

One of the things I've been taught since the dawn of my RDBMS time is that dynamic cursors are a performance pig – I've found this not to always be the case. This seems to be particularly true when the underlying tables are not very large in size. If you think about it for a while, you might be able to come up with why a dynamic cursor can actually be slightly faster in terms of raw speed.

My guess as to what's driving this is the use of `tempdb` *for keyset cursors. While a lot more work has to be done with each* `FETCH` *in order to deal with a dynamic cursor, the data for the re-query will often be completely in cache (depending on the sizing and loading of your system). This means the dynamic cursor gets to work largely from RAM. The keyset cursor, on the other hand, is stored in* `tempdb`*, which is on disk (i.e. much, much slower) for most systems.*

As your table size gets larger, there is more diverse traffic hitting your server, the memory allocated to SQL Server gets smaller, and the more that keyset-driven cursors are going to have something of an advantage over dynamic cursors. In addition, raw speed isn't everything – you really need to think about concurrency issues too (we will look at the options for concurrency in detail later in the chapter), which can be more problematic in dynamic cursors. Still, don't count out dynamic cursors for speed alone if you're dealing with a server-side cursor with small data sets.

Let's go ahead and rerun our last script with only one modification – the change from `KEYSET` to `DYNAMIC`:

```
USE Northwind
/* Build the table that we'll be playing with this time */
SELECT OrderID, CustomerID
INTO CursorTable
FROM Orders
WHERE OrderID BETWEEN 10701 AND 10705

-- Now create a unique index on it in the form of a primary key
ALTER TABLE CursorTable
      ADD CONSTRAINT PKCursor
      PRIMARY KEY (OrderID)

/* The IDENTITY property was automatically brought over when
** we did our SELECT INTO, but I want to use my own OrderID
** value, so I'm going to turn IDENTITY_INSERT on so that I
** can override the identity value.
*/
SET IDENTITY_INSERT CursorTable ON

-- Declare our cursor
DECLARE CursorTest CURSOR
GLOBAL              -- So we can manipulate it outside the batch
SCROLL              -- So we can scroll back and see if the changes are there
DYNAMIC             -- This is what we're testing this time
FOR
SELECT OrderID, CustomerID
FROM CursorTable

-- Declare our two holding variables
DECLARE @OrderID      int
DECLARE @CustomerID   varchar(5)

-- Get the cursor open and the first record fetched
OPEN CursorTest
FETCH NEXT FROM CursorTest INTO @OrderID, @CustomerID
```

```
-- Now loop through them all
WHILE @@FETCH_STATUS=0
BEGIN
     PRINT CONVERT(varchar(5),@OrderID) + '    ' +  @CustomerID
     FETCH NEXT FROM CursorTest INTO @OrderID, @CustomerID
END

-- Make a change. We'll see that it does affect the cursor this time.
UPDATE CursorTable
       SET CustomerID = 'XXXXX'
       WHERE OrderID = 10703

-- Now we'll delete a record so we can see how to deal with that
DELETE CursorTable
       WHERE OrderID = 10704

-- Now Insert a record. We'll see that the cursor is oblivious to it.
INSERT INTO CursorTable
       (OrderID, CustomerID)
VALUES
       (99999, 'IIIII')

-- Now look at the table to show that the update is really there.
SELECT OrderID, CustomerID
FROM CursorTable

-- Now go back to the top. We can do this since we have a scrollable cursor
FETCH FIRST FROM CursorTest INTO @OrderID, @CustomerID

/* And loop through again.
** This time, notice that we changed what we're testing for.
** Since we have the possibility of rows being missing (deleted)
** before we get to the end of the actual cursor, we need to do
** a little bit more refined testing of the status of the cursor.
*/
WHILE @@FETCH_STATUS != -1
BEGIN
     IF @@FETCH_STATUS = -2
     BEGIN
          PRINT '  MISSING! It probably was deleted.'
     END
     ELSE
     BEGIN
          PRINT CONVERT(varchar(5),@OrderID) + '    ' +  @CustomerID
     END
     FETCH NEXT FROM CursorTest INTO @OrderID, @CustomerID
END


-- Now it's time to clean up after ourselves
CLOSE CursorTest

DEALLOCATE CursorTest

DROP TABLE CursorTable
```

And the results:

```
(5 row(s) affected)

10701        HUNGO
10702        ALFKI
10703        FOLKO
10704        QUEEN
10705        HILAA

(1 row(s) affected)


(1 row(s) affected)


(1 row(s) affected)

OrderID      CustomerID
------------ -----------
10701        HUNGO
10702        ALFKI
10703        XXXXX
10705        HILAA
99999        IIIII

(5 row(s) affected)

10701        HUNGO
10702        ALFKI
10703        XXXXX
10705        HILAA
99999        IIIII
```

The first two recordsets look exactly as they did last time. The change comes when we get to the third (and final) resultset:

- There is no indication of a failed fetch, even though we deleted a record (no notification)
- The updated record shows the update (just as it did with a keyset)
- The inserted record now shows up in the cursor set

Dynamic cursors are the most sensitive of all cursors. They are affected by everything you do to the underlying data. The downside is that they can provide some extra concurrency problems, and they can pound the system when dealing with larger data sets.

Technically speaking, and unlike a keyset cursor, a dynamic cursor can operate on a non-unique index. Avoid this at all costs (in my opinion, it should prevent you from doing this and throw an error). Under certain circumstances, it is quite possible to create an infinite loop because the dynamic cursor cannot keep track of where it is in the cursor set. The only sure-fire way of avoiding this is to either stay away from dynamic cursors or only work on tables with a truly unique index available.

FAST_FORWARD Cursors

Fast is the operative word (from a cursor standpoint – queries make this or any other cursor look like a snail) on this one. This one is the epitome of the term "Firehose Cursor" that is often used around forward-only cursors. I've always taken the analogy to imply the way that the data sort of spews forth – once out, you can't put it back in. In short, you're simply awash with data. With `FAST_FORWARD` cursors, you open the cursor, and do nothing else but deal with the data, move forward, and deallocate it (note that I didn't say close it).

Now, it's safe to say that calling this a cursor "type" is something of a misnomer. This kind of cursor has several different circumstances where it is automatically converted to other cursor types, but I think of them as being most like a keyset-driven cursor in the sense that membership is fixed – once the members of the cursor are established, no new records are added. Deleted rows show up as a missing record (`@@FETCH_STATUS` of `-2`). Keep in mind though that, if the cursor is converted to something else (via automatic conversion), it will take on the behavior of that new cursor type.

The nasty side here is that SQL Server doesn't tell you that the conversion has happened unless you have the `TYPE_WARNING` option added to your cursor definition.

As I said before, there are a number of circumstances where a `FAST_FORWARD` cursor is implicitly converted to another cursor type. Below is a table that outlines these conversions:

Condition	Converted to
The underlying query requires that a temporary table be built	Static
The underlying query is distributed in nature	Keyset
The cursor is declared as `FOR UPDATE`	Dynamic
A condition exists that would convert to keyset driven, but at least one underlying table does not have a unique index	Static

I've heard that there are other circumstances where a cursor will be converted, but I haven't seen any documentation of this, and I haven't run into it myself.

> **If you find that you are getting that most dreadful of all computer-related terms (unpredictable results), you can make use of `sp_describe_cursor` (a system stored procedure) to list out all the currently active options for your cursor.**

It's worth noting that all `FAST_FORWARD` cursors are read-only in nature. You can explicitly set the cursor to have the `FOR UPDATE` option, but, as suggested in the implicit conversion table above, the cursor will be implicitly converted to dynamic.

OK, so what exactly does a `FAST_FORWARD` cursor have that any of the other cursors wouldn't have if they were declared as being `FORWARD_ONLY`? Well, a `FAST_FORWARD` cursor will implement at least one of two tricks to help things along:

- The first is to pre-fetch data. That is, at the same time that you open the cursor, it automatically fetches the first row – this means that you save a round trip to the server if you are operating in a client-server environment using ODBC. Unfortunately, this is only available under ODBC.
- The second is the one that is a sure thing – auto-closing of the cursor. Since you are running a cursor that is forward-only, SQL Server can assume that you want the cursor closed once you reach the end of the recordset. Again, this saves a round trip and squeezes out a tiny bit of additional performance.

Oddly enough, cursors declared as being `FAST_FORWARD` are not allowed to also be declared as `FORWARD_ONLY` (or `SCROLL` for that matter) – you need to leave the scrolling vs forward-only option out when specifying a cursor of type `FAST_FORWARD`.

Choosing a cursor type is one of the most critical decisions when structuring a cursor. Choices that have little apparent difference in the actual output of the cursor task can have major differences in performance. Other affects can be seen in sensitivity to changes, concurrency issues, and updatability.

Concurrency Options

We got our first taste of concurrency issues back in our chapter on transactions and locks. As you recall, we deal with concurrency issues whenever there are issues surrounding two or more processes trying to get to the same data at essentially the same time. When dealing with cursors, however, the issue becomes just slightly stickier.

The problem is multi-fold:

- The operation tends to last longer (more time to have a concurrency problem)
- Each row is read at the time of the fetch, but someone may try to edit it before you get a chance to do your update
- You may scroll forward and backward through the resultset for what could be an essentially unlimited amount of time (I hope you never do that, but it's possible to do)

As with all concurrency issues, this tends to be more of a problem in a transaction environment than when running in a single statement situation. The longer the transaction, the more likely you are to have concurrency problems.

SQL Server gives us three different options for dealing with this issue:

- READ_ONLY
- SCROLL_LOCKS (equates to Pessimistic in most terminologies)
- OPTIMISTIC

Each of these bring their own thing to the party, so let's look at them one by one.

READ_ONLY

In a read-only situation, you don't have to worry about whether your cursor is going to try and obtain any kind of update or exclusive lock. You also don't have to worry about whether anyone has edited the data while you've been busy making changes of your own. Both of these make life considerably easier.

READ_ONLY is just what it sounds like. When you choose this option, you cannot update any of the data, but you also skip most (but not all) of the notion of concurrency entirely.

SCROLL_LOCKS

Scroll locks equate to what is more typically referred to as pessimistic locking in the various APIs and object models. In its simplest form, it means that, as long as you are editing this record, no one else is allowed to edit it. The specifics of implementation of duration, of this, vary depending on:

- Whether you're in a transaction or not
- What transaction isolation level you've set

Note that this can be different from what we saw with update locks back in our locking and transaction chapter.

With update locks, we prevented other users from updating the data. This lock was held for the duration of the transaction. If it was a single statement transaction, then the lock was not released until every row affected by the update was complete.

Scroll locks work identically to update locks with only one significant exception – the duration the lock is held. With scroll locks, there is much more of a variance depending on whether the cursor is participating in a multi-statement transaction or not. Assuming for the moment that you do not have a transaction wrapped around the cursor, then the lock is held only on the current record in the cursor. That is, from the time the record is first fetched until the next record (or end of the resultset) is fetched. Once you move on to the next record, the lock is removed from the prior record.

Let's take a look at this through a significantly pared down version of the script we've been using throughout much of this chapter:

```
USE Northwind
/* Build the table that we'll be playing with this time */

SELECT OrderID, CustomerID
INTO CursorTable
FROM Orders
WHERE OrderID BETWEEN 10701 AND 10705

-- Now create a unique index on it in the form of a primary key
ALTER TABLE CursorTable
      ADD CONSTRAINT PKCursor
      PRIMARY KEY (OrderID)

/* The IDENTITY property was automatically brought over when
** we did our SELECT INTO, but I want to use my own OrderID
** value, so I'm going to turn IDENTITY_INSERT on so that I
** can override the identity value.
*/
SET IDENTITY_INSERT CursorTable ON

-- Declare our cursor
DECLARE CursorTest CURSOR
GLOBAL                -- So we can manipulate it outside the batch
SCROLL                -- So we can scroll back and see if the changes are there
DYNAMIC               -- This is what we're testing this time
SCROLL_LOCKS
FOR
SELECT OrderID, CustomerID
FROM CursorTable

-- Declare our two holding variables
DECLARE @OrderID      int
DECLARE @CustomerID   varchar(5)

-- Get the cursor open and the first record fetched
OPEN CursorTest
FETCH NEXT FROM CursorTest INTO @OrderID, @CustomerID
```

You'll not see much of our usual gray (to indicate that changes were made on that line) because only one line was added. The remainder of the changes were deletions of lines, so there's nothing for me to make gray for you. Just make sure that you've made the appropriate changes if you're going to try and run this one.

What we've done is toss out most of the things that were happening, and we've refocused ourselves back on the cursor. Perhaps the biggest thing to notice though is a couple of key things that we have deliberately omitted even though they are things that would normally cause problems if we try to operate without them:

- We do not have a CLOSE on our cursor, nor do we deallocate it at this point
- We don't even scroll any farther than getting the first row fetched

The reason we've left the cursor open is to create a situation where the state of the cursor being open lasts long enough to play around with the locks somewhat. In addition, we only fetch the first row because we want to make sure that there is an active row (the way we had things before, we would have been to the end of the set before we started running with other, possibly conflicting, statements).

What you want to do is execute the previous and then open a completely separate connection window with `Northwind` active. Then run a simple test in the new connection window:

```
SELECT * FROM CursorTable
```

If you haven't been grasping what I've been saying in this section, you might be a tad surprised by the results:

```
OrderID          CustomerID
---------------- ----------------
10701            HUNGO
10702            ALFKI
10703            FOLKO
10704            QUEEN
10705            HILAA

(5 row(s) affected)
```

Based on what we know about locks (from our chapter on the subject), you would probably expect the `SELECT` statement above to be blocked by the locks on the current record. Not so with scroll locks. The lock is only on the record that is currently in the cursor, and, perhaps more importantly, the lock only prevents updates to the record. Any `SELECT` statements (such as ours) can see the contents of the cursor without any problems.

Now that we've seen how things work, go back to the original window and run the code to clean things up. This is back to the same code we've worked with for much of this chapter:

```
-- Now it's time to clean up after ourselves
CLOSE CursorTest

DEALLOCATE CursorTest

DROP TABLE CursorTable
```

Don't forget to run the clean up code above!!! If you forget, then you'll have an open transaction sitting in your system until you terminate the connection. SQL Server should clean up any open transactions (by rolling them back) when the connection is broken, but I've seen situations where you run the database consistency checker (DBCC) and find that you have some really old transactions – SQL Server missed cleaning up after itself.

OPTIMISTIC

Optimistic locking creates a situation where no scroll locks of any kind are set on the cursor. The assumption is that, if you do an update, you want people to still be able to get at your data. You're being optimistic because you are essentially guessing (hoping may be a better word) that no-one will edit your data between when you fetched it into the cursor and when you applied your update.

The optimism is not necessarily misplaced. If you have a lot of records and not that many users, then the chances of two people trying to edit the same record at the same time are very small (depending on the nature of your business processes). Still, if you get this optimistic, then you need to also be prepared for the possibility that you will be wrong – that is, that someone has altered the data in between when you performed the fetch and when you went to actually update the database.

If you happen to run into this problem, SQL Server will issue an error with a value in @@ERROR of 16394. When this happens, you need to completely re-fetch the data from the cursor (so you know what changes were being made) and either rollback the transaction or try the update again.

Detecting Conversion of Cursor Types: TYPE_WARNING

This one is really pretty simple. If you add this option to your cursor, then you will be notified if an implicit conversion is made on your cursor. Without this statement, the conversion just happens with no notification. If the conversion wasn't an anticipated behavior, then there's a good chance that you're going to see the most dreaded of all computer terms (unpredictable results).

This is one of those that is perhaps best understood with an example, so let's go back and run a variation again of the cursor that we've been using throughout most of the chapter.

In this instance, we're going to take out the piece of code that creates a key for the table. Remember that without a unique index on a table, a keyset will be implicitly converted to a static cursor:

```
USE Northwind
/* Build the table that we'll be playing with this time */
SELECT OrderID, CustomerID
INTO CursorTable
FROM Orders
WHERE OrderID BETWEEN 10701 AND 10705

-- Declare our cursor
DECLARE CursorTest CURSOR
GLOBAL               -- So we can manipulate it outside the batch
SCROLL               -- So we can scroll back and see the changes
KEYSET
TYPE_WARNING
FOR
SELECT OrderID, CustomerID
FROM CursorTable

-- Declare our two holding variables
DECLARE @OrderID      int
DECLARE @CustomerID   varchar(5)

-- Get the cursor open and the first record fetched
OPEN CursorTest
FETCH NEXT FROM CursorTest INTO @OrderID, @CustomerID

-- Now loop through them all
WHILE @@FETCH_STATUS=0
BEGIN
     PRINT CONVERT(varchar(5),@OrderID) + '    ' + @CustomerID
     FETCH NEXT FROM CursorTest INTO @OrderID, @CustomerID
END

-- Now it's time to clean up after ourselves
CLOSE CursorTest

DEALLOCATE CursorTest

DROP TABLE CursorTable
```

There's nothing particularly special about this one. I'm considering it to be something of a complete rewrite only because we've deleted so much from the original and it's been so long since we've seen it. The creation of the table and cursor is pretty much the same as when we did our keyset-driven cursor much earlier in the chapter. The major changes are the removal of blocks of code that we don't need for this illustration along with the addition of the `TYPE_WARNING` option in the cursor declaration.

Now we come up with some interesting results:

```
(5 row(s) affected)

Cursor created was not of the requested type.
10701       HUNGO
10702       ALFKI
10703       FOLKO
10704       QUEEN
10705       HILAA
```

Everything ran OK – we just saw a statement that was meant solely as a warning. The results may not be what you expected given that the cursor was converted.

> *The down side here is that you get a message sent out, but no error. Programmatically speaking, there is essentially no way to tell that you received this message – which makes this option fairly useless in a production environment. Still, it can often be quite handy when you're trying to debug a cursor to determine why it isn't behaving in the expected fashion.*

FOR <SELECT>

This section of the cursor declaration is at the very heart of the matter. This is a section that is required under even the most basic of cursor syntax, and that's because it's the one and only clause that determines what data should be placed in the cursor.

Almost any `SELECT` statement is valid – even those including an `ORDER BY` clause. As long as your `SELECT` statement provides a single result set, you should be fine. Examples of options that would create problems would be any of the summary options such as a `CUBE` or `ROLLUP`.

FOR UPDATE

By default, any cursor that is updateable at all is completely updateable – that is, if one column can be edited then any of them can.

The `FOR UPDATE <column list>` option allows you to specify that only certain columns are to be editable within this cursor. If you include this option, then only the columns in your column list will be allowed to be updateable. Any columns not explicitly mentioned will be considered to be read-only.

Navigating the Cursor: The FETCH Statement

I figure that whoever first created the SQL cursor syntax must have really liked dogs. They probably decided to think of the data they were after as being the bone, with SQL Server the faithful bloodhound. From this I'm guessing, the `FETCH` keyword was born.

It's an apt term if you think about it. In a nutshell, it tells SQL Server to "go get it boy!" With that, our faithful mutt (in the form of SQL Server) is off to find the particular bone (row) we were after. We've gotten a bit of a taste for the `FETCH` statement in some of the previous cursors in this chapter, but it's time to look at this very important statement more closely.

`FETCH` actually has many more options than what we've seen so far. Up to this point, we've seen three different options for `FETCH` (`NEXT`, `PREVIOUS`, and `FIRST`). These really aren't a bad start. Indeed, we really only need to add one more for the most basic set of cursor navigation commands, and a few after that for the complete set.

Let's look at each of the cursor navigation commands and see what they do for us:

FETCH Option	Description
`NEXT`	This moves you forward exactly one row in the result set, and is the backbone option. 90% or more of your cursors won't need any more than this. Keep this in mind when deciding to declare as `FORWARD_ONLY` or not. When you try to do a `FETCH NEXT` and it results in moving beyond the last record, you will have a `@@FETCH_STATUS` of `-1`.
`PRIOR`	As you have probably surmised, this one is the functional opposite of `NEXT`. This moves backwards exactly one row. If you performed a `FETCH PRIOR` when you were at the first row in the result set, then you will get a `@@FETCH_STATUS` of `-1` just as if you had moved beyond the end of the file.
`FIRST`	Like most cursor options, this one says what it is pretty clearly. If you perform a `FETCH FIRST` then you will be at the first record in the recordset. The only time this option should generate a `@@FETCH_STATUS` of `-1` is if the result set is empty.
`LAST`	The functional opposite of `FIRST`, `FETCH LAST` moves you to the last record in the result set. Again, the only way you'll get a `-1` for `@@FETCH_STATUS` on this one is if you have an empty result set.
`ABSOLUTE`	With this one, you supply an integer value that indicates how many rows you want from the beginning of the cursor. If the value supplied is negative, then it is that many rows from the end of the cursor. Note that this option is not supported with dynamic cursors (since the membership in the cursor is redone with every fetch, you can "really know where you're at"). This equates roughly to navigating to a specific "absolute position" in a few of the client access object models.
`RELATIVE`	No – this isn't your mother-in-law kind of thing. Instead, this is about navigating by moving a specified number of rows forward or backwards relative to the current row.

We've already gotten a fair look at a few of these in our previous cursors. The other navigational choices work pretty much the same.

Altering Data within Your Cursor

Up 'til now, we've kind of glossed over the notion of changing data directly in the cursor. Now it's time to take a look at updating and deleting records within a cursor.

Since we're dealing with a specific row rather than set data, we need some special syntax to tell SQL Server that we want to update. Happily, this syntax is actually quite easy given that you already know how to perform an UPDATE or DELETE.

Essentially, we're going to update or delete data in the table that is underlying our cursor. To do this, it's as simple as running the same UPDATE and DELETE statements that we're now used to, but qualifying them with a WHERE clause that matches our cursor row. We just add one line of syntax to our DELETE or UPDATE statement:

```
WHERE CURRENT OF <cursor name>
```

Nothing remarkable about it at all. Just for grins though, we'll go ahead and implement a cursor using this syntax:

```
USE Northwind
/* Build the table that we'll be playing with this time */
SELECT OrderID, CustomerID
INTO CursorTable
FROM Orders
WHERE OrderID BETWEEN 10701 AND 10705

-- Now create a unique index on it in the form of a primary key
ALTER TABLE CursorTable
      ADD CONSTRAINT PKCursor
      PRIMARY KEY (OrderID)

/* The IDENTITY property was automatically brought over when
** we did our SELECT INTO, but I want to use my own OrderID
** value, so I'm going to turn IDENTITY_INSERT on so that I
** can override the identity value.
*/
SET IDENTITY_INSERT CursorTable ON

-- Declare our cursor
DECLARE CursorTest CURSOR
SCROLL              -- So we can scroll back and see if the changes are there
KEYSET
FOR
SELECT OrderID, CustomerID
FROM CursorTable

-- Declare our two holding variables
DECLARE @OrderID      int
DECLARE @CustomerID   varchar(5)

-- Get the cursor open and the first record fetched
OPEN CursorTest
FETCH NEXT FROM CursorTest INTO @OrderID, @CustomerID
```

```
-- Now loop through them all
WHILE @@FETCH_STATUS=0
BEGIN
     IF (@OrderID % 2 = 0)     -- Even number, so we'll update it
     BEGIN
          -- Make a change. This time though, we'll do it using cursor syntax
          UPDATE CursorTable
                 SET CustomerID = 'EVEN'
                 WHERE CURRENT OF CursorTest
     END

     ELSE                         -- Must be odd, so we'll delete it.
     BEGIN
          -- Now we'll delete a record so we can see how to deal with that
          DELETE CursorTable
                 WHERE CURRENT OF CursorTest
     END
     FETCH NEXT FROM CursorTest INTO @OrderID, @CustomerID
END

-- Now go back to the top. We can do this since we have a scrollable cursor
FETCH FIRST FROM CursorTest INTO @OrderID, @CustomerID

-- And loop through again.
WHILE @@FETCH_STATUS != -1
BEGIN
     IF @@FETCH_STATUS = -2
     BEGIN
          PRINT '  MISSING! It probably was deleted.'
     END
     ELSE
     BEGIN
          PRINT CONVERT(varchar(5),@OrderID) + '    ' +  @CustomerID
     END
     FETCH NEXT FROM CursorTest INTO @OrderID, @CustomerID
END

-- Now it's time to clean up after ourselves
CLOSE CursorTest

DEALLOCATE CursorTest

DROP TABLE CursorTable
```

Again, I'm treating this one as an entirely new cursor. We've done enough deletions, additions, and updates that I suspect you'll find it easier to just key things in a second time rather than having to look through row by row to see what you might have missed.

We are also again using the modulus operator (%) that we saw earlier in the book. Remember that it gives us nothing but the remainder. Therefore, if the remainder of any number divided by 2 is zero, then we know the number was an even number.

The rest of the nuts and bolts of this don't require any rocket science, yet we can quickly tell that we got some results:

```
(5 row(s) affected)

(1 row(s) affected)

(1 row(s) affected)

(1 row(s) affected)

(1 row(s) affected)

(1 row(s) affected)

  MISSING! It probably was deleted.
10702   EVEN
  MISSING! It probably was deleted.
10704   EVEN
  MISSING! It probably was deleted.
```

You can see the multiple "1 row affected" that is the returned message for any row that was affected by the `UPDATE` and `DELETE` statements. When we get down to the last result set enumeration, you can quickly tell that we deleted all the odd numbers (which is what we told our code to do), and that we updated the even numbered rows with a new `CustomerID`.

No tricks – just a `WHERE` clause that makes use of the `WHERE CURRENT` argument.

Summary

Cursors give us those memories of the old days – when we could address things row by row. Ahhh, it sounds so romantic with that "old days" kind of thought. WRONG! I'd stick to set operations any day if I thought I could get away with it.

The fact is that set operations can't do everything. Cursors are going to be the answer anytime a solution must be done on a row-by-row basis. Notice that I used the word "must" in there, and that's the way you should think of it. Cursors are great at taking care of some problems that can't be solved by any other means.

That being said, remember to avoid cursor use wherever possible. Cursors are a resource pig, and will almost always produce 100 times or worse negative performance impact. It is extremely tempting – especially if you come from the mainframe world or from a dBase background – to just keep thinking in that row by row method. Don't fall into that trap! Cursors are meant to be used only when no other options are available.

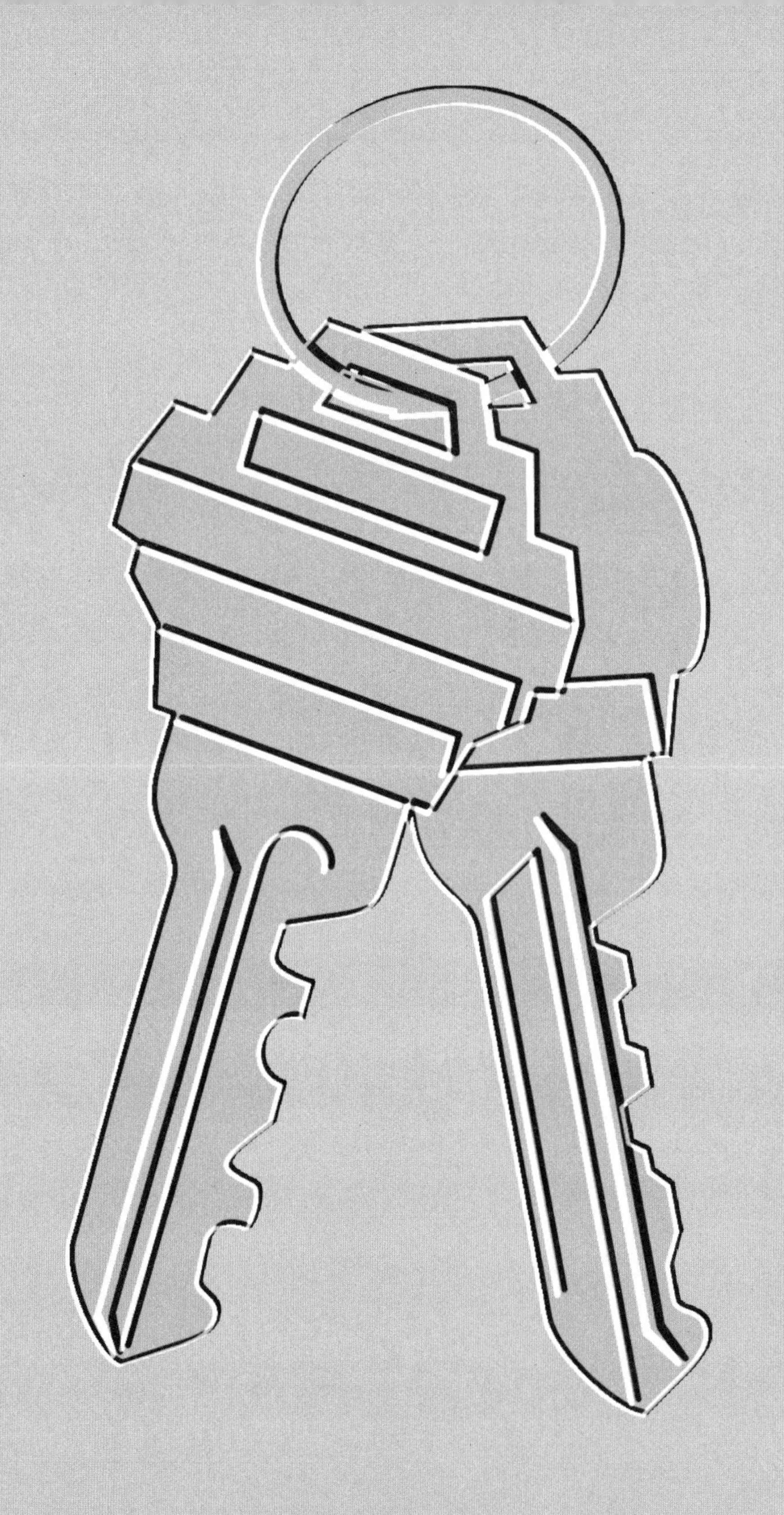

18

Making a Change... Bulk Copy Program & Data Transformation Services

Overview

Sometimes, the easiest way to understand SQL Server is to imagine it operating in a network vacuum. It's simpler to focus on server and application components and keep the outside world's direct influence to a minimum. Data comes into the server only through data entry applications; data leaves the server only through end-user reports and data requests.

Unfortunately, the real world doesn't work that way. There will be times when you need to move around large blocks of data. You need to bring in data that's in the wrong format or that's sitting in another application's data files. Sometimes, reality just gets in the way. The good thing is, SQL Server 7.0 has two tools to do this for you - the **bulk copy program** (**bcp**) and **Data Transformation Services** (**DTS**).

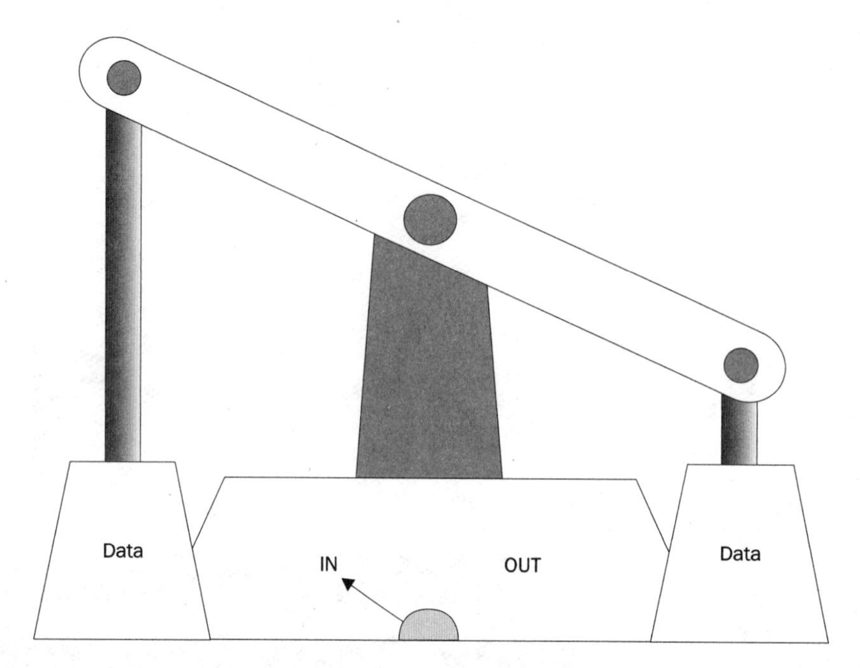

Bcp is used for transferring text and SQL Server native format data to and from SQL Server tables. Yes, that same old bcp you've seen if you've worked with SQL Server in the past. You can think of bcp as being like a data pump, moving data into and out of text (and native) files. Native files, in case you're wondering, are files containing data output from a SQL Server using native data types, such as ASCII flat files (`.txt`, `.csv`), or Binary data files (`.mdb`). Bcp is a powerful tool, but it can't always meet all of your needs.

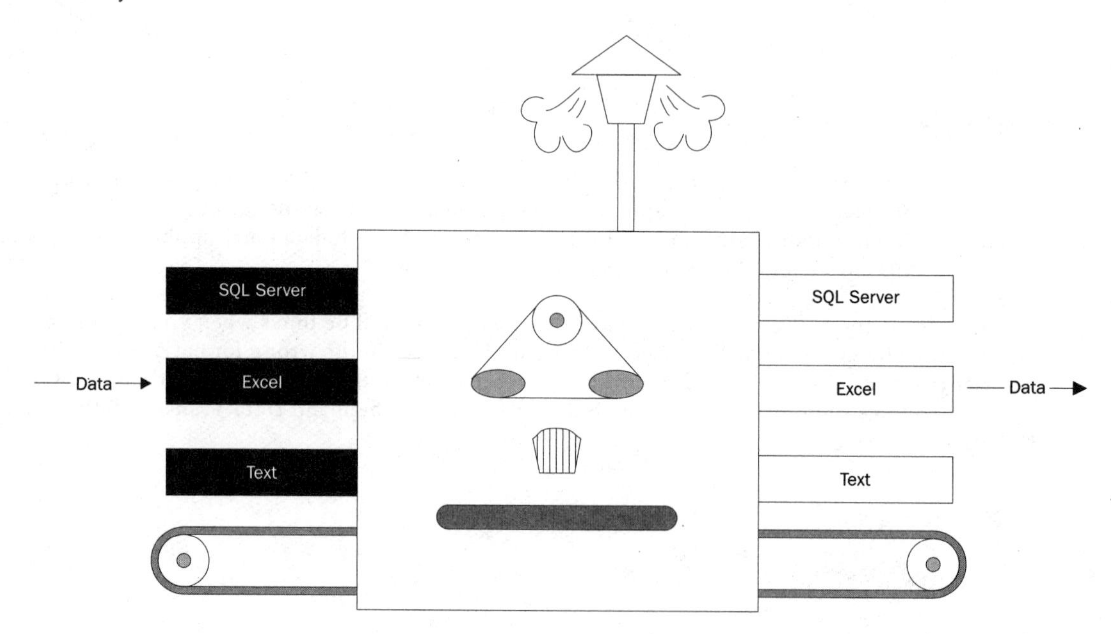

If you want to think of bcp as a data pump, then DTS is more like a data engine. DTS accepts data from a wide variety of sources, lets you remap and massage the data as necessary, then sends the data out to any of a number of destinations. The Import and Export Wizards walk you through setting up the transformation. The DTS Designer gives you even more control and flexibility, letting you take control behind the scenes.

Data Transfer and Transformation

You need to move data into or out of SQL Server. It may be that you need to transfer data between SQL Server and other applications or between several SQL Servers. Both bcp and DTS can do this for you. The one you choose depends on the situation and your personal preference.

Bcp is a legacy utility that has been updated to support Unicode text and SQL Server 7.0 data types. It's most commonly used when working with text files or using native format to move data between servers. It can be used to move data back and forth between SQL Server and other applications, as long as you can put up with passing the data through a text file as part of the process.

DTS is much more flexible, but can be more complicated to use. With DTS, you can move data directly between servers or directly between SQL Server and other applications. There is no need to go through the text file step.

Suppose you wanted to import the contents of an Excel spreadsheet into a SQL Server table. With bcp, you would need to save the spreadsheet as a text file, such as `.csv`, then run bcp to import the contents of that file into the table. With DTS, you could select Microsoft Excel as your data source, SQL Server as your destination, and directly transfer the data.

Data transfer is a relatively easy process with either bcp or DTS, assuming a close match between the source and destination. What if they don't match? Well if it's just a problem with column or field order, you can still you use bcp if you want. If you need to do more than that, then DTS will quickly become your tool of choice. In short, your general rule of thumb should be that bcp is for data imports, DTS is for data migration.

Of course, the only way you're going to be able to make an informed decision is if you're well informed. So, let's get you informed, starting with bcp.

And by the way...

Don't assume that you're going to get it right the first time. There are likely to be times when you need complicated transformations updating tables with complex relationships.

What's the key to success? Test and verify.

Do not, especially on your first attempts, directly update your production databases. Set up working copies on which you can test data transfer and transformations first, to make sure you've got everything working properly. If that's not possible, try setting up an Access database to mimic your production database and test DTS transfers against that.

If complex transformations and data scrubbing are involved, you should consider having a staging area that receives the data before updating the production databases. This can be a worthwhile idea even when you've already tested the transformations. You never know when something in the source data file can cause you problems.

Finally, before any transfers or transformations, *always* back up your production database. Run a full backup and keep it readily available in case you have to recover quickly. A good way to manage this is by backing up to a temporary disk backup file.

BCP Utility

Bcp runs from an operating system command prompt to import or export native data (specific to SQL Server), ASCII text, or Unicode text. This means that you can execute bcp from an operating system batch file or user-defined stored procedure, as well as from other places. Bcp can also be run as part of a scheduled job, or executed from a COM-based object.

Options can be specified using a hyphen (-) or forward slash (/). Watch carefully when specifying options. Unlike most DOS or Windows family utilities, option switches are case sensitive.

The kind of circumstances in which you might prefer to use bcp rather than DTS include working with legacy applications that are based on bcp.

BCP Syntax

```
bcp [[database_name.][owner].]table_name|view_name|"query"
in|out|queryout|format data_file
[-m max_errors] [-f format_file] [-e error_file] [-F first_row] [-L
last_row] [-b batch_size]
[-n] [-c] [-w] [-N] [-6] [-q] [-C code_page] [-t field_terminator] [-r
row_terminator]
[-i input_file] [-o output_file] [-a packet_size] [-S server_name] [-U
user_name] [-P password]
[-T] [-v] [-R] [-k] [-E] [-h "hint [,...]]
```

Now comes the dry part. Yes, bcp has a lot of option switches, and yes, we're going to go through all of them. Don't worry, we'll keep it as painless as possible.

Parameter	Description
database_name	When specifying a table or view, this is the database in which the table or view is located. If not specified, the user's default database is assumed.
owner	If the user running bcp owns the table or view, it is not necessary to specify the owner. If the user running bcp does not own the table and the owner is not specified, bcp will fail.

Parameter	Description
	Pick one – table, view, or query.
table_name	This is the input destination or output source view.
view_name	This is the input destination or output source view. As is always the case, all destination columns must be in the same table.
"*query*"	A SQL Server query can only be used as a bcp output source, and only when queryout is specified. If the query returns multiple result sets, only the first result set is used by bcp.
-q	Use -q to specify that a table or view name includes non-ANSI characters. The fully qualified name, database, owner, and table or view, must be enclosed in double quotation marks, in the format "*database_name.owner.table*".
in *data_file*	Pick one, as well as a source and destination.
out *data_file* queryout *data_file* format *data_file*	Use **in** to specify importing data into a table or view, **out** to output from a table or view. Use **queryout** only for output using a query as its source. Use **format** to create a format file based on the format option you've selected. You must also specify -f, as well as format options (-n, -c, -w, -6, or-N) or answer prompts from interactive bcp.
	The source or destination path and filename is specified as *data_file*, and cannot include more than 255 characters.
-n	Native data types (SQL Server data types) are used for the copy operation. This option provides support for SQL Server version 6.5 if combined with option -6.
-c	This specifies that the operation uses character data (text). A tab character is assumed as field delimiter and new line character as row separator, unless you specify different terminator values. Terminator values are discussed in Chapter 20.
-w	The -w option specifies Unicode data type. A tab character is assumed as field delimiter and new line character as row separator. This option cannot be used with SQL Server version 6.5 or earlier.
-N	Native data types (database data types) are used for non-character data and Unicode is used for character data copy. This option cannot be used with SQL Server version 6.5 or earlier.

Table Continued on Following Page

Parameter	Description
-6	Use this option to force bcp to use SQL Server 6.0 or 6.5 data types. This option is used in conjunction with the -c or -n format options.
-C ACP|OEM|RAW|*value*	This option is used to specify the code page for the data file data. It is only necessary to use this option with char, varchar, or text data having character values less than 32 or greater than 127. A code page value of ACP specifies ANSI/Microsoft Windows (ISO 1252). OEM specifies the default client code page. If RAW is specified, there will be no code page conversion. You also have the option of providing a specific code page value.
-t *field_terminator*	This option allows you to override the default field terminator. The default terminator is \t, the tab character. You can specify the terminator as tab (\t), new line (\n), carriage return (\r), backslash (\\), null terminator (\0), any printable character, or a string of up to ten printable characters. For example, you would use -t, for a comma-delimited text file.
-r *row_terminator*	This option allows you to override the default row terminator. The default terminator is \n, the newline character. You can specify the terminator as tab (\t), new line (\n), carriage return (\r), backslash (\\), null terminator (\0), any printable character, or a string of up to ten printable characters.
-R	Use this option to specify that the regional format for clients' local settings is used when copying currency, date, and time data. The default is that regional settings are ignored.
-k	Use this option to override the use of column default values during bulk copy, ignoring any default constraints. Empty columns will retain a null value rather than the column default.
-E	This option is used during import when the import source file contains identity column values. If not specified, SQL Server will ignore the values supplied in the source file and automatically generate identity column values. You can use the format file to skip the identity column when importing data from a source that does not include identity values and have SQL Server generate the values.

Parameter	Description
-f *format_file*	A format file contains stored responses from a previous bcp operation on the same table or view. Replace *format_file* with the full path and filename. This option is also used with the format option to specify the path and filename when creating a format file.
-e *error_file*	You can specify the full path and filename for an error file to store any rows that bcp is not able to transfer. Otherwise, no error file is created. Any error messages will be displayed at the client station.
-m *max_errors*	You can specify a maximum number of errors that you will allow before SQL Server cancels the bulk copy operation, defaulting to 10 errors. Each row that cannot be copied by bcp is counted as one error.
-b *batch_size*	You can specify the number of rows copied as a batch, defaulting to all source data. A batch is copied as a single transaction. When SQL Server commits the transaction, all rows in the batch are committed. If a failure occurs and SQL Server rolls back the transaction, all rows are rolled back. Do not use the -b option with the -h "ROWS_PER_BATCH=*nn*" option.
-F *first_row*	Use this option if you want to specify the first row to be copied by the bulk copy operation. If not specified, bcp defaults to a value of 1 and begins copying with the first row in the source data file.
-L *last_row*	Use this option if you want to specify the last row to be copied by the bulk copy operation. If not specified, bcp defaults to a value of 0, the last row in the source file.
-S *server_name*	If running bcp from a server, the default is the local SQL Server. This option lets you specify a different server and is required in a network environment when running bcp from a remote system.
-U *login_name*	Unless connecting to SQL Server through a trusted connection, you must provide a valid username for login.
-P *password*	When you supply a username, you must also supply a password. Otherwise, you will be prompted for a password. Include -P as your last option with no password to specify a null password.
-T	You have the option of connecting to the server using network user credentials through a trusted connection. If a trusted connection is specified, there is no need to provide a *login_name* or *password* for the connection.

Table Continued on Following Page

Parameter	Description
-v	When this option is used, bcp returns version number and copyright information.
-i *input_file*	You have the option of specifying a response file, as *input_file*, containing the responses to be used when running bcp in interactive mode.
-o *output_file*	You can redirect bcp output from the command prompt to an output file. This gives you a way to capture command output and results when executing bcp from an unattended batch or stored procedure.
-a *packet_size*	You have the option of overriding the default packet size for data transfers across the network. The specified value must be between 4096 and 65535, inclusive. The default packet size is 4096 bytes, unless modified for the server through SQL Server Enterprise Manager or the sp_configure system stored procedure.
-h "*hint*[, ...]"	The hint option lets you specify one or more hints to be used by the bulk copy operation. Option -h is not supported for SQL Server version 6.5 or earlier.
ORDER *column* [ASC|DESC]	You can use this hint to improve performance when the sort order of the source data file matches the clustered index in the destination table. If the destination table does not have a clustered index or if the data is sorted in a different order the `ORDER` hint is ignored.
ROWS_PER_BATCH=*nn*	This can be used in place of the -b option to specify the number of rows to be transferred as a batch. Do not use this hint with the -b option.
KILOBYTES_PER_BATCH=*nn*	You can optionally specify batch size as the approximate number of kilobytes of data to be transferred in a batch.
TABLOCK	This will cause a table-level lock to be acquired for the duration of the operation. Default locking behavior is set by the table lock on bulk load table option.
CHECK_CONSTRAINTS	By default, check constraints are ignored during an import operation. This hint forces check constraints to be checked during import.

Bcp runs in interactive mode, prompting for format information, unless `-f`, `-c`, `-n`, `-w`, `-6`, or `-N` is specified when the command is executed. When running in interactive mode, bcp will also prompt to create a format file after receiving the format information.

A Quick Word on Security

Security is discussed later in this book, but it might be worth the time to give you a quick thumbnail description (and review) before we go much further. SQL Server supports two methods for authenticating logins, Windows NT authentication and SQL Server authentication.

With Windows NT authentication, the user is authenticated when he or she logs onto the Windows NT domain. SQL Server trusts this authentication, so it isn't necessary for the server to authenticate the user again. Hence the name, trusted connection. With SQL Server authentication, the server authenticates the login and password. The login and password must be passed explicitly to the server for authentication.

Something to keep in mind is that Windows NT authentication, and therefore trusted connections, are not supported for SQL Servers running on Windows 95/98. This means you must supply a login name and password when running bcp to update a Windows 95/98-based server.

Surprised by the security options? You shouldn't be. Did you really think that, just because you're working from an operating system prompt, you would be able bypass SQL Server security? You still need the permission before you can access the server and server data.

Do you use SQL Server Authorization (login and password) or a trusted connection to run bcp? How do you decide? Take this simple test. If you were going to launch Query Analyzer from this workstation, which method would you use? Use the same option for running bcp.

BCP Import

Ready to get started? Probably the most common use of bcp is to import bulk data into existing SQL Server tables and views. To import data, you must have access permissions to the server, either through a login ID or a trusted connection, and you must have `INSERT` and `SELECT` permissions on the destination table or view.

The source file can contain native code, ASCII characters, Unicode, or mixed native and Unicode data. Remember to use the appropriate option to describe the source data. Also, for the data file to be usable, you must be able to describe the field and row terminators. Terminators are discussed in Chapter 20.

Be sure you know your destination before you start. Bcp has a few quirks that can affect data import. Values supplied for timestamp or computed columns are ignored. If you have values for those columns in the source file, they'll be ignored. If the source file doesn't have values for these columns, you'll need a format file so you can skip over them. Don't worry, you'll see how to use format files a little later in the chapter.

Any triggers or rules are also ignored, as are check constraints unless the `CHECK_CONSTRAINTS` hint is specified. Unique constraints, indexes, and primary/foreign key constraints are enforced. Default constraints are enforced unless the `-k` option is specified.

By default, users will be able to access the destination table during bcp operations, but it's not really a good idea if it can be avoided. Typically, bcp is used during periods of minimal user activity. It is also a good idea to back up a database before running bcp.

Data Import Example

The easiest way to see how bcp import works is to look at an example. Let's start with a simple example, a tab delimited file containing shipper information for the `Northwind` database. Here's how the data looks:

```
47	Readyship	(503)555-1234
48	MyShipper	(503)555-3443
```

To import this into the `Shippers` table using a trusted connection at the local server, you run:

```
bcp northwind.dbo.shippers in d:\data\newship.txt -c -T
```

Because the first column in the `Shippers` table is an identity column and the `-E` option wasn't specified, SQL Server will ignore the identity values in the file and generate new values. The `-c` option identifies the source data as character data and `-T` specifies to use a trusted connection.

Now let's look at a more involved example. This time, the file is a comma-delimited file (in the same format as a `.csv` file) with new customer information. This time, the file looks like:

```
XWALL,Wally's World,Wally Smith,Owner,,,,,,(503)555-8448,,
XGENE,Generic Sales and Services,Al Smith,,,,,,,(503)555-9339,,
XMORE,More for You,Paul Johnston,President,,,,,,(573)555-3227,,
```

You are going to run bcp to import the data from a remote system. The command this time is:

```
bcp northwind.dbo.customers in d:\data\newcust.txt -c -t, -r\n
-Saristotle -Usa -P
```

The line wrapping shown here was added to make the command string easier to read. Do *not* press *ENTER* to wrap if you try this example yourself. Type the command as a single string and allow it to wrap itself inside the command prompt.

Once again, the data is being identified as character data. The `-t`, option identifies the file as comma delimited (terminated) data and `-r\n` identifies the new line character as the row delimiter. Server connection information is also provided, using `sa` as your login with no password. The sample files, `NEWSHIP.TXT` and `NEWCUST.TXT`, can be downloaded from the Wrox website at `www.wrox.com`, along with the other sample files mentioned in this chapter.

What's with all the commas in the source file? Those are place holders for columns in the `Customers` table. The source file doesn't provide values for all of the columns, so commas are used to skip over those columns. This isn't the only way to handle a source file that doesn't provide values for all of the columns. You can use a format file to map the source data to the destination. We'll be covering format files in a little bit.

Logged vs. Non-logged

Bcp can run in either fast mode (not logged) or slow mode (logged operation). Each has its advantages. Fast mode gives you the best performance, but slow mode provides maximum recoverability. Since slow mode is logged, you can run a quick transaction log backup immediately after the import and be able to recover the database should there be a failure.

Fast mode is usually your best option when you need to transfer large amounts of data. Not only does the transfer run faster, since the operation isn't logged you don't have to worry about running out of space in the transaction log. What's the catch? There are several conditions that must be met for bcp to run as non-logged:

- The select into/bulkcopy option must be set to true
- The target table cannot be replicated
- If the target table is indexed, it must not currently have any rows
- If the target table already has rows, it must not have any indexes
- The `TABLOCK` hint is specified

Obviously, if you want to do a fast mode copy into an indexed table with data, you will need to:

- Drop the indexes
- Run bcp
- Reindex the target table

You need to immediately back up the destination database after a non-logged bcp operation.

If the target table doesn't meet the requirements for fast bcp, then the operation will be logged. This means that you can run the risk of filling the transaction log when transferring large amounts of data. You can run `BACKUP LOG` using the `WITH TRUNCATE_ONLY` option to clear the transaction log. The `TRUNCATE_ONLY` option truncates the inactive portion of the log without backing up any data.

Format File

The use of format files was mentioned earlier. Format files can be thought of as import templates and make it easier to support recurring import operations when:

- Source file and target table structures do not match
- You want to skip columns in the target table

To get a better idea of how format files work, let's look at some specific examples. First you'll see how the file is structured when the source and destination match. Next, you can compare this to situations where the number of source file fields don't match the number of table columns and where source fields are ordered differently than the table columns.

You can create a default format file to use as your source when you run bcp in interactive mode. After prompting for column value information, you're given the option of saving the file. The default filename is `bcp.fmt`, but you can give the format file any valid filename.

To create a default format like this for the `Northwind` database `Customers` table, you could run:

```
bcp northwind.dbo.customers out c:\cust.txt -Saristotle -Usa -P
```

This is a handy way of creating a quick format file that you can then edit as needed. You can do this with any table, so you can use bcp to get a jump start on your format file needs.

Of course, you would have to supply your own server, user, and password information. Enter prefix length and data length information and, in this case, a comma as the field terminator and `\n` as the row terminator. SQL Server will prompt you to save the format file after you've entered all of the format information. You can then edit the format file to meet your particular needs with any text editor, such as Windows Notepad.

Host and Target Match

First, let's look at a format file where there is a direct match between the host (source) and target:

```
7.0
11
1     SQLCHAR    0    5     ","        1     CustomerID
2     SQLCHAR    0    40    ","        2     CompanyName
3     SQLCHAR    0    30    ","        3     ContactName
4     SQLCHAR    0    30    ","        4     ContactTitle
5     SQLCHAR    0    60    ","        5     Address
6     SQLCHAR    0    15    ","        6     City
7     SQLCHAR    0    15    ","        7     Region
8     SQLCHAR    0    10    ","        8     PostalCode
9     SQLCHAR    0    15    ","        9     Country
10    SQLCHAR    0    24    ","        10    Phone
11    SQLCHAR    0    24    "\r\n"     11    Fax
```

The first two lines in the file identify the bcp version number and the number of fields in the host file. The remaining lines describe the host data file and how the fields match up with target columns.

The first column is the host file field number. Numbering starts with 1 through the total number of fields. Next is the host file data type. The example file is an ASCII text file, so the data type of all fields is `SQLCHAR`. The next two columns describe the prefix and data length for the data fields. The prefix is the number of prefix characters in the field. The data field is the maximum length of the data stored in the field. This is followed by the terminator (delimiter). In this case, a command is used as the field terminator and new line as the row terminator. The last two columns describe the target table columns with the server column order and server column name. Since there is a direct match between the server columns and host fields in this example, the column and field numbers are the same. This format file can be downloaded from the Wrox website as `CUST.FMT`.

Host File with Fewer Fields

When the host file has fewer fields than the destination table, modify the format file to identify which columns do not exist in the data file and which table columns should be ignored. This is done by setting the prefix and data length to 0 for each missing field and the table column number to 0 for each missing column.

For example, if the host data only has `CustomerID`, `CompanyName`, `ContactName`, `ContactTitle`, `Phone`, and `Fax`, you would modify the file as:

```
7.0
11
1       SQLCHAR     0     5      ","        1      CustomerID
2       SQLCHAR     0     40     ","        2      CompanyName
3       SQLCHAR     0     30     ","        3      ContactName
4       SQLCHAR     0     30     ","        4      ContactTitle
5       SQLCHAR     0     0      ""         0      Address
6       SQLCHAR     0     0      ""         0      City
7       SQLCHAR     0     0      ""         0      Region
8       SQLCHAR     0     0      ""         0      PostalCode
9       SQLCHAR     0     0      ""         0      Country
10      SQLCHAR     0     24     ","        10     Phone
11      SQLCHAR     0     24     "\r\n"     11     Fax
```

As you can see, the `Address`, `City`, `Region`, `PostalCode` and `Country` fields and columns have been zeroed out. This format file can be downloaded from the Wrox web site as `SHRTCUST.FMT`.

Host File with More Fields

What about a host file that has more fields than the target table? You need to add column information for the additional fields, but the prefix length, data length, and column number fields are all set to 0:

```
7.0
11
1       SQLCHAR     0     5      ","        1      CustomerID
2       SQLCHAR     0     40     ","        2      CompanyName
3       SQLCHAR     0     30     ","        3      ContactName
4       SQLCHAR     0     30     ","        4      ContactTitle
5       SQLCHAR     0     60     ","        5      Address
6       SQLCHAR     0     15     ","        6      City
7       SQLCHAR     0     15     ","        7      Region
8       SQLCHAR     0     10     ","        8      PostalCode
9       SQLCHAR     0     15     ","        9      Country
10      SQLCHAR     0     24     ","        10     Phone
11      SQLCHAR     0     24     ","        11     Fax
12      SQLCHAR     0     0      ","        0      Email
13      SQLCHAR     0     0      "\r\n"     0      SalesContact
```

This time, the host file includes fields for an e-mail address and a sales contact. The target table doesn't have any columns to receive this information. The fields are added to the original format file, as well as two dummy columns with a column number of 0. This will force bcp to ignore the fields. This format file can be downloaded from the Wrox web site as `MORECUST.FMT`.

Mismatched Field Order

Another possibility is that the host and target have the same fields, but the field orders don't match. This is corrected by changing the server column order to match the host file order:

```
7.0
11
1       SQLCHAR     0     5      ","        1      CustomerID
2       SQLCHAR     0     40     ","        2      CompanyName
3       SQLCHAR     0     30     ","        4      ContactName
4       SQLCHAR     0     30     ","        3      ContactTitle
5       SQLCHAR     0     60     ","        5      Address
6       SQLCHAR     0     15     ","        6      City
7       SQLCHAR     0     15     ","        7      Region
8       SQLCHAR     0     10     ","        8      PostalCode
9       SQLCHAR     0     15     ","        9      Country
10      SQLCHAR     0     24     ","        10     Phone
11      SQLCHAR     0     24     "\r\n"     11     Fax
```

In this case, the contact title is listed before the contact name in the host file. The server column order has been changed to reflect this. Notice, the order in which the server columns are listed has not changed, but the server column numbers have been swapped. This format file is available for download from the Wrox web site as MIXCUST.FMT.

Using Format Files

As an example, let's use a format file for an import. This command will copy records into the Customers table based on a format file named shrtcust.txt:

```
bcp northwind.dbo.customers in d:\data\shrtcust.txt -fd:\data\shrtcust.fmt
-Saristotle -Usa -P
```

The sample files used in this example, SHRTCUST.TXT and SHRTCUST.FMT, are available for download from the Wrox web site.

Maximizing Import Performance

One obvious way of maximizing bcp performance is to make sure that the target table meets all the requirements for running bcp as a non-logged operation. This may mean having to drop indexes before running bcp and then reindexing after the operation. The TABLOCK hint is also required. Not only is this required for non-logged operation, it helps to improve performance since lock contention on the table is reduced.

If you're looking for additional improvement when importing data into a table, you can run parallel loads from multiple clients. To do this, you must:

- Drop any existing indexes on the target table
- Set the select into/bulkcopy option on

How would this work? Rather than importing one very large file, break it up into smaller files. Then you launch bcp from multiple client systems, each client importing one of the smaller files. Obviously, you will only be interested in doing this if the expected performance increase saves more time on the import than you'll spend preparing the source files and copying them to the clients.

The TABLOCK option is not required for parallel loads, but is strongly suggested. Parallel loads are not supported for SQL Server 6.5 or earlier.

With either of these operations, it will be necessary to recreate any indexes on the target table after completing the operation. Recreate the target table clustered index (if any) before any non-clustered indexes.

You can get additional performance improvement by letting SQL Server ignore check constraints, the default option. Keep in mind that this can result in loading data that violates the table's check constraints.

BCP Export

You can export data from a table, a view, or a query. You must specify a destination filename, and if an existing file is specified, it will be overwritten. You cannot skip columns during export, and index, timestamp, and computed columns export in the same manner as any other SQL Server columns. To run an export, you must have access to the source server. You'll also need `SELECT` permission on the source table, as well as the `sysobjects`, `syscolumns`, and `sysindexes` tables.

Data Export Example

Let's look at a couple of quick examples using the `Northwind Shippers` table. To export to a default data file, you could run:

```
bcp northwind.dbo.shippers out d:\data\shipout.txt -c -Saristotle -Usa -P
```

This would create a file that looks like:

```
1    Speedy Express    (503) 555-9831
2    United Package    (503) 555-3199
3    Federal Shipping  (503) 555-9931
4    Readyship   (503)555-1234
5    MyShipper   (503)555-3443
```

This creates an ASCII text file with tab as a field terminator and new line as the row terminator. To modify this to create a comma-delimited file, you could run:

```
bcp northwind.dbo.shippers out d:\data\shipout.txt -c -t, -Saristotle -Usa -P
```

This would give you:

```
1,Speedy Express,(503) 555-9831
2,United Package,(503) 555-3199
3,Federal Shipping,(503) 555-9931
4,Readyship,(503)555-1234
5,MyShipper,(503)555-3443
```

Keep in mind that the destination file will be overwritten if it already exists. Bcp will overwrite the file without prompting you. The output file in this second example, `SHIPOUT.TXT`, is available for download from the Wrox web site.

Data Transformation Services (DTS)

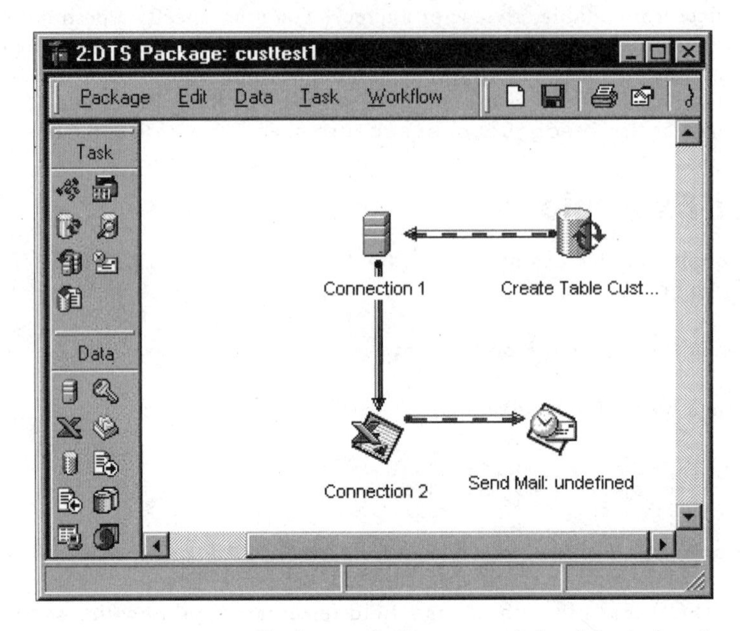

This is where it starts to get exciting. You've probably guessed that bcp isn't going to meet all of your needs. It's too limited and can require too much overhead to manage data before or after transfer. Not only that, it can sometimes be difficult to even get the data into a form that is acceptable to bcp.

You need something that's more powerful and more flexible than bcp. That something is Data Transformation Services (DTS). DTS lets you move data between a wide variety of sources and destinations, and if necessary, transform the data along the way. You can even use DTS to transfer SQL Server objects between servers.

Simple data transfers and transformations can be handled through the DTS Import and Export Wizard. If you need more control over the process, you can have even more flexibility and control through the DTS Designer. You can even create custom transformation objects that can be integrated into other applications through the use of DTS COM objects.

How are you going to use DTS? What do you need and how far can your imagination take you? Simple import and export is just the beginning. Some other ideas include:

- Scrubbing data before loading SQL Server tables
- Automatically transfer data into data marts and data warehouses
- Automatically transfer data on a periodic basis to other application formats to meet analysis and reporting requirements
- Transferring working copies of databases between servers

Here's an example for you. You performed a one-machine upgrade of SQL Server 6.5 to 7.0. You want to do some testing without affecting the production server, so you would like to put copies of selected databases on your laptop where you are running SQL Server 7.0 desktop on Windows 98. With DTS, you can run this as a simple transfer.

It's likely that the more you use DTS, the more potential uses you are going to find for it.

What if you have data transfer and transformation needs that don't include SQL Server? DTS is still your answer. You don't have to specify SQL Server as your source or destination. This means you can use DTS to transfer data directly between different application formats. For example, you could use DTS to create Excel spreadsheets directly from dBase III database data. I don't know why you would still want to be pulling data out of a dBase III database, but you can do it.

Sources and Destinations

Let's take a look at the "from where" and "to where" part of the equation. DTS supports a wide variety of sources and destinations, with Microsoft OLE DB provider for SQL Server as the default for source and destination. Access is provided to both OLE DB connections and ODBC connections, as well as text files. When you specify a source or destination, you also have to provide connection information.

SQL Server Connection

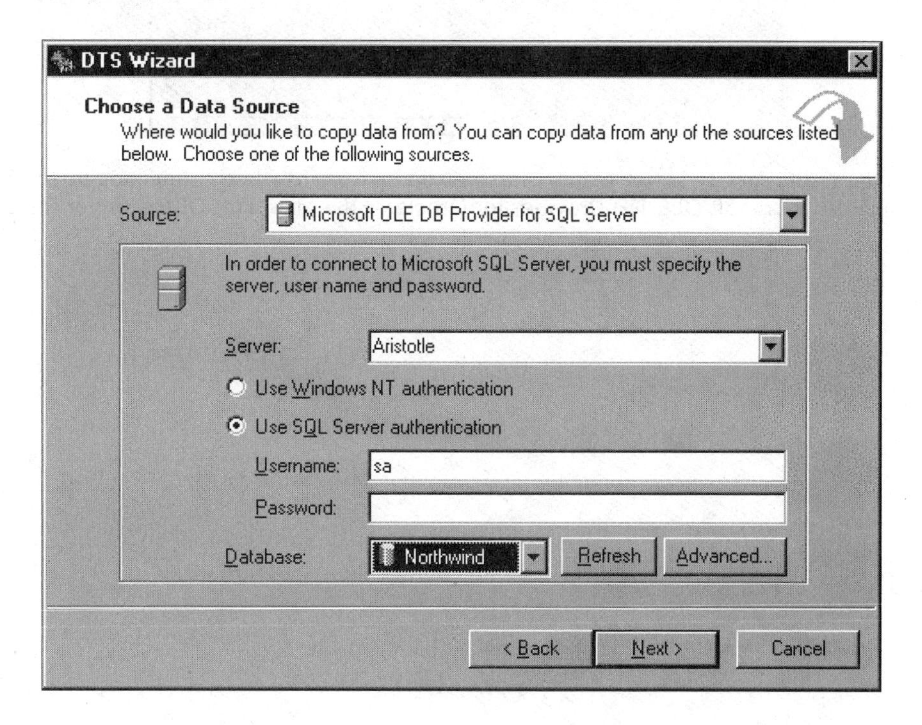

Most transfers will probably include SQL Server at one end or the other. When connecting to Microsoft OLE DB Provider for SQL Server or Microsoft ODBC Provider for SQL Server you must specify:

- Server name or (local) for a local server
- Connection security information, either Windows NT authentication or a username and password
- Database name or default database

You may need to click on the Refresh button to retrieve a list of available databases after specifying the server name.

Oracle Connection

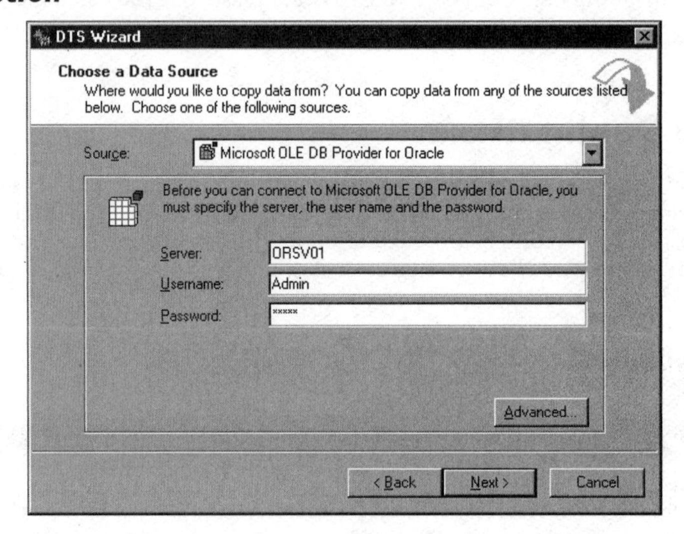

You are required to specify server name, username and password when connecting to an Oracle server using the Microsoft OLE DB Provider for Oracle or the Microsoft ODBC driver for Oracle.

File Connection

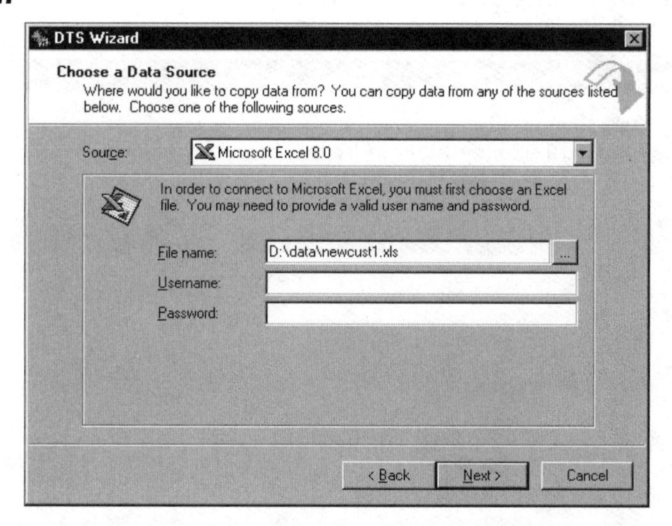

Path and filename information is required when connecting to dBase III, dBase IV, dBase V, Microsoft Access, Microsoft Excel 3.0, Microsoft Excel 4.0, Microsoft Excel 5.0, Microsoft Excel 8.0, Paradox 3.x, Paradox 4.x, Paradox 5.x, and text files. With any of these connection types, *except* text file, you can also enter user and password information. Depending on the connection, you may also have to supply connection-specific format information.

Visual FoxPro or other ODBC

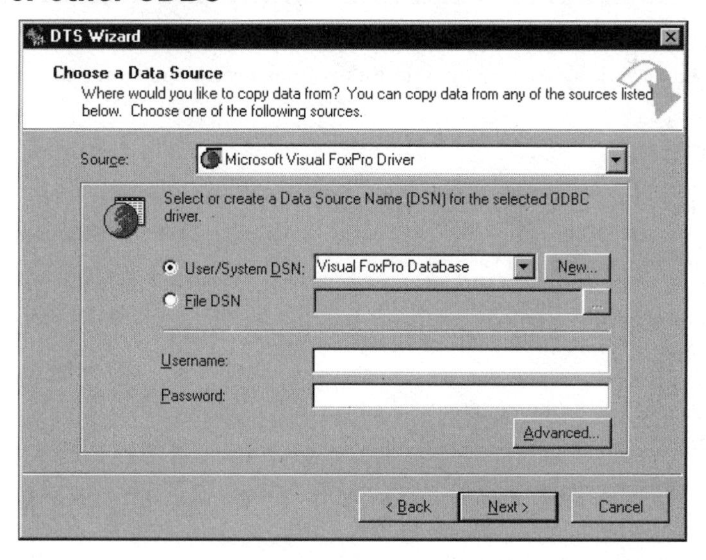

When you are connecting to Visual FoxPro, or any other ODBC source (other than SQL Server or Oracle), you are prompted for either a User/System data source name (DSN) or a File DSN. You can also provide username and password information.

Microsoft Data Link Connection

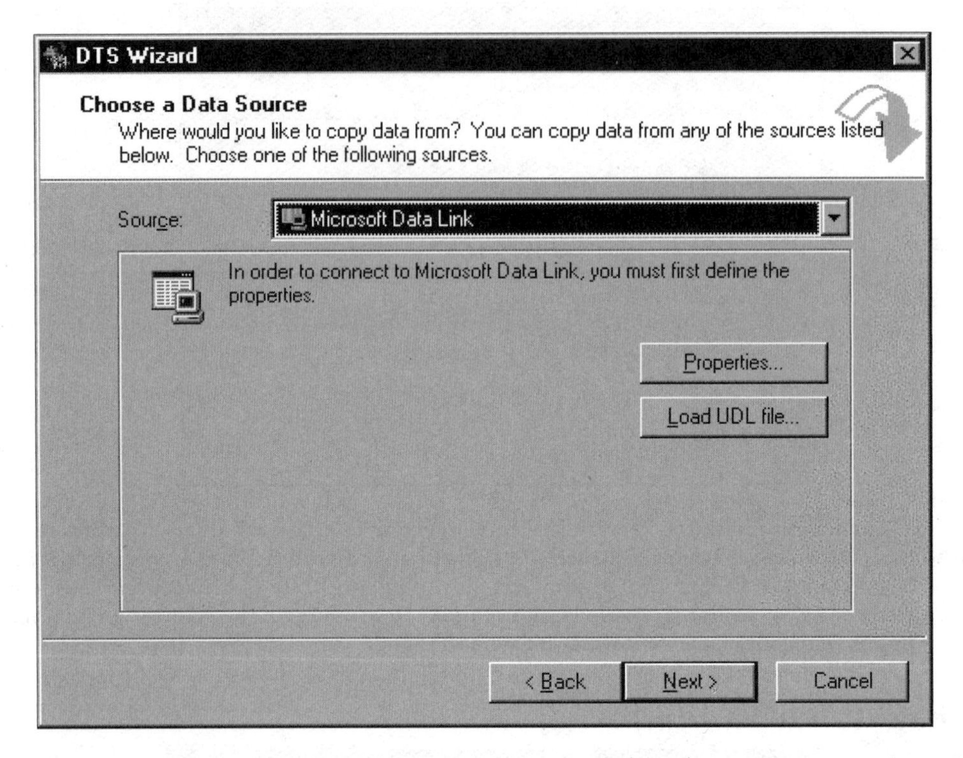

Microsoft Data Link lets you specify an existing data link file (UDL). In addition, you have the option of defining a new data link by specifying data link properties for the connection.

Transformations

Data transformation is the process of reformatting data to meet your needs. The DTS Wizard lets you write DTS transformation scripts in VB Script or in JScript. The DTS Designer gives you the option of creating ActiveX transformation scripts.

What kind of transformations can you perform? It might be better to ask what kind of transformations you need. For example, you can:

- Validate data before loading it into the destination
- Perform calculations to generate new values for loading
- Combine multiple columns into a single column
- Break a single column into multiple columns
- Reformat and manipulate text data
- Convert between data types

In short, if you can script it, you can change it. Since DTS gives you the option of saving your transformation package, you can also reuse it. This is just what you need if you have to periodically update your server (or another destination) from a data source with data that doesn't quite fit.

DTS Packages

When you define a DTS transformation, you are defining a DTS package. A DTS package contains all the information necessary to connect to your source and destination and perform the data transformations.

Once you've defined a DTS package, you can:

- Run the package immediately
- Create a DTS package for replication
- Schedule the package for later execution

If you want to schedule a package for later execution, you will be required to save the package. You may also want to save DTS packages for reuse later.

You also have the option of saving the package to:

- SQL Server
- Microsoft Repository
- Operating system file

Many of your transfers and transformations are going to be one-time operations. For example, you may use DTS for initial database load from various legacy source files. Once you've completed your initial data load, you (hopefully) won't be going back to these files.

Some transfers are going to be periodic transfers. For example, you may be supporting a data warehouse that requires regular updates. You might need to have Excel spreadsheets periodically prepared for distribution to selected users. If there's a chance you might need to reuse a package, you're going to want to save it.

About the DTS Wizard

To say that you are going to use the DTS Wizard for "simple" transfers would be misleading. Yes, it is relatively easy to use, but it also gives you a great deal of power and flexibility.

- You have access to all of the DTS connection types
- You can remap and transform data
- You can transfer objects between servers
- You can save your packages for later use

What if you find out later that a package you saved through the DTS Wizard doesn't quite do what you need. That's easy enough to fix. You've got the DTS Designer.

About the DTS Designer

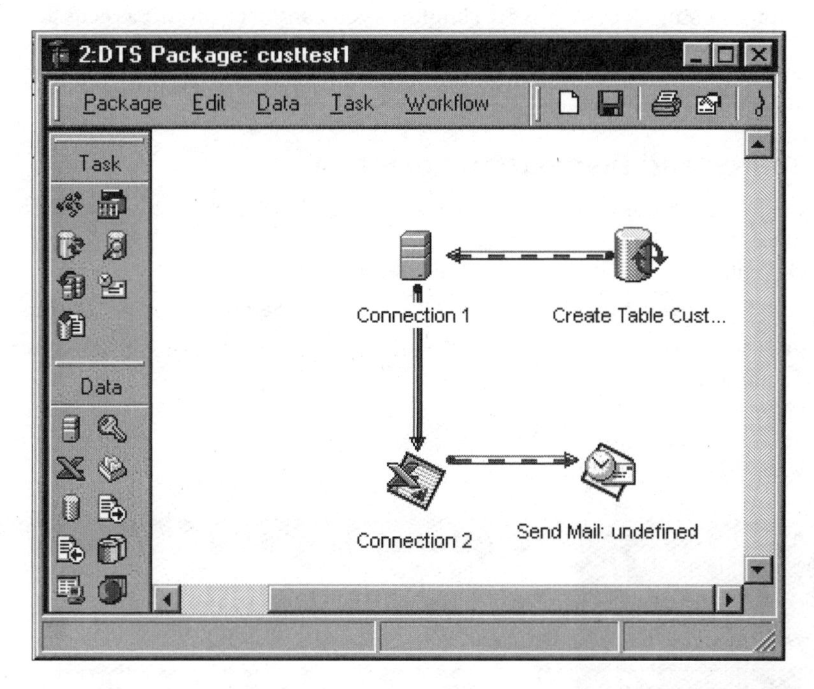

If the DTS Wizard is so powerful, then why do you need the DTS Designer? Because there are things you are going to need to do during a transformation that you simply cannot do with the DTS Wizard. The DTS Designer gives you greater flexibility. It gives you more control over package execution. You can execute tasks, including launching other applications, based on the completion, success, or failure of other tasks.

Power and flexibility comes with a price. DTS Designer can be more difficult to use until you have a little experience designing packages. A good way to start learning to use the DTS Designer is to save packages created through the DTS Wizard, then open the packages under DTS Designer. This gives you some examples that actually work for you to review while you're learning to use the designer. It also provides an excellent starting point for building your own packages by modifying those you've created with the Wizard.

DTS Wizard

You will likely find that the DTS Wizard meets most of your data transfer and transformation requirements. It's especially useful for doing one-time, ad hoc transfers. Its ease of use makes it preferable over the DTS Designer in most situations, especially if you're relatively new to using DTS.

The easiest way to get an idea of what you can do with the DTS Wizard is to walk through its use.

Importing Text Example

This first example is going to be relatively simple so you can focus on the screens and the basic steps for using the DTS wizard. We're going to import an ASCII text file into a SQL Server table. It is going to require a little bit of remapping as we go through, but we're not going to need to do any data transformations.

Launching/Source and Destination Selection

The first step is to launch the wizard. You have several options for launching the DTS Wizard:

- From command line or Run command, run dtswiz
- From the Start menu, Start | Programs | Microsoft SQL Server 7.0 | Import and Export Data
- From Enterprise Manager, run Tools | Wizards, expand Data Transformation Services and run DTS Export Wizard or DTS Import Wizard

All methods take you to the opening Wizard screen. The opening screen gives you a quick overview of DTS and what you can do with the DTS Wizard:

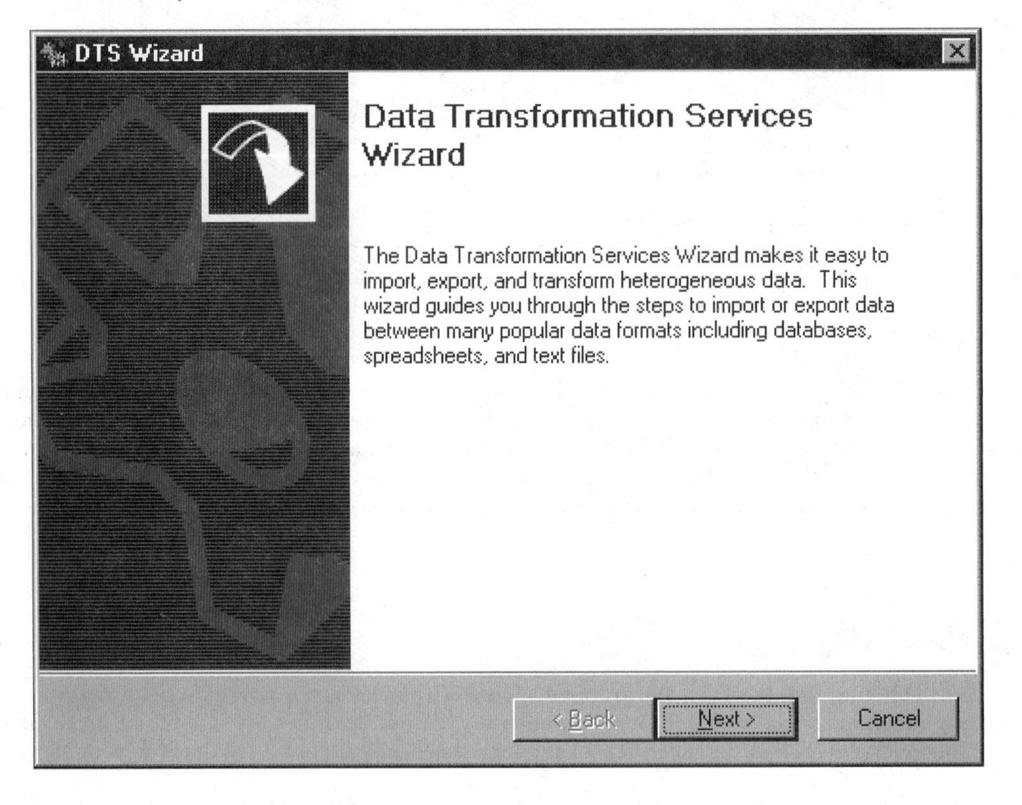

The next screen prompts you for your data source, defaulting to the OLE DB Provider for SQL Server:

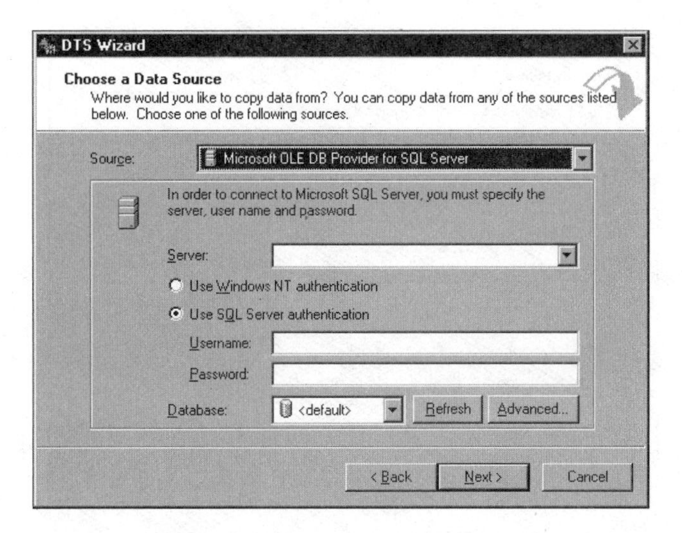

The drop-down list lets you pick from other available sources. Since we're importing an ASCII text file, we'll pick Text File as our source:

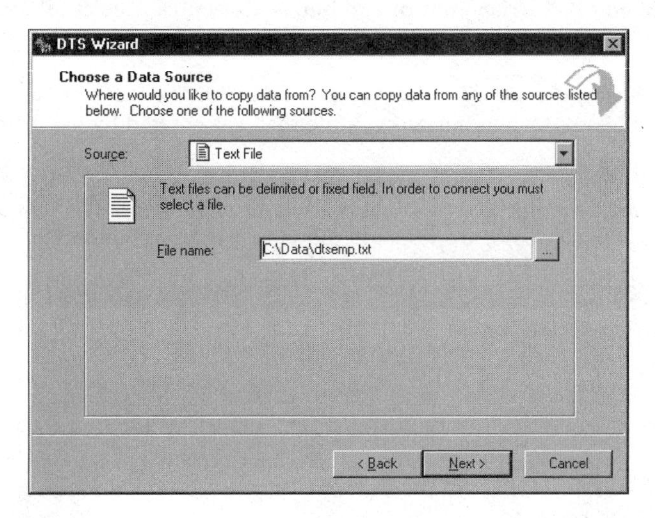

The only thing you need to provide for a text file is the filename and its location. You can type in the path and filename or click on the Browse button to the right to locate the file.

This example uses a sample file named DTSEMP.TXT. In case you want to try for yourself, the file is available from the Wrox web site.

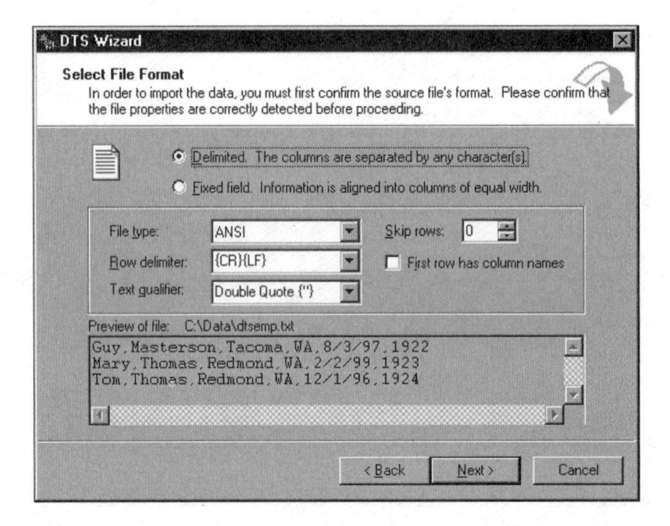

The DTS Wizard needs to know how the text file is formatted for import. The Wizard will open and read the file to try to determine how it is formatted. In this example, we have a delimited file with the row delimiter identified as a carriage return and line feed. You can select to skip rows at the beginning of the file and identify if the first row has the column names.

The file type in this example is ANSI. OEM (native) and Unicode file types are also supported. The OEM file type would be used when importing a file that was created by exporting from bcp in native format.

In this usage, the terms delimiter and terminator are interchangeable. The bcp utility referred to field and row terminators. The DTS Wizard refers to the same values as column and row delimiters.

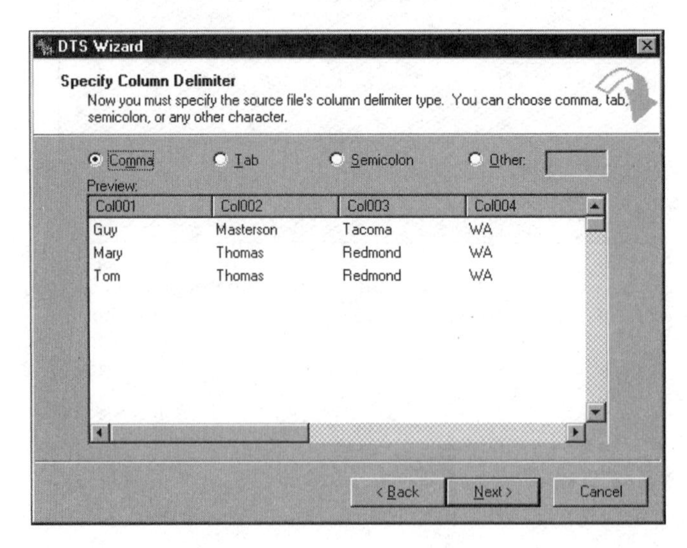

You have to identify, or at least verify, the delimiter (terminator) for delimited files. Once again, the DTS Wizard will attempt to identify the delimiter for you. In this case, we have a comma-delimited file.

And you thought text files were easy, right? The DTS Wizard forces you to pay attention to the details.

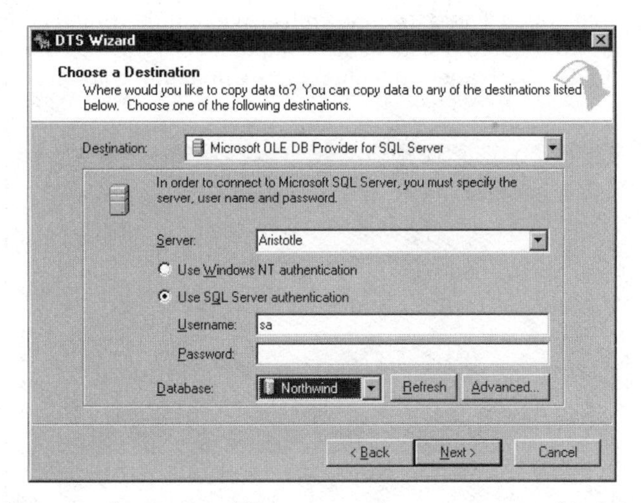

Next, we need to select our destination. This time, we're going to use the default destination type since we're importing data into SQL Server. If you are running the Wizard at the server, you can identify the server as (local). Otherwise, you have to supply the server name. The DTS Wizard supports Windows NT and SQL Server authentication. SQL Server authentication requires you to supply a username and password for login. You will probably find it easier to go ahead and pick your destination database at this point.

The Advanced button lets you set advanced options for the OLE DB Provider for SQL Server. Any driver that supports advanced options, such as connection timeout values, will give you access to the options through an Advanced button.

Mappings and Transformation

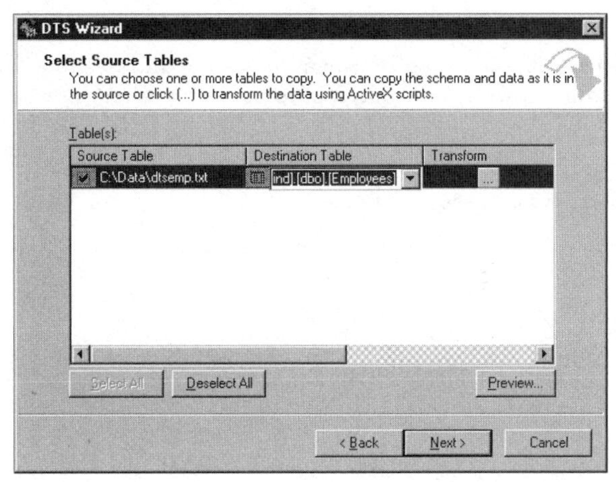

Now you need to select your source and destination tables. A text file is treated as a single source table. Other source types such as Excel, Access, and SQL Server, will have you choose from multiple tables.

Pay close attention to the Destination Table column. The default is to create a new destination table based on the source. If you want to import data into an existing table, you have to select your destination from the Destination Table drop-down list. We're importing data into the `Employees` table. Be careful making your column selections. Column names can be difficult to read in the drop-down list. The button under the Transform column lets you define column mappings and transformations.

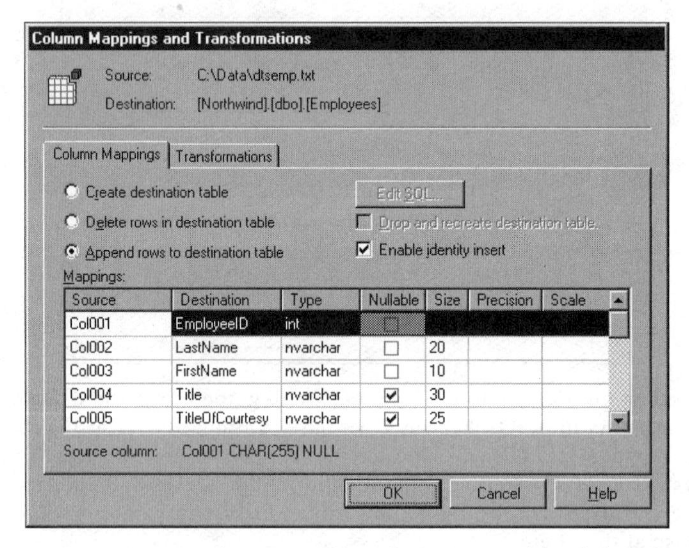

Under column mappings, you can select to create a destination table, delete the existing rows before import, or append the rows to the destination table. We're going with the default, appending the rows. If you choose to create the destination table and the table already exists, you'll have to drop and recreate the destination table.

For tables having an identity column, you can also enable identity insert so that you can import identity values.

The DTS Wizard assumes a direct match between the source and destination columns. Since they don't match up in our column, we need to do a little mapping. First, here's what the source looks like:

```
Guy,Masterson,Tacoma,WA,8/3/97,1922
Mary,Thomas,Redmond,WA,2/2/99,1923
Tom,Thomas,Redmond,WA,12/1/96,1924
```

We have the employee ID, the employee's first name, last name, city, state, and hire date. You remap the columns by clicking on each source column to display a drop-down list, and selecting the correct source for the destination. Here's what the Wizard looks like after our mappings:

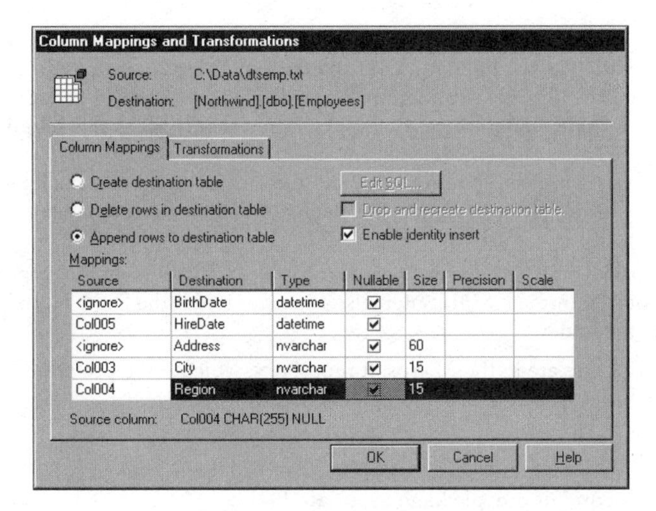

We can see part of the columns in the sample figure. You can see part of the mappings as Col005 to HireDate, Col003 to City and Col004 to Region. We don't need to do any data transformations in this example, so we can continue. Scrolling up, you could see the other mappings, Col006 is mapped to EmployeeID, column Col002 is mapped to the LastName column, and Col001 is mapped to the FirstName column. When you click on OK, you will be returned to the Select Source Tables dialog. You will need to click Next at that dialog to continue.

Finishing the Transfer

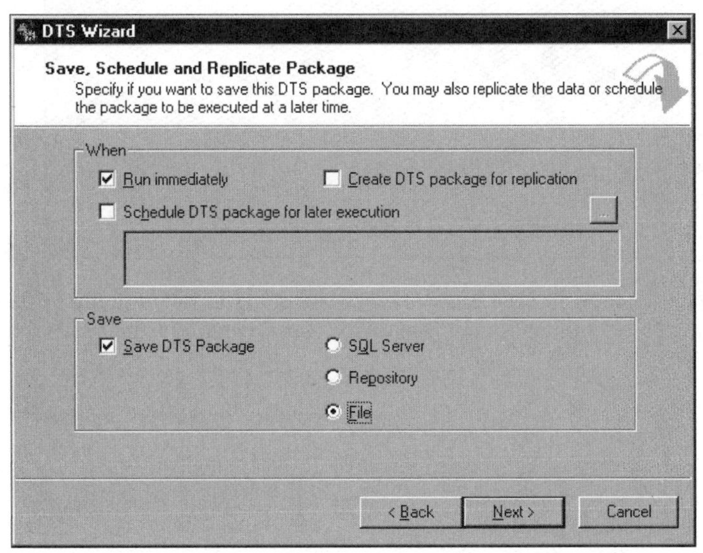

Okay, now that you've got a package, what are you going to do with it? You need to provide information on when to run the package. If you want to save the package, you also have to provide information on how to save the package.

The default is to run the package immediately. You can also create a DTS package for replication to other servers or schedule the package for later execution. Selecting to create a DTS package for replication will launch the Create Publication Wizard. If you choose to schedule for later execution, you can choose to run the package once, or have it run periodically on a schedule you set.

By default, the package is not saved. You have the option of saving the package. If you schedule the package for later execution, you must save the package. When saving packages:

- SQL Server packages are stored as binary large objects (BLOBs) in the `sysdtspackages` table and can be viewed through SQL Enterprise Manager under the Data Transformation Services Local Packages folder
- Repository packages are in the Microsoft repository, which is the preferred method in data warehousing support since it provides data lineage for packages
- File storage lets you set the file as a COM-structured data file

We're going to save a copy of our package as a data file:

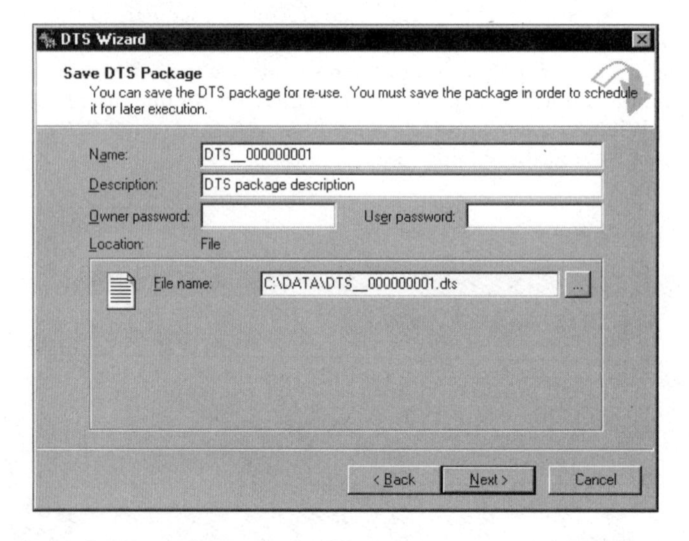

The default filename is shown in the example. We are going to save the file to `C:\DATA`, using the default filename. A copy of this package is available for download from the Wrox web site as `DTS_000000001.dts`.

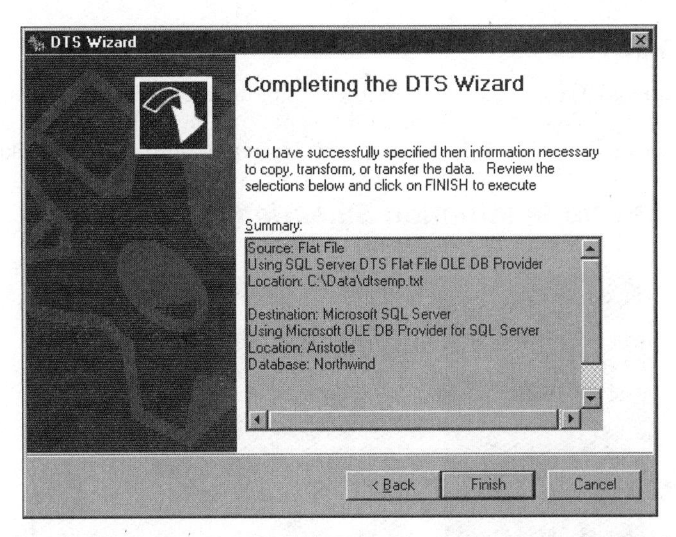

Now we're ready to complete the transfer. The Wizard gives you a summary of the transfer information you entered as a review:

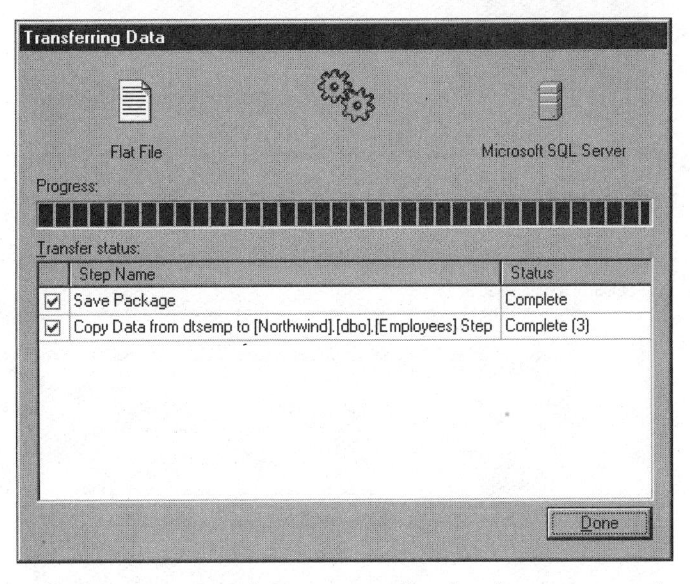

The DTS Wizard will advise you as each step is completed and prompt you after the transfer. If any errors occur, you can double-click on the step generating the error for a detailed error message.

Importing from Excel

Let's go ahead and look at a second example, importing data from Excel. This time, we're going to need to specify some simple data transformations as part of the process. Many of the screens are exactly the same, so we'll be able to go through this example a little more quickly.

Launching/Source and Destination Selection

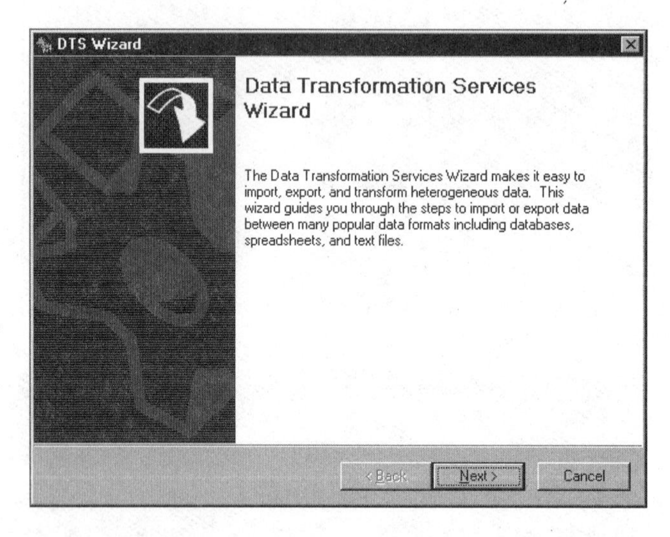

Once again, we start with the opening screen.

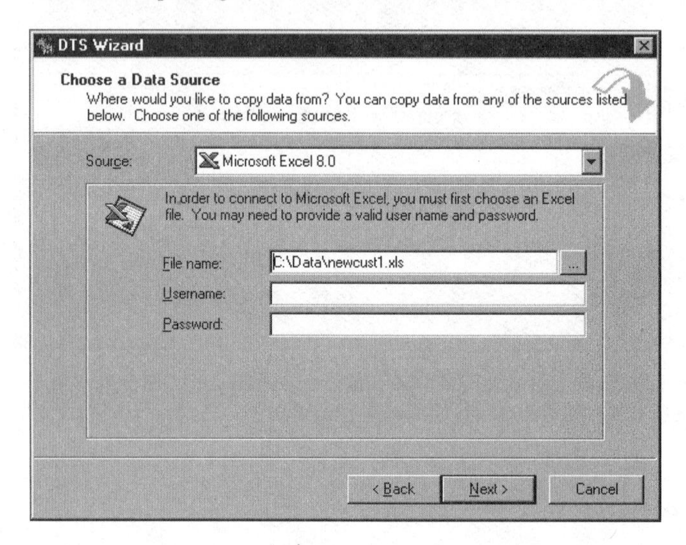

This time, we're selecting a Microsoft Excel document as the source. You have to provide the file name and, if necessary to access the file, a user name and password. We're importing data from a spreadsheet named `newcust1.xls`. The source file used in this example may be downloaded from the Wrox web site.

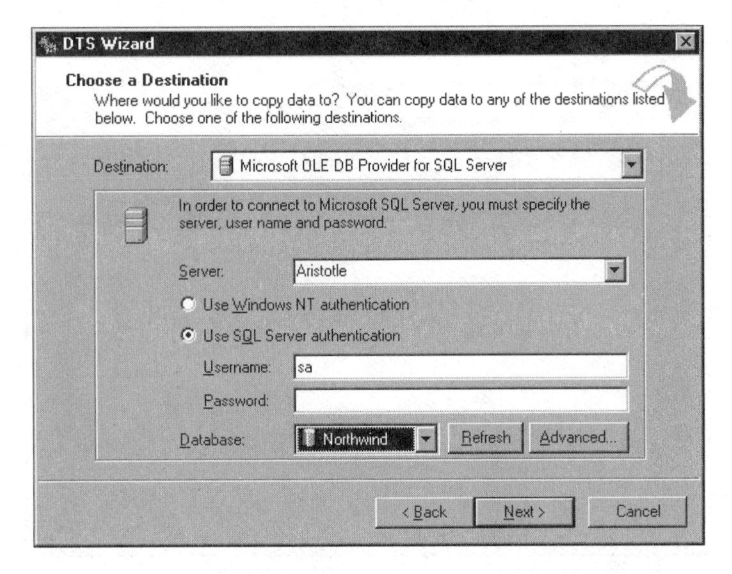

We're picking the `Northwind` database on Aristotle as our destination again.

Mappings and Transformation

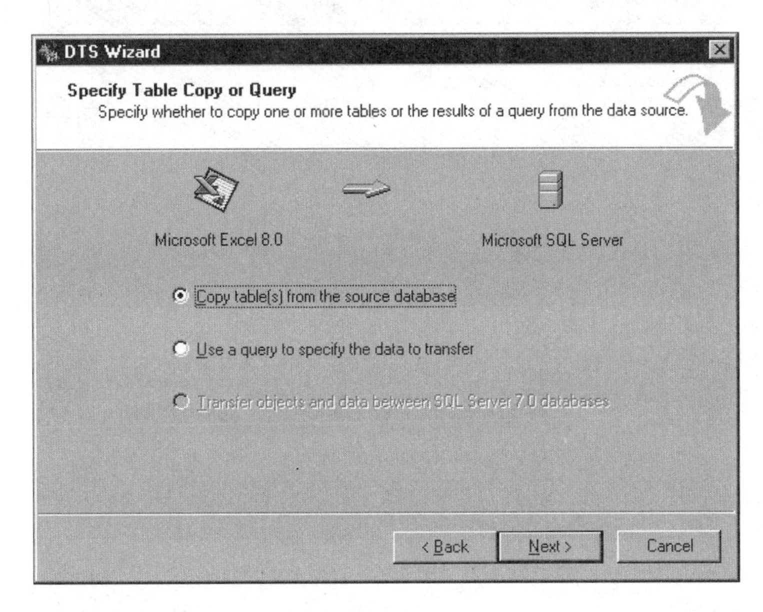

This time we see a new prompt, selecting whether we want to copy data directly from tables or use a query to specify the data to be copied. If we chose to build a query, we'd be taken to the Query Builder. Since we want all of the data from the spreadsheet, we'll choose to copy the table.

You can use a carefully designed query to perform some of your mappings (by changing column order) and simple transformations for you. However, you will often find it easier to script transformations and will be required to script more involved transformations.

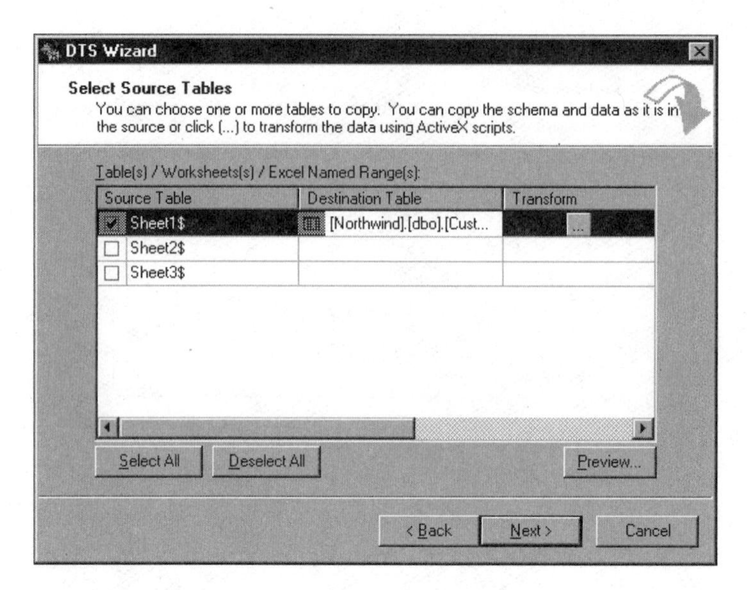

We are going to be transferring data from the first worksheet only. The default is to create a new table, but we'll be using the `Customers` table as our destination. The Transform button lets us complete our mappings and data transformation.

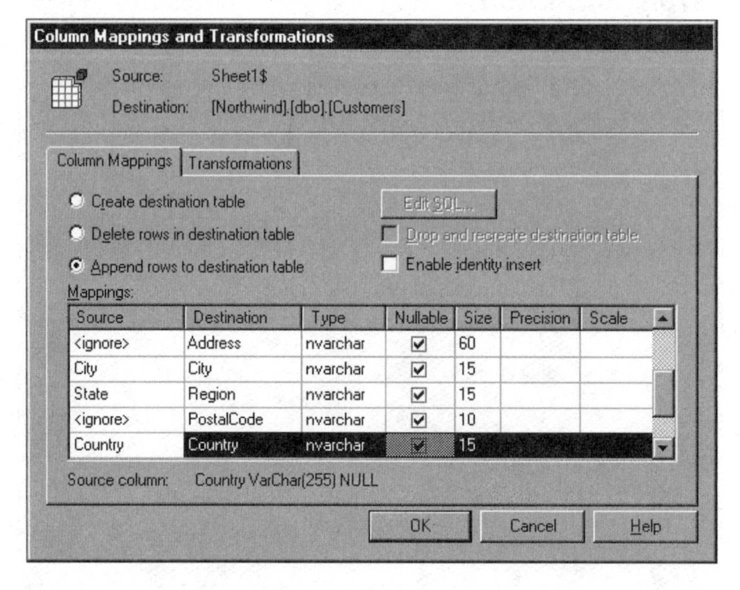

Just like in the earlier example, a one-to-one match is assumed. We've already remapped the column in the example figure. Now, on to data transformation:

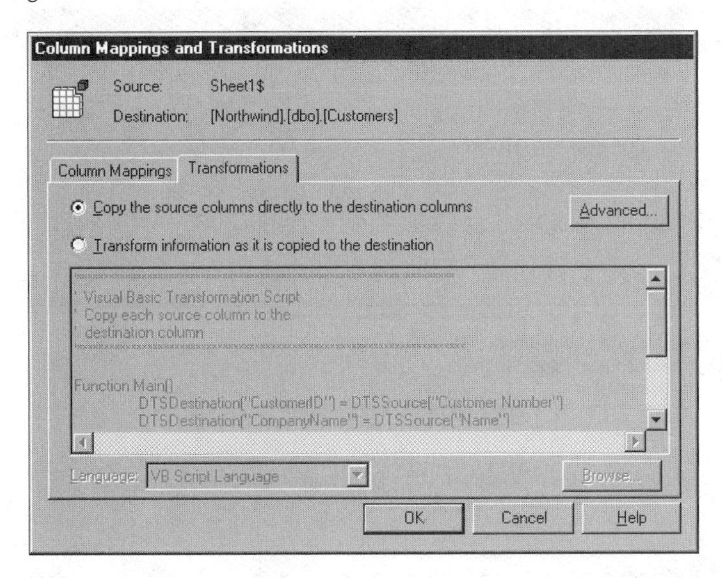

The default is to copy the source columns directly into the destination columns. The other option is to edit the transformation script to transform data as it is copied. The Advanced button lets you define the transformation flags:

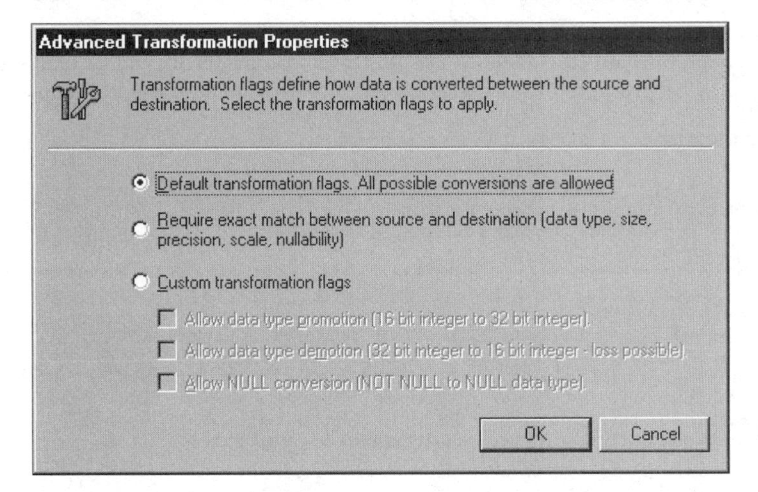

You can use default transformation flags, which will allow all possible conversions. You can require an exact match between the source and destination. You can also set custom flags for:

- Allow data type promotion from 16-bit to 32-bit integer
- Allow data demotion from 32-bit to 16-bit integer, which may result in loss of precision
- Allow `NULL` conversion from `NOT NULL` data type to `NULL` data type

We're going to leave the transformation flags at default.

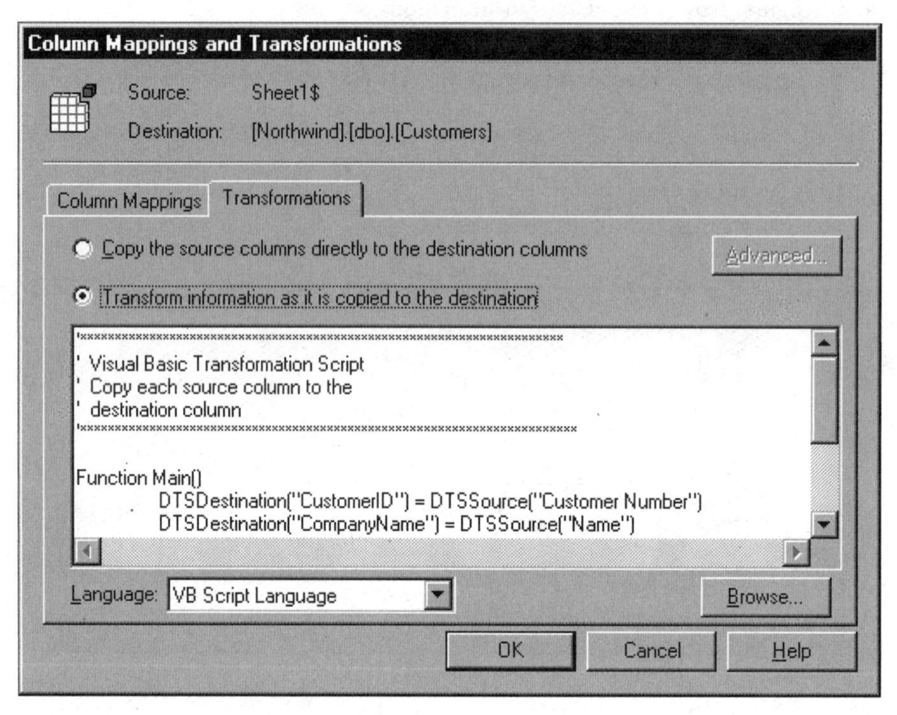

When you select to transfer information you are able to edit the transformation script. By default, the script is in VBScript, but you can select to use JScript if you prefer. If you've changed column mappings, you may be prompted to let DTS Wizard create a default script.

Here's our default script:

```
'**********************************************************************
'  Visual Basic Transformation Script
'  Copy each source column to the
'  destination column
'************************************************************************

Function Main()
     DTSDestination("CustomerID") = DTSSource("Customer Number")
     DTSDestination("CompanyName") = DTSSource("Name")
     DTSDestination("ContactName") = DTSSource("Contact Name")
     DTSDestination("City") = DTSSource("City")
     DTSDestination("Region") = DTSSource("State")
     DTSDestination("Country") = DTSSource("Country")
     Main = DTSTransformStat_OK
End Function
```

The `State` and `Country` columns in our source are in lowercase characters. We want them converted to uppercase before transfer, so we need to make a couple of minor modifications to the script:

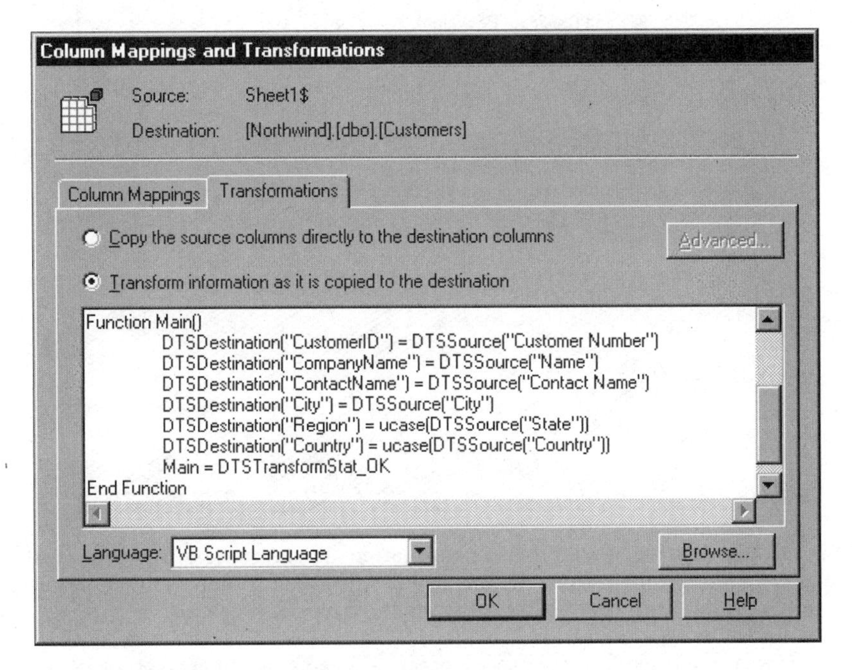

Here are the full contents of the modified script:

```
'**********************************************************************
'  Visual Basic Transformation Script
'  Copy each source column to the
'  destination column
'************************************************************************

Function Main()
     DTSDestination("CustomerID") = DTSSource("Customer Number")
     DTSDestination("CompanyName") = DTSSource("Name")
     DTSDestination("ContactName") = DTSSource("Contact Name")
     DTSDestination("City") = DTSSource("City")
     DTSDestination("Region") = ucase(DTSSource("State"))
     DTSDestination("Country") = ucase(DTSSource("Country"))
     Main = DTSTransformStat_OK
End Function
```

Finishing the Transfer

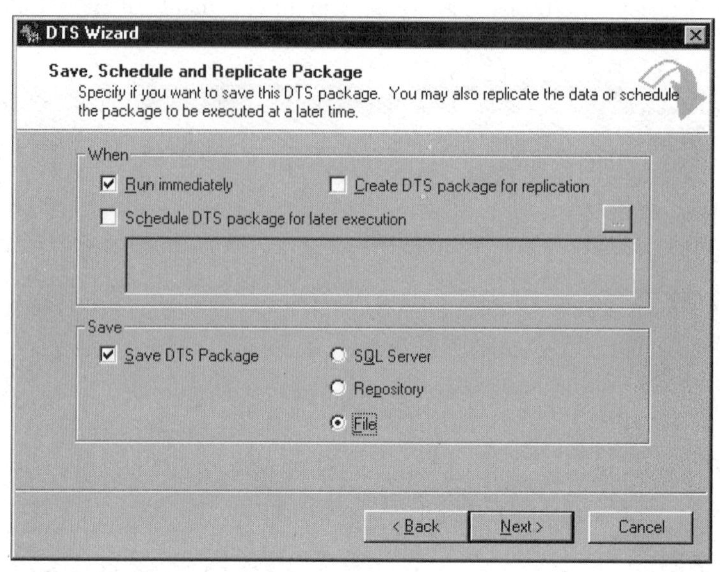

Now you need to decide when to run the transformation. We're going to run the transfer immediately. We're also going to save the package to `C:\DATA`. A copy of this import package may be downloaded from the Wrox web site as `NEWCUST1.DTS`.

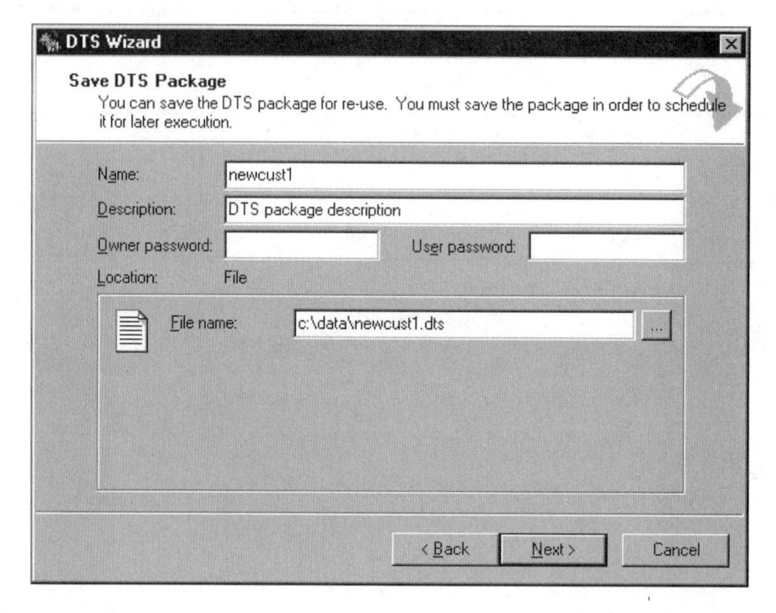

Unlike the last example, this time we're providing a filename for the package, `NEWCUST1.DTS`.

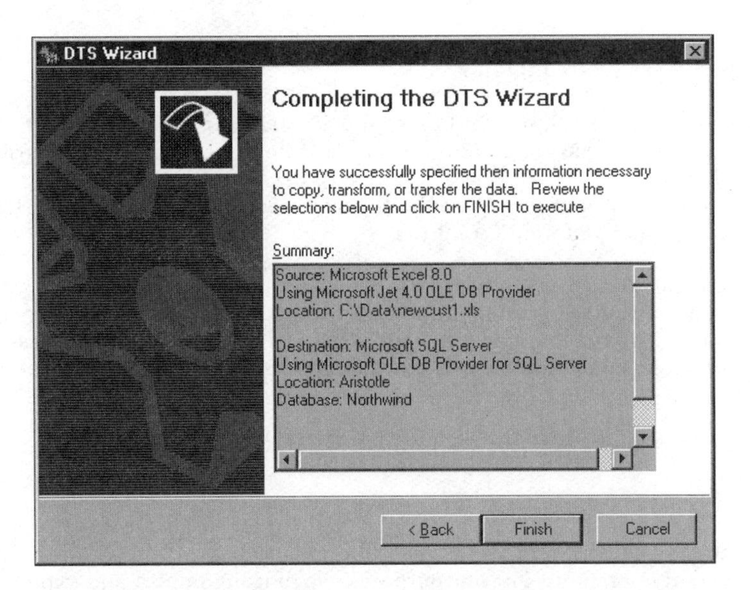

Be sure to review the summary before completing the transformation.

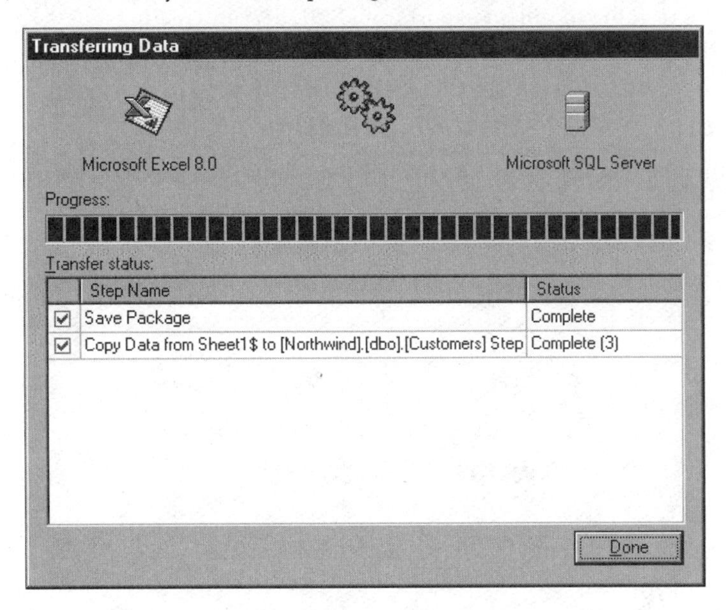

Once again, there are two steps in the transformation. The package is saved to disk, then data is transferred from the Excel spreadsheet to the destination table.

> **Let me guess what you're thinking.**
>
> **These are nice examples, but aren't they kind of "made up"? Sure, I might have to load a spreadsheet as part of an initial load, but I don't need to save the package.**
>
> **Well, you're right. You probably wouldn't need to save this package, but let me give you an example that you would want to save.**
>
> **You've got a normalized database that supports a transaction processing system. You need a denormalized version of the data for analysis purposes that's updated on a weekly basis. How are you going to do it? Create a DTS package that creates a new version of the analysis table and schedule it to run every week.**

Data Export

You may have already guessed that the terms "import" and "export" aren't always an accurate way to describe DTS Wizard operations. For our purposes, we're using import and export in reference to SQL Server. Keep in mind that you don't necessarily have to have SQL Server as either your source or destination. We're going to run an export from SQL Server, creating a new Excel spreadsheet based on the `Northwind` database `Employees` table.

Launching/Source and Destination Selection

Continue past the opening screen to select your data source and destination.

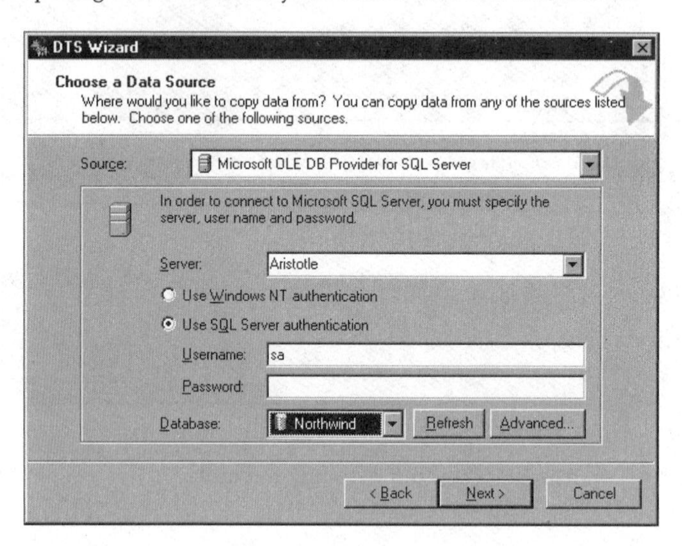

This time, we're using SQL Server as our source. The prompts are the same as when we specified a SQL Server destination.

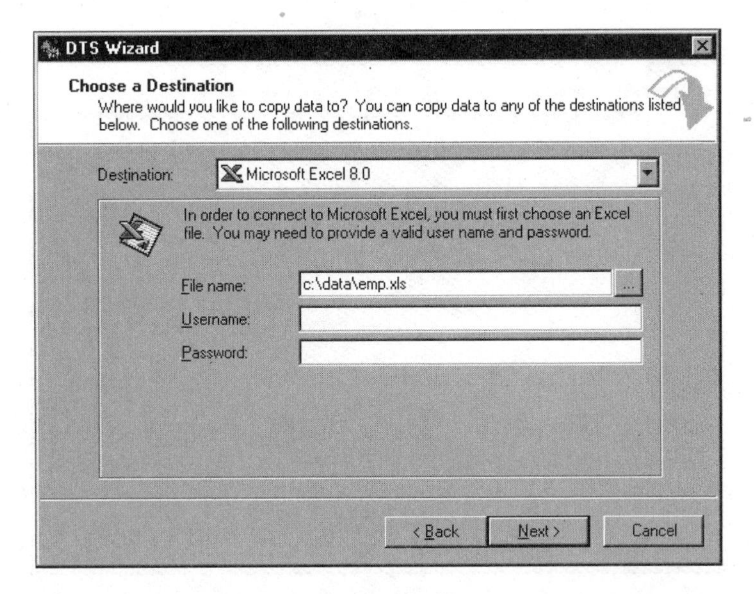

Next, we are specifying Excel 8.0 as our destination. We're providing a filename that doesn't already exist.

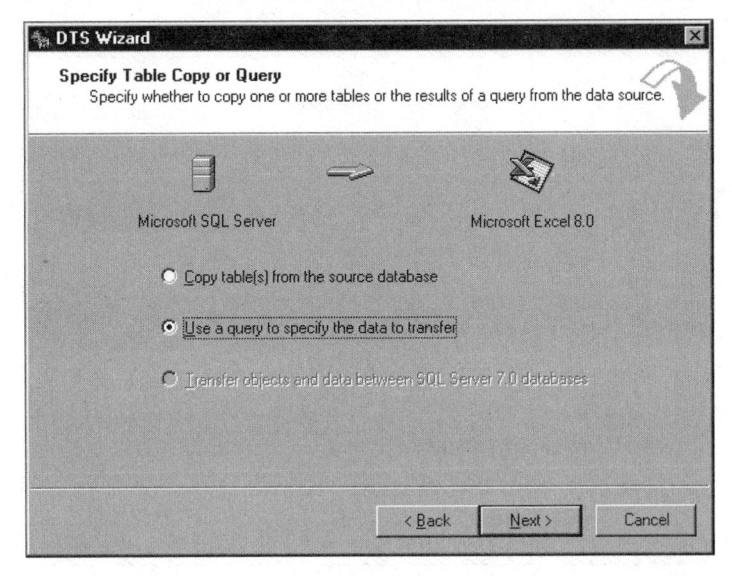

We only want a few columns out of the `Employees` table, so we're going to use a query to specify the data to transfer.

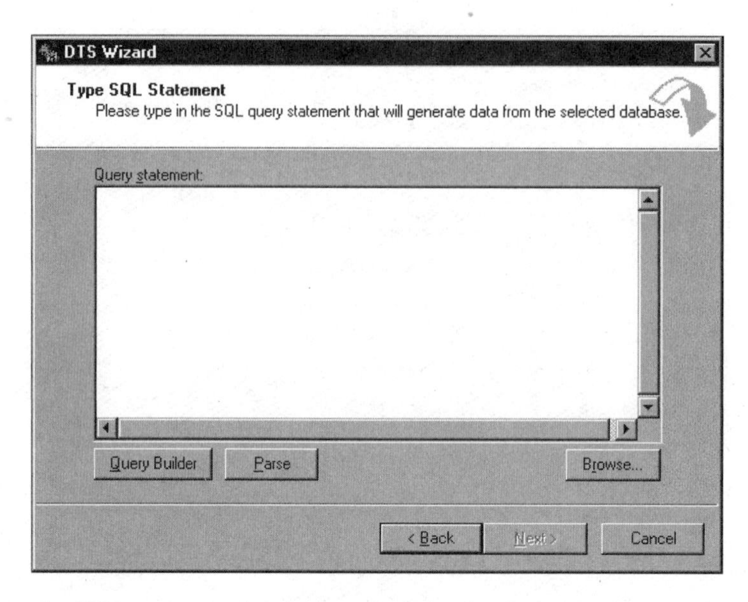

You can type in the SQL statement for the query or use the Query Builder. We're going to use the Query Builder so that DTS can prompt us with valid column names.

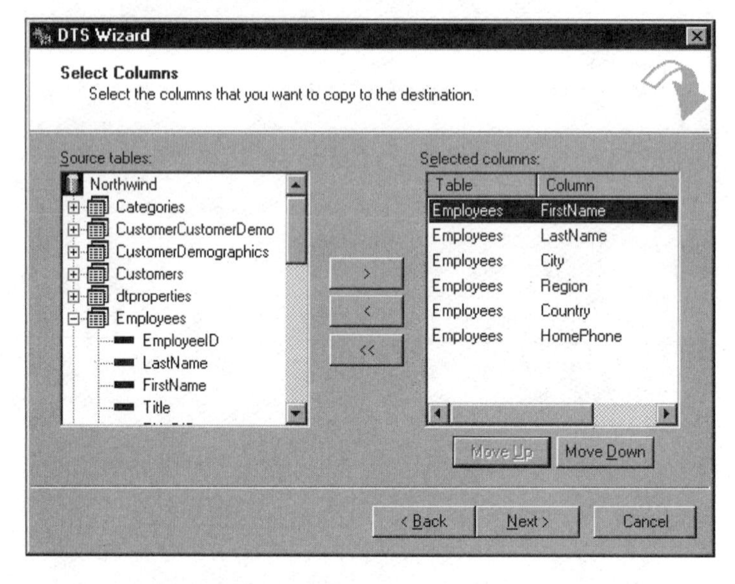

The query builder lets you select the columns you want to copy. You can select columns in any order, which can help you reduce the need for remapping later.

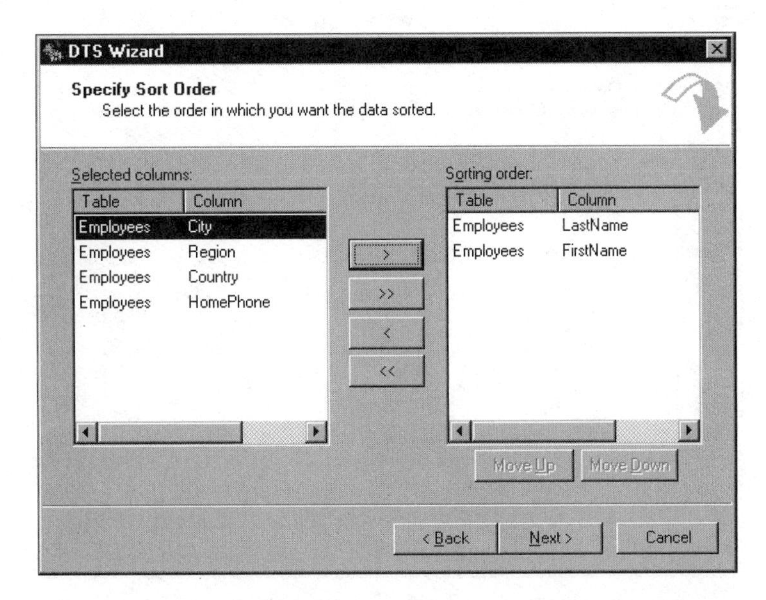

You also get to select your sort order for the data. We're sorting by last and first name.

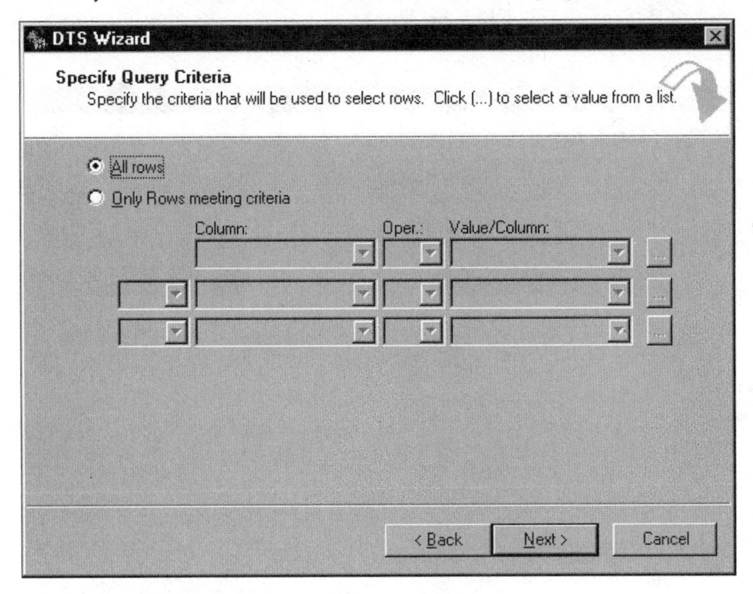

You can set selection criteria, defining the `WHERE` clause for your SQL statement. We're going to accept all rows as qualifying.

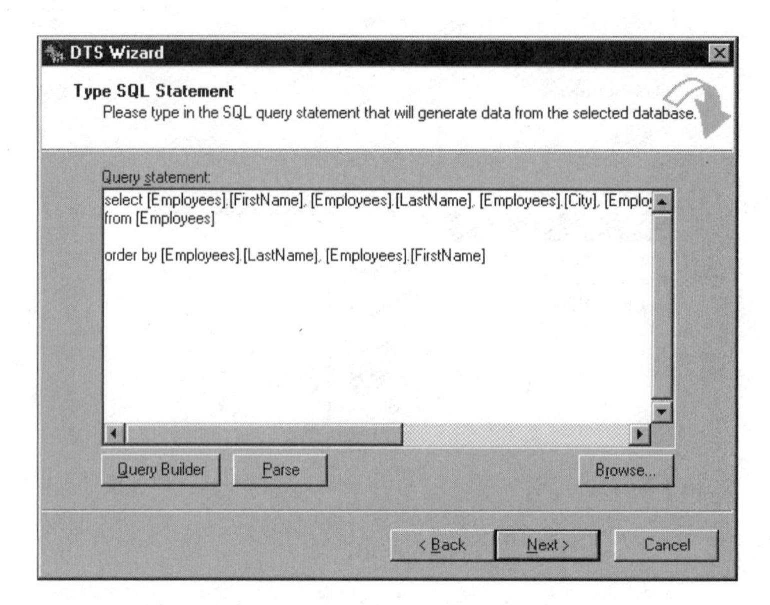

This will take you back to the SQL Statement dialog. If you want, you can make further changes by directly editing the SQL Statement. Click on Parse to parse the statement and check for syntax errors.

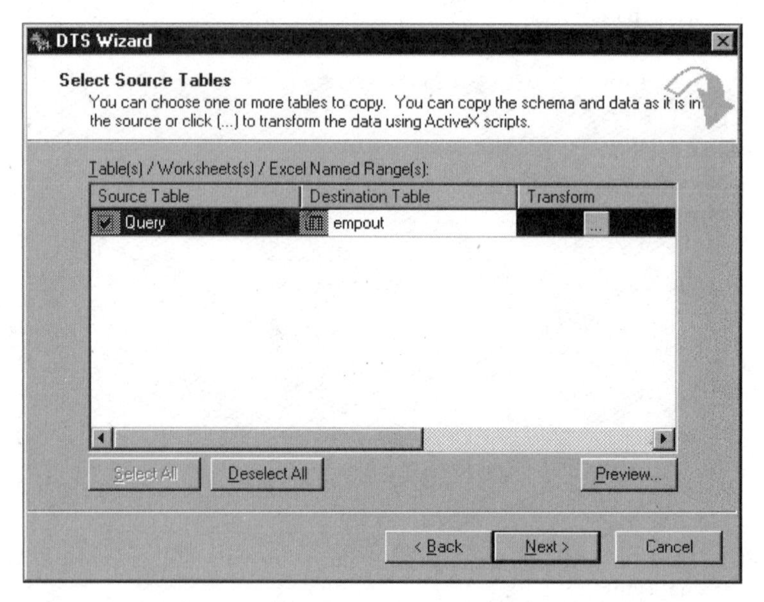

We're going to use the default this time and create a new destination. We are, however, overwriting the default table name. We're also going to take a quick look at column mappings and transformations.

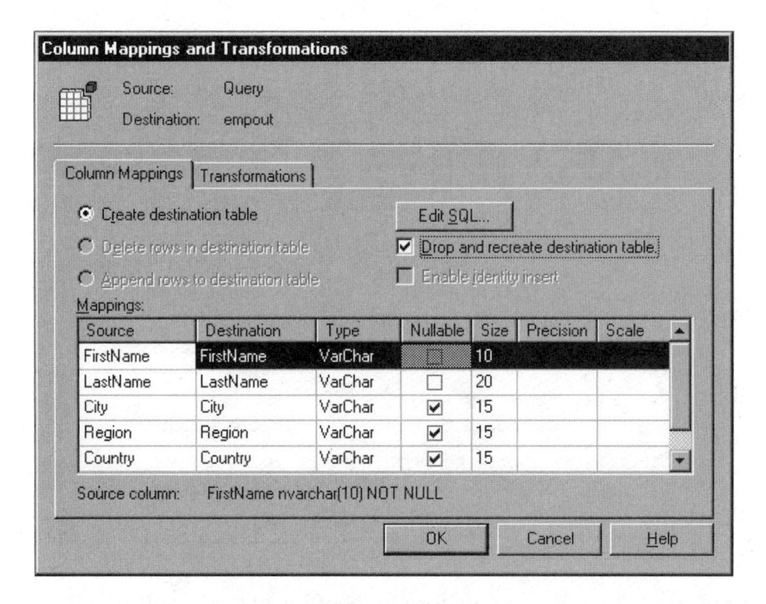

This time, we have the option of editing the SQL statement being used to create the destination. Even though this will be the first time we've run the transformation, we plan to use this on a periodic basis. We've chosen to drop and recreate the destination so that it can be recreated each time the package runs.

Completing the Transfer

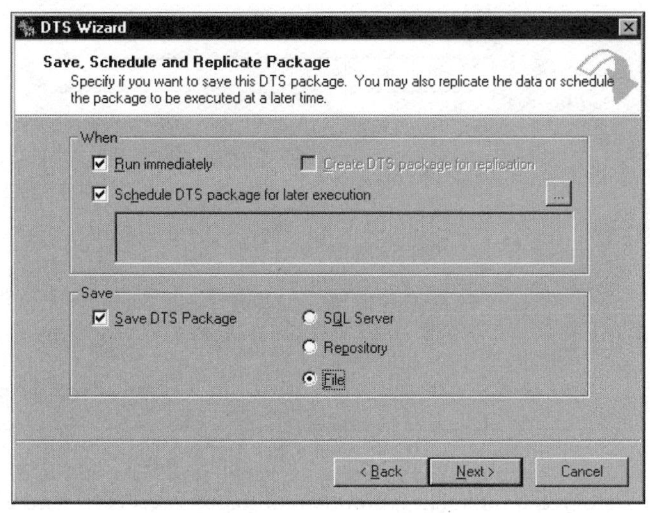

This time, we're going to both run the package immediately and schedule for later execution. We're going to save the package as a file named `EMPSUM.DTS`.

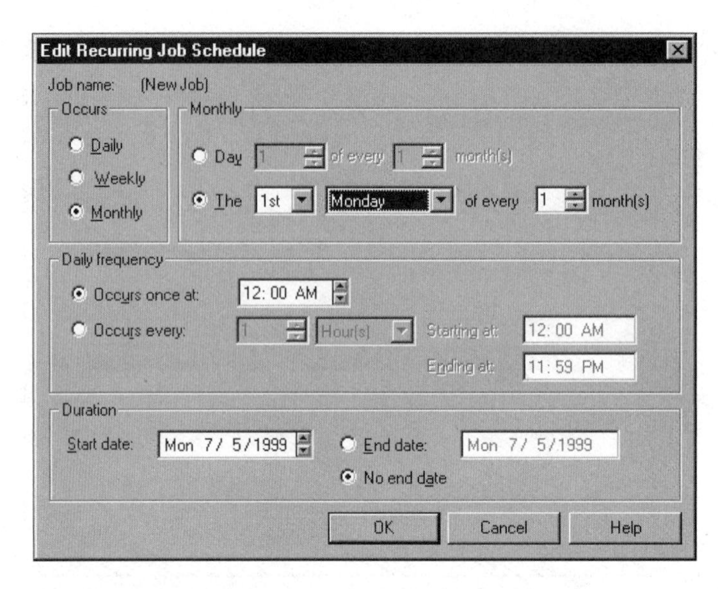

We have to edit the recurring job schedule to set when this package will run. We're going to have the package run monthly, on the first Monday of every month. Since we're not sure for how long we need to keep generating this summary, we won't set an end date.

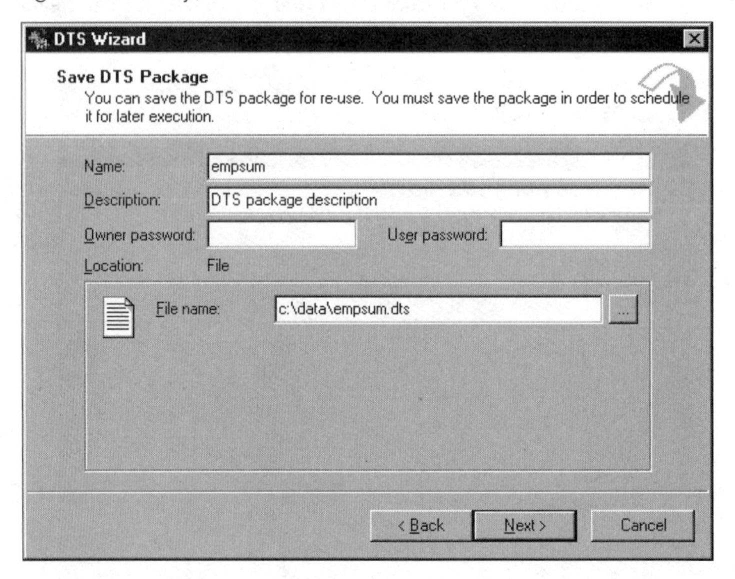

We also need to provide a filename for saving the package and a destination directory. You will receive a warning if the SQLServerAgent is stopped on the target server. You will need to make sure that the agent is running for scheduled execution. The package will still be able to execute immediately even if the agent isn't running.

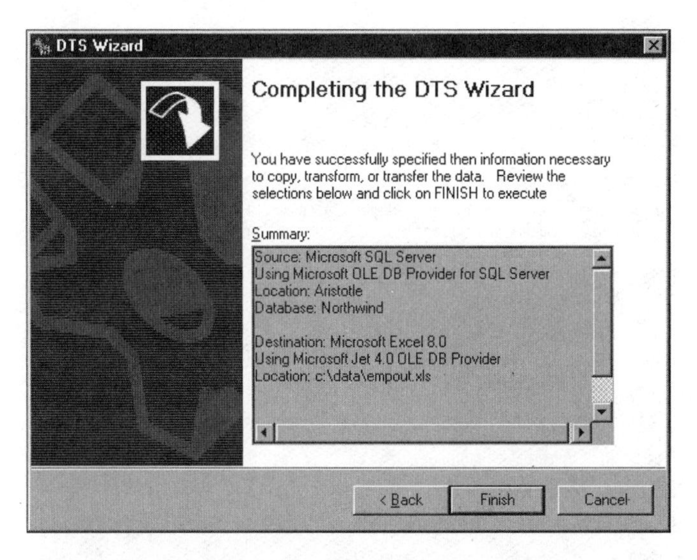

We're ready to review the summary and complete the transformation.

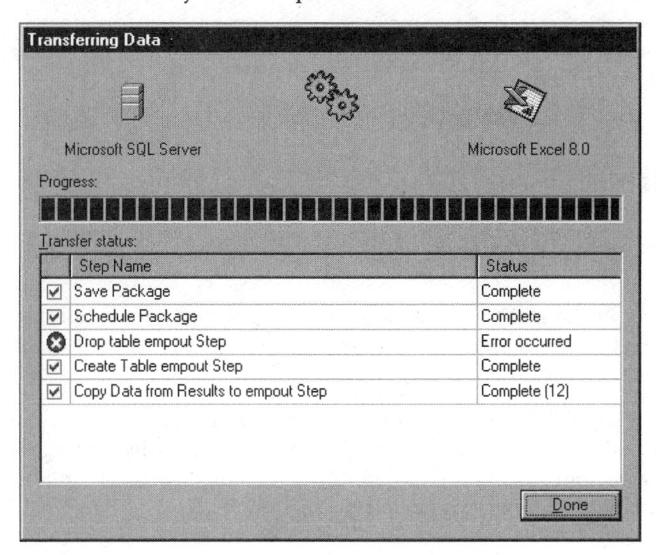

This time, there are five steps involved. DTS Wizard has to:

- Save the package
- Schedule the package
- Drop the existing table
- Create the new table
- Copy data into the new table

As you can see, we got an error on the create table step. This is a valid error. Since this is the first time we've run the transformation, the table doesn't exist. The next time it runs, the package should run without any errors.

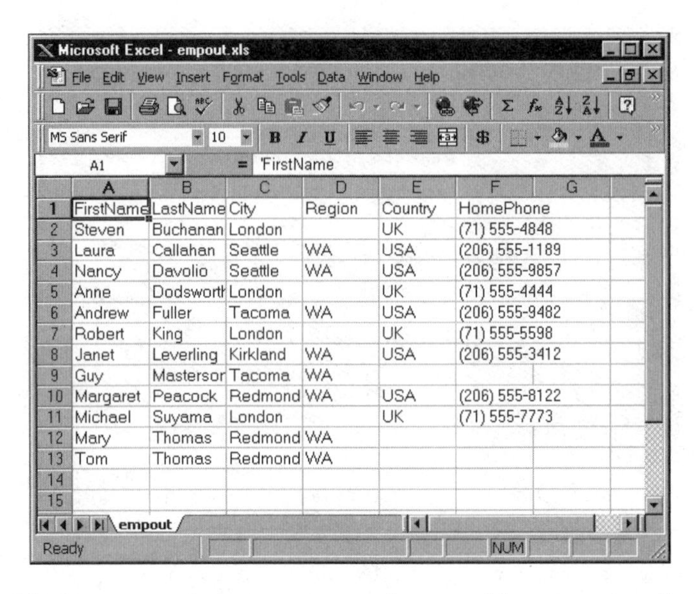

	A	B	C	D	E	F	G
1	FirstName	LastName	City	Region	Country	HomePhone	
2	Steven	Buchanan	London		UK	(71) 555-4848	
3	Laura	Callahan	Seattle	WA	USA	(206) 555-1189	
4	Nancy	Davolio	Seattle	WA	USA	(206) 555-9857	
5	Anne	Dodsworth	London		UK	(71) 555-4444	
6	Andrew	Fuller	Tacoma	WA	USA	(206) 555-9482	
7	Robert	King	London		UK	(71) 555-5598	
8	Janet	Leverling	Kirkland	WA	USA	(206) 555-3412	
9	Guy	Masterson	Tacoma	WA			
10	Margaret	Peacock	Redmond	WA	USA	(206) 555-8122	
11	Michael	Suyama	London		UK	(71) 555-7773	
12	Mary	Thomas	Redmond	WA			
13	Tom	Thomas	Redmond	WA			

Here's the spreadsheet we created. As you can see, the spreadsheet contains all of our query columns. The sample export package and spreadsheet from this example, EMPOUT.XLS and EMPSUM.DTS, are available for download from the Wrox web site.

DTS Designer

Okay, now it's time. You know it was going to happen sooner or later. We're ready to talk about the DTS Designer.

DTS Designer gives you the ability to handle more complicated data validation and transformation. Not only can you use DTS Designer to create new packages, you can edit existing packages, including packages created and saved through DTS Wizard.

Before we take a look at DTS Designer, you need to realize that this is a very powerful utility, but it is also more complex than the DTS Wizard. DTS Designer could easily be the subject of a book this size all by itself. For our purposes, we're going to have to limit ourselves to a quick overview giving you some of the highlights and basic procedures.

The basic steps for working with DTS Designer are:

- Creating or opening a package
- Editing the package
- Saving the package
- Executing the package or scheduling execution
- Deleting the package

We'll be looking at these steps, but we ought to begin with a few concepts and a look at DTS Designer components.

Designer Concepts and Components

A DTS package typically consists of connections, data transformations, tasks, and precedence constraints:

- A **connection** is a connection to any OLE DB data source. You can specify multiple connections as part of your package.
- **Data transformations** refers to the movement of data between source and destination connections. Even if there is a one-to-one relationship between the source and destination, the transfer is still referred to as a data transformation.
- **Tasks** are operations to be performed by the DTS package. Tasks can be linked by precedence constraints.
- **Precedence constraints** provide the order between tasks.

Precedence constraints are defined as:

- On Success, which means task 1 must run successfully before task 2 can execute
- On Failure, which means task 1 must fail before task 2 can execute
- On Completion, which means task 2 will run as soon as task 1 is completed, whether it succeeds or fails

Now, let's take a quick look at the DTS Designer interface :

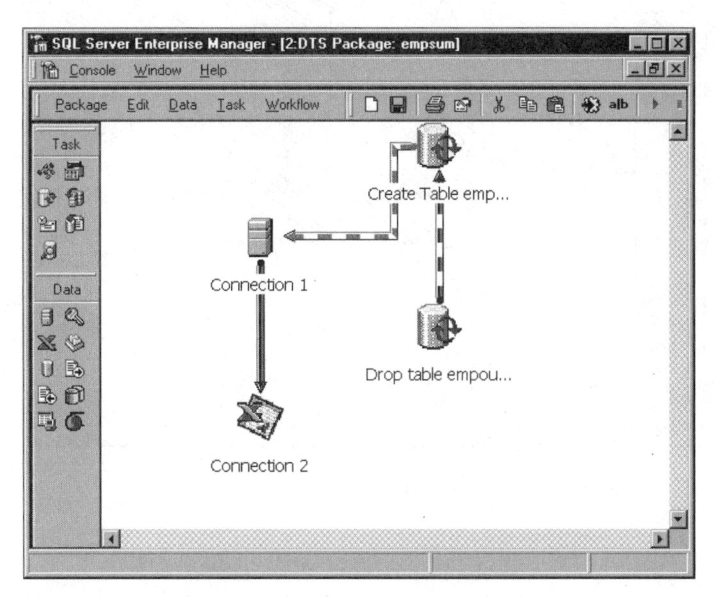

The example above shows an open package. The Task icons let you select from available tasks. The Data icons are used to select data connections. Tasks and data connections can also be selected from menu commands. There are also package commands to save, print, or execute the package and workflow commands for managing precedence constraints.

Working with Packages

The first step is to open a package or create a new package. You can open an existing Local or Repository package by double-clicking on the package or by selecting the package and running Action | Design Package. To open a package stored as a file, you select the Data Transformation Services folder and run Action | All Tasks | Open Package. This will open a dialog through which you can choose a package.

To create a new package, select the Data Transformation Services folder (or one of its subfolders) and run Action | New Package, or right-click and run New Package from the pop-up menu.

The easiest way to see the steps is to work with a package, so let's use the export package we created earlier.

Opening Packages

Since the package was saved as a COM file, we run Action | All Tasks | Open Package to open the package. This will open the package in the Design window.

Editing Packages

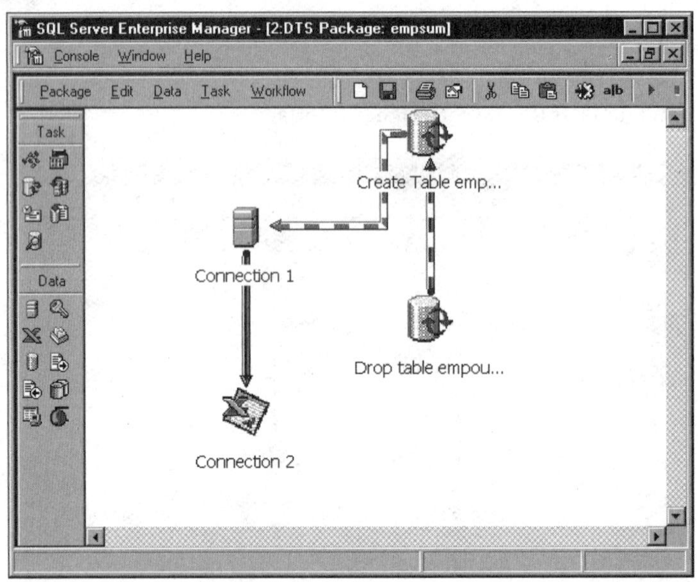

Once the package is open, you can edit the package by adding or modifying connections, tasks, and precedence constraints. In our example, we have two tasks and two connections. The first task is to drop the `Empout.xls` table. Next is the step to create the new `Empout.xls` table. The precedence between these is to create the new table on completion of dropping the old table. Here are the properties for the workflow between these two tasks:

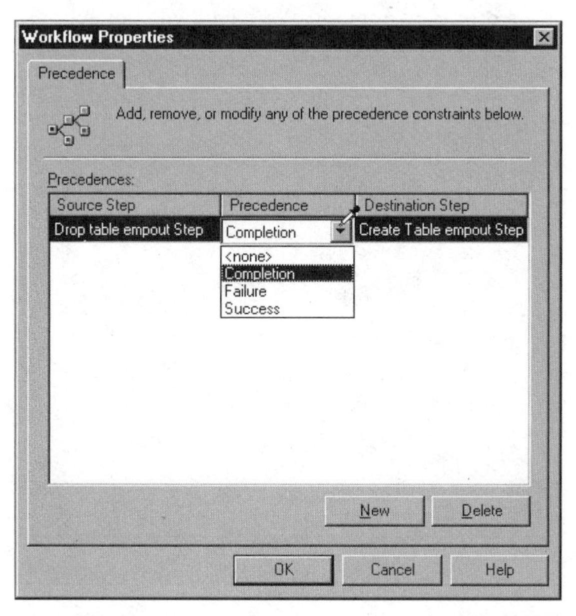

We can use the Precedence drop-down to change this from on Completion to on Success, requiring that the old table be dropped before the new table can be created.

You can tell the precedence between two tasks in the design window by color. On completion is blue, on success is green, and on failure is red.

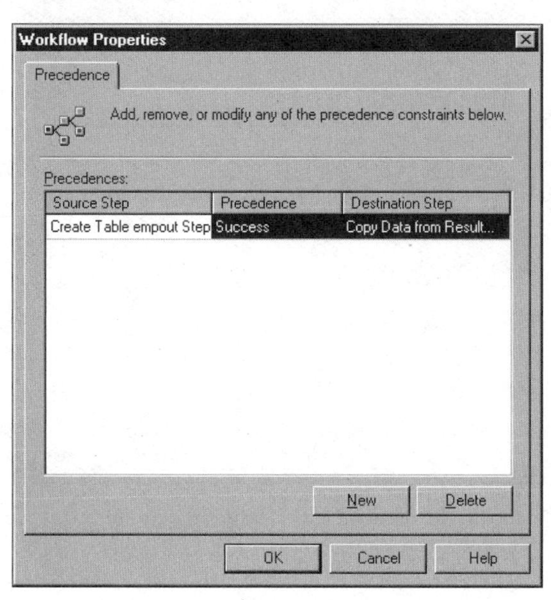

The precedence between the new table and the first connection is already set as on Success. It controls the Destination Step of copying data from the result set and will only run if the table is created.

You can get information about either connection by double-clicking on its icon or right-clicking and running Properties from the drop-down menu. We have two connections.

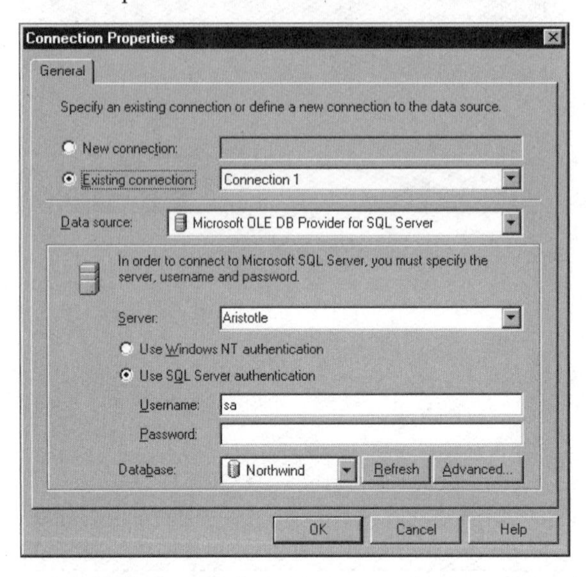

The first connection is to our SQL Server. As you can see, the connection information was taken from the information we entered in the DTS Wizard.

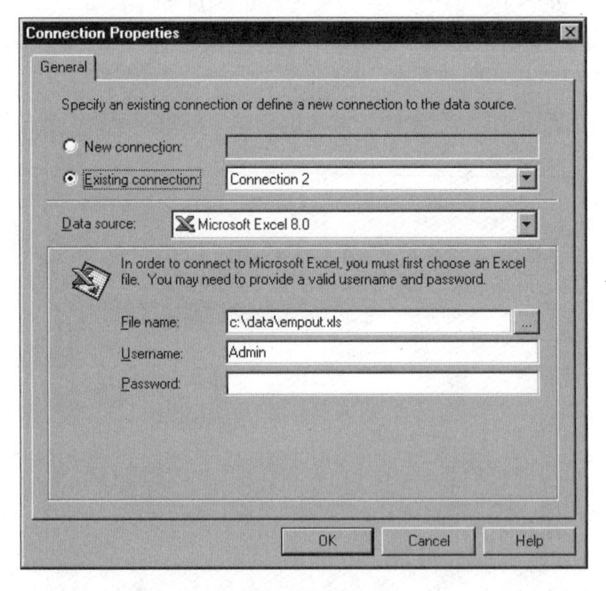

The second connection is to the destination Excel file. Once again, this was generated for us by the Wizard.

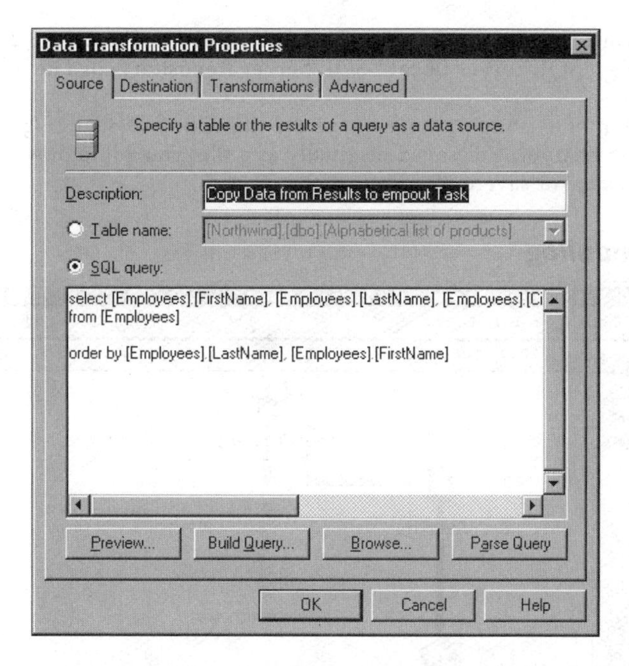

Between the two connections is our data transformation, using a SQL query to copy data from the source table to the Excel spreadsheet. The Destination tab describes the destination table, the Transformations tab describes any transformations that must be performed as well as source to destination mappings, and the Advanced tab sets options for error handling and data movement. We'll be looking at these in more detail a little later.

Saving a Package

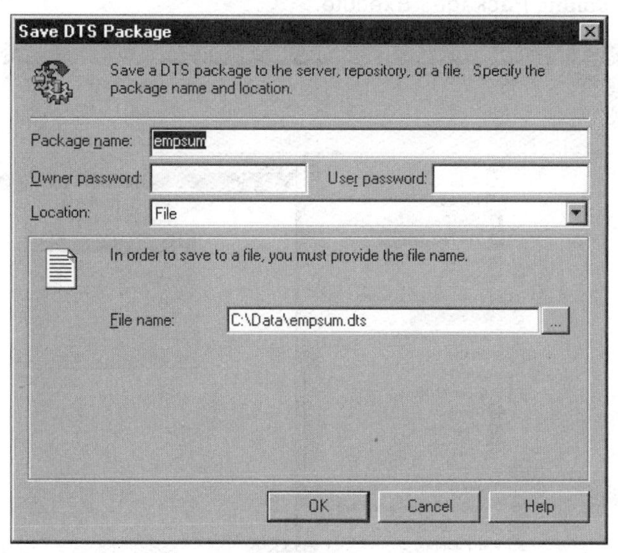

Once you've made your changes you can run Package | Save or Package | Save As to save your changes. You can select SQL Server (local), SQL Server Repository, or File as the destination.

If you run Save as for an existing package, you have the option of changing the location. For example, even though empsum was saved originally as a file, you could now save the package as a local SQL Server package or save to the Repository.

Executing or Scheduling

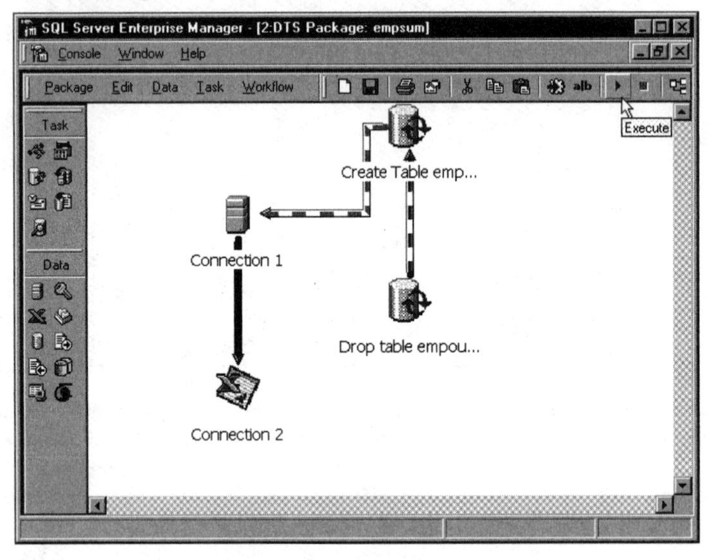

You can immediately execute an open package by clicking on the Execute button (the green arrow) in the toolbar or by running Package | Execute.

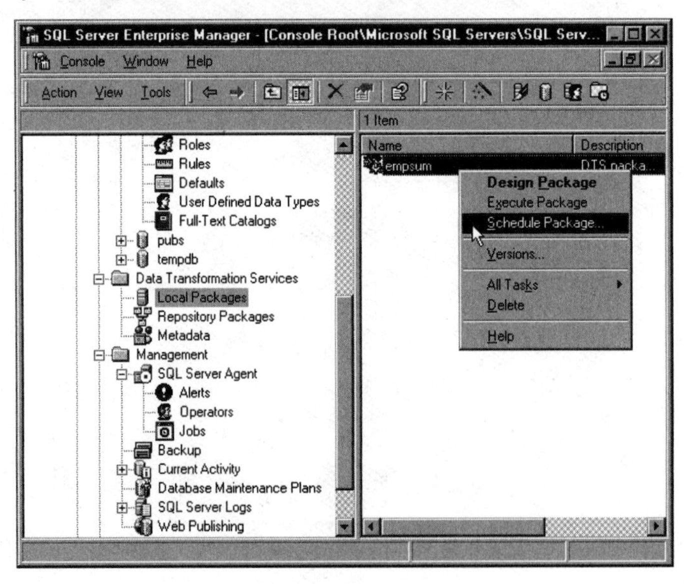

After storing a package on SQL Server or in the Repository, you can use Enterprise Manager to schedule the package. Select the package and run Action | Schedule Package or right-click on the package and run Schedule Package. The Edit Recurring Job Schedule dialog is the same as we saw earlier.

Using DTSRUN

You also have the option of using the DTSRUN utility to execute a DTS package. DTSRUN lets you execute a package from a command line or inside of a batch. The general syntax for the command is:

dtsrun [/? | /[~]S *server_name* /[~]U *username* /[~]P *password* | /E
| /[~]F *filename* /[~]R *repository_database* /.[~]N *package_name* [/M[~] *package_password*]
| [/[~] *package_string*] | [/[~]V *package_version_string*] [/!X] [/!D] [/!Y] [/!C]]

Unless your option switches specify otherwise, the package will run immediately when DTSRUN executes. Let's take a look at the option switches you have available:

Parameter	Description
/?	You can use ? to display a list of available option switches.
~	A tilde specifies that the next parameter is a hexadecimal value used to represent the encrypted value of the parameter. This increases security by encrypting server name, user name, and so forth.
/S *server_name*	This specifies the server to which you want to connect.
/U *username*	When using SQL Server Authentication, you must supply a username as the server login ID.
/P *password*	This is the password required for *username* login and validation.
/E	The /E option specifies a trusted connection. If you use /E, you don't need to supply a login ID.
/N *package_name*	This is the name assigned to the packages when it was created.
/M *package_password*	If there is a password associated with the package, use this option to specify the password.
/G *package_string*	This is a globally unique identifier (GUID) package ID assigned to the package when it was created.
/V *package_version_string*	This is a GUID version ID that was assigned to the package the first time it was saved or executed.

Table Continued on Following Page

Parameter	Description
/F *filename*	This is the path and filename of the package you want to execute. It allows you to execute DTS packages stored as COM-structured data files. If a *server_name* is also specified, then the contents of the file will be overwritten with the package retrieved from the server. You can specify the path as a drive ID and directory path and filename or UNC path and filename. In most cases, it is considered more reliable, especially when using DTSRUN in a batch or stored command string, to use a UNC path and filename. This avoids the potential problem of changes in shared drive IDs.
/R *repository_database*	You can use this option to specify the name of the repository database that contains DTS packages. If not specified, the default is assumed.
/!X	With this option, you can retrieve a package from the server and use it to overwrite the contents of *filename* without executing the package.
/!D	Use this option to delete DTS packages from the Local Packages or Repository Packages folders. You cannot use DTSRUN to delete a COM-structured data file. You can, however, use the `/F` and `/S` options to overwrite the file.
/!Y	This is used to display the encrypted command used to execute the package, but without executing the package.
/!C	The DTSRUN command is copied to the Windows clipboard. This option can be used with the `/!X` and `/!Y` options.

If you ran the package from the previous example, you would get results similar to the following:

```
C:\>dtsrun /S aristotle /N empsum /U sa /P
DTSRun:  Loading...
DTSRun:  Executing...
DTSRun OnStart:  Drop table empout Step
DTSRun OnFinish:  Drop table empout Step
DTSRun OnStart:  Create Table empout Step
DTSRun OnFinish:  Create Table empout Step
DTSRun OnStart:  Copy Data from Results to empout Step
DTSRun OnProgress:  Copy Data from Results to empout Step; 12 Rows have been tra
nsformed or copied.; PercentComplete = 0; ProgressCount = 12
DTSRun OnFinish:  Copy Data from Results to empout Step
DTSRun:  Package execution complete.
```

Deleting a Package

To delete a package from the Local Packages or Repository Packages folders, select the package and run Action | Delete or right-click on the package and run Delete from the pop-up menu.

You will be prompted to verify your action before the package is deleted.

You can also use DTSRUN with the /!D option to delete packages from the Local Packages and Repository Packages folders. COM-structured files can be deleted through the operating system.

Creating a Package

Feeling brave? Ready to take the plunge? Good! Let's create a new package. We start by selecting the Data Transformation Services folder and running Action | New Package.

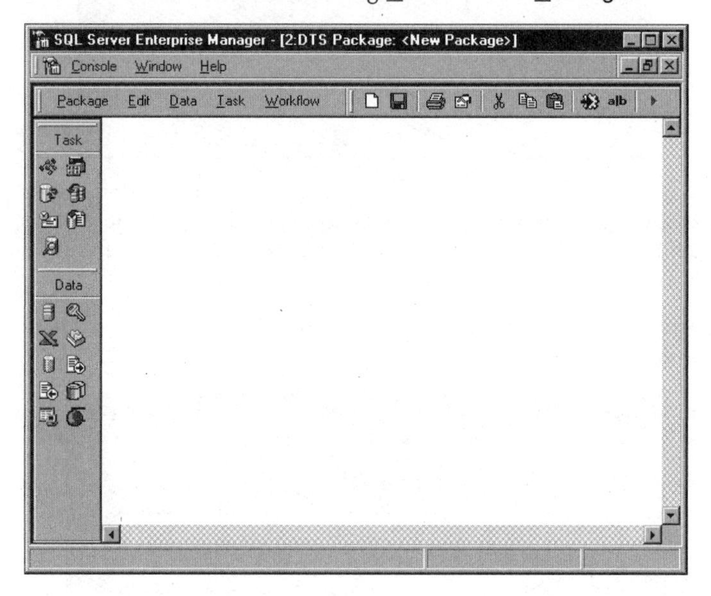

We need to define our connections. We're going to copy from an Excel spreadsheet to a SQL Server table. We'll run Data | 3 Microsoft Excel 8.0 to create our first connection. Optionally, we could select the connection from the Data icons.

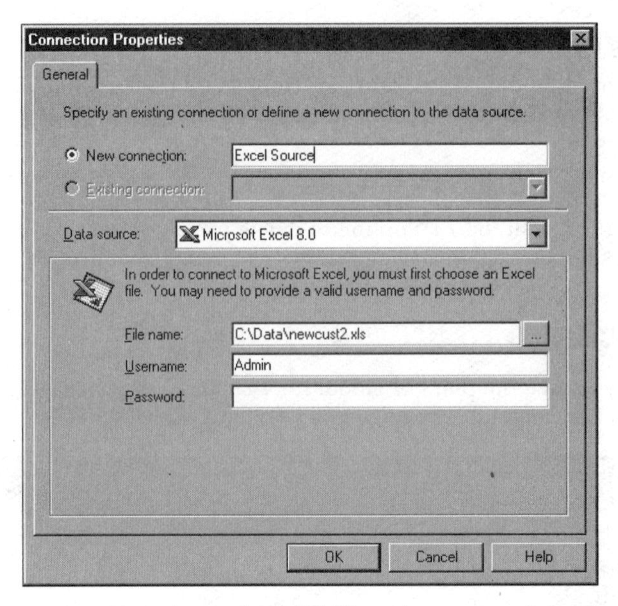

The connection prompt is very similar to the DTS Wizard source and destination prompts. The only real difference is that we need to name the connection. The default name is Microsoft Excel 8.0, but we'll call ours Excel Source. We're going to use the file `NEWCUST2.XLS` as the source file. `NEWCUST2.XLS` is available for download from the Wrox web site.

We also need a destination. We can select the connection from the Data icons or from the Data menu to create a SQL Server connection.

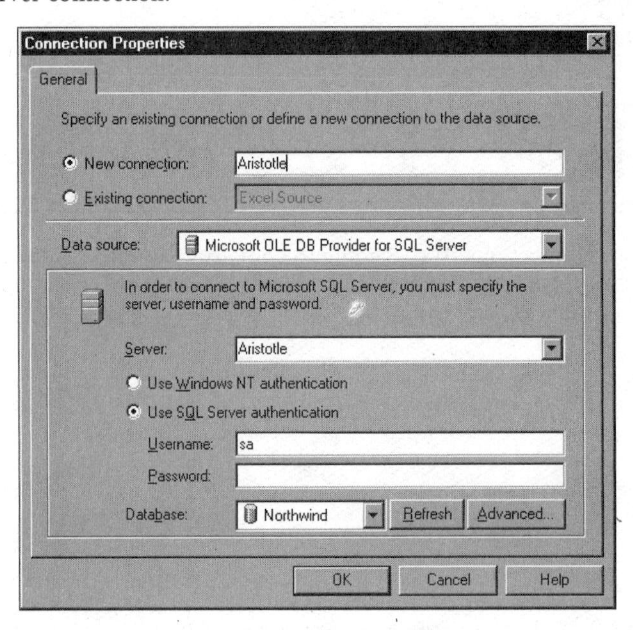

Once again, the prompts are similar to those we saw for DTS Wizard. We're going to name the connection Aristotle and select Northwind as our database.

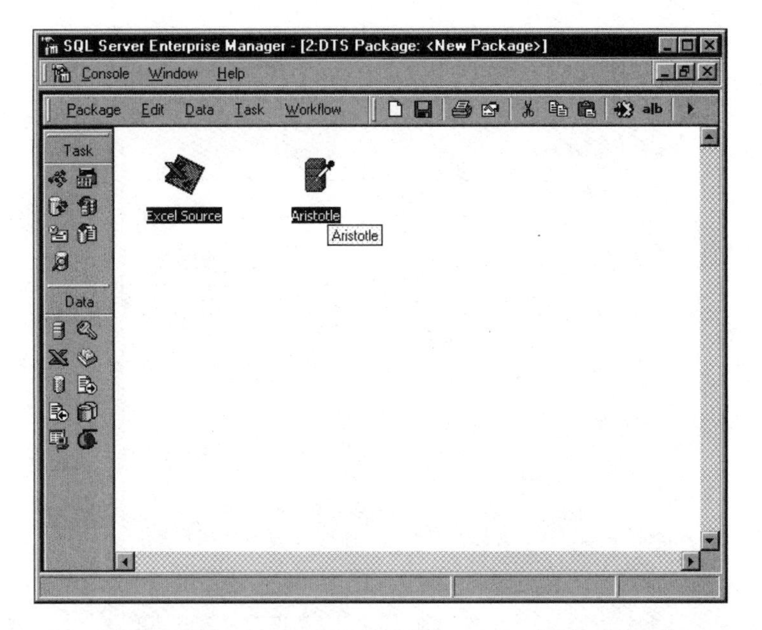

Now we're ready to add our transformation. Select the source (Excel Source) first, then press *Shift* while clicking to select Aristotle.

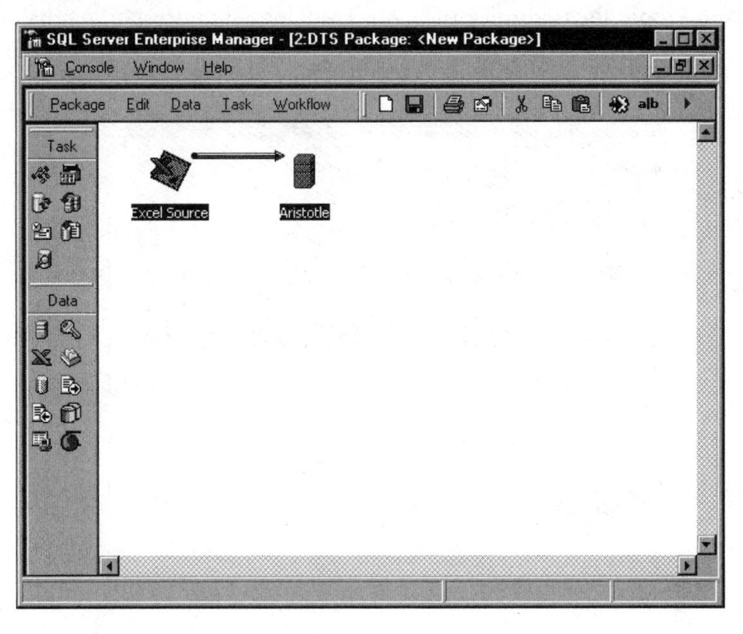

Run Add Transform from the Workflow menu. This will add a Data Pump (Data Transformation) task to the package.

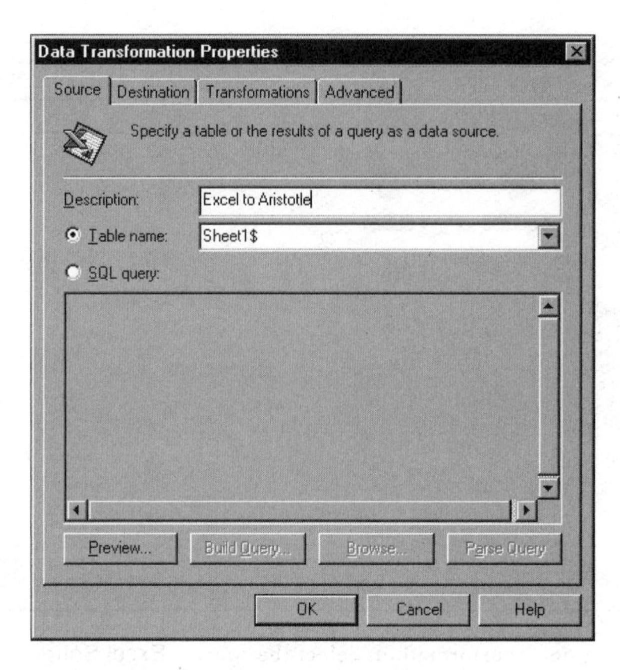

We still need to define the transformation. Select the transformation and run Package | Properties or right-click and run Properties to display the Data Transformation Properties dialog.

We're going to name the transformation Excel to Aristotle and select Sheet1$ as the source.

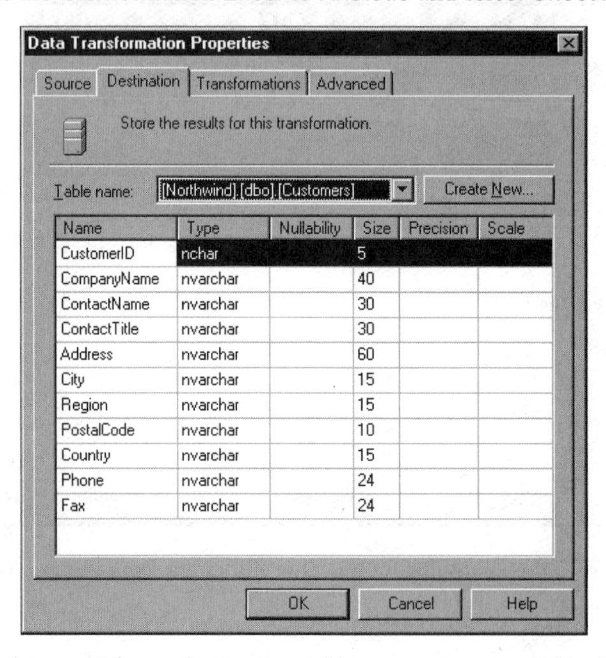

The Destination tab lets us pick our destination table or create a new table. We're going to pick `Customers` as our destination.

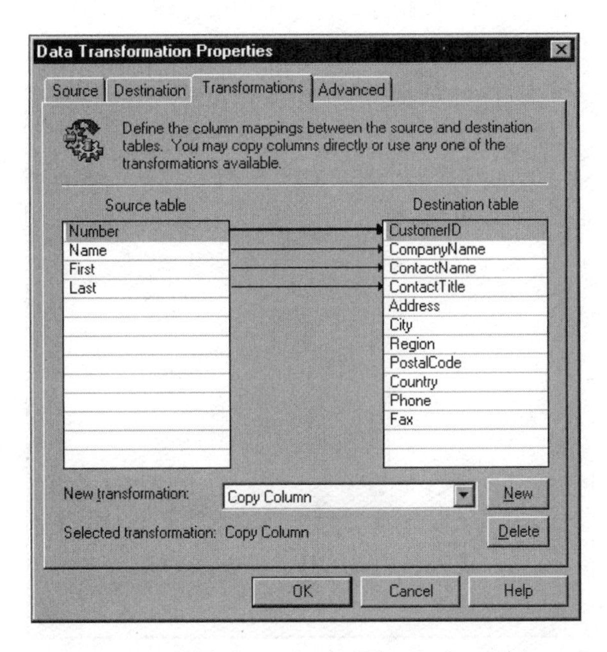

The default transformation is a simple column copy. We need to make a data transformation, however, to combine the `First` and `Last` name Excel columns into one for loading into the `ContactName` column.

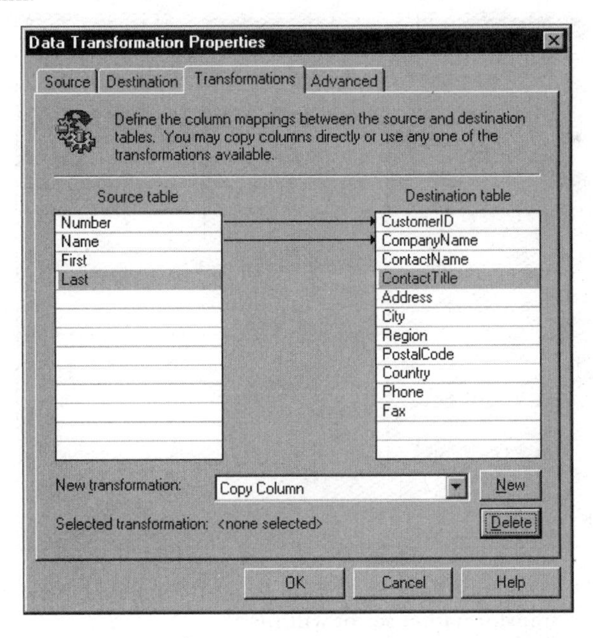

Firstly, we will have to select and delete the Copy Column transformations for First and Last.

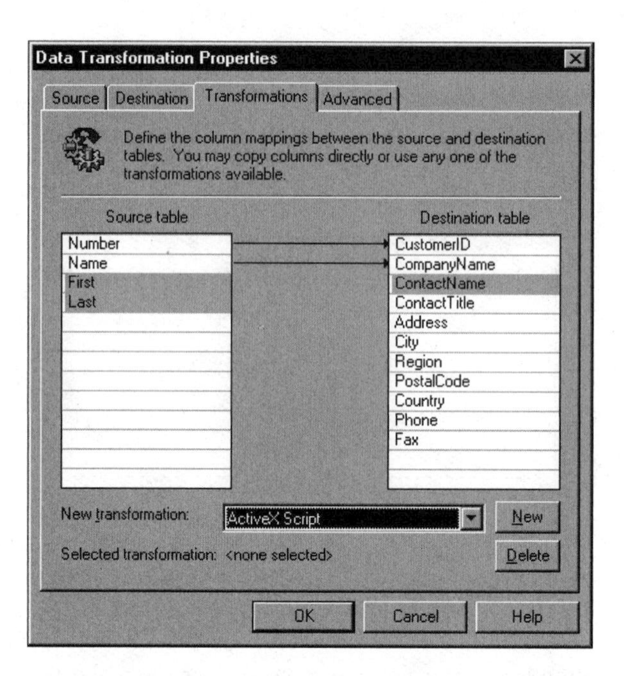

Now, we select First and Last as our source, then ContactName as our destination. We pick ActiveX Script from the New transformation drop-down box and click on New.

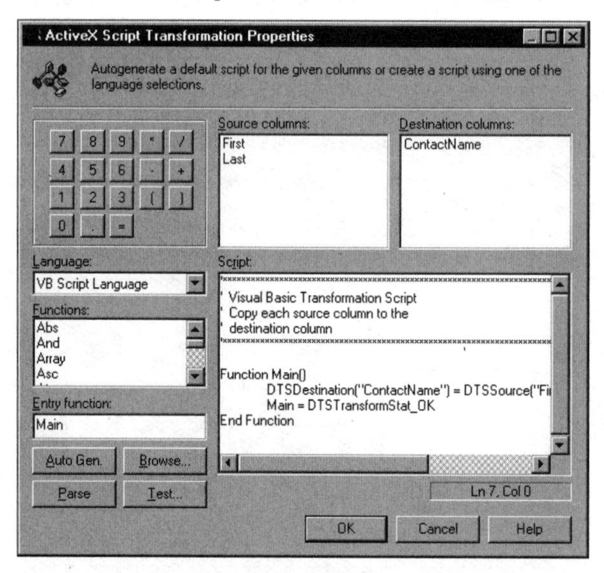

This takes us to the ActiveX Script Transformation Properties dialog. Now we can edit the script for our transformation. Our transformation script will read:

```
'**********************************************************************
'  Visual Basic Transformation Script
'  Copy each source column to the
'  destination column
'************************************************************************
```

```
Function Main()
     DTSDestination("ContactName") = DTSSource("First") + " " + DTSSource("Last")
     Main = DTSTransformStat_OK
End Function
```

This will concatenate the `First` and `Last` name columns as a single column.

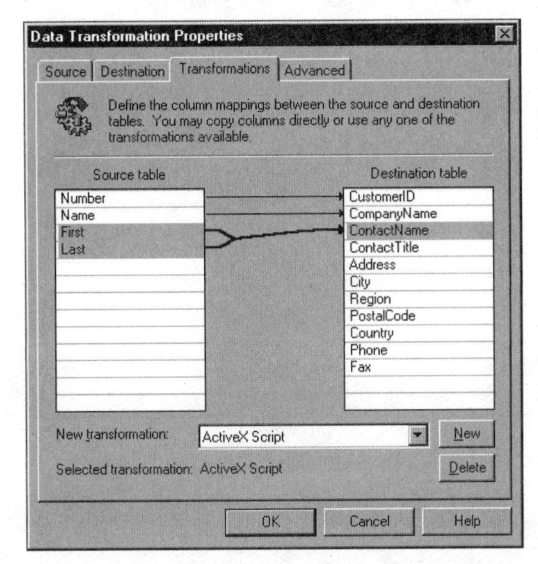

Our transformation now shows both First and Last pointing into the ContactName column.

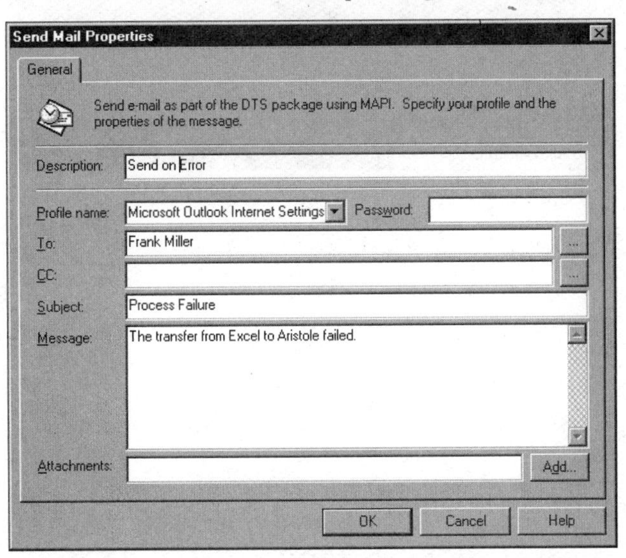

We're going to add one more task to our package so that a mail message will be sent should there be a problem during the transfer. We run Task | 5 Send Mail to add a Send Mail task. We're going to call the task Send on Error and add our mail information to send a message to Frank Miller if the procedure fails.

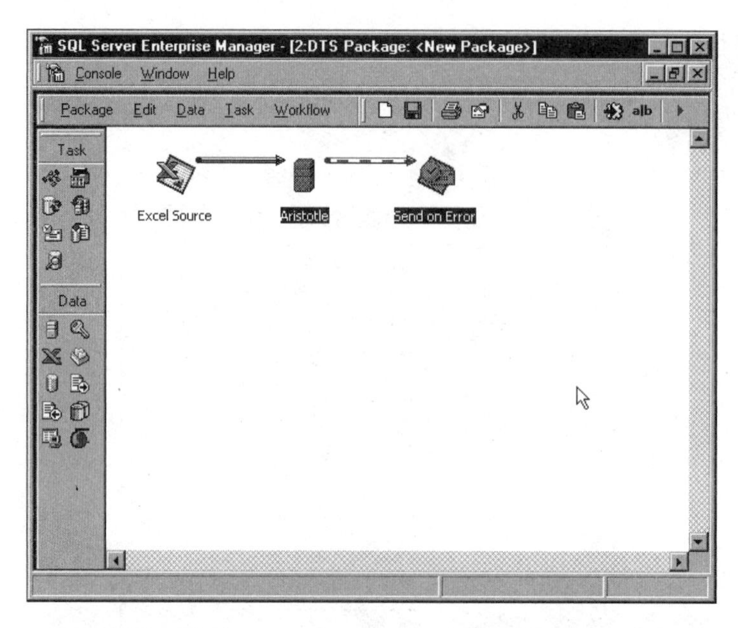

Select Aristotle and Send on Error, then run Workflow | On Failure.

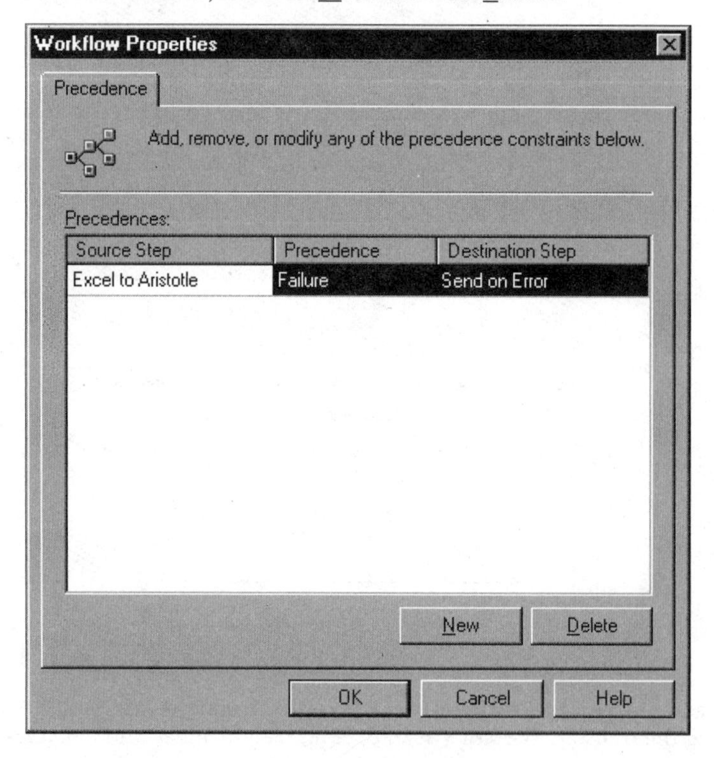

This sets the Source Step as Excel to Aristotle, the Precedence to Failure, and the Destination Step to Send on Error.

With that, we're done. At least, we're done defining the package. Now we can execute the package or save it for later execution. After saving the package, we have the option of scheduling it for execution.

This package is available from the Wrox web site as `SENDMAIL.DTS`. The example package is based on a specific mail configuration.

Let's go ahead and run the package and see what happens.

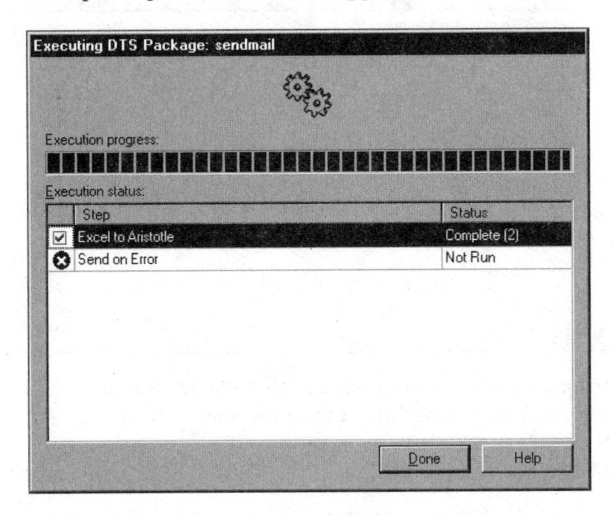

Here's what the dialog looks like on a successful transfer. The Send on Error task is shown as having not run.

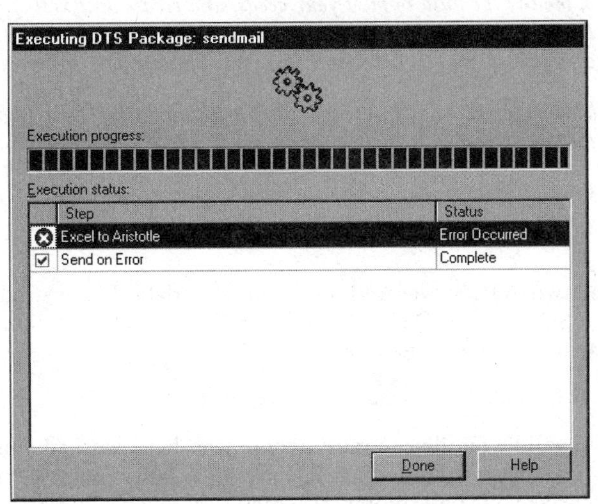

Should an error occur, the task will automatically generate a mail message. This time, the Send Mail task did execute. If you want to run and test this example, you will need to modify the Send Mail task with your e-mail information.

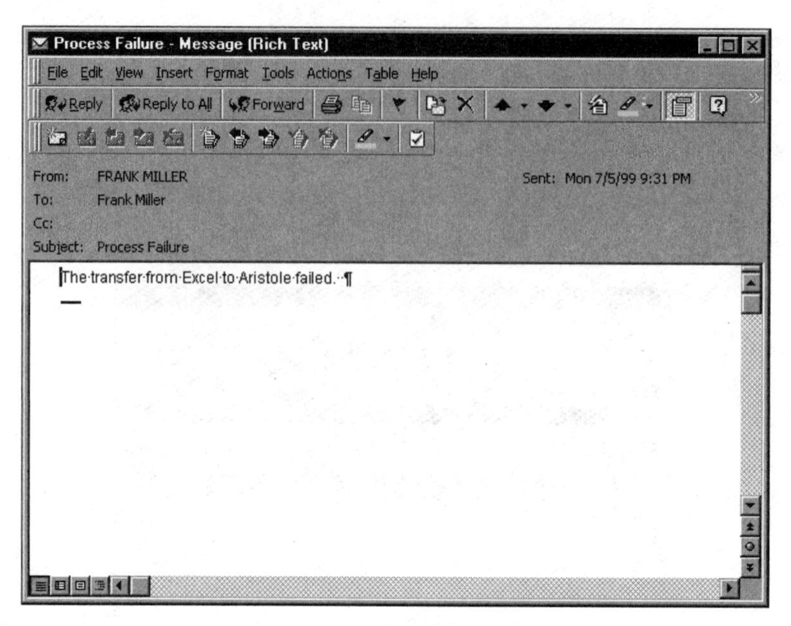

In case you're wondering, here's the mail message that was generated by the transformation package. The destination address has been erased from the message.

Is that all there is? Not even close. In fact, we've just scratched the surface of what you can do with DTS.

How's this sound for an example of what you could do? You could create a package to connect to an Access database, modify the data to meet your needs, and create an Excel spreadsheet. Okay, except the Access database part, you've already seen this, right? How about this, you could also add an On Success *task to launch Excel and open the database you just created.*

I won't say that the sky's the limit, but once you start working with DTS Designer, you may be surprised by how far you can go.

Summary

This chapter discussed two SQL Server options for moving data. Bcp is used primarily for importing text files into or out of SQL Server. DTS, on the other hand, can be used for moving data between any of its supported sources and destinations.

To put it simply, bcp is for data imports, and DTS is for data migration.

As a legacy utility, bcp will be familiar to most people who have worked with SQL Server for any length of time. Since it has been modified for SQL Server 7.0, it remains a viable option for data transfer, though not always your best option. Still, bcp can be a useful part of your utility toolkit. It's a fast, easy way to import into or export out of SQL Server tables.

DTS gives you the option of defining transformation packages through DTS Wizard or DTS Designer. Most situations are going to call for DTS Wizard, but there are going to be situations where you need to use DTS Designer to meet your transformation needs. DTS is going to be your utility of choice in situations where bcp just can't meet you needs.

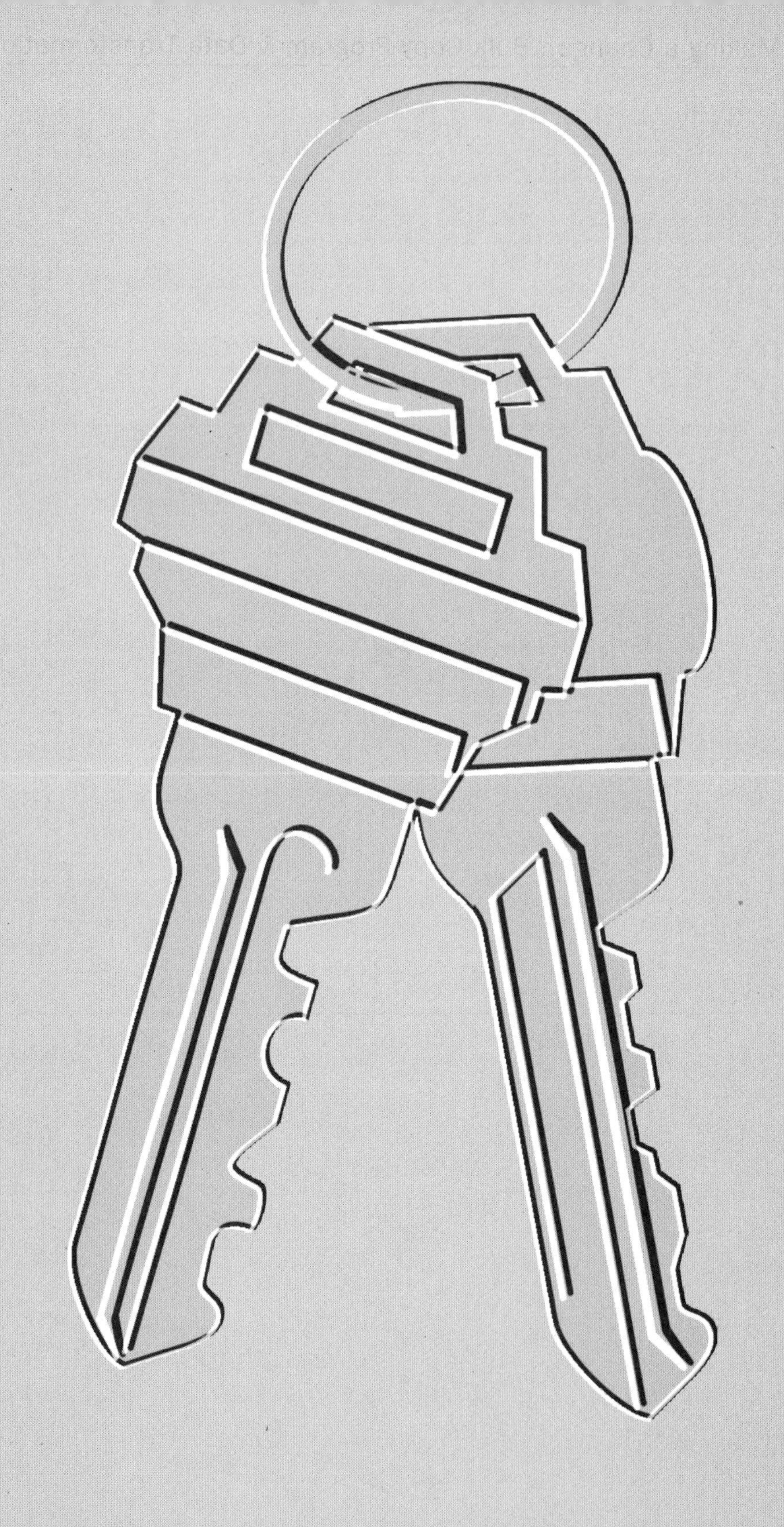

19

Replication

The problem seems relatively straightforward. You've got multiple SQL Servers and you want to keep data between the servers current and accurate. Data Transformation Services (DTS) or the bulk copy program (bcp) might work, but they would require too much interaction and overhead. You've considered doing everything through distributed transactions, but there are timing, bandwidth and reliability issues going out to the remote links. Trying to manage the process through careful use of backups and restores is out of the question.

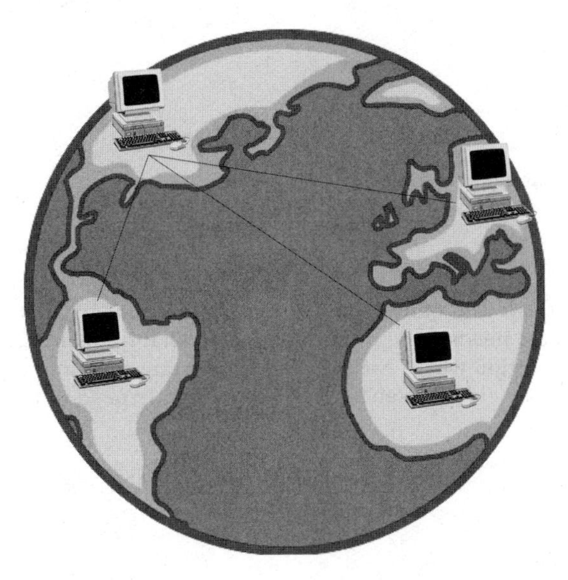

Does this sound familiar to you? The problem is distributed data. The solution, quite often, is **replication**. In most cases, Microsoft SQL Server will provide the functionality and flexibility to support your distributed data environment.

Supporting Distributed Data

You may be wondering how you ended up supporting distributed data in the first place. It could be that you started with autonomous servers and later discovered a need to duplicate data between servers. It could come about as an organization grows and you want to keep data geographically close to the users. It might even have been planned that way from the outset, but it's probably more likely that distributed data requirements "just happened".

If you're just at the planning stage, you actually have an advantage. You can design your databases from the beginning with replication in mind. If you're working with existing servers, you're going to find yourself working around design decisions that were made in the past. You'll probably have to make some changes to the way data is organized on some of the servers.

What changes? That will depend on how you implement replication. As I said at the beginning of the chapter, the problem "seems" relatively straightforward. "Seems" is the key word here.

Considerations when Planning for Replication

If you've come this far, then you've probably decided that you need to at least consider replication. Even if you don't need it now, you may have a need for it in the future.

That decided, let's start looking at some of the details. First, what are some of the factors that you have to consider when planning for replication? Key considerations include:

- Autonomy
- Latency
- Data consistency

Let's take a quick look at each of these.

Autonomy

You have to consider the level of **autonomy** or **server independence** that you want to support at each site. Determine what data needs to be replicated and at what frequency. For example, you could be supporting a sales application where each site keeps separate customer records. You would want to have these replicated to a central database, but you may only need to make daily updates.

Latency

Latency refers to the time delay between updates. The higher the autonomy between sites, the greater the latency between updates. You need to determine the acceptable delay. This will typically depend on the particular data and different latency values that may be acceptable for different types of data.

Data Consistency

Obviously, **data consistency** is going to be critical. Data consistency can be accomplished through data convergence or transactional consistency:

- **Data convergence** means that all sites eventually end up with the same values. However, the values aren't necessarily the same as they would be if all of the changes had taken place on one server.
- **Transactional consistency** is a little different. The results at any server are the same as if all transactions were executed on a single server.

Replication can ensure data consistency, but you will have to keep potential latency in mind. How data consistency is managed and maintained is somewhat dependent on the replication method you select.

SQL Server version 6.x referred to transactional consistency using the terms tight and loose consistency. Tight consistency is now called immediate transactional consistency. It depends on real time transaction processing to ensure that all servers see the same data at the same time. For example, distributed transactions provide immediate transactional consistency. With loose transactional consistency, all servers will see the same data at some time. Loose transactional consistency involves a delay in updates.

Why bring this up now? Just to make sure that, in case you encounter these terms, you know what they mean and how they are related.

Other Considerations

Finally, you have to consider the geographic locations of your servers, the type of connection between the servers, and the connection bandwidth. You're not going to want to constantly saturate your connection with replication traffic, so you may need to adjust your initial autonomy and latency decisions to match real-world capabilities.

The Publishing Metaphor

Before we can look more closely at how replication works, you need to understand some of the basic terms and concepts. Replication is built around a **publishing metaphor** for distributing data.

The source database is maintained at the **Publisher**, which also owns the source data. The Publisher identifies the data to be published (made available for replication) and sends changes to the Distributor.

The **Distributor** can be on the same server as the Publisher or can be set up on a different server, as in the following figure. Note that one Distributor can support multiple Publishers:

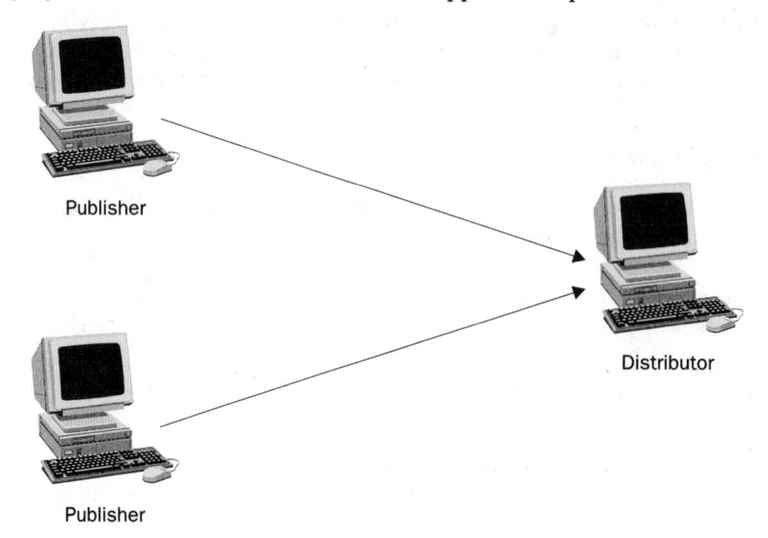

Changes to published data are stored on the Distributor where they are held until forwarded to **Subscribers**. Not only can a Distributor support multiple Publishers, it can also support multiple Subscribers:

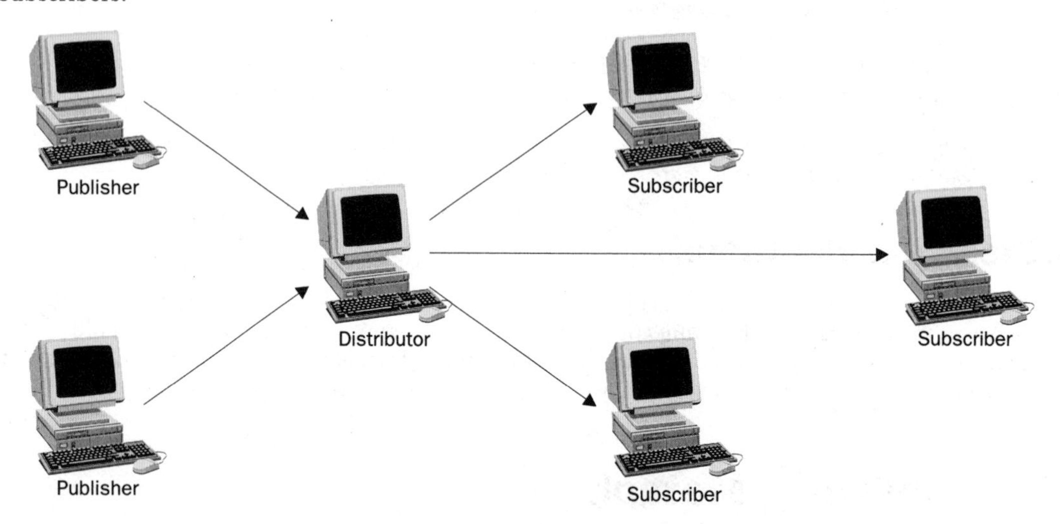

A key component of the Distributor is the **distribution database**. The distribution database stores any transactions awaiting distribution and tracks the replication status.

A copy of the published data is maintained on the Subscriber. Changes to the data are sent to the Subscriber on a periodic basis. In some situations, you may want to configure replication so that changes can occur on both the Publisher and Subscriber.

Subscriptions

Under SQL Server 7.0, the subscriptions that the Subscriber receives are called **publications**. A publication will contain one or more **articles**. An article is most commonly a table or part of the data from a table, but it can be a stored procedure or a group of stored procedures. By subscribing to a publication, the Subscriber is subscribing to all of the articles in the publication - the Subscriber cannot subscribe to individual articles alone.

SQL Server version 6.x supported subscriptions to individual articles, and in fact, was based on article subscriptions. This is maintained to allow backward compatibility with existing applications, but the SQL Server 7.0 Enterprise Manager will not let you directly subscribe to an article.

Subscriptions can be set up as **push** subscriptions or **pull** subscriptions.

With push subscriptions:

- The Publisher determines when updates go out to the Subscriber
- You usually want to keep latency to a minimum or you want to keep full control at the Publisher

With pull subscriptions:

- The Subscriber requests updates
- Allow for a higher level of autonomy since the Subscriber decides when updates occur

A publication can simultaneously support both push and pull subscriptions. However, any one Subscriber can either have a push or pull subscription to a publication, but cannot have both to the same publication.

Types of Subscribers

SQL Server supports three types of Subscribers:

- The default is a **local** Subscriber. The Publisher is the only server that knows the Subscriber. Local Subscribers are often used as a security mechanism or when you want to maximize autonomy between servers.
- You can also have **global** Subscribers, where all servers know the Subscribers. Global Subscribers are commonly used in a multi-server environment where you want to be able to combine data from different Publishers at the Subscriber.
- Finally, you can have **anonymous** Subscribers. The Publisher is only aware of an anonymous Subscriber while it is connected. This is useful when setting up Internet-based applications.

Filtering Data

You aren't just limited to publishing an entire table as an article. You have the option of horizontally or vertically filtering tables.

Horizontal filtering (you may come across the term **horizontal partitioning** for this as well) identifies rows within the table for publication. For example, you could divide inventory information by warehouse as a way of maintaining separate warehouse totals.

Vertical filtering (also known as **vertical partitioning**) identifies the columns to be replicated. For example, you might want to publish quantity-on-hand information from an inventory table, but not quantity-on-order.

Types of Replication

SQL Server supports various types of replication, letting you pick the type that best meets your needs. From highest to lowest autonomy they are:

- Snapshot replication
- Transactional replication
- Merge replication

We're going to look at potential benefits and drawbacks of each replication type, situations where it would be an appropriate solution, and outline any data concerns that might arise.

It's important for you to know that you can mix and match the replication types as necessary to meet your implementation requirements. There are going to be some publications where you want to allow greater autonomy between sites. There will be other publications where minimizing latency is critical.

Snapshot Replication

With **snapshot replication**, a "picture" is taken at the source of all of the data to be replicated. This is used to replace the data at the destination server.

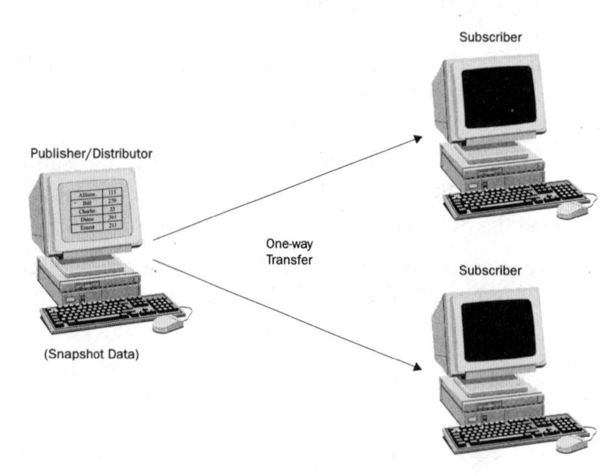

Snapshot replication can be the easiest type of replication to set up and manage. Complete tables or table segments (for partitioned tables) are written to the Subscribers during replication. Since updates occur on a periodic basis only, most of the time there is minimal server or network overhead required to support replication.

In its simplest form, snapshot replication is used to update read-only tables on Subscriber systems. It allows for a high level of autonomy at the Subscriber, but at the cost of relatively high latency.

You are able to keep tight control on when periodic updates occur when using snapshot replication. This means that you can schedule updates to occur when network and server activity is at a lull.

There is a potential concern about the time and resources to complete replication during the periodic updates. As source tables grow, the amount of data that has to be transferred during each update increases. Over time it may become necessary to either change the replication type or partition the table to reduce the amount of data replicated to keep traffic to manageable levels.

> *A variation of snapshot replication is* ***snapshot replication with immediate-updating subscribers****. With this, changes can be made to the data at the Subscriber. Those changes are sent to the publishing server on a periodic basis.*

How Snapshot Replication Works

Replication is implemented through **replication agents**. Each plays a vital role in the replication process.

Snapshot Agent

The **Snapshot Agent** supports snapshot replication and initial synchronization of data tables for replication. All types of replication require that the source and destination tables must be synchronized, either by the replication agents or through manual synchronization, before replication can begin. In either case, the Snapshot Agent has the same responsibility. It takes the "picture" of the published data and stores the files on the Distributor.

Distribution Agent

The **Distribution Agent** is responsible for moving transactions and snapshots from the Publisher to the Subscriber(s). The Distribution Agent is used for moving data for initial synchronization and snapshot replication (and, as we'll see later, for transactional replication). For push subscriptions, the Distribution Agent runs on the Distributor. For pull subscriptions, the Distribution Agent runs on the Subscriber.

The Process of Snapshot Replication

Snapshot replication uses periodic updates. During the updates, schema and data files are created and sent to the Subscribers. Let's step through the basic procedure:

- The Snapshot Agent places a shared lock on all articles in the publication to be replicated, ensuring data consistency
- A copy of each article's table schema is written to the distribution working folder on the Distributor
- A snapshot copy of table data is written to the distribution working folder
- The Snapshot Agent releases the shared locks from the publication articles
- The Distribution Agent creates the destination tables and database objects, such as indexes, on the Subscriber and copies in the snapshot data, overwriting the existing tables, if any

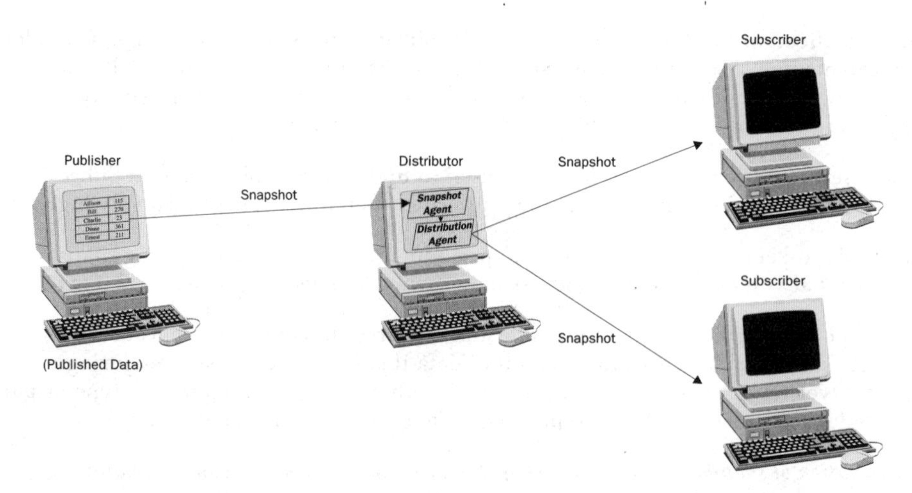

Snapshot data is stored as a native bcp file if all of the Subscribers are Microsoft SQL Servers. Character data snapshots, instead of SQL Server native data snapshots, will be created if you are supporting heterogeneous (non-SQL Server) Subscribers.

When to Use Snapshot Replication

Use snapshot replication to update look-up data or read-only copies of data on remote servers. You can use snapshot replication when you want (or need) to connect to the Publisher intermittently.

Think of how servers might be managed for a chain of garden supply stores. You have stores in several cities. Some larger cities have multiple stores. What are some good candidates for snapshot replication?

Customer records are an obvious choice. A customer, such as a landscape gardener, may turn up at different locations. In most cases, it won't matter if there's a delay updating customer information. This would also give you a way to make sure that only users who have access to the publishing server can change customer records.

Inventory records could be a little more of a problem. The items you keep in inventory are somewhat constant with most changes taking place by season. Even then, you would probably keep the items on file, but with a zero quantity on hand. The problem is, you may want to replicate more up-to-date inventory records between stores. This would let you search for items you might not have on hand without having to call each of the stores. Timely updates would most likely mean transactional replication.

Special Planning Requirements

An important issue when setting up snapshot replication is timing. You need to make sure that users are not going to need write access to any published tables when the Snapshot Agent is generating its snapshot. You also want to be sure that the traffic generated by replication does not interfere with other network operations.

Storage space can also become an issue as published tables grow. You have to verify that you have enough physical disk space available on the Distributor to support the snapshot folder.

Transactional Replication

The difference between transactional and snapshot replication is that incremental changes, rather than full tables, are replicated to the Subscribers during **transactional replication**. Any logged changes to published articles, such as `INSERT`, `UPDATE` and `DELETE` statements, are tracked and replicated to Subscribers. In transactional replication, only changed table data is distributed, maintaining the transaction sequence. In other words, all transactions are applied to the Subscriber in the same order that they were applied to the Publisher.

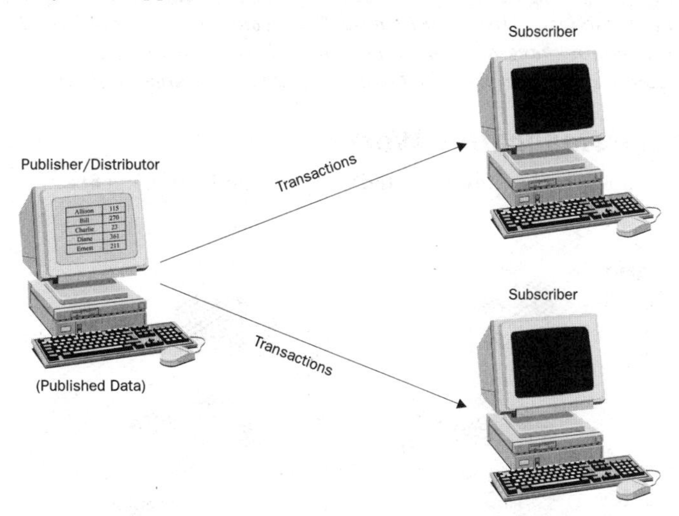

In its simplest form, changes can only be made at the Publisher. Changes can be replicated to Subscribers at set intervals or as near-real-time updates. While you may have less control over when replication occurs, you are typically moving less data with each replication. Updates are occurring much more often and latency is kept to a minimum. Reliable and consistent near-real-time Subscriber updates (immediate transactional consistency) require a network connection between the Publisher and Subscriber.

Before transactional replication can take place, the published articles must be initially synchronized between the Publisher and the Subscriber. This is typically managed through automatic synchronization using snapshot replication. In situations where automatic synchronization is neither practical nor efficient, manual synchronization can be used to prepare the Subscriber. This is a relatively simple process:

- Run `BACKUP DATABASE` to back up the Publisher database
- Deliver the tape backup to the Subscriber system
- Run `RESTORE DATABASE` to create the database and database objects, and to load the data

The Publisher and Subscriber are synchronized as of the point when the backup was run.

Transactional replication can also be used to replicate stored procedures. In its simplest implementation, changes can only be made at the publishing server. This means that you don't have any worries about conflicts.

You can also implement transactional replication as ***transactional replication with immediate-updating subscribers****. This means that changes can be made at the Publisher or at the Subscriber. Transactions occurring at the Subscriber are treated as distributed transactions. MS DTC (Microsoft Distributed Transaction Coordinator) is used to ensure that both the local data and data on the Publisher are updated at the same time to avoid update conflicts.*

Note that you would have to implement distributed transactions to get a lower latency than that provided with transactional replication with immediate-updating subscribers. You still have the distribution delay in getting changes posted at the Publisher, either locally or from a Subscriber, out to all of the Subscribers. Distributed transactions would provide near immediate updates to all servers when data is changed at any server. Depending on the connection speed between servers, this could result in performance problems, including locking conflicts.

How Transactional Replication Works

Transactional replication is also implemented through **replication agents**.

Log Reader Agent

The **Log Reader Agent** is used in transactional replication. After a database is set up for transactional replication, its transaction log is monitored for changes to published tables. It's the Log Reader Agent's responsibility to copy the transactions marked for replication from the Publisher to the Distributor.

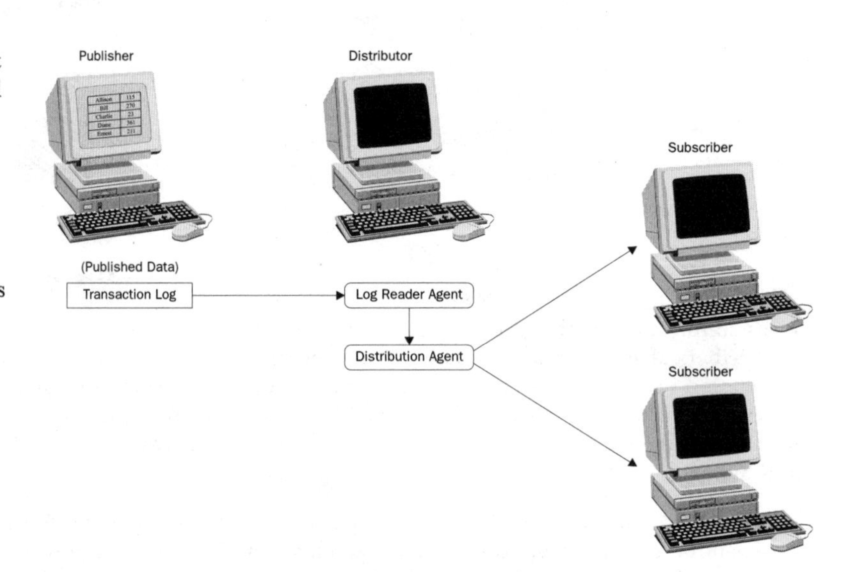

Distribution Agent

The **Distribution Agent** is also used in transactional replication and is responsible for moving transactions from the Publisher to the Subscriber(s).

The Process of Transactional Replication

Assuming that initial synchronization has already taken place, transactional replication follows these basic steps:

- Modifications are posted to the Publisher's transaction log
- The Log Reader Agent reads the transaction log and identifies changes marked for replication
- Changes taken from the transaction log are written to the distribution database on the Distributor
- The Distribution Agent applies the changes to the appropriate database tables

You can set up the Log Reader Agent to read the transaction log continuously or on a schedule that you specify. As before, the Distribution Agent runs at the Publisher for push subscriptions and at the Subscriber for pull subscriptions.

When to Use Transactional Replication

Use transactional replication when you want to reduce latency and provide Subscribers with relatively up-to-date information. Near-real-time updates usually require a local area network connection, but scheduled replication can often be managed through scheduled updates. If you choose to use scheduled updates, latency increases, but you gain control over when replication occurs.

Let's go back to our garden supply store and the inventory problem discussed earlier. You want each of the stores to have up-to-date, or at the very least, relatively up-to-date inventory information. You would probably use scheduled replication to pass data to the Subscribers.

Now let's see if we can make things a little more difficult. Not only do you have a chain of stores, you also have traveling sales people who visit and take orders from your largest customers. They need to have at least relatively up-to-date inventory information, but can't spend their days sitting around and waiting for updates from the Publisher. For systems of this type, you may want to use pull subscriptions, letting the sales people decide when they connect to the server and download recent transactions.

You've probably noticed a potential problem in both of these scenarios. The remote servers can receive data, but they are not able to make any changes to the data. We'll cover that problem a little later. Transactional replication, when implemented in this manner, is used to support read-only copies of the data at Subscriber systems.

Special Planning Requirements

Space is an important issue when planning for transactional replication. You have to make sure that you allow for adequate space for the transaction log on the Publisher and for the distribution database on the Distributor.

Check each of the tables that you are planning to publish. For a table to be published under transactional replication, it must have a primary key. There are also potential concerns if you are supporting text or image data types in any of the tables. `INSERT`, `UPDATE` and `DELETE` are supported as for any data type, but you must be sure to use the `WITH LOG` option if using `WRITETEXT` or `UPDATETEXT` to update a published table.

You may encounter problems with the `max text repl size` *parameter, which sets the maximum size of text or image data that can be replicated. Make sure that this parameter is set to a high enough value to support your replication requirements.*

Immediate-Update Subscribers

You have the option of setting up Subscribers to snapshot or transactional publications as immediate-update subscribers. Immediate-update subscribers have the ability to update subscribed data, as long as the updates can be immediately reflected at the Publisher. This is accomplished using the two-phase commit protocol managed by the MS DTC.

There is, effectively, no latency in updating the Publisher. Updates to other Subscribers are made normally, as if the change was initiated at the Publisher, so latency when going to other Subscribers will depend on the rate at which they are updated.

You should consider immediate-updating subscribers when you need to post changes to replicated data at one or more Subscribers and propagate near-immediate updates. You might be using multiple servers to support an online transaction processing (OLTP) application as a way of improving performance and providing near-real-time redundancy. When a transaction is posted to any server, it will be sent to the Publishers, and through the Publisher, to the remaining servers.

There is a possibility of conflicts arising when using immediate-updating subscribers. A timestamp column will be added to any published tables that do not already have one.

Here's how the timestamp column is used. You have two Subscribers, SubOne and SubTwo. SubOne sends an immediate-update transaction to the Publisher. Before that transaction will be sent to SubTwo, the Publisher will check the timestamp value on any effected row to verify that it has not changed since it was replicated to SubTwo. In other words, it won't change a row that has been modified locally.

A high-speed, *reliable* connection is required between the Publisher and any immediate-updating Subscribers, such as a local area network connection.

Merge Replication

Another way of managing data changes taking place at multiple servers, is through the use of **merge replication**. The changes from all of the sites are merged when they are received by the Publisher. Updates take place either periodically or on demand:

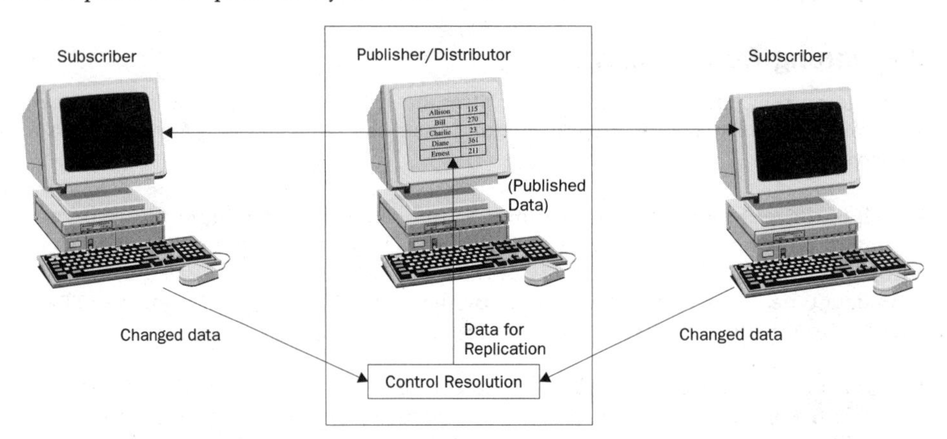

Merge replication has the highest autonomy, but also has the highest latency and runs a risk of lower transactional consistency.

In a way, roles tend to get somewhat blurred in merge replication. The Publisher is the initial source for the merge data, but changes can be made at the Publisher or at the Subscribers. Changes can be tracked by row or by column. Transactional consistency is not guaranteed because conflicts can occur when different systems make updates to the same row. Data consistency is maintained through conflict resolution based on criteria you establish. You can determine whether conflicts are recognized by row or by column.

As with transactional replication, the Snapshot Agent prepares the initial snapshot for synchronization. The synchronization process is different, however, in that the Merge Agent performs synchronization. It will also apply any changes made since the initial snapshot.

How Merge Replication Works

As with the other forms of replication, an agent implements the replication.

Merge Agent

The **Merge Agent** is used with merge replication. It copies the changes from all Subscribers and applies them to the Publisher. The Merge Agent copies all changes at the Publisher (including those made by the Merge Agent) to the Subscribers. The Merge Agent runs on the Distributor for push subscriptions and on the Subscriber for pull subscriptions:

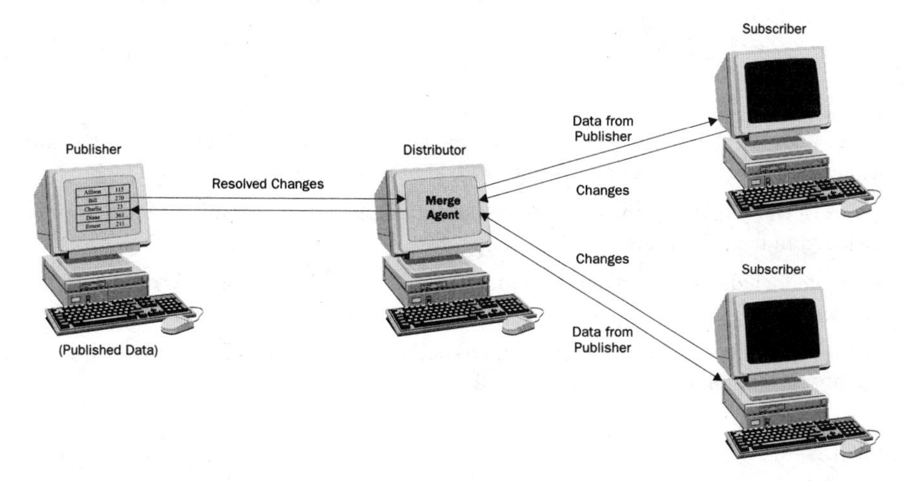

The Process of Merge Replication

Assuming that the initial synchronization has already taken place, here's what happens during merge replication:

- Triggers installed by SQL Server track changes to published data
- Changes from the Publisher are applied to Subscribers
- Changes from Subscribers are applied to the Publisher and any conflicts resolved

Note that merge triggers do not interfere with the placement or use of user-defined triggers.

Changes, whether occurring at the Publisher or Subscriber, are applied by the Merge Agent. Conflicts are resolved automatically through the Merge Agent. The Merge Agent tracks every row update for conflicts at the row or column level, depending on how you have configured conflict resolution. You will define the priority scheme to be used when conflicts occur between new (arriving) and current data values.

When to Use Merge Replication

One way of using merge replication is to support partitioned tables. Going back to the garden supply business, you could set up filtering (partitioning) so that each store can view inventory information for any store, but would only be able to directly update its own inventory. Changes would be propagated through merge replication. Data can only be filtered horizontally. Merge replication does not support vertical filtering. You can exclude rows from being replicated from a table, but you cannot exclude any table columns. Merge replication watches for changes to any column in a replicated row.

Special Planning Requirements

When implementing merge replication, there are checks that you need to make to ensure that your data is ready for replication. While setting up merge replication, some changes will be made automatically by SQL Server to your data files.

You Need to...

- Remove any `timestamp` columns from published tables. Values in `timestamp` columns are server unique values rather than globally unique values. You cannot overwrite `timestamp` values from one server with timestamp values with another server.
- Use care when selecting the tables to be published. Any tables required for data validation must be included in the publication.
- If a table includes a foreign key, you must include the table that it is referencing as part of the publication.
- Do not use `WRITETEXT` or `UPDATE` text to update text or image data. Only changes made using the `UPDATE` statement will be recognized and propagated.

The Server Will...

SQL Server will identify a column as a globally unique identifier for each row in a published table. If the table already has a `uniqueidentifier` column, SQL Server will automatically use that column. Otherwise, it will add a `rowguid` column to the table and create an index based on the column.

There will be triggers created on the published tables at both the Publisher and the Subscribers. These are used to allow the Merge Agent to track data changes based on row or column changes.

There will also be several tables added for tracking purposes. These tables are used by the server to manage:

- Conflict detection and resolution
- Data tracking
- Synchronization
- Reporting

For example, conflicts are detected through a column in the `MSmerge_contents` table, one of the tables created when you set up merge replication.

Mixing Replication Types

You can mix and match replication types as needed. Not only can you have different replication types on the same server, you can even have different replication types for the same table.

Here's a possible situation where you might want to publish a table in different ways. A heavy equipment warehouse wants to have up-to-date inventory information and reference copies of invoices available at each of its locations. Each location has its own local SQL Server. Invoices are posted to a central location using an Internet-based application. These are replicated to all local servers through transactional replication so that inventory records are updated.

You want to have invoice and inventory information replication updated on a separate server weekly. This information is used for business analysis and running weekly reports. This server is updated weekly through a separate snapshot publication referencing the same tables.

Replication Model Scenarios

Microsoft has defined a number of replication topology models (which represent the logical and physical connectivity) to describe how replication can be implemented. These are provided as reliable topology suggestions, not as hard and fast rules for implementation. It is not only possible to mix and modify these models; it's actually quite common.

Your decisions about the type of replication you need to use and your replication model topology can be made somewhat independent of each other. That said; there is a chance that restrictions imposed by your physical topology, such as transmission bandwidth, will influence your decisions.

Standard Models

Let's start with a look at the standard models. Once you've got the basic idea, we can move on to some variations.

Central Publisher/Distributor

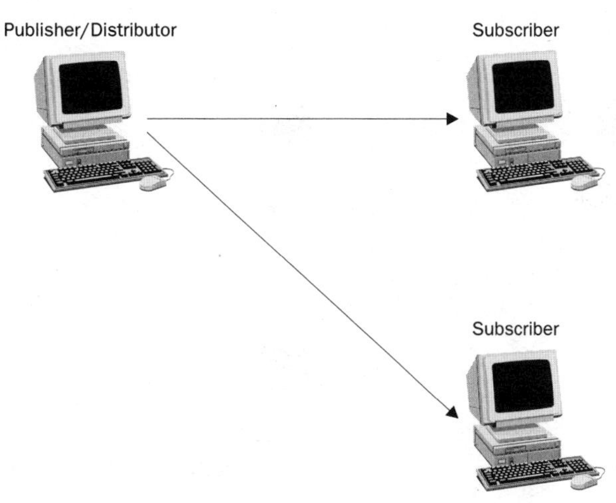

This is the default SQL Server model. You have one system acting as Publisher and as its own Distributor. This Publisher/Distributor supports any number of Subscribers. The Publisher owns all replicated data and is the sole data source for replication. The most basic model assumes that all data is being published to the Subscribers as read-only data. Read-only access can be enforced at the Subscriber by giving users `SELECT` permission only on the replicated tables.

Since this is the easiest model to set up and manage, you should consider its use in any situation where it fits. If you have a single Publisher, one or more Subscribers, and read-only access to data at the Subscriber, this is your best choice.

Central Publisher/Remote Distributor

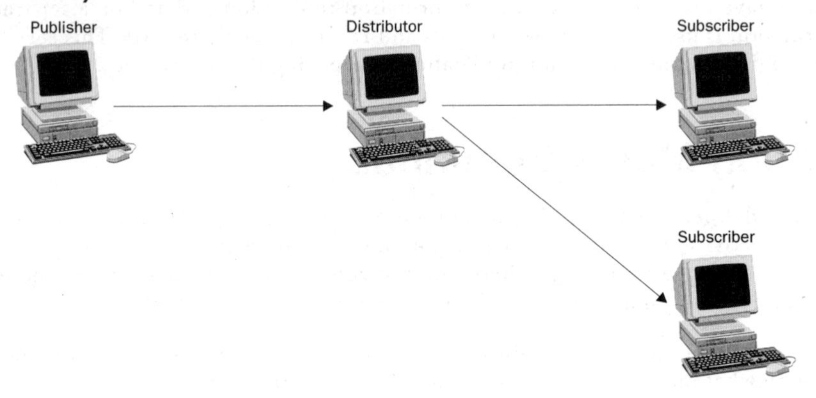

Depending upon the volume of replicated data and the amount of activity at the Publisher, it may be necessary to implement the Publisher and Distributor as separate systems. Operationally, this is effectively the same as the Publisher/Distributor model. The Publisher is still the owner of and only source for replicated data. Once again, the basic model assumes that the data will be treated as read-only at the Subscriber.

Obviously, you will use this model when a single Publisher/Distributor cannot handle both production activity and replication to Subscribers.

Central Subscriber

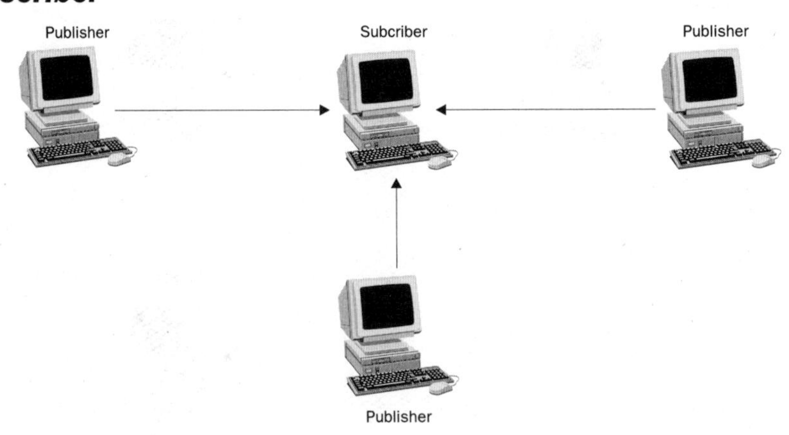

In this model, you only have one Subscriber receiving data, but you have multiple Publishers. The Publishers can be configured as Publisher/Distributor systems. This model provides a way to keep just local data at the local server, but still have a way of consolidating the data at one central location. Horizontal filtering may be necessary to keep Publishers from overwriting each other's data at the Subscriber.

This is the model to use when you have data consolidation requirements.

Mixed Models

Now let's look at a few variations to the basic models. These are just suggestions and are not meant to imply a complete list of possibilities.

Publishing Subscriber

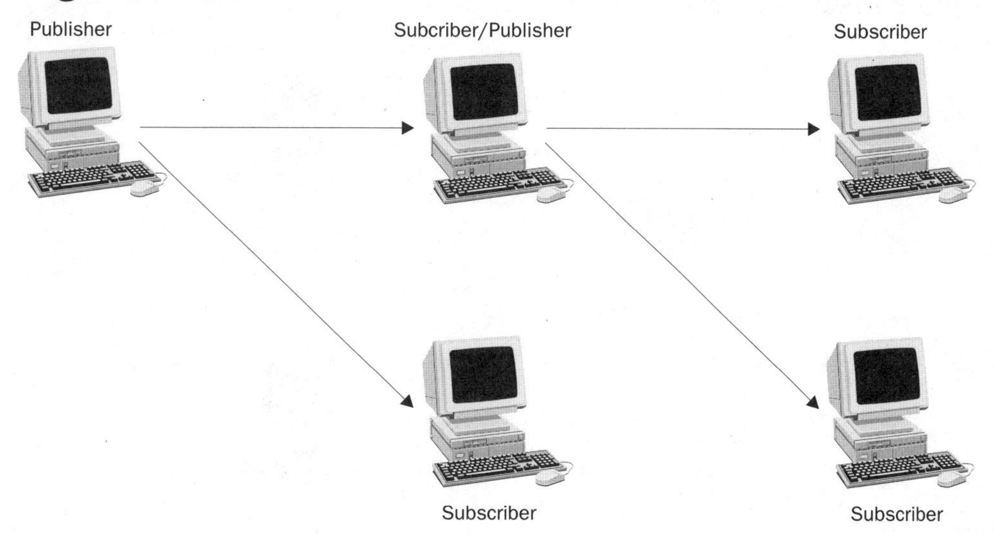

Publishing Subscribers (that is Subscribers which are also configured as Publishers) can be added to any of the basic models. This model has two Publishers publishing the same data. The original Publisher replicates data to its Subscribers, one of which is a Publishing Subscriber. The Publishing Subscriber can then pass the same data along to its Subscribers.

This model is useful when you have pockets of servers or when you have an especially slow or expensive link between servers. Another possibility is that you don't have a direct link between the initial Publisher and all of the potential Subscribers. The Publisher only needs to pass data to one system on the far side of the link, and the Publisher Subscriber can then pass the data along to the other subscribers.

Publisher/Subscriber

This is another case where you have SQL Servers acting as both Publishers and Subscribers. Each server has its own set of data for which it is responsible. This model can be used when you have data changes taking place at both locations and you want to keep both servers updated. This is different than Publishing Subscribers in that each server is generating its own data, not just passing along updates received from another server.

Multiple Subscribers/Multiple Publishers

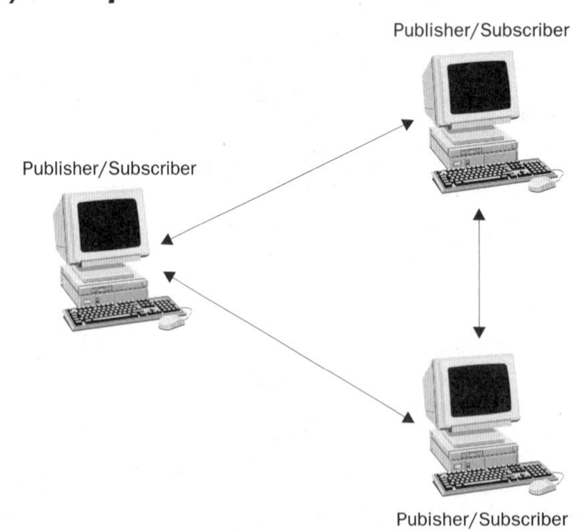

This is where things can start getting complicated. You have multiple Publishers and multiple Subscribers. Systems may or may not act as a Publisher/Subscriber or Publishing Subscriber. This model requires very careful planning to provide optimum communications and to ensure data consistency.

One More Issue...

Before leaving topology models there is another issue that needs to be raised.

Publish to Self

SQL Server allows a server to subscribe to its own published articles. Before you dismiss this as just an interesting quirk, there are a number of situations where this could be a part of a business solution. One obvious example is that you want to segregate the data used for online transaction processing from the data used for decision-making. You can use replication to make separate read-only copies of your data (updated on any schedule you consider appropriate) to be used as a reference.

Implementation Examples

Ready to try some examples of how you might put these replication types and topology models into practice to build a business solution? Note that the sample solutions provided here are not necessarily the only possible solutions to the problem.

Contractor Supply

Contractor Supply has three warehouses in addition to its home office in San Francisco. The warehouses are located in Los Angeles, Denver and Boston. Currently, each warehouse manages its own sales and inventory. If there is a request for an out-of-stock item, the warehouse will dial into each of the other warehouses through RAS servers to check inventory levels and request an overnight shipment.

Proposed Changes

It's been decided that each warehouse will continue to manage its inventory, customer and sales information. All business activity needs to be reported to the home office on a weekly basis for analysis and reporting. Each warehouse's business will be kept in a separate database at the home office.

Proposed Solution

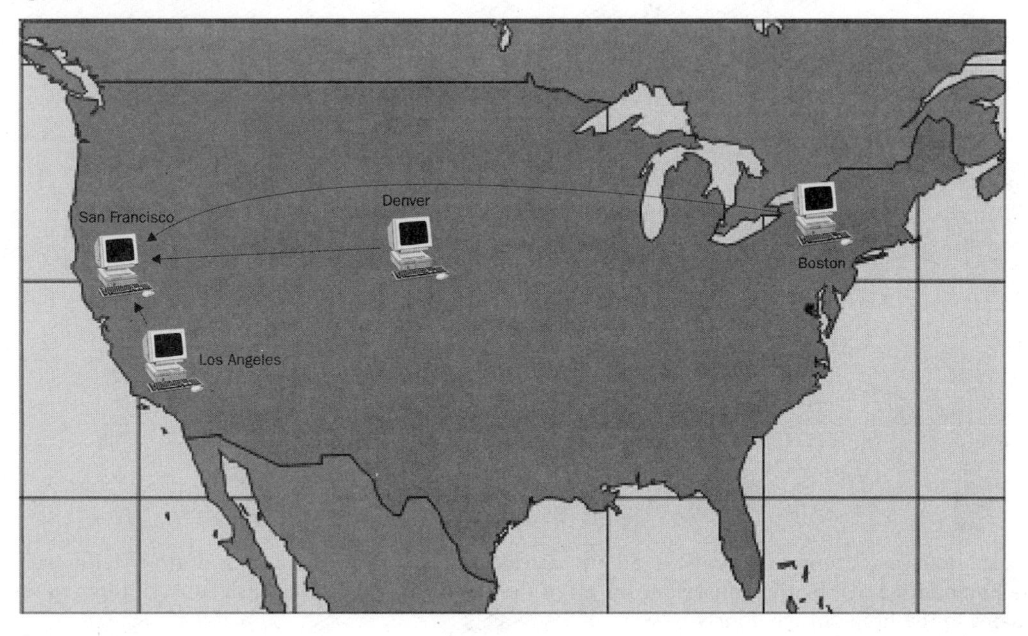

Set up each of the warehouses as Publisher/Distributors. Create a snapshot publication on each warehouse server containing all of the business activity tables. Define push subscriptions from each of the warehouses to separate databases on a server at the home office with updates going out on a weekly basis.

Cleanzeazy

Cleanzeazy is a cleaning service with its main office in New York and satellite offices along the United States eastern seaboard. Currently, the satellite offices send hard copies of customer invoices to the home office daily by overnight mail. Updated customer information is e-mailed as an Excel spreadsheet weekly.

Proposed Changes

Cleanzeazy is installing SQL Server desktop version at each of the satellite offices. Customer invoices will be posted locally as they are created. The invoices do not update local copies of customer balances. All updates take place at the home office. Updated customer records need to go out to the satellite offices nightly.

Proposed Solution

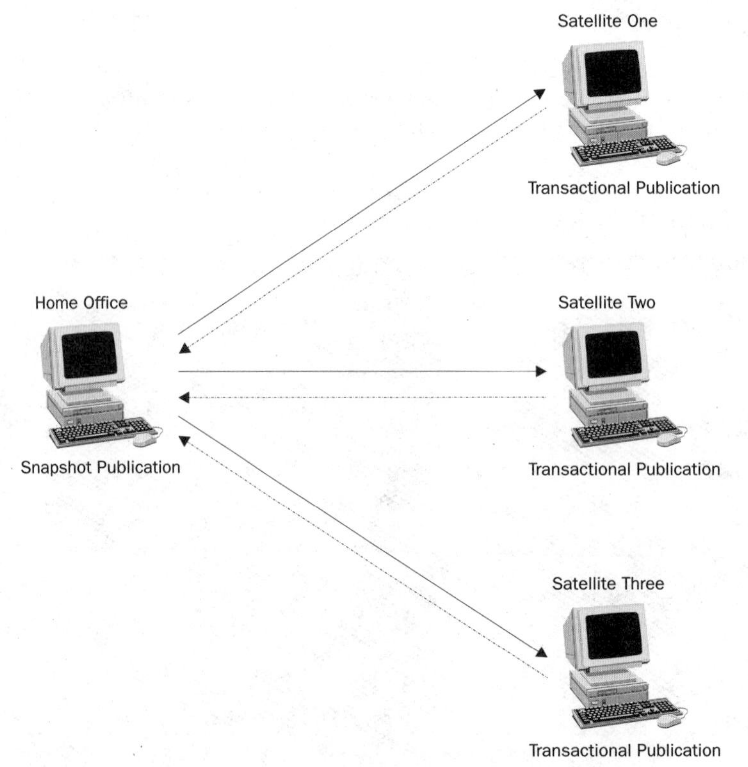

This solution is a little more involved. Set up transactional replication on each of the satellite servers. The home office will be the Subscriber for all of the satellites. Configure push subscriptions to send updates to the home office hourly.

> **Depending on the traffic levels generated by the transactional updates, you may want to stagger the updates so that they arrive at different times.**

Set up the customer table at the home offices as a snapshot publication. Create push subscriptions to each of the satellite offices to run nightly.

Planning for Replication

Now we're ready to step through the procedures for setting up replication. The first step *must* be planning. The time you spend in planning will more than pay off in the long run. Planning considerations include:

- Replication data
- Replication type
- Replication model

Along with these are other factors that will influence your decision, such as current network topologies, current server configurations, server growth potential, activity levels, and so forth.

Data Concerns

First, you have to consider what you are going to publish and to whom. You need to identify your articles (tables to be published) and how you plan to organize them into publications. In addition, there are some other data issues of which you need to be aware. Some of these have already been mentioned, but it's worth our time to review them here.

timestamp

Whether or not your published tables should have a `timestamp` column depends on how they are being published. Include a `timestamp` column for transaction publications. That gives you a way of detecting conflicts on updates. By having a `timestamp` column already in place, you've already met part of the requirements for adding immediate-updating Subscribers.

The opposite is true if setting up merge replication. You will need to remove the `timestamp` column from any published table.

uniqueidentifier

A unique index and globally unique identifier is required for merge replication. Remember, if a published table doesn't have a `uniqueidentifier` column, a globally unique identifier column will be added.

User-Defined Data Types

User-defined data types are not supported unless they exist on the Subscriber destination database. Alternatively, you can have user-defined data types converted to base data types during synchronization.

NOT FOR REPLICATION

The `NOT FOR REPLICATION` clause lets you disable table features on Subscribers. You can disable:

- The `IDENTIFY` property
- `CHECK` constraints
- Triggers

These features are disabled when replication processes data on the Subscriber. The features remain enabled when user applications change data.

Replication Type

It may be more accurate to say that you need to consider replication types. It's not uncommon to be supporting more than one type of replication.

Replication Wizards

We're almost ready to start setting up replication. SQL Server Enterprise Manager provides several wizards to help simplify the process:

- Configure Publishing and Distribution Wizard
- Create Publication Wizard
- Disable Publishing and Distribution Wizard
- Pull Subscription Wizard
- Push Subscription Wizard

To launch any of the replication wizards, select your database in the Enterprise Manager tree and run Tools | Wizards. Expand the Replication list and select the wizard that you want to run.

Enabling Publishing and Distribution

The first step is setting up your Distributor. You can do this through the **Configure Publishing and Distribution Wizard**. You can also use the Configure Publishing and Distribution Wizard to modify Distributor and Publisher properties. Launch the wizard from the Select Wizard dialog or run Tools | Replication | Configure Publishing and Subscribers:

Starting the Wizard

The opening screen lists your options. You can use the Configure Publishing and Distribution Wizard to:

- ❑ Specify a server as a Distributor
- ❑ Configure Distributor properties
- ❑ Configure Publishing properties

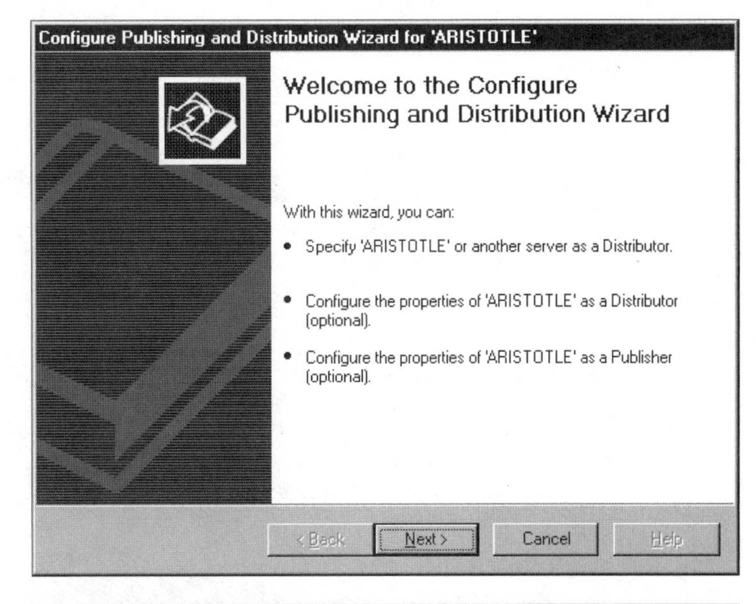

First, you have to identify the system that you are configuring as a Distributor. You can specify the default server or another registered server. You can also select to register servers from this dialog if you've chosen to use a different server:

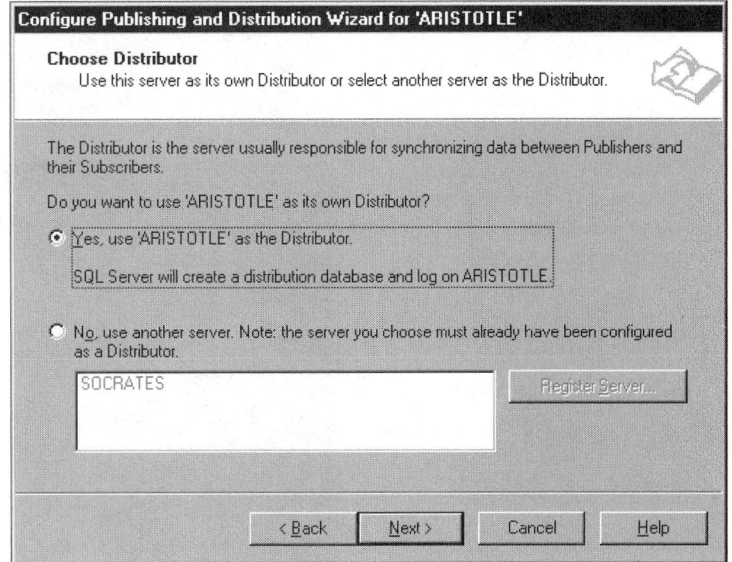

Default Configuration

The Wizard prompts you to set up the default configuration, which is to:

- Configure the server as a Distributor
- Configure all registered servers as Subscribers
- Name the distribution database `distribution` and create it on `C:\MSSQL7\data`
- Enable the specified server to use itself as Distributor when configured later as a Publisher

This figure shows configuration information based on SQL Server installed to the standard destination directory on drive `C:`. The default location will be the SQL Server 7.0 directory on the installation drive, wherever that might actually be:

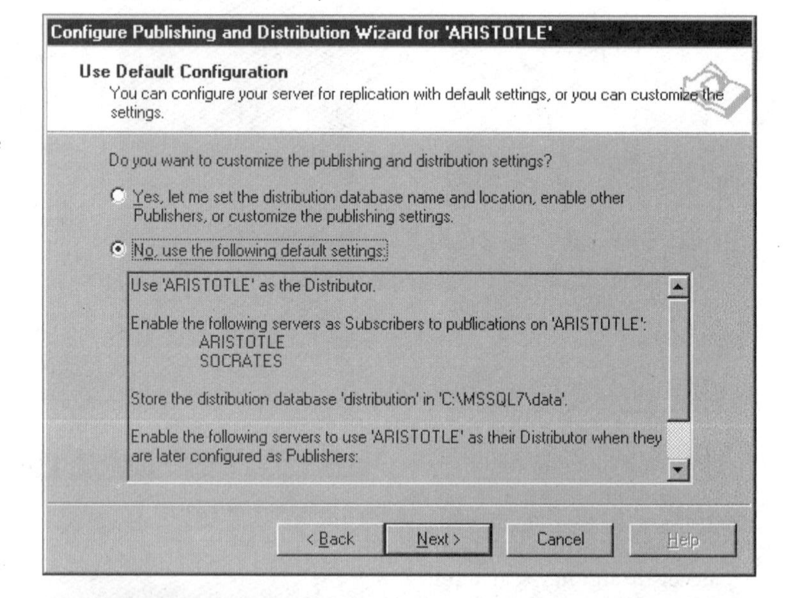

If you continue on at this point, the Wizard will prompt you to complete configuration:

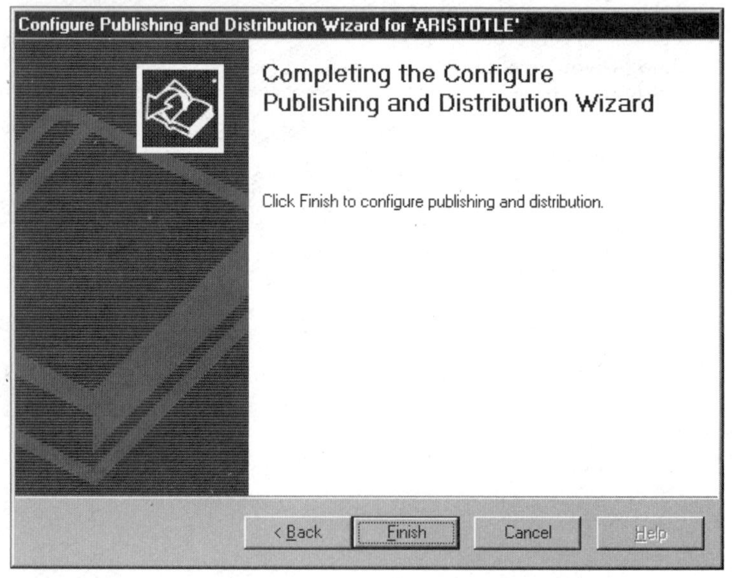

The Wizard steps through the configuration steps as it configures the server as a Distributor and prompts you when finished.

You will be prompted if the SQL Server Agent service is not configured to start automatically on your server. Click on Yes to configure the SQL Server Agent service to start automatically. SQL Server will also add the Replication Monitor to your Enterprise Manager tree after it finishes configuring the server:

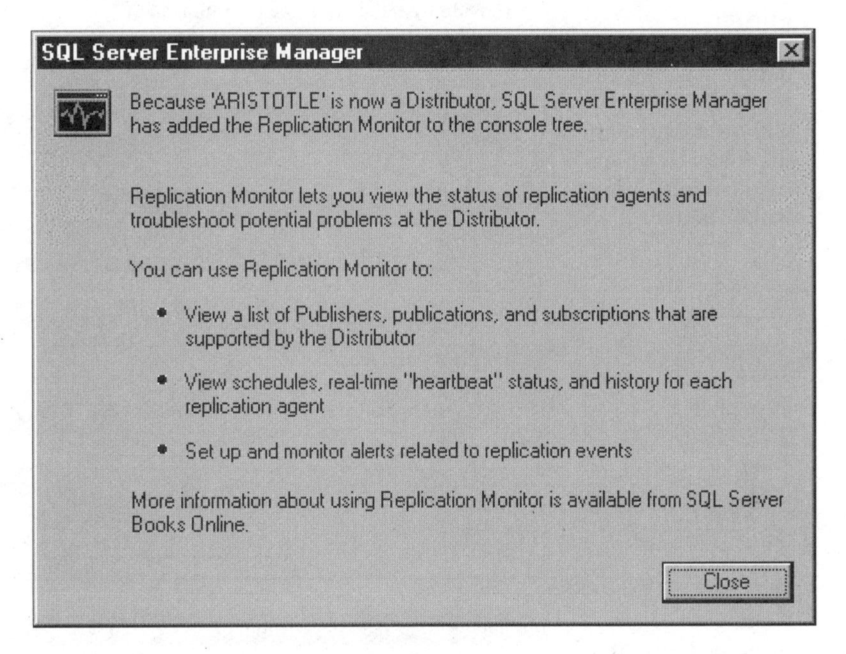

Custom Configuration

If you choose to set configuration information, you are taken through a separate series of prompts:

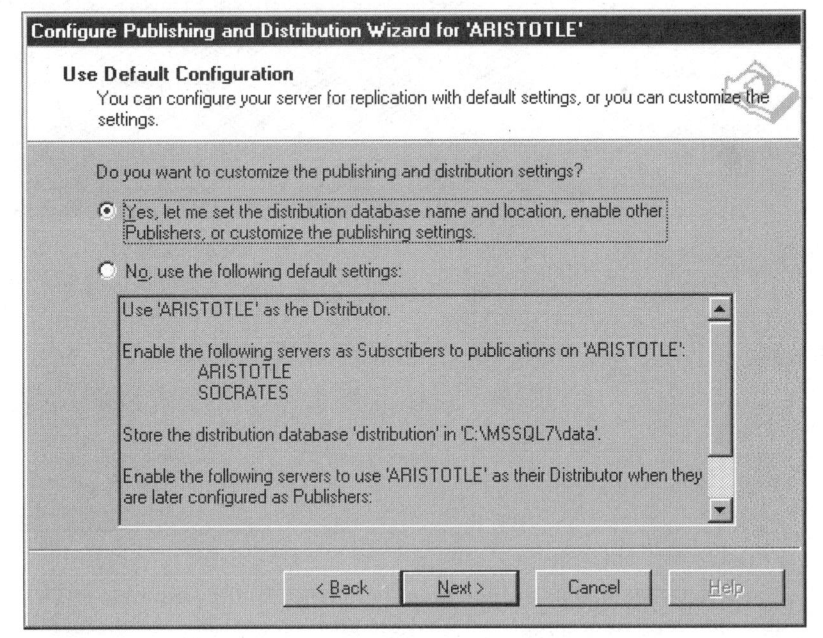

First, you are prompted to provide the distribution database name, the folder in which it will be stored, and the folder in which the distribution log will be stored:

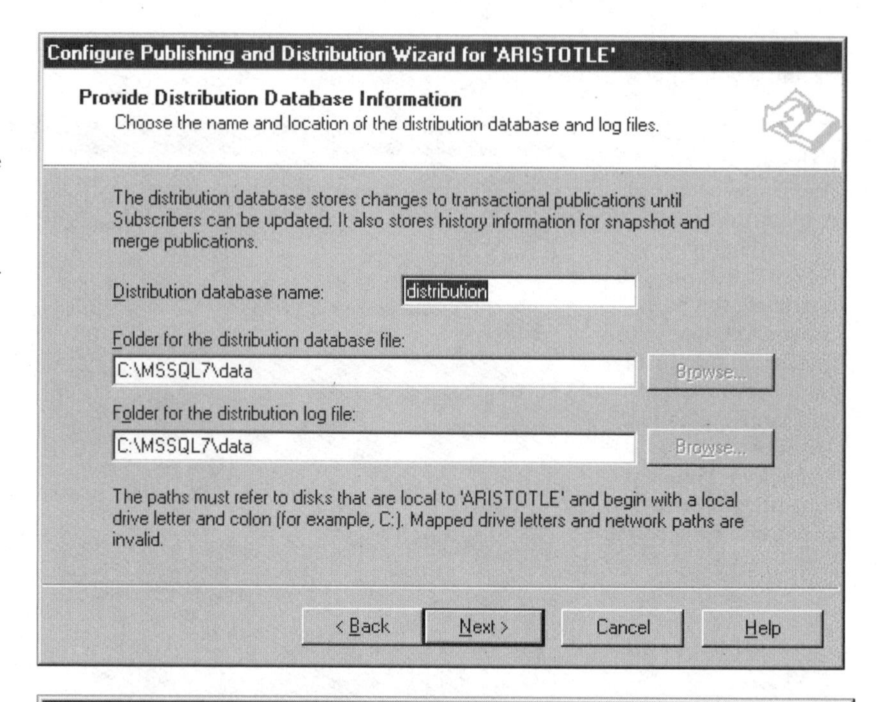

Next, you are prompted to enable Publishers. Click on the properties button (see the mouse pointer in the figure) to display server Properties:

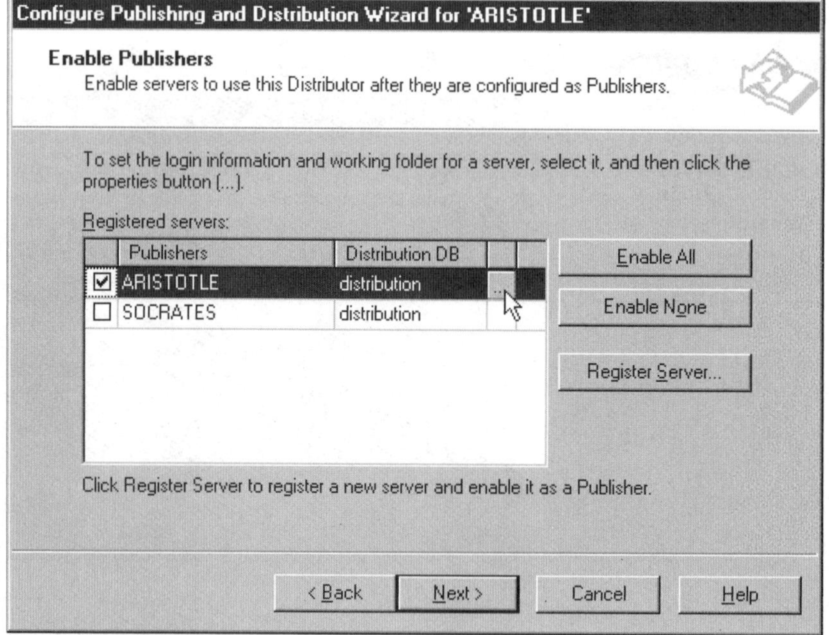

The Properties dialog lets you identify the distribution database to be used as well as the location of the snapshot folder. Make sure that the location specified for the snapshot folder has sufficient space to meet your storage requirements.

You can also specify how replication agents log into the Publisher, either by impersonating the SQL Server agent account through a trusted connection or by using a SQL Server Authentication connection:

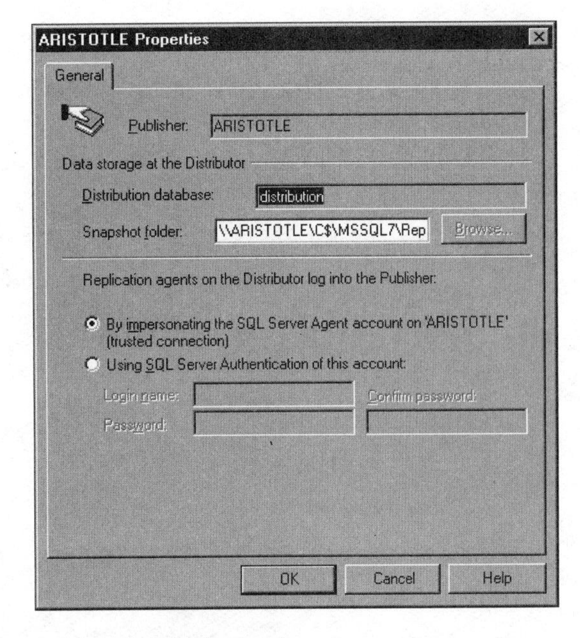

Next, you need to enable databases for replication. You can enable a database for transactional replication, merge replication, or both. Enabling a database for transactional replication also enables the database for snapshot replication.

> **SQL Server 7.0 Desktop edition does not support publishing via transactional replication. You can only have snapshot and merge running from a SQL Server Desktop Publisher. SQL Server Desktop Subscribers can subscribe to transactional replication publications.**

The figure shows the `Northwind` database enabled for both transactional and merge replication:

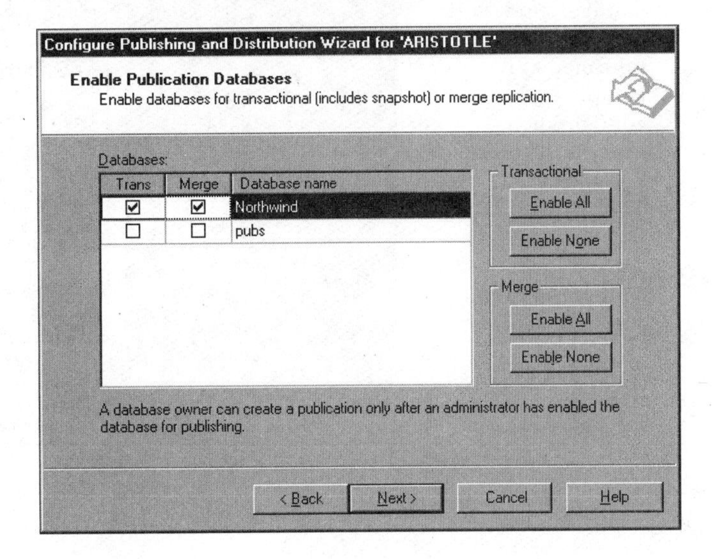

You can also identify authorized subscribers to the database. You can choose from a list of registered servers. Click on Register Server if you want to register additional servers:

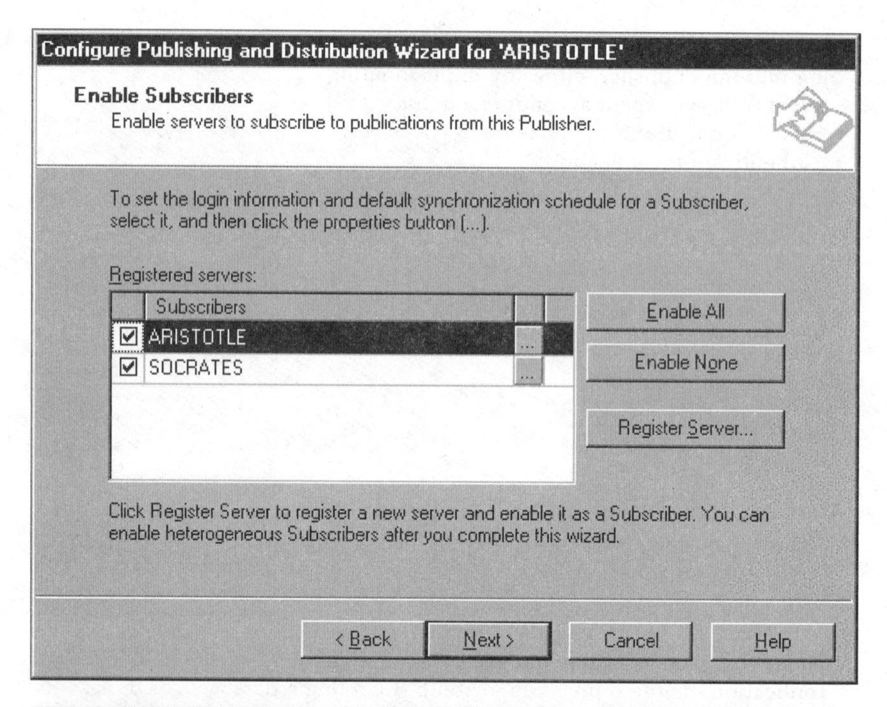

Now you're ready to finish configuration based on your configuration settings. The dialog describes your configuration. SQL Server keeps you informed as it completes the configuration process. As before, you will be prompted if the SQL Server Agent service is not configured to start automatically:

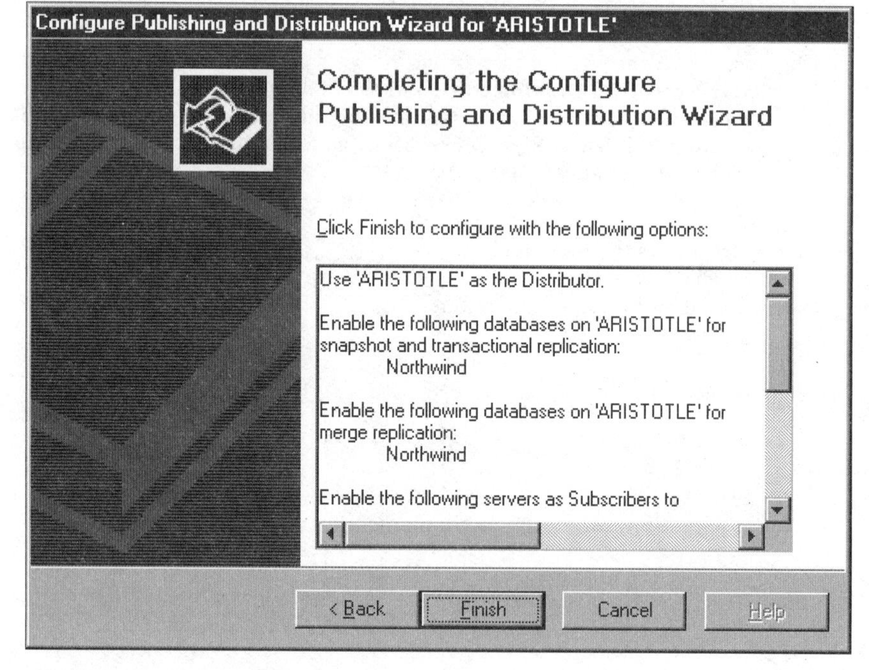

After Configuration

Once you identify a database as publishing, the Enterprise Manager will show the database as shared. You can also see the Replication Monitor in the Enterprise Manager tree:

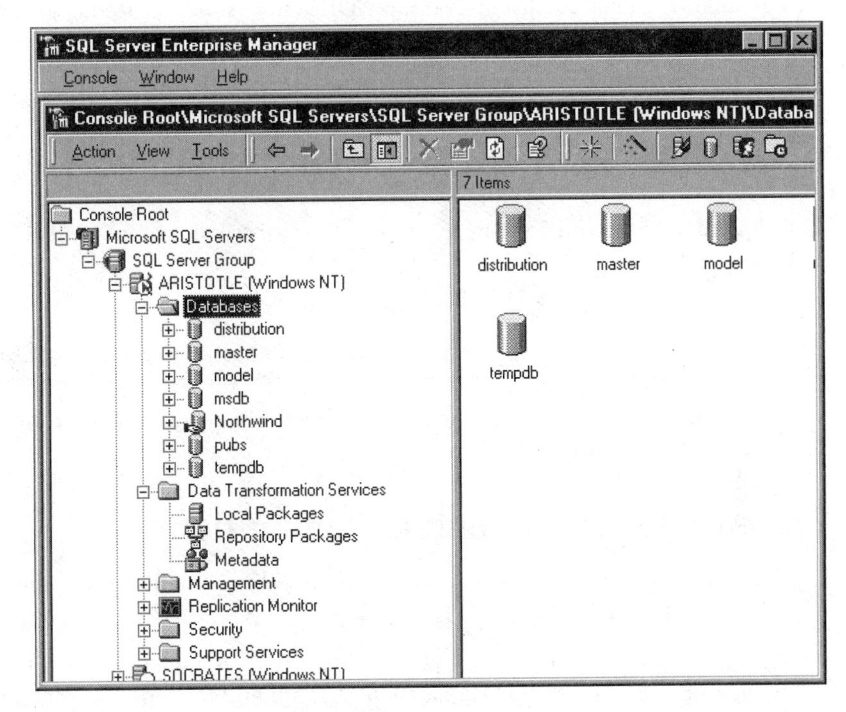

A Distributor can be uninstalled using the **Disable Publishing and Distribution Wizard**. Uninstalling a Distributor will automatically delete its distribution databases and disable any Publishers using the Distributor. Subscribers and publications on disabled Publishers are deleted. Any data that has been replicated to Subscribers is not deleted from the Subscribers. To launch this Wizard, select your database in Enterprise Manager and run Tools | Replication | Disable Publishing, or select Disable Publishing and Distribution Wizard from the Select Wizard dialog.

You can review and modify Publisher and Distributor properties at any time. Run Tools | Replication | Configure Publishing, Subscribers, and Distribution to display the property pages. You can view and modify the following property pages:

- Distributor – Distribution databases and replication agent profiles
- Publishers – Properties for all Publishers including snapshot folder and login method for Distribution Agents
- Publication Databases – Enable or disable databases for publication
- Subscribers – Register or remove Subscribers

In the examples throughout the rest of this chapter, we will walk through the process of configuring publications and articles, as well as setting up Subscribers. We'll cover transactional and snapshot replication first, then merge replication.

Transact-SQL Procedures

The following table is a list of Transact-SQL system stored procedures that you can use to set up Publishers and Distributors, as well as identifying Subscribers:

Stored Procedure	Description
`sp_adddistributor`	Run `sp_adddistributor` at the server to configure the server as a Distributor.
`sp_adddistributiondb`	Run at the Distributor to create the distribution database(s).
`sp_adddistpublisher`	Run at each server that you will be configuring as a Publisher to identify its Distributor.
`sp_addsubscriber`	Run at the Publisher to register a Subscriber.

These stored procedures have extensive input parameters and options; please refer to SQL Server Books Online for detailed information about these procedures.

Transactional/Snapshot Publications

Note that you will see the same prompts when setting up either a snapshot or transactional publication.

You can create publications by launching the **Create Publication Wizard** from the Select Wizard dialog or by running Tools | Replication | Create and Manage Publications.

Create and Manage Publications

First, you need to select the database for which you want to define publications, then click on Create Publication to continue:

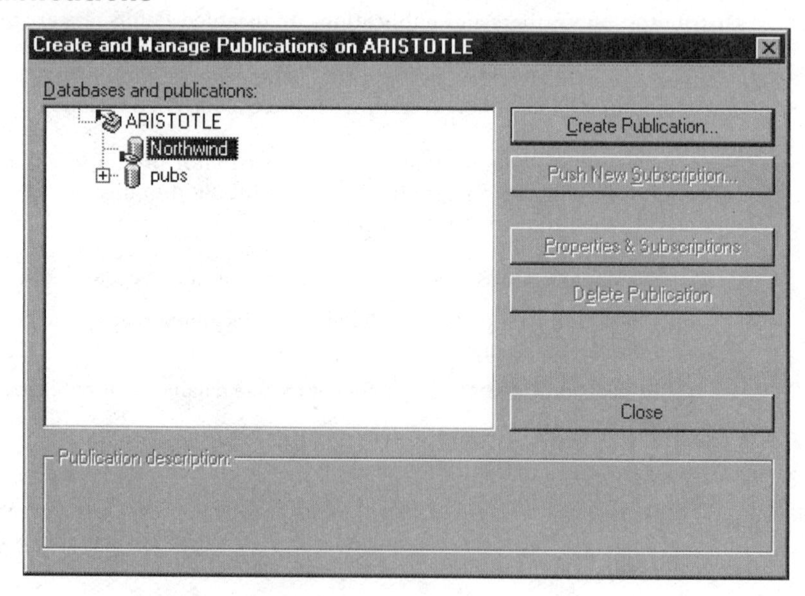

The opening Wizard dialog explains that you can create a publication, filter data, and set publication properties through the Wizard:

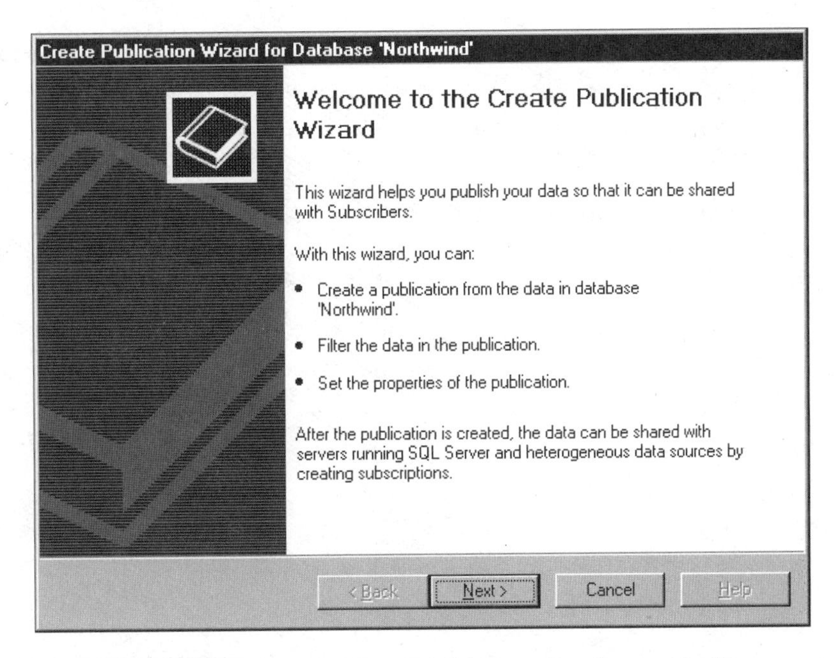

If you have already created a publication for this database, you will be prompted as to whether or not to use the existing publication as a template for the new publication.

You can select to create a snapshot, transactional, or merge publication. That is, of course, unless you're running SQL Server Desktop edition. SQL Server Desktop cannot be configured to publish for transactional replication.

We're going to choose transactional for this example:

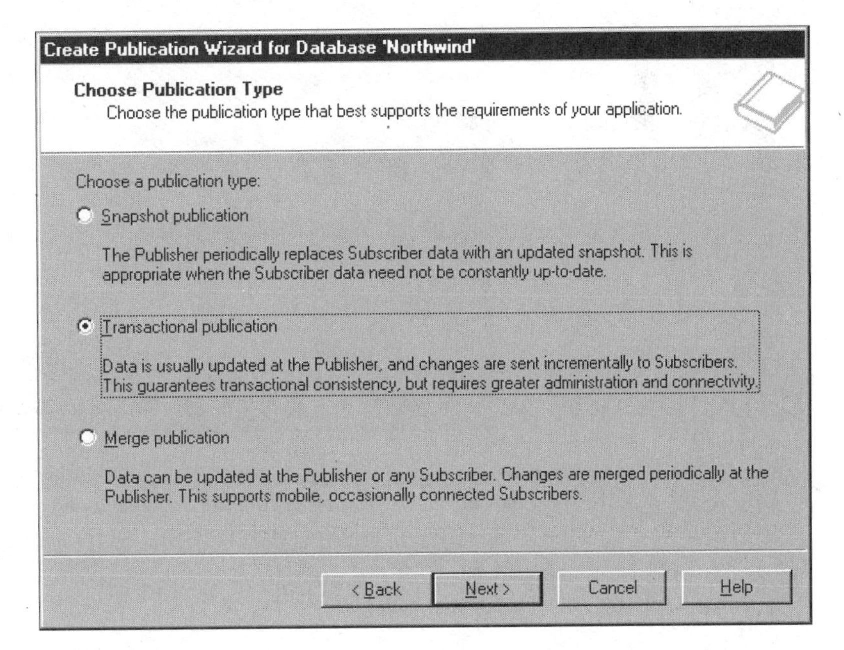

You have to decide whether or not you are going to support immediate-updating subscriptions. We're not supporting immediate-updates for this example:

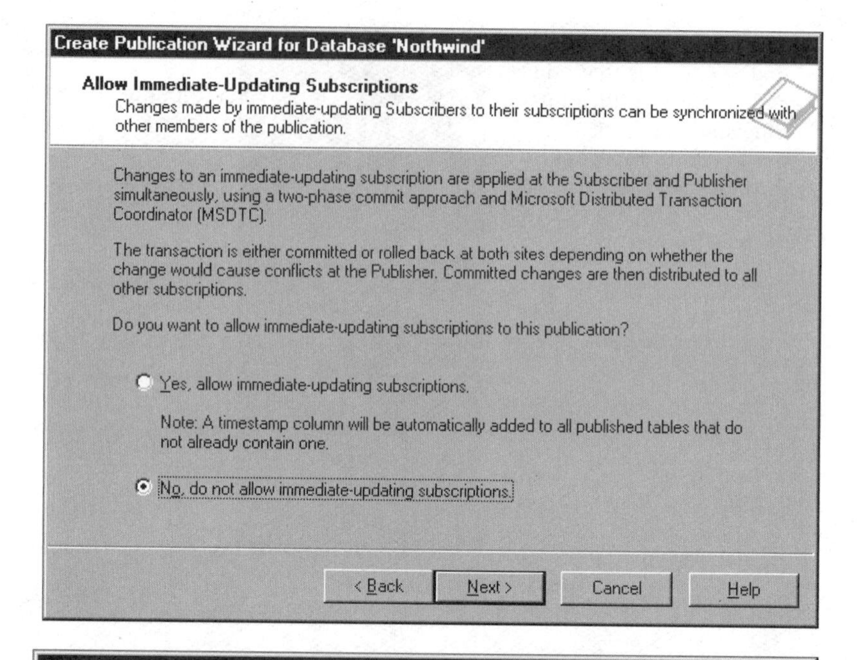

You also have to let SQL Server know if any of the subscribers will be a database server other than SQL Server. This makes it relatively easy to set up replication support in a heterogeneous networking environment. All of our subscribers are running SQL Server:

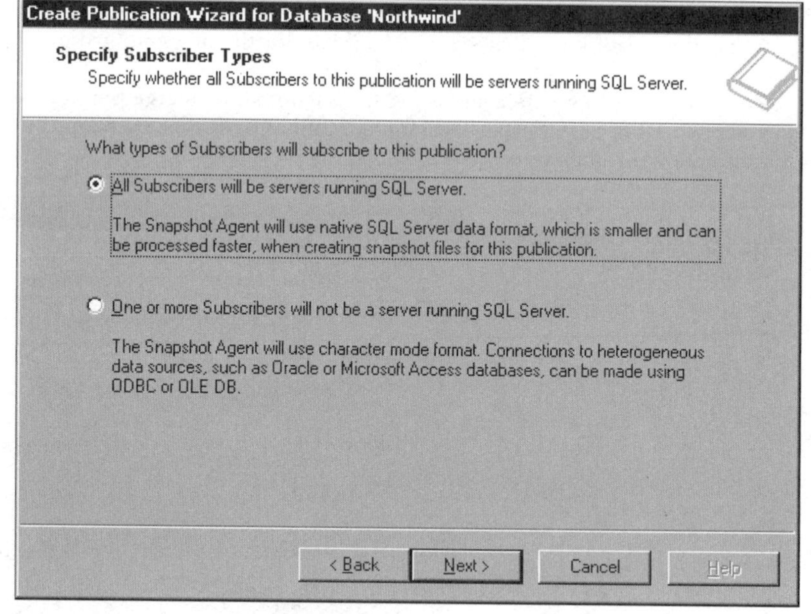

Now you're ready to select the tables to be published. For this example, we're going to publish the `Employees` table. You can choose whether to include tables, stored procedures, or both in your publication. We're limiting the publication to tables.

By default, the dialog lists all user-defined tables in the database. If you select the Only published objects option under Filter list to show, only tables marked for publication will be displayed in the list.

As a special note on stored procedures, you may be creating stored procedures at some time that will be used for filtering tables and will only be executed by replication. When creating stored procedures of this type, be sure to specify the `FOR REPLICATION` option as part of your `CREATE PROCEDURE` statement.

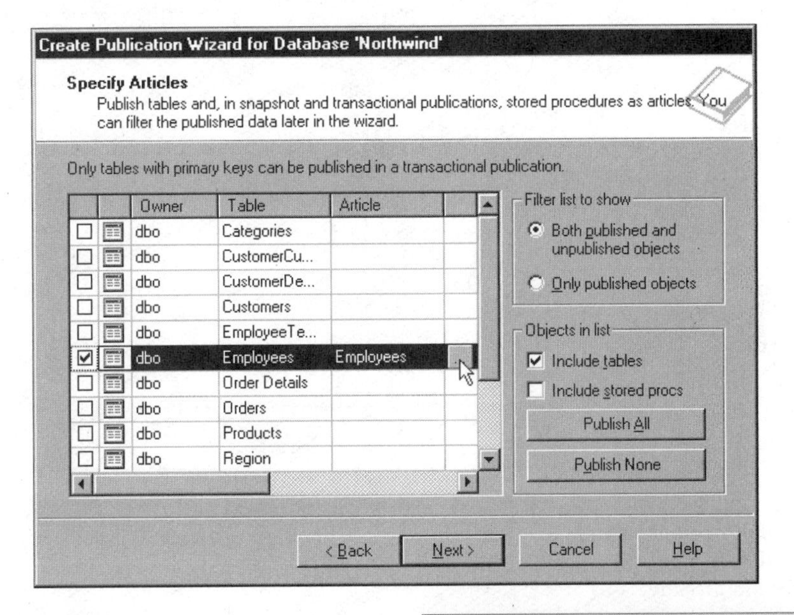

Click on the properties button to view article properties. The General tab includes the article name and table information. You can change the article name and destination table name. You can also specify an owner for the destination table:

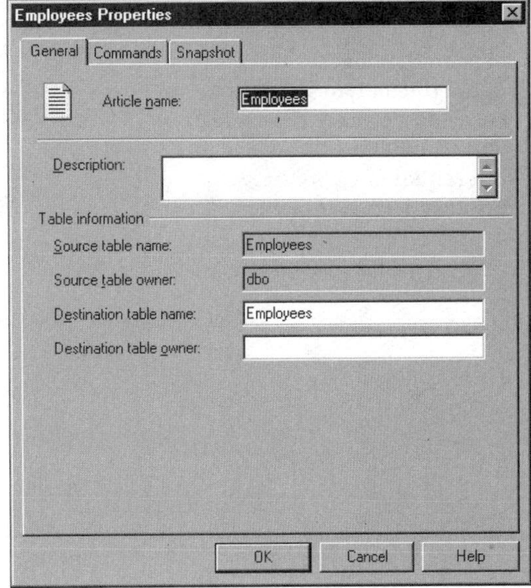

The Commands tab shows the stored procedures that will be used instead of `INSERT`, `DELETE` and `UPDATE` commands at the Subscriber. The stored procedures will be created at the Subscriber during synchronization:

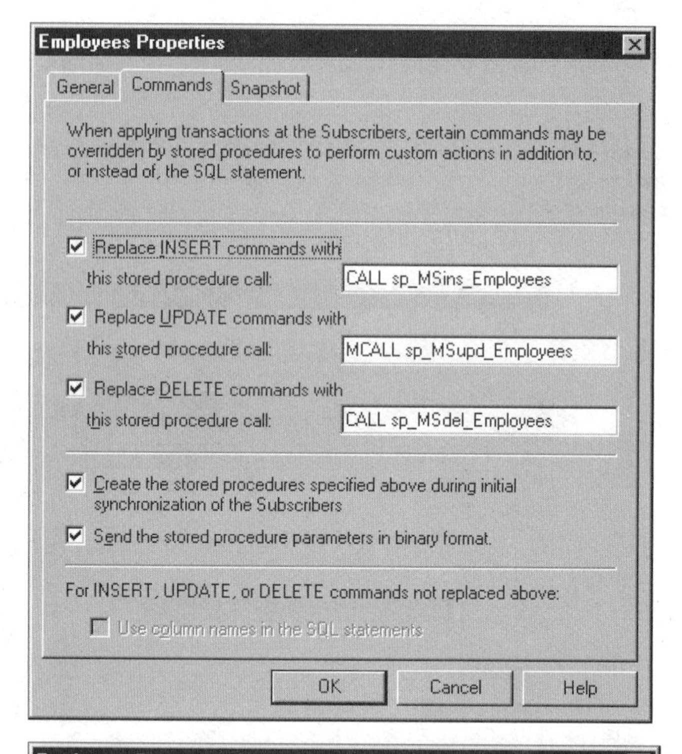

The Snapshot tab lets you modify snapshot options. You can specify what to do if the destination table already exists, identify whether to copy clustered and non-clustered indexes, set if user-defined data types should be converted to base data types, and whether declared referential integrity on primary keys is included:

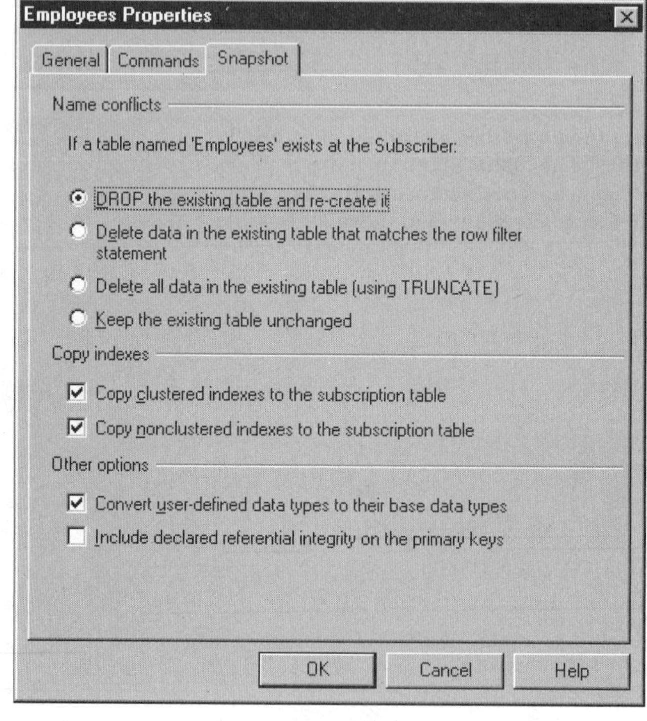

The publication name defaults to the database name. We're changing the name to NorthTran here to allow us to easily recognize the publication. You can name your publication as you wish. If you are going to be supporting several publications, pick names that will help remind you what is being published. It will probably be helpful to include the source database name, and possibly, the name of one of the source tables, as part of the publication name:

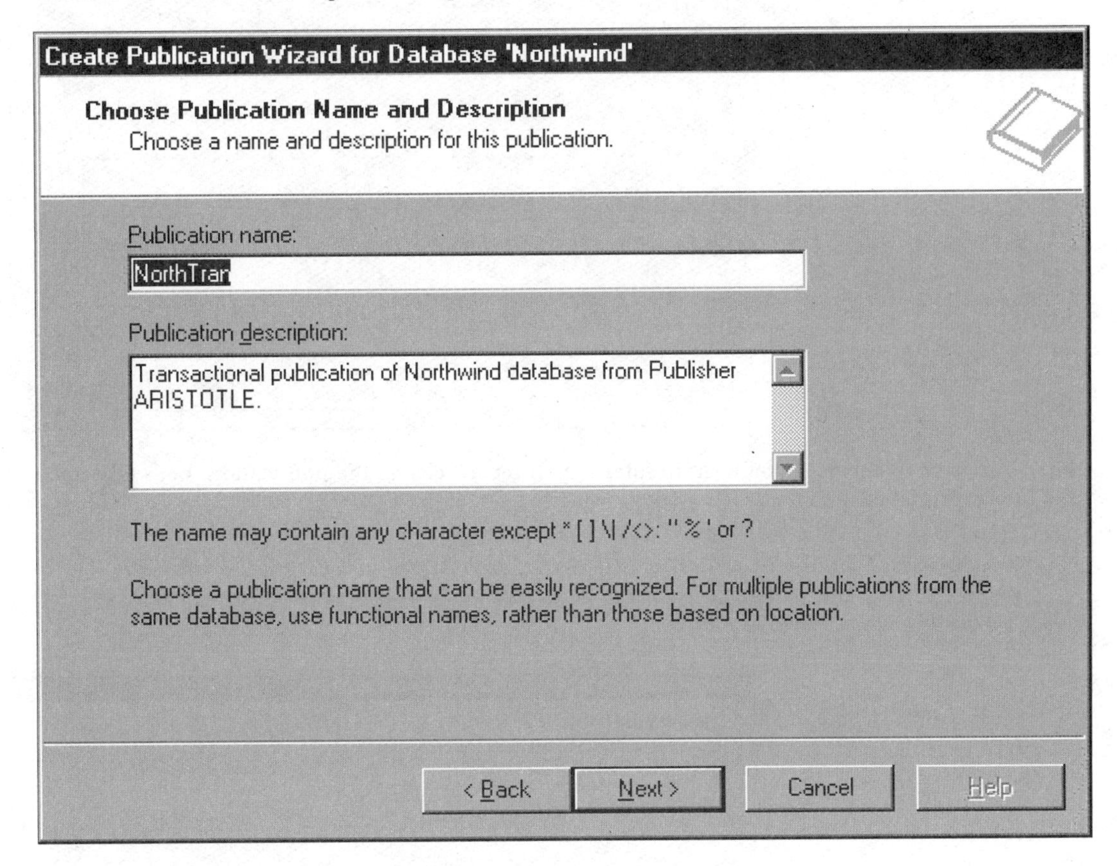

You can accept default properties for the article or set custom properties. Default properties include:

- Do not filter the publication
- Do not allow anonymous Subscribers to create pull subscriptions
- Run the snapshot once at 11:30 PM

We're going to define custom options for our publication:

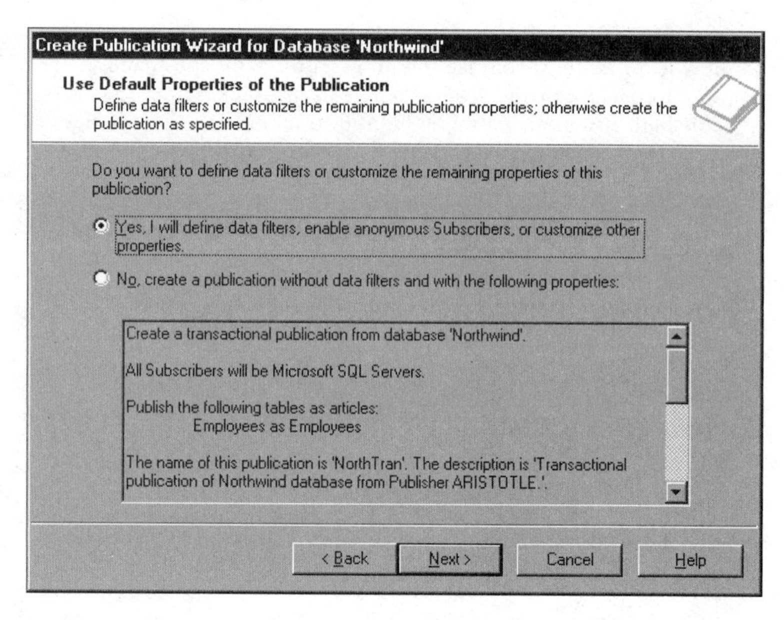

First, you have to decide if you want to filter any of the articles in the publication. Let's take a look at the filtering options.

If you've worked with earlier versions of SQL Server, don't forget that what is being referred to now as "filtering" was previously referred to as "partitioning". When you see "filter", think "partition" and you should be fine.

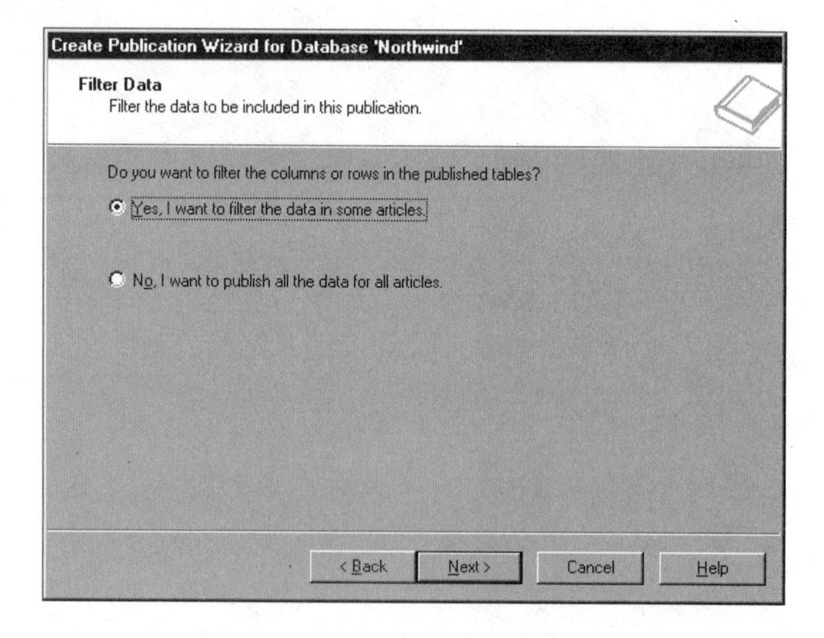

To filter columns (vertical filtering) to not be included in the article, remove the check from any undesired columns. We're filtering out the columns containing mailing address information, such as address, city, state, and so on:

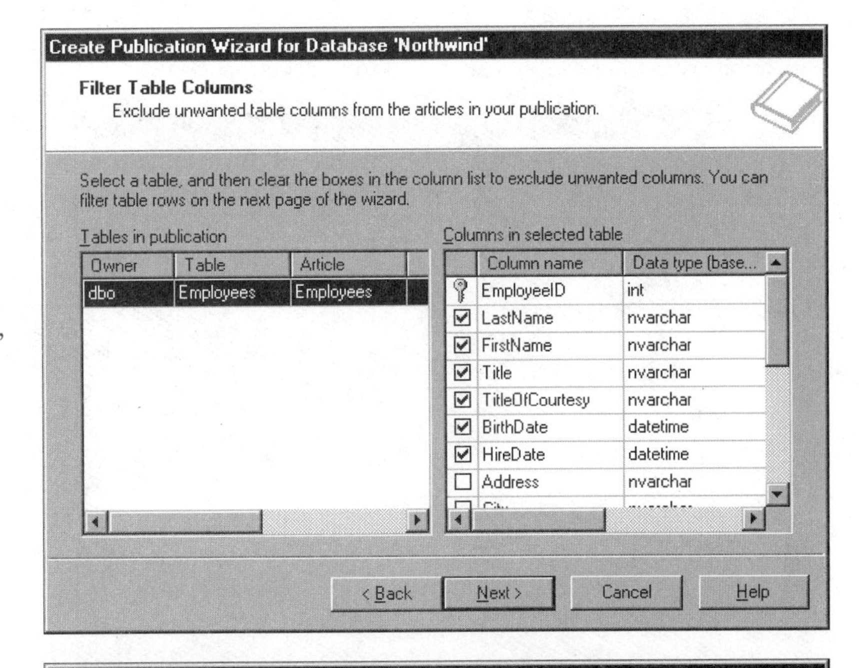

Row (horizontal) filtering is selected on the next screen. Click on the button next to the filtering clause to define filters:

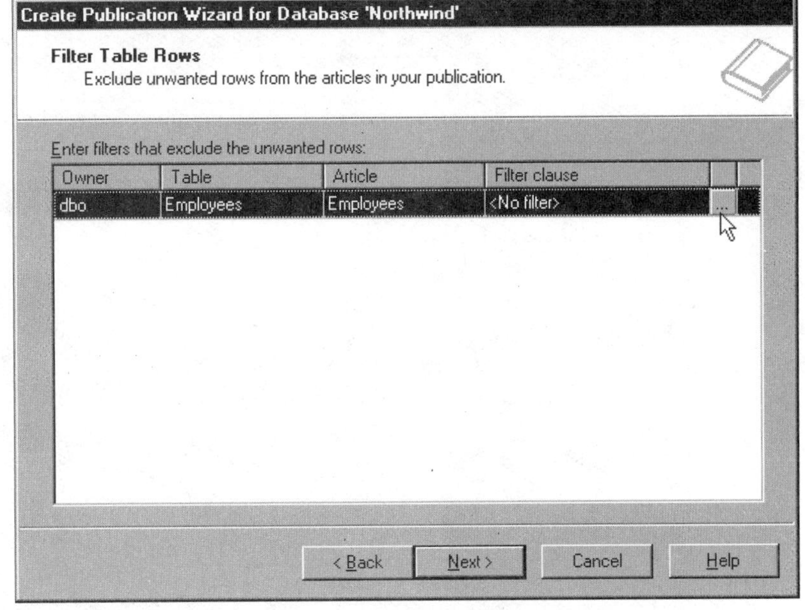

Row filtering is defined by entering a filtering clause as a `WHERE` clause in a `SELECT` statement. We're not using any row filtering in this example.

Note that the Create and Manage Publications Wizard uses the term column filtering to refer to vertical filtering and row filtering to refer to horizontal filtering.

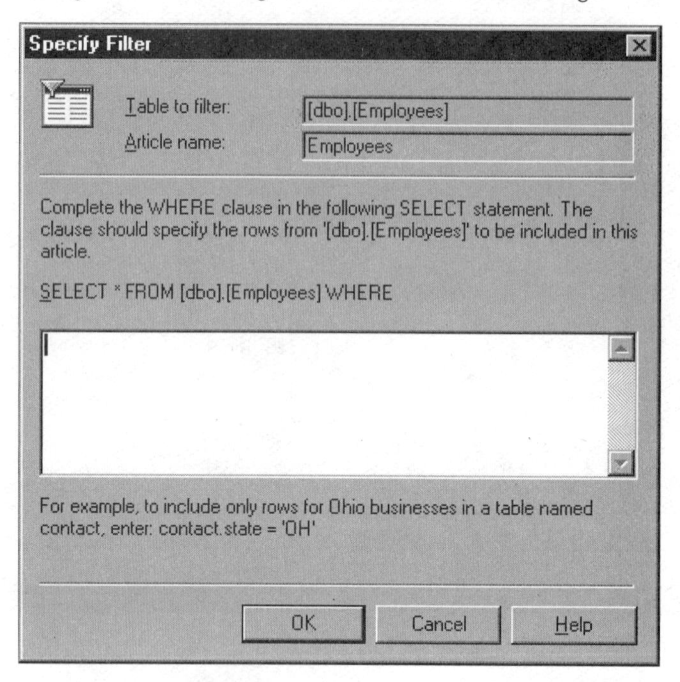

You can also allow or disallow subscriptions from anonymous Subscribers. We're not going to allow anonymous Subscribers in this example:

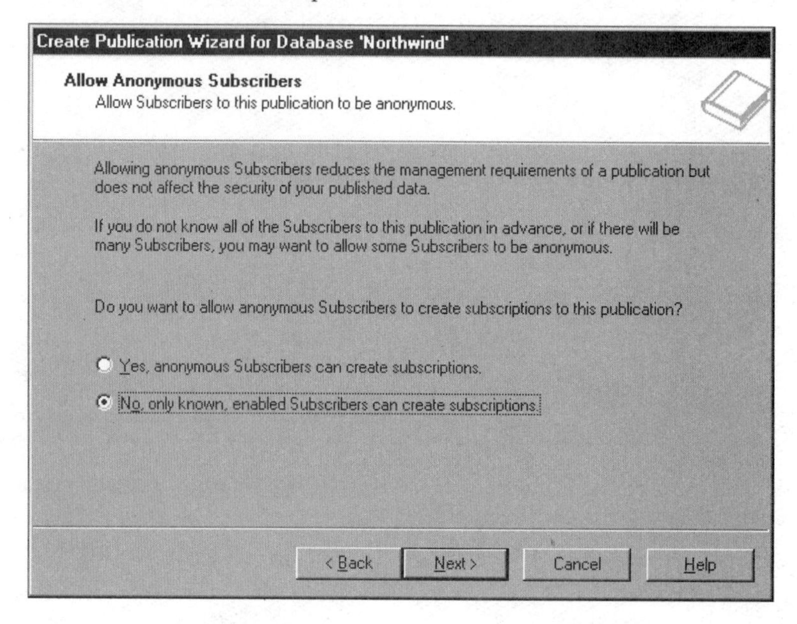

You also need to set the Snapshot Agent schedule. Click on Change to make changes to the default schedule.

Notice also that, by default, the first snapshot will be created at the first scheduled run of the Snapshot Agent. In our example, we've chosen to have the first snapshot created immediately:

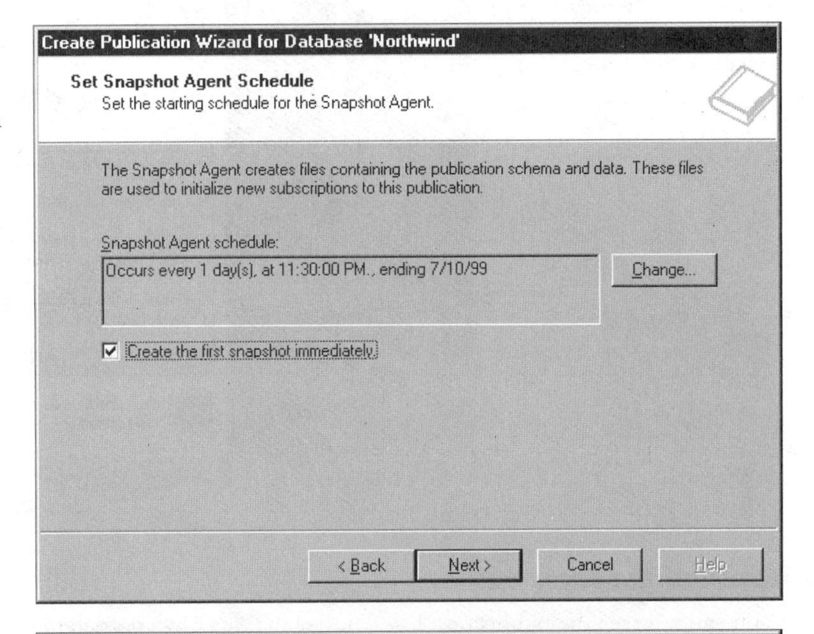

You can have replication occur daily, weekly, or monthly, as well as set the time of day for replication. You can also define the start and end date. Here we're leaving the settings at their defaults.

This dialog can be used to configure a recurring snapshot, even if you are supporting transactional replication. This will force periodic resynchronization between the Publisher and Subscriber:

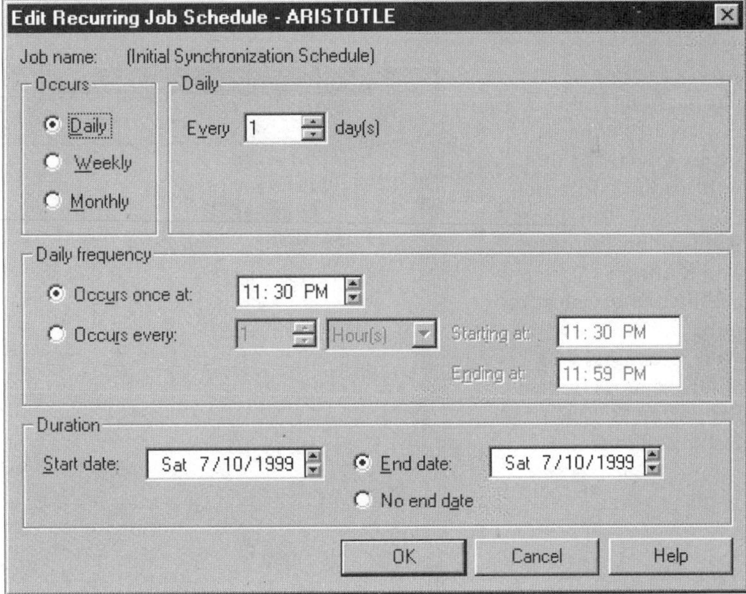

Now, you're ready to create the publication. The Wizard summarizes the options you've selected for your review:

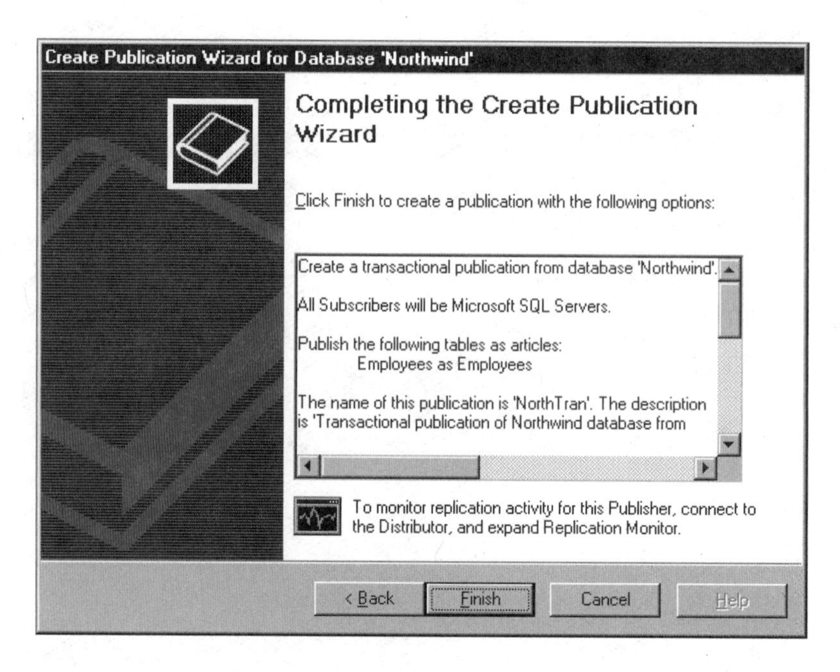

After Configuration

You can now see the publication listed under the `Northwind` database. From here, you can push a subscription out to Subscribers, modify properties and subscriptions, or delete the publication:

After creating a publication, you can display its property pages to view or modify publication and article properties. Run Tools | Replication | Create and Manage Publications. Select the publication you wish to view from under its database and click on Properties & Subscriptions:

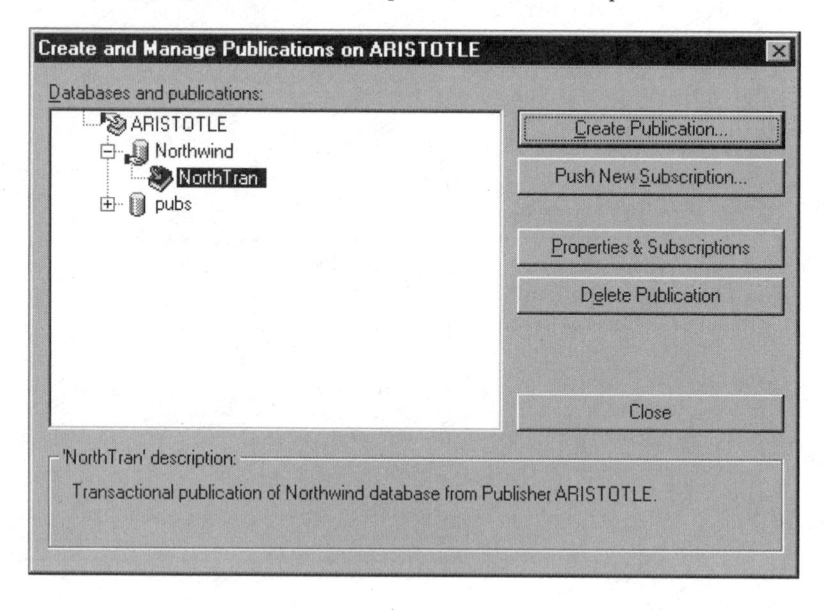

The property pages include:

- **General** – Publication identification, description, and snapshot file properties
- **Articles** – Modify properties for published articles, add articles to the publication, and delete articles
- **Filter Columns** – View, add, or modify vertical filtering
- **Filter Rows** – View, add, or modify horizontal filtering
- **Subscriptions** – View subscription properties, create new push subscriptions, delete subscriptions, and force resynchronization between the Publisher and Subscribers
- **Subscription Options** – View and set subscription options, including Internet support
- **Publication Access List** – View and modify logins used by pull and immediate-update subscriptions
- **Status** – View Snapshot Agent and service status information, run the Snapshot Agent, and start services
- **Scripts** – View and modify script options and format

You will have to remove any subscriptions from the publication to be able to modify some publication options.

Transact-SQL Procedures

The following system stored procedures are used to definesnapshot and transactional publications and articles:

Stored Procedure	Description
`sp_replicationdboption`	Run this procedure to enable publication of the current database.
`sp_addpublication`	Use this procedure to define a publication in the current database.
`sp_addpublication_snapshot`	This is used to create a Snapshot Agent and place the schema and data into the replication working directory for running synchronization.
`sp_addarticle`	Run for each article you wish to add to the publication.
`Sp_articlefilter`	This procedure lets you set up horizontal filtering for an article.
`sp_articlecolumn`	Use this procedure to set up vertical filtering for an article.
`sp_articleview`	This is used to create the synchronization object for a filtered article.

As before, refer to SQL Server Books Online for detailed information about these procedures.

Merge Publications

Now we're going to step through creating a merge publication.

You can create publications by launching the Create Publication Wizard from the Select Wizard dialog or by running Tools | Replication | Create and Manage Publications.

Create and Manage Publications Wizard

You start out the same, by selecting the database from which you want to publish. The opening screen of the Wizard is also the same, so we won't show these here. This time, we're selecting to create a merge publication:

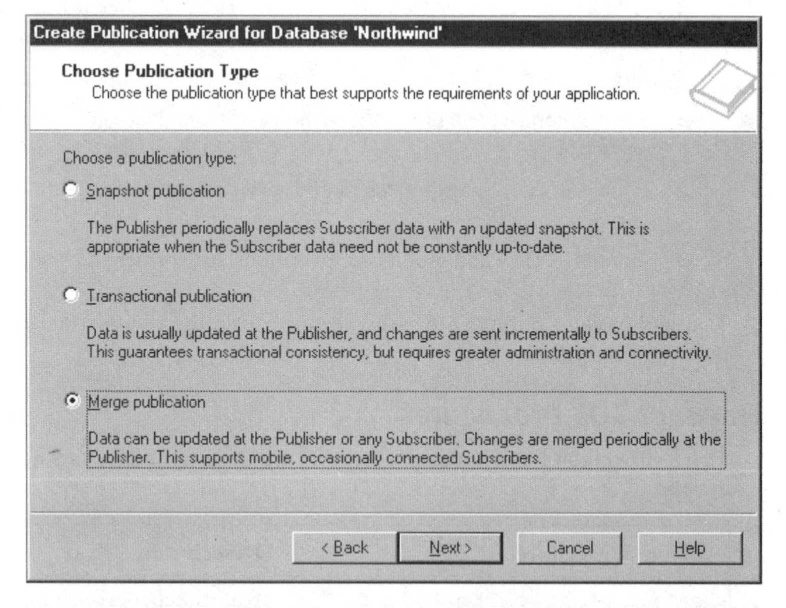

As before, you have to identify whether or not all of the Subscribers are running Microsoft SQL Server:

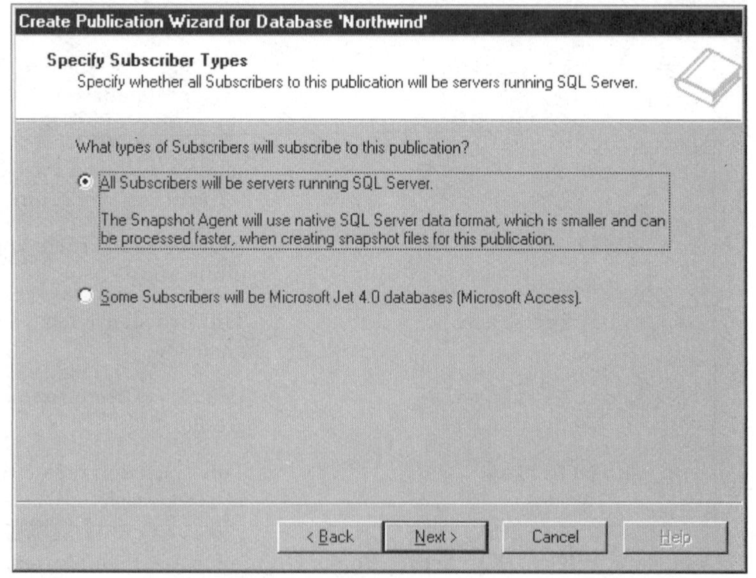

You also have to identify the tables that you wish to publish. When defining a merge publication you can only select to publish tables. Don't forget, a table can be identified as an article in more than one publication:

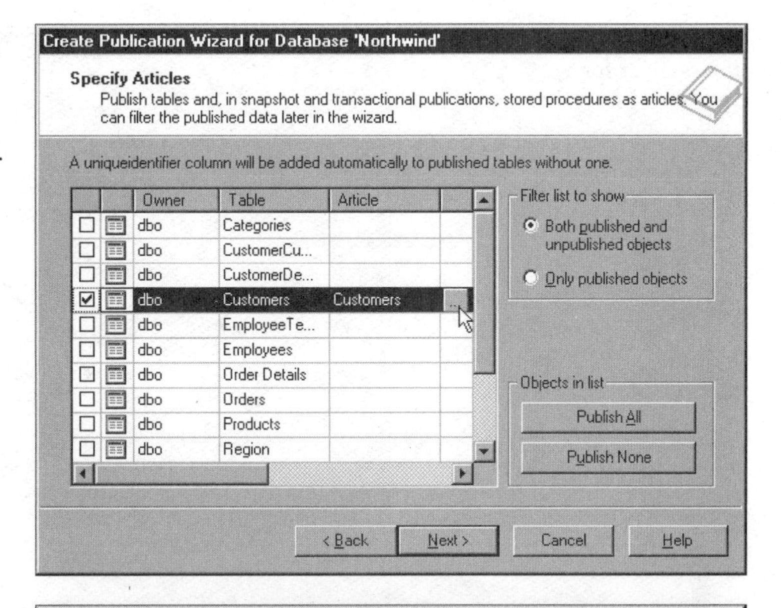

The article properties are a little different for merge publications. The General tab lets you determine whether changes to the same row, or changes to the same column in a row, are considered conflicts:

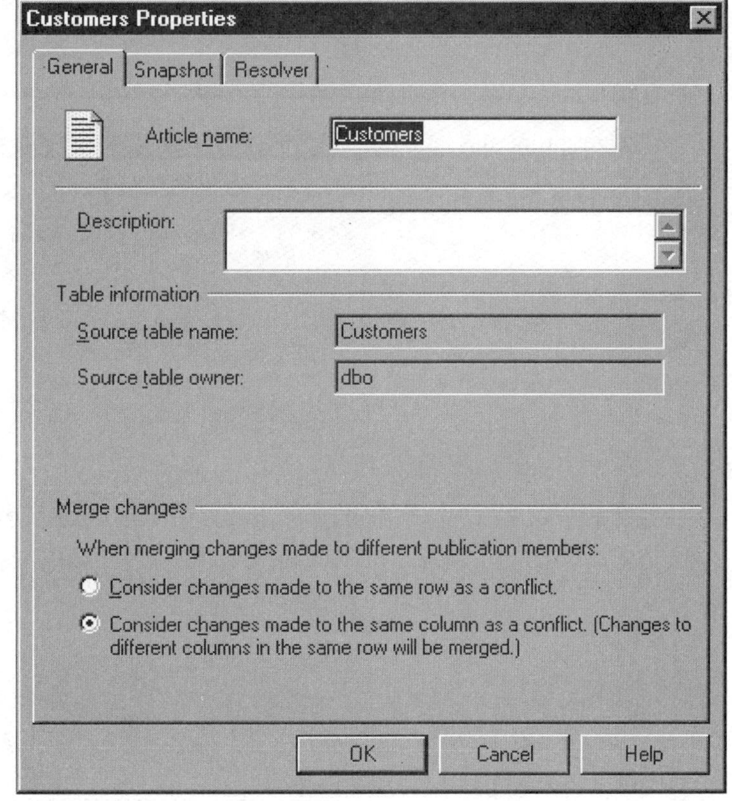

The Snapshot properties are the same as for snapshot/transactional replication:

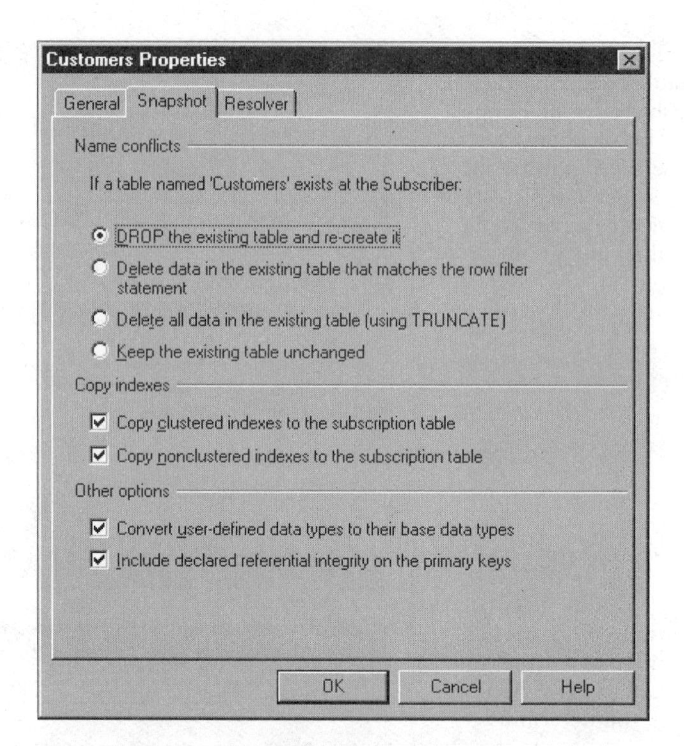

The Resolver properties let you choose to either use the default resolver or a custom resolver:

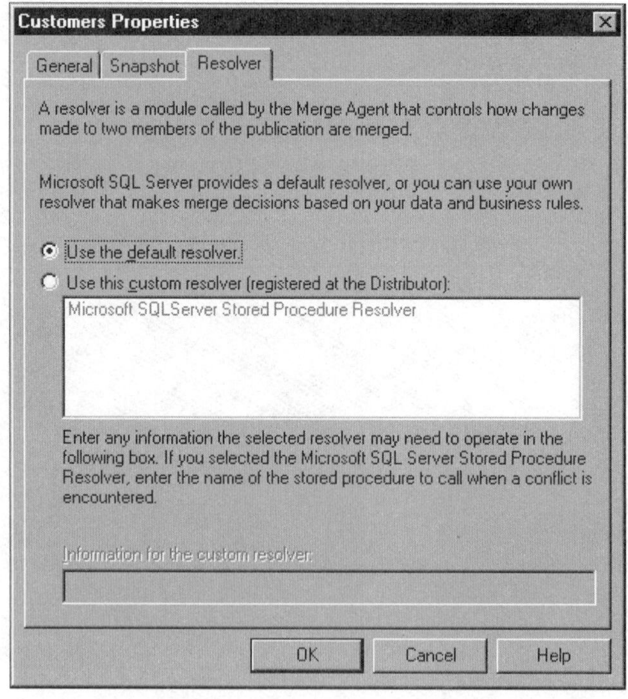

If any of the published tables do not include a `uniqueidentifier` column, you will be prompted that the column will be created for you:

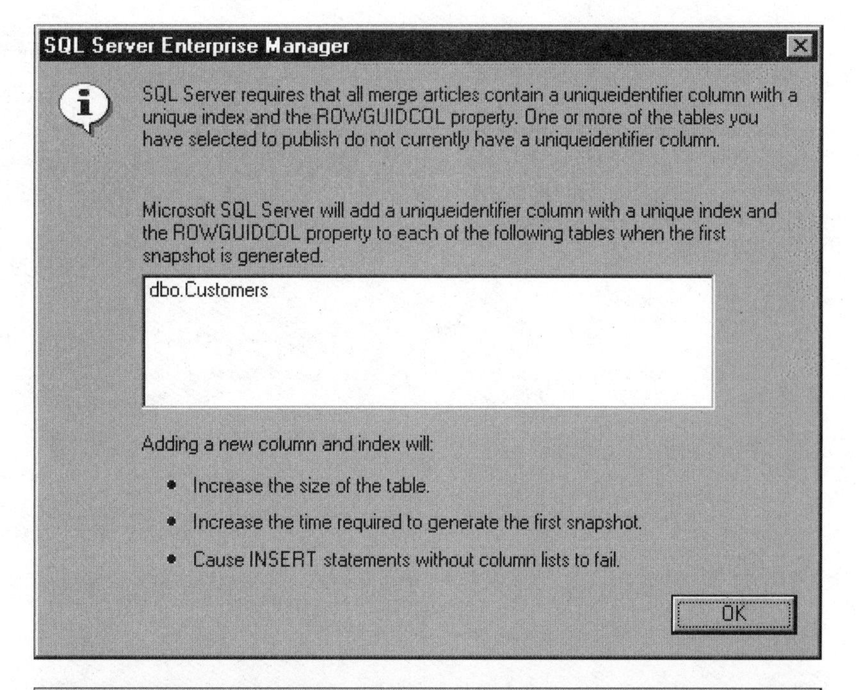

As in the last example, the article needs to be given a name and description. This time, we're calling the article NorthMerge:

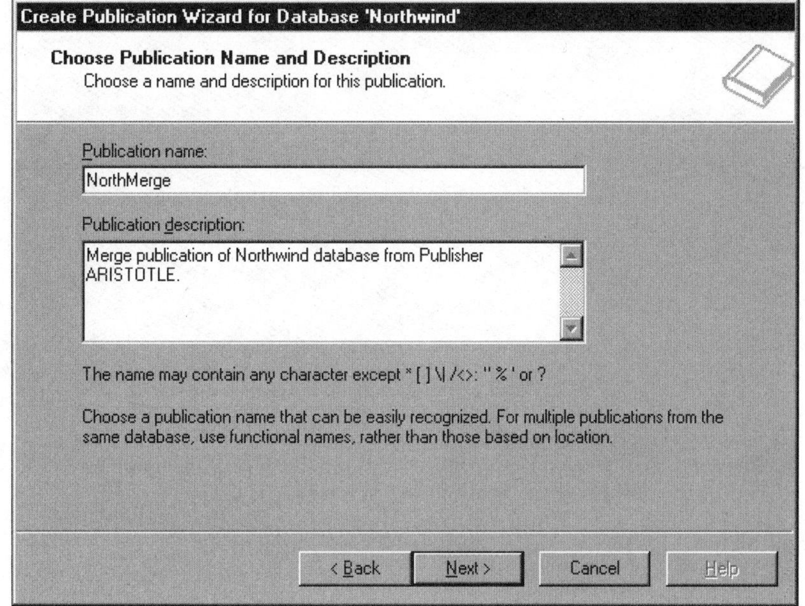

You can create the publication using the default properties or define customized properties. You'll see very nearly the same screens as for snapshot and transactional publications, except for the filtering screens:

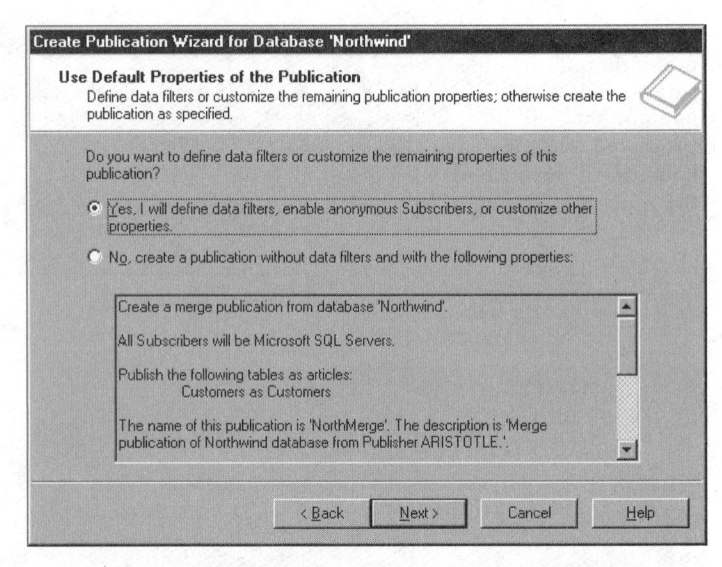

The default is that you want to use filtering:

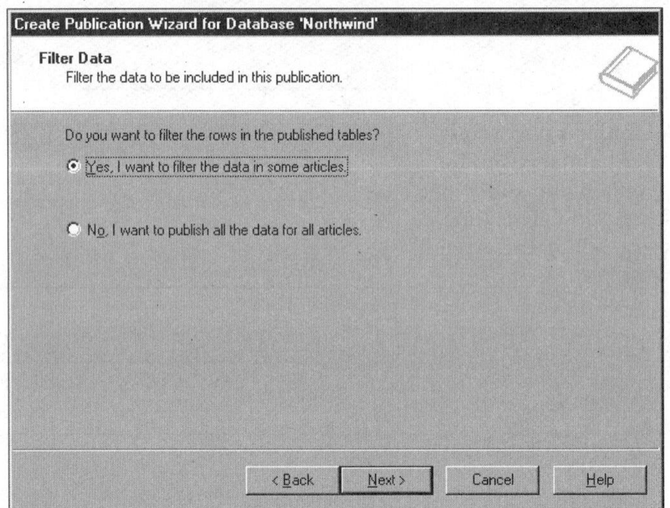

You have to pick either static or dynamic filters. A static filter sends the same data to all subscribers. If you want to send different parts of the data to different subscribers, you need to use dynamic filters. For this example, we're going to use static filters:

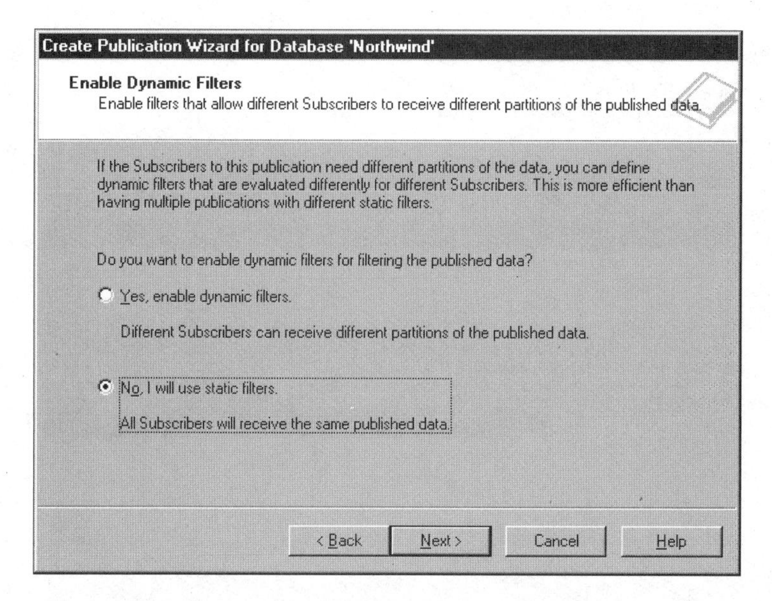

We're going to create a static filter limiting the rows to just those customers in the USA. SQL Server will create the filters for you before continuing to the next Wizard prompt:

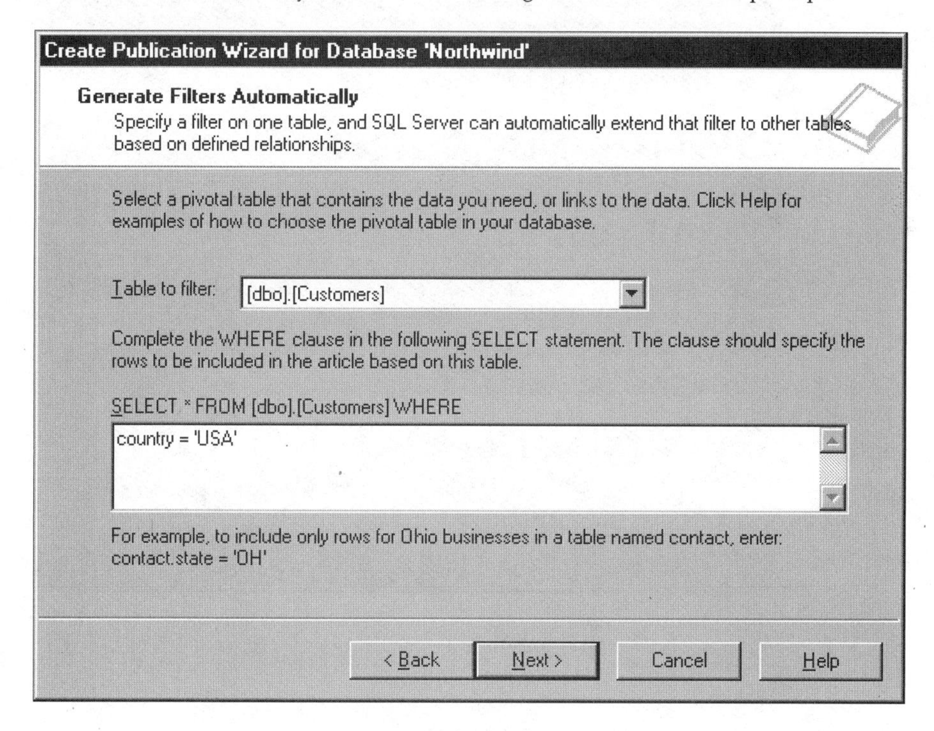

You can also set up joins between filtered tables. We're not making any join specifications:

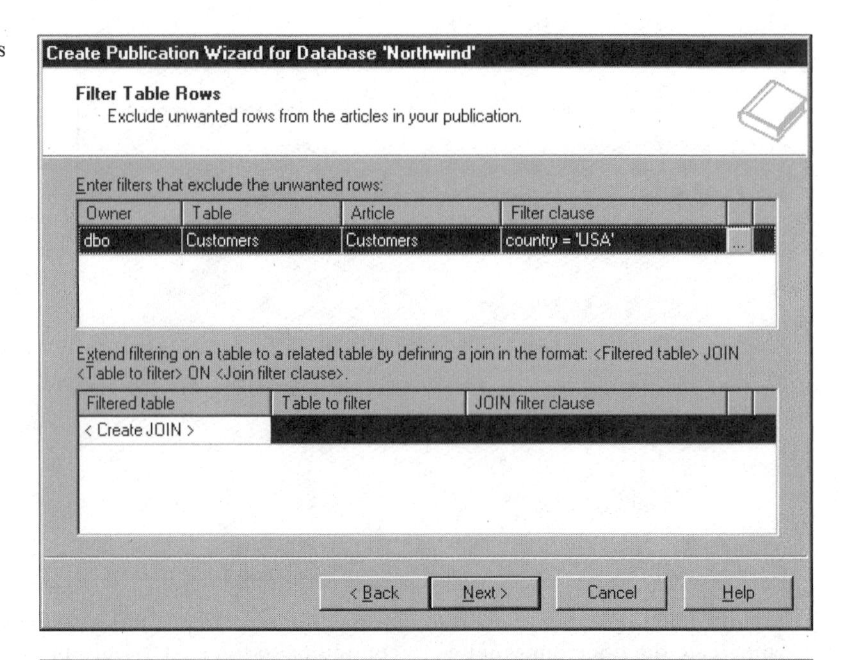

As before, you can choose whether or not you want to support anonymous subscribers:

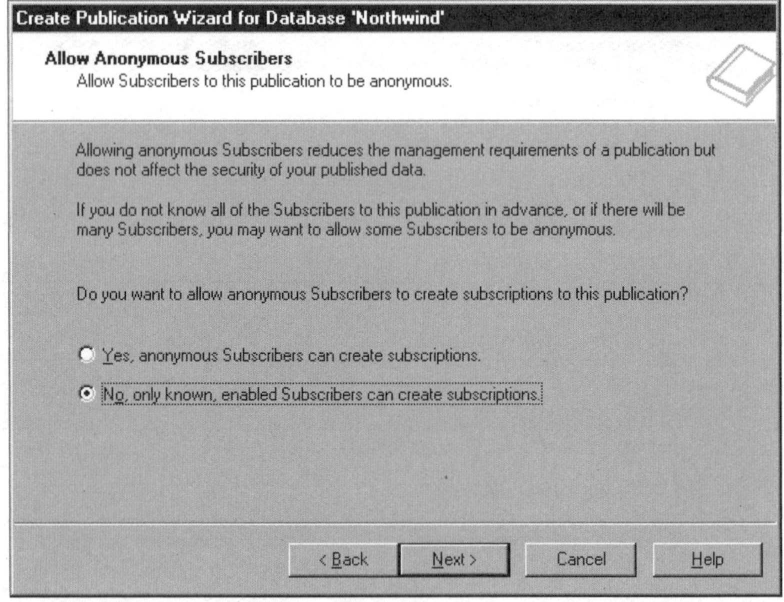

You can also make changes to the default snapshot schedule. By default, the snapshot will only run once:

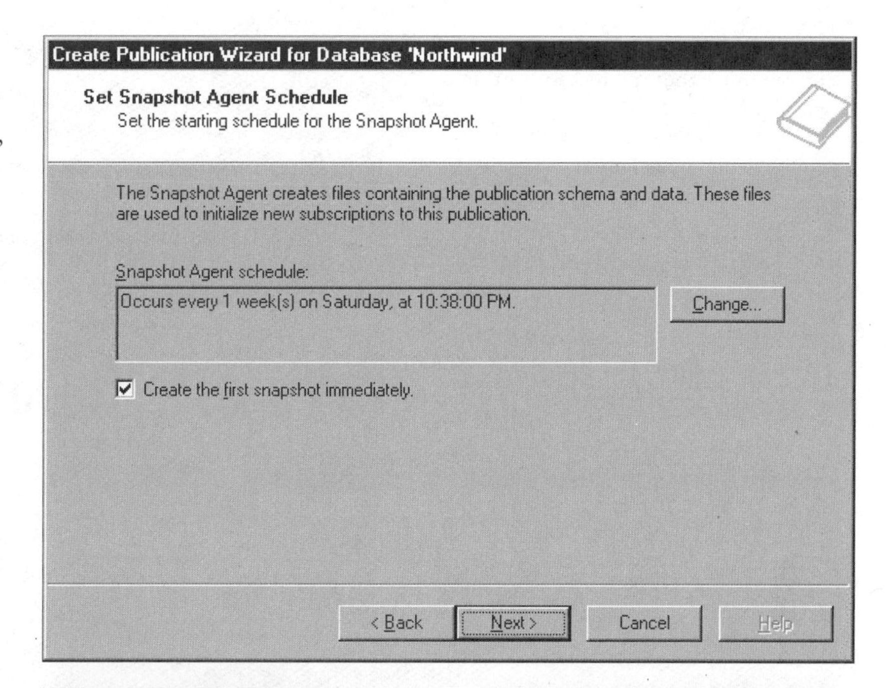

Now you're ready to create the publication. SQL Server will show you as it completes each step of the process:

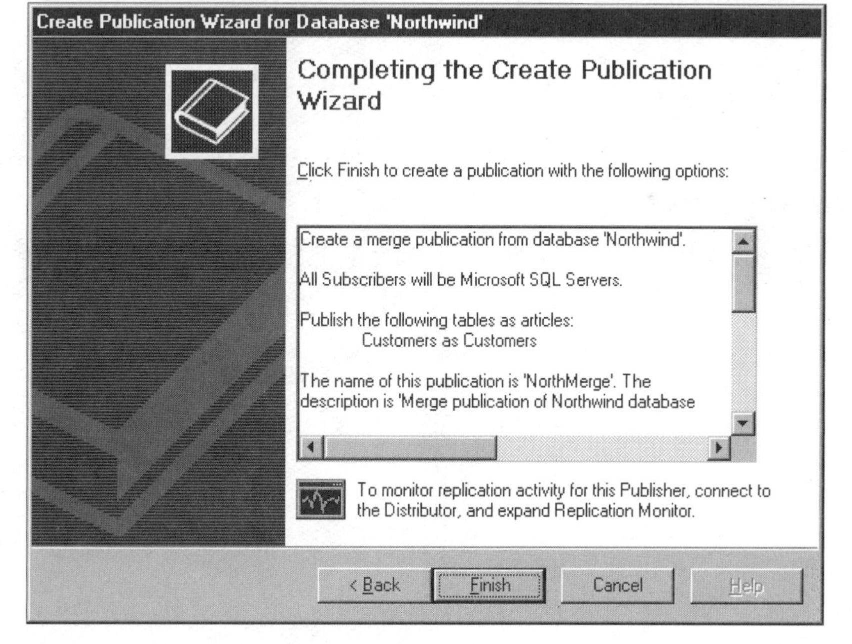

You will be informed of any errors or anything that might result in data corruption:

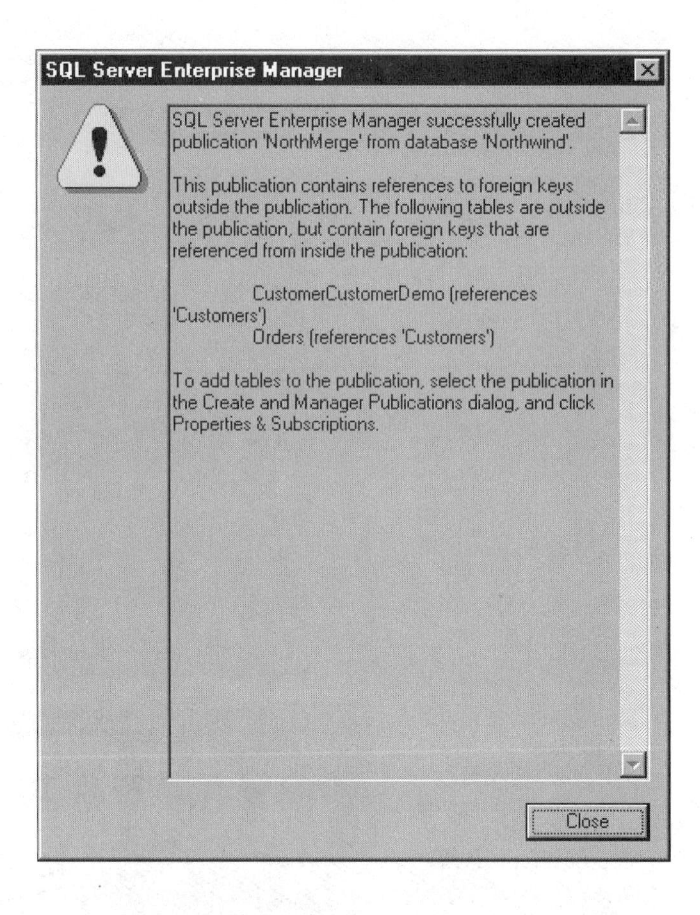

After Configuration

As you can see, NorthMerge is now listed as a publication:

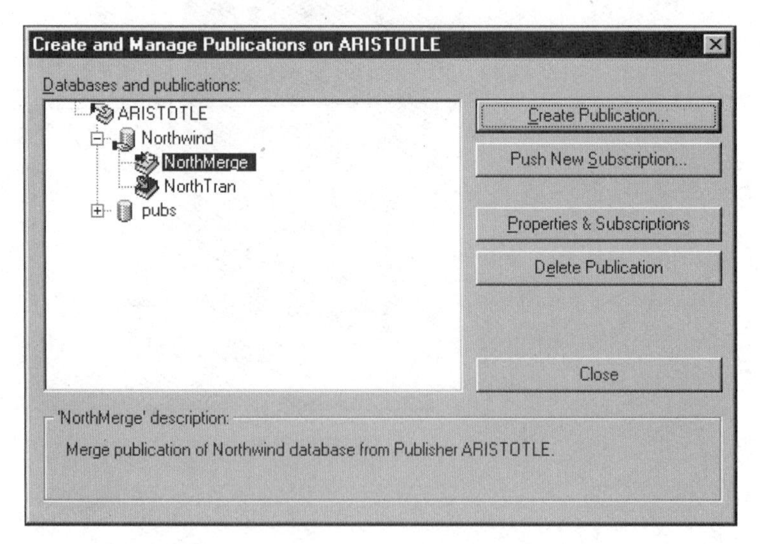

After creating a publication, you can display its property pages to view or modify publication and article properties. Run Tools | Replication | Create and Manage Publications. Select the publication you wish to view from under its database and click on Properties & Subscriptions. The property pages include:

- General – Publication identification, description, and snapshot file properties
- Articles – Modify properties for published articles, add articles to the publication, and delete articles
- Filter Rows – View, add, or modify horizontal filtering
- Subscriptions – View subscription properties, create new push subscriptions, delete subscriptions, and force resynchronization between the Publisher and Subscribers
- Subscription Options – View and set subscription options, including Internet support
- Publication Access List – View and modify logins used by pull and immediate-update subscriptions
- Status – View Snapshot Agent and service status information, run the Snapshot Agent, and start services
- Scripts – View and modify script options and format

You will have to remove any subscriptions from the publication to be able to modify some publication options.

Transact-SQL Procedures

The following system stored procedures are used to define merge publications and articles:

Stored Procedure	Description
`sp_replicationdboption`	Run this procedure to enable publication of the current database.
`sp_addmergepublication`	Use this procedure to define a publication in the current database.
`sp_addpublication_snapshot`	This is used to create a Snapshot Agent and place the schema and data into the replication working directory for running synchronization.
`sp_addmergearticle`	Run for each article you wish to add to the publication.
`sp_addmergefilter`	This procedure lets you set up horizontal filtering for an article. Merge articles do not support vertical filtering.

Refer to SQL Server Books Online for detailed information about these procedures.

Push Subscriptions

You can configure push subscriptions by selecting the **Push Subscription Wizard** from the Select Wizard dialog or by running Tools | Replication | Push Subscriptions to Others.

Push Subscription Wizard

Select the publication for which you want to push a subscription:

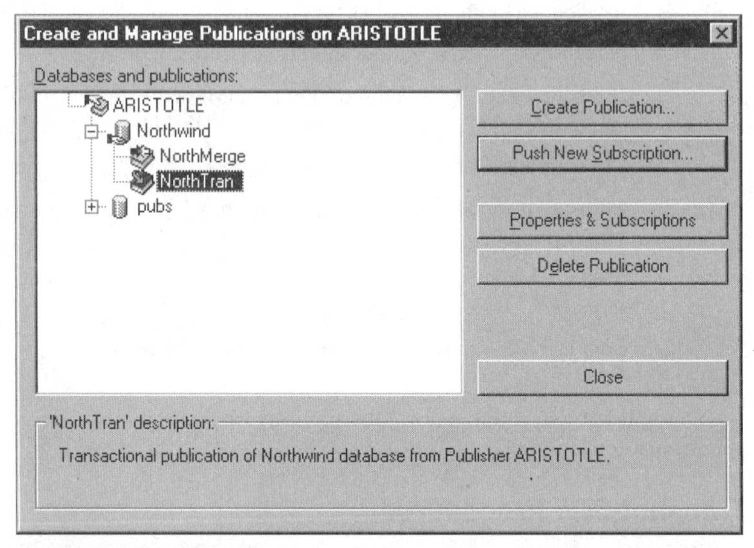

The Push Subscription Wizard lets you:

- Select Subscribers
- Select the destination database
- Set the initialization and synchronization schedule
- Set subscription properties

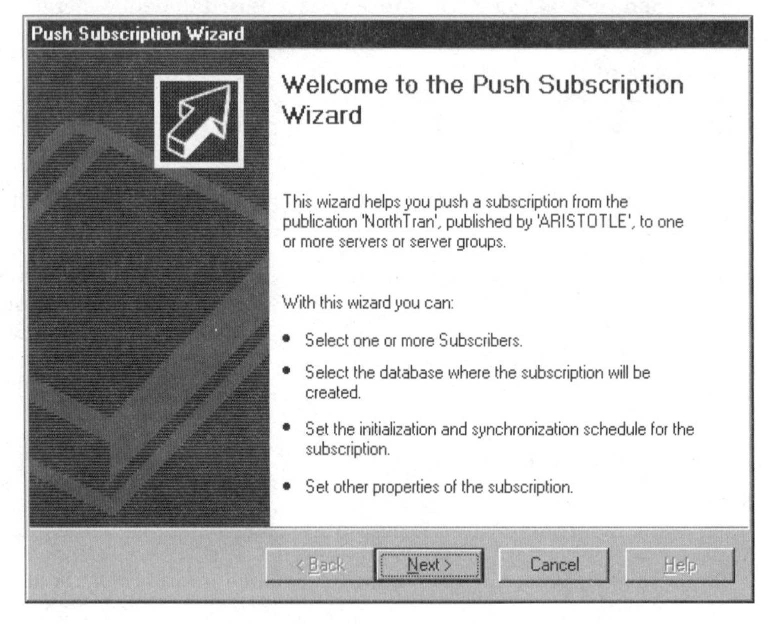

You are prompted to select Subscribers. Selecting a server group will select all of the servers in that group:

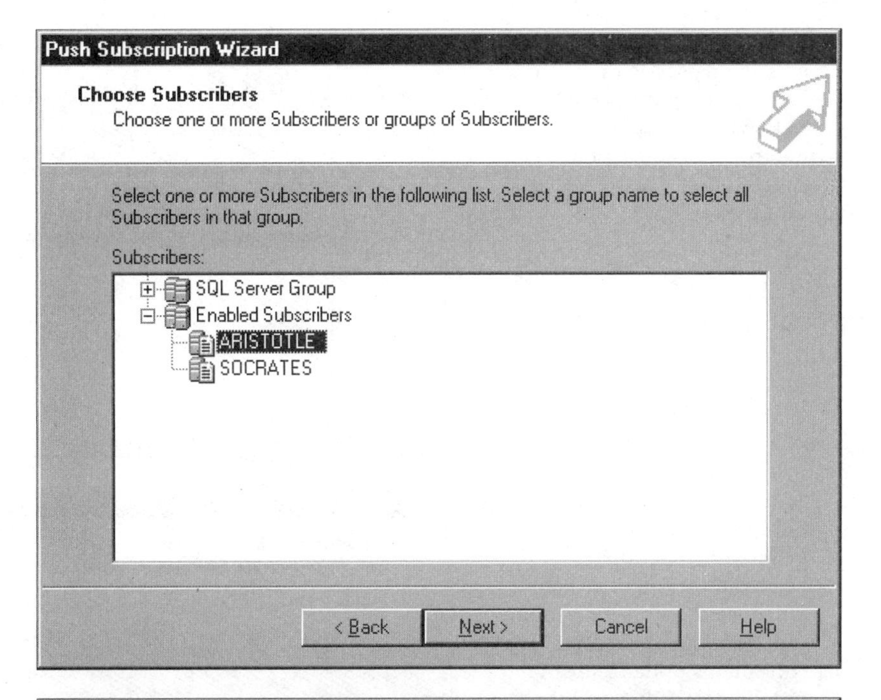

Next, you need to select the destination database. Click on Browse Databases to view a list of available databases:

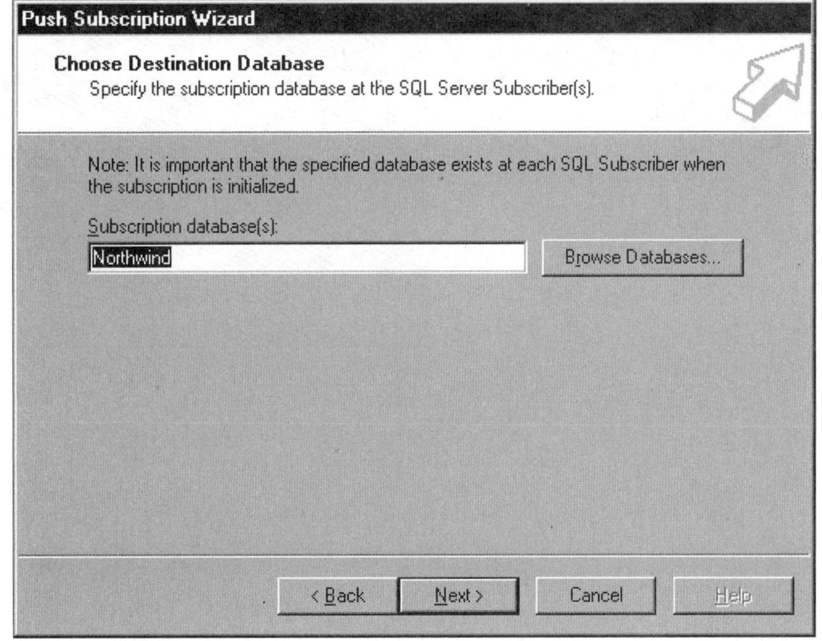

You can either pick from an existing database or create a new database on the Subscriber. Create a new database for testing our subscription, PushTest, and select that:

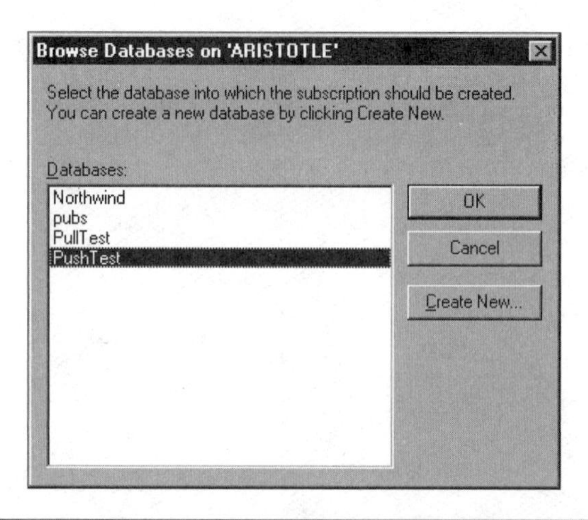

This is a transactional publication, so we're prompted to set the Distribution Agent schedule. Since we're publishing to the same server, we'll select continuous updates for our test. The default schedule is to update every 5 minutes, but you can set the schedule to meet your particular needs and available network bandwidth:

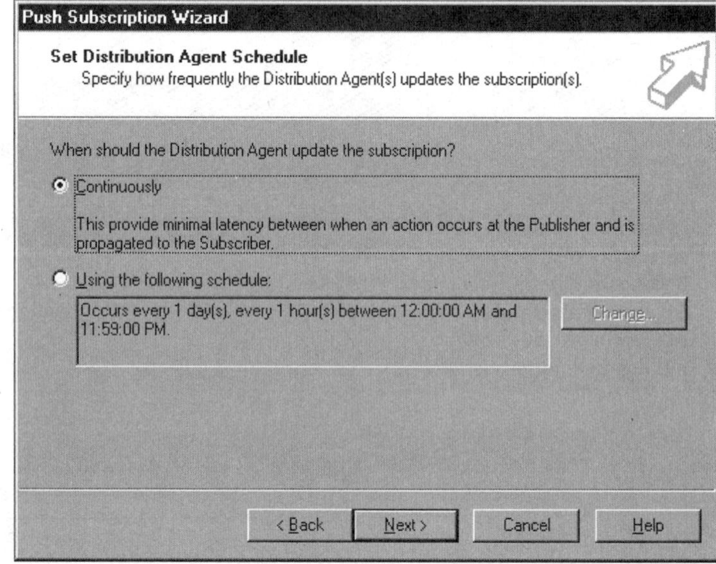

You also need to set the initialization schedule. The default is to initialize the Subscriber. We've also selected to start the process immediately. If you are using manual synchronization, you will select that the Subscriber already has the schema and data:

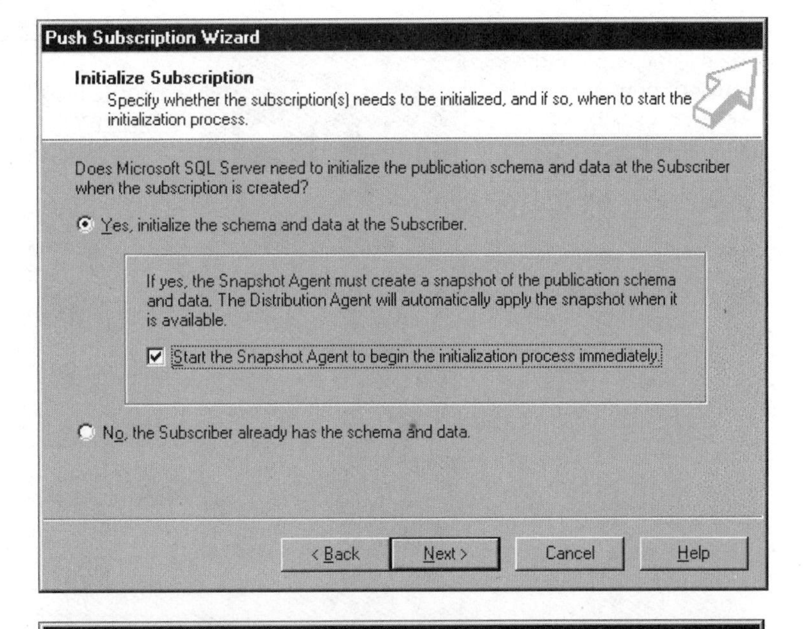

Services that need to be running for the subscription will be listed. The check indicates that the service will be started automatically if it is not already running:

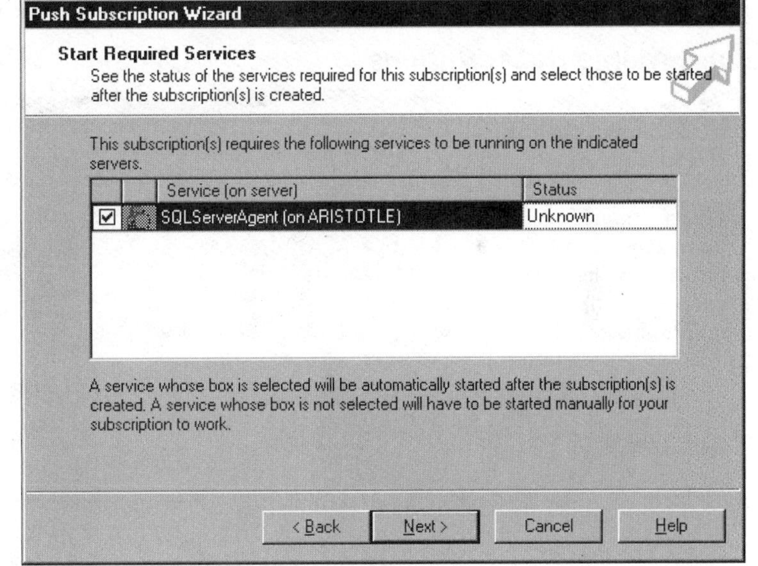

The Wizard is now ready to complete the subscription. You will receive a verifying dialog when the subscription is created:

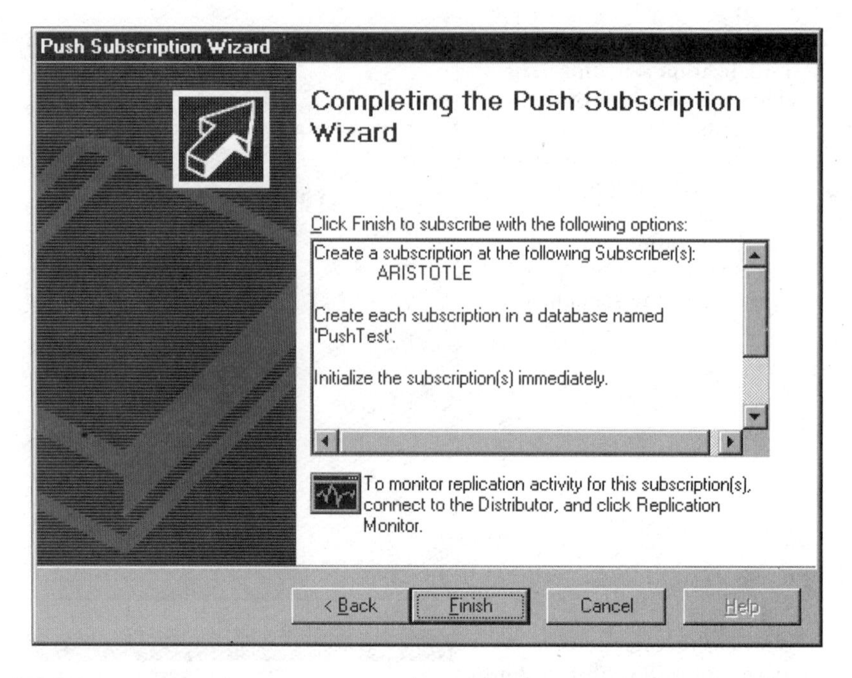

About Merge Subscriptions

You are going to see an additional prompt when configuring a merge push subscription. You will be prompted to set the priority for resolving conflicts using either the Publisher setting or a different value that you specify:

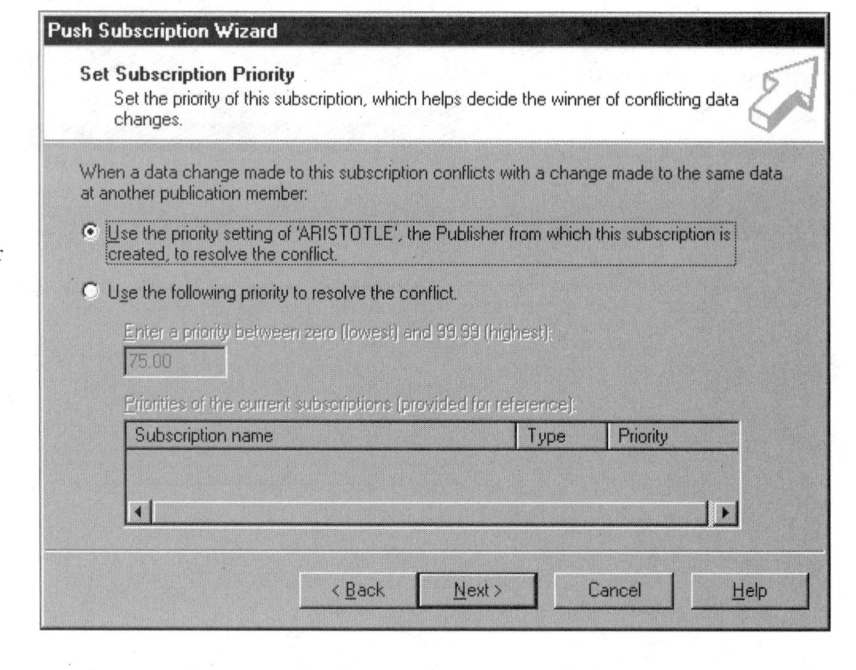

Transact-SQL Procedures

The following system stored procedures are used to define push subscriptions:

Stored Procedure	Description
sp_addsubscription	Run at the Publisher to create a snapshot or transactional push subscription.
sp_addmergesubscription	Run at the Publisher to create a merge push subscription.

Refer to SQL Server Books Online for detailed information about these procedures.

Pull Subscriptions

Pull subscriptions, as the name implies, are initiated from the Subscriber. Select the **Pull Subscription Wizard** from the Select Wizard dialog or run Tools | Replication | Pull Subscriptions.

A Subscriber can only have one subscription to an article. If the Subscriber is already subscribed through a push subscription, the subscription must be deleted before a pull subscription can be created. To drop a push subscription, run Tools | Replication | Create and Manage Publications, select the database containing the publication, click on Properties & Subscriptions, then on the Subscriptions tab. This will display the push subscriptions list. Click on the subscription you want to delete, then on Delete.

Pull Subscription Wizard

The first step is to select a database - click on Pull New Subscription:

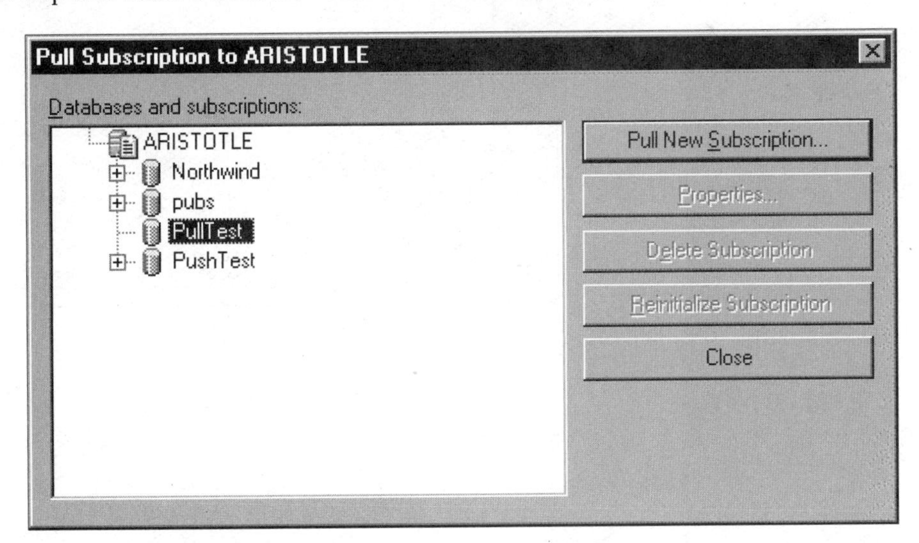

The Pull Subscription Wizard lets you:

- ❑ Select the Publisher and publication
- ❑ Select the destination database
- ❑ Set the initialization and synchronization schedule
- ❑ Set subscription properties

You have to select a publication to which you want to subscribe. This tree will only list Publishers that recognize the destination server as a Subscriber and servers that allow anonymous Subscribers:

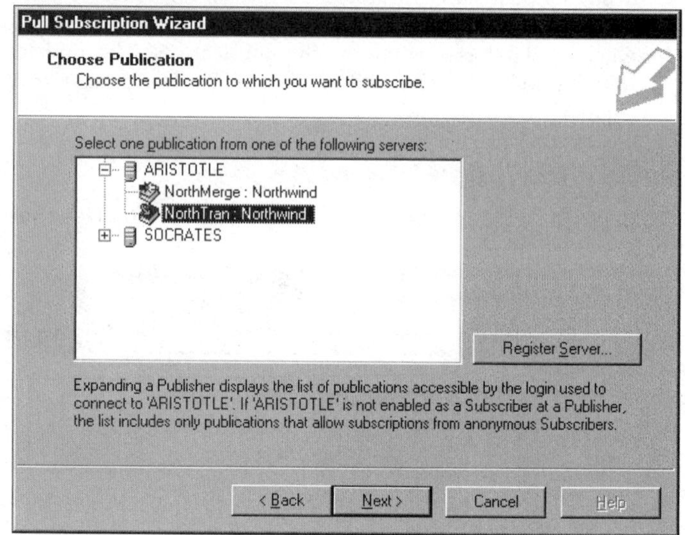

If the Publisher is set up for SQL Server Authorization, you will be prompted for login information. Otherwise, you will be taken directly to a list of available databases. Select the destination database from this list. If you wish, you can click on New Database to create a new database on the Subscriber:

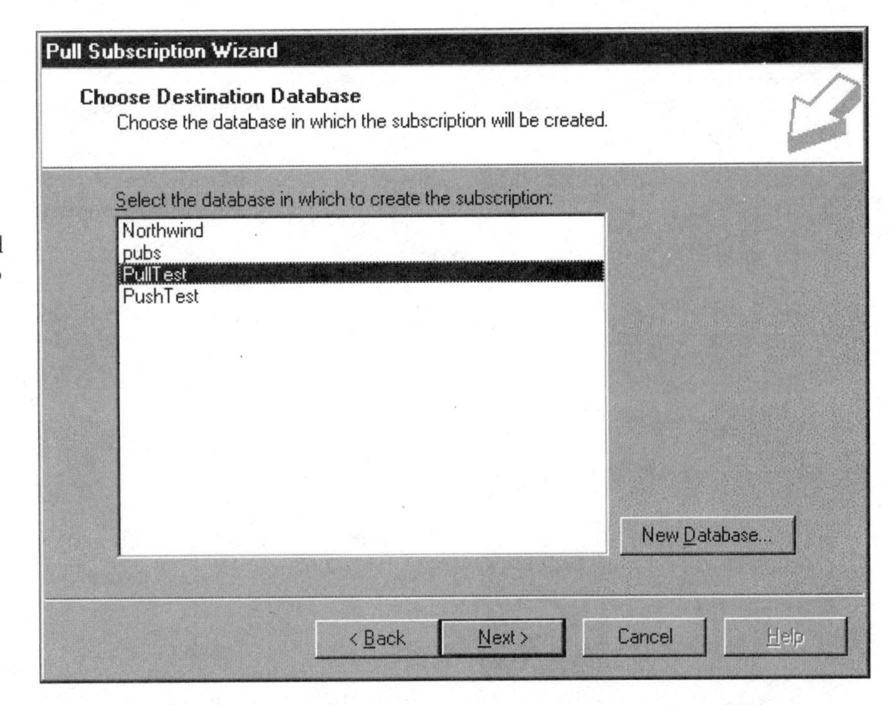

The remaining dialogs are the same as for a push subscription, as shown earlier. You will be prompted to:

- Initialize the subscription
- Set the Distribution Agent schedule
- Configure required services to start
- Create the subscription

If you are creating a merge subscription, you will also be prompted to set subscription priority.

Transact-SQL Procedures

The following system stored procedures are used to add pull subscriptions:

Stored Procedure	Description
`sp_addsubscription`	Run at the Publisher to create a subscription.
`sp_addpullsubscription`	Run at the Subscriber to create the pull subscription.
`sp_addpullsubscription_agent`	This procedure will create a scheduled job for the Subscriber's Distribution Agent. Run this procedure at the Subscriber.

Table Continued on Following Page

Stored Procedure	Description
sp_addmergesubscription.	Run at the Publisher to create a subscription.
sp_addmergepullsubscription	This procedure is run at the Subscriber to create a merge subscription.
sp_addmergepullsubscription_agent	This procedure will create a scheduled job for the Subscriber's Distribution Agent. Run this procedure at the Subscriber.

Refer to SQL Server Books Online for detailed information about these procedures.

Managing Replication

Before we can leave the subject of replication, there are a few additional issues that deserve special mention.

Replication Scripts

SQL Server gives you a way of generating **replication scripts**, Transact-SQL scripts, based on your replication configuration. Replication scripts let you document your configuration and give you an easy way to recover and reinstall replication. If you need to set up multiple servers with identical configurations, you can set up one server, generate a script, and use the script to configure the remaining servers.

Run Tools | Replication | Generate Replication Scripts to generate a replication script. You have the option of previewing the script before it is created.

Supporting Heterogeneous Replication

SQL Server supports replication with other databases, including Microsoft Access databases, Oracle databases, as well as other databases as long as they comply with SQL Server ODBC Subscriber requirements. The ODBC driver for Subscribers must:

- Allow updates
- Support transactions
- Support Transact-SQL data definition language statements (such as CREATE, ALTER and DROP)
- Conform to ODBC level 1
- Be 32-bit and thread-safe

Only SQL Server subscribers can request pull subscriptions. All other subscribers are supported by push subscriptions.

This isn't to say there aren't potential problems with heterogeneous Subscribers. For example, where there are differences in data types supported, data is mapped to the nearest match on the Subscriber. Depending on naming conventions, you can even run into problems just trying to configure Subscribers. The Subscriber ODBC data source name (DSN) must be a valid SQL Server identifier.

Publishing to the Internet

SQL Server supports replication across the Internet, but publishing to the Internet requires careful planning. You need to understand the requirements and restrictions before you start.

First, there are some basic requirements for all subscriptions. An obvious one is TCP/IP. TCP/IP is required for Internet communications. You have to make sure that the Publisher and Distributor, if installed on separate systems, have a direct network connection and are on the same side of your firewall.

Pull subscriptions are supported through FTP. This means that the Distributor and Microsoft Internet Information Server must be installed on the same system with the FTP home directory set to the distribution working folder. The Subscriber Distribution and Merge Agents will need the FTP's IP address.

You need to make some changes to the Subscription Options tab in the Properties dialog for a publication to allow it to support Internet subscriptions. Run Tools | Replication | Create and Manage Publications, select the publication from its database, and click on Properties & Subscriptions. Set the properties to:

- Allow anonymous Subscribers to pull subscriptions
- Allow snapshots to be downloaded using FTP

You will need to drop any existing subscriptions from the publication before you can configure an independent Distribution Agent. Don't forget to recreate any subscriptions after you are finished.

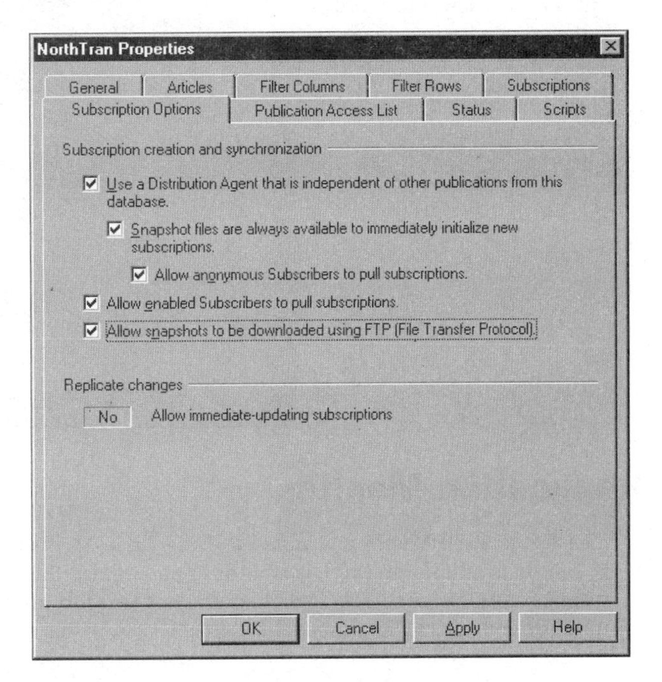

After you've set up a publication to support pull subscriptions over the Internet, you will see additional prompts when running the Pull Subscription Wizard. You will be asked whether or not the Subscriber will be using FTP to copy the snapshot files:

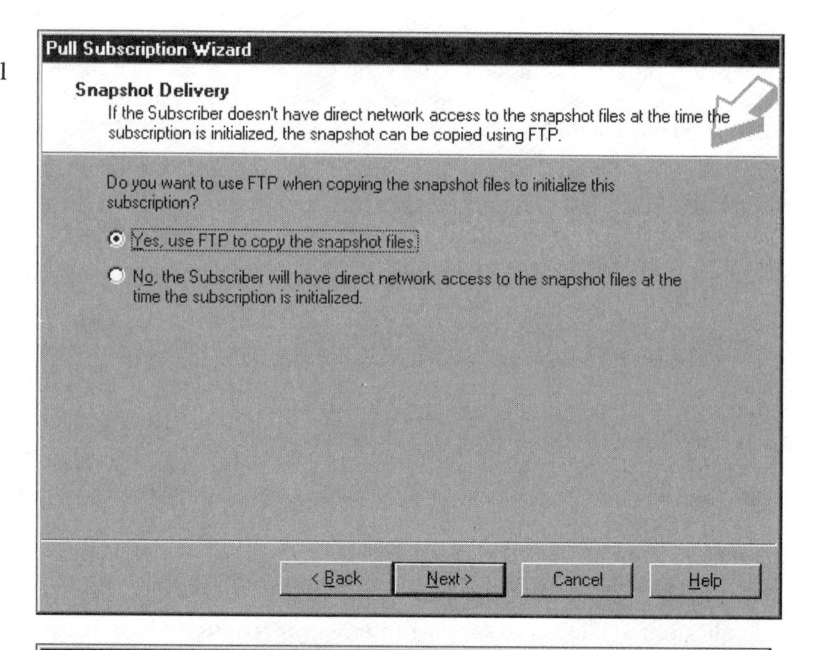

The other new screen isn't specific to Internet subscriptions only. It appears any time you allow anonymous pull subscriptions and lets you determine whether or not this will be an anonymous subscription:

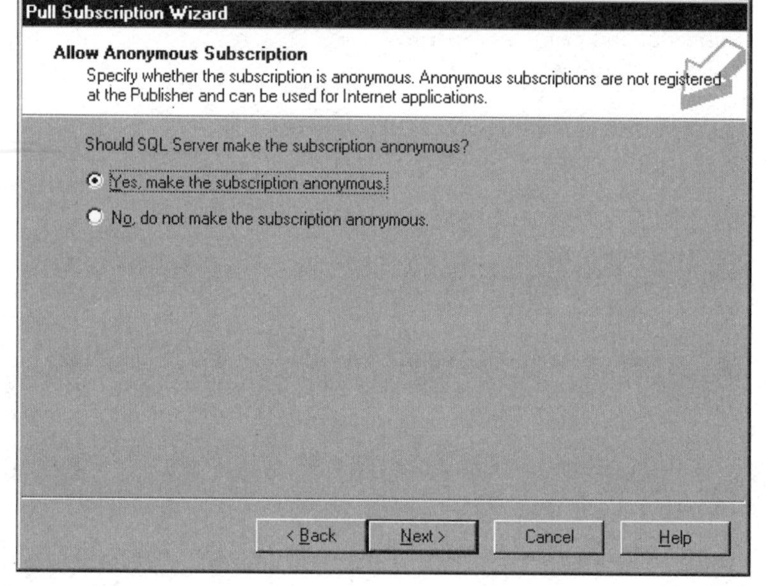

Replication Monitor

The **Replication Monitor** is added to Enterprise Monitor when a server is configured as a Distributor. It is only available on the Distributor. You can use the Replication Monitor to view Publishers, publications, Subscribers, agents, and agent and job history. You can also set agent priorities, and set up and monitor replication event alerts:

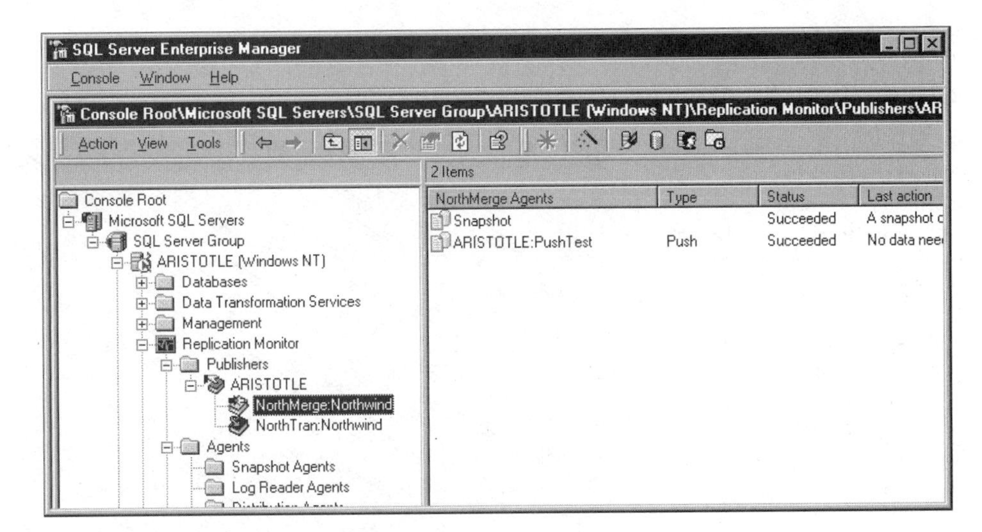

Selecting a Publisher, publication, or agent will display information about the selected component in the Enterprise Manager window. You can also display this information in a separate window by running Action | New window from here or right-clicking on the Publisher, publication, or agents and running New window from here:

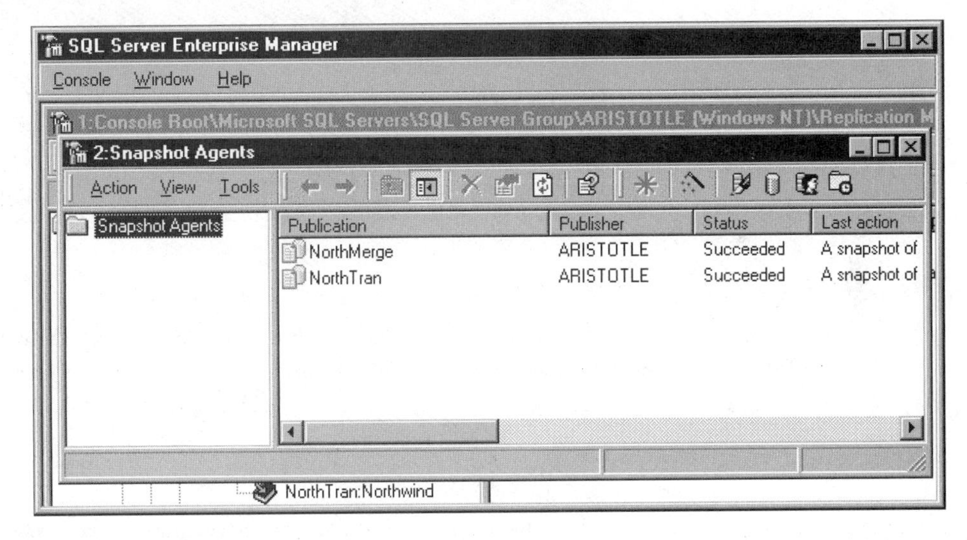

Selecting an agent displays history information for that agent. You can also view agent history by querying the agent histories in the distribution database. These are:

- MSsnapshot_history
- MSlogreader_history
- MSdistribution_history
- MSmerge_history

Each table includes entries for the local distributor. Table columns track agent-specific information, including date and time stamps for each row. By querying the table, you can view activity over a period of time, as well as check for specific conditions.

You can modify the Replication Monitor refresh rate and performance monitor information. Select a Publisher, publication, or agent and run Action | Refresh Rate and Settings or right-click and run Refresh Rate and Settings. The General tab sets the refresh rate and inactivity threshold. The Performance Monitor tab sets the path to the file containing settings that Performance Monitor will use to monitor replication performance:

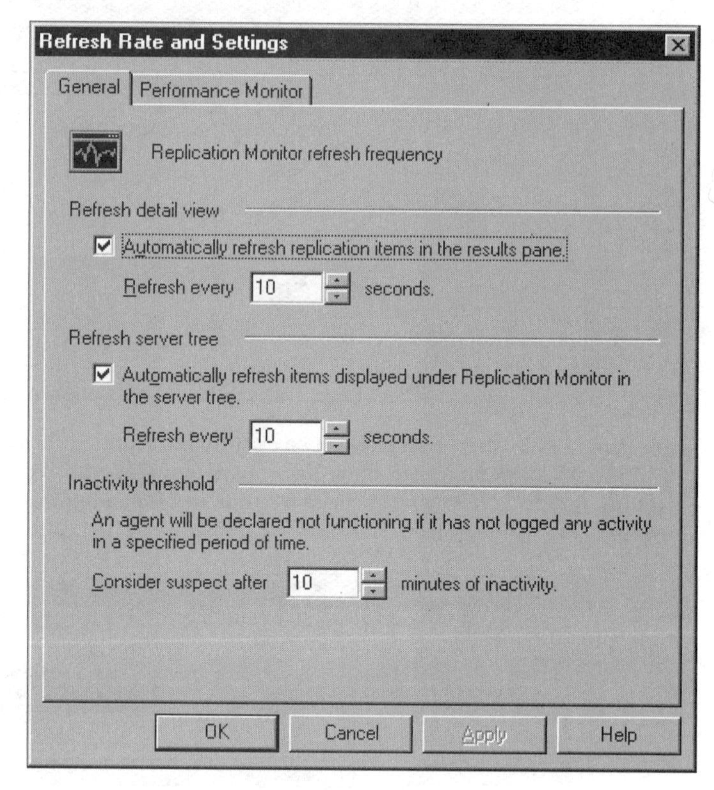

Keeping it Going

Of course, there's more to keeping replication running smoothly than checking Replication Monitor on occasion. Replication may be an automatic process, but unfortunately, some of its required upkeep isn't.

Disk Space

SQL Server Agents clean up after themselves on a regular basis to help keep storage space requirements to a minimum. You need to check the clean-up jobs on occasion to make sure that they are running.

In addition, you need to keep an eye on the distribution database and transaction log to keep them from growing too large. You can help keep the distribution database to a manageable size by adjusting the retention period.

You can limit the size and growth characteristics of the distribution database as in any other database. However, you need to exercise caution to make sure it is large enough to store all of your replication jobs.

Error Logs

Sooner or later, you can expect that problems will arise with replication. When they do, it helps to know where to look for information. You've already been introduced to Replication Monitor, but you have other sources available.

One source is the SQL Server Agent Error Log. Right-click on the SQL Server Agent node under the Management node in Enterprise Manager and run Display Error Log. Entries are identified as errors, warnings, and informational messages:

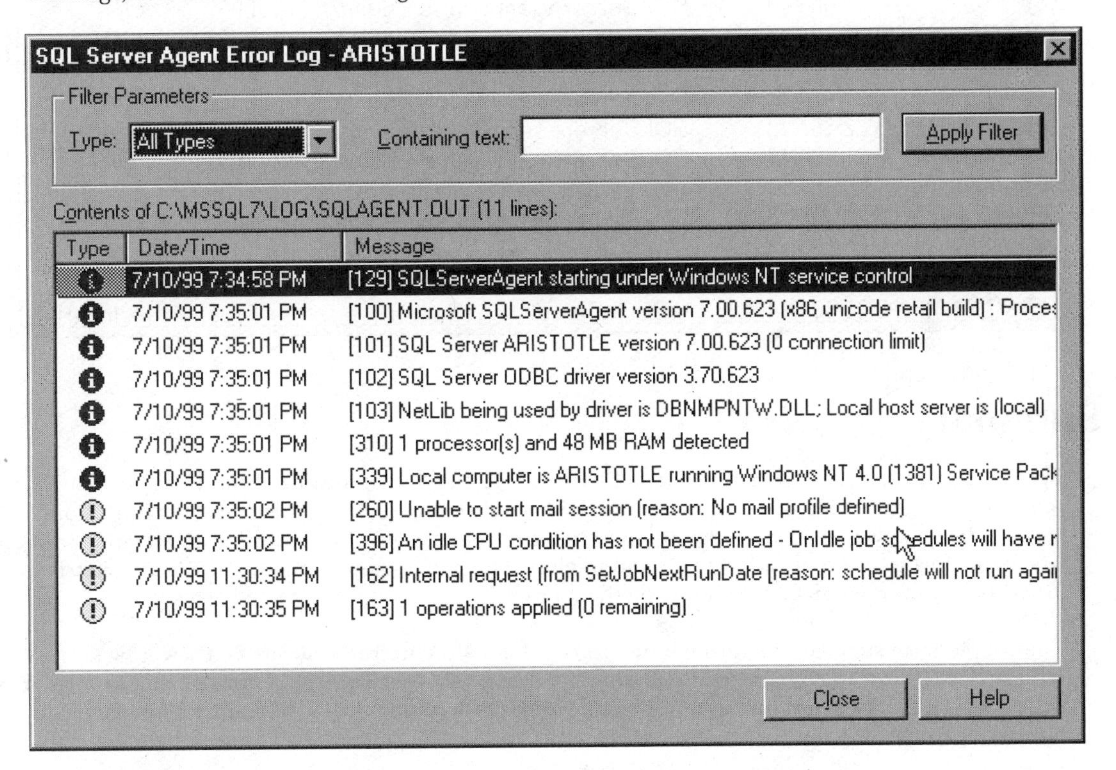

You can get detailed information about server activity through the agent logs in Enterprise Manager. Click on an agent to view the activity log. You can run Actions | New window from here or right-click on a log and run New window from here to open the log in a separate window.

A source that is sometimes overlooked is the Windows NT Event Viewer. You can find SQL Server information and error messages by selecting Log | Application from Event Viewer's menu:

Event Viewer - Application Log on \\ARISTOTLE

Log View Options Help

Date	Time	Source	Category	Event	User
9/7/99	5:30:06 PM	MSSQLServer	Server	17055	N/A
9/7/99	5:27:08 PM	SQLServerAgent	Job Engine	203	N/A
9/7/99	5:25:58 PM	SQLServerAgent	Job Engine	203	N/A
9/7/99	5:24:48 PM	SQLServerAgent	Job Engine	203	N/A
9/7/99	5:23:41 PM	SQLServerAgent	Job Engine	203	N/A
9/7/99	5:22:35 PM	SQLServerAgent	Job Engine	203	N/A
9/7/99	5:21:25 PM	SQLServerAgent	Job Engine	203	N/A
9/7/99	5:20:36 PM	MSSQLServer	Server	17055	SYSTEM
9/7/99	5:20:22 PM	SQLServerAgent	Job Engine	203	N/A
9/7/99	5:20:06 PM	SQLServerAgent	Service Control	101	N/A
9/7/99	5:18:10 PM	SQLServerAgent	Service Control	101	N/A
9/7/99	5:08:56 PM	MSSQLServer	Server	17055	Administ

Summary

This chapter gave you a relatively detailed look at SQL Server replication. You were introduced to some general terms and concepts, including the terms relating to components in the replication publishing metaphor. You saw how different types of replication work and were given guidelines on when and how to use replication types and models. This included data requirements and restrictions for snapshot, transactional, and merge publications.

The chapter also stepped you through the process for setting up replication. You saw how to use the replication Wizards to configure Distributors, Publishers, Subscribers, publications, and articles. You were also given a brief introduction to heterogeneous environments and the procedures for publishing to the Internet.

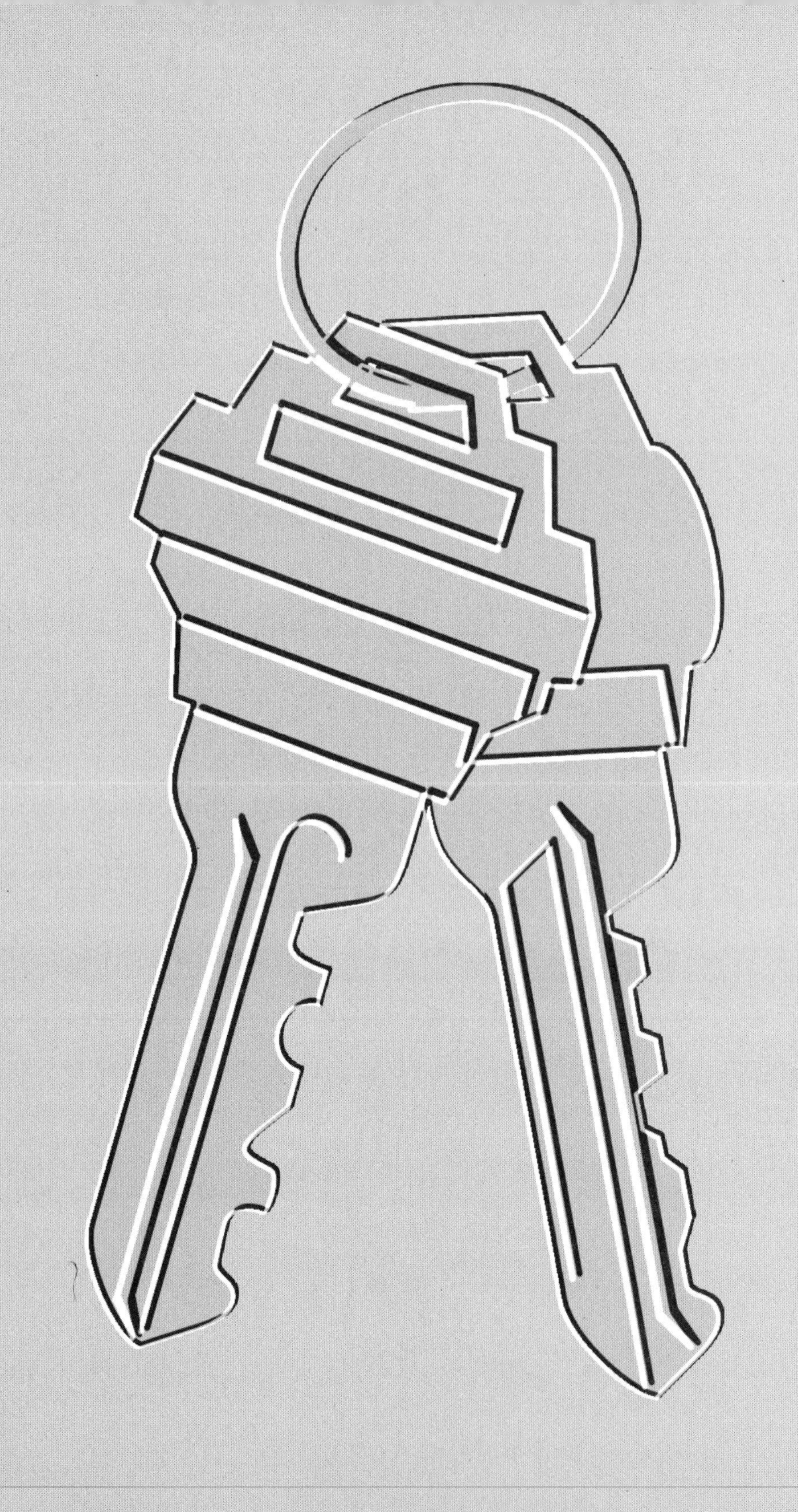

20

Advanced Design

OK, so now you're an expert – right? I mean, we've looked at all sorts of stuff up to this point: Normalization, sprocs, triggers, views, transactions, linked servers. Hard to believe we still have five chapters to go, eh? That's the way the database thing is though – it's a big thing to swallow. What's worse, you really need to understand a significant percentage of it before you can be truly productive.

In this chapter, we'll be adding to the database design issues that we've talked about thus far. Most (but not quite all) of what we'll deal with after this chapter sits on the periphery of our database design, so it seems like a good time to try and pull some of what we've learned together to the point of seeing how to deal with certain situations. This chapter is going to be about identifying solutions to several common database problems, and seeing how we can mix and match the functionality within SQL Server to end up with good answers to some tough problems.

Some of the scenarios we'll look over in this chapter include:

- More on Diagramming
- Logical vs. Physical Design
- Dealing with large file-based information
- Sub-Categories
- Database reusability

More on Diagramming And Relationships

As I said way back in Chapter 8, SQL Server doesn't really give us all that much in terms of diagramming tools (before SQL Server 7.0, they didn't give us anything at all), and what there is doesn't adhere to either of the most common diagramming paradigms – IE, and IDEF1X. You'll find both of these in widespread use, but I'm going to limit things here to a once over of the basics of IE (also called Information Engineering). For the record, IDEF1X is a perfectly good diagramming paradigm, and was put forth by the US AirForce. IE is, however, the method I use personally, and I do so for just one reason – it is far more intuitive for the inexperienced reviewer of your diagrams.

So why, if SQL Server doesn't provide anything to do this, am I providing information on IE? Well, even if you're using the da Vinci tools to do your diagramming, I'm going to strongly encourage you to create a logical model for all your databases. Since the da Vinci tools don't have a mechanism for logical modeling, I'm going to give you some of the rules of the road in case you decide to:

- Draw them out by hand
- Using a simple diagramming program such as Visio
- Upgrade to a real Entity Relationship Diagram (ERD) tool

If nothing else, it will really help you out when you're working on the white board with a co-worker.

I can't say enough about the importance of having the right tools. While the da Vinci tools are a tremendous step forward from what we had before, it is largely because we didn't have anything before. We'll be talking in this chapter about the importance of physical modeling – well, da Vinci has absolutely nothing in the way of logical modeling – just physical.

ERD tools are anything but cheap – running from somewhere over $1,000 to just under $3,500 (that's per seat!). They are also something of a language unto themselves. Don't plan on just sitting down and going to work with any of the major ER tools – you had better figure on some preparation time to get it to do what you expect.

Don't let the high price of these tools keep you from building a logical model. While Visio (the low cost editions anyway) is not the answer to the world's database design problems, it does do OK in a pinch for light logical modeling. That said, if you're serious about database design, and going to be doing a lot of it, you really need to find the budget for a real ERD tool.

Expense aside, there is no comparison between the productivity possible in the 3rd party tools out there and the built-in tools. Depending on the ER tool you select, they give you the capability to do things like:

- Create logical models, then switch back and forth between the logical and physical model
- Work on the diagram off-line – then propagate all your changes to the physical database at one time (when you're ready, and opposed to when you need to log off)

- Reverse engineer your database from any one of a number of mainstream RDBMS systems (even some ISAM databases), then forward engineer them to a completely different RDBMS
- Create your physical model on numerous different systems

This really just scratches the surface. We review some of these tools a bit further in Appendix C – but I wanted to hop on the soapbox here to make sure that you don't forget to look at what you're missing!

A Couple Of Relationship Types

Before we get going too far into more diagramming concepts, we want to explore two types of relationships: Identifying and Non-Identifying.

Identifying Relationships

For some of you, I'm sure the term "Identifying Relationship" brings back memories of some boyfriend or girlfriend you've had in the past that got just a little over-possessive – this is not that kind of relationship. Instead, we're dealing with the relationships that are defined by foreign keys.

An identifying relationship is one where the column or columns (remember, there can be more than one) being referenced (in the parent table) are used as all or part of the referencing (child) table's primary key. Since a primary key serves as the identity for the rows in a table, and all or part of the primary key for the child table is dependent on the parent table – the child table can be said to, at least in part, be "Identified" by the parent table.

Non-Indentifying Relationships

Non-identifying relationships are those that are created when you establish a foreign key that does not serve as part of the referencing (child) table's primary key. This is extremely common in situations where you are referencing a domain table – where essentially the sole purpose of the referenced table is to limit the referencing field to a set list of possible choices.

The Entity Box

One of the many big differences you'll see in both IE and IDEF1X vs. SQL Server's own brand of diagramming comes in the **entity box**. The entity box, depending on whether you're dealing with logical or physical models, equates roughly to a table. By looking over the entity box, you should be able to easily identify the entity's Name, primary key, and any attributes (effectively columns) that entity has. In addition, the diagram may expose other information such as the attributes data type or whether it has a foreign key defined for it. As an example, the entity box for our Orders table from back in Chapter 8 (remember all that first design and normalization stuff?):

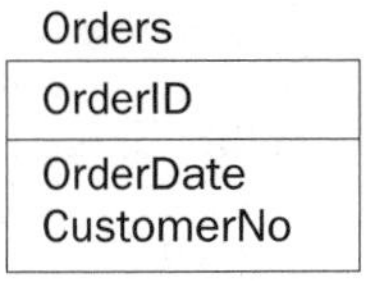

Orders

OrderID
OrderDate CustomerNo

The name of our entity is kept on the top outside the box. Then, in the top area of the overall box, but in a separate box of its own, we have the primary key (we'll look at an example with more than one column in the primary key shortly), and last, but not least, come the attributes of the entity.

Let's look at a slightly different entity:

OrderDetails
LineItem TEXT(50) OrderID INT (FK)
PartNo Text(5) Qty INT UnitPrice CURRENCY

Several new things appear:

- The data types (I've turned on the appropriate option)
- Foreign keys (If any – again I've turned on the option to make this show)
- We have multiple columns in the primary key (everything above the line is part of the primary key)
- This time, the entity is rounded on the corners (this tells us that this table is identified (remember identifying relationships?) by at least one other table)

Depending on the ER tool, the data types can be defined right within the ER diagram. Also, as we draw the lines that form our relationships (we'll look at those shortly), we are able to define foreign keys which can also be shown. For most available ER tools, you can even tell the tool to automatically define the referenced field(s) in the foreign key relationship as being part (or possibly all) of the primary key in the referencing table.

The Relationship Line

There are two kinds, and they match 100% with our relationship types:

A solid line indicates an identifying relationship: ________________

A broken or dashed line indicates a non-identifying relationship: - - - - - - - - - - - - - - - -

Terminators

Ahh, this is where things become slightly more interesting. The terminators we're talking about here are, of course, not the kind you'd see Arnold Schwarzeneggar play in a movie – they are the end caps that we put on our relationship lines.

The terminators on our lines will communicate as much or more about the nature of our database as the entities themselves will. They are the thing that will tell us the most information about the true nature of the relationship, including the **cardinality** of the relationship.

Cardinality is, in its most basic form, the number of records on both sides of the relationship. When we say it is a one-to-many relationship, then we are indicating cardinality. Cardinality can, however, be much more specific than the zero, one, or many naming conventions that we use more generically. Cardinality can address specifics, and is often augmented in a diagram with two numbers and a colon, such as:

- 1:M
- 1:6 (which, while meeting a one-to-many criteria, is more specific and says there is a maximum of 6 records on that side of the relationship

Let's walk through a couple of the parts of a terminator and examine what they mean:

Just as a reminder, the terminators that follow are the ones from the IE diagramming methodology. There is another diagramming standard that is in widespread use (though I see it much less than IE) called IDEF1X. While it's entity boxes are much like IE's, it's terminators on the relationship lines are entirely different.

For the top half of the terminator, it is indicating the first half of our relationship. In this case, we have a zero. For the bottom half, we are indicating the second half of our relationship – in this case, a many. In this example, then, we have a zero, one, or many side of a relationship.

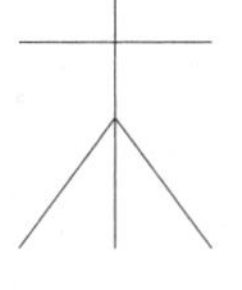

This time, we're not allowing nulls at this end of the relationship – this is a one or many end to a relationship.

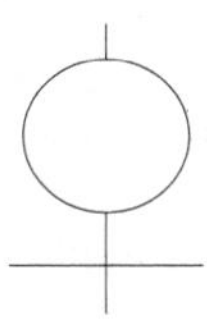

This time around, we're back to allowing a zero at this end of the relationship, but we are now allowing a maximum of one. This is a zero or one side of a relationship.

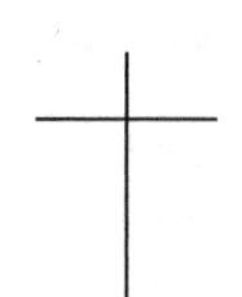

And this one is pretty restrictive – it's simply a "one" side of a relationship.

Since it's probably pretty confusing to look at these just by themselves, let's look at a couple of example tables and relationships.

First, we'll stick with our original couple of tables from when we were working with normalization back in Chapter 8:

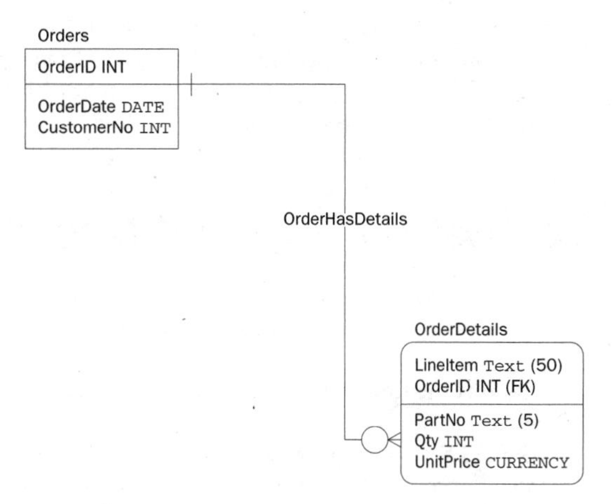

This is a diagram that shows not only our Orders and OrderDetails tables, but also depicts a one (the Orders side)-to-zero, one, or many (the OrderDetails side) relationship between the two tables. The relationship is an identifying relationship (solid, rather than dashed line), and the relationship is called OrderHasDetails.

Now, let's toss in the Products table:

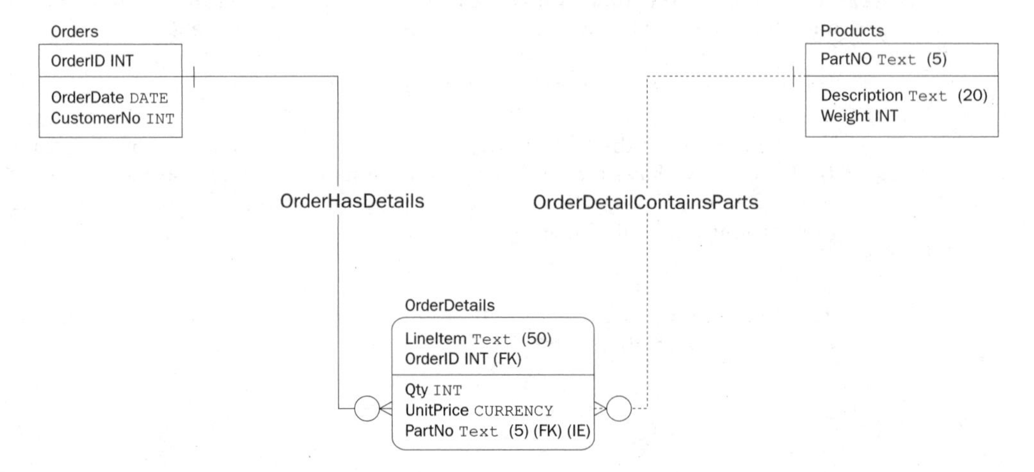

This new relationship is very similar to the relationship that we already looked at. It is again a one (Products this time)-to-zero, one or many (OrderDetails again) relationship, but this is it is non-identifying (as represented by the broken line). The "IE" indicates that, for this table, PartNo is an Inversion Entry – back in Chapter 9 we called this Alternate Keys (which is a more common terminology, but apparently not what Visio uses). The alternate key has been added since it usually makes sense to have an index on a field that is a foreign key (since it is a frequent target of lookups).

By looking at all three together, we can see that there is a many-to-many relationship between Orders and Products by virtue of their relationship through the OrderDetails table.

As I've indicated before, we are still really only scratching the surface of the different information that your ER diagrams can convey. Still, by now you should have a good idea of the fact that the more accepted methodologies out there have an awful lot more information to convey than what is offered by the tools in SQL Server. In addition, just the nature of how tables are displayed makes information such as keys more visible and easier to read.

Logical Vs Physical Design

As you move forward in your database endeavors, you're likely to hear about the concepts of logical vs. physical models. In this section, we'll be exploring the differences between the two.

The physical model is one that's probably pretty easy to grasp. It is essentially what you have been working with up to this point in the book. You can think of anything that you can perform a CREATE statement on as being part of the physical model. Indeed – if you run any statements in SQL Server on it at all then it must be part of the physical model.

That being said, a logical model is a means to a number of different things – the physical model in particular. This means that, as you work on the logical model, you are working your way towards being able to generate DDL (Data Definition Language) – or things like `CREATE`, `ALTER` and `DROP` statements.

Purpose Of A Logical Model

The first thing to understand about logical models is that they have somewhat different goals than physical models do. A logical model does several things for you:

- Allows you to begin to build abstracts of complex, data-related business issues as well as provide an high-level beginning effort at identifying your entities
- Use these abstracts to effectively communicate about business rules and content as relates to data
- Represent the purest form of the data (before you start introducing the realities of what will really work)
- Serves as a major piece of documentation in the data requirements portion of your project

Because logical models aren't strictly rooted in the exact syntax to create the database, they give you a flexibility that you can't obtain from a physical model. You can attach dialog and rules to the logical model regardless of whether your particular RDBMS will support those rules or not. In short, it let's you squeeze in all the facts before you start paring down your design to a more specific implementation.

What's nice about this is that logical models allow you to capture all of your data rules in one place regardless of where that rule will be actually implemented. You will frequently run into situations where you cannot sensibly implement your rules in the databases. The rules in question may be data related, but due to some constraint or requirement, you need to implement them using more procedural code in your client or in some form of middle tier. With logical models – you go ahead and include the data related rules anyway.

Regardless of its source, you include all data related information in a first logical design to create one or more abstracts of the data in your system. These abstracts can then be used as a representation to your customer about what you really are intending to store and what rules you believe you have captured. Using such a representation early (and often), can save your projects valuable time and money by opening extra doors of communication. Even a customer who is not very data savvy can often look at the highest level diagrams and say things like "Where are the purchase requisitions?" Usually, you have some handy dandy explanation of why you called them something else and you can point to them on the diagram – other times, however, you find yourself uttering those most fearsome of words – "Oops!" I don't know about you, but I'd rather utter those words in the first weeks of a project rather than the first weeks of deployment – logical modeling, when properly shared with the customer, can help avoid those deployment time "Oops" statements.

I can't do enough to stress the importance of sharing your logical design (there had better be one!) with your customer both early and often. With a little education of the customer in how to read your logical model (this should also include good documentation on cause and purpose of the entities and relationships of the model), you can save a fortune in both time and money.

I haven't met a developer with any real experience who hadn't, at least once (and probably far more often than that), learned the hard way about the cost of late changes to your system. Changing code is very expensive, but that typically doesn't even begin to touch what happens when you need to change your database late in a project. If you haven't done a good job of abstracting your database (3-tier or n-tier design), then every change you make to your database is going to cascade through tons of code. In other words, one little change in your database can potentially cost several – possibly hundreds or even thousands (depending on the size of the system) of changes in the code that accesses the database.

In short, communication is everything, and logical modeling should be a huge part of your tool set for communicating with your customer.

Parts Of A Logical Model

A logical model contains three major parts:

- Structure
- Constraints
- Rules

The combination of these three should completely describe the requirements of the data in your system, but they may not translate entirely to the physical model. Some of the issues identified in the logical model may need to be implemented in some procedural form (such as in a middle tier component). Other times, the entire logical model can be implemented through the various features of your RDBMS.

This is a really important highpoint, and I want to stress it again – just because it's in your logical model doesn't mean that it will be in your physical database. A logical model should take into account all of your data requirements – even those that are not possible to implement in your RDBMS. Having everything in your logical model allows you to plan the physical design in such a way that you can be sure that you have addressed all data issues – not just those that will physically reside in the database.

Structure

Structure is that part of the logical design that deals with the concept of actually storing the data. When we deal with the structure of the database, we're talking about the tables that will store our data, and the particular columns were are going to need to maintain the atomicity of our data.

Constraints

Constraints, from a logical model standpoint, are a bit more broad than the way that we've used the word "constraint" up until now. Prior to now, when we used the word constraint, we were talking about a specific set of features to limit data to certain values.

From a logical standpoint, a constraint is anything that defines the "what" question for our data – that is, what data is valid. A logical model includes constraints, which is to say that it includes things like:

- Data Types (notice that this is really a separate thought from the notion that even notices that a column needs to exist or what the name of that column should be).
- Constraints in the form we're used to up until now – that is, Check constraints, Foreign Keys – even Primary Keys and Unique constraints (alternate keys). Each of these provides a logical definition of what data can exist in our database. This area would also include things like domain tables (which we would reference using foreign keys) – which restrict the values in a column to a particular "domain" list.

Rules

If constraints were the "what" in our data, then rules are the "when and how much" in our data.

When you define logical rules, you're defining things like "Do we require a value on this one?" (which equates to a "do we allow nulls?") and "How many of these do we allow" (which defines the cardinality of our data – do we accept one or many?).

It's worth noting again that any of these parts may not be implemented in the physical part of our database – we may decide that the restrictions that we want to place on things will be handled entirely at the client – regardless of where the requirement is implemented, it should still be part of our comprehensive logical data model. It is only when we achieve this complete modeling of our data that we can really know that we have addressed all the issues (regardless of where we addressed them).

Dealing With File Based Information

BLOBs. You haven't really seen enough to them to hate them yet – and I do mean yet. BLOBs, or Binary Large Objects, are slow – very slow and big. Hey, did I mention they were slow?

BLOBs are nice in the sense that they let you break the 8K barrier on row size (BLOBs can be up to about 2GB in size). The problem is that they are painfully slow (I know, I'm repeating myself, but I suspect I'm also making a point here). In the race between the BLOB and the tortoise (the sequel to the Tortoise and the Hare), the BLOB won only after the tortoise stopped for a nap.

OK, so we've beaten the slow thing into the ground, and you still need to store large blocks of text or binary information. Normally, you'd do that using a BLOB – but we're not going to. We're going to go around the problem by storing things as files instead.

OK, so by now some of you have to be asking the question of "Isn't a database going to be a faster way of accessing data than the file system?" My answer is quite simply – "No." There is an exception to this that I'll get to before the chapter is done, but, by and large, using files is going to be much faster.

I'm going to warn you right up front that, in order to pull this off, you need to be planning for this in your client – this isn't a database server only kind of thing to do. Indeed, we'll be removing most of the work from the database server and putting it into your middle tiers and file system.

Let's start by looking at what we need to do on the server's file system side. The only thing that we need is to make sure that we have at least one directory to store the information in. Depending on the nature of our application, we may also need to have logic in a middle tier object that will allow it to create additional directories as needed.

All of the Windows operating systems have limits on the number of files they can store in one directory. As such, you need to think about how many files you're going to be storing. If it will be many (say, over 500), then you'll want to create a mechanism in the object that stores your BLOB so that it can create new directories either on an as needed basis, or based on some other logical criteria.

Your business component will be in charge of copying the BLOB information to the file you're going to store it in. If it is already is some defined file format, you're on easy street – just run your language's equivalent to a copy command (with a twist we'll go over shortly) and you're in business. If it is streamed data, then you'll need to put the logic in your component to store the information in a logical format (such as COM structured storage) for later retrieval.

One big issue with this implementation is that of security. Since you're storing the information in a file that's outside of SQL Server's realm, that means that it is also outside SQL Server's protection security wise. Instead, you have to rely on your network security.

There are several "Wow, that's scary!" things that should come to mind for you here. First, if someone's going to read data out of the directory that you're storing all this in, doesn't that mean they can see other files that are stored in there? Yes, it does (if you wanted to get really tricky, you could get around this by changing the NT security for each file, but it would be very tedious indeed). Second, since you'd have to give people rights to copy the file into the directory, wouldn't there be a risk of someone altering the file directly rather than using the database (potentially causing your database to be out of synch with the file)? Absolutely.

> **The answer to these and the many other questions that you could probably come up with lies in your data access layer (I'm assuming an n-tier approach here). Using MTS, you can have the access component run under a different security context than the end user. This means that you can create a situation where the user can access their data – but only when they are using the data access component to do it (they don't have any rights to the directory themselves – indeed, they probably don't even know where the files are stored).**
>
> **Doing things this way in not nearly as difficult as it may first sound, and Wrox has a number of good books on MTS to help you figure it out.**

So then, where does SQL Server come into play in all this? It keeps track of where you stored the information in question. Theoretically, the reason why you were trying to store this information in the databases in the first place is because it relates to some other information in the row you were going to store it as part of. But instead of saving the actual data in the row in the form of a BLOB, you will now store a path to the file that you saved. The process for storage will look something like this:

1. Determine the name you're going to store it as
2. Copy the file to the location that you're going to store it at
3. Save the full name and path in a varchar(255) (which also happens to be the maximum size for a name in a Windows directory at the moment) along with the rest of the data for that row

To retrive the data:

1. Run your query much as you would have if you were going to retrieve the data direct from the table, only this time, retrieve the path to where the actual BLOB data is stored.
2. Retrieve the data from the file system

In general, this approach will run approximately 2-3 times faster than if we were using BLOBs. There are, however, some exceptions to the rule of wanting to use this approach:

- The BLOBs you are saving are consistently small (less than 64K) in size.
- The data is text and you want to be able to perform Full Text searches against it

If the size of your BLOBs are consistently less than 64K, then the data is able to all fit on one data page. This significantly minimizes the overhead in dealing with your BLOB. While the file system approach is still probably going to be faster, the benefits will be sharply reduced such that it doesn't make as much sense. If you're in this scenario, and speed is everything, then all I can suggest is to experiment.

If you want to perform Full Text searches, you're probably going to be better off going ahead and storing the large blocks of text as a TEXT data type (which is a BLOB) in SQL Server. Don't get me wrong, it's still very possible to do Full Text searches against the text in the file, but you're going to have to do substantially more coding to keep your relationships in tack if you want non-BLOB data from the same functional row. In addition, you're most likely going to wind up having to program your middle tier to make use of Index Server (which is what supports SQL Server's Full Text search also).

If push comes to shove, and you need to make a Full Text search against file system based information, you could take a look at accessing the Index Server via a query directly. Remember from our chapter on remote queries that we can potentially access any OLE DB datasource – well, the Index Server service has an OLE DB provider and can be used at the target as a linked server or in an OPENQUERY.

Sub-Categories

Sub-categories are a logical construct that provides us another type of relationship (sometimes called a "Supertype" or "SubType" relationship) to work with. On the physical side of the model, a sub-category is implemented using a mix the types of relationships that we've already talked about (we'll see the specifics of that before we're done).

A sub-category deals with the situation where you have a number of what may at first seem like different entities, but which share some, although not all, things in common.

I think the best way to get across the concept of a sub-category is to show you one. To do this, we'll take the example of a document in a company.

A document has a number of attributes that are common to any kind of document. For example:

- Title
- Author
- Date Created
- Date Last Modified
- Storage Location

I'm sure there are more. Note that I'm not saying that every document has the same title, rather that every document has a title. Every document has an author (possibly more than one actually, but, for this example, we'll assume a limit of one). Every document was created on some date. You get the picture – we're dealing with the attributes of the concept of a document, not any particular instance of a document.

But there are lots of different kinds of documents. From things like legal forms (say your mortgage documents) to office memos, to report cards – there are lots of document types. Still, each of these can still be considered to be a document – or a sub-category of a document. Let's consider a few examples:

For our first example, we'll look at a lease. A lease has all the characteristics that we expect to find our in documents category, but it also has information that is particular to a lease. A lease has things like:

- Lessor
- Lessee
- Term (how long the lease is for)
- Rate (how much per month or week)
- Security Deposit
- Start Date
- Expiration Date
- Option (with usually offers an extension at a set price for a set additional term)

The fact that a lease has all of these attributes does not preclude the fact that it is still a document.

We can come up with a few more examples, and I'll stay with my legal document trend – let's start with a divorce document. It has attributes such as:

- Plaintiff (the person suing for a divorce)
- Defendant (the plaintiff's spouse)
- Separation Date
- Date the plaintiff files for the divorce
- Date the divorce was considered "final"
- Alimony (if any)
- Child support (if any)

We could also have a bill of sale – our bill of sale might include attributes such as:

- Date of Sale
- Amount of the Sale
- Seller
- Purchaser
- Warranty Period (if any)

Again, the fact that divorces and bills of sale both have their own attributes does not change the fact that they are documents.

In each case – leases, divorces, and bills of sale – we have what is really a sub-category of the category of "documents". A document really has little or no meaning without also belonging to a sub-category. Likewise, any instance of a sub-category has little meaning without the parent information that is found only in the super-category – documents.

Types of Sub-categories

Subcategories fall into two separate classifications of their own – exclusive and non-exlcusive.

When we refer to a sub-category as simply a "sub-category", then we are usually referring to a sub-category arrangement where we have a record in a table that represents the super-category (a document in our previous example), and a matching record in at least one of the sub-categories.

This kind of sub-category is represented with a symbol that appears rather odd as compared to those we've seen thus far:

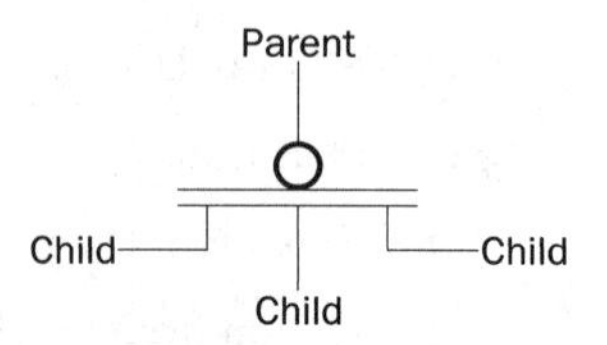

Even though there are three subcategories depicted both here and in the document example, don't misconstrue this as being any kind of official limit to the number of sub-categories – there isn't one. You could have a single sub-category or 10 of them – it doesn't really make any difference.

Far more common is the situation where we have an **exclusive sub-category**. An exlcusive sub-category works exactly as a category did with only one exception – for every record in the super-category, there is only one matching record in any of the sub-categories. Each sub-category is deemed to be mutually exclusive, so a record to match the super-category exists as exactly one row in exactly one of the sub-category tables.

The diagramming for an exclusive sub-type looks even a little more odd yet:

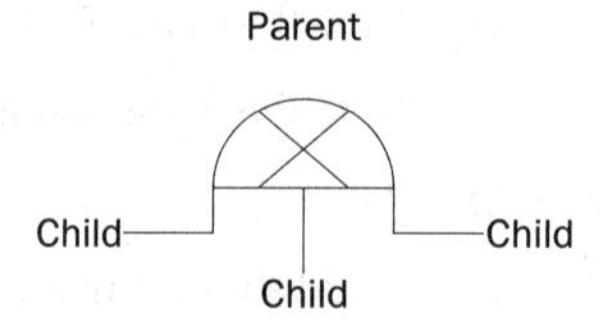

Keeping Track Of What's What – Implementing Sub-categories

The thing that's really cool about sub-categories is that they allow you to store all of a similar construct in one place. Before learning this concept, we would have taken one of two approaches to implement our document model:

- Add all of the attributes into one column and just leave the columns null for the information that doesn't fit the specific type of document we're interested in for a given record.
- Have separate tables for each type of document. The columns that are essentially the same between document types would be repeated for each table (each table stores its own copy of the document information as it applies to the records in that particular table).

Using the notion of a sub-category, we can now store all documents, regardless of type, such that they all begin in one place. Any query that you have that is looking for information about all the documents in your system can now run against just one table instead of having to do something like using the UNION operator on 3 (maybe more, maybe less) different tables. It probably goes without saying, then, that implementing this kind of situation using a sub-category can provide a serious performance enhancement over the other options.

There is a catch though (you knew there would be, right?) – you need to provide some mechanism to point to the rest of the information for that document. Your query of all documents may provide the base information on the specific document that you're looking for, but when you want the rest of the information for that document (the things that are unique to that document type), then how does your application know which of the sub-category tables to search for the matching record in? To do this, just add a field to your super-category that indicates what the sub-category is for that record. In our example, we would probably implement another column in our documents table called `DocumentType`. From that type, we would know which of our other tables to look through for the matching record with more information. Furthermore, we might implement this using a domain table – a table to limit the values in our `DocumentType` column to just those types that we have subcategories for – and a foreign key to that table.

> *Keep in mind that, while what we're talking about here is the physical storage and retrieval of the data, there is no reason why you couldn't abstract this using either a sproc or a series of views (or both). For example, you could have a stored procedure call that would pull together the information from the* `Documents` *table and then join to the appropriate sub-category.*
>
> *Oh - for those of you who are thinking "Wait, didn't that other text that I read about n-tier architecture say to never use sprocs? Well, that's a garbage recommendation in my not so humble option (which I indicated to some degree back in Chapter 12). It's foolish not to use the performance tools available – just remember to only access them through your data access layer – don't allow middle tier or client components to even know your sprocs exist.*

In addition to establishing a pointer to the type of document, we also need to determine whether we're dealing with a plain sub-category or an exclusive sub-category. In our document example, we have what should be designed as an exclusive sub-category. We may have lots of documents, but we do not have documents that are both a lease and a divorce (a non-exclusive sub-category would allow any mix of our sub-categories). Even if we had a lease with a purchase option, the bill of sale would be a separate document created at the time the lease option was exercised.

So now we're ready to implement our logical model:

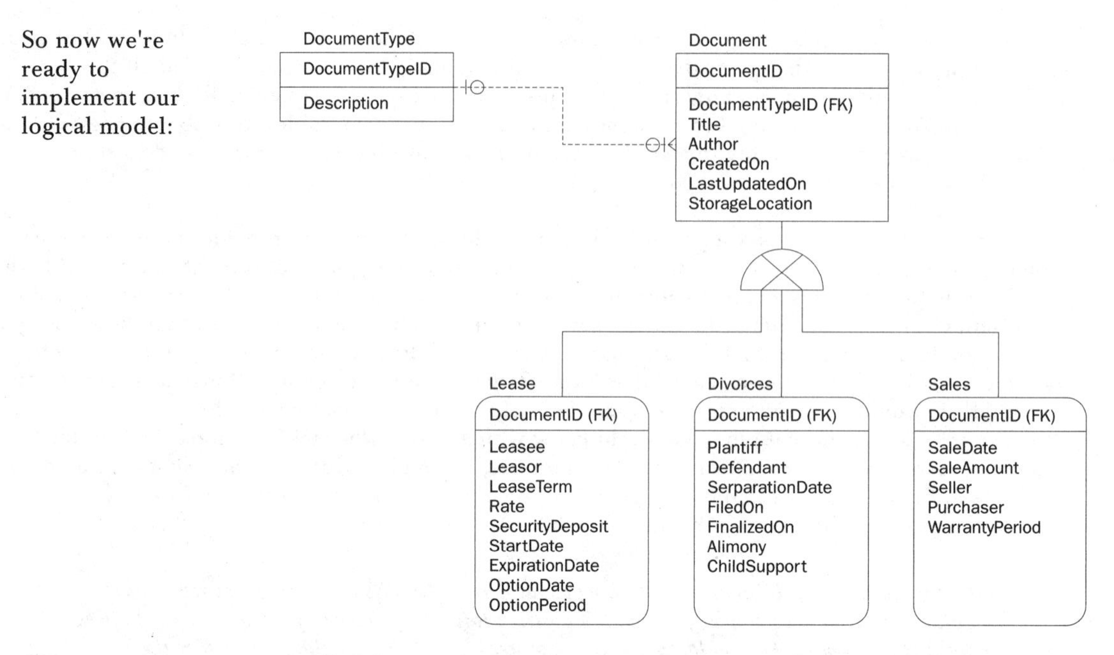

OK, so we have an entity called documents. These documents are of a specific type, and that type is limited to a domain – the boundaries of that domain are set by `DocumentType`. In addition, each of the types are represented by its own entity – or sub-category. The symbol in the middle of it all (the half circle with an "X" through it), tells us that the three sub-categories are exclusive in nature (you have one, and only one for each instance of a document).

This is an excellent place to step back and reflect on what our logical model can do for us. As we discussed earlier in the chapter, our logical model, among other things, provides us with a way to communicate the business rules and requirements of our data. In this case, with a little explanation, someone (a customer perhaps?) can look at this and recognize the concept that we are saying that Leases, Divorces, and Sales are all variations on a theme – that they are really the same thing. This gives the viewer the chance to say "Wait – no, those aren't really the same thing." Or perhaps something like "Oh, I see – you know, we also have will and power-of-attorney documents – they are pretty much the same, aren't they?" These are little pieces of information that can save you a bundle of time and money later.

Let's Get Physical – The Physical Implementation of Sub-categories

On the physical side of things, there's nothing quite as neat and clean as it looks in the logical model. Indeed, all we do for the physical side is implement a series of one-to-zero or one relationships. We do, however, draw them out as being part of a single, multi-table relationship:

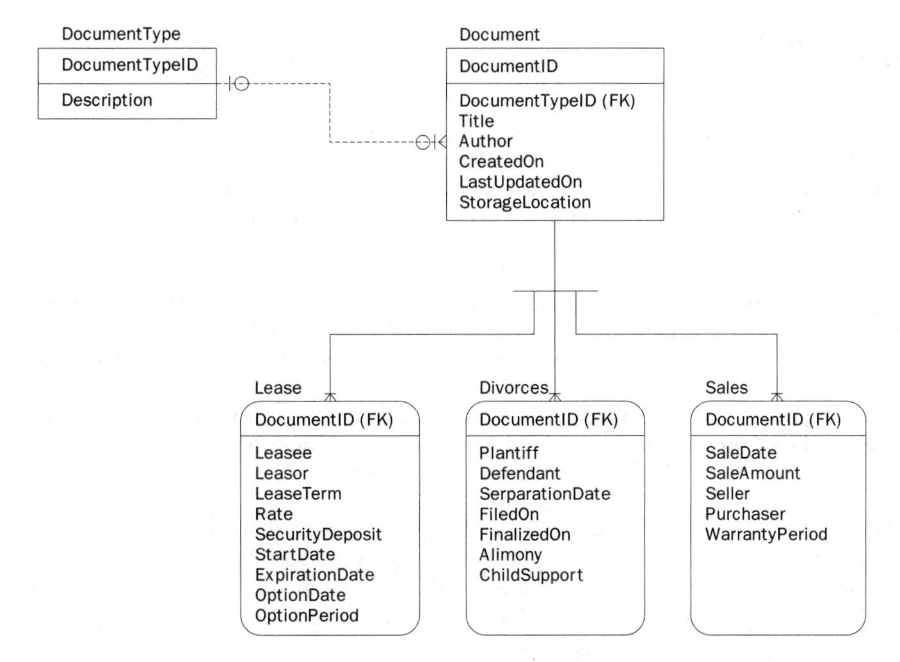

The only real trick in the game occurs if you have an exclusive sub-category (which is actually the case much more often than not). In this case, you also need to put some logic into the sub-category tables (in the form of triggers) to insure that, if any row is to be inserted, there is not already another matching row in one of the other sub-categories. For example, you would need to place an insert trigger in Leases that queried the Divorces and Sales tables for records with the same DocumentID. If one was found, then the trigger should reject inserted record with an appropriate error message and a `ROLLBACK`.

How Sub-categories Add To Extensibility

Sub-categories are one of those concepts that can make a huge difference in the success of your database design. If used when appropriate, you can cut significant time off your queries and significantly simplify pulling together aggregate information for related but different pieces of information. Yet these aren't the only benefits to sub-categories.

Sub-categories can provide a pathway to making your database more extensible. If you need to add another sub-category, the only queries you need to deal with are those that are specific to your new sub-category. Any of your queries that worked only with the parent table will still work fine – what's more, they'll pick up the information on your new sub-category without any changes!

In short, you're picking up two major scalability benefits:

- The information for your super-category (documents in the example) can be scanned from just one table rather than using a `UNION` operator. This means less joins and faster query performance especially as your tables grow larger or you have more and more sub-categories.
- The addition of new sub-categories often does not take as much development time as it would have if you where developing the framework for that category from scratch.

Database Reuse

This is almost never thought of, but you can create databases that facilitate reusability. Why do I say that it's almost never thought of? Well, just trust me on this – developers think of things like reusable components. Things such as objects to validate credit cards, distribute mail, stream binary information in and out – these are all things that you would immediately think about placing in a repository and using over and over again. For whatever reason, however, databases just don't seem to get thought of in that way.

Perhaps one reason for this is that databases, by definition, store data. Data is normally thought of as being unique to one company or industry and, most of all, as being private. I'm guessing that we then automatically think of the storage container for that data as also being personal – who knows?

Contrary to popular belief, however, databases can be built to be reusable. Surprisingly, to do this you apply a lot of the same concepts that make code components reusable – most of all compartmentalization and the use of common interfaces.

Much as many of the concepts of how to implement reusability of code components also apply to database reuse, so too does the concept of efficiency in the cost and time departments. Databases that are already designed save the design time and the associated costs. This can shorten product schedules and help in the ever present battle with the budget.

Candidates For Reusable Databases

The databases that have the best chance at being reusable are those that can be broken up into separate subject areas (much like components are usually broken up into functional groupings). Each subject area is kept as generic as is feasible. An example would be something like an `accounting` database. You could have separate subject areas that match up with the functional areas in accounting:

- Purchasing
- Accounts Receivable (which in turn may be broken up into Invoicing and Cash Receipts)
- Inventory
- Accounts Payable
- General Ledger
- Cash Management

The list could go on. One can also take the approach down to a more granular level and create many, many databases down to the level of things like Persons, commercial entities (ever noticed how similar customers are to vendors), Orders – there are lots of things that have base constructs that are used repeatedly. You can roll these up into their own "mini-database", then plug them into a larger logical model (tied together using sprocs, views, or other components of your data access layer).

How To Break Things Up

This is where the logical vs. physical modeling really starts to show its stuff. When we're dealing with databases that we're trying to make reusable, we often have one logical database (that contains all the different subject areas) which contains many physical databases. Sometimes we'll choose to implement our logical design by referencing each of the physical implementations directly. Other times we may choose an approach that does a better job of hiding the way that we've implemented the database – we can create what amounts to a "virtual" database in that it holds nothing but views that reference the data from the appropriate physical database.

> *Let me digress long enough to point out that this process is essentially just like encapsulation in object oriented programming. By using the views, we are hiding the actual implementation of our database from the users of the view. This means that we can remove one subject area in our database and replace it with an entirely different design – the only trick in doing this is to map the new design to our views – from that point on, the client application and users are oblivious to the change in implementation.*

Breaking things up into separate physical databases and/or virtualizing the database places certain restrictions on us, and many of these restrictions contribute to the idea of being able to separate one subject area from the whole, and reuse it in another environment:

Some of the things to do include:

- Minimize or eliminate direct references to other functional areas. If you've implemented the view approach, connect each physically separate piece of the database to the logical whole only through the views.
- Don't use Foreign Key constraints - where necessary, use triggers instead. Foreign Key constraints can't span databases, but triggers can.

The High Price Of Reusability

All this reuse comes at a price. Many of the adjustments that you make to your design in order to facilitate reuse have negative performance impacts. Some of these include:

- Foreign Key Constraints are faster than Triggers overall
- Using views means two levels of optimization run on all your queries (one to get at the underlying query and mesh that into your original query, another to sort out the best way to provide the end result) – that's more overhead and it slows things down.
- If not using the virtual database approach (one database that has views that map to all the other databases), maintaining user rights across many databases can be problematic.

In short, don't look for things to run as fast unless you're dealing with splitting the data across more servers than you can with the single database model.

Reusing your database can make lots of sense in terms of reduced development time and cost, but you need to balance those benefits against the fact that you may suffer to some degree in the performance category.

Summary

In this chapter, we've added some more things to think about in your database designs. We've seen how a logical model can help us truly understand our database rules and requirements before we are committed to a physical database design. We also looked into an alternative way of storing large file based information. Using this alternative method will often yield you increased throughput and performance. We've taken a solid look at sub-categories and the very important role the can and should play in your database design strategy. Last, but certainly not least, we tool a look over some of the concepts of reusability of databases. Frankly, the number of different things to think about in design is virtually unlimited, but, hopefully, you now have some additional tools in our attempts to make the right choices about your database design.

In our next chapter, we'll toss in more design information yet. We'll be checking into the concepts that surround Online Analytical Processing rather than the Online Transaction Processing that has so dominated the book thus far. We'll see that the needs of OLAP are wildly different than those of an OLTP environment. Hopefully, by the time we're done, you'll see why you need to thing in terms of OLTP and OLAP as two completely separate problems, and you'll refuse to yield to the user to solve them both with one solution (it just doesn't work).

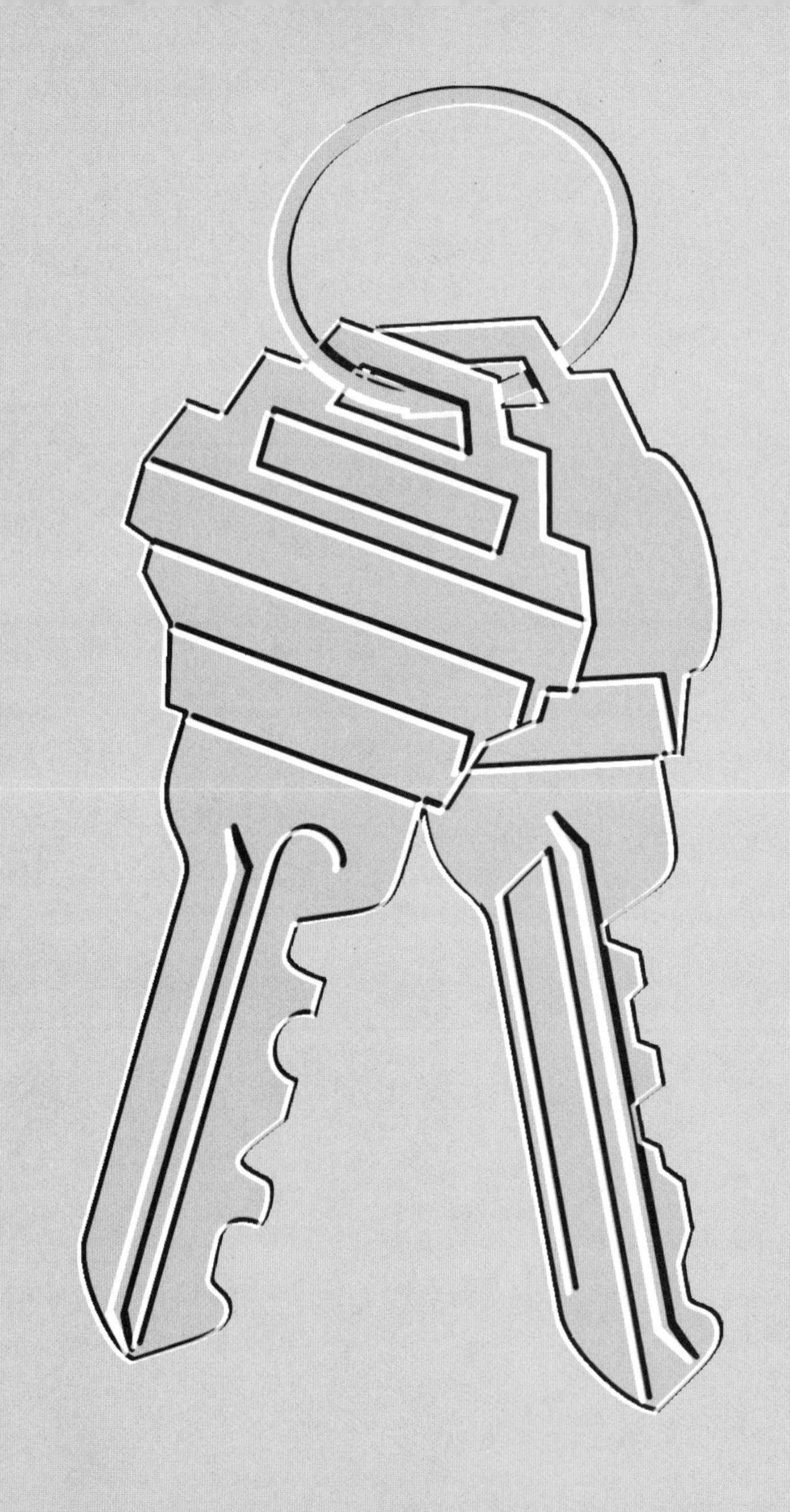

21

OLAP

Here we are 21 chapters in. You've learned all the great and fantastic stuff – now forget most of it.

Up to this point, we've been thinking in terms of transactions – we've been working primarily in the world of **Online Transaction Processing**, or **OLTP**. Now, however, it's time to get dimensional – to start thinking in terms of analysis and **Online Analytical Processing**, or **OLAP**.

In this chapter we will:

- Discuss the differences between the needs of transaction processing versus analysis processing
- Discuss how these differences necessarily lead to substantially different solutions
- Dispel the myth that your OLTP solution can also work as a great OLAP solution
- Define the concept of a data cube, and indicate how they can help provide a solution to the special requirements of an OLAP environment
- Look at the basic new OLAP Services that now come as part of SQL Server 7.0

The Requirements of End Users

As corporations build business applications and store their daily data in back-end databases associated with their applications, the databases swell in size. This swelling eventually has negative impacts on the applications themselves - slowing them down, hampering concurrency, reducing scalability, and even causing them to crash at times.

End users may use the data sources differently from one another. Two main categories of users can be distinguished:

- Those who want to access the data sources on a daily basis, retrieving certain records, adding new records, updating, or deleting existing records
- Those who want to make sense of the enormous amounts of data piling in the database, generating reports that will help them come up with the right decisions for the corporation and give it the competitive edge that will make it succeed in the marketplace

Two separate systems, Online Transaction Processing (OLTP) and Online Analytical Processing (OLAP), help satisfy the different requirements of the two categories of users. The following sections present the characteristics of the two systems. A comparison is then drawn between the two systems to come up with common rules that govern the creation of such systems.

Online Transaction Processing (OLTP)

Just as I mentioned in the previous section, OLTP systems are designed to allow for high concurrency making it possible for many users to access the same data source and conduct the processing they need. As the name implies, these systems allow for transactions to be processed against the database. Transactions mean controlled changes to the data in the tables due to inserts, updates and deletes during the conduction of business processes. The following figure depicts a basic OLTP system:

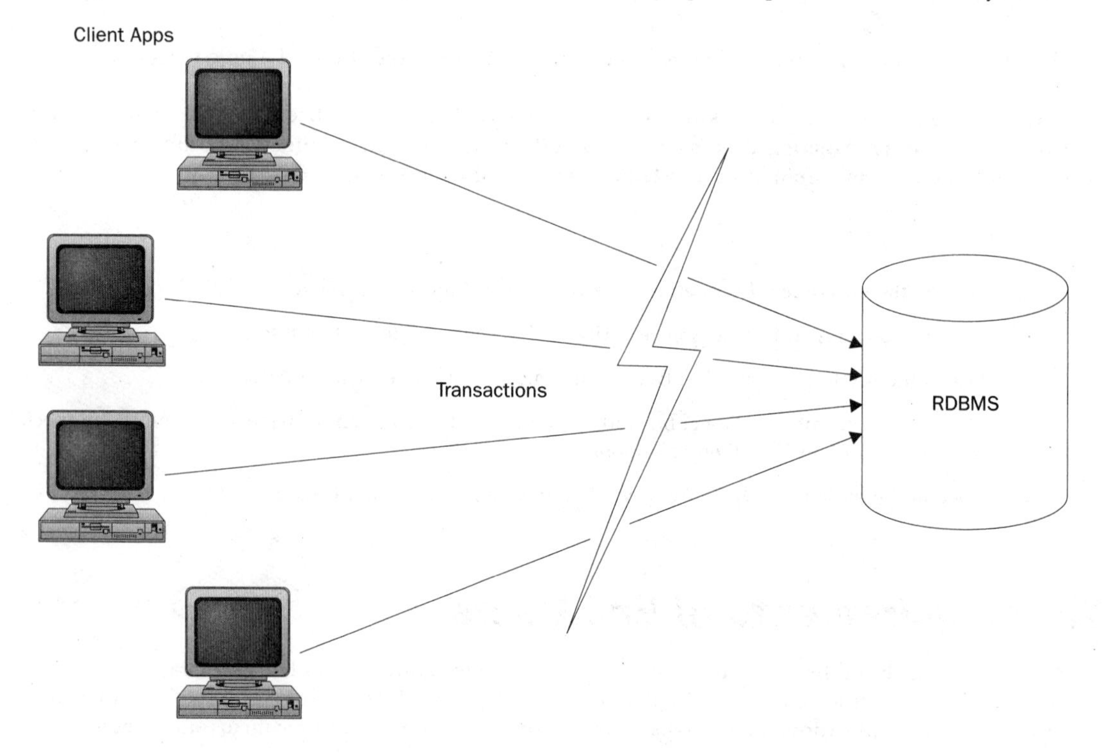

The figure shows that numerous client applications are accessing the database to get small pieces of information, add new data, update, or delete existing data. The broken line between the client applications and the server symbolizes that such a connection can physically take place in many different ways. For instance, client applications could be accessing the database through a transaction monitor, or they could be connected directly through the network.

Examples of OLTP systems include data-entry programs, such as, banking, ticket reservation, online sales applications, etc. No matter what the application is, OLTP systems are usually built with the following objectives in mind:

- Process data generated by transactions
- Maintain a high degree of accuracy by eliminating data redundancy
- Ensure data and information integrity
- Produce timely documents and reports, such as receipts and invoices
- Increase work efficiency
- Improve and enhance offered services to build and maintain customer loyalty

These objectives are usually accomplished by keeping the database in third normal form (or better), eliminating redundancy in the system, and maximizing relationships among the business entities as represented by the tables.

Online Analytical Processing (OLAP)

OLAP systems fall under the broader scope of **Decision Support Systems (DSS)** and **Executive Information Systems (EIS)**. The goal of OLAP systems is analyzing huge amounts of data, generating summaries and aggregations in many different ways to help decision makers find patterns and trends that would allow them to improve the performance of their corporations, gain competitive edge, and optimize business processes.

With OLAP systems, you need to forget about nicely keeping your relational database in the third normal form. You'll need to break this form and de-normalize the database (or flatten it) allowing for some redundancy with improving query performance in mind. This is because data stored in OLAP systems rarely undergoes edits and changes. The data is kept there for query purposes; to generate reports that would help decision makers plan the future of their enterprises. With this established, the database no longer conforms to the relational database definition and conditions; it becomes what is called a **dimensional database**. These databases are used to build **data cubes**, which are multi-dimensional representations of the data that facilitate online business analysis and query performance. The dimensions of a cube represent distinct categories for analyzing business data. Such categories include time, geography, or product line among others.

SQL Server 7.0's OLAP Manager allows you to build up to 64 dimensions for each data cube.

Later, we will discuss data cubes and dimensions in more detail. For now, let's just see how these concepts serve DSS and EIS in a more useful manner than OLTP.

OLTP or OLAP?

Now that you have seen the general ideas behind the two systems of OLAP and OLTP, let's consider the following example.

Let's take the banking business for example. During the bank work hours, bank tellers help customers perform their much needed transactions, like depositing funds into their accounts, transferring funds between accounts, and withdrawing funds from these accounts. The customers may also conduct their own transactions using an automatic teller machine (ATM) or phone-based and/or computer-based banking service. In other words, such transactions are not limited to a particular part of the day but can take place around the clock. All of these operations lead to changes in the data stored in the database. These changes could be inserts of new records, updating, or deleting existing records.

OLTP is built to allow these transactions to be made by a large number of users accessing the database concurrently. Databases serving OLTP systems are usually relational and in the third normal form, and their table indexes need to be selected carefully for the right fields. OLTP databases should be built to promote performance, allow high frequency of transactions, and represent tables in a relational fashion with parent-child relationships. Transactions held in such systems include inserts, updates, deletes, and selects.

Let's now look at a different scenario with the banking example. Suppose that the bank managers are conducting future planning. They definitely need to look at the current and historical performance data of the bank. If they were to query the database that is used for the OLTP system, they will face big difficulties and cause major problems to other users who are conducting their transactions.

These issues arise because the queries used to build management reports will usually be summary, or aggregation queries. For example, they might want to know the total amount of transactions conducted by all customers in a certain region. Such queries will have to sift through large amounts of data that is fragmented and scattered over many joined tables. For example, an accounting general ledger transaction could be stored in a dozen different tables. The queries will have to pull fields from these joined tables to build the views needed by the management, grouping and performing aggregations as it does so. All of this will impose a large overhead on the database management system (DBMS) slowing down the OLTP applications and the report generation process for the managers as well.

To face these challenges, it was necessary to separate the managers who use existing bank data to build their future outlook and planning, and have them use a different system based on OLAP principals. This means creating two different systems: an OLTP system for transaction processing by bank staff and customers, and an OLAP system to help with the decision-making.

Now we have two different systems, should these systems use the same database with separate tables for each system, or should they use two completely different databases? The answer to this question depends on how much effect one of the systems will have on the performance of the other. It is very likely that the two systems will be used at the same time. This causes performance problems even if the tables are separate. This is because the two systems still share many resources on the database server, and these resources may be depleted quickly with the two systems in use. These two systems are usually optimized differently. If we optimize for OLAP, we may adversely affect the performance of the OLTP system, and vice versa. Therefore, even though it is theoretically possible to tap into the same database, it is a good idea to keep separate databases on separate database servers for the two systems. With this, each system will have its own resources, and optimizing it will not affect the other system.

Querying an OLTP System

Although the relational model allows for great flexibility in defining ways to look at and process the data in the database, we often find that the way data is processed in a business solution is different, especially by decision makers. Decision makers are not interested in the details of every single transaction recorded in the database; they are interested in looking at the big picture instead. Let's consider a `sales` database for a bookseller, for instance. The database is likely to include a `sales` table, such as the one presented here:

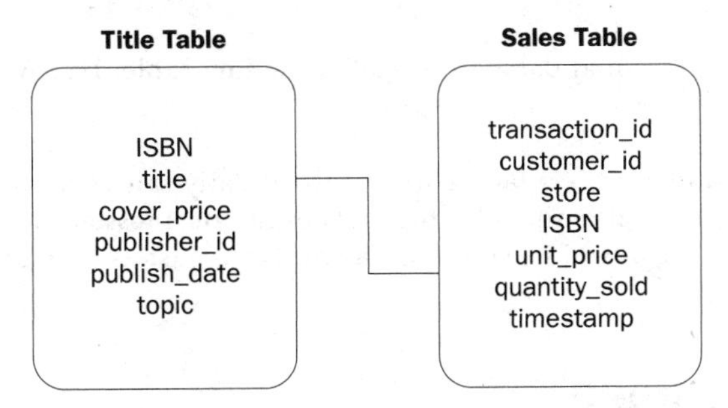

As the OLTP system is used over time, the table grows in size and becomes full of sales data, sometimes for the same customers, buying the same goods at different prices. Thus, the table becomes a good candidate for analysis.

The business analyst may be interested in finding out the effect the price had on the sales of programming-related books. In this case, she would be looking for the results in a table or even graph format similar to the chart below:

Price	Quantity Sold	Revenue
$20	7,000	140,000
$30	3,500	105,000
$40	2,500	100,000
$50	2,000	100,000

To get such results, the business analyst may ask a SQL developer to write a complex query for her that would extract the data from the OLTP system and put it in the format she wants. Such query may look like the code presented below:

```
SELECT     unit_price AS Price,
           SUM(quantity_sold) AS 'Quantity Sold',
           unit_price * SUM(quantity_sold) AS Revenue
FROM       sales, title
WHERE      title.ISBN = sales.ISBN
      AND  title.topic = 'programming book'
GROUP BY   unit_price
```

Needless to say, it's very time and resource consuming for the business analyst to have to follow this path whenever she wants to get some summaries and aggregations of data. Yet, this is a simplified version of what could happen in the real world. In production OLTP systems, such a query may be much larger, involving many table joins that would effect the speed at which the results will return and effect the performance of other users of the database.

Dimensional Databases

The solution to the problems inherent with requesting complex queries from OLTP systems is to build a separate database that would represent the business facts more accurately. The structure of this database will not be relational; instead, it will be **dimensional**.

The Fact Table

The central table of a dimensional database is called the **fact table**. Its rows are known as **facts** and they are **measures** of activities.

For example, we may build a `sales` fact table to record daily sales transactions of products offered by a given store. The `sales` table includes the facts of the business activities. `quantity` and `total_price` are the measures of facts in the `sales` table, just as they usually are in a typical relational database.

The Dimension Tables

Dimensions help put the facts in context and represent such things as time, product, customer, and location. The dimensions describe the data in the fact table. Continuing with our sales example, it would make sense to have time, store, customer, and product line dimensions.

The fact table, `sales`, captures transactions on a daily level for each store, for all customers, and for all books. This table, therefore, will grow to be very large. To improve the efficiency with which data is retrieved from the database, aggregates are pre-computed at different levels and stored in the database or in an optimized format, as we will see later in the chapter.

The tables linked to the fact table are called **dimension tables** and each represents a dimension. They are used to generate the aggregations from the fact table. For instance, we could find the total monthly sales of all books to all customers by all stores if we were to query the `sales` table grouping by month of the year. Alternatively, we could find the total sales by state at all times, for all customers, and for all books if we queried the `sales` table grouping on state. We can also have aggregations on a combination of the dimensions in the `sales` fact table. For example, we could find the total sales for a particular book category by state on a monthly basis for a certain type of customer by grouping on state and month and adding the appropriate criteria in the `WHERE` clause for the customer and book category.

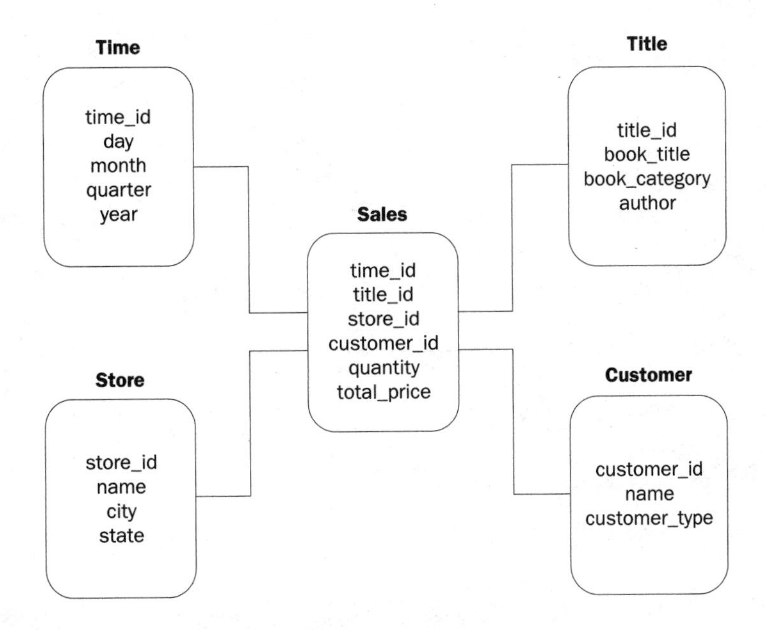

The Star and Snowflake Schemas

The database schema above, where there is a single fact table with a number of dimension tables linked directly to it, is an example of the **star schema**.

Another schema the dimensional database can follow is the **snowflake schema**. In a snowflake schema, multiple tables define one or more of the dimensions. What this means is that the snowflake schema is an extension of the star schema, where extra dimension tables are linked, not to the fact table directly, but to dimension tables.

Data Cubes

The example we have just seen is often represented as a **data cube**. The dimensions of the cube represent the dimensions of the fact table. Each cell in the cube represents a fact corresponding to a level of detail for the different dimensions of the cube. Although the graphical representation of the cube can only show three dimensions, a data cube can have up to 64 dimensions when using SQL Server's OLAP services. The following figure shows a representation of a data cube for the `sales` table with the store, title, and time dimensions shown:

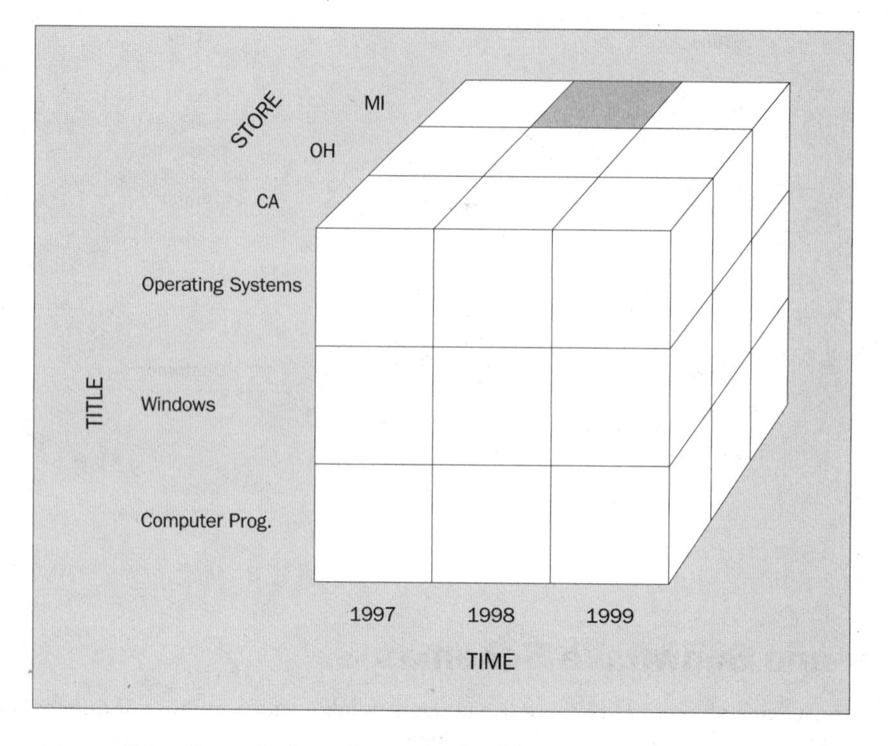

If you want to use this cube to find out the total sales for stores in Michigan during 1998 for the Operating Systems book category, you need to look at the shaded cell in the figure, which is the resulting cell from the intersection of those three dimensions. That cell should contain the quantity of books sold and the total price, which are the facts identified in the fact table.

Microsoft's OLAP Services allows you to build your cube from any source of data that has an OLE DB provider. This source can be a relational database in any database management system that has an ODBC driver (such as Oracle or Sybase SQL Server) or has a native OLE DB provider (such as SQL Server, or MS Access). The data source for the cube can also be a dimensional database, text files or LDAP data source.

OLAP Storage Types

Based on the cube data storage method, three options of OLAP are supported by the decision support systems that ship with SQL Server 7.0. These options are:

- Multi-dimensional OLAP (MOLAP)
- Relational OLAP (ROLAP)
- A hybrid of the previous two options (HOLAP)

Each of these options provides certain benefits, depending on the size of your database and how the data will be used.

MOLAP

MOLAP is a high-performance, multi-dimensional data storage format. The data supporting the cubes is stored with this option on the OLAP server as a multi-dimensional database. MOLAP gives the best query performance, because it is specifically optimized for multi-dimensional data queries. Performance gains stem from the fact that the fact tables are compressed with this option and bitmap indexing is used for them.

Since MOLAP requires that all of the data be copied, converting its format appropriately to fit the multi-dimensional data store, MOLAP is appropriate for small to medium-sized data sets. Copying all of the data for such data sets would not require significant loading time or utilize large amounts of disk space.

ROLAP

Relational OLAP storage keeps the data that feeds the cubes in the original relational tables. A separate set of relational tables is used to store and reference aggregation data in this OLAP system. These tables are not downloaded to the DSS server. The tables that hold the aggregations of the data are called **materialized views**. These tables store data aggregations as defined by the dimensions when the cube is created.

With this option, aggregation tables have fields for each dimension and measure. Each dimension column is indexed. A composite index is also created for all of the dimension fields. Due to its nature, ROLAP is ideal for large databases or legacy data that is infrequently queried.

HOLAP

A combination of MOLAP and ROLAP is also supported by the DSS server. This combination is referred to as **HOLAP**. With HOLAP, the original data is kept in its relational database tables similar to ROLAP. Aggregations of the data are performed and stored in a multi-dimensional format. An advantage of this system is that HOLAP provides connectivity to large data sets in relational tables while taking advantage of the faster performance of the multi-dimensional aggregation storage. A disadvantage of this option is that the amount of processing between the ROLAP and MOLAP systems may affect its efficiency.

Data Warehouse Concepts

Now we have seen what OLAP and dimensional databases are, let's define what a data warehouse is, and how it can be built in SQL Server 7.0.

A **data warehouse** is a data store that holds the data collected during the company's conduction of business over a long period of time. The data warehouse uses the OLTP systems that collect the data from everyday activities and transactions as its source. The data warehouse concept also includes the processes that scrub (see Data Scrubbing later in the chapter) and transform the data, making it ready for the data warehouse. It also includes the repository of summary tables and statistics, as well as the dimensional database. Finally, it also includes the tools needed by the business analysts to present and use the data. These tools include OLAP tools (such as SQL Server's OLAP Manager), as well as data mining and reporting tools. The following figure depicts the conceptual structure and components of a data warehouse solution:

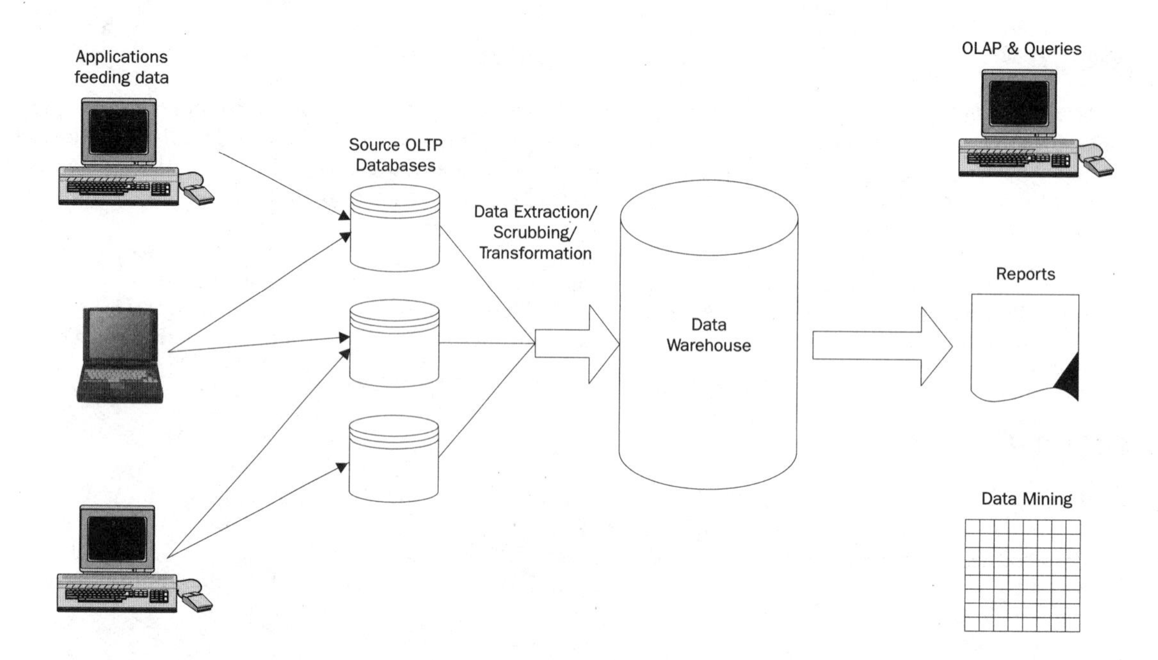

Data Warehouse Characteristics

A data warehouse is usually built to support decision-making and online analysis (OLAP) because it is designed with the following unique characteristics:

- **Consolidated and consistent data**: In a data warehouse, data is collected from different sources, consolidated and made consistent in many ways, including the use of naming conventions, measurements, physical attributes and semantics. This is important because business analysts accessing the data warehouse and using its data for their decision-making process, have to use consistent standards. For example, date formats may all follow one standard, showing day, month, quarter and year. Data should be stored in the data warehouse in a single, acceptable format. This allows for the referencing, consolidating, and cross-referencing of data from numerous heterogeneous sources, such as legacy data on mainframes, data in spreadsheets, or even data from the Internet, giving the analysts a better understanding of the business.

- **Subject-oriented data**: The data warehouse organizes key business information from OLTP sources so that it is available for business analysis. In the process, it weeds out irrelevant data that might exist in the source data store. The organization takes place based on the subject of the data, separating customer information from product information, which may have been intermingled in the source data store.

- **Historical data**: Unlike OLTP systems, the data warehouse represents historical data. In other words, when you query the data warehouse, you use data that had been collected using the OLTP system in the past. The historical data could be over a long period of time, compared to the OLTP system, which contains current data that accurately describes the system for the most part.

- **Read-only data**: After data has been moved to the data warehouse, you may not be able to change it unless the data was incorrect in the first place. The data in the data warehouse cannot be updated because it represents historical data, which cannot be changed. Deletes, inserts, and updates (other than those involved in the data loading process) are not applicable in a data warehouse. The only operations that occur in a data warehouse once it has been set up, are loading of additional data and querying.

Data Marts

You may find out, after building your data warehouse, that many people in your organization only access certain portions of the data in the data warehouse. For instance, the sales managers may only access data relevant to their departments. Alternatively, they may only access data for the last year. In this case, it would be inefficient to have these people query the whole data warehouse to get their reports. Instead, it would be wise to partition the data warehouse in smaller units, called **data marts**, which are based on their business needs.

In addition, some people in your organization may want to be able to access the data in the data warehouse in remote areas far from the company buildings. For instance, a sales manager may want to access data about products and sales particular to his or her market area while on a sales venture. People such as this would benefit from a data mart, as they would be able to carry a section of the data warehouse on their laptop computers, allowing them to access the data they need at any time.

Of course, with data marts, the data should be kept in synch with the data warehouse at all times. This can be done in a variety of ways, such as using DTS, ActiveX scripting or programs. The following diagram shows the structure of the data warehouse concept with data marts included:

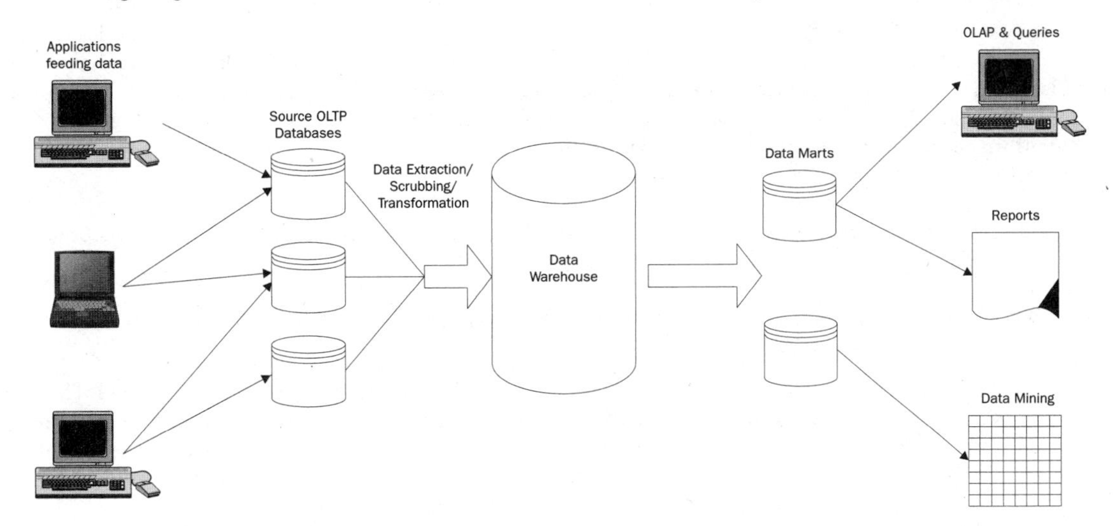

Data Transformation Services

Many organizations need to centralize data to improve decision-making. However, this data can be stored in a large variety of formats in a number of different sources. The row data that exists in these sources has to be reconciled and transformed in many cases before it can be stored in the data warehouse. **Data transformation services** (DTS), which we saw back in Chapter 18, conducts this function, providing a means to move data from the source OLTP database to the destination data warehouse while validating, cleaning up, consolidating and transforming the data when needed.

Data Validation

Conducting **data validation** before the data is extracted from the source OLTP databases and transferred to the destination data warehouse is extremely important. If the data is not valid, the integrity of the business analysis conducted based on it will be in question. For example, if one of the fields is a currency field, and the OLTP data sources exist in multiple countries around the globe, one has to make sure that the data in this currency field is always transferred in the currency of the destination data warehouse. If you transfer 500 French Franks as 500 US dollars, you will be misrepresenting the data in the data warehouse, and any report that includes this value will not be valid.

Another thing you need to pay close attention to when validating the data, is information related to geographical regions; you need to make sure that referenced cities are in the right countries as the `country` field states. Yet another example of validating data is that you need to make sure that the products (books in our example) are represented in a similar manner in all data sources.

Data Scrubbing

Data reconciliation has to take place between multiple sources feeding the same data warehouse. The reconciliation process is referred to as **data scrubbing**. For example, if the book mentioned above is classified in one OLTP database under the category, database, and in another OLTP database under a category called, database systems, aggregations in the data warehouse involving this category will yield inaccurate results, unless the two data sources have been reconciled during the data transformation process.

Data scrubbing can be achieved in different ways. These ways are beyond the scope of this book, but are mentioned here:

- Using DTS import and export wizards to modify data as it is copied from the source to the destination data store
- By writing a Microsoft ActiveX script or program. Such a script or program may use the DTS API to connect to the data source and scrub the data. This method is not the easiest method to perform data scrubbing, but it provides a great deal of flexibility, because it uses the power of the scripting or programming language to access the data, which can often provide a tremendous amount of control and manipulation across heterogeneous data sources.
- DTS Lookup provides the ability to perform queries using one or more named, parameterized query strings. This allows for building custom transformation schemes to retrieve data from locations other than the immediate source or destination row being transformed.

Data Migration

Ideally, when migrating data from OLTP data sources to a data warehouse, data is copied to an intermediate database before it is finally copied to the data warehouse. This intermediate process is necessary to allow for data scrubbing and validation to occur.

Special care should be taken when performing the **data migration**. The migration process should be performed during periods of low activity at the operational OLTP system to minimize the impact on the users of that system. If the migration is done from multiple data sources that are replicas or participate in replication processes, the migration should happen when all these sources are synchronized to make sure that consistent data is copied from these sources.

A commonly deployed strategy is to execute data migration procedures after the nightly database backups occur. This ensures that if a migration procedure crashes the system, the backup was just performed.

Data Transformation

When you move the data from the source OLTP databases to the destination data warehouse, you may find yourself performing many transformations of existing data to make it more operational and practical when used in the destination warehouse. Below are examples of **data transformations** you may want to consider when moving data from the OLTP databases to the data warehouse:

- You may break a column into multiple columns, such as dividing a date or timestamp field into its components of day, month, quarter and year
- You may also find yourself having to calculate new fields based on the values in source fields, such as creating a `total_price` field in the destination data warehouse, which is a result of multiplying the `unit_price` by the `quantity_sold` fields in the source database
- You may need to merge separate fields into one field, such as merging the `first_name` and `last_name` fields in the source database in one `name` column in the destination data warehouse
- You may also want to map data from one representation to another, such as translation of code to literal values and converting values from decimal numerical values (1, 2, 3, etc.) to Roman numerals (I, II, III, etc.)

DTS Components

Data transformation services (DTS) is comprised of the import wizard, the export wizard, and COM programming interfaces that allow for the creation of custom import/export and transformation applications. A detailed discussion of these topics was presented in Chapter 18.

Metadata and the Repository

Metadata is, by definition, data about data. In other words, the information about the way storage is structured in the data warehouse, OLAP and DTS services is all kept as metadata, which is stored in the Microsoft Repository. The repository is built to maintain such technical information about the data sources involved with the services mentioned above.

Repository information is stored in the SQL Server `msdb` database. The repository is the preferred means of storing DTS packages in a data warehousing scenario because it is the only method of providing data lineage for packages.

Access to the repository is possible through the interfaces exposed by the OLAP Manager's graphical user interface (GUI). Metadata can also be accessed through the **Decision Support Objects** (**DSO**), and through programs that use interfaces to the repository. However, Microsoft recommends only using the DSO or OLAP Manager's GUI to access the metadata, because the repository is subject to change in next releases, which may render any programs you build to access the repository directly unusable.

Note that multiple repositories can exist in a single SQL Server installation. However, DTS supports only a single repository database per server in the Enterprise Manager tree.

Decision Support Systems

Decision Support Systems is the general name given to tools that provide decision support. Microsoft's suite of decision support tools is called **Decision Support Services** (**DSS**) and consists of the DSS Analysis server and the PivotTable Service. These tools are used in both the storage and user tools to extract and manipulate the data in the data warehouse environment. The DSS Analysis server can utilize heterogeneous data sources across the organization for analysis and querying. DSS Analysis server gives you the option to optimize for query performance, or to optimize for disk storage requirements. Several tools, including English Query and Microsoft Office (especially MS Excel and MS Access) work with the DSS Analysis server accessing its cubes through the PivotTable Service. This gives the user a great advantage, because she/he is usually familiar with these tools, and can use them efficiently for the data analysis.

PivotTable Service was added to SQL Server 7.0 after being tested for quite a long time in Microsoft Excel and Access. This service allows the user to create cross-tab tables on the fly by specifying the columns and rows on which aggregations should be made.

OLAP Manager

OLAP Manager is installed separately from the SQL Server CD ROM after installing SQL Server. This tool is a graphical user interface that allows the user to build an OLAP solution based on existing data sources. This section will demonstrate how this tool can be used while presenting an OLAP solution example at the same time.

To run OLAP Manager, you need to select the Microsoft SQL Server 7.0 group from the Start | Programs menu, then select OLAP Services | OLAP Manager. You'll see the following screen:

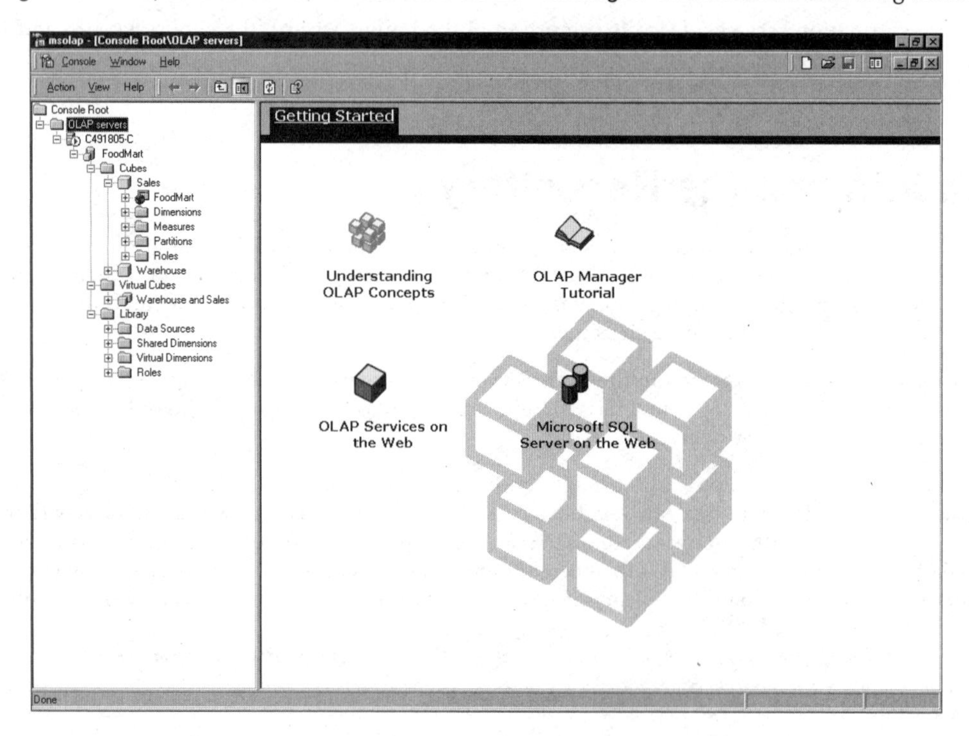

OLAP Manger is a snap-in of the Microsoft Management Console. Like the Enterprise Manager, it consists of two panes. The left pane contains a tree structure that depicts the available OLAP servers, databases, cubes, etc. The right pane contains details of the selected items in the left pane, whenever such details are available.

To add and/or remove existing snap-in items in MMC screen, select Console | Add/Remove Snap-in. Click on the Add button and you'll see the following Add Standalone Snap-in dialog:

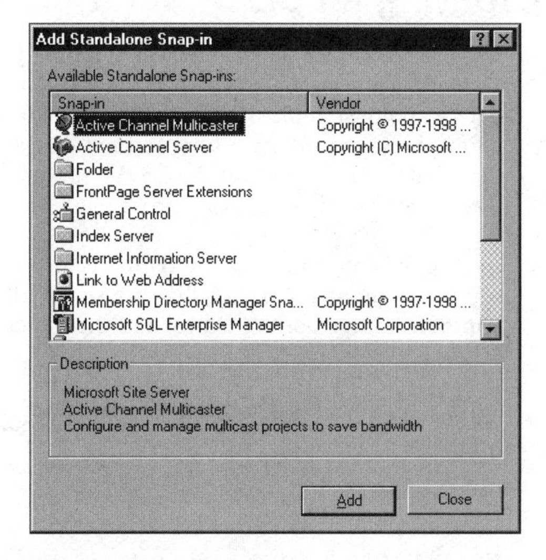

Select the Microsoft SQL Enterprise Manager snap-in and click the Add button, then close the dialog. As a result, you will see a screen similar to this:

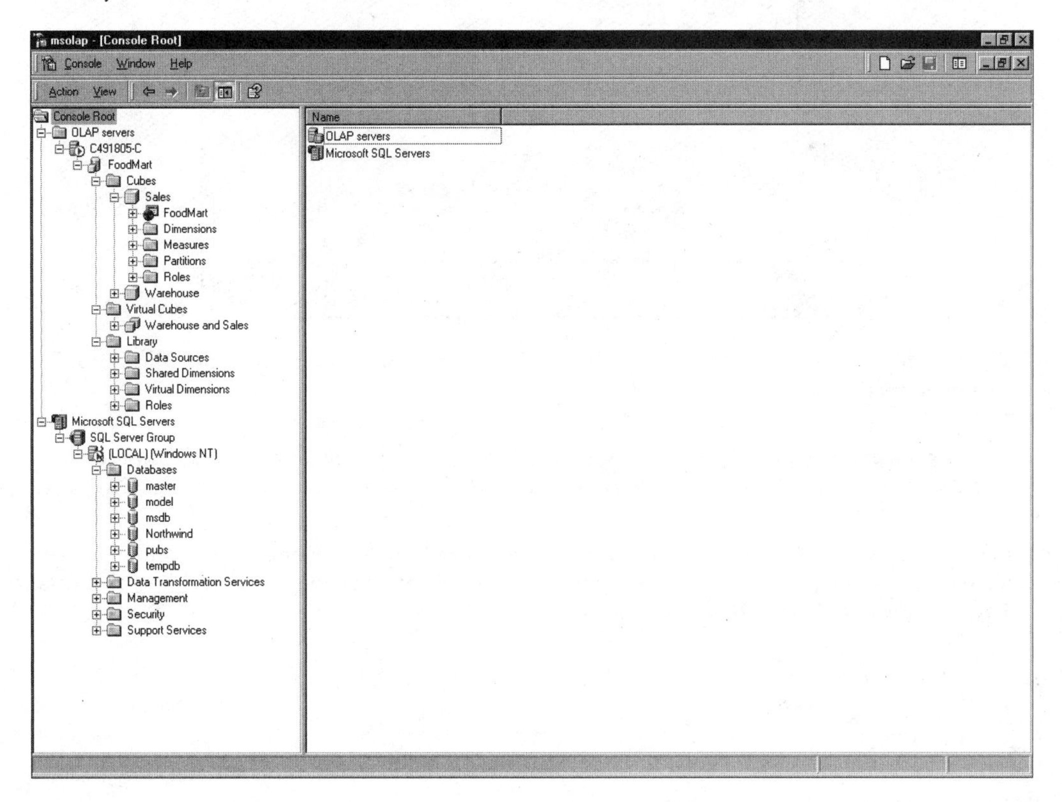

In summary, the OLAP Manager allows you to manage databases, data sources, cubes, dimensions, measures etc.

Creating an OLAP Solution

In this section, we will look at an example OLAP database that ships with SQL Server 7.0 OLAP services. This database is already full of data that can be used to show how the different OLAP and data warehouse tools work together. The database is called `FoodMart` and contains information about the sales and inventory of a national food chain. The database is an Access database that is installed when you install the OLAP server, and its default location is `C:\Program Files\OLAP Services\Samples\FoodMart.mdb`.

An ODBC data source name (DSN) is also created for this database at the time you install the OLAP services. The name of the DSN is also `FoodMart`. To verify that this DSN exists, select the ODBC32 applet from the Control Panel and then click on the System DSN tab, you'll see a screen similar to this:

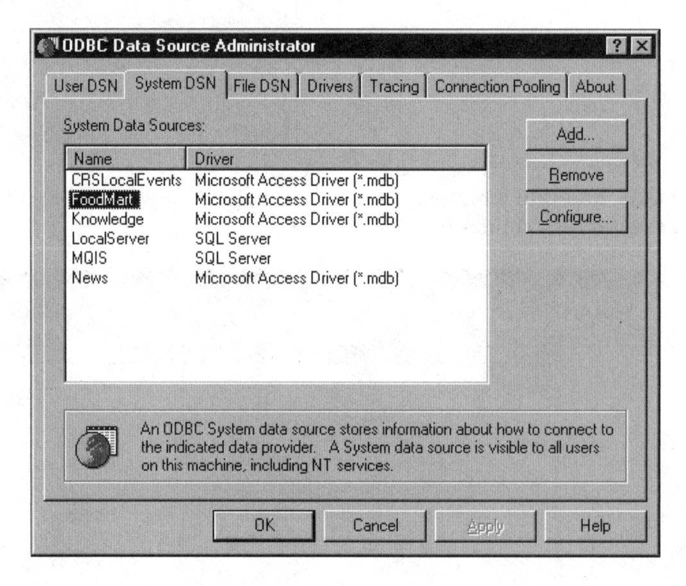

The goal here is to present the sales data for the stores, broken down by region, product, date, and customer for the year 1998.

> *If you want to look at the database in Microsoft Access, you need to close the OLAP Services Manager first, because when it is open, it accesses the `FoodMart` database in an exclusive mode.*

Let's now examine the database tables that we will need for our example. We will have a fact table for the year 1998 linked to the dimension tables: `product`, `store`, `time_by_day` and `customer`. The `product` table is also linked to a `product_class` table.

The fact table (`sales_fact_1998`) is the main table with which we need to concern ourselves. This table contains the fields that link it to the dimension tables mentioned above, as well as the measures we need to find eventually. These measures are the `store_sales`, `store_cost` and `unit_sale`. The following screenshot shows the database schema that we will need to use:

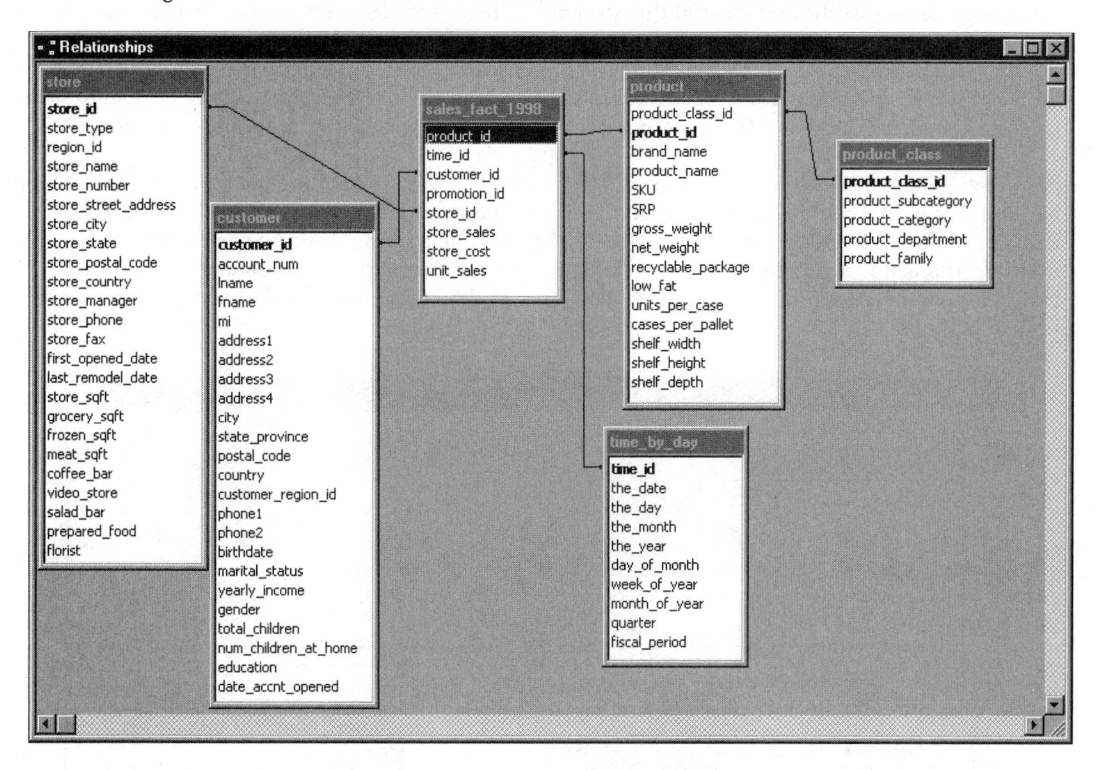

The links that the fact table has to the dimension tables allow us to produce the aggregations we want, rolling up the data to any level of these dimensions, as we shall see later in the chapter.

Before we move to the next section, notice that in the `customer` dimension table, there is no field that holds the customer name. Instead, there is a field for first name (`fname`), a field for middle initial (`mi`), and a field for last name (`lname`). It would be better to combine these three fields in one field called `name`. This makes it easier to define the levels of the dimension later on `country`, `state`, `city`, and `name`. To do this, create a new field called `name`, and update its value by running the following query in the `FoodMart` MS Access database:

```
/* To add the new field, run the following query */
ALTER TABLE customer ADD name text(180);
/* To update the name column, run the next query */
UPDATE customer SET customer.name = [fname] & ' ' & [mi] & ' ' & [lname];
```

Once you have run the two queries in MS Access, you will see that a new field, called `name`, has been created and populated the way we wanted by concatenating the first name, middle initial, and last name fields.

How Did We Get to this Schema?

You may be wondering how the schema shown above was reached. It is most likely that the original production database was a relational database in the third normal form. This means that it is likely that the store table did not exist in this structure. The store.store_manager field was probably called store_manager_id originally, and linked to a table that held the employee information, maybe called employee. In such a table, the information about the employees would be stored, including their titles. When the store table linked to the employee table, it only needed to have the employee_id field as a foreign key pointing to the primary key in the employee table.

Also in the same table are the fields, grocery_sqft, frozen_sqft and meat_sqft. These fields were probably in a middle table between the store table and another table, perhaps called departments. The relationship between the store table and the departments table is a many-to-many relationship. A middle table would be used to transform the many-to-many relationship into two one-to-many relationships. The structure of the middle table and its relationships might have looked like this:

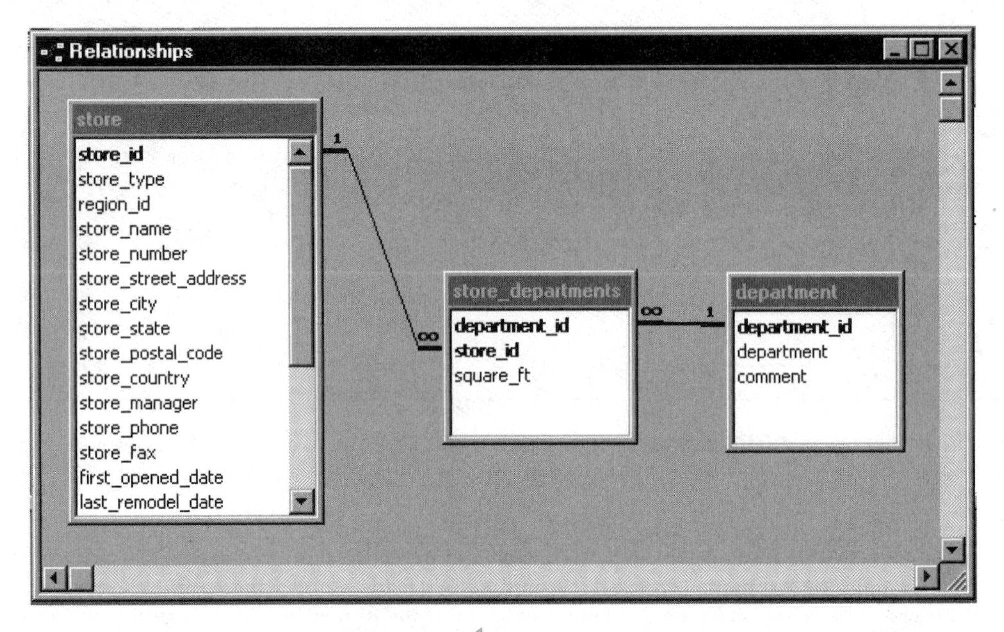

The kind of de-normalization in this particular case is described as de-normalization by flattening the data structures.

In summary, you can analyze the remaining dimension tables and normalize them to reach a relational database. The resulting database would represent the production database responsible for feeding the data warehouse.

Creating the OLAP Database in the OLAP Manager

To create the database we will be using, right-click the OLAP server name (which happens to be the same name as your machine) in the left pane of the OLAP Manager, and select New Database. Add the following information:

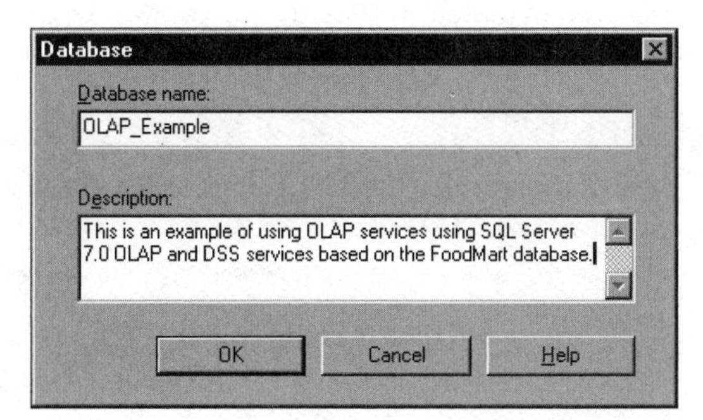

The new database will appear in the tree-view pane of the OLAP Manager. The database will have no cubes yet, no dimensions, no measures, etc. This will become apparent as you expand the tree view for the database by clicking on the + signs that correspond to it and its components:

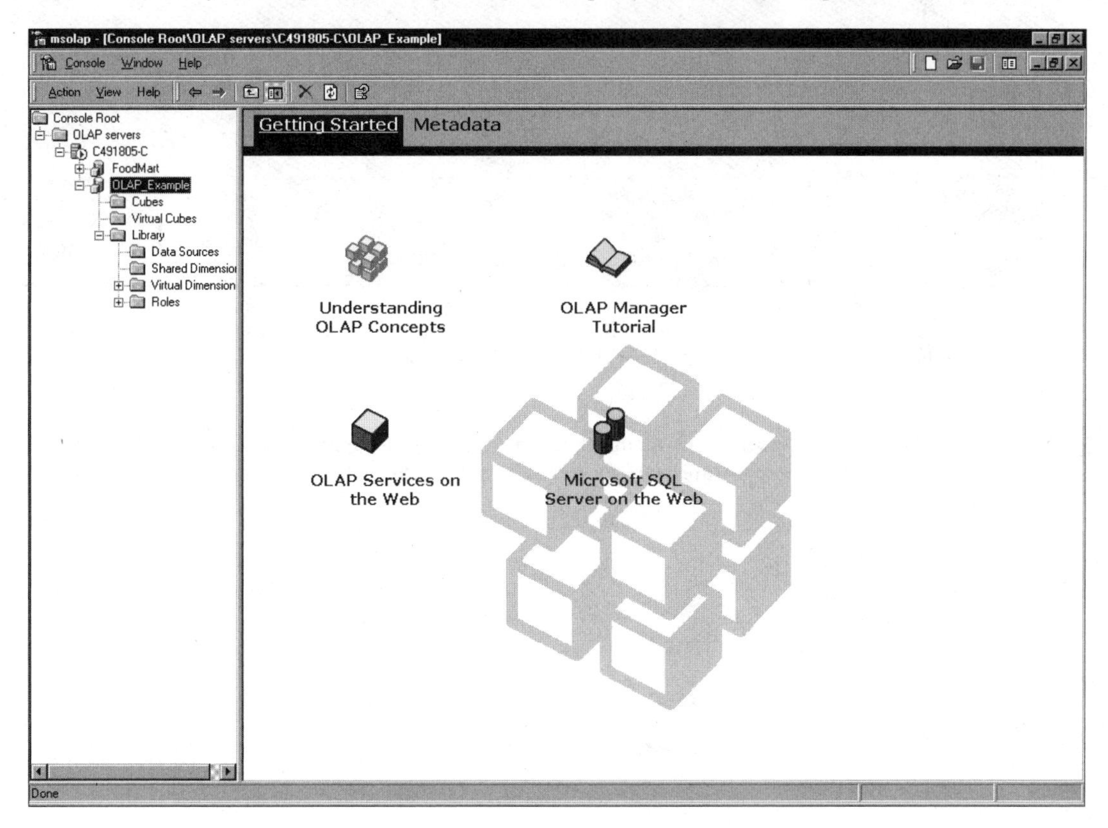

Adding the Data Sales Cube

To add the first data cube in the database we just created, you need to right-click on the Cubes item in the left pane underneath the OLAP_Example database we have just created, and select New Cube from the context-sensitive menu. You will be presented with a submenu that has the two commands: Wizard and Editor (which is grayed out). Select Wizard, and you will be presented with the first screen of the Cube Wizard:

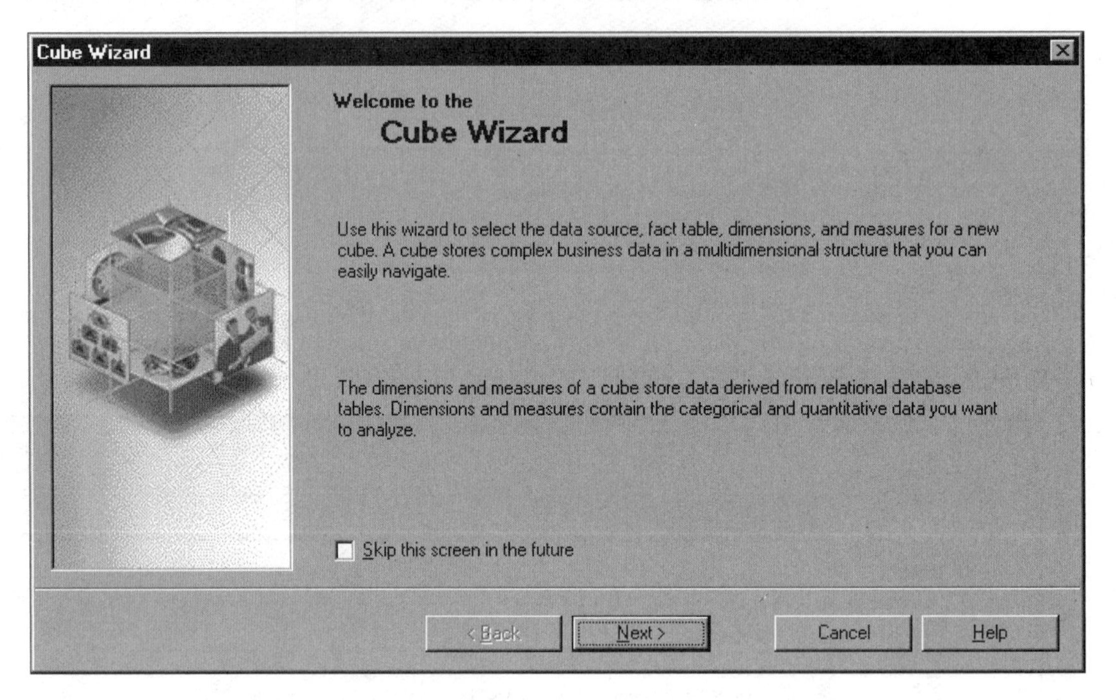

On the first screen of the Cube Wizard, click the Next button. The following screen will allow you to add a new data source to use for building the data cube, or use an existing data source for this purpose.

You can also add new data sources outside this wizard by right-clicking the Data Sources item in the left pane of the OLAP Manager and selecting New Data Source. This will lead you directly to the Data Link Properties screen.

As for our example, click the New Data Source button on the wizard screen:

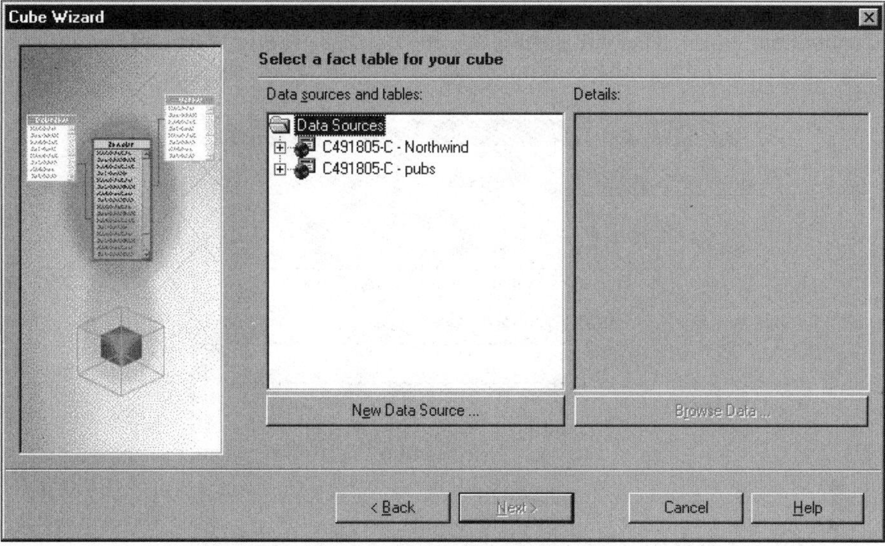

The Data Link Properties dialog will appear, allowing you to set up a data link using an OLE DB provider you have selected from the list. Select the OLE DB provider for Microsoft JET 3.51 or 4.0, and click the Next button:

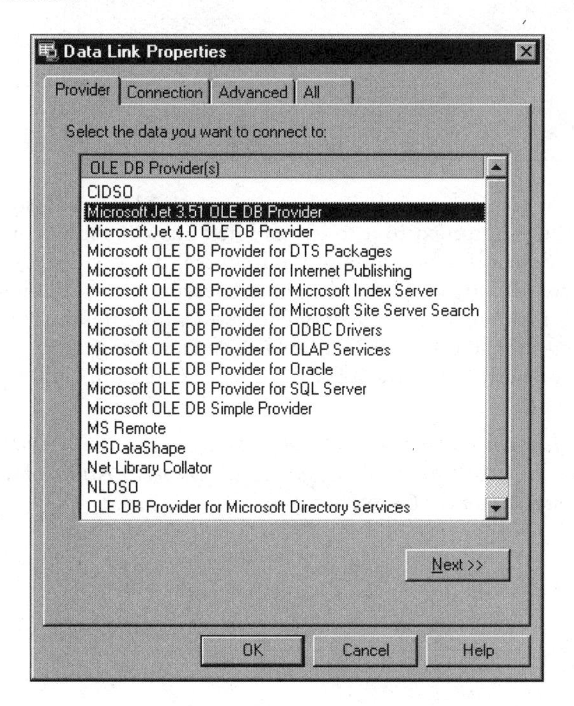

When you do so, you will be presented with the same dialog set to the Connection tab. This tab allows you to specify the properties of the connection or data link, such as the database name, user name and password. Once you have connected to `FoodMart.mdb`, test the connection by clicking on the Test Connection button. This will ensure that the database server is up and running, that the database name is valid, and that the user name and password are also valid:

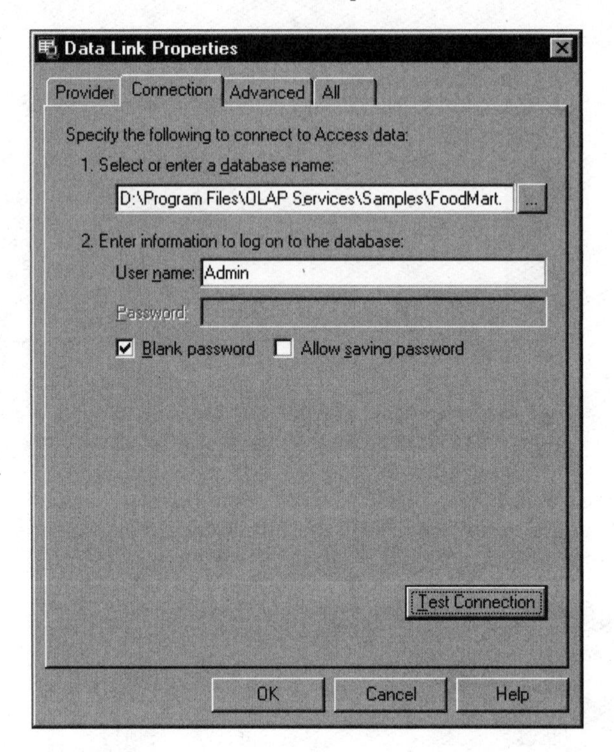

Click OK after testing the connection, and then select the newly added data source on the Cube Wizard screen, then click the + sign next to it to expand it. This will show you all the tables available from the selected database. Select the fact table of your choice, `sales_fact_1998` in our case. As you do so, you will notice that the right side of the wizard screen shows the fields existing in the selected fact table. You will also see a button called Browse Data. Clicking this button will actually bring a spreadsheet showing the data in your fact table. You can navigate through the records at this point. However, let's proceed with the Cube Wizard for now. Click the Next button.

Make sure you set your Microsoft Management Console (MMC) so you are in Author Mode. To do this, select Options *from the* Console *menu and make sure you select* Author Mode *from the* Console Mode *drop down list on the* Console *tab.*

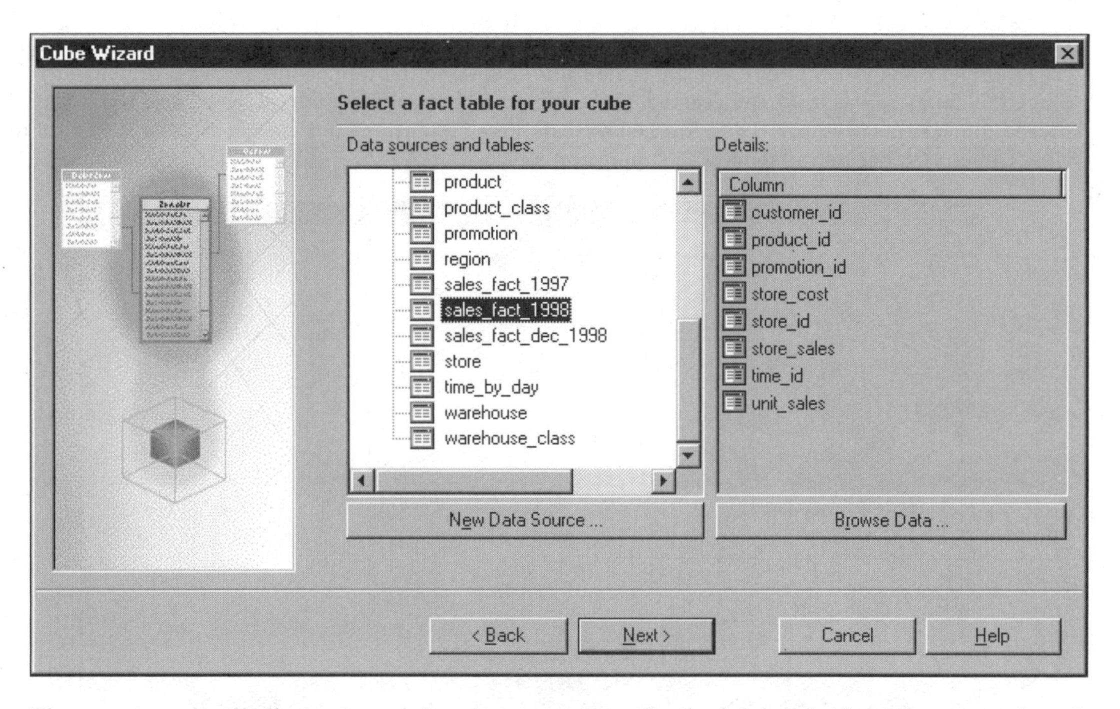

The next screen will allow you to define your measures. On the left-hand side of the screen there is a list of available columns in the fact table. Select the fields store_cost, store_sales and unit_sales individually, double-clicking each one to transfer it to the right-hand side list, the Cube measures list:

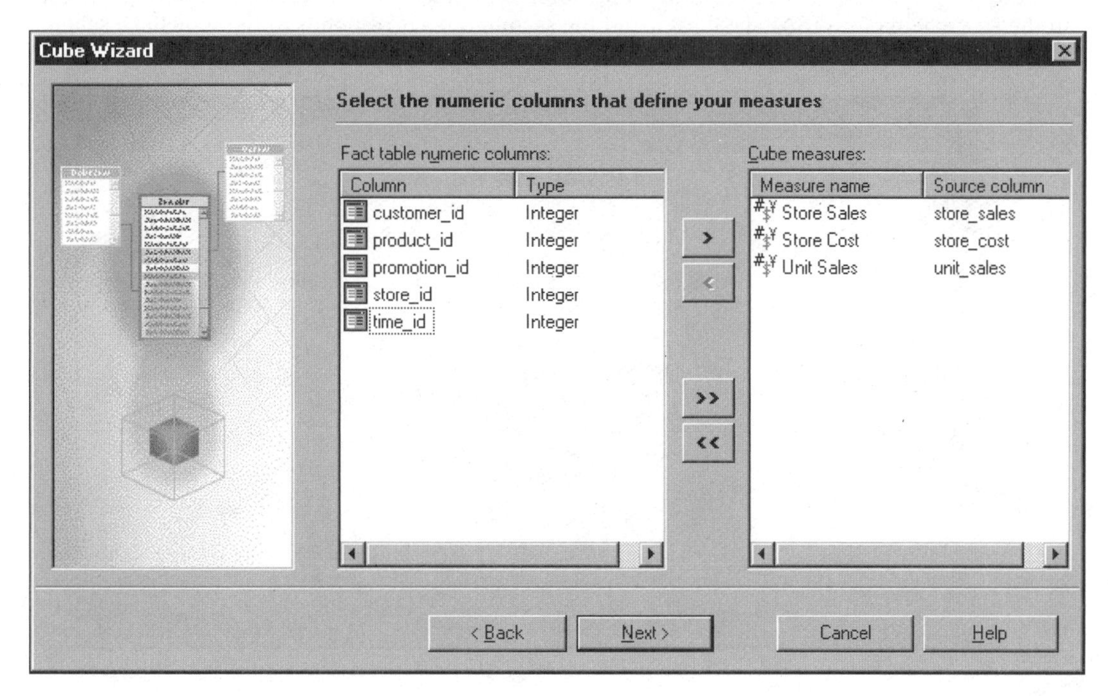

Click the Next button. The next screen will allow you to establish the cube dimensions. When you create dimensions for a cube, you have the option of making the dimension a shared dimension. Since the database has just been created, there are no dimensions defined in it yet, and the list of shared dimensions is empty. Therefore, let's create new dimensions to use for our cube. Click on the New Dimension button to launch the Dimension Wizard:

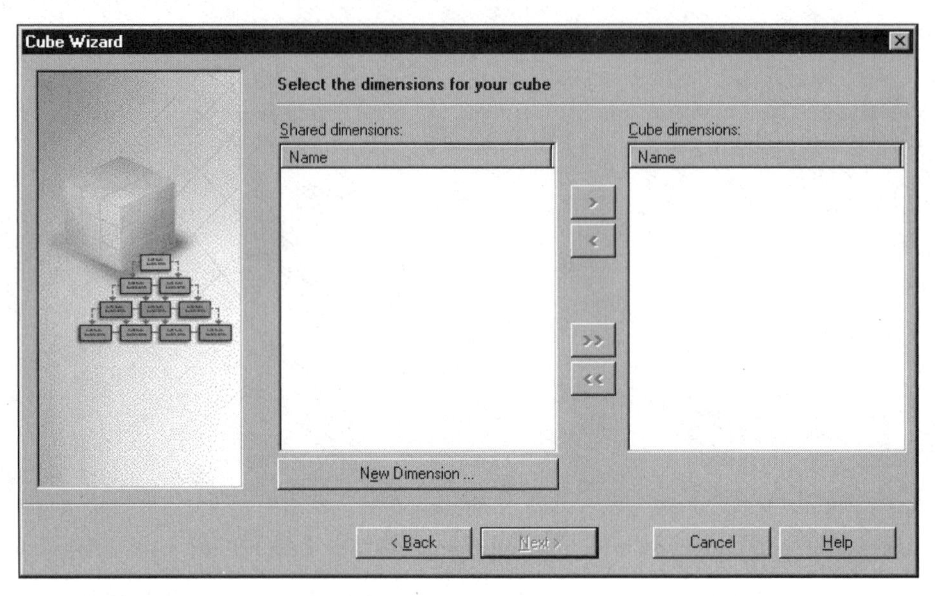

The first screen in the Dimension Wizard, allows you to specify whether the dimension you are creating will be based on a single dimension table, or on multiple tables. The first option corresponds to the star schema for OLAP databases, and the second one corresponds to the snowflake schema. Let's select the first option, A single dimension table, and click the Next button:

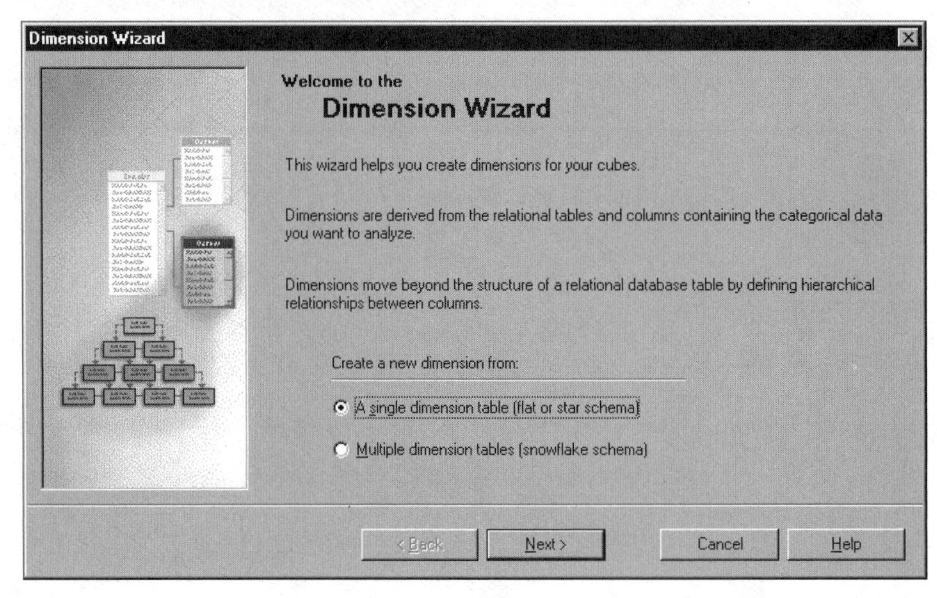

The next screen in the Dimension Wizard, allows you to select the dimension table. A list on the left-hand side shows all the available tables from which you can pick. Once a table is selected, a list on the right-hand side shows the fields in the selected table. Similar to the fact table, a Browse Data button allows you to browse the data in the selected dimension table in a spreadsheet format when you click it. For our example, select the customer table, and click the Next button:

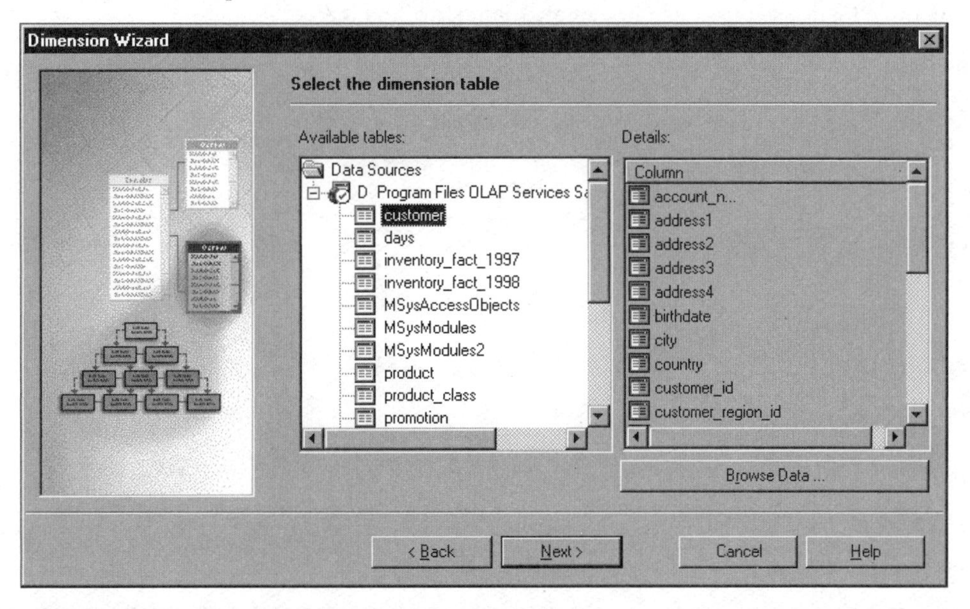

The next screen asks you whether the dimension you selected is a time or a standard dimension. Select Standard dimension and click the Next button:

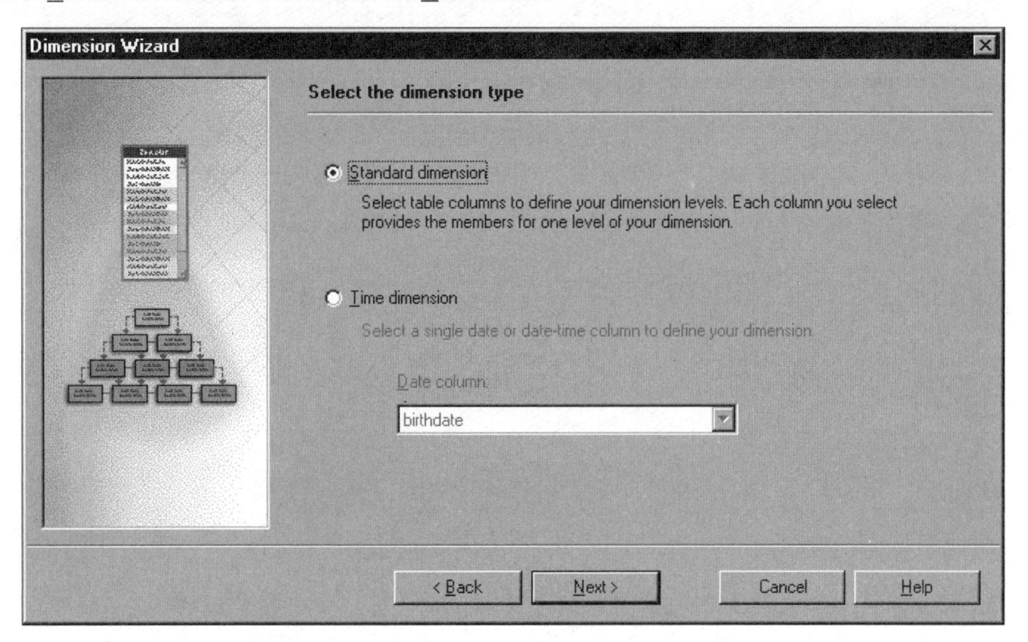

The next screen allows you to select the fields you want to use for your dimension levels. The fields in the customer table are presented on the left-hand list. Select the country, state_province, city and name fields, double-clicking them individually to transfer them to the Dimension levels list on the right-hand side. Note the name field that we added prior to creating our OLAP database and running the Cube Wizard. It makes more sense to select this field for our dimension level than selecting any of the three fields used to create it, namely fname, mi, and lname:

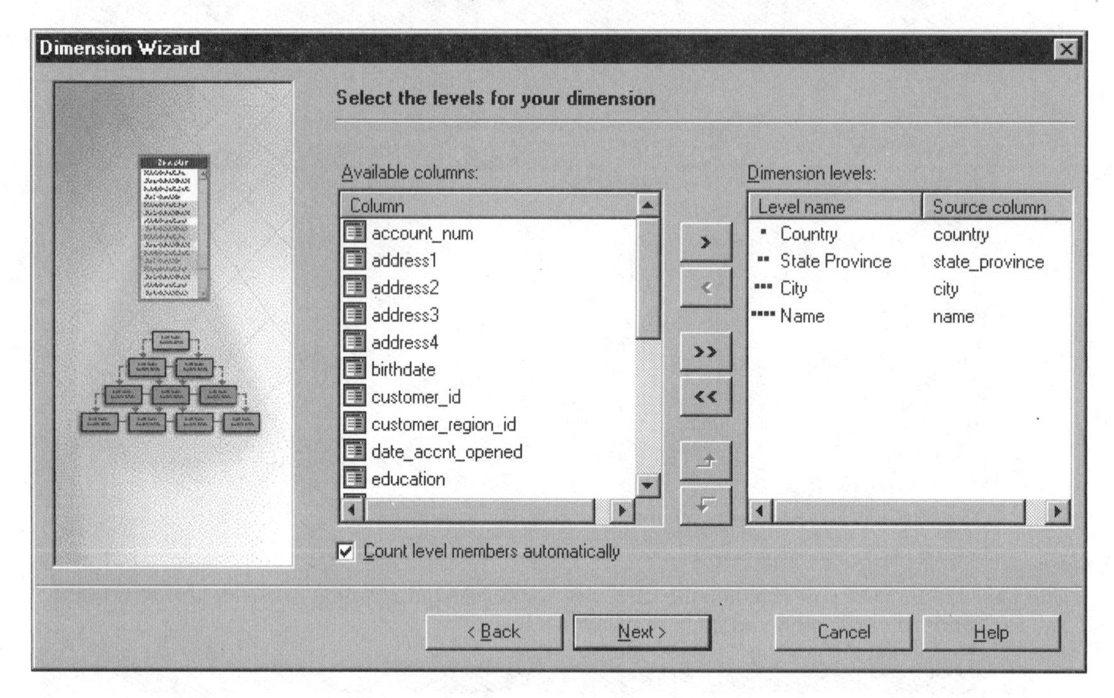

The next screen in the Dimension Wizard lets you select a name for the newly created dimension. Let's call it customer. Notice how a small window within the screen allows you to preview the data in the `customer` table in terms of the levels you selected. If you click the + signs to expand the view, you can clearly see the hierarchy that follows the selected levels for the dimension starting with the country at the top level, followed by the state/province, city, then name at the lowest level. This view shows you that three countries exist in the `customer` dimension table and that California is one of the US states for which there is data in the table. The cities within California that have related customers are shown. When you select one of these cities, you can see a list of the customers whose addresses are in that city.

Please note the checkbox that asks you whether you want to Share this dimension with other cubes in the database. Make sure it is checked, because it is always a good idea to share these dimensions, rather than re-inventing the wheel every time you need to create a similar dimension:

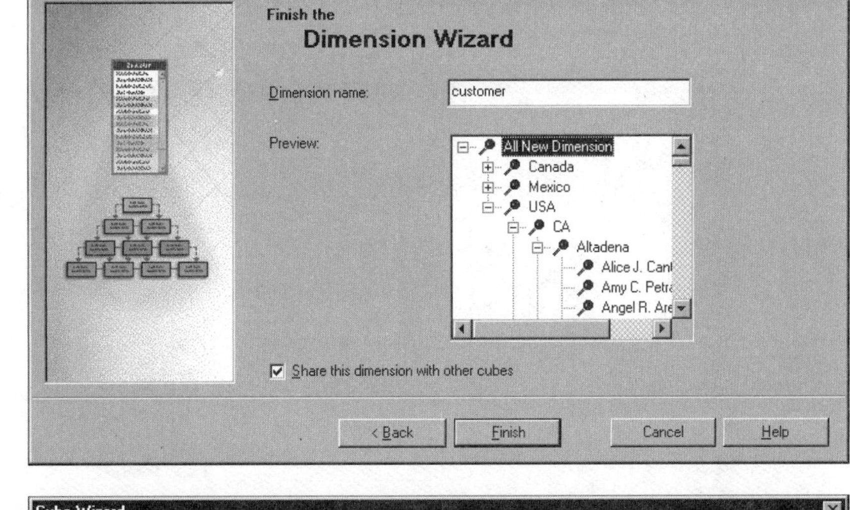

When you click on the Finish button, you are brought back to the Cube Wizard, specifically at the screen where you started the Dimension Wizard, with the new dimension already selected in the right-hand list of dimensions:

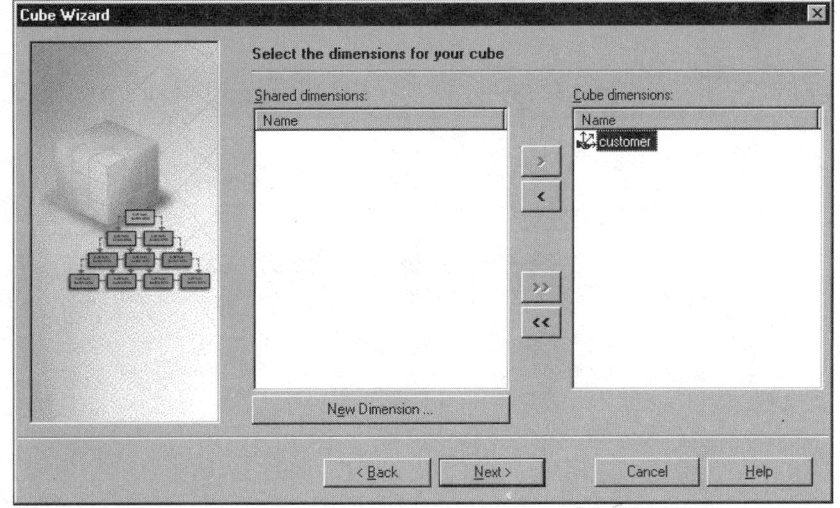

Follow the same steps we have just done to create the customer dimension, to create the store dimension. Make sure you select the following levels for the store dimension: store_country, store_state, store_city, and store_name.

Creating the time dimension is a little different in the Dimension Wizard. From the Select the dimension table screen, select the time_by_day table from the Available tables list to be the table for the `time` dimension, and click the Next button:

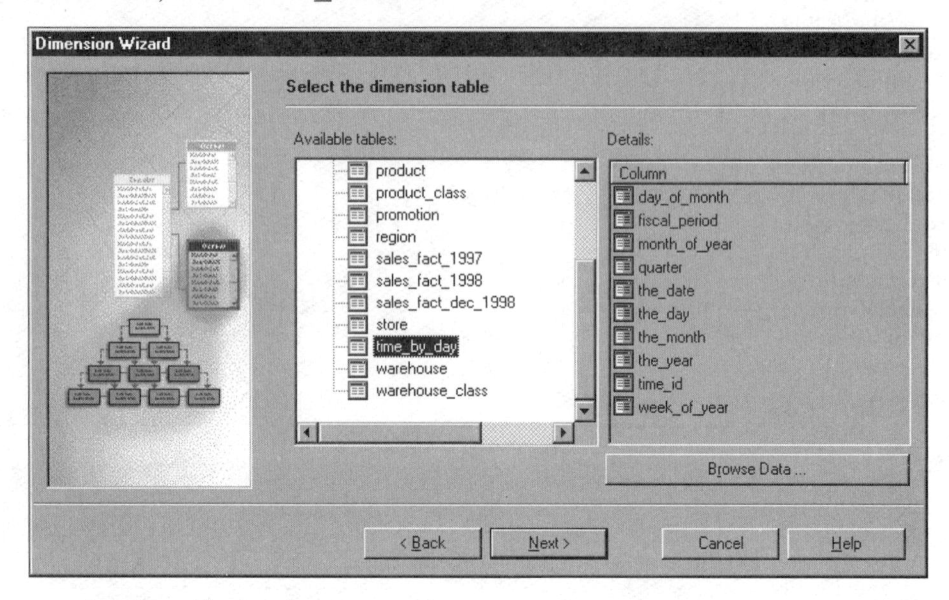

The screen asking you whether this is a time dimension or a standard dimension will pop up. Select the Time dimension radio button, make sure the date-formatted column, the_date is selected in the Date column drop-down list, and click the Next button:

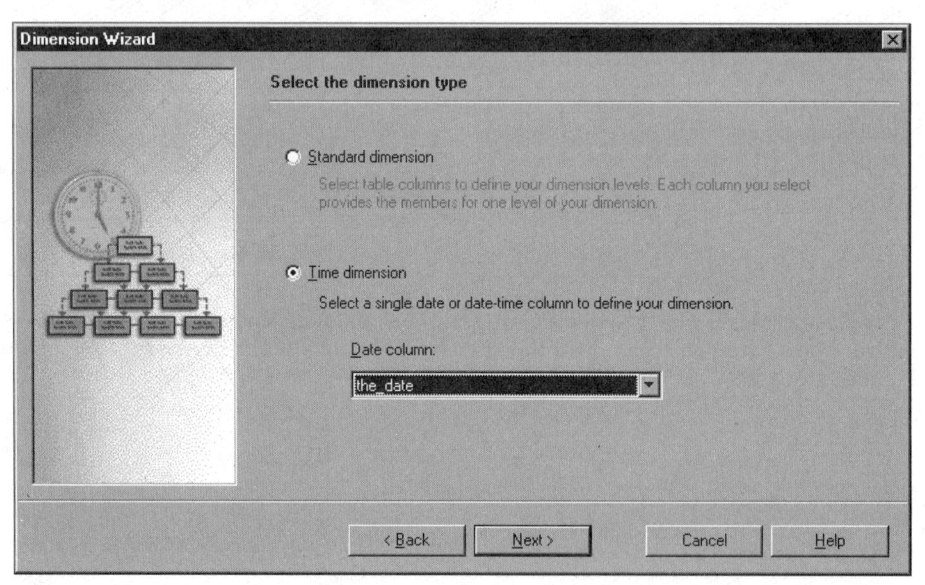

The next screen allows you to define the time dimension levels. From the Select time levels drop-down list, select Year, Quarter, Month, Day. A list below the drop-down list will then show you the dimension structure.

Two drop-down lists called Year starts on allow you to specify the month and day of the start of the fiscal year, in case they are different from the calendar year. This is a great feature. Just imagine how much work this feature will save you compared to having to program this yourself. Let's select the defaults and click the Next button:

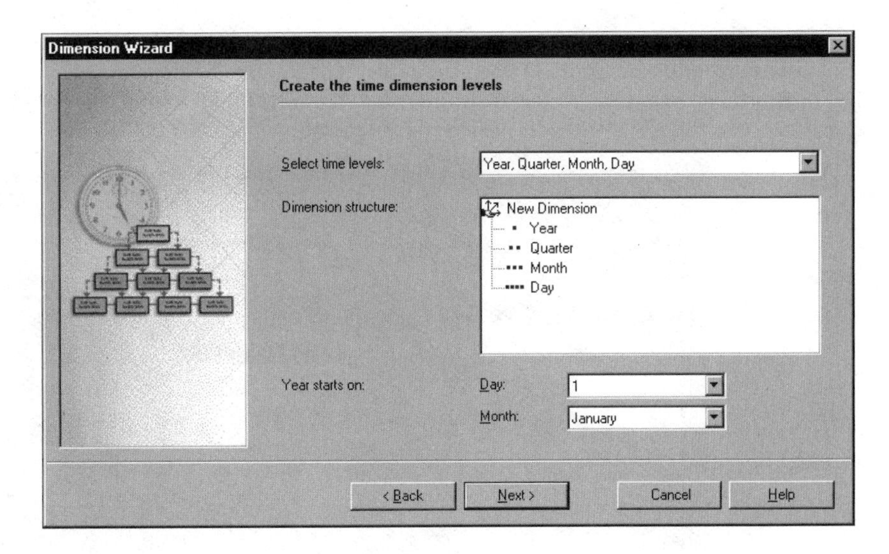

Name the dimension as the time dimension, then continue until you get back to the Cube Wizard screen that launched the Dimension Wizard. Once you get back to that screen, you should see three dimensions selected in the Cube dimensions list.

Launch the Dimension Wizard one last time to create the product dimension. On the first screen of the Dimension Wizard, select Multiple dimension tables because the levels we will be selecting exist in two tables, `product` and `product_class`. This is a good example of the snowflake schema, because we have the `product_class` dimension indirectly linked to the fact table. Clicking the Next button after you make the selection mentioned above will lead you to the following screen:

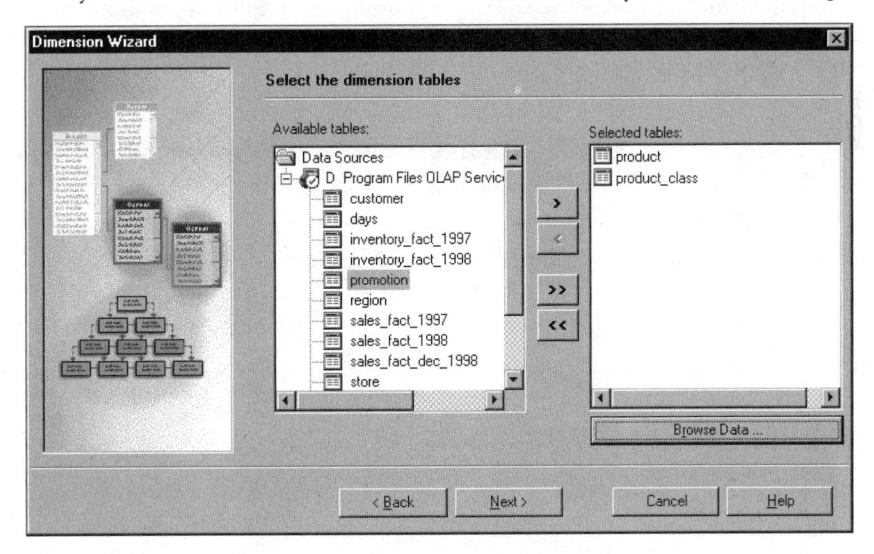

Select the product and product_class tables from the Available tables list, and click on the Next button.

At this point, you will be presented with the following screen. This screen allows you to specify and/or modify the join between the tables selected in the previous step. Since we don't need to make any changes to the join between the product and product_class tables (they're joined on the product_class_id field), let's click the Next button:

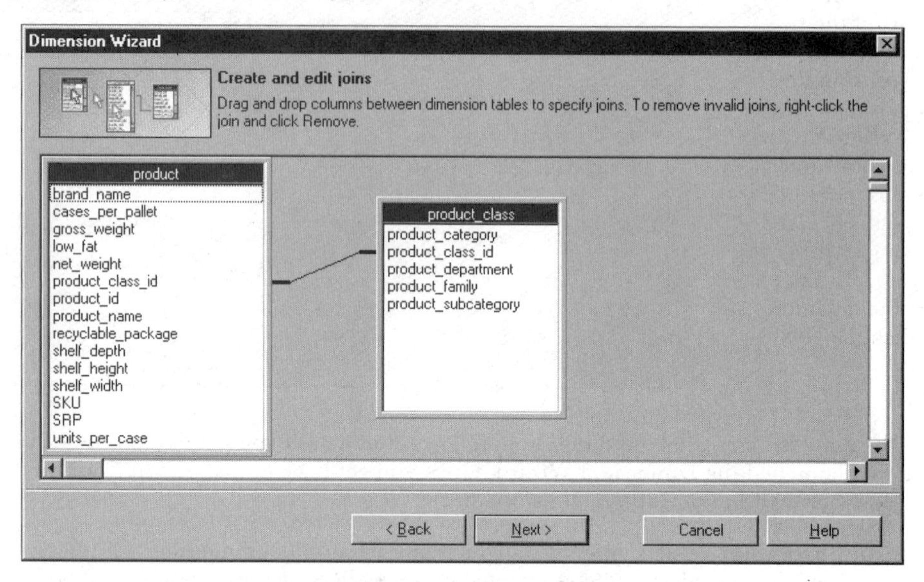

The next screen will allow you to specify the levels of the product dimension. These levels are: Product Family, Product Department, Product Category, Product Subcategory, Brand Name and Product Name. The number of blue dots shown to the left of the selected levels in the selected level list, indicates the ordinal number for the corresponding level. For our example, the first level is the Product Family whereas the fifth level is the Brand Name. Click the Next button to name the dimension as product, and proceed with creating the dimension until you reach the Cube Wizard again:

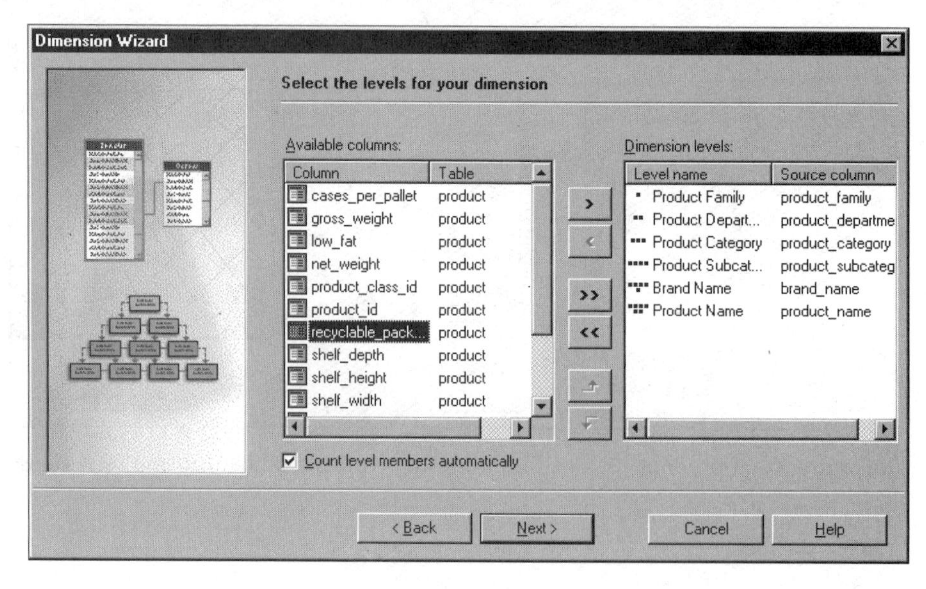

Clicking the Next button on the Cube Wizard screen will lead you to the screen where you can name your cube. Let's name it sales_1998. Notice the small window that shows you the structure of the newly created cube on this screen. You can expand and collapse the view to make sure you did everything correctly:

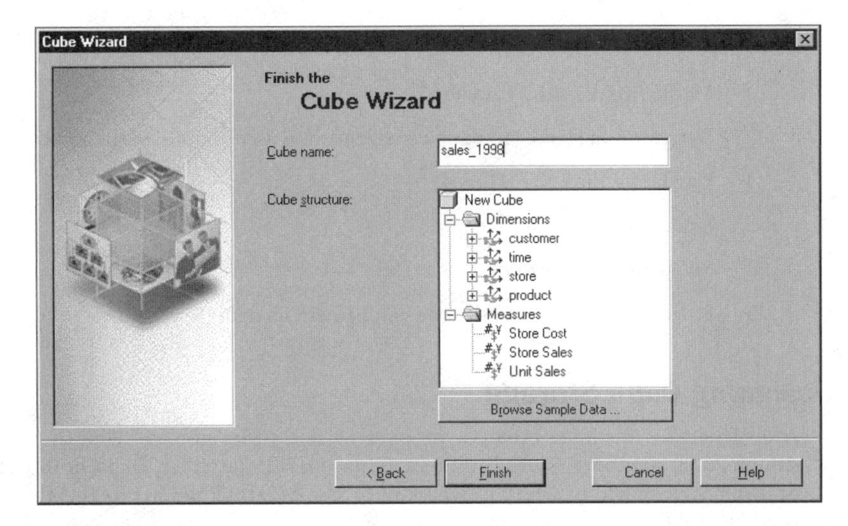

When you click the Finish button on the Cube Wizard screen, you get the Cube Editor screen:

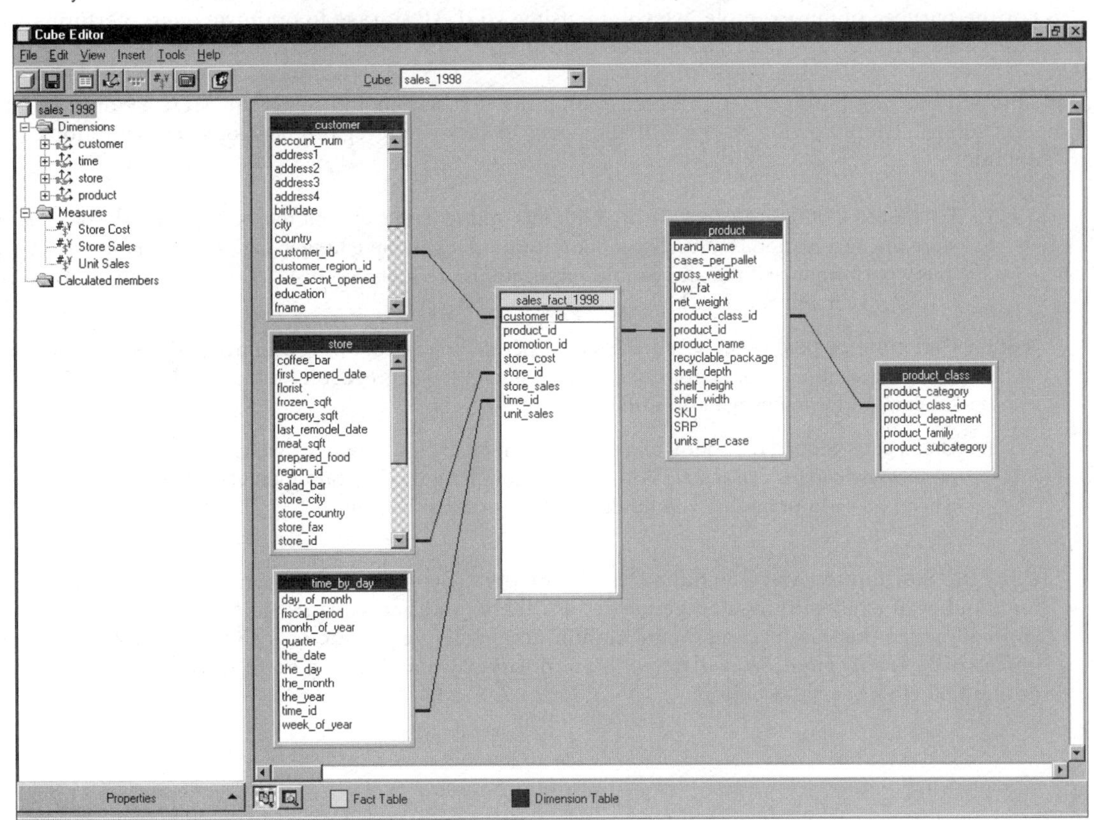

As the name implies, this editor can be used for many useful tasks, such as:

- Modifying the cube structure
- Designing the cube storage (we will see how this is done in the next section)
- Validating the cube schema
- Optimizing the cube schema
- Managing the cube roles
- Processing the cube so that we can browse its data

Designing Cube Storage

After the cube has been created, we need to design its storage. Will the cube data be kept in a new dimensional database, stored in the original OLTP database, or in both databases. These three options correspond to whether we want to use MOLAP versus ROLAP storage, or a hybrid of the two, HOLAP.

For the purpose of our example, we will be using MOLAP storage to optimize query performance. To design the storage, select the Tools | Design Storage from the Cube Editor menu.

This will start the Storage Design Wizard. Skip the first screen and select the MOLAP option in the next screen. The following screen will allow you to set the aggregation options. These options include:

- Estimated storage reaches x MB: With this option, you can limit the amount of disk space used to store the aggregation results. This option is useful if you have limited disk space, but it may effect query performance if not all possible aggregations are saved on disk. With this option SQL Server's OLAP server will choose which aggregates will be stored.
- Performance gain reaches x%: This means, that you are allowing as much disk space as needed to store aggregations, until performance gains due to the aggregation storage reaches x% of the original performance with no storage.
- Until I click Stop: This option allows you to manually set the points which disk storage and performance gains can reach. You do so by watching the Performance vs Size graph and clicking when you see a point that you think would be optimal for you.

Click the Start button and watch the Performance vs. Size graph change, indicating at the bottom, the number of aggregations, storage needed for them, and performance gains. At the end of the run, you will notice that in our case, the maximum number of aggregations is 332. The needed disk space is 43.8 MB. At this point, we will get 100% performance gains. Based on this, let's select the default option and click the Next button:

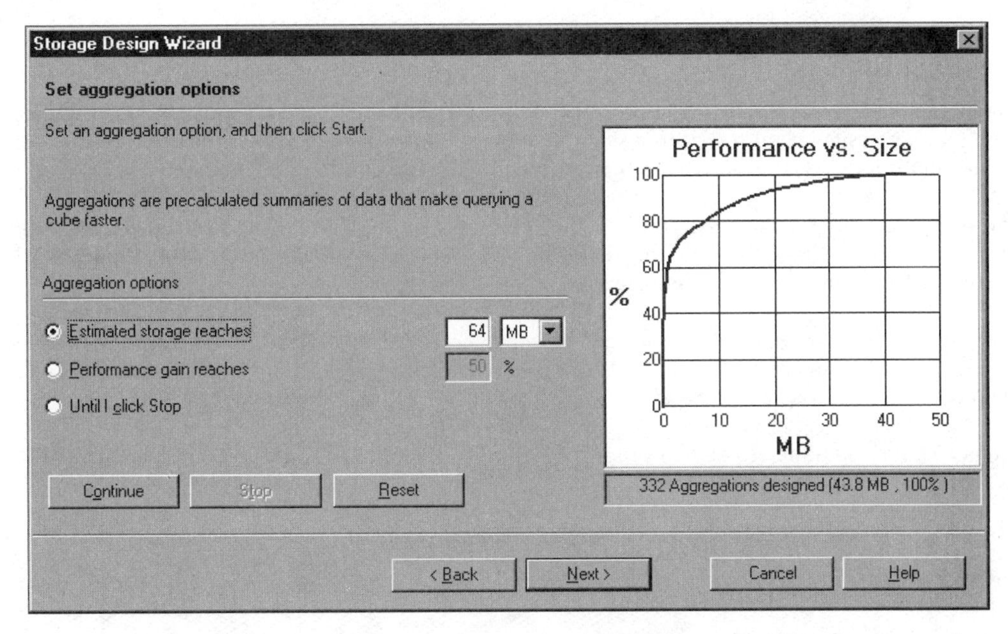

The next screen will ask you whether you want to process the data, or just save the storage design (and process the aggregations later). Processing the data actually both creates and stores the aggregations for you. Let's choose Process now.

While processing the data, the Wizard will show you a screen that includes information on the progress of the operation:

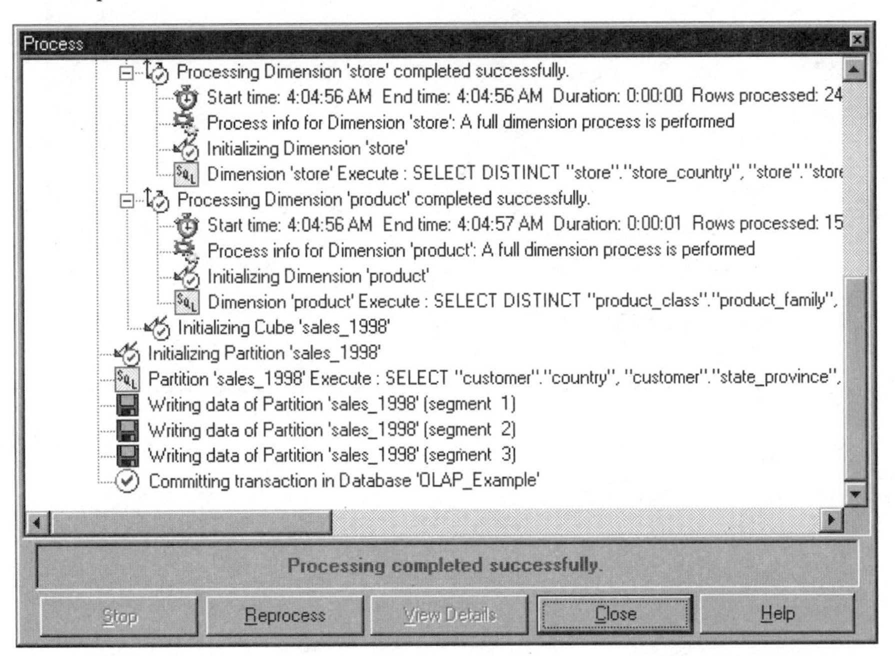

Cube Security

Since the data presented by the cube could be sensitive historical data about the performance of your company, you may want to set up a security scheme as to who can access the cube and use it, and who cannot do so. Cube security is tightly integrated with Windows NT security.

To set up security for the cube you have just created, you need to create a **role**. The role will have certain access privileges to the cube. The role will then be assigned to groups of Windows NT users, setting permissions for them accordingly.

Let's create a new role. To do so, we can either select Tools | Manage Roles from the menu bar of the Cube Editor, or we can close the Cube Editor and add a role to the Roles folder in the OLAP Manager's tree view.

Select Tools | Manage Roles from the Cube Editor's menu bar. This will launch a Manage Role wizard:

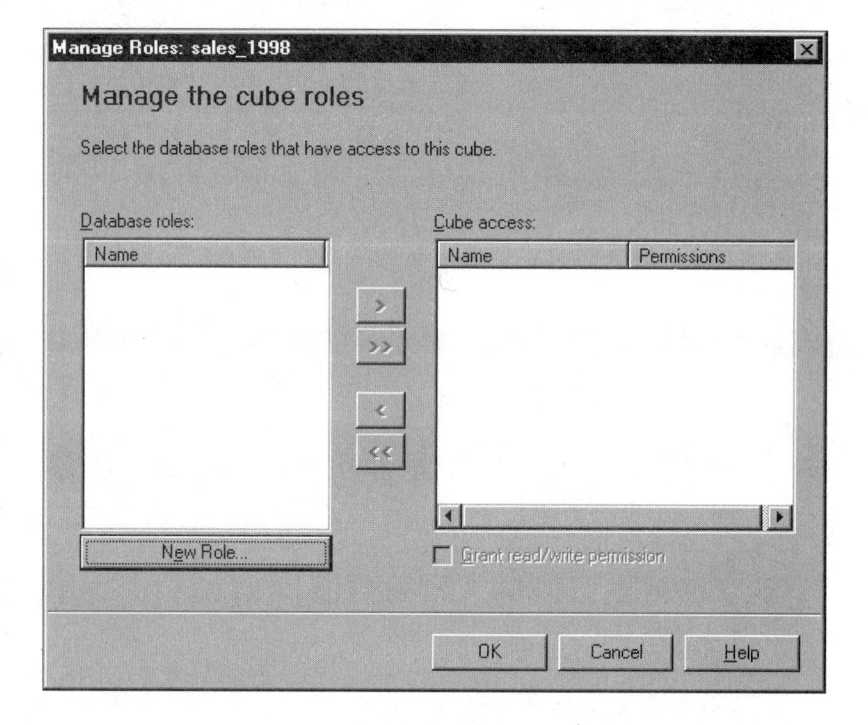

Click on the New Role button and you will presented with the dialog shown here:

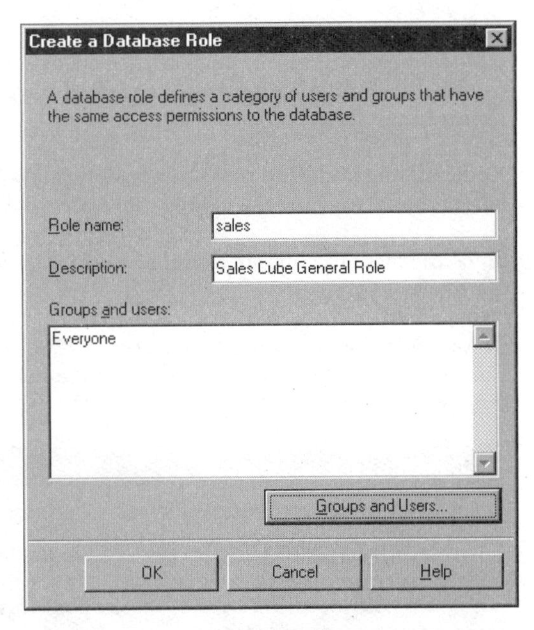

In this screen, you can click the Groups and Users button to add Windows NT users and/or groups. Let's add the Everyone group, then click OK to close the dialog. The new role will then be seen on the Manage Role wizard in the Cube access list with read-only permission. You can grant read/write permissions by checking the option box on the screen. However, for our purposes, we will keep it read-only.

Browsing the Cube Data

Now the `sales_1998` cube has been created, its storage set up, and security taken care of, let's browse the data in it so we can see how the aggregations have been done.

Right-click the sales_1998 cube from the OLAP Manager's tree view menu, and click Browse Data. The following dialog will be shown:

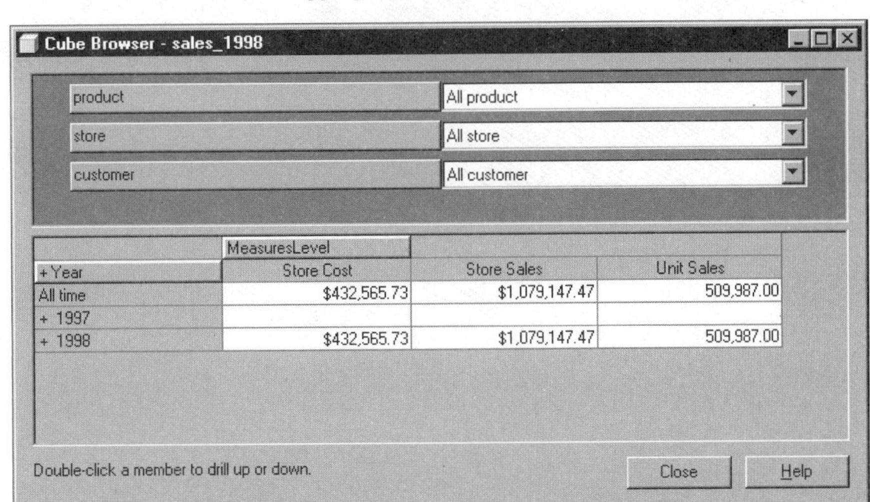

This dialog shows you a spreadsheet with the values of the measure in which we are interested. The left column of the spreadsheet represents one of the dimensions (`time` in this case) and on top, you can see the remaining dimensions created for the `sales_1998` cube. These dimensions are `product`, `store`, and `customer`.

You can drag and drop these dimensions the way you like onto the spreadsheet to show them to the left, and to show how the aggregations are taking place.

Since the fact table in our example stores data for 1998 only, we can see that the measures for 1997 are blank.

To see the measure values by quarter of 1998 for food products, sold in stores in Los Angeles, California to customers, you need to make the selections shown in the drop-down lists and in the time dimension column as shown:

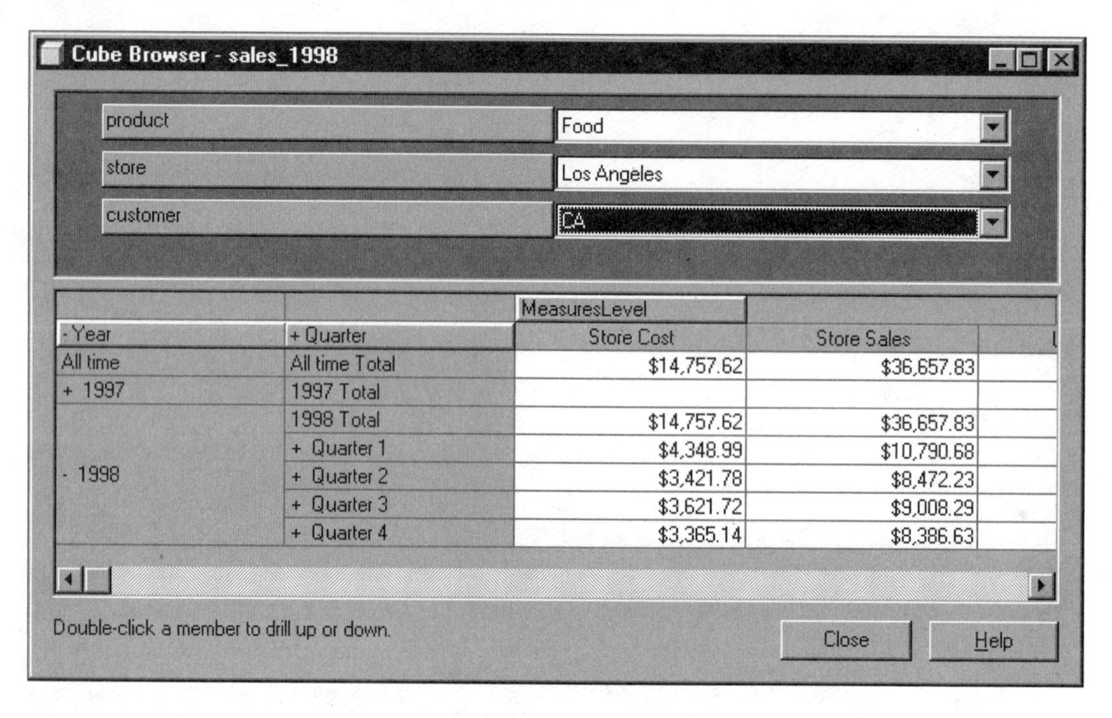

You can also browse data by quarter, by product family, and store country by dragging the product and store dimensions to the spreadsheet and expanding them appropriately, as shown:

Cube Browser - sales_1998

customer | CA

MeasuresLevel

- Year	+ Quarter	+ Product Family	+ Store Country	Store Cost	Store Sales	Unit Sales
+ 1998	1998 Total	All product	+ USA	$61,936.33	$154,513.49	73,017.00
		+ Drink	All store	$5,523.57	$13,755.12	6,871.00
			+ Canada			
			+ Mexico			
			+ USA	$5,523.57	$13,755.12	6,871.00
		+ Food	All store	$44,676.82	$111,467.82	52,515.00
			+ Canada			
			+ Mexico			
			+ USA	$44,676.82	$111,467.82	52,515.00
		+ Non-Consumable	All store	$11,735.95	$29,290.55	13,631.00
			+ Canada			
			+ Mexico			
			+ USA	$11,735.95	$29,290.55	13,631.00
- 1998	+ Quarter 1	All product	All store	$17,007.27	$42,396.97	19,969.00
			+ Canada			
			+ Mexico			
			+ USA	$17,007.27	$42,396.97	19,969.00
		+ Drink	All store	$1,506.30	$3,767.55	1,855.00
			+ Canada			
			+ Mexico			
			+ USA	$1,506.30	$3,767.55	1,855.00
		+ Food	All store	$12,282.25	$30,594.05	14,383.00
			+ Canada			
			+ Mexico			
			+ USA	$12,282.25	$30,594.05	14,383.00
		+ Non-Consumable	All store	$3,218.73	$8,035.37	3,731.00
			+ Canada			
			+ Mexico			
			+ USA	$3,218.73	$8,035.37	3,731.00
	+ Quarter 2	All product	All store	$14,879.27	$37,028.41	17,546.00
			+ Canada			
			+ Mexico			
			+ USA	$14,879.27	$37,028.41	17,546.00
		+ Drink	All store	$1,400.16	$3,464.49	1,695.00
			+ Canada			
			+ Mexico			

Double-click a member to drill up or down.

Close | Help

Summary

This was an introductory chapter about OLAP services in SQL Server 7.0. OLAP services and data warehousing in SQL Server really deserve much more than one chapter. There are many more topics I wish I could cover. These topics include data mining, using MDX, the SQL language equivalent for data cubes and using programming languages to build custom cube browsers. However, I hope that this chapter will only be a start for you and entice you learn more about this powerful technology and the powerful tools that come with it.

We covered the basics of data warehousing and OLAP at the beginning of the chapter, then I introduced you to the Microsoft SQL Server OLAP Manager and the great wizards and tools that come with it, using an example. The example was detailed and probably looked like a tutorial in some instances, but I hope that it will put you on the right track in your endeavor to explore this technology more.

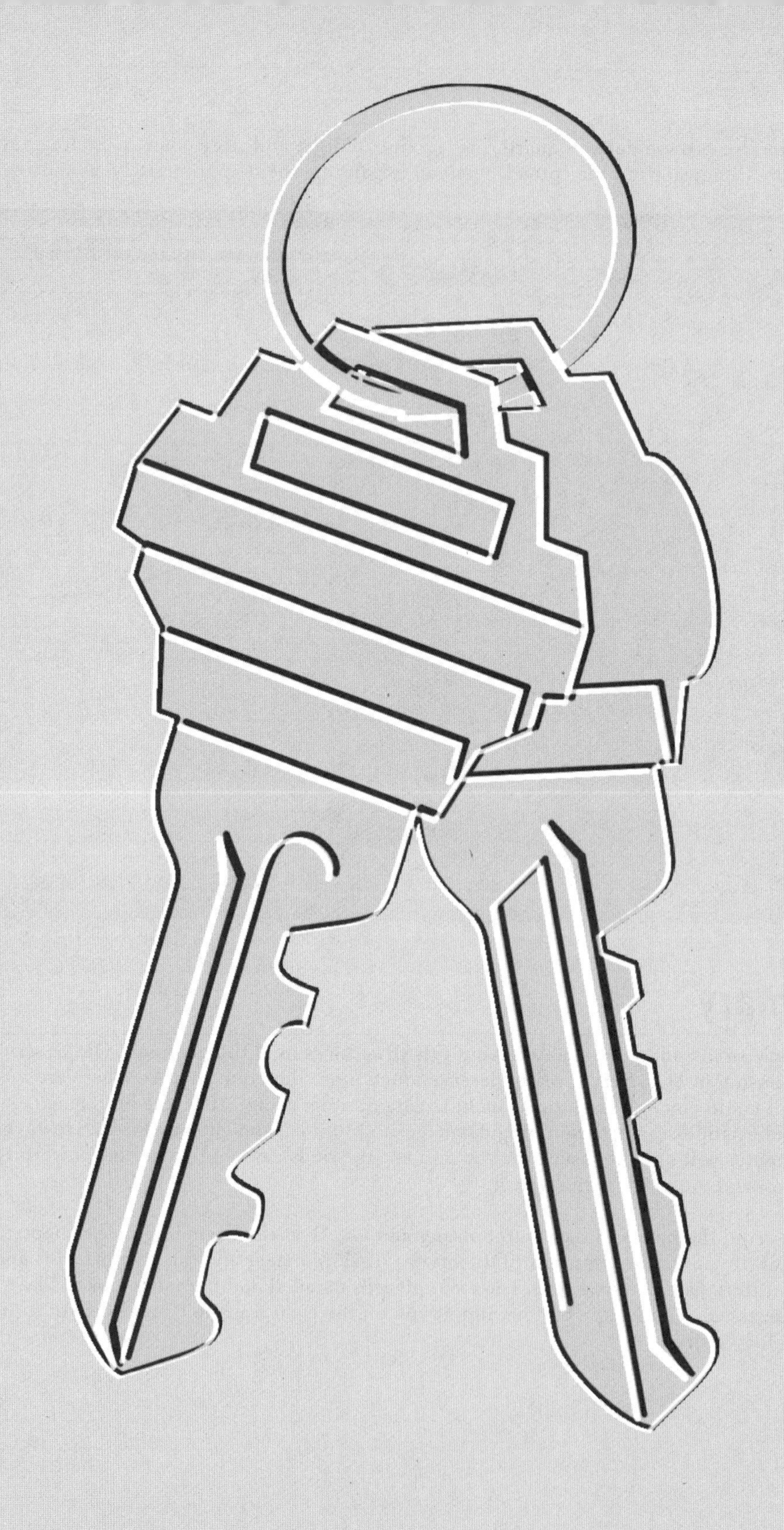

22

English Query and Full-Text Search

SQL Server 7.0 includes two important features that allow you to build applications that provide users with more flexible and powerful data retrieval capabilities than is possible using standard Transact-SQL. These capabilities are **English Query** and **Full-Text Search**.

This chapter will introduce both of these technologies and provide you with the fundamentals for implementing them. The discussion will focus on:

- The benefits and uses of English Query
- The architecture of an English Query application
- Rules for designing a database that works reliably with English Query
- How to define the semantics for an English Query application
- How to compile and deploy an English Query application
- How to use an English Query application
- The benefits and uses of Full-Text Search
- How to create a Full-Text Search catalog
- How to schedule repopulation of a Full-Text Search catalog
- How to create queries that use a Full-Text Search catalog

What is English Query?

English Query allows application and Web site developers to provide users with the ability to retrieve data from a database by asking questions in plain English. It must be used in conjunction with a data access technology, such as ActiveX Data Objects (ADO) or Remote Data Objects (RDO). The illustration shows the role of the English Query Engine and an English Query application. The graphic shows the communication that takes place between a client application, the English Query Engine, and the English Query Application (`.eqd` file) created by a developer using the English Query Domain Editor:

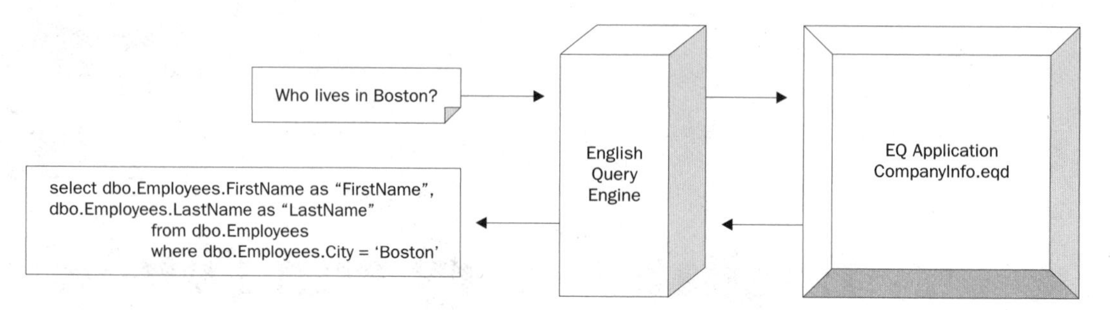

As you can see, the user asks a question in normal English, such as, "Who lives in Boston?" The client application passes the user's question to the English Query Engine, which then uses the English Query Application's knowledge about the database and its semantics to generate a Transact-SQL statement. That statement is passed back to the client application. The client application must then issue the query against the database to retrieve a result set.

I use the term "client application" to refer to the application that utilizes the services of the English Query Engine. As you'll see later in the chapter, this client application can be built in any Automation controller, such as Visual Basic, Visual C++, or Active Server Pages. It can run on the client workstation or it can run as an ActiveX component on an application or database server.

The Benefits of English Query

English Query can provide an important enhancement to applications that allows users to retrieve information about a data source. Implementing English Query support provides the following benefits:

- Users can interact with the application in a more natural way
- Users can retrieve the information they really want
- Users can get answers to more complicated questions
- Developers do not have to write complicated joins for every combination of data users might need

Another scenario to consider when using English Query is one that involves speech recognition. By using English Query, in conjunction with speech recognition technology, developers can provide users with the ability to ask questions about a data source, almost as naturally as they would ask another person. This provides a distinct advantage for supporting visually impaired users, users with other disabilities, and users who suffer from repetitive motion disorders.

The Limitations of English Query

Although English Query opens the door to some exciting possibilities, it is not a panacea. It involves more overhead than a predesigned query and much more overhead than a stored procedure. This means that it should only be used in situations that can benefit from the type of flexibility it offers users. If the users of your application will typically perform the same query over and over again, you will want to provide them with a faster way to execute it. For example, if ninety percent of the time, the users are interested in retrieving a particular report, you will want to create a stored procedure to generate that report. This does not mean that English Query is not appropriate for use in that application. If the other ten percent of the information required is diverse, you may want to implement the ability to retrieve it through English Query.

When evaluating English Query for use in your solution, it is important that you understand the trade-offs. English Query cannot take advantage of the highly tuned stored procedures you might develop to address common data access requirements. This means that queries generated by English Query will often take longer to execute. However, from the users' perspective, performance requirements are not always met by increasing the speed of query execution. When the needs of the customer are met by the ability to ask any question about the data in natural English, using English Query will give them what they want.

This doesn't mean that you can't tune your SQL Server for English Query. Carefully selected indexes become even more important when queries are generated by English Query and cannot be precompiled.

Another limitation is that English Query does what its name implies – it translates English to a query. At this time, there are no equivalent implementations in other languages.

It is also important to realize that building an effective English Query application is not a trivial task. It requires a careful consideration of how the entities and relationships in your database can be used to answer questions. Testing your application well is essential to ensuring that users won't be frustrated by questions that can't be answered. This chapter will give you some understanding of the work involved in creating an English Query application so that you can make an informed choice about whether the effort will create a sufficient return on your investment.

Installing English Query

The following screen shows the list of English Query components that you can select to install during a custom installation:

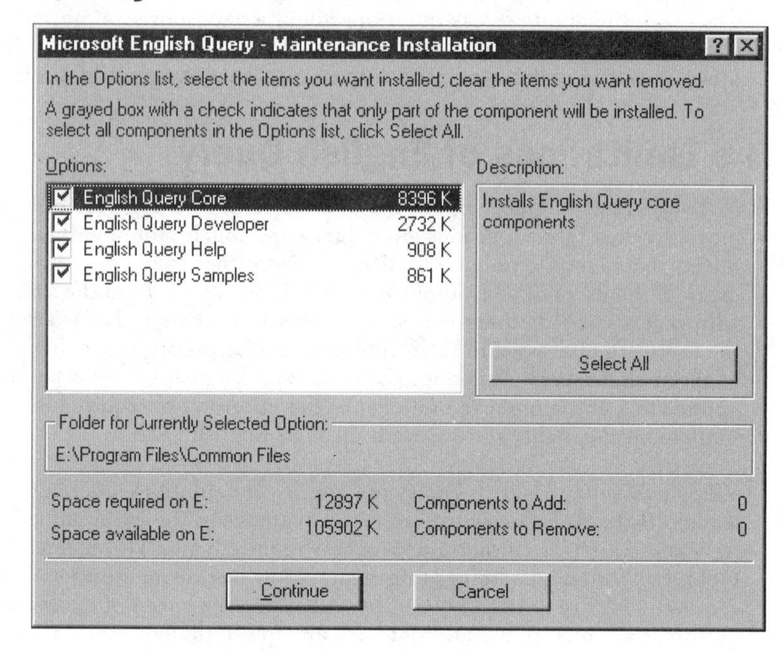

English Query was originally released as part of the SQL Server 6.5, Enterprise Edition. With SQL Server 7.0, it is included in both the Standard edition and the Enterprise edition. However, it is installed separately from any version of SQL Server, by selecting English Query from the opening installation menu. English Query can be installed on Windows 95, Windows 98, Windows NT, or Windows 2000.

By default, English Query installs the files for both the English Query Engine and the English Query Domain Editor (`mseqdev.exe`). The domain editor is required only on systems where you will be building English Query applications. The English Query Engine files will be required on any computer where you will execute an English Query application. Applications and ActiveX components that utilize the services of English Query should package and install the core files. Otherwise, English Query installation will need to be run on those computers. Since the English Query engine does not communicate directly with SQL Server when translating queries, English Query does not need to be installed on the SQL Server. The specific requirements for deploying an English Query application will be discussed later in the chapter.

The Architecture of an English Query Application

Before looking at the specifics of how to build an English Query application, let's look at its contents. An English Query application requires two types of information: the database schema and information about how that schema maps to semantic objects.

A **semantic object** can be either an entity (a noun) or a relationship between entities. There are two types of entities, major entities (which are represented by tables) and minor entities (which are represented by a column in that table). You will also find that some minor entities are known as **traits**. Relationships are expressed as phrases, corresponding to a particular sentence structure. Let's look at a very simple example:

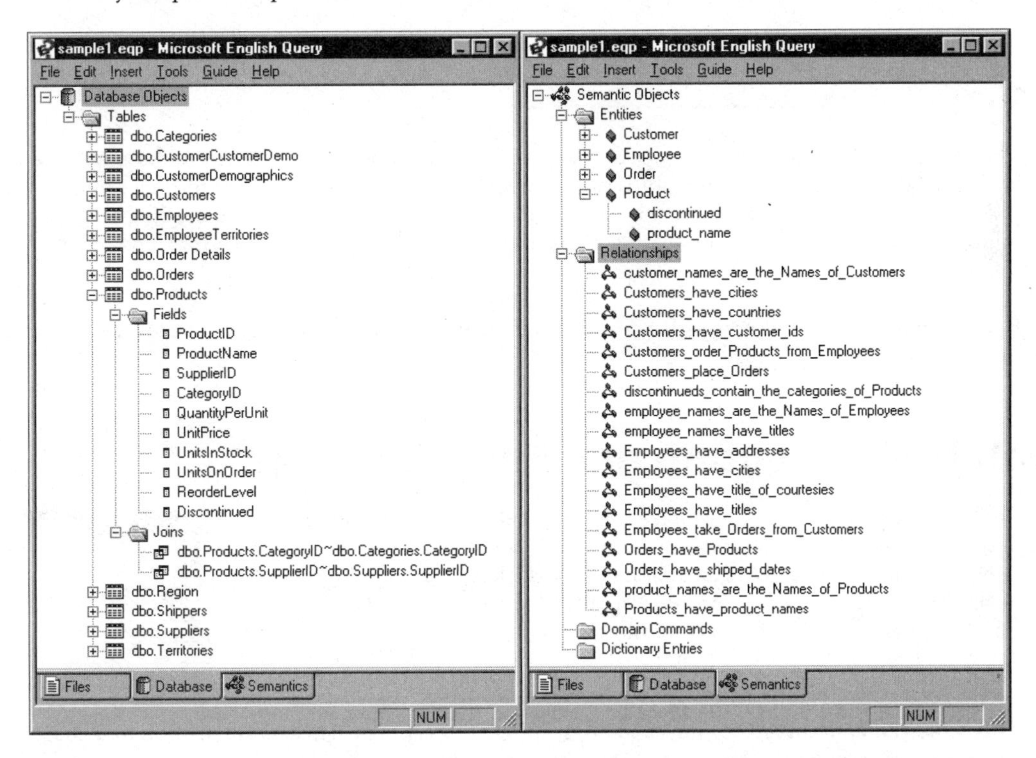

In the screenshot above, the major entities are Customer, Employee, Order and Product (which relate to tables of a similar name). The Product entity has two minor entities called discontinued and product_name, which are taken from columns in the `Products` table. There are also numerous relationships such as Customers_have_cities and product_names_are_the_Names_of_Products.

Semantic Objects - A Simple Example

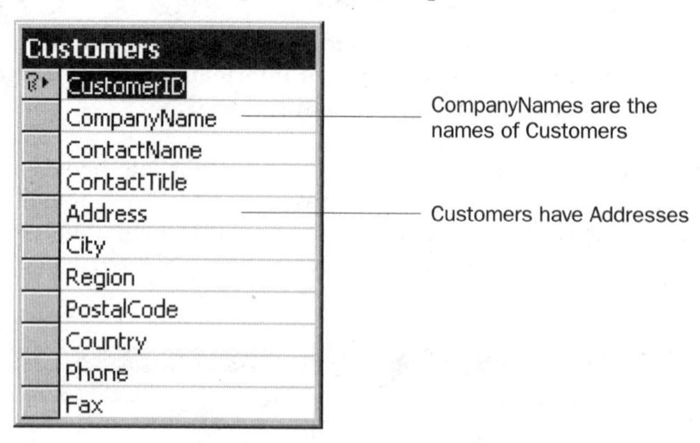

The `Customers` table can be mapped to the major entity `Customer`. When looking at the attributes of the table, two types of relationships are immediately obvious. The `CompanyName` field contains the names of the customers and each customer has a set of characteristics, including an address. Some minor entities like `Address` are called traits and are defined by a "*major entities* have *traits*" relationship.

Relationships can be defined within a particular table or between tables. Relationships that exist between tables require joins.

Database Structure and English Query

English Query depends on a precise mapping between nouns and database objects, and relationships between those objects that can be unequivocally defined. This means that it works best against a highly normalized database. Let's consider the problems presented when English Query is used against the following table:

This table can contain entries for cats, dogs, birds, and reptiles. These animals don't all share the same traits. For example, John Doe might have a cockatiel, a dachshund and a basset hound. He wants to find out if either of his dogs is due for a rabies vaccination. When he asks the question, "Which of John Doe's pets have not received a rabies shot this year?" the cockatiel's name would appear on the list. Since birds don't get rabies vaccinations, the cockatiel would not be due for one. An even more nonsensical situation is created by the fact that "grooming" entails different activities for each species. For dogs, it means a haircut; for cats, it means a flea dip and combing; and for birds, it means getting their wings clipped. In order to make the application friendly for English Query, we'd need to assign a variety of synonyms to the `GroomedOn` field to account for each of these procedures. This could result in some amusing (but incorrect) results when a user asks, "Show me when John Doe's pets had their wings clipped."

Another problem arises when multiple instances of a trait are listed in the same row. Consider the following example:

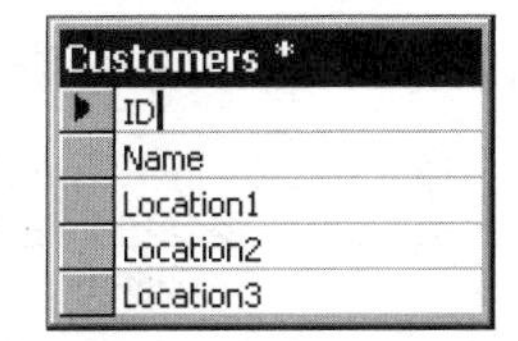

In this case, the user would need to ask the question in a very cumbersome manner to retrieve the locations for a particular customer. Instead of, "Where is SuperMart located?" The user would need to ask, "Where is the first location, the second location, and the third location for SuperMart?"

Creating an English Query Project

Now that you understand the fundamental concepts behind English Query, it's time to look at what's involved in creating an English Query project. The steps you need to take to build an English Query project are:

1. Create a new project
2. Define a Data Source Name (DSN) for your connection
3. Define entities
4. Define relationships
5. Test your project
6. Define more entities and relationships
7. Test again
8. Compile and distribute your application

If you have used case documents or Unified Modeling Language (UML) documentation for your application, you will be able to use these as a starting point for defining the entities and relationships in your English Query application. However, you will also need significant input from your users. Survey them to determine what questions they are likely to want to ask when analyzing the data and pay particular attention to how they phrase their questions. Your design documentation may refer to `Customer` *objects, but the salespeople may call them Clients and the accounting department may call them Accounts. If you are going to build an application allows users to ask questions in their own way, you will need to consider these differences.*

Testing and refining your project will be an iterative process. It's a good idea to get users involved in the testing. When working with the product, they may ask questions they didn't think about during the initial design phase. When you and the group of users whose help you have enlisted are satisfied that your application can answer all of the questions a user will pose, you can compile and distribute your application.

Let's take a close look at the steps involved in building an application. The sample application we will build in this chapter will use the `Northwind` database.

Create a New Project

When the English Query Domain Editor is installed, a shortcut is created in Start | Programs | Microsoft SQL Server 7.0 | English Query (provided you have placed English Query in the default location). When the English Query Domain Editor is launched, a dialog is displayed, prompting us to create a new project or open an existing project:

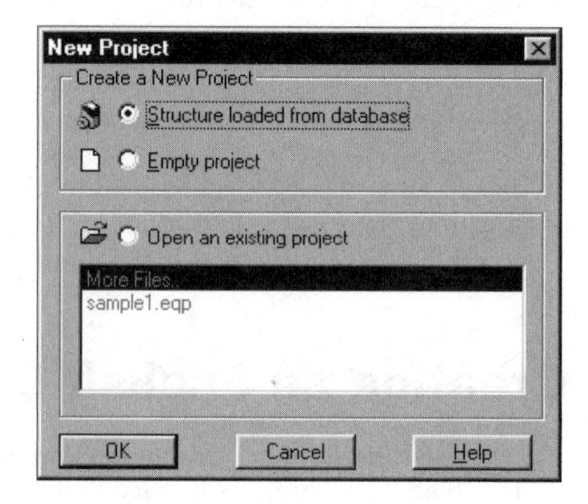

When creating a new project, you can select to load the structure from a database or create an empty project. If you select to create an empty project, you will need to import tables using the File | Import New Tables command after the English Query Domain Editor opens. This option allows you to select only certain tables of a particular database to include in your domain. The first time the Import New Tables command is run, you will be prompted to select a Data Source Name (DSN).

If you select to load the structure from a database, you will also be prompted to select a DSN. If no DSN has been defined for the database, you will need to define one.

If you're following along with me, select Structure loaded from database and click on OK. Define a DSN for the `Northwind` database and then select it from the Select Data Source dialog. Click on OK.

At this point, the database schema for the database or tables we've selected will be read into the project. The Database tab will allow us to view the objects available in the database, including tables, fields and joins:

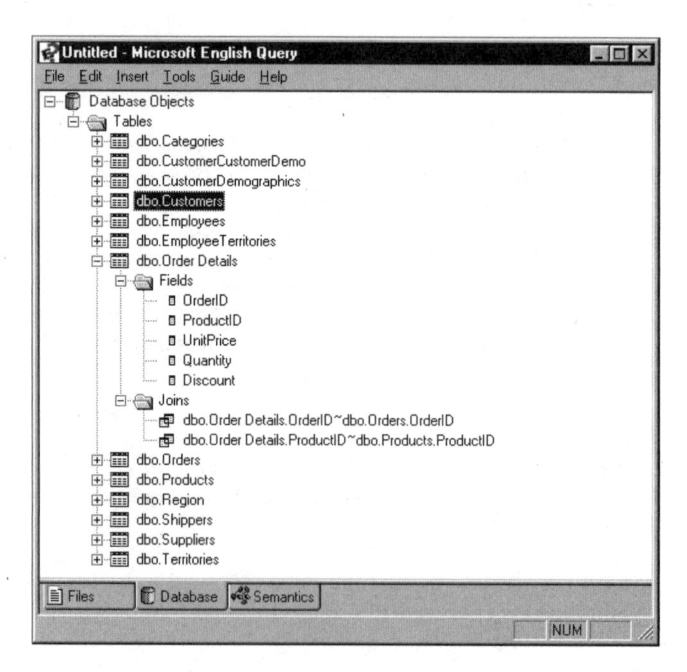

Defining a Major Entity

Next, we want to begin defining our entities. Entities and relationships are listed on the Semantics tab. When a project is first created, there will be no semantic objects defined. It is up to us to specify how the objects in our database are described using the English language:

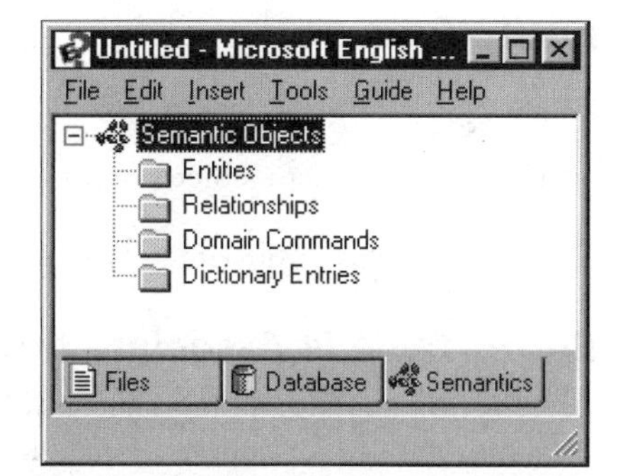

Let's begin by defining a major entity. A major entity corresponds to a table or view in the database. For example, if we are building an English Query application that will allow users to gather information about customers and the orders they have placed, we will probably want to define a major entity named `Customer`. To do so, run Insert | Entity; the New Entity dialog will appear:

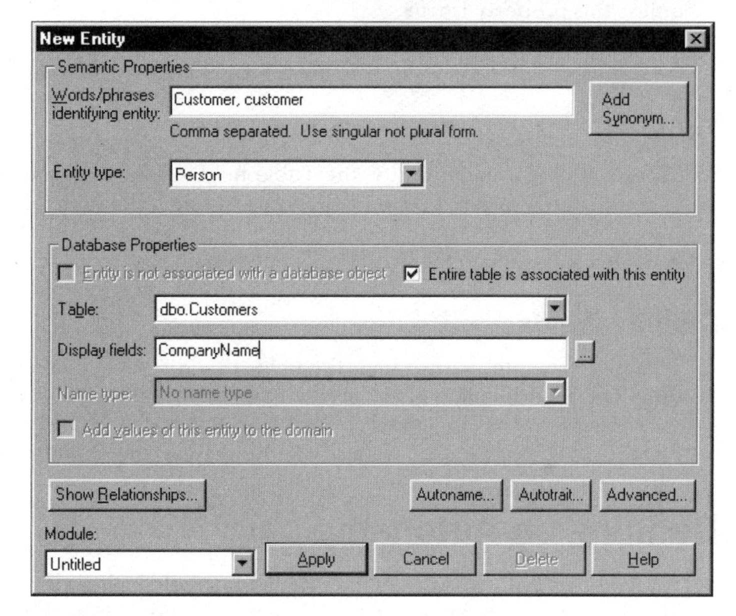

Next, we need to set the properties for the object. The properties you will need to set are described below.

Words/Phrases Identifying the Entity

The words we type here are the nouns the user will use to reference the entity in the question.

> **Make sure that you type the word in its singular form. In addition, these words are case-sensitive. If users are likely to use various cases when entering the question, make sure to list all cases of the word here.**

Synonyms for the word should also be listed, separated by commas. An entity phrase can be used instead of a single word. A phrase should not be enclosed in quotes or brackets. Some guidelines for choosing good synonyms will be discussed later in the chapter.

In our case, we need to specify Customer, customer as in the screenshot above.

Entity Type

An entity type defines whether the entity can be used to answer a "Who" question, a "Where" question, a "What" question, or a "When" question. A major entity is usually going to be defined as a person, an animate object, or a physical object. Only a field can have the date/time entity type.

Select Person as the Entity type.

Entire Table is Associated with this Entity

This property should be selected when defining major entities. Otherwise, you will not be able to add minor entities for columns beneath it. The Autoname and Autotrait buttons are also not enabled unless this property is true.

As `Customer` is a major entity, make sure that you check this box.

Table

When defining a major entity, the Table field allows us to select the table associated with that entity. When defining a trait, this field allows us to select the table to which the trait belongs.

We need to associate the `Customer` entity with the `Customers` table so select dbo.Customers.

Display Fields

This property allows us to limit the fields that display when a query using that entity is performed. If this field is left blank, a query involving a major entity will display all fields.

For the `Customer` entity, we just want to display the CompanyName field.

Defining an Autoname

An Autoname allows us to define the field or fields with which the name of a major entity is identified. Defining an Autoname creates a relationship with the phrasing "*major entity* names are the Names of *Major Entity*". While this is not required, it does allow users to ask questions about the names of major entities. For example, defining an Autoname property for the `Customer` entity results in a relationship of "*customer names are the Names of Customers*". This allows users to ask questions such as:

- "What are the names of the customers?"
- "List the customers by name."
- "Which customers are named Bella Ristorante?"

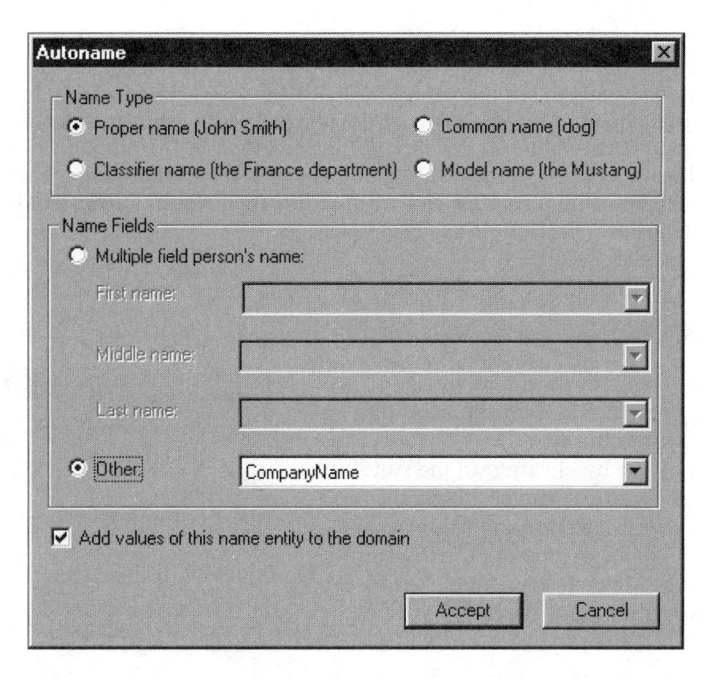

Identifying the appropriate name type helps the query engine understand when a value for the name entity is being specified. For example, a proper name is usually capitalized and is not preceded by articles or used to modify nouns. You would not expect a user to ask a question about a company like, "Where is *the* IBM?" Therefore, the customer name should have a name type of Proper Name.

Defining an Autoname is particularly important when a person's name spans multiple fields. Suppose we create an `Employee` entity and associate it with the `Employees` table. An employee may sometimes be referenced by first name, sometimes by last name, and sometimes by his or her full name. By creating an Autoname property that includes a first name and last name field, the query generated will automatically check both fields, allowing users to use the first name, the last name, or both names to locate a match. For example, the table below shows the queries that will be generated if an `Employee` entity contains an Autoname property mapped to first name and last name:

English	SQL
Which employees are named Steven?	`SELECT dbo.Employees.FirstName AS "FirstName", dbo.Employees.LastName AS "LastName" FROM dbo.Employees WHERE dbo.Employees.FirstName='Steven' OR dbo.Employees.LastName='Steven'`
Who is Steven Buchanan?	`SELECT dbo.Employees.FirstName AS "FirstName", dbo.Employees.LastName AS "LastName" FROM dbo.Employees WHERE dbo.Employees.LastName='Buchanan' AND dbo.Employees.FirstName='Steven'`

Although the second query is a little obvious, if more entities and relationships were defined, it would allow users to ask about Steven Buchanan's address, title, or salary.

The Add values of this name entity to this domain option is checked by default. Checking this option causes the values in the column associated with this entity to be added to the domain for each row of the table. Keeping this option checked is recommended. If the values of entities are not included in the domain, some questions involving these values will be untranslatable or ambiguous. Turning this option off will result in a smaller application, but the English Query Engine will not be able to translate some questions users pose.

Defining Traits

A trait is a characteristic of an entity. Just as a physical object or person has multiple traits, an entity can have many traits as well. We can define a trait for an entity either by clicking on the Autotrait button or (if the entity already exists) by right-clicking on the entity in the Domain Editor and running Autotrait. A dialog showing the fields in the table with which the entity is associated that have not yet been assigned to a name or trait will be displayed:

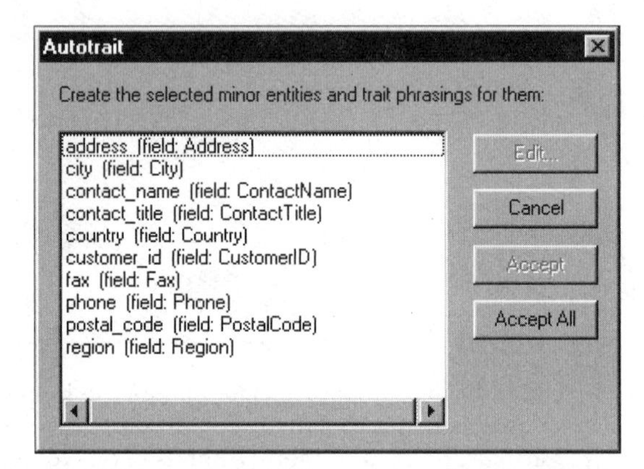

If you click on Accept All, a minor entity (trait) will be created for each field in the database. If you don't want all of the fields to be traits of the entity, you can accept each field separately. You can also edit the properties of each trait before creating it. Select the city trait and click on Edit:

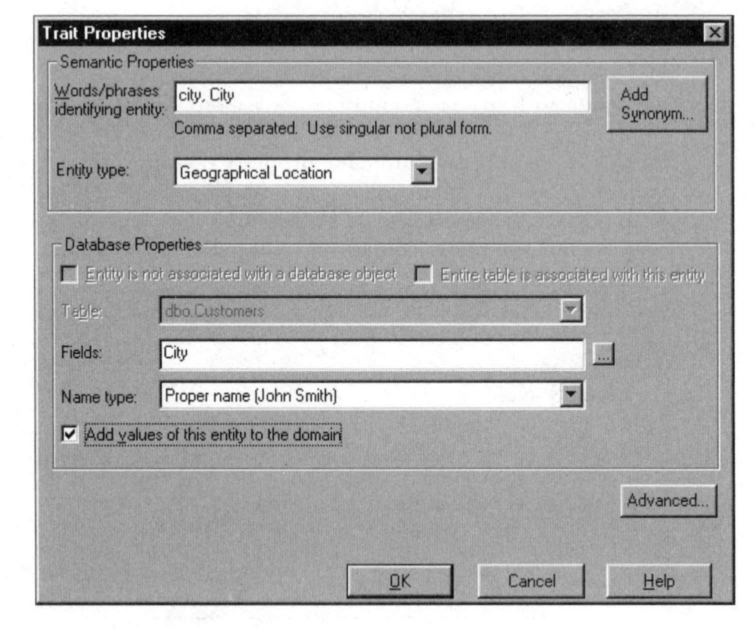

Make sure that you have set the city trait's properties as shown in the figure.

Trait properties are similar to entity properties. Notice that the example in the graphic shows city as an entity of the type Geographical Location. Unfortunately, this is not sufficient to allow a user to ask a question like, "Where is Taco Bell?" When a trait is added to an entity, a relationship of the form "*major entities* have a *trait*" is created. This allows a user to ask questions such as, "List the customers by city." or, "How many London customers are there?" However, to allow the user to ask questions about the location of the customers in a more natural manner, we need to define some alternative phrasings. Let's look at how that is done.

Defining Phrasings

When a trait is defined, a "have a" relationship will be added to the Relationships folder of the main English Query dialog. This type of relationship is known as a **trait phrasing**. We have also seen an example of a **Name/ID phrasing**. A Name/ID phrasing is created when you define an Autoname for a major entity. To define additional phrasings for that entity pair, go back to the main dialog (making sure that you accept the new `city` trait). Now, double-click on the "have a" relationship and select the Phrasings tab. Click on Add, the following dialog will appear:

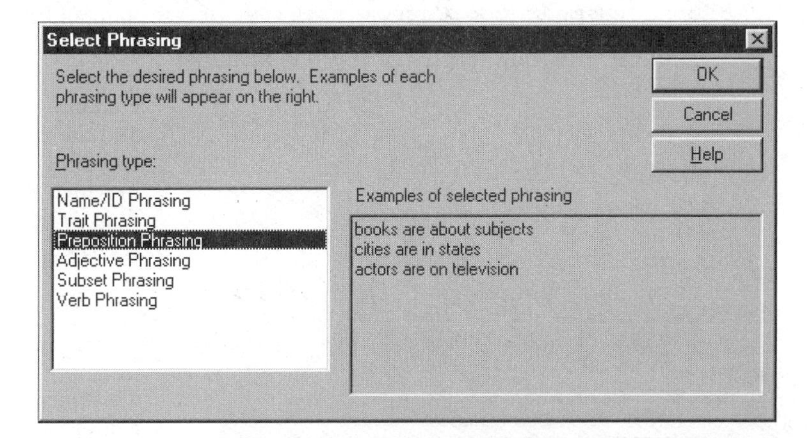

Select the type of phrasing you would like to define. In this case, we want to be able to answer questions like, "Which customers are in London?" Since "in London" is a prepositional phrase, we must double-click on Preposition Phrasing:

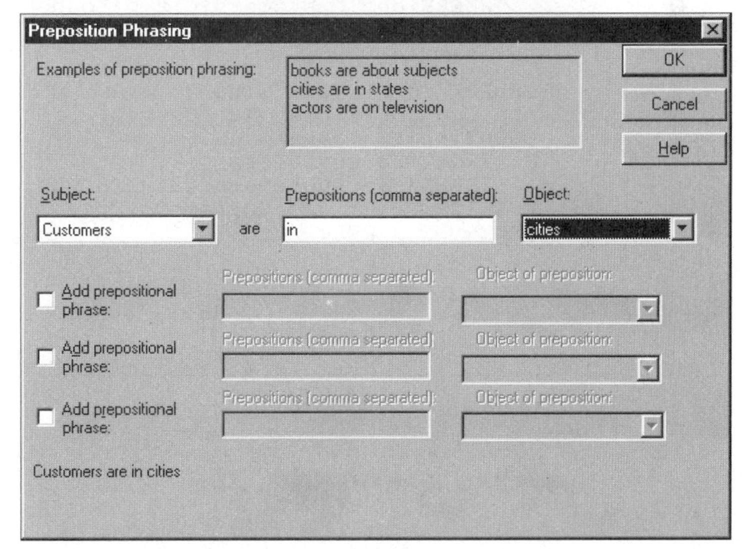

Next, we need to define the prepositional phrases that apply to the pair of entities. Since customers are *in* cities, this would be the only prepositional phrase that would apply.

> *Since the `City` entity was defined as a geographical location when the trait was defined, you will receive a hint here, suggesting that you add `City` to the* Time/Location *tab. This tab allows you to define where particular events occur. The* Time/Location *tab will be covered a little later in the chapter.*

Once you have defined this phrasing, users will be able to get information about customer locations using more natural questions. The table below shows some potential questions and the SQL that is returned by English Query. The comments column describes some of the clauses and functions in the English Query-generated SQL queries:

English	SQL	Comments
Where are the customers located?	`SELECT dbo.Customers.CompanyName AS "CompanyName", dbo.Customers.City AS "City" FROM dbo.Customers WHERE dbo.Customers.City IS NOT NULL`	Since `CompanyName` is defined as the Autoname property for `Customer`, this query will return a result set containing the company name and the city where the company is located. Only rows in which the `city` column does not contain `NULL` will be returned.
Which customers are in London?	`SELECT dbo.Customers.CompanyName AS "CompanyName" FROM dbo.Customers WHERE dbo.Customers.City='London'`	
How many customers are in London?	`SELECT COUNT(*) AS "count" FROM dbo.Customers WHERE dbo.Customers.City='London'`	This query uses the `COUNT` aggregate to determine how many customers are in the city of London.
Which city has the most customers?	`SELECT TOP 1 WITH TIES dbo.Customers.City AS "City", COUNT(*) AS "count" FROM dbo.Customers WHERE dbo.Customers.City IS NOT NULL GROUP BY dbo.Customers.City ORDER BY 2 DESC`	The SQL generated to answer this question returns a result set with two columns, the first is the contents of the `City` column. The second is the number of customers in that city. It then sorts the customers in descending order, by the value in the second column returned (hence the 2).

English	SQL	Comments
How many customers are in each city?	`SELECT dbo.Customers.City AS "City", COUNT(*) AS "count" FROM dbo.Customers WHERE dbo.Customers.City IS NOT NULL GROUP BY dbo.Customers.City`	Since this question asks for a sum of customers in each city, the SQL generated uses the `COUNT` aggregate, in conjunction with the `GROUP BY` clause to cause the number of customers to be tallied for each city. The `GROUP BY` clause ensures that there is only one row per city, regardless of how many times the city appears in the database.
List the customers in London or France.	`SELECT dbo.Customers.CompanyName AS "CompanyName", dbo.Customers.City AS "City" FROM dbo.Customers WHERE dbo.Customers.City='London' OR dbo.Customers.City='France'`	

As you can see, adding a verb phrasing to a relationship provides a great deal more flexibility and allows users to ask more natural questions. The example also shows how much intelligence is actually built into English Query. Notice that English Query can answer quantitative questions as well as simply searching on defined criteria. This capability is built into the engine and works automatically when you have defined traits that can be used for categorization.

One new Transact-SQL clause is worth mentioning. Notice that the question, "Which city has the most customers?" generates SQL code that includes the `WITH TIES` clause. `WITH TIES` is used to include records that are ranked equally in the result set. For example, in this case, if two cities were tied for the most customers, both would be listed. If the `WITH TIES` clause was omitted, only the first customer in the list would be included in the result set. It is important to note that English Query uses the `WITH TIES` clause by default. This means that even if the customer requests a particular number of records by asking a question like, "Which ten cities have the most customers?" the application that calls the English Query application and handles the result set cannot count on exactly ten records being returned.

Defining Relationships between Tables

Since the power in relational databases lies in the ability to generate queries across multiple tables, English Query becomes even more powerful as multiple major entities and the relationships between them are defined. English Query relationships between tables require a join. Implicit joins exist whenever there is a primary key/foreign key relationship in the database:

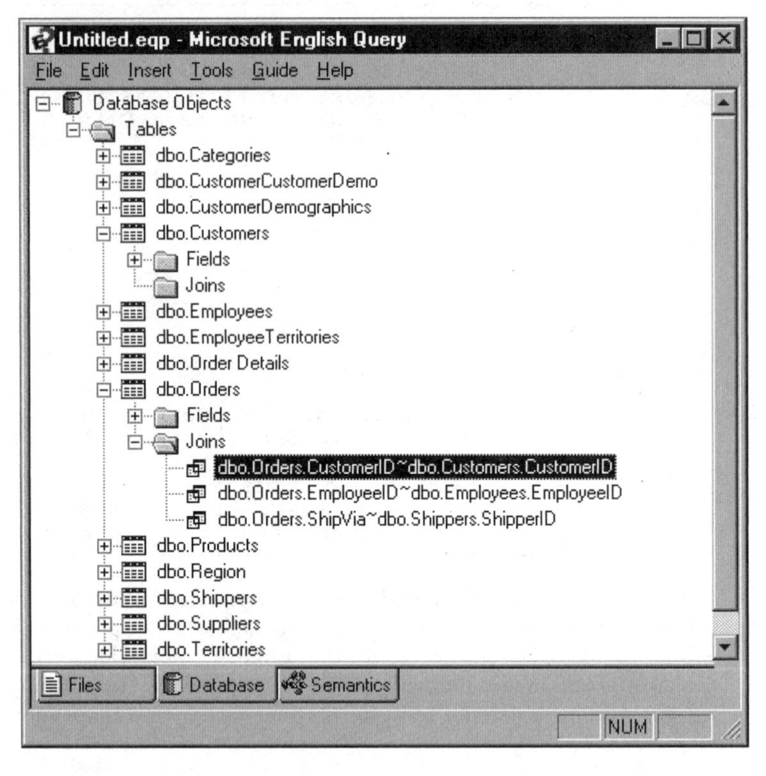

In the case of the `Northwind` database, the `Orders` table and the `Customers` table are joined by the `CustomerID` field. You can also explicitly define joins between tables in your application if you require relationships that are not already defined by the database schema.

Let's look at how to describe the relationship between `Customers` and `Orders` in plain English. First, we need to add a major entity called `Order`. Since it is a major entity, we need to associate the entire table with the entity. If we expected users to ask questions such as, "What are the names on the orders?" we would also want to define an Autoname for the entity. In this case, the only column that could feasibly be used to answer that question would be the `ShipName` field. However, if the `Orders` table had both `ShipName` and `BillName` columns, we would need to make a choice between them, depending on our business requirements.

Next, run Insert | Relationship to identify the relationship between the `Customer` and `Order` entities. Add the Customer entity and the Order entity on the Entities tab. Click on Phrasings and then on the Add button. In this case, we want to define the relationship "Customers place Orders". This type of phrasing is a verb phrasing because *place* is a verb. Double-click on Verb Phrasing.

Now we need to identify the sentence type of the phrasing we are adding. The supported sentence types are listed below, along with an example and the type of question that verb phrasing might answer.

Sentence Type	Example	Answers Question
Subject Verb	Customers shop.	Who shops the most?
Subject Verb Object	Customers place orders.	Who placed the most orders?
Subject Verb Object Object	Employees sell customers products.	Which employees sold Taco Bell the most Corny Tortillas?
Object are Verb	Products are ordered.	How many Corny Tortillas were ordered?
Object are Verb Object	Customers are shipped products.	Who has been shipped Ole Guacamole?

In this case, select Subject Verb Object. Next, select Customers as the subject, type place as the verb, and select Orders as the object. The completed phrasing is shown below:

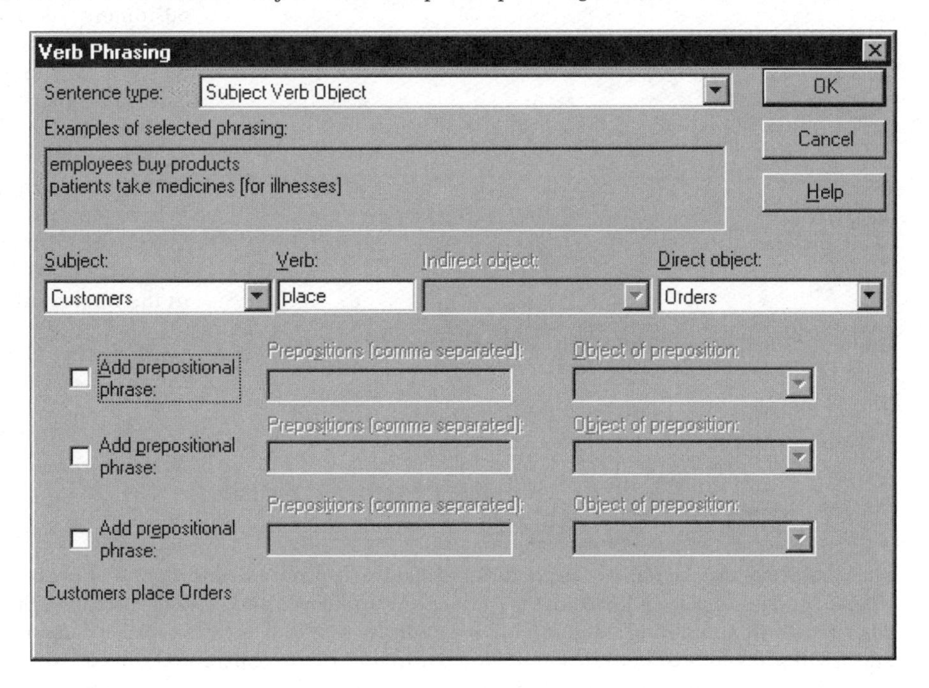

At this point, our application will be able to translate questions such as those shown below:

English	SQL	Comments
Who placed the most orders?	`SELECT TOP 1 WITH TIES dbo.Customers.CompanyName AS "CompanyName", COUNT(*) AS "count" FROM dbo.Orders, dbo.Customers WHERE dbo.Orders.CustomerID=dbo.Customers.CustomerID GROUP BY dbo.Orders.CustomerID, dbo.Customers.CompanyName ORDER BY 2 DESC`	
Which customers have not placed an order?	`SELECT dbo.Customers.CompanyName AS "CompanyName" FROM dbo.Customers WHERE dbo.Customers.CustomerID NOT IN (SELECT dbo.Orders.CustomerID FROM dbo.Orders)`	In this case, the English Query engine creates a non-correlated subquery. When this query is executed, first a result set containing a list of customer IDs of all customers who have placed orders is generated. This query is the inner query. The outer query uses that result set to compare it against each `CustomerID` in the `Customers` table. Where a match is not found, the customer's `CompanyName` is included in the final result set.
How many times has Around the Horn placed an order?	`SELECT COUNT(*) AS "count" FROM dbo.Customers, dbo.Orders WHERE dbo.Customers.CompanyName='Around the Horn' AND dbo.Customers.CustomerID=dbo.Orders.CustomerID`	

Notice that the phrasing also allows us to add prepositional phrases. Adding the appropriate prepositional phrases to a verb phrasing can allow our application to answer questions that qualify when, where, or how something happened. For example, to allow questions like, "How many orders were placed with Steven?" to be translated we need to add the prepositional phrase "with Employees". Note that before you can add this prepositional phrase to the phrasing, you need to add the `Employee` entity to the relationship. Let's look at how that's done.

If you are following along with the example and haven't already created an `Employee` entity, you will need to do that now. Set the Autoname of the entity to be a proper name, using both the `FirstName` and `LastName` fields.

Adding a Prepositional Phrase to a Verb Phrasing

To add a prepositional phrase to the "Customers place Orders" verb phrasing, we first need to add the `Employee` entity to the relationship. This is done by clicking on Add Entity on the Entities tab of the Relationship dialog. Select Employee from the list. Next, click on the Phrasings tab and edit the Customers place Orders phrasing:

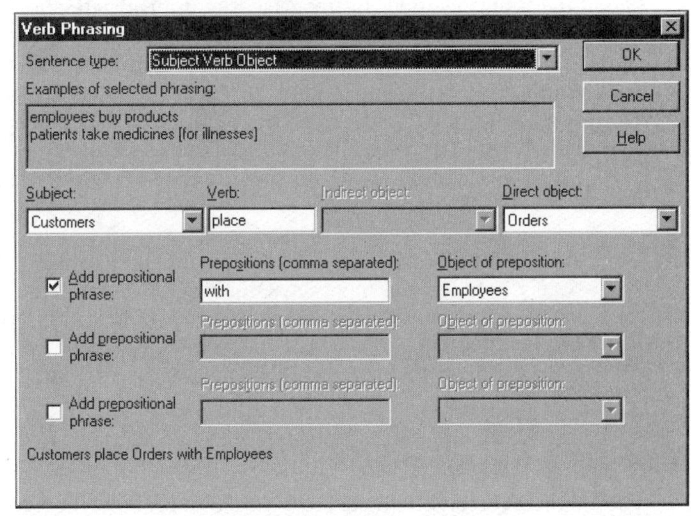

Place a check mark in Add prepositional phrase box. Type the preposition or prepositions that users will use to describe this relationship and select the object of the preposition from the drop-down list. In this case, we are interested in the prepositional phrase "with Employees".

Supporting Questions about Time

We can also add support for questions about the time at which a particular relationship occurs. For example, we may want the users to be able to enquire about the number of orders placed in a particular month or year. To do this, we add the appropriate entity to the relationship. Since the `Orders` table includes an `OrderDate` field, we can define an `order_date` trait for the `Order` entity. Next, add the `order_date` entity to the `Customers_place_Orders_with_Employees` relationship. Display the Time/Location tab:

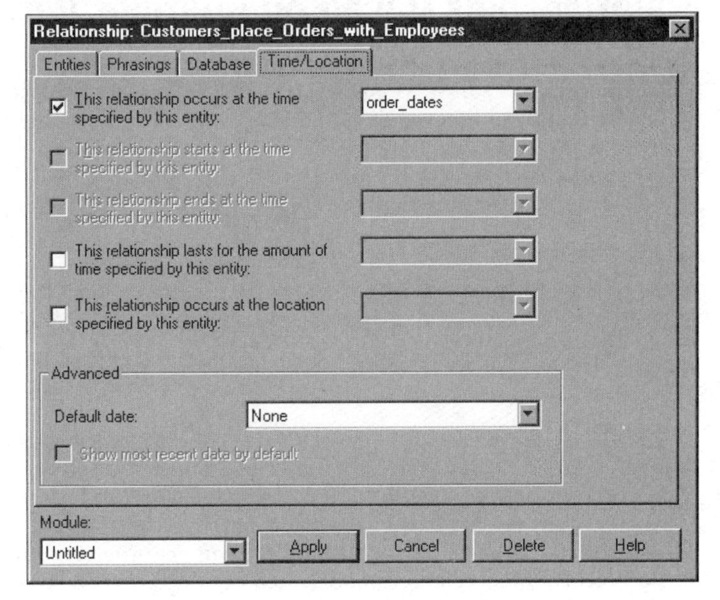

Here we can define whether the relationship *occurs* at the time specified, *starts* at the time specified, or *ends* at the time specified. In this case, the appropriate choice is that the relationship *occurs* at the time specified by the `order_dates` entity. If you want the query to be limited to a particular date, if none is specified in the question, you can select a Default date setting. The available choices are None, This Month, This Year, and Today. If the Default date is set to None, the field associated with the date entity will not be qualified in the query. When the query is executed, the results for all dates will be included. If the default date is set to Today, the query will limit the results to those for which the `order_date` was today when no specific date is included in the user's question.

Be careful when setting defaults in your application. Make sure that users are aware of any defaults you have set. Otherwise, a user might think he is asking for a specific set of orders placed over all time, when in fact only the orders placed that day will be returned.

Transitive Relationships

The English Query Engine is fairly intelligent about the way defined relationships flow into each other. For example, since it knows that Customers are in Cities and Customers place Orders, it can figure out that Customers place Orders in Cities. This intelligence allows users to ask questions such as, "Where were the most orders placed?" In this case, the transition flows from a relationship defined between tables to a relationship defined by traits.

Relationships Based on Multiple Joins

Because English Query understands the schema of the database, it is also intelligent enough to handle relationships that involve joins across multiple tables. In fact, we don't even need to define the intermediary tables as entities. The best way to understand this is through an example:

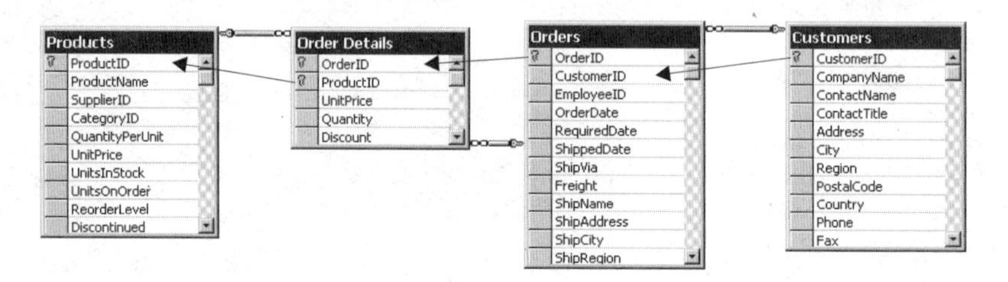

Customers order Products

In order to support questions like, "Which customers ordered Ole Guacamole?" we need to define a major entity for the `Products` table and a relationship between the `Customer` and `Product` entities that uses the verb phrasing "Customers order Products". Although there is no direct foreign key/primary key relationship between the `Customers` table and the `Products` table, English Query can analyze the schema and generate SQL that performs the appropriate join. The following table shows some of the questions that a user can ask based on this relationship and the complex queries they generate:

English	SQL

Who ordered Camembert Pierrot?	`SELECT DISTINCT dbo.Customers.CompanyName AS "CompanyName"`
	`FROM dbo.Products, dbo."Order Details", dbo.Orders, dbo.Customers`
	`WHERE dbo.Products.ProductName='Camembert Pierrot'`
	`AND dbo."Order Details".OrderID=dbo.Orders.OrderID`
	`AND dbo.Products.ProductID=dbo."Order Details".ProductID`
	`AND dbo.Orders.CustomerID=dbo.Customers.CustomerID`

Which ten products were ordered by the most customers?	`SELECT TOP 10 WITH TIES dbo.Products.ProductName AS "ProductName", COUNT(distinct dbo.Orders.CustomerID) AS "count"`
	`FROM dbo."Order Details", dbo.Orders, dbo.Products`
	`WHERE dbo."Order Details".OrderID=dbo.Orders.OrderID`
	`AND dbo."Order Details".ProductID=dbo.Products.ProductID`
	`GROUP BY dbo."Order Details".ProductID,`
	`dbo.Products.ProductName ORDER BY 2 DESC`

Which products did Around the Horn order?	`SELECT DISTINCT dbo.Products.ProductName AS "ProductName"`
	`FROM dbo.Customers, dbo."Order Details", dbo.Orders, dbo.Products`
	`WHERE dbo.Customers.CompanyName='Around the Horn'`
	`AND dbo."Order Details".OrderID=dbo.Orders.OrderID`
	`AND dbo.Customers.CustomerID=dbo.Orders.CustomerID`
	`AND dbo."Order Details".ProductID=dbo.Products.ProductID`

Complex queries like these involve joins between a number of tables (in this case four). In order to improve performance, you will need to give careful consideration to how your indexes are built.

Defining Subset Phrasings

If you want to allow users to ask questions that categorize entities, you need to identify the appropriate subset phrasings. Let's look at an example.

The `Northwind` database includes a `Categories` table that contains various descriptive categories for the types of products in the `Products` table. In order to allow users to ask questions like, "Which products are beverages?" we need to define a major entity based on the `Categories` table. Set its Autoname to map to the `CategoryName` field and define it as a Common Name. Next, establish a relationship between the `Category` entity and the `Product` entity. Display the Phrasings tab. Click on Add and select Subset Phrasing:

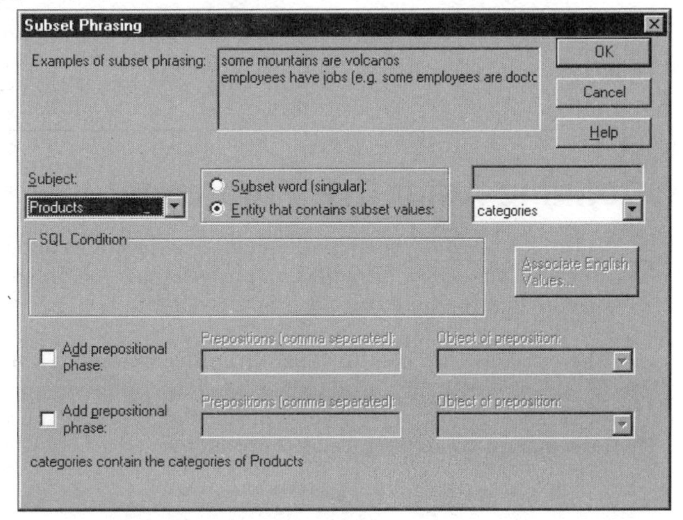

In this case, we will want to select **Products** as the subject and **Categories** as the entity that contains subset values. This subset phrasing, along with the other entities and relationships we've created so far, will allow us to translate questions like those shown in the table below:

English	SQL
Who ordered the most seafood?	SELECT TOP 1 WITH TIES dbo.Customers.CompanyName AS "CompanyName", COUNT(DISTINCT dbo."Order Details".ProductID) AS "count" FROM dbo."Order Details", dbo.Orders, dbo.Categories, dbo.Products, dbo.Customers WHERE dbo."Order Details".OrderID=dbo.Orders.OrderID AND dbo.Categories.CategoryName='Seafood' AND dbo.Categories.CategoryID=dbo.Products.CategoryID AND dbo."Order Details".ProductID=dbo.Products.ProductID AND dbo.Orders.CustomerID=dbo.Customers.CustomerID GROUP BY dbo.Orders.CustomerID, dbo.Customers.CompanyName ORDER BY 2 DESC
Which customers ordered dairy products?	SELECT DISTINCT dbo.Customers.CompanyName AS "CompanyName" FROM dbo.Categories, dbo.Products, dbo."Order Details", dbo.Orders, dbo.Customers WHERE dbo.Categories.CategoryName='Dairy Products' AND dbo.Categories.CategoryID=dbo.Products.CategoryID AND dbo."Order Details".OrderID=dbo.Orders.OrderID AND dbo.Products.ProductID=dbo."Order Details".ProductID AND dbo.Orders.CustomerID=dbo.Customers.CustomerID
Which cities did not order beverages?	SELECT DISTINCT dbo.Customers.City AS "City" FROM dbo.Customers WHERE dbo.Customers.CustomerID NOT IN (SELECT dbo.Orders.CustomerID FROM dbo.Categories, dbo.Products, dbo."Order Details", dbo.Orders WHERE dbo.Categories.CategoryName='Beverages' AND dbo.Categories.CategoryID=dbo.Products.CategoryID AND dbo."Order Details".OrderID=dbo.Orders.OrderID AND dbo.Products.ProductID=dbo."Order Details".ProductID)

Defining Adjective Phrasings

In order to enable users to ask qualitative questions about the entities, we need to define some adjective phrasings. An adjective phrasing may be based on the value of a particular entity or it might be a qualitative word, such as best or worst.

The `Product` table in the `Northwind` database has a `Discontinued` field that is of the `bit` data type. It is set to 1 if a product has been discontinued and 0 if it has not been discontinued. Let's look at how that field can be used to provide an adjective phrasing that allows users to retrieve information about discontinued products.

Create a relationship and add `Product` as the only entity. Display the Phrasing tab and double-click on Adjective Phrasing:

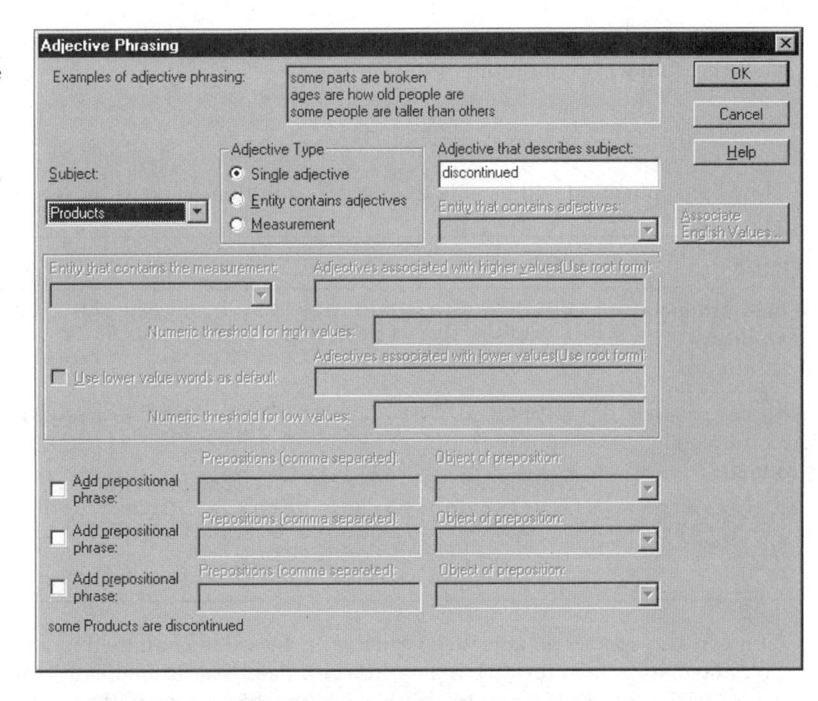

Select Products as the Subject and select Single adjective as the Adjective Type. Enter the word discontinued to describe the subject. Click on OK to close the dialog.

Now we need to let the query engine know under what circumstances the adjective discontinued will describe the product. We will do this on the Database tab of the relationship property dialog:

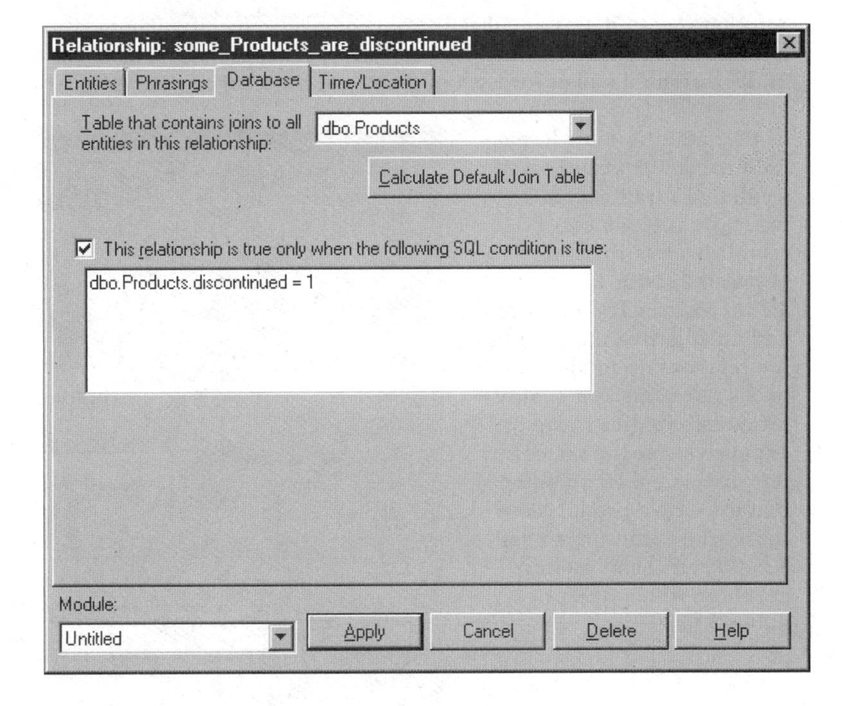

Check the checkbox for This relationship is true only when the following SQL condition is true and enter the following condition:

```
dbo.Products.discontinued = 1
```

Now the application will be able to interpret questions such as those shown in the table:

English	SQL
Which products have been discontinued?	`SELECT dbo.Products.ProductName AS "ProductName" FROM dbo.Products WHERE dbo.Products.Discontinued=1`
Who has ordered discontinued products?	`SELECT DISTINCT dbo.Customers.CompanyName AS "CompanyName" FROM dbo.Products, dbo."Order Details", dbo.Orders, dbo.Customers WHERE dbo.Products.Discontinued=1 AND dbo."Order Details".OrderID=dbo.Orders.OrderID AND dbo.Products.ProductID=dbo."Order Details".ProductID AND dbo.Orders.CustomerID=dbo.Customers.CustomerID`

You can also specify an adjective type that is the value contained in a particular entity. For example, you may have a field for `Color` in a `Houses` database. In that case, you could define an entity for both `Color` and `House` and establish a relationship between them with an adjective phrase. This would allow users to ask questions like, "Which houses are brown?"

Another way to define an adjective phrasing is by specifying a measurement type. This adjective type is a little more complex than the other two because it allows us to set high and low adjectives, as well as the threshold values for each of them. Let's look at an example.

The `Products` table has a field named `UnitPrice`. If we define a trait called `unit_price`, we can establish a relationship between `Product` and `unit_price`. Then we can add an adjective phrasing to the relationship to allow users to ask questions that qualify products as either cheap or expensive. For the sake of this discussion, let's assume that expensive products are those with a unit price over $25.00 and cheap products are those with a unit price under $10.00.

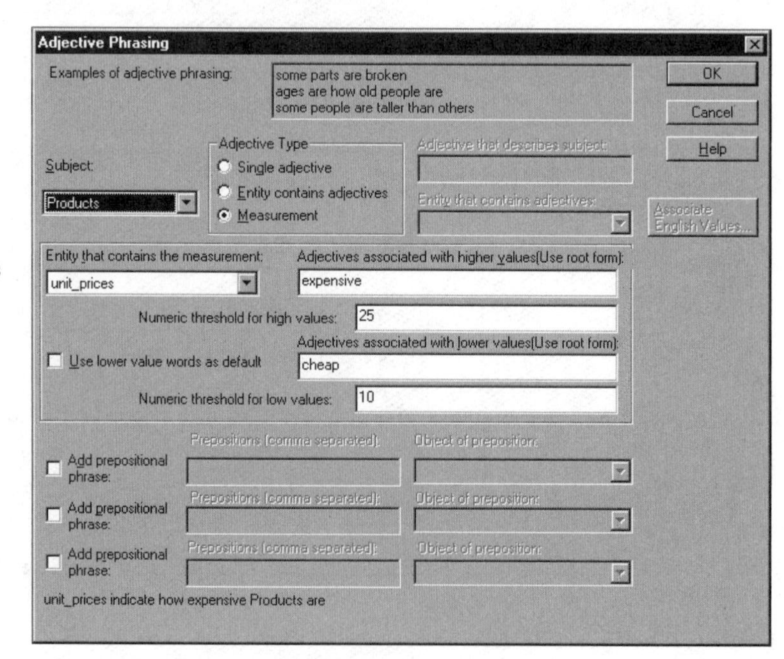

To set up this adjective phrasing, specify an Adjective Type of Measurement. Select unit_prices as the Entity that contains the measurement. Next, enter the adjective that will describe the values over the threshold. You can also enter synonyms by separating them with commas. Enter the threshold for the high values. You must also specify the adjective and threshold for the low values. While these thresholds may sometimes be the same, in this case they are different because there are also medium price products that are neither cheap nor expensive.

The table below shows questions about the cost of products and the SQL that is generated:

English	SQL
Which products are expensive?	`SELECT dbo.Products.ProductName AS "ProductName", dbo.Products.UnitPrice as "UnitPrice" FROM dbo.Products WHERE dbo.Products.UnitPrice>25`
Which products are cheap?	`SELECT dbo.Products.ProductName AS "ProductName", dbo.Products.UnitPrice AS "UnitPrice" FROM dbo.Products WHERE dbo.Products.UnitPrice<10`
Which products are neither expensive nor cheap?	`SELECT dbo.Products.ProductName AS "ProductName", dbo.Products.UnitPrice AS "UnitPrice" FROM dbo.Products WHERE dbo.Products.UnitPrice>=10 AND dbo.Products.UnitPrice<=25`

Notice that the Use lower value words as default checkbox is not checked. If it had been, the queries generated would have been significantly different. Let's look at the effect it would have:

English	SQL
Which products are expensive?	`SELECT dbo.Products.ProductName AS "ProductName", dbo.Products.UnitPrice AS "UnitPrice" FROM dbo.Products WHERE dbo.Products.UnitPrice>10`
Which products are cheap?	`SELECT dbo.Products.ProductName AS "ProductName", dbo.Products.UnitPrice AS "UnitPrice" FROM dbo.Products WHERE dbo.Products.UnitPrice<25`
Which products are neither expensive nor cheap?	`SELECT dbo.Products.ProductName AS "ProductName", dbo.Products.UnitPrice AS "UnitPrice" FROM dbo.Products WHERE dbo.Products.UnitPrice>=25 AND dbo.Products.UnitPrice<=10`

Turning on the Use lower value words as default option causes the low threshold to be used with the high adjective and the high threshold to be used with the low adjective. In this case, this is not an appropriate choice because it results in products being described as both expensive and cheap. The Use lower value words option is appropriate in situations where the high adjective and the low adjective are not opposites. For example, consider the words affordable and deluxe. Perhaps deluxe items are considered those that cost $10.00 or more and affordable items are those that cost $25.00 or under. In this case, an item that costs between $10.00 and $25.00 are both affordable and deluxe.

Defining Synonyms

A synonym is a word that means the same thing as another word. It is essential that you try to account for the synonyms your users will use to describe entities, relationships, and other words they will use in their queries. As you're building your application, you may want to consult a thesaurus for a list of common synonyms. Keep in mind regional differences. Consider, for example, an `Employees` table that includes a termination date. When a company releases employees in order to cut costs, users in the United States would refer to that person as "laid off". Users in the United Kingdom would refer to that employee as "made redundant". As you think about the different ways users will refer to items, consider the geographic scope of your application and get as much advice from users in those locations as possible.

Synonyms for Entities

You have already seen that entity words are case-sensitive. Different cases can be accounted for by separating the words with commas in the words/phrases identifying the entity field. In a loose sense of the term, you are defining synonyms. You use the same technique to list additional synonyms for entities. For example, you may want to add the synonym "merchandise" to the list of words that identify the `Product` entity.

Synonyms for Verbs

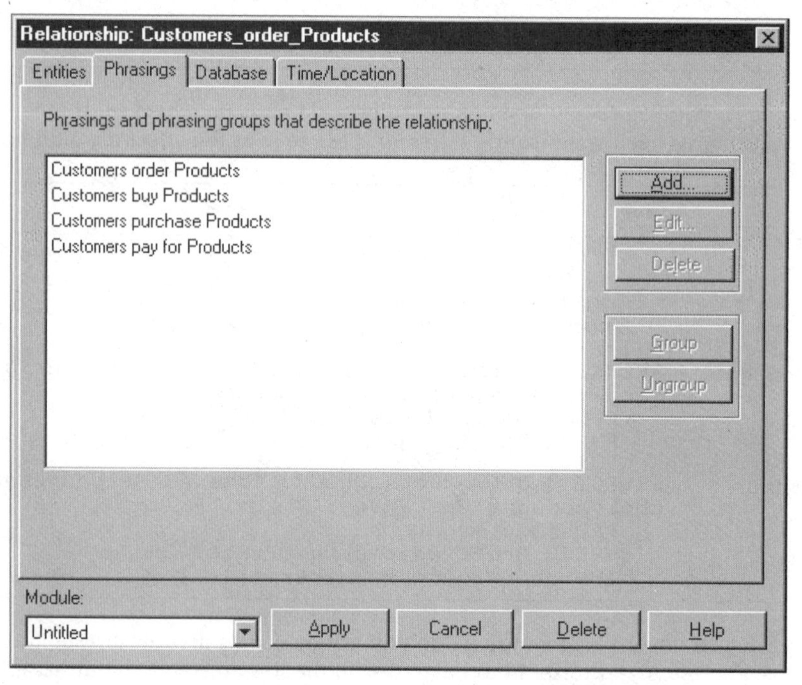

Synonyms for verbs are defined by adding phrasings. You should think about the different ways users will ask about a set of entities and add phrasings to account for each of them. In the graphic shown above, four alternate phrasings have been provided to allow customers to ask the same question four different ways. If you are walking through the example, please add these phrasings to your English Query project.

Keep in mind that the synonyms you define are application-specific. Depending on the way the database tracks data, customers ordering products and paying for products may not always mean the same thing.

Dictionary Entries

The dictionary contains words, phrasings, and their synonyms that are commonly used when forming English questions and statements. You can add words and synonyms to your application's dictionary. While you can do this instead of identifying synonyms and synonymous verb phrasings, keep in mind that the changes you make here are applicable throughout your entire application. They do not depend on the context of an entity or relationship.

Dictionary entries are useful for defining industry-specific jargon words and acronyms, particularly if they use irregular conjugation. English Query is fairly tolerant of incorrect conjugations when generating queries. It will generally try most conjugation rules against a root and if any of them match the word in the question, it will be used. For example, to generate a past tense of a word, it will add "d" to the root and "ed" to the root, even if it knows that the correct conjugation is irregular. This enables English Query to work well even for users who do not remember irregular conjugations. The table shows how English Query restates the user's questions when "pay" is conjugated correctly and incorrectly. In this case, the primary phrasing is "Customers order Products" and one of the secondary phrasings is "Customers pay for Products":

Question	English Query Conjugation	Restatement
Which customers paid for seafood?	Default dictionary conjugation	Which customers paid for seafoods?
Which customers payed for seafood?	Pay + ed	Which customers paid for seafoods?
Which customers payd for seafood?	Pay + d	Which customers paid for seafoods?

Notice that English Query is able to parse the question. Since the irregular conjugation of pay is included in the built-in dictionary, the restatement and the answer text will contain the correctly conjugated form of the word.

However, this answer points out a different problem. The English Query engine is applying standard conjugation rules to the word "seafood". If we want the restatement and the answer text to return the correct plural for seafood, we will need to define a dictionary entry.

To define a dictionary entry, run Insert | Dictionary Entry:

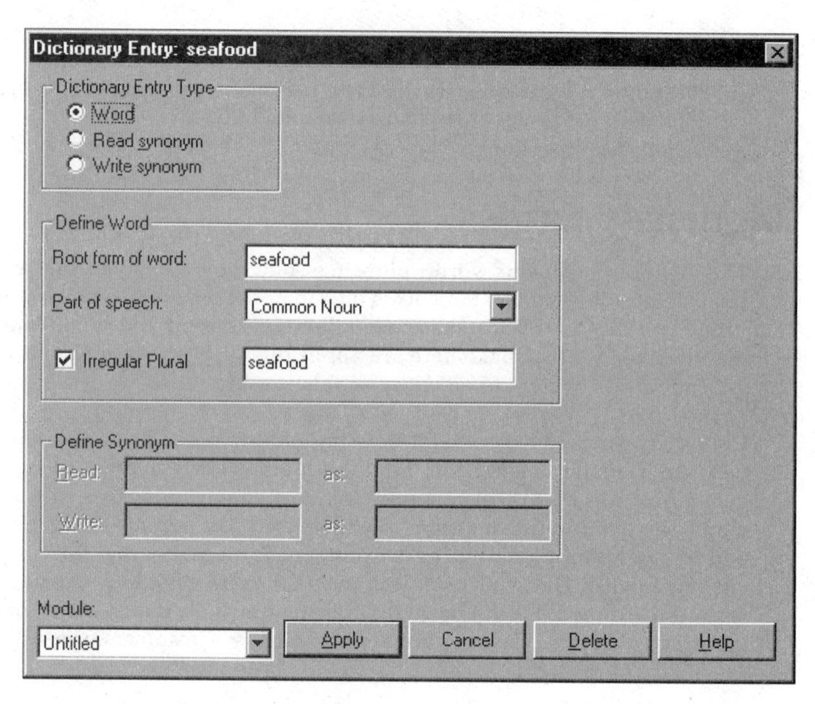

Since we need to define an irregular plural conjugation, we need to select Word as the Dictionary Entry Type. Next, define the root form of the word, the part of speech, in this case a Common Noun. Check the Irregular Plural box and enter the correct conjugation for seafood. You can only enter irregular conjugations for Common Nouns and Verbs.

We can also add dictionary entries for Read synonyms and Write synonyms. A Read synonym tells the English Query engine that when a particular word is encountered in a question, it should be *read* as its synonym. For example, if we want the word "fish" to be interpreted as "seafood" every time it is encountered in a question, we would enter it as a Read synonym.

A Write synonym tells the English Query engine that when a particular word would generally be used in the answer text, to substitute the write synonym instead. One use of this is to account for terms that appear plural in the database. Consider the product categories in the `Northwind` database. The category name of Condiments is used to identify spices and sauces. When English Query generates the answer text for a question like, "Show me the condiments," it tries to pluralize "condiments" by adding an "es". This results in the answer text, "The condimentses are:" To correct this problem, add a Write synonym to the dictionary. Define the synonym as *Write condimentses as condiment*s. Now the correct answer text will be generated.

Testing Our Application

Thorough testing of our application is essential to minimize the number of questions that return no results, or worse yet, incorrect results. The English Query domain editor provides us with two ways to test our English Query application:

- An interactive testing tool
- An automated regression test

Both are useful for specific purposes.

Automated Regression Testing

The automated regression test reads questions from an ASCII file, runs them through the query application, and outputs the results to another ASCII file. It includes a feature that allows us to compare a previous regression test with the current test. Because it is driven by an ASCII file, it allows us to quickly test a large set of questions.

One way to use this capability is to ask the users to prepare a list of questions they would like the stored data to be able to answer. You can then consolidate these questions into the ASCII file and run them through a regression test to identify whether your application meets the users' expectations. Another important use is for testing a new version of the application to ensure that none of your modifications caused existing functionality to break.

Let's look at how this tool is used.

Setting Filenames

The filenames for the question file, the output file, and the reference file used to perform compares are set on the Global Properties dialog. This dialog is displayed by running Edit | Global Properties.

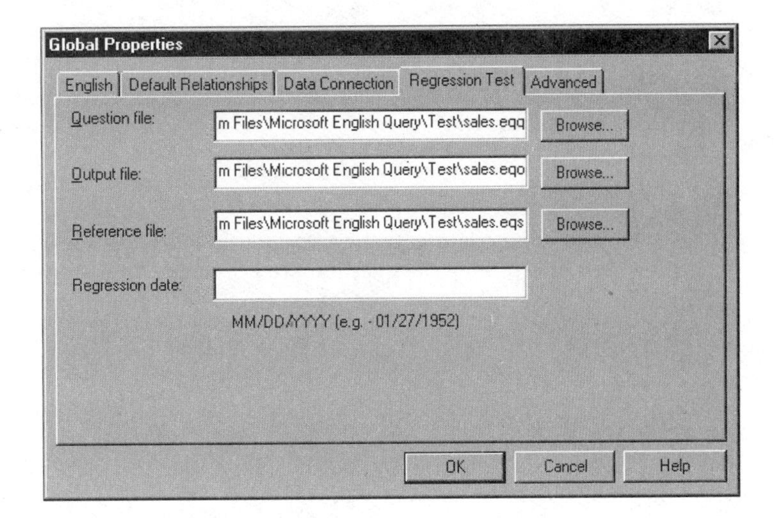

By default, the question file is named `project_name.eqq`, the output file is named `project_name.eqo`, and the reference file is named `project_name.eqs` and they are stored in the path that contains your project files. However, you can name them anything you'd like. This dialog also allows you to specify a regression date. The regression date runs your application as if that date were the current system date. This may be helpful when you need to test the application's ability to translate questions about events that occurred on a date relative to the current date like, "Which customers ordered discontinued products last week?"

File Contents

The question file is an ASCII file with the questions separated by a single carriage return. It can be created and edited in any text editor, such as Notepad. In addition, the domain editor's interactive testing tool allows you to create and add questions to this file. If you do not have an ASCII file when you begin testing, configure the file name for the file and begin testing through the interactive tool. You can select to add the questions you test to the question file. You'll see an example of this a little later in the chapter.

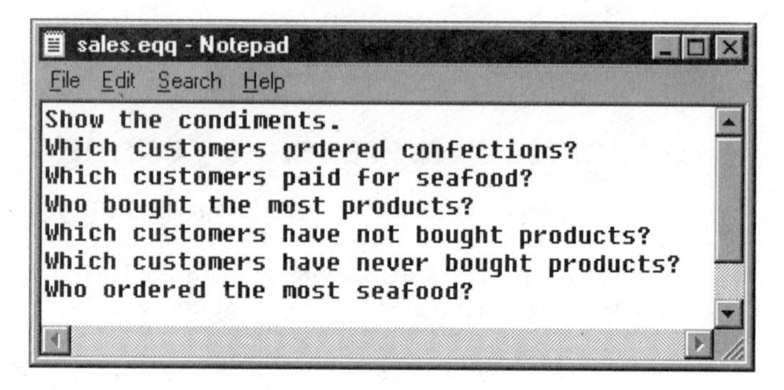

The output file is also an ASCII file. It is generated automatically when you run a regression test. It includes the following information for each question in the question file that the application was able to translate:

- The question
- The English Query restatement of the question
- The Answer text
- The SQL query generated by English Query

For questions that could not be translated, the question and a description of the problem English Query had interpreting the question are provided. An example output file is shown opposite:

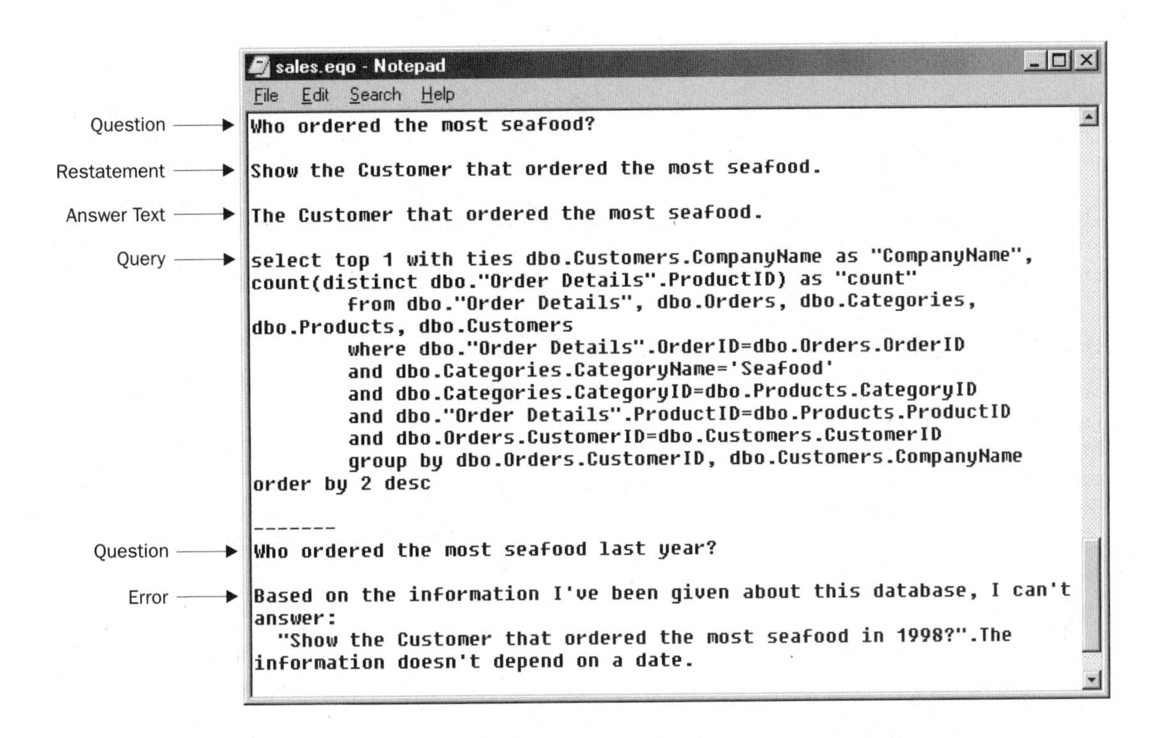

> **The reference file is actually just an output file, renamed with the `.eqs` extension. The reference file is NOT created automatically. After you have run a regression test, you should change the output file's name to match that specified in the Global Properties dialog for the reference file.**

Running a Regression Test

Once the filenames have been set and the question file has been populated, you can run a regression test against your application. To run a regression test, run Tools | Regression Test:

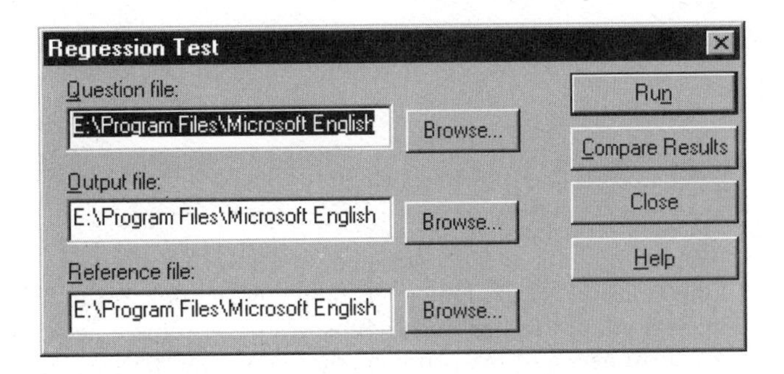

Verify that the filenames are correct and click on Run. The application's dictionary and forms will be loaded into memory and each question in the question file can be run through the application.

Analyzing the Output File

Just because English Query is able to translate a question into a query it does not mean the query is correct. The first time you run a regression test against a set of questions, you should check the syntax of each generated query carefully to ensure that it correctly reflects the way you believe the question should be answered. You should also look for inefficient queries, such as those that involve joins based on non-indexed columns. You might even consider copying some of the queries and running them in Query Analyzer to view the execution plan. It is particularly important to check for queries that don't do what you expect. Consider the following example:

Question	Restatement	Answer Text	SQL
Which customers have not bought products?	Which Customers have not ordered Products?	The Customers that have not ordered Products are:	`SELECT dbo.Customers.CompanyName AS "CompanyName" FROM dbo.Customers WHERE dbo.Customers.CustomerID NOT IN (SELECT dbo.Orders.CustomerID FROM dbo.Products, dbo."Order Details", dbo.Orders WHERE dbo."Order Details".OrderID=dbo.Orders.Order ID AND dbo.Products.ProductID=dbo."Order Details".ProductID)`
Which customers have never bought products?	Which Customers have never ordered Products?	The Customers that have never ordered Products are:	`SELECT DISTINCT dbo.Customers.CompanyName AS "CompanyName", dbo.Products.ProductName AS "ProductName" FROM dbo.Products, dbo."Order Details", dbo.Orders, dbo.Customers WHERE dbo."Order Details".OrderID=dbo.Orders.Order ID AND dbo.Products.ProductID=dbo."Order Details".ProductID AND dbo.Orders.CustomerID=dbo.Custome rs.CustomerID`

When you look at the restatement and the answer text, it seems like English Query interpreted both questions correctly. However, take a close look at the SQL generated for the second question. This query will not return a list of customers who have never bought products. Instead, it will return a list of customers and the products they have purchased. This example emphasizes how important it is not to assume that if one phrasing works, a slightly different one will work as well.

In this case, the solution to the problem is quite simple. We need to add *never* to the dictionary as a Read synonym for *not.*

Comparing Regression Test Results

Once you believe you have solved the problems revealed by your first run of a regression test, you should rename your output file to the name specified for the reference file and run the test again.

After it has finished running, click on Compare Results to compare the most recent regression test against the saved reference file. The first difference between the two files will be highlighted as shown below:

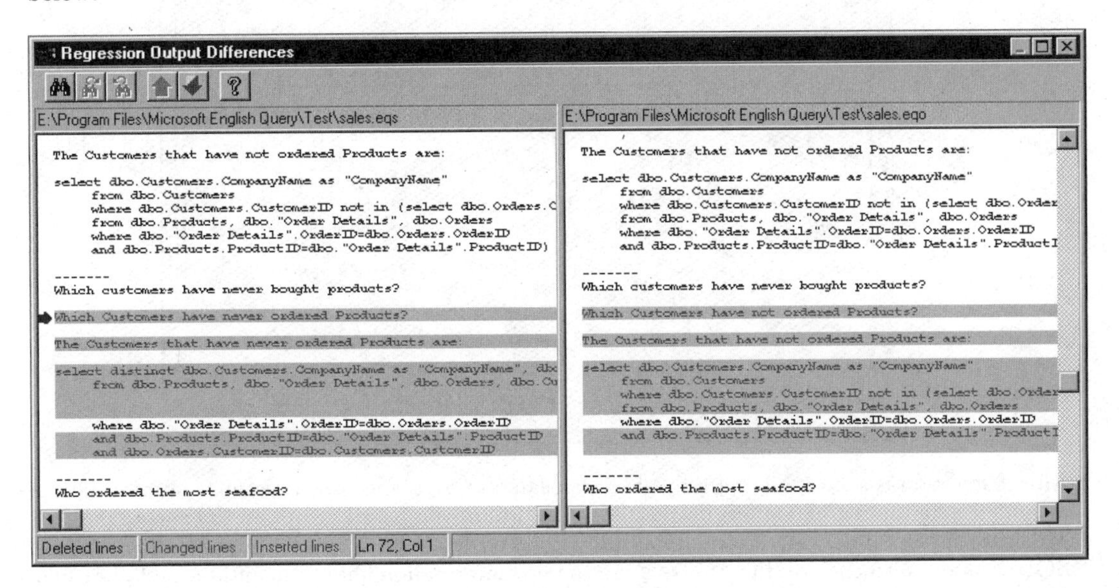

Text that has been deleted will be shown in blue, text that has changed will be shown in red, and new text will be shown in green. You can click on the button with the down arrow icon to display the next difference between the files. This capability allows you to quickly check the questions that generated different results due to the changes you have made. Check the differences carefully. Sometimes a change can have unexpected repercussions in the way other questions are interpreted.

Interactive Testing Tool

When you're developing an English Query application, it is useful to be able to test questions interactively, make a change, then test again. The English Query domain editor provides a tool to allow you to do that. The test tool is launched by running Tools | Test Application.

The test application allows you to submit questions by typing them into the question field and clicking on Submit. Questions that are submitted are saved in the drop-down list for later use.

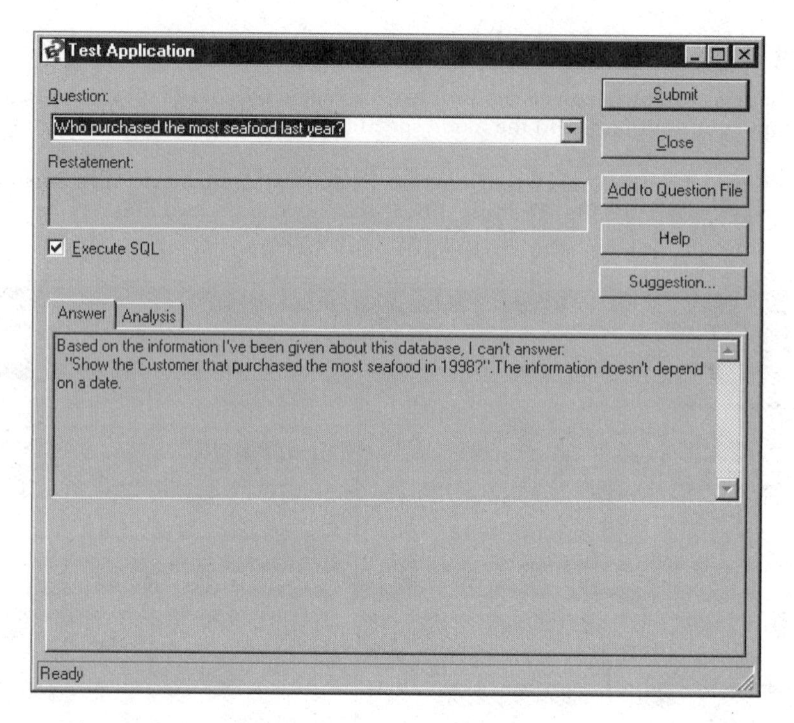

After a question is submitted, the English is translated to SQL and the same types of information are provided as in the regression test output file. In addition, you have the option to execute the SQL. This can be helpful because it sometimes allows you to detect problems without needing to read the SQL. You can also click on the Analysis tab to view information about the entities and phrasings that were used to generate the query.

When a question cannot be interpreted, the Suggestion button helps you determine the changes you need to make. When you click on it, you are prompted to identify each entity that English Query cannot interpret.

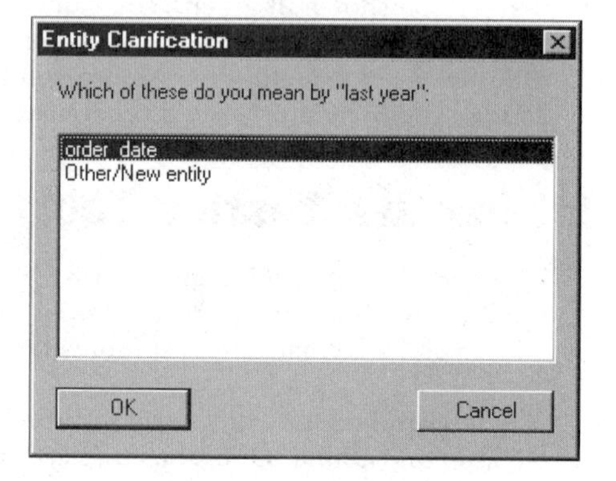

English Query suggests the entities it suspects are the most likely candidates. In this case, since English Query knows that "last year" generally refers to a time or date, it is suggesting the only date/time entity that has been defined. We also have the option of choosing an entity that is not listed or creating a new one. Since the entity order_date is what the question is looking for, select it and click on OK.

Once all of the entities have been identified, you will be prompted to create a new relationship for these entities:

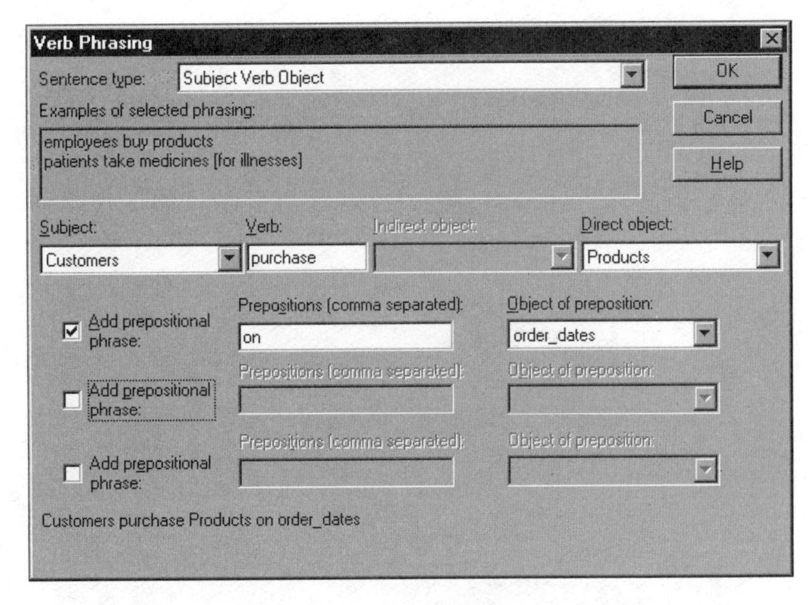

In this case, the phrasing is the verb phrasing, "Customers purchase Products on order_dates".

It is important to keep in mind that this is a new relationship. In this case, since the application already has a "Customers order Products" relationship defined that includes multiple verb phrasings, it would actually be better to click on Cancel here and modify the existing "Customers order Products" relationship. English Query will work either way, but defining them using different phrasings of the same relationship will make your application more maintainable.

Since `order_date` maps to the time an event occurs, we can simply add it as an entity and modify the Time/Location tab for the relationship. By configuring it in this manner, we are allowing the change to be reflected across all of the verb phrasings identified for that relationship:

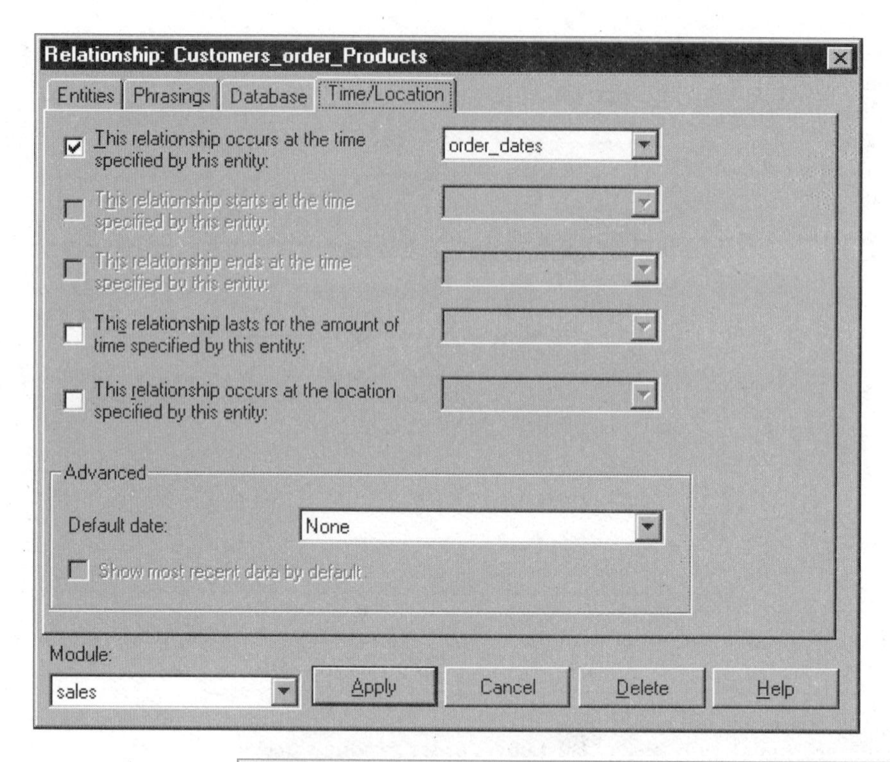

Once the entities and relationships have been defined, submit the query again. This time it is able to execute with no problem:

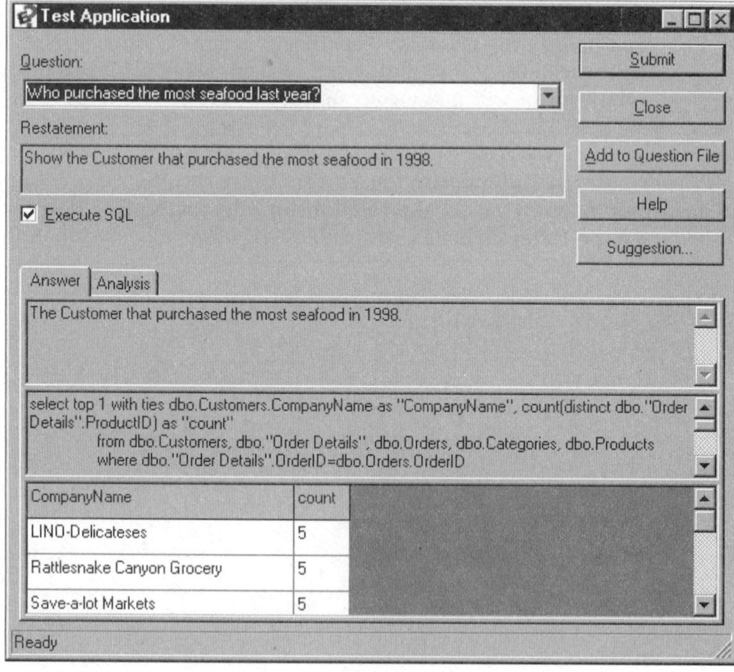

Since the Execute SQL option is enabled, the query is executed and the result set is displayed at the bottom of the dialog. While viewing the result set can sometimes help you spot problems more quickly, you should also take a close look at the SQL generated. You can do this on screen, or click on Add to Question File to add the question to the .eqq file for regression testing.

It's a good idea to add all questions you troubleshoot interactively to the question file. Remember, sometimes a change you make to fix one problem may have unexpected repercussions.

The Analysis tab allows you to view the entities and phrasings used to build the query. This can provide you with additional information when troubleshooting a question:

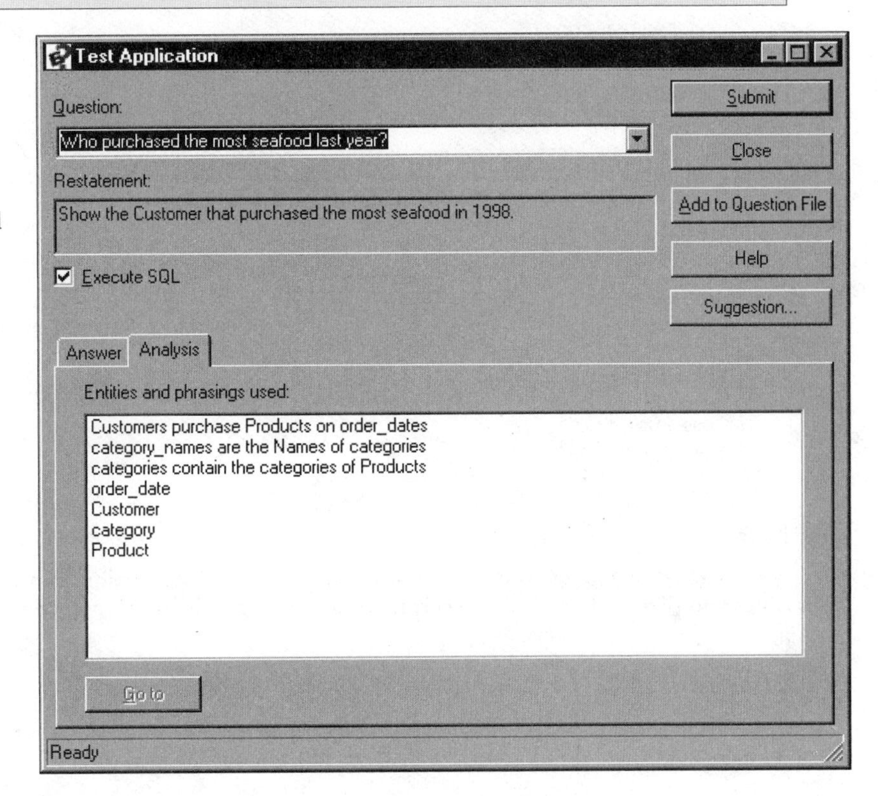

Deploying an English Query Application

Once you have defined your entities and relationships and tested your application thoroughly, you are ready to deploy your English Query application. Deploying an application consists of the following steps:

- Building your English Query application
- Writing code that uses your English Query application
- Distributing the English Query application and the English Query engine

We'll look at each of these steps. However, first, let's examine the files in an English Query project.

Project Files

While in development, an English Query project is composed of the following three files:

EQP File

This file is called the **project file**. It contains database connection information and the settings for global variables, such as the names of the regression files. A sample .eqp file is shown below:

```
Project: "sales.eqp";
EQVersion: 7.0;

Module: "sales", "sales.eqm";

Globals {
   Database: "DRIVER=SQL Server;SERVER=(local);APP=Microsoft® English
Query;WSID=BRAIN;DATABASE=Northwind;TranslationName=Yes;QueryLogFile=Yes";
   DBMSType: "SQL Server";
   DBMSVersion: "07.00.0623";
   UserContext: Yes;
   OuterJoins: Yes;
   RegressionQuestFile: "sales.eqq";
   RegressionOutFile: "sales.eqo";
   RegressionSaveFile: "sales.eqs";
   TestLoadSampleData: Yes;
   TestLoadWords: Yes;
   TestAddWords: "500";
   DBMaxRows: "100";
   DBTimeOut: "120";
   DefaultModule: "sales";
   }
```

EQM File

The .eqm file is the **module file**. It contains definitions of tables, fields, joins, entities, relationships, phrasings and dictionary entries. Excerpts from the .eqm file are shown below:

```
Module: "sales";
EQVersion: 7.0;
Table "dbo.Customers" {
   Fields: "CustomerID", "CompanyName", "ContactName", "ContactTitle", "Address",
"City", "Region", "PostalCode", "Country", "Phone", "Fax";
   Keys: "CustomerID";
   }
```

Each database table that is included in the project is listed, along with the fields it contains.

The field attributes are described in detail directly below the table definition:

```
Field "CustomerID" {
   Table: "dbo.Customers";
   DataType: String;
   Nullable: No;
   }

Field "CompanyName" {
   Table: "dbo.Customers";
   DataType: String;
   Nullable: No;
   Capitalization: First_Letter_Of_Each_Word;
   }
```

The field attributes listed are based on the database schema. The capitalization attribute is discovered based on the data in the fields when the field or the table that contains it is added to the project. It can be modified by editing the field properties on the **Database** tab of the domain editor.

Join information is determined by examining the primary key and foreign key relationships in the database:

```
Join "dbo.Orders.CustomerID~dbo.Customers.CustomerID"[0] {
   SourceTable: "dbo.Orders";
   SourceField: "CustomerID";
   DestinationTable: "dbo.Customers";
   DestinationField: "CustomerID";
   }
```

Entity information includes values you specifically define, such as the words used to reference the entity and the fields the entity includes. It also may include information discovered from the database, such as a sampling of the data. This sampling helps the English Query engine parse the query.

```
Entity "Customer" {
   Isa: Person;
   Words: "Customer", "customer";
   DBObject: Yes;
   TableIsEntity: Yes;
   Table: "dbo.Customers";
   Fields: "CompanyName";
   }


Entity "customer_name" {
   Words: "customer name";
   DBObject: Yes;
   TableIsEntity: No;
   NameType: ProperNoun;
   MemorizeNames: Yes;
   Table: "dbo.Customers";
   Fields: "CompanyName";
   SampleData: "Alfreds Futterkiste", "Ana Trujillo Emparedados y helados",
"Antonio Moreno Taquería", "Around the Horn";
   }
```

Relationship information includes the table containing the join on which the relationship is based and a list of entities included in the relationship:

```
Relationship "Customers_order_Products" {
   JoinTable: "dbo.Order Details";
   When: "Customers_order_Products"[2];
   }

EntsInRel "Customers_order_Products"[0] {
   Entity: "Product";
   }

EntsInRel "Customers_order_Products"[1] {
   Entity: "Customer";
   }

EntsInRel "Customers_order_Products"[2] {
   Entity: "order_date";
   }
```

```
Phrasing "Customers_order_Products"[0] {
   SVOPhrasing;
   Subject: "Customers_order_Products"[1];
   Verb: "order";
   Object: "Customers_order_Products"[0];
   }

Phrasing "Customers_order_Products"[1] {
   SVOPhrasing;
   Subject: "Customers_order_Products"[1];
   Verb: "purchase";
   Object: "Customers_order_Products"[0];
   }

Phrasing "Customers_order_Products"[2] {
   SVPhrasing;
   Subject: "Customers_order_Products"[1];
   Verb: "pay";
   Prep: "for";
   PrepObj: "Customers_order_Products"[0];
   }
```

If any of these entities have special properties, such as designating when an event occurs (time entity) or a SQL condition it depends on, these properties will also be listed. An example of this is:

```
   When: "Customers_order_Products"[2];
```

Notice that the `[2]` subscript refers to the `order_date` entity.

Dictionary entries are listed as language properties. Notice that a new word entry includes all of the information you defined. A synonym will either be a `ReadAs` or `WriteAs` synonym. In the example shown, the word *fish* would be read as *seafood*:

```
LanguageProperty seafood {
   Type: NewWord;
   PartOfSpeech: CommonNoun;
   Word: "seafood";
   IrregularType: Plural;
   IrregularForm: "seafood";
   }

LanguageProperty fish {
   Type: ReadAs;
   Word: "fish";
   Associate: "seafood";
   }
```

The `.eqp` and `.eqm` files are ASCII files and may be edited directly. However, unless you are very comfortable with what you're doing, editing these files may cause unwanted repercussions. It is generally better to use the domain editor to modify your application.

EQC File

The `.eqc` file is a **compiled connection file**. Although it is an ASCII file, it should not be edited directly. This file is used when testing your English Query application. Although it may be used when creating a session with the English Query engine, this is not recommended. Using the `.eqc` file to establish an English Query application is not as efficient as using a fully built binary English Query application. In addition, entity values that should be added to the domain are not added until the application is built.

Building an English Query Application

The English Query domain editor allows you to build a binary `.eqd` file by running Tools | Build Application. If you have selected to include values for a number of entities and your database has a lot of data, this may take some time. In addition, make sure you have enough disk space. The size of the `.eqd` file will increase dramatically with the amount of data it needs to include.

Using an English Query Application

A session with an English Query application is established through an in-process ActiveX server, `MSEQOLE.DLL`. This means that you can use your English Query application in any environment that allows you to use COM automation servers. These environments include:

- Active Server Pages
- Visual Basic
- Visual C++

When choosing the development environment, keep in mind the tools with which your developers have experience, as well as other application and business requirements. If you are using English Query as part of a Web solution, you may find that Active Server Pages will meet your needs. However, for performance and scalability, you may be better off building an ActiveX component with either Visual Basic or Visual C++. Let's walk through an example using Visual Basic as the COM controller.

> **Although the example is provided in Visual Basic, using the `MSEQOLE.DLL` objects from any other COM controller is very similar.**
>
> **The example provided here includes only the most fundamental coding in order to demonstrate the key steps involved in creating an application that can use an English Query application. Code to gracefully handle all possible user input will be much more involved.**

Setting a Reference to the Library

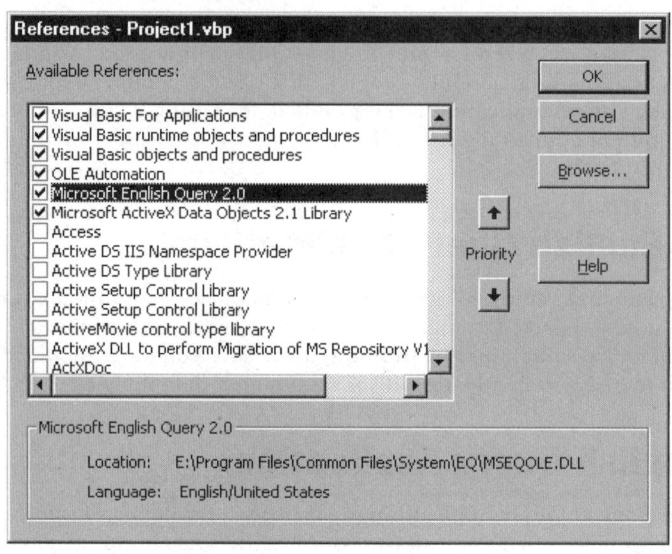

When writing the application in Visual Basic, a reference to the Microsoft English Query 2.0 library or Microsoft English Query Type Library is set by running Project | References. Before you can reference the English Query library, the English Query core components must first be installed on your Visual Basic development machine. If this is the same machine you have been using to build your English Query application, using the Domain Editor, the files will already be installed. Otherwise, you will need to select them by running SQL Server installation.

> **Notice that a reference to the Microsoft ActiveX Data Objects 2.1 Library is also set. ADO, OLE DB, RDO, or ODBC is required in order to actually run the query returned by Microsoft English Query (MSEQ).**

Project Overview

The Visual Basic project has two forms, `frmMain` and `frmClarify`. `frmMain` is shown below:

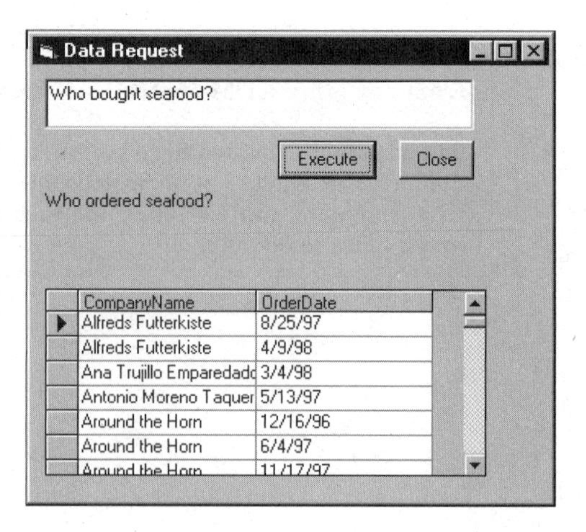

The controls on frmMain are described in this table:

Control Class	Control Name
TextBox	txtEnglish
CommandButton	cmdExecute
CommandButton	cmdClose
Label	lblAnswer
DataGrid	DataGrid1

You will need to add the Microsoft DataGrid Control 6.0 to your toolbox. To do this, right-click on the toolbox and run Components.

The sample application will use ADO to execute the queries. We want to prevent users from clicking on the cmdExecute button until the open recordset has been closed. For that reason, code will be added to disable the cmdExecute button after a query has been executed. We'll see that code a little later. To close the recordset and enable the cmdExecute button, the following code has been added to the cmdClose_Click event:

```
Private Sub cmdClose_Click()
   rs.Close
   cmdExecute.Enabled = True
End Sub
```

The other form in the project is frmClarify. It is displayed when clarification about an entity is needed. It is shown:

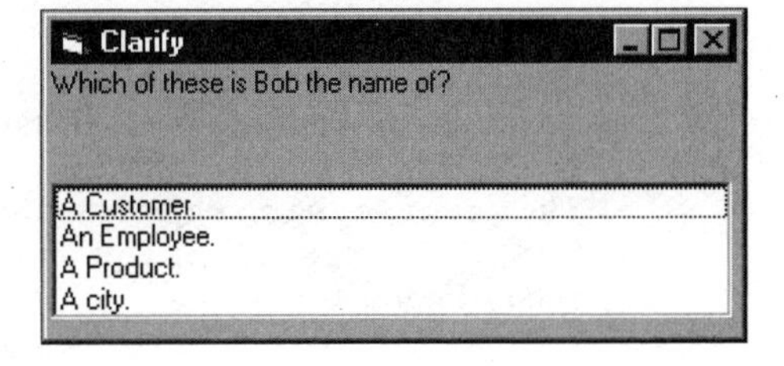

The controls on frmClarify are described here:

Control Class	Control Name
Label	lblClarify
ListBox	lstChoices

Opening a Session

At minimum, we need to declare a Session object and a Response object variable. The Session object is used to initiate the domain and parse the request. The Response object will hold the results of the ParseRequest method. Their ProgIDs are Mseq.Session and Mseq.Response, respectively. These variables should be declared in the General Declarations section of the frmMain form module. These are declared as shown below:

```
Private eqs As Mseq.Session
Public eqr As Mseq.Response
'Public because it will be referenced from another form

Private rs As ADODB.Recordset
Private conn As ADODB.Connection
```

Before we can use the Session object, we will need to create an instance of it. The code below, which should be added to frmMain, shows how the CreateObject function is used to instantiate the Session object. The Response object does not need to be instantiated because it is not externally creatable. The only way to set a reference to a Response object is through the ParseRequest method of the Session object:

```
Private Sub Form_Load()
   Set eqs = CreateObject("Mseq.session")
   eqs.InitDomain (App.Path & "\sales.eqd")
   Set conn = CreateObject("ADODB.Connection")
   Set rs = CreateObject("ADODB.Recordset")
   conn.CursorLocation = adUseClient
   conn.Open("DRIVER=SQL Server;SERVER=(local);DATABASE=Northwind")
   Set rs.ActiveConnection = conn
   rs.CursorType = adOpenStatic
End Sub
```

> **If are using the English Query application from an ASP, you need to use `Server.CreateObject` to instantiate the `Mseq.Session` object.**
>
> **The `Mseq.Session` object should not be confused with the** Session **object provided by ASP. The `Mseq.Session` object is used to create a session with the English Query Engine.**

The InitDomain method of the Session object is used to establish a session with a particular application. You need to provide the path and filename of either the .eqd file or the .eqc file. In this example, the Path property of the Visual Basic App object was used to indicate that the sales.eqd file is in the same directory as the executable.

> **The declarations and instantiations for the ADO objects are also shown in order to help you understand the code in the following sections.**

Parsing a Request

After a user enters an English sentence and requests that a query be executed, the first thing we need to do is call the `ParseRequest` method of the `Session` object as shown below:

```
Private Sub cmdExecute_Click()
   Dim doneParsing As Boolean

   Set eqr = eqs.ParseRequest(txtEnglish.Text)
   Do Until doneParsing = True
      doneParsing = HandleResponse
   Loop
End Sub
```

The method accepts the English string to be translated as its only argument. In this case, the string is in the `Text` property of the `txtEnglish` control. The `ParseRequest` method returns a reference to a `Response` object. The `Response` object may be an `ErrorResponse`, a `CommandResponse`, or a `UserClarifyResponse` object.

Handling a Response

The `ErrorResponse`, `CommandResponse`, and `UserClarifyResponse` objects all inherit from the `Response` object. This means that they all implement the `Type` property. It also means that a generic `Response` object can hold references to each of them. However, the `ErrorResponse`, `CommandResponse`, and `UserClarifyResponse` objects implement very different properties and methods. If you want to reference these unique properties and methods through the generic `Response` object, you will need to code very carefully to avoid runtime errors. Always check the `Type` property of the `Response` object before referencing any other property, method, or event.

The `Type` property lets us know what type of `Response` object the variable references. Its possible values are stored in the `nlResponse` enumeration. The three values that concern us here are:

Constant	Value	Response object type
`nlResponseCommand`	0	`CommandResponse`
`nlResponseError`	2	`ErrorResponse`
`nlResponseUserclarify`	3	`UserClarifyResponse`

The code below shows how the `ErrorResponse`, `CommandResponse`, and `UserClarifyResponse` objects can be declared and references to them set to the generic `Response` object, based on the value of the `Type` property (add the code overleaf to `frmMain`):

```
Public Function HandleResponse() As Boolean
   Dim eqCR As Mseq.CommandResponse
   Dim eqUCR As Mseq.UserClarifyResponse
   Dim eqErr As Mseq.ErrorResponse

   Select Case eqr.Type
      Case nlResponseCommand
         Set eqCR = eqr
         HandleResponse = True
      Case nlResponseError
         Set eqErr = eqr
         HandleResponse = True
      Case nlResponseUserclarify
         Set eqUCR = eqr
         HandleResponse = False
   End Select
End Function
```

The `HandleResponse` function returns `True` if the `CommandResponse` is of type `nlResponseCommand` or `nlResponseError`. If the `CommandResponse` object is of type `nlResponseUserClarify`, the function returns `False`. You'll see how the return value of this function is used in the application a little later. First, let's take a look at the code that needs to execute for each type of response. As each type of response is discussed, more code will be added to this function.

CommandResponse

A `CommandResponse` is returned when English Query was able to translate the English into SQL or answer the question directly. An example of the latter is a question that does not depend on the database, such as "What time is it?"

The `CommandResponse` object exposes a `Commands` collection, a `Restatement` property, and a `Type` property. The `Commands` collection contains `AnswerCommand` objects and `Command` objects. The `CmdID` property identifies the type of object. The code below shows how the `CmdID` property is checked to determine if the command returned contains a SQL query or if it is an `AnswerCommand`. If the command is a query, the following occurs:

- The `Restatement` property is displayed in the `lblAnswer` control
- The query is executed and the results returned to the `rs` variable
- The DataGrid control's `DataSource` is set to the result set that was returned
- The `cmdExecute` control's `Enabled` property is set to `False`

> **Disabling the `cmdExecute` button prevents users from trying to execute another query before the recordset has been closed (by clicking on the Close button). The `cmdClose_Click` event procedure was shown earlier.**

If the command is an `AnswerCommand`, the answer is displayed in the `lblAnswer` control:

```
Public Function HandleResponse() As Boolean
   Dim eqCR As Mseq.CommandResponse
   Dim eqUCR As Mseq.UserClarifyResponse
   Dim eqErr As Mseq.ErrorResponse

   Select Case eqr.Type
      Case nlResponseCommand
         Set eqCR = eqr
         If eqCR.Commands(0).CmdID = nlCmdQuery Then
            lblAnswer.Caption = eqCR.Restatement
            rs.Open (eqCR.Commands(0).SQL)
            Set DataGrid1.DataSource = rs
            cmdExecute.Enabled = False
         ElseIf eqCR.Commands(0).CmdID = nlCmdAnswer Then
            lblAnswer.Caption = eqCR.Commands(0).Answer
         End If
         HandleResponse = True
      Case nlResponseError
         Set eqErr = eqr
         HandleResponse = True
      Case nlResponseUserclarify
         Set eqUCR = eqr
         HandleResponse = False
   End Select
End Function
```

It is important to note that the `CommandResponse` object contains a collection of `Command` objects. A sophisticated application will handle every `Command` object in the collection. For simplicity's sake, the code shown here extracts information from only the first instance of the `Command` object.

The handling of the returned data has been simplified by using ADO and the DataGrid control. In a more fully functional application, you would need to iterate through the recordset and check for column names, data types, and values.

ErrorResponse

A reference to an `ErrorResponse` object is returned when English Query is unable to parse the question. This occurs when the question contains entities or verbs the English Query application doesn't know about. The `ErrorResponse` object has a `Description` property that contains a detailed description of the reason English Query could not translate the question. The code on the next page shows how the error description can be displayed in the `lblAnswer` control:

```
Public Function HandleResponse() As Boolean
   Dim eqCR As Mseq.CommandResponse
   Dim eqUCR As Mseq.UserClarifyResponse
   Dim eqErr As Mseq.ErrorResponse

   Select Case eqr.Type
      Case nlResponseCommand
         Set eqCR = eqr
         If eqCR.Commands(0).CmdID = nlCmdQuery Then
            lblAnswer.Caption = eqCR.Restatement
            rs.Open (eqCR.Commands(0).SQL)
            Set DataGrid1.DataSource = rs
            cmdExecute.Enabled = False
         ElseIf eqCR.Commands(0).CmdID = nlCmdAnswer Then
            lblAnswer.Caption = eqCR.Commands(0).Answer
         End If
         HandleResponse = True
      Case nlResponseError
         Set eqErr = eqr
         lblAnswer.Caption = eqErr.Description
         HandleResponse = True
      Case nlResponseUserclarify
         Set eqUCR = eqr
         HandleResponse = False
   End Select
End Function
```

UserClarifyResponse

In some situations, a user may need to be asked to clarify what is meant by certain words or phrases in the question. One situation in which this might occur is if an entity's meaning is ambiguous. Ambiguity is frequently the result of an entity that was defined without including its values in the domain. However, it may also result from new entries that have been added to the database after the English Query application was built and distributed. For example, suppose the `Employee` entity and the `Customer` entity both have relationships that define where they are located. If you ask the question, "Where is John Doe?" English Query will examine the domain to determine whether John Doe is an employee or a customer. If it cannot make that determination, a reference to a `UserClarifyResponse` object will be returned.

> **It is important to point out that a question may require more than one clarification. For this reason, it is important to continue processing clarifications until the `ParseRequest` method returns a reference to either an `ErrorResponse` or a `CommandResponse` object.**

A `UserClarifyResponse` object contains a collection of `UserInput` objects. As with the `Response` object, the `UserInput` property may contain a reference to one of three object types: the `ListInput`, `StaticInput`, and `TextInput` objects. The `StaticInput` object contains static informational text that is used in a clarification. The `TextInput` object is used when the user must enter a value for the clarification. For example, if the user asks, "Who are the new employee?" English Query may ask for a definition of what makes an employee new. The `ListInput` object is used when the clarification requires a user to choose from a list of entities. Let's look at an example of how code can be added to the `HandleResponse` function to deal with a `ListInput` clarification:

```
Public Function HandleResponse() As Boolean
   Dim i As Integer
   Dim Items() As Variant
   Dim eqCR As Mseq.CommandResponse
   Dim eqUCR As Mseq.UserClarifyResponse
   Dim eqErr As Mseq.ErrorResponse

   Dim eqUI As Mseq.UserInput

   Select Case eqr.Type
      Case nlResponseCommand
         Set eqCR = eqr
         If eqCR.Commands(0).CmdID = nlCmdQuery Then
            lblAnswer.Caption = eqCR.Restatement
            rs.Open (eqCR.Commands(0).SQL)
            Set DataGrid1.DataSource = rs
            cmdExecute.Enabled = False
         ElseIf eqCR.Commands(0).CmdID = nlCmdAnswer Then
            lblAnswer.Caption = eqCR.Commands(0).Answer
         End If
         HandleResponse = True

      Case nlResponseError
         Set eqErr = eqr
         lblAnswer.Caption = eqErr.Description
         HandleResponse = True

      Case nlResponseUserclarify
         Set eqUCR = eqr
         Set eqUI = eqUCR.UserInputs(0)
         If eqUI.Type = nlInputList Then
            frmClarify.lblClarify = eqUI.Caption
            For i = 0 To eqUI.ItemCount - 1
               Items = eqUI.Items
               frmClarify.lstChoices.AddItem Items(i)
            Next
            frmClarify.Show vbModal
            Set frmClarify = Nothing
         End If
         HandleResponse = False

   End Select
End Function
```

This example tests the value of the `Type` property of the `UserInput` object to ensure that it is an `InputList`. It then displays the `Caption` property in `lblControl` on the `frmClarify` form. The list of choices is stored in an array of variants named `Items`. The `ItemCount` property of the `UserInput` object returns the number of items in the array. The code iterates through the `Items` array, adding each string to the `ListBox` control on `frmClarify`. Finally, `frmClarify` is displayed as a modal dialog:

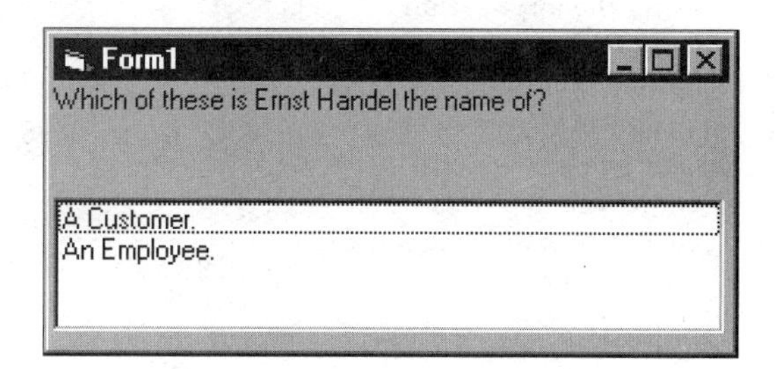

Notice that a new variable of the type `Mseq.UserInput` is declared and set to reference the first item in the `UserInputs` collection of the `UserClarifyResponse` object. In addition, notice that a reference to the `Items` array is stored in a variant variable named `Items`. This syntax is necessary because the following code generates an error:

```
frmClarify.lstChoices.AddItem eqUCR.UserInputs(0).Items(i)
```

After the user selects the appropriate entity, we need to add that information to the request. To do so, we set the `Selection` property of the `UserInput` object, then call the `Reply` method of the `Response` object (or `UserClarifyResponse` object). Make sure to set the `Response` object equal to the new reference. The code below shows the syntax for doing this:

```
Private Sub lstChoices_DblClick()
   frmMain.eqr.UserInputs(0).Selection = lstChoices.ListIndex
   Set frmMain.eqr = frmMain.eqr.Reply
   Me.Hide
End Sub
```

In this case, the code is added to the `DblClick` event procedure of the `lstChoices` control on `frmClarify`.

Now the new `Response` object should be processed to determine whether it contains a query, an answer, an error, or another clarification request.

Distribution

Both `MSEQOLE.DLL` and your `.eqd` file must be distributed as part of the application. If you are using the application from within an application built in Visual Basic, you can use the Package and Deployment Wizard to ensure that the correct files are included, as shown:

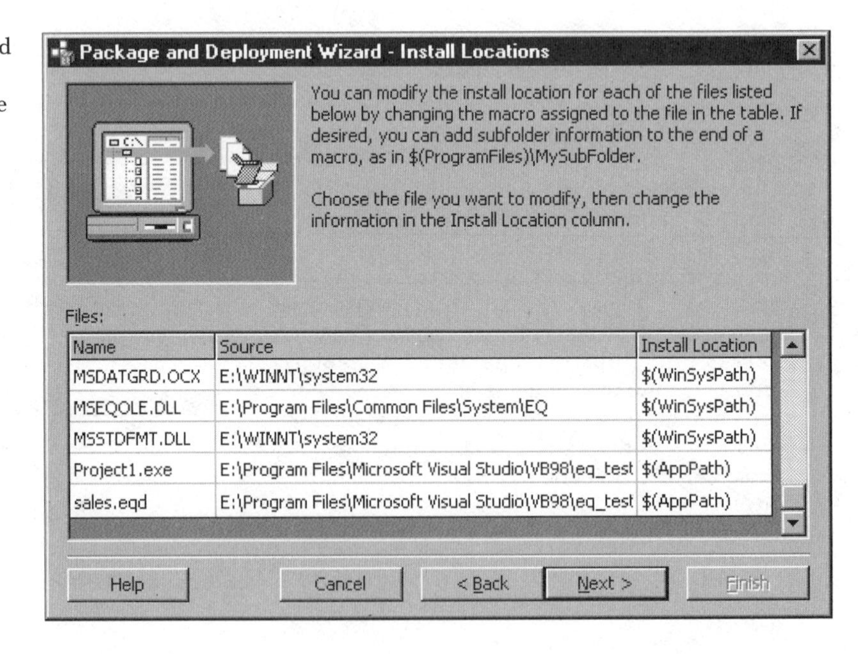

Notice that MSEQOLE.DLL will be installed to the WinSysPath location. You can select to install your .eqd file anywhere you want. However, in this case, it should be installed to the same path as the application because the example used the Path property of the App object to locate it in the call to InitDomain.

Regardless of the method you use to build the Setup program, you will need to ensure that MSEQOLE.DLL is properly installed and registered on the server where the application that uses English Query is being run. If you are planning to access English Query from within an ASP, you will need to install MSEQOLE.DLL on the Web server.

The location of the .eqd file depends on the implementation inside your code. In an application that is compiled and distributed, you will most likely want to install it to the application directory or a subdirectory beneath it. If you are deploying through ASP, you will locate the sales.eqd file inside a virtual directory.

What is Full-Text Search?

SQL Server 7.0 Standard edition and Enterprise edition provide the ability to perform a full-text search on information stored in a SQL database. This allows relational database information to be queried based on keywords and keyword proximity. It also provides the ability to search on inflected forms of words, such as plurals and various verb tenses. This provides enhanced information retrieval capabilities over what is possible through standard Transact-SQL pattern matching.

Full-Text Search is not installed during a Typical or Minimum installation. You must perform a Custom installation and select Full-Text Search.

Full-Text Search is implemented by the Microsoft Search Service. This service is installed when Full-Text Search's capabilities are installed on a Windows NT Server. It is not installed with the Desktop version of SQL Server. When installed, it is configured to start automatically using the local system account.

The Microsoft Search Service is responsible for creating and populating the full-text search catalog files. However, creation and population is requested through the SQL Server Enterprise Manager:

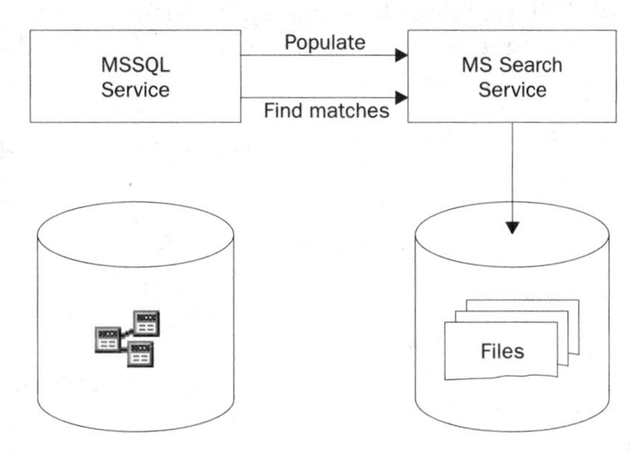

The Microsoft Search Service is also responsible for locating records that match a full-text search query and returning their unique identifiers to the MSSQL service:

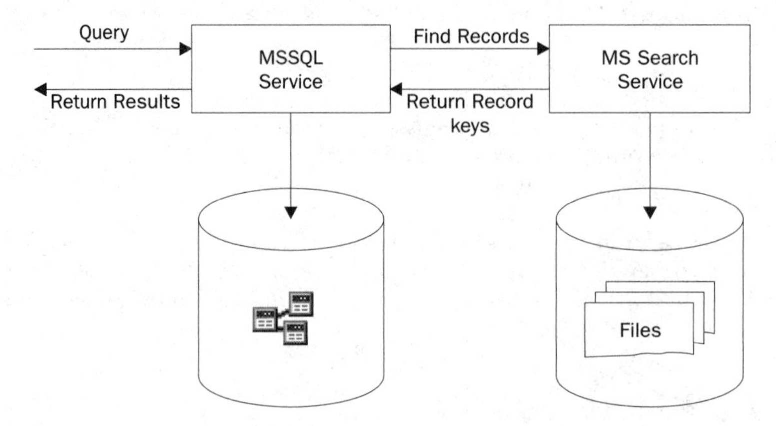

It is important to note that the full-text search catalog files are not stored in the relational database. Therefore, they are not backed up when the database is backed up. The correct procedure for disaster recovery when using Full-Text Search will be covered later in the chapter.

Benefits of Full-Text Search

Full-Text Search is an appropriate tool to use when you want to allow users to search a database for keywords that are part of a field. Obvious examples include columns that store descriptions, comments, and background information. A column that is enabled for full-text search can enable powerful searches for both exact values and more *fuzzy* data. The search can include any inflectional form of the word and the Boolean operators AND, AND NOT, and OR can be applied. In addition, when matches are found, you can specify that a rank value be returned along with the row identifier. This is helpful with large amounts of data because it allows you to sort the result set so that the most likely matches are at the top.

Limitations of Full-Text Search

As previously mentioned, Full-Text Search is only available on Windows NT Server. This means that Full-Text Search cannot be used in an environment where data is stored on the desktop computer. However, you can issue full-text queries from any client.

Another limitation is that a full-text catalog cannot span multiple databases. It also cannot index data from a column of a view.

Creating and Populating a Catalog

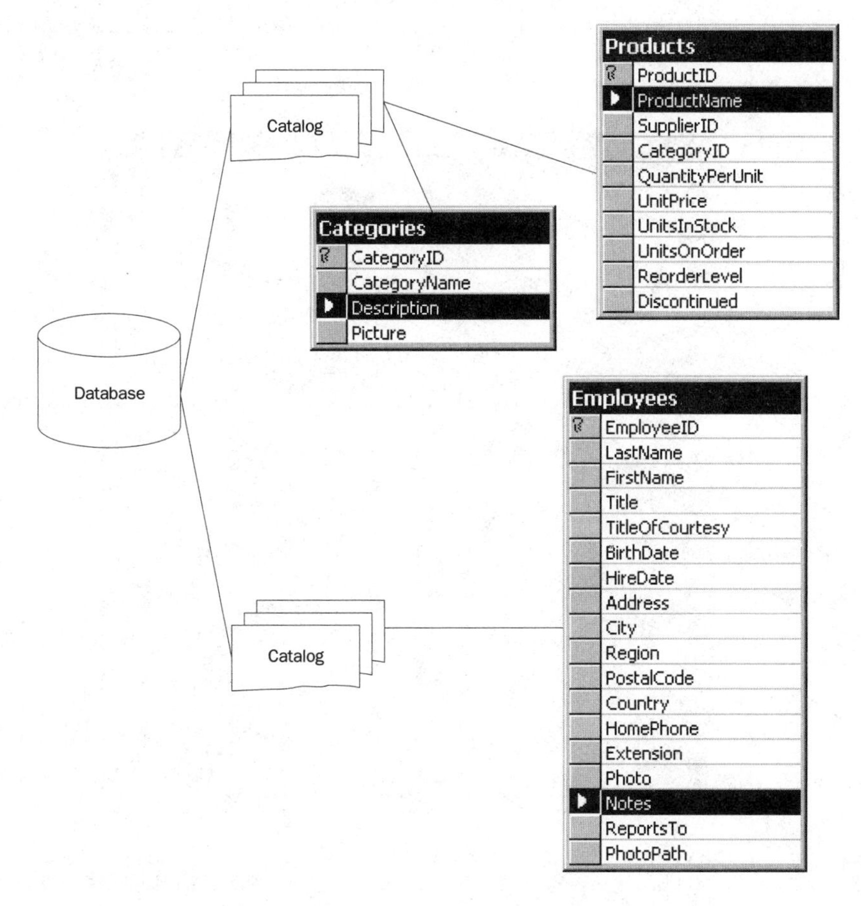

Each database that supports Full-Text Search can have one or more catalogs. However, a catalog cannot contain full-text indexes for multiple databases. Each catalog can contain full-text indexes to one or more tables. However, a table can only be included in a single full-text catalog. Each table that is indexed requires at least two columns:

- A unique identifier
- One or more character-based columns to be searchable through full-text search

Full-Text Search can be configured either through the SQL Server Enterprise Manager or by running stored procedures. Let's look at an example, using both methods.

Creating a Full-Text Catalog

Let's create a full-text catalog for the `Northwind` database through the SQL Server Enterprise Manager. Begin by expanding the Northwind node, then locate and right-click on the Full-Text Catalogs container. Run the New Full-Text Catalog command.

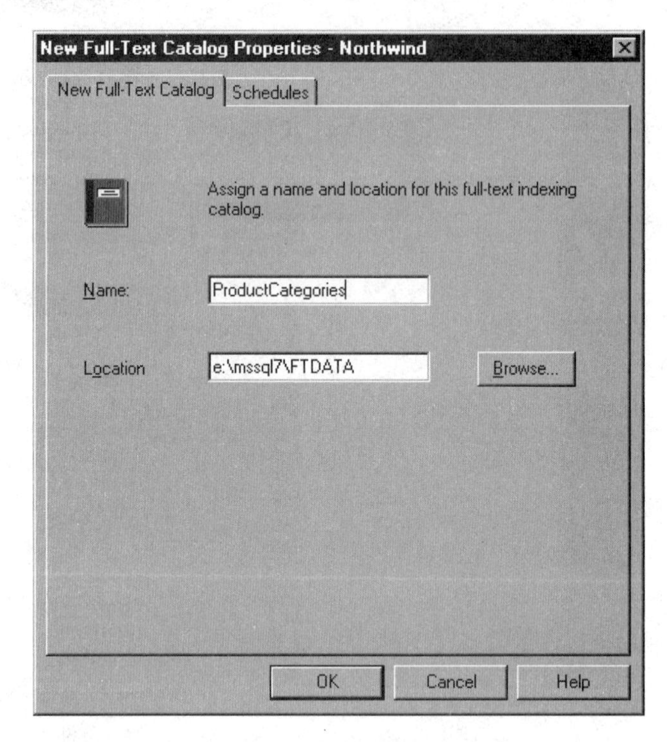

Provide a name for the catalog (in this case ProductCategories) and specify the location at which you'd like to store the catalog files. By default, catalog files are stored in the `MSSQL7\FTDATA` directory. Catalog files must be stored on the local computer and must be on non-removable media. The path specified here must be a directory path, not a network path specified using the Universal Naming Convention (UNC). Click on OK when you are finished.

Full-Text Search catalogs can be rather large. You need to ensure that you have sufficient disk space available on the drive you select.

Creating a Catalog with a Stored Procedure

The `sp_fulltext_catalog` stored procedure allows us to create a catalog, drop a catalog, populate a catalog, or rebuild a catalog. Its general syntax is shown below:

```
sp_fulltext_catalog [@ftcat =] 'fulltext_catalog_name',
[@action =] 'action'
[,[@path =] 'root_directory']
```

The three arguments to the stored procedure are as follows:

Argument	Description	Possible Values	
`ftcat`	This required argument defines the name of the catalog. Each catalog in a database must have a unique name.	Any unique string. You will want to name it using a descriptive name for the type of data it contains. You may want to precede the name with an `ft_` to differentiate it as a Full-Text catalog.	
`action`	This required argument specifies which action the stored procedure should take. Any of the following values can be specified:	`create`	Creates a new catalog. A row listing the catalog is added to `sysfulltextcatalogs`.
		`drop`	Drops an existing catalog by deleting the files and removing the reference in `sysfulltextcatalogs`. This command will only succeed for catalogs that do not contain table metadata.
		`rebuild`	Deletes, then recreates, an existing catalog. This command does not repopulate the catalog.
		`start_full`	This command initiates a full repopulation.
		`start_incremental`	This command initiates an incremental repopulation.
		`stop`	This command halts a repopulation that is in progress.
path	This optional argument specifies the path to the root directory that will contain the catalog. If the path is not specified, it is the `\MSSQL7\FTDATA` directory.	The fully-qualified path to a directory on the local computer. The directory must already exist.	

For example, to create a catalog named `Employees` in the default directory, we would execute the following:

```
USE Northwind

EXEC sp_fulltext_catalog 'Employees', 'create'
```

sysfulltextcatalogs

The sysfulltextcatalogs system table contains references to each catalog that has been created. After creating the ProductCategories catalog and the Employees catalog, run the following statement:

```
Select * from sysfulltextcatalogs
```

The following results will be returned:

Ftcatid	Name	Status	Path
5	ProductCategories	0	NULL
6	Employees	0	NULL

The ftcatid column is a unique identifier for the column. It is used to identify the folder containing the files for that specific catalog. Since the catalogs were created at the default path, the Path column contains NULL.

The graphic below shows the folders that were created to contain these catalogs. Notice that one directory name ends with the number 5 and the other ends with the number 6. These numbers correlate to the ftcatid in sysfulltextcatalogs:

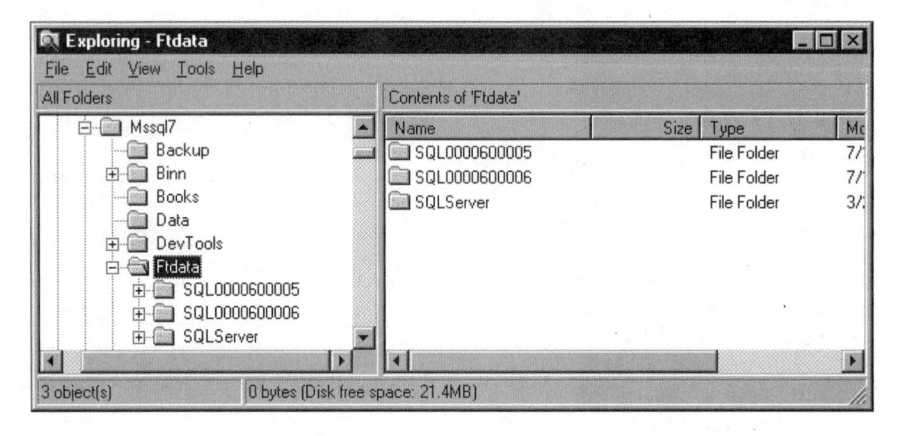

Enabling Full-Text Search on a Table

Once a catalog has been created, we need to enable full-text indexing on the appropriate tables. To do so, locate the table you'd like to index (in this case `ProductCategories`) and right-click on it. Run Full-Text Index Table | Define Full-Text Indexing on a Table. The Full-Text Indexing Wizard will be launched:

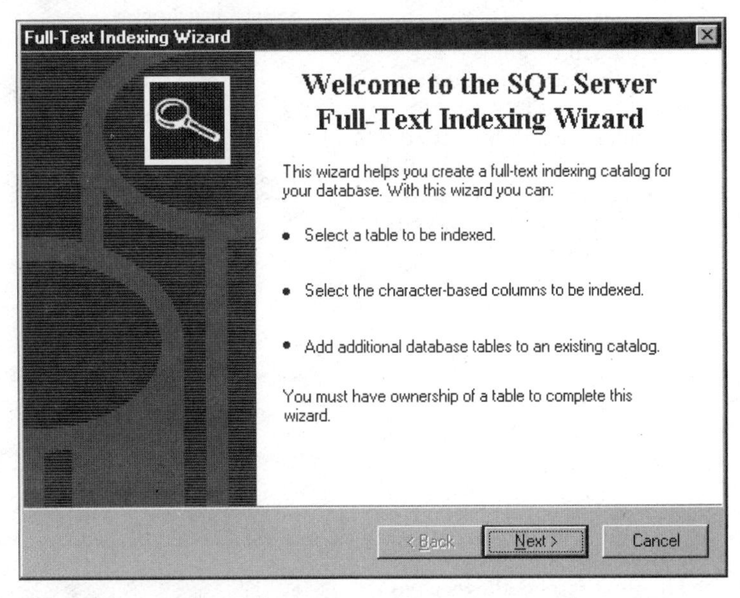

The opening screen of the wizard describes the steps in the process. Keep in mind that you must be a member of the `db_owner` role in order to add full-text indexing to a table. Click on Next to continue.

The next screen requires us to select a unique index. The index specified here will uniquely identify the row that contains a match. The column used as an index must be unique and cannot contain nulls. Usually, you will want to use the table's primary key as the unique identifier. Let's do that now by keeping the default of PK_Categories, then click on Next:

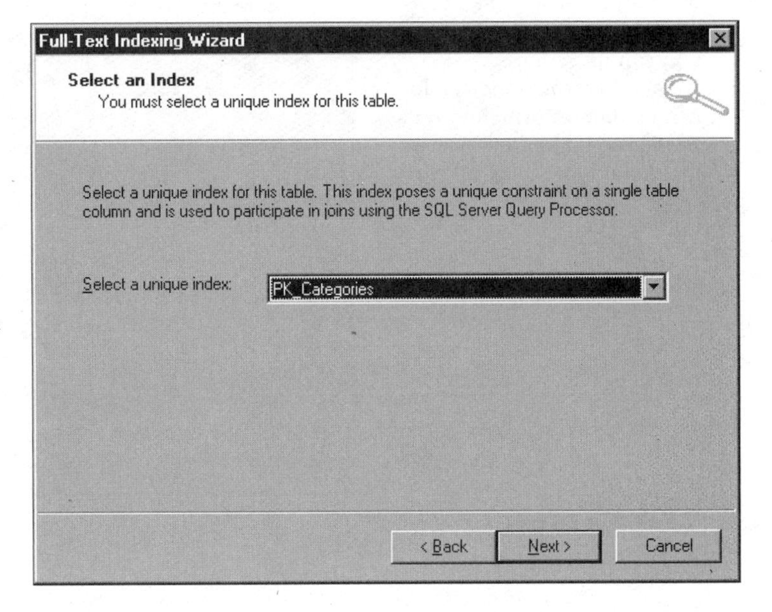

On the next screen, we add the column(s) that we would like included in the full-text catalog. All columns that have a character-based data type are listed in Available columns. To add them to the catalog, select them and click on Add. Add both columns to the Added columns list and click on Next:

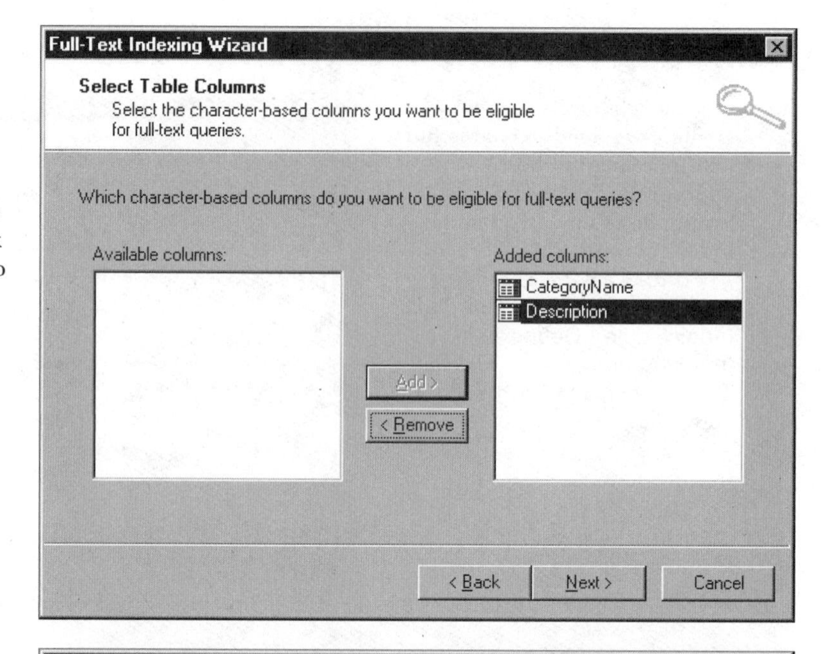

The next screen allows us to select the full-text catalog that should contain the data from this table. If you have not already created the catalog, you can do so here. Remember, only one catalog can contain information on a particular table. Let's accept the default and click on Next:

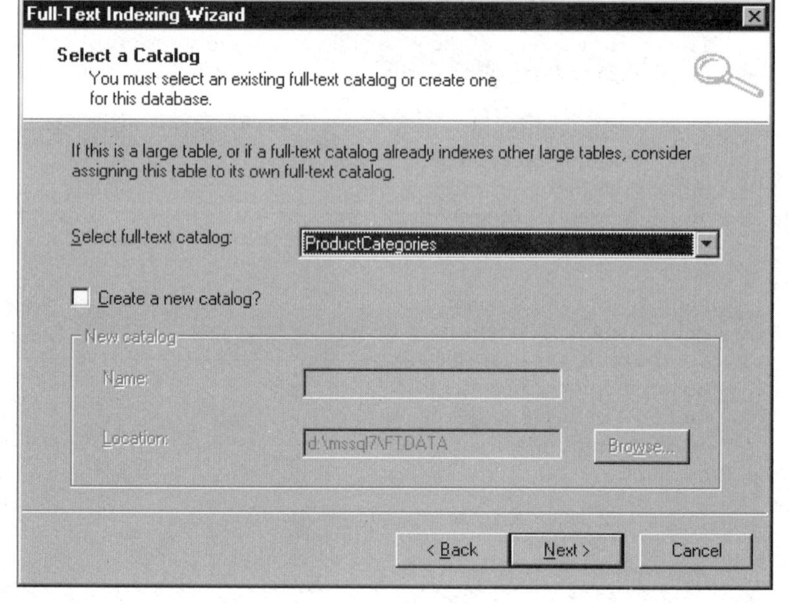

The next screen allows us to define population schedules. Population schedules will be discussed a little later in the chapter so for now just click on Next:

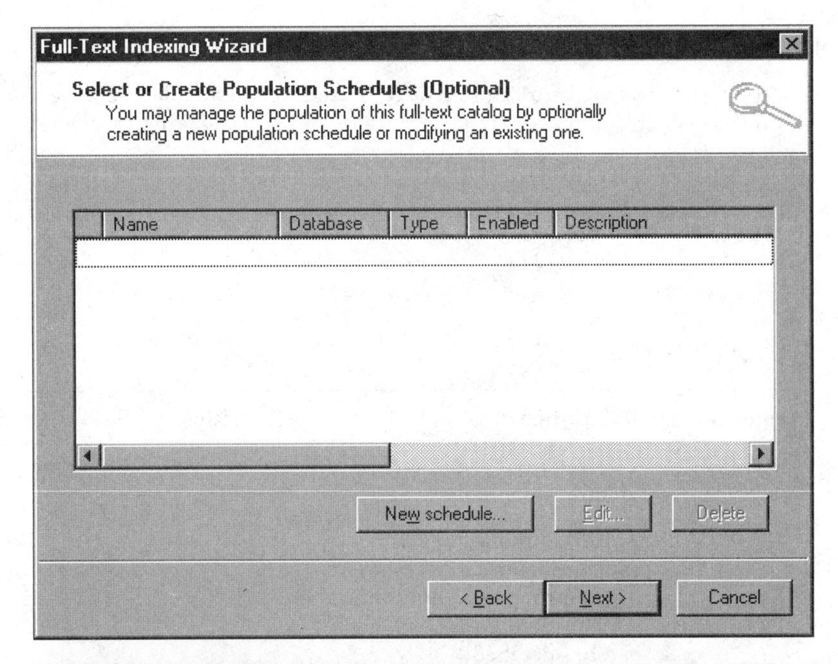

The final screen shows a summary of our selections. Click on Finish to add the table to the catalog. At this point, information about the table's schema is added to the catalog. However, the catalog has not been populated with any data:

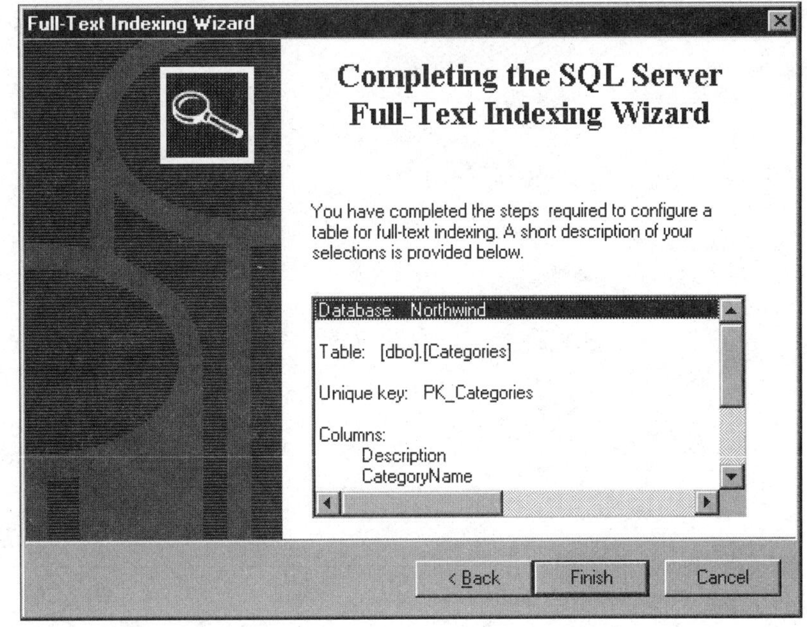

Before looking at how a catalog is populated, let's take a look at how we can add a table to a catalog using a stored procedures, `sp_fulltext_table` and `sp_fulltext_column`.

sp_fulltext_table

The sp_fulltext_table procedure is used to add a table's schema to a catalog, drop its schema from the catalog, and activate or deactivate full-text indexing for the table. Its general syntax is shown below:

```
sp_fulltext_table [@tabname =] 'qualified_table_name',
[@action =] 'action'
[,[@ftcat =] 'fulltext_catalog_name',
[@keyname =] 'unique_index_name']
```

The four arguments to the stored procedure are as follows:

Argument	Description	Possible Values	
tabname	This required argument identifies the table.	Any valid table name	
action	This required argument specifies which action the stored procedure should take. Any of the following values can be specified.	activate	Enables full-text indexing for the table by registering the table with the full-text catalog so that it will be indexed during the next population. This action cannot be taken until at least one character-based column has been added.
		create	Adds the table's metadata to the catalog. After performing the create action, you need to add one or more columns, then perform the activate action.
		deactivate	Prevents the table from participating in full-text indexing. However, the metadata is not removed from the catalog. The table can easily be reactivated and repopulated at a later time.

Argument	Description	Possible Values	
		drop	Removes the table's metadata from the catalog. If the table is active, it also deactivates it. You need to drop each table from a catalog before you can drop a catalog.
ftcat	This optional argument identifies the catalog.	Any valid catalog name. The catalog must already exist. This value must be supplied when creating a catalog, but should be NULL for all other actions.	
keyname	The column name of the unique index.	The name of a unique index. The index must be unique, not-nullable, and composed of a single column.	

sp_fulltext_column

The sp_fulltext_column procedure is used to add columns to and drop tables from a catalog. When columns are added, they are only registered for indexing. Indexing does not actually occur until population. The general syntax for sp_fulltext_column is shown below:

```
sp_fulltext_column [@tabname =] 'qualified_table_name',
[@colname =] 'column_name',
[@action =] 'action'
```

The three arguments to the stored procedure are as follows:

Argument	Description	Possible Values	
tabname	This required argument identifies the table.	Any valid table name	
colname	This required argument identifies the column being added.	Any name for a character-based column in the table.	
action	This required argument specifies which action the stored procedure should take. Any of the following values can be specified.	add	Adds a column to the full-text catalog associated with the table.
		drop	Removes a column from the full-text catalog associated with the table.

Example Using Stored Procedures

The following example shows how to associate the `Employees` table with the `Employees` catalog. The table's primary key will be used as the unique index. The `Notes` and `Title` columns will be added to the catalog for indexing:

```
EXEC sp_fulltext_table 'Employees', 'create', 'Employees', 'PK_Employees'
EXEC sp_fulltext_column 'Employees', 'Notes', 'add'
EXEC sp_fulltext_column 'Employees', 'Title', 'add'
EXEC sp_fulltext_table 'Employees', 'activate'
```

While creating a catalog and adding tables to it can be accomplished either through the SQL Server Enterprise Manger or by executing stored procedures, behind the scenes these two methods act somewhat differently. When stored procedures are used, the full directory and file structure for the index is built. When the wizards are used, only the `Build` directory is added. This causes a different behavior if a query requiring the catalog is run prior to initial population. A catalog created with stored procedures will simply return a zero-record result set. A catalog created with the wizards will generate the error:

Server: Msg 7623, Level 17, State 1, Line 1
Full-text query failed because full-text catalog 'Products' is not yet ready for queries.

Populating a Catalog

Indexing for full-text search is a processor-intensive activity. Therefore, unlike SQL Server indexes, a full-text search index is not created and modified in real-time. Instead, you need to explicitly populate a full-text catalog, both when it is first created and periodically in order to keep it as up-to-date with the database as possible. There are two types of population:

- Full population
- Incremental population

Let's look at their characteristics and requirements.

Full Population

Full population should be performed on a new catalog or if the schema of a table in the catalog changes. It is also the only type of population that can be performed for tables that do not include a `timestamp` column. As with most other full-text capabilities, full population can be performed either through the SQL Server Enterprise Manager or through running a stored procedure.

To initiate full population through the SQL Server Enterprise Manager, right-click on the catalog you'd like to populate and run Start Population | Full Population.

Full population can also be initiated by calling the sp_fulltext_catalog stored procedure with the start_full action as shown below:

```
EXEC sp_fulltext_catalog 'Employees', 'start_full'
```

Incremental Population

Incremental population is used to keep a full-text catalog up-to-date with changes that have occurred to the database. During incremental population, rows that have been added and modified since the last repopulation are indexed. Rows that have been deleted are removed from the catalog. In order for incremental population to be run, a table must include a timestamp column. If a table does not include a timestamp column, full population will occur.

As with most other full-text capabilities, incremental population can be performed either through the SQL Server Enterprise Manager or through running a stored procedure.

To initiate incremental population through the SQL Server Enterprise Manager, right-click on the catalog you'd like to populate and run Start Population | Incremental Population.

Incremental population can also be initiated by calling the sp_fulltext_catalog stored procedure with the start_incremental action as shown below:

```
EXEC sp_fulltext_catalog 'Employees', 'start_incremental'
```

Because population is disk and processor intensive, you will probably want to perform population during non-peak hours. Fortunately, you can schedule when you'd like population to occur, both for one-time and for periodic populations.

Scheduling Population

Scheduled population events are defined on the Schedule tab of the catalog's property pages. This can be accessed by double-clicking on the catalog or running Properties from the catalog's popup menu, then clicking on the Schedules tab. It can also be accessed directly by running Schedules from the catalog's popup menu.

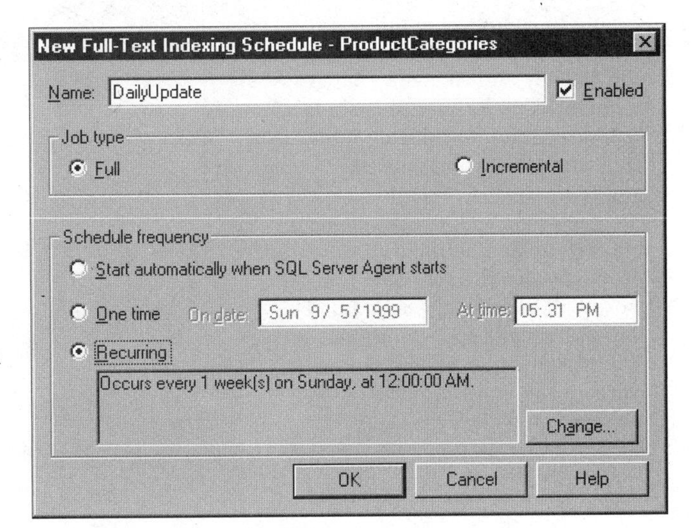

To add a scheduled population, click on New schedule. The following dialog will be displayed:

This dialog allows you to name the scheduled event, select whether it is a full or incremental population, and schedule how frequently you'd like the update to occur. By default, the frequency is a One time update, occurring at the time the dialog is displayed. If this is the first population, or a full population to adjust for some one-time modification, you may want to enter a later date and time. You can also select to have the population occur every time SQL Server agent starts or on a recurring basis. The default interval for a recurring population is once a week. You can modify the interval by clicking on Change:

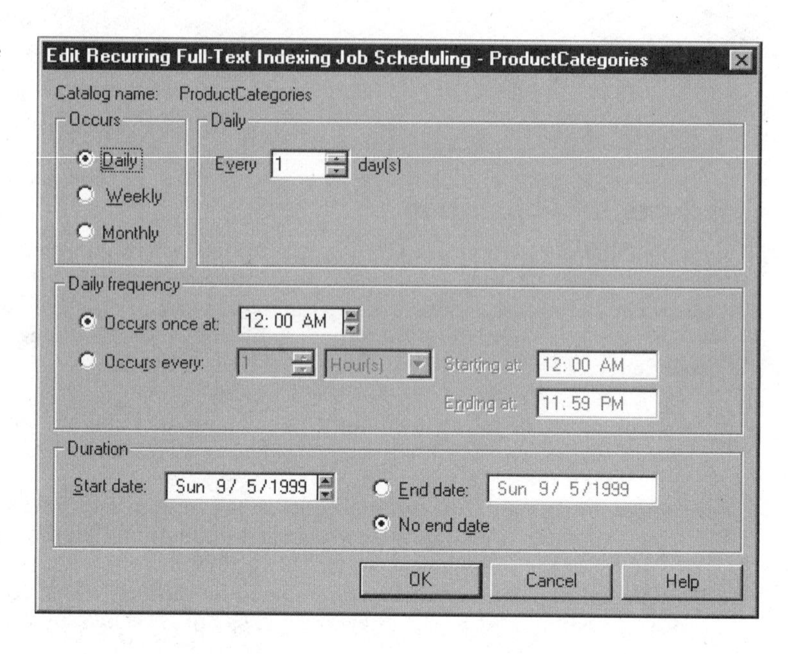

The interval you select should be based on how frequently the underlying data changes, the level of consistency required between the database and the full-text search capabilities, and the amount of processor time you can afford to devote to keeping the full-text catalog current. If you need high consistency and the data changes frequently, make sure to include a timestamp column in each table and schedule an incremental population.

Once you have configured the properties for the schedule and closed all dialogs, the scheduled population will appear on the Schedules tab as shown below. It can later be modified or deleted as required:

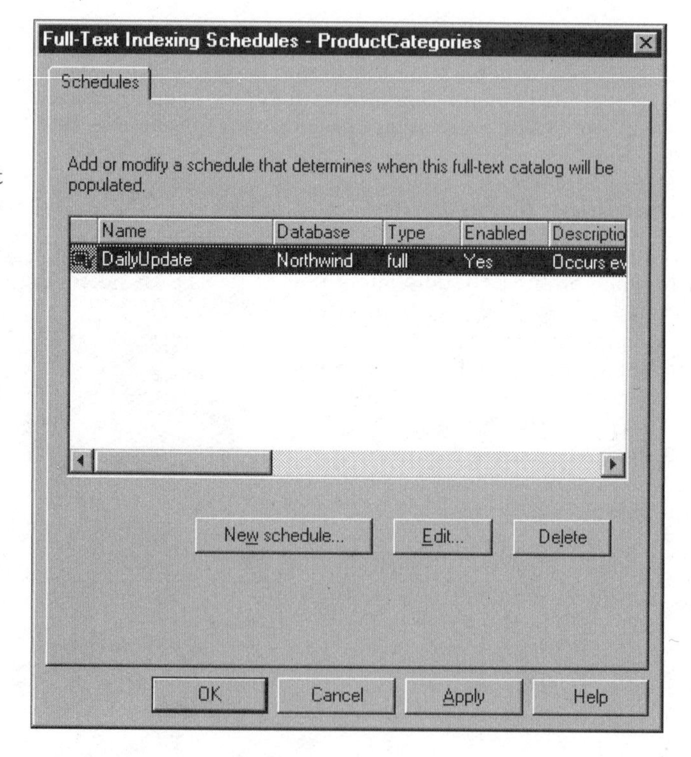

Noise Words

When a catalog is populated, the data in the character-based columns enabled for full-text indexing is gathered and any noise words it contains are deleted. Noise words are words that are unlikely to be important during a search, such as articles, prepositions, and the letters of the alphabet. Language-specific noise files are stored in the `MSSQL7\ftData\SQLServer\Config` directory. The language used is specified by the Unicode collation locale identifier you selected during SQL Server installation.

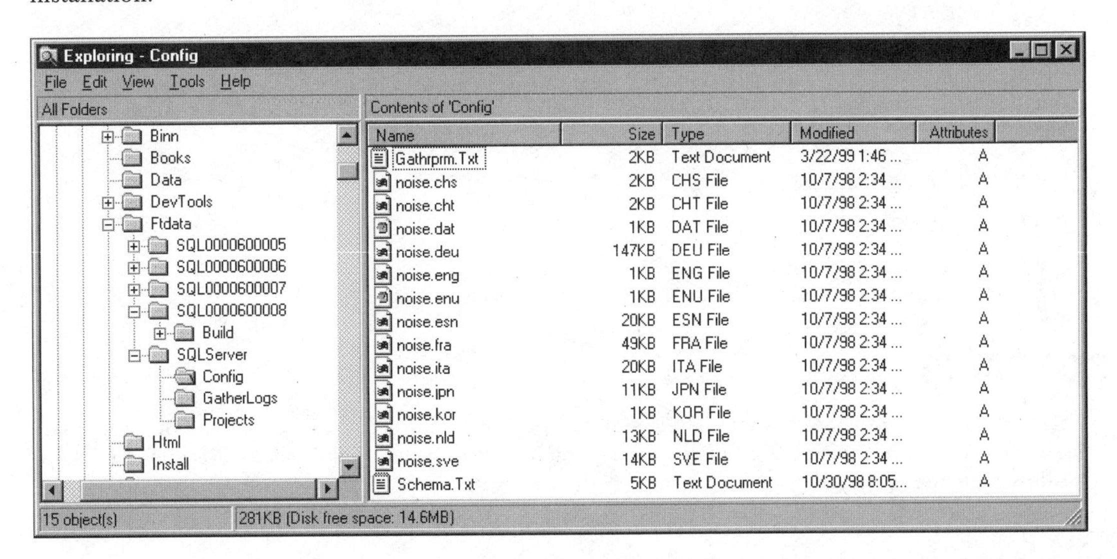

Noise files are ASCII files and may be modified in Notepad. For example, your database may have words that appear frequently enough that they are not relevant to searches. Adding these words to the noise file will prevent instances of them from being stored in the index. Keep in mind, however, that these noise word files are global to the SQL Server, not local to a specific catalog. After editing a noise file, you should run a full population.

> **The `noise.eng` file contains entries for UK English. The `noise.enu` file contains entries for US English. Although there is no initial difference between these files, if you are going to edit one, you will want to make sure to edit the one that corresponds to the Unicode locale identifier selected during SQL Server installation.**
>
> **One interesting point to note is that the word "while" appears in both the UK and US English files. The word "whilst" does not occur in either file.**

Executing Queries Using Full-Text Search

SQL Server 7.0 provides two SELECT statement predicates and two functions that can be used to execute queries against a full-text search catalog. These predicates can be used in a stored procedure or in a query passed to SQL Server from a Visual Basic, Visual C++, or Active Server Pages application. The two predicates are:

- CONTAINS
- FREETEXT

The two functions are:

- CONTAINSTABLE
- FREETEXTTABLE

Let's look at each, beginning with CONTAINS and CONTAINSTABLE.

CONTAINS

The CONTAINS predicate allows us to search the full-text catalog for a match based on particular criteria. The criteria used can require an exact match or an inflectional match. It is specified using the following general syntax:

```
CONTAINS
({column|*}, <'contains_search_condition'>)
```

The *column* can be any column on which full-text search has been enabled. If you'd like to search all columns in a particular catalog, use the asterisk (*). If the catalog contains information about multiple tables, you will need to qualify the asterisk with the table name. For example, if the ProductCategories catalog contained a full-text index for the Products table and for the Categories table, but you were only interested in searching for a match in the Categories table, you would use Categories.* as the column identifier.

At a bare minimum, the *contains_search_condition* is the word or phrase that should be located in the catalog. Let's look at a very simple example. Suppose you want to locate all of the employees who have obtained a Bachelor of Arts degree. Short biographies for the employees, including the degrees they have earned are stored in the Notes field. The Notes field is enabled for full-text search. To obtain a list of their first and last names, and the contents of the Notes field, we would perform a query as follows:

```
SELECT FirstName, LastName, Notes FROM Employees WHERE CONTAINS (Notes, 'BA')
```

Executing this query against the Employees table of the Northwind database returns the following results:

FirstName	LastName	Notes
Nancy	Davolio	Education includes a BA in psychology from Colorado State University in 1970. She also completed "The Art of the Cold Call." Nancy is a member of Toastmasters International.
Margaret	Peacock	Margaret holds a BA in English literature from Concordia College (1958) and an MA from the American Institute of Culinary Arts (1966). She was assigned to the London office temporarily from July through November 1992.
Anne	Dodsworth	Anne has a BA degree in English from St. Lawrence College. She is fluent in French and German.
Laura	Callahan	Laura received a BA in psychology from the University of Washington. She has also completed a course in business French. She reads and writes French.

To search for a phrase instead of a single word, enclose the phrase in quotes. For example, to locate members of Toastmasters International, we could perform the following query:

```
SELECT FirstName, LastName, Notes FROM Employees
WHERE CONTAINS (Notes, '"Toastmasters International"')
```

This query returns a result containing only Nancy Davolio's data.

Boolean operators can be used to perform more elaborate searches. For example, suppose that we are interested in the employees who earned any Bachelors degree. In this case, we could use the `OR` operator as follows:

```
SELECT FirstName, LastName, Notes FROM Employees
WHERE CONTAINS (Notes, 'BA OR BS')
```

This query returns a result set containing all of the employees where the `Notes` field contains 'BA' and all of the employees where the `Notes` field contains 'BS'.

The `AND` operator allows us to locate only records that contain both keywords. For example, suppose we were interested in locating an employee with a BA who also speaks French. In this case, we execute the query:

```
SELECT FirstName, LastName, Notes FROM Employees
WHERE CONTAINS (Notes, 'BA AND French')
```

This query returns information on Anne Dodsworth and Laura Callahan, the only two employees with a `Notes` field that contains 'BA' and 'French'.

The AND NOT operator allows us to locate records that contain one keyword, but not another. For example, we may be interested in locating the employees who have earned a BA, but not an MA. This query would be performed as follows:

```
SELECT FirstName, LastName, Notes FROM Employees
WHERE CONTAINS (Notes, 'BA AND NOT MA')
```

This query returns the result set shown below. Notice that Margaret Peacock is missing because she has also earned an MA:

FirstName	LastName	Notes
Nancy	Davolio	Education includes a BA in psychology from Colorado State University in 1970. She also completed "The Art of the Cold Call." Nancy is a member of Toastmasters International.
Anne	Dodsworth	Anne has a BA degree in English from St. Lawrence College. She is fluent in French and German.
Laura	Callahan	Laura received a BA in psychology from the University of Washington. She has also completed a course in business French. She reads and writes French.

We can also perform a wildcard search, based on a field containing words that start with a particular pattern. For example, suppose we were interested in obtaining a list of all employees who studied psychology, psychobiology, or psychiatry. We could execute the following query:

```
SELECT FirstName, LastName, Notes FROM Employees
WHERE CONTAINS (Notes, '"psych*"')
```

In the case of the Northwind database, two employees studied psychology, but there are no other instances of the psych prefix, so only two names will be returned.

The Microsoft Search Service understands grammatical inflections. Therefore, we can use the FORMSOF clause with the INFLECTIONAL keyword to search for any form of a particular word. This is helpful for locating words that may have been entered in either singular or plural form and for locating different tenses of a verb. For example, we may want to search for any graduates or people who hold degrees. To do so, we could execute an inflectional search as follows:

```
SELECT FirstName, LastName, Notes FROM Employees
WHERE CONTAINS (Notes, 'FORMSOF (INFLECTIONAL, graduate, degree)')
```

This query returns the following results:

FirstName	LastName	Notes
Janet	Leverling	Janet has a BS degree in chemistry from Boston College (1984). She has also completed a certificate program in food retailing management. Janet was hired as a sales associate in 1991 and promoted to sales representative in February 1992.
Michael	Suyama	Michael is a graduate of Sussex University (MA, economics, 1983) and the University of California at Los Angeles (MBA, marketing, 1986). He has also taken the courses "Multi-Cultural Selling" and "Time Management for the Sales Professional." He is fluent...
Anne	Dodsworth	Anne has a BA degree in English from St. Lawrence College. She is fluent in French and German.
Robert	King	Robert King served in the Peace Corps and traveled extensively before completing his degree in English at the University of Michigan in 1992, the year he joined the company. After completing a course entitled "Selling in Europe," he was transferred to the...
Steven	Buchanan	Steven Buchanan graduated from St. Andrews University, Scotland, with a BSC degree in 1976. Upon joining the company as a sales representative in 1992, he spent 6 months in an orientation program at the Seattle office and then returned to his permanent...

Notice that records containing the words degree, graduate, and graduated are all returned from the query.

The `FORMSOF` clause requires that word `INFLECTIONAL` precede the list of terms. Otherwise, you will receive an error.

We can also perform a search based on words being in near proximity to each other. For example, suppose we were interested obtaining a list of employees who graduated from a college or university in Colorado. In this case, we could execute the following query:

```
SELECT FirstName, LastName, Notes FROM Employees
WHERE CONTAINS (Notes, 'College NEAR Colorado OR University NEAR Colorado')
```

Although the number is not documented, MS Search seems to qualify nearness by being within 11 words.

When the `NEAR` keyword is used, Microsoft Search Service also returns a ranking that indicates how close together the keywords were. If the ranking is 0, the record's index is not returned.

> *If you are interested in capturing the rank of a returned index, you should use the `CONTAINSTABLE` function.*

If we want to control how the rank is determined, we can use the `ISABOUT` keyword and assign a weight to each word specified. A weight is a value between 0 and 1. For example, to execute a query that returns all records with MA, BA, or BS, but that rank MA the highest, we would execute a query like this:

```
SELECT FirstName, LastName, Notes FROM Employees
WHERE CONTAINS
      (Notes, 'ISABOUT (BA WEIGHT (.2), BS WEIGHT (.4), MA WEIGHT (.8) )' )
```

As with the `NEAR` keyword, it is best to use `CONTAINSTABLE` to perform this query, so you can order the results by rank.

CONTAINSTABLE

The `CONTAINSTABLE` function returns a table with a column containing the unique index of any matching records and a column containing that index's rank. In order for this information to be used in a meaningful way, it must be joined with the table containing the actual data. Let's look at an example.

```
SELECT k.Rank, e.FirstName, e.LastName, e.Notes FROM Employees AS e INNER JOIN
CONTAINSTABLE
   (Employees, Notes, 'College NEAR Colorado OR University NEAR Colorado')
    AS k
ON k.[Key] = e.EmployeeID
```

Notice that the syntax of `CONTAINSTABLE` is very similar to that of `CONTAINS`. The only difference is that the table name is passed as the first argument. The more notable difference is that the `CONTAINSTABLE` function is used as one component in an `INNER JOIN`.

A more useful example and one that will better illustrate the importance of rank is a weighted query. Suppose we are looking for an employee who has at least a BA or BS, but preferably also has an MA. In this case, we can use `CONTAINSTABLE` to issue a weighted query, as follows:

```
SELECT k.Rank, e.FirstName, e.LastName, e.Notes FROM Employees AS e INNER JOIN
CONTAINSTABLE (Employees, Notes,
   'ISABOUT (BA WEIGHT (.2), BS WEIGHT (.4), MA WEIGHT (.8) )' ) AS k
ON k.[Key] = e.EmployeeID ORDER BY k.Rank DESC
```

This query will result in a result set in which the first record has the highest rank. The relative rank orders for this query are shown in the table below:

MA (0.8)	BS (0.4)	BA (0.2)	Rank
X	X	X	Highest
X	X		
X		X	
X			
	X	X	
	X		
		X	Lowest

The table below shows the results returned from executing the query:

Rank	FirstName	LastName	Notes
56	Margaret	Peacock	Margaret holds a BA in English literature from Concordia College (1958) and an MA from the American Institute of Culinary Arts (1966). She was assigned to the London office temporarily from July through November 1992.
47	Michael	Suyama	Michael is a graduate of Sussex University (MA, economics, 1983) and the University of California at Los Angeles (MBA, marketing, 1986). He has also taken the courses "Multi-Cultural Selling" and "Time Management for the Sales Professional." He is fluent...
31	Janet	Leverling	Janet has a BS degree in chemistry from Boston College (1984). She has also completed a certificate program in food retailing management. Janet was hired as a sales associate in 1991 and promoted to sales representative in February 1992.
7	Nancy	Davolio	Education includes a BA in psychology from Colorado State University in 1970. She also completed "The Art of the Cold Call." Nancy is a member of Toastmasters International.
7	Laura	Callahan	Laura received a BA in psychology from the University of Washington. She has also completed a course in business French. She reads and writes French.
7	Anne	Dodsworth	Anne has a BA degree in English from St. Lawrence College. She is fluent in French and German.

Notice that the top ranking individual has both MA and BA in her `Notes` field. The employee at the next rank has only MA. The employee at the next rank has a BS degree. The three employees with the lowest rank have BA degrees.

FREETEXT

As its name suggests, the `FREETEXT` predicate allows us to specify a much more free-form search than the `CONTAINS` predicate. The `FREETEXT` predicate has the following syntax:

```
FREETEXT ({column|*}, 'freetext_string')
```

The *freetext_string* argument allows you to enter any string. The string you enter is parsed by the Microsoft Search Service and the most important keywords are identified. A match occurs when a full-text enabled column contains any one of those keywords. For example, the following query will locate any record with the word London, Scotland, or Paris in the `Notes` field:

```
SELECT FirstName, LastName, Notes FROM Employees
WHERE FREETEXT(Notes, "has been to London, Scotland, OR Paris")
```

Although this seems to be the easiest way to search a full-text catalog, keep in mind that this simple search may be very misleading. Microsoft Search Service merely extracts the keywords from the freetext string. It does not attempt to translate what the sentence is really asking. For example, consider the following query:

```
SELECT FirstName, LastName, Notes FROM Employees
WHERE FREETEXT(Notes, "graduated in London, Scotland, OR Paris")
```

This query will actually return the index for any record that contains the word graduated (or any of its forms), London, Scotland, or Paris.

FREETEXTTABLE

Like `CONTAINSTABLE`, the `FREETEXTTABLE` function returns a table that contains one column for the key and another for the row's relevance ranking. It has the following syntax:

```
FREETEXTTABLE (table, {column|*}, 'freetext_string')
```

For example, the following query will return a list of matches with the highest ranking matches listed first:

```
SELECT KT.Rank, FirstName, LastName, Notes FROM Employees AS e INNER JOIN
FREETEXTTABLE(Employees, Notes, "graduated in London, Scotland, OR Paris") AS KT
ON KT.[Key] = e.EmployeeID ORDER BY KT.Rank DESC
```

Maintenance and Failure Recovery

Ensuring that your full-text search functionality is operational and that it utilizes system resources in a way that is most optimal for your environment is essential. This final section looks at three special areas of concern:

- Dropping catalogs
- Backup and recovery
- System resources and performance

Dropping Catalogs

A catalog can be deleted either through the SQL Server Enterprise Manager or by running stored procedures. For example, to delete the `Employees` catalog through SQL Server Enterprise Manager, run Delete from its popup menu. A warning dialog will be displayed:

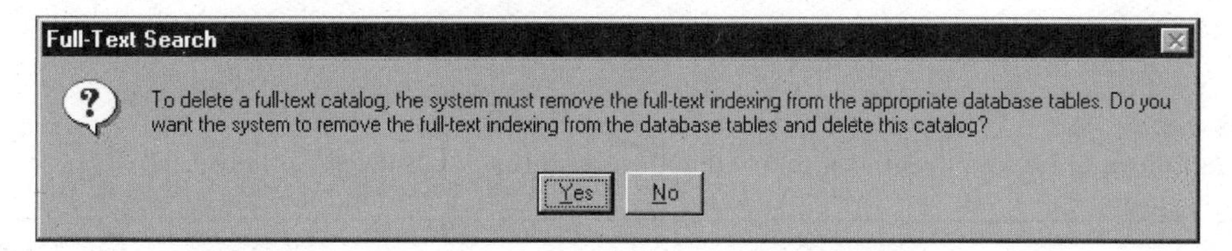

When you click on Yes, full-text indexing for all tables in the catalog will be deactivated, the row containing information about this table will be removed from `sysfulltextcatalogs`, and the files containing the catalog will be deleted from the file system.

> **When a catalog is dropped through the SQL Server Enterprise Manager, the directory that contained the catalog files (`SQL000060000x`) will remain on the hard drive, along with the `Build` and `Indexer` subdirectories. These directories will be empty.**

In order to drop a catalog using stored procedures, you must first disable full-text search on any of the tables it contains. Failure to do so will result in the following error message:

Server: Msg 15604, Level 16, State 1, Line 0
Cannot drop full-text catalog 'ProductCategories' because it contains a full-text index.

Tables are dropped from a catalog by specifying the `drop` action in the call to the `sp_fulltext_table` stored procedure. Once a catalog contains no tables, it can be dropped by specifying the `drop` action in a call to the `sp_fulltext_catalog` stored procedure. The following code illustrates how the `ProductCategories` catalog that contains full-text indexing for the `Categories` table can be dropped:

```
EXEC sp_fulltext_table 'Categories', 'drop'
EXEC sp_fulltext_catalog 'ProductCategories', 'drop'
```

Dropping catalogs using stored procedures does a more thorough job of deleting directories. The directory associated with the catalog and all of its subdirectories are dropped.

Backup and Recovery

Since full-text catalogs are stored in the file system instead of in the database, they cannot be backed up and restored through normal SQL Server backup and restore routines. Catalog information and the metadata about the tables and columns they index are backed up. After the database has been restored, run a full population to allow full-text search to work.

System Resources and Performance

The `sp_fulltext_service` stored procedure allows you to adjust factors that influence how full-text search uses system resources. It has the following syntax:

```
sp_fulltext_service [@action =] 'action'
[,[@value =] 'value']
```

The following table shows the supported actions and the values applicable to each:

Action	Description	Supported values	Default
`clean_up`	This action compares the `sysfulltext` catalogs table with the file system and deletes any catalog files and directories that don't belong to a catalog in `sysfulltext`. This type of inconsistency may occur when the Microsoft Search Service is not running when a catalog or database is dropped.	NULL	
`connect_timeout`	This action sets a timeout value for the Microsoft Search Service to connect to SQL Server during full repopulation. You may want to increase this value if SQL Server is always very busy, particularly if you suspect that population is not occurring. However, a better solution if possible would be to reschedule your populations for a period in which SQL Server is less busy.	1 to 32767 seconds	20 seconds

Action	Description	Supported values	Default
resource_usage	This action sets a relative value for the amount of system resources Microsoft Search Service can use. By default, it is set to 3. A value of 1 causes the MS Search Service to run in the background. A value of 5 causes system resources to be dedicated to running it. The best setting will depend on how the percentage of work done by your database server includes full-text search queries. If the server is primarily used for OLTP applications, you will want to set this value to 1 or 2. If the server is primarily used to support full-text queries, you will want to set this value to 4 or 5.	1 to 5	3

Summary

This chapter provided a discussion of two ways in which SQL Server 7.0 allows you to build applications that can allow users to retrieve information in a very intuitive way. You saw appropriate uses for these technologies and examples showing their implementation.

English Query is a powerful way to provide natural language queries against relational data. You saw how an English Query application can be built, tested, deployed, and used in a client application.

Full-Text Search provides a way to search character-based fields for precise and less precise values. You saw how to build and populate full-text catalogs and learned the syntax for issuing queries that utilize them.

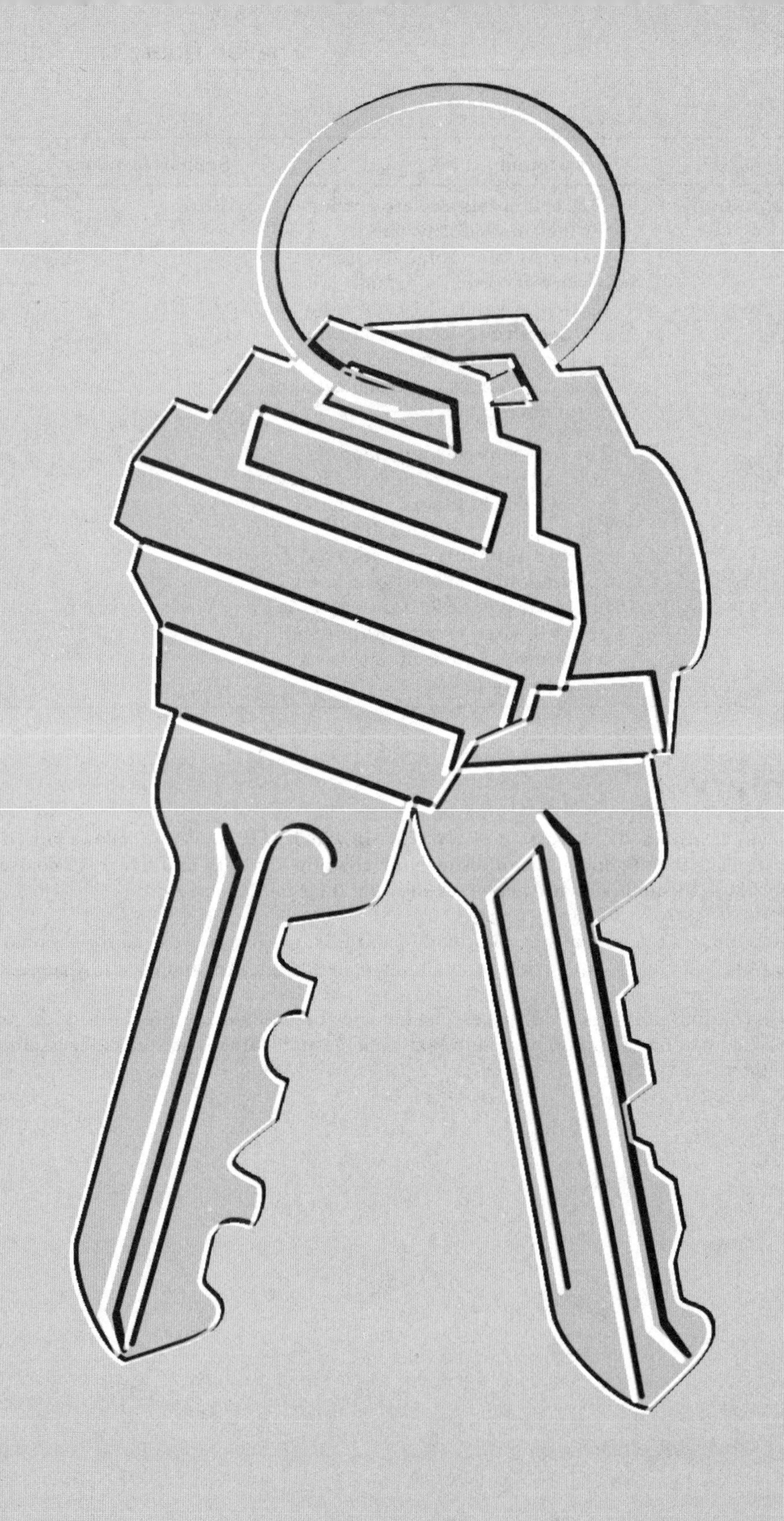

23

Security

There are probably as many ideas on security as there are programmers. It's one of those things where there isn't necessarily a right way to do it, but there are definitely plenty of wrong ones.

The first thing to understand about security is that there is no such thing as a totally secure application. If you can make it secure, rest assured that someone, somewhere, can defeat your efforts and "hack" into the system.

Even with this knowledge, the goal still needs to be to keep unwanted intruders out of your system. The happy news about security is that, for most instances, you can, fairly easily, make it such a hassle that 99.999% of people out there won't want to bother with it. For the other .001%, I can only encourage you to make sure that all your employees have a life so they fall into the 99.999%. The .001% will hopefully find someplace else to go.

In this chapter, we're going to cover:

- Security basics
- SQL Server security options
- Database and server roles
- Application roles
- More advanced security

What we'll discover is that there's a lot of different ways to approach the security problem. Security goes way beyond giving someone a user ID number and a password – we'll see many of the things that you need to think about.

Security Basics

I'm sure that a fair amount of what we're going to look into in this section is going to seem exceedingly stupid – I mean, doesn't everyone know this stuff? Judging by how often I see violations of even the most simple of these rules, I would say, "No, apparently they don't." All I can ask is that you bear with me, and don't skip ahead. As seemingly obvious as some of this stuff is, you'd be amazed how often it gets forgotten or just plain ignored.

Among the different basics that we'll look at here are:

- One person, one login ID, one password
- Password expirations
- Password length and makeup
- Number of attempts to log in
- Storage of user ID and password information

One Person, One Login, One Password

It never ceases to shock me how, everywhere I go, I almost never fail to find that the establishment has at least one "global" user – some login into the network or particular applications which is usually known by nearly everyone in the department or even the whole company. Often, this "global" user has carte blanche (i.e. everything) access. For SQL Server, the common no-no is that many installations haven't even bothered to change the `sa` password from the default of no password to some discrete value. Even if they have changed it, you'll often find that seemingly everyone knows what the password is. This is a very bad scenario indeed.

The first basic point then is that if everyone has access to a user ID which is essentially anonymous (if everyone knows it, it could have been anyone who used it), and has access to everything, then you've defeated your security model – entirely. The only real benefit that's left is being able to tell who's who as far as who is connected at any point in time (assuming that they are really using their individual login rather than the global login).

Users who have carte blanche access should be limited to just one or two people. Ideally, if you need passwords with carte blanche access, then you would want two separate logins which each have the access, but only one person knows the password for each login.

You'll find that users will often share their passwords with someone else in order to let the other user temporarily gain some level of access (usually because the owner of the login ID is out of the office or doesn't have time to bother with doing it themselves at the time) – you should make this nothing short of a hanging offense if possible.

The problem created by password sharing is multifold. First, someone is getting access to something which you've previously decided not to give them (otherwise, why don't they have it on their own password?) – if you didn't want them to have access before, why do you want them to have it now? Second, the user that's not supposed to have access will probably always now have that access. Since users almost never change their passwords (unless forced to), the person they gave the password to will probably be able to use that login ID indefinitely – and, I assure you, they will! Third, you lose auditing. You may have something that tracks which user did what based on the login ID. If more than one person has the password for that login ID, how can you be sure which person was logged into that login ID at the time?

In short – sharing passwords should be nothing short of a firing offense if you can arrange it that way.

To summarize, stay away from global use accounts whenever possible. If you must use them, keep their use limited to as few people as at all possible – usually this should be kept to just two (one to be a main user, and one person as a backup if the first person isn't available). If you really must have more than one person with significant access, then consider creating multiple accounts (one per user) that have the level of access necessary. By following these simple steps, you'll find you can do a lot for both the security and auditability of the system.

Password Expirations

Using expiration of passwords tends to be either abused or ignored. Too bad – it's a good idea that often goes wrong.

The concept here is to set up your system to have passwords which automatically expire after a certain period of time. After that time, the user must change their password to continue having access to the account. The concept has been around many years, and, if you work in a larger corporation, there's a good chance that the auditors from your accounting firm are already insisting you implement some form of password expiration.

The problem is that SQL Server does not, natively speaking, support any kind of automatic expiration of passwords. If you want to have automatic password expiration, you have to either use NT-based security (more on that in the next section), or you will have to build your own expiration model into your application.

One other caveat here – NT doesn't really enforce the password expiration. It will come up and tell the user they have to change their password, but the user can, if they choose, just enter the exact same password in and NT will take it.

What Do You Get for Your Effort?

So, what does password expiration get you? Well, remember when, in the final part of the previous section, I said that once a password is shared, the user it was shared with would have that access forever? Well, this is the exception. If you expire passwords, then you refresh the level of your security – at least temporarily. The password would have to be shared a second time in order for the user who isn't supposed to have access to regain access. While this is a far cry from foolproof (often, the owner of the login ID will be more than happy to share it again), it does deal with the situation where the password sharing was really just intended for one-time use. Often, users who share their passwords don't even realize that months later, the other user still has the password, and may be using it on occasion to gain access to something they would not have on their own security.

Now the Bad News

It is possible to get too much of a good thing. I mentioned earlier how many audit firms will expect their clients to implement a model where a user's password expires every 30 days – this is a very bad idea indeed.

Every installation I've seen that does this – without exception – has *worse* security after implementing a 30-day expiration policy. The problem is, as you might expect, multifold in nature.

First, tech-support calls go way up. When users change passwords that often, they simply can't keep them all memorized. They can't remember which month's password they are supposed to use, so they are constantly calling for support to reset the password because they forgot what it is.

Second, and much larger, in scale users get tired of both thinking of new passwords and remembering them. Experience has shown me that, for better than 90% of the users I've worked with in installations that use a 30 day expiration, users change their passwords to incredibly predictable (and, therefore, hackable) words or word/number combinations. Indeed, this often gets to a level where perhaps 50% or more of your users will have the same password – they are all using things like MMMYY where MMM is the month and YY is the year. For example, for January 1996 they might have used JAN96 for their password. Pretty soon, everyone in the place is doing something like that.

> *I've seen some companies try and deal with this by implementing something of a password sniffer – it checks the password when you go to change it. The sniffing process looks for passwords that incorporate your name or start with a month prefix. These mechanisms are weak at best.*
>
> *Users are far smarter than we often give them credit for. It takes about a week for most users to circumvent the first one of these password sniffers I saw – they simply changed their passwords to have an "X" prefix on them, and otherwise stayed with the same MMMYY format they had been using before. In short, the sniffer wound up doing next to nothing.*

The bottom line here is not to get carried away with your expiration policy. Have it be short enough to get reasonable turnover and deal with shared or stolen passwords, but don't make it so often that users rebel and start using weak passwords. Personally, I suggest nothing more frequent than 90 days, and nothing longer than 180 days.

Growing Your Own

If you decide you want to implement this functionality on your own, I suggest a couple of things:

- Track old passwords at least ten passwords back – don't let the user use the same password twice for at least 10 times. You might also consider checking the first several characters of the new password against old passwords – this can help prevent the user from getting away with only slight changes to the password (changing "hotdog" to "hotdogs" doesn't get you much in the security category)
- Track the date the password was changed (as part of the user information), and allow for a system-wide variable that states the number of days that a password can be valid – you can then use the `DATEDIFF()` function every time the user logs on to your application to make sure the password has been set recently (this assumes that the user has a separate login for each application)

Password Length and Makeup

This is a toughie from the standpoint of both SQL Server and NT-based security. Currently, the only real way to implement this is to make your application the single available route to access the database.

Technically speaking, there is only one way to make your application the sole route into the database. You need to embed the information for a login and password that is dedicated to the application; then store your user and password information completely outside the normal security structure of SQL Server. This is something of a real pain. It means that you must manage user access entirely within your application.

The reason why SQL Server or NT security can't limit access to being only through your application is that they key off the login ID – not the application which passed through that login information. If you are giving users rights to tables and procedures for use with your application, be aware that the users will have those same rights if they log in through the Query Analyzer.

Password Length

If you do indeed make all access driven by your application, then you can implement restrictions on the nature of the password. Realize that, for each possible alpha-numeric digit the user includes in their password, they are increasing the number of possible passwords by a factor of 36. That means there are only 36 possible single character passwords, but 1,296 possible two-character passwords. Go up to three characters and you increase the possibilities to 46,656. By the time you add a fourth character, you're well over a million possibilities. The permutations just keep going up as you require more and more characters. The downside, though, is that it becomes more and more difficult for your users to actually remember what their password was and to think up passwords. Indeed, I suspect that you'll find that requiring anything more than 4 or 5 characters will generate a full-scale revolt from your end users.

Password Makeup

All right, so I've pointed out that, if you required at least 4 alpha-numeric characters, you've created a situation where there are over a million possible password combinations. The problem comes when you realize that people aren't really going to use all those combinations – they are going to use words or names they are familiar with. Considering that the average person only uses about 25,000 words on a regular basis, that doesn't leave you with very many words to try out if you're a hacker.

If you're implementing your own user ID and password scheme, then consider requiring that at least one character be alpha in nature (no numbers, just letters), and that at least one character be numeric. This rules out simple numbers that are easy to guess (people really like to use their social security, telephone number or birthdays) and all words. The user can still create things that are easy to remember for them – say "77pizzas" – but the password can't be pulled out of a dictionary. Any hacker is forced to truly try each permutation in order to try and break in.

Number of Attempts to Log in

Regardless of how you're physically storing the user and password information, your login screen should have logic to it which limits the number of tries that someone gets to login. The response if they go over the limit can differ in strength, but you want to make sure you throw in some sort of device that makes it difficult to set up a routine to try out all the passwords programmatically.

How many tries to allow isn't really that important as long as it's a reasonably small number – I usually use 3 times, but I've seen 4 and 5 in some places and that's fine too.

What to Do about it

So, what if they go over? Then what? Well, there are a few different possibilities depending on what extreme you want to go to and how many tech support calls you want:

- Stop giving them chances: This is what I most commonly use. I give them their maximum number of tries – each time telling them about their mistake and bringing back up the login dialog. When they hit the limit of failed attempts, I either tell them that was their last chance and close the application, or I just take away the login dialog and make them close the app and restart it on their own. In either case, what I'm trying to do is not stop them from logging in (they can just re-run the app and get another 3 tries), but rather be enough of a nuisance that they'll want to remember their password correctly next time
- Disable the login ID: You can only do this once if you are using your own security arrangement or if you are using NT/2000. For the former, you can either send a message from the client to set something in the database on the third attempt, or you can actually increment a "failed attempts" counter in the user's login information

I much prefer the latter of these two choices in this situation. If you're going to go so far as to say that someone's login is disabled on the third failed attempt, then you might as well truly enforce it. If you just send an update from the client to disable login on the final attempt, then it's easy to get around the limit – the user just needs to try one less than the limit, then manually close the application, then start the whole process over again. Each time they close the app it will lose track of the attempts already made. Updating a "failed attempts" column after each such failure ensures that you truly "remember" about all the failed attempts.

Storage of User and Password Information

For the most part, there's no rocket science in how to store user profile and password information. There are, however, a few things to think about:

- Since you need to be able to get at the information initially, you will have to either compile a password right into the client application or component (and then make sure that the proper login and password is created on any server that you install your app on), or you'll need something of a double password situation – one to get the user as far as the regular password information, and one to get them to the real application. Forcing a user into two logins is generally unacceptable, which pushes you back to the first option in most cases
- If you go with a double password scenario, you'll want the access for the first login to be limited to just a stored procedure execution if possible. By doing this, you can allow the first login to obtain the validation it needs while not revealing anything to anyone that tries to login through the Query Analyzer. Have your sproc accept a user ID and password, and simply pass back either a Boolean (true/false that they can log in), or pass back a recordset that lists what screens and functions the user can see at the client end. If you use a raw `SELECT` statement, you won't be able to restrict what they can see

  One solution I've implemented close to this scenario was to have a view that mapped the current SQL Server login to other login information. In this case, an application role was used that gave the application complete access to everything – the application had to know what the user could and couldn't do. All that the user's login had a right to do was to execute a stored procedure to request a listing of their rights. The sproc looked something like this:

```
CREATE PROC GetUserRights
AS

DECLARE @User varchar(128)
SELECT @User = USER_NAME()
SELECT * FROM UserPermissions WHERE LoginID = @User
```

- If you're going to store password information in the system – encrypt it!!! I can't say enough about the importance of this. Most users will use their passwords for more than one thing – it just makes life a lot easier when you have less to remember. By encrypting the data before you put it in the database, you ensure that no one is going to stumble across a user's password information – even accidentally. They may see it, but what they see is not usable unless they have the key to decrypt it.

Security Options

As far as built-in options go, you now have only two choices in how to set up security under SQL Server. Prior to version 7.0, there were three choices. Just for backward compatibility's sake, let's look at all three types of security that were available for SQL Server 6.x:

- NT (or Win 2000) integrated security: The user logs into NT not SQL Server. Authentication is done via NT with trusted connections.
- Standard security: The user logs into SQL Server separately from logging into NT. Authentication is done by SQL Server.
- Mixed security: An environment in which some users use NT integrated security and others use standard security.

Only the first and last of these are still available. You can still choose a security option that lets you run things as you did with standard security under 6.5 and older versions – it's just that you also have to leave NT security as an option. That is, you can now choose from:

- NT (or Win 2000) integrated security
- Mix of NT and SQL Server security

However, you can no longer go only for the old SQL Server only form of security.

Let's take a look at the two security options available for SQL Server 7.

SQL Server Security

We'll start with SQL Server's built-in login model, as it will have some relevance when we talk about how NT security has worked in the past.

With SQL Server security, you create a **login ID** which is completely separate from your network login information. Some of the pros for using SQL Server security include:

- The user doesn't necessarily have to be a domain user in order to gain access to the system
- It's easier to gain programmatic control over the user information
- In the past, it was much easier to maintain than NT-based or mixed security

Some of the cons are:

- Your users have to login twice or more – once into whatever network access they have, and once into the SQL Server for each connection they create from a separate application.
- Two logins mean more maintenance for your DBA.
- The passwords can easily get out of synch, and that leads to an awful lot of failed logins or forgotten passwords (Does this sound familiar? "Let's see now, which one was it for this login?")

An example of logging in using SQL Server security would be the use of the `sa` account that you've probably been using for much of this book. It doesn't matter how you've logged into your network, you log into the SQL Server using a login ID of `sa` and a separate password (which will be empty if you haven't changed it).

On an on-going basis, you really don't want to be doing things day-to-day logged in as `sa`. Why? Well, it will probably only take you a minute or two of thought to figure out many of the terrible things you can do by sheer accident when you're using the `sa` account. Using `sa` means you have complete access to everything, that means the `DROP TABLE` statement you execute when you are in the wrong database will actually do what you told it – drop that table!!! About all you'll be left to say is "oops!" Your boss will probably be saying something completely different.

Even if you do want to always have carte blanche access, just use the `sa` account to make your regular user account a member of the `sysadmins` server role. That gives you the power of `sa`, but gains you the extra security of separate passwords and the audit trail (in Profiler or when looking at system activity) of who is currently logged into the system.

Creating a New SQL Server Login

There are three ways to create logins on a SQL Server:

- By using `sp_addlogin`
- By using the Enterprise Manager
- By using SQL Distributed Management Objects (DMO)

SQL DMO is beyond out of the scope of this book, but let's take a look at the other two options.

sp_addlogin

This sproc does exactly what it says. It only requires one parameter, but most of the time you'll use two or three. There are a couple of additional parameters, but you'll find that you use those far more rarely. The syntax looks like this:

```
EXEC sp_addlogin [@loginame =] <'login'>
     [,[@passwd =] <'password'>]
     [,[@defdb =] <'database'>]
     [,[@deflanguage =] <'language'>]
     [,[@sid =] 'sid']
     [,[@encryptopt =] <'encryption_option'>]
```

Parameter	Description
`@loginame`	Just what it sounds like – this is the login ID that will be used.
`@passwd`	Even more what it sounds like – the password that is used to login using the aforementioned login ID.
`@defdb`	The default database. This defines what is the first "current" database when the user logs in. Normally, this will be the main database your app uses. If left unspecified, the default will be the `master` database (you usually don't want that, so be sure to provide this parameter).
`@deflanguage`	The default language for this user. You can use this to override the system default if you are supporting localization.
`@sid`	A binary number that becomes the **system identifier** (**SID**) for your login ID. If you don't supply a SID, SQL Server generates one for you. Since SIDs must be unique, any SID you supply must not already exist in the system. Using a specific SID can be handy when you are restoring your database to a different server or are otherwise migrating login information.
`@encryptopt`	The user's login ID and password information is stored in the `sysusers` table in the `master` database. The `@encryptopt` determines whether the password stored in the `master` database is encrypted or not. By default, (or if you provide a `NULL` in this parameter), the password is indeed encrypted. The other options are `skip_encryption`, which does just what it says – the password is not encrypted; and `skip_encryption_old`, which is only there for backward compatibility, and should not be used.

`sp_addlogin` gives you the ability to add users as more of a batch function, or to script it right into a client-side administration tool (you could also use SQL DMO for this).

Let's do a quick example with this one:

```
EXEC sp_addlogin UserFromSP, 'password', Northwind
```

Now create a new connection using the new login of `UserFromSP` and password of `password`, and you should be logged in with `Northwind` as the first database that shows as current.

> *Just for ease of use as you go through these exercises, there are two ways in which you can create a new connection. You can either open up a new instance of Query Analyzer, or you can go to the File/Connect menu option. While the second option can often be easier since you only need to manage windows rather than toggling between QA instances, you must also be careful with it. It's very easy when you use this connect option with multiple logins or servers to forget which one is which and do something that you didn't intend.*

sp_password

Once you have that login created, you'll still need to provide a mechanism for changing the password information. The tool to use if you want to do it in T-SQL is `sp_password`. The syntax is pretty straightforward:

```
sp_password [[@old =] <'old password'>,]
    [@new =] <'new password'>
    [,[@loginame =] <'login'>]
```

The new and old password parameters work, of course, just exactly as you would expect. You need to accept those from the user and pass them into the sproc. Note, however, that the login is an optional parameter. If you don't supply it, then it will assume that you want to change the password on the current connection. Also note that `sp_password` can't be executed as part of a transaction.

> *You might be thinking something like, "Don't most systems require you to enter the new password twice?" Indeed they do. So the follow-up question is, "How come `sp_password` doesn't do that?" The answer is a simple one – because they leave that up to you. You would build that logic in to check for a double entry of the new password in before you ever got as far as using `sp_password`.*

Adding SQL Server Logins Using Enterprise Manager

The most common way in which users are added to a SQL Server is with the Enterprise Manager.

To add a login in EM, just open Enterprise Manager and navigate to the server to which you want to add the login. Expand that server's tree, and the Security node. Then right-click on Logins and select New Login:

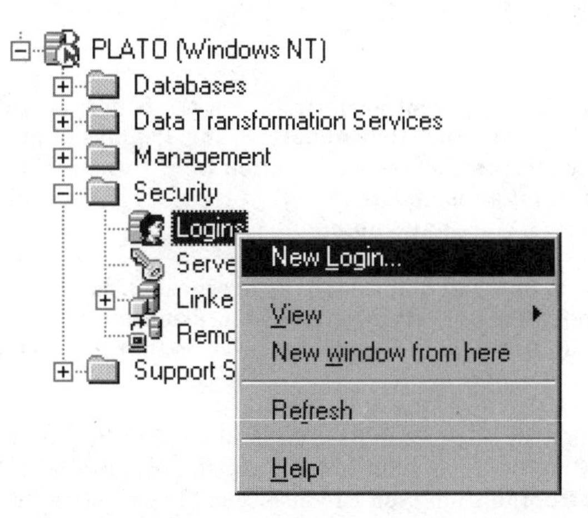

This brings up the New Login dialog box:

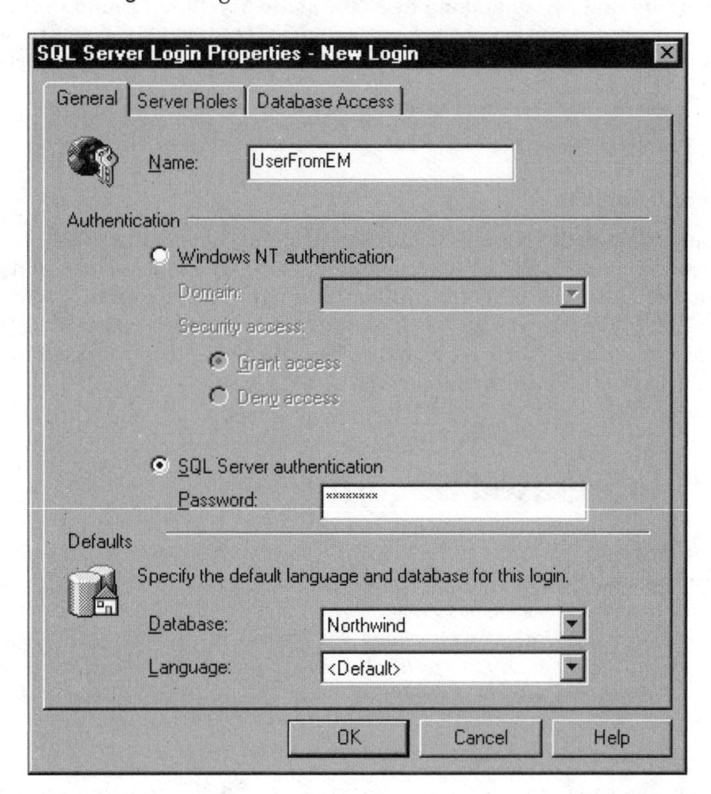

Fill out the fields to match the picture above except use a password of "password". For now, just stick with the defaults on the other two tabs – we'll get to those in the next section.

When you click on OK, you should get another dialog prompting you to re-type the password. This is to be doubly sure that the password you wanted is the one that is really created. Just type the same password in, click on OK, and the login will be created. Now, when you click on the Logins node, you should see the UserFromEM login ID listed in the right-hand pane.

> **In order to improve the apparent performance of the Enterprise Manager, Microsoft changed the way that they update all the displays of information. Under 6.5 and earlier, the information for each section in EM was constantly refreshed. Under 7.0, the information is updated the first time it's needed, and is then assumed to be stable – that is, EM assumes nothing has changed.**
>
> **The benefit of this is that you don't have the overhead of constantly reloading and checking the membership of certain groups of information (logins, databases, tables within the database, etc). The downside, however, is that the lists are often totally unaware of changes on your server.**
>
> **If you're certain that some changes have been made, but they don't show up in the proper listing, try right-clicking on that node of the tree in the left pane of EM, and then select the Refresh option (you can also select the node you're interested in and then press *F5*). This will usually clear things up. Note, also, that you'll occasionally bump into errors that say something like "Database MyDB not found in Databases collection". This is a symptom of the same problem. Quit whatever you're doing, right-click on the Databases node and refresh – then try whatever you were doing again.**

Changing a Password Using EM

Just as there's a quick and easy way in EM to create a login, there is also a quick and easy way to change a password. Navigate to the Logins node in the left pane – just as you did when you were creating the login, then just select the node rather than right-clicking on it. Then look in the right-hand pane of the EM window, and right-click on the login for which you want to change the password. Choose Properties. You'll get exactly the same dialog that you used to create the login. Just type in the new password information and click OK – you'll get a simple dialog to enter the password again to confirm.

NT (or 2000) Integrated Security

I'm going to do the rather odd thing of starting this section with a comment before we get right down to the nitty-gritty. Prior to 7.0 – NT integrated security was a great idea gone awry (although mixed was even worse). The concept is pretty simple, yet the hassles in both implementation and, in particular, maintenance, rarely made it worth the price of admission. I'm happy to say that this appears to be well taken care of in 7.0. The model for implementation is much easier to understand and, in short, works a heck of a lot better. That said, let's get down to it.

NT security gives us the capability to map logins from trusted NT domains into our SQL Server. I can't tell you how cool this notion is, but I can tell you some of the problems it solves, the things it simplifies, and why, under SQL Server 7.0, it's just plainly the way to go in many situations.

In this section, we'll look at:

- What is NT security?
- How do we set it up?
- What does (and doesn't) it do for us?

In the end, if you're new to SQL Server, I suspect that you'll think that NT security is pretty cool, and, if you're a user of a previous version, then you'll think, "Wow, they finally fixed it!"

What Is NT Security?

NT security is simply a model where you take existing NT domain user accounts or groups and provide SQL Server rights to them directly rather than forcing users to keep separate passwords and make separate logins. Let's again look at examples using both T-SQL and EM.

Granting Access to NT User Accounts

Actually, this is painfully easy, and works pretty much as it did for SQL Server security. The only real trick is that you need to provide a full domain path to the user profile to which you want to grant access. This is provided through the syntax of:

```
sp_grantlogin [@loginname = ]'<Domain Name>\<NT User Name>'
```

This is one of those things that's perhaps best understood by actually doing it, so let's get right to it.

> *In order to follow along with this example, you're going to have to have the authority to create users and grant them rights in an NT domain. The domain does not necessarily need to be the main domain which you use at your workplace (for which there's a good chance that you don't have this level of administrative rights), but could be the local domain for your machine if you have administrative rights to it. You should be able to do this example in any domain as long as you have administrative access to some account that you can substitute in the place of the TestAccount that we're going to create.*

We'll need to start by creating an account with which to test access (we could just use some existing account in a domain somewhere, but I want to be sure of what we're getting, for our purposes in this example). Call the new account `TestAccount`, and don't give it any special rights of any kind (by default, it will belong to the `Everyone` built-in NT group).

As soon as we have that account, we're ready to grant some access to it. My `TestAccount` is in a domain called `Aristotle`, so I'll need to prefix that domain name when I create the NT login mapping (you will need to replace `Aristotle` with whatever the name of your NT domain is):

```
EXEC sp_grantlogin 'ARISTOTLE\TestAccount'
```

When you execute sp_grantlogin, you should get a message back indicating that access has been given. However, note that the new user will, by default, not have access to much, if anything, depending on:

- If any NT group the login belongs to has SQL Server access granted to it
- The status of the guest account

We'll look at the specifics of each of these later in the chapter, but, if you haven't changed anything security-wise on the server since it was installed, then our NT user TestAccount will have access to the following databases:

- Master
- Msdb
- Northwind
- Pubs
- tempdb

For our case, the access is accidental – we haven't granted anything explicitly, so we end up defaulting to the level of access granted to the guest user. We want to eliminate the access to the Northwind database so we can do some testing (you'll find out later about the reasons why I recommend removing all access from guest). To do this in EM, navigate to the Users node under the Northwind database. Right-click on guest, and then choose Delete (we'll add it back later).

After you've removed the guest access, log into NT using the TestAccount user (or whatever user you're substituting for that account), and start up the Query Analyzer. This time, when you get the login box, choose NT security, and click OK to log in. Try changing to the Northwind database – you shouldn't be allowed access (if you have, then guest must not have been disabled, or some other configuration change has been made).

You now have a valid NT login with SQL Server access – you just don't have a lot you can do with it. This will be the norm on most SQL Servers when you first create a login depending on the factors I mentioned earlier (NT groups, guest account). The login is there, but it has little or no access.

Granting SQL Server access to an NT user account in EM works exactly the same as it did when we were creating SQL Server login accounts. The only difference is that you need to provide the full domain path of the user just as we did with sp_grantlogin.

Why Use NT Security?

Prior to Version 7.0, NT-based security for SQL Server really seemed like nothing more than an afterthought – something of a castaway that nobody really took too seriously. With 7.0, things have become much more usable. Indeed, Microsoft has hinted at several events that they'd like to see most installations move to using NT security. As we move into the Windows 2000 era, the notion is to have a far more integrated security environment. This makes sense of course – the fewer the logins the tighter and easier it is to maintain security. What's more, it's just plain easier in the long run.

NT Security now allows:

- You to maintain much more of a user's access from just one place
- Granting of SQL Server rights by simply adding a user to an NT group (this means that you often don't have to even go into SQL Server in order to grant access to a user)
- Your users only have to remember one password and login

The long and the short of it is that NT security now works, for the most part, as it always should have worked.

That being said, let's take a look at how to grant specific rights to specific users.

User Rights

The simplest definition of what a **user right** is would be something like, "What a user can and can't do." In this case, the simple definition is a pretty good one.

User rights fall into three categories:

- The right to login (we've pretty much seen that one already)
- The right to access a specific database
- The right to perform specific actions on particular objects within that database

Since we've already looked at creating logins, we'll focus here on the specific rights that a login can have.

Granting Access to a Specific Database

The first thing that you need to do if you want a user to have access to a database is to grant them the right to access that database. This can be done in EM by adding them to the Users member of the Databases node of your server. To add them using T-SQL, you need to use the `sp_grantdbaccess` in the form of:

```
sp_grantdbaccess [@loginame =] <'login'>
```

Note that the access granted will be to the current database – that is, you need to make sure that the database you want them to have access to is the current database when you issue the command.

To grant access to the `Northwind` database to our `Aristotle\TestAccount` NT user, we need to use this stored procedure call:

```
USE Northwind
EXEC sp_grantdbaccess 'Aristotle\TestAccount'
```

If you run this (changing the domain name as appropriate), you should get a confirmation message back that access was granted.

Removing access to a database works pretty much the same – for this, we use the `sp_revokedbaccess` system sproc:

```
sp_revokedbaccess [@name_in_db =] <'login'>
```

To remove the access we just granted to the `Northwind` database, we would execute:

```
USE Northwind
EXEC sp_revokedbaccess 'Aristotle\TestAccount'
```

You'll get a message back indicating that the user was "dropped" from the database.

The login that we just revoked access from is the one we're going to be using as an example throughout the remainder of this chapter. As such, if you're following along with the examples, you'll want to make sure that you grant access back to the user, or none of the rest of the examples will work.

Granting Object Permissions within the Database

OK, so the user has a login and access to the database you want them to have access to, so now everything's done – right? Ahh, if it were that simple! We are, of course, not done yet.

SQL Server gives us a pretty fine degree of control over what our users can access. Most of the time, you have some information that you want your users to be able to get to, but you also have other information in the database to which you don't want them to have access. For example, you might have a customer service person who has to be able to look at and maintain order information – but you probably don't want them messing around with the salary information. The opposite is also probably true – you need your human resource people to be able to edit employee records, but you don't want them giving somebody a major discount on a sale.

SQL Server allows you to assign a separate set of rights to some of the different objects within SQL Server. The objects you can assign rights to include tables, views and stored procedures. Triggers are implied to have the rights of the person who creates them.

User rights on objects fall into six different types:

User Right	Description
`SELECT`	Allows a user to "see" the data. If a user has this permission, the user has the right to run a `SELECT` statement against the table or view on which the permission is granted.
`INSERT`	Allows a user to create new data. Users with this permission can run an `INSERT` statement. Note that, unlike many systems, having `INSERT` capability does not necessarily mean that you have `SELECT` rights.

User Right	Description
UPDATE	Allows a user to modify existing data. Users with this permission can run an UPDATE statement. Like the INSERT statement, having UPDATE capability does not necessarily mean that you have SELECT rights.
DELETE	Allows a user to create new data. Users with this permission can run a DELETE statement. Again, having DELETE capability does not necessarily mean that you have SELECT rights.
REFERENCES	Allows a user to insert rows where the table that is being inserting into has a foreign key constraint, which references another table to which that user doesn't have SELECT rights.
EXECUTE	Allows a user to EXECUTE a specified stored procedure.

You can mix and match these rights as needed on the particular table, view or sproc to which you're assigning rights.

You can assign these rights in EM by simply navigating to the Logins option of the Security node of your server. Just right-click on the user and choose Properties. You'll be presented with a different dialog depending on whether you're in the database or security node, but, in either case, you'll have the option of setting permissions. Assigning rights using T-SQL uses three commands that are good to know even if you're only going to assign rights through EM (the terminology is the same).

GRANT

GRANT gives the specified user or role the access specified for the object that is the subject of the GRANT statement.

The syntax for a GRANT statement looks like this:

```
GRANT
    ALL [PRIVILEGES] | <permission>[,...n]
    ON
    <table or view name>[(<column name>[,...n])]
       |<stored or extended stored procedure name>
    TO <login or role name>[,...n]
    [WITH GRANT OPTION]
    [AS <role name>]
```

The ALL keyword indicates that you want to grant all the rights that are applicable for that object type (EXECUTE *never* applies to a table). If you don't use the ALL keyword, then you need to supply one or more specific permissions which you want granted for that object.

PRIVILEGES is a new keyword that has no real function other than to improve ANSI-92 compatibility.

The ON keyword just serves as a placeholder to say that what comes next is the object on which you want the permissions granted. Note that, if you are granting rights on a table, you can specify permissions down to the column level by specifying a column list to be affected – if you don't supply specific columns, then it's assumed to affect all columns.

Microsoft appears to have done something of an about face in their opinion of column level permissions. Being able to say that a user can do a `SELECT` *on a particular table, but only on certain columns seems like a cool idea, but it really convolutes the security process both in its use and in the work it takes Microsoft to implement it. As such, recent literature on the subject, plus what I've been told by insiders, seems to indicate that Microsoft wishes that column level security would go away. They have recommended against its use – if you need to restrict a user to seeing particular columns, consider using a view instead.*

The `TO` statement is what it looks like – it specifies to whom you want this access granted. It can be a login ID or a role name.

`WITH GRANT OPTION` allows the user to whom you're granting access, to also grant access to other users.

I recommend against the use of this option since it can quickly become a pain to keep track of who has got access to what. Sure, you can always go into EM and look at the permissions for that object, but then you're in a reactive mode rather than a proactive one – you're looking for what's wrong with the current access levels rather than stopping unwanted access up front.

Last, but not least, is the `AS` keyword. This one deals with the issue of a login belonging to multiple roles.

Let's go ahead and move on to an example or two. We'll see later that the `TestAccount` we created already has some access based on being a member of the `Public` role – something that every database user belongs to, and from which you can't remove them. There are, however, a large number of items to which `TestAccount` doesn't have access (because `Public` is the only role it belongs to, and `Public` doesn't have rights either).

Start by logging in with the `TestAccount` user. Then try a `SELECT` statement against the `Region` table:

```
SELECT * FROM Region
```

You'll quickly get a message from SQL Server telling you that you are a scoundrel and attempting to go to places you shouldn't be going:

```
Server: Msg 229, Level 14, State 5, Line 1
SELECT permission denied on object 'Region', database 'Northwind', owner 'dbo'.
```

Login separately as `sa` – you can do this in the same instance of QA if you like by choosing the File | Connect menu choice. Then select SQL Server security for the new connection and log in as `sa` with the appropriate password. Now execute a `GRANT` statement:

```
USE Northwind
GRANT SELECT ON Region TO [Aristotle\TestAccount]
```

Now switch back to the TestAccount connection (remember, the information for which user you're connected in as, is in the Title Bar of the connection window), and try that SELECT statement again. This time, you get better results:

```
RegionID       RegionDescription
-------------- ------------------------
1              Eastern
2              Western
3              Northern
4              Southern

(4 row(s) affected)
```

Let's go ahead and try another one. This time, let's run the same tests and commands against the EmployeeTerritories table:

```
SELECT * FROM EmployeeTerritories
```

This one fails – again, we don't have rights to it, so let's grant the rights:

```
USE Northwind
GRANT SELECT ON EmployeeTerritories TO [Aristotle\TestAccount]
```

Now, if you re-run the select statement, things work just fine:

```
EmployeeID  TerritoryID
----------- -----------
1           06897
1           19713
...
...
...
9           48304
9           55113
9           55439

(49 row(s) affected)
```

To add an additional twist, however, let's try an INSERT into this table:

```
INSERT INTO EmployeeTerritories
VALUES
     (1, '01581')
```

SQL Server wastes to time in telling us to get lost – we don't have the required permissions, so let's grant them (using the sa connection):

```
USE Northwind
GRANT INSERT ON EmployeeTerritories TO [Aristotle\TestAccount]
```

Now try that INSERT statement again:

```
INSERT INTO EmployeeTerritories
VALUES
    (1, '01581')
```

Everything works great.

DENY

DENY explicitly prevents the user from getting the access specified on the targeted object. The key to DENY is that it overrides any GRANT statements. Since a user can belong to multiple roles (discussed shortly), it's possible for a user to be part of a role that's granted access, but also have a DENY in effect. If a DENY and a GRANT both exist in a user's mix of individual and role based rights, then the DENY wins every time. In short, if the user or any role the user belongs to has a DENY for the right in question, then the user will not be able to make use of that access on that object.

The syntax looks an awful lot like the GRANT statement:

```
DENY
   ALL [PRIVILEGES]|<permission>[,...n]
   ON
   <table or view name>[(column[,...n])]
     |<stored or extended stored procedure name>
   TO <login ID or roll name>[,...n]
   [CASCADE]
```

Again, the ALL keyword indicates that you want to deny all the rights which are applicable for that object type (EXECUTE *never* applies to a table). If you don't use the ALL keyword, then you need to supply one or more specific permissions that you want to be denied for that object.

PRIVILEGES is still a new keyword and has no real function other than to improve ANSI-92 compatibility.

The ON keyword just serves as a placeholder to say that what comes next is the object on which you want the permissions denied.

Everything has worked pretty much the same as with a GRANT statement until now. The CASCADE keyword matches up with the WITH GRANT OPTION that was in the GRANT statement. CASCADE tells SQL Server that you also want to deny access to anyone that this user granted access to under the rules of the WITH GRANT OPTION.

To run an example on DENY, let's try a simple SELECT statement using the TestAccount login:

```
USE Northwind
SELECT * FROM Employees
```

This should get you nine records or so. How did you get access when we haven't granted it to TestAccount? TestAccount belongs to Public, and Public has been granted access to Employees.

Let's say that we don't want TestUser to have access. For whatever reason, TestUser is the exception, and we don't want that user snooping in the data – we just issue our DENY statement (remember to issue the DENY using the sa login):

```
USE Northwind
DENY ALL ON Employees TO [Aristotle\TestAccount]
```

When you run the SELECT statement again using TestAccount, you'll get an error – you no longer have access. Note also that, since we used the ALL keyword, the INSERT, DELETE and UPDATE access that Public has, is now also denied from TestAccount.

Note that DENY is new to SQL Server 7.0. The concept of a deny was there in 6.5, but it was implemented differently. Instead of DENY, you would issue a REVOKE statement twice. The new DENY keyword makes things much clearer.

REVOKE

REVOKE eliminates the effects of a previously issued GRANT or DENY statement. Think of this one as something of a targeted "Undo" statement.

The syntax is a mix of the GRANT and DENY statements:

```
REVOKE [GRANT OPTION FOR]
   ALL [PRIVILEGES] | <permission>[,...n]
   ON
   <table or view name>[(column name [,...n])]
       |<stored or extended stored procedure name>
   TO | FROM <login ID or roll name>[,...n]
   [CASCADE]
   [AS <role name>]
```

The explanations here are virtually identical to those of the GRANT and DENY statements – I put them here again in case you're pulling the book back off the shelf for a quick lookup on REVOKE.

Once again, the ALL keyword indicates that you want to revoke all the rights which are applicable for that object type. If you don't use the ALL keyword, then you need to supply one or more specific permissions that you want to be revoked for that object.

PRIVILEGES still has no real function other than to improve ANSI-92 compatibility.

The ON keyword just serves as a placeholder to say that what comes next is the object on which you want the permissions revoked.

The CASCADE keyword matches up with the WITH GRANT OPTION that was in the GRANT statement. CASCADE tells SQL Server that you want also revoke access from anyone this user granted access to under the rules of the WITH GRANT OPTION.

The AS keyword again just specifies which role you want to issue this command based on.

Using the sa connection, let's undo the access that we granted to the Region table in Northwind:

```
REVOKE ALL ON Region FROM [Aristotle\TestAccount]
```

After executing this, our TestAccount can no longer run a SELECT statement against the Region table.

In order to remove a DENY, we also issue a REVOKE statement. This time, we'll regain access to the Employees table:

```
USE Northwind
REVOKE ALL ON Employees TO [Aristotle\TestAccount]
```

Now that we've seen how all the commands to control access work for individual users, let's take a look at the way we can greatly simplify management of these rights by managing in groupings.

User Rights and Statement-Level Permissions

User permissions don't just stop with the objects in your database – they also extend to certain statements that aren't immediately tied to any particular object. SQL Server gives you control over permissions to run several different statements, including:

- CREATE DATABASE
- CREATE DEFAULT
- CREATE PROCEDURE
- CREATE RULE
- CREATE TABLE
- CREATE VIEW
- BACKUP DATABASE
- BACKUP LOG

At this point, we've already seen all of these commands at work except for the two backup commands – what those are about is pretty self-explanatory, so I'm not going to spend any time on them here (we'll look at them in Chapter 25) – just keep in mind that they are something you can control at the statement level.

OK, so how do we assign these permissions? Actually, now that you've already seen GRANT, REVOKE and DENY in action for objects, you're pretty much already schooled on statement-level permissions too. Syntactically speaking, they work just the same as object-level permissions except that they are even simpler (you don't have to fill in as much). The syntax looks like this:

```
GRANT <ALL | statement[,...n]> TO <login ID>[,...n]
```

Easy, hey? To do a quick test, let's start by verifying that our test user doesn't have CREATE authority already. Make sure you are logged in as your TestAccount, and then run the following command (don't forget to switch your domain name for Aristotle below):

```
USE Northwind

CREATE TABLE TestCreate
(
   Col1 int Primary Key
)
```

This gets us nowhere fast:

Server: Msg 262, Level 14, State 1, Line 2
CREATE TABLE permission denied, database 'Northwind', owner 'dbo'.

Now log into SQL Server using the sa account (or another account with dbo authority for Northwind). Then run our command to grant permissions:

```
GRANT CREATE TABLE To [Aristotle\TestAccount]
```

You should get confirmation that your command completed successfully. Then just try running the CREATE statement again (remember to log back in using the TestAccount):

```
USE Northwind

CREATE TABLE TestCreate
(
   Col1 int Primary Key
)
```

This time everything works.

DENY and REVOKE also work the same way as they did for object-level permissions.

Server and Database Roles

Prior to version 7.0, SQL Server had the concept of a "group" – a grouping of user rights that you can assign all at once by simply assigning the user to that group – but it didn't work anything like NT groups do. A user can belong to more than one NT group, so you can mix and match them as needed. SQL Server 6.5 and prior only allowed a user to belong to one group per database.

The fallout from the pre 7.0 way of doing things were groups which fell into one of three categories:

- Were frequently modified by user-level permissions
- Were only a slight variation of the main group
- Had more access than required so the DBA wouldn't have to think about it much

Basically, they were one great big hassle, albeit a rather necessary one.

Along came version 7.0 and some very big changes. Instead of a group, a user now belongs to a **role**. A role is, in the most general sense, the same thing as a group.

> **A role is a collection of access rights that can be assigned to a user en masse simply by assigning a user to that role.**

The differences begin to fade there, though. With roles, a user can belong to several at one time. This can be incredibly handy since you can group access rights into smaller and more logical groups, and then mix and match them into the formula that fits a user best.

Roles fall into two categories:

- Server Roles
- Database Roles

We'll soon see a third thing that's also called role – I wish Microsoft had chosen another name. Application roles (the third role form we shall look at) are really more of a special way to alias a user into a different set of permissions. An application role isn't something you assign a user to, it's more a way of having an application have a different set of rights than the user does. For this reason, I don't usually think of application roles as a "role" in the true sense of the word.

Server roles are limited to those that are already built into SQL Server when it ships, and are primarily there for the maintenance of the system as well as granting the capability to do non database-specific things like creating login accounts and creating linked servers.

Much like server roles, there are a number of built-in (or "fixed") database roles, but you can also define your own database roles to meet your particular needs. Database roles are for setting up and grouping specific user rights within a single given database.

Let's look at both of these types of roles individually.

Server Roles

All server roles available are "fixed" roles and are there right from the beginning – all the server roles that you're ever going to have existed from the moment your SQL Server was installed.

Role	Nature
sysadmin	This role can perform any activity on your SQL Server. Anyone with this role is essentially an sa for that server. The creation of this server role provides Microsoft with the capability to one day eliminate the sa login – indeed, the Books Online refers to sa as being legacy in nature. It's worth noting that the NT Administrators group on the SQL Server is automatically mapped into the sysadmin role. This means that anyone who is a member of your server's Administrators group also has sa-level access to your SQL data. You can, if you need to, remove the NT administrators group from the sysadmin role to tighten that security loophole.
serveradmin	This one can set server-wide configuration options or shut down the server. It's rather limited in scope, yet the functions controlled by members of this role can have a very significant impact on the performance of your server.
setupadmin	This one is limited to managing linked servers and startup procedures.
securityadmin	This one is very handy for logins that you create specifically to manage logins, read error logs, and CREATE DATABASE permissions. In many ways, this one is the classic system operator role – it can handle most of the day-to-day stuff, but doesn't have the kind of global access that a true omnipotent superuser would have.
processadmin	Has the capability to manage processes running in SQL Server – this one can kill long running processes if necessary.
dbcreator	Is limited to creating and altering databases.
diskadmin	Manages disk files (what filegroup things are assigned to, attaching and detaching databases, etc).

You can mix and match these roles to individual users who are responsible for administration roles on your server. In general, I suspect that only the very largest of database shops will use more than the sysadmin and securityadmin roles, but they're still handy to have around.

Earlier in this chapter, I got into a lengthy soapbox diatribe on the evils of global users. It probably comes as no surprise to you to learn that I was positively ecstatic about the new sysadmin role. The addition of this role means that, on an ongoing basis, you should not need to have anyone have the sa login – just let the users who need that level of access become members of the sysadmins role, and they shouldn't ever need to login as sa.

Database Roles

Database roles are limited in scope to just one database – just because a user belongs to the db_datareader role in one database it doesn't mean that he belongs to that role in another database. Database roles fall into two subcategories: fixed and user-defined.

Fixed Database Roles

Much as there are several fixed server roles, there are also a number of fixed database roles. Some of them have a special nature to them that isn't duplicable using the normal statements (you couldn't create a user-defined role that had the same functionality), but most are just there to deal with the more common situations and make things easier for you.

Role	Nature
db_owner	This role performs as if it were a member of all the other database roles. Using this role, you can create a situation where multiple users can perform the same functions and tasks as if they were the database owner.
db_accessadmin	Performs a portion of the functions similar to the securityadmin server role, except this role is limited to the individual database where it is assigned to, and the creation of users (not individual rights). It cannot create new SQL Server logins, but members of this role can add NT users and groups as well as existing SQL Server logins into the database.
db_datareader	Can issue a SELECT statement on all user tables in the database.
db_datawriter	Can issue INSERT, UPDATE, and DELETE statements on all user tables in the database.
db_ddladmin	Can add, modify, or drop objects in the database.
db_securityadmin	The other part of the database-level equivalent of the securityadmin server role. This database role cannot create new users in the database, but does manage roles and members of database roles as well as manage statements and object permissions in the database.
db_backupoperator	Backs up the database (gee, bet you wouldn't have guessed that one!).
db_denydatareader	Provides the equivalent of a DENY SELECT on every table and view in the database.
db_denydatawriter	Similar to db_denydatareader, only affects INSERT, UPDATE, and DELETE statements.

Much like the fixed server roles, you're probably not going to see all of these used in anything but the largest of database shops. Some of the roles are not replaceable with your own establishments of rights, and others are just very handy to deal with the quick and dirty situations that seem to frequently come up.

User-Defined Database Roles

The fixed roles that are available are really only meant to be there to help you get started. The real mainstay of your security is going to be the creation and assignment of user-defined database roles. For these roles, you decide which permissions they include.

With user-defined roles, you can GRANT, DENY, and REVOKE in exactly the same fashion as we did for individual users. The nice thing about using roles is that users tend to fall into categories of access needs – by using roles you can make a change in one place and have it propagate to all similar users (at least the ones that you have assigned to that role).

Creating a User-Defined Role

To create our own role, we use the sp_addrole system sproc. The syntax is pretty simple:

```
sp_addrole [@rolename =] <'role name'>
    [, [@ownername =] <'owner'>]
```

The *role name* is simply what you want to call that role. Examples of common naming schema would include by department (Accounting, Sales, Marketing, etc) or by specific job (CustomerService, Salesperson, President, etc). Using roles like this can make it a real snap to add new users to the system. If your accounting department hires someone new, you can just add them to the Accounting role (or, if you're being more specific, it might even be the AccountsPayable role) and forget it – no researching "What should this person have for rights?"

The *owner* is the same thing as it is for all other objects in the system. The default is the database owner, and I strongly suggest leaving it that way (in other words, just ignore this optional parameter).

Let's go ahead and create ourselves a role:

```
USE Northwind
EXEC sp_addrole 'OurTestRole'
```

When you execute this, you should get back a nice and friendly message telling you that the new role has been added.

Now, we need to add some value to this role in the form of it actually having some rights assigned to it. To do this, we use our GRANT, DENY, or REVOKE statements just as we did for actual users earlier in the chapter:

```
USE Northwind
GRANT SELECT ON Territories TO OurTestRole
```

Anyone who belongs to our role now has SELECT access to the Territories table (unless they have a DENY somewhere else in their security information).

At this point, you're ready to start adding users.

Adding Users to a Role

Having all these roles around is great, but they are of positively no use if they don't have anyone assigned to them. Adding a user to a role is as simple as using the `sp_addrolemember` system sproc and providing the database name and login ID:

```
sp_addrolemember [@rolename =] <role name>,
   [@membername =] <Login ID>
```

Everything is pretty self-explanatory on the parameters for this one, so let's move right into an example.

Let's start off by verifying that our `TestAccount` doesn't have access to the `Territories` table:

```
SELECT * FROM Territories
```

Sure enough, we are rejected (No access yet):

Server: Msg 229, Level 14, State 5, Line 1
SELECT permission denied on object 'Territories', database 'Northwind', owner 'dbo'.

Now we'll go ahead and add our `TestAccount` NT user to our `OurTestRole` role:

```
USE Northwind
EXEC sp_addrolemember OurTestRole, [Aristotle\TestAccount]
```

Again, we get a friendly confirmation that things have worked properly:

'Aristotle\TestAccount' added to role 'OurTestRole'.

It's time to try and run the `SELECT` statement again – this time with much more success (you should get about 53 rows back).

Removing a User from a Role

What goes up, must come down, and users who are added to a role will also inevitably be removed from roles.

Removing a user from a role works almost exactly as adding them does, except we use a different system sproc called `sp_droprolemember` in the form of:

```
sp_droprolemember [@rolename =] <role name>,
   [@membername =] <security account>
```

So let's go right back to our example and remove the `TestAccount` from the `OurTestRole` database role:

```
USE Northwind
EXEC sp_droprolemember OurTestRole, [Aristotle\TestAccount]
```

You should receive another friendly confirmation that things have gone well, now try our SELECT statement again:

```
SELECT * FROM Territories
```

And, sure enough, we are again given the error that we don't have access.

You can add and drop users from any role this way – it doesn't matter whether the role is user-defined or fixed, or whether it's a system or database role. In any case, they work pretty much the same.

Note also that you can do all of this through EM. To change the rights associated with a role, just click on the Roles member of the database node, and assign permissions by using the checkboxes. When you want to add a user to the role, just go to the user properties, select either the server or database roles tab, and then put a checkmark in all the roles you want that user to have.

Dropping Roles

Dropping a role is as easy as adding one. The syntax is simply

```
EXEC sp_droprole <'role name'>
```

And it's gone.

Application Roles

Application roles are something of a different animal than are database and server roles. Indeed, the fact that the term "role" is used would make you think that they are closely related – they aren't.

Applications roles are really much more like a security alias for the user. Application roles allow you to define an access list (made up of individual rights or groupings of databases). They are also similar to a user in the aspect that they have their own password. They are, however, different from a user login because they cannot "login" as such – a user account must first login, then they can activate the application role.

So what do we need application roles for? For applications – what else? Time and time again, you'll run into the situation where you would like a user to have a separate set of rights depending on under what context they are accessing the database. With an application role, you can do things like grant a user no more than read-only access to the database (SELECT statements only), but still allow them to modify data when they do so within the confines of your application.

Note that application roles are a one-way trip – that is, once you've established an application role as being active for a given connection, you can't go back to the user's own security on that connection. In order for users to go back to their own security information, they must terminate the connection and login again.

The process works like this:

1. The user logs in (presumably using a login screen provided by your application).
2. The login is validated, and the user has whatever his or her rights have been set up as.
3. The application executes a system sproc called `sp_setapprole` and provides a role name and password.
4. The application role is validated, and the connection is switched to the context of that application role (all the rights the user had are gone – he or she may now have more or less depending on what rights the application role has).
5. The user continues with access based on the application role rather than his or her personal login throughout the duration of the connection – the user cannot go back to his or her own access information.

One would only want to use application roles as part of a true application situation. You would build the code to set the application role right into the app. You would also compile the required password into the app or store the information in some local file to be accessed when it is needed.

Creating Application Roles

To create an application role, we use a new system sproc called `sp_addapprole`. This is another pretty easy one to use, and its syntax looks like this:

```
sp_addapprole [@rolename =] <role name>,
   [@password =] <'password'>
```

Much like many of the sprocs in this chapter, the parameters are pretty self-explanatory, so let's move right on to using it by creating ourselves an app role:

```
EXEC sp_addapprole OurAppRole, 'password'
```

Just that quick, our app role is created.

Adding Permissions to the App Role

Adding permissions to app roles works just like adding permissions to anything else. Just substitute the app role name anywhere that you would use a login ID or regular server or database role.

Again, we'll move to the quick example:

```
GRANT SELECT ON Region TO OurAppRole
```

Our app role now has `SELECT` rights on the `Region` table – it doesn't, as yet, have access to anything else.

Using the App Role

Using the app role is a matter of calling a system sproc (sp_setapprole) and providing both the app role name and the password for that app role. The syntax looks like this:

```
sp_setapprole [@rolename =] <role name>,
   [@password =] {Encrypt N'password'}|'password'
   [,[@encrypt =] '<encryption style>']
```

The *role name* is simply the name of whatever app role you want to activate.

The *password* can either be supplied straightforward or encrypted using the ODBC encrypt function. If you're going to encrypt the password, then you need to enclose the password in quotes after the Encrypt keyword and precede the password with a capital N – this indicates to SQL Server that you're dealing with a Unicode string, and it will be treated accordingly. Note the use of a curly braces { } rather than parentheses for the encryption parameter. If you don't want encryption, then just supply the password without using the Encrypt keyword.

The *encryption style* is only needed if you chose the encryption option for the password parameter. If you are encrypting, then supply "ODBC" as the encryption style.

It's worth noting that encryption is only an option with ODBC and OLE DB clients. You cannot use DB-Lib with encryption.

Moving right into the example category, let's start by verifying a couple of things about the status of our TestAccount user. At this point in the chapter (assuming you've been following along with all the examples), your TestAccount user should not be able to access the Region table, but should be able to access the EmployeeTerritories table. You can verify this to be the case by running a couple of SELECT statements:

```
SELECT * FROM Region
SELECT * FROM EmployeeTerritories
```

The first SELECT should give you an error, and the second should return around 50 rows or so.

Now let's activate the app role that we created a short time ago, type this in using TestAccount user:

```
sp_setapprole OurAppRole, {Encrypt N'password'}, 'odbc'
```

When you execute this, you should get back a confirmation that your application role is now "active".

Try it out by running our two SELECT statements – you'll find that what does and doesn't work has been exactly reversed. That is, TestAccount had access to EmployeeTerritories, but that was lost when we went to the application role. TestAccount did not have access to the Regions table, but the application role now provides that access.

There is no way to terminate the application role for the current connection, so you can go ahead and terminate your TestAccount connection. Then, create a new connection with NT security for your TestAccount. Try running those SELECT statements again and you'll find that your original set of rights has been restored.

Getting Rid of App Roles

When you no longer need the app role on your server, you can use `sp_dropapprole` to eliminate it from the system. The syntax is as follows:

```
sp_dropapprole [@rolename =] <role name>
```

To eliminate our application role from the system, we would just issue the command (from `sa`):

```
EXEC sp_dropapprole OurAppRole
```

More Advanced Security

This section is really nothing more than an "extra things to think about" section. All of these fall outside the defined set of rules, but they address ways around some problems and also how to close some common loopholes in your system.

What to Do about the guest Account

The `guest` account provides a way of having default access. When you have the `guest` account active, then several things happen:

- Logins gain `guest`-level access to any database to which they are not explicitly given access
- Outside users can login through the `guest` account to gain access. This requires that they know the password for `guest`, but they'll already have an advantage by the fact that they know the user exists (although, they probably also know that the `sa` account exists too)

Personally, one of the first things I do with my SQL Server is to eliminate every ounce of access the `guest` account has. It's a loophole, and it ends up providing access in a way you don't intuitively think of. (You probably think that when you assign rights to someone – that's all the rights they have. With `guest` active, that isn't necessarily so.) I recommend that you do the same.

TCP/IP Port Settings

By default when using TCP/IP, SQL Server uses port number 1433. A port can be thought of as something like a radio channel – it doesn't matter what channel you're broadcasting on, it won't do you any good if no one is listening to that channel.

Leaving things with the default value of 1433 can be very convenient – all of your clients will automatically use port 1433 unless you specify otherwise, so this means that you have one less thing to worry about if you leave this as a default.

The problem, however, is that just about any potential SQL Server hacker also knows that port 1433 is the one to which 99% of all SQL Servers are listening. If your SQL Server has a direct connection to the Internet, I strongly recommend changing to a non-standard port number – check with your network administrator for what he/she recommends as an available port. Just remember that, when you change what the server is "listening" to, you'll also need to change what all the IP based clients are using. For example, if we were going to change to using port 1402, we would go into the Client Network Utility and set up a specific entry for our server with 1402 as the IP port to use:

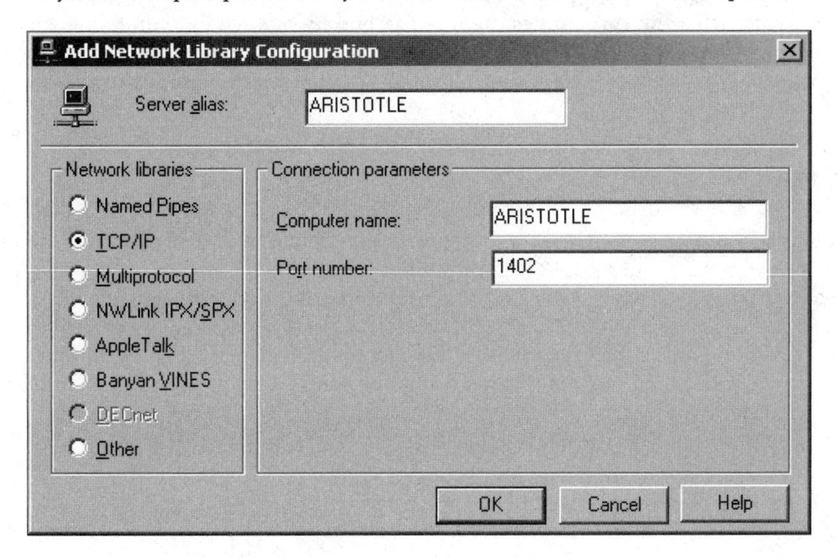

Don't Use the sa Password

Everyone who's studied SQL Server for more than about 10 minutes knows about the system administrator account. Now that SQL Server has the `sysadmins` fixed server role, I strongly suggest adding true logins to that role, then changing the `sa` password to something very long and very incomprehensible – something not worth spending the time to hack into.

Keep xp_cmdshell under Wraps

I already mentioned this one back in Chapter 12, but remember to be careful about who you grant access to use `xp_cmdshell`. It will run any DOS or NT Command Prompt command. The amount of authority that it grants to your users depends on what account SQL Server is running under. If it is a system account (as the majority are), then the users of `xp_cmdshell` will have very significant access to your server (they could, for example, copy files onto the server from elsewhere on the network, then execute those files). Let's raise the stakes a bit though – there are also a fair number of servers running out there under the context of an NT domain administrator account. Yuck! Anyone with `xp_cmdshell` now has fairly open access to your entire network!!!

The short rendition here is not to give anyone access to `xp_cmdshell` that you wouldn't give administrative rights to for your server or possibly even your domain.

Don't Forget Views and Sprocs as Security Tools

Remember that views and sprocs both have a lot to offer in terms of hiding data. Views can usually take the place of column-level security. They can do wonders to make a user think they have access to an entire table, when they in reality have access to only a subset of the entire data (remember our example of filtering out sensitive employee information, such as salary?). Sprocs can do much the same – you can grant `EXECUTE` rights to a sproc, but that doesn't mean they get all the data from a table (they only get what the sproc gives them) – the end user may not even know what underlying table is supplying the data. In addition, views and sprocs have implied authority to them – that is, just because views and sprocs use a table it doesn't mean that the user has rights to that table directly.

Summary

Security is one of those areas that tend to be ignored by developers. Unfortunately much of the backbone for how secure your system is going to be is determined by how your application handles things, so there's only so much a DBA can do after you've shipped your app.

Treat security as though it is the lifeblood for the success or failure of your system at your customer site (which, if you're building internal projects, may be your site) – it probably is indeed a critical factor.

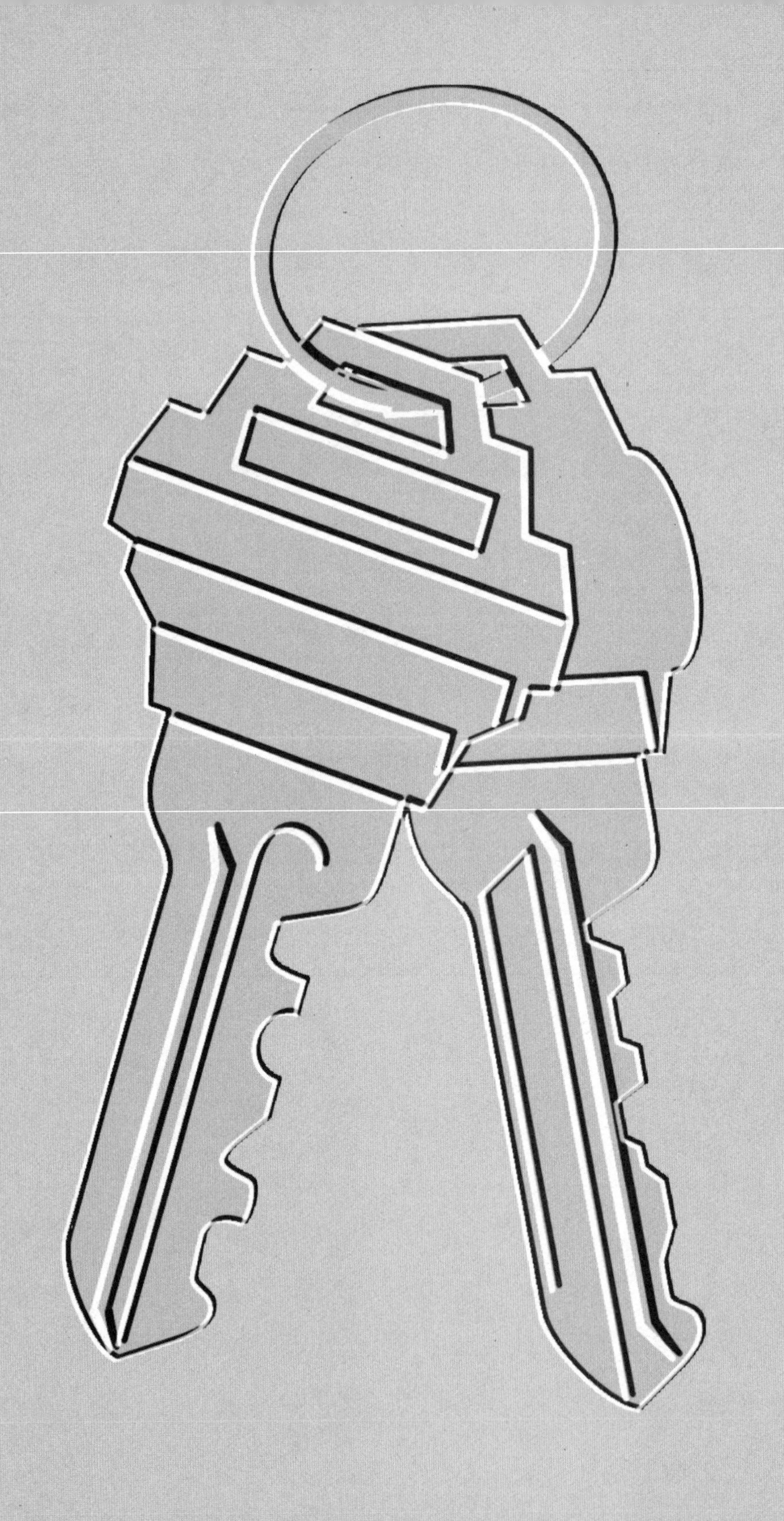

24

Performance Tuning

This is probably the toughest chapter in the book from my perspective as the author, but not for the normal reasons. Usually, the issue is how to relate complex information in a manner that's easy to understand. As we're getting near the end of the book, I hope that I've succeeded there. At this point, you have a solid foundation in everything we're going to discuss in this chapter. That means I'm relatively free to get to the nitty-gritty and not worry quite as much about confusion.

Why then would this be a tough chapter for me to write? Well, because deciding exactly what to put into this chapter is difficult. You see, this isn't a book on performance tuning – that can easily be a book unto itself. It is, however, a book about making you successful in your experience developing with SQL Server. Having a well-performing system is critical to that success. The problem lies in a line from Bob Seger, "What to leave in, what to leave out." What can we focus on here that's going to get you the most bang for your buck?

Perhaps the most important thing to understand about performance tuning is that you are never going to know everything there is to know about it. If you're the average SQL developer, you're going to be lucky if you know 20% of what there is to know. Fortunately, performance tuning is one of those areas where the old 80-20 rule (80% of the benefit comes from the right 20% of the work) definitely applies.

With that in mind, we're going to be roaming around quite a bit in this chapter, topically speaking. Everything we talk about is going to be performance related in some fashion, but we'll touch on a wide range of ways to squeeze the most out of the system performance wise. The topics we'll go into include both new and old subjects. In many cases, it will be a subject we've already covered, but with a particular eye on performance. Some of the places we'll focus on include:

- Index choices
- Client vs server-side processing
- Strategic de-normalization
- Routine maintenance
- Organizing your sprocs
- Uses for temporary tables
- Small gains in repetitive processes vs big gains in long-running processes
- Hardware configuration issues
- Trouble-shooting

Even though we're going to touch on these, there is what is a more important concept to be sure that you get – this is only the beginning. The biggest thing in performance is really just to stop and think about it. There is, for some strange reason, a tendency when working with SQL to just use the first thing that comes to mind that will work. You need to give the same kind of thought to your queries, sprocs, database designs – whatever – that you would give to any other development work that you're doing.

Index Choices

Again, this is something that was covered in extreme depth previously, but the topic still deserves something more than a mention here because of its shear importance to query performance.

People tend to go to extremes with **indexes** – I'm encouraging you not to follow any one rule, but to instead think about the full range of items that your index choices impact upon.

Any table that has a primary key (and with very rare exception, all tables should have a primary key) has at least one index. This doesn't mean, however, that it is a very useful index from a performance perspective. Indexes should be considered for any column that you're going to be frequently using as a target in a `WHERE` or `ORDER BY` clause.

Remember though, that the more indexes you have, the slower your inserts are going to be. When you insert a record, one or more entries (depending on what's going on in the non-leaf levels of the B-Tree) have to be made for that index. That means more indexes and also more for SQL Server to do on inserts. In an OLTP environment (where you tend to have a lot of inserts, updates and deletes), this can be a killer. In an OLAP environment, this is probably no big deal since your OLAP data is usually relatively stable (few inserts), and what inserts are made are usually done through a highly repetitive batch process (doesn't have quite the lack of predictability that users have).

Technically speaking, having additional indexes can also have an impact on updates similar to that for inserts. The problem is, however, to a much smaller degree. Your indexes only need to be updated if the column that was changed is part of the key for that index. If you do indeed need to update the index though, think about it as a delete and insert – that means that you're exposed to page splits again.

So, what then about deletes? Well, again, when you delete a record you're going to need to go and delete all the entries from your indexes too, so you do add some additional overhead. The bright spot is that you don't have to worry about page splits.

The bottom line here is that if you're doing a lot more querying than modifying, then more indexes are OK. However, if you're doing lots of modifications to your data keep your indexes for high use columns.

If you're treating this book as more of a reference than a full "learn how" book and haven't taken the time to read the index chapter yet – do it!

Don't Forget the Index Tuning Wizard

New with Version 7.0 of SQL Server is the **Index Tuning Wizard**. With this tool, you use the SQL Server Profiler to create what's called a **workload file**. A workload file is a trace of all the server activity over a given time period. You can place a number of different filters on it (most notably, what database you want to trace), and it "records" what's really happening on the server. What's great about that is that the Index Tuning Wizard can then use that file to help determine what indexes are going to get the biggest bang for the buck.

The Index Tuning Wizard goes through the workload and runs the query optimizer against every query that was run in the workload file. It runs the optimizer not just once, but several times to investigate how the cost estimates would change if there was a change to the indexes on the underlying table(s). If the wizard finds that new indexes might improve the results of the cost estimate; then it balances that information against things such as how many `INSERT` statements the new index would affect. If there are many `INSERT`s and the new index offers only minimal performance improvement; then the recommendation to add that index might not be made. If, however, the index provides substantial improvement, then it will add it to a list of recommended indexes. The wizard then gives you the opportunity to implement the suggested indexes at the click of a button. Even better – you don't have to make the change right away – SQL Server gives you the chance to either schedule a job to make the change or to generate a script that you could run at your leisure.

Client vs Server-Side Processing

Where you decide to "do the work" can have a very serious impact – for better or worse – on overall system performance.

When **client/server computing** first came along, the assumption was that you would get more/faster/cheaper by "distributing" the computing. For some tasks, this is true. For others though, you lose more than you gain.

Here's a quick review of some preferences as to which end to do things at:

Static cursors	Usually much better on the client. Since the data isn't going to change, you want to package it up and send it all to the client in one pass – thus limiting round trips and network impact. The obvious exception is if the cursor is generated for the sole purpose of modifying other records. In such a case, you should try and do the entire process at the server-side – again eliminating round trips.
Forward-only, read-only cursors	Client-side again. The ODBC libraries can take special advantage of the `FAST_FORWARD` cursor type to gain maximum performance. Just let the server spew the records into the client cursor and then move on with life.
`HOLDLOCK` situations	Most transactioning works much better on the server than on the client. MTS mitigates a lot of this, but direct client/server transactioning through the different object models are a real pain. RDO is not that bad, but ADO is very problematic – particularly when you are dealing with multiple connections.
Processes that require working tables	This is another of those situations where you want to try to have the finished product created before you attempt to move records to the client. If you keep all of the data server-side until it is really ready to be used, you minimize round trips to the server and speed performance.
Minimizing client installations	OK, so this isn't "performance" as such, but it can be a significant cost factor. If you want to minimize the number of client installations you have to do, then keep as much of the business logic out of the client as possible. Either perform that logic in sprocs, or, much better yet, look at using component-based development with MTS (Wrox has a very good book on MTS called *Professional MTS and MSMQ with VB and ASP*).

Significant filtering and/or re-sorting	Use ADO. It has a great set of tools for receiving the data from the server just once (fewer round trips!), then applying filters and sorts locally using the ADO engine. If you wanted the data filtered or sorted differently by SQL Server, it would run an entirely new query using the new criteria. It doesn't take a rocket scientist to figure out that the overhead on that can get rather expensive. Note, however, that with very large result sets, your client computer may not have the wherewithal to deal with the filters and sorts effectively– you may be forced to go back to the server. If you want to learn more about ADO, please refer to the ADO 2.1 Programmer's Reference from Wrox Press.

These really just scratch the surface. The big thing to remember is that round-trips are a killer. What you need to do is move the smallest amount of data back and forth – and only move it once. Usually this means that you'll pre-process the data as much as possible on the server-side, and then move the entire result to the client if possible.

Keep in mind, though, that you need to be sure that your client is going to be able to handle what you give it. Servers are usually much better equipped to handle the resource demands of larger queries. By the same token, you also have to remember that the server is going to be doing this for multiple users – that means the server needs to have adequate resources to store all of the server-side activity for that number of users. If you take a process that was too big for the client to handle and move it server-side for resource reasons, just remember that you may also run out of resources on the server, if more than one client goes to use that process at one time. The best thing is to try to keep result sets and processes the smallest size possible.

Strategic De-Normalization

This could also be called, "When following the rules can kill you." Normalized data tends to work for both data integrity and performance in an OLTP environment. The problem is that not everything that goes on in an OLTP database is necessarily transaction processing related. Even OLTP systems have to do a little bit of reporting (a summary of transactions entered that day for example).

Often, adding just one extra column to a table can prevent a large join, or worse, a join involving several tables. I've seen situations where adding one column made the difference between a two-table join and a nine-table join. We're talking the difference between 100,000 records being involved and several million. This one change made the difference in a query dropping from a run-time of several minutes down to just seconds.

Like most things, however, this isn't something with which you should get carried away. Normalization is the way that most things are implemented for a reason. It adds a lot to data integrity, and can make a big positive difference performance wise in many situations. Don't de-normalize just for the sake of it. Know exactly what you're trying to accomplish, and test to make sure that it had the expected impact. If it didn't, then look at going back to the original way of doing things.

Routine Maintenance

I hate it when good systems go bad. It happens on a regular basis though. It usually happens when people buy or build systems, put them into operation, then forget about them.

Maintenance is as much about performance as it is about system integrity. Query plans get out of date, index pages get full (so you have a lot of page splits), fragmentation happens, the best indexes have to have changes as usage and the amount of data in various tables changes.

Watch the newsgroups. Talk to a few people who have older systems running. You'll hear the same story over and over again. "My system used to run great, but it just keeps getting slower and slower – we haven't changed anything, so what happened?" Well, systems will naturally become slower as the amount of data they have to search over increases; however, the change doesn't have to be all that remarkable and usually it shouldn't be. Instead, the cause is usually that the performance enhancements you put in place when you first installed the system don't really apply anymore, as the way your users use the system and the amount of data has changed, so has the mix of things that will give you the best performance.

We'll be looking at maintenance quite a bit in the next chapter. However, we've discussed it here for two reasons. Firstly, to help if you are checking out this chapter because you have a specific performance problem. Secondly, and perhaps more importantly, because there is a tendency to just think about maintenance as being something you do to prevent the system from going down and to ensure backups are available should the worst happen. This simply isn't the case. Maintenance is also a key from a performance perspective.

Organizing Your Sprocs Well

I'm not talking from the outside (naming conventions and such are important, but that's not what I'm getting at here), but rather from a "how they operate" standpoint. Remember to:

Keep Transactions Short

Long transactions can not only cause deadlock situations, but also basic blocking. Any time you have a process that is blocked – even if it will eventually be able to continue after the blocking transaction is complete – you are delaying, and therefore hurting the performance of, that blocked procedure. There is nothing that has a more immediate effect on performance than that a process has to simply stop and wait.

Use the Least Restrictive Transaction Isolation Level Possible

The tighter you hold those locks, the more likely that you're going to wind up blocking another process. You need to be sure that you take the amount of locks that you really need to ensure data integrity – but try not to take any more than that.

If you need more information on isolation levels, check out the chapter on transactions and locks earlier in the book.

Implement Multiple Solutions if Necessary

An example here is a search query that accepts multiple parameters but doesn't require all of them. It's quite possible to write your sproc so that it just uses one query, regardless of how many parameters were actually supplied– a "one size fits all" kind of approach. This can be a real timesaver from a development perspective, but it is really deadly from a performance point of view. More than likely, it means that you are joining several unnecessary tables for every run of the sproc!

The thing to do here is add a few `IF…ELSE` statements to check things out. This is more of a "look before you leap" kind of approach. It means that you will have to write multiple queries to deal with each possible mix of supplied parameters, but once you have the first one written, the others can often be cloned and then altered from the first one.

> *This is a real problem area in lots of code out there. Developers are a fickle bunch. We generally only like doing things as long as they are interesting. If you take the example above, you can probably see that it would get very boring very quickly to be writing what amounts to a very similar query over and over to deal with the nuances of what parameters were supplied.*
>
> *All I can say about this is – well, not everything can be fun, or everyone would want to be a software developer! Sometimes you just have to grin and bear it for the sake of the finished product.*

Avoid Cursors if Possible

If you're a programmer who has come from an ISAM or VSAM environment, doing things by cursor is probably going to be something towards which you'll naturally gravitate. After all, the cursor process works an awful lot more like what you're used to in those environments.

Don't go there!

Almost all things that are first thought of as something you can do by cursors can actually be done as a set operation. Sometimes it takes some pretty careful thought, but it usually can be done.

By way of illustration, I was asked a while back for a way to take a multi-line cursor-based operation and make it into a single statement if possible. The existing process ran something like 20 minutes. The run-time was definitely problematic, but the customer wasn't really looking to do this for performance reasons (they had accepted that the process was going to take that long). Instead, they were just trying to simplify the code.

They had a large product database and they were trying to set things up to automatically price their available products based on cost. If the markup had been a flat percentage (say 10%) then the `UPDATE` statement would have been easy – say something like:

```
UPDATE Products
SET UnitPrice = UnitCost * 1.1
```

The problem was that it wasn't a straight markup – there was a logic pattern to it. The logic went something like this:

- If the pennies on the product after the markup were greater than or equal to .50, then price it at .95
- If the pennies were below .50, then mark it at .49

The pseudocode to do this by cursor would look something like:

```
Declare and open the cursor
Fetch the first record
Begin Loop Until the end of the result set
Multiply cost * 1.1
If result has cents of < .50
   Change cents to .49
Else
   Change cents to .95
Loop
```

This is, of course, an extremely simplified version of things. There would actually be about 30-40 lines of code to get this done. Instead, we changed it around to work with one single correlated sub-query (which had a `CASE` statement embedded in it). The run-time dropped down to something like 12 seconds.

The point here, of course, is that, by eliminating cursors wherever reasonably possible, we can really give a boost to not only complexity (as was the original goal here), but also to performance.

Uses for Temporary Tables

The use of **temporary tables** can sometimes help performance – usually by allowing the elimination of cursors.

As we've seen before, cursors can be the very bane of our existence. Using temporary tables, we can sometimes eliminate the cursor by processing the operation as a series of two or more set operations. An initial query creates a working dataset. Then another process comes along and operates on that working data.

We can actually make use of the pricing example we laid out in the last section to illustrate the temporary table concept too. This solution wouldn't be quite as good as the correlated sub-query, but it is still quite workable and much faster than the cursor option. The steps would look something like:

```
SELECT ProductID, FLOOR(UnitCost * 1.1) + .49 AS TempUnitPrice
     INTO #WorkingData
     FROM Products
     WHERE (UnitCost * 1.1) - FLOOR(UnitCost * 1.1) < .50
INSERT INTO #WorkingData
SELECT ProductID, FLOOR(UnitCost * 1.1) + .95 AS TempUnitPrice
     FROM Products
     WHERE (UnitCost * 1.1) - FLOOR(UnitCost * 1.1) >= .50
UPDATE p
     SET p.UnitPrice = t.TempUnitPrice
     FROM Product p
     JOIN #WorkingData t
       ON p.ProductID = t.ProductID
```

With this, we wind up with three steps instead of thirty or forty. This won't operate quite as fast as the correlated sub-query would, but it still positively screams in comparison to the cursor solution.

Keep this little interim step using temporary tables in mind when you run into complex problems that you think are going to require cursors. Try to avoid the temptation of just automatically taking this route – look for the single statement query before choosing this option – but if all else fails, this can really save you a lot of time vs a cursor option.

Sometimes, it's the Little Things...

A common mistake in all programming for performance efforts is to ignore the small things. Whenever you're trying to squeeze performance, the natural line of thinking is that you want to work on the long running stuff.

It's true that the long running processes are the ones on which you stand the biggest chance of getting big one-time performance gains. It's too bad that this often leads people to forget that it's the total time saved that they're interested in – that is, how much time when the process is really live.

While it's definitely true that a single change in a query can often turn a several minute query into seconds (I've actually seen a few that took literally days trimmed to just seconds by index and query tuning), the biggest gains for your application often lie in getting just a little bit more out of what already seems like a fast query. These are usually tied to often-repeated functions or items that are often executed within a loop.

Think about this for a bit. Say you have a query that currently takes 3 seconds to run, and this query is used every time an order taker looks up a part for possible sale - say 5000 items looked up a day. Now imagine that you are able to squeeze 1 second off the query time. That's 5000 seconds, or over an hour and 20 minutes!

Hardware Considerations

Forgive me if I get too bland here – I'll try to keep it interesting, but if you're like the average developer, you'll probably already know enough about this to make it very boring, yet not enough about it to save yourself a degree of grief.

Hardware prices have been falling like a rock over the last few years – unfortunately, so has what your manager or customer is probably budgeting for your hardware purchases. When deciding on a budget for your hardware, remember:

- Once you've deployed, the hardware is what's keeping your data safe – just how much is that data worth?
- Once you've deployed, you're likely to have many users – if you're creating a public website, it's possible that you'll have tens of thousands of users active on your system 24 hours per day. What is it going to cost you in terms of productivity loss, lost sales, loss of face, and just general credibility loss if that server is unavailable or – worse – you lose some of your data?
- Maintaining your system will quickly cost more than the system itself. Dollars spent early on a mainstream system that is going to have fewer quirks may save you a ton of money in the long run.

There's a lot to think about when deciding who to purchase from and what specific equipment to buy. Forgetting the budget for a moment, some of the questions to ask yourself include:

- Will the box be used exclusively as a database server?
- Will the activity on the system be processor or I/O intensive? (For databases, it's almost always the latter, but there are exceptions.)
- Am I going to be running more than one production database? If so, is the other database of a different type (OLTP vs OLAP)?
- Will the server be on-site at my location, or do I have to travel to do maintenance on it?
- What are my risks if the system goes down?
- What are my risks if I lose data?
- Is performance "everything"?
- What kind of long-term driver support can you expect as your O/S and supporting systems are upgraded?

Again, we're just scratching the surface of things – but we've got a good start. Let's look at what these issues mean to us.

Exclusive Use of the Server

I suppose it doesn't take a rocket scientist to figure out that, in most cases, having your SQL Server hardware dedicated to just SQL Server and having other applications reside on totally separate system(s) is the best way to go. Note, however, that this isn't always the case.

If you're running a relatively small and simple application that works with other subsystems (say IIS as a web server for example), then you may actually be better off, performance wise, to stay with one box. Why? Well, if there are large amounts of data going back and forth between the two subsystems (your database in SQL Server and your web pages or whatever in a separate process), then memory space to memory space communications are going to be much faster than the bottleneck that the network can create – even in a relatively dedicated network backbone environment.

Remember that this is the exception, not the rule though. The instance where this works best usually meets the following criteria:

- The systems have a very high level of interaction
- The systems have little to do beyond their interactions (the activity that's causing all the interaction is the main thing that the systems do)
- Only one of the two processes is CPU intensive and only one is I/O intensive

If in doubt, go with conventional thinking on this and separate the processing into two or more systems.

I/O vs CPU Intensive

I can just hear a bunch of you out there yelling "Both!" If that's the case, then I hope you have a very large budget – but we'll talk about that scenario too.

If your system is already installed and running, then you can use a combination of NT's perfmon (short for Performance Monitor) and SQL Server Profiler to figure out just where your bottlenecks are – in CPU utilization or I/O. CPU utilization can be considered to be high as it starts approaching a consistent 60% level. Some would argue and say that this number should be as high as 80%, but I'm a believer in the idea that a person's time is more expensive than the CPU's, so I tend to set my thresholds a little lower. I/O depends a lot more on the performance characteristics of your drives and controller.

If you haven't installed yet, then it's a lot more guesswork. While almost anything you do in SQL Server is data based, and will, therefore, certainly require a degree of I/O, how much of a burden your CPU is under varies widely on the types of queries you're running.

Low CPU Load	High CPU Load
Simple, single table queries and updates	Large joins
Joined queries over relatively small tables	Aggregations (`SUM`, `AVG`, etc)
	Sorting of large resultsets

With this in mind, let's focus a little closer on each situation.

I/O Intensive

I/O intensive tasks should cause you to focus your budget more on the drive array than on the CPU(s). Notice that I said the drive "array" – I'm not laying that out as an option. In my not so humble opinion on this matter, if you don't have some sort of redundancy arrangement on your database storage mechanism then you have certainly lost your mind. Any data worth saving at all is worth protecting – we'll talk about the options there in just a moment.

Before we get into talking about the options on I/O, let's look briefly into what I mean by I/O intensive. In short, I mean that a lot of data retrieval is going on, but the processes being run on the system are almost exclusively queries (not complex business processes) and those do not include updates that require wild calculations. Remember – your hard drives are, more than likely, the slowest thing in your system (short of a CD-ROM) in terms of moving data around.

A Brief Look at RAID

RAID; it brings images of barbarian tribes raining terror down on the masses. Actually, most of the RAID levels are there for creating something of a fail-safe mechanism against the attack of the barbarian called "lost data." If you're not a RAID aficionado, then it might surprise you to learn that not all RAID levels provide protection against lost data.

RAID originally stood for **Redundant Array of Inexpensive Disks**. The notion was fairly simple – at the time, using a lot of little disks was cheaper than one great big one. In addition, an array of disks meant that you had multiple drive heads at work and could also build in (if desired) redundancy.

Since drive prices have come down so much (I'd be guessing, but I'd bet that drive prices are, dollar per meg, less than 1% of what they were when the term RAID was coined), I've started to hear new renditions of what RAID stands for. The most common are Random Array of Independent Disks (this one seems like a contradiction in terms to me) and Random Array of Individual Disks (this one's not that bad). The thing to remember, no matter what you think it's an acronym for, is that you have two or more drives working together – usually for the goal of some balance between performance and safety.

There are lots of places you can get information on RAID, but let's take a look at the three levels that are most commonly considered:

RAID Level	Description
RAID 0	aka Disk Striping Without Parity. Out of the three that we are examining here, this is the one you are least likely to know. This requires at least three drives to work just as RAID 5 does. Unlike RAID 5, however, you get no safety net from lost data. (Parity is a special checksum value that allows reconstruction of lost data in some circumstances – as indicated by the time, RAID 0 doesn't have parity.) RAID 0's big claim to fame is giving you maximum performance without loosing any drive space. With RAID 0, the data you store is spread across all the drives in the array (at least 3). While this may seem odd, it has the advantage of meaning that you always have three or more disk drives reading or writing your data for you at once. Under mirroring, the data is all on one drive (with a copy stored on a separate drive). This means that you'll just have to wait for that one head to do the work for you.
RAID 1	aka Mirroring. For each active drive in the system, there is a second drive that "mirrors" (keeps an exact copy of) the information. The two drives are usually identical in size and type, and store all the information to each drive at the same time. (Windows NT has software-based RAID that can mirror any two volumes as long as they are the same size.) Mirroring provides no performance increase when writing data (you still have to write to both drives), but can, depending on your controller arrangement, double your read performance since it will use both drives for the read. What's nice about mirroring is that as long as only one of the two mirrored drives fails, the other will go on running with no loss of data or performance (well, reads may be slower if you have a controller that does parallel reads). The biggest knock on mirroring is that you have to buy two drives to every one in order to have the disk space you need.

RAID Level	Description
RAID 5	The most commonly used. Although, technically speaking, mirroring is a RAID (RAID 1); when people refer to using RAID, they usually mean RAID 5. RAID 5 works exactly as RAID 0 does with one very significant exception – parity information is kept for all the data in the array. Let's say for example that you have a 5-drive array. For any given write, data is stored across all 5 of the drives, but a percentage of each drive (the sum of which adds up to the space of one drive) is set aside to store parity information. Contrary to popular belief, no one drive is the parity drive. Instead, some of the parity information is written to all the drives – it's just that the parity information for a given byte of data is not stored on the same drive as the actual data is. If any one drive is lost, then the parity information from the other drives can be used to re-construct the data that was lost. The great thing about RAID 5 is that you get the multi-drive read performance. The downside is that you lose one drive worth of space (if you have a 3-drive array, you'll see the space of 2, if it's a 7-drive array, you'll see the space of 6). It's not as bad as mirroring in the price per megabyte category, but you still see great performance.

The long and the short of it is that RAID 5 is the de-facto standard for database installations, and I couldn't agree more. That being said, if you have a loose budget, then I'd actually suggest mixing things up a bit.

What you'd like to have is a RAID 5 setup for your main databases, but a completely separate mirrored set for your logs. People who manage to do both usually put both NT and the logs on the mirror set and the physical databases on the RAID 5 array. Since I'm sure inquiring minds want to know why you would want to do this, let's make a brief digression into how log data is read and written.

Unlike database information, which can be read in parallel (thus why RAID 4 or 5 works so well performance wise), the transaction log is chronology dependent – that is, it needs to be written and read serially to be certain of integrity. I'm not necessarily saying that physically ordering the data in a constant stream is required; rather, I'm saying that everything needs to be logically done in a stream. As such, it actually works quite well if you can get the logs into their own drive situation where the head of the drive will only seldom have to move from the stream from which it is currently reading and writing. The upshot of this is that you really want your logs to be in a different physical device than your data, so the reading and writing of data won't upset the reading and writing of the log.

Logs, however, don't usually take up nearly as much space as the read data does. With mirroring, we can just buy two drives and have our redundancy. With RAID 5, we would have to buy three, but we don't see any read benefit from the parallel read nature of RAID 5. When you look at these facts together, it doesn't make much sense to go with RAID 5 for the logs or O/S.

You can have all the RAID arrays in the world, and they still wouldn't surpass a good backup in terms of long-term safety of your data. Backups are easy to take off-site, and are not subject to mechanical failure. RAID units, while redundant and very reliable, also become worthless if two (instead of just one) drives fail. Another issue – what if there's a fire? Probably all the drives will burn up – again, without a backup, you're in serious trouble. We'll look into how to backup your databases in our next chapter.

CPU Intensive

On a SQL Server box, you'll almost always want to make sure that you go multi-processor (assuming your O/S will utilize them – Win 9x won't), even for a relatively low utilization machine. This goes a long way to preventing little "pauses" in the system that will drive your users positively nuts, so consider this part of things to be a given, even if the CPU wasn't your primary focus.

The next big issue is whether to go with Intel or another NT supported platform. The only real candidate in the mainstream here would be Alpha. These are true RISC processors and are blazingly fast – if you really do need the most out of one box, then this may be a viable choice for you. The hard part in this camp is in the area of support. Since there is so much less experience with the Alpha platform, trying to find someone who really knows what they are doing can be a real challenge when you have problems. In addition, Microsoft has announced that NT service pack 5 is the end of the line for support for Alpha. It was supported through RC1 of Win2K, but Microsoft has announced that there will not be a production version of Win2K for Alpha.

Perhaps the biggest issue of all though is memory. This is definitely one area that you don't want to short change. In addition, remember that if you are in a multiprocessor environment (and you should be), then you are going to have more things going on at once in memory. No SQL Server worth installing should ever be configured with less than 128MB of RAM – even in a development environment. Production servers should be equipped with no less than 256MB of RAM – quite possibly more.

Things to think about when deciding how much RAM to use include:

- How many user connections will there be at one time (each one takes up space)? Each connection takes up about 24K of memory (it used to be even higher). This isn't really a killer since 1000 users would only take up 24MB, but it's still something to think about.
- Will you be doing a lot of aggregations and/or sorts? This can be a killer depending on the size of the dataset you're working with in your query.
- How large is my largest database? If your database is only 500MB (and, actually, most databases are much smaller than people think), then having 1GB of RAM probably doesn't make much sense.
- The standard edition of SQL Server for Intel (for Alpha, this is a non-issue) only supports addressing of memory up to 2GB. If you need more than this, you'll need to go with the Enterprise edition.

In addition, once you're in operation – or when you get a fully populated test system up and running – you may want to take a look at your cache-hit ratio in perfmon. We'll talk about how this number is calculated a little bit later in the chapter. For now, it's sufficient to say that this can serve as something of a measurement for how often we are succeeding at getting things out of memory rather than off disk (memory is going to run much, much faster than disk). A low cache-hit ratio is usually a certain indication that more memory is needed. Keep in mind though, that a high ratio does not necessarily mean that you shouldn't add more memory. The read-ahead feature of SQL Server may create what is an artificially high cache hit ratio and may disguise the need for additional memory.

OLTP vs OLAP

The needs between these two systems are often at odds with each other. In any case, I'm going to keep my recommendation short here:

> **If you are running databases to support both of these kinds of needs, run them on different servers – it's just that simple.**

On-Site vs Off-Site

It used to be that anything that would be SQL Server based would be running on-site to those who were responsible for its care and upkeep. If the system went down, people were right there to worry about reloads and to trouble-shoot.

In the Internet era, many installations are co-located to an ISP. The ISP is responsible for making sure that the entire system is backed up – they will even restore according to your directions – but they do not take responsibility for your code. This can be very problematic when you run into a catastrophic bug in your system. While you can always connect remotely to work on it, you're going to run into several configuration and performance issues including:

- Security - remote access being open to you means that you're also making it somewhat more open to others who you may not be interested in having access. My two bits worth on this is to make sure that you have very tight routing restrictions in place. For those of you not all that network savvy (which includes me), this means that you restrict what IP addresses are allowed to be routed to the remote server.
- Performance - you're probably going to be used to the 10Mb to 100Mb network speeds that you have around the home office. Now you're communicating via VPN over the Internet or, worse, dialup and you are starting to hate life (things are SLOW!).
- Responsiveness - it's a bit upsetting when you're running some e-commerce site or whatever and you can't get someone at your ISP to answer the phone, or they say that they will get on it right away and hours later you're still down. Make sure you investigate your remote hosting company very closely – don't assume that they'll still think you're important after the sale.
- Many co-hosting facilities will not do hardware work for you. If you have a failure that requires more than a reloading, you may have to travel to the site yourself or call yet another party to do the maintenance – that means that your application will be offline for hours or possibly days.

If you're a small shop doing this with an Internet site, then off-site can actually be something of a saving grace. It's expensive, but you'll usually get lots of bandwidth plus someone to make sure that the backups actually get done – just make sure that you really check out your ISP. Many of them don't know anything about SQL Server, so make sure that expertise is there.

The Risks of Being Down

This may seem like a silly question. When I ask it, I often get this incredulous look. For some installations, the answer is obvious – they can't afford to be down, period. This number is not, however, as high as it might seem. You see, the only true life and death kind of applications are the ones that are in acute medical applications or are immediately tied to safety operations. Other installations may lose money – they may even cause bankruptcy if they go down – but that's not life and death either.

That being said, it's really not as black and white as all that. There is really something of a continuum in how critical downtime is. It ranges from the aforementioned medical applications at the high end, to data-mining operations on old legacy systems at the low end (usually – for some companies, it may be all they have). The thing that pretty much everyone can agree on for every system is that downtime is highly undesirable.

So the question becomes one of just how undesirable is it? How do we quantify that?

If you have a bunch of bean counters (I can get away with saying that since I was one) working for you, it shouldn't take you all that long to figure out that there are a lot of measurable costs to downtime. For example, if you have a bunch of employees sitting around saying that they can't do anything until the system comes back up, then the number of affected employees times their hourly cost (remember, the cost of an employee is more than just their wages) equals the cost of the system being down from a productivity standpoint. But wait, there's more. If you're running something that has online sales – how many sales did you lose because you couldn't be properly responsive to your customers? Oops – more cost. If you're running a plant with your system, then how many goods couldn't be produced because the system was down – or, even if you could still build them, did you lose quality assurance or other information that might cost you down the line?

I think by now you should be able to both see and sell to your boss the notion that downtime is very expensive – how expensive depends on your specific situation. Now the thing to do is to determine just how much you're willing to spend to make sure that it doesn't happen.

Lost Data

There's probably no measuring this one. In some cases, you can quantify this by the amount of cost you're going to incur reconstructing the data. Sometimes you simply can't reconstruct it, in which case you'll probably never know for sure just how much it cost you.

Again, how much you want to prevent this should affect your budget for redundant systems as well as things like back up tape drives and off-site archival services.

Is Performance Everything?

More often than not, the answer is no. It's important, but just how important has something of diminishing returns to it. For example, if buying those extra 100Mhz of CPU power is going to save you 2 seconds per transaction – that may be a big deal if you have 50 data entry clerks trying to enter as much as they can a day. Over the course of a day, seemingly small amounts of time saved can add up. If each of those 50 clerks are performing 500 transactions a day, then saving 2 seconds per transaction adds up to over 13 man hours (that's over one person working all day!). Saving that time may allow you to delay a little longer in adding staff. The savings in wages will probably easily pay for the extra power.

The company next door may look at the situation a little differently though – they may only have one or two employees; furthermore, the process that they are working on might be one where they spend a lengthy period of time just filing out the form – the actual transaction that stores it isn't that big a deal. In such a case, your extra dollars for the additional speed may not be worth it.

Driver Support

Let's start off by cutting to the chase – I don't at all recommend that you save a few dollars (or even a lot of dollars) when buying your server by purchasing it from some company like "Bob's Pretty Fine Computers". Remember, all those risks? Now, try introducing a strange mix of hardware and driver sets. Now, imagine when you have a problem – you're quickly going to find all those companies pointing the finger at each other saying, "It's their fault!" Do you really want to be stuck in the middle?

What you want is the tried and true – the tested – the known. Servers – particularly data servers – are an area to stick with well-known, trusted names. I'm not advocating anyone in particular (no ads in this book!), but I'm talking very mainstream people like Compaq, IBM, HP, etc. If you need to go to very large systems that are going to exceed the typical 4 processor limit, then you can look at names like Unisys, Tandem, and Sequent just to name a few (a couple of these are now subsidiaries of names I've already mentioned, but they really operate as a separate unit). Note that, when I say well-known, trusted names, I mean names that are known in servers. Just because someone sells a billion desktops a year doesn't mean they know anything about servers – it's almost like apples and oranges. They are terribly different.

By staying with well-known equipment, in addition to making sure that you have proper support when something fails, it also means that you're more likely to have that equipment survive upgrades well into the future. Each new version of the O/S only explicitly supports just so many pieces of equipment – you want to be sure that yours is one of them.

The Ideal System

Let me preface this by saying that there is no one ideal system. That being said, there is a general configuration (size excluded) that I and a very large number of other so called "experts" seem to almost universally push as where you'd like to be if you had the budget for it. What we're talking about is drive arrangements here (the CPU and memory tends to be relative chicken feed budget and setup wise).

What you'd like to have is a mix of mirroring and RAID 5. You place the O/S and the logs on the mirrored drives. You place the data on the RAID 5 array. That way, the O/S and logs – which both tend to do a lot of serial operations – have a drive setup all of their own without being interfered with by the reads and writes of the actual data. The data has a multi-head read/write arrangement for maximum performance while maintaining a level of redundancy.

Trouble-shooting

SQL Server offers a number of options to help with the prevention, detection and measurement of long running queries. The options range from a passive approach of measuring actual performance so you know what's doing what, to a more active approach of employing a query "governor" to automatically kill queries that run over a length of time you choose. These tools are very often ignored or used only sparingly – which is something of a tragedy – they can save hours of trouble-shooting by often leading you right to the problem query and even the specific portion of your query that is creating the performance issues.

Tools to take a look at include:

- `SHOWPLAN TEXT|ALL` and Graphical showplan - looked at in this chapter
- `STATISTICS IO` - also in this chapter
- DBCC - in this chapter
- The Query Governor - covered in this chapter
- `sp_lock` - check out the cool replacement for this in Chapter 13
- The `sysprocesses` table - this is where SQL Server keeps track of what's happening!
- The SQL Server Profiler - in this chapter

Many people are caught up in just using one of these, but the reality is that there is little to no (depending on which two you're comparing) overlap between them. This means that developers and DBAs who try to rely on just one of them are actually missing out on a lot of potentially important information.

Also, keep in mind that many of these are still useful in some form even if you are writing in a client-side language and sending the queries to the server (no sprocs). You can either watch the query come through to your server using the SQL Server Profiler, or you could even test the query in QA before moving it back to your client code.

The Various Showplans and STATISTICS

SQL Server gives you a few different `SHOWPLAN` options. The information that they provide varies a bit depending on what option you choose, but this is one area where there is a fair amount of overlap between your options; however, each one definitely has its own unique thing that it brings to the picture. In addition, there are a number of options available to show query statistics.

Here are the options and what they do:

SHOWPLAN TEXT|ALL

When either of these two SHOWPLAN options (they are mutually exclusive) is executed, SQL Server changes what results you get for your query. Indeed, the NOEXEC option (which says to figure out the query plan but don't actually do it) is put in place, and you receive no results other than those put out by the SHOWPLAN.

The syntax for turning the SHOWPLAN on and off is pretty straightforward:

```
SET SHOWPLAN TEXT|ALL ON|OFF
```

When you use the TEXT option, you get back the query plan along with the estimated costs of running that plan. Since the NOEXEC option automatically goes with SHOWPLAN, you won't see any query results.

When you use the ALL option, you receive everything you received with the TEXT option, plus a slew of additional statistical information including such things as:

- The actual physical and logical operations planned
- Estimated row counts
- Estimated CPU usage
- Estimated I/O
- Average row size
- Whether the query will be run in parallel or not

Let's go run a very brief query utilizing (one at a time) both of these options:

```
SET SHOWPLAN_TEXT ON
GO

SELECT *
FROM Orders
GO

SET SHOWPLAN_TEXT OFF
GO

SET SHOWPLAN_ALL ON
GO

SELECT *
FROM Orders
GO

SET SHOWPLAN_ALL OFF
GO
```

Notice that every statement is followed by a GO – thus making it part of its own batch. The batches that contain the actual query could have had an unlimited number of statements, but the statements setting the SHOWPLAN option have to be in a batch by themselves.

The SHOWPLAN_TEXT portion of the results should look something like this:

```
StmtText
---------------------------

SELECT *
FROM Orders

(1 row(s) affected)

StmtText
--------------------------------------------------------------------------
  |--Clustered Index Scan(OBJECT:([Northwind].[dbo].[Orders].[PK_Orders]))
```

If we had been running a larger query – say something with several joins, the additional sub-processes would have been listed with indentations to indicate hierarchy.

I'm going to skip including the ALL results here since they simply will not fit in a book format (it's about 800 characters wide, and won't fit in any readable form in a book – even if we flipped things sideways), but it included a host of other information. Which one of these to use is essentially dependent on just how much information you want to be flooded with. If you just want to know the basic plan – such as, is it using a merge or hash join, you probably just want to use the TEXT option. If you really want to know where the costs are and such, then you want the ALL option.

Since the SHOWPLAN options imply the NOEXEC – that means nothing in your query is actually being executed. Before you do anything else, you need to set the option back to off – that even includes switching from one showplan option to the other (e.g. SET SHOWPLAN_ALL ON wouldn't have any effect if you had already run SET SHOWPLAN_TEXT ON and hadn't yet turned it off).

I like to make sure that every script I run that has a SET SHOWPLAN statement in it has both the on and off within that same script. It goes along way towards keeping me from forgetting that I have it turned on and being confused when things aren't working the way I expect.

Graphical Showplan

The graphical showplan tool combines bits and pieces of the SHOWPLAN_ALL and wraps them up into a single graphical format. We looked at this briefly when we were looking at the Query Analyzer back in Chapter 3. Part of the reason for looking at it there is that it is a Query Analyzer-only tool. It is selected through options in the QA rather than through T-SQL syntax – this means that it is only available when using QA.

We have three options to start the graphical showplan tool:

- Select the Show Execution Plan option from the Query menu
- Select Show Execution Plan from the Execute mode drop-down list on the toolbar (both this and the option above will execute the query and show the plan)
- Click on the Display Estimated Execution Plan button on the toolbar (this option just shows us the plan with the NOEXEC option active)

Personally, I like the option of having the graphical showplan in addition to my normal query run. While it means that I have to put the actual hit of the query on my system, it also means that the numbers I get are no longer just estimates, but based on the actual cost numbers. Indeed, if you run the showplan both ways and wind up with wildly different results, then you may want to take a look at the last time your statistics were updated on the tables on which the query is based. If necessary, you can then update them manually and try the process again.

The hierarchy of the different sub-processes is then shown graphically. In order to see the costs and other specifics about any sub-process, just hover your mouse over that part of the graphical showplan and a Tooltip will come up with the information:

```
Query 1: Query cost (relative to the batch): 100.00%
Query text: SELECT *   FROM Orders
```

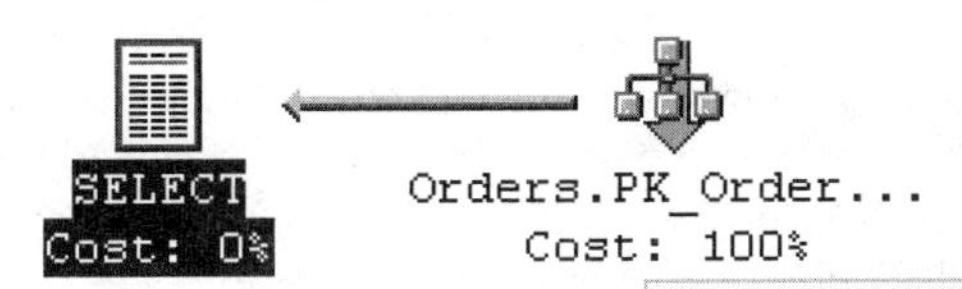

Clustered Index Scan

Scanning a clustered index, entirely or only a range.

Physical operation:	Clustered Index Scan
Logical operation:	Clustered Index Scan
Estimated row count:	830
Estimated row size:	240
Estimated I/O cost:	0.0516
Estimated CPU cost:	0.000991
Estimated number of executes:	1.0
Estimated cost:	0.052644(100%)
Estimated subtree cost:	0.0526

Argument:
OBJECT:([Northwind].[dbo].[Orders].[PK_Orders])

This arrangement can often make it much easier to sort out the different pieces of the plan. The downside is that you can't print it out for reporting the way that you can with the text versions.

STATISTICS

In addition to using the graphical showplan with actual execution of the query, you have a couple of other options for retrieving the "real" information on the statistics of your query – using SQL Server Profiler and turning on `STATISTICS PROFILE`.

`STATISTICS` actually has a couple of options that can be very handy in trouble-shooting query performance including:

SET STATISTICS IO ON|OFF

This one is a very commonly used tool to figure out where and how the query is performing. I find that I'm actually missing the old graphical version of this that used to exist in version 6.5.

`STATISTICS IO` provides several key pieces of information regarding the actual work necessary to perform your query. Information provided includes:

- **Physical Reads**. This represents the actual physical pages read from disk. It is never any more than, and is usually smaller than, the number for logical reads. This one can be very misleading in the sense that it will usually change (be less than the first run) the second time that you run your query. Any page that is already in the buffer cache will not have a physical read done on it, so, the second time you run the query in reasonably short succession, the pages involved will, more than likely, still be in cache. In addition, this number will not be incremented if the page has already been read due to the read ahead mechanism that is part of SQL Server. This means that your query may be responsible for loading the page physically into cache, but it still may not show up as part of the physical reads.
- **Logical Reads**. This is the number of times that the page was actually looked at – regardless of from where it came. That is, any page already in the memory cache will still create a logical read if the query makes use of it. Note that I said it is how many times the page was looked at – that means that you may have several logical reads for a single page if the page is needed several times (say for a nested loop that affects a page that has several rows on it).
- **Read Ahead Reads**. This is the number of pages that SQL Server read into the cache as a result of the read ahead mechanism anticipating that they will be needed. The page may actually be used – or it may not. In either case, the read still counts as a read ahead. Read aheads are very similar to physical reads in the sense that they represent data being physically read from disk. The problem is that the number you get is based on the optimistic nature of the read ahead mechanism, and does not necessarily mean that all that work was actually put to use.
- **Scan Count**. The scan count represents the number of times that a table was accessed. This is somewhat different from logical reads, which was focused on page access. This is another situation where a nested loop is a good example. The outer table that is forming the basis for the condition on the query that is on the inside may only have a scan count of 1, where the inner loop table would have a scan count added for every time through the loop – that is, every record in the outer table.

Some of the same information that forms the basis for `STATISTICS IO` is the information that feeds your cache-hit ratio if you look in Performance Monitor. The cache-hit ratio is based on the number of logical reads, less the physical reads, and then divide that into the total actual reads (logical reads).

The thing to look for with `STATISTICS IO` is for any one table that seems disproportionately high in either physical or logical reads.

A very high physical read count could indicate that the data from the table is being pushed out of the buffer-cache by other processes. If this is a table that you are going to be accessing with some regularity, then you may want to look at purchasing (or, if you're an ISV developing a SQL Server product, recommending) more memory for your system.

If the logical reads are very high, then the issue may be more one of proper indexing. I'll give an example here from a client I had some time back. A query was taking approximately 15 seconds to run on an otherwise unloaded system. Since the system was to be a true OLTP system, this was an unacceptable time for the user to have to wait for information (the query was actually a fairly simple lookup that happened to require a 4 table join). In order to find the problem, I used what amounted to `STATISTICS IO` – it happened to be the old graphical version that came with 6.5, but the data was much the same. After running the query just once, I could see that the process was requiring less than 20 logical reads from three of the tables, but it was performing over 45,000 logical reads from the fourth table. This is what I liked about the old graphical version, it took about a half a second to see that the bar on one table stretched all the way across the screen when the others were just a few pixels! From there, we knew right where to focus – in about two minutes, I had an index built to support a foreign key (remember, they aren't built by default), and the response time dropped to less than a second. The entire trouble-shooting process on this one took literally minutes. Not every performance trouble-shooting effort is that easy, but using the right tools can often help a lot.

SET STATISTICS TIME ON|OFF

This one is amazingly little known. It shows the actual CPU time required to execute the query. Personally, I often use a simple `SELECT GETDATE()` before and after the query I'm testing – as we've done throughout most of the book – but this one can be handy because it separates out the time to parse and plan the query vs. the time to actually execute the query. It's also nice to not have to figure things out for yourself (it will calculate the time in milliseconds – using `GETDATE()` you have to do that yourself).

The Database Consistency Checker (DBCC)

The Database Consistency Checker (or DBCC) has a number of different options available to allow you to check the integrity and structural makeup of your database. This is far more the realm of the DBA than the developer, so I am, for the most part, considering the DBCC to be out of scope for this book. The most notable exceptions come in the maintenance of indexes – those are discussed in the next chapter, so I will address DBCC no further at this time.

The Query Governor

The query governor is a tool that's easiest found in Enterprise Manager (you can also set it using `sp_configure`). This sets the maximum amount of time a query can be estimated to take and still have SQL Server execute the query – that is, if the estimated cost of running the query exceeds that allowed in the query governor, then the query will not be allowed to run.

To get to the query governor in EM, right-click on your server and choose Properties. Then choose the Server Settings tab:

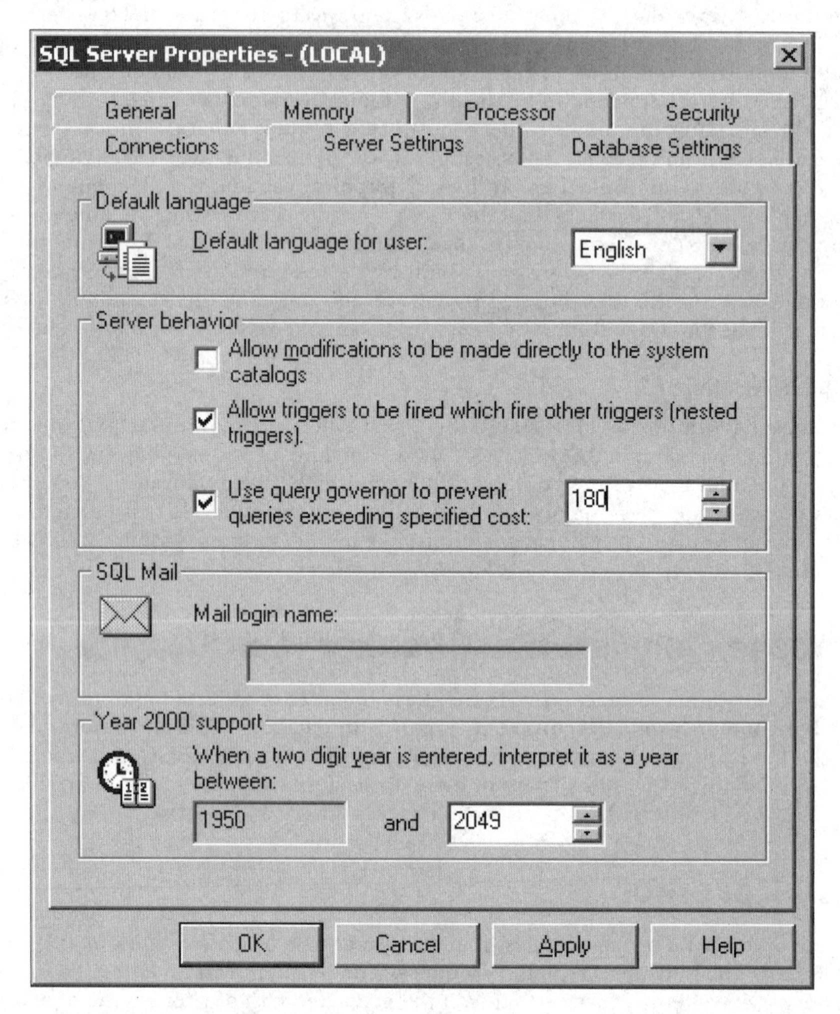

The number you enter into the query governor field loosely (*very* loosely) equates to number of seconds. So, theoretically, if you set it to 180, that's about 3 minutes. Queries that are estimated to run longer than 3 minutes would not be allowed to run. This can be very handy for keeping just a few rather long queries from taking over your system.

Did you happen to notice that I slipped the word theoretically in the paragraphs above? There's a very important reason for that – the time is just an estimate. What really drives the limit is what the optimizer calculates as the estimated "cost" for that query. The problem is that the time is an estimate based on how cost equates to time. The values used are based on a single test box at Microsoft. You can expect that, as systems get faster, the equation between the query governor setting and the real time factor will get less and less reliable.

The SQL Server Profiler

The true lifesaver among the tools provided with SQL Server.

For those of you familiar with SQL Server 6.5, the Profiler used to be called SQL Trace. This version definitely has its differences, but they are much the same in the sense that they let you "sniff out" what's really going on with the server.

Profiler can be started remotely if you're in EM (although found in the Tools menu, it still runs as a separate app), or from the Start menu in Windows. When you first start it up, you can either load an existing profile template, or create a new one.

Let's take a look at some of the key points by walking through a brief example.

Start by choosing New | Trace from the File menu. Log into the server you've been working with, and you should be presented with the following dialog box:

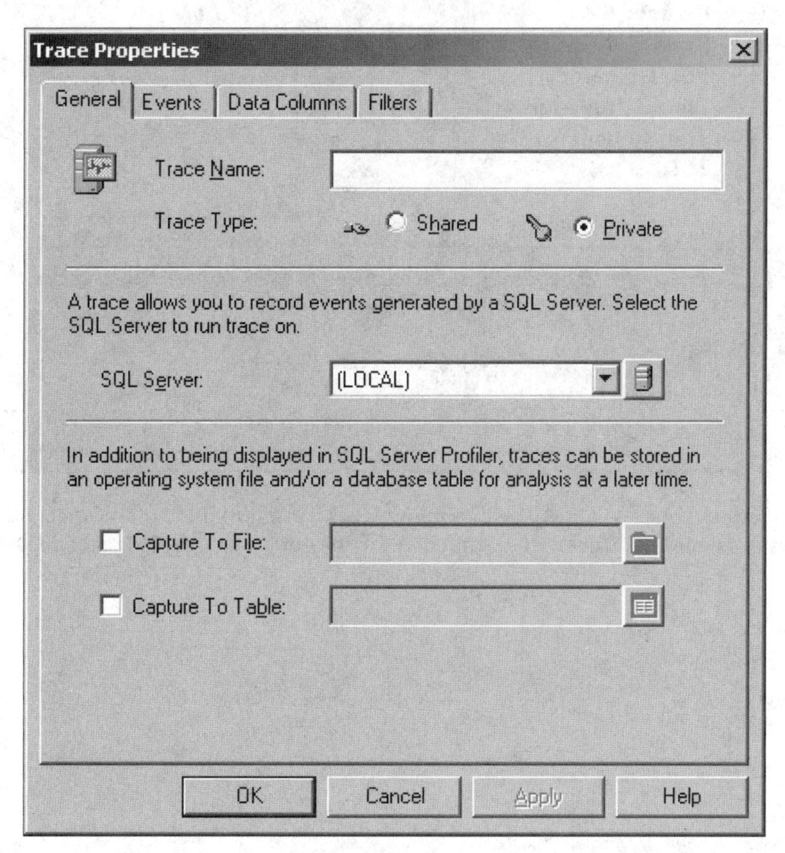

The trace name is probably obvious enough, but the trace type might not be. If you set the trace up as Private, then only the current user will be able to make use of that trace; as Shared, anyone can. You can also choose here whether to capture the trace to a file on disk or a table in the database.

Things get somewhat more interesting on the dialog that comes next:

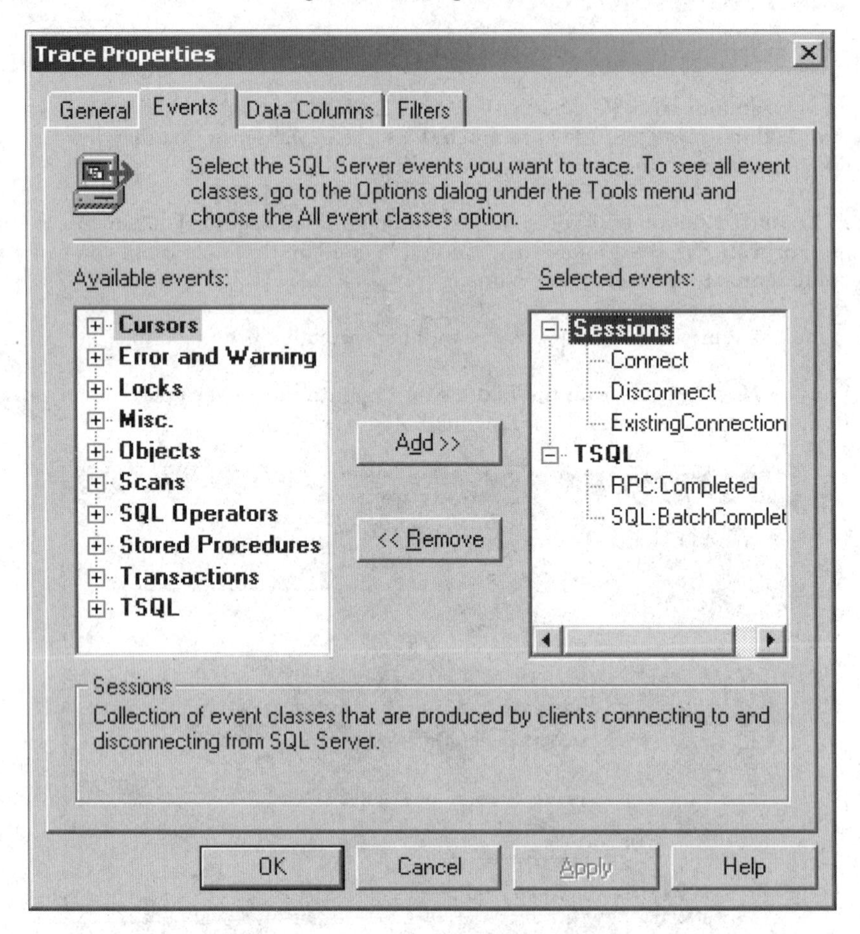

This one is all about what events you are going to track, and, as you can see, there's quite a range. The initial setup is one that tracks what's needed for the Index Tuning Wizard plus a bit more.

For this example, I'm going actually leave things just the way they are and move on to the next tab:

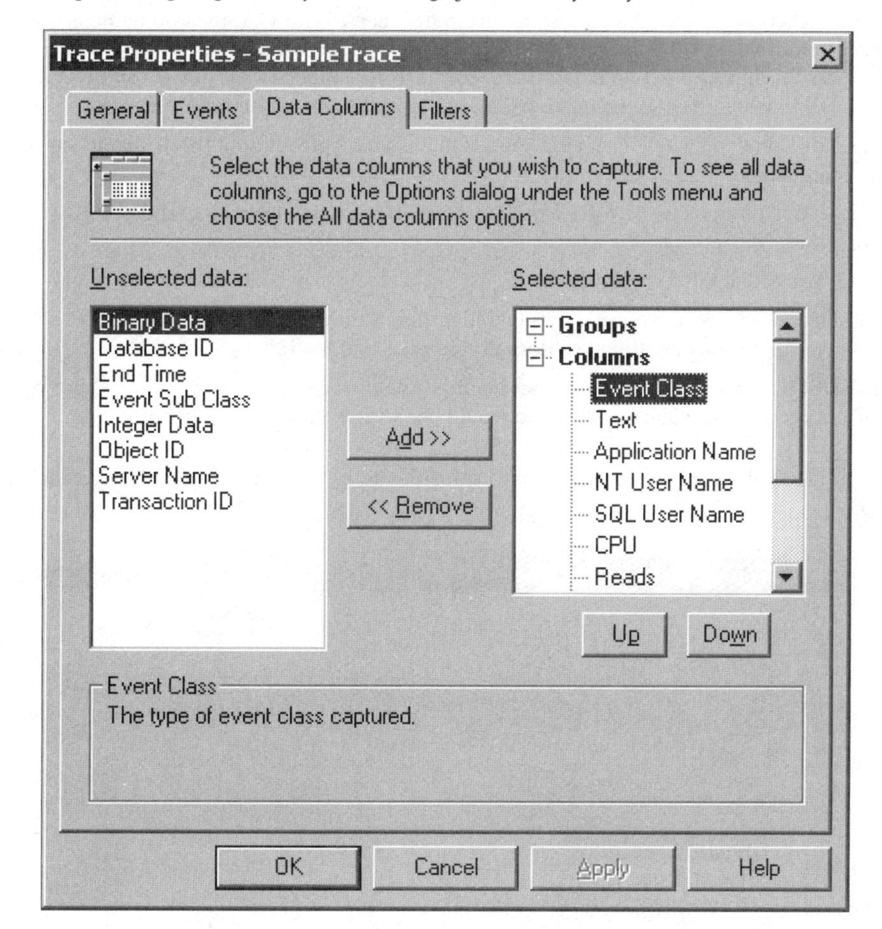

This one is about what information you want to be kept as part of your trace. The temptation here is just to select everything under the sun so you'll be sure to have all the information. There are a couple of reasons not to do this. First, it means that a lot of additional text has to come back down the pipe to your server. Remember that SQL Server Profiler has to place some audits in the system, and this means that your system is having an additional burden placed on it whenever the Profiler is running – the bigger the trace the bigger the burden. Second, it often means lower productivity for you since you have to wade through a huge morass of data – much of which you probably won't need.

In this particular case, I'm again going to take the defaults, but I want to point out a couple of key fields here before we move on:

- Text: This is the actual text of the statement that the Profiler happens to have added to the trace at that moment in time.

- Application Name: Another of those highly under-utilized features. The app name is something you can set when you create the connection from the client. With QA, the app name is Query Analyzer, but if you're using ADO or some other data object model and underlying connection method, you can pass the application name as a parameter in your connection string. It can be quite handy for your DBAs when they are trying to trouble-shoot problems in the system.
- NT User Name: This one is what it sounds like – what's great about this is that it can provide a level of accountability.
- SQL User Name: Same as NT User Name - only used when operating under SQL Server Security rather than NT Security.
- CPU: The actual CPU cycles used.
- Duration: How long the query ran – includes time waiting for locks and such (where the CPU may not have been doing anything, so doesn't reference that load).
- SPID (SQL Process ID): This one can be nice if your trace reveals something where you want to kill a process – this is the number you would use with your `KILL` statement.

Moving right along, let's take a look at what I consider to be one of the most important tabs – the Filters tab:

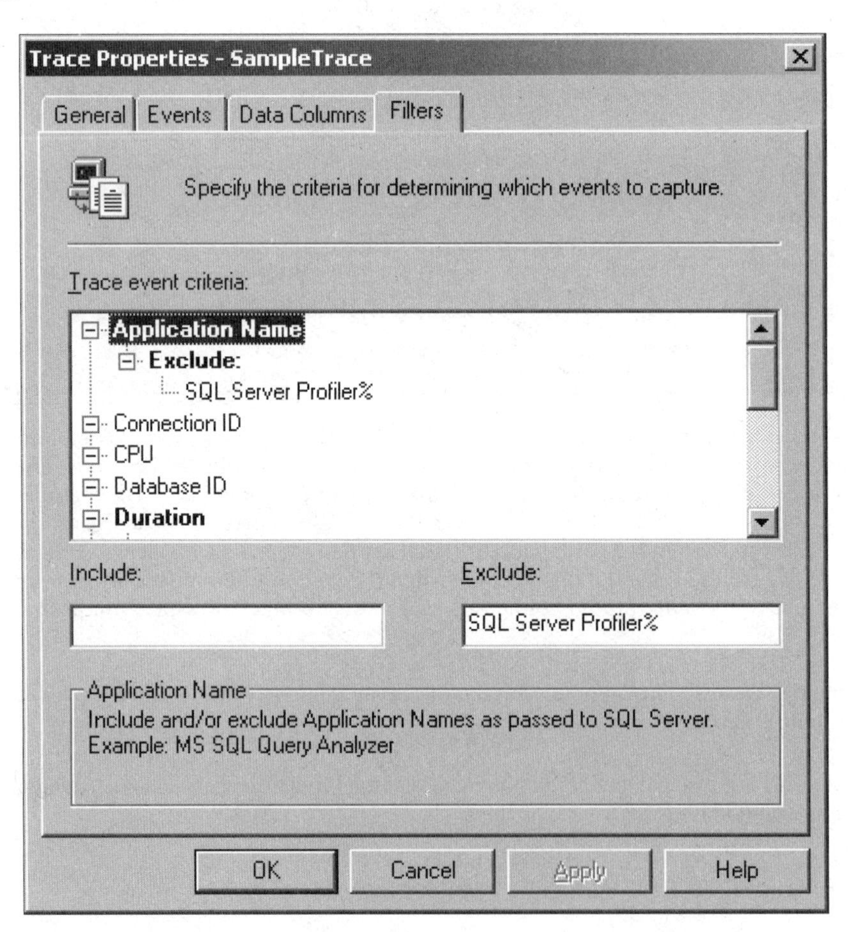

This is the one that makes sure that, on a production server, you don't get buried in several thousand pages of garbage just by opening a trace up for a few minutes.

With the Filters tab, you can select from a number of different options to use to filter out data and limit the size of your result set. By default, Profiler automatically sets up to exclude its own percentage in order to try to reduce the Profiler's impact on the end numbers. For our example here, I'm adding in a Duration value where I've set the minimum to 3000 milliseconds with no maximum.

Odds are that, if you run this with a query against the `Northwind` `Orders` table, you're not going to see it appear in the trace. Why is that? Because that query will probably run very fast and not meet the criteria for being included in our trace – this is an example of how you might set up a trace to capture the query text and user name of someone who has been running very long running queries on the system. Now try running something a little longer – such as a query that joins the `Customers`, `Orders` and `Order Details` tables. There's a good chance that you'll now exceed the duration threshold, and your query will show up in the Profiler (if not, then try adjusting down the duration expectation that you set in Profiler).

I can't say enough about how important this tool is in solving performance and other problems. Too many times to count have I been thinking that my sproc was running down one logic path only to find that a totally different branch was being executed. How did I originally find out? I watched it execute in Profiler.

The Performance Monitor (PerfMon)

The **Performance Monitor** (which is sometimes called **perfmon** because of the executable's file name - `perfmon.exe`) that you'll find included in the Microsoft SQL Server 7.0 menu group is actually just a set of connections into the NT Performance Monitor.

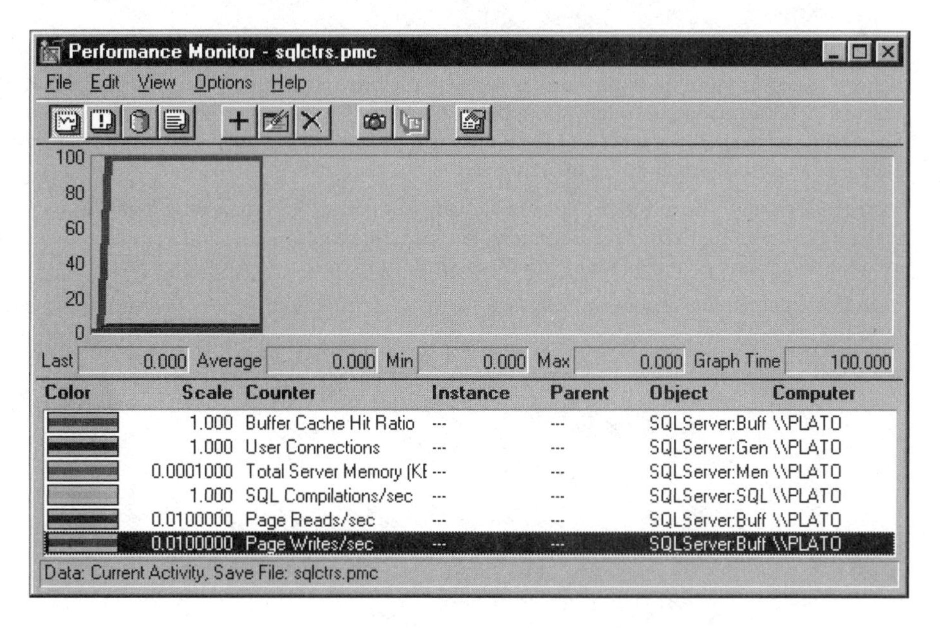

What's different is twofold:

- A number of SQL Server specific choices have been added to your object combo box
- Some of the most commonly used choices are already added to your monitor list

Actually, the extra objects were added to the Performance Monitor when SQL Server was installed on your server. After SQL Server installation, these are available in NT Performance Monitor regardless of how perfmon gets started (from the SQL Server menu choice or the choice you'll find under NT's own Administrative Tools (Common) menu choice).

The biggest difference then is what counters are selected by default. SQL Server will choose six for you right off the bat:

- Buffer Hit Cache Ratio - This is the number of pages that were able to be read from the buffer cache rather than having to issue a physical read from disk. The thing to watch out for here is that this number can be thrown off depending on how effective the read-ahead mechanism was – anything that the read-ahead mechanism got to and put in cache before the query actually needed it is counted as a buffer-cache hit – even though there really was a physical read related to the query. Still, this one is going to give you a decent idea of how efficient your memory usage is. You want to see really high numbers here (in the 90+% range) for maximum performance. Generally speaking, a low buffer hit cache ratio is indicative of needing more memory.
- User Connections - Pretty much as it sounds, this is the number of user connections currently active in the system.
- Total Server Memory - The total amount of dynamic memory that the SQL Server is currently using. As you might expect, when this number is high relative to the amount of memory available in your system (remember to leave some for the O/S!), then you need to seriously consider adding more RAM.
- SQL Compilations/sec - This is telling you how often SQL Server needs to compile things (sprocs, triggers). Keep in mind that this number will also include recompiles (due to changes in index statistics or because a recompile was explicitly requested). When your server is first getting started, this number may spike for a bit, but it should become stable after your server has been running for a while at a constant set and rate of activities.
- Page Reads/sec - The number of physical reads from disk for your server. You'd like to see a relatively low number here. Unfortunately, because the requirements and activities of each system are different, I can't give you a benchmark to work from here.
- Page Writes/sec - The number of physical writes performed to disk for your server. Again, you'd like a low number here.

If you want to change any of these, just click on the plus (+) sign up on the tool bar. You'll be presented with a dialog that lets you choose between all the different objects and counters available on your system (not just those related to SQL Server):

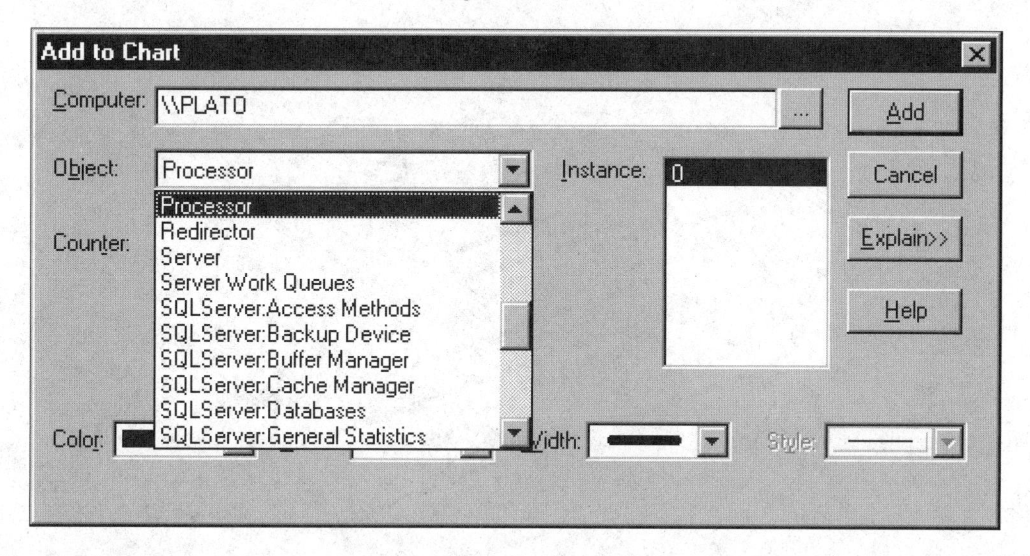

The big thing here is to realize that you can mix and match a wide variety of counters to be able to reach a better understanding of what's going on with your server and make the appropriate adjustments. Much of the time, this kind of a task is going to have more to do with the DBA than the developer, but many of these stats can be helpful to you when you are doing load testing for your application.

Summary

Performance could be, and should be, in a book by itself. There's simply just too much to cover and get acquainted with to do it all in one or even several chapters. The way I've tried to address this is by pointing out performance issues throughout the book so you could take them on a piece at a time.

In this chapter, we've reviewed a number of the performance considerations touched on throughout the book, plus added several new tools and ideas to consider.

In our next chapter, we'll be taking a look at administration issues. As you've seen through some of the portions of this chapter, proper administration can also be a key ingredient to performance.

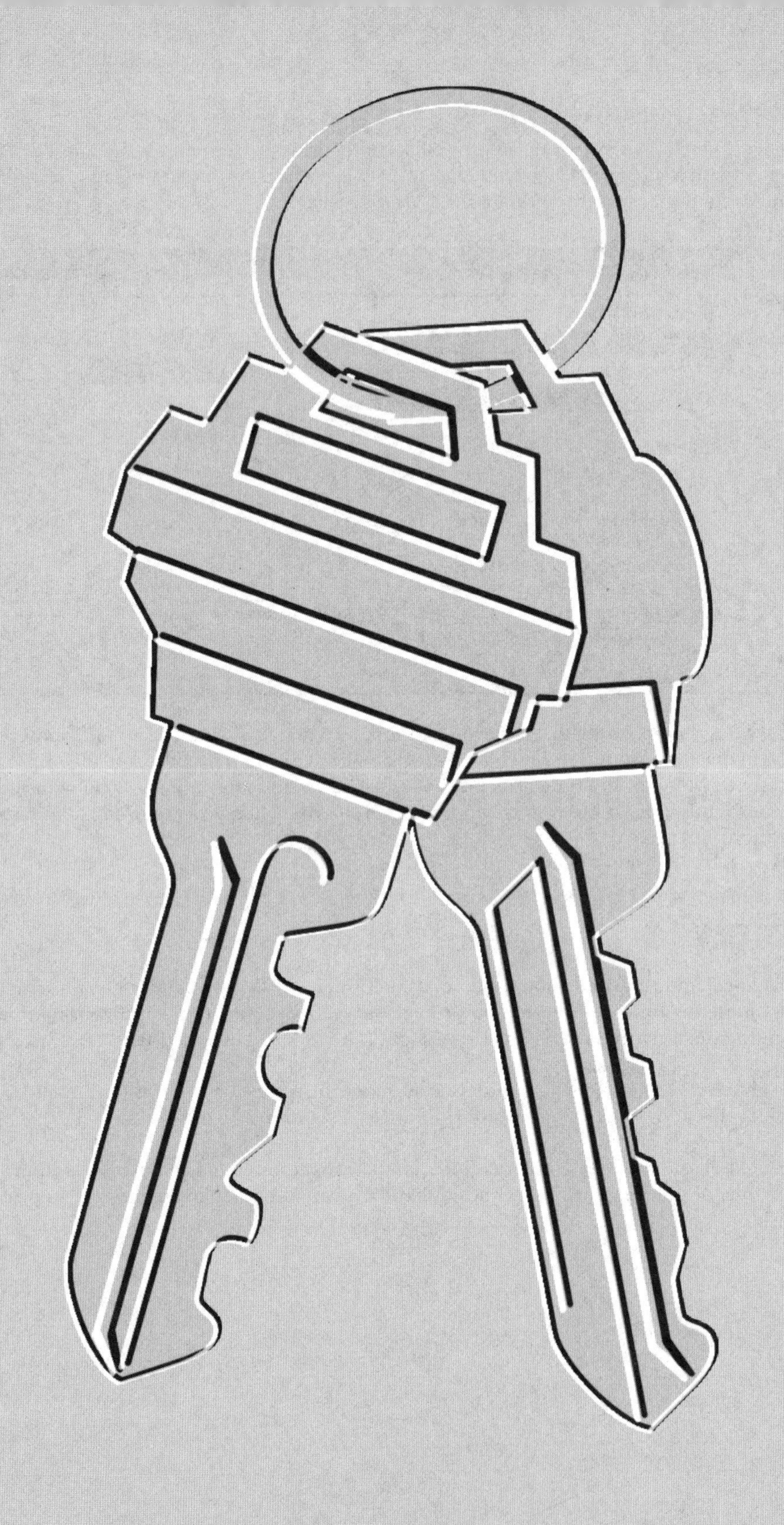

25

Administration Overview

OK, so you're a developer. That means that there's a good chance that one of your highest goals in life is to not get sucked into the role of being the permanent DBA for your application. If you're building a shrink-wrap kind of product or otherwise building a system to be used by a different company, then you're probably reasonably safe in the long-run (but not the short-run). If you're building a system for in-house use, then you'll find yourself constantly being sucked into some level of problem solving for the system that has little or nothing to do with the code. While this situation is a real pain, I have only three words for you: Get over it!

The fact is that, no matter how well you avoid being cast in the DBA role, you're going to need to know a lot of DBA kinds of things in order to build a system that has maximum performance and can be easily administered. Indeed, throughout this book we've already seen how to look into many functions and issues that are more typically thought of as being in the DBA's realm. In each case we've either focused on the issue in question because it has performance impacts that need to be taken into account in the development of the product; or because not realizing how things work can really make it near impossible to administer the system once it's up and running.

In this chapter, we're going to try and do a round up of a number of the administration issues that face any system. While some of these seem more like day-to-day things that the DBA will have to handle, you'll want to know about them too, so you can deal with these issues in your operations and setup documentation. If you're in a consulting role, you'll also find that you will invariably end up doing the initial setup of and training on any scheduled tasks – that means you better get it done right!

We'll be focusing in on:

- Scheduling jobs
- Backup and restore
- Alerts
- Full-Text Catalog population
- Carrying data from one place to another
- Index rebuilding
- Archival of data

These are really just some of the basics – administration issues could create a list of topics hundreds if not thousands of entries long, but that's for another book. In looking at these, we'll cover most of the issues that frequently come up, and allow you to plan for them when you are designing your system, so the DBAs that eventually are put in charge of your system will come to love rather than hate you.

Scheduling Jobs

Many of the tasks that we'll go over in the remainder of the chapter can be **scheduled**. Scheduling jobs allows you to run tasks that place a load on the system at off-peak hours. It also assures that you don't forget to take care of things. From index rebuilds to back-ups you'll hear of horror stories over and over about shops that "forgot" to do that, or thought they had set up a scheduled job but never checked on it.

SQL Server has always had a job-scheduling tool, but they really beefed things up with the **SQL Server Agent** (previously **SQL Executive**) in version 7.0.

> *If your background is in Windows NT, and you have scheduled other jobs using the Windows NT Scheduler service, you could utilize that scheduling engine to support SQL Server.*

With this version, you now have two terms to think about instead of one: Jobs and Tasks

- **Tasks**: These are a single process that is to be executed or batch of commands that are to be run. Tasks are no longer independent – they exist only as members of jobs.
- **Jobs**: Jobs are a grouping of one or more tasks that should be run together. You can, however, set up dependencies and branching depending on the success or failure of individual tasks (for example, task A runs if the previous task succeeds; but task B runs if the previous task fails).

Jobs can be scheduled based on:

- Daily, weekly or monthly schedules
- A specific time of the day
- A specific frequency (say, every 10 minutes, or every 1 hour)
- When the CPU becomes idle for a period of time
- When the SQL Agent starts
- In response to an alert

Tasks are run by virtue of being part of a job and based on the branching rules you define for your job. Just because a job runs, it doesn't mean that all the tasks that are part of that job will run – some may be executed and others not depending on the success or failure of previous tasks in the job and what **branching rules** you have established.

It is this later branching process within a job that is the new and cool thing. Previously, developers and DBAs would use a series of tricks to simulate this functionality. The most common approach was to schedule dependent tasks at intervals that were much farther apart than would immediately seem necessary. Task A might run for 2 minutes, but Task B that is depending on Task A might not be scheduled to run for an hour – this would be done so that the person who scheduled the job could be absolutely sure that the previous job was complete. The beginning of the second task would often have logic built in to try and detect if the previous job succeeded or failed. It probably doesn't take a rocket scientist to figure out that this kind of approach was problematic at best (and disastrous at worst). First of all, you wind up wasting tremendous amounts of time just from the "buffer" that you place between jobs running. If you had 10 or 15 different dependencies, trying to run all this as a night job could become rather problematic – especially if some of the processes were naturally long-running.

The new scenario addresses this quite well. SQL Server not only allows one task to automatically fire when another finishes – it also allows for doing something entirely different (such as running some sort of recovery task) if the current task fails.

In addition to branching you can, depending on what happens, also tell SQL Server to:

- Provide notification of the success or failure of a job to an operator. You're allowed to send a separate notification for a network message (which would pop-up on a user's screen as long as he/she is logged in - NT only), a pager, and an e-mail address to one operator each.
- Write the information to the NT Event Log (assuming you're running NT).
- Automatically delete the job (to prevent executing it later and generally "clean-up").

Let's take a quick look at how to create operators and tasks using both EM and T-SQL.

Creating an Operator

If you're going to make use of the notification features of the SQL Agent, then you must have an operator set up to define the specifics for who is notified. This side of things – the creation of operators - isn't typically done through any kind of automated process or as part of the developed code, these are usually created manually by the DBA. We'll go ahead and take a rather brief look at it here just to understand how it works in relation to the scheduling of tasks.

Creating an Operator Using EM

To create an operator using EM, you need to navigate to the SQL Server Agent sub-node of the Management node of the server for which you're creating the operator. Right-click on the Operators member, and choose New Operator...

You should be presented with the following dialog box (mine is partially filled out for example):

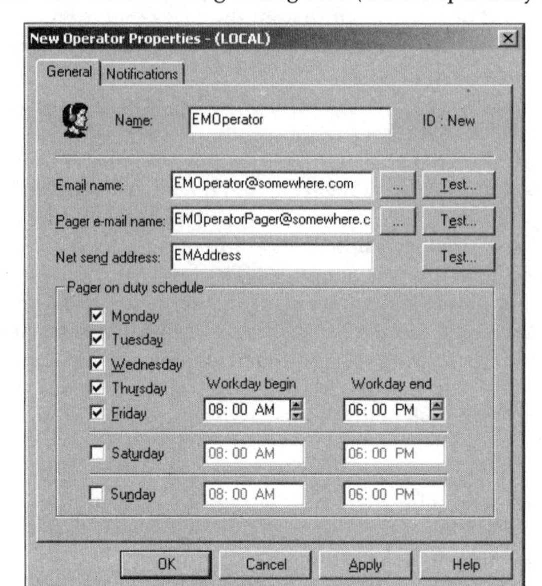

Note that the Pager on duty schedule won't be enabled until you supply some form of pager e-mail address. You can then fill out a schedule for what times this operator is to receive e-mail notifications for certain kinds of errors that we'll see on the Notifications tab.

Speaking of that Notifications tab, go ahead and click over to that tab:

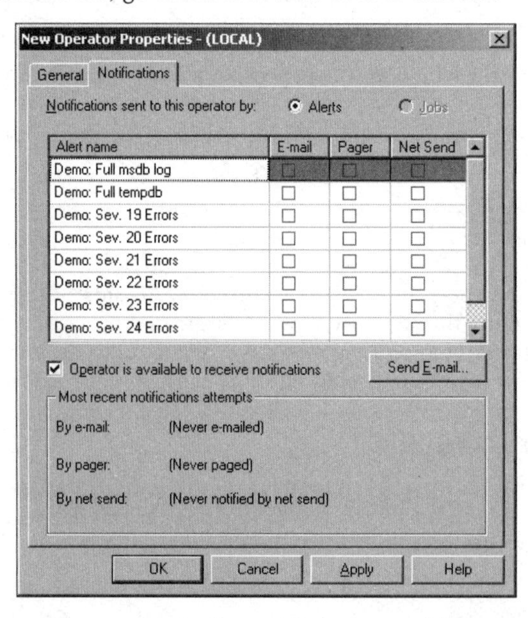

Notice that the operator can be automatically notified of any of the critical system errors that occur (anything above Severity 18). They will only be notified of those messages that you check in this dialog tab.

Creating an Operator Using T-SQL

If you do decide to create operators programmatically, you can make use of the sp_add_operator system sproc. Note that, since this is a SQL Server Agent sproc, you'll find it only in the msdb database.

After seeing all the different things you need to choose in EM, it probably won't surprise you to find out that this sproc has a ton of different parameters. Fortunately, a number of them are optional, so you only need to supply them if you're going to make use of them. The syntax looks like this:

```
sp_add_operator [@name =] '<operator name>'
[, [@enabled =] <0 for no, 1 for yes>]
[, [@email_address =] '<email alias or address>']
[, [@pager_address =] '<pager_address>']
[, [@weekday_pager_start_time =] <weekday pager start time>]
[, [@weekday_pager_end_time =] <weekday pager end time>]
[, [@saturday_pager_start_time =] <Saturday pager start time>]
[, [@saturday_pager_end_time =] <Saturday pager end time>]
[, [@sunday_pager_start_time =] <Sunday pager start time>]
[, [@sunday_pager_end_time =] <Sunday pager end time>]
[, [@pager_days =] <pager days>]
[, [@netsend_address =] '<netsend address>']
[, [@category_name =] '<category name>']
```

Most of the parameters in this sproc are self-describing, but there are a few we need to take a closer look at:

- @enabled: This is a Boolean value and works just like you would typically use a bit flag – 0 means disable this operator and 1 means enable the operator.
- @email_address: This one is just a little tricky. In order to use e-mail with your SQL Server, you need to configure SQL Mail to be operational using a specific mail server. This parameter assumes that whatever value you supply is an alias on that mail server. If you are providing the more classic e-mail address type (somebody@SomeDomain.com), then you need to enclose it in braces – like [somebody@SomeDomain.com]. Note that the entire address – including the brackets – must still be enclosed in quotes.
- @pager_days: This is a number that indicates the days that the operator is available for pages. This is probably the toughest of all the parameters. This uses a single-byte bit-flag approach similar to what we saw with the @@OPTIONS global variable that we looked at earlier in the book (and is also described in the globals appendix at the back of the book). You simply add the values together for all the values that you want to set as active days for this operator. The options are:

Value	Day of Week
Sunday	1
Monday	2
Tuesday	4
Wednesday	8
Thursday	16
Friday	32
Saturday	64

OK, so let's go ahead and create our operator using sp_add_operator. We'll keep the parameters down since many of them are redundant:

```
USE msdb

DECLARE @PageDays int

SELECT @PageDays = 2 + 8 + 32

EXEC sp_add_operator @name = 'TSQLOperator',
       @Enabled = 1,
       @pager_address = 'YourEmail@YourDomain.com',
       @weekday_pager_start_time = 080000,
       @weekday_pager_end_time = 170000,
       @pager_days = @PageDays
```

Now go back into EM and refresh your Operators list. You should see your new operator there – double-click in it to look at the properties:

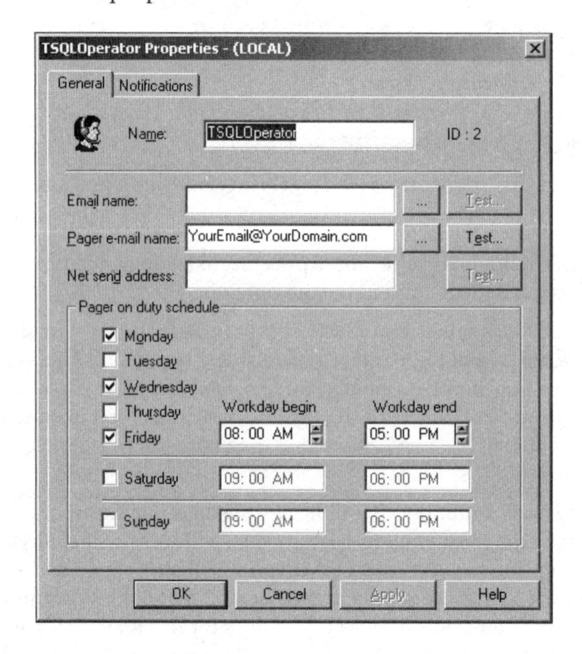

Notice that all our information is exactly as we set it – even the days of the week only include Monday, Wednesday and Friday, just as we planned in our sproc.

There are three other sprocs that you need to make use of in order to have power over your operator from T-SQL:

- sp_help_operator: Provides information on the current settings for the operator
- sp_update_operator: Accepts all the same information at sp_add_operator – the new information completely replaces the old information
- sp_delete_operator: Removes the specified operator from the system

Now that we've seen how to create operators, let's take a look at creating actual jobs and tasks.

Creating Jobs and Tasks

As I mentioned earlier, jobs are a collection of one or more tasks. A task is a logical unit of work, such as backing up one database or running a T-SQL script to meet a specific need such as rebuilding all your indexes.

Even though a job can contain several tasks, this is no guarantee that every task in a job will run. They will either run or not run depending on the success or failure of other tasks in the job and what you've defined to be the response in each success or failure case. For example, you might cancel the remainder of the job if one of the tasks fails.

Just like operators, jobs can be created in EM, T-SQL, and DMO (Distributed Management Objects). In this book, we'll cover the quick and dirty creation of tasks and jobs in EM and the automated nature of T-SQL.

Creating Jobs and Tasks Using EM

EM makes it very easy to create scheduled jobs. Just navigate to the SQL Server Agent sub-node of the Management node of your server in EM. Then right click on the Jobs member and select New Job... You should get a four-tab dialog box that will help you build the job one step at a time:

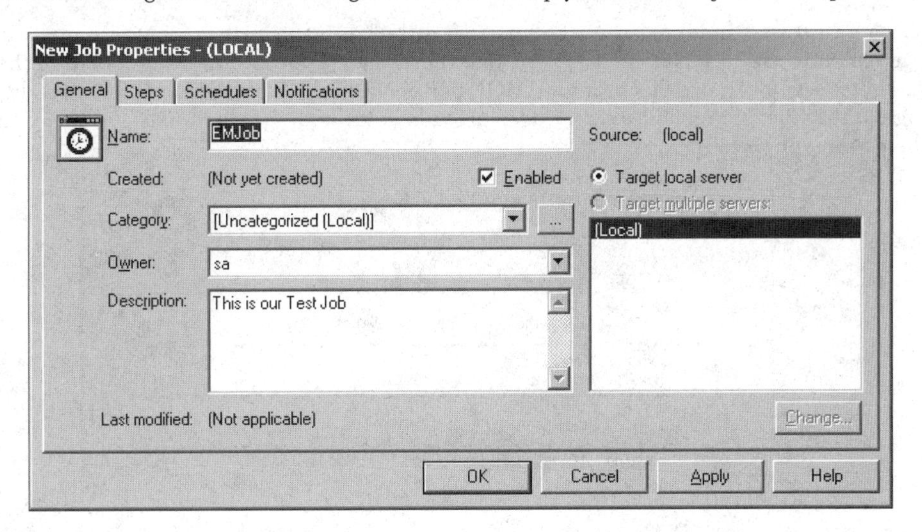

The name can be whatever you like as long as it adheres to the SQL Server rules for naming as discussed back in Chapter 2.

Most of the rest of the information is, again, self-explanatory with a couple of exceptions:

- Category: Is just one way of grouping together jobs. Most of the time this is going to be Uncategorized, although you will probably on occasion run into instances where you want to create Web Assistant or Replication Jobs – those go into their own category for easy identification.
- The Target local server vs. Target multiple servers option buttons are only enabled if you've configured remote servers. This is an administrator-only requirement in 99.9% of situations, so we won't cover it here.

We can then move on to tab two. This is the place where we tell SQL Server to start creating our new tasks that will be part of this job. To add a new task, we just click on the New... button and fill in the new dialog box:

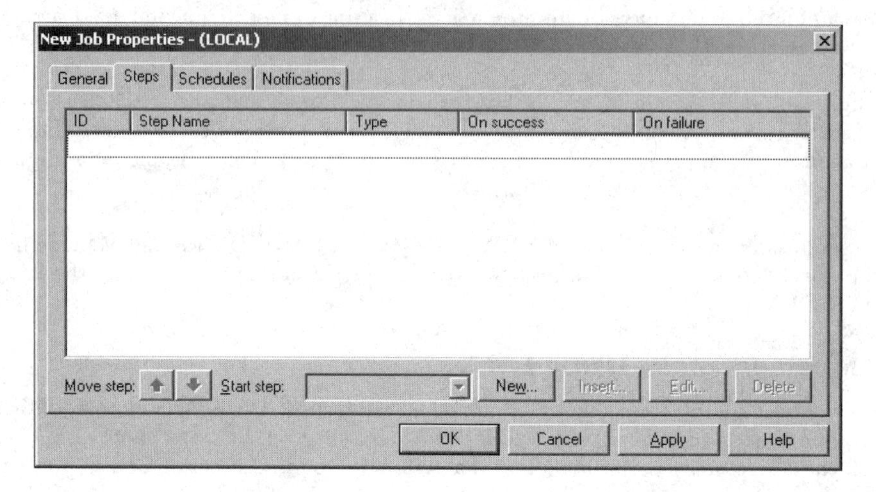

We'll use a T-SQL statement to raise a bogus error just so we can see that things are really happening when we schedule this job. Notice, however, that there is an Open... button to the left of the command box – you can use this to import SQL Scripts that you have saved in files. It's also worth pointing out that the command box here does provide color-coding (much like QA does), so you get a bit of help with your editing:

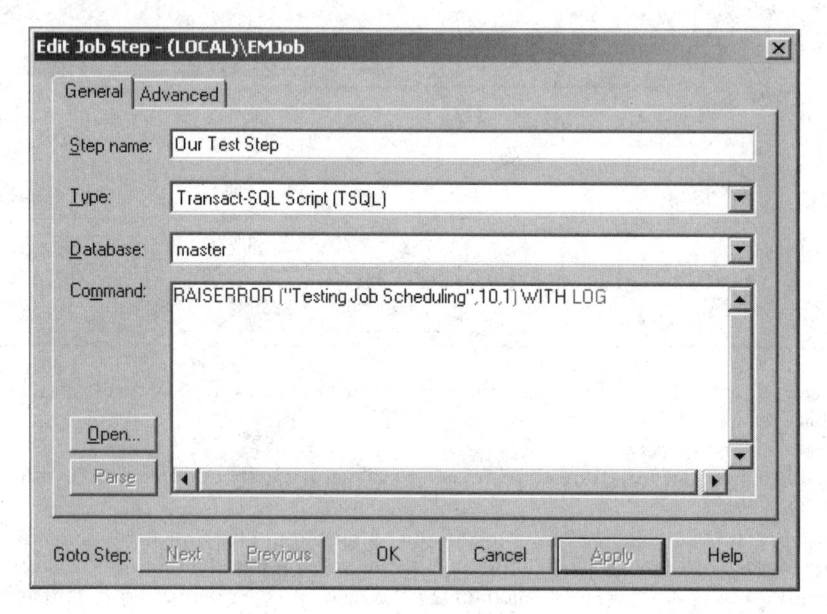

Let's go ahead and move on to the Advanced tab for this dialog – it's here that we really start to see some of the functionality that is new with SQL Server 7.0:

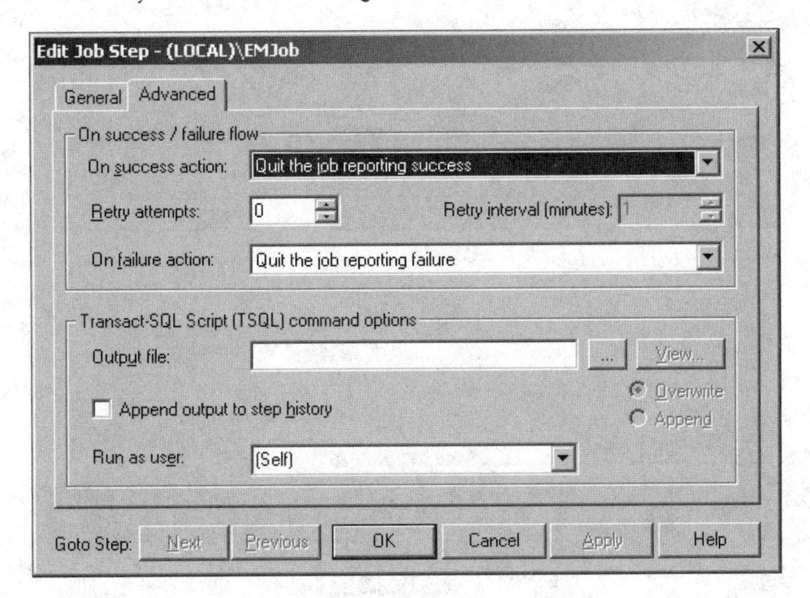

Notice several things in this dialog:

- You can automatically retry at a specific interval if the task fails.
- You can choose what to do if the job succeeds or fails. For each result, you can:
  - Quit reporting success
  - Quit reporting failure
  - Move on to the next step
- You can output results to a file. (This is very nice for auditing.)
- You can impersonate another user (for rights purposes) – note that you have to have rights to that user. Since we're logged in as `sa`, we can run the job as the `dbo` or using the `guest` account. The average user would probably only have the guest account available (unless they were the `dbo`) – but, hey, in most cases a general user shouldn't be scheduling their own jobs this way anyway (let your client application provide that functionality).

OK, so there's little chance that our `RAISERROR` statement is going to fail, so we'll just take the default of Quit the job reporting success on this one (we'll see other possibilities later in the chapter as we work on backups).

That moves us back to the New Job Properties dialog, and we're now ready to move on to the Schedules tab:

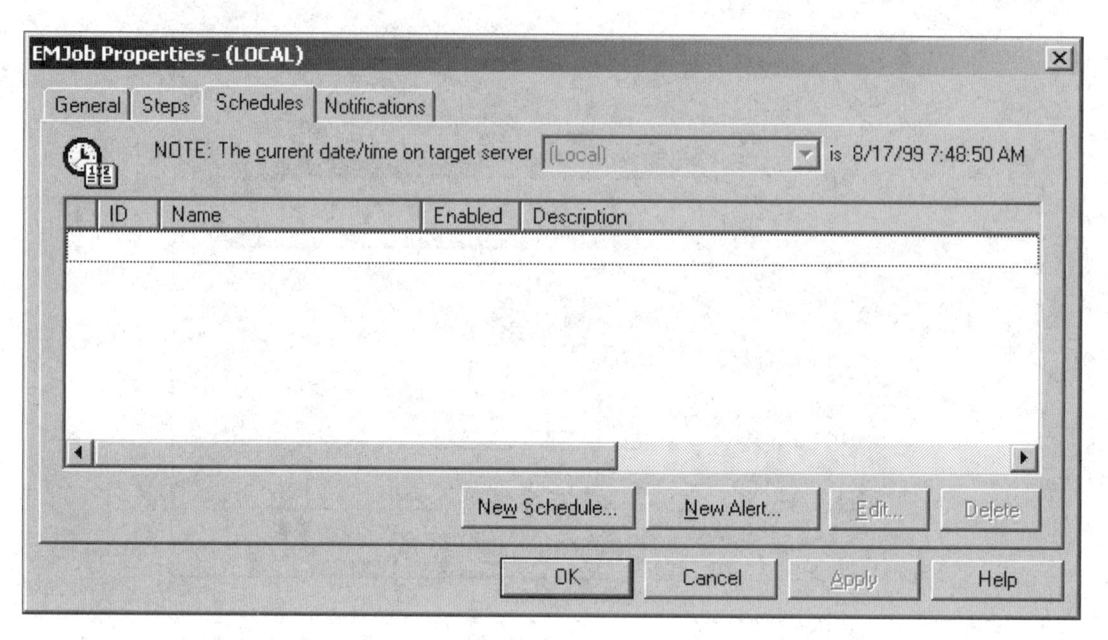

In this dialog, we can manage one or more scheduled times for this job to run. To actually create a new scheduled time for the job to run, we need to click on the New Schedule... button. That brings us up yet another dialog:

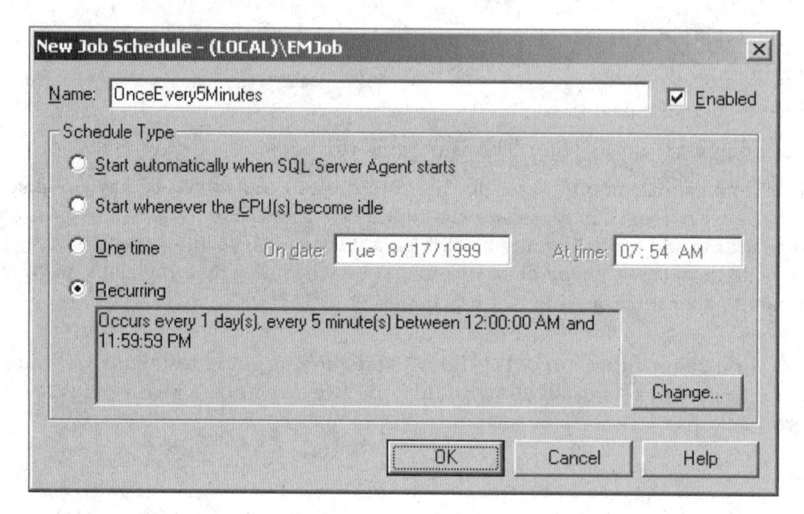

It is from this dialog that we begin the process of creating a new schedule for this job. The first three options can be set entirely from this screen. If you want the job to be recurring, then you need to choose that option and click on the Change button, which takes you to a dialog where you can set how frequently you want the job to run:

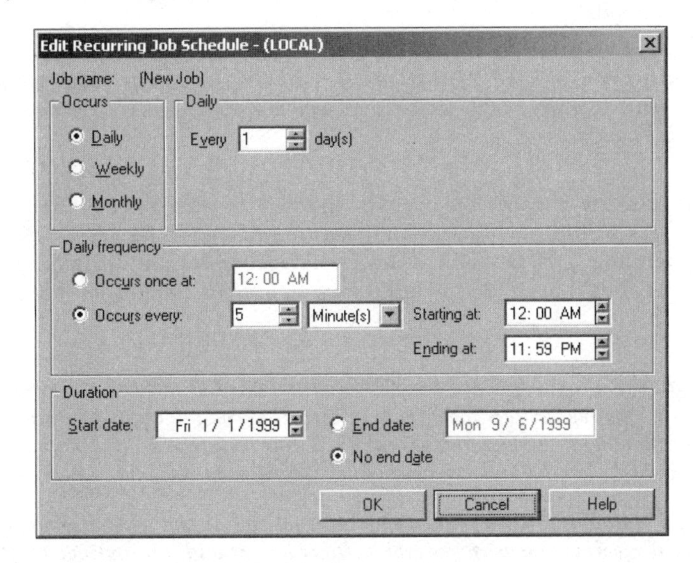

The frequency side of things can be a bit confusing because of the funny way that they've worded things. If you want something to run at multiple times every day, then you need to set the job to Occur Daily – every 1 day. This seems like it would run only once a day, but then you also have the option of setting whether it runs once or on an interval. In our case, we want to set our job to run every 5 minutes.

Now we're ready to move on to the final tab of our job properties:

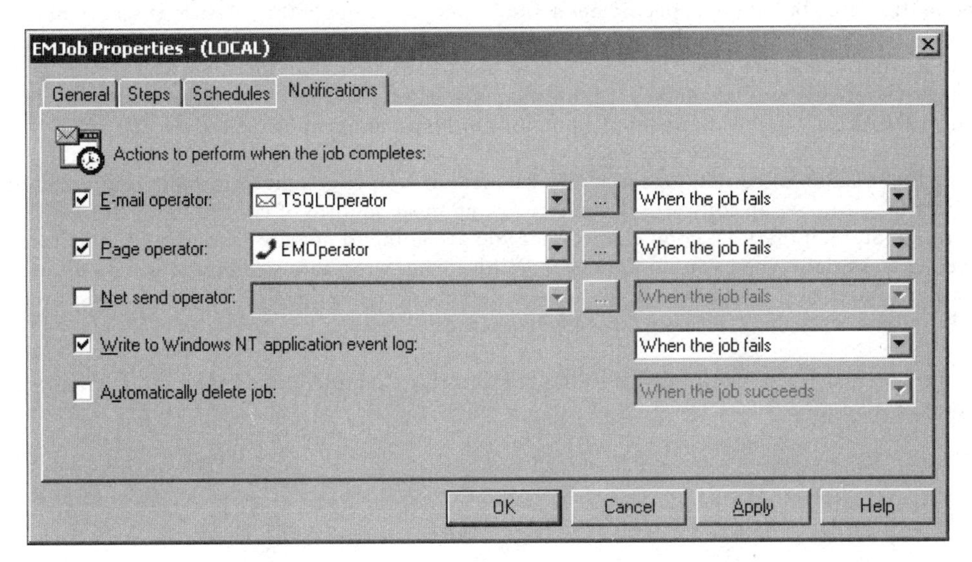

On this last tab, we can select what notifications we want to make depending on what happens. Notice that I was able to choose the couple of operators that we created earlier in the chapter. It is through the definitions of these operators that the SQL Server Agent knows what e-mail address or net send address to make the notification to. Also notice that we have control on the right hand side for when the notification is made.

Since you probably don't have SQL Mail set up (see your DBA about this), and the standard e-mail channels cannot be used as SQL Mail defines how to reach these, I'd recommend turning the notifications other than net send off for now.

At this point, you are ready to apply the changes and exit the dialog. You'll need to wait a few minutes before the task will fire, but you should start to see log entries appear every five minutes in the **Windows NT event log**. You can look at this by navigating to Start | Programs | Administrative Tools | Event Viewer. You'll need to switch the view to use the Application log rather than the default System log.

Don't forget that, if you're going to be running scheduled tasks like this one, you need to have the SQL Server Agent running in order for them to be executed. You can check the status of the SQL Server Agent by running the Service Manager and selecting the SQL Server Agent service, or by navigating to the SQL Server Agent sub-node of the Management Node for your server in EM.

Also, don't forget to disable this job (right click on the job in EM and select Disable Job) after you've seen that it's working the way you expect. Otherwise, it will just continue to sit there and create entries in your Application log – eventually, the Application Log will fill up and you can have problems with your system.

Creating Jobs and Tasks Using T-SQL

Before we get started, I want to point out that using T-SQL for this kind of stuff (creating scheduled jobs and tasks) is not usually the way things are done on a day-to-day basis. Most jobs wind up being scheduled by the DBA based on a specific need and a specific schedule they desire. If you're not in a situation where you need to script the installation of tasks, then you may want to just skip this section (it's a lot to learn if you aren't going to use it!). That being said, there can be times where your end users won't have a DBA handy (small shops, for example, often don't have anything even remotely resembling a DBA), so you'll want to script some jobs to help out unsophisticated users.

Automating the creation of certain jobs is a very frequent area of oversight in installation procedures – particularly for shrink-wrap software. If you're working in some form of consulting or private IS shop environment, then there's a good chance that you are going to need to take care of scheduling all the needed tasks right when you do the install. With shrink-wrap software however, you often aren't at all in control of the installation process – indeed, you're often 100s or 1000s of miles away from the install and may not even know that it's happening.

How then do you make sure that basic tasks (like backups for example) get done? You can make it part of your installation process.

Jobs can be added to SQL Server using T-SQL by using three different stored procedures:

- sp_add_job: This creates the actual job.
- sp_add_job_step: This creates a task within the above job.
- sp_add_jobschedule: This determines when the job will run.

Each of these builds a piece of the overall execution of the scheduled task much as the different tabs in EM did. Let's look at each individually.

sp_add_job

This one creates the top-level of a hierarchy and establishes who owns the job and how notifications should be handled. There are quite a few parameters, but most of them are fairly easy to figure out:

```
sp_add_job [@job_name =] '<job name>'
[,[@enabled =] <0 for no, 1 for yes>]
[,[@description =] '<description of the job>']
[,[@start_step_id =] <ID of the step you want to start at>]
[,[@category_name =] '<category>']
[,[@category_id =] <category ID>]
[,[@owner_login_name =] '<login>']
[,[@notify_level_eventlog =] <eventlog level>]
[,[@notify_level_email =] <email level>]
[,[@notify_level_netsend =] <netsend level>]
[,[@notify_level_page =] <page level>]
[,[@notify_email_operator_name =]
                '<name of operator to email>']
[,[@notify_netsend_operator_name =]
                '<name of operator for network message>']
[,[@notify_page_operator_name =] '<name of operator to page>']
[,[@delete_level =] <delete level>]
[,[@job_id =] <job id> OUTPUT]
```

Again, most of the parameters here are self-describing, but let's touch on some of the more sticky ones:

- @start_step_id: This one is going to default to 1, and that's almost always going to be the place to leave it. We'll be adding steps shortly, but those steps will have identifiers to them, and this just lets the SQL Server Agent know where to begin the job.
- @category_name: This one equates directly with the category we saw in the EM. It will often be none, but could be a Database Maintenance (another common choice), Full Text, Web Assistant or Replication category.
- @category_id: This is just a way of providing a category without being dependent on a particular language.

- `@notify_level_eventlog`: For each type of notification, this determines under what condition the notification occurs. In EM, this was the far right combo box in the Notifications tab. To use this sproc though, we need to supply some constant values to indicate when we want the notification to happen. The constants are:

Constant Value	When the Notification Occurs
0	Never
1	When the task succeeds
2	When the task fails (this is the default)
3	Every time the task runs

- `@job_id`: This is just a way of finding out what job ID was assigned to your newly created job – you'll need this value when you go to create job steps and the job schedule(s). The big things on this one is to remember to:
    - Receive the value into a variable so you can re-use it.
    - Remember that the variable needs to be of type `uniqueidentifier` rather than the types you might be more familiar with at this point.

Note that all the non-level "notify" parameters are expecting an operator name – you should create your operators before running this sproc.

So, let's create a job to test this process out. What we're going to do here is create a job that's near identical to our EM-created job. We will use EM as we create the job and the steps so we can watch it come together.

First, we need to create our top-level job. All we're going to do for notifications is to send a message on failure to the NT Event log. If you have got SQL Mail set-up, then feel free to add in notification parameters for your operator.

```
USE msdb

DECLARE @JobID  uniqueidentifier

EXEC sp_add_job
   @job_name = 'TSQLCreatedTestJob',
   @enabled = 1,
   @notify_level_eventlog = 3,
   @job_id = @JobID OUTPUT

SELECT "JobID is " + CONVERT(varchar(128),@JobID)
```

Now, execute this, you should wind up with something like this:

```
-----------------------------------------------------------------
JobID is 83369994-6C5B-45FA-A702-3511214A2F8A

(1 row(s) affected)
```

Note that your particular GUID will be different from the one I got here (remember that GUIDs are effectively guaranteed to be unique across time and space). You can either use this value or you can use the job name to refer to the job later (I happen to find this a lot easier, but it can create problems when dealing with multiple servers).

sp_add_jobserver

This is a quick and dirty one. We've now got ourselves a job, but we don't have anything assigned for it to run against. You see, you can create a job on one server, but still run it against a completely different server if you choose.

In order to target a particular server, we'll use a sproc (in msdb still) called sp_add_jobserver. The syntax is the easiest by far of any we'll be looking at in this section, and looks like this:

```
sp_add_jobserver [@job_id =] <job id>|[@job_name =] '<job name>',
[@server_name =] '<server>'
```

Note that you supply either the job ID or the job name – not both.

So, to assign a target server for our job, we need to run a quick command:

```
USE msdb
EXEC sp_add_jobserver
   @job_name = 'TSQLCreatedTestJob',
   @server_name = "(local)"
```

Note that this will just point at the local server regardless of what that server is named. We could have also put the name of another valid SQL Server in to be targeted.

sp_add_jobstep

The second step in the process is to tell the job specifically what it is going to do. At the moment, all we have in our example is just the shell of a job – it doesn't have any tasks to perform, and that makes it a very useless job indeed. There is a flip side to this though – a step can't even be created without some job to assign it to.

The next step then is to run sp_add_job_step. This is essentially adding a task to the job. If we had multiple steps we wanted the job to do, then we would run this particular sproc multiple times.

The syntax looks like this:

```
sp_add_jobstep [@job_id =] <job ID> | [@job_name =] '<job name>']
[,[@step_id =] <step ID>]
{,[@step_name =] '<step name>']
[,[@subsystem =] '<subsystem>']
[,[@command =] '<command>']
[,[@additional_parameters =] '<parameters>']
[,[@cmdexec_success_code =] <code>]
[,[@on_success_action =] <success action>]
[,[@on_success_step_id =] <success step ID>]
[,[@on_fail_action =] <fail action>]
[,[@on_fail_step_id =] <fail step ID>]
[,[@server =] '<server>']
```

```
[, [@database_name =] '<database>']
[, [@database_user_name =] '<user>']
[, [@retry_attempts =] <retry attempts>]
[, [@retry_interval =] <retry interval>]
[, [@os_run_priority =] <run priority>]
[, [@output_file_name =] '<file name>']
[, [@flags =] <flags>]
```

Not as many of the parameters are self-describing here, so let's look at the more confusing ones in the list:

- `@job_id` vs. `@job_name`: This is actually a rather odd sproc in the sense that it expects you to enter one of the first two parameters, but not both. You can either attach this step to a job by its GUID (which we saved from the last sproc run) or by the job name.
- `@step_id`: All the steps in any job have an ID. SQL Server assigns these IDs automatically as you insert the steps. So why, if it does it automatically, do we have a parameter for it? That's in case we want to insert a step in the middle of everything. If there are already numbers 1-5 in the job, and we insert a new step and provide a step ID of 3, then our new step will be assigned to position number 3. The previous step 3 will be moved to position 4 with each succeeding step being incremented by 1 to make room for the previous step.
- `@step_name`: Is what it says – the name of that particular task. Just be aware that there is no default here – you must provide a step name.
- @subsystem: This ties in very closely to job categories, and determines which subsystem within SQL Server (such as the replication engine, or the command line (DOS prompt), or VB Script engine) is responsible for executing the script. The default is that you're running a set of T-SQL statements. The possible subsystems are:

Subsystem	Description
`ACTIVESCRIPTING`	The scripting engine (VB Script)
`CMDEXEC`	Gives you the capability to execute compiled programs or batch files from a command (DOS) prompt
`DISTRIBUTION`	The Replication Distribution Agent
`LOGREADER`	Replication Log Reader Agent
`MERGE`	The Replication Merge Agent
`SNAPSHOT`	The Replication Snapshot Agent
`TSQL`	A T-SQL batch, this is the default

- `@command`: This is the actual command you're issuing to a specific subsystem. In our example, this is going to be the `RAISERROR` command just like we issued when using EM, but it could be most any T-SQL commands. What's cool here is that there are some system supplied values you can use in your commands. You place these in the middle of your scripts as needed, and they are replaced at run-time (we'll make use of this in our example). The possible system supplied values are:

Tag	Description
[A-DBN]	Substitutes in the database name.
[A-SVR]	Substitutes the server name in the place of the tag.
[A-ERR]	Error number.
[A-SEV]	Error severity.
[A-MSG]	The message text from the error
[DATE]	Supplies the current date (in YYYYMMDD format).
[JOBID]	Supplies the current job ID.
[MACH]	The current computer name.
[MSSA]	Master SQL Server Agent name.
[SQLDIR]	The directory in which SQL Server is installed (usually `C:\Mssql7`).
[STEPCT]	A count of the number of times this step has executed (excluding retires). You could use this one to keep count of the number of executions and force the termination of a multistep loop.
[STEPID]	Step ID.
[TIME]	The current time in HHMMSS format.
[STRTTM]	The start time for the job in HHMMSS format.
[STRTDT]	The start date for the job in YYYYMMDD format.

- `@cmdexec_success_code`: This is the value you expect to be returned by whatever command interpreter ran your job if the job ran successfully (only applies to command prompt subsystem). The default is zero.

- `@on_success_action` and `@on_fail_action`: This is what you say what to actually do at the success or failure of your step. Remember that at the job level we define what notifications we want to happen, but, at the step level, we can define how we want processing to continue (or end). For this parameter, you need to supply one of the following constant values:

Value	Description
1	Quit with success. This is the default for successful task executions.
2	Quit with failure. This is the default for failed tasks.
3	Go to the next step.
4	Go to a specific step as defined in `on_success_step_id` or `on_fail_step_id`.

- `@on_success_step_id` and `@on_fail_step_id`: What step you want to run next if you've selected option four above.
- `@server`: The server the task is to be run against (you can run tasks on multiple target servers from a single master server).
- `@database_name`: The database to be set as current when the task runs.
- `@retry_interval`: This is set in minutes.
- `@os_run_priority`: Ahhh, an undocumented feature. The default here is normal, but you can adjust how important NT is going to think that your `cmdExec` (command line) scheduled task is. The possible values are:

Value	Priority
-15	Run at idle only
-1	Below normal
0	Normal (this is the default)
1	Above normal
15	Time critical

I just can't help but think of the old "Lost In Space" TV show here and the robot saying, "DANGER Will Robinson - DANGER!" Don't take messing with these values lightly. If you're not familiar with the issues surrounding NT thread priorities, I'd suggest staying as far away from this one as possible. Going with the higher values, in particular, can have a very detrimental impact on your system - including creating significant instabilities. When you say that this is the most important thing, remember that you are taking away some of the importance of things like operating system functions - not something that's smart to do... Stay clear of this unless you really know what you're doing.

- `@flags`: This one relates to the Output File parameter, and indicates whether to overwrite or append your output information to the existing file. The options are:

Value	Description
0	No option specified (currently, this means your file will be overwritten every time)
2	Append information to the existing file (if one exists)
4	Explicitly overwrite the file

OK, now that we've looked at the parameters, let's add a step to the job we created a short time ago:

```
sp_add_jobstep
   @job_name = 'TSQLCreatedTestJob',
   @step_nme = 'This Is The Step',
   @command = "RAISERROR
      ('RAISERROR ('TSQL Task is Job ID [JOBID] .',10,1) WITH LOG',10,1)
      WITH LOG",
   @database_name = 'Northwind',
   @retry_attempts = 3 ,
   @retry_interval = 5
```

Technically speaking – our job should be able to be run at this point. The reason I say "technically speaking" is because we haven't scheduled the job, so the only way to run it is to manually tell the job to run. Let's take care of the scheduling issue, and then we'll be done.

sp_add_jobschedule

This is the last piece of the puzzle – we need to tell our job when to run. To do this, we'll make use of `sp_add_jobschedule`, which, like all the other sprocs we've worked on in this section, can only be found in the `msdb` database. Note that we could submit an entry from this sproc multiple times to create multiple schedules for our job. Keep in mind though that getting too many jobs scheduled can lead to a great deal of confusion, so schedule jobs wisely (for example, don't schedule one job for every day of the week when you can schedule a single job that knows to run daily).

The syntax has some similarities to what we've already been working with, but adds some new pieces to the puzzle:

```
sp_add_jobschedule
[@job_id =] <job ID>, | [@job_name =] '<job name>',
[@name =] '<name>'
[, [@enabled =] <0 for no, 1 for yes>]
[, [@freq_type =] <frequency type>]
[, [@freq_interval =] <frequency interval>]
[, [@freq_subday_type =] <frequency subday type>]
[, [@freq_subday_interval =] <frequency subday interval>]
[, [@freq_relative_interval =] <frequency relative interval>]
[, [@freq_recurrence_factor =] <frequency recurrence factor>]
[, [@active_start_date =] <active start date>]
[, [@active_end_date =] <active end date>]
[, [@active_start_time =] <active start time>]
[, [@active_end_time =] <active end time>]
```

Again, let's look at some of these parameters:

- `@freq_type`: The just defines the nature of the intervals that are set up in the following parameters. This is another of those parameters that uses bit flags (although you should only use one at a time). Some of the choices are clear, but some aren't until you get to `@freq_interval` (which is next). Your choices are:

Value	Frequency
1	Once
4	Daily
8	Weekly
16	Monthly (fixed day)
32	Monthly (relative to `@freq_interval`)
64	Run at start of SQL Server Agent
128	Run when CPU is idle

- `@freq_interval`: Decides the exact days that the job is executed, but the nature of this value depends entirely on `@freq_type` (above). This one can get kind of confusing, just keep in mind that it works with both `@freq_type` and `@frequency_relative_interval`. The interpretation works like this:

Frequency Type Value	Matching Frequency Interval Values
1(once)	Not used
4(daily)	Runs every x days, where x is the value in the Frequency Interval
8(weekly)	Frequency Interval is one or more of the following: 1 (Sunday) 2 (Monday) 4 (Tuesday) 8 (Wednesday) 16 (Thursday) 32 (Friday) 64 (Saturday)

Frequency Type Value	Matching Frequency Interval Values
16(monthly - fixed)	Runs on the exact day of the month specified in the frequency interval
32(monthly - relative)	Runs on exactly one of the following: 1 (Sunday) 2 (Monday) 3 (Tuesday) 4 (Wednesday) 5 (Thursday) 6 (Friday) 7 (Saturday) 8 (Specific day) 9 (Every weekday) 10 (Every weekend day)
64(run at Agent startup)	Not used
128(run at CPU idle)	Not used

- `@freq_subday_type`: Is the units for `@freq_subday_interval`. If you're running daily, then you can set a frequency to run within a given day. The possible value here are:

Value	Description
1	At the specified time.
4	Every x minutes, where x is the value of the Frequency Sub-day Interval.
8	Every x hours, where x is the value of the Frequency Sub-day Interval.

- `@freq_subday_interval`: This is the number of `@freq_subday_type` periods to occur between each execution of the job (x in the above table).
- `@freq_relative_interval`: This is only used if the Frequency Type is Monthly Relative (32). If this is the case, then this value determines in what week a specific day of week job is run or flags things to be run on the last day of the month. The possible values are:

Value	Description
1	First Week
2	Second Week
4	Third Week
8	Fourth Week
16	Last Week or Day

- `@freq_recurrence_factor`: How many weeks or months between execution. The exact treatment depends on the Frequency Type and is only applicable if the type was weekly or monthly (either one). This is an integer value, and, for example, if your frequency type was 8 (Weekly) and the Frequency Recurrence Factor was 3, then the job would run on the specified day of the week every third week.

The default for each of these parameters is 0.

OK, so let's move on to getting that job scheduled to run every five minutes as we did when using EM:

```
sp_add_jobschedule
   @job_name = 'TSQLCreatedTestJob',
   @name = 'Every 5 Minutes',
   @freq_type = 4,
   @freq_interval = 1,
   @freq_subday_type = 4,
   @freq_subday_interval = 5,
   @active_start_date = 19990101
```

Now, if you go and take a look at the job in EM, you'll find that you have a job that is (other than the name) identical to the job we created directly in EM. Our job has been fully implemented using T-SQL this time.

Maintaining and Deleting Jobs and Tasks

Maintaining jobs in EM is pretty simple – just double-click on the job and edit it just as if you were creating a new job. Deleting jobs and tasks in EM is more simple – just highlight the job and press the delete button. After one confirmation, your job is gone.

Checking out what you have, editing it, and deleting it are all slightly more tricky in T-SQL. The good news, however, is that maintaining jobs, tasks, and schedules works pretty much as creating did, and that deleting any of them is a snap.

Editing and Deleting Jobs with T-SQL

To edit or delete each of the four steps we just covered for T-SQL, you just use (with one exception) the corresponding update – the information provided to the update sproc completely replaces that of the original add (or prior updates) - or delete sproc. The parameters are the same as the add sproc for each:

If the Add was	Then Update with	And Delete with
sp_add_job	sp_update_job	sp_delete_job
sp_add_jobserver	None (Drop and Add)	sp_delete_jobserver
sp_add_jobstep	sp_update_jobstep	sp_delete_jobstep
sp_add_jobschedule	sp_update_jobschedule	sp_delete_jobschedule

Backup and Restore Operations

I'm not sure there can be a more fundamental administration role than backing up and restoring, but you would truly be amazed at the percentage of database operations that I've gone into that don't have any kind of reliable backup. Tisk, Tisk.

There is one simple rule to follow regarding backups – do it early and often. The follow up to this to not just backup to a file on the same disk and forget it. You need to make sure that a copy moves to a completely separate place (ideally off-site) to be sure that it's safe. I've personally seen servers catch fire (the stench was terrible, as were all the freaked out staff). You don't want to find out that your backups went up in the same smoke that your original data did.

Backups have been substantially improved with version 7.0 in the sense that they run much faster, put less of a load on the system, and are a little easier to operate with. Restore operations have seen similar improvements. There are three areas to deal with in dealing with backups:

- Backup media and devices
- Backup operations
- Restore operations

Let's look at how to backup your data, and, of course, how to get it back when you need it.

Backup Media

SQL Server doesn't really care all that much whether your backup is to tape or to a physical hard drive. Still, it does prefer that you pre-define where your backup data is going. This isn't a hard and fast requirement (you can backup directly to a filename if you wish), but it's the way things are supposed to work.

This pre-defined destination for your backup is referred to as a **device**. A device is really nothing more than an alias to help insulate SQL Server from whether you're using a tape drive or a disk file. You can create the backup "device" from T-SQL, EM, and DMO.

Creating a Device Using EM

To create a backup device using EM, right-click on the Backup member of the Management node for your server. Choose New Backup Device... and you'll be presented with a dialog box:

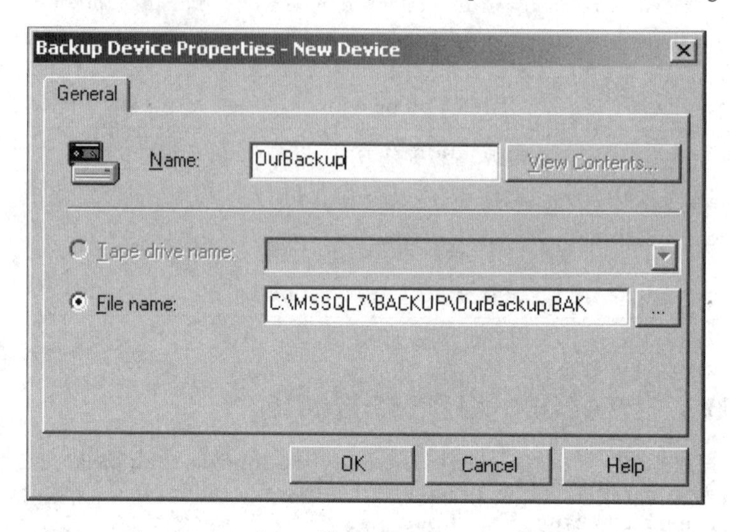

You can see there is no rocket science here. You simply name the device in the top text box, and choose a file name or tape drive from below (mine is grayed out because this system doesn't have a table drive in it). Be sure to notice the default location and name for your backup – you don't want to delete these by accident. You can also feel free to change them at this point (before they are created).

Click OK and you're done!

Creating a Device Using T-SQL

Creating a device using T-SQL is almost as easy and brings a touch of nostalgia compared to the older versions of SQL server when a backup was still called a **dump**. A dump is now a backup – it's that simple. To create the backup device, we use a legacy system sproc called `sp_adddumpdevice`. The syntax looks like this:

```
sp_addumpdevice
[@devtype =] '<type>',
[@logicalname =] '<logical name>',
[@physicalname =] '<physical name>'
```

The *type* is going to be one of the following:

- Disk: A local hard drive
- Pipe: A named pipe – can be used for network backups, but not doesn't work well (the connection or dump fails quite often in my experience)
- Tape: A tape drive

The *logical name* is the name that you will use in the BACKUP and RESTORE statements that we will look at shortly.

The *physical name* is either the name of the tape device (must be one on the local server) or the physical path to the disk volume you're backing up to.

As an example, we'll create a backup device called TSQLBackupDevice:

```
EXEC sp_addumpdevice 'DISK', 'TSQLBackupDevice',
                     'C:\MSSQL7\BACKUP\TSQLBackupDevice.bak'
```

And we're done!

Backing Up

Backing Up Using EM

To backup the database in EM, just right-click on the database, select All Tasks... and then Backup Database. You'll get one of EM's all too common dialog boxes:

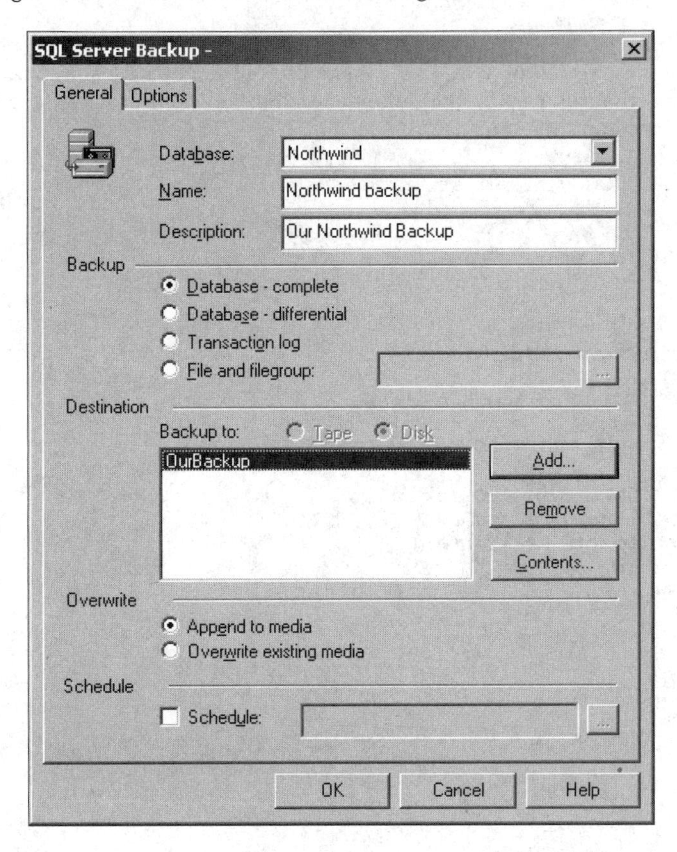

This dialog has everything you need for most situations. We fill it out with the Northwind database, what we want to call our backup, the type of backup, and the destination. The destination will be whatever device(s) we want to backup to. Just click on Add to choose between the existing devices, or to define an on-the-fly file to backup to.

Perhaps one of the coolest features of this dialog is that it will let you create a scheduled backup right from here. You can set that scheduled job to be a one-time or a repetitive task, and it will automatically be added to your job list.

Backing up of the logs is just a matter of changing which option button you're selecting.

There are also two other options here for types of backups – differential and filegroup.

A differential backup allows you to backup only what has changed since the last backup – we'll cover this further when we look at backing up using T-SQL.

A filegroup backup allows you to backup just one filegroup, as opposed to the entire database.

Backing Up Using T-SQL

To back up the database or log in T-SQL, we make use of the BACKUP command. The syntax for BACKUP works almost, but not quite, the same depending on whether you're backing up the database or the log. The syntax looks like this:

```
BACKUP DATABASE|LOG <database name>
-- Next two lines for logs only
{WITH
NO_LOG|TRUNCATE_ONLY}
TO <backup device> [,...n]
[WITH
[BLOCKSIZE = <block size>]
[[,] DESCRIPTION = <description>]
[[,] DIFFERENTIAL]
[[,] EXPIREDATE = <expiration date>
| RETAINDAYS = <days>]
[[,] FORMAT|NOFORMAT]
[[,] INIT|NOINIT]
[[,] MEDIADESCRIPTION = <description>]
[[,] MEDIANAME = <media name>]
[[,] [NAME = <backup set name>]
[[,] NOSKIP|SKIP]
[[,] NOUNLOAD|UNLOAD]
[[,] RESTART]
[[,] STATS [= percentage]]
]
```

Let's look at some of the parameters:

- `<backup_device>`: That's right, you can backup to more than one device. This creates what's called a **media set**. These can really speed up your backups if the media is spread over several disks, as it creates a parallel load situation – you're not bound by the I/O limitations of any of the individual devices. Be aware, however, that you must have the entire media set intact to restore from this kind backup.
- `BLOCKSIZE`: This is automatically determined in a hard drive backup, but, for tape, you need to provide the correct block size – contact your vendor for help on this one.
- `DIFFERENTIAL`: This is to perform a **differential backup**. A differential backup only backs up the data that is changed since your last full backup. Any log or other differential backup are ignored – any row/column changed, added, or deleted since the last full backup is included in the new backup. Differential backups have the advantage of being much faster to create than a full backup and much faster to restore than applying each individual log when restoring.
- `EXPIREDATE/RETAINDAYS`: You can have your backup media expire after a certain time. Doing so lets SQL Server know when it can overwrite the older media.
- `FORMAT/NOFORMAT`: Determines whether the media header (required for tapes) should be re-written or not. Be aware that formatting affects the entire device – this means that formatting for one backup on a device destroys all the other backups on that device as well.
- `INIT/NOINIT`: Overwrites the device data, but leaves the header intact.
- `MEDIADESCRIPTION` and `MEDIANAME`: Just describe and name the media – maximum of 255 characters for description and 128 for a name.
- `SKIP/NOSKIP`: Decides whether or not to pay attention to the expiration information from previous backups on the tape. If `SKIP` is active, then the expiration is ignored so the tape can be overwritten.
- `UNLOAD/NOUNLOAD`: Used for tape only – determines whether to rewind and eject the tape (`UNLOAD`) or leave it in its current position (`NOUNLOAD`) after the backup is complete.
- `RESTART`: Picks up where a previously interrupted backup left off.
- `STATS`: Displays a progress bar indicating progress as the backup runs.

Now let's try one out for a true backup:

```
BACKUP DATABASE Northwind
TO TSQLBackupDevice
   WITH
      DESCRIPTION = 'My what a nice backup!',
      STATS
```

We now have a backup of our `Northwind` database. It's that simple, so let's follow it up with a simple backup of the log:

```
BACKUP LOG Northwind
TO TSQLBackupDevice
   WITH
      DESCRIPTION = 'My what a nice backup of a log!',
      STATS
```

It's worth noting that you can't do a backup of a log while the Truncate On Checkpoint database option is active. (To turn this off right-click on the Northwind database, select Properties and the Options tab.) If you think about it, this makes sense given that your log is always going to be essentially empty of any committed transactions.

It's also worth noting that backups work just fine while there are users in your database. SQL Server is able to reconcile the changes that are being made by knowing the exact point in the log that the backup was begun, and using that as a reference point for the rest of the backup.

Restoring Data

We always hope that we'll never need to restore from backup – the reality, of course, works much differently. You can use EM or T-SQL (or DMO) for restoring a database, and the restoration process for each is very much like the backup was.

Restoring Data Using EM

Restoration of data using EM works almost identically to backing up your data. Right-click on your database and select All Tasks|Restore Database.... It will, as EM usually does, bring up a handy dialog box:

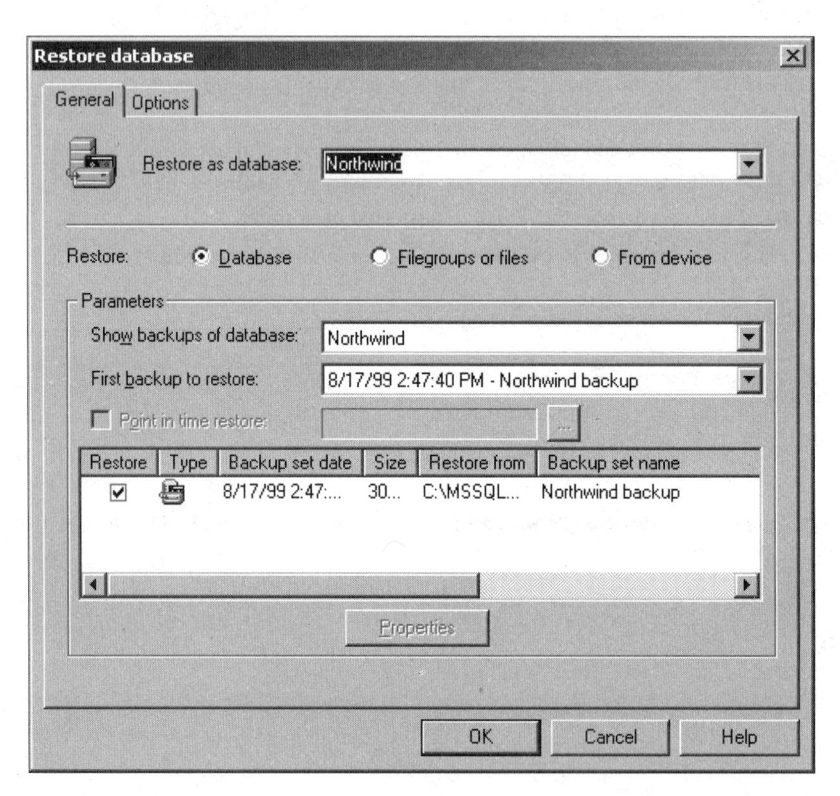

As you can see, EM pretty much holds your hand all the way through this one. If you click on the First backup to restore combo box, you'll probably see additional backups in there from which we could restore.

If you have an existing database that you want to restore over, just click on the Options tab and select Force restore over existing database. It probably goes without saying that this is something you want to be very careful with – once the restore starts, the database that you are restoring over is lost (there isn't any "undo" button for this one!).

> **Because I don't want to risk overwriting your `Northwind` database at this juncture, I recommend just choosing Cancel in this dialog box. We'll have another opportunity when we look at the T-SQL restoration to see restore in action.**

Restoring Data Using T-SQL

We use the `RESTORE` command to recover the data that we have in our backups. The syntax looks like this:

```
RESTORE DATABASE|LOG <database name>
[FROM <backup_device> [,...n]]
[WITH
[DBO_ONLY]
[[,] FILE = <file number>]
[[,] MEDIANAME = <media name>]
[[,] MOVE '<logical file name>' TO
        '<operating system file name>'][,...n]
[[,] NORECOVERY | RECOVERY | STANDBY = <undo file name>}]
[[,] {NOUNLOAD | UNLOAD}]
[[,] REPLACE]
[[,] RESTART]
[[,] STATS [= percentage]]]
```

Let's look at some of these options:

- `DBO_ONLY`: When the restore is done, the database will be set with the `dbo_only` database option turned on. This gives the `dbo` a chance to look around and test things out before allowing users back into the system.

> **This is a biggie, and I very strongly recommend that you always use it. You would be amazed at how quickly users will be back in the system once it's back up for even a moment. When a system is down, you'll find users are very impatient to get back to work. They'll constantly be trying to log in, and they won't bother to ask if it's OK or not – they'll assume that, when it's up, it's OK to go into it.**

- `FILE`: You can backup multiple times to the same media. This option lets you select a specific version to restore. If this one isn't supplied, SQL Server will assume that you want to restore from the most recent backup.

- MOVE: Allows you to restore the database to a different physical file that the database was using when it was originally backed up.
- NORECOVERY/RECOVERY/STANDBY: RECOVERY and NORECOVERY are mutually exclusive. STANDBY works in conjunction with NORECOVERY. They work as follows:

Option	Description
NORECOVERY	Restores the database, but keeps it marked as off-line. Uncommitted transactions are left intact. This allows you to continue further with the recovery process – for example, if you still have additional logs to apply.
RECOVERY	As soon as the restore command is done successfully, the database is marked as active again. Data can again be changed. Any uncommitted transactions are rolled back. This is the default if none of the options are specified.
STANDBY	STANDBY allows you to create an undo file so that the effects of a recovery can be undone. STANDBY allows you to bring the database up for read-only access before you have issued a RECOVERY (which means at least part of your data's been restored, but you aren't considering the restoration process complete yet). This allows users to make use of the system in a read-only mode while you verify the restoration process.

- REPLACE: Overrides the safety feature that prevents you from restoring over the top of an existing database.
- RESTART: Tells SQL Server to continue a previously interrupted restoration process.

I'm going to go ahead and give you an example run of restoring the Northwind database. Do not do this yourself unless you are absolutely certain that your backup was successful and is intact.

First, I'm going to drop the existing Northwind database:

```
USE master
DROP DATABASE Northwind
```

Once that's done, I'll try and restore it back using my RESTORE command:

```
RESTORE DATABASE Northwind
   FROM TSQLBackupDevice
   WITH
      DBO_ONLY,
      NORECOVERY,
      STATS
```

I did my restore with NORECOVERY because I want to add another piece to the puzzle. My log will contain any transactions that happened between when my database or log was last backed up and when this log was backed up. I'm going to "apply" this log, and that should bring my database as up-to-date as I can make it:

```
RESTORE LOG Northwind
   FROM TSQLBackupDevice
   WITH
      DBO_ONLY,
      NORECOVERY,
      STATS
```

Note that if I had several logs to apply from this one device, then I would have to name them as I wanted to apply them. They would also need to be applied in the order in which they were backed up.

Now, I could have turned everything on there, but I wanted to hold off for a bit before making the database active again. Even though I don't have any more logs to apply, I still need to re-run the RESTORE statement to make the database active again:

```
RESTORE LOG Northwind WITH RECOVERY
```

I should now be able to test out my database:

```
USE Northwind
SELECT * FROM Region
```

And, sure enough, I get the results I'm looking for:

```
RegionID       RegionDescription
-------------- ------------------------
1              Eastern
2              Western
3              Northern
4              Southern

(4 row(s) affected)
```

We're not done yet though. Remember that I chose the DBO_ONLY option for all this. If we run sp_dboption we'll see that no one else is able to get in:

```
EXEC sp_dboption
```

Look for the dbo use only:

```
Settable database options:
-----------------------------------
ANSI null default
ANSI nulls
ANSI warnings
auto create statistics
auto update statistics
```

```
autoclose
autoshrink
concat null yields null
cursor close on commit
dbo use only
default to local cursor
merge publish
offline
published
quoted identifier
read only
recursive triggers
select into/bulkcopy
single user
subscribed
torn page detection
trunc. log on chkpt.
```

You must remember to turn that option off or your users won't be able to get in the system:

```
EXEC sp_dboption Northwind, 'dbo use only', 'false'
```

You now have yourself a restored and active database.

Alerts

This tends to be even more of a true DBA task than job scheduling was, but you should know that **alerts** are there and you might even consider adding a few into your installation routines to deal with things like nearly full logs or databases.

Alerts have a definite relationship to jobs in the sense that they define an action that is to take place. The difference is in what causes the defined action to happen. For jobs, the action happened as a result of some schedule being met, but, for alerts, the action is taking place as a result of something else happening in the system. The actions that tell an alert to happen are typically an error or performance condition. When you define the alert, the system monitors for the condition you have specified. Examples of what conditions can be based on include:

- Error numbers
- Severity levels
- Specific databases that the error occurred in
- Specific event messages
- Counters (say, exceeding a certain number of active connections)
- Specific instances (say, just one server process ID – aka a spid)

You can set any of these up to fire your alert, and then choose how to respond to it by firing a job or notifying an operator.

Creating an Alert in EM

Creating alerts in EM is pretty straightforward. Right-click on the Alerts member in the SQL Server Agent sub-node of the Management node for your server and choose New Alert... You'll be greeted with a dialog box:

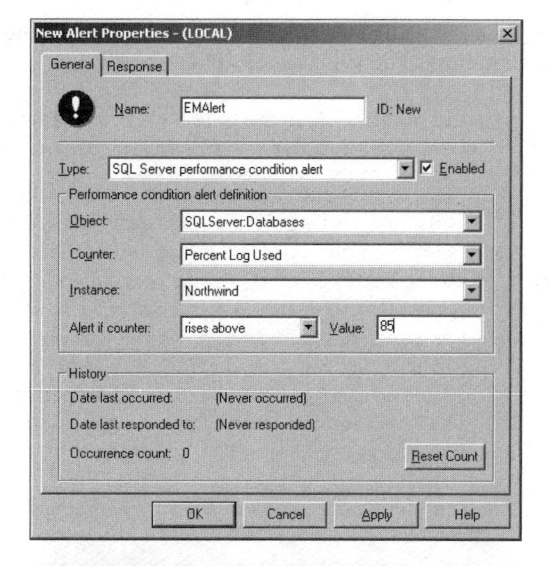

In this case, I have set up an alert that is based on how full the log for the Northwind database is. If the log rises above 85% of capacity, then my alert will be fired. We can then click on the Response tab to declare what our alert is supposed to do:

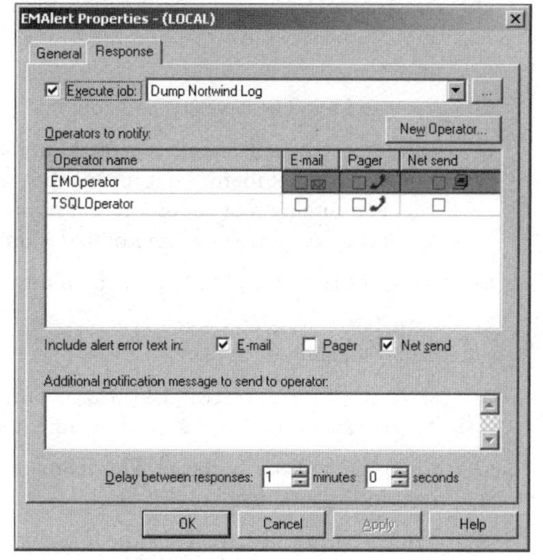

I've created a special job to automatically dump the log if it becomes 85% full before I do my normal backups. Although I haven't done it here, I should probably make sure that I turn on notification to an operator so they know to check things – like maybe they should increase the size of the log or back it up more often.

Creating an Alert in T-SQL

To create an alert in T-SQL, we make use of the sp_addalerts sproc that can be found in the msdb database. The syntax looks like this:

```
sp_add_alert [@name =] '<alert name>'
[, [@message_id =] <message ID from master..sysmessages>]
[, [@severity =]<severity>]
[, [@enabled =] <enabled>]
[, [@delay_between_responses =] <delay between responses>]
[, [@notification_message =] '<notification message>']
[, [@include_event_description_in =] <include event description in>]
[, [@database_name =] '<database>']
[, [@event_description_keyword =] '<event description>']
[, {[@job_id =] <job ID> | [@job_name =] '<job name>'}]
[, [@raise_snmp_trap =] <raise snmp trap>]
[, [@performance_condition =] '<performance condition>']
[, [@category_name =] '<category name>']
```

As usual, let's take a look at the more obscure parameters:

- @message_id: This would be the system message ID. You can create custom messages just as you do custom errors using sp_addmessage. Creating messages is discussed in detail in the chapter on sprocs.
- @severity: The severity (1 through 25) that the message has to be at before your alert will fire.
- @delay_between_responses: Many alerts are set against items that won't change until we do something about them. That means that, if we don't tell the SQL Server Agent to give it a rest, it will keep finding that condition and notifying us over and over again. This interval value tells the Agent that, once we've been notified, don't tell us again for the specified period of time in seconds.
- @notification_message: The message you want sent with any notifications.
- @include_event_description_in: This just says whether to include the event description in the notification or not.
- @event_description_keyword: This is the word or phrase that you're saying the alert message (the one that fires the alert, not the one it sends) has to match up with.
- @job_id and @job_name: The ID or name (one or the other, but not both) of the job that you want to fire as a result of this alert.
- @raise_snmp_trap: This one is bogus for this release – just ignore it.
- @performance_condition: The is the full evaluator (up to 512 characters in Unicode) to find out if the performance condition is met or not. These can be a real bear to figure out, but as an example, our performance condition from our EM example would look like this:

```
SQLServer:Databases|Percent Log Used|Northwind|>|85
```

So, to create an example just like the one we did in EM (except for the percentage), the sproc would look like this:

```
sp_add_alert
   @name = 'Our T-SQL Alert',
   @enabled = 1,
   @delay_between_responses = 300,
   @job_name = 'Dump Northwind Log',
   @performance_condition =
         'SQLServer:Databases|Percent Log Used|Northwind|>|65'
```

SQL Server is smart enough to keep you from creating duplicate performance alerts – even if they have different names. Be aware that if you, for some bizarre reason (for instance, you're trying to give a demo), want to have two alerts that do exactly the same thing, you're out of luck. You'll need to vary them slightly (as I did by changing to 65% instead of 85%).

Full-Text Catalog Population

This was covered very well back in Chapter 22, but I want to touch on it very briefly here because it can be a major stumbling point in the admin side of things.

Backup and Restore

Don't forget that full-text catalogs are completely separate from your database. While they can't be backed up on their own, they also are not and cannot be, backed up with your regular database. In short – they can't be backed up.

Any time you need to restore your database, you will need to populate your full-text catalogs immediately after the recovery is complete. If you fail to do this, your users will be performing full-text queries that return nothing even though there should be matches in the database.

Schedule Your Populations

Now that we've seen how to schedule tasks, make sure that you schedule the re-population of your full-text catalogs. You've probably already taken care of this since the full-text catalog wizards will try and help guide you through setting up such a job, but go check it and make sure. Another key pitfall that often traps unsuspecting developers and DBAs is a full text catalog that has been populated once. It returns some data – but fails to return rows you think it should because it doesn't know anything about the new rows that have been added or changes made to the existing rows in the database.

Carrying Data from One Place to Another

In the past, you would have done this by carrying out a backup and restoring at the new location. You can still do that, but there's now another way – `sp_detach_db` and `sp_attach_db`.

`sp_detach_db` removes the database from your database entry list – so you don't want to do this on an in-production database. The advantage, though, is that it is very quick in comparison to backup and restore. It's great for development databases. The syntax looks like this:

```
sp_detach_db [@dbname =] '<database name>'
[@skipchecks =] '<true|false>']
```

Making `@skipchecks` true just means that `UPDATE STATISTICS` won't automatically be run as the database is detached.

You can then copy the file and carry it to another location. The syntax for reattaching the database is:

```
sp_attach_db [@dbname =] '<database name>',
[@filename1 =] '<physical filename>' [,...16]
```

You can re-attach multiple files, and they become active immediately as long you have a complete set (which you must have for everything to work at all).

Index Rebuilding

This should be part of a set of scripts you include with your application regardless of what kind of development you're doing. You want to correct any `FILLFACTOR` problems (too full or too empty) as well as fragmentation issues on a regular basis. How often this is necessary varies by the degree and nature of the activity that goes on in the database. This is one of those things which is often forgotten, and it's frequently the source of performance issues. I hear comments such as, "Gee, our database used to run great, but it's turned into a dog recently." You ask questions like, "Did this happen slowly, or all at once?" The response is usually that they just noticed it, but that it's probably been going on for a while. The answer – no maintenance!

Just run this script (it combines many of the skills we've learned in this book, and is actually straight out of Chapter 17) in your database on a weekly or monthly basis as seems appropriate:

```
DECLARE @TableName varchar(255)
DECLARE TableCursor CURSOR FOR
   SELECT TABLE_NAME FROM INFORMATION_SCHEMA.TABLES
      WHERE TABLE_TYPE = 'BASE TABLE'
DECLARE @Command varchar(255)

OPEN TableCursor
FETCH NEXT FROM TableCursor INTO @TableName
WHILE @@FETCH_STATUS = 0
BEGIN
   PRINT "Reindexing " + @Tablename
   DBCC DBREINDEX(@TableName)
   FETCH NEXT FROM TableCursor INTO @TableName
END
CLOSE TableCursor
DEALLOCATE TableCursor
```

It rebuilds all the indexes in your tables. They should go back to whatever padding level your established when the table was created.

Archival of Data

Oooooh – here's a tricky one. There are as many ways of archiving data as there are database engineers. The OLAP database idea that you saw in Chapter 21 should address what you need to know as far as archiving for long-term reporting goes – but you also need to deal with the issue of when your OLTP data becomes simply too voluminous for your system to perform well.

As I said, there are just too many ways to go about archiving because every database is a little bit different. The key is to think about archival needs at the time that you create your database. Realize that, as you start to delete records, you're going to be hitting referential integrity constraints and/or orphaning records – design in a logical path to delete/move records at archival time. Here are some things to think about as you write your archival scripts:

- If you already have the data in an OLAP database, then you probably don't need to worry about saving it anywhere else – talk to your boss and your attorney on that one.
- How often is the data really used? Is it worth keeping? Human beings are natural born pack rats in a larger size. Simply put, we hate giving things up – that includes our data. If you're only worried about legal requirements, think about just saving a copy of never or rarely used data to tape (I'd suggest multiple backups for archival data) and reducing the amount of data you have online – your users will love you for it when they see improved performance.
- Don't leave orphans. As you start deleting data, your referential integrity constraints should keep you from leaving very many orphans, but you'll wind up with some referential integrity that didn't apply. This situation can lead to serious system errors.
- Realize that your archival program will probably be long running – plan on running it at a time where your system will have little or no use for a lengthy period of time.
- TEST! TEST! TEST!

Summary

Well, that gives you a few things to think about. It's really easy to, as a developer, think about many administrative tasks and establish what the *Hitchhiker's Guide To The Galaxy* called an "SEP" field. That's something that makes things like administration seem invisible because it's, "Somebody else's problem." Don't go there! Think about administration issues as you're doing your design and especially in your deployment plan. If you plan ahead to simplify the administration of your system, you'll find that you system is much more successful – that usually translates into rewards for the developer (i.e. you!).

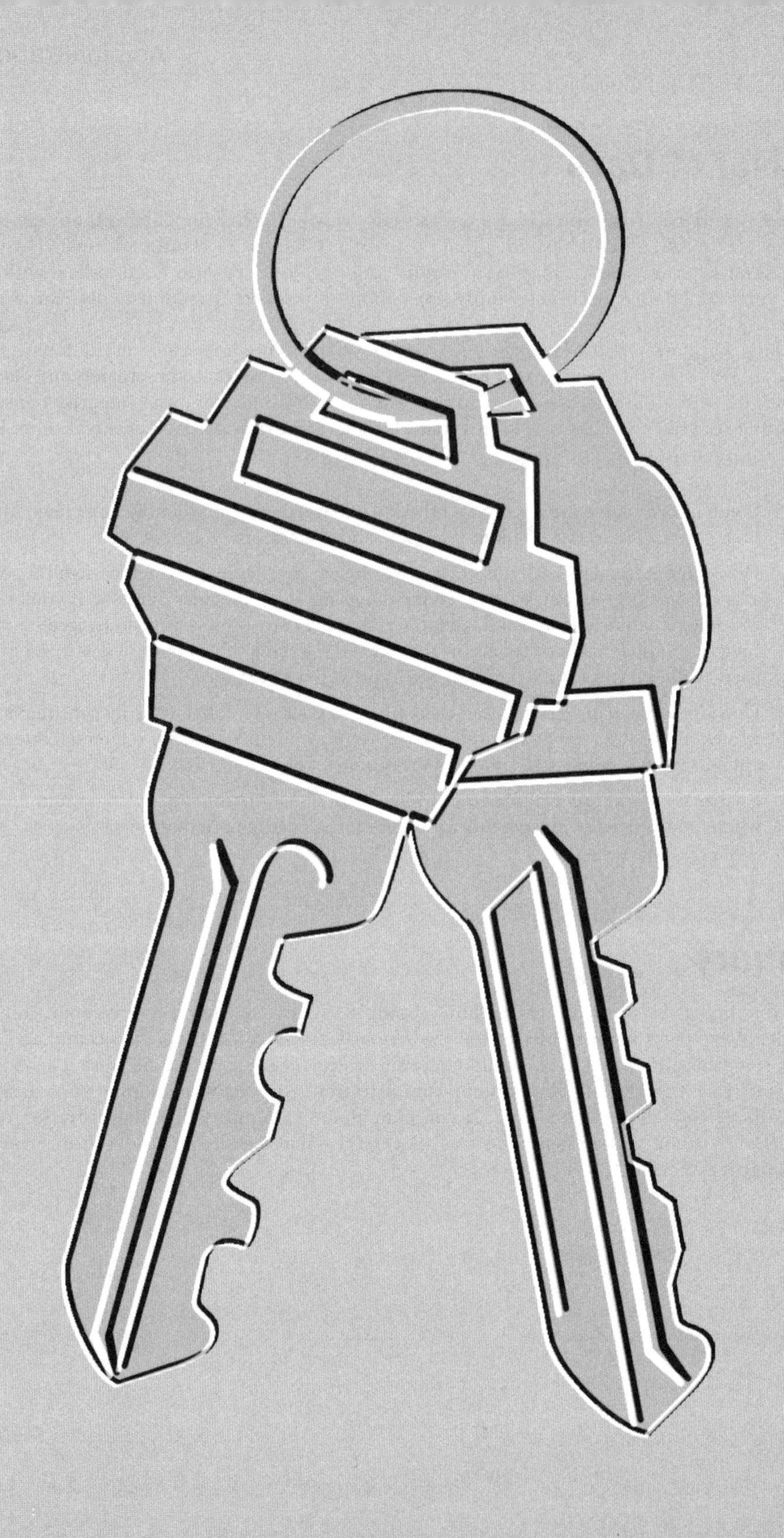

Global Variables

In the paragraphs below, I strive to clarify each of the documented global variables in SQL Server 7.0. Some of them are more useful than others, but each has its own little bit to offer.

@@CONNECTIONS

Returns the number of connections attempted since the last time your SQL Server was started.

This one is the total of all connection *attempts* made since the last time your SQL Server was started. The key thing to remember here is that we are talking about attempts, not actual connections, and that we are talking about connections as opposed to users.

Every attempt made to create a connection increments this counter regardless of whether that connection was successful or not. The only catch with this is that the connection attempt has to have made it as far as the server. If the connection failed because of Netlib differences or some other network issue, then your SQL Server wouldn't even know that it needed to increase the count – it only counts if the server saw the connection attempt. Whether the attempt succeeded or failed does not matter.

It's also important to understand that we're talking about connections instead of login attempts. Depending on your app, you may create several connections to your server, but you'll probably only ask the user for information once. Indeed, even Query Analyzer does this. When you click for a new window, it automatically creates another connection based on the same login information.

@@CPU_BUSY

Returns the time in milliseconds that the CPU has been actively doing work since SQL Server was last started. This number is based on the resolution of the system timer – which can vary – and can therefore vary in accuracy.

This is another of the "since the server started" kind of globals. This means that you can't always count on the number going up as your app runs. It's possible, based on this number, to figure out a CPU percentage that your SQL Server is taking up; but, realistically, I'd rather tap right into the Performance Monitor for that if I had some dire need for it. The bottom line is that this is one of those really cool things from a "gee, isn't it swell to know that" point of view, but doesn't have all that many practical uses in most applications.

@@CURSOR_ROWS

How many rows are currently in the last cursor set opened on the current connection.

Keep in mind that this number is reset every time you open a new cursor. If you need to open more than one cursor at a time, and you need to know the number of rows in the first cursor, then you'll need to move this value into a holding variable before opening subsequent cursors.

It's possible to use this to set up a counter to control your `WHILE` loop when dealing with cursors, but I strongly recommend against this practice – the value contained in this global can change depending on the cursor type and whether SQL Server is populating the cursor asynchronously or not. Using `@@FETCH_STATUS` is going to be far more reliable and at least as easy to use.

@@DATEFIRST

Returns the numeric value that corresponds to the day of the week that the system considers being the first day of the week.

The default in the US is 7, which equates to Sunday. The values convert as follows:

- 1 – Monday (the first day for most of the world)
- 2 – Tuesday
- 3 – Wednesday
- 4 – Thursday
- 5 – Friday
- 6 – Saturday
- 7 – Sunday

This can be really handy when dealing with localization issues so you can properly lay out any calendar or other day of week dependent information you have.

@@DBTS

Returns the last used timestamp for the current database

At first look this one seems to act an awful lot like `@@IDENTITY` in that it gives you the chance to get back the last value set by the system (this time, it's the last timestamp instead of the last identity value). The things to watch out for on this one include:

- The value changes based on any change in the database, not just the table you're working on.
- The value is more of a true global than is `@@IDENTITY` – *any* timestamp change in the database is reflected, not just those for the current connection.

Because you can't count on this value truly being the last one that you used (someone else may have done something that would change it), I personally find very little practical use for this one.

@@ERROR

Returns the error code for the last T-SQL statement ran on the current connection. If there is no error, then the value will be zero.

If you're going to be writing stored procedures or triggers, this is a bread and butter kind of global – you pretty much can't live without it.

> **The thing to remember with `@@ERROR` is that its life span is just one statement. This means that, if you want to use it to check for an error after a given statement, then you either need to make your test the very next statement, or you need to move it into a holding variable.**

For a listing of all the system errors, see Appendix D. Don't forget that you can also view this using the `sysmessages` system table in the `master` database.

To create your own custom errors, use `sp_addmessage`.

@@FETCH_STATUS

Returns an indicator of the status of the last cursor `FETCH` operation.

If you're using cursors, you're going to be using `@@FETCH_STATUS`. This one is how you know the success or failure of your attempt to navigate to a record in your cursor. It will return a constant depending on whether SQL Server succeeded in your last `FETCH` operation or not, and, if the `FETCH` failed, why. The constants are:

- 0 – Success
- -1 – Failed. Usually because you are beyond either the beginning or end of the cursorset
- -2 – Failed. The row you were fetching wasn't found, usually because it was deleted between when the cursorset was created and when you navigated to the current row. Should only occur in scrollable, non-dynamic cursors.

For purposes of readability, I often will set up some constants prior to using @@FETCH_STATUS.

For example:

```
DECLARE @NOTFOUND int
DECLARE @BEGINEND int

SELECT @NOTFOUND = -2
SELECT @BEGINEND = -1
```

I can then used these in my conditional in the WHILE statement of my cursor loop instead of just the row integer. This can make the code quite a bit more readable.

@@IDENTITY

Returns the last identity value created by the current connection.

If you're using identity columns and then referencing them as a foreign key in another table, you'll find yourself using this one all the time. You can create the parent record (usually the one with the identity you need to retrieve), then select @@IDENTITY to know what value you need to relate child records to.

If you perform inserts into multiple tables with identity values, remember that the value in @@IDENTITY will only be for the *last* identity value inserted – anything before that will have been lost, unless you move the value into a holding variable after each insert. Also, if the last column you inserted into didn't have an identity column, then @@IDENTITY will be set to NULL.

@@IDLE

Returns the time in milliseconds (based on the resolution of the system timer) that SQL Server has been idle since it was last started

You can think of this one as being something of the inverse of @@CPU_BUSY. Essentially, it tells you how much time your SQL Server has spent doing nothing. If anyone finds a programmatic use for this one, send me an e-mail – I'd love to hear about it (I can't think of one).

@@IO_BUSY

Returns the time in milliseconds (based on the resolution of the system timer) that SQL Server has spent doing input and output operations since it was last started. This value is reset every time SQL Server is started.

This one doesn't really have any rocket science to it, and it is another one of those that I find falls into the "no real programmatic use" category.

@@LANGID and @@LANGUAGE

Respectively return the ID and the name of the language currently in use.

This one can be handy for figuring out if your product has been installed in a localization situation or not, and, if so, what language is the default.

For a full listing of the languages currently supported by SQL Server, run a `SELECT *` on the `syslanguages` table.

@@LOCK_TIMEOUT

Returns the current amount of time in milliseconds before the system will time-out waiting on a blocked resource.

If a resource (a page, a row, a table, whatever) is blocked, your process will stop and wait for the block to clear. This determines just how long your process will wait.

The default time to wait is zero (which equates to indefinite) unless someone has changed it at the system level (using `sp_configure`). Regardless of how the system default is set, you will get a value of –1 from this global unless you have manually set the value for the current connection using `SET LOCK_TIMEOUT`.

@@MAX_CONNECTIONS

Returns the maximum number of simultaneous user connections allowed on your SQL Server

Don't mistake this one to mean the same thing as you would see under the Maximum Connections property in the Enterprise Manager. This one is based on licensing, and will show a very high number if you have selected "Per Seat" licensing.

Note that the actual number of user connections allowed also depends on the version of SQL Server you are using and the limits of your application(s) and hardware.

@@MAX_PRECISION

Returns the level of precision currently set for decimal and numeric data types.

The default is 28 places, but the value can be changed by using the `/p` option when you start your SQL Server. The `/p` can be added by starting SQL Server from a command line, or by adding it in the Startup Parameters for the MSSQLServer service in the Windows NT or 2000 Services applet (if you're running NT or 2000)

@@NESTLEVEL

Returns the current nesting level for nested stored procedures

The first stored procedure (sproc) to run has an `@@NESTLEVEL` of 1. If that sproc calls another, then the second sproc is said to be nested in the first sproc (and `@@NESTLEVEL` is incremented to a value of 2). Likewise, the second sproc may call a third, and so on up to maximum of 32 levels deep.

Again, `@@NESTLEVEL` Returns 1 for non-nested stored procedures, and a higher number for each additional nesting level.

@@OPTIONS

Returns information about options that have been applied using the SET command.

Since you only get one value back, but can have many options set, SQL Server uses binary flags to indicate what values are set. In order to test whether the option you are interested in is set, you must use the option value together with a bitwise operator. For example:

```
IF (@@OPTIONS & 2)
```

evaluated to true, then you would know that IMPLICIT_TRANSACTIONS had been turned on for the current connection. The values are:

Bit	SET Option	Description
1	DISABLE_DEF_CNST_CHK	Interim vs. deferred constraint checking.
2	IMPLICIT_TRANSACTIONS	A transaction is started implicitly when a statement is executed.
4	CURSOR_CLOSE_ON_COMMIT	Controls behavior of cursors after a COMMIT operation has been performed.
8	ANSI_WARNINGS	Warns of truncation and NULL in aggregates.
16	ANSI_PADDING	Controls padding of fixed-length variables.
32	ANSI_NULLS	Determines handling of NULLs when using equality operators.
64	ARITHABORT	Terminates a query when an overflow or divide-by-zero error occurs during query execution.
128	ARITHIGNORE	Returns NULL when an overflow or divide-by-zero error occurs during a query.
256	QUOTED_IDENTIFIER	Differentiates between single and double quotation marks when evaluating an expression.
512	NOCOUNT	Turns off the row(s) affected message returned at the end of each statement.
1024	ANSI_NULL_DFLT_ON	Alters the session's behavior to use ANSI compatibility for nullability. Columns created with new tables or added to old tables without explicit null option settings are defined to allow nulls. Mutually exclusive with ANSI_NULL_DFLT_OFF.
2048	ANSI_NULL_DFLT_OFF	Alters the session's behavior not to use ANSI compatibility for nullability. New columns defined without explicit nullability are defined not to allow nulls. Mutually exclusive with ANSI_NULL_DFLT_ON.

@@PACK_RECEIVED and @@PACK_SENT

Respectively return the number of input packets read/written from/to the network by SQL Server since it was last started.

Primarily a trouble-shooting tool.

@@PACKET_ERRORS

Returns the number of network packet errors that have occurred on connections to your SQL Server since the last time the SQL Server was started.

Primarily a trouble-shooting tool.

@@PROCID

Returns the stored procedure ID of the currently running procedure

Primarily a trouble-shooting tool.

@@REMSERVER

Returns the value of the server (as it appears in the login record) that called the stored procedure.

Used only in stored procedures. This one is handy when you want the sproc to behave differently depending on what remote server (often a geographic location) the sproc was called from.

@@ROWCOUNT

Returns the number of rows affected by the last statement

One of the most used globals, my most common use for this one is to check for non run-time errors – that is, items that are logically errors to your program, but that SQL Server isn't going to see any problem with. An example would be a situation where you are performing an update based on a condition, but you find that it affects zero rows. Odds are that, if your client submitted a modification for a particular row, then it was expecting that row to match the criteria given – zero rows affected is indicative of something being wrong.

@@SERVERNAME

Returns the name of the local server that the script is running from.

@@SERVICENAME

Returns the name of the registry key under which SQL Server is running.

Only returns something under Windows NT/2000, and, under either of these, should always return MSSQLService unless you've been playing games in the registry. Should return nothing if running under Win 9x (Win 9x doesn't have services, so SQL Server can't run as one).

@@SPID

Returns the server process ID (SPID) of the current user process.

This equates to the same process ID that you see if you run `sp_who`. What's nice is that you can tell the SPID for your current connection.

@@TEXTSIZE

Returns the current value of the `TEXTSIZE` option of the `SET` statement, which specifies the maximum length, in bytes, returned by a `SELECT` statement when dealing with text or image data.

The default is 4096 bytes (4KB). You can change this value by using the `SET TEXTSIZE` statement.

@@TIMETICKS

Returns the number of microseconds per tick. This varies by machines and is another of those that falls under the category of "No real programmatic use".

@@TOTAL_ERRORS

Returns the number of disk read/write errors encountered by the SQL Server since it was last started.

Don't confuse this with run-time errors or as having any relation to `@@ERROR`. This is about problems with physical I/O. This one is another of those of the "No real programmatic use" variety. The primary use here would be more along the lines of system diagnostic scripts. Generally speaking, I would use Performance Monitor for this instead.

@@TOTAL_READ and @@TOTAL_WRITE

Respectively return the total number of disk reads/writes by SQL Server since it was last started.

The names here are a little misleading, as these do not include any reads from cache – they are only physical I/O.

@@TRANCOUNT

Returns the number of active transactions – essentially the transaction nesting level – for the current connection

This is a very big one when you are doing transactioning. I'm not normally a big fan of nested transactions, but there are times where they are difficult to avoid. As such, it can be important to know just where you are in the transaction nesting side of things (for example, you may have logic that only starts a transaction if you're not already in one).

If you're not in a transaction, then @@TRANCOUNT is zero. From there, let's look at a brief example:

```
SELECT @@TRANCOUNT As TransactionNestLevel     --This will be zero at this point

BEGIN TRAN
SELECT @@TRANCOUNT As TransactionNestLevel     --This will be one at this point
     BEGIN TRAN
          SELECT @@TRANCOUNT As TransactionNestLevel --This will be two at this
                                                     --point
     COMMIT TRAN
SELECT @@TRANCOUNT As TransactionNestLevel     --This will be back to one at this
point
ROLLBACK TRAN
SELECT @@TRANCOUNT As TransactionNestLevel     --This will be back to zero at this
point
```

Note that, in this example, the @@TRANCOUNT at the end would also have reached zero if we had a COMMIT as our last statement.

@@VERSION

Returns the current version of SQL Server as well as the processor type and OS architecture

For example:

```
SELECT @@VERSION
```

gives:

```
--------------------------------------------------------------------------------
Microsoft SQL Server  7.00 - 7.00.623 (Intel X86)
     Nov 27 1998 22:20:07
     Copyright (c) 1988-1998 Microsoft Corporation
     Standard Edition on Windows NT 5.0 (Build 2072: )
```

Unfortunately, this doesn't return the information into any kind of structured field arrangement, so you have to parse it if you want to use it to test for specific information.

Consider using the xp_msver system sproc instead – it returns information in such a way that you can more easily retrieve specific information from the results.

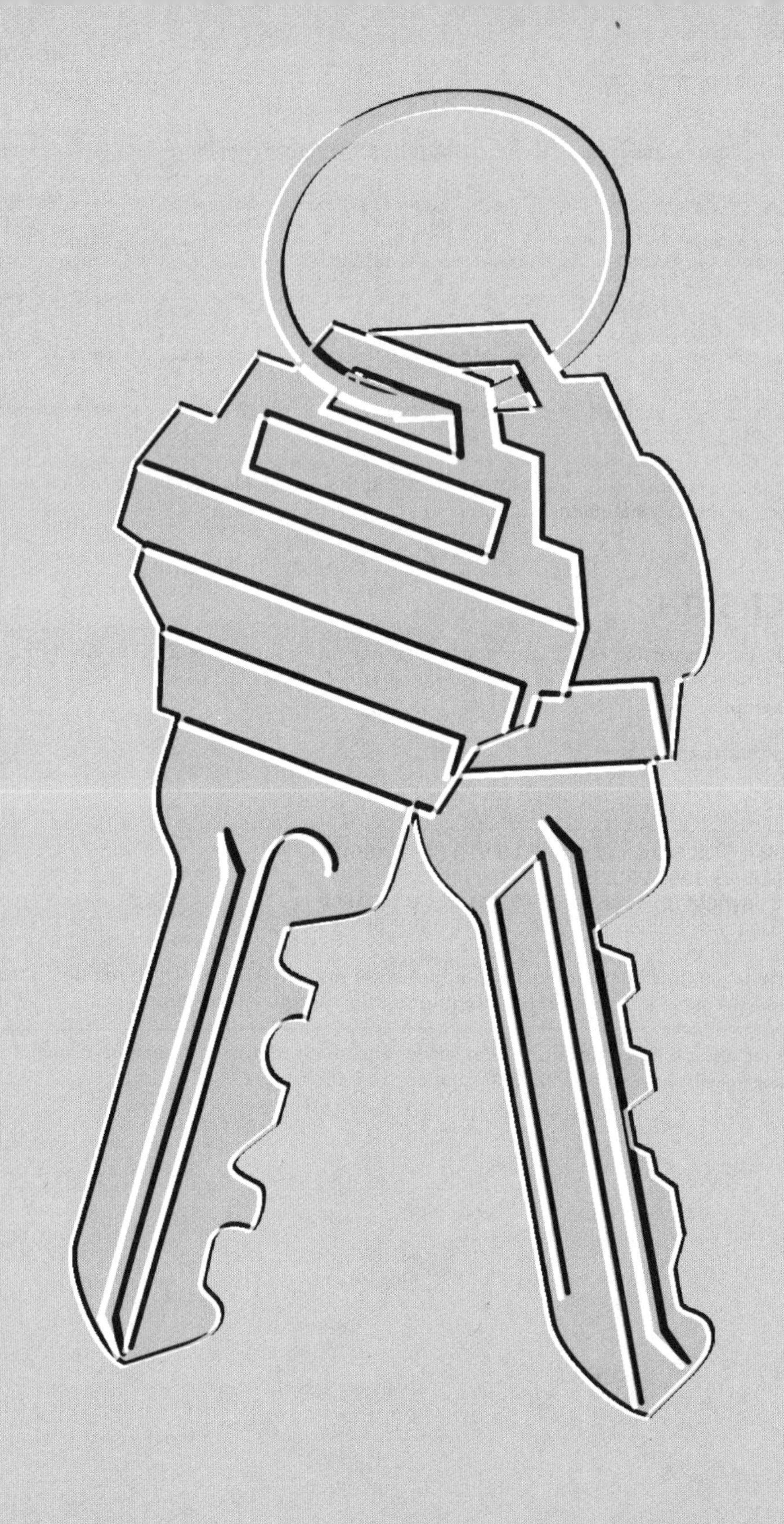

Function Listing

The T-SQL functions available in SQL Server 7 fall into 10 categories:

- Aggregate functions
- Cursor functions
- Date and time functions
- Mathematical functions
- Metadata functions
- Rowset functions
- Security functions
- String functions
- System functions
- Text and image functions

Aggregate Functions

Aggregate functions are applied to sets of records rather than a single record. The information in the multiple records is processed in a particular manner and then is displayed in a single-record answer. Aggregate functions are often used in conjunction with the GROUP BY clause.

The aggregate functions are:

- AVG
- COUNT
- GROUPING
- MAX
- MIN
- SUM
- STDEV
- STDEVP
- VAR
- VARP

In most aggregate functions, the ALL or DISTINCT can be used. The ALL argument is the default and will apply the function to all the values in expression, even if a value appears numerous times. The DISTINCT argument means that a value will only be included in the function once, even if it occurs several times.

Aggregate functions cannot be nested. The *expression* cannot be a subquery.

AVG

AVG returns the average of the values in *expression*. The syntax is as follows:

```
AVG([ALL | DISTINCT] <expression>)
```

The *expression* must contain numeric values. Null values are ignored.

COUNT

COUNT returns the number of items in *expression*. The syntax is as follows:

```
COUNT
(
   [ALL | DISTINCT] <expression> | *
)
```

The *expression* cannot be of the uniqueidentifier, text, image or ntext data type. The * argument returns the number of rows in the table, it does not eliminate duplicate or NULL values.

GROUPING

GROUPING adds an extra column to the output of a SELECT statement. The GROUPING function is used in conjunction with CUBE or ROLLUP to distinguish between normal NULL values and those added as a result of CUBE and ROLLUP operations. Its syntax is:

```
GROUPING (<column_name>)
```

GROUPING is only used in the SELECT list. Its argument is a column that is used in the GROUP BY clause and which is to be checked for NULL values.

MAX

The MAX function returns the maximum value from *expression*. The syntax is as follows:

```
MAX([ALL | DISTINCT] <expression>)
```

MAX ignores any NULL values.

MIN

The MIN function returns the smallest value from *expression*. The syntax is as follows:

```
MIN([ALL | DISTINCT] <expression>)
```

MIN ignores NULL values.

SUM

The SUM function will return the total of all values in *expression*. The syntax is as follows:

```
SUM([ALL | DISTINCT] <expression>)
```

SUM ignores NULL values.

STDEV

The STDEV function returns the standard deviation of all values in *expression*. The syntax is as follows:

```
STDEV(<expression>)
```

STDEV ignores NULL values.

STDEVP

The STDEVP function returns the standard deviation for the population of all values in *expression*. The syntax is as follows:

```
STDEVP(<expression>)
```

STDEVP ignores NULL values.

VAR

The VAR function returns the variance of all values in *expression*. The syntax is as follows:

```
VAR(<expression>)
```

VAR ignores NULL values.

VARP

The VARP function returns the variance for the population of all values in *expression*. The syntax is as follows:

```
VARP(<expression>)
```

VARP ignores NULL values.

Cursor Functions

There is only one cursor function (CURSOR_STATUS) and it provides information about cursors.

CURSOR_STATUS

The CURSOR_STATUS function allows the caller of a stored procedure to determine if that procedure has returned a cursor and result set. The syntax is as follows:

```
CURSOR_STATUS
    (
        {'<local>', '<cursor_name>'}
        | {'<global'>, '<cursor_name>'}
        | {'<variable>', '<cursor_variable>'}
    )
```

local, *global* and *variable* all specify constants that indicate the source of the cursor. *local* equates to a local cursor name, *global* to a global cursor name and *variable* to a local variable.

If you are using the *cursor_name* form then there are four possible return values:

- 1 - The cursor is open. If the cursor is dynamic, its result set has zero or more rows. If the cursor is not dynamic, it has one or more rows.
- 0 - The result set of the cursor is empty.
- -1 - The cursor is closed.
- -3 - A cursor of *cursor_name* does not exist.

If you are using the *cursor_variable* form, there are five possible return values:

- 1 - The cursor is open. If the cursor is dynamic, its result set has zero or more rows. If the cursor is not dynamic, it has one or more rows.
- 0 - The result set is empty.
- -1 - The cursor is closed.
- -2 - There is no cursor assigned to the *cursor_variable*.
- -3 - The variable with name *cursor_variable* does not exist, or if it does exist, has not had a cursor allocated to it yet.

Date and Time Functions

The date and time functions perform operations on values that have `datetime` and `smalldatetime` data types or which are character data types in a date form. They are:

- DATEADD
- DATEDIFF
- DATENAME
- DATEPART
- DAY
- GETDATE
- MONTH
- YEAR

SQL Server recognizes eleven "dateparts" and their abbreviations as shown in the following table:

Datepart	Abbreviations
year	yy, yyyy
quarter	qq, q
month	mm, m
dayofyear	dy, y
day	dd, d
week	wk, ww
weekday	dw
hour	hh
minute	mi, n
second	ss, s
millisecond	ms

DATEADD

The DATEADD function adds an interval to a date and returns a new date. The syntax is as follows:

```
DATEADD(<datepart>, <number>, <date>)
```

The *datepart* argument specifies time scale of the interval (day, week, month, etc) and may be any of the dateparts recognized by SQL Server. The *number* argument is the number of *dateparts* that should be added to the *date*.

DATEDIFF

The DATEDIFF function returns the difference between two specified dates in a specified unit of time (e.g. hours, days, weeks). The syntax is as follows:

```
DATEDIFF(<datepart>, <startdate>, <enddate>)
```

The *datepart* argument may be any of the dateparts recognized by SQL Server and specifies the unit of time to be used.

DATENAME

The DATENAME function returns a string representing the name of the specified *datepart* (e.g. 1999, Thursday, July) of the specified *date*. The syntax is as follows:

```
DATENAME(<datepart>, <date>)
```

DATEPART

The DATEPART function returns an integer that represents the specified *datepart* of the specified *date*. The syntax is as follows:

```
DATEPART(<datepart>, <date>)
```

The DAY function is equivalent to DATEPART(dd, <*date*>); MONTH is equivalent to DATEPART(mm, <*date*>); YEAR is equivalent to DATEPART(yy, <*date*>).

DAY

The DAY function returns an integer representing the day part of the specified date. The syntax is as follows:

```
DAY(<date>)
```

The DAY function is equivalent to DATEPART(dd, <*date*>).

GETDATE

The GETDATE function returns the current system date and time. The syntax is as follows:

```
GETDATE()
```

MONTH

The MONTH function returns an integer that represents the month part of the specified date. The syntax is as follows:

```
MONTH(<date>)
```

The MONTH function is equivalent to DATEPART(mm, <*date*>).

YEAR

The YEAR function returns an integer that represents the year part of the specified date. The syntax is as follows:

```
YEAR(<date>)
```

The YEAR function is equivalent to DATEPART(yy, <*date*>).

Mathematical Functions

The mathematical functions perform calculations. They are:

- ABS
- ACOS
- ASIN
- ATAN
- ATN2
- CEILING
- COS
- COT
- DEGREES
- EXP
- FLOOR
- LOG
- LOG10

- PI
- POWER
- RADIANS
- RAND
- ROUND
- SIGN
- SIN
- SQUARE
- SQRT
- TAN

ABS

The ABS function returns the positive, absolute value of *numeric_expression*. The syntax is as follows:

```
ABS(<numeric_expression>)
```

ACOS

The ACOS function returns the angle in radians for which the cosine is the *expression* (i.e. it returns the arccosine of *expression*). The syntax is as follows:

```
ACOS(<expression>)
```

The value of *expression* must be between -1 and 1 and be of the float data type.

ASIN

The ASIN function returns the angle in radians for which the sine is the *expression* (i.e. it returns the arcsine of *expression*). The syntax is as follows:

```
ASIN(<expression>)
```

The value of *expression* must be between -1 and 1 and be of the float data type.

ATAN

The ATAN function returns the angle in radians for which the tangent is *expression* (i.e. it returns the arctangent of *expression*). The syntax is as follows:

```
ATAN(<expression>)
```

The expression must be of the float data type.

ATN2

The `ATN2` function returns the angle in radians for which the tangent is between the two expressions provided (i.e. it returns the arctangent of the two expressions). The syntax is as follows:

```
ATN2(<expression1>, <expression2>)
```

Both *expression1* and *expression2* must be of the `float` data type.

CEILING

The `CEILING` function returns the smallest integer that is equal to or greater than the specified expression. The syntax is as follows:

```
CEILING(<expression>)
```

COS

The `COS` function returns the cosine of the angle specified in `expression`. The syntax is as follows:

```
COS(<expression>)
```

The angle given should be in radians and *expression* must be of the `float` data type.

COT

The `COT` function returns the cotangent of the angle specified in `expression`. The syntax is as follows:

```
COT(<expression>)
```

The angle given should be in radians and `expression` must be of the `float` data type.

DEGREES

The `DEGREES` function takes an angle given in radians (*expression*) and returns the angle in degrees. The syntax is as follows:

```
DEGREES(<expression>)
```

EXP

The `EXP` function returns the exponential value of the value given in *expression*. The syntax is as follows:

```
EXP(<expression>)
```

The *expression* has to be of the `float` data type.

FLOOR

The `FLOOR` function returns the largest integer that is equal to or less than the value specified in *expression*. The syntax is as follows:

```
FLOOR(<expression>)
```

LOG

The `LOG` function returns the natural logarithm of the value specified in *expression*. The syntax is as follows:

```
LOG(<expression>)
```

The *expression* is of the `float` data type.

LOG10

The `LOG10` function returns the base 10 logarithm of the value specified in *expression*. The syntax is as follows:

```
LOG10(<expression>)
```

The *expression* must be of the `float` data type.

PI

The `PI` function returns the value of the constant π. The syntax is as follows:

```
PI()
```

POWER

The `POWER` function raises the value of the specified *expression* to the specified *power*. The syntax is as follows:

```
POWER(<expression>, <power>)
```

RADIANS

The `RADIANS` function returns an angle in radians corresponding to the angle in degrees specified in *expression*. The syntax is as follows:

```
RADIANS(<expression>)
```

RAND

The `RAND` function returns a random value between 0 and 1. The syntax is as follows:

```
RAND([<seed>])
```

The *seed* value is an integer expression, which specifies the start value.

ROUND

The `ROUND` function takes a number specified in *expression* and rounds it to the specified length. The syntax is as follows:

```
ROUND(<expression>, <length> [, <function>])
```

The *length* parameter specifies the precision to which *expression* should be rounded. The *length* parameter should be of the `tinyint`, `smallint` or `int` data type. The optional *function* parameter can be used to specify whether the number should be rounded or truncated. If a *function* value is omitted or is equal to 0 (the default) the value in *expression* will be rounded. If any value other than 0 is provided, the value in *expression* will be truncated

SIGN

The `SIGN` function returns the sign of the `expression`. The possible return values are `+1` for a positive number, `0` for zero and `-1` for a negative number. The syntax is as follows:

```
SIGN(<expression>)
```

SIN

The `SIN` function returns the sine of an angle. The syntax is as follows:

```
SIN(<angle>)
```

The *angle* should be in radians and should be of the `float` data type. The return value will also be of the `float` data type.

SQUARE

The `SQUARE` function returns the square of the value given in *expression*. The syntax is as follows:

```
SQUARE(<expression>)
```

The *expression* should be of the `float` data type.

SQRT

The `SQRT` function returns the square root of the value given in *expression*. The syntax is as follows:

```
SQRT(<expression>)
```

The *expression* must be of the `float` data type.

TAN

The `TAN` function returns the tangent of the value specified in *expression*. The syntax is as follows:

```
TAN(<expression>)
```

The *expression* parameter specifies the number of radians and must be of the `float` or `real` data type.

Metadata Functions

The metadata functions provide information about the database and database objects. They are:

- COL_LENGTH
- COL_NAME
- COLUMNPROPERTY
- DATABASEPROPERTY
- DB_ID
- DB_NAME
- FILE_ID
- FILE_NAME
- FILEGROUP_ID
- FILEGROUP_NAME
- FILEGROUPPROPERTY
- FILEPROPERTY
- FULLTEXTCATALOGPROPERTY
- FULLTEXTSERVICEPROPERTY
- INDEX_COL
- INDEXPROPERTY
- OBJECT_ID
- OBJECT_NAME
- OBJECTPROPERTY
- TYPEPROPERTY

COL_LENGTH

The `COL_LENGTH` function returns the defined length of a column. The syntax is as follows:

```
COL_LENGTH('<table>', '<column>')
```

The *`column`* parameter specifies the name of the column for which the length is to be determined. The *`table`* parameter specifies the name of the table that contains that column.

COL_NAME

The `COL_NAME` function takes a table ID number and a column ID number and returns the name of the database column. The syntax is as follows:

```
COL_NAME(<table_id>, <column_id>)
```

The *`column_id`* parameter specifies the ID number of the column. The *`table_id`* parameter specifies the ID number of the table that contains that column.

COLUMNPROPERTY

The `COLUMNPROPERTY` function returns data about a column or procedure parameter. The syntax is as follows:

```
COLUMNPROPERTY(<id>, <column>, <property>)
```

The *`id`* parameter specifies the ID of the table/procedure. The *`column`* parameter specifies the name of the column/parameter. The *`property`* parameter specifies the data that should be returned for the column or procedure parameter. The *`property`* parameter can be one of the following values:

- `AllowsNull` - allows `NULL` values
- `IsComputed` - the column is a computed column
- `IsCursorType` - the procedure is of type `CURSOR`
- `IsFullTextIndexed` - the column has been Full-Text indexed
- `IsIdentity` - the column is an `IDENTITY` column
- `IsIdNotForRepl` - the column checks for `IDENTITY NOT FOR REPLICATION`
- `IsOutParam` - the procedure parameter is an output parameter
- `IsRowGuidCol` - the column is a `ROWGUIDCOL` column
- `Precision` - the precision for the data type of the column or parameter
- `Scale` - the scale for the data type of the column or parameter
- `UseAnsiTrim` - the ANSI padding setting was `ON` when the table was created

The return value from this function will be `1` for true, `0` for false and `NULL` if the input was not valid - except for `Precision` (where the precision for the data type will be returned) and `Scale` (where the scale will be returned).

DATABASEPROPERTY

The `DATABASEPROPERTY` function returns the setting for the specified database and property name. The syntax is as follows:

```
DATABASEPROPERTY('<database>', '<property>')
```

The *`database`* parameter specifies the name of the database for which data on the named property will be returned. The *`property`* parameter contains the name of a database property and can be one of the following values:

- `IsAnsiNullDefault` - the database follows the ANSI-92 standard for `NULL` values
- `IsAnsiNullsEnabled` - all comparisons made with a `NULL` cannot be evaluated
- `IsAnsiWarningsEnabled` - warning messages are issued when standard error conditions occur
- `IsAutoClose` - the database frees resources after the last user has exited
- `IsAutoShrink` - database files can be shrunk automatically and periodically
- `IsAutoUpdateStatistics` - the autoupdate statistics option has been enabled
- `IsBulkCopy` - the database allows non-logged operations (such as those performed with the bulk copy program)
- `IsCloseCursorsOnCommitEnabled` - any cursors that are open when a transaction is committed will be closed
- `IsDboOnly` - the database is only accessible to the `dbo`
- `IsDetached` - the database was detached by a detach operation
- `IsEmergencyMode` - the database is in emergency mode
- `IsFulltextEnabled` - the database has been Full-Text enabled
- `IsInLoad` - the database is loading
- `IsInRecovery` - the database is recovering
- `IsInStandby` - the database is read-only and restore log is allowed
- `IsLocalCursorsDefault` - cursor declarations default to `LOCAL`
- `IsNotRecovered` - the database failed to recover
- `IsNullConcat` - concatenating to a `NULL` results in a `NULL`
- `IsOffline` - the database is offline
- `IsQuotedIdentifiersEnabled` - identifiers can be delimited by double quotation marks
- `IsReadOnly` - the database is in a read-only mode
- `IsRecursiveTriggersEnabled` - the recursive firing of triggers is enabled
- `IsShutDown` - the database encountered a problem during startup
- `IsSingleUser` - the database is in single-user mode
- `IsSuspect` - the database is suspect
- `IsTruncLog` - the database truncates its log on checkpoints
- `Version` - the internal version number of the SQL Server code with which the database was created

The return value from this function will be 1 for true, 0 for false and NULL if the input was not valid - except for Version (where the function will return the version number if the database is open and NULL if the database is closed).

DB_ID

The DB_ID function returns the database ID number. The syntax is as follows:

```
DB_ID(['<database_name>'])
```

The optional *database_name* parameter specifies which database's ID number is required. If the *database_name* is not given, the current database will be used instead.

DB_NAME

The DB_NAME function returns the name of the database that has the specified ID number. The syntax is as follows:

```
DB_NAME([<database_id>])
```

The optional *database_id* parameter specifies which database's name is to be returned. If no *database_id* is given, the name of the current database will be returned.

FILE_ID

The FILE_ID function returns the file ID number for the specified file name in the current database. The syntax is as follows:

```
FILE_ID('<file_name>')
```

The *file_name* parameter specifies the name of the file for which the ID is required.

FILE_NAME

The FILE_NAME function returns the file name for the file with the specified file ID number. The syntax is as follows:

```
FILE_NAME(<file_id>)
```

The *file_id* parameter specifies the ID number of the file for which the name is required.

FILEGROUP_ID

The FILEGROUP_ID function returns the filegroup ID number for the specified filegroup name. The syntax is as follows:

```
FILEGROUP_ID('<filegroup_name>')
```

The *filegroup_name* parameter specifies the filegroup name of the required filegroup ID.

FILEGROUP_NAME

The FILEGROUP_NAME function returns the filegroup name for the specified filegroup ID number. The syntax is as follows:

```
FILEGROUP_NAME(<filegroup_id>)
```

The *filegroup_id* parameter specifies the filegroup ID of the required filegroup name.

FILEGROUPPROPERTY

The FILEGROUPPROPERTY returns the setting of a specified filegroup property, given the filegroup and property name. The syntax is as follows:

```
FILEGROUPPROPERTY(<filegroup_name>, <property>)
```

The *filegroup_name* parameter specifies the name of the filegroup that contains the property being queried. The *property* parameter specifies the property being queried and can be one of the following values:

- IsReadOnly - the filegroup name is read-only
- IsUserDefinedFG - the filegroup name is a user-defined filegroup
- IsDefault - the filegroup name is the default filegroup

The return value from this function will be 1 for true, 0 for false and NULL if the input was not valid.

FILEPROPERTY

The FILEPROPERTY function returns the setting of a specified file name property, given the file name and property name. The syntax is as follows:

```
FILEPROPERTY(<file_name>, <property>)
```

The *file_name* parameter specifies the name of the filegroup that contains the property being queried. The *property* parameter specifies the property being queried and can be one of the following values:

- IsReadOnly - the file is read-only
- IsPrimaryFile - the file is the primary file
- IsLogFile - the file is a log file
- SpaceUsed - the amount of space used by the specified file

The return value from this function will be 1 for true, 0 for false and NULL if the input was not valid, except for SpaceUsed (which will return the number of pages allocated in the file).

FULLTEXTCATALOGPROPERTY

The `FULLTEXTCATALOGPROPERTY` function returns data about the Full-Text catalog properties. The syntax is as follows:

```
FULLTEXTCATALOGPROPERTY(<catalog_name>, <property>)
```

The *`catalog_name`* parameter specifies the name of the Full-Text catalog. The *`property`* parameter specifies the property that is being queried. The properties that can be queried are:

- `PopulateStatus` - for which the possible return values are: `0` (Idle), `1` (Population in progress), `2` (Paused), `3` (Throttled), `4` (Recovering), `5` (Shutdown), `6` (Incremental population in progress), `7` (Updating index)
- `ItemCount` - returns the number of Full-Text indexed items currently in the Full-Text catalog
- `IndexSize` - returns the size of the Full-Text index in megabytes
- `UniqueKeyCount` - returns the number of unique words that make up the Full-Text index in this catalog
- `LogSize` - returns the size (in bytes) of the combined set of error logs associated with a Full-Text catalog
- `PopulateCompletionAge` - returns the difference (in seconds) between the completion of the last Full-Text index population and 01/01/1990 00:00:00

FULLTEXTSERVICEPROPERTY

The `FULLTEXTSERVICEPROPERTY` function returns data about the Full-Text service-level properties. The syntax is as follows:

```
FULLTEXTSERVICEPROPERTY(<property>)
```

The *`property`* parameter specifies the name of the service-level property that is to be queried. The *`property`* parameter may be one of the following values:

- `ResourceUsage` - returns a value from `1` (background) to `5` (dedicated)
- `ConnectTimeOut` - returns the number of seconds that the Search Service will wait for all connections to SQL Server for Full-Text index population before timing out
- `IsFulltextInstalled` - returns `1` if Full-Text Service is installed on the computer and a `0` otherwise

INDEX_COL

The `INDEX_COL` function returns the indexed column name. The syntax is as follows:

```
INDEX_COL('<table>', <index_id>, <key_id>)
```

The *`'table'`* parameter specifies the name of the table, *`index_id`* specifies the ID of the index and *`key_id`* specifies the ID of the key.

INDEXPROPERTY

The INDEXPROPERTY function returns the setting of a specified index property, given the table ID, index name and property name. The syntax is as follows:

```
INDEXPROPERTY(<table_ID>, <index>, <property>)
```

The *property* parameter specifies the property of the index that is to be queried. The *property* parameter can be one of these possible values:

- IndexDepth - the depth of the index
- IsAutoStatistic - the index was created by the auto create statistics option of sp_dboption
- IsClustered - the index is clustered
- IsStatistics - the index was created by the CREATE STATISTICS statement or by the auto create statistics option of sp_dboption
- IsUnique - the index is unique
- IndexFillFactor - the index specifies its own fill factor
- IsPadIndex - the index specifies space to leave open on each interior node
- IsFulltextKey - the index is the Full-Text key for a table
- IsHypothetical - the index is hypothetical and cannot be used directly as a data access path

The return value from this function will be 1 for true, 0 for false and NULL if the input was not valid, except for IndexDepth (which will return the number of levels the index has) and IndexFillFactor (which will return the fill factor used when the index was created or last rebuilt).

OBJECT_ID

The OBJECT_ID function returns the specified database object's ID number. The syntax is as follows:

```
OBJECT_ID('<object>')
```

OBJECT_NAME

The OBJECT_NAME function returns the name of the specified database object. The syntax is as follows:

```
OBJECT_NAME(<object_id>)
```

OBJECTPROPERTY

The `OBJECTPROPERTY` function returns data about objects in the current database. The syntax is as follows:

```
OBJECTPROPERTY(<id>, <property>)
```

The *id* parameter specifies the ID of the object required. The *property* parameter specifies the information required on the object. The following *property* values are allowed:

```
CnstIsClustKey                 CnstIsColumn
CnstIsDisabled                 CnstIsNonclustKey
CnstIsNotRepl                  ExecIsAnsiNullsOn
ExecIsDeleteTrigger            ExecIsInsertTrigger
ExecIsQuotedIdentOn            ExecIsStartup
ExecIsTriggerDisabled          ExecIsUpdateTrigger
IsCheckCnst                    IsConstraint
IsDefault                      IsDefaultCnst
IsExecuted                     IsExtendedProc
IsForeignKey                   IsMSShipped
IsPrimaryKey                   IsProcedure
IsReplProc                     IsRule
IsSystemTable                  IsTable
IsTrigger                      IsUniqueCnst
IsUserTable                    IsView
OwnerId                        TableDeleteTrigger
TableDeleteTriggerCount        TableFulltextCatalogId
TableFulltextKeyColumn         TableHasActiveFulltextIndex
TableHasCheckCnst              TableHasClustIndex
TableHasDefaultCnst            TableHasDeleteTrigger
TableHasForeignKey             TableHasForeignRef
TableHasIdentity               TableHasIndex
TableHasInsertTrigger          TableHasNonclustIndex
TableHasPrimaryKey             TableHasRowGuidCol
TableHasTextImage              TableHasTimestamp
TableHasUniqueCnst             TableHasUpdateTrigger
TableInsertTrigger             TableInsertTriggerCount
TableIsFake                    TableIsPinned
TableUpdateTrigger             TableUpdateTriggerCount
TriggerDeleteOrder             TriggerInsertOrder
TriggerUpdateOrder
```

The return value from this function will be `1` for true, `0` for false and `NULL` if the input was not valid, except for:

- `OwnerId` (which will return the database user ID of the object owner)
- `TableDeleteTrigger`, `TableDeleteTriggerCount`, `TableInsertTrigger`, `TableInsertTriggerCount`, `TableUpdateTrigger`, `TableUpdateTriggerCount` (all of which will return the ID of the first trigger with the given type)
- `TableFulltextCatalogId` and `TableFulltextKeyColumn` (both of which will return the Full-Text catalog ID, or a `0` to indicate that the table has not been Full-Text indexed or a `NULL` to indicate that the input was invalid)

TYPEPROPERTY

The `TYPEPROPERTY` function returns information about a data type. The syntax is as follows:

```
TYPEPROPERTY(<type>, <property>)
```

The *type* parameter specifies the name of the data type. The *property* parameter specifies the property of the data type that is to queried; it can be one of the following values:

- `Precision` - returns the number of digits/characters
- `Scale` - returns the number of decimal places
- `AllowsNull` - returns `1` for true and `0` for false
- `UsesAnsiTrim` - returns `1` for true and `0` for false

Rowset Functions

The rowset functions return an object that can be used in place of a table reference in a T-SQL statement. The rowset functions are:

- `CONTAINSTABLE`
- `FREETEXTTABLE`
- `OPENQUERY`
- `OPENROWSET`

CONTAINSTABLE

The `CONTAINSTABLE` function is used in Full-Text queries. Please refer to Chapter 22 for an example of its usage. The syntax is as follows:

```
CONTAINSTABLE (<table>, {<column> | *}, '<contains_search_condition>')
```

FREETEXTTABLE

The `FREETEXTTABLE` function is used in Full-Text queries. Please refer to Chapter 22 for an example of its usage. The syntax is as follows:

```
FREETEXTTABLE (<table>, {<column> | *}, '<freetext_string>')
```

OPENQUERY

The `OPENQUERY` function executes the specified pass-through *query* on the specified *linked_server*. The syntax is as follows:

```
OPENQUERY(<linked_server>, '<query>')
```

OPENROWSET

The OPENROWSET function accesses remote data from an OLE DB data source. The syntax is as follows:

```
OPENROWSET('<provider_name>'
    {
     '<datasource>';'<user_id>';'<password>'
     | '<provider_string>'
    },
    {
       [<catalog.>][<schema.>]<object>
       | '<query>'
    })
```

The *provider_name* parameter is a string representing the friendly name of the OLE DB provided as specified in the registry. The *data_source* parameter is a string corresponding to the required OLE DB data source. The *user_id* parameter is a relevant username to be passed to the OLE DB provider. The *password* parameter is the password associated with the *user_id*.

The *provider_string* parameter is a provider-specific connection string and is used in place of the *datasource*, *user_id* and *password* combination.

The *catalog* parameter is the name of catalog/database that contains the required object. The *schema* parameter is the name of the schema or object owner of the required object. The *object* parameter is the object name.

The *query* parameter is a string that is executed by the provider and is used instead of a combination of *catalog*, *schema* and *object*.

Security Functions

The security functions return information about users and roles. They are:

- IS_MEMBER
- IS_SRVROLEMEMBER
- SUSER_ID
- SUSER_NAME
- SUSER_SID
- SUSER_SNAME
- USER_ID
- USER

IS_MEMBER

The `IS_MEMBER` function returns whether the current user is a member of the specified Windows NT group/SQL Server role. The syntax is as follows:

```
IS_MEMBER ({'<group>' | '<role>'})
```

The *group* parameter specifies the name of the NT group and must be in the form *domain\group*. The *role* parameter specifies the name of the SQL Server role. The role can be a database fixed role or a user-defined role but cannot be a server role.

This function will return a `1` if the current user is a member of the specified group or role, a `0` if the current user is not a member of the specified group or role and `NULL` if the specified group or role is invalid.

IS_SRVROLEMEMBER

The `IS_SRVROLEMEMBER` function returns whether a user is a member of the specified server role. The syntax is as follows:

```
IS_SRVROLEMEMBER ('<role>' [,'<login>'])
```

The optional *login* parameter is the name of the login account to check - the default is the current user. The *role* parameter specifies the server role and must be one of the following possible values:

- sysadmin
- dbcreator
- diskadmin
- processadmin
- serveradmin
- setupadmin
- securityadmin

This function returns a `1` if the specified login account is a member of the specified role, a `0` if the login is not a member of the role and a `NULL` if the role or login is invalid.

SUSER_ID

The `SUSER_ID` function returns the specified user's login ID number. The syntax is as follows:

```
SUSER_ID(['<login>'])
```

The *login* parameter is the specified user's login ID name. If no value for *login* is provided, the default of the current user will be used instead.

> *The `SUSER_ID` system function is included in SQL Server 7 for backward compatibility, so if possible you should use `SUSER_SID` instead.*

SUSER_NAME

The `SUSER_NAME` function returns the specified user's login ID name. The syntax is as follows:

```
SUSER_NAME([<server_user_id>])
```

The *server_name_id* parameter is the specified user's login ID number. If no value for *server_user_id* is provided, the default of the current user will be used instead.

> *The `SUSER_NAME` system function is included in SQL Server 7 for backward compatibility only, so if possible you should use `SUSER_SNAME` instead.*

SUSER_SID

The `SUSER_SID` function returns the security identification number (SID) for the specified user. The syntax is as follows:

```
SUSER_SID(['<login>'])
```

The *login* parameter is the user's login name. If no value for login is provided, the current user will be used instead.

SUSER_SNAME

The `SUSER_SNAME` function returns the login ID name for the specified security identification number (SID). The syntax is as follows:

```
SUSER_SNAME([<server_user_sid>])
```

The *server_user_sid* parameter is the user's SID. If no value for the *server_user_sid* is provided, the current user's will be used instead.

USER_ID

The `USER_ID` function returns the specified user's database ID number. The syntax is a follows:

```
USER_ID(['<user>'])
```

The *user* parameter is the username to be used. If no value for *user* is provided, the current user is used.

USER

The `USER` function allows a system-supplied value for the current user's database username to be inserted into a table if no default has been supplied. The syntax is as follows:

```
USER
```

String Functions

The string functions perform actions on string values and return strings or numeric values. The string functions are:

- ASCII
- CHAR
- CHARINDEX
- DIFFERENCE
- LEFT
- LEN
- LOWER
- LTRIM
- NCHAR
- PATINDEX
- REPLACE
- QUOTENAME
- REPLICATE
- REVERSE
- RIGHT
- RTRIM
- SOUNDEX
- SPACE
- STR
- STUFF
- SUBSTRING
- UNICODE
- UPPER

ASCII

The `ASCII` function returns the ASCII code value of the left-most character in *character_expression*. The syntax is as follows:

```
ASCII(<character_expression>)
```

CHAR

The `CHAR` function converts an ASCII code (specified in expression) into a string. The syntax is as follows:

```
CHAR(<expression>)
```

The expression can be any integer between 0 and 255.

CHARINDEX

The `CHARINDEX` function returns the starting position of an *expression* in a *character_string*. The syntax is as follows:

```
CHARINDEX(<expression>, <character_string> [, <start_location>])
```

The *expression* parameter is the string, which is to be found. The *character_string* is the string to be searched, usually a column. The *start_location* is the character position to begin the search, if this is anything other than a positive number, the search will begin at the start of *character_string*.

DIFFERENCE

The `DIFFERENCE` function returns the difference between the SOUNDEX values of two expressions as an integer. The syntax is as follows:

```
DIFFERENCE(<expression1>, <expression2>)
```

This function returns an integer value between `0` and `4`. If the two expressions sound identical (e.g. blue and blew) a value of `4` will be returned. If there is no similarity a value of `0` is returned.

LEFT

The `LEFT` function returns the leftmost part of an expression, starting a specified number of characters from the left. The syntax is as follows:

```
LEFT(<expression>, <integer>)
```

The *expression* parameter contains the character data from which the leftmost section will be extracted. The *integer* parameter specifies the number of characters from the left to begin - it must be a positive integer.

LEN

The `LEN` function returns the number of characters in the specified *expression*. The syntax is as follows:

```
LEN(<expression>)
```

LOWER

The LOWER function converts any uppercase characters in the *expression* into lowercase characters. The syntax is as follows:

```
LOWER(<expression>)
```

LTRIM

The LTRIM function removes any leading blanks from a *character_expression*. The syntax is as follows:

```
LTRIM(<character_expression>)
```

NCHAR

The NCHAR function returns the Unicode character that has the specified *integer_code*. The syntax is as follows:

```
NCHAR(<integer_code>)
```

The *integer_code* parameter must be a positive whole number from 0 to 65535.

PATINDEX

The PATINDEX function returns the starting position of the first occurrence of a pattern in a specified expression or zero if the pattern was not found. The syntax is as follows:

```
PATINDEX('<%pattern%>', <expression>)
```

The *pattern* parameter is a string that will be searched for. Wildcard characters can be used, but the % characters must surround the pattern. The *expression* parameter is character data in which the pattern is being searched for - usually a column.

REPLACE

The REPLACE function replaces all instances of second specified string in the first specified string with a third specified string. The syntax is as follows:

```
REPLACE('<string_expression1>', '<string_expression2>',
'<string_expression3>')
```

The *string_expression1* parameter is the expression in which to search. The *string_expression2* parameter is the expression to search for in *string_expression1*. The *string_expression3* parameter is the expression with which to replace all instances of *string_expression2*.

QUOTENAME

The `QUOTENAME` function returns a Unicode string with delimiters added to make the specified string a valid SQL Server delimited identifier. The syntax is as follows:

```
QUOTENAME('<character_string>'[, '<quote_character>'])
```

The *character_string* parameter is Unicode string. The *quote_character* parameter is a one-character string that will be used as a delimiter. The *quote_character* parameter can be a single quotation mark ('), a left or a right bracket ([]) or a double quotation mark (") - the default is for brackets to be used.

REPLICATE

The `REPLICATE` function repeats a *character_expression* a specified number of times. The syntax is as follows:

```
REPLICATE(<character_expression>, <integer>)
```

REVERSE

The `REVERSE` function returns the reverse of the specified *character_expression*. The syntax is as follows:

```
REVERSE(<character_expression>)
```

RIGHT

The `RIGHT` function returns the rightmost part of the specified *character_expression*, starting a specified number of characters (given by *integer*) from the right. The syntax is as follows:

```
RIGHT(<character_expression>, <integer>)
```

The *integer* parameter must be positive whole number.

RTRIM

The `RTRIM` function removes all the trailing blanks from a specified *character_expression*. The syntax is as follows:

```
RTRIM(<character_expression>)
```

SOUNDEX

The `SOUNDEX` function returns a four-character (SOUNDEX) code, which can be used to evaluate the similarity of two strings. The syntax is as follows:

```
SOUNDEX(<character_expression>)
```

SPACE

The SPACE function returns a string of repeated spaces, the length of which is indicated by *integer*. The syntax is as follows:

```
SPACE(<integer>)
```

STR

The STR function converts numeric data into character data. The syntax is as follows:

```
STR(<numeric_expression>[, <length>[, <decimal>]])
```

The *numeric_expression* parameter is a numeric expression with a decimal point. The *length* parameter is the total length including decimal point, digits and spaces. The *decimal* parameter is the number of places to the right of the decimal point.

STUFF

The STUFF function deletes a specified length of characters and inserts another set of characters in their place. The syntax is as follows:

```
STUFF(<expression>, <start>, <length>, <characters>)
```

The *expression* parameter is the string of characters in which some will be deleted and new ones added. The *start* parameter specifies where to begin deletion and insertion of characters. The *length* parameter specifies the number of characters to delete. The *characters* parameter specifies the new set of characters that is to be inserted into the expression.

SUBSTRING

The SUBSTRING function returns part of an expression. The syntax is as follows:

```
SUBSTRING(<expression>, <start>, <length>)
```

The *expression* parameter specifies the data from which the substring will be taken, can be a character string, binary string, text or an expression that includes a table. The *start* parameter is an integer that specifies where to begin the substring. The *length* parameter specifies how long the substring is.

UNICODE

The UNICODE function returns the Unicode number that represents the first character in *character_expression*. The syntax is as follows:

```
UNICODE('<character_expression>')
```

UPPER

The `UPPER` function converts all the lowercase characters in *`character_expression`* into uppercase characters. The syntax is as follows:

```
UPPER(<character_expression>)
```

System Functions

The system functions can be used to return information about values, objects and settings with SQL Server. The functions are as follows:

- `APP_NAME`
- `CASE`
- `CAST and CONVERT`
- `COALESCE`
- `CURRENT_TIMESTAMP`
- `CURRENT_USER`
- `DATALENGTH`
- `FORMATMESSAGE`
- `GETANSINULL`
- `HOST_ID`
- `HOST_NAME`
- `INDENT_INCR`
- `INDENT_SEED`
- `IDENTITY`
- `ISDATE`
- `ISNULL`
- `ISNUMERIC`
- `NEWID`
- `NULLIF`
- `PARSENAME`
- `PERMISSIONS`
- `SESSION_USER`
- `STATS_DATE`
- `SYSTEM_USER`
- `USER_NAME`

APP_NAME

The APP_NAME function returns the application name for the current session if one has been set by the application as an nvarchar type. It has the following syntax:

```
APP_NAME()
```

CASE

The CASE function evaluates a list of conditions and returns one of multiple possible results. It also has two formats:

- The simple CASE function compares an expression to a set of simple expressions to determine the result
- The searched CASE function evaluates a set of Boolean expressions to determine the result

Both formats support an optional ELSE argument.

Simple CASE function:

```
CASE <input_expression>
   WHEN <when_expression> THEN <result_expression>


   ELSE <else_result_expression>
END
```

Searched CASE function:

```
CASE
    WHEN <Boolean_expression> THEN <result_expression>


    ELSE <else_result_expression>
END
```

CAST and CONVERT

These two functions provide similar functionality in that they convert one data type into another type.

Using CAST:

```
CAST(<expression> AS <data_type>)
```

Using CONVERT:

```
CONVERT (<data_type>[(<length>)], <expression> [, <style>])
```

Where *style* refers to the style of date format when converting to a character data type.

COALESCE

The COALESCE function is passed an undefined number of arguments and it tests for the first non-null expression among them. Its syntax is:

```
COALESCE(<expression> [,...n])
```

If all arguments are NULL the COALESCE returns NULL.

CURRENT_TIMESTAMP

The CURRENT_TIMESTAMP function simply returns the current data and time as a datetime type. It is equivalent to GETDATE(). The syntax is as follows:

```
CURRENT_TIMESTAMP
```

CURRENT_USER

The CURRENT_USER function simply returns the current user as a sysname type. It is equivalent to USER_NAME(). The syntax is as follows:

```
CURRENT_USER
```

DATALENGTH

The DATALENGTH function returns the number of bytes used to represent *expression* as an integer. It is especially useful with varchar, varbinary, text, image, nvarchar, and ntext data types because these data types can store variable-length data. The syntax is as follows:

```
DATALENGTH(<expression>)
```

FORMATMESSAGE

The FORMATMESSAGE function uses existing messages in sysmessages to construct a message. The syntax is as follows:

```
FORMATMESSAGE(<msg_number>, <param_value>[,...n])
```

Where *msg_number* is the ID of the message in sysmessages.

FORMATMESSAGE looks up the message in the current language of the user. If there is no localized version of the message, the U.S. English version is used.

GETANSINULL

The `GETANSINULL` function returns the default nullability for a database as an integer. The syntax is as follows:

```
GETANSINULL(['<database>'])
```

The *database* parameter is the name of the database for which to return nullability information.

When the nullability of the given database allows `NULL` values and the column or data type nullability is not explicitly defined, `GETANSINULL` returns 1. This is the ANSI NULL default.

HOST_ID

The `HOST_ID` function returns the ID of the workstation. The syntax is as follows:

```
HOST_ID()
```

HOST_NAME

The `HOST_NAME` function returns the name of the workstation. The syntax is as follows:

```
HOST_NAME()
```

IDENT_INCR

The `IDENT_INCR` function returns the increment value specified during the creation of an identity column from a table or view that has an identity column. The syntax is as follows:

```
IDENT_INCR('<table_or_view>')
```

The *table_or_view* parameter is an expression specifying the table or view to check for a valid identity increment value.

IDENT_SEED

The `IDENT_SEED` function returns the seed value specified during the creation of an identity column from a table or a view that has an identity column. The syntax is as follows:

```
IDENT_SEED('<table_or_view>')
```

The *table_or_view* parameter is an expression specifying the table or view to check for a valid identity increment value.

IDENTITY

The IDENTITY function is used to insert an identity column into a new table. It is used only with a SELECT statement with an INTO table clause. The syntax is as follows:

```
IDENTITY(<data_type>[, <seed>, <increment>]) AS <column_name>
```

Where:

- *data_type* is the data type of the identity column.
- *seed* is the value to be assigned to the first row in the table. Each subsequent row is assigned the next identity value, which is equal to the last IDENTITY value plus the *increment* value. If neither *seed* nor *increment* is specified, both default to 1.
- *increment* is the increment to add to the *seed* value for successive rows in the table.
- *column_name* is the name of the column that is to be inserted into the new table.

ISDATE

The ISDATE function determines whether an input expression is a valid date. The syntax is as follows:

```
ISDATE(<expression>)
```

ISNULL

The ISNULL function checks an expression for a NULL value and replaces it with a specified replacement value. The syntax is as follows:

```
ISNULL(<check_expression>, <replacement_value>)
```

ISNUMERIC

The ISNUMERIC function determines whether an expression is a valid numeric type. The syntax is as follows:

```
ISNUMERIC(<expression>)
```

NEWID

The NEWID function creates a unique value of type uniqueidentifier. The syntax is as follows:

```
NEWID()
```

NULLIF

The NULLIF function compares two expressions and returns a NULL value. The syntax is as follows:

```
NULLIF(<expression1>, <expression2>)
```

PARSENAME

The PARSENAME function returns the specified part of an object name. The syntax is as follows:

```
PARSENAME('<object_name>', <object_piece>)
```

The *object_name* parameter specifies the object name from which a part is to be retrieved. The *object_piece* parameter specifies the part of the object to return. The *object_piece* parameter takes one of these possible values:

- 1 = Object name
- 2 = Owner name
- 3 = Database name
- 4 = Server name

PERMISSIONS

The PERMISSIONS function returns a value containing a bitmap, which indicates the statement, object, or column permissions for the current user. The syntax is as follows:

```
PERMISSIONS([<objectid> [, '<column>']])
```

The *object_id* parameter specifies the ID of an object. The optional *column* parameter specifies the name of the column for which permission information is being returned.

SESSION_USER

The SESSION_USER function allows a system-supplied value for the current session's username to be inserted into a table if no default value has been specified. The syntax is as follows:

```
SESSION_USER
```

STATS_DATE

The STATS_DATE function returns the date that the statistics for the specified index were last updated. The syntax is as follows:

```
STATS_DATE(<table_id>, <index_id>)
```

SYSTEM_USER

The SYSTEM_USER function allows a system-supplied value for the current system username to be inserted into a table if no default value has been specified. The syntax is as follows:

```
SYSTEM_USER
```

USER_NAME

The USER_NAME returns a database username. The syntax is as follows:

```
USER_NAME([<id>])
```

The *id* parameter specifies the ID number of the required username, if no value is given the current user is assumed.

Text and Image Functions

The text and image functions perform operations on text or image data. They are:

- PATINDEX (this was covered in the String Functions section)
- TEXTPTR
- TEXTVALID

TEXTPTR

The TEXTPTR function checks the value of the text pointer that corresponds to a text, ntext or image column and returns a varbinary value. The text pointer should be checked to ensure that it points to the first text page before running READTEXT, WRITETEXT and UPDATE statements. The syntax is as follows:

```
TEXTPTR(<column>)
```

TEXTVALID

The TEXTVALID function checks whether a specified text pointer is valid. The syntax is as follows:

```
TEXTVALID('<table.column>', <text_ptr>)
```

The *table.column* parameter specifies the name of the table and column to be used. The *text_ptr* parameter specifies the text pointer to be checked.

This function will return 0 if the pointer is invalid and 1 if the pointer is valid.

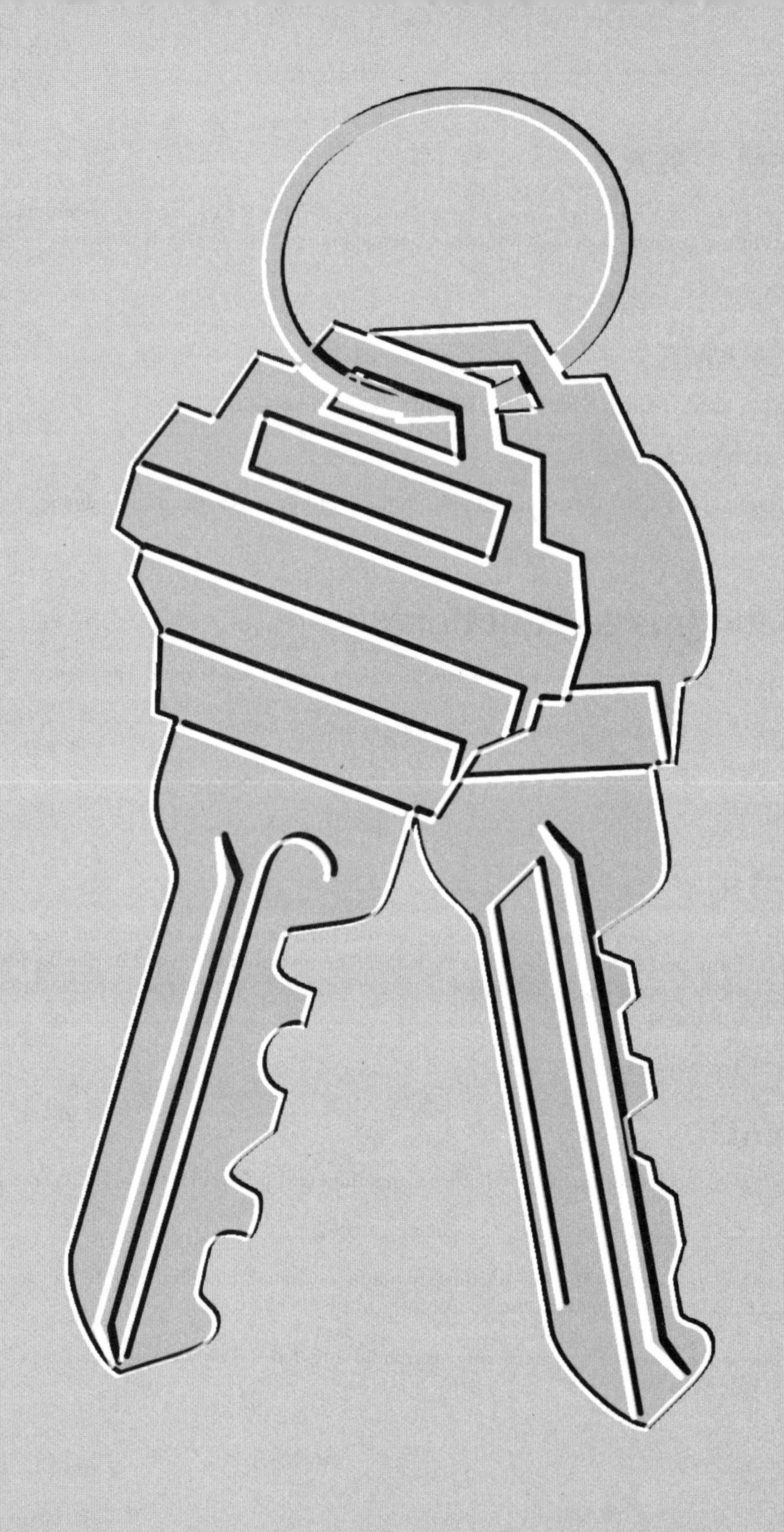

C

Tools for Our Time

So, here it is - tool time.

I need to start off this appendix by calming expectations a bit. You are not going to hear me make some "Oh, you *have* to buy this product!" kind of recommendation. Indeed, you're going to find me trying fairly hard to keep from favoring any particular product.

What I'm after in this chapter is more just to show you some of the tools and features that are out there - essentially, I want to show you the possibilities. Realistically speaking, it doesn't matter to me which tool you use as long as you are getting the most from your experience with SQL that you can (a sentimental kind of comment, I know - but a sincere one).

In this appendix, we're going to look at just a couple of the types of different tools that you should be considering adding to your arsenal. The ones I'll touch on here are:

- ERD (Diagramming) Tools
- Code Tools
- Backup Utilities

ERD Tools

ERD stands for Entity Relationship Diagram. This is the cornerstone of both understanding and relating to others your database design. If you're serious about database development, then buy a serious ERD tool - end of story.

Now that I've gone and said that, I should probably brace you for what you're going to pay – figure on a $1,000 minimum, and probably double that or more (I'm aware of at least one that goes up to $15K per seat – but it's also a *very* powerful product). What exactly these tools offer you vary by product, but let's take a look at some specific items so you get an idea of what these products can do for you.

Logical and Physical Designs

All of the major products support the concept of the separation of logical vs. physical design. Logical vs. physical modelling is given a serious overview in Chapter 20 of the book, and I can't stress enough the importance of understanding your logical model before trying to build your physical model.

Your ER tool should facilitate this process. It should allow you to have entities and relationships in the logical model that do not necessarily need to exist in the physical side of things. In Chapter 20, I explained the notion that you may have things that are really part of your data model that can't (or, in some cases, just don't) reside in the traditional database. These can range from query components that are implemented instead of stored procedures, to working tables that only exist in memory somewhere (perhaps using the new `In Memory Database` (`IMDB`) that is part of Win2K). Your logical model should be able to pull all of these data constructs together in your logical model, and still be able to easily separate those that won't be in the physical database from those that will.

General Scripting

Pretty much all of the ER tools are capable of converting your physical diagram into scripts to generate your database. Perhaps what's the greatest about this is that most of them also support multiple platforms – this means that you can develop your entity relationships once, but be able to generate the script for multiple back-end servers. You'll find that most support SQL Server, Oracle, and Sybase. Still most, but a fewer number, support DB/2, Access, and Informix. This can be a real time saver when you have to deal with multiple platforms.

Reverse Engineering

OK, so you've been able to create a diagram and generate a database from it – but what if you want to go the other way? The tool you choose should support the notion of "Reverse Engineering" a database – that is, connect to a database, scan it, and generate a diagram that properly reflects all the tables, views, triggers, constraints, indexes and relationships.

Fortunately, most of the high-end tools I'm talking about in this section will do this for you and actually do a very good job of it. Some will even import sprocs for you.

Synchronization

One of the biggest problem areas in database work is changes once you have created the physical database. This is even more of a problem once you start getting live data loaded into the database. In short, they are usually a monumental hassle to take care of.

Just the issue of trying to keep track of what you've changed in the model and what has actually been propagated out to the database can be very tedious at best – it is incredibly simple to not get a change out to a database. That's the first place a ERD tool with synchronization can help.

Several of the major ERD vendors have products that will look over your database, compare that to your physical model, and then give you a list of discrepancies. This can be a real lifesaver as you continue to make changes both small (sometimes these are the most dangerous – you tend to forget about them) and large to your database. But wait – there's more:

Once you recognize that you have a difference in your design (which should be reflected in the ERD), you have to write the code to make the actual change.

At first, writing the code to make the change to the database may not seem like too big a deal. Indeed, if what you're doing is adding one more column to the end of a table, then it's no big deal at all. Imagine, however, that you want to add a column, but you want it to be in the middle of the column order. Hmmm. That means that you have to

1. Create the table with the new layout using a different name
2. Copy all the data to the appropriate columns of the new table
3. Delete the old table
4. Rename the new table

That's a few steps – and it's already a hassle. Now let's add a little more reality check to it. Now think about if you have foreign keys that reference the old table. Hmmm, again. Those are going to have to be dropped before the table can be deleted (Number 3 above), plus they are going to have to be recreated again. Now what have we got?

1. Create the table with the new layout using a different name
2. Copy all the data to the appropriate columns of the new table
3. Drop the foreign keys from any table that is referencing the old table
4. Delete the old table
5. Rename the new table
6. Re-create the foreign keys for all those tables that we just dropped them from.

This is starting to get pretty complex, eh?

OK, so that takes us back to the "more" I mentioned before. Some (not all) of the major ERD tools will script this for you. After the comparison phase of the synchronization is complete, they'll give you a dialog to compare – one side for the ERD, and one side for the database. You get to decide which side of the diagram wins for each difference– do you propogate the ERD to the database, or do you accept the difference in the database as needing to be part of the ERD?

In short, this kind of thing can save hours and hours of work.

Now, after saying all that, I have to give you a word of caution – these tools are NOT foolproof in the way they script the changes. If you're running update scripts against a live database, make sure that you have thoroughly tested the script the ERD tools generate against test databases before you run the change on your live data.

Macros

Some of the tools give you the capability to build macros in your ERD. These may be used for simplifying repetitive tasks, but they can also do things like automate the generation of stored procedures and triggers by automatically substituting the data names and data types into trigger and sproc templates you create.

The really great thing about macro-based development is how flexible it is to change – when you change the table, then your sprocs and triggers are also automatically changed (depending on how well you've utilized the macro language).

On the down side of this one is learning time. It takes a while to get to know the macro language (which is proprietary), and it takes even longer to fully grasp everywhere you can make use of macros once you've learned the language.

Integration with Other Tools (Code Generation)

Yep – you can even get versions of ER tools that either have some code generating capabilities of their own, or they integrate with other tools to do so. This can be really useful from a couple of perspectives – prototyping and integration to logical model.

Let's say, for example, that you have a logical model that calls for several non-database data objects – the tool can generate template code for you for those objects. For example, it can create the code to expose properties and provide stubs for method calls. This eliminates a ton of rather tedious work.

Just like the synchronization above, you need to be a little careful of these tools. Don't just assume that everything in them is going to be correct – proof the code that was generated and make sure that everything that you expect is there. Even with the time spent looking it over, you can still pick up quite a time saving using these code generators.

Other Things

Some other items to think of or watch out for include:

- **Automatic loading of domain data**: Most databases have several domain tables that need to have data loaded into them that will be constant (a table containing all the states or a list of countries are common examples of this). The problem is that, every time you regenerate your database, you have to reload the domain data. Some of the tools will allow you to build "pre-load" scripts right into the ERD – when you generate the database, these tables are preloaded with the desired data every time.
- **Cut & Paste**: Some of the tools do not support linking and embedding – that is, you can't cut them out of the ERD tool and paste them into Word or some other word processor. Needless to say, this can be a huge hassle when you go to document your database.
- **Diagram methodologies supported**: You'll find that the two most common methodologies – IDEF1X and IE – are supported by pretty much all the tools. What's different is the level that they support these methodologies. For example, at least one of the major tools accepts using IE for the physical database, but won't allow it for the logical database (instead, forcing you to use their own proprietary methodology). If you don't mind this – then no big deal; however, be sure you know what you're getting.
- **Subject areas**: Some databases get positively huge in the number of separate entities that they have. This can make managing your ERD on a computer screen (which is usually no more that 21" at most – and that's only for the luckier of you out there) virtually impossible. One way that some of the tools get around this is through the concept of subject areas. Subject areas allow you to effectively filter the main drawing. You decide what tables are going to appear in the subject area. This means that you can manage different parts of the database in smaller sections.
- **Integration** with source control: Only the truly high end ($10,000+ a seat) tools seem to have a decent level of integration with source control utilities (such as Source Safe or PVCS). We can, however, hope this improves in the future.

Coding Tools

In C++, Visual Basic, or any of the other modern programming languages, we have begun to expect very robust development environments. High integration with source controls and excellent debugging tools are just the beginning of the things that we now pretty much expect to be there in mainstream development tools. For SQL however, this is an area that is really just beginning to blossom.

Don't expect too much from these areas yet, but there are now tools out there that do things like validate code, integrate with Source Safe (hey, source control for your sprocs – what a novel idea!), and even provide debugging capabilities.

It is this last area – debugging – that is winning over the hearts of many SQL developers. Debugging triggers, for example, is about as painful as any part of development can be. You can't invoke the code directly (it only fires when you do something to the table the trigger is attached to), and, even then, you can't really see what's going on inside the trigger. Some of the newer tools out there will not only let you debug – they will also allow step debugging (walk through one line of code at a time), break points (preset places to stop and look at things), and watch windows (check variable values as of the current line of code). This is a positively huge feature for both sprocs and triggers.

These tools have a much wider range in cost. To some extent, you can find this functionality free as part of the Visual Studio package (if you already have it), but even better implementations can be found ranging in price from $299 up to $15,000 (the latter is a complete suite of tools that also includes ER tools amongst other things).

Backup Utilities

OK, so this is more of a DBA thing than a developer thing, but I would argue that developers still need to think about things like backups. Why? Well, for a lot more than just making sure that you don't lose the data on your development system. Instead, I would argue the biggest motivation here should be to help out your end users – particularly if what you're developing is likely to go into an installation that won't have a true DBA.

SQL Server has its own backup options – just like it has its own ways to diagram a database and enter code. However, some of the major backup tools provide a much more useful user interface. In addition, many of these tools will allow you to backup to a tape directly over a network (which SQL Server won't currently do by itself) – this means that you don't have to have a tape drive on every SQL Server that you own.

Backup utilities are not, as a developer, the first place I would spend my money. But I still recommend that you take a look at what's available so you're prepared to make recommendations to your customers.

Summary

The tools for SQL Server work pretty much as tools for anything do – you don't necessarily have to have the right tool for the job, but it sure can make a huge difference in both productivity and the level of satisfaction (vs. frustration) you have in your job and in the end product.

Take the time to look at what's available on the market. Even though some of the tools may seem expensive, be sure you think about what they might save you – as how much that saving is worth. I suspect you'll be buying one or more of the tools listed in this chapter.

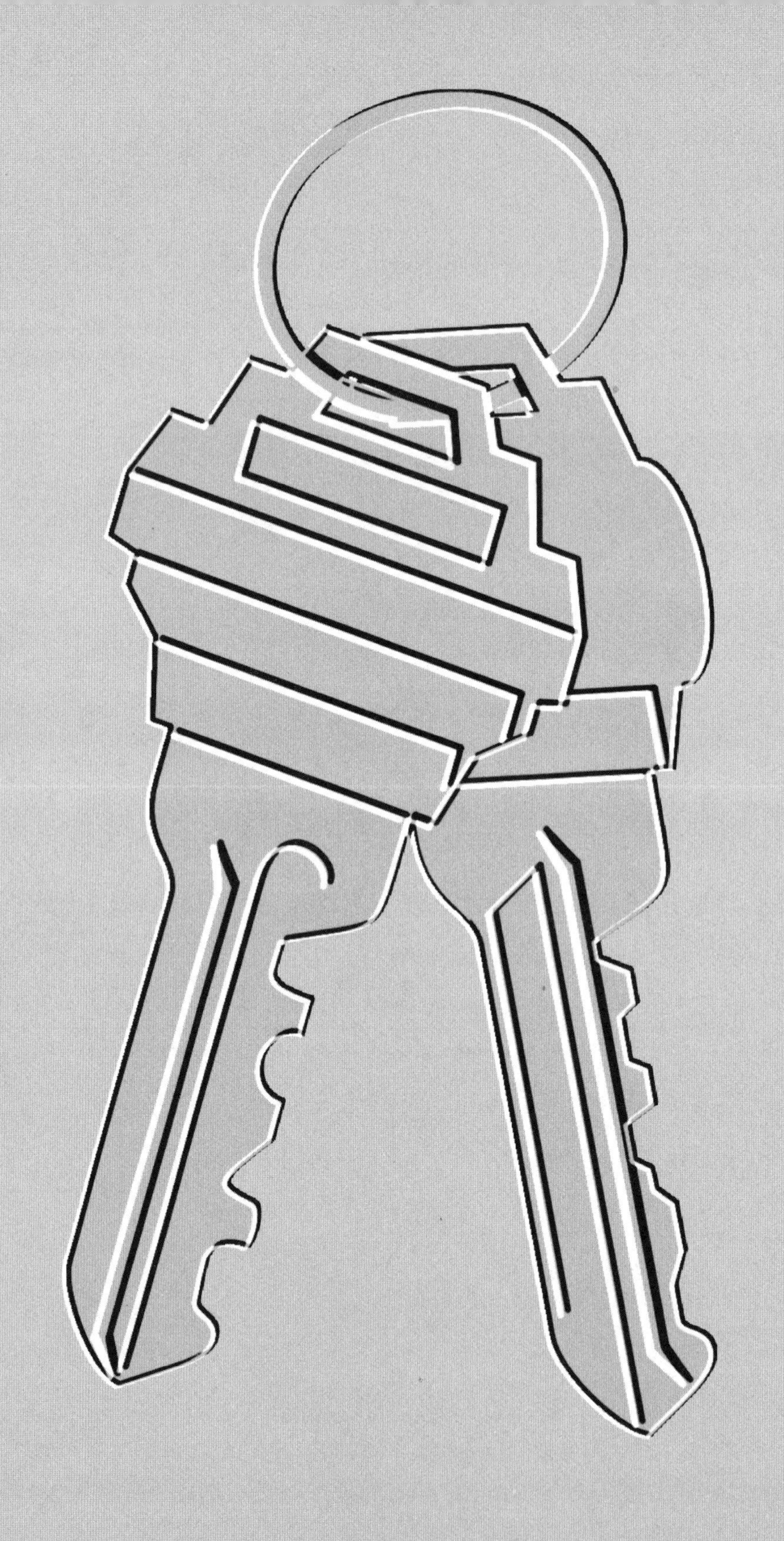

D

Error Listing

Error	Severity	Description
1	10	Version date of last upgrade: 10/11/90.
21	10	Warning: Fatal error %d occurred at %S_DATE. Note the error and time, and contact your system administrator.
102	15	Incorrect syntax near '%.*ls'.
103	15	The %S_MSG that starts with '%.*ls' is too long. Maximum length is %d.
104	15	ORDER BY items must appear in the select list if the statement contains a UNION operator.
105	15	Unclosed quotation mark before the character string '%.*ls'.
106	16	Too many table names in the query. The maximum allowable is %d.
107	15	The column prefix '%.*ls' does not match with a table name or alias name used in the query.
108	15	The ORDER BY position number %ld is out of range of the number of items in the select list.
109	15	There are more columns in the INSERT statement than values specified in the VALUES clause. The number of values in the VALUES clause must match the number of columns specified in the INSERT statement.

Error	Severity	Description
110	15	There are fewer columns in the INSERT statement than values specified in the VALUES clause. The number of values in the VALUES clause must match the number of columns specified in the INSERT statement.
111	15	'%ls' must be the first statement in a query batch.
112	15	Variables are not allowed in the %ls statement.
113	15	Missing end comment mark '*/'.
114	15	Browse mode is invalid for a statement that assigns values to a variable.
116	15	Only one expression can be specified in the select list when the subquery is not introduced with EXISTS.
117	15	The %S_MSG name '%.*ls' contains more than the maximum number of prefixes. The maximum is %d.
118	15	Only members of the sysadmin role can specify the %ls option for the %ls statement.
119	15	Must pass parameter number %d and subsequent parameters as '@name = value'. After the form '@name = value' has been used, all subsequent parameters must be passed in the form '@name = value'.
120	15	The select list for the INSERT statement contains fewer items than the insert list. The number of SELECT values must match the number of INSERT columns.
121	15	The select list for the INSERT statement contains more items than the insert list. The number of SELECT values must match the number of INSERT columns.
123	15	Batch/procedure exceeds maximum length of %d characters.
124	15	CREATE PROCEDURE contains no statements.
125	15	Case expressions may only be nested to level %d.
128	15	The name '%.*ls' is not permitted in this context. Only constants, expressions, or variables allowed here. Column names are not permitted.
129	15	Fillfactor %d is not a valid percentage; fillfactor must be between 1 and 100.
130	16	Cannot perform an aggregate function on an expression containing an aggregate or a subquery.
131	15	The size (%d) given to the %S_MSG '%.*ls' exceeds the maximum. The largest size allowed is %d.
132	15	The label '%.*ls' has already been declared. Label names must be unique within a query batch or stored procedure.

Error	Severity	Description
133	15	A GOTO statement references the label '%.*ls' but the label has not been declared.
134	15	The variable name '%.*ls' has already been declared. Variable names must be unique within a query batch or stored procedure.
135	15	Cannot use a BREAK statement outside the scope of a WHILE statement.
136	15	Cannot use a CONTINUE statement outside the scope of a WHILE statement.
137	15	Must declare the variable '%.*ls'.
138	15	Correlation clause in a subquery not permitted.
139	15	Cannot assign a default value to a local variable.
140	15	Can only use IF UPDATE within a CREATE TRIGGER statement.
141	15	A SELECT statement that assigns a value to a variable must not be combined with data-retrieval operations.
142	15	Incorrect syntax for definition of the '%ls' constraint.
143	15	A COMPUTE BY item was not found in the order by list. All expressions in the compute by list must also be present in the order by list.
144	15	Cannot use an aggregate or a subquery in an expression used for the group by list of a GROUP BY clause.
145	15	ORDER BY items must appear in the select list if SELECT DISTINCT is specified.
146	15	Could not allocate ancillary table for a subquery. Maximum number of tables in a query (%d) exceeded.
147	15	An aggregate may not appear in the WHERE clause unless it is in a subquery contained in a HAVING clause or a select list, and the column being aggregated is an outer reference.
148	15	Incorrect time syntax in time string '%.*ls' used with WAITFOR.
149	15	Time value '%.*ls' used with WAITFOR is not a valid value. Check date/time syntax.
150	15	Both terms of an outer join must contain columns.
151	15	'%.*ls' is an invalid money value.
153	15	Invalid usage of the option %.*ls in the %ls statement.
154	15	%S_MSG is not allowed in %S_MSG.
155	15	'%.*ls' is not a recognized %ls option.

Error	Severity	Description
156	15	Incorrect syntax near the keyword '%.*ls'.
157	15	An aggregate may not appear in the set list of an UPDATE statement.
159	15	For DROP INDEX, you must give both the table and the index name, in the form tablename.indexname.
160	15	Rule does not contain a variable.
161	15	Rule contains more than one variable.
163	15	The compute by list does not match the order by list.
164	15	GROUP BY expressions must refer to column names that appear in the select list.
165	16	Privilege %ls may not be granted or revoked.
166	15	'%ls' does not allow specifying the database name as a prefix to the object name.
167	16	Cannot create a trigger on a temporary object.
168	15	The %S_MSG '%.*ls' is out of the range of computer representation (%d bytes).
169	15	A column has been specified more than once in the order by list. Columns in the order by list must be unique.
170	15	Line %d: Incorrect syntax near '%.*ls'.
171	15	Cannot use SELECT INTO in browse mode.
172	15	Cannot use HOLDLOCK in browse mode.
173	15	The definition for column '%.*ls' must include a data type.
174	15	The %ls function requires %d arguments.
177	15	The IDENTITY function can only be used when the SELECT statement has an INTO clause.
178	15	A RETURN statement with a return status can only be used in a stored procedure.
179	15	Cannot use the OUTPUT option when passing a constant to a stored procedure.
180	15	There are too many parameters in this %ls statement. The maximum number is %d.
181	15	Cannot use the OUTPUT option in a DECLARE statement.
182	15	Table and column names must be supplied for the READTEXT or WRITETEXT utility.
183	15	The scale (%d) for column '%.*ls' must be within the range %d to %d.

Error	Severity	Description
185	15	Data stream is invalid for WRITETEXT statement in bulk form.
186	15	Data stream missing from WRITETEXT statement.
188	15	Cannot specify a log device in a CREATE DATABASE statement without also specifying at least one non-log device.
189	15	The %ls function requires %d to %d arguments.
190	15	Cannot update the function '%.*ls'.
191	15	Some part of your SQL statement is nested too deeply. Rewrite the query or break it up into smaller queries.
192	16	The scale must be less than or equal to the precision.
193	15	The object or column name starting with '%.*ls' is too long. The maximum length is %d characters.
194	15	A SELECT INTO statement cannot contain a SELECT statement that assigns values to a variable.
195	15	'%.*ls' is not a recognized %S_MSG.
196	15	SELECT INTO must be the first query in an SQL statement containing a UNION operator.
198	15	Browse mode is invalid for statements containing a UNION operator.
199	15	An INSERT statement cannot contain a SELECT statement that assigns values to a variable.
201	16	Procedure '%.*ls' expects parameter '%.*ls', which was not supplied.
203	16	The name '%.*ls' is not a valid identifier.
204	20	Normalization error in node %ls.
205	16	All queries in an SQL statement containing a UNION operator must have an equal number of expressions in their target lists.
206	16	Operand type clash: %ls is incompatible with %ls
207	16	Invalid column name '%.*ls'.
208	16	Invalid object name '%.*ls'.
209	16	Ambiguous column name '%.*ls'.
210	16	Syntax error converting datetime from binary/varbinary string.
212	16	Expression result length exceeds the maximum. %d max, %d found.
213	16	Insert Error: Column name or number of supplied values does not match table definition.
214	16	Cannot convert parameter '%ls' to %ls data type expected by procedure.

Error	Severity	Description
217	16	Maximum stored procedure nesting level exceeded (limit %d).
220	16	Arithmetic overflow error for data type %ls, value = %ld.
221	10	FIPS Warning: Implicit conversion from %ls to %ls.
223	11	Object ID %ld specified as a default for table ID %ld, column ID %d is missing or not of type default.
224	11	Object ID %ld specified as a rule for table ID %ld, column ID %d is missing or not of type default.
226	16	%ls statement not allowed within multi-statement transaction.
229	14	%ls permission denied on object '%.*ls', database '%.*ls', owner '%.*ls'.
230	14	%ls permission denied on column '%.*ls' of object '%.*ls', database '%.*ls', owner '%.*ls'.
231	11	No such default. ID = %ld, database ID = %d.
232	16	Arithmetic overflow error for type %ls, value = %f.
233	16	The column '%.*ls' in table '%.*ls' cannot be null.
234	16	There is insufficient result space to convert a money value to %ls.
235	16	Cannot convert a char value to money. The char value has incorrect syntax.
236	16	The conversion from char data type to money resulted in a money overflow error.
237	16	There is insufficient result space to convert a money value to %ls.
238	16	There is insufficient result space to convert the %ls value (= %d) to the money data type.
241	16	Syntax error converting datetime from character string.
242	16	The conversion of a char data type to a datetime data type resulted in an out-of-range datetime value.
243	16	Type %.*ls is not a defined system type.
244	16	The conversion of the %ls value '%.*ls' overflowed an %hs column. Use a larger integer column.
245	16	Syntax error converting the %ls value '%.*ls' to a column of data type %ls.
248	16	The conversion of the %ls value '%.*ls' overflowed an int column. Maximum integer value exceeded.
251	16	Could not allocate ancillary table for query optimization. Maximum number of tables in a query (%d) exceeded.

Error	Severity	Description
252	16	Cannot group by a bit column.
256	16	The data type %ls is invalid for the %ls function. Allowed types are: char/varchar, nchar/nvarchar, and binary/varbinary.
257	16	Implicit conversion from data type %ls to %ls is not allowed. Use the CONVERT function to run this query.
259	16	Ad hoc updates to system catalogs are not enabled. The system administrator must reconfigure SQL Server to allow this.
260	16	Disallowed implicit conversion from data type %ls to data type %ls, table '%ls', column '%ls'. Use the CONVERT function to run this query.
261	16	'%.*ls' is not a recognized function.
262	16	%ls permission denied, database '%.*ls', owner '%.*ls'.
263	16	Must specify table to select from.
264	16	Column name '%.*ls' appears more than once in the result column list.
266	16	Transaction count after EXECUTE indicates that a COMMIT or ROLLBACK TRANSACTION statement is missing. Previous count = %ld, current count = %ld.
267	16	Object '%.*ls' cannot be found.
268	16	Cannot run SELECT INTO in this database. The database owner must run sp_dboption to enable this option.
270	16	Table '%.*ls' cannot be modified.
271	16	Column '%.*ls' cannot be modified because it is a computed column.
272	16	Cannot update a timestamp column.
273	16	Cannot insert a non-null value into a timestamp column. Use INSERT with a column list or with a default of NULL for the timestamp column.
278	16	The text, ntext, and image data types cannot be used in a GROUP BY clause.
279	16	The text, ntext, and image data types are invalid in this subquery or aggregate expression.
280	16	Only text, ntext, and image data types are valid with the TEXTPTR function.
281	16	%d is not a valid style number when converting from datetime to a character string.
282	10	The '%.*ls' procedure attempted to return a status of NULL, which is not allowed. A status of 0 will be returned instead.
284	16	Rules cannot be bound to text, ntext, or image data types.

Error	Severity	Description
285	16	The READTEXT and WRITETEXT statements cannot be used with views.
286	16	The logical tables INSERTED and DELETED cannot be updated.
287	16	The %ls statement is not allowed within a trigger.
288	16	The PATINDEX function operates on char, nchar, varchar, nvarchar, text, and ntext data types only.
292	16	There is insufficient result space to convert a smallmoney value to %ls.
293	16	Cannot convert char value to smallmoney. The char value has incorrect syntax.
294	16	The conversion from char data type to smallmoney data type resulted in a smallmoney overflow error.
295	16	Syntax error converting character string to smalldatetime data type.
296	16	The conversion of char data type to smalldatetime data type resulted in an out-of-range smalldatetime value.
298	16	The conversion from datetime data type to smalldatetime data type resulted in a smalldatetime overflow error.
299	16	The DATEADD function was called with bad type %ls.
301	16	Query contains an outer-join request that is not permitted.
303	16	The table '%.*ls' is an inner member of an outer-join clause. This is not allowed if the table also participates in a regular join clause.
306	16	The text, ntext, and image data types cannot be used in the WHERE, HAVING, or ON clause, except with the LIKE or IS NULL predicates.
307	16	Index ID %d on table '%.*ls' (specified in the FROM clause) does not exist.
308	16	Index '%.*ls' on table '%.*ls' (specified in the FROM clause) does not exist.
310	16	Invalid escape sequence. Valid characters after ESC are: an ESC pair, underscore, percent sign.
311	16	Cannot use text, ntext, or image columns in the 'inserted' and 'deleted' tables.
312	16	Cannot reference text, ntext, or image columns in a filter stored procedure.
401	16	Unimplemented statement or expression %ls.
403	16	Invalid operator for data type. Operator equals %ls, type equals %ls.
409	16	The %ls operation cannot take a %ls data type as an argument.

Error	Severity	Description
410	20	COMPUTE clause #%d 'BY' expression #%d is not in the order by list.
411	20	COMPUTE clause #%d, aggregate expression #%d is not in the select list.
420	16	The text, ntext, and image data types cannot be used in an ORDER BY clause.
425	16	Data type %ls of receiving variable is not equal to the data type %ls of column '%.*ls'.
426	16	The length %d of the receiving variable is less than the length %d of the column '%.*ls'.
427	20	Could not load sysprocedures entries for constraint ID %d in database ID %d.
428	20	Could not find row in sysconstraints for constraint ID %d in database ID %d.
429	20	Could not find new constraint ID %d in sysconstraints, database ID %d, at compile time.
430	20	Could not resolve table name for object ID %d, database ID %d, when compiling foreign key.
431	19	Could not bind foreign key constraint. Too many tables involved in the query.
433	20	Could not find CHECK constraint for '%.*ls', although the table is flagged as having one.
436	20	Could not open referenced table ID %d in database ID %d.
437	20	Could not resolve the referenced column name in table ID %d.
438	20	Could not resolve the referencing column name in table ID %d.
439	20	Could not find FOREIGN KEY constraints for table '%.*ls' in database ID %d although the table is flagged as having them.
441	16	Cannot use the '%ls' function on a remote data source.
505	16	Current user account was invoked with SETUSER. Changing databases is not allowed.
506	16	Invalid ESCAPE character '%.*hs' has been specified in a LIKE predicate.
507	16	Invalid argument %d specified for SET ROWCOUNT.
509	11	User name '%.*ls' not found.
510	16	Cannot create a work table row larger than allowable maximum. Resubmit your query with the ROBUST PLAN hint.

Error	Severity	Description
511	16	Cannot create a row of size %d which is greater than the allowable maximum of %d.
512	16	Subquery returned more than 1 value. This is not permitted when the subquery follows =, !=, <, <= , >, >= or when the subquery is used as an expression.
513	16	A column insert or update conflicts with a rule imposed by a previous CREATE RULE statement. The statement was terminated. The conflict occurred in database '%.*ls', table '%.*ls', column '%.*ls'.
515	16	Cannot insert the value NULL into column '%.*ls', table '%.*ls'; column does not allow nulls. %ls fails.
516	18	Could not get system date/time.
517	16	Adding a value to a '%ls' column caused overflow.
518	16	Cannot convert data type %ls to %ls.
528	20	System error detected during attempt to use the 'upsleep' system function.
529	16	Explicit conversion from data type %ls to %ls is not allowed.
532	16	The timestamp (changed to %S_TS) shows that the row has been updated by another user.
535	16	Difference of two datetime columns caused overflow at runtime.
536	16	Invalid length parameter passed to the substring function.
538	16	Cannot find '%.*ls'. This language may have been dropped. Contact your system administrator.
542	16	An invalid datetime value was encountered. Value exceeds the year 9999.
544	16	Cannot insert explicit value for identity column in table '%.*ls' when IDENTITY_INSERT is set to OFF.
545	16	Explicit value must be specified for identity column in table '%.*ls' when IDENTITY_INSERT is set to ON.
547	16	%ls statement conflicted with %ls %ls constraint '%.*ls'. The conflict occurred in database '%.*ls', table '%.*ls'%ls%.*ls%ls.
548	16	Cannot perform direct %ls to range maintained by replication. The conflict occurred in database '%.*ls', table '%.*ls'%ls%.*ls%ls.
550	16	The attempted insert or update failed because the target view either specifies WITH CHECK OPTION or spans a view that specifies WITH CHECK OPTION and one or more rows resulting from the operation did not qualify under the CHECK OPTION constraint.

Error	Severity	Description
551	16	The checksum has changed to %d. This shows that the row has been updated by another user.
553	16	%hs over nullable side of outer join query on table '%ls'.
555	16	User-defined functions are not yet enabled.
556	16	INSERT EXEC failed because the stored procedure altered the schema of the target table.
601	12	Could not continue scan with NOLOCK due to data movement.
602	21	Could not find row in sysindexes for database ID %d, object ID %ld, index ID %d. Run DBCC CHECKTABLE on sysindexes.
604	21	Could not find row in sysobjects for object ID %ld in database '%.*ls'. Run DBCC CHECKTABLE on sysobjects.
605	21	Attempt to fetch logical page %S_PGID in database '%.*ls' belongs to object '%.*ls', not to object '%.*ls'.
607	21	Insufficient room was allocated for search arguments in the session descriptor for object '%.*ls'. Only %d search arguments were anticipated.
615	21	Could not find database table ID %d, name '%.*ls'.
617	20	Descriptor for object ID %ld in database ID %d not found in the hash table during attempt to unhash it.
618	21	A varno of %d was passed to the opentable system function. The largest valid value is %d.
623	21	Could not retrieve row from page by RID because logical page %S_PGID is not a data page. %S_RID. %S_PAGE.
624	21	Could not retrieve row from page by RID because the requested RID has a higher number than the last RID on the page. %S_RID.%S_PAGE, DBID %d.
625	21	Could not retrieve row from logical page %S_PGID by RID because the entry in the offset table (%d) for that RID (%d) is less than or equal to 0.
626	16	Cannot use ROLLBACK with a savepoint within a distributed transaction.
627	16	Cannot use SAVE TRANSACTION within a distributed transaction.
628	13	Cannot issue SAVE TRANSACTION when there is no active transaction.
635	20	Process %d tried to remove DES resource lock %S_DES, which it does not hold.
637	20	Index shrink program returned invalid status of 0.

Error	Severity	Description
639	21	Could not fetch logical page %S_PGID, database ID %d. The page is not currently allocated.
644	21	Could not find the index entry for RID '%.*hs' in index page %S_PGID, index ID %d, database '%.*ls'.
649	21	Could not find the clustered index entry for page %S_PGID, object ID %ld, status 0x%x. Index page %S_PGID, in database '%.*ls', was searched for this entry.
650	16	You can only specify the READPAST lock in the READ COMMITTED or REPEATABLE READ isolation levels.
651	16	Cannot use %hs granularity hint on table '%.*ls' because locking at the specified granularity is inhibited.
652	16	Index ID %d for table '%.*ls' resides on a read-only filegroup which cannot be modified.
653	20	Two buffers are conflicting for the same keep slot in table '%.*ls'.
654	20	No slots are free to keep buffers for table '%.*ls'.
655	20	Expected to find buffer in keep slot for table '%.*ls'.
666	16	Maximum system-generated unique value for a duplicate group exceeded for table ID %d, index ID %d. Dropping and re-creating the index may fix the problem; otherwise use another clustering key.
701	19	There is insufficient system memory to run this query.
708	10	Warning: Due to low virtual memory, special reserved memory used %d times since startup. Increase virtual memory on server.
802	17	No more buffers can be stolen.
804	20	Could not find buffer 0x%lx holding logical page %S_PGID in the SDES 0x%lx kept buffer pool for object '%.*ls'.
809	20	Buffer 0x%lx, allocation page %S_PGID, in database '%.*ls' is not in allocation buffer pool in PSS (process status structure). Contact Technical Support.
813	20	Logical page %S_PGID in database ID %d is already hashed.
816	20	Process ID %d tried to remove a buffer resource lock %S_BUF that it does not hold in SDES %S_SDES. Contact Technical Support.
818	19	There is no room to hold the buffer resource lock %S_BUF in SDES %S_SDES. Contact Technical Support.
821	20	Could not unhash buffer at 0x%lx with a buffer page number of %S_PGID and database ID %d with HASHED status set. The buffer was not found. %S_PAGE.
822	21	Could not start I/O for request %S_BLKIOPTR.

Error	Severity	Description
823	24	I/O error %ls detected during %S_MSG of %S_BUF.
834	21	The bufclean system function was called on dirty buffer (page %S_PGID, stat %#x/%#x, objid %#x, sstat%#x).
840	17	Device '%.*ls' (physical name '%.*ls', virtual device number %d) is not available. Contact the system administrator for assistance.
844	10	Time out occurred while waiting for buffer latch type %d, bp %#x, page %S_PGID, stat %#x, object ID %d:%d:%d, waittime %d. Continuing to wait.
845	17	Time out occurred while waiting for buffer latch type %d for page %S_PGID, database ID %d, object ID %d, index ID %d.
901	21	Could not find descriptor for database ID %d, object ID %ld in hash table after hashing it.
903	22	Could not find row in sysindexes for clustered index on system catalog %ld in database ID %d. This index should exist in all databases. Run DBCC CHECKTABLE on sysindexes in the database.
906	22	Could not locate row in sysobjects for system catalog '%.*ls' in database '%.*ls'. This system catalog should exist in all databases. Run DBCC CHECKTABLE on sysobjects in this database.
911	16	Could not locate entry in sysdatabases for database '%.*ls'. No entry found with that name. Make sure that the name is entered correctly.
913	22	Could not find database ID %d. Database may not be activated yet or may be in transition.
916	14	Server user '%.*ls' is not a valid user in database '%.*ls'.
921	14	Database '%.*ls' has not been recovered yet. Wait and try again.
922	14	Database '%.*ls' is being recovered. Waiting until recovery is finished.
923	14	User %d not allowed in database '%.*ls'. Only the owner can access this database.
924	14	Database '%.*ls' is already open and can only have one user at a time.
925	19	Maximum number of databases used for each query has been exceeded. The maximum allowed is %d.
926	14	Database '%.*ls' cannot be opened. It has been marked SUSPECT by recovery. See the SQL Server errorlog for more information.
927	14	Database '%.*ls' cannot be opened. It is in the middle of a restore.
929	20	Attempting to close a database that is not already open. Contact Technical Support.
941	14	Cannot open database '%.*ls'. It has not been upgraded to the latest format.

Error	Severity	Description
942	14	Database '%.*ls' cannot be opened because it is offline.
943	14	Database '%.*ls' cannot be opened because its version (%d) is later than the current server version (%d).
944	10	Converting database '%.*ls' from version %d to the current version %d.
945	16	Database '%.*ls' cannot be opened because some of the files could not be activated.
946	14	Cannot open database '%.*ls' version %d. Upgrade the database to the latest version.
947	16	Error while closing database '%.*ls' cleanly.
1001	16	Line %d: Length or precision specification %d is invalid.
1002	16	Line %d: Specified scale %d is invalid.
1003	15	Line %d: %ls clause allowed only for %ls.
1005	15	Line %d: Invalid procedure number (%d). Must be between 1 and 32767.
1006	15	CREATE TRIGGER contains no statements.
1007	15	The %S_MSG '%.*ls' is out of the range for numeric representation (maximum precision %d).
1008	15	The SELECT item identified by the ORDER BY number %d contains a variable as part of the expression identifying a column position. Variables are only allowed when ordering by an expression referencing a column name.
1010	15	Invalid escape character '%.*ls'.
1011	15	The correlation name '%.*ls' is specified multiple times in a FROM clause.
1012	15	The correlation name '%.*ls' has the same exposed name as table '%.*ls'.
1013	15	Tables '%.*ls' and '%.*ls' have the same exposed names. Use correlation names to distinguish them.
1015	15	An aggregate cannot appear in an ON clause unless it is in a subquery contained in a HAVING clause or select list, and the column being aggregated is an outer reference.
1016	15	Outer join operators cannot be specified in a query containing joined tables.
1019	15	Invalid column list after object name in GRANT/REVOKE statement.
1020	15	Cannot specify column list for INSERT/DELETE/EXECUTE privileges in the GRANT/REVOKE statement.

Error	Severity	Description
1021	10	FIPS Warning: Line %d has the non-ANSI statement '%ls'.
1022	10	FIPS Warning: Line %d has the non-ANSI clause '%ls'.
1023	15	Invalid parameter %d specified for %ls.
1024	10	FIPS Warning: Line %d has the non-ANSI function '%ls'.
1025	10	FIPS Warning: The length of identifier '%.*ls' exceeds 18.
1027	15	Too many expressions are specified in the GROUP BY clause. The maximum number is %d when either CUBE or ROLLUP is specified.
1028	15	The CUBE and ROLLUP options are not allowed in a GROUP BY ALL clause.
1029	15	Browse mode is invalid for subqueries and derived tables.
1031	15	Percent values must be between 0 and 100.
1032	16	Cannot use the column prefix '%.*ls'. This must match the object in the UPDATE clause '%.*ls'.
1033	16	An ORDER BY clause is invalid in views, derived tables, and subqueries unless TOP is also specified.
1035	15	Incorrect syntax near '%.*ls', expected '%.*ls'.
1036	15	File option %hs is required in this CREATE/ALTER DATABASE statement.
1037	15	The CASCADE, WITH GRANT or AS options cannot be specified with statement permissions.
1038	15	Cannot use empty object or column names. Use a single space if necessary.
1039	15	SHOWPLAN is not available. Use SHOWPLAN_TEXT or SHOWPLAN_ALL instead.
1040	15	Mixing old and new syntax in CREATE/ALTER DATABASE statement is not allowed.
1041	15	Option %.*ls is not allowed for a LOG file.
1042	15	Conflicting %ls optimizer hints specified.
1043	15	'%hs' is not yet implemented.
1044	15	Cannot use an existing function name to specify a stored procedure name.
1045	15	Aggregates are not allowed in this context. Only scalar expressions are allowed.
1046	15	Subqueries are not allowed in this context. Only scalar expressions are allowed.

Error	Severity	Description
1047	15	Conflicting locking hints specified.
1048	15	Conflicting cursor options %ls and %ls.
1049	15	Mixing old and new syntax to specify cursor options is not allowed.
1050	15	This syntax is only allowed within the stored procedure sp_executesql.
1051	15	Cursor parameters in a stored procedure must be declared with OUTPUT and VARYING options, and they must be specified in the order CURSOR VARYING OUTPUT.
1052	15	Conflicting %ls options %ls and %ls.
1053	15	For DROP STATISTICS, you must give both the table and the column name in the form 'tablename.column'.
1055	15	'%.*ls' is an invalid name because it contains a NULL character.
1056	15	The maximum number of elements in the select list is %d and you have supplied %d.
1057	15	The IDENTITY function cannot be used with a SELECT INTO statement containing a UNION operator.
1058	15	Cannot specify both READ_ONLY and FOR READ ONLY on a cursor declaration.
1059	15	Cannot set or reset the %ls option within a procedure.
1060	15	The number of rows in the TOP clause must be an integer.
1061	16	The text/ntext/image constants are not yet implemented.
1062	16	The TOP N WITH TIES clause is not allowed without a corresponding ORDER BY clause.
1063	16	A filegroup cannot be added using ALTER DATABASE ADD FILE. Use ALTER DATABASE ADD FILEGROUP.
1064	16	A filegroup cannot be used with log files.
1065	15	The NOLOCK, READUNCOMMITTED, and READPAST lock hints are only allowed in a SELECT statement.
1066	10	Warning. Line %d: The option '%ls' is obsolete and has no effect.
1067	15	The SET SHOWPLAN statements must be the only statements in the batch.
1068	16	Only one list of index hints per table is allowed.
1069	16	Index hints are only allowed in a FROM clause.
1070	15	CREATE INDEX option '%.*ls' is no longer supported.
1071	16	Cannot specify a JOIN algorithm with a remote JOIN.

Error	Severity	Description
1072	16	A REMOTE hint can only be specified with an INNER JOIN clause.
1073	15	'%.*ls' is not a recognized cursor option for cursor %.*ls.
1101	17	Could not allocate new page for database '%.*ls'. There are no more pages available in filegroup %.*ls. Space can be created by dropping objects, adding additional files, or allowing file growth.
1102	22	IAM page %S_PGID for object ID %ld is incorrect. The %S_MSG ID on page is %ld; should be %ld. The entry in sysindexes may be incorrect or the IAM page may be corrupt.
1103	21	Allocation page %S_PGID in database '%.*ls' has different segment ID than that of the object which is being allocated to. Run DBCC CHECKALLOC.
1105	17	Could not allocate space for object '%.*ls' in database '%.*ls' because the '%.*ls' filegroup is full.
1109	21	Could not read allocation page %S_PGID because either the object ID (%ld) is not correct, or the page ID (%S_PGID) is not correct.
1201	20	The page_lock system function was called with a mode %d that is not permitted.
1203	20	Process ID %d attempting to unlock unowned resource %.*ls.
1204	19	SQL Server has run out of LOCKS. Rerun your statement when there are fewer active users, or ask the system administrator to reconfigure SQL Server with more LOCKS.
1205	13	Your transaction (process ID #%d) was deadlocked with another process and has been chosen as the deadlock victim. Rerun your transaction.
1211	13	Process ID %d was chosen as the deadlock victim with P_BACKOUT bit set.
1220	17	No more lock classes available from transaction.
1221	20	Invalid lock class for release call.
1222	13	Lock request time out period exceeded.
1501	20	Sort failure.
1505	14	CREATE UNIQUE INDEX terminated because a duplicate key was found. Most significant primary key is '%S_KEY'.
1507	10	Warning: Deleted duplicate row. Primary key is '%S_KEY'.
1508	14	CREATE INDEX terminated because a duplicate row was found. Primary key is '%S_KEY'.
1509	20	Row compare failure.
1510	17	Sort failed. Out of space or locks in database '%.*ls'.

Error	Severity	Description
1511	20	Sort cannot be reconciled with transaction log.
1522	20	Sort failure. Prevented overwriting of allocation page in database '%.*ls' by terminating sort.
1523	20	Sort failure. Prevented incorrect extent deallocation by aborting sort.
1528	21	Character data comparison failure. An unrecognized Sort-Map-Element type (%d) was found in the server-wide default sort table at SMEL entry [%d].
1529	21	Character data comparison failure. A list of Sort-Map-Elements from the server-wide default sort table does not end properly. This list begins at SMEL entry [%d].
1530	16	CREATE INDEX with DROP_EXISTING was aborted because a row was out of order. Most significant offending primary key is '%S_KEY'. Explicitly drop and create the index instead.
1531	16	The SORTED_DATA_REORG option cannot be used for a nonclustered index if the keys are not unique within the table. CREATE INDEX was aborted because of duplicate keys. Primary key is '%S_KEY'.
1532	20	New sort run starting on page %S_PGID found extent not marked as shared.
1533	20	Cannot share extent %S_PGID among more than eight sort runs.
1534	20	Extent %S_PGID not found in shared extent directory.
1535	20	Cannot share extent %S_PGID with shared extent directory full.
1536	20	Cannot build a nonclustered index on a memory-only work table.
1537	20	Cannot suspend a sort not in row input phase.
1538	20	Cannot insert into a sort not in row input phase.
1540	16	Cannot sort a row of size %d, which is greater than the allowable maximum of %d.
1619	21	Could not open tempdb. Cannot continue.
1701	16	Creation of table '%.*ls' failed because the row size would be %d, including internal overhead. This exceeds the maximum allowable table row size, %d.
1702	16	CREATE TABLE failed because column '%.*ls' in table '%.*ls' exceeds the maximum of %d columns.
1703	17	Could not allocate disk space for a work table in database '%.*ls'. You may be able to free up space by using BACKUP LOG, or you may want to extend the size of the database by using ALTER DATABASE.

Error	Severity	Description
1704	16	Only members of the sysadmin role can create the system table '%.*ls'.
1705	16	You must create system table '%.*ls' in the master database.
1706	16	System table '%.*ls' was not created, because ad hoc updates to system catalogs are not enabled.
1708	10	The total row size (%d) for table '%.*ls' exceeds the maximum number of bytes per row (%d). Rows that exceed the maximum number of bytes will not be added.
1709	16	Cannot use TEXTIMAGE_ON when a table has no text, ntext, or image columns.
1750	10	Could not create constraint. See previous errors.
1752	16	Could not create DEFAULT for column '%.*ls' as it is not a valid column in the table '%.*ls'.
1753	16	Column '%.*ls.%.*ls' is not the same length as referencing column '%.*ls.%.*ls' in foreign key '%.*ls'.
1754	16	Defaults cannot be created on columns with an IDENTITY attribute. Table '%.*ls', column '%.*ls'.
1755	16	Defaults cannot be created on columns of data type timestamp. Table '%.*ls', column '%.*ls'.
1756	10	Skipping FOREIGN KEY constraint '%.*ls' definition for temporary table.
1759	16	Invalid column '%.*ls' specified in constraint definition.
1760	16	Constraints of type %ls cannot be created on columns of type %ls.
1763	16	Cross-database foreign key references are not supported. Foreign key '%.*ls'.
1766	16	Foreign key references to temporary tables are not supported. Foreign key '%.*ls'.
1767	16	Foreign key '%.*ls' references invalid table '%.*ls'.
1768	16	Foreign key '%.*ls' references object '%.*ls' which is not a user table.
1769	16	Foreign key '%.*ls' references invalid column '%.*ls' in referencing table '%.*ls'.
1770	16	Foreign key '%.*ls' references invalid column '%.*ls' in referenced table '%.*ls'.
1772	16	Foreign key '%.*ls' defines an invalid relationship between a user table and system table.
1773	16	Foreign key '%.*ls' has implicit reference to object '%.*ls' which does not have a primary key defined on it.

Error	Severity	Description
1774	16	The number of columns in the referencing column list for foreign key '%.*ls' does not match those of the primary key in the referenced table '%.*ls'.
1776	16	There are no primary or candidate keys in the referenced table '%.*ls' that match the referencing column list in the foreign key '%.*ls'.
1777	14	User does not have correct permissions on referenced table '%.*ls' to create foreign key '%.*ls'.
1778	16	Column '%.*ls.%.*ls' is not the same data type as referencing column '%.*ls.%.*ls' in foreign key '%.*ls'.
1779	16	Table '%.*ls' already has a primary key defined on it.
1780	20	Could not find column ID %d in syscolumns for object ID %d in database ID %d.
1781	16	Column already has a DEFAULT bound to it.
1801	16	Database '%.*ls' already exists.
1802	11	CREATE DATABASE failed. Some file names listed could not be created. Check previous errors.
1803	17	CREATE DATABASE failed. Could not allocate enough disk space for a new database on the named disks. Total space allocated must be at least %d MB to a accommodate copy of the model database.
1804	10	There is no disk named '%.*ls'. Checking other disk names.
1805	10	The CREATE DATABASE process is allocating %.2f MB on disk '%.*ls'.
1807	17	Could not obtain exclusive lock on database '%.*ls'. Retry the operation later.
1808	21	Default devices are not supported.
1811	16	'%.*ls' is the wrong type of device for CREATE DATABASE or ALTER DATABASE. Check sysdevices. The statement is aborted.
1813	16	Could not open new database '%.*ls'. CREATE DATABASE is aborted.
1814	10	Could not create tempdb. If space is low, extend the amount of space and restart.
1816	16	Could not attach the database because the character set, sort order, or Unicode collation for the database differs from this server.
1817	10	Warning: %ls %ld in database differs from server %ls of %ld.
1818	16	Primary log file '%ls' is missing and the database was not cleanly shut down so it cannot be rebuilt.
1819	10	Could not create default log file because the name was too long.

Error	Severity	Description
1820	16	Disk '%.*ls' is already completely used by other databases. It can be expanded with DISK RESIZE.
1826	16	User-defined filegroups are not allowed on '%hs'.
1827	16	CREATE/ALTER DATABASE failed because the resulting cumulative database size would exceed your licensed limit of %d MB per %S_MSG.
1828	16	The file named '%.*ls' is already in use. Choose another name.
1829	16	The FOR ATTACH option requires that at least the primary file be specified.
1830	16	The files '%.*ls' and '%.*ls' are both primary files. A database can only have one primary file.
1831	10	Successfully %ls database '%.*ls'.
1832	20	Could not attach database '%.*ls' to file '%.*ls'.
1901	16	Column '%.*ls'. Cannot create index on a column of bit data type.
1902	16	Cannot create more than one clustered index on table '%.*ls'. Drop the existing clustered index '%.*ls' before creating another.
1903	16	%d is the maximum allowable size of an index. The composite index specified is %d bytes.
1904	16	Cannot specify more than %d column names for index key list. %d specified.
1905	21	Could not find 'zero' row for index '%.*ls' the table in sysindexes.
1906	11	Cannot create an index on table '%.*ls', because this table does not exist in database '%.*ls'.
1909	16	Cannot use duplicate column names in index key list. Column name '%.*ls' listed more than once.
1910	16	Cannot create more than %d indexes or column statistics on one table.
1911	16	Column name '%.*ls' does not exist in the target table.
1913	16	There is already an index on table '%.*ls' named '%.*ls'.
1914	16	Cannot create index on object '%.*ls' because it is not a user table.
1915	16	Only members of the sysadmin role or the owner of table '%.*ls' can create an index on it.
1916	16	CREATE INDEX options %ls and %ls are mutually exclusive.
1918	10	Index (ID = %d) is being rebuilt.

Error	Severity	Description
1919	16	Column '%.*ls'. Cannot create index on a column of text, ntext, or image data type.
1920	10	Skipping rebuild of index ID %d, which is on a read-only filegroup.
1921	16	Invalid filegroup '%.*ls' specified.
1922	16	Filegroup '%.*ls' has no files assigned to it. Tables, indexes, and text, ntext, and image columns cannot be created on this filegroup.
1923	10	The clustered index has been dropped.
1924	16	Filegroup '%.*ls' is read-only.
1925	16	Cannot convert a clustered index to a nonclustered index using the DROP_EXISTING option.
1926	16	Cannot create a clustered index because nonclustered index ID %d is on a read-only filegroup.
1927	16	There are already statistics on table '%.*ls' named '%.*ls'.
1928	16	Cannot create statistics on table '%.*ls' because this table does not exist in database '%.*ls'.
1929	16	Cannot create statistics on table '%.*ls' because it is not a user table.
1930	16	Only the owner of table '%.*ls' or a member of the sysadmin fixed server role can create statistics on it.
2001	10	Cannot use duplicate parameter names. Parameter name '%.*ls' listed more than once.
2004	16	Procedure '%.*ls' has already been created with group number %d. Create procedure with an unused group number.
2007	11	Cannot add rows to sysdepends for the current stored procedure because it depends on the missing object '%.*ls'. The stored procedure will still be created.
2008	16	The object '%.*ls' is not a procedure so you cannot create another procedure under that group name.
2009	10	Procedure '%.*ls' was created despite delayed name resolution warnings (if any).
2010	16	Cannot use ALTER %ls with %.*ls because %.*ls is a %S_MSG.
2106	11	Cannot create a trigger on table '%.*ls', because this table does not exist in database '%.*ls'.
2108	16	Cannot create a trigger on table '%.*ls' because you can only create a trigger on a table in the current database.
2110	16	Cannot alter trigger '%.*ls' for table '%.*ls' because this trigger does not belong to this table.

Error	Severity	Description
2501	16	Could not find table named '%.*ls'. Check sysobjects.
2502	16	Could not start transaction.
2503	10	Successfully deleted the physical file '%ls'.
2504	16	Could not delete the physical file '%ls'. The DeleteFile system function returned error %ls.
2505	16	The device '%.*ls' does not exist. Use sp_helpdevice to show available devices.
2511	16	Table Corrupt: Object ID %d, Index ID %d. Keys out of order on page %S_PGID, slots %d and %d.
2513	16	Table Corrupt: Object ID %ld (object '%.*ls') does not match between '%.*ls' and '%.*ls'.
2514	16	Table Corrupt: Data type %ld (type '%.*ls') does not match between '%.*ls' and '%.*ls'.
2520	16	Could not find database '%.*ls'. Check sysdatabases.
2521	16	Could not find database ID %d. Check sysdatabases.
2526	16	Incorrect DBCC statement. Check the documentation for the correct DBCC syntax and options.
2528	10	DBCC execution completed. If DBCC printed error messages, contact your system administrator.
2532	16	DBCC SHRINKFILE could not shrink file %ls. Log files are not supported.
2535	16	Table Corrupt: Page %S_PGID is allocated to object ID %d, index ID %d, not to object ID %d, index ID %d found in page header.
2536	10	DBCC results for '%.*ls'.
2538	10	Allocation page %S_PGID. Number of extents = %ld, used pages = %ld, referenced pages = %ld.
2539	10	Total number of extents = %ld, used pages = %ld, referenced pages = %ld in this database.
2540	10	The system cannot self repair this error.
2541	10	DBCC UPDATEUSAGE: sysindexes row updated for table '%.*ls' (index ID %ld):
2542	10	DATA pages: Changed from (%ld) to (%ld) pages.
2543	10	USED pages: Changed from (%ld) to (%ld) pages.
2544	10	RSVD pages: Changed from (%ld) to (%ld) pages.
2545	10	ROWS count: Changed from (%I64d) to (%I64d) rows.

Error	Severity	Description
2557	16	Only the owner of object '%.*ls' can run DBCC %ls on it.
2560	16	Parameter %d is incorrect for this DBCC statement.
2562	16	'%ls' cannot access object '%.*ls' because it is not a table.
2566	14	DBCC DBREINDEX cannot be used on system tables.
2568	16	Page %S_PGID is out of range for this database or is in a log file.
2571	10	Only members of the sysadmin role can use the DBCC statement %.*ls.
2573	16	Database '%.*ls' is not marked suspect. You cannot drop it with DBCC.
2574	10	Object ID %d, index ID %d: Page %S_PGID is empty. This is not permitted at level %d of the B-tree.
2583	16	An incorrect number of parameters was given to the DBCC statement.
2588	16	Page %S_PGID was expected to be the first page of a text, ntext, or image value.
2591	16	Could not find row in sysindexes with index ID %d for table '%.*ls'.
2592	10	%ls index successfully restored for object '%.*ls' in database '%.*ls'.
2593	10	There are %I64d rows in %ld pages for object '%.*ls'.
2594	16	Invalid index ID (%d) specified.
2595	16	Database '%.*ls' must be set to single user mode before executing this statement.
2597	16	The database is not open. Execute a 'USE %.*ls' statement and rerun the DBCC statement.
2598	16	Clustered indexes on sysobjects and sysindexes cannot be re-created.
2601	14	Cannot insert duplicate key row in object '%.*ls' with unique index '%.*ls'.
2603	21	No space left on logical page %S_PGID of index ID %d for object '%.*ls' when inserting row on an index page. This situation should have been handled while traversing the index.
2617	20	Buffer holding logical page %S_PGID not found in keep pool in SDES for object '%.*ls'. Contact Technical Support.
2624	21	Could not insert into table %S_DES because row length %d is less than the minimum length %d.
2627	14	Violation of %ls constraint '%.*ls'. Cannot insert duplicate key in object '%.*ls'.
2701	10	Database name '%.*ls' ignored, referencing object in tempdb.

Error	Severity	Description
2702	16	Database '%.*ls' does not exist.
2705	16	Column names in each table must be unique. Column name '%.*ls' in table '%.*ls' is specified more than once.
2706	11	Table '%.*ls' does not exist.
2710	16	You are not the owner specified for the object '%.*ls' in this statement (CREATE, ALTER, TRUNCATE, UPDATE STATISTICS or BULK INSERT).
2714	16	There is already an object named '%.*ls' in the database.
2715	16	Column or parameter #%d: Cannot find data type %.*ls.
2716	16	Column or parameter #%d: Cannot specify a column width on data type %.*ls.
2717	16	Column or parameter #%d: Specified column width too large for data type %.*ls.
2718	16	Column or parameter #%d: Cannot specify null values on a column of data type bit.
2721	11	Could not find a default segment to create the table on. Ask your system administrator to specify a default segment in syssegments.
2724	10	Parameter '%.*ls' has an invalid data type.
2727	11	Cannot find index '%.*ls'.
2729	16	Procedure '%.*ls' group number 1 already exists in the database. Choose another procedure name.
2730	11	Cannot create procedure '%.*ls' with a group number of %d because a procedure with the same name and a group number of 1 does not currently exist in the database. Must execute CREATE PROCEDURE '%.*ls';1 first.
2732	16	User error number %ld is invalid. The number must be between %ld and %ld.
2734	16	The user name '%.*ls' does not exist in sysusers.
2736	16	Owner name specified is a group name. Objects cannot be owned by groups.
2737	16	Message passed to %hs must be of type char, varchar, nchar, or nvarchar.
2738	16	A table can only have one timestamp column. Because table '%.*ls' already has one, the column '%.*ls' cannot be added.
2739	16	The text, ntext, and image data types are invalid for local variables.
2740	16	SET LANGUAGE failed because '%.*ls' is not an official language name or a language alias on this SQL Server.

Error	Severity	Description
2741	16	SET DATEFORMAT date order '%.*ls' is invalid.
2742	16	SET DATEFIRST %d is out of range.
2743	16	%ls statement requires %S_MSG parameter.
2744	16	Multiple identity columns specified for table '%.*ls'. Only one identity column per table is allowed.
2745	10	Process ID %d has raised user error %d, severity %d. SQL Server is terminating this process.
2746	16	Cannot specify user error format string with a length exceeding %d bytes.
2747	16	Too many substitution parameters for RAISERROR. Cannot exceed %d substitution parameters.
2748	16	Cannot specify %ls data type (RAISERROR parameter %d) as a substitution parameter for RAISERRROR.
2749	16	Identity column '%.*ls' must be of data type int, smallint, tinyint, or decimal or numeric with scale of 0, and constrained to be nonnullable.
2750	16	Column or parameter #%d: Specified column precision %d is greater than the maximum precision of %d.
2751	16	Column or parameter #%d: Specified column scale %d is greater than the specified precision of %d.
2752	16	Identity column '%.*ls' contains invalid SEED.
2753	16	Identity column '%.*ls' contains invalid INCREMENT.
2754	16	Error severity levels greater than %d can only be specified by members of the sysadmin role, using the WITH LOG option.
2755	16	SET DEADLOCK_PRIORITY option '%.*ls' is invalid.
2756	16	Invalid value %d for state. Valid range is from %d to %d.
2757	16	RAISERROR failed due to invalid parameter substitution(s) for error %d, severity %d, state %d.
2758	16	%hs could not locate entry for error %d in sysmessages.
2759	0	CREATE SCHEMA failed due to previous errors.
2760	16	Specified owner name '%.*ls' either does not exist or you do not have permission to use it.
2761	16	The ROWGUIDCOL property can only be specified on the uniqueidentifier data type.
2762	16	sp_setapprole was not invoked correctly. Refer to the documentation for more information.

Error	Severity	Description
2763	16	Could not find application role '%.*ls'.
2764	16	Incorrect password supplied for application role '%.*ls'.
2765	15	Could not locate statistics for column '%.*ls' in the system catalogs.
2766	16	The definition for user-defined data type '%.*ls' has changed.
2767	15	Could not locate statistics '%.*ls' in the system catalogs.
2768	15	Statistics for %ls '%.*ls'.
2769	15	Column '%.*ls'. Cannot create statistics on a column of data type %ls.
2770	16	The SELECT INTO statement cannot have same source and destination tables.
2771	16	Cannot create statistics on table '%.*ls'. This table is a virtual system table.
2809	18	The request for %S_MSG '%.*ls' failed because '%.*ls' is a %S_MSG object.
2812	16	Could not find stored procedure '%.*ls'.
3009	16	Could not insert a backup or restore history/detail record in the msdb database. This may indicate a problem with the msdb database. The backup/restore operation was still successful.
3013	16	Backup or restore operation terminating abnormally.
3014	10	Backup or restore operation successfully processed %d pages in %d.%03d seconds (%d.%03d MB/sec).
3015	10	%hs is not yet implemented.
3016	16	File '%ls' of database '%ls' has been removed or shrunk since this backup or restore operation was interrupted. The operation cannot be restarted.
3017	16	Could not resume interrupted backup or restore operation. See the SQL Server error log for more information.
3018	16	There is no interrupted backup or restore operation to restart. Reissue the statement without the RESTART clause.
3019	16	The checkpoint file was for a different backup or restore operation. Reissue the statement without the RESTART clause.
3020	16	The backup operation cannot be restarted as the log has been truncated. Reissue the statement without the RESTART clause.
3021	16	Cannot perform a backup or restore operation within a transaction.

Error	Severity	Description
3023	16	Backup, CHECKALLOC, bulk copy, SELECT INTO, and file manipulation (such as CREATE FILE) operations on a database must be serialized. Reissue the statement after the current backup, CHECKALLOC, or file manipulation operation is completed.
3024	16	You can only perform a full backup of the master database. Use BACKUP DATABASE to back up the entire master database.
3025	16	Missing database name. Reissue the statement specifying a valid database name.
3026	16	Could not find filegroup ID %d in sysfilegroups for database '%ls'.
3027	16	Could not find filegroup '%.*ls' in sysfilegroups for database '%.*ls'.
3028	16	Operation checkpoint file is invalid. Could not restart operation. Reissue the statement without the RESTART option.
3029	16	Database file '%ls' is subject to logical recovery and must be among the files to be backed up as part of the file or filegroup backup.
3030	16	Database file '%ls' is subject to logical recovery and must be among the files to be restored.
3031	16	The statement has inconsistent or conflicting options. Remove the conflicting option and reissue the statement.
3032	16	One or more of the options is not supported for this statement. Review the documentation for supported options.
3033	16	BACKUP DATABASE cannot be used on a database opened in emergency mode.
3034	16	No files were selected to be processed. You may have selected one or more filegroups that have no members.
3035	16	Cannot perform a differential backup for database '%ls', because a current database backup does not exist. Reissue the statement omitting the WITH DIFFERENTIAL option.
3036	16	Database '%ls' is in warm-standby state (set by executing RESTORE WITH STANDBY) and cannot be backed up until the entire load sequence is completed.
3101	16	Database in use. The system administrator must have exclusive use of the database to run the restore operation.
3106	16	The specified file '%ls' is in an obsolete backup database format (version %d) and cannot be upgraded to current server version %d.
3108	16	RESTORE DATABASE must be used in single user mode when trying to restore the master database.
3110	14	Only members of the sysadmin role or the database owner of '%.*ls' can run RESTORE DATABASE.

Error	Severity	Description
3112	16	Cannot restore any database other than master when the server is in single user mode.
3113	21	The database owner (DBO) does not have an entry in sysusers in database '%.*ls'.
3114	21	Database '%.*ls' does not have an entry in sysdatabases.
3115	10	User '%.*ls' in database '%.*ls' has SUID %d, which is the same as the SUID of the database owner (as defined in sysdatabases). User '%.*ls' will be given SUID %d.
3116	10	When all restore transactions have been completed for database '%.*ls', user '%.*ls' should be given the next available SUID.
3117	10	Database '%.*ls' already has a user with SUID %d.
3120	16	The database you are attempting to restore was backed up under a different sort order ID (%d) than the one currently running on this server (%d), and at least one of them is a non-binary sort order.
3123	16	Invalid database name '%.*ls' specified for backup or restore operation.
3127	16	Temporary Message: The backup set does not contain pages for file '%ls'.
3128	16	File '%ls' has an unsupported page size (%d).
3129	16	Temporary Message: File '%ls' has changed size from %d to %d bytes.
3132	16	The RAID set for database '%ls' is missing member number %d.
3133	16	The volume on device '%ls' is not a member of the media family.
3135	16	Cannot use the backup set in file '%ls' for this restore operation.
3136	16	Cannot apply the differential backup on device '%ls' to database '%ls'.
3138	16	One or more files in the backup set are no longer part of database '%ls'.
3140	16	Could not adjust the space allocation for file '%ls'.
3141	16	The database to be restored was named '%ls'. Reissue the statement using the WITH REPLACE option to overwrite the '%ls' database.
3142	16	One or more devices or files already exist. Reissue the statement using the WITH REPLACE option to overwrite these files and devices.
3143	16	The data set on device '%ls' is not a SQL Server backup set.
3144	16	File '%.*ls' was not backed up in file %d on device '%ls'. The file cannot be restored from this backup set.

Error	Severity	Description
3145	16	The STOPAT option is not supported for RESTORE DATABASE. You can use the STOPAT option with RESTORE LOG.
3146	16	None of the newly-restored files had been modified after the backup was taken, so no further recovery actions are required. The database is now available for use.
3147	16	Backup and restore operations are not allowed on database tempdb.
3148	16	Media recovery for ALTER DATABASE is not yet implemented. The database cannot be rolled forward.
3149	16	The database you are attempting to restore was backed up under a different Unicode locale ID (%d) or Unicode comparison style (%d) than the Unicode locale ID (%d) or Unicode comparison style (%d) currently running on this server.
3150	10	The master database has been successfully restored. Shutting down SQL Server.
3151	21	The master database failed to restore. Use the rebuildm utility to rebuild the master database. Shutting down SQL Server.
3152	16	Cannot overwrite file '%ls' because it is marked as read-only.
3153	16	The database is already fully recovered.
3154	16	The backup set holds a backup of a database other than the existing '%ls' database.
3155	16	The RESTORE operation cannot proceed because one or more files have been added or dropped from the database since the backup set was created.
3156	16	The file '%ls' cannot be used by RESTORE. Consider using the WITH MOVE option to identify a valid location for the file.
3157	16	The logical file (%d) is named '%ls'. RESTORE will not overwrite it from '%ls'.
3158	16	Could not create one or more files. Consider using the WITH MOVE option to identify valid locations.
3159	16	The tail of the log for database '%ls' has not been backed up. Back up the log and rerun the RESTORE statement specifying the FILE clause.
3160	16	Could not update primary file information in sysdatabases.
3161	16	The primary file is unavailable. It must be restored or otherwise made available.
3162	16	The database has on-disk structure version %d. The server supports version %d and can only restore such a database that was inactive when it was backed up. This database was not inactive.

Error	Severity	Description
3163	16	The transaction log was damaged. All data files must be restored before RESTORE LOG can be attempted.
3164	16	Cannot roll forward the database with on-disk structure version %d. The server supports version %d. Reissue the RESTORE statement WITH RECOVERY.
3165	16	Could not adjust the replication state of database '%ls'. The database was successfully restored, however its replication state is indeterminate. See the Troubleshooting Replication section in SQL Server Books Online.
3166	16	RESTORE DATABASE could not drop database '%ls'. Drop the database and then reissue the RESTORE DATABASE statement.
3167	16	RESTORE could not start database '%ls'.
3201	16	Cannot open backup device '%ls'. Device error or device off-line. See the SQL Server error log for more details.
3202	16	Write on '%ls' failed, status = %ld. See the SQL Server error log for more details.
3203	16	Read on '%ls' failed, status = %ld. See the SQL Server error log for more details.
3204	16	Operator aborted backup or restore. See the error messages returned to the console for more details.
3205	16	Too many backup devices specified for backup or restore; only %d are allowed.
3206	16	No entry in sysdevices for backup device '%.*ls'. Update sysdevices and rerun statement.
3207	16	Backup or restore requires at least one backup device. Rerun your statement specifying a backup device.
3208	16	Unexpected end of file while reading beginning of backup set. Confirm that the media contains a valid SQL Server backup set, and see the console error log for more details.
3209	16	'%.*ls' is not a backup device. Check sysdevices.
3211	10	%d percent %hs.
3217	16	Invalid value specified for %ls parameter.
3221	16	The ReadFileEx system function executed on file '%ls' only read %d bytes, expected %d.
3222	16	The WriteFileEx system function executed on file '%ls' only wrote %d bytes, expected %d.
3227	16	The volume on device '%ls' is a duplicate of stripe set member %d.

Error	Severity	Description
3229	16	Request for device '%ls' timed out.
3230	16	Operation on device '%ls' exceeded retry count.
3234	16	File '%.*ls' is not a database file for database '%ls'.
3235	16	File '%ls' is not part of database '%ls'. You can only list files that are members of this database.
3237	16	Option not supported for Named Pipe-based backup sets.
3239	16	The backup set on device '%ls' uses a feature of the Microsoft Tape Format not supported by SQL Server.
3241	16	The media family on device '%ls' is incorrectly formed. SQL Server cannot process this media family.
3242	16	The file on device '%ls' is not a valid Microsoft Tape Format backup set.
3243	16	The media family on device '%ls' was created using Microsoft Tape Format version %d.%d. SQL Server supports version %d.%d.
3244	16	Descriptor block size exceeds %d bytes. Use a shorter name and/or description string and retry the operation.
3245	16	Could not convert a string to or from Unicode, %ls.
3246	16	The media family on device '%ls' is marked as nonappendable. Reissue the statement using the INIT option to overwrite the media.
3247	16	The volume on device '%ls' has the wrong media sequence number (%d). Remove it and insert volume %d.
3248	25	>>> VOLUME SWITCH <<< (not for output!)
3249	16	The volume on device '%ls' is a continuation volume for the backup set. Remove it and insert the volume holding the start of the backup set.
3250	16	The value '%d' is not within range for the %ls parameter.
3251	10	The RAID stream on device '%ls' has been finished. The device will now be reused for one of the remaining RAID streams.
3252	16	Passwords on media and/or data sets are not supported in this release of SQL Server.
3253	16	The block size parameter must supply a value that is a power of 2.
3254	16	The volume on device '%ls' is empty.
3255	16	The data set on device '%ls' is a SQL Server backup set not compatible with this version of SQL Server.

Error	Severity	Description
3256	16	The backup set on device '%ls' was terminated while it was being created and is incomplete. RESTORE sequence is terminated abnormally.
3257	16	There is insufficient free space on disk volume '%ls' to create the database. The database requires %I64u additional free bytes, while only %I64u bytes are available.
3258	16	The volume on device '%ls' belongs to a different media set.
3259	16	The volume on device '%ls' is not part of a multifamily (RAID) media set. Use WITH FORMAT to form a new RAID set.
3260	16	An internal buffer has become full.
3261	16	SQL Server cannot use the virtual device configuration.
3262	10	The backup set is valid.
3263	16	Cannot use the volume on device '%ls' as a continuation volume. It is sequence number %d of family %d for the current media set. Insert a new volume, or sequence number %d of family %d for the current set.
3264	16	The operation did not proceed far enough to allow RESTART. Reissue the statement without the RESTART qualifier.
3265	16	The login has insufficient authority. Membership of the sysadmin role is required to use VIRTUAL_DEVICE with BACKUP or RESTORE.
3266	10	The Microsoft Tape Format (MTF) soft filemark database on backup device '%ls' cannot be read, inhibiting random access.
3267	16	Insufficient resources to create UMS scheduler.
3268	16	Cannot use the backup file '%ls' because it was originally formatted with sector size %d and is now on a device with sector size %d.
3269	16	Cannot restore the file '%ls' because it was originally written with sector size %d; '%ls' is now on a device with sector size %d.
3270	16	An internal consistency error occurred. Contact Technical Support for assistance.
3271	16	Nonrecoverable I/O error occurred on file '%ls'.
3272	16	The '%ls' device has a hardware sector size of %d, but the block size parameter specifies an incompatible override value of %d. Reissue the statement using a compatible block size.
3301	21	Invalid log record found in the transaction log (logop %d).
3307	21	Process %d was expected to hold logical lock on page %S_PGID.
3313	21	Error while redoing logged operation in database '%.*ls'. Error at log record ID %S_LSN.

Error	Severity	Description
3314	21	Error while undoing logged operation in database '%.*ls'. Error at log record ID %S_LSN.
3405	10	Recovering database '%.*ls'.
3406	10	%d transactions rolled forward in database '%.*ls' (%d).
3407	10	%d transactions rolled back in database '%.*ls' (%d).
3408	10	Recovery complete.
3413	21	Database ID %d. Could not mark database as suspect. Getnext NC scan on sysdatabases.dbid failed.
3414	10	Database '%.*ls' (database ID %d) could not recover. Contact Technical Support.
3415	16	Read-only database '%.*ls' must be made writable before it can be upgraded.
3417	21	Cannot recover the master database. Exiting.
3429	10	Warning: The outcome of transaction %S_XID, named '%.*ls' in database '%.*ls' (database ID %d), could not be determined because the coordinating database (database ID %d) could not be opened. The transaction was assumed to be committed.
3430	10	Warning: Could not determine the outcome of transaction %S_XID, named '%.*ls' in database '%.*ls' (with ID %d) because the coordinating database (ID %d) did not contain the outcome. The transaction was assumed to be committed.
3431	21	Could not recover database '%.*ls' (database ID %d) due to unresolved transaction outcomes.
3432	16	Warning: syslanguages is missing.
3433	16	Name is truncated to '%.*ls'. The maximum name length is %d.
3434	20	Cannot change sort order or locale. Server shutting down. Restart SQL Server to continue with sort order unchanged.
3435	20	Sort order or locale cannot be changed because user objects or user databases exist.
3436	20	Cannot rebuild index ID %d for the '%.*ls' table in the '%.*ls' database.
3437	21	Error recovering database '%.*ls'. Could not connect to MSDTC to check the completion status of transaction %S_XID.
3438	10	Database '%.*ls' (database ID %d) failed to recover because transaction first LSN is not equal to LSN in checkpoint. Contact Technical Support.
3439	10	Database '%.*ls' (database ID %d). The DBCC RECOVERDB statement failed due to previous errors.

Error	Severity	Description
3440	21	Database '%.*ls' (database ID %d). The DBCC RECOVERDB statement can only be run after a RESTORE statement that used the WITH NORECOVERY option.
3441	21	Database '%.*ls' (database ID %d). The RESTORE statement could not access file '%ls'. Error was '%ls'.
3442	21	Database '%.*ls' (database ID %d). The size of the undo file is insufficient.
3443	21	Database '%.*ls' (database ID %d) was marked for standby or read-only use, but has been modified. The RESTORE LOG statement cannot be performed.
3444	21	Database '%.*ls' (database ID %d). Could not find start of previous recovery operation. The RESTORE LOG statement cannot be performed.
3445	21	Database '%.*ls' (database ID %d). The file '%ls' is not a valid undo file.
3446	16	Primary file not available for database '%.*ls'.
3447	16	Could not activate or scan all of the log files for database '%.*ls'.
3448	21	Could not undo log record %S_LSN, for transaction ID %S_XID, on page %S_PGID, database '%.*ls' (database ID %d). Page information: LSN = %S_LSN, type = %ld. Log information: OpCode = %ld, context %ld.
3449	21	An error has occurred indicating potential database corruption. SQL Server is shutting down so that recovery can be performed on database ID %d.
3450	10	Recovery progress on database '%.*ls' (%d): %d percent.
3451	16	Recovery has failed because reexecution of CREATE INDEX found inconsistencies between target filegroup '%ls' (%d) and source filegroup '%ls' (%d). Restore both filegroups before attempting further RESTORE LOG operations.
3452	10	Recovery of database '%.*ls' (%d) detected possible identity value inconsistency in table ID %d. Run DBCC CHECKIDENT ('%.*ls').
3453	21	Recovery has failed because a nonlogged operation could not be redone. Use the RESTORE statement to restore all data in filegroup '%ls' (%d) to a point beyond the nonlogged changes.
3501	21	Could not find row in sysdatabases for database ID %d at checkpoint time.
3505	14	Only the owner of database '%.*ls' can run the CHECKPOINT statement.

Error	Severity	Description
3508	25	Could not get an exclusive lock on the database '%.*ls'. Make sure that no other users are currently using this database, and rerun the CHECKPOINT statement.
3509	14	Could not set database '%.*ls' %ls read-only user mode because you could not exclusively lock the database.
3510	16	Database '%.*ls' cannot be changed from read-only because the primary and/or log file(s) are not writable.
3604	10	Duplicate key was ignored.
3605	10	Duplicate row was ignored.
3606	10	Arithmetic overflow occurred.
3607	10	Division by zero occurred.
3608	16	Cannot allocate a GUID for the token.
3612	10	%hsSQL Server Execution Times:%hs CPU time = %lu ms, elapsed time = %lu ms.
3613	10	SQL Server parse and compile time: %hs CPU time = %lu ms, elapsed time = %lu ms.
3615	10	Table '%.*ls'. Scan count %d, logical reads %d, physical reads %d, read-ahead reads %d.
3618	10	The transaction has been terminated.
3619	10	Could not write a CHECKPOINT record in database ID %d because the log is out of space.
3620	10	Automatic checkpointing is disabled in database '%.*ls' because the log is out of space. It will continue when the database owner successfully checkpoints the database. Free up some space or extend the database and then run the CHECKPOINT statement.
3621	10	The statement has been terminated.
3622	10	A domain error occurred.
3623	10	A transaction on a no_log table was undone. See the SQL Server errorlog for details.
3625	20	'%hs' is not yet implemented.
3627	16	Could not create worker thread.
3701	11	Cannot drop the %S_MSG '%.*ls', because it does not exist in the system catalog.
3702	16	Cannot drop the %S_MSG '%.*ls' because it is currently in use.
3704	16	Only the owner or members of the sysadmin role can drop the %S_MSG '%.*ls'.

Error	Severity	Description
3705	16	Cannot use DROP %ls with '%.*ls' because '%.*ls' is a %S_MSG. Use DROP %ls.
3708	16	Cannot drop the %S_MSG '%.*ls' because it is a system %S_MSG.
3716	16	The %S_MSG '%.*ls' cannot be dropped because it is bound to one or more %S_MSG.
3718	11	Could not drop index '%.*ls' because the table or clustered index entry cannot be found in the sysindexes system table.
3723	16	An explicit DROP INDEX is not allowed on index '%.*ls'. It is being used for %ls constraint enforcement.
3724	16	Cannot drop the %S_MSG '%.*ls' because it is published for replication.
3725	16	The constraint '%.*ls' is being referenced by table '%.*ls', foreign key constraint '%.*ls'.
3726	16	Could not drop object '%.*ls' because it is referenced by a FOREIGN KEY constraint.
3727	10	Could not drop constraint. See previous errors.
3728	16	'%.*ls' is not a constraint.
3733	16	Constraint '%.*ls' does not belong to table '%.*ls'.
3736	16	Cannot drop the %S_MSG '%.*ls' because it is being used for distribution.
3737	16	Could not delete file '%ls'. See the SQL Server error log for more information.
3738	16	Deleting database file '%ls'.
3739	15	Cannot %ls the index '%.*ls' because it is not a statistics collection.
3740	16	Cannot drop the %S_MSG '%.*ls' because at least part of the table resides on a read-only filegroup.
3902	13	The COMMIT TRANSACTION request has no corresponding BEGIN TRANSACTION.
3903	13	The ROLLBACK TRANSACTION request has no corresponding BEGIN TRANSACTION.
3904	21	Cannot unsplit logical page %S_PGID in object '%.*ls', in database '%.*ls'. Both pages together contain more data than will fit on one page.
3906	16	Could not run BEGIN TRANSACTION in database '%.*ls' because the database is read-only.
3908	16	Could not run BEGIN TRANSACTION in database '%.*ls' because the database is in bypass recovery mode.

Error	Severity	Description
3909	16	Session binding token is invalid or corrupt.
3910	16	Transaction context in use by another session.
3912	16	Cannot bind using an XP token while the server is not in an XP call.
3914	16	The data type '%s' is invalid for transaction names or savepoint names. Allowed data types are char, varchar, nchar, or nvarchar.
3915	16	Cannot use the ROLLBACK statement within an INSERT-EXEC statement.
3916	16	Cannot use the COMMIT statement within an INSERT-EXEC statement unless BEGIN TRANSACTION is used first.
3917	16	Session is bound to a transaction context that is in use. Other statements in the batch were ignored.
4003	21	ODS error. Server is terminating this connection.
4004	16	ntext data cannot be sent to clients using DB-Library (such as ISQL) or ODBC version 3.7 or earlier.
4015	16	Language requested in login '%.*ls' is not an official name on this SQL Server. Using server-wide default %.*ls instead.
4016	16	Language requested in 'login %.*ls' is not an official name on this SQL Server. Using user default %.*ls instead.
4017	16	Neither the language requested in 'login %.*ls' nor user default language %.*ls is an official language name on this SQL Server. Using server-wide default %.*ls instead.
4018	16	User default language %.*ls is not an official language name on this SQL Server. Using server-wide default %.*ls instead.
4019	16	Language requested in login '%.*ls' is not an official language name on this SQL Server. Login fails.
4020	16	Default date order '%.*ls' for language %.*ls is invalid. Using mdy instead.
4027	16	Mount tape for %hs of database '%ls'.
4028	16	End of tape has been reached. Remove tape '%ls' and mount next tape for %hs of database '%ls'.
4030	10	The medium on device '%ls' expires on %hs and cannot be overwritten.
4035	10	Processed %d pages for database '%ls', file '%ls' on file %d.
4037	16	User-specified volume ID '%ls' does not match the volume ID '%ls' of the device '%ls'.
4038	16	Cannot find file ID %d on device '%ls'.

Error	Severity	Description
4060	11	Cannot open database requested in login '%.*ls'. Login fails.
4061	11	Cannot open either database requested in login (%.*ls) or user default database (%.*ls). Using master database instead.
4062	11	Cannot open user default database '%.*ls'. Using master database instead.
4063	11	Cannot open database requested in login (%.*ls). Using user default '%.*ls' instead.
4207	16	BACKUP LOG is not allowed while the select into/bulkcopy option is enabled. Use BACKUP DATABASE or disable the option using sp_dboption.
4208	16	BACKUP LOG is not allowed while the trunc. log on chkpt. option is enabled. Use BACKUP DATABASE or disable the option using sp_dboption.
4212	16	Cannot back up the log of the master database. Use BACKUP DATABASE instead.
4213	16	Cannot allow BACKUP LOG because file '%ls' has been subjected to nonlogged updates and cannot be rolled forward. Perform a full database, or differential database, backup.
4214	10	There is no current database backup. This log backup cannot be used to roll forward a preceding database backup.
4215	10	The log was not truncated because records at the beginning of the log are pending replication. Ensure the Log Reader Agent is running or use sp_repldone to mark transactions as distributed.
4301	16	Database in use. The system administrator must have exclusive use of the database to restore the log.
4304	16	A USER ATTENTION signal raised during RESTORE LOG is being ignored until the current restore completes.
4305	16	This backup set cannot be restored because the database has not been rolled forward far enough. You must first restore all earlier logs before restoring this log.
4306	16	The preceding restore operation did not specify WITH NORECOVERY or WITH STANDBY. Restart the restore sequence, specifying WITH NORECOVERY or WITH STANDBY for all but the final step.
4312	16	Only members of the sysadmin role or owner of database '%.*ls' can run RESTORE LOG.
4316	16	Can only RESTORE LOG in the master database if SQL Server is in single user mode.

Error	Severity	Description
4318	16	File '%ls' has been rolled forward to LSN %.*ls. This log terminates at LSN %.*ls, which is too early to apply the WITH RECOVERY option. Reissue the RESTORE LOG statement WITH NORECOVERY.
4319	16	Cannot use the STOPAT and NORECOVERY options together. Reissue the statement specifying WITH RECOVERY to roll the database forward to a specific point in time.
4320	16	File '%ls' was only partially restored by a database or file restore. The entire file must be successfully restored before applying the log.
4321	16	The minimum recovery point of the database is beyond the specified point-in-time. Reissue this statement without specifying STOPAT.
4322	10	This log file contains records logged before the designated point-in-time. The database is being left in load state so you can apply another log file.
4323	16	The database is marked suspect. Transaction logs cannot be restored. Use RESTORE DATABASE to recover the database.
4324	10	Backup history older than %ls has been deleted.
4325	16	Could not delete entries for backup set ID '%ls'.
4403	16	View '%.*ls' is not updatable because it contains aggregates.
4404	16	View '%.*ls' is not updatable because the definition contains the DISTINCT clause.
4405	16	View '%.*ls' is not updatable because the FROM clause names multiple tables.
4406	16	View '%.*ls' is not updatable because a column of the view is derived or constant.
4408	19	The query and the views in it exceed the limit of %d tables.
4413	16	Could not use view '%.*ls' because of previous binding errors.
4414	16	Could not allocate ancillary table for view resolution. The maximum number of tables in a query (%d) was exceeded.
4415	16	View '%.*ls' is not updatable because either it was created WITH CHECK OPTION or it spans a view created WITH CHECK OPTION and the target table is referenced multiple times in the resulting query.
4416	16	View '%.*ls' is not updatable because the definition contains a UNION operator.
4417	16	Derived table '%.*ls' is not updatable because the definition contains a UNION operator.
4418	16	Derived table '%.*ls' is not updatable because it contains aggregates.

Error	Severity	Description
4419	16	Derived table '%.*ls' is not updatable because the definition contains the DISTINCT clause.
4420	16	Derived table '%.*ls' is not updatable because the FROM clause names multiple tables.
4421	16	Derived table '%.*ls' is not updatable because a column of the derived table is derived or constant.
4424	16	Joined tables cannot be specified in a query containing outer join operators. View '%.*ls' contains joined tables.
4425	16	Cannot specify outer join operators in a query containing joined tables. View '%.*ls' contains outer join operators.
4427	16	The view '%.*ls' is not updatable because the definition contains the TOP clause.
4428	16	The derived table '%.*ls' is not updatable because the definition contains the TOP clause.
4429	16	View '%.*ls' contains a self-reference. Views cannot reference themselves directly or indirectly.
4430	10	Warning: Index hints supplied for view '%.*ls' will be ignored.
4501	16	View '%.*ls' has more columns defined than column names given.
4502	16	View '%.*ls' has more column names specified than columns defined.
4504	16	Could not perform CREATE TABLE because there was not enough space to allocate memory for the table.
4505	16	CREATE VIEW failed because column '%.*ls' in view '%.*ls' exceeds the maximum of %d columns.
4506	10	Column names in each view must be unique. Column name '%.*ls' in view '%.*ls' is specified more than once.
4508	16	Views are not allowed on temporary tables. Table names that begin with '#' denote temporary tables.
4510	16	Could not perform CREATE VIEW because WITH CHECK OPTION was specified and the view is not updatable.
4511	16	Could not perform CREATE VIEW because no column name was specified for column %d.
4602	14	Only members of the sysadmin role can grant or revoke the CREATE DATABASE permission.
4603	14	Only the owner of the current database can grant or revoke this permission.
4604	16	There is no such user or group '%.*ls'.
4606	16	Granted or revoked privilege %ls is not compatible with object.

Error	Severity	Description
4610	16	You can only grant or revoke permissions on objects in the current database.
4611	16	To revoke grantable privileges, specify the CASCADE option with REVOKE.
4613	16	Grantor does not have GRANT permission.
4615	16	Invalid column name '%.*ls'.
4617	16	Cannot grant, deny or revoke permissions to or from special roles.
4618	16	You do not have permission to use %.*ls in the AS clause.
4619	16	CREATE DATABASE permission can only be granted in the master database.
4701	11	Could not truncate table '%.*ls' because this table does not exist in database '%.*ls'.
4706	17	Could not truncate table '%.*ls' because there is not enough room in the log to record the deallocation of all the index and data pages.
4707	16	Could not truncate object '%.*ls' because it or one of its indexes resides on a READONLY filegroup.
4708	16	Could not truncate object '%.*ls' because it is not a table.
4709	16	You are not allowed to truncate the system table '%.*ls'.
4710	16	Only the owner or members of the sysadmin role can truncate table '%.*ls'.
4711	16	Cannot truncate table '%.*ls' because it is published for replication.
4712	16	Cannot truncate table '%.*ls' because it is being referenced by a FOREIGN KEY constraint.
4801	20	Bulk_main: The opentable system function on BULK INSERT table failed. Database ID %d, name '%.*ls'.
4803	21	Received invalid row length %d from bcp client. Maximum row size is %d.
4804	21	Premature end-of-message while reading current row from host. Host program may have terminated.
4805	17	The front-end tool you are using does not support the feature of bulk insert from host. Use the proper tools for this command.
4807	21	Received invalid row length %d from bcp client. Minimum row size is %d.
4810	16	Expected the TEXT token in data stream for bulk copy of text or image data.

Error	Severity	Description
4811	16	Expected the column offset in data stream for bulk copy of text or image data.
4812	16	Expected the row offset in data stream for bulk copy of text or image data.
4813	16	Expected the text length in data stream for bulk copy of text, ntext, or image data.
4815	21	Received invalid column length from bcp client.
4817	16	Could not bulk insert. Invalid sorted column '%.*ls'. Assuming data stream is not sorted.
4818	16	Could not bulk insert. Sorted column '%.*ls' was specified more than once. Assuming data stream is not sorted.
4819	16	Could not bulk insert. Bulk data stream was incorrectly specified as sorted.
4820	16	Could not bulk insert. Unknown version of format file '%s'.
4821	16	Could not bulk insert. Error reading the number of columns from format file '%s'.
4822	16	Could not bulk insert. Invalid number of columns in format file '%s'.
4823	16	Could not bulk insert. Invalid column number in format file '%s'.
4824	16	Could not bulk insert. Invalid data type for column number %d in format file '%s'.
4825	16	Could not bulk insert. Invalid prefix for column number %d in format file '%s'.
4826	16	Could not bulk insert. Invalid column length for column number %d in format file '%s'.
4827	16	Could not bulk insert. Invalid column terminator for column number %d in format file '%s'.
4828	16	Could not bulk insert. Invalid destination table column number for source column %d in format file '%s'.
4829	16	Could not bulk insert. Error reading destination table column name for source column %d in format file '%s'.
4830	10	Bulk Insert: DataFileType was incorrectly specified as char. DataFileType will be assumed to be widechar because the data file has a Unicode signature.
4831	10	Bulk Insert: DataFileType was incorrectly specified as widechar. DataFileType will be assumed to be char because the data file does not have a Unicode signature.
4832	16	Bulk Insert: Unexpected end-of-file (EOF) encountered in data file.

Error	Severity	Description
4833	16	Bulk Insert: Version mismatch between the provider dynamic link library and the server executable.
4834	16	Permission denied. Only members of the sysadmin role can use the BULK INSERT statement.
4835	16	Bulk copying into a table with computed columns is not supported for downlevel clients.
4836	10	Warning: Table '%s' is published for merge replication. Reinitialize affected subscribers or execute sp_addtabletocontents to ensure that data added is included in the next sychronization.
4837	16	Error: Cannot bulk copy into a table '%s' enabled for immediate-updating subscriptions
4849	16	Could not import table '%ls'. Error %d.
4850	10	Data import: Table '%ls' is already locked by another user.
4851	10	Data import: Table '%ls' already has data. Skipping to next table.
4852	10	Data import: Table '%ls' does not exist or it is not a user table.
4853	10	%hs
4854	21	%hs
4860	16	Could not bulk insert. File '%ls' does not exist.
4861	16	Could not bulk insert because file '%ls' could not be opened. Operating system error code %ls.
4862	16	Could not bulk insert because file '%ls' could not be read. Operating system error code %ls.
4863	16	Bulk insert data conversion error (truncation) for row %d, column %d (%ls).
4864	16	Bulk insert data conversion error (type mismatch) for row %d, column %d (%ls).
4865	16	Could not bulk insert because the maximum number of errors (%d) was exceeded.
4866	16	Could not bulk insert because column too long in data file. Make sure FieldTerminator and RowTerminator were specified correctly.
4867	16	Bulk insert data conversion error (overflow) for row %d, column %d (%ls).
4901	16	ALTER TABLE only allows columns to be added that can contain nulls or have a DEFAULT definition specified. Column '%.*ls' cannot be added to table '%.*ls' because it does not allow nulls and does not specify a DEFAULT definition.

Error	Severity	Description
4902	11	Cannot alter table '%.*ls' because this table does not exist in database '%.*ls'.
4909	16	Cannot alter '%.*ls' because it is not a table.
4910	16	Only the owner or members of the sysadmin role can alter table '%.*ls'.
4916	16	Could not enable or disable the constraint. See previous errors.
4917	16	Constraint '%.*ls' does not exist.
4920	16	ALTER TABLE failed because trigger '%.*ls' on table '%.*ls' does not exist.
4921	16	ALTER TABLE failed because trigger '%.*ls' does not belong to table '%.*ls'.
4922	16	%ls %.*ls failed because %ls %.*ls accesses this column.
4923	16	ALTER TABLE DROP COLUMN failed because '%.*ls' is the only data column in table '%.*ls'. A table must have at least one data column.
4924	16	%ls failed because column '%.*ls' does not exist in table '%.*ls'.
4925	16	ALTER TABLE ALTER COLUMN ADD ROWGUIDCOL failed because a column already exists in table '%.*ls' with ROWGUIDCOL property.
4926	16	ALTER TABLE ALTER COLUMN DROP ROWGUIDCOL failed because a column does not exist in table '%.*ls' with ROWGUIDCOL property.
4927	16	Cannot alter column '%.*ls' to be data type %.*ls.
4928	16	Cannot alter column '%.*ls' because it is '%ls'.
4929	16	Cannot alter the %S_MSG '%.*ls' because it is being published for replication.
4930	10	Warning: Columns added to the replicated table %S_MSG '%.*ls' will be ignored by existing articles.
4931	16	Cannot add columns to %S_MSG '%.*ls' because it is being published for merge replication.
5001	16	User must be in the master database.
5002	16	Database '%.*ls' does not exist. Check sysdatabases.
5004	16	Database must be in state where it can be checkpointed to use ALTER DATABASE.
5005	10	Extending database by %.2f MB on disk '%.*ls'.
5006	16	Could not get exclusive use of %S_MSG '%.*ls' to perform the requested operation.

Error	Severity	Description
5008	16	ALTER DATABASE option not implemented yet.
5009	16	ALTER DATABASE failed. Some disk names listed in the statement were not found. Check that the names exist and are spelled correctly before rerunning the statement.
5011	14	Only members of the sysadmin role or owner of database '%.*ls' can alter it.
5013	16	The master and model databases cannot have files added to them. ALTER DATABASE was aborted.
5014	16	The %S_MSG '%.*ls' does not exist in database '%.*ls'.
5015	16	ALTER DATABASE failed. The total size specified must be 1 MB or greater.
5017	16	ALTER DATABASE failed. Database '%.*ls' was not created with 'FOR LOAD' option.
5018	0	File '%.*ls' modified in sysaltfiles. Delete old file after restarting SQL Server.
5019	16	Could not find entry in sysaltfiles for file '%.*ls'.
5020	16	The primary data or log file cannot be removed from a database.
5021	16	MAXSIZE cannot be larger than the maximum database size of %ld MB.
5022	16	Log file '%ls' for this database is already active.
5023	16	Database must be put in bypass recovery mode to rebuild the log.
5024	16	No entry found for the primary log file in sysfiles1. Could not rebuild the log.
5025	16	The file '%ls' already exists. It should be renamed or deleted so that a new log file can be created.
5026	16	Could not create a new log file with file '%.*ls'. See previous errors.
5027	16	System databases master, model, and tempdb cannot have their logs rebuilt.
5028	16	The system could not activate enough of the database to rebuild the log.
5029	10	Warning: The log for database '%.*ls' has been rebuilt. Transactional consistency has been lost. DBCC CHECKDB should be run to validate physical consistency. Database options will have to be reset, and extra log files may need to be deleted.
5030	16	The database could not be exclusively locked to perform the operation.

Error	Severity	Description
5031	16	Cannot remove the file '%.*ls' because it is the only file in the DEFAULT filegroup.
5035	16	Filegroup '%.*ls' already exists in this database.
5036	16	MODIFY FILE failed. Specify logical name.
5037	16	MODIFY FILE failed. Do not specify physical name.
5038	16	MODIFY FILE failed. Only modify one file and one property at a time.
5039	16	MODIFY FILE failed. Specified size is less than current size.
5040	16	MODIFY FILE failed. Size is greater than MAXSIZE.
5041	16	MODIFY FILE failed. File '%.*ls' does not exist.
5042	16	The %S_MSG '%.*ls' cannot be removed because it is not empty.
5043	16	The %S_MSG '%.*ls' cannot be found in %ls.
5044	10	The %S_MSG '%.*ls' has been removed.
5045	16	The %S_MSG already has the '%ls' property set.
5046	10	The %S_MSG property '%ls' has been set.
5047	16	Cannot change the READONLY property of the PRIMARY filegroup.
5048	16	Cannot %ls file in read-only filegroup '%.*ls'.
5049	16	Cannot extend file '%ls' using this syntax as it was not created with DISK INIT. Use ALTER DATABASE MODIFY FILE.
5050	16	Cannot change the properties of empty filegroup '%.*ls'. The filegroup must contain at least one file.
5051	16	Cannot have a filegroup with the name 'DEFAULT'.
5053	16	The maximum of %ld filegroups per database has been exceeded.
5054	16	Could not cleanup worktable IAM chains to allow shrink or remove file operation. Please try again when tempdb is idle.
5055	16	Cannot %ls read-only file '%.*ls'.
5101	15	You must supply parameters for the DISK %hs statement. Usage: %hs.
5102	15	No such statement DISK %.*ls.
5103	16	MAXSIZE cannot be less than SIZE for file '%ls'.
5104	16	File '%.*ls' already used.
5105	16	Device activation error. The physical file name '%.*ls' may be incorrect.
5106	15	Parameter '%hs' requires value of data type '%hs'.

Error	Severity	Description
5107	15	Value is wrong data type for parameter '%hs' (requires data type '%hs').
5109	16	No such parameter '%.*ls'.
5116	14	Permission denied. Only members of the sysadmin role can run DISK statements.
5117	16	Could not run DISK statement. You must be in the master database to run this statement.
5122	10	Each disk file size must be greater than or equal to 1 MB.
5123	16	CREATE FILE encountered operating system error %ls while attempting to open or create the physical file '%.*ls'.
5126	16	The logical device '%.*ls' does not exist in sysdevices.
5146	16	The %hs of %d is out of range. It must be between %d and %d.
5148	16	Could not set the file size to the desired amount. The operating system file size limit may have been reached.
5149	16	MODIFY FILE encountered operating system error %ls while attempting to expand the physical file.
5150	16	The size of a single log file must not be greater than 2 TB.
5151	16	The %hs statement is obsolete and no longer supported.
5154	16	Device '%.*ls' is not open.
5156	16	Usage: DBCC DEVCONTROL(devname,ONLINE|OFFLINE)
5157	16	I/O error encountered in the writelog system function during backout.
5158	10	Warning: Media in device '%.*ls' may have been changed.
5159	16	Operating system error %.*ls on device '%.*ls' during %ls.
5160	16	Cannot take '%.*ls' offline because the database is in use.
5162	16	Cannot find '%.*ls' in sysdatabases.
5163	16	Cannot open '%.*ls' to take offline.
5164	16	Usage: DBCC DBCONTROL(dbname,ONLINE|OFFLINE)
5165	16	Cannot explicitly open or close master database.
5167	16	Database '%.*ls' is already offline.
5168	16	File '%.*ls' is on a network drive, which is not allowed.
5169	16	FILEGROWTH cannot be greater than MAXSIZE for file '%.*ls'.
5170	16	Cannot create file '%ls' because it already exists.
5171	16	%.*ls is not a primary database file.

Error	Severity	Description
5172	16	The header for file '%ls' is not a valid database file header. The %ls property is incorrect.
5173	16	Cannot associate files with different databases.
5174	10	Each file size must be greater than or equal to 512 KB.
5175	10	The file '%.*ls' has been expanded to prevent recovery from failing. Contact the system administrator for further assistance.
5176	10	The file '%.*ls' has been expanded beyond its maximum size to prevent recovery from failing. Contact the system administrator for further assistance.
5177	16	Encountered an unexpected error while checking the sector size for file '%.*ls'. Check the SQL Server error log for more information.
5178	16	Cannot use file '%.*ls' because it was originally formatted with sector size %d and is now on a device with sector size %d.
5179	16	Cannot use file '%.*ls', which is on a device with sector size %d. SQL Server supports a maximum sector size of 4096 bytes.
5180	22	Could not open FCB for invalid file ID %d in database '%.*ls'. Table or database may be corrupted.
5181	16	Could not restart database '%.*ls'. Reverting back to old status.
5701	10	Changed database context to '%.*ls'.
5702	10	SQL Server is terminating this process.
5703	10	Changed language setting to %.*ls.
5803	10	Unknown config number (%d) in sysconfigures.
5805	16	Too few locks specified. Minimum %d.
5807	16	Recovery intervals above %d minutes not recommended. Use the RECONFIGURE WITH OVERRIDE statement to force this configuration.
5808	16	Ad hoc updates to system catalogs not recommended. Use the RECONFIGURE WITH OVERRIDE statement to force this configuration.
5809	16	Average time slices above %d milliseconds not recommended. Use the RECONFIGURE WITH OVERRIDE statement to force this configuration.
5810	16	Valid values for the fill factor are 0 to 100.
5812	14	Permission denied. Only members of the sysadmin role can run RECONFIGURE.
5823	16	Cannot reconfigure SQL Server to use sort order ID %d, because the row for that sort order does not exist in syscharsets.

Error	Severity	Description
5824	16	Cannot reconfigure SQL Server to use sort order ID %d, because the row for its underlying character set (ID %d) does not exist in syscharsets.
5825	16	Cannot reconfigure the server's sort order because the syscharsets table does not exist. You must upgrade your server prior to attempting this.
5826	10	You have just reconfigured SQL Server's sort order. Table indexes on columns of type char or varchar will be rebuilt when SQL Server is restarted.
5827	10	By changing the default sort order, you have also reconfigured SQL Server's default character set.
5828	16	User connections are limited to %d.
5829	16	The specified user options value is invalid.
5830	10	You have just reconfigured SQL Server's Unicode collation. Table indexes on columns of type nchar or nvarchar will be rebuilt when SQL Server is restarted.
5831	16	Minimum server memory value (%d) must be less than or equal to the maximum value (%d).
5904	17	Background checkpoint process suspended until locks are available.
6001	10	SHUTDOWN is waiting for %d process(es) to complete.
6002	10	SHUTDOWN is in progress. Log off.
6004	10	SHUTDOWN can only be used by members of the sysadmin role.
6005	10	SHUTDOWN is in progress.
6006	10	Server shut down by request.
6007	10	The SHUTDOWN statement cannot be executed within a transaction or by a stored procedure.
6101	16	Process ID %d is not a valid process ID. Choose a number between 1 and %d.
6102	14	Only members of the sysadmin role can use the KILL statement.
6103	17	Could not do cleanup for the killed process. Received message %d.
6104	16	Cannot use KILL to kill your own process.
6106	16	Process ID %d is not an active process ID.
6107	14	Only user processes can be killed.
6108	16	KILL WITH COMMIT/ABORT can only be used with waiting distributed transactions.

Error	Severity	Description
6401	16	Cannot roll back %.*ls. No transaction or savepoint of that name was found.
7101	17	Could not allocate new text, ntext, or image node in database ID %d.
7102	20	SQL Server Internal Error. Text manager cannot continue with current statement.
7105	22	Page %S_PGID, slot %d for text, ntext, or image node does not exist.
7116	25	Offset %d is not in the range of available text, ntext, or image data.
7122	16	Invalid text, ntext, or image pointer type. Must be binary(16).
7123	16	Invalid text, ntext, or image pointer value %hs.
7124	16	The offset and length specified in the READTEXT statement is greater than the actual data length of %ld.
7125	16	The text, ntext, or image pointer value conflicts with the column name specified.
7126	16	The text, ntext, or image pointer value references a data page with an invalid text, ntext, or image status.
7127	16	The text, ntext, or image pointer value references a data page with an invalid timestamp.
7128	16	The text, ntext, or image pointer value references a data page that is no longer allocated.
7130	16	%ls WITH NO LOG is not valid at this time. Use sp_dboption to set the 'select into/bulkcopy' option on for database '%.*ls'.
7133	16	NULL textptr (text, ntext, or image pointer) passed to %ls function.
7135	16	Deletion length %ld is not in the range of available text, ntext, or image data.
7136	16	%ls WITH NO LOG is not valid when the column is being replicated.
7139	16	Length of text, ntext, or image data (%ld) to be replicated exceeds configured maximum %ld.
7140	16	Text has been padded with 0 due to dirty read.
7141	16	Must create orphaned text inside a user transaction.
7142	16	Must drop orphaned text before committing the transaction.
7143	16	Invalid locator de-referenced.
7201	17	Could not execute procedure on remote server '%.*ls' because SQL Server is not configured for remote access. Ask your system administrator to reconfigure SQL Server to allow remote access.

Error	Severity	Description
7202	11	Could not find server '%.*ls' in sysservers. Execute sp_addlinkedserver to add the server to sysservers.
7204	20	Could not obtain or use interface %hs from Microsoft OLE DB provider for ODBC. Microsoft OLE DB provider for ODBC not registered. Remote procedures cannot be executed.
7212	16	Could not execute procedure '%.*ls' on remote server '%.*ls'.
7213	20	Could not set up parameter for remote server '%.*ls'.
7214	16	Remote procedure time out of %d seconds exceeded. Remote procedure '%.*ls' is canceled.
7221	16	Could not relay results of procedure '%.*ls' from remote server '%.*ls'.
7300	16	OLE DB error trace [%ls].
7301	16	Could not obtain a required interface from OLE DB provider '%ls'.
7302	16	Could not create an instance of OLE DB provider '%ls'.
7303	16	Could not initialize data source object of OLE DB provider '%ls'. %ls
7304	16	Could not create a new session on OLE DB provider '%ls'.
7305	16	Could not create a statement object using OLE DB provider '%ls'.
7306	16	Could not open table '%ls' from OLE DB provider '%ls'. %ls
7307	16	Could not obtain the data source of a session from OLE DB provider '%ls'. This action must be supported by the provider.
7310	16	Could not obtain the schema options for OLE DB provider '%ls'. The provider supports the interface, but returns a failure code when it is used.
7311	16	Could not obtain the schema rowset for OLE DB provider '%ls'. The provider supports the interface, but returns a failure code when it is used.
7312	16	Invalid use of schema and/or catalog for OLE DB provider '%ls'. A four-part name was supplied, but the provider does not expose the necessary interfaces to use a catalog and/or schema.
7313	16	Invalid schema or catalog specified for provider '%ls'.
7314	16	OLE DB provider '%ls' does not contain table '%ls'.
7315	16	OLE DB provider '%ls' contains multiple tables that match the name '%ls'.
7316	16	Could not use qualified table names (schema or catalog) with OLE DB provider '%ls' because it does not implement required functionality.
7317	16	OLE DB provider '%ls' returned an invalid schema definition.

Error	Severity	Description
7318	16	OLE DB provider '%ls' returned an invalid column definition.
7319	16	OLE DB provider '%ls' returned a '%ls' index '%ls' with incorrect bookmark ordinal %d.
7320	16	Could not execute query against OLE DB provider '%ls'. %ls
7321	16	An error occurred while preparing a query for execution against OLE DB provider '%ls'. %ls
7322	16	A failure occurred while giving parameter information to OLE DB provider '%ls'. %ls
7323	16	An error occurred while submitting the query text to OLE DB provider '%ls'. %ls
7330	16	Could not fetch a row from OLE DB provider '%ls'. %ls
7331	16	Could not release a row from OLE DB provider '%ls'. %ls
7332	16	Could not rescan the result set from OLE DB provider '%ls'. %ls
7333	16	Could not fetch a row using a bookmark from OLE DB provider '%ls'. %ls
7340	16	Could not create a column accessor for OLE DB provider '%ls'. %ls
7341	16	Could not get the current row value of column '%ls.%ls' from the OLE DB provider '%ls'. %ls
7342	16	Unexpected NULL value returned for column '%ls.%ls' from the OLE DB provider '%ls'. This column cannot be NULL.
7343	16	OLE DB provider '%ls' could not %ls table '%ls'. %ls
7344	16	OLE DB provider '%ls' could not %ls table '%ls' because of column '%ls'. %ls
7345	16	OLE DB provider '%ls' could not delete from table '%ls'. %ls
7346	16	Could not get the data of the row from the OLE DB provider '%ls'. %ls
7347	16	OLE DB provider '%ls' returned an unexpected data length for the fixed-length column '%ls.%ls'. The expected data length is %ls, while the returned data length is %ls.
7348	16	OLE DB provider '%ls' could not set range for table '%ls'.%ls
7349	16	OLE DB provider '%ls' could not set range for table '%ls' because of column '%ls'.%ls
7350	16	Could not get the column information from the OLE DB provider '%ls'.
7351	16	OLE DB provider '%ls' could not map ordinals for one or more columns of object '%ls'.

Error	Severity	Description
7352	16	OLE DB provider '%ls' supplied inconsistent metadata. The object '%ls' was missing expected column '%ls'.
7353	16	OLE DB provider '%ls' supplied inconsistent metadata. An extra column was supplied during execution that was not found at compile time.
7354	16	OLE DB provider '%ls' supplied invalid metadata for column '%ls'. %ls
7355	16	OLE DB provider '%ls' supplied inconsistent metadata for a column. The name was changed at execution time.
7356	16	OLE DB provider '%ls' supplied inconsistent metadata for a column. Metadata information was changed at execution time.
7357	16	Could not process object '%ls'. The OLE DB provider '%ls' indicates that the object has no columns.
7358	16	Could not execute query. The OLE DB provider '%ls' did not provide an appropriate interface to access the text, ntext, or image column '%ls.%ls'.
7360	16	Could not get the length of a storage object from the OLE DB provider '%ls' for table '%ls', column '%ls'.
7361	16	Could not read a storage object from the OLE DB provider '%ls', for table '%ls', column '%ls'.
7370	16	One or more properties could not be set on the query for OLE DB provider '%ls'. %ls
7371	16	One or more properties could not be set on the table for OLE DB provider '%ls'.
7373	16	Could not set the initialization properties for the OLE DB provider '%ls'.
7375	16	Could not open index '%ls' on table '%ls' from OLE DB provider '%ls'. %ls
7376	16	Could not enforce the remote join hint for this query.
7390	16	The requested operation could not be performed because the OLE DB provider '%ls' does not support the required transaction interface.
7391	16	The operation could not be performed because the OLE DB provider '%ls' does not support distributed transactions.
7392	16	Could not start a transaction for OLE DB provider '%ls'.
7393	16	OLE DB provider '%ls' reported an error aborting the current transaction.
7394	16	OLE DB provider '%ls' reported an error committing the current transaction.

Error	Severity	Description
7399	16	OLE DB provider '%ls' reported an error. %ls
7401	16	Cannot create OLE DB provider enumeration object installed with SQL Server. Verify installation.
7403	16	Could not locate registry entry for OLE DB provider '%ls'.
7404	16	The server could not load DCOM on startup (-O command-line used to force startup). Heterogeneous queries and remote RPC are disabled.
7405	16	Heterogeneous queries require the ANSI_NULLS and ANSI_WARNINGS options to be set for the connection. This ensures consistent query semantics. Enable these options and then reissue your query.
7410	16	Remote access not allowed for Windows NT user activated by SETUSER.
7411	16	Server '%.*ls' is not configured for %ls.
7413	16	Could not perform a Windows NT authenticated login because delegation is not available.
7414	16	Invalid number of parameters. Rowset '%ls' expects %d parameter(s).
7415	16	Ad hoc access to OLE DB provider '%ls' has been denied. You must access this provider through a linked server.
7416	16	Access to the remote server is denied because no login-mapping exists.
7417	16	Remote tables are not allowed in GROUP BY ALL operations.
7601	16	Cannot use a CONTAINS or FREETEXT predicate on %S_MSG '%.*ls' because it is not full-text indexed.
7602	16	The Full-Text Service (Microsoft Search) is not available. The system administrator must start this service.
7603	15	Syntax error in search condition '%ls'.
7604	17	Full-text operation failed due to a time out.
7605	17	Full-text catalog '%ls' has been lost. Use sp_fulltext_catalog to rebuild and to repopulate this full-text catalog.
7606	17	Could not find full-text index for database ID %d, table ID %d. Use sp_fulltext_table to deactivate then activate this index.
7607	17	Search on full-text catalog '%ls' for database ID %d, table ID %d with search condition '%ls' failed with unknown result (%x).
7608	17	An unknown full-text failure (%x) occurred in function %hs on full-text catalog '%ls'.
7609	17	Could not load the Full-Text Search component (SQLFTQRY.DLL).

Error	Severity	Description
7610	16	Could not create full-text catalog because '%ls' is an invalid file path.
7611	10	Warning: Request to start a population in full-text catalog '%ls' ignored because a crawl is currently active for this full-text catalog.
7612	16	%d is not a valid value for full-text system resource usage.
7613	16	Cannot drop index '%.*ls' because it enforces the full-text key for table '%.*ls'.
7614	16	Cannot alter or drop column '%.*ls' because it is enabled for Full-Text Search.
7615	16	A CONTAINS or FREETEXT predicate can only operate on one table. Qualify the use of * with a table name.
7616	16	Full-Text Search is not enabled for the current database. Use sp_fulltext_database to enable full-text search for the database.
7617	16	Query does not reference the fulltext indexed table.
7618	16	%d is not a valid value for a full-text connection time out.
7620	16	Conversion to data type %ls failed for full-text search key value 0x%ls.
7621	16	Invalid use of full-text predicate in the HAVING clause.
7622	17	Full-text catalog '%ls' lacks sufficient disk space to complete this operation.
7623	17	Full-text query failed because full-text catalog '%ls' is not yet ready for queries.
7624	17	Full-text catalog '%ls' is in a unusable state. Drop and re-create this full-text catalog.
7908	10	The table '%.*ls' was created with the NO_LOG option.
7909	10	A transaction involving the NO_LOG table '%.*ls' was undone. This may have left the table in an inconsistent state. Rebuild the table.
7910	10	Repair: Page %S_PGID has been allocated to object ID %d, index ID %d.
7911	10	Repair: Page %S_PGID has been deallocated from object ID %d, index ID %d.
7912	10	Repair: Extent %S_PGID has been allocated to object ID %d, index ID %d.
7913	10	Repair: Extent %S_PGID has been deallocated from object ID %d, index ID %d.
7914	10	Repair: %ls page at %S_PGID has been rebuilt.
7915	10	Repair: IAM chain for object ID %d, index ID %d, has been truncated before page %S_PGID and will be rebuilt.

Error	Severity	Description
7916	10	Repair: Deleted record for object ID %d, index ID %d, on page %S_PGID, slot %d. Indexes will be rebuilt.
7917	10	Repair: Converted forwarded record for object ID %d, index ID %d, at page %S_PGID, slot %d to a data row.
7918	10	Repair: Page %S_PGID next and %S_PGID previous pointers have been set to match each other in object ID %d, index ID %d.
7919	16	Repair statement not processed. Database needs to be in single user mode.
7920	10	Processed %ld entries in sysindexes for database ID %d.
7922	16	**
7923	10	Table %.*ls Object ID %ld.
7924	10	Index ID %ld FirstIAM %S_PGID Root %S_PGID Dpages %ld Sort %d.
7925	16	Index ID %d. %ld index pages in %ld extents.
7926	16	Data level %d. %ld data pages in %ld extents.
7927	16	Total number of extents is %ld.
7932	16	The indexes for '%.*ls' are already correct. They will not be rebuilt.
7933	16	One or more indexes are corrupt. They will be rebuilt.
7934	16	The table '%.*ls' has no indexes.
7935	16	REINDEX received an exception. Statement terminated.
7937	16	The data in table '%.*ls' is possibly corrupt. REINDEX terminated. Run DBCC CHECKTABLE and report errors to your system administrator.
7939	16	Cannot detach database '%.*ls' because it does not exist.
7940	16	System databases master, model, and tempdb cannot be detached.
7941	10	Trace option(s) not enabled for this connection. Use 'DBCC TRACEON()'.
7942	10	DBCC %ls scanning '%.*ls' table...
7943	10	Table: '%.*ls' (%d); index ID: %d, database ID: %d
7944	10	%ls level scan performed.
7945	10	- Pages Scanned................................: %lu
7946	10	- Extents Scanned..............................: %lu
7947	10	- Extent Switches..............................: %lu
7948	10	- Avg. Pages per Extent........................: %3.1f

Error	Severity	Description
7949	10	- Scan Density [Best Count:Actual Count].......: %4.2f%ls [%lu:%lu]
7950	10	- Logical Scan Fragmentation ....: %4.2f%ls
7951	10	- Physical Scan Fragmentation ....: %4.2f%ls
7952	10	- Extent Scan Fragmentation ....: %4.2f%ls
7953	10	- Avg. Bytes Free per Page.....................: %3.1f
7954	10	- Avg. Page Density (full).....................: %4.2f%ls
7955	10	Invalid SPID %d specified.
7956	10	Permission to execute DBCC %ls denied.
7957	10	Cannot display the specified SPID's buffer; in transition.
7958	10	The specified SPID does not process input/output data streams.
7959	10	The DBCC statement is not supported in this release.
7962	16	Upgrade requires SQL Server to be started in single user mode. Restart SQL Server with the -m flag.
7963	16	Upgrade encountered a fatal error. See the SQL Server errorlog for more information.
7965	16	Table corrupt: Could not check object ID %d, index ID %d due to invalid allocation (IAM) page(s).
7966	10	Warning: NO_INDEX option of %ls being used. Checks on non-system indexes will be skipped.
7968	10	Transaction information for database '%.*ls'.
7969	10	No active open transactions.
7970	10	%hsOldest active transaction:
7971	10	SPID (server process ID) : %d
7972	10	UID (user ID) : %d
7974	10	Name : %.*ls
7975	10	LSN : (%d:%d:%d)
7977	10	Start time : %.*ls
7979	10	%hsReplicated Transaction Information:
7980	10	Oldest distributed LSN : (%d:%d:%d)
7982	10	Oldest non-distributed LSN : (%d:%d:%d)
7983	14	Only the owner of database '%.*ls' can run the DBCC %ls statement.
7984	16	Invalid object name '%.*ls'.

Error	Severity	Description
7985	16	The object name '%.*ls' contains more than the maximum number of prefixes. The maximum is %d.
7986	16	Warning: Pinning tables should be carefully considered. If a pinned table is larger, or grows larger, than the available data cache, the server may need to be restarted and the table unpinned.
7991	16	System table mismatch: Table '%.*ls', object ID %d has index ID 1 in sysindexes but the status in sysobjects does not have the clustered bit set. The table will be checked as a heap.
7992	16	Cannot shrink 'read only' database '%.*ls'.
7993	10	Cannot shrink file '%d' in database '%.*ls' to %d pages as it only contains %d pages.
7994	16	Object ID %d, index ID %d: FirstIAM field in sysindexes is %S_PGID. FirstIAM for statistics only and dummy index entries should be (0:0).
7995	16	Database '%ls' consistency errors in sysobjects, sysindexes, syscolumns, or systypes prevent further %ls processing.
7996	16	Extended stored procedures can only be created in the master database.
7997	16	'%.*ls' does not contain an identity column.
7998	16	Checking identity information: current identity value '%.*hs', current column value '%.*hs'.
7999	16	Could not find any index named '%.*ls' for table '%.*ls'.
8101	16	An explicit value for the identity column in table '%.*ls' can only be specified when a column list is used and IDENTITY_INSERT is ON.
8102	16	Cannot update identity column '%.*ls'.
8103	16	Table '%.*ls' does not exist or cannot be opened for SET operation.
8104	16	The current user is not the database or object owner of table '%.*ls'. Cannot perform SET operation.
8105	16	'%.*ls' is not a user table. Cannot perform SET operation.
8106	16	Table '%.*ls' does not have the identity property. Cannot perform SET operation.
8107	16	IDENTITY_INSERT is already ON for table '%.*ls.%.*ls.%.*ls'. Cannot perform SET operation for table '%.*ls'.
8108	16	Cannot add identity column, using the SELECT INTO statement, to table '%.*ls', which already has column '%.*ls' that inherits the identity property.
8109	16	Attempting to add multiple identity columns to table '%.*ls' using the SELECT INTO statement.

Error	Severity	Description
8110	16	Cannot add multiple PRIMARY KEY constraints to table '%.*ls'.
8111	16	Cannot define PRIMARY KEY constraint on nullable column in table '%.*ls'.
8112	16	Cannot add more than one clustered index for constraints on table '%.*ls'.
8114	16	Error converting data type %ls to %ls.
8115	16	Arithmetic overflow error converting %ls to data type %ls.
8116	16	Argument data type %ls is invalid for argument %d of %ls function.
8117	16	Operand data type %ls is invalid for %ls operator.
8118	16	Column '%.*ls.%.*ls' is invalid in the select list because it is not contained in an aggregate function and there is no GROUP BY clause.
8119	16	Column '%.*ls.%.*ls' is invalid in the HAVING clause because it is not contained in an aggregate function and there is no GROUP BY clause.
8120	16	Column '%.*ls.%.*ls' is invalid in the select list because it is not contained in either an aggregate function or the GROUP BY clause.
8121	16	Column '%.*ls.%.*ls' is invalid in the HAVING clause because it is not contained in either an aggregate function or the GROUP BY clause.
8122	16	Only the first query in a UNION statement can have a SELECT with an assignment.
8123	16	A correlated expression is invalid because it is not in a GROUP BY clause.
8124	16	Multiple columns are specified in an aggregated expression containing an outer reference. If an expression being aggregated contains an outer reference, then that outer reference must be the only column referenced in the expression.
8125	16	An aggregated expression containing an outer reference must be contained in either the select list, or a HAVING clause subquery in the query whose FROM clause contains the table with the column being aggregated.
8126	16	Column name '%.*ls.%.*ls' is invalid in the ORDER BY clause because it is not contained in an aggregate function and there is no GROUP BY clause.
8127	16	Column name '%.*ls.%.*ls' is invalid in the ORDER BY clause because it is not contained in either an aggregate function or the GROUP BY clause.
8128	10	Using '%s' version '%s' to execute extended stored procedure '%s'.
8129	16	The new disk size must be greater than %d. Consider using DBCC SHRINKDB.

Error	Severity	Description
8130	16	The device is not a database device. Only database devices can be expanded.
8131	10	Extended stored procedure DLL '%s' does not export __GetXpVersion(). Refer to the topic "Backward Compatibility Details (Level 1) - Open Data Services" in the documentation for more information.
8132	10	Extended stored procedure DLL '%s' reports its version is %d.%d. Server expects version %d.%d.
8133	16	None of the result expressions in a CASE specification can be NULL.
8134	16	Divide by zero error encountered.
8135	16	Table level constraint does not specify column list, table '%.*ls'.
8136	16	Duplicate columns specified in %ls constraint key list, table '%.*ls'.
8138	16	More than 16 columns specified in foreign key column list, table '%.*ls'.
8139	16	Number of referencing columns in foreign key differs from number of referenced columns, table '%.*ls'.
8140	16	More than one key specified in column level %ls constraint, table '%.*ls'.
8141	16	Column %ls constraint for column '%.*ls' references another column, table '%.*ls'.
8142	16	Subqueries are not supported in %ls constraints, table '%.*ls'.
8143	16	Parameter '%.*ls' was supplied multiple times.
8144	16	Too many arguments were supplied for procedure %.*ls.
8145	16	%.*ls is not a parameter for procedure %.*ls.
8146	16	Procedure %.*ls has no parameters and arguments were supplied.
8147	16	Could not create IDENTITY attribute on nullable column '%.*ls', table '%.*ls'.
8148	16	More than one column %ls constraint specified for column '%.*ls', table '%.*ls'.
8150	16	Multiple NULL constraints were specified for column '%.*ls', table '%.*ls'.
8151	16	Both a PRIMARY KEY and UNIQUE constraint have been defined for column '%.*ls', table '%.*ls'. Only one is allowed.
8152	16	String or binary data would be truncated.
8153	0	Warning: Null value eliminated from aggregate.

Error	Severity	Description
8154	15	The table '%.*ls' is ambiguous.
8155	15	No column was specified for column %d of '%.*ls'.
8156	15	The column '%.*ls' was specified multiple times for '%.*ls'.
8157	15	All the queries in a query expression containing a UNION operator must have the same number of expressions in their select lists.
8158	15	'%.*ls' has more columns than were specified in the column list.
8159	15	'%.*ls' has fewer columns than were specified in the column list.
8160	15	A grouping function can only be specified when either CUBE or ROLLUP is specified in the GROUP BY clause.
8161	15	A grouping function argument does not match any of the expressions in the GROUP BY clause.
8162	16	Formal parameter '%.*ls' was defined as OUTPUT but the actual parameter not declared OUTPUT.
8163	16	The text, ntext, or image data type cannot be selected as DISTINCT.
8164	16	An INSERT EXEC statement cannot be nested.
8166	16	Constraint name '%.*ls' not permitted. Constraint names cannot begin with a number sign (#).
8168	16	Cannot create two constraints named '%.*ls'. Duplicate constraint names are not allowed.
8169	16	Syntax error converting from a character string to uniqueidentifier.
8170	16	Insufficient result space to convert uniqueidentifier value to char.
8175	10	Could not find table %.*ls. Will try to resolve this table name later.
8177	16	Cannot use a column in the %hs clause unless it is contained in either an aggregate function or the GROUP BY clause.
8178	16	Prepared statement '%.*ls' expects parameter %.*ls, which was not supplied.
8179	16	Could not find prepared statement with handle %d.
8180	16	Statement(s) could not be prepared.
8181	16	Text for '%.*ls' is missing from syscomments. The object must be dropped and re-created before it can be used.
8190	16	Cannot compile replication filter procedure without defining table being filtered.
8191	16	Replication filter procedures can only contain SELECT, GOTO, IF, WHILE, RETURN, and DECLARE statements.
8192	16	Replication filter procedures cannot have parameters.

Error	Severity	Description
8193	16	Cannot execute a procedure marked FOR REPLICATION.
8194	16	Cannot execute a USE statement while an application role is active.
8196	16	Duplicate column specified as ROWGUIDCOL.
8197	16	Windows NT user '%.*ls' does not have server access.
8198	16	Could not obtain information about Windows NT group/user '%ls'.
8199	16	In EXECUTE <procname>, procname can only be a literal or variable of type char, varchar, nchar, or nvarchar.
8501	16	MSDTC on server '%.*ls' is unavailable.
8502	20	Unknown MSDTC token '0x%x' received.
8504	20	Invalid transaction import buffer.
8506	20	Invalid transaction state change requested from %hs to %hs.
8508	20	QueryInterface failed for '%hs': %hs.
8509	20	Import of MSDTC transaction failed: %hs.
8510	20	Enlist of MSDTC transaction failed: %hs.
8511	20	Unknown isolation level %d requested from MSDTC.
8512	20	MSDTC Commit acknowledgement failed: %hs.
8513	20	MSDTC Abort acknowledgement failed: %hs.
8514	20	MSDTC PREPARE acknowledgement failed: %hs.
8515	20	MSDTC Global state is invalid.
8517	20	Failed to get MSDTC PREPARE information: %hs.
8518	20	MSDTC BEGIN TRANSACTION failed: %hs.
8519	16	Current MSDTC transaction must be committed by remote client.
8520	20	Commit of internal MSDTC transaction failed: %hs.
8521	20	Invalid awakening state. Slept in %hs; awoke in %hs.
8522	20	Distributed transaction aborted by MSDTC.
8523	15	PREPARE TRAN statement not allowed on MSDTC transaction.
8524	16	The current transaction could not be exported to the remote provider. It has been rolled back.
8525	16	Distributed transaction completed. Either enlist this session in a new transaction or the NULL transaction.
8601	17	Internal Query Processor Error: The query processor could not obtain access to a required interface.

Error	Severity	Description
8602	16	The Index Tuning Wizard cannot process queries which contain index hints. Remove the index hints which reference table '%.*ls'.
8616	10	The index hints for table '%.*ls' were ignored because the table was considered a fact table in the star join.
8617	17	Invalid Query: CUBE and ROLLUP cannot compute distinct aggregates.
8618	17	Warning: The query processor could not produce a query plan from the optimizer because the total length of all the columns in the GROUP BY clause exceeds 8000 bytes.
8619	17	Warning: The query processor could not produce a query plan from the optimizer because the maximum row size of an intermediate result was too large to fit into a work table. Resubmit your query without the ROBUST PLAN hint.
8620	17	Internal Query Processor Error: The query processor encountered an internal limit overflow.
8621	16	Internal Query Processor Error: The query processor ran out of stack space during query optimization.
8622	16	Query processor could not produce a query plan because of the hints defined in this query. Resubmit the query without specifying any hints and without using SET FORCEPLAN.
8623	16	Internal Query Processor Error: The query processor could not produce a query plan.
8624	16	Internal SQL Server error.
8625	16	Warning: The join order has been enforced because a local join hint is used.
8626	16	Only text pointers are allowed in work tables, never text, ntext, or image columns. The query processor produced a query plan that required a text, ntext, or image column in a work table.
8627	16	The query processor could not produce a query plan because of the combination of hints and text, ntext, or image data passing through operators using work tables.
8628	17	A time out occurred while waiting to optimize the query. Rerun the query.
8629	16	The query processor could not produce a query plan from the optimizer because a query cannot update a text, ntext, or image column and a clustering key at the same time.
8630	17	Internal Query Processor Error: The query processor encountered an unexpected error during execution.

Error	Severity	Description
8640	17	Internal Query Processor Error: The query processor encountered an unexpected work table error during execution.
8642	17	The query processor could not start the necessary thread resources for parallel query execution.
8644	16	Internal Query Processor Error: The plan selected for execution does not support the invoked given execution routine.
8645	17	A time out occurred while waiting for memory resources to execute the query. Rerun the query.
8646	21	The index entry for row ID %.*hs was not found in index ID %d, of table %d, in database '%.*ls'.
8647	20	Scan on sysindexes for database ID %d, object ID %ld, returned a duplicate index ID %d. Run DBCC CHECKTABLE on sysindexes.
8648	20	Could not insert a row larger than the page size into a hash table. Resubmit the query with the ROBUSTPLAN hint.
8649	17	The query has been canceled because the estimated cost of this query (%d) exceeds the configured threshold of %d. Contact the system administrator.
8650	13	Intra-query parallelism caused your server command (process ID #%d) to deadlock. Rerun the query without intra-query parallelism by using the query hint option (maxdop 1).
8651	17	Could not perform the requested operation because the minimum query memory is not available. Decrease the configured value for the 'min memory per query' server configuration option.
8680	17	Internal Query Processor Error: The query processor encountered an unexpected error during the processing of a remote query phase.
8901	13	Deadlock detected during DBCC. Complete the transaction in progress and retry this statement.
8902	17	Memory allocation error during DBCC processing.
8903	16	Extent %S_PGID in database ID %d is allocated in both GAM %S_PGID and SGAM %S_PGID.
8904	16	Extent %S_PGID in database ID %d is allocated by more than one allocation object.
8905	16	Extent %S_PGID in database ID %d is marked allocated in the GAM, but no SGAM or IAM has allocated it.
8906	16	Page %S_PGID in database ID %d is allocated in the SGAM %S_PGID and PFS %S_PGID, but was not allocated in any IAM. PFS flags '%hs'.
8907	16	Mixed extent %S_PGID in database ID %d has %d free pages. It should be included in the SGAM %S_PGID.

Error	Severity	Description
8908	16	Table Corrupt: Database ID %d, object ID %d, index ID %d. Chain linkage mismatch. %S_PGID->next = %S_PGID, but %S_PGID->prev = %S_PGID.
8909	16	Table Corrupt: Object ID %d, index ID %d, page ID %S_PGID. The PageId in the page header = %S_PGID.
8910	16	Page %S_PGID in database ID %d is allocated to both object ID %d, index ID %d, and object ID %d, index ID %d.
8911	10	The error has been repaired.
8912	10	%.*ls fixed %d allocation errors and %d consistency errors in database '%ls'.
8913	16	Extent %S_PGID is allocated to '%ls' and at least one other object.
8914	10	Incorrect PFS free space information for page %S_PGID, object ID %d, index ID %d, in database ID %d. Expected value %hs, actual value %hs.
8915	10	%S_PGID (number of mixed extents = %ld, mixed pages = %ld).
8916	10	Object ID %ld, Index ID %ld, data extents %ld, pages %ld, mixed extent pages %ld.
8917	10	Object ID %ld, Index ID %ld, index extents %ld, pages %ld, mixed extent pages %ld.
8918	10	(number of mixed extents = %ld, mixed pages = %ld) in this database.
8919	16	Single page allocation %S_PGID in table %ls, object ID %d, index ID %d is not allocated in PFS page ID %S_PGID.
8920	16	Cannot perform a %ls operation inside a user transaction. Terminate the transaction and reissue the statement.
8921	16	CHECKTABLE terminated. A failure was detected while collecting facts. Possibly tempdb out of space or a system table is corrupt. Check previous errors.
8922	10	Could not repair this error.
8923	10	The repair level on the DBCC statement caused this repair to be bypassed.
8924	10	Repairing this error requires other errors to be corrected first.
8925	16	Table Corrupt: Cross object linkage: Page %S_PGID, slot %d, in object ID %d, index ID %d, refers to page %S_PGID, slot %d, in object ID %d, index ID %d.
8926	16	Table Corrupt: Cross object linkage: Parent page %S_PGID, slot %d, in object ID %d, index ID %d, and page %S_PGID, slot %d, in object ID %d, index ID %d, next refer to page %S_PGID but are not in the same object.

Error	Severity	Description
8927	16	Object ID %d, index ID %d: The ghosted record count (%d) in the header does not match the number of ghosted records (%d) found on page %S_PGID.
8928	16	Object ID %d, index ID %d: Page %S_PGID could not be processed. See other errors for details.
8929	16	Object ID %d: Errors found in text ID %I64d owned by data record identified by %.*ls.
8930	16	Table Corrupt: Object ID %d, index ID %d cross-object chain linkage. Page %S_PGID points to %S_PGID in object ID %d, index ID %d.
8931	16	Table Corrupt: Object ID %d, index ID %d B-tree level mismatch, page %S_PGID. Level %d does not match level %d from parent %S_PGID or previous %S_PGID.
8932	16	Table Corrupt: Object ID %d, index ID %d, column '%.*ls'. The column ID %d is not valid for this table. The valid range is from 1 to %d. System table corruption.
8933	16	Table Corrupt: Object ID %d, index ID %d. The low key value on page %S_PGID (level %d) is not %ls the key value in the parent %S_PGID slot %d.
8934	16	Table Corrupt: Object ID %d, index ID %d. The high key value on page %S_PGID (level %d) is not less than the low key value in the parent %S_PGID, slot %d of the next page %S_PGID.
8935	16	Table Corrupt: Object ID %d, index ID %d. The previous link %S_PGID on page %S_PGID does not match the previous page %S_PGID that the parent %S_PGID, slot %d expects for this page.
8936	16	Table Corrupt: Object ID %d, index ID %d. B-tree chain linkage mismatch. %S_PGID->next = %S_PGID, but %S_PGID->Prev = %S_PGID.
8937	16	Table Corrupt: Object ID %d, index ID %d. B-tree page %S_PGID has two parent nodes %S_PGID, slot %d and %S_PGID, slot %d.
8938	16	Table Corrupt: Page %S_PGID corrupt. Object ID %d, index ID %d. Unexpected page type %d.
8939	16	Table Corrupt: Object ID %d, index ID %d, page %S_PGID. Test (%hs) failed. Values are %ld and %ld.
8940	16	Table Corrupt: Object ID %d, index ID %d, page %S_PGID. Test (%hs) failed. Address 0x%x is not aligned.
8941	16	Table Corrupt: Object ID %d, index ID %d, page %S_PGID. Test (%hs) failed. Slot %d, offset 0x%x is invalid.
8942	16	Table Corrupt: Object ID %d, index ID %d, page %S_PGID. Test (%hs) failed. Slot %d, offset 0x%x overlaps with the prior row.

Error	Severity	Description
8943	16	Table Corrupt: Object ID %d, index ID %d, page %S_PGID. Test (%hs) failed. Slot %d, row extends into freespace at 0x%x.
8944	16	Table Corrupt: Object ID %d, index ID %d, page %S_PGID, row %d. Test (%hs) failed. Values are %ld and %ld.
8945	16	Table Corrupt: Object ID %d, index ID %d will be rebuilt.
8946	16	Table Corrupt: Allocation page %S_PGID has invalid %ls page header values. Type is %d. Check type, object ID and page ID on the page.
8947	16	Table Corrupt: Multiple IAM pages for object ID %d, index ID %d contain allocations for the same interval. IAM pages %S_PGID and %S_PGID.
8948	16	Database Corrupt: Page %S_PGID is marked with the wrong type in PFS page %S_PGID. PFS status 0x%x expected 0x%x.
8949	10	%.*ls fixed %d allocation errors and %d consistency errors in table '%ls' (object ID %d).
8950	16	%.*ls fixed %d allocation errors and %d consistency errors not associated with any single object.
8951	16	Table Corrupt: Table '%ls' (ID %d). Missing or invalid key in index '%ls' (ID %d) for the row:
8952	16	Table Corrupt: Database '%ls', index '%ls.%ls' (ID %d) (index ID %d). Extra or invalid key for the keys:
8953	10	Repair: Deleted text column, text ID %I64d, for object ID %d on page %S_PGID, slot %d.
8954	10	%.*ls found %d allocation errors and %d consistency errors not associated with any single object.
8955	16	Data row (%d:%d:%d) identified by (%ls) has index values (%ls).
8956	16	Index row (%d:%d:%d) with values (%ls) points to the data row identified by (%ls).
8957	10	DBCC %ls (%ls%ls%ls) executed by %ls found %d errors and repaired %d errors.
8958	10	%ls is the minimum repair level for the errors found by DBCC %ls (%ls %ls).
8959	16	Table Corrupt: IAM page %S_PGID for object ID %d, index ID %d is linked in the IAM chain for object ID %d, index ID %d by page %S_PGID.
8960	23	Table Corrupt: Page %S_PGID, slot %d, column %d is not a valid complex column.

Error	Severity	Description
8961	23	Table Corrupt: Object ID %d. The text, ntext, or image node at page %S_PGID, slot %d, text ID %I64d does not match its reference from page %S_PGID, slot %d.
8962	23	Table Corrupt: The text, ntext, or image node at page %S_PGID, slot %d, text ID %I64d has incorrect node type %d.
8963	23	Table Corrupt: The text, ntext, or image node at page %S_PGID, slot %d, text ID %I64d has type %d. It cannot be placed on a page of type %d.
8964	23	Table Corrupt: Object ID %d. The text, ntext, or image node at page %S_PGID, slot %d, text ID %I64d is not referenced.
8965	23	Table Corrupt: Object ID %d. The text, ntext, or image node at page %S_PGID, slot %d, text ID %I64d is referenced by page %S_PGID, slot %d, but was not seen in the scan.
8966	22	Could not read and latch page %S_PGID with latch type %ls. %ls failed.
8967	16	Table Corrupt: Invalid value detected in %ls for Object ID %d, index ID %d. Row skipped.
8968	16	Table Corrupt: %ls page %S_PGID (object ID %d, index ID %d) is out of the range of this database.
8969	16	Table Corrupt: IAM chain linkage error: Object ID %d, index ID %d. The next page for IAM page %S_PGID is %S_PGID, but the previous link for page %S_PGID is %S_PGID.
8970	16	Row corrupt: Object ID %d, index ID %d, page ID %S_PGID, row ID %d. Column '%.*ls' was created NOT NULL, but is NULL in the row.
8971	16	Forwarded row mismatch: Object ID %d, page %S_PGID, slot %d points to forwarded row page %S_PGID, slot %d; the forwarded row points back to page %S_PGID, slot %d.
8972	16	Forwarded row referenced by more than one row. Object ID %d, page %d, slot %d incorrectly points to forwarded row page %S_PGID, slot %d; the forwarded row correctly refers back to page %S_PGID, slot %d.
8973	16	CHECKTABLE processing of object ID %d, index ID %d encountered page %S_PGID, slot %d twice. Possible internal error or allocation fault.
8974	16	Text node referenced by more than one node. Object ID %d, text, ntext, or image node page %S_PGID, slot %d, text ID %I64d is pointed to by page %S_PGID, slot %d and by page %S_PGID, slot %d.
8975	16	Page referenced by more than one page: Object ID %d, index ID %d. Page %S_PGID->next is an unmatched linkage to page %S_PGID. %S_PGID->next matches the previous linkage of the page.

Error	Severity	Description
8976	16	Table Corrupt: Object ID %d, index ID %d. Page %S_PGID not allocated or corrupt. Parent %S_PGID and previous %S_PGID refer to it.
8977	16	Table Corrupt: Object ID %d, index ID %d. Parent node for page %S_PGID was not encountered.
8978	16	Table Corrupt: Object ID %d, index ID %d. Page %S_PGID is missing a reference from previous page %S_PGID. Possible chain linkage problem.
8979	16	Table Corrupt: Object ID %d, index ID %d. Page %S_PGID is missing references from parent (unknown) and previous (page %S_PGID) nodes. Possible bad root entry in sysindexes.
8980	16	Table Corrupt: Object ID %d, index ID %d. Index node page %S_PGID, slot %d refers to child page %S_PGID and previous child %S_PGID, but they were not encountered.
8981	16	Table Corrupt: Object ID %d, index ID %d. The next pointer of %S_PGID refers to page %S_PGID. Neither %S_PGID nor its parent were encountered. Possible bad chain linkage.
8982	16	Table Corrupt: Cross object linkage. Page %S_PGID->next in object ID %d, index ID %d refers to page %S_PGID in object ID %d, index ID %d but is not in the same index.
8983	10	Allocation page %S_PGID. Extents %d, used pages %d, referenced pages %d, mixed extents %d, mixed pages %d.
8984	10	Object ID %d, index ID %d. Allocations for %S_PGID. IAM %S_PGID, extents %d, used pages %d, mixed pages %d.
8985	16	Could not locate file '%.*ls' in sysfiles.
8986	16	Too many errors found (%d) for object ID %d. To see all error messages rerun the statement using "WITH ALL_ERRORMSGS".
8987	16	No help available for DBCC statement '%.*ls'.
8988	10	The schema for database '%ls' is changing. May find spurious allocation problems due to schema changes in progress.
8989	10	%.*ls found %d allocation errors and %d consistency errors in database '%ls'.
8990	10	%.*ls found %d allocation errors and %d consistency errors in table '%ls' (object ID %d).
8991	16	0x%.8x + 0x%.8x bytes is not a valid address range.
8992	16	Database ID %d, object '%ls' (ID %d). Loop in data chain detected at %S_PGID.

Error	Severity	Description
8993	16	Object ID %d, forwarding row page %S_PGID, slot %d points to page %S_PGID, slot %d. Did not encounter forwarded row. Possible allocation error.
8994	16	Object ID %d, forwarded row page %S_PGID, slot %d should be pointed to by forwarding row page %S_PGID, slot %d. Did not encounter forwarding row. Possible allocation error.
8995	16	System table '%.*ls' (object ID %d, index ID %d) is in filegroup %d. All system tables must be in filegroup %d.
8996	16	IAM page %S_PGID for object ID %d, index ID %d controls pages in filegroup %d, that should be in filegroup %d.
8997	16	Single page allocation %S_PGID for object ID %d, index ID %d is in filegroup %d; it should be in filegroup %d.
8998	16	Page corruptions on the GAM, SGAM, or PFS pages do not allow CHECKALLOC to verify database ID %d pages from %S_PGID to %S_PGID. See other errors for cause.
8999	10	Database tempdb allocation errors prevent further %ls processing.
9001	10	The log for database '%.*ls' is not available.
9002	19	The log file for database '%.*ls' is full. Back up the transaction log for the database to free up some log space.
9003	20	The LSN %S_LSN passed to log scan in database '%.*ls' is invalid.
9004	21	The log for database '%.*ls' is corrupt.
10000	16	Unknown provider error.
10001	16	The provider reported an unexpected catastrophic failure.
10002	16	The provider did not implement the functionality.
10003	16	The provider ran out of memory.
10004	16	One or more arguments were reported invalid by the provider.
10005	16	The provider did not support an interface.
10006	16	The provider indicated an invalid pointer was used.
10007	16	The provider indicated an invalid handle was used.
10008	16	The provider terminated the operation.
10009	16	The provider did not give any information about the error.
10010	16	The data necessary to complete this operation was not yet available to the provider.
10021	16	Execution terminated by the provider because a resource limit was reached.

Error	Severity	Description
10022	16	The provider called a method from IRowsetNotify in the consumer, and the method has not yet returned.
10023	16	The provider does not support the necessary method.
10024	16	The provider indicates that the user did not have the permission to perform the operation.
10031	16	An error occurred because one or more properties could not be set.
10032	16	Cannot return multiple result sets (not supported by the provider).
10033	16	The specified index does not exist or the provider does not support an index scan on this data source.
10034	16	The specified table does not exist.
10035	16	No value was given for one or more of the required parameters.
10041	16	Could not set any property values.
10042	16	Cannot set any properties while there is an open rowset.
10051	16	An error occurred while setting the data.
10052	16	The insertion was canceled by the provider during notification.
10053	16	Could not convert the data value due to reasons other than sign mismatch or overflow.
10054	16	The data value for one or more columns overflowed the type used by the provider.
10055	16	The data violated the integrity constraints for one or more columns.
10056	16	The number of rows that have pending changes has exceeded the limit specified by the DBPROP_MAXPENDINGROWS property.
10057	16	Cannot create the row. Would exceed the total number of active rows supported by the rowset.
10058	16	The consumer cannot insert a new row before releasing previously-retrieved row handles.
10061	16	An error occurred while setting data for one or more columns.
10062	16	The change was canceled by the provider during notification.
10063	16	Could not convert the data value due to reasons other than sign mismatch or overflow.
10064	16	The data value for one or more columns overflowed the type used by the provider.
10065	16	The data violated the integrity constraints for one or more columns.
10066	16	The number of rows that have pending changes has exceeded the limit specified by the DBPROP_MAXPENDINGROWS property.

Error	Severity	Description
10067	16	The rowset was using optimistic concurrency and the value of a column has been changed after the containing row was last fetched or resynchronized.
10068	16	The consumer could not delete the row. A deletion is pending or has already been transmitted to the data source.
10069	16	The consumer could not delete the row. The insertion has been transmitted to the data source.
10075	16	An error occurred while deleting the row.
10081	16	The rowset uses integrated indexes and there is no current index.
10085	16	RestartPosition on the table was canceled during notification.
10086	16	The table was built over a live data stream and the position cannot be restarted.
10087	16	The provider did not release some of the existing rows.
10088	16	The order of the columns was not specified in the object that created the rowset. The provider had to reexecute the command to reposition the next fetch position to its initial position, and the order of the columns changed.
11000	16	Unknown status code for this column.
11001	16	Non-NULL value successfully returned.
11002	16	Deferred accessor validation occurred. Invalid binding for this column.
11003	16	Could not convert the data value due to reasons other than sign mismatch or overflow.
11004	16	Successfully returned a NULL value.
11005	16	Successfully returned a truncated value.
11006	16	Could not convert the data type because of a sign mismatch.
11007	16	Conversion failed because the data value overflowed the data type used by the provider.
11008	16	The provider cannot allocate memory or open another storage object on this column.
11009	16	The provider cannot determine the value for this column.
11010	16	The user did not have permission to write to the column.
11011	16	The data value violated the integrity constraints for the column.
11012	16	The data value violated the schema for the column.
11013	16	The column had a bad status.
11014	16	The column used the default value.

Error	Severity	Description
11015	16	The column was skipped when setting data.
11031	16	The row was successfully deleted.
11032	16	The table was in immediate-update mode, and deleting a single row caused more than one row to be deleted in the data source.
11033	16	The row was released even though it had a pending change.
11034	16	Deletion of the row was canceled during notification.
11036	16	The rowset was using optimistic concurrency and the value of a column has been changed after the containing row was last fetched or resynchronized.
11037	16	The row has a pending delete or the deletion had been transmitted to the data source.
11038	16	The row is a pending insert row.
11039	16	DBPROP_CHANGEINSERTEDROWS was VARIANT_FALSE and the insertion for the row has been transmitted to the data source.
11040	16	Deleting the row violated the integrity constraints for the column or table.
11041	16	The row handle was invalid or was a row handle to which the current thread does not have access rights.
11042	16	Deleting the row would exceed the limit for pending changes specified by the rowset property DBPROP_MAXPENDINGROWS.
11043	16	The row has a storage object open.
11044	16	The provider ran out of memory and could not fetch the row.
11045	16	User did not have sufficient permission to delete the row.
11046	16	The table was in immediate-update mode and the row was not deleted due to reaching a limit on the server, such as query execution timing out.
11047	16	Updating did not meet the schema requirements.
11048	16	There was a recoverable, provider-specific error, such as an RPC failure.
11100	16	The provider indicates that conflicts occurred with other properties or requirements.
11101	16	Could not obtain an interface required for text, ntext, or image access.
11102	16	The provider could not support a required row lookup interface.
11103	16	The provider could not support an interface required for the UPDATE/DELETE/INSERT statements.

Error	Severity	Description
11104	16	The provider could not support insertion on this table.
11105	16	The provider could not support updates on this table.
11106	16	The provider could not support deletion on this table.
11107	16	The provider could not support a row lookup position.
11108	16	The provider could not support a required property.
11109	16	The provider does not support an index scan on this data source.
13001	10	data page
13002	10	index page
13003	10	leaf page
13004	10	last
13005	10	root
13006	10	read from
13007	10	send to
13008	10	receive
13009	10	send
13010	10	read
13011	10	wait
13012	10	a USE database statement
13013	10	a procedure or trigger
13014	10	a DISTINCT clause
13015	10	a view
13016	10	an INTO clause
13017	10	an ORDER BY clause
13018	10	a COMPUTE clause
13019	10	a SELECT INTO statement
13020	10	option
13021	10	offset option
13022	10	statistics option
13023	10	parameter option
13024	10	function name

Error	Severity	Description
13026	10	parameter
13027	10	convert specification
13028	10	index
13029	10	table
13030	10	database
13031	10	procedure
13032	10	trigger
13033	10	view
13034	10	default
13035	10	rule
13036	10	system
13037	10	unknown type
13038	10	SET statement
13039	10	column
13040	10	type
13041	10	character string
13042	10	integer
13043	10	identifier
13044	10	number
13045	10	integer value
13046	10	floating point value
13047	10	object
13048	10	column heading
13076	10	an assignment
13077	10	a cursor declaration
13078	10	replication filter
13079	10	variable assignment
13080	10	statistics
13081	10	file
13082	10	filegroup

Error	Severity	Description
13083	10	server
13084	0	write
14001	16	The destination table must not be qualified.
14002	16	Could not find the 'Sync' subsystem with the task ID %ld.
14003	16	You must supply a publication name.
14004	16	%s must be in the current database.
14005	16	Could not drop publication. A subscription exists on it.
14006	16	Could not drop the publication.
14008	11	There are no publications.
14009	11	There are no articles for publication '%s'.
14010	16	The remote server is not defined as a subscription server.
14012	16	The @status parameter value must be either 'active' or 'inactive'.
14013	16	This database is not enabled for publication.
14014	16	The synchronization method (@sync_method) must be either '[bcp] native' or '[bcp] character'.
14015	16	The replication frequency (@repl_freq) must be either 'continuous' or 'snapshot'.
14016	16	The publication '%s' already exists.
14017	16	Invalid @restricted parameter value. Valid options are 'true' or 'false'.
14018	16	Could not create the publication.
14019	16	The @operation parameter value must be either 'add' or 'drop'.
14020	16	Could not obtain the column ID for the specified column. The column was not correctly added to the article.
14021	16	The column was not correctly added to the article.
14022	16	The @property parameter value must be either 'description', 'sync_object', 'type', 'ins_cmd', 'del_cmd', 'upd_cmd', 'filter', 'dest_table', 'dest_object', 'creation_script', 'pre_creation_cmd', 'status', 'schema_option', or 'destination_owner'.
14023	16	The type must be 'logbased', 'logbased manualfilter', 'logbased manualview', or 'logbased manualboth'.
14025	10	The article was successfully updated.
14027	11	%s does not exist in the current database.
14028	16	Only user tables and procedures can be published.

Error	Severity	Description
14029	16	The vertical partition switch must be either 'true' or 'false'.
14030	16	The article '%s' already exists in publication '%s'.
14031	16	User tables and views are the only valid synchronization objects.
14032	16	The value of parameter %s cannot be 'all'. It is reserved by replication stored procedures.
14033	16	Could not change replication frequency because there are active subscriptions on the publication.
14034	16	The publication name (@publication) cannot be the keyword 'all'.
14035	16	The replication option '%s' of database '%s' has already been set to true.
14036	16	Could not enable database for publishing.
14037	16	The replication option '%s' of database '%s' has already been set to false.
14038	16	Could not disable database for publishing.
14039	16	Could not construct column clause for article view. Reduce the number of columns or create the view manually.
14040	16	The server '%s' is already a subscriber.
14042	16	Could not create Subscriber.
14043	16	The parameter %s cannot be NULL.
14044	16	Owner-qualified %s names are not allowed.
14046	16	Could not drop article. A subscription exists on it.
14047	16	Could not drop %s.
14048	16	The server '%s' is not a Subscriber.
14049	16	Stored procedures for replication are the only objects that can be used as a filter.
14050	11	You do not have a subscription on this publication or article.
14051	16	The parameter value must be 'sync_type' or 'dest_db'.
14052	16	The @sync_type parameter value must be 'automatic' or 'none'.
14053	16	The subscription could not be updated at this time.
14054	10	The subscription was successfully updated.
14055	10	The subscription does not exist.
14056	16	The subscription could not be dropped at this time.
14057	16	The subscription could not be created.

Error	Severity	Description
14058	16	The subscription already exists.
14061	16	The @pre_creation_cmd parameter value must be 'none', 'drop', 'delete', or 'truncate'.
14062	10	The Subscriber was dropped.
14063	11	The remote server does not exist or has not been designated as a valid Subscriber.
14065	16	The @status parameter value must be 'active', 'inactive', or 'subscribed'.
14066	16	The previous status must be 'active', 'inactive', or 'subscribed'.
14067	16	The status value is the same as the previous status value.
14068	16	Could not update sysobjects. The subscription status could not be changed.
14069	16	Could not update sysarticles. The subscription status could not be changed.
14070	16	Could not update the distribution database subscription table. The subscription status could not be changed.
14071	16	Could not find the Distributor, or the distribution database, for the local server. The Distributor may not be installed, or the local server may not be configured as a Distribution Publisher at the Distributor.
14074	16	The server '%s' is already listed as a Publisher.
14075	16	The Publisher could not be created at this time.
14076	16	Could not grant replication login privilege to '%s'.
14077	10	The publication was successfully updated.
14078	16	The parameter must be 'description', 'taskid', 'sync_method', 'status', 'repl_freq', 'restricted', 'retention', 'immediate_sync', 'enabled_for_internet', 'allow_push', 'allow_pull', 'allow_anonymous', or 'retention'.
14079	16	Do not qualify the destination object name with a database. Use the 'dest_db' property of sp_changesubscription to specify a destination database.
14080	11	The remote server does not exist or has not been designated as a valid Publisher.
14085	16	The Subscriber information could not be obtained from the Distributor.
14088	16	The table '%s' must have a primary key in order to be published using the transaction-based method.
14091	16	The @type parameter passed to sp_helpreplicationdb must be either 'pub' or 'sub'.

Error	Severity	Description
14092	16	Could not change article because there is an existing subscription to the article.
14093	16	Cannot grant or revoke access directly on publication '%s' because it uses the default publication access list.
14094	16	Could not subscribe to article '%s' because the ODBC Subscriber '%s' does not support the @pre_creation_cmd parameter value 'truncate'.
14095	16	Could not subscribe to publication '%s' because ODBC Subscriber '%s' only supports the @sync_method parameter value 'bcp character' .
14096	16	The path and name of the table creation script must be specified if the @pre_creation_cmd parameter value is 'drop'.
14097	16	The @type parameter value must be 'no column names', 'include column names', 'string literals', or 'parameters'.
14098	16	Cannot drop Distribution Publisher '%s'. The remote Publisher is using '%s' as Distributor.
14099	16	The server '%s' is already defined as a Distributor.
14101	16	The publication '%s' already has a Snapshot Agent defined.
14105	10	You have successfully updated the distribution database property '%s'.
14106	10	Distribution retention periods must be greater than 0.
14107	10	The @max_distretention value must be larger than the @min_distretention value.
14108	10	Removed %ld history records from %s.
14109	10	The @security_mode parameter value must be 0 (SQL Server Authentication) or 1 (Windows NT Authentication).
14110	16	For stored procedure articles, the @property parameter value must be either 'description', 'dest_table', 'dest_object', 'creation_script', 'pre_creation_cmd', 'schema_option', or 'destination_owner'.
14111	16	The @pre_creation_cmd parameter value must be 'none' or 'drop'.
14112	16	This procedure can only be executed against table-based articles.
14113	16	Could not execute '%s'. Check '%s' in the install directory.
14114	16	'%s' is not configured as a Distributor.
14115	16	The property parameter value must be %s.
14117	16	'%s' is not configured as a distribution database.
14118	16	The @type parameter value must be 'proc exec', or 'serializable proc exec'.

Error	Severity	Description
14119	16	Could not add the distribution database '%s'. This distribution database already exists.
14120	16	Could not drop the distribution database '%s'. This distributor database is associated with a Publisher.
14121	16	Could not drop the Distributor '%s'. This Distributor has associated distribution databases.
14122	16	The @article parameter value must be 'all' for immediate_sync publications.
14123	16	The subscription @sync_type parameter value 'manual' is no longer supported.
14124	16	An immediate_sync publication must have at least one article before it can be subscribed to.
14126	16	You do not have the required permissions to complete the operation.
14128	16	Invalid @subscription_type parameter value. Valid options are 'push' or 'pull'.
14129	16	The @status parameter value must be NULL for 'automatic' sync_type when you add subscriptions to an immediate_sync publication.
14135	16	There is no subscription on Publisher '%s', publisher database '%s', publication '%s'.
14136	16	The keyword 'all' is reserved by replication stored procedures.
14137	16	The @value parameter value must be either 'true' or 'false'.
14138	16	The @optname parameter value must be either 'publish' or 'merge publish'.
14139	16	The replication system table '%s' already exists.
14143	16	Cannot drop Distributor Publisher '%s'. There are Subscribers associated with it in the distribution database '%s'.
14144	16	Cannot drop Subscriber '%s'. There are subscriptions from it in the published database '%s'.
14146	16	The article parameter '@schema_option' cannot be NULL.
14147	16	Restricted publications are no longer supported.
14148	16	Invalid '%s' value. Valid values are 'true' or 'false'.
14149	10	Removed %ld replication history records in %s seconds (%ld row/secs).
14150	10	Replication-%s: agent %s succeeded. %s
14151	18	Replication-%s: agent %s failed. %s

Error	Severity	Description
14152	10	Replication-%s: agent %s scheduled for retry. %s
14153	10	Replication-%s: agent %s warning. %s
14154	16	The Distributor parameter must be '@heartbeat_interval'.
14155	16	Invalid article ID specified for procedure script generation.
14156	16	The custom stored procedure was not specified in the article definition.
14157	10	The subscription created by Subscriber '%s' to publication '%s' has expired and has been dropped.
14158	10	Replication-%s: agent %s: %s.
14159	16	Could not change property '%s' for article '%s' because there is an existing subscription to the article.
14200	16	The specified '%s' is invalid.
14201	10	0 (all steps) ..
14202	10	before or after @active_start_time
14203	10	sp_helplogins [excluding Windows NT groups]
14204	10	0 (non-idle), 1 (executing), 2 (waiting for thread), 3 (between retries), 4 (idle), 5 (suspended), 7 (performing completion actions)
14205	10	(unknown)
14206	10	0..n seconds
14207	10	-1 [no maximum], 0..n
14208	10	1..7 [1 = E-mail, 2 = Pager, 4 = NetSend]
14209	10	0..127 [1 = Sunday .. 64 = Saturday]
14210	10	notification
14211	10	server
14212	10	(all jobs)
14213	16	Core Job Details:
14214	16	Job Steps:
14215	16	Job Schedules:
14216	16	Job Target Servers:
14217	16	SQL Server Warning: '%s' has performed a forced defection of TSX server '%s'. Run sp_delete_targetserver at the MSX in order to complete the defection.
14218	10	hour

Error	Severity	Description
14219	10	minute
14220	10	second
14221	16	This job has one or more notifications to operators other than '%s'. The job cannot be targeted at remote servers as currently defined.
14222	16	Cannot rename the '%s' operator.
14223	16	Cannot modify or delete operator '%s' while this server is a %s.
14224	0	Warning: The server name given is not the current MSX server ('%s').
14225	16	Warning: Could not determine local machine name. This prevents MSX operations from being posted.
14226	0	%ld history entries purged.
14227	0	Server defected from MSX '%s'. %ld job(s) deleted.
14228	0	Server MSX enlistment changed from '%s' to '%s'.
14229	0	Server enlisted into MSX '%s'.
14230	0	SP_POST_MSX_OPERATION: %ld %s download instruction(s) posted.
14231	0	SP_POST_MSX_OPERATION Warning: The specified %s ('%s') is not involved in a multiserver job.
14232	16	Specify either a job_name, job_id, or an originating_server.
14233	16	Specify a valid job_id (or 0x00 for all jobs).
14234	16	The specified '%s' is invalid (valid values are returned by %s).
14235	16	The specified '%s' is invalid (valid values are greater than 0 but excluding %ld).
14236	0	Warning: Non-existent step referenced by %s.
14237	16	When an action of 'REASSIGN' is specified, the New Login parameter must also be supplied.
14238	0	%ld jobs deleted.
14239	0	%ld jobs reassigned to %s.
14240	0	Job applied to %ld new servers.
14241	0	Job removed from %ld servers.
14242	16	Only a system administrator can reassign ownership of a job.
14243	0	Job '%s' started successfully.
14244	16	Only a system administrator can reassign tasks.

Error	Severity	Description
14245	16	Specify either the @name, @id, or @loginname of the task(s) to be deleted.
14246	16	Specify either the @currentname or @id of the task to be updated.
14247	16	Only a system administrator can view tasks owned by others.
14248	16	This login is the owner of %ld job(s). You must delete or reassign these jobs before the login can be dropped.
14249	16	Specify either @taskname or @oldloginname when reassigning a task.
14250	16	The specified %s is too long. It must contain no more than %ld characters.
14251	16	Cannot specify '%s' as the operator to be notified.
14252	16	Cannot perform this action on a job you do not own.
14253	0	%ld (of %ld) job(s) stopped successfully.
14254	0	Job '%s' stopped successfully.
14255	16	The owner ('%s') of this job is either an invalid login, or is not a valid user of database '%s'.
14256	16	Cannot start job '%s' (ID %s) because it does not have any job server(s) defined.
14257	16	Cannot stop job '%s' (ID %s) because it does not have any job server(s) defined.
14258	16	Cannot perform this operation while SQLServerAgent is starting. Try again later.
14259	16	A schedule (ID %ld, '%s') for this job with this definition already exists.
14260	16	You do not have sufficient permission to run this command.
14261	16	The specified %s ('%s') already exists.
14262	16	The specified %s ('%s') does not exist.
14263	16	Target server '%s' is already a member of group '%s'.
14264	16	Target server '%s' is not a member of group '%s'.
14265	25	The MSSQLServer service terminated unexpectedly.
14266	16	The specified '%s' is invalid (valid values are: %s).
14267	16	Cannot add a job to the '%s' job category.
14268	16	There are no jobs at this server that originated from server '%s'.
14269	16	Job '%s' is already targeted at server '%s'.
14270	16	Job '%s' is not currently targeted at server '%s'.

Error	Severity	Description
14271	16	A target server cannot be named '%s'.
14272	16	Object-type and object-name must be supplied as a pair.
14273	16	You must provide either @job_id or @job_name (and, optionally, @schedule_name), or @schedule_id.
14274	16	Cannot add, update, or delete a job (or its steps or schedules) that originated from an MSX server.
14275	16	The originating server must be either '(local)' or '%s'.
14276	16	'%s' is a permanent %s category and cannot be deleted.
14277	16	The command script does not destroy all the objects that it creates. Revise the command script.
14278	16	The schedule for this job is invalid (reason: %s).
14279	16	Supply either @job_name or @originating_server.
14280	16	Supply either a job name (and job aspect), or one or more job filter parameters.
14281	0	Warning: The @new_owner_login_name parameter is not necessary when specifying a 'DELETE' action.
14282	16	Supply either a date (created or last modified) and a data comparator, or no date parameters at all.
14283	16	Supply @target_server_groups or @target_servers, or both.
14284	16	Cannot specify a job ID for a new job. An ID will be assigned by the procedure.
14285	16	Cannot add a local job to a multiserver job category.
14286	16	Cannot add a multiserver job to a local job category.
14287	16	The '%s' supplied has an invalid %s.
14288	16	%s cannot be less than %s.
14289	16	%s cannot contain '%s' characters.
14290	16	This job is currently targeted at the local server so cannot also be targeted at a remote server.
14291	16	This job is currently targeted at a remote server so cannot also be targeted at the local server.
14292	16	There are two or more tasks named '%s'. Specify %s instead of %s to uniquely identify the task.
14293	16	There are two or more jobs named '%s'. Specify %s instead of %s to uniquely identify the job.
14294	16	Supply either %s or %s to identify the job.

Error	Severity	Description
14295	16	Frequency Type 0x2 (OnDemand) is no longer supported.
14296	16	This server is already enlisted into MSX '%s'.
14297	16	Cannot enlist into the local machine.
14298	16	This server is not currently enlisted into an MSX.
14299	16	Server '%s' is an MSX. Cannot enlist one MSX into another MSX.
14300	16	Circular dependencies exist. Dependency evaluation cannot continue.
14301	16	Logins other than the current user can only be seen by members of the sysadmin role.
14302	16	You must upgrade your client to version 6.5 of SQL-DMO and SQL Server Enterprise Manager to connect to this server. The upgraded versions will administer both SQL Server version 6.5 and 6.0 (if sqlole65.sql is run).
14500	16	Supply either a non-zero message ID, non-zero severity, or non-null performance condition.
14501	16	An alert ('%s') has already been defined on this condition.
14502	16	The @target_name parameter must be supplied when specifying an @enum_type of 'TARGET'.
14503	16	The @target_name parameter should not be supplied when specifying an @enum_type of 'ALL' or 'ACTUAL'.
14504	16	'%s' is the fail-safe operator. You must make another operator the fail-safe operator before '%s' can be dropped.
14505	16	Specify a null %s when supplying a performance condition.
14506	16	Cannot set alerts on message ID %ld.
14507	16	A performance condition must be formatted as: 'object_name|counter_name|instance_name|comparator(> or < or =)|numeric value'.
14539	16	Only a Standard or Enterprise edition of SQL Server can be enlisted into an MSX.
14540	16	Only a SQL Server running on Microsoft Windows NT can be enlisted into an MSX.
14541	16	The version of the MSX (%s) is not recent enough to support this TSX. Version %s or later is required at the MSX.
14542	16	It is invalid for any TSQL step of a multiserver job to have a non-null %s value.
14543	16	Login '%s' owns one or more multiserver jobs. Ownership of these jobs can only be assigned to members of the %s role.

Error	Severity	Description
14544	16	This job is owned by '%s'. Only a job owned by a member of the %s role can be a multiserver job.
14545	16	The %s parameter is not valid for a job step of type '%s'.
14546	16	The %s parameter is not supported on Windows 95/98 platforms.
14547	10	Warning: This change will not be downloaded by the target server(s) until an %s for the job is posted using %s.
14548	10	Target server '%s' does not have any jobs assigned to it.
14549	10	(Description not requested.)
14550	10	Command-Line Subsystem
14551	10	Replication Snapshot Subsystem
14552	10	Replication Transaction-Log Reader Subsystem
14553	10	Replication Distribution Subsystem
14554	10	Replication Merge Subsystem
14555	10	Active Scripting Subsystem
14556	10	Transact-SQL Subsystem
14557	10	[Internal]
14558	10	(encrypted command)
14559	10	(append output file)
14560	10	(include results in history)
14561	10	(normal)
14562	10	(quit with success)
14563	10	(quit with failure)
14564	10	(goto next step)
14565	10	(goto step)
14566	10	(idle)
14567	10	(below normal)
14568	10	(above normal)
14569	10	(time critical)
14570	10	(Job outcome)
14571	10	No description available.
14572	10	@freq_interval must be at least 1 for a daily job.

Error	Severity	Description
14573	10	@freq_interval must be a valid day of the week bitmask [Sunday = 1 .. Saturday = 64] for a weekly job.
14574	10	@freq_interval must be between 1 and 31 for a monthly job.
14575	10	@freq_relative_interval must be one of 1st (0x1), 2nd (0x2), 3rd [0x4], 4th (0x8) or Last (0x10).
14576	10	@freq_interval must be between 1 and 10 (1 = Sunday .. 7 = Saturday, 8 = Day, 9 = Weekday, 10 = Weekend-day) for a monthly-relative job.
14577	10	@freq_recurrence_factor must be at least 1.
14578	10	Starts whenever the CPU usage has remained below %ld percent for %ld seconds.
14579	10	Automatically starts when SQLServerAgent starts.
14580	10	job
14585	16	Only the owner of DTS Package '%s' or a member of the sysadmin role may reassign its ownership.
14586	16	Only the owner of DTS Package '%s' or a member of the sysadmin role may create new versions of it.
14587	16	Only the owner of DTS Package '%s' or a member of the sysadmin role may drop it or any of its versions.
14588	10	ID.VersionID =
14589	10	[not specified]
14590	16	DTS Package '%s' already exists with a different ID in this category.
14591	16	DTS Category '%s' already exists in the specified parent category.
14592	16	DTS Category '%s' was found in multiple parent categories. You must uniquely specify the category to be dropped.
14593	16	DTS Category '%s' contains packages and/or other categories. You must drop these first, or specify a recursive drop.
14594	10	DTS Package
14595	16	DTS Package '%s' exists in different categories. You must uniquely specify the package.
14596	16	DTS Package '%s' exists in another category.
14597	16	DTS Package ID '%s' already exists with a different name.
14598	16	Cannot drop the Local, Repository, or LocalDefault DTS categories.
14599	10	Name

Error	Severity	Description
15000	16	Only members of the sysadmin role or the database owner can execute this stored procedure.
15001	16	%s does not exist.
15002	16	The procedure '%s' cannot be executed within a transaction.
15003	16	Only members of the %s role can execute this stored procedure.
15004	16	Name cannot be NULL.
15005	0	Statistics for all tables have been updated.
15006	16	'%s' is not a valid name because it contains invalid characters.
15007	16	The login '%s' does not exist.
15008	16	User '%s' does not exist in the current database.
15009	16	The object '%s' does not exist in database '%s'.
15010	16	The database '%s' does not exist. Use sp_helpdb to show available databases.
15011	16	Database option '%s' does not exist.
15012	16	The device '%s' does not exist. Use sp_helpdevice to show available devices.
15013	0	Table '%s': No columns without statistics found.
15014	16	The role '%s' does not exist in the current database.
15015	16	The server '%s' does not exist. Use sp_helpserver to show available servers.
15016	16	The default '%s' does not exist.
15017	16	The rule '%s' does not exist.
15018	0	Table '%s': Creating statistics for the following columns:
15019	16	The extended stored procedure '%s' does not exist.
15020	0	Statistics have been created for the %d listed columns of the above tables.
15021	16	There are no remote users mapped to any local user from remote server '%s'.
15022	16	The specified user name is already aliased.
15023	16	User or role '%s' already exists in the current database.
15024	16	The group '%s' already exists in the current database.
15025	16	The login '%s' already exists.
15026	16	Logical device '%s' already exists.

Error	Severity	Description
15027	16	There are no remote users mapped to local user '%s' from remote server '%s'.
15028	16	The server '%s' already exists.
15029	16	The data type '%s' already exists in the current database.
15030	16	The read-only bit cannot be turned off because the database is in standby mode.
15031	0	'Virtual_device' device added.
15032	16	The database '%s' already exists.
15033	16	'%s' is not a valid official language name.
15034	16	The application role password must not be NULL.
15035	16	'%s' is not a database device.
15036	16	The data type '%s' does not exist.
15037	16	The physical data type '%s' does not allow nulls.
15038	16	User-defined data types based on timestamp are not allowed.
15039	16	The language %s already exists in syslanguages.
15040	16	User-defined error messages must have an ID greater than 50000.
15041	16	User-defined error messages must have a severity level between 1 and 25.
15042	16	Only members of the sysadmin role can add messages with severity levels greater than 18 or those which use the TRUE (for WITH_LOG) option.
15043	16	You must specify 'REPLACE' to overwrite an existing message.
15044	16	'%s' is an unknown device type. Use 'disk', 'tape', or 'pipe'.
15045	16	The logical name cannot be NULL.
15046	16	The physical name cannot be NULL.
15047	16	The only permitted options for a tape device are 'skip' and 'noskip'.
15048	0	Valid values of database compatibility level are %d, %d, or %d.
15049	11	Cannot unbind from '%s'. Use ALTER TABLE DROP CONSTRAINT.
15050	11	Cannot bind default '%s'. The default must be created using the CREATE DEFAULT statement.
15051	11	Cannot rename the table because it is published for replication.
15052	0	Prior to updating sysdatabases entry for database '%s', mode = %d and status = %d (status suspect_bit = %d).

Error	Severity	Description
15053	16	Objects exist which are not owned by the database owner.
15054	0	The current compatibility level is %d.
15055	11	Error. Updating sysdatabases returned @@error <> 0.
15056	0	No row in sysdatabases was updated because mode and status are already correctly reset. No error and no changes made.
15057	16	List of %s name contains spaces, which are not allowed.
15058	16	List of %s has too few names.
15059	16	List of %s has too many names.
15060	16	List of %s names contains name(s) which have '%s' non-alphabetic characters.
15061	16	Add device request denied. A physical device named '%s' already exists.
15062	16	The guest user cannot be mapped to a login name.
15063	16	The login already has an account under a different user name.
15064	11	PRIMARY KEY and UNIQUE KEY constraints do not have space allocated.
15065	16	All user IDs have been assigned.
15066	16	A default-name mapping of a remote login from remote server '%s' already exists.
15067	16	'%s' is not a local user. Remote login denied.
15068	16	A remote user '%s' already exists for remote server '%s'.
15069	16	One or more users are using the database. The requested operation cannot be completed.
15070	0	Object '%s' was successfully marked for recompilation.
15071	16	Usage: sp_addmessage <msgnum>,<severity>,<msgtext> [,<language> [,FALSE | TRUE [,REPLACE]]]
15072	16	Usage: sp_addremotelogin remoteserver [, loginame [,remotename]]
15073	0	For row in sysdatabases for database '%s', the status bit %d was forced off and mode was forced to 0.
15074	0	Warning: You must recover this database prior to access.
15075	16	The data type '%s' is reserved for future use.
15076	16	Default, table, and user data types must be in the current database.
15077	16	Rule, table, and user data type must be in the current database.

Error	Severity	Description
15078	16	The table or view must be in the current database.
15079	10	Queries processed: %d.
15082	11	NULL is not an acceptable parameter value for this procedure. Use a percent sign instead.
15084	16	The column or user data type must be in the current database.
15085	16	Usage: sp_addtype name, 'data type' [,'NULL' | 'NOT NULL']
15086	16	Invalid precision specified. Precision must be between 1 and 38.
15087	16	Invalid scale specified. Scale must be less than precision and positive.
15088	16	The physical data type is fixed length. You cannot specify the length.
15089	11	Cannot change the '%s' option of a database while another user is in the database.
15090	16	There is already a local server.
15091	16	You must specify a length with this physical data type.
15092	16	Invalid length specified. Length must be between 1 and 8000 bytes.
15093	16	'%s' is not a valid date order.
15094	16	'%s' is not a valid first day.
15095	16	Insert into syslanguages failed. Language not added.
15096	16	Only members of the sysadmin role or '%s' can change the default language for '%s'.
15100	16	Usage: sp_bindefault defaultname, objectname [, 'futureonly']
15101	16	Cannot bind a default to a column of data type timestamp.
15102	16	Cannot bind a default to an identity column.
15103	16	Cannot bind a default to a column created with or altered to have a default value.
15104	16	You do not own a table named '%s' that has a column named '%s'.
15105	16	You do not own a data type with that name.
15106	16	Usage: sp_bindrule rulename, objectname [, 'futureonly']
15107	16	Cannot bind a rule to a column of data type text, ntext, image, or timestamp.
15108	16	Only members of the sysadmin role can change the owner of a database.
15109	16	Cannot change the owner of the master database.
15110	16	The proposed new database owner is already a user in the database.

Error	Severity	Description
15111	16	The proposed new database owner is already aliased in the database.
15123	16	The configuration option '%s' does not exist, or it may be an advanced option.
15124	16	The configuration option '%s' is not unique.
15125	16	Only members of the sysadmin role can change configuration parameters.
15127	16	Cannot set the default language to a language ID not defined in syslanguages.
15129	16	'%d' is not a valid value for configuration option '%s'.
15131	16	Usage: sp_dbremove <dbname> [,dropdev]
15132	16	Cannot change default database belonging to someone else.
15134	16	No alias exists for the specified user.
15139	16	The device is a RAM disk and cannot be used as a default device.
15140	16	Usage: sp_diskdefault logicalname {defaulton | defaultoff}
15142	16	Cannot drop the role '%s'.
15143	16	'%s' is not a valid option for the @updateusage parameter. Enter either 'true' or 'false'.
15144	16	The role has members. It must be empty before it can be dropped.
15174	16	Login '%s' owns one or more database(s). Change the owner of the following database(s) before dropping login:
15175	16	Login '%s' is aliased or mapped to a user in one or more database(s). Drop the user or alias before dropping the login.
15176	16	The only valid @parameter value is 'WITH_LOG'.
15177	16	Usage: sp_dropmessage <msg number> [,<language> | 'ALL']
15178	16	Cannot drop a message with an ID less than 50000.
15179	16	Message number %u does not exist.
15180	16	Cannot drop. The data type is being used.
15181	16	Cannot drop the database owner.
15182	16	Cannot drop the guest user from master or tempdb.
15183	16	The user owns objects in the database and cannot be dropped.
15184	16	The user owns data types in the database and cannot be dropped.
15185	16	There is no remote user '%s' mapped to local user '%s' from the remote server '%s'.

Error	Severity	Description
15190	16	There are still remote logins for the server '%s'.
15191	16	Usage: sp_dropserver server [, droplogins]
15193	16	This procedure can only be used on system tables.
15194	16	Cannot re-create index on this table.
15197	16	There is no text for object '%s'.
15198	16	The name supplied (%s) is not a user, role, or aliased login.
15200	16	There are no remote servers defined.
15201	16	There are no remote logins for the remote server '%s'.
15202	16	There are no remote logins defined.
15203	16	There are no remote logins for '%s'.
15204	16	There are no remote logins for '%s' on remote server '%s'.
15205	16	There are no servers defined.
15206	16	Invalid Remote Server Option: '%s'.
15210	16	Only members of the sysadmin role can use the loginame option. The password was not changed.
15211	16	Old (current) password incorrect for user. The password was not changed.
15216	16	'%s' is not a valid option for the @delfile parameter.
15218	16	Object '%s' is not a table.
15219	16	You do not own table '%s'. Only members of the sysadmin role or the table owner may perform this action.
15220	16	Usage: sp_remoteoption [remoteserver, loginame, remotename, optname, {true | false}]
15221	16	Remote login option does not exist or cannot be set by user. Run sp_remoteoption with no parameters to see options.
15222	16	Remote login option '%s' is not unique.
15223	11	Error: The input parameter '%s' is not allowed to be null.
15224	11	Error: The value for the @newname parameter contains invalid characters or violates a basic restriction (%s).
15225	11	No item by the name of '%s' could be found in the current database '%s', given that @itemtype was input as '%s'.
15226	16	Only members of the sysadmin role can change the name of a database.

Error	Severity	Description
15227	16	The database '%s' cannot be renamed.
15228	16	A member of the sysadmin role must set database '%s' to single user mode with sp_dboption before it can be renamed.
15229	16	Usage: sp_serveroption [server [,optname [,'true' | 'false']]]
15230	16	Server option '%s' does not exist or cannot be set by user. Run sp_serveroption with no parameters to see options.
15231	16	Server option '%s' is not unique.
15232	16	Only members of the sysadmin role may set server options.
15234	16	Object is stored in sysprocedures and has no space allocated directly.
15235	16	Views do not have space allocated.
15236	16	Column '%s' has no default.
15237	16	User data type '%s' has no default.
15238	16	Column '%s' has no rule.
15239	16	User data type '%s' has no rule.
15241	16	Usage: sp_dboption [dbname [,optname [,'true' | 'false']]]
15242	16	Database option '%s' is not unique.
15243	16	The option '%s' cannot be changed for the master database.
15244	16	Only members of the sysadmin role or the database owner may set database options.
15245	16	DBCC DBCONTROL error. Database was not placed offline.
15248	11	Error: The parameter @oldname is either ambiguous or the claimed @itemtype (%s) was wrong.
15249	11	Error: Explicit @itemtype '%s' is unrecognized (%d).
15250	16	The database name component of the object qualifier must be the name of the current database.
15251	16	Invalid '%s' specified. It must be %s.
15252	16	The primary or foreign key table name must be given.
15253	11	Syntax error parsing SQL identifier '%s'.
15254	16	Users other than the database owner or guest exist in the database. Drop them before removing the database.
15255	11	'%s' is not a valid value for @autofix. The only valid value is 'auto'.
15256	16	Usage: sp_certify_removable <dbname> [,'auto']

Error	Severity	Description
15257	16	The database that you are attempting to certify cannot be in use at the same time.
15258	16	The database must be owned by a member of the sysadmin role before it can be removed.
15261	16	Usage: sp_create_removable <dbname>,<syslogical>,<sysphysical>,<syssize>,<loglogical>,<logphysical>,<logsize>,<datalogical1>,<dataphysical1>,<datasize1> [,<datalogical2>,<dataphysical2>,<datasize2>...<datalogical16>,<dataphysical16>,<datasize16>]
15262	0	Invalid file size entered. All files must be at least 1 MB.
15264	16	Could not create the '%s' portion of the database.
15266	16	Cannot make '%s' database removable.
15269	16	Logical data device '%s' not created.
15270	16	You cannot specify a length for user data types based on sysname.
15271	16	Invalid @with_log parameter value. Valid values are 'true' or 'false'.
15275	16	FOREIGN KEY constraints do not have space allocated.
15277	16	The only valid @parameter_value values are 'true' or 'false'.
15278	16	Login '%s' is already mapped to user '%s' in database '%s'.
15279	16	You must add the us_english version of this message before you can add the '%s' version.
15280	16	All localized versions of this message must be dropped before the us_english version can be dropped.
15283	16	The name '%s' contains too many characters.
15284	16	The user has granted or revoked privileges to the following in the database and cannot be dropped.
15285	16	The special word '%s' cannot be used for a logical device name.
15286	16	Terminating this procedure. The @action '%s' is unrecognized. Try 'REPORT', 'UPDATE_ONE', or 'AUTO_FIX'.
15287	16	Terminating this procedure. '%s' is a forbidden value for the login name parameter in this procedure.
15288	16	Terminating this procedure. Only %s has the permissions to run the action '%s'.
15289	16	Terminating this procedure. Cannot have an open transaction when this is run.
15290	16	Terminating this procedure. The Action '%s' is incompatible with the other parameter values ('%s', '%s').

Error	Severity	Description
15291	16	Terminating this procedure. The %s name '%s' is absent or invalid.
15292	0	The row for user '%s' will be fixed by updating its login link to a login already in existence.
15293	0	Barring a conflict, the row for user '%s' will be fixed by updating its link to a new login. Consider changing the new password from null.
15294	0	The number of orphaned users fixed by adding new logins and then updating users was %d.
15295	0	The number of orphaned users fixed by updating users was %d.
15298	0	New login created.
15300	11	No recognized letter is contained in the parameter value for General Permission Type (%s). Valid letters are in this set: %s .
15302	11	Database_Name should not be used to qualify owner.object for the parameter into this procedure.
15303	11	The "user options" config value (%d) was rejected because it would set incompatible options.
15304	16	The severity level of the '%s' version of this message must be the same as the severity level (%ld) of the us_english version.
15305	16	The @TriggerType parameter value must be 'insert', 'update', or 'delete'.
15306	16	Cannot change the compatibility level of replicated or distributed databases.
15307	16	Could not change the merge publish option because the server is not set up for replication.
15308	16	You must set database '%s' to single user mode with sp_dboption before fixing indexes on system tables.
15311	16	The file named '%s' does not exist.
15312	16	The file named '%s' is a primary file and cannot be removed.
15318	0	All fragments for database '%s' on device '%s' are now dedicated for log usage only.
15319	17	Error: DBCC DBREPAIR REMAP failed for database '%s' (device '%s').
15321	16	There was some problem removing '%s' from sysaltfiles.
15322	0	File '%s' was removed from tempdb, and will take effect upon server restart.
15323	16	The selected index does not exist on table '%s'.
15324	16	The option %s cannot be changed for the '%s' database.

Error	Severity	Description
15325	16	The current database does not contain a %s named '%ls'.
15326	0	No extended stored procedures exist.
15327	0	The database is now offline.
15328	0	The database is offline already.
15330	11	There are no matching rows on which to report.
15331	11	The user '%s' cannot take the action auto_fix because another user has SUID = %d.
15333	11	Error: The qualified @oldname references a database (%s) other than the current database.
15334	11	Error: Only members of the sysadmin role or the database owner can rename items they do not own.
15335	11	Error: The @newname value '%s' is already in use as a %s name and would cause a duplicate that is not permitted.
15337	0	Caution: sysdepends shows that other objects (views, procedures and so on) are referencing this object by its old name. These objects will become invalid, and should be dropped and re-created promptly.
15338	0	The %s was renamed to '%s'.
15339	0	Creating '%s'.
15340	0	Alias user added.
15341	0	Granted database access to '%s'.
15342	0	Replacing message.
15343	0	New message added.
15354	0	Usage: sp_detachdb <dbname>, [TRUE|FALSE]
15358	0	User-defined filegroups should be made read-only.
15363	16	The role '%s' already exists in the current database.
15379	11	The server option value '%s' supplied is unrecognized.
15386	11	For input parameter @OptionName you entered the value '%s'. The number of valid option names matching this value is %d (not equal to 1). Terminating this procedure.
15387	11	If the qualified object name specifies a database, that database must be the current database.
15388	11	There are no objects matching the input name '%s' in the current database.
15389	11	The value '%s' for the @OptionValue parameter is unrecognized.

Error	Severity	Description
15390	11	Only members of the sysadmin role or the database owner can modify '%s' settings for objects owned by other users.
15391	0	All %d matched objects now have their '%s' setting as '%s'. Updates were required for %d objects.
15392	11	Only members of the sysadmin role can modify the settings for option %s.
15393	16	Commit service transaction (XACT) ID does not exist.
15395	11	The qualified old name could not be found for item type '%s'.
15396	11	Cannot change option %s for an object without first performing a DROP statement then a CREATE statement.
15397	11	Could not change option %s. Not more than one object can be changed per execution for this option. %d objects match the parameter values in the current attempt.
15398	11	Only objects in the master database and owned by a member of the sysadmin role can have the setting changed for option %s.
15399	11	Could not change option %s. This type of change is restricted to objects that have no parameters or columns.
15400	11	Could not change an object of type %s. The setting of option %s cannot be changed for objects of this type. Bypassing object '%s'. Other valid, matching objects will be processed now.
15401	11	Windows NT user or group '%s' not found. Check the name again.
15402	11	'%s' is not a fixed server role.
15403	11	Insufficient permission to add a member to the fixed role '%s'.
15405	11	Cannot use the reserved user or role name '%s'.
15407	11	'%s' is not a valid Windows NT name. Give the complete name: <domain\username>.
15409	11	'%s' is not a role.
15410	11	User or role '%s' does not exist in this database.
15412	11	'%s' is not a known fixed role.
15413	11	Cannot make a role a member of itself.
15415	11	User is a member of more than one group. sp_changegroup is set up for backward compatibility and expects membership in one group at most.
15416	16	Usage: sp_dbcmptlevel [dbname [, compatibilitylevel]]
15417	16	Insufficient permission to change the compatibility level of the '%s' database.

Error	Severity	Description
15418	16	Only members of the sysadmin role or the database owner may set the database compatibility level.
15419	16	Supplied parameter @sid should be binary(16).
15420	16	The group '%s' does not exist in this database.
15421	16	The user owns role(s) in the database and cannot be dropped.
15422	16	Application roles can only be activated at the ad hoc level.
15423	0	The password for application role '%s' has been changed.
15424	0	New role added.
15425	0	New application role added.
15426	16	You must specify a provider name with this set of properties.
15427	16	You must specify a provider name for unknown product '%ls'.
15428	16	You cannot specify a provider or any properties for product '%ls'.
15429	16	'%ls' is an invalid product name.
15430	19	Limit exceeded for number of servers.
15431	16	You must specify the @rolename parameter.
15432	16	Stored procedure '%s' can only be executed at the ad hoc level.
15433	16	Supplied parameter @sid is in use.
15434	16	Could not drop login '%s' as the user is currently logged in.
15435	0	Database successfully published.
15436	0	Database successfully enabled for subscriptions.
15437	0	Database successfully published using merge replication.
15438	0	Database is already online.
15439	0	Database is now online.
15440	0	Database is no longer published.
15441	0	Database is no longer enabled for subscriptions.
15442	0	Database is no longer enabled for merge publications.
15443	0	Checkpointing database that was changed.
15444	0	'Disk' device added.
15445	0	'Diskette' device added.
15446	0	'Tape' device added.
15447	0	'Pipe' device added.

Error	Severity	Description
15448	0	New remote login created.
15449	0	Type added.
15450	0	New language inserted.
15451	0	%s messages altered.
15452	0	No alternate languages are available.
15453	0	us_english is always available, even though it is not in syslanguages.
15454	0	Language deleted.
15456	0	Valid configuration options are:
15457	0	Configuration option changed. Run the RECONFIGURE statement to install.
15458	0	Database removed.
15459	0	In the current database, the specified object references the following:
15460	0	In the current database, the specified object is referenced by the following:
15461	0	Object does not reference any object, and no objects reference it.
15462	0	File '%s' closed.
15463	0	Device dropped.
15466	0	Message dropped.
15467	0	Type has been dropped.
15468	0	Remote login dropped.
15469	0	No constraints have been defined for this object.
15470	0	No foreign keys reference this table.
15471	0	The object comments have been encrypted.
15472	0	The object does not have any indexes.
15473	0	Settable remote login options.
15474	11	Only members of the sysadmin role can set remote login options.
15475	0	The database is renamed and in single user mode.
15476	0	A member of the sysadmin role must reset the database to multiuser mode with sp_dboption.
15477	0	Caution: Changing any part of an object name could break scripts and stored procedures.
15478	0	Password changed.

Error	Severity	Description
15479	0	Login dropped.
15480	0	Could not grant login access to '%s'.
15481	0	Granted login access to '%s'.
15482	0	Could not deny login access to '%s'.
15483	0	Denied login access to '%s'.
15484	0	Could not revoke login access from '%s'.
15485	0	Revoked login access from '%s'.
15486	0	Default database changed.
15487	0	%s's default language is changed to %s.
15488	0	'%s' added to role '%s'.
15489	0	'%s' dropped from role '%s'.
15490	0	The dependent aliases were also dropped.
15491	0	User has been dropped from current database.
15492	0	Alias user dropped.
15493	0	Role dropped.
15494	0	The application role '%s' is now active.
15495	0	Application role dropped.
15496	0	Group changed.
15497	0	Could not add login using sp_addlogin (user = %s). Terminating this procedure.
15498	17	Inside txn_1a_, update failed. Will roll back (1a1).
15499	0	The dependent aliases were mapped to the new database owner.
15500	0	The dependent aliases were dropped.
15501	0	Database owner changed.
15502	0	Setting database owner to SA.
15503	0	Giving ownership of all objects to the database owner.
15504	0	Deleting users except guest and the database owner from sysusers.
15505	0	The object owner has been changed.
15506	0	Server added.
15507	0	Remote logins for remote server '%s' have been dropped.
15508	0	Server dropped.

Error	Severity	Description
15509	0	Settable server options.
15510	0	Server network name set.
15511	0	Default bound to column.
15512	0	Default bound to data type.
15513	0	The new default has been bound to columns(s) of the specified user data type.
15514	0	Rule bound to table column.
15515	0	Rule bound to data type.
15516	0	The new rule has been bound to column(s) of the specified user data type.
15517	0	Option %s turned on.
15518	0	Option %s turned off.
15519	0	Default unbound from table column.
15520	0	Default unbound from data type.
15521	0	Columns of the specified user data type had their defaults unbound.
15522	0	Rule unbound from table column.
15523	0	Rule unbound from data type.
15524	0	Columns of the specified user data type had their rules unbound.
15525	0	sp_checknames is used to search for non 7-bit ASCII characters.
15526	0	in several important columns of system tables. The following
15527	0	columns are searched:
15528	0	In master:
15536	0	In all databases:
15543	0	Looking for non 7-bit ASCII characters in the system tables of database '%s'.
15544	0	Table.column '%s'
15545	0	The following database names contain non 7-bit ASCII characters.
15546	0	If you wish to change these names, use '%s'.
15547	0	The following logins have default database names that contain
15548	0	non 7-bit ASCII characters. If you wish to change these names use
15549	0	sp_defaultdb.

Error	Severity	Description
15550	0	The following servers have 'initialization file' names that contain
15551	0	non 7-bit ASCII characters. If you wish to change these names,
15552	0	use UPDATE.
15553	0	Database '%s' has no object, user, and so on
15554	0	names that contain non 7-bit ASCII characters.
15555	0	The database name provided '%s' must be the current database when executing this stored procedure.
15564	0	The following device names contain non 7-bit ASCII characters.
15565	0	The following login names contain non 7-bit ASCII characters.
15566	0	The following remote login names contain non 7-bit ASCII characters.
15567	0	The following server names contain non 7-bit ASCII characters.
15568	0	The following column and parameter names contain non 7-bit ASCII characters.
15569	0	The following index names contain non 7-bit ASCII characters.
15570	0	The following object names contain non 7-bit ASCII characters.
15571	0	The following segment names contain non 7-bit ASCII characters.
15572	0	The following data type names contain non 7-bit ASCII characters.
15573	0	The following user or role names contain non 7-bit ASCII characters.
15600	15	An invalid parameter or option was specified for procedure '%s'.
15601	16	Fulltext Search is not enabled for the current database. Use sp_fulltext_database to enable full-text search.
15602	16	Full-Text catalog '%ls' does not exist.
15603	16	A full-text catalog named '%ls' already exists in this database.
15604	16	Cannot drop full-text catalog '%ls' because it contains a full-text index.
15605	16	A full-text index for table '%ls' has already been created.
15606	16	You must first create a full-text index on table '%ls'.
15607	16	'%ls' is not a valid index to enforce a full-text search key. You must specify a unique, non-nullable, single-column index.
15608	16	Full-text search has already been activated for table '%ls'.
15609	16	Cannot activate full-text search for table '%ls' because no columns have been enabled for full-text search.
15610	16	You must deactivate full-text search on table '%ls' before adding columns to or removing columns from the full-text index.

Error	Severity	Description
15611	16	Column '%ls' of table '%ls' cannot be used for full-text search because it is not a character-based column.
15612	16	DBCC DBCONTROL error. Database was not made read-only.
15613	0	The database is now read-only.
15614	0	The database already is read-only.
15615	16	DBCC DBCONTROL error. Database was not made single user.
15616	0	The database is now single user.
15617	0	The database already is single user.
15618	0	The database is now read/write.
15619	0	The database already is read/write.
15620	0	The database is now multiuser.
15621	0	The database already is multiuser.
15622	10	No permission to access database '%s'.
16801	11	sp_dropwebtask requires at least one defined parameter @outputfile or @procname.
16802	11	sp_dropwebtask cannot find the specified task.
16803	11	sp_runwebtask requires at least one defined parameter @outputfile or @procname.
16804	11	SQL Web Assistant: Could not establish a local connection to SQL Server.
16805	11	SQL Web Assistant: Could not execute the SQL statement.
16806	11	SQL Web Assistant: Could not bind the parameter to the SQL statement.
16807	11	SQL Web Assistant: Could not obtain a bind token.
16808	11	SQL Web Assistant: Could not find the existing trigger. This could be due to encryption.
16809	11	SQL Web Assistant failed on the call to SQLGetData.
16810	11	SQL Web Assistant failed on the call to SQLFetch.
16811	11	SQL Web Assistant failed to bind a results column.
16812	11	SQL Web Assistant: The @query parameter must be specified.
16813	11	SQL Web Assistant: Parameters can be passed either by name or position.
16814	11	SQL Web Assistant: Invalid parameter.

Error	Severity	Description
16815	11	SQL Web Assistant: @procname is not valid.
16816	11	SQL Web Assistant: @outputfile is not valid.
16817	11	SQL Web Assistant: Could not read the given file.
16820	11	SQL Web Assistant failed because the state of the Web task in msdb..MSwebtasks is invalid.
16821	11	SQL Web Assistant: Could not open the output file.
16822	11	SQL Web Assistant: Could not open the template file.
16823	11	SQL Web Assistant: Could not allocate enough memory to satisfy this request.
16824	11	SQL Web Assistant: The template file specified in the Web task has a bad size.
16825	11	SQL Web Assistant: Could not read the template file.
16826	11	SQL Web Assistant: Could not find the specified marker for data insertion in the template file.
16827	11	SQL Web Assistant: Could not write to the output file.
16828	11	SQL Web Assistant: @tabborder must be tinyint.
16829	11	SQL Web Assistant: @singlerow must be 0 or 1. Cannot specify this parameter with @nrowsperpage.
16830	11	SQL Web Assistant: The @blobfmt parameter specification is invalid.
16831	11	SQL Web Assistant: The output file name is mandatory for every column specified in the @blobfmt parameter.
16832	11	SQL Web Assistant: Procedure called with too many parameters.
16833	11	SQL Web Assistant: @nrowsperpage must be a positive number and it cannot be used with @singlerow.
16834	11	SQL Web Assistant: Read/write operation on text, ntext, or image column failed.
16838	11	SQL Web Assistant: Could not find the table in the HTML file.
16839	11	SQL Web Assistant: Could not find the matching end table tag in the HTML file.
16841	11	SQL Web Assistant: The @datachg parameter cannot be specified with the given @whentype value.
16842	11	SQL Web Assistant: Could not find and drop the necessary trigger for updating the Web page.

Error	Severity	Description
16843	11	SQL Web Assistant: Could not add the necessary trigger for the @datachg parameter. There could be an existing trigger on the table with missing or encrypted text.
16844	11	SQL Web Assistant: Incorrect syntax for the @datachg parameter.
16845	11	SQL Web Assistant: @datachg must be specified for the given @whentype option.
16846	11	SQL Web Assistant: @unittype and/or @numunits must be specified for the given @whentype option.
16847	11	SQL Web Assistant: @fixedfont must be 0 or 1.
16848	11	SQL Web Assistant: @bold must be 0 or 1.
16849	11	SQL Web Assistant: @italic must be 0 or 1.
16850	11	SQL Web Assistant: @colheaders must be 0 or 1.
16851	11	SQL Web Assistant: @lastupdated must be 0 or 1.
16852	11	SQL Web Assistant: @HTMLheader must be in the range 1 to 6.
16853	11	SQL Web Assistant: @username is not valid.
16854	11	SQL Web Assistant: @dbname is not valid.
16855	11	SQL Web Assistant: @whentype must be in the range 1 to 9.
16856	11	SQL Web Assistant: @unittype must be in the range 1 to 4.
16857	11	SQL Web Assistant: @targetdate is invalid. It must be a valid date after 1900-01-01.
16858	11	SQL Web Assistant: The @targettime parameter must be between 0 and 240000.
16859	11	SQL Web Assistant: @dayflags must be 1, 2, 4, 8, 16, 32, or 64.
16860	11	SQL Web Assistant: @numunits must be greater than 0.
16861	11	SQL Web Assistant: @targetdate must be specified for the given @whentype option.
16862	11	SQL Web Assistant: @dayflags must be specified for the given @whentype option.
16863	11	SQL Web Assistant: URL specification is invalid.
16864	11	SQL Web Assistant: @blobfmt is invalid. The file must include the full path to the output_file location.
16865	11	SQL Web Assistant: URL hyperlink text column must not be of the image data type.
16866	11	SQL Web Assistant: Could not obtain the number of columns in @query.

Error	Severity	Description
16867	11	SQL Web Assistant: URL hyperlink text column is missing in @query.
16868	11	SQL Web Assistant failed on the call to SQLColAttribute.
16869	11	SQL Web Assistant: Columns of data type image cannot have a template.
16870	11	SQL Web Assistant: Internal error. Could not read @ parameters.
16871	11	SQL Web Assistant: Invalid @charset. Execute sp_enumcodepages for a list of character sets.
16873	11	SQL Web Assistant: Invalid @codepage. Execute sp_enumcodepages for a list of code pages.
16874	11	SQL Web Assistant: Internal error. Cannot translate to the specified code page.
16875	11	SQL Web Assistant: Translation to the desired code page is unavailable on this system.
16876	11	SQL Web Assistant: Internal error. Could not obtain COM interface ID.
16877	11	SQL Web Assistant: Internal error. Could not obtain COM language ID.
16878	11	SQL Web Assistant: Internal error. Could not initialize COM library.
16879	11	SQL Web Assistant: Internal error. Could not translate from Unicode to the specified code page.
16880	11	SQL Web Assistant: Internal error. Could not create translation object. Make sure that the file MLang.dll is in your system directory.
16881	16	SQL Web Assistant: This version is not supported on Win32s of Windows 3.1.
16882	16	SQL Web Assistant: Web task not found. Verify the name of the task for possible errors.
16883	16	SQL Web Assistant: Could not list Web task parameters. xp_readwebtask requires @procname.
16884	16	SQL Web Assistant: Procedure name is required to convert Web tasks.
16885	16	SQL Web Assistant: Could not upgrade the Web task to 7.0. The Web task will remain in 6.5 format and will need to be re-created.
16886	16	SQL Web Assistant: Could not update Web tasks system table. The Web task remains in 6.5 format.
16887	16	SQL Web Assistant: @procname parameter is missing. The parameter is required to upgrade a Web task to 7.0.

Error	Severity	Description
16888	16	SQL Web Assistant: Source code page is not supported on the system. Ensure @charset and @codepage language files are installed on your system.
16889	16	SQL Web Assistant: Could not send Web task row to the client.
16890	16	SQL Web Assistant: ODS error occurred. Could not send Web task parameters.
16901	16	%hs: This feature has not been implemented yet.
16902	16	%hs: The value of parameter %hs is invalid.
16903	16	%hs procedure called with incorrect number of parameters.
16904	16	sp_cursor: optype: You can only specify ABSOLUTE in conjunction with DELETE or UPDATE.
16905	16	The cursor is already open.
16907	16	%hs is not allowed in cursor statements.
16909	16	%hs: The cursor identifier value provided (%x) is not valid.
16911	16	%hs: The fetch type %hs cannot be used with forward only cursors.
16914	16	%hs procedure called with too many parameters.
16915	16	A cursor with the name '%.*ls' already exists.
16916	16	A cursor with the name '%.*ls' does not exist.
16917	16	Cursor is not open.
16922	16	Cursor Fetch: Implicit conversion from data type %s to %s is not allowed.
16924	16	Cursorfetch: The number of variables declared in the INTO list must match that of selected columns.
16925	16	The fetch type %hs cannot be used with dynamic cursors.
16926	16	sp_cursoroption: The column ID (%d) does not correspond to a text, ntext, or image column.
16927	16	sp_cursoroption: The cursor already has a name.
16929	16	The cursor is READ ONLY.
16930	16	The requested row is not in the fetch buffer.
16931	16	There are no rows in the current fetch buffer.
16932	16	The cursor has a FOR UPDATE list and the requested column to be updated is not in this list.
16933	16	The cursor does not include the table being modified.

Error	Severity	Description
16934	16	Optimistic concurrency check failed. The row was modified outside of this cursor.
16935	16	No parameter values were specified for the sp_cursor-%hs statement.
16936	16	sp_cursor: One or more values parameters were invalid.
16937	16	A server cursor is not allowed on a stored procedure with more than one SELECT statement. Use a default result set or client cursor.
16938	16	sp_cursoropen/sp_cursorprepare: The statement parameter can only be a single select or a single stored procedure.
16940	16	Cannot specify UPDLOCK or TABLOCKX with READ ONLY or INSENSITIVE cursors.
16941	16	Cursor updates are not allowed on tables opened with the NOLOCK option.
16942	16	Could not generate asynchronous keyset. The cursor has been deallocated.
16943	16	Could not complete cursor operation because the table schema changed after the cursor was declared.
16944	16	Cannot specify UPDLOCK or TABLOCKX on a read-only table in a cursor.
16945	16	The cursor was not declared.
16946	16	Could not open the cursor because one or more of its tables have gone out of scope.
16947	10	No rows were updated or deleted.
16948	16	The variable '%.*ls' is not a cursor variable, but it is used in a place where a cursor variable is expected.
16949	16	The variable '%.*ls' is a cursor variable, but it is used in a place where a cursor variable is not valid.
16950	10	The variable '%.*ls' does not currently have a cursor allocated to it.
16951	16	The variable '%.*ls' cannot be used as a parameter because a CURSOR OUTPUT parameter must not have a cursor allocated to it before execution of the procedure.
16952	16	A cursor variable cannot be used as a parameter to a remote procedure call.
16953	10	Updatable keyset cursors on remote tables require a transaction with the REPEATABLE_READ or SERIALIZABLE isolation level.
16954	16	Executing SQL directly; no cursor.
16955	16	Could not create an acceptable cursor.

Error	Severity	Description
16956	10	Cursor created was not of the requested type.
16997	16	Could not create cursor because worktable rows of size %d exceed maximum rowsize of %d bytes. Use fewer columns in the declaration.
16998	20	Internal Cursor Error: A cursor work table operation failed.
16999	20	Internal Cursor Error: The cursor is in an invalid state.
17000	10	Usage: sp_autostats <table_name> [, {ON|OFF} [, <index_name>]]
17026	10	Using '%1' version '%2'.
17050	16	initerrlog: Could not open error log file '%1'. Operating system error = %2.
17052	10	%1
17053	16	%1: Operating system error %2 encountered.
17054	16	LogEvent: Failed to report the current event. Operating system error = %1.
17055	16	%1 :%n%2
17059	16	Operating system error %1!d!.
17065	16	SQL Server Assertion: File: <%1>, line = %2!d! %nFailed Assertion = '%3' %4.
17066	16	SQL Server Assertion: File: <%1>, line=%2!d! %nFailed Assertion = '%3'.
17067	16	SQL Server Assertion: File: <%1>, line = %2!d! %n%3.
17068	10	PrintStack Request
17112	16	Invalid command option %1!c!.
17113	16	initconfig: Error %2 opening '%1' for configuration information.
17114	16	initconfig: Error %2 reading configuration information from '%1'.
17117	10	initconfig: Number of user connections reduced to %1!ld!.
17118	10	upinit: Warning: Could not raise priority of %1 thread.
17119	10	initconfig: Number of server processes reduced to %1!ld!.
17120	16	SQL Server could not spawn %1 process.
17121	16	SQL Server could not spawn first connection handler.
17122	16	initdata: Warning: Could not set working set size to %1!d! KB.
17123	16	initdata: Could not create thread local storage.
17127	16	initdata: No memory for kernel buffer hash table.

Error	Severity	Description
17128	16	initdata: No memory for kernel buffers.
17130	16	initdata: No memory for kernel locks.
17131	16	initdata: Not enough memory for descriptor hash tables.
17132	16	initdata: Not enough memory for descriptors.
17134	16	initmaster: Could not allocate process status structure (PSS).
17138	16	Could not allocate enough memory for data initialization.
17140	16	Could not dispatch SQL Server by Service Control Manager. Operating system error = %1.
17141	16	Could not register Service Control Handler. Operating system error = %1.
17142	16	SQL Server has been paused. No new connections will be allowed.
17143	16	%1: Could not set Service Control Status. Operating system error = %2.
17144	10	SQL Server is disallowing new connections due to 'pause' request from Service Control Manager.
17145	10	Service Control Handler received an invalid control code = %1!d!.
17146	10	SQL Server is allowing new connections due to 'continue' request from Service Control Manager.
17147	10	SQL Server terminating because of system shutdown.
17148	10	SQL Server is terminating due to 'stop' request from Service Control Manager.
17150	16	%1: Error in spawning console process.
17151	10	Maximum number of pages in batch I/O is limited to %1!ld!.
17154	16	initdata: Not enough memory for procedure cache/hash table.
17156	16	initeventlog: Could not initiate the EventLog Service for the key '%1'.
17157	16	%1: Could not initialize Communication Layer.
17158	16	Could not use OPENDSNT.DLL version '%1'. OPENDSNT.DLL version '%2' was expected.
17160	16	Could not use SQLEVN70.DLL version '%1'. SQLEVN70.DLL version '%2' was expected.
17161	10	Master device sector size is %1!d!. SQL Server cannot use the NO_BUFFERING option during I/O.
17162	10	SQL Server is starting at priority class '%1'(%2!d! %3 detected).

Error	Severity	Description
17168	16	SQL Server shut down because configured codepage %1!d! is not supported by the
17204	16	%1: Could not open device %2 for virtual device number (VDN) %3!d!.
17207	16	%1: Operating system error %3 during the creation/opening of physical device %2.
17208	16	%1: File '%2' has an incorrect size (%3!d! MB, should be %4!d! MB).
17218	16	%1: Operating system error %2 on device '%3' (virtual page %4).
17249	16	%1: Negative outstanding I/O count in process ID = %2!d!.
17252	16	%1: Actual bytes transferred (%2!d!) does not match requested amount (%3!d!) on device '%4' (virtual page %5).
17253	10	The sector size for device %1 is %2!d!. SQL Server cannot use the NO_BUFFERING option during I/O on this device.
17254	10	Warning: Cannot use NO_BUFFERING option on '%1'. Operating system error %2.
17300	16	Not enough memory for process status structure (PSS) allocation.
17302	16	The maximum limit for connections has been reached.
17303	16	freepss: Bad process status structure (PSS) value.
17304	10	Warning: Clean_process system function called from another thread. Outstanding I/O may not complete.
17308	16	%1: Process %2!d! generated an access violation. SQL Server is terminating this process.
17309	16	The current contents of process' input buffer are '%1'.
17310	16	%1: Process %2!d! generated fatal exception %3!lx! %4. SQL Server is terminating this process.
17311	16	SQL Server is aborting. Fatal exception %1!lx! caught.
17402	10	Database '%1' set to single user mode.
17422	16	closetable: Called with null session descriptor (SDES), server process ID (SPID) %1!d!.
17423	16	closetable: Table already closed for session descriptor (SDES) %1!08lx!.
17424	10	Warning: OPEN OBJECTS parameter may be too low.
17426	16	Run sp_configure to increase the parameter value.
17429	16	The srchindex system function failed for index ID = %1!d!, sridoff = %2!d!.

Error	Severity	Description
17430	10	Database '%1' set to read only mode.
17550	10	DBCC TRACEON %d, server process ID (SPID) %d.
17551	10	DBCC TRACEOFF %d, server process ID (SPID) %d.
17557	16	DBCC DBRECOVER failed for database ID %d.
17558	10	%*** Bypassing recovery for database ID %d.
17560	10	DBCC DBREPAIR: '%ls' index restored for '%ls.%ls'.
17561	10	'%ls' index restored for '%ls.%ls'.
17569	16	DBCC cannot find the library initialization function %ls.
17570	16	DBCC cannot find the function %ls in the library %ls.
17571	20	DBCC function %ls in the library %ls generated an access violation. SQL Server is terminating process %d.
17572	16	DBCC cannot free DLL %ls. SQL Server depends on this DLL to function properly.
17654	10	Warning: Process status structure (PSS) found with open session descriptor (SDES). PSPID %1!d!, PSUID %2!d!, PCURDB %3!d!, range entry %4!d!, SDESP 0x%5!lx!, object ID %6!ld!.
17657	10	Attempting to change default sort order ID from %1!d! to %2!d!.
17658	10	SQL Server started in single user mode. Updates allowed to system catalogs.
17660	10	Starting without recovery.
17661	10	Recovering all databases but not clearing tempdb.
17669	10	Table still open. Database ID %1!d!, table ID %2!ld!.
17674	10	Login: %1 %2, server process ID (SPID): %3!d!, kernel process ID (KPID): %4!d!.
17676	10	SQL Server shutdown due to Ctrl-C or Ctrl-Break signal.
17750	16	Cannot load the DLL %ls, or one of the DLLs it references. Reason: %ls.
17751	16	Cannot find the function %ls in the library %ls. Reason: %ls.
17752	16	Extended procedure memory allocation failed for '%ls'.
17753	16	%.*ls can only be executed in the master database.
17801	16	Unknown internal error value.
17802	16	Could not create server event thread.
17803	16	Insufficient memory available.

Error	Severity	Description
17804	16	Invalid 'nbytes' value.
17805	16	Invalid buffer received from client.
17806	16	Invalid event specification.
17807	16	Invalid event '%1!ld!'.
17808	16	Invalid starting position specified.
17809	10	Could not connect. The maximum number of '%1!ld!' configured user connections are already connected. The system administrator can change the maximum to a higher value using sp_configure.
17810	16	Could not set up Named Pipe.
17811	16	Requested data-conversion does not exist.
17812	16	Data conversion resulted in overflow.
17813	16	Could not convert data due to syntax error in source field.
17814	16	Invalid function parameter.
17815	10	No longer waiting for client connections using '%1!hs!'.
17816	16	No active RPC or parameter value out of range.
17817	16	No active RPC or no parameters.
17818	16	No active RPC or parameter name not found.
17819	16	No active RPC.
17820	16	Invalid data type parameter.
17821	16	Could not set up subchannel.
17822	16	Could not load ListenOn Net-Library '%1!hs!'.
17823	16	Could not read from ListenOn connection.
17824	16	Could not write to ListenOn connection '%1!hs!', loginname '%2!ls!', hostname '%3!ls!'. Connection closed.
17825	16	Could not close ListenOn connection.
17826	16	Could not set up ListenOn connection '%1!hs!'.
17827	10	The maximum number of '%1!ld!' remote connections are currently in use.
17828	16	Could not read from local subchannel Named Pipe.
17829	16	Could not copy buffer to subchannel thread, subchannel closed.
17830	16	A subchannel protocol error has occurred.

Error	Severity	Description
17831	16	Could not load ListenOn Net-Library '%1!hs!' version '%2!hs!'. Need Net-Library version '%3!hs!' or greater.
17832	16	Connection opened but invalid login packet(s) sent. Connection closed.
17833	16	ListenOn connection '%1!hs!' is already in use.
17834	10	Using '%1!hs!' version '%2!hs!' to listen on '%3!hs!'.
17835	16	Configured for local access only.
17836	16	Could not create I/O completion port.
17837	16	char data type%0
17838	16	variable-length char data type%0
17839	16	binary data type%0
17840	16	variable-length binary data type%0
17841	16	1-byte integer data type%0
17842	16	2-byte integer data type%0
17843	16	4-byte integer data type%0
17844	16	bit data type%0
17845	16	datetime data type%0
17846	16	datetime data type, nulls allowed%0
17847	16	money data type%0
17848	16	money data type, nulls allowed%0
17849	16	4-byte float data type, nulls allowed%0
17850	16	8-byte float data type%0
17851	16	8-byte float data type, nulls allowed%0
17852	16	4-byte datetime data type, nulls allowed%0
17853	16	4-byte money data type%0
17854	16	event type%0
17855	16	done packet status field%0
17856	16	error severity type%0
17857	16	4-byte integer data type, nulls allowed%0
17858	16	image data type%0
17859	16	text data type%0

Error	Severity	Description
17868	16	numeric data type%0
17869	16	numeric data type, nulls allowed%0
17870	16	decimal data type%0
17871	16	decimal data type, nulls allowed%0
17872	16	bit data type, nulls allowed%0
17873	16	8000-byte variable-length binary data type%0
17874	16	8000-byte variable-length character data type%0
17875	16	8000-byte binary data type%0
17876	16	8000-byte character data type%0
17877	16	8000-byte Unicode character data type%0
17878	16	8000-byte Unicode variable-length character data type%0
17879	16	Unicode text data type%0
17880	16	uniqueidentifier data type%0
18002	20	Stored function '%.*ls' in the library '%.*ls' generated an access violation. SQL Server is terminating process %d.
18052	16	Error: %1!d!, Severity: %2!d!, State: %3!d!.
18053	16	Error: %1!d!, Severity: %2!d!, State: %3!d!%n%4%5.
18100	10	Process ID %d killed by hostname %.*ls, host process ID %d.
18101	10	Non-Unicode sort order being reconfigured:
18102	10	old value = %d new value = %d
18103	10	Non-Unicode character set also being reconfigured:
18112	10	Non-Unicode sort order successfully changed.
18113	10	SQL Server shutdown after verifying system indexes.
18114	16	Cannot install '%1' because there can be at most %2!d! languages in cache.
18122	10	Unicode locale ID being reconfigured:
18123	10	Unicode comparison style being reconfigured:
18124	10	Unicode collation successfully changed.
18200	16	%1: Backup device ID %2!d! out of range.
18201	16	ksconsole: Cannot create ConsBufMutex: %1.

Error	Severity	Description
18203	16	ksconsole: Cannot create %1 : %2.
18204	16	%1: Backup device '%2' failed to %3. Operating system error = %4.
18205	16	%1: Could not initialize console operation.
18207	16	%1: Null request packet.
18208	16	%1: Backup device ID %2!d! is not active.
18209	16	ksconsole: Could not send request to console client.
18210	16	%1: %2 failure on backup device '%3'. Operating system error %4.
18211	16	ksconsole: Could not receive request from console client.
18213	16	ksconsole: Console input request for type 0x%1!x!, ID 0x%2!x! failed.
18214	16	%1: Server console thread not running.
18215	16	%1: Response type 0x%2!x!, ID 0x%3!x! not found in request.
18216	16	%1: Could not access console mutex. Operating system error %2.
18217	16	%1: Type 0x%2!x! not implemented.
18218	16	%1: Incorrect number of parameters: %2!d!.
18219	16	ksconsole: Could not close console connection.
18221	10	ksconsole: Reinitializing the console.
18223	16	%1: No console client connected. Start CONSOLE.EXE.
18225	10	Tape '%1' (Family ID: %2, sequence %3) mounted on tape drive '%4'.
18227	10	Unnamed tape (Family ID: %1, sequence %2) mounted on tape drive '%3'.
18257	10	%1: Device or media does not support %2.
18264	10	Database backed up with following information: Database: %1, creation date and time: %2(%3), pages dumped: %4!d!, first LSN: %5, last LSN: %6, sort order: %7!d!, striped: %8, number of dump devices: %9!d!, device information: (%10).
18265	10	Log backed up with following information: Database: %1, creation date and time: %2(%3), first LSN: %4, last LSN: %5, striped: %6, number of dump devices: %7!d!, device information: (%8).
18266	10	Database file backed up with following information: Database: %1, creation date and time: %2(%3), file list: (%4), pages dumped: %5!d!, sort order: %6!d!, striped: %7, number of dump devices: %8!d!, device information: (%9).

Error	Severity	Description
18267	10	Database restored: Database: %1, creation date and time: %2(%3), first LSN: %4, last LSN: %5, striped: %6, number of dump devices: %7!d!, device information: (%8).
18268	10	Log restored: Database: %1, creation date and time: %2(%3), first LSN: %4, last LSN: %5, striped: %6, number of dump devices: %7!d!, device information: (%8).
18269	10	Database file restored: Database: %1, creation date and time: %2(%3), file list: (%4), striped: %5, number of dump devices: %6!d!, device information: (%7).
18270	10	Database incremental changes backed up with following information: Database: %1, creation date and time: %2(%3), pages dumped: %4!d!, first LSN: %5, last LSN: %6, full backup LSN: %7, sort order: %8!d!, striped: %9, number of dump devices: %10!d!, device
18271	10	Database incremental changes restored: Database: %1, creation date and time: %2(%3), first LSN: %4, last LSN: %5, striped: %6, number of dump devices: %7!d!, device information: (%8).
18272	16	I/O error on backup or restore restart-checkpoint file '%1'. Operating system error %2. The statement is proceeding but is non-restartable.
18400	16	Checkpoint process is terminating due to a fatal exception.
18450	14	Login failed for user '%ls'. Reason: Not defined as a valid user of a trusted SQL Server connection.
18452	14	Login failed for user '%ls'. Reason: Not associated with a trusted SQL Server connection.
18453	14	Login succeeded for user '%ls'. Connection: Trusted.
18454	14	Login succeeded for user '%ls'. Connection: Non-Trusted.
18455	14	Login succeeded for user '%ls'.
18456	14	Login failed for user '%ls'.
18457	14	Login failed for user '%ls'. Reason: User name contains a mapping character or is longer than 30 characters.
18458	14	Login failed. The maximum simultaneous user count of %d licenses for this server has been exceeded. Additional licenses should be obtained and registered through the Licensing application in the Windows NT Control Panel.
18459	14	Login failed. The maximum workstation licensing limit for SQL Server access has been exceeded.
18460	14	Login failed. The maximum simultaneous user count of %d licenses for this '%ls' server has been exceeded. Additional licenses should be obtained and installed or you should upgrade to a full version.

Error	Severity	Description
18482	16	Could not connect to server '%ls' because '%ls' is not defined as a remote server.
18483	16	Could not connect to server '%ls' because '%ls' is not defined as a remote login at the server.
18485	16	Could not connect to server '%ls' because it is not configured for remote access.
18490	16	Maximum number of processors supported is '%1!ld!'.
18491	16	Could not start due to invalid serial number.
18492	16	The license agreement has been violated for this '%1' version of SQL Server. Cannot start.
18500	16	Could not load startup handler DLL '%1'.
18501	16	Could not load startup handler function '%1'.
18502	16	Could not add startup handler '%1'.
18666	17	Could not free up descriptor in rel_desclosed() system function.
18750	16	%ls: The parameter '%ls' is invalid.
18751	16	%ls procedure called with incorrect number of parameters.
18752	16	Another log reader is replicating the database.
18754	16	Could not open table %d.
18755	16	Could not allocate memory for replication.
18756	16	Could not get replication information for table %d.
18757	16	The database is not published.
18759	16	Replication failure. File '%ls', line %d.
18760	16	Invalid %ls statement for article %d.
18761	16	Commit record at (%ls) has already been distributed. Check DBTABLE.
18762	16	Invalid begin LSN (%ls) for commit record (%ls). Check DBTABLE.
18763	16	Commit record (%ls) reports oldest active LSN as (0:0:0).
18764	16	Execution of filter stored procedure %d failed. See the SQL Server errorlog for more information.
18765	16	Begin LSN specified for replication log scan is invalid.
18766	16	The replbeginlsn field in the DBTABLE is invalid.
18767	16	The specified begin LSN (%ls) for replication log scan occurs before replbeginlsn (%ls).

Error	Severity	Description
18768	16	The specified LSN (%ls) for repldone log scan occurs before the current start of log (%ls).
18769	16	The specified LSN (%ls) for repldone log scan is not a replicated commit record.
18770	16	The specified LSN (%ls) for repldone log scan is not present in the transaction log.
18831	16	;// Database ID %d. Could not find object descriptor for object ID %ld.
18833	16	Database ID %d. Could not find clustered index on system table ID %ld. This index should exist in all databases. Run DBCC CHECKTABLE on sysindexes in the database.
18836	16	Database ID %d. Could not find object ID %ld in sysobjects. This system catalog should exist in all databases. Run DBCC CHECKTABLE on sysobjects in this database.
18841	16	Could not locate entry in sysdatabases for database '%.*ls'. No entry found with that name.
18843	16	Could not find database ID %d in sysdatabases.
18872	16	Rec_finish: getnext SCAN_NOINDEX on sysdatabases.dbid=%d failed.
18874	16	Rec_complete: Could not open controlling database (ID %d) of controlling database in multi-database transaction
18875	16	Recovering database '%.*s'.
18876	16	%d transactions rolled forward in database '%.*ls' (%d).
18877	16	%d transactions rolled back in database '%.*ls' (%d).
18878	16	Recovery complete.
18883	16	;//Database ID %d: Attempt to mark database SUSPECT. Getnext NC scan on sysobjects.dbid failed.
18884	16	;//Database '%.*s' (ID %d). Recovery failed. Run DBCC.
18885	16	Page #%lx from table ID #%ld, database ID #%d, not found in cache.
18886	16	Page #%lx from sysindexes in database ID #%X not in cache after reading it into cache.
18887	16	Cannot recover the master database. Exiting.
18892	16	Extent ID %ld which should belong to syslogs belongs to object ID %ld.
18894	16	No more room in the transaction table.
18895	16	Transaction (%d, %d) not found in the transaction table.

Error	Severity	Description
18901	16	Could not build an allocation map for the database '%.*s'. Database does not have a DBINFO structure.
19000	16	ODBC error encountered, State = %1, native error = %2, error message = %3.
19001	16	Windows NT Error encountered, %1.
19002	16	MS SQL SNMP Extension Agent starting, %1, version %2.
19003	16	MS SQL SNMP Extension Agent reconnecting.
19004	16	MS SQL SNMP Extension Agent stopping.
19020	16	RPC Net-Library listening on: %1.
20001	0	There is no nickname for article '%s' in publication '%s'.
20002	0	The filter '%s' already exists for article '%s' in publication '%s'.
20003	0	Could not generate nickname for '%s'.
20007	16	The system tables for merge replication could not be dropped successfully.
20008	16	The system tables for merge replication could not be created successfully.
20009	16	The article '%s' could not be added to the publication '%s'.
20010	16	The Snapshot Agent corresponding to the publication '%s' could not be dropped.
20011	16	Cannot set incompatible publication properties. The 'allow_anonymous' property of a publication depends on the 'immediate_sync' property.
20012	16	The subscription type '%s' is not allowed on publication '%s'.
20013	16	The publication property '%s' cannot be changed when there are subscriptions on it.
20014	16	Invalid @schema_option value.
20015	16	Could not remove directory '%ls'. Check the security context of xp_cmdshell and close other processes that may be accessing the directory.
20016	16	Invalid @subscription_type value. Valid values are 'pull' or 'anonymous'.
20017	16	The Subscriber side subscription does not exist.
20018	16	The @optional_command_line is too long. Use an agent definition file.

Error	Severity	Description
20019	16	The value must be 'name', 'description', 'subset_filterclause', 'column_tracking', 'article_resolver', 'resolver_procedure', 'status', 'pre_creation_command', 'creation_script', or 'schema_option'.
20020	16	The article resolver supplied is either invalid or nonexistent.
20021	16	The subscription could not be found.
20023	16	Invalid @subscriber_type value. Valid options are 'local', 'global', 'anonymous', or 'repub'.
20025	16	The publication name must be unique. The specified publication name '%s' has already been used.
20026	16	The publication '%s' does not exist.
20027	16	The article '%s' does not exist.
20028	16	The Distributor has not been installed correctly. Could not enable database for publishing.
20029	16	The Distributor has not been installed correctly. Could not disable database for publishing.
20030	16	The article '%s' already exists in another publication with a different column tracking option.
20031	16	Could not delete the row could because it was not present.
20032	16	'%s' is not defined as a Subscriber for '%s'.
20033	16	Invalid publication type.
20034	16	Publication '%s' does not support '%s' subscriptions.
20036	16	The Distributor has not been installed correctly.
20037	16	The article '%s' already exists in another publication with a different article resolver.
20038	16	The article filter could not be added to the article '%s' in the publication '%s'.
20039	16	The article filter could not be dropped from the article '%s' in the publication '%s'.
20040	16	Could not drop the article(s) from the publication '%s'.
20041	16	Transaction rolled back. Could not execute trigger. Retry your transaction.
20043	16	Could not change the article '%s' because the publication has already been activated.
20044	16	The priority property is invalid for local subscribers.
20045	16	You must supply an article name.

Error	Severity	Description
20046	16	The article does not exist.
20047	16	You are not authorized to perform this operation.
20049	16	The priority value should not be larger than 100.0.
20050	16	The retention period must be greater than or equal to %d.
20051	16	The Subscriber is not a registered Subscriber.
20054	16	Current database is not enabled for publishing.
20055	16	Table '%s' cannot be published for merge replication because it has a timestamp column.
20056	16	Table '%s' cannot be republished.
20057	16	The profile name '%s' already exists for the specified agent type.
20058	16	The @agent_type must be 1 (Snapshot), 2 (Logreader), 3 (Distribution), or 4 (Merge)
20059	16	The @profile_type must be 0 (system) or 1 (Custom)
20060	16	Compatibility level can not be smaller than 60.
20061	16	The compatibility level of this database must be set to 70 or higher to be enabled for merge publishing.
20062	16	Update of columns with the rowguidcol property is not allowed.
20064	16	Cannot drop profile. Either it is not defined, or is defined as the default profile.
20065	16	Cannot drop profile, because it is in use.
20066	16	Profile not defined.
20067	16	The parameter name '%s' already exists for the specified profile.
20068	16	The article cannot be created on table '%s' because it has more than %d columns.
20069	16	Cannot validate a merge article that uses looping join filters.
20070	16	Cannot update subscription row.
20072	16	Cannot update Subscriber information row.
20073	16	Articles can only be added or changed at the publisher.
20074	16	Only tables can be published for merge replication.
20075	16	The 'status' parameter value must be either 'active' or 'unsynced'.
20076	16	The @sync_mode parameter value must be 'native' or 'character'.
20077	16	Problem encountered generating replica nickname.

Error	Severity	Description
20078	16	The @property parameter value must be 'sync_type', 'priority', or 'description'.
20079	16	Invalid @subscription_type parameter value. Valid options are 'push', 'pull', or 'both'.
20081	16	Publication property '%s' cannot be NULL.
20084	16	Publication '%s' cannot be subscribed to by Subscriber database '%s'.
20086	16	Publication '%s' does not support the nosync type because it contains a table that does not have a rowguidcol column.
20087	16	You cannot push an anonymous subscription.
20088	16	You can only assign priorities that are greater than or equal to 0 and less than 100.
20089	16	Could not get license information correctly.
20090	16	Could not get version information correctly.
20091	16	sp_mergesubscription_cleanup is used to clean up push subscriptions. Use sp_dropmergepullsubscription to clean up pull or anonymous subscriptions.
20100	16	Cannot drop Subscriber '%s'. There are existing subscriptions.
20500	16	The updatable Subscriber stored procedure '%s' does not exist in sysobjects.
20501	16	Could not insert into sysarticleupdates using sp_articlecolumn.
20502	16	Invalid '%s' value. Valid values are 'read only' or 'sync tran'.
20503	16	Invalid '%s' value in '%s'. The publication is not enabled for updatable Subscribers.
20505	16	Could not drop synchronous update stored procedure '%s' in '%s'.
20506	16	Source table '%s' not found in '%s'.
20507	16	Table '%s' not found in '%s'.
20508	16	Updatable Subscribers: The text/ntext/image values inserted at Subscriber will be NULL.
20509	16	Updatable Subscribers: The text/ntext/image values cannot be updated at Subscriber.
20510	16	Updatable Subscribers: Cannot update identity columns.
20511	16	Updatable Subscribers: Cannot update timestamp columns.
20512	16	Updatable Subscribers: Rolling back transaction.
20515	16	Updatable Subscribers: Rows do not match between Publisher and Subscriber. Refresh rows at Subscriber.

Error	Severity	Description
20516	16	Updatable Subscribers: Replica is not updatable.
20517	16	Updatable Subscribers: Update of replica's primary key is not allowed unless published table has a timestamp column.
20518	16	Updatable Subscribers: INSERT and DELETE operations are not supported unless published table has a timestamp column.
20519	16	Updatable Subscribers: INSERT operations on tables with identity or timestamp columns are not allowed unless a primary key is defined at the Subscriber.
20520	16	Updatable Subscribers: UPDATE operations on tables with identity or timestamp columns are not allowed unless a primary key is defined at the Subscriber.
20521	16	sp_MSmark_proc_norepl: Must be a member of the db_owner or sysadmin roles.
20522	16	sp_MSmark_proc_norepl: Invalid object name '%s'.
20523	16	Could not validate the article '%s'. It is not activated.
20524	10	Table '%s' may be out of synchronization. Rowcount difference (actual: %d, expected: %d). Rowcount method %d used (0 = Full, 1 = Fast).
20525	10	Table '%s' is out of synchronization. Rowcounts (actual: %d, expected %d). Checksum difference (actual: %s, expected: %s).
20526	10	Table '%s' passed rowcount (%d) validation. Rowcount method %d used (0 = Full, 1 = Fast).
20527	10	Table '%s' passed rowcount (%d) and checksum validation. (Note: checksum is not compared for any text and image columns.)
20528	10	Log agent startup message.
20529	10	Starting agent.
20530	10	Run agent.
20531	10	Detect nonlogged agent shutdown.
20532	10	Replication Agent Schedule.
20533	10	Replication agents checkup
20534	10	Detects replication agents that are not actively logging history.
20535	10	Removes replication agent history from the distribution database.
20536	10	Replication: Agent failure
20537	10	Replication: Agent retry
20538	10	Replication: Expired subscription dropped

Error	Severity	Description
20540	10	Replication: Agent success
20541	10	Removes replicated transactions from the distribution database.
20542	10	Detects and removes expired subscriptions from published databases.
20545	10	Default agent profile
20546	10	Verbose history agent profile.
20547	10	Agent profile for detailed history logging.
20548	10	Slow link agent profile.
20549	10	Agent profile for low bandwidth connections.
20550	10	Windows Synchronization Manager profile
20551	10	Profile used by the Windows Synchronization Manager.
20552	10	Could not clean up the distribution transaction tables.
20553	10	Could not clean up the distribution history tables.
20554	10	The agent is suspect. No response within last %ld minutes.
20555	10	6.x publication.
20556	10	Heartbeats detected for all running replication agents.
20557	10	Agent shutdown. For more information see the SQL Server Agent job history for job '%s'.
20558	10	Table '%s' passed full rowcount validation after failing the fast check. DBCC UPDATEUSAGE will be automatically initiated.
20559	10	Conditional Fast Rowcount method requested without specifying an expected count. Fast method will be used.
20560	10	An expected checksum value was passed, but checksums will not be compared because rowcount only checking was requested.
20561	10	Generated expected rowcount value of %d for %s.
20562	10	User delete.
20563	10	No longer belongs in this partial.
20564	10	System delete.
20565	10	Replication: Subscriber has failed data validation
20566	10	Replication: Subscriber has passed data validation
20567	10	Agent history clean up: %s
20568	10	Distribution clean up: %s
20569	10	Expired subscription clean up

Error	Severity	Description
20570	10	Reinitialize subscriptions having data validation failures
20571	10	Reinitializes all subscriptions that have data validation failures.
20572	10	Subscriber '%s' subscription to article '%s' in publication '%s' has been reinitialized after a validation failure.
20573	10	Replication: Subscription reinitialized after validation failure
20574	10	Subscriber '%s' subscription to article '%s' in publication '%s' failed data validation.
20575	10	Subscriber '%s' subscription to article '%s' in publication '%s' passed data validation.
20576	10	Subscriber '%s' subscription to article '%s' in publication '%s' has been reinitialized after a synchronization failure.
20577	10	No entries were found in msdb..sysreplicationalerts.
20578	10	Replication: Agent custom shutdown
20579	10	Generated expected rowcount value of %d and expected checksum value of %s for %s.
20580	10	Heartbeats not detected for some replication agents. The status of these agents have been changed to 'Failed'.
20581	10	Cannot drop server '%s' because it is used as a Distributor in replication.
20582	10	Cannot drop server '%s' because it is used as a Publisher in replication.
20583	10	Cannot drop server '%s' because it is used as a Subscriber in replication.
20584	10	Cannot drop server '%s' because it is used as a Subscriber to Remote Publisher '%s' in replication.
21000	16	Cannot subscribe to an inactive publication.
21001	16	Cannot add a Distribution Agent at the Subscriber for a push subscription.
21002	16	The Distribution Agent for this subscription already exists (%s).
21003	16	Changing publication names is no longer supported.
21004	16	Cannot publish the stored procedure '%s' because it is encrypted.
21005	10	For backward compatibility, sp_addpublisher can be used to add a Distribution Publisher. However, you should use sp_adddistpublisher, which is more flexible.
21006	16	Cannot use sp_addpublisher to add a Distribution Publisher this time. Use sp_adddistpublisher instead.

Error	Severity	Description
21007	16	Cannot add the remote Distributor at this time. Make sure that the local server is configured as a Distribution Publisher at the Distributor.
21008	16	Cannot uninstall the Distributor because there are Subscribers defined.
21009	16	The specified filter procedure is already associated with a table.
21010	16	Removed %ld replicated transactions consisting of %ld statements in %ld seconds (%ld rows/sec).
21011	16	Deactivated subscriptions.
21012	16	Cannot change the 'allow_push' property of the publication to false. There are push subscriptions on it.
21013	16	Cannot change the 'allow_pull' property of the publication to false. There are pull subscriptions on it.
21014	16	The @optname parameter value must be 'transactional' or 'merge'.
21015	16	The replication option '%s' has been set to TRUE already.
21016	16	The replication option '%s' has been set to FALSE already.
21018	16	There are too many consecutive snapshot transactions in the distribution database. Rerun the Log Reader Agent or clean up the distribution database.
21021	16	Drop the Distributor first before you uninstall replication.
21022	16	Cannot set incompatible publication properties. The 'immediate_sync' property of a publication is dependent on the 'independent agent' property of a publication.
21023	16	'%s' is no longer supported.
21024	16	The stored procedure '%s' is already published as an incompatible type.
21025	16	The string being encrypted cannot have null characters.
21026	16	Cannot have an anonymous subscription on a publication that does not have an independent agent.
21027	16	'%s' replication stored procedures are not installed. Use sp_replicationoption to install them first.
21028	16	Replication components are not installed on this server. Run SQL Server Setup again and select the option to install replication.
21029	16	Cannot drop a push subscription entry at the subscriber unless @drop_push is 'true'.
21030	16	Names of SQL Server replication agents cannot be changed.
21031	16	'post_script' is not supported for stored procedure articles.

Error	Severity	Description
21032	16	Could not subscribe because non-SQL Server Subscriber '%s' does not support 'sync tran' update mode.
21033	16	Cannot drop server '%s' as Distribution Publisher because there are databases enabled for replication on that server.
21034	16	Rows inserted or updated at the Subscriber are not allowed to be outside the article partition.
21035	16	You have successfully updated the Distribution Publisher property '%s'.
21036	16	Another %s agent for the subscription(s) is running.
21037	16	Invalid working directory '%s'.
21038	16	Windows NT Authentication mode is not supported by the server.
21039	16	The destination owner name is not supported for publications that can have heterogeneous Subscribers. Use native mode bcp for this functionality.
21040	16	Publication '%s' does not exist.
21041	16	A remote Distribution Publisher is not allowed on this server version.
21042	16	The Distribution Publisher property, 'distributor_password', has no usage and is not supported for a Distributor running on Windows NT.
21043	16	The Distributor is not installed.
21044	16	Cannot ignore the remote Distributor (@ignore_remote_distributor cannot be 1) when enabling the database for publishing or merge publishing.
21045	16	Cannot uninstall the Distributor because there are databases enabled for publishing or merge publishing.
21046	16	Cannot change Distribution Publisher property 'distribution_db' because the remote Publisher is using the current distribution database.
21047	16	Cannot drop the local Distribution Publisher because there are Subscribers defined.
21048	16	Cannot add login '%s' to the publication access list because it does not have access to the distribution server '%s'.
21049	16	The login '%s' does not have access permission on publication '%s'.
21050	16	Only members of the sysadmin or db_owner roles can perform this operation.
21051	16	Could not subscribe because non-SQL Server Subscriber '%s' does not support custom stored procedures.

Error	Severity	Description
21053	16	The parameter must be 'description', 'status', 'retention', 'sync_mode', 'allow_push', 'allow_pull', 'allow_anonymous', 'enabled_for_internet', 'centralized_conflicts', or 'snapshot_ready'.
21054	16	Updatable Subscribers: RPC to Publisher failed.
21055	15	Invalid parameter %s specified for %s.
21056	16	The subscription to publication '%s' has expired or does not exist.
21057	16	Anonymous Subscribers are not allowed to have updatable subscriptions.
21058	16	An updatable subscription to publication '%s' on Subscriber '%s' already exists.
21059	16	Cannot reinitialize subscriptions of non-immediate_sync publications.
21060	16	Could not subscribe because non-SQL Server Subscriber '%s' does not support parameterized statements.
21061	16	Invalid article status %d specified when adding article '%s'.
21062	16	The row size of table '%s' exceeds the replication limitation of 6000 bytes.
21063	16	Table '%s' cannot participate in updatable subscriptions because it is published for merge replication.
21070	16	This subscription does not support automatic reinitialization (subscribed with the 'no sync' option). To reinitialize this subscription, you must drop and re-create the subscription.
21071	10	Cannot reinitialize article '%s' in subscription '%s:%s' to publication '%s' (subscribed with the 'no sync' option).
21072	16	The subscription has not been synchronized within the maximum retention period. You must reinitialize the subscription to receive data.
21073	16	The publication specified does not exist.
21074	16	The subscription has expired and must be reinitialized at the Publisher.
21075	10	The initial snapshot for publication '%s' is not yet available.
21076	10	The inital snapshot for article '%s' is not yet available.
21077	10	Deactivated initial snapshot for anonymous publication(s). New subscriptions must wait for the next scheduled snapshot.
21078	16	Table '%s' does not exist in the Subscriber database.
21079	16	The RPC security information for the Publisher is missing or invalid. Use sp_link_publication to set it.

Error	Severity	Description
21080	16	The timestamp column has to be in the vertical partition of the article that is enabled for updatable subscriptions.
21081	16	Server setting 'Allow triggers to be fired which fire other triggers (nested triggers)' has to be on at updatable subscribers.
21082	16	Database property 'IsRecursiveTriggersEnabled' has to be true for subscribing databases at updatable subscribers.
21083	16	Database compatibility level at immediate-updating Subscribers cannot be less than 7.0.
21084	16	Publication '%s' does not allow anonymous subscriptions.
21085	16	The retention period must be less than retention period for the distribution database.
21086	16	The retention period for the distribution database must be greater than the retention period of any existing non-merge publications.
21087	16	Anonymous Subscribers or Subscribers at this server are not allowed to create merge publications.
21088	10	The initial snapshot for the publication is not yet available.
21107	16	'%ls' is not a table or view.
21108	16	This edition of SQL Server does not support transactional publications.
21109	16	The parameters @xact_seqno_start and @xact_seqno_end must be identical if @command_id is specified.
21110	16	All parameters must be specified if @command_id is specified.
21111	16	'%s' is not a valid parameter for the Snapshot Agent.
21112	16	'%s' is not a valid parameter for the Log Reader Agent.
21113	16	'%s' is not a valid parameter for the Distribution Agent.
21114	16	'%s' is not a valid parameter for the Merge Agent.
21115	16	'%s' is not a valid value for the '%s' parameter. The value must be a positive integer.
21116	16	'%s' is not a valid value for the '%s' parameter. The value must be 1, 2, or 3.
21117	16	'%s' is not a valid value for the '%s' parameter. The value must be 0, 1, or 2.
21118	16	'%s' is not a valid value for the '%s' parameter. The value must be greater than or equal to 0 and less than or equal to 10000.

Error	Severity	Description
21119	16	'%s' is not a valid value for the '%s' parameter. The value must be a non-negative integer.
21120	16	Only members of the sysadmin fixed server role and db_owner fixed database role can drop subscription '%s' to publication '%s'.
21121	16	Only members of the sysadmin fixed server role and '%s' can drop the pull subscription to the publication '%s'.
21122	16	Cannot drop the distribution database '%s' because it is currently in use.
21123	16	The agent profile '%s' could not be found at the Distributor.
21124	16	Cannot find the table name or the table owner corresponding to the alternative table id(nickname) '%d' in sysmergearticles.
21125	16	A table used in merge replication must have at least one non-computed column.
21126	16	Pull subscriptions cannot be created in the same database as the publication.
21127	16	Only global merge subscriptions can be added to database '%s'.
21128	16	Aborting immediate-updating insert trigger because it is not the first trigger to fire.
21129	16	Aborting immediate-updating update trigger because it is not the first trigger to fire.
21130	16	Aborting immediate-updating delete trigger because it is not the first trigger to fire.
21131	16	There are existing subscriptions to heterogeneous publication '%s'. In order to add new articles, you must first drop the existing subscriptions to the publication.
21132	16	Cannot create transactional subscription to merge publication '%s'. The publication type should be either transactional(0) or snapshot(1) for this operation.
21133	16	Publication '%s' is not enabled to use an independent agent.

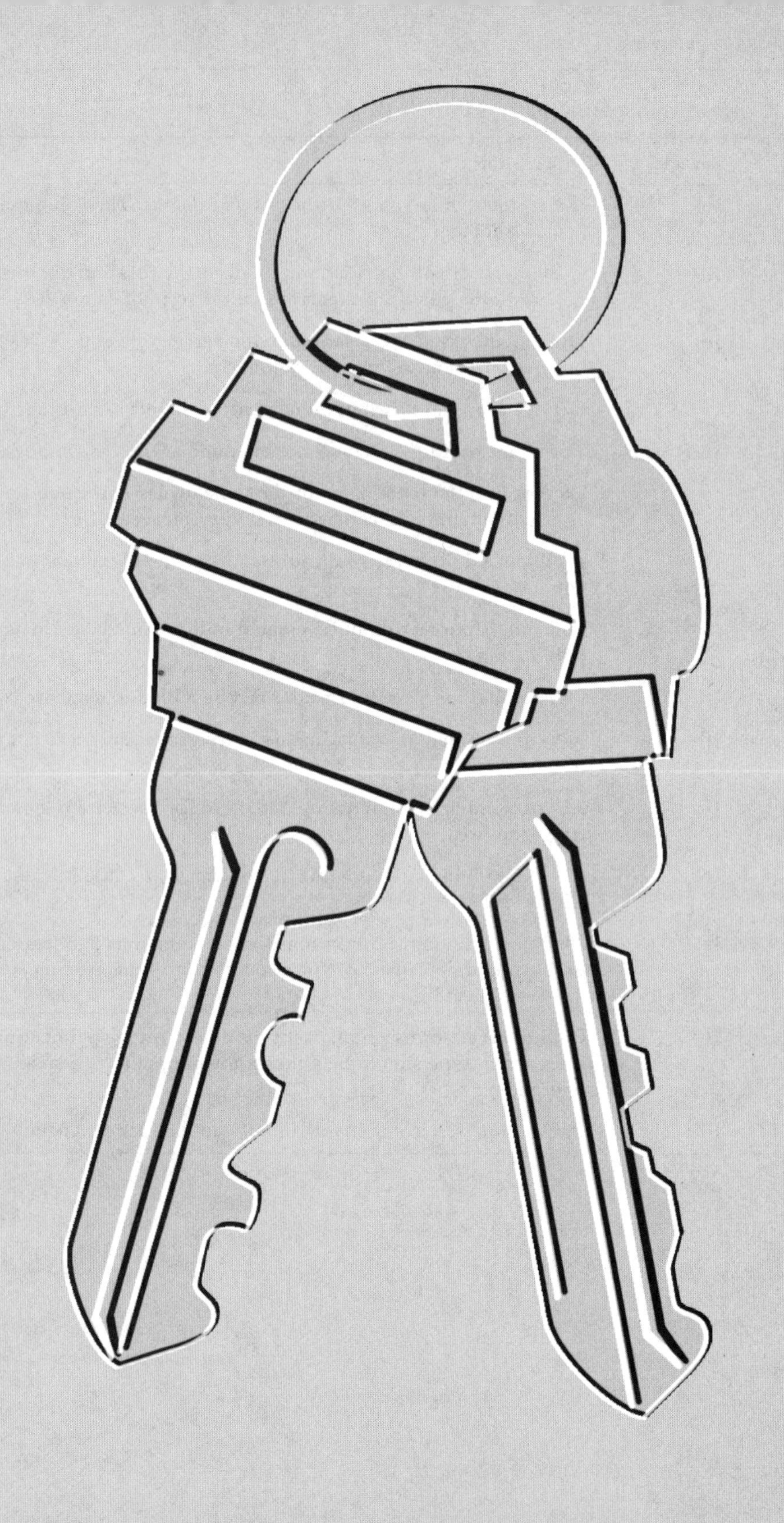

E

Access Upsizing

If you've started out on Access, and have now decided that it's just not meeting your needs anymore – you're not the first. Don't take that as a bad mark on Access, it's just that Access tends to be used often in places it was never intended for. It starts out honestly enough – we design a simple little database that we're going to use to keep track of some things. After all, there's no sense in going to the expense of a big RDBMS if you already have Access – right?

Then the problems start. Your work colleague figures out that you have some information they want, and so you give them access to your database. Then you decide to add a couple of features, and a few more people want to have access too. It doesn't take long before your database is growing too large, too fast, with too many users connected to it all at once.

Fortunately, a few years ago, Microsoft decided to save us all from ourselves. They created the Access Upsizing Wizard. This chapter is all about walking you through a quick demonstration of using that wizard.

> *Most of the wizard is self-guiding – that is, you don't really have to think about all that much. As such, I'm just going to get you familiar with it by walking through a quick example, and pointing out things where you are most likely to have questions.*

OK, let's start by opening up the `Contact` sample database that is included in Access 2000.

> *If you're still running Access '97 and don't have `Contact`, don't worry too much. Much of the wizard is the same, and you should be able to use pretty much any Access database (it's the concepts that matter, not the specific database). Just use whatever database you have and follow along as best you can.*

Make sure that no forms or anything apart from the database window open.

Using The Wizard

To start the wizard, navigate to the Tools menu and the Database Utilities submenu:

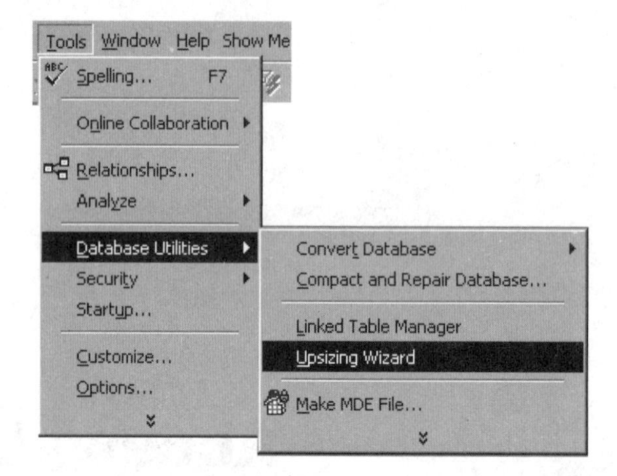

If this is the first time that you've used the Upsizing Wizard, then you are probably going to get a message indicating that it isn't installed.

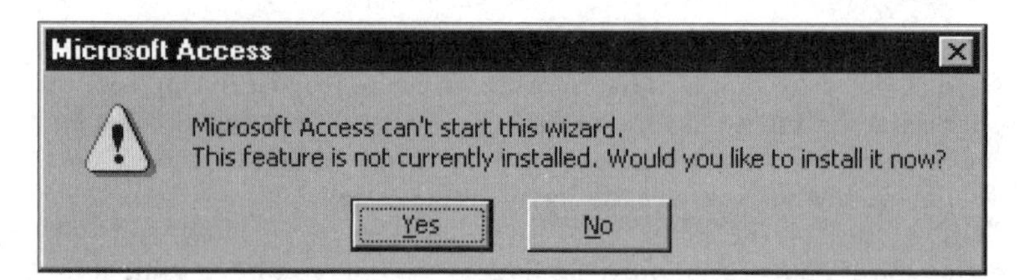

Choose yes, and follow the instructions to load the wizard (you will probably have to insert your Office CD).

After it's installed you should get the following dialog (if you get an error about database objects being open, close all forms except for the database window).

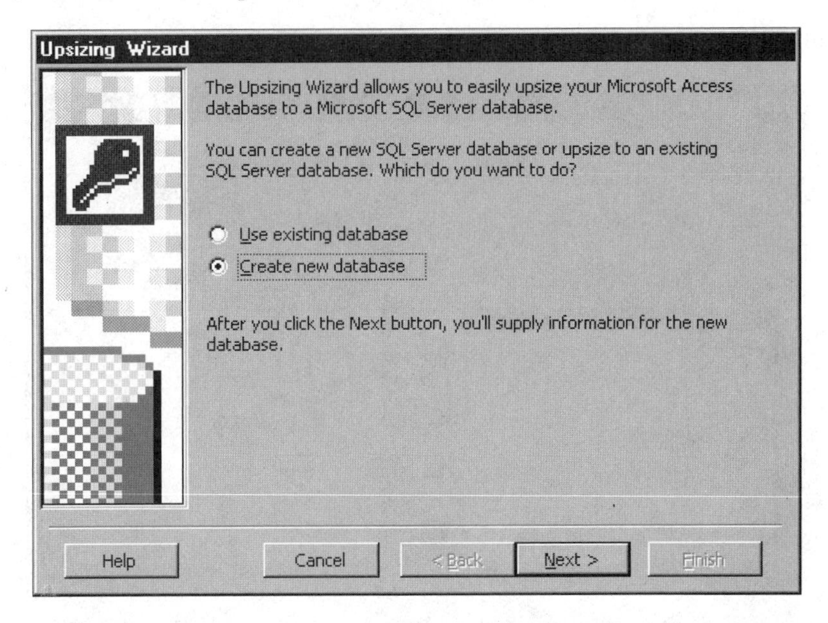

You can either create an entirely new database from right within the wizard, or you can have the wizard move your database objects into an existing database.

I'm going to choose Create new database here since I don't have any database set up to accept the contents of this database. This choice causes a dialog to come up to ask us about the server and the database we want to create on that server:

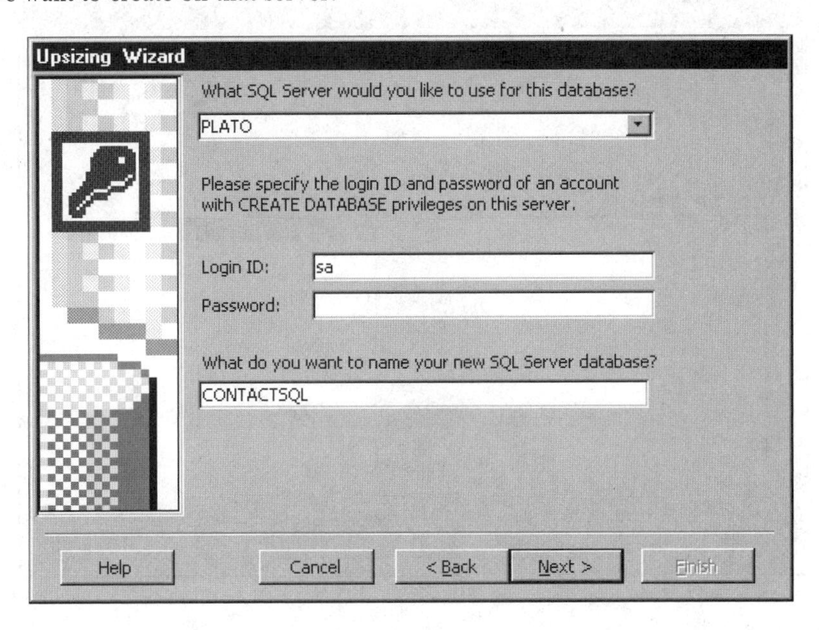

Enter in your server and login information (remember that the login that you use will need to have proper authority granted to it to be able to create a database).

The Upsizing Wizard then prompts you for the tables that you want to upsize:

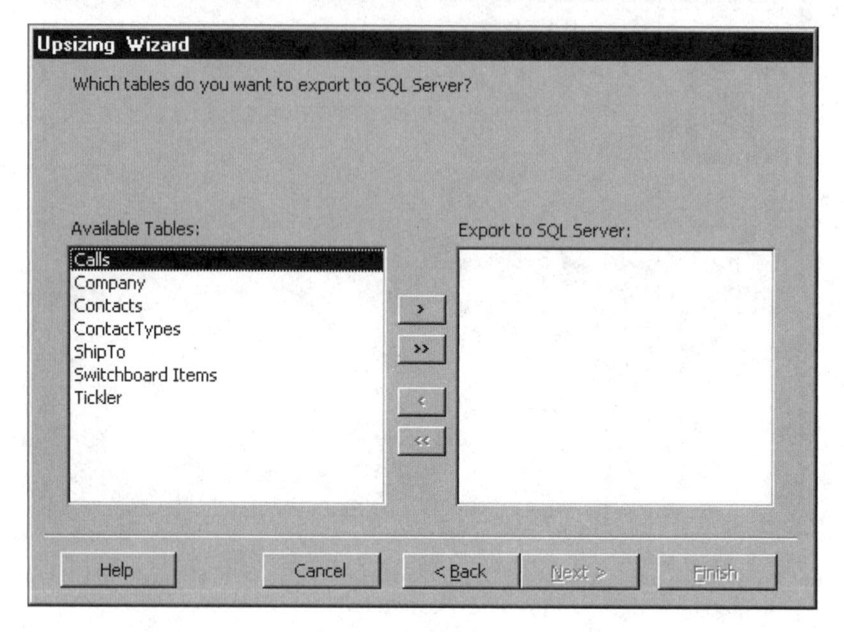

We're going to choose to move all of the tables over – so just click on the double-chevron that points to the right (>>):

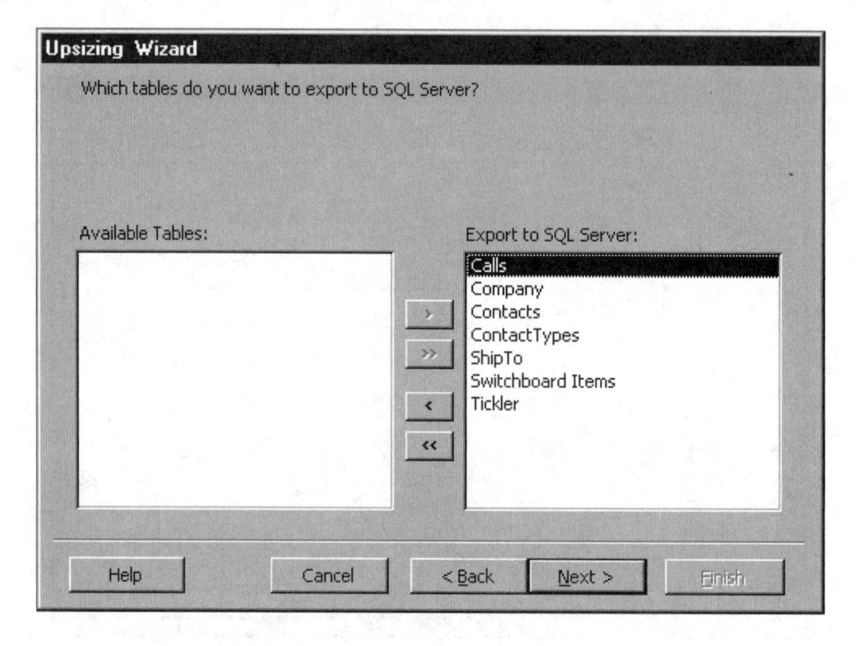

Next, SQL Server wants to know just how much information about these tables we want to migrate to the SQL Server:

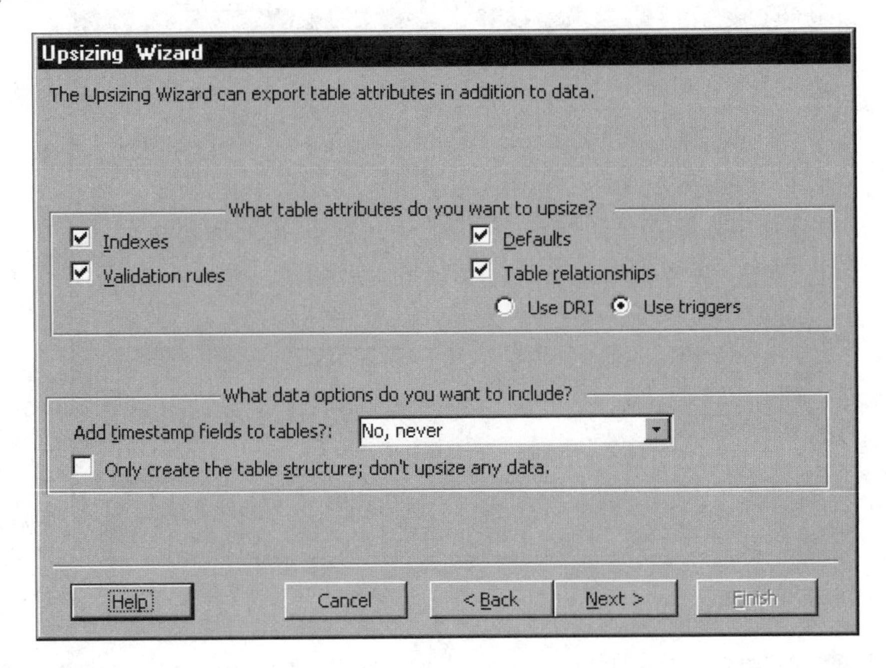

Let's pause long enough at this point to look these over:

- Tables Attributes: This allows us to decide what constraints and indexes we want to migrate. Notice that it gives you both options for referential integrity – Foreign Key constraints and triggers. The catch here is that it is an all or nothing kind of approach. If you select triggers, then you'll be using triggers for everything. If you select Foreign Keys, then you'll use them for everything – the problem with this later approach is that you will lose any cascading deletes and updates that you've set up in your Access database (remember, SQL Server foreign keys don't currently support cascading).
- Data Options: You get to decide on two things – first, whether to use timestamps or not. This actually has three options to it: No timestamps, timestamps if the wizard thinks you need them, and timestamps on everything. Whether you need these or not depends on the way you are accessing your data – the answer is probably not with modern access methods. The second thing to be set is whether you want to upsize your data or not. This gives you the option of migrating only the design, not the data.

I've selected to migrate all the table attributes, and to use triggers for referential integrity. I've also elected to migrate the data (I've ignored the Only create the table structure... option).

Next up, we decide how we're going to connect with things in the future (after it's been upsized).

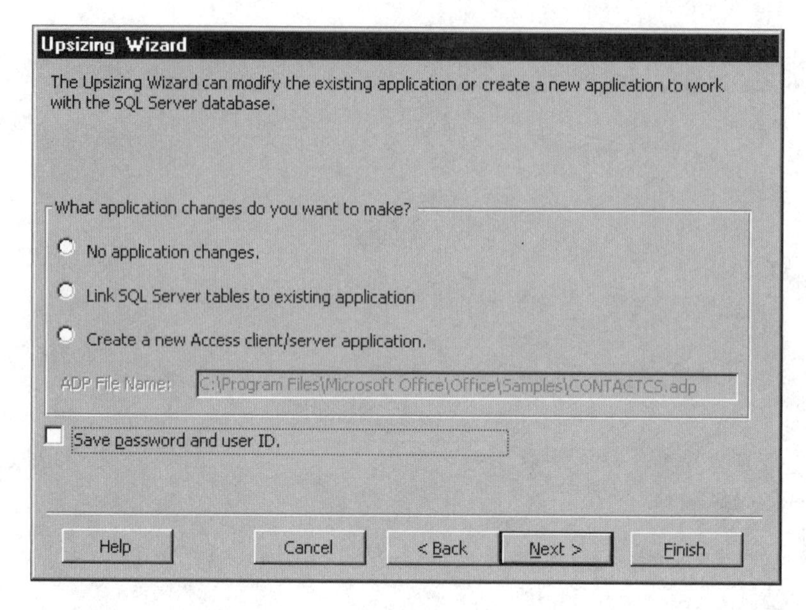

Let's again look at each of these:

- No application changes: This leaves everything exact the way it is code and data wise. All we'll be doing is essentially copying the data to the SQL Server. The Access database will be otherwise unchanged.
- Link SQL Server tables to existing application: This is the quick and dirty upsizing approach. Depending on the exact implementation of your code in Access, your application should have a high compatibility with the new approach to storing the data (in the SQL Server), but you still gain that advantage of having the data in the SQL Server.
- Create a new Access client/server application: Helps create a totally new application using the new client/server features that Access has for working with SQL Server.
- Save password and user ID information: Stores away user ID and login information. In Access, quite often you don't have to actually "logon" as such. This option allows the SQL Server user information to be stored away so you can maintain things the way you're used to with Access (i.e. no login – its login is automatically based on the stored information).

I'm going to choose to have no application changes, and move on to the final dialog before the upsizing occurs:

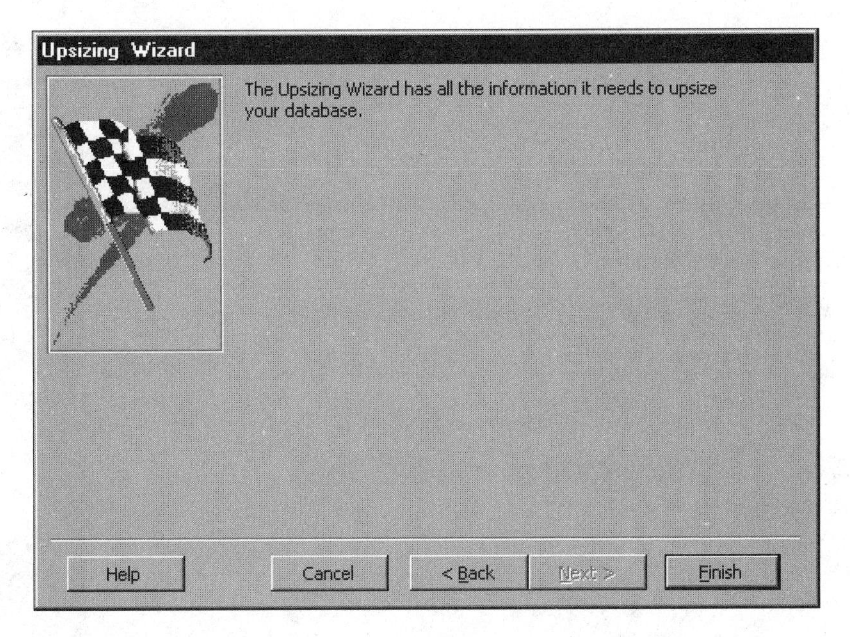

This is just a last minute chance to cancel – Access is ready to do the upsizing.

Choose Finish, and Access begin the process, and provides us with progress information:

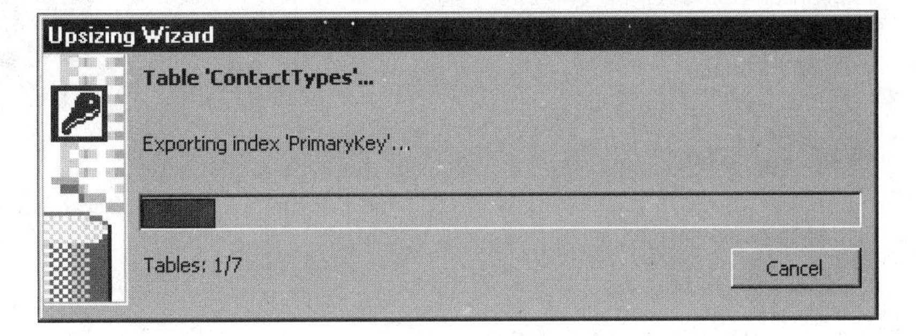

When Access is all done, it provides you with a report so you know how things went with the upsizing process and what exactly was done:

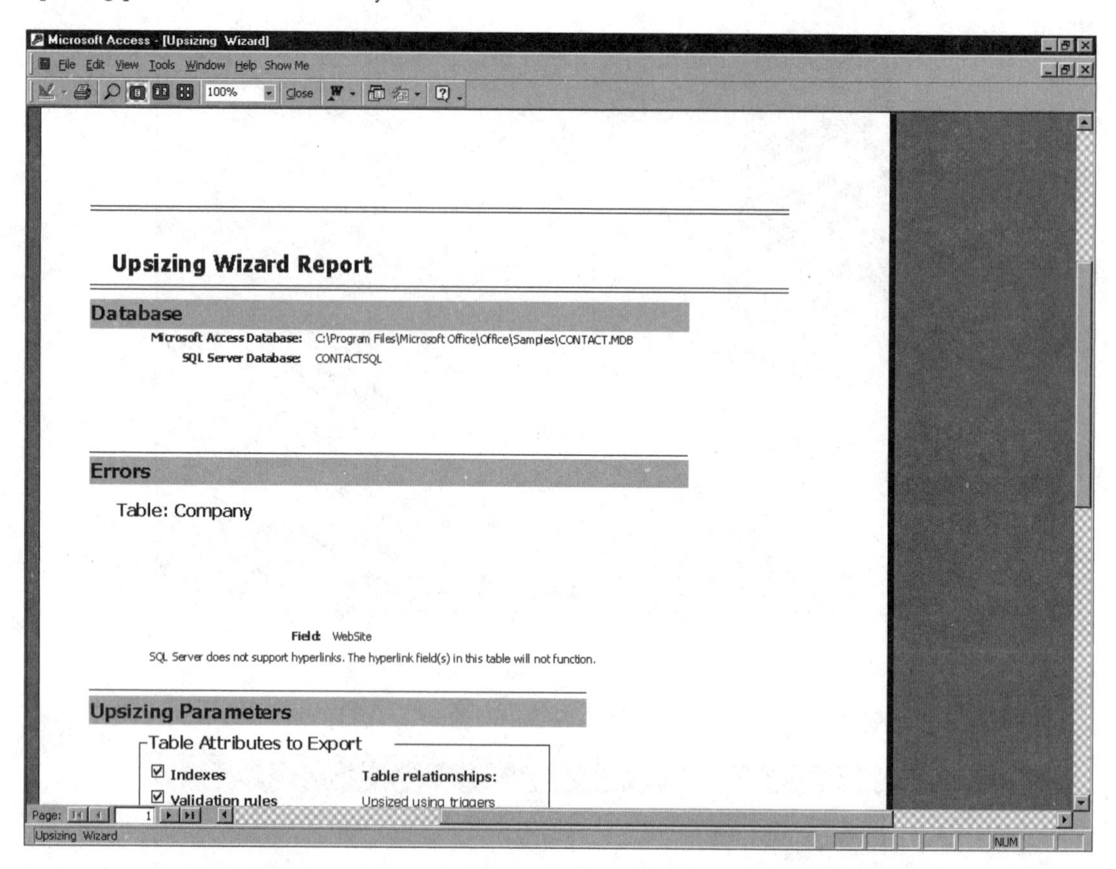

For me, the report was about 15 pages long, and reported just one error (SQL Server doesn't have the new Access `Hyperlink` data type, so it is converted to text).

Checking The Work

Don't just assume that the report tells you whether everything got there or not – go check both your data and your other objects (the triggers for instance?).

Start off by logging into the Query Analyzer and selecting the CONTACTSQL database.

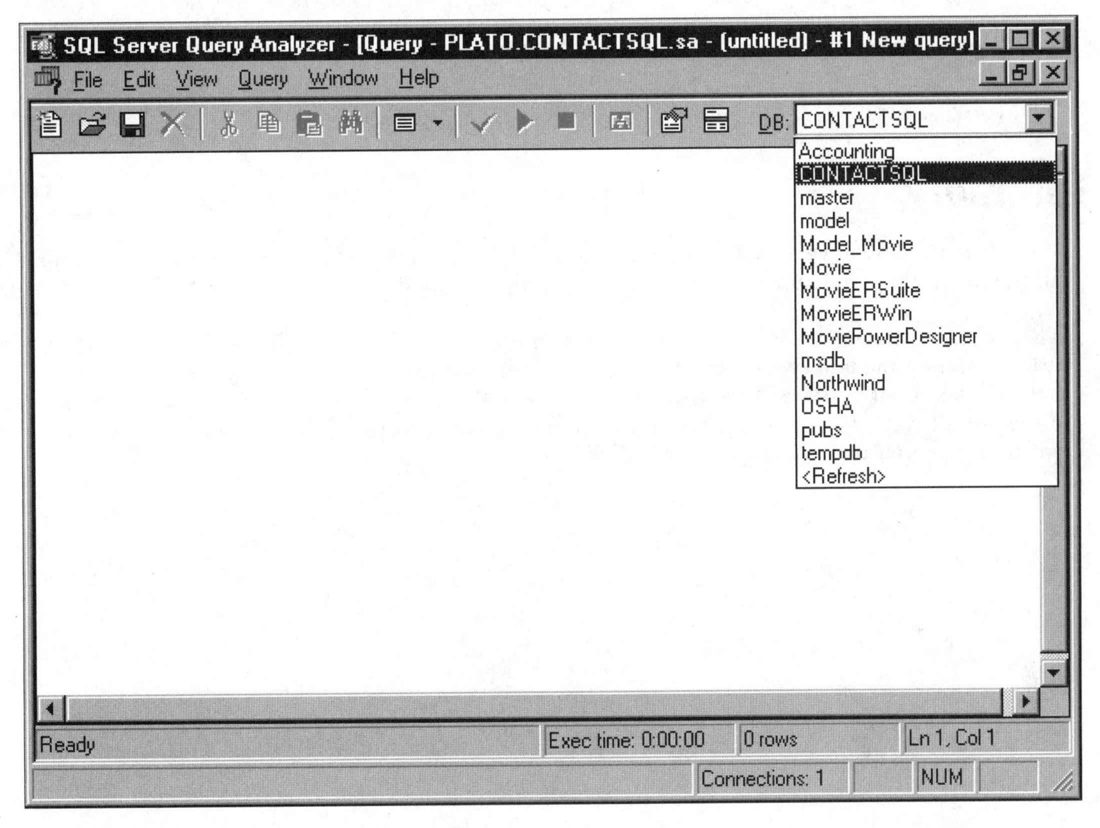

Let's check out how big it decided to make our database (remember – it didn't ask us for any of that information in the wizard).

```
EXEC sp_helpdb CONTACTSQL
```

If you look over the results (they are too wide to fit in a book), you'll see that it created only a 4MB database – including the log (2MB each for database and log). It also allows for a 10% growth factor, so, as the database grows in size, we don't have to worry too much about that 4MB size.

Next, let's look over a table:

```
EXEC sp_help company
```

Again, we see that our table appears to have been created as expected, and has all the columns that existed in the original Access database. `CompanyID` has been created as an identity column (it was an `AutoNumber` field in Access), as well as the proper primary key and indexes.

One down note here – the wizard doesn't pick up on duplicate indexes. For example, in this table (`company`*), there was a primary key and an index set separately on* `CompanyID`*. This means that two indexes were created on SQL Server (one by default with the primary key, the other explicitly based on the separate index). Watch out for these kinds of situations, and make sure you delete the duplicate index if you find one.*

Summary

Well, that didn't take very long, did it? The process is actually amazingly simple when you consider all the things that are happening to achieve the end result.

The Access Upsizing Wizard makes the migration much easier – but don't think that it's as simple as this illustration made it seem. You would still want to look over your code and retest thoroughly before releasing it to users. Also, consider a time like this an excellent opportunity to re-examine the design of the database – does it need more upgrading than just the platform it's running on? In other words, remember this is a tool – not a crutch.

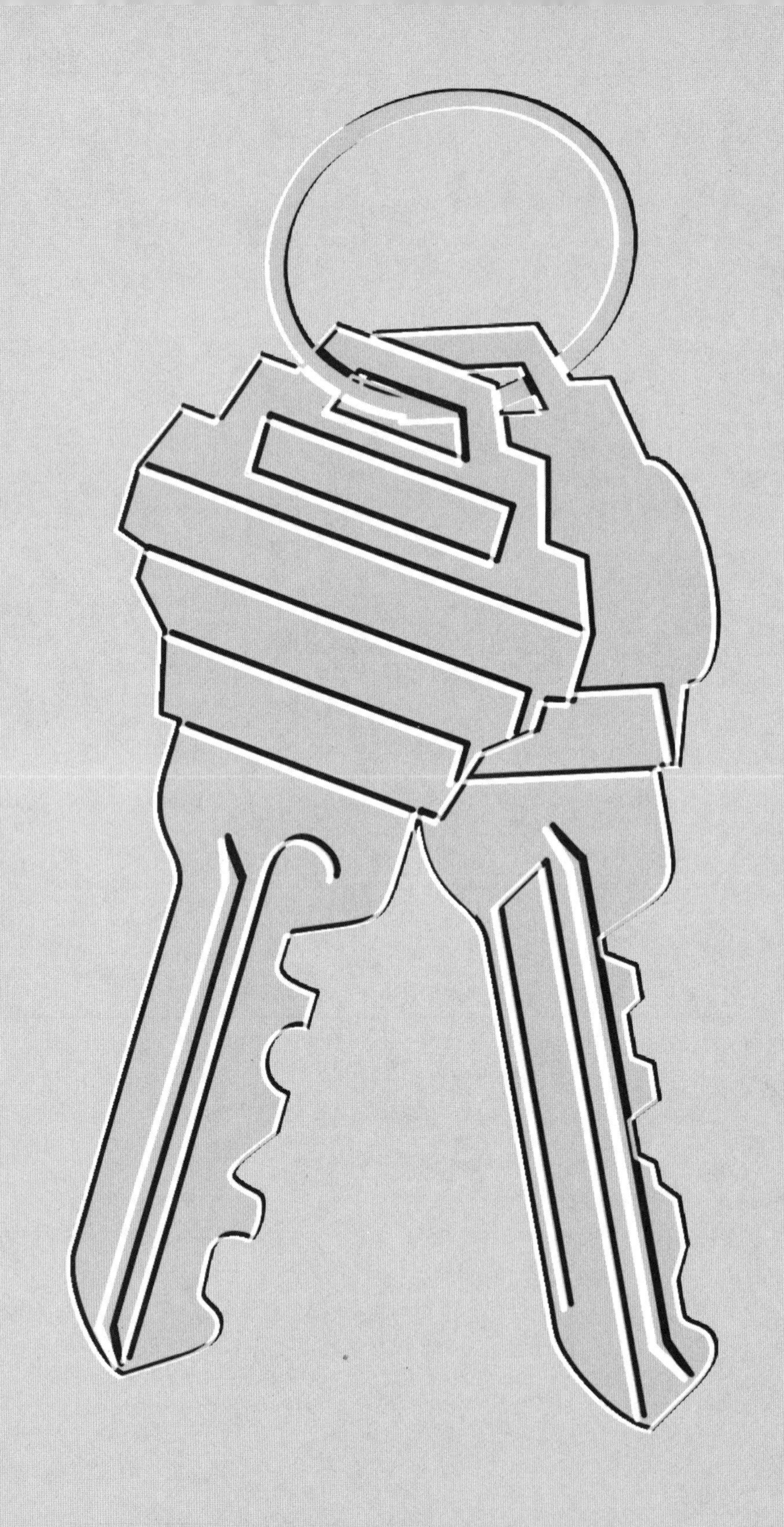

Index

Symbols

F

G

H

I

O

P

Q

S

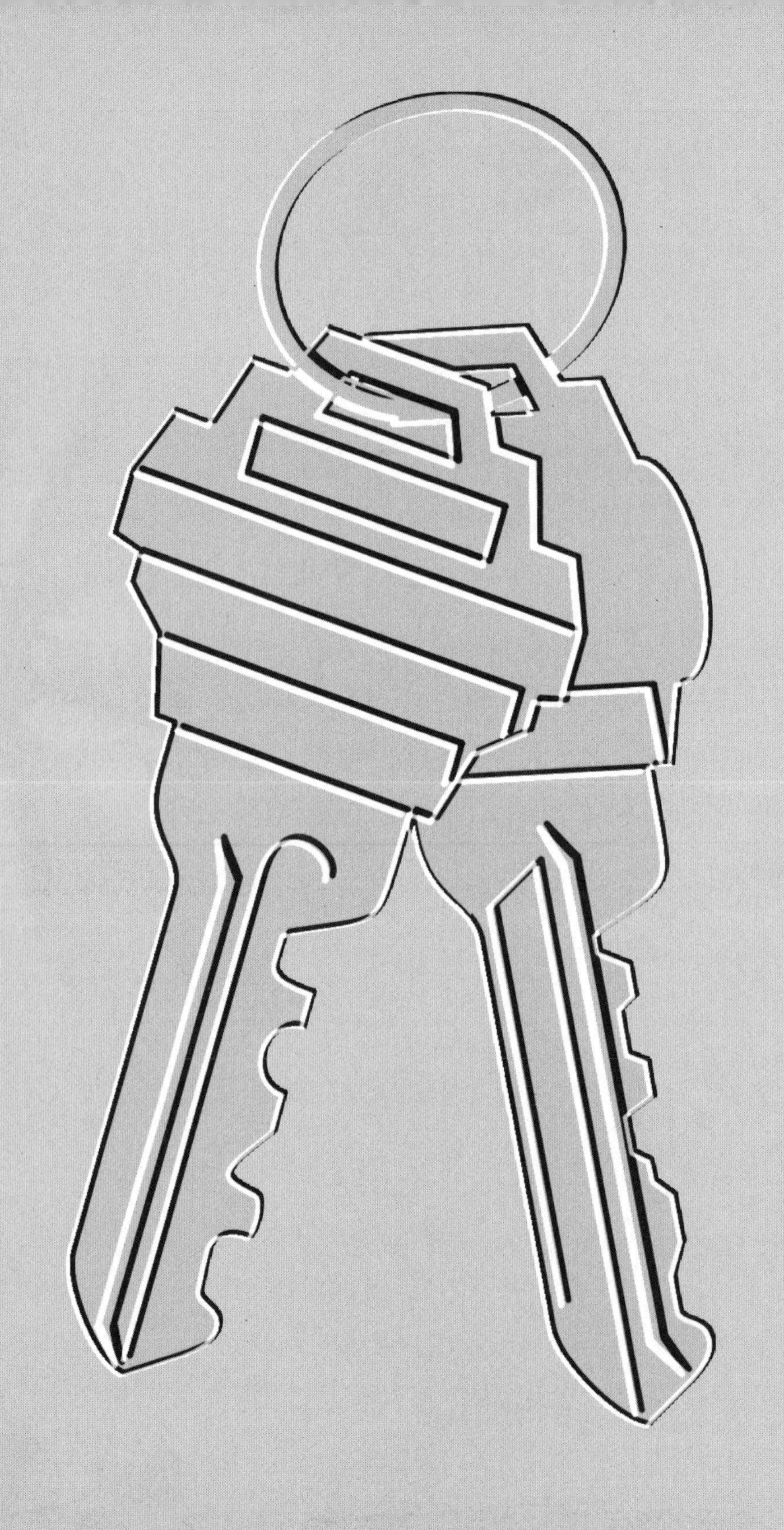